MW00879011

Given In Full Measure...
Cradling Grenades

To Dr. Ken Gleitsmann,

Your service and patient care
give proof to your USMC bloodline!

With respect,

Terence W. Barrett

04-15-22

Given In Full Measure...
Cradling Grenades

VOLUME I

✳✳✳

Terence W. Barrett PhD

AmR

First published in 2017 by Aftermath Research, P.O. Box 5551, Fargo, ND, 58102.
Copyright © 2017 by Terence W. Barrett PhD

The accounts in this book are factual. All efforts were made to validate details, in most cases from two or more sources. Some unverified details have been excluded from the text. Suppositions are noted with such words as "likely" and "probably" or explained in the End Notes. Any errors of fact discovered in this rendering are solely the author's responsibility.

Library of Congress Cataloging-in-Publication Data
Barrett, Terence W., 1949–

Includes bibliographical references.
ISBN–10: 1545162379
ISBN–13: 9781545162378
Library of Congress Control Number: 2017905401
CreateSpace Independent Publishing Platform
North Charleston, South Carolina

1. Medal of Honor. 2. Biography. 3. United States Marine Corps. 4. Military History. 5. Banana Wars. 6. World War II.

Front cover image is a Japanese Nambu Type 97 hand grenade.
Medal of Honor image used with permission of Carol Cepregi, Congressional Medal of Honor Society, Mount Pleasant, South Carolina.

Back Cover image is Department of Defense Photo (USMC) 71921, February 1, 1944, 1:05 PM. From their perspective on Roi Island's Beach Red 3, a squad of 23d Marines looks past Namur Island's Yokohama Pier at the blockhouse explosion that killed twenty men of Company F, 2d Battalion, 24th Marines.

Printed in the United States of America

"I was very interested in Terence Barrett's project when he first contacted me and was pleased to help where I could. Reading through his discoveries, experiencing a flood of memories, there were moments when I cried and others when I laughed. His account of Donald Truesdell and his family is very much the story of many American families from the mid-eighteenth century to the present. Immigrants seeking better lives, fighting in the wars that created and sustained the identity of our nation, working hard, rearing families, worshipping freely, and in the process becoming Americans. Most of the men and women who fought in our many wars were brave and heroic, but certain acts stood out and were awarded the Congressional Medal of Honor. My father's sacrifice of his right hand is recognized anew in this detailed account of his life and times. Such humanizing is helpful in giving us the perspective to evaluate our history. I am amazed that Barrett also shows how complex people can be—products of their times, cultural background, and events over which they had no control or responsibility. Kudos to Terence for a well-done history."

—Donna Truesdell

"I applaud the diligence and depth Terry put into this research and his outstanding effort to get the facts straight. My father talked little about his time in the Corps or in Nicaragua or about his Medal of Honor. I suppose he thought it was all in the past. This book introduces aspects of my father's life and military service I didn't know. The writing highlights the exterior influences affecting the individual and possible effects on others, matching the ability of authors like John Barry, Rick Atkinson, and James Reston to portray a character in a full historical context. Terry draws out details not well reported in other histories—my father's affinity for the impoverished Nicaraguan natives, the level of violence by the Guardia troops against the Marines, the command climate that resulted in mutinies, and the number of suicides. Terry was also able to make sense of the complicated Truesdell genealogy, and he depicts our family life and times in Lugoff in an honest way. I was honored to contribute to this most excellent work."

—Stephen Truesdell

"I am honored that Terence wrote about my father. This is fascinating and enjoyable reading. Through my father, I was fortunate in my life to meet many Medal of Honor recipients at conventions, other events, and, sadly enough, at funerals. Some of the men became personal friends. This book clearly portrays the influences and lessons my father taught me and how his life impacted my own life, like the importance and rewards of community involvement, responsibility, and hard work. I was happy to contribute to this meaningful endeavor."

—Robert William Sorenson

"When I received Dr. Barrett's letter about writing biographies of USMC Medal of Honor recipients, I noticed the return label on the envelope had a USMC emblem. So, I understood his bond with other Marines and was happy to answer any questions he had about my father. I am very proud of my father and of everyone who sacrificed so much for our country. Personally, Richard K. Sorenson was my hero just for being my loving father. I was in college when I fully realized how significant his sacrifice on the grenade had been, because it had impacted so many lives, even those of the next generation. I hope that reading about the heroism of all the men in this book will inspire people in the same way my father inspired me."

—Wendy Sorenson Thorson

"I didn't have any idea that Dad was a hero until I was 10 years old. I learned about what he did from my teacher in history class. I was shocked that Dad never told us. So, that night I asked him, and he looked embarrassed. He told me in a soft voice that 'You just don't talk about those kinds of things.'"

—Debby Sorenson Hanaway

"I have read many articles and stories about my father over the years, and no one has even approached the incredible detail that Terry Barrett gave to this fantastic work. I am impressed with his thoroughness and painstaking research. The work is skillfully written, a tapestry of incredible facts woven into flowing story, reminding me of *Unbroken*, Laura Hillenbrand's biography of Louis Zamperini. He brings to light so many facts concerning these heroes that the reading was fascinating and enlightening for me. The greater picture of the events going on at the time these men served our country benefits the reader immensely. I salute the kindness Terry demonstrates in extending a tribute to my father and all the brave men introduced in this masterful book. He has performed a wonderful labor of love in telling their stories."

—James Sorenson

"How interesting it was to learn that Terry was writing about my father. I was more than willing to help. My memories of my Dad have always been from my childhood and teenage years, as I was a college junior when he passed from this life. I was in college on a Medal of Honor scholarship and got to know a number of other students whose fathers were also Medal holders. It always strikes me to realize that these men are often viewed differently, admired as heroes. They were just our dads! I appreciate all the hard work Terry put into this writing. The first time I read through it, my first thought was 'Wow!' It means a lot that someone far from Lindenwold, New Jersey, wants our nation to remember men like my Dad."

—Jacquelyn A. Rouh Govan

Also by Terence W. Barrett, PhD:

The Search For The Forgotten Thirty-Four: Honored By The U.S. Marines, Unheralded In Their Hometowns?

Remembering James Edmund Johnson, USMC: Pocatello's "Number One Hero Of The Korean War"

Remembering Douglas Eugene Dickey, USMC: "Reaching the Finest and Most Noble Heights"

Life After Suicide: The Survivor's Grief Experience, Revised Edition

To all our Wounded Warriors and their families who find in their hearts and spirits the will to prevail.

Contents

Acknowledgments

✳✳✳

I WISH TO THANK THOSE who shared a part in this tribute to United States Marine Corps Medal of Honor recipients.

My heartfelt *thank you* goes to my wife, Rachel Dittmer Barrett, for her interest in the discoveries about these Marines and for her thoughtful and creative suggestions.

Donna Truesdell, Stephen Truesdell, Gayle Truesdell Lilly, Robert William Sorenson, Wendy Sorenson Thorson, Debby Sorenson Hanaway, James Sorenson, Thomas Sorenson, and Jacquelyn A. Rouh Govan reviewed portions of the text and provided personal recollections of their fathers and early family life. Without their welcome contributions, the accounts of their fathers would have been limited to public sources.

Special thanks go those who helped research materials otherwise unavailable to me. Their contributions are described in the text and Notes. Lois Monson assisted in researching background information. In the order in which they are included in the chapters, others are: Emmett Becker, Lisa Coffman, and Tammy Kuddes; Rickie Good; Vickie Wendel, Gwendolyn Poore, Lynn Ann Rone, Phyllis (Beard) Robertus, Pam Sigurdson, Marilyn Anderson, and Pam Leindecker; Kathryn Carroll and Brenda Roach; Amy O'Neal; Herbert Edwards, Nelson A. Francisco, Eric R. Powers, Jodi L. Foor, Jason Gibbs, Jennifer Brewington Taylor, Katie McLain, Christine Moraetes, Jerry V. Stahl, and Karen Carlson Loving.

Major General James E. Livingston, USMC (Ret.), Medal of Honor recipient, Brigadier General Thomas V. Draude, USMC (Ret.), Jack Lengyel, United States Naval Academy Director of Athletics (Ret.), Robert Sharp, Darke County Educational History, and Kenneth A. Steffel, Marine Corps League Detachment #758, have promoted the importance of remembering the dedication and sacrifices of heroic Marines, no matter their ranks and medals.

Many thanks go to my family. My parents, sisters, brothers, nephews and nieces have all played a part in my understanding of bravery: William J. Barrett (1919–1999), Mary J. Barrett, Mary Anne Cody, Timothy and Jan Barrett, Susanne Barrett Kazmer (1955–2011), Dennis Barrett (1957–2016), David Cody, Shawn and Anne Cody, Mike and Caryn Cody, Scot and Kathy Cody, Leslie and Josh Hall, Katie and Joe Nowak, Heather Kazmer, Jillian and Jake Gaydosh and Shanna Kazmer. The interest Rachel's family has expressed in Medal of Honor Marines has also made a difference in writing these biographies: Raymond (1933–2017) and Mary DeRidder, Bill and SueAnn Dittmer, Rollie and Ruth Ann Helgerson, Kevin and Martha Larson, and Arnold and Pamela Dittmer.

I am indebted to longtime friends whose interest in this research and boundless humor make a difference: Paul and Patty Becka, Eric and Pati Walz, Joe Arnold, James Barry, grandson of a WWI Belleau Wood Marine who was recommended for a Medal of Honor, Tom and Susan Boardman, Richard Clark, Tim Cleary, proud son of a WWII Marine who fought on Saipan and Okinawa, Thomas M. Coughlin (1949–2016), Gerald Fallon, Michael Feighan, Tim Harkness, retired USAF pilot, Kevin Keegan, Ed Kihm, Mike Kolody, Ron and Kitty Maltarich, Regis McGann, Tim McManamon, Kevin O'Malley, Daniel and Cheri Reed, John Richilano, Dennis and Maureen Salettel, and Don and Pam Sandborg.

Neighbors have been supportive, perhaps without knowing their part: Lyle Andvik, a Navy aviator who flew close air support missions in the OV-10A over Viet Nam with Light Attack Squadron Four (VAL-4), and his wife, Kathleen; Kevin and Sandy Metzger; Seth and Deborah Sauvageau; Mark and Becca Sperry; and Brian and Emily Teberg.

Credit goes to Andrew Bennett, CreateSpace sales account manager, for his assistance in paying tribute to these Marines.

I extend my appreciation to Timothy Teig, Denise Leeby, Kari Appletoft, Nicholas Gard, James Cronin, and Christy Karst of the Fargo VET Center for their continued commitment to support the men and women who have returned from war and guide them in the adjustments to coming home.

Terence W. Barrett
Fargo, North Dakota
2017

Foreword

✳✳✳

HISTORY HAS ALWAYS BEEN AN interest of mine. Born in Albany, New York, I was eight years old, living in Locust, New Jersey, when Pearl Harbor was attacked. World War II ended before I finished elementary school. I attended high school at The Gunnery in Washington, Connecticut, preparing to go on to college. The faculty and curriculum there focused on serious learning, developing confidence, and instilling a sure, moral compass—not just to be a success in college and life, but to be a person who would contribute to the greater society. The North Korean tanks crossed the 38th Parallel, starting the Korean War in the summer before my sophomore year began. I had just finished high school when the Armistice was signed and the fighting ended in July 1953.

I went on to Princeton University and graduated in 1956 with a Bachelor of Arts degree in History. From college, I went to Marine Corps Base Quantico. As a newly commissioned second lieutenant, I attended The Basic School at Camp Barrett and was indoctrinated into the Marine Corps philosophy. Of course, there was the physical fitness program, but the true emphasis was on leadership and military skills. Academics included the Corps' history and the lessons of such battles as Guadalcanal, Iwo Jima, Okinawa, and the Chosin Reservoir. The names General Alexander Archer Vandegrift, Lieutenant Colonel Aquilla James Dyess, Lieutenant Baldomero Lopez, Jr., Major Reginald Myers and Gunny Dan Daly became familiar examples of inspiring leadership under fire. Military law was of particular fascination for me.

The Corps' training was strict and seriously rigorous, teaching young boys to become men, and I have a deep admiration for anyone able to go through that regimen. During my time, the instructors, WWII and Korean War veterans, would have no part in mollycoddling those who might go to war to stand up for our way of life. I came to believe that every young man should have the experience of being a Marine or serving in the military.

I was an infantry officer, living in a little house for married officers at Camp Lejeune. Egypt had just nationalized the Suez Canal in July 1956. Trouble brewed in the Middle East as Jordanian and Syrian governments faced military coups and Lebanon reported massive border incursions. Israel attacked Egypt in October.

I count myself fortunate to have been sent to the Army Ranger's school at Fort Benning, Georgia. The patrols and marches into the swamps were memorable, and I might have enjoyed jump school had I not been called back to Lejeune for a deployment. Afterward, people might roll their eyes, but I was never deterred from singing out "I want to be an airborne ranger, live the life of guts and danger . . . .," a lyric second only to "From the Halls of Montezuma . . . ."

I had the pleasure of sailing the Atlantic with a company of Marines when the Sixth Fleet moved forces into the Eastern Mediterranean to demonstrate American support for King Hussein. Cyprus was a paradise belying the tensions in the region.

The Corps was a wonderful experience, giving me a confidence to pursue objectives and conquer obstacles. I would have stayed except for family obligations. I resigned my first lieutenant's commission in mid-1958 and went on to studies at Rutgers University Law School, earning my LL.B. in 1961. For several years, I had a private law practice in Monmouth County, New Jersey, then served as counsel to the Monmouth County Board of Social Services. I retired in 1991 and moved to Saratoga Springs, New York, with my wife, Mary, having time, then, to enjoy reading, gardening and traveling. Stephen E. Ambrose's histories and biographies have been favorites.

In conversations with Terry Barrett over the years, neither of us made much of our time in the Marine Corps: a question or two every now and then, a brief answer, and more about our full lives. His regard for Marines, something I share, is made evident in his writing.

When I read his *Search For The Forgotten Thirty-Four* in 2011, it was like returning to The Basic School. The book was replete with stories of heroic individuals and the long history of the Medal of Honor. Then followed *Remembering James Edmund Johnson* and *Remembering Douglas Eugene Dickey*. I read them cover to cover. Each is a study of heroic bravery. That Terry traces the roots of valor back into a young man's ancestry to pre-Colonial America, describing Revolutionary War militias retreating down Lake Champlain to the Crown Point Fort in New York, gave me pause to consider my own ancestors.

Garett DeRidder arrived from Holland before 1730 and was among the first permanent settlers in Saratoga County. His five sons, Walter, Simon, Hendrick, Killian, and Evert, developed their land around Schuylerville and Easton on either side of the Hudson River and operated ferries. Brigadier General Simon DeRidder led a militia in the decisive American victory over the British at the two Battles of Saratoga in September and October 1777. He also led the three regiments of the 16th Brigade in the War of 1812. His son, Colonel Walter DeRidder, later commanded the 156th Infantry Regiment, New York State Militia. Simon's sword and scabbard are kept at the Fort Ticonderoga Museum, and much of his battle correspondence is in a collection at the New York State Library in Albany.

I appreciate that Terry remembers "ordinary" Marines and was honored that he asked me to write a Foreword to *Given in Full Measure*. I must admit that my health challenged my reading through these chapters, and I had trouble writing out my thoughts, but his writing could hold my attention and interest for hours at a time. The ball was in my court to finish a Foreword.

Like his others, this book is a glimpse into America's history, as well as the lives of five Medal of Honor holders. The detailed accounts of courage and the character of young men sharpened in the culture of their times take the reader beyond official dispatches, award citations, and newspaper reports. Terry makes clear the resilience combat veterans must possess to adjust to life once home from war and the commitment to be of service that earning a Medal of Honor brings to men who survive their battles.

Medal recipients believe they represent the brave men who fought and died beside them. Throughout this book, Terry introduces the Marines who Donald Truesdale, Richard

Sorenson, Carlton Rouh, Jack Lucas, and Richard Bush never forgot. His portrayal of a Marine's life is insightful. His description of days in the holds of a "sailing troop coffin" took me back to my cruise to Cyprus. His narrative will bring many surprises for the reader. The stories of Princeton University alumni, Second Lieutenant Charles McAllister, Class of 1942, and Silver Star recipient First Lieutenant Richard Rhea Patton Goheen, Class of 1936, held special meaning for me.

There will be many rewards in reading *Given in Full Measure* for anyone interested in WWII and the United States Marine Corps.

Vestra frui vita.

Raymond Budington Deridder, Esq. (1933–2017)
Princeton University, Class of 1956
USMC, 1956–1958
Attorney at Law, Monmouth County, New Jersey, (Ret.)

List of Recipients

✳✳✳

Second Nicaragua—Donald Leroy Truesdell (Survived)

World War II (27)—Richard Beatty Anderson * Lewis Kenneth Bausell * Charles Joseph Berry * Richard Earl Bush (Surv) * William Robert Caddy * Anthony Peter Damato * Harold Glenn Epperson * William Adelbert Foster * Harold Gonsalves * Henry Gurke * Elbert Luther Kinser * Richard Edward Kraus * James Dennis Labelle * Jacklyn Harrell Lucas (Surv) * John Dury New * Joseph William Ozbourn * Wesley Phelps * George Phillips * Charles Howard Roan * Carlton Robert Rouh (Surv) * Donald Jack Ruhl * Richard Keith Sorenson (Surv) * Herbert Joseph Thomas Jr. * Frederick Timmerman * John Peter Fardy * William Gary Walsh * Robert Lee Wilson

Korean War (16)—William Bernard Baugh * Hector Albert Cafferata Jr. (Surv) * David Bernard Champagne * Jack Arden Davenport * Duane Edgar Dewey (Surv) * Fernando Luis Garcia * Edward Gomez * Jack William Kelso * Robert Sidney Kennemore (Surv) * Herbert A. Littleton * Baldomero Lopez Jr. * Whitt Lloyd Moreland * Robert Dale Reem * Robert Ernest Simanek (Surv) * Sherrod Emerson Skinner Jr. * Lewis George Watkins

Vietnam War (23)—James Anderson Jr. * Richard Allen Anderson * Oscar Palmer Austin * Jedh Colby Barker * Daniel Dean Bruce * Bruce Wayne Carter * Ronald Leroy Coker * Peter Spencer Connor * Thomas Elbert Creek * Rodney Maxwell Davis * Emilio Albert DeLaGarza * Douglas Eugene Dickey * Paul Hellstrom Foster * James Donnie Howe * Robert Henry Jenkins Jr. * Ralph Henry Johnson * Allan Jay Kellogg Jr. (Surv) * William Thomas Perkins Jr. * Jimmy Phipps * Roy Mitchell Wheat * DeWayne Thomas Williams * Alfred Mac Wilson * Kenneth Lee Worley

Iraq and Afghanistan (3) — William Kyle Carpenter (Surv) * Jason L. Dunham * Rafael Peralta (Silver Star)

CHAPTER 1

Introduction

✳✳✳

"A warrior must learn to make every act count, since he is going to be here in this world for only a short while, in fact, too short for witnessing all the marvels of it." [1]

—CARLOS CASTANEDA, 1925–1998

WHEN ONE IS BLESSED TO live a long life, it is natural to wonder about how life might have turned out for a friend or family member who died in his or her youth. It is especially common among combat veterans who came home from a war. The comrades who gave their lives on foreign soil are seldom far from their thoughts.

"Every morning when I first look in the mirror, I thank George Phillips for another day." That is what Robert Eugene "Bob" McLanahan said in 1990, forty-five years after he was saved from a grenade blast. Bob was remembering a United States Marine Corps Medal of Honor recipient.

George Phillips had acted heroically brave in circumstances in which large numbers of individuals were being generally brave. One historical document provides an account of his actions. Like all Medal of Honor Citations, the document provides brief biographical data about George and synopsis-like information about the event. [2] Other participants in the actions, like Bob McLanahan, are not named. Obviously, heroic bravery does not occur in the absence of other individuals nor separate from a larger circumstance. To provide context to George's actions and to learn more about his life, available public sources were reviewed, including archival records, newspaper articles, and WWII histories.

George did not have time to make friends in Rich Hill, Bates County, Missouri. He was born there on July 14, 1926, near the border with Kansas, where the land is formed by the Ozarks and cut by the Maris Des Cygnes River. The youngest of six children, named after his mother's brother, he also did not have much chance to get to know his parents or his brothers and sister.

Isaac "Fred" Phillips married 16-year-old Elizabeth "Lizzie" Dunnahay on April 3, 1912, in Miller County, in the center of Missouri. Perry was their first child, a New Year's baby, born on January 1, 1914. Both mother and baby survived. That was a relief, given the U.S. infant mortality rates of the time. When Perry took his first breath, an average of 105 babies out of every 1,000 live births died in their first year of life.

Lizzie's parents and brothers had moved to Rich Hill, as there seemed to be work for laborers, prompting the Phillips to relocate. Fred moved the family west to Bates County, on the Kansas border, where a tragedy not unfamiliar to the Ozarks struck on January 6, 1915. Two minutes after Lizzie gave birth at home, the baby boy died of an unknown cause. The unnamed infant was buried in Papinville Cemetery that day without the services of an undertaker. [3]

Leslie (Lester) George Phillips was born on September 3, 1916, and Frankie Richard was born in Webb City, Jasper County, on December 15, 1917. The two brothers remained close for forty-eight years, until Frank died in a broadside, two-car accident in Pasco, southeastern Washington, after a Memorial Day visit to his older brother.

Fred moved the family again, up to Wyandotte County. He rented a house at 823 South Fifth Street in a Kansas City working-class neighborhood, and took a job as a janitor at a packinghouse. The home was shared with a 65-year-old Missouri woman, who did the house-keeping. Residents on the block had come from Alabama, Missouri, Texas, Kansas, Arkansas, Louisiana, and New York.

The racial mixture on the street and in the neighborhood included White, Mulatto, and Black people. Those who were employed had jobs at the packinghouse. Several doors down the street lived a man from Wales who had a job as a beef pusher and spoke Welsh at work. A large, Spanish-speaking family of Mexican laborers lived a couple of houses up the same block from the Phillips.

Arzetta Phillips, Fred and Lizzie's only daughter, was born in Kansas City on May 18, 1920. George's next closest sibling, Carlisle "Carl" Phillips was born on December 14, 1923, after their father had moved the family down Route 69 to Treece, Cherokee County, in the corner Kansas shares with Missouri and Oklahoma. Staying only through several seasons, Fred moved the family back to Rich Hill, so that Lizzie could be close to her own parents. George was born shortly after the return to Missouri.

Perry Phillips was just age 14, starting off to work, and George was not yet two, when their grandfather was inflicted with influenza. The family worried it was consumption. In a time before antibiotics, consumption and flu could be fatal. Alfred "Alf" Dunnahay, 63, suf-fered a "complete collapse of the lung" on January 5, 1928, and died of pulmonary tuberculo-sis. He was buried in Papinville Cemetery.

Lizzie, 32, followed her father to the cemetery. She also departed this life in 1928, possibly killed in a car accident. She was buried in Papinville Cemetery. Then, her brother, George Dunnahay, 21, employed as a miner, was killed in a car accident on November 24, 1929, in Rich Hill. He died of a broken neck. He was buried in Papinville Cemetery.

Caring for six children under the ages of 14 years was more than widowed Fred Phillips or Grandma Frances (Witt), 60, could keep up with. The children were sent to live with various aunts and uncles. Lester and Frank went to live with Bennie and Bena (Phillips) Rodden. Carl first resided with Phillip and Linnie (Dunnahay) Hymer on Walnut Street. Grandma Frances also lived there. Arzetta lived with George and Lavona (Witt) Wilson.

Fred died in January 1930 in Kansas City, Wyandotte County, of pulmonary tuberculo-sis. [4] The Phillips children were officially orphans.

George, the youngest, was taken in by his father's sister, Lillian O'Brien, in Labadie, Franklin County, a small farming community on the Missouri River—"out in the sticks" west of St. Louis. His Uncle James O'Brien worked on a section crew for the Missouri–Pacific Railroad. George was 3 years 9 months old when the enumerator wrote his name as "Philip George" in the 1930 Census on May 1. His relationship to James was recorded as "Adopted Son." Again, he was the youngest in the family. In the next census, he would be listed as "Nephew." [5]

George's older cousins became his foster sister and two brothers. Edna Lucinda Penelope O'Brien, 19, had already graduated from Kirkwood High School and was considering Julius Dutton's marriage proposal. [6] Earl O'Brien was 18, living out of the home, and Arthur Eugene O'Brien was 12 years old. Around town, George was known as "Junior O'Brien."

The O'Brien's lived in town, down the hill and within a football-field distance of Labadie Grade School. That proved a benefit for George, who later earned certificates for perfect attendance and for never being tardy.

"Junior" is remembered as a quiet and shy child, always wearing overalls. His favorite holiday was Christmas. He liked school, had friends in Labadie, and wanted to be a professional baseball player, apparently having had enough talent to be competitive on the sandlot. Maybe he dreamed of playing with the *Gas House Gang* of the St. Louis *Cardinals*—certainly not the St. Louis *Browns*, who had never enjoyed a winning season in all George's childhood years in Labadie until 1942. He attended the Methodist Church regularly, joined the Boy Scouts, and enjoyed every opportunity to go hunting and fishing. He was never in any kind of trouble, never wanting to raise hell. [7]

Emmett Becker was a grade behind Junior in school and a close friend. The two engaged in wild corncob wars on the Becker farm when they had free time to frolic. One favorite pastime for the boys was to go up old Route 47, through Truesdale, to the woods and rolling meadows around Hawk Point, Lincoln County. The many small lakes and streams and branches of Coon Creek, Turkey Creek, and the Bailey Branch provided ample spots for a hunting expedition or a quiet day of fishing.

The times being as they were, after Junior and his two classmates graduated from grade school, rather than go on to high school, he went right to work. Emmett and his six classmates had another year of grade school.

How much Lillian kept her nephew apprised of his biological family is unknown. His maternal Grandma Frances Dunnahay died of a cerebral embolism attributed to a vascular disease on June 14, 1937, in Rich Hill. Perry had moved back to the family pioneer lands in Glaze Township where the Phillips, Witts, and Dunnahays worked as laborers and farmers.

Brothers Lester and Frank had moved to the Oregon–Washington State–Idaho area to find work. The regions along the Snake, Columbia, and Yakima rivers provided potato and sugar laborers a lot to do during the Depression years. On August 11, 1940, Frank married Mildred Dalphnee. Lester married Lois Lorraine Chastain. The two families lived in Gooding, Idaho, between Mountain Home and Twin Falls.

A lot of extended Phillips family resided in Yakima, and Lester and Lois Phillips settled there in 1942. They had two daughters—Junior's nieces—Lorraine and Patricia. [8]

George was "a good old boy" working a variety of jobs on nearby farms until he was hired as a painter for the Shell Oil Company pipeline. He was 15 years old when Pearl Harbor was attacked.

Patriotism was a common characteristic of the Labadie community. George's eldest foster brother, Earl Robert, married to Marie J., was already serving in the Army. Arthur Eugene had married Wilma Hurst in 1936 and was getting ready to enlist—his 22-year-old bride, Wilma, was living with the O'Brien's.

Family tragedies continued to unfold. For months, the church sermons in southwest Missouri had been about the 1943 coal miners' strike and problems with the draft board. Prayer requests went out for Jimmy Woodall, who was struck by lightning on Friday, June 4, while he was swimming in a Rich Hill watering hole during a rain downpour. The local Methodist pastor searched for the appropriate message when it came to Carl Phillips' death.

Carl, 19, employed as a general laborer, died of a self-inflicted gunshot wound to the chest on September 1, 1943, at 5th and Cedar in Rich Hill, the home of his maternal uncle, Richard Sylvester Dunnahay, where he had lived for fourteen years. Coroner John G. Underwood determined the death to have been by external cause—suicide. Carl was buried near his mother and infant brother.

Three months short of turning 18 years old, slender in build and 6 feet tall, Junior went over to Jefferson City, got a copy of his birth certificate, and enlisted in the Marine Corps from Labadie on April 25, 1944.

By then, Junior was an uncle to at least five nephews. Perry had married Georgia T. Shelton and lived for years on his brother-in-law's farm, putting in sixty-hour weeks. His son, Morris Lynn, was born in June 1939. Perry Jr. was born in October 1943. Arzetta, had married Amos Glen Guthrie on January 15, 1939, and had two sons, Robert Glenn and Donald Lee. Amos worked in road construction, and the young family lived with his older brother, a coal miner, on East Rollins Street in Moberly City, Randolph County. Arzetta was living 110 miles northwest of Labadie, sixty miles north of Jefferson City on Route 63. Adrian Richard Phillips was born to Frank and Mildred on November 17, 1943.

Private Phillips celebrated his 18th birthday in San Diego. He sailed from the States just before Christmas and joined F Company, 2nd Battalion, 28th Marines, 5th Division, in Hilo, Hawaii. The 28th Marines had been on Saipan and Tinian Islands in June and July and were training for their next island campaign. Private Phillips was among combat veterans, most them a few years older than he was. Combat veteran Private First Class Donald Jack Ruhl joined the same battalion in September. Three years apart in age, they ended up sharing common experiences.

Four men of the 28th Marines would earn Medals of Honor on Iwo Jima, three of them posthumously.

Before Private Phillips saw any combat, the *Gooding Leader* printed a newspaper article about the Services for Young Mother of Two. In August 1944, Arzetta Guthrie moved with her husband and her children, Robert, 5, and Donald, 4, to live in Gooding, near her brother Frank in the Magic Valley. She became seriously ill in mid-October and was admitted to the Gooding Hospital. Arzetta, aged 24, died on Tuesday, October 17. Besides her husband and children, the only other survivor mentioned in her obituary was Frank. [9] Whoever wrote her obituary did not mention her other surviving brothers: Perry, Lester, and George.

Arzetta's funeral services were held the next Tuesday at the Thompson Chapel. The Reverend Roy M. Franklin of the Nazarene church officiated. Frank Hammond, Cecil Hammond, Fay Hoyt, Howard Lawler, Art McGee, and H. F. Hahrowald carried her casket to her gravesite in Elmwood Cemetery. [10]

Whether the news of her niece's death reached Lillian O'Brien in Labadie, she was on record as Pvt Phillips' Next-of-Kin and would receive a telegram about her nephew in four months.

Private Phillips went ashore on Iwo Jima's Green Beach 1, on February 19, 1945, and joined the fight to cross the island and take Mount Suribachi. Corporal Tony Stein of the 1st Battalion died the first day of the assault. PFC Ruhl died on top of a grenade on the third day.

After Suribachi was secured, Pvt Phillips maneuvered up the western flank of Iwo, taking part in some of the most difficult fighting in late February and early March. He survived the terrain, Hill 362-A, and Nishi Ridge. The battalions of the 28th Marines continued up the coast toward Kitano point, fighting every day for a football length or two of volcanic soil.

On the night of March 14, members of his squad tried to get some rest and sleep in the lull of battle—bayonets fixed and ready—while Pvt Phillips stood watch. The men had spent the night as they had previous nights, exchanging hand grenades with enemy soldiers trying to infiltrate the lines. Private Phillips was the only Marine awake in the foxhole. A sputtering, sparkling Japanese grenade was tossed into their midst. He was the only one aware of its presence.

Private Phillips, 18 years old, shouted a warning to his four squad mates, grabbed the grenade with both hands and threw himself onto the projectile, covering it with his chest. He absorbed "the shattering violence of the exploding charge in his own body," and "willingly yielded his own life." He was the last Marine to dive onto a grenade to save other Marines on Iwo Jima. His remains were buried in the 5th Marine Division Cemetery on the island. [11]

Aunt Lillian would never learn of the full circumstances of Junior's heroism. A month after the telegram arrived cryptically informing the O'Brien's that Junior had been killed in action, Lillian Inez (Phillips) O'Brien was taken to St. Francis Hospital in Washington, ten miles west of home, on June 4, 1945. A month before her 59th birthday, she died of a heart attack due to coronary occlusion and arteriosclerosis on June 9. She was buried in Bethel Cemetery, two miles west of Labadie.

Private Phillips' Medal of Honor was presented to his Uncle James in Labadie on February 17, 1946. He was brought home in 1948, and re-interred in Bethel Cemetery, across from the Bethel Methodist Church on State Highway T.

Emmett Becker visited his friend's grave often over the years. The standard, flat, bronze military marker with the MOH symbol did not seem an adequate-enough tribute for Junior. The Commander of American Legion Post 565 formed a committee and got busy planning a monument befitting the "one famous internment" in Bethel Cemetery.

The Private George Phillips Memorial was dedicated in July 1990 at Bethel Cemetery. The four-foot-tall monument stands at the top of the hill, to the right of the front gate, and faces out to HWY T. "Old Glory" waves on the flagpole over the memorial, with a light shining on it at night. Affixed to the stone is a polished bronze plaque. At the top, Private Phillips' image in his dress blue uniform looks toward the church he attended on Sundays. Details of his life and his Medal Citation fill the lower plaque area. [12]

All four of Private Phillips' squad mates returned home. Private Robert Eugene "Bob" McLanahan, 21, from Collinsville, Illinois, was one of the Marines saved from the grenade blast. He attended the dedication and had a long talk with Emmett. Bob kept Junior's photograph on the wall in his home and thanked George Phillips every morning for another day. [13]

Behind George Phillips' original WWII marker now stands a white marble stone similar to Arlington National Cemetery markers. Marine Corps League Detachment #1214 in Ballwin, on St. Louis' west side, is named in his honor, and the Detachment holds an annual birthday celebration in Labadie for their namesake. The July 14 ceremony is held to remember Junior's heroic sacrifice for his country. A festive luncheon follows the ceremony.

The lasting image of Private George Phillips is of a young man months short of his 19th birthday—never to enjoy the company of friends and comrades again, never to attend a reunion, never to grow old, and never to be forgotten. He was in extraordinary circumstances, his bravery reached the level of heroic, and his highest character emerged and prevailed. He should be remembered.

The comradeship he experienced in two World Wars deeply touched Ernest Taylor "Ernie" Pyle, America's favorite WWII combat correspondent. So did the roster of men killed in action in WWII. He dedicated his 1944 book to them. "IN SOLEMN SALUTE TO THOSE THOUSANDS OF OUR COMRADES—GREAT, BRAVE MEN THAT THEY WERE—FOR WHOM THERE WILL BE NO HOMECOMING, EVER." [14]

Just like Bob McLanahan, the men who came home from WWII brought with them the memories of friends and unit comrades who had died beside them. The images were etched forever in their minds and brought a sadness to their hearts whenever thoughts returned of the ones who never made it back. Many tried to form a "mental block" against who made it and who did not. "More than a few hairs raised" when the images intruded in quiet moments.

Nick Barack, of Crete, Illinois, served in the famous Carlson's 2d Raider Battalion and fought in WWII Pacific Island battles. After the war, he was a truck driver—thirty-one years on the Chicago to Denver route. Forty-four years after he came home, he wrote a note. "So many times I think of those young men we left in the Pacific who never had a chance to get old." [15]

So it is in every war. In March 1965, Second Lieutenant Philip J. Caputo landed at Da Nang with the first Marine ground combat unit deployed to Viet Nam. Six months later in early September, Second Lieutenant Walter Neville Levy, 26, from New York, New York, landed in-country. He was 2d Platoon Commander, Company C, 1st Battalion, 1st Marines, 3d MARDIV, III MAF, and had been one of Lieutenant Caputo's closest friends in "H" Company, Class 4–64, at the U.S. Marine Corps Officers Basic School (TBS).

Lieutenant Levy's platoon went out on a patrol on September 18, two weeks after he had arrived. A corpsman was hit with small-arms fire through the head. Lieutenant Levy rushed to the rescue and was killed by a sniper. He was the first, but not the last, of Lieutenant Caputo's TBS classmates to die in combat.

His friend's ghost haunted Lieutenant Caputo. He wrote a eulogy to Lieutenant Levy eleven years after he learned of the death. "So much was lost with you, so much talent and intelligence and decency. . . . you embodied the best that was in us. You were a part of us, and a part of us died with you, the small part that was still young, that had not yet grown cynical, grown bitter and old with death. Your courage was an example to us." [16]

Reasonable questions arise when a man of character who died young is remembered. Philip Caputo wondered what Walt Levy would have accomplished in his life after Vietnam. Later in Emmett Becker's life, whenever he saw teenagers around Labadie, he remembered how young George looked when he left town for the war and would wonder what his friend's life might have been like had he survived the grenade blast.

What if this brave young man had returned to Missouri after having his photograph taken wearing a Medal of Honor around his neck and standing with President Harry Truman on the White House lawn? What if Labadie, or even St. Louis, had held a parade in his honor as he sat in the back seat of a jeep in 1945, humbled by all the attention?

The purpose of this writing is, first and foremost, to pay tribute to men who in moments of extreme peril, rose above natural fear and acted honorably; second, to provide examples of the kind of bravery that "ordinary" people can demonstrate; and third, to better understand the kind of lives heroically brave men lead after returning from war. They provide examples of what the lives of other brave, young men might have been like if they had not died on foreign battlefields.

The writer and reader of history is challenged to accurately understand heroism under fire. The experience is best told by men who faced enemy guns. Lowell V. Bulger, WWII and U.S. Marine Raider Regiment veteran, provided his insight.

"The real story of any battle is what goes on inside a man in battle. No one man can tell it so his listener will feel it exactly like he did and does." [17]

Another challenge in this endeavor is that we tend to idealize our heroes, sometimes putting them into a light they find uncomfortable. The men described throughout this book were in extraordinary circumstances. While public attention might celebrate them as heroes, they recognized their own flaws, human frailties, and weaknesses. Among those whose actions raised them to a hero's status in their nation's eyes, most would admit there is no perfect man wearing a Medal of Honor.

This being reality, we must avoid diminishing our view of these men and their accomplishments should we discover questionable elements in their backgrounds or personal imperfections or just plain ordinariness. That a Medal recipient seemed ordinary or troubled at times in life is not a justification for ignoring or disregarding his brave actions.

As General Walter E. Boomer wrote of Major General Merritt A. Edson, "less than perfect in his personal life . . . his human frailty allows us to better appreciate him as a person, not a mythological hero." [18]

CHAPTER 2

Given In Full Measure

✳✳✳

"The brave man may fall, but cannot yield." [1]

THE PARTICULARS OF COMBAT HAVE historically included one side throwing explosive projectiles at the other side. Over time and across wars, the explosives got larger and were projected farther. War planners and tacticians then realized that explosives could also be useful in close-in encounters with the other side. So, "bombs" and projectiles were downsized for close-in combat.

Hand grenades have been a weapon of war since the 15th Century and became more a part of combat during the Napoleonic Wars. Eventually, hand grenades were designed to be convenient enough for the individual infantryman to carry as an "accessory" to his primary weapon. Some men went into battle with a small arsenal of grenades strung from a belt or stuffed in a pack.

Hand grenades were the primary weapon in the First World War trench battles. In a twelve-and-a-half-hour battle on Pozieres Heights during the night of July 26–27, 1916, the Germans and Australians tossed nearly 30,000 grenades at each other. The United States Marines went ashore at St. Nazaire, France, on June 27, 1917, and for seventeen months faced blazing machine guns and bursting artillery shells and tossed live grenades, their own and the enemy's, from trenches and foxholes.

Hand-grenade exchanges were frequent in the jungle and hostile environments in which Marines have fought since then. Grenades have impelled Marines to make critical decisions about surviving or saving comrades; their explosions have accounted for a high number of the fatalities and injured casualties.

Marines like Private George Phillips are not the only combatants to have protected comrades from grenades. According to the Center for Military History, of the more than 3,497 Medal of Honor recipients, no fewer than 146 men across services have earned the award by cradling a grenade. [2] Pharmacist's Mate 1st Class John Harlan Willis is an example.

Corpsman Willis was born on June 10, 1921, in Columbia, Tennessee. He was a platoon corpsman for the 3d Battalion, 27th Marines, 5th Marine Division, and landed with them on Iwo Jima. On February 28, 1945, the Marines were taking casualties from heavy artillery and mortar fire from enemy positions on Hill 362. "Doc" Willis steadfastly administered first aid to as many of the wounded as he could reach. During the ferocious close-in fighting, shrapnel wounded him. He was ordered to withdraw to an aid station. Once treated, without waiting for medical release, he returned to his company. [3]

Corpsman Willis then made his way up to the front line, where the Marines were engaged in fending off an enemy counterattack in hand-to-hand fighting. Enemy mortars and sniper fire swept the area. "Doc" Willis found a wounded Marine lying in a shell hole and immediately began administering blood plasma. As he worked calmly to save the Marine's life, an enemy grenade landed in the hole with them. He quickly snatched it up and tossed it back toward the enemy advance. "Doc" ignored the danger to himself and remained with the Marine, though hostile grenades continued to be tossed at them. He returned seven more of the explosive devices to the enemy in quick succession.

When the corpsman picked up the ninth grenade to throw back, it exploded in his hand. Pharmacist's Mate 1st Class Willis, 23, was killed instantly. According to his Citation, his death rallied the Marines who witnessed his efforts to save one of their comrades and inspired them to aggressively push back and stifle the enemy counterattack.

All men and women who leave their homes and go to war are brave. Yet, there is no argument that people in the same situation respond differently to unfolding events. Put 4,000 brave men on a beach and order them to assault concrete fortifications with hostile machine guns and cannons pointed at them, and they will act bravely in different ways.

Bravery can be experienced in certain degrees or levels and obviously takes different forms among those who find themselves in life-threatening situations. Danger can unintentionally immobilize an individual, especially when it occurs suddenly and unexpectedly. A threat to survival can momentarily hold even the bravest in check. Overcoming natural hesitancy is an element of bravery.

The inner forces that propel courageous individuals into action vary. For example, historian Jon T. Hoffman provides a distinction among men recognized as brave in combat situations: some resolutely override their nervous systems to act bravely; others get so caught up in the adrenaline flows triggered by events that they disregard all dangers; and, then, others lacking any noticeable fear of death, or perhaps seeking death, seem to relish putting themselves into situations in which death is a very real possibility. [4]

Marines in battle situations, by nature of their training and character, fight with valor. Among the hundreds of thousands who have been in combat since the Corps' inception on November 10, 1775, a group of men have been recognized for bravery exceptional enough to be considered heroic. From the Civil War to today, 295 Marines have earned Medals of Honor, the nation's highest award for valor, primarily for actions in combat against an enemy force. They might have seemed ordinary to those who knew them before they were Marines, but these men rose above natural fear and acted honorably in moments of extreme peril.

Private Phillips and "Doc" Willis demonstrated bravery. Senior military officers recommended them for the Medal based on the Navy's and Corps' established standards. Their actions were investigated and scrutinized. Generally, their valor had to have been exemplary enough to clearly exceed the obligations of duty and markedly distinct from other common acts of bravery in combat. Their actions were uncontested by those present, beyond any justified criticism, and attested to by at least two eyewitnesses. Their bravery involved actions that unquestionably placed their lives at risk.

Recommendations for a Medal of Honor must provide proof that the Marine went "above and beyond the call of duty." The determination that the individual "acted fearlessly and unfalteringly in the face of certain death" is often cited. Such statements imply that he deliberately placed himself into a circumstance in which the outcome, death, was a certainty. Investigators seek certitude. The President of the United States will finally authorize this award only when its justification has been confirmed.

Did the Marine believe at the time that his actions would likely result in his death and act anyway? Did he give his own "certain death" a thought? Did he truly act deliberately or react impulsively and spontaneously?

Obviously, if the Marine survived the event, he might be able afterwards to relay what he was thinking at the time of his actions.

Examination of their Medal Citations suggests that 295 Marines repeatedly performed in certain ways to earn the nation's highest award for bravery in battle. They did what was asked for, or required, and more. Each volunteered for a challenging task potentially dangerous to his survival. They fended off enemy assaults, often of unequal odds. They initiated assaults that turned the outcome of enemy engagements. They demonstrated leadership that inspired others to act despite imminent danger. They sustained deliberateness of purpose despite extended duress. Each typically carried on his duties despite grievous, debilitating, and life-threatening wounds. They put themselves in harm's way, disregarding danger, to rescue others. And, they acted in defense of fellow combatants, even to their own risk.

Most Marine MOH recipients acted in defense of fellow combatants. Of the many ways to defend others in combat, sixty-nine recipients from World War II to the Afghanistan War covered a grenade with their bodies.

When It Comes to Grenades.

The U.S.-made Mark II ("Deuce"), manufactured from 1918 into the 1960s, was a recognizable hand grenade to the average American. Also called the Pineapple, the explosive was a 1.3-pound fragmentation grenade shaped like a lemon, but with a skin that looked like a pineapple. The cast iron grenade body, made to fit into an average-sized hand, had forty segments divided into a standard eight columns and five rows. Internally, the grenade was filled with an explosive like TNT and a fuse that served as a detonator.

The Mark II was designed with safety features for the protection of friendly troops. A safety lever, or "spoon" also serving as a "fly-off" lever, topped the grenade body. A safety pin and pull ring pierced the spoon, preventing it from striking the fuse and inadvertently charging the grenade. To free the safety lever, the pin had to be pulled out by the ring. Once the pin was pulled, the lever could be held compressed in the palm, preventing charging and detonation. If necessary, the pin could be repositioned into the handle, rendering the grenade safe again.

When the pin was pulled, the grenade could be thrown with the spoon still attached, and it would "fly off" as the weapon left the thrower's grasp. Releasing the spoon made a distinguishable sound, alerting the user that the fuse was charged and the detonation sequence initiated. Once the burn of the fuse started, it could not be halted. And, few Mark IIs were duds.

The normal fuse burn was four to four-point-eight seconds once the fly-off lever was released. By that point in time, the person who pulled the pin and released the handle was expected to have tossed the projectile a safe distance away, protecting the combatant from the explosion of metal shrapnel. The accepted throwing range was thirty-five to forty yards.

The TNT ignited at the end of the fuse burn, blasting away the forty iron segments in a high velocity projection. Normally, it was the metal fragments, or shrapnel, that were lethal, not the explosion itself. Fatal wounds became more probable the closer an individual was to the detonation. The odds of surviving the grenade's blast within an arm's length away were very low, because the Mark II had a certain killing radius of five to ten yards. Potentially, the projected metal fragments could be lethal out to fifty yards.

Whether enemy or friendly hands toss the deadly weapons, the concussion an exploding grenade creates is stunning and disorienting, the burst deafening, and the flash blinding.

All Marines are trained to handle and throw grenades at adversaries. Having observed such weapons detonate, most hope to never be in the proximity of an exploding grenade.

When Private Phillips and "Doc" Willis saw live grenades at their feet, they could be sure that the pending detonation would likely be deadly to nearby comrades.

If a Marine were alone in a trench and a grenade was lobbed in and landed at his feet, or if he dropped a live grenade in the trench as he tried to throw it, his reflexive actions would be predictable. No trained Marine alone in such a circumstance would feel the impulse to smother the explosion by jumping on top of the grenade. He would either quickly grab for the device to throw it from the trench, or he would just as quickly leap out of the trench to avoid the explosion. Marines do not look forward to one day jumping on a grenade.

Of the eighty-two Marines awarded the Medal of Honor in World War II, twenty-seven hurled themselves onto grenades to save fellow Marines. Twenty-three awards were presented posthumously. Of the forty-two Marines in the Korean War awarded Medals of Honor, sixteen dived onto grenades to save comrades. Twenty-three Marines saved others from grenades in Viet Nam. Two Marines have more recently earned Medals of Honor cradling grenades to preserve the lives of others in Iraq and Afghanistan. The life of each of these men provides a perspective into the nature of heroic bravery.

The first MOH Citation mentioning a Marine's life-threatening encounter with a grenade occurred during the Nicaraguan expedition, between the two World Wars. [5]

CHAPTER 3

A Medal Easier To Win Than To Wear

✳✳✳

"Fight or Die. That's what people do." [1]

—ERNEST HEMINGWAY

THE REALITY IN LIFE FOR some people is unquestionably to fight, escape, retreat, or die. Maybe the reaction is to the overall circumstances in the person's life, or to a series of experiences across a specific period, or maybe just to a one-time, powerful event. For Corporal Donald Leroy "Roy" Truesdell, all these influences seem to have melded together.

He called rural Lugoff his hometown—a small, populated place, "a community rooted in strong local traditions" in Kershaw County, southwest of Camden, South Carolina. [2] The county takes up about 781 square miles of southern land. Most of the people Donald knew, relatives and neighbors, belonged to farming families growing corn, the old, tough, yellow corn used to feed the animals and for canning for the winter. Lugoff is not considered prime farmland, but ample rain falls year-round, and the soils can also sustain wheat for grain, soybeans, peaches, tomatoes, and blackberries. From April to October, the "pickers" were in their fields harvesting crops. Pecan trees and walnut trees in the yards provided shade as well as nuts.

If Lugoff is notable outside of South Carolina today, it might be because it was also the hometown of rock and roll and rhythm and blues singer and songwriter Brook Benton (1931–1988). Today, few people would know that Don Truesdell and Brook Benton knew each other; in fact, they lived down the road from each other for a time.

According to the family histories recorded in Bibles and church rosters, Don could trace back five generations of relatives living in South Carolina. He and his five siblings were in the sixth generation.

It's in the Blood

The Truesdales left England in 1650 as part of Cromwell's invasion to drive the native Irish off their lands. They found fertile lowlands and isolated, rugged landscapes in the valleys around County Down, Province of Ulster, in the northeast regions of the island. They cleared the woodlands, drained bogs, built roads, fortified towns, and cultivated large plantations on the River Bann. Over the next century, the Presbyterian Truesdale families spread around Rathfriland and Kinghill Townland in Clonduff Parish, between Newry and Downpatrick. Colonists, tenants, and patent owners, their property holdings included mountain, marshland, pasture, and excellent arable cropland.

John Truesdale Jr., 20, married Mary "Molly" Hollingsworth, 18, in Kinghill in 1763. [3] The couple sailed for the American Colonies aboard the 250-ton brigantine *Free Mason* in

October 1772 to take advantage of King George's offer of 250 acres per family to settle in the Carolinas. Three children boarded with them: James, five years old, Sarah, four years old, and John III, three years old. [4] Their eldest boy, six-year-old Robert, did not immigrate to America with them, but stayed in Ireland with relatives. "Molly" delivered twin boys during the voyage. One they named Hollingsworth, after her maiden name. The other infant was stillborn, given the name "Seaborn," and was buried at sea before the family landed at the port of Charleston, South Carolina, in December.

It is uncertain if any of John's brothers—Samuel, Thomas, James, and Robert—ever left Ireland behind to seek a new life in the Colonies.

John, a Presbyterian farmer, was unable to pay the 250-acre warrant. He chose to settle his family on grant land in north-central South Carolina beneath the North Carolina border. The homestead was on a branch of Lynches Creek in the Flat Rock township between Camden, the present Kershaw County seat, and Heath Springs.

The Truesdales added another daughter to the family. Mary was born in 1774. Then, their last child, Jesse, was born in 1776, just as the Colonists were planning a rebellion.

Hoping to join his family in South Carolina, John Jr's 16-year-old son, Robert, left Ireland in 1782, during the American Revolutionary War. He was never heard from again and is believed to have died and been buried at sea. John and Molly would not learn of Robert's death until an exchange of letters with family in Kinghill in 1792.

John joined the Colonists as a private in Colonel Joseph Kershaw's Regiment, South Carolina Militia. Serving forty days in 1783, fighting against England and the Tories, Private Truesdale received 300 acres of "Bounty Land" on June 5, 1786. The acres were on Hanging Rock Creek, west of Kershaw Town.

Both of John and Molly's daughters married before he died and provided him many grandchildren. Neither daughter stayed in Kershaw. Sarah married Samuel Jones, had a son and four daughters, and relocated to Alabama before any consideration of breaking up the newly formed states stirred in the lands she had migrated to as a child. Mary Truesdale married Sterling Horton around 1800, and they had twelve children. Sterling moved the family down to Taylor County in west central Georgia.

Little is known of twin Hollingsworth's life. He married Eleanor Small shortly after 1800, and their first son was born in Kershaw County in 1806. He acquired land across the line in Lancaster County and bought a portion of the original family land on September 18, 1817. By the 1820 Census, he and Eleanor had eight children at home and five laborers. Hollingsworth did not own slaves. After 1820, he moved his family to Lauderdale County, in the northwest corner of Alabama. In the 1830 Census, he is recorded to have a family of six free white males and three free white females. He died in late 1849. The *Florence Gazetter* announced on February 9, 1850, that his son, John N. Truesdel, had been appointed administrator for Hollingsworth Truesdel's estate. [6]

Patriarch Truesdale's two older boys had large families, and many of their children did not get to know their grandfather. Raised in the life of a "Planter," James Rembert Truesdale (1767–1859) became a Methodist. In 1797, he married Rebecca Ussery (1785–1860) from King William County, Virginia, and settled in Pleasant Hill, Lancaster County. Census records note that they had fifteen children.

According to a family Bible, John III (1769–1852) married Nancy McDonald in 1797 and remained a Presbyterian like his father, farming on several plantations. He held the original immigrant grant land. Of his eight children, seven survived to adulthood and lived out their lives in Flat Rock.

John Truesdale Jr. died in 1806.

In the 1810 Census, the Widow Molly was living with John III. In addition to farming, her son had a mill and produced 170 yards of cloth annually. He owned eight slaves.

Molly joined her husband in death in 1815. She and John Jr. are buried in unmarked graves at Robert Floyd's home place above Kershaw toward Heath Springs.

By 1840, John III owned extensive holdings and fifty-six slaves. When he wrote out his *Last Will and Testament* before his death in 1852, he owned a house, plantations, hundreds of acres, and 107 slaves. [5] There were no Cherokee Indians in his household. He bequeathed "to my wife Nancy the dwelling house and 200 acres, 100 bought of John Chestnut and 100 of Robert Mahaffey, lying on creek below Hanging Rock bridge." John and Nancy Truesdel are buried in Hanging Rock Churchyard.

John Henry Truesdale was James and Rebecca's fifth child, born to them in 1807. John Henry got around Kershaw and Heath Springs and got along very well with the Thomas and Nancy Cauthen family. Thomas was a Revolutionary War patriot who happened to have eight girls and four boys at home. Once reaching manhood, J. Henry married Druscilla Cauthen. Their first child, James, was born in 1830, and they would have eleven more children, the last born in 1856. It turned out that the twelve would also have a good number of half-siblings.

Druscilla's older sister, Mary Matilda Cauthen, had been married to Joseph West. In April 1825, Matilda was pregnant for the first time, and her father provided her a negro woman named Jensey (Jenney) under a Deed of Gift. Shortly after Cynthia Louisa West was born, Joseph left Matilda a widow. Records indicate that said Matilda afterwards intermarried to John Truesdell and had three boys and four daughters. Their first child was born in 1832, and the birth records make it appear that Matilda gave birth in between the years that Druscilla had her babies. Matilda's last child was born in 1845. [7] Cynthia Louisa married James R. Hunter, who would serve as the Lancaster County Sheriff for a long time.

A reflection of the antebellum era, John Truesdell, by virtue of his marital rights, took possession of negro Jenney and her increase (nine children and six grandchildren) and retained and kept possession of them. Jenney's children were Phill, Charity, Jack, Mose, Sarah, Peter, Essex, Ellen, and Lenina. Charity's children were Jane, Mary, Mariah, Milley, and Amanda. Sarah had one child named Martha. [8]

South Carolinians had been advocating secessionist impulses as early as 1830 and continued to protest "Northern anti-slavery" aggression into the early 1850s when the crisis smoldered nearly to a boil.

James counseled his sons, all of them slave holders. Rebecca as much worried for her children as she did for the state leaving the Union. Sixteen-year-old Sarah "Sallie" had married Samuel King Jones on Christmas Eve 1818 and began having a newborn every other year—eleven sons and five daughters. With their first eleven children, Sam and Sallie moved down to Opelika in east-central Alabama, near the Georgia border. Their older two daughters both died at age 29: Elizabeth in 1850 and Rebecca in 1854. Then, Sallie died four days after her 36th wedding anniversary in 1854. She would not learn of her boys putting on the Gray to fight for the Confederacy.

As decisions about the Mason-Dixon Line closed in on the southern states, John Henry Truesdale died on February 2, 1858. Lewis M. Cauthen, the administrator of his estate, had to determine who were the distributees and heirs at law. In addition to widow Matilda, slaves were to be given and advanced to the "Truesdell" sons and married daughters: wives of C.L. Duncan, James Hunter, John Stover, and William Stover. Four of the Truesdell children were not of age to inherit property. Per the final Agreement and Terms of Settlement that all the involved parties signed and X'd on May 23, 1858, James and Cynthia Louisa Hunter gave up all claim, wanting to take no part or share of the named negroes, releasing them into the ownership of other heirs.

James Truesdale went to his eternal rest in 1859 and Rebecca to hers on September 11, 1860. They had departed Pleasant Hill and were buried in Hanging Rock United Methodist Church Cemetery.

Two months after Rebecca's burial, South Carolina's congressmen declared Abraham Lincoln's election a hostile act. A secession convention was convened on December 17, 1860, and three days later South Carolina became the first southern state to severe affiliation with the United States.

Three of J. Henry and Druscilla's boys would serve honorably in the Confederate forces. One of J. Henry and Mary Matilda's boys died before the national turmoil began and their sons went to war. Mary also died in 1860, months before Confederate canons fired on Fort Sumter in Charleston Harbor.

The Truesdale family lines blurred a bit, as fathers, sons, brothers, uncles, nephews and cousins answered the muster calls.

Confederate War Turmoils

Colonel J.B. Kershaw began organizing the 2d South Carolina Volunteers (S.C.V.) in February 1861. Young men from the Kershaw, Lancaster, Richland, and Charleston counties mustered in. [9]

Second Lieutenant James Thomas Truesdale/Truesdell (1830–1919) served first in the 2d S.C.V., then as a member of Troup K, 7th South Carolina Calvary. Known as "Squire" Truesdell, he farmed in Westville, Kershaw County, after the war. He held the office of Magistrate in Flat Rock for nearly half a century and "was known as the terror of evil doers." [10] Having been widowed and remarried, he applied for a Pension for Service on May 12, 1919. His widow Mary (Gay) reapplied for his pension on January 4, 1921.

His battle-scarred brother, John Rutledge Truesdale (1834–1916) was remembered as one of Kershaw's bravest, having given four years of valiant service to the Confederate cause. [11]

Their younger brother, J. Henry Truesdale Jr. (1845–1926), later of West Wateree, Camden, served first in the 2d S.C.V., then with Troup K, 7th South Carolina Calvary. [12] On February 29, 1872, Henry married Sallie Ella Parker (1853–1938), a girl from Lugoff. They had three daughters. Their son, Willie Truesdale, died in 1896 at age 10 years. Henry, one of the few "gallant old Confederate veterans" in the county, applied for his Pension for Service on April 3, 1919. Henry and Sallie, their children, and twenty-one other Truesdales are buried in Quaker Cemetery in Camden.

James T. Truesdale was J. Henry and Mary Matilda's fourth child, born in 1839 in Kershaw County. He had married Martha Ann Rollings before the hostilities erupted with the North. He was among the 3,650 Union and Confederate soldiers killed along Antietam Creek in Sharpsburg, northwestern Maryland, on September 17, 1862—the bloodiest one-day battle of the Civil War. [13]

Jesse Erasmus Truesdale (1834–1885), born in Flat Rock, was a distant cousin, the sixth child of a farmer and a great-grandson of John Jr. of North Ireland. He was an original member of the Flat Rock Guards, then, joined a company of the 2d S.C.V. on January 16, 1861. He mustered in to the Confederate Army at Camp Davis near Richmond, Virginia, on May 22, 1861, and was promoted to 3d Lieutenant before the year ended. On May 13, 1862, he was elected to 1st Lieutenant.

Lieutenant Truesdale's younger brother, William Jasper Truesdale, was eighth born in the family. He mustered in as a private in Company G, 2d S.C.V., on April 24, 1861. A month later, on May 22, he was with the Confederate Army at Richmond, Virginia, and was promoted to corporal on December 21.

In June 1862, General Robert E. Lee's Army of Northern Virginia prepared to stop Union Major General George B. McClellan's Union Army of the Potomac advance on Richmond. Generals Stonewall Jackson, D. H. Hill, and A. P. Hill met with Lee at the Dabbs House headquarters. The Seven Days Battles began on June 25. Within days, McClellan's army was in a general withdrawal to the James River. The Battle of Savage's Station took place on June 29. Kershaw's brigade advanced on the Union forces in late afternoon. Corporal W. J. Truesdale, 21, was killed in the action, dying "of face wounds."

1st Lieutenant Jesse Truesdale was severely wounded in action at Gettysburg on July 2, 1862. He remained in the service and was promoted to a captain's rank on July 4, 1863. Invalided home to Flat Rock in August 1863, he last presented for muster roll on June 30, 1864. Jesse married Amanda Elizabeth Stephenson on January 25, 1865, and they raised seven Truesdale children in Buffalo Township, Kershaw County. After the war, he was known as a well-to-do farmer.

A company of 16-year-old boys from Lancaster and Kershaw counties formed when it was decided in the summer of 1864, that all males between the ages of 16 and 60 were liable for service. Third Sergeant James Truesdale, born in 1848, served in Company I, 3rd Regiment, Junior Reserves, South Carolina State Troops. [14] The company stood guard and picket duty in various places in the state. Third Sergeant Truesdale served from November 1864 to early April 1865.

Private George C. Truesdell joined Company E, Evan's Tramp Brigade, 17th South Carolina Infantry Regiment, out of York County. He was promoted to second lieutenant and was among the Confederate casualties at Hewlett's Farm and Ware Bottom Church, Virginia, on May 20, 1864, before the siege of Petersburg. He was paroled with the Army of Northern Virginia at the Appomattox Court House on April 9, 1865.

Southerners experienced the agonies associated to having been defeated in war. For most people in the decimated South there was no money in circulation. Beyond the loss of sons and economic disaster, the miseries also included humiliation and loss of dignity. While Northerners recovered from the war, maybe even gloated, Southerners grieved.

One way they adapted and learned to manage was to "soldier on" and to "suffer on bravely." There was no point in complaining or whining—neither of those outlets changed a thing. Character demanded going on, doing what had to be done until a new day dawned, with the expectation that the new day would be no different than the current day. Many, despairing and depleted of any resilience, eventually did not wait for the new day. The vanquished do not bounce back in a single generation.

Zachariah Taylor "Zack" Truesdale (1847) was born in Hanging Rock, the ninth-born child of John Henry and Mary Truesdale, and their fifth boy. He was 13 years old when his mother died. When the Civil War erupted, his two oldest brothers had already married and moved from the family dwelling. Zack had celebrated his 17th birthday on June 22, 1864, when the Confederacy declared him liable for service. The conflict was resolved before he had to stand picket duty. He married Mittie Emma Parker in Hanging Rock, and they had eight children. Earl Trantham, born in 1882, was their fifth child. At times, the men wrote their surname as it was pronounced—Truesdell.

Zack was a business partner with his brother, Henry, in a West Wateree plantation and a Camden mercantile business. Neighbors believed that he and his wife were "in very comfortable circumstances."

Measured by post war standards, the Truesdales were relatively well off. [15] Photographs showed them to be handsome men and lovely ladies, and they had good-looking children. Yet, there was little in their lives to smile about. Humor was tenuous at best. The Truesdales kept their emotions to themselves. Life was as it was. A person did what had to be done. Farm life meant that there was always some pet dying or something being killed. [16] Each generation managed the loss of family members and funeral services at gravesites. As the men lived out their years, they tended toward drawn and defeated facial expressions and looked older than their ages.

Zack and Mittie raised their crops and reared their children in the two-floor "Big House" in West Wateree. A nice staircase led up to the second floor. Due to the danger of fire created by wood burning stoves, the kitchen was away from the house and connected by a covered walkway. Since there was no refrigeration, a small, low, spring house built over a spring in the back yard kept food as cool as possible. A jostling board on the front porch gave young people a place to sit and bounce.

The property also had a smoke house, with an attached laundry area, a barn with stalls for horses, mules, and cows, storage for hay for the animals, and a chicken coop one could stoop down to go into to gather the eggs. Down in a field, out of sight of the house, was a small house used for the black people who "helped out." They received their housing and food and small wages.

The family ate many meatless meals, despite having livestock. In addition to the horses and mules that plowed and pulled the wagon for hauling crops and going to town, the Truesdales raised cows, pigs, and chickens. The cows provided milk and were seldom butchered. The one or two calves each cow birthed in a year had greater value than meat on the table. The pigs were spared as well for the litters they could farrow. Around the yard, a rooster or two kept the chickens producing fertilized eggs that hatched into more chicks. So, it was chicken or pork when the family did have meat. Zack kept whatever hams he could salt and smoke hanging in the smokehouse.

On weekly wash day, a couple of black women would take the huge black pot out of the barn, place it on an open fire, fill it with water, add some sort of soap and dirty clothes, and then stir the mixture with a long stick until the clothes were clean. It was exhausting work.

Eli Manning and Sarah Henrietta (Moseley) Lee had migrated from Sumter County with their children and lived near the Truesdales. Much poorer than the neighbors, they had ten children—too many to feed. Margaret Elizabeth "Maggie" Lee (1880) was their third child, the second oldest of five girls. As a child, she was sent to live with a more affluent family. Living for some time with a family with food to spare, she had seen a better way of life.

When "Maggie" returned to the Lee family, some of her sisters thought that she put on airs and acted like she was better than the rest of them. She preferred to be called Miss Margaret and was not amused with family addressing her by the less formal name. She had learned that there was a better life, and, for the rest of her days, she did her best to keep up her Southern Lady appearances.

If the family stayed in contact with their distant relatives, they would have known that J. Henry's stepdaughter, Cynthia Louisa, had died. James R. Hunter, 66, the Lancaster jailer, survived her and had lived as "almost an invalid" for two years. Word spread like wildfire on

June 4, 1888, that he had committed suicide at 4-o'clock in the morning; shooting himself through the head with a 44-caliber Smith & Wesson pistol, "for the purpose of ending his sufferings." The news "was received with saddest regrets," especially by his many children, one of whom was the present county sheriff. [17]

The Truesdales and Lees and all their children got together on Sundays. When the wagon left from the Truesdales to visit the Lees, everyone went. The same was true when the Lees visited at the Big House. Margaret Lee was most impressed with the Truesdale's house and pinned her hopes on getting engaged to Ernest Truesdale, who had his hopes on becoming a physician. Ernest's younger brother, Earl, took a liking to "Maggie."

Earl T. had three little sisters; Sallie Daisy was the youngest, born on July 7, 1890. Earl had his 9th birthday in February 1891. During that year around the Big House and in the fields, he heard vague whispers, strange words, which he did not understand. His father had made some sort of attempt. Earl had no idea what "aberration of mind" meant. He would not understand the words any better in September.

On a Friday morning, a year after his last child was born, Zachariah Truesdale, aged 44, ran out of resilience for life, and his earthly career came to a close. He gained his eternal rest on September 4, 1891. The short notice in the newspaper reported that he had committed suicide with a shotgun. [18] His was the second interment in Saint John's Methodist Cemetery in Lugoff—the first in the family to be buried there.

Zachariah's tombstone, easily identified by the hand grasping a broken chain engraved at the top, stands taller than the brick wall that now encloses half of the small cemetery. Mittie outlived him by forty-two years and was buried beside him in 1933. Over the decades, three of their daughters and one son would be interred near them. [19]

Irishmen

The Rosborough ancestors were Irishmen who had spread out through Fairfield County, miles above Lugoff. They were true-blue Southerners and proud Confederates. James Thomas Rosborough, son of a doctor, had enlisted as a private in Company D, Sixth North Carolina Infantry, when he was attending a military school. He fought at the battles of Bull Run and Gettysburg, was promoted to a captain's rank, and was wounded at Malvern Hill and Sharpsburg. He served with the Confederate Army until May 20, 1865.

In 1861, Samuel Yongue Rosborough, 30, had joined the Cedar Creek Rifles, Company C, 12th Regiment, South Carolina Infantry, and served as a first lieutenant. Samuel C. Rosborough was a neighbor to the Truesdales. He had served under P.W. Goodwin's Orangeburg Company C, 6th South Carolina Cavalry Regiment, CSA, known as "The Carolina Guerrillas."

James A. Rosborough was not quite four years old when the Civil War ended. As a grown man, he earned a reputation as a "Woodman of the World" and had his eye on Zack and Mittie's second daughter. Jim, 34, married 20-year-old Leila Brewer Truesdale. Their first son, Edward, was born in 1894. At that time, Leila's brother, Earl T. was near his adolescent years. Karl Rosborough was born to the couple in 1896, and their third boy, James Jr, was born in 1901.

Much to Margaret Lee's disappointment, Ernest Truesdale, did not become her beau. One day, Ernie took a train ride and had a water stop in Bethune, a very small town chartered in 1900, twelve miles east of Lugoff on the Lynches River. Daniel Murdock Bethune, his brother, and other family were Scotsmen—pioneer men who had come to till the South Carolina soils with others like the McCaskills, McLaurins, McNaulls, and Shaws. When the Seaboard Railroad was laying down track toward Columbia, it had crossed Daniel's property, thus the town's new name.

Ernest met the Bethunes and married the refined Christine Cornelia Bethune (1883), "a woman of noble and Christian character." He went down to Charleston to attend the Medical College of South Carolina. By the time the doctor had "slipped away," Margaret had already married his younger brother.

Margaret E. Lee married the slightly younger Earl Trantham Truesdale on Wednesday, February 18, 1902, six days after his 21st birthday. The story the Lee family passed down is that, while out horseback riding, "Maggie" went to the parsonage on a dare, and she and Earl married on horseback in front of the minister. Her life did not turn out as genteel as she would have liked. While the Truesdales owned land, they were not affluent.

They named their first child Earl Jr. The infant died on March 10, 1903, the day he was born, and was buried in Saint John's Methodist Cemetery near his paternal grandfather. Earl and Margaret's first daughter, Edna, was born on August 19, 1905. She would be a big sister before her first birthday. Margaret was soon expecting her third child and wanting a better life than the one she had.

Earl was not a farmer by interest or ability. He also faced the impact of forces that had taken place 36,000 years earlier.

The Atlantic Ocean had reached to Columbia before the last great ice age began. As ocean water gradually transformed into glaciers, massive ice sheets blanketed the north, and global sea levels dropped, the oceans retreated into their basins. Starting along the U.S. 1 corridor through the Carolinas, seven sandy beach areas terraced the flat lands between Columbia and the modern shoreline. The fine, white sands made the porous soil nutrient-poor, and only hearty, well-adapted plants, like scrub vegetation and various species of pine and oak trees, prospered naturally. Peach trees could do well, but the sandy soil was not good for growing crops. Farming required significant irrigation. The Truesdale property in Lugoff sits on one of the old beaches. [20]

Options were limited for Earl, but his family had to eat. So, he and Margaret worked hard, doing things they did not like, all to keep the family going. The farming family was very poor. Growing a cash crop of cotton was the only way to get money. The black laborers helped plant, chop, harvest, and bale the cotton—hard, backbreaking work done in the heat and humidity of summer. There were no tractors. Plowing was done behind a mule or horse pulling the plow. Hot, dirty, mind-numbing work. Cotton sales covered taxes, seed for the next crop, the laborers' wages, and any food staples that could not be grown. After that, ready cash was in short supply.

Breakfast was the important meal. Margaret was up early, lighting a kerosene lantern so she could prepare breakfast over a wood-burning stove before she had to get Earl out the door to plow, hoe, deal with large animals, and manage the farm. Then, she would collect eggs from the chicken coop: a nasty business. Chickens do not give up eggs peacefully. They flew up and fluttered around her head with feathers and dust flying all over as she reached into the nest.

Egg gathering accomplished, Margaret milked the cows in the barn. Back to the house to deal with her baby, straighten house, do the canning and preserving and baking, and prepare the midday meal. Another big meal to fuel up for the afternoon's labors. Southerners called it dinner.

Margaret heated up her iron on the stove to get the wrinkles out of clothing. Soon pregnant again, she would have more clothes to stitch and sew. Whenever she sat down, she was mending, crocheting, or churning. There was no spring near Earl and Margaret's property, no springhouse to keep food or milk cool, so she had to plan and prepare the menu to coincide with meal times. As afternoon faded, she turned her attention to getting supper ready.

The third meal of the day was smaller, because bedtime came early. Everyone had to be rested and ready to repeat the tiring routine the next day. On Sundays, she killed, cleaned, and picked a chicken or two for the afternoon dinner. Of course, then, the family dined on fried chicken.

Both Earl Truesdale and Margaret Lee had been born after the war, but had relatives who had lived through the violence, depravation, deaths, and destruction, and who passed stories down to the younger generations. Margaret would tell her children and grandchildren the stories of who had ridden along local stretches of road announcing the arrival of Yankees in the area and where the family had found hiding places for their silver.

Margaret let her dignity drop occasionally, but only a little. She never said "Yankee" without disdain and prefacing the label with "Damn." [21]

The Truesdales were Methodist. Earl had helped build St. John's Methodist Church just south of Highway 1 in Lugoff. The men voted Democrat, since the Yankees and Abe Lincoln had been Republicans. Margaret, all women, and the black citizens had no rights to cast their votes.

The Truesdale and Lee families joined together for another marriage when Earl's younger sister, Mittie Emma Truesdale, married John Kershaw Lee, Margaret's younger brother.

Margaret had been a Truesdale wife for four years on April 18, 1906, and she was five months along with another child. At 8:12 AM, she and Earl had been busy with farm chores for hours. Lugoff is 2,711 miles east of San Francisco, so they did not feel it.

A 7.8-magnitude earthquake struck San Francisco at 5:12 AM Northern California time. Fires ravaged the city of 410,000 residents for three days. More than 3,000 people died, and over 80% of the city was destroyed in the disaster. In addition to the death toll, between 227,000 and 300,000 people were made homeless.

That was all very newsworthy and made the front pages of *The Kershaw News-Era* and the daily Columbia *The State*. But, the earthquake and San Francisco great fire was not a topic of discussion at any of the Truesdale meal times. There were no cars and no newspaper delivery. There was no electricity, no electric lights, and no radios or television. On the rare occasion when they drove a wagon seven miles into Camden, they did not "waste" money on a newspaper. They were not much interested in San Francisco. The focus was on working hard and surviving. Food, shelter, clothing. Realistic as that might be, Margaret would have reason later, when her first boy was a man, to fear that he was much closer, possibly in the midst of, a devastating Pacific coast earthquake.

Donald Leroy "Roy" Truesdale was born on August 26, 1906, in Lugoff.

Three months after Roy's birth, on November 6, 1906, Republican President Theodore "Teddy" Roosevelt, the 26th U.S. President, started a 17-day trip to the Panama Canal Zone to check on the progress of his "Great Enterprise" under construction since 1904. It was the first time a sitting U.S. president traveled outside the continental United States to make an official diplomatic tour while in office.

No one in Lugoff had any appreciation for Teddy Roosevelt. The Truesdales could not have known that the president's policies would personally affect their family in the future. Donald Truesdale would sail to that region twenty-five years later to protect Americans against dangerous bandits.

In the heat of the next summer, 1907, the attention of the extended families concentrated on matters close to home. Typhoid fever would claim the lives of Truesdale and Lee kin. Maggie's 22-year-old brother, Robert, died of the fever on July 2, 1907. A week later, Earl's nephew, Leila's first boy, Edward Rosborough, died on July 8, two days before his 13th birthday. Then, 23-year-old Christine Bethune Truesdale fell ill and was taken to the hospital in Columbia for treatment. She held on to life for three months, hoping to get home to her husband and infant son. She died on September 21, 1907, leaving behind a host of relatives and dear friends. [22]

Fewer than two years later, still reeling from the death of her son, Earl's sister was made a widow. James Rosborough, 60, died on May 20, 1909. Leila was left with the farm and two boys to raise.

Life around Lugoff was pragmatic and hardly romantic. Everyone in Kershaw County understood that a farming life is more productive when the responsibilities are divided between a husband and wife. Widows and widowers both tended to remarry very shortly after the death of a spouse.

Thomas Orren Lee was Margaret's oldest sibling. He served in the United States Army and was 22 years old when an explosion sank the Battleship Maine in Havana Harbor on February 15, 1898. The United States declared war on Spain on April 25. The Treaty of Paris ended the Spanish-American War on December 10, 1898. T. Orren served out his time after the war and returned to farm in Lugoff.

Leila Brewer Truesdale Rosborough and T. Orren married. They had one son.

Doctor Ernest Truesdale graduated as a physician four years after his wife had died. He established his medical practice in Bethune and married Christine's older sister, Catherine Isabell "Kate" Bethune (1881–1974), a Winthrop College graduate. They had a son together. [23]

Life went on. "Roy" was a big brother three times, having two little sisters and a brother: Lois (1908), Marguerite (1910), and Ebin Trantham (1912). With two paternal uncles and four aunts and three maternal uncles and four aunts spread throughout Kershaw and Lancaster counties, he also had many Truesdale and Lee cousins.

All the Truesdale children walked to school, either in Lugoff or to the one in Camden. It was a childhood experience they would recall when they were adults with their own families. When the relatives gathered later, they talked a lot about walking and told the younger generations great stories about their walks. A favorite was how one day they were walking home from school as darkness was falling. They came upon a man who was also walking, but he had no head.

Roy's older sister was the most serious among the six siblings. When the story was told within the hearing of nieces and nephews, Aunt Edna vouched for its authenticity. That knitted the natural conclusion. "So, it must be true." [24]

Since getting around was generally on foot, and blackberries grew wild on bushes along the roadside and in the woods, Roy and the Truesdale kids picked them to take home. Margaret made the berries into jams, jellies, and pies for the family. She harvested tomatoes, sweet potatoes and Irish potatoes, carrots, collard greens, green beans, peas, and various other vegetables from her "kitchen garden" canning for the winter, "putting up" food to see the family through until there was another crop. There was no electricity, no air conditioning. Margaret worked over the wood-burning, iron "stove," day in and day out, all summer long.

She was a proud woman, wanting always to better her family. Married for ten years, her life was all about working, and she never had enough to keep her growing family in the style she fancied. She kept up appearances, making sure she and Edna had a couple sets of nice clothes. They were the two to represent the family in public at church, funerals, and weddings, giving her some opportunities to wear her pearl necklace. Very much a Southern Lady, she never raised her voice: did not have to, because she could give a look that scared everyone anyway. Earl and the rest of the children stayed home to hide how poor the family remained.

As the children grew up, Margaret was watchful for symptoms of any infectious or dietary diseases that they might catch, like beriberi and scurvy. Outbreaks of those calamitous illnesses were known to be associated with South Carolina poverty. Pellagra cases, another nutritional deficiency disease, occurred in the late spring before the summer crops had been harvested. When it turned hot and humid and rainy, mothers who had heard of the Civil War epidemics worried about dysentery—"the bloody flux."

Roy was eight years old in 1914.

At first, no one paid much attention. Weakness, fatigue, muscle aches, sweating, and headaches seemed common elements in the farming life. More alarm sounded when adults and children in the county started having low fevers, severe abdominal pains, and diarrhea and constipation. When word spread of neighbors becoming delirious, so did the panic.

Doctor Ernest Truesdale worked diligently day and night to treat anyone who contracted a fever. All in the family survived the 1914 typhoid epidemic that swept through eastern Kershaw County.

Roy, Lois, Marguerite, and E.T. had a limited existence—work and a little schooling. They did not go anywhere. Maybe on a Sunday when a horse or mule was not needed for work, the family would hitch up a wagon and go somewhere to visit. They did not know anything. Everyone did what was necessary to get by. When the two young boys needed disciplining, a belt or switch whipping was Earl's tool for teaching lessons. He was not one to "spare the rod." Although Truesdale's did not whine or complain about their fair in life, none of the children could say that they had a happy childhood.

To have something to play with, Lois once made a doll from a corn cob. She viewed their existence to be not much better than the animals around the farm. Lois was so mortified about her childhood, that when she married Stephen C. Clyburn in 1930 and had her first baby at the Camden hospital, she told the staff that she was an orphan. [25]

The Truesdales survived another epidemic when Roy was 11 years old. South Carolina experienced its first serious outbreak of influenza in spring 1918, during the widespread WWI flu epidemic.

Being big for his age and physically strong did not make growing up in Lugoff easier for Roy. He was not much interested in a school education. Instead, he wanted to contribute pennies to the family funds. He quit walking to school after four years.

Earl woke him up before dawn, and the two walked miles together to work at a local sawmill. Roy carried slabs and earned 6 cents an hour, working 10-hour days—amounting to a 60¢ day's wage. Maybe a pittance, but plenty of people waited for the work anytime he felt like quitting. [26] He stayed.

On days off, Roy liked to explore and hunt in the vast woods. Deer, gophers, geese, and ducks were abundant in the wilds. Thick forests of oaks, pines, myrtles, dogwoods, sweetgum, maple, and magnolia trees accounted for about 70% of the county's land. The trees shared ground with shrubs, grass, ferns, mosses, and lichens.

Roy grew adept at picking out barberry, holly, paperbush, peashrub, sphagnum moss, willows, and cordgrass. He traversed swamps, marshes, and bogs in the wetlands and liked to follow the Twenty-Five Mile Creek until it flowed into the Wateree River. In his boyhood, he learned to survive alone in the wild, drinking water from the streams and cooking squirrels.

Hunting for rabbits and squirrels for dinner was like a pastime for him. His comfort as a woodsman was going to serve him well.

Severe poverty continued to plague the Truesdales and the people of the South. Earl relocated his family up to Baltimore around World War I to find work in a shipyard or factory. [27] Maryland was one of the border states that had strong sympathies toward both the Confederate and Union sides during the Civil War. What a change. At the time, Baltimore was ranked eighth in size in the United States, in the range of 733,826 residents, and the urban population in the city's twenty wards was diverse.

Having migrated to the congested northern city, the Truesdales encountered families of all sorts of racial and ethnic backgrounds, the largest being African Americans. Germans, Irish, English, French, Greek, Eastern Europeans, and Romani families from Hungary and Spain clustered into their own neighborhoods. Small pockets of Chinese and Japanese-born immigrants also joined the work force. Even descendants of the original Piscataway and Cherokee tribes resided on their own blocks.

Earl found a place to live on West Saratoga Street, just above the city's north-south dividing line. Predominantly residential, block after block of row homes and single-family houses, the street ran from downtown to the railroad yards, factory district, and Gwynns Falls stream on the western edge of the city.

For a boy at home in 473,000 acres of forests and wetlands, the big city was a drastic change for Roy. Whenever he had a chance, he took his sisters and brother on a North Fulton Avenue streetcar to play up in Druid Hill Park, north of downtown. The old city park provided more than 700 acres of trails, fields, rolling hills, gardens, a lake and ponds, and the Baltimore City Zoo. While there, the children could believe for a while that they were back in Kershaw County.

The Truesdales did not stay long in Baltimore.

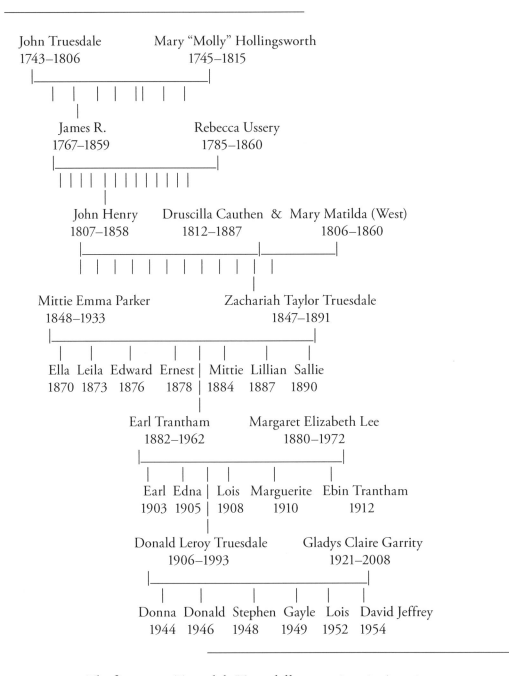

John Truesdale   Mary "Molly" Hollingsworth
1743–1806   1745–1815

James R.   Rebecca Ussery
1767–1859   1785–1860

John Henry   Druscilla Cauthen & Mary Matilda (West)
1807–1858   1812–1887   1806–1860

Mittie Emma Parker   Zachariah Taylor Truesdale
1848–1933   1847–1891

Ella   Leila Edward   Ernest │ Mittie Lillian Sallie
1870 1873   1876   1878   │ 1884   1887   1890

Earl Trantham   Margaret Elizabeth Lee
1882–1962   1880–1972

Earl Edna │ Lois Marguerite Ebin Trantham
1903 1905 │ 1908 1910   1912

Donald Leroy Truesdale   Gladys Claire Garrity
1906–1993   1921–2008

Donna Donald Stephen Gayle Lois David Jeffrey
1944   1946   1948   1949   1952 1954

The first seven Truesdale/Truesdell generations in America.

CHAPTER 4

Proud to Claim the Title

✳✳✳

"There's no such thing as a former Marine."

—General James F. Amos, 35th Commandant of the Marine Corps
April 2011

DONALD TRUESDALE WAS NOT YET a teenager when the United States Marines demonstrated valor in the fields and trenches during World War I. His cousin Private First Class Karl T. Rosborough had served with the South Carolina National Guard, and was assigned to Company A, 306th Ammunition Train Headquarters & Military Police. The soldiers were at Camp Mills, New York, training for deployment to France, and sailed from the States in May 1918, en route to Liverpool, England.

After a brief stay in a rest camp, PFC Rosborough embarked at Southampton for Le Havre. From June to September he participated in the occupation of the Lagney Sector, the Lucey Sector, and the Marbache Sector of Lorraine. Then he participated in the St-Mihiel and the Meuse-Argonne operations. He stayed in France for six months after the Armistice and returned to the U.S. for demobilization in May 1919. Don was 12 years old when his cousin returned to Lugoff.

Five years later in 1924, Don had the idea of joining the Navy. Enlistments in the Navy and Marine Corps had been four years long. The law changed on July 1, 1924, making enlistments for two-, three-, four-, or six-year terms. Proportionate benefits were established for reenlisting after a discharge of service. Any man under the age of 21 years making application had to show proof of age and written consent of his parent or guardian.

Earl drove his son, three months past his 18th birthday, the thirty miles over to Columbia to enlist. The Navy recruiter was gone from the station for the day, but a Marine recruiter was on duty. On the wall over his shoulder, a WWI poster advertised the office to be a DEVIL DOG RECRUITING STATION. A fierce bulldog with an eagle, globe, and anchor emblem on his helmet chased a frightened, black dachshund, tail between his legs and wearing a spiked helmet with the German eagle coat of arms insignia, off the side of the poster. The poster declared that the Germans had nicknamed the U.S. Marines the "Teufel Hunden." [1]

The recruiter took a good look at the strapping young man, standing 6 feet tall, weighing in just under two hundred pounds, wanting to join the Navy. He saw Marine material. And, as they are known to do, the recruiter made a convincing case for joining his Corps. The pay was the same as the Navy's, and Don and Earl would not have to drive back and forth again to catch the Navy recruiter at work. [2] Marines stayed on the job past quitting time. And, Parris Island would be "a cake walk" for a strong boy right off the farm.

Parris Island, 160 road miles from the Truesdale farm, had a history. The first Marines had landed in the area on November 2, 1861, to seize the port and secure it for the Union Navy to use during the Civil War. That was back in the day when the Union had "wooden ships manned by iron men." In November 1910, plans were circulated to change the base's mission from a detention center to a training depot for three companies of recruits. Then, beginning in 1917, to meet the demands of the ongoing World War, the depot installations underwent expansion, and training instructions were revamped to ready raw Marines for trench warfare. The depot was officially designated as Marine Barracks, Parris Island. [3]

The recruits at Parris Island would be reminded of the *Leathernecks* who had distinguished themselves on the front lines in France and of the many accounts of glory. On July 25, 1924, three months before Don and Earl walked into the recruiting office, Major General John A. Lejeune, 13th Commandant of the Marine Corps, had presided over a ceremony, unveiling a bronze statue on Panama Street near the Depot's Taylor Shop.

Iron Mike, 8 feet tall and dressed for battle, stood atop a white stone monument, sleeves rolled up to his elbows, his outstretched left hand defiantly pointing a pistol at the sky, and his right hand holding a Colt–Vickers M1915 machine gun slung over his shoulder. The statue was dedicated to the Marines who had fought, and died, in France and would inspire the columns of recruits who marched past it.

The Marine recruiter even pitched the idea of boot camp with a little humor.

One Boot said to another, "I hear that the drill sergeant called you a blockhead."

"No," his pal answered. "He didn't make it that strong."

"What did he actually say?"

"Put on your hat, here comes a woodpecker." [4]

Whether the legendary tales about the rigors of Marine Corps training were factual, fables, exaggerations, or understatements, it did not matter; Don was more impressed with heroism than intimidated by boot camp. He entered the USMC as a private on November 25, 1924, and relocated to a two-story wooden barracks to spend twelve weeks with six platoons of men.

The peacetime Depot routine was divided into three phases of four weeks each. [5] In the first phase, Private Truesdale was introduced to marching, physical exercise, and swimming, and to preliminary and basic military instruction conducted in the East Wing. He sat in a field classroom and listened to instructors tell of the combat lessons learned in France, the First Nicaraguan Campaign, and of the United States' interests in Central America. The lessons included renditions about the actions of eight Marines who had earned Medals of Honor during WWI, in addition to the two from St. Louis who then wore the Medal for actions in the Second Haitian Campaign of 1919–1920.

Since the turn of the century, American companies had purchased the rights to vast tracts of plantations in banana country and timber lands on the Republic of Nicaragua's east coast. Gradually, the companies also controlled transportation along rivers, port facilities, gold mines in the mountain regions, and coffee plantations in the western interior.

During the civil unrest of 1909, Marines landed on the east coast and occupied the capital city of Bluefields to protect American property and reinforce the Nicaraguan army. Withdrawn the next year, the Marines returned in 1912 to suppress another rebellion and kept a legation of 100 Marines in Managua, the nation's capital city for the next twenty-three years. [6]

Private Truesdale was introduced to tales of one Marine who had led American troops in Nicaragua. Brigadier General Smedley Darlington Butler, "The Fighting Quaker" from West Chester, Pennsylvania, was becoming a much-loved legend in the Corps. There was no question about his bravery, having earned two Medals of Honor: his first for April 22, 1914, actions in Vera Cruz, Mexico, and the second for actions on November 17, 1915, during the

U.S. invasion and occupation of Haiti. President Thomas Woodrow Wilson had signed both awards.

As a distinguished officer, he had led three expeditions to Nicaragua. Promoted to Brigadier General, "Ol' Gimlet Eye" Butler was dispatched to France as WWI neared its end. He took command of Camp Pontanezen in Brest, the main American replacement depot, and cleaned it up. The general was on the dock to see the Marines depart from the Continent after the November 11, 1918, Armistice. When he returned stateside, General Butler assumed command of the Marine Barracks at Quantico, Virginia. He transformed the developing wartime camp into a permanent Marine Corps Base.

When Private Truesdale first learned of General Butler, the tales had grown. The years of Prohibition were at their height and the corruption rampant in the big cities was all the news. Philadelphia's newly elected mayor was aware of General Butler's reputation for "cleaning things up." He asked the general to leave the Marines and serve as the Director of Public Safety, taking charge of the city's police and fire departments. President Calvin Coolidge got involved, authorizing the combat veteran to take leave from the Corps and go to Philadelphia. General Butler had departed from Quantico in January 1924 and would be in his civilian post until December 1925.

At the time, there was no way Private Truesdale could understand the influence the general would have on his own Marine Corps career. Having lived a short time in Baltimore, he had his own opinions of big city life. He could not have known that he would later catch the attention of a grandmother on the streets of Philadelphia. His P.I. drill instructors definitely made no connection between the recruit from Lugoff and "Ol' Gimlet Eye."

In the second phase of recruit training, the platoons hiked each day from the East Wing to the rifle range for marksmanship practice. Private Truesdale had a noon meal at the range, prepared by the field kitchen, then returned to the barracks after completing the day's firing. His marksmanship earned an Expert Marksmanship Badge, something he would treasure and find pride in for the rest of his life. [7]

The third, and final, phase involved intensive instruction in close-order and extended-order drilling, interior-guard duties, bayonet instruction, personal combat, wall scaling, rope climbing, and other skills required in modern warfare. The strength of two good arms was pertinent. Not all the recruits who processed in with the platoons could perfect the necessary skills, and about thirty percent were discharged from the service. Private Truesdale successfully completed basic training and graduated into the Corps' active forces.

Private Truesdale went home for a visit before going to his first duty station—a teenager with his formerly thick black hair completely shorn in Corps style. One mid-day, he sat on the

ground beside a brick wall, legs outstretched, arms crossed against his abdomen, wearing a sleeveless t-shirt under a South Carolina Pindo palm. Someone took a photograph at ground level, the soles of his studded boots captured in the foreground.

The profile of a pretty, fashionable woman's face, in the manner of "Mother," was tattooed on his right deltoid. A tattoo of what looked like an eagle in flight was on his left bicep. Private Truesdale also had a tattoo on his right forearm: what might have been the USMC emblem. Mrs. Margaret Truesdale was not pleased with her son adopting the Leathernecks' practice of marking their bodies with indelible ink images and symbols, but she did keep the photo. For that, she would be grateful, because when he returned to Lugoff years later, he would no longer have the USMC tattoo.

The Marines remained in Nicaragua when Pvt Truesdale finished his training. The Legation was withdrawn in August 1925 and another rebellion erupted. The U.S. Navy with Marines on board kept an anchorage off Balboa on the Pacific side of the Panama Canal and patrolled off Colon, the Caribbean terminus of the canal. The 51st Company Marines garrisoned various outposts in Nicaragua. Marines forces were again dispatched to Bluefields in May and August 1926.

The civil disturbance escalated as bandits attempted to overthrow the government. Augusto Cesar Sandino, using the city of San Rafael del Norte for his operational center, took armed outlaws into the difficult countryside of Nueva Segovia, pillaging mines and towns and harassing Americans. A Marine expeditionary force was sent to help quell the insurrection, focusing the mission on the central mountains and the Northern Area.

Marines landed on the east coast of the Central American isthmus in December and took over four major ports.

1927

On January 6, 1927, the Marines landed more forces at Corinto, on the west coast, and moved a battalion to Managua to reestablish the Legation Guard. The Legation buildings were within the government section of the city, five blocks north of Campo de Marte. The camp was a Nicaraguan government reservation located on the south-central edge of the city (now a small park beside the Hugo Chávez Roundabout). The twenty-two-acre military complex had been laid out in the late eighteenth century and enclosed the old presidential palace.

The battalion set up headquarters in the palace, where most of the officers were quartered. The enlisted Marines were bivouacked in a corner of the camp in tents and in the old, run-down, garrison barracks previously used by the Nicaraguan Army. The main gate was off the intersection of Central Avenue West and 5 A Street South. [8] That was a short five-block walk to Central Street, or ten blocks to the plaza and Dario Park on the north side of town under the railroad line. A short three-block walk west was the Viejo Cementerio, and three blocks past the cemetery was the penitenciario. Commanders encouraged their men to remain close to camp, learn some Spanish, and take in the local culture. They might be in the tropics, but they were not there for rest and recreation.

The Marines immediately began orienting to the region. They studied their tactical maps, noting the passages and roads around the lakes and active volcanoes. Just south of the camp's back gate was the prominent La Loma fortress, on the heights of the Laguna de Tiscapa, an extinct volcanic crater. Locals encouraged hikes to La Loma and the "azul precioso lago de crater" ("precious blue crater lake") during their daily liberty periods. Few Marines would have been reading the third edition of *The Origin of Continents and Oceans*, a thick book that had generated hostile and scathing ridicule of the author by geologists and fellow scientists. [9] Unbeknownst to all, if a volcano was nearby, extinct or not, Campo De Marte was in a rift valley and near a fault line.

Having seen some of the sights, most Marines spent their free time wandering the barrios de miseria and drinking large amounts of cheap bebida alcohólica at the many cantinas. Legation Marines were commonly restricted to campgrounds after a night of not so friendly brawling with the National Guardsmen, often a fracas over a *muy bonita señorita*.

A bloody battle between the government forces and the revolutionary forces in January 1927 laid carnage to the town of Chinandega. Propagandists circulated anti-Yankee vitriol.

The Nicaraguan president appealed for more Marines to guard against further sabotage and to disarm the rival armies.

President Calvin Coolidge had no more patience for the rebel cause. Their disregard for American lives, property, and production had gone too far. He informed Congress on January 10, that protecting American interests in Nicaragua had become a priority. That same day, 2d Battalion, 5th Marines, arrived at Bluefields on Nicaragua's east coast. After establishing a neutral zone along the Escondido River, the battalion sailed from Bluefields through the Panama Canal to Corinto, leaving the 51st Company inland at Rama, where the Río Mico and the Río Rama joined the Escondido.

The USS *Henderson* steamed out from Quantico carrying over a thousand reinforcements for the 5th Regiment on February 19.

A reinforced Marine rifle company left Managua to garrison ruined Chinandega. Together with landing parties from three cruisers, they manned an outpost on the edge of town to watch over a railway bridge. Major Ross E. Rowell led six VO-1M DeHavillands to Corinto, landed, and quickly loaded the aircraft on train flatcars to clatter down to Managua.

Brigadier General Logan Feland arrived at Corinto on March 7 to command the now 2,000 Marines serving in Nicaragua.

The Marines began training a constabulary, the Guardia Nacional de Nicaragua (GNN), otherwise known as *La Guardia*, on May 8, 1927. On paper, the National Guard forces were entirely distinct from the Marine companies stationed in the country.

On May 9, the 11th Marine Regiment with two battalions was activated and organized as an infantry regiment for service of brief duration in Nicaragua.

Having demonstrated leadership and been promoted, CPL Truesdale oversaw a rifle squad in the Marine Detachment sailing on the dreadnought battleship USS *Arkansas* (BB-33). The ship was berthed in Guantanimo, Cuba, when the order to proceed south and "maintain order and stability" in Nicaragua was wired from Washington, D.C.

Corporal Truesdale was a proud member of the *Fighting Fifth*. The regiment had earned its place in history during WWI. In spring 1918, the 5th Marines was involved in the fierce battle of Belleau Wood and participated in the offensive campaigns at Aisne, the Battle of Saint-Mihiel, and in the Meuse-Argonne offensive—all places CPL Truesdale's cousin, Karl Rosborough, would have known. The Marine regiments came home with the nickname *Devil Dogs*. Before returning to Lugoff, CPL Truesdale was going to share one distinction earned by the legendary Sergeant Major Daniel "Dan" Daly, who a Major General once described as "The fightin'est Marine I ever knew!"

The U.S. Scouting Fleet's battleships USS *Arkansas* and USS *Florida* (BB-30) sailed south for Colon, passed through the Panama Canal, and steamed up the Pacific coast. Eighty-three Marines of the 5th Marine Regiment were on board. The cruisers USS *Milwaukee* (CL-5) and USS *Galveston* (CL-19) also carried regimental landing forces. Captain Franklin Augustus "Frank" Hart was in command of the Marine Detachment on the *Milwaukee*. The ships arrived off Corinto. [10]

The roving rebels were creating turmoil, interrupting traffic along important railroad lines. Captain Hart landed ashore, went north, and set up his Marines in an outpost at Chinandega. The headquarters of one of the guerilla chieftains at El Viejo was north of their position.

On Saturday, May 14, Captain Hart and four Marines rode their horses up to El Viejo to discuss disarmament with the bandit leader, Francisco Sequeira. The talks were continued back at Chinandega.

On Sunday, the detachment of forty-five Marines from the USS *Arkansas* was dispatched ashore under the command of 34-year-old Captain Richard Bell Buchanan of Carbondale, Illinois. They railed south to La Paz Centro, a railroad village of 4,000 residents between the large cities of León and Managua, the capital city, and west of Lake Managua.

Corporal Truesdale had arrived in the República de Nicaragua for the first time. He would be deployed there three times in the next six years. He was certain of their purpose in being dispatched to the war-torn country. "We went down there, not to harm them," he would recall later, "but to make peace—to help those people. That's why we went in." [11] He was going to see the first two Marines shed their blood in combat and die in the Second Nicaraguan Campaign—the first serious casualties the Marines suffered since they had arrived in January.

Captain Buchanan's detachment camped across the Corinto-Managua tracks 300 yards north of La Paz. It did not escape their attention that farmers labored in their fields with rifles slung over their shoulders.

On Monday, "General" Sequeira departed the Chinandega outpost at 2:00 PM and withdrew to his headquarters. Reports of an incident at La Paz reached Captain Hart that afternoon.

A small band of revolutionary guerrillas had raided the village and looted the shops and a saloon without warning. The town's people pleaded for help from Captain Buchanan. Just before 1:00 AM on Monday, gunfire rang out in the town in the general direction of the Marine camp. Captain Buchanan ordered "Call to Arms" to be bugled, and he formed up a platoon of forty Marines into an advance column. He left First Sergeant Dennis W. Green and eight Company Headquarters men to guard the camp.

Moving south, Captain Buchanan entered the darkened town at the forward position with seven Marines. His second in command was fifty yards behind the Marine skipper. Second Lieutenant Clarence Joseph "C.J." Chappell Jr., 26, from Macon, Georgia, had landed with the USS *Florida* detachment. He led two squads in the main body of the patrol formation on the streets north of Main Street. [12]

Corporal Truesdale's squad covered the right flank on the east side of the town. Sergeant Glendell L. Fitzgerald led a half-squad of four Marines on the left flank, covering Main Street.

Three blocks into La Paz, about seventy-five mounted outlaws brought heavy rifle and machine-gun fire to bear on the left flank. Sergeant Fitzgerald and his men took cover under a raised wooden walkway and behind a pile of railroad ties on Main Street. The rebels took shelter in houses and a cantina.

At 6 feet 2 inches tall and weighing 180 pounds, Private Marvin Andrew Jackson, 20, from the USS *Florida* detachment, had to really crouch down behind the railroad ties. He had been resolute about enlisting in the Marines. Private Jackson was born in Jacksonville, Florida, but years before the Nicaraguan campaign began, he was living with his mother, Mrs. Nellie C. Everett, at 627 Fullerton Parkway in the Lincoln Park neighborhood on Chicago's North Side. He had an easy walk to Lake Michigan and Wrigley Field. Getting to school on time required a ride, because Senn High School, on Glenwood Avenue in the Edgewater neighborhood, was four-and-a-half miles north of the Everett's rowhome. [13]

Marvin, 17 years old, had decided to join the Marines with his mother's permission. "He was always such a good boy," she would tell a reporter. "And, so interested in military matters. As soon as he got out of school he tried to get into the Marines." He was initially turned down for physical defects. Nellie and her husband sent him to doctors to have his tonsils taken out and to have an operation to correct a very slight flat foot. Marvin took his enlistment oath in September 1925 and traveled to Parris Island, nearly a year after CPL Truesdale.

Captain Buchanan immediately swung the point element left in the direction of the barrage to flank the bandits. Advancing a block and a half, the point was forced to take cover under fire. Captain Buchanan moved forward, leading the point another twenty-five yards to join Sergeant Fitzgerald's flankers. Private First Class William F. Simon Jr., was hit; the index finger on his right hand was completely shot away.

The captain ordered Lieutenant Chappell to move his two squads on line to the left of where the point was then located. Corporal Truesdale's squad was now covering the rear of the line. The patrol was outnumbered and under fire from three sides, from houses, behind buildings, and from the saloon.

Sergeant Fitzgerald was directing his men to fire on a house harboring the rebels. Private Jackson, "heedless of great personal danger, fighting in a cool and effective manner," attempted to secure a better position. He was hit through his head by a bullet and several more in his side before he could be dragged behind the railroad ties.

Corporal Anthony Joseph Rausch, of Philadelphia, and PFC Joseph H. Downs attempted to get to Sergeant Fitzgerald's position. Corporal Rausch was struck and badly wounded in the chest and arm, but continued fighting. A bullet hit PFC Downs' rifle and drove a piece of his rifle butt plate into his side. His injury did not prove serious. Around 2:00 AM, Captain Buchanan charged across the main street to take up a better position. Fire from the house window hit and seriously wounded him in the side.

Three PFCs entered and cleared the house, killing seven rebels. Sergeant Fitzgerald and CPL Gavins Strickland, who had been at the point of the column, carried the captain into the house, and the men inside administered first aid treatment to their commander, in very critical condition. Practically unable to talk, he encouraged the Marines to keep up the fight. Private Jackson was moved into the house and received first aid. The house became the strong point.

Lieutenant Chappell, now in command, and CPL Rausch, bleeding from his wounds, made their way to the post office, one block from the fighting. Lieutenant Chappell telephoned Captain Woodward, informed him of the fighting, and requested medical aid as soon as possible. While they were at the post office, Captain Buchanan died at 2:30 AM.

The intense fighting went on. The Marines reorganized and took the offensive deployed along the main street. The heavy barrage they put on the houses forced the rebels to cease firing at about 3:00 AM. They began to retreat from the village in small bands.

When the La Paz streets were secured, CPL Truesdale entered the house and saw an image he would always remember. His bloodied captain was dead. Private Jackson, shot through the brain, was struggling to hold on to life.

"That was one boy that didn't want to die," he would say. "His brains were sticking out of that bullet hole, and he didn't want to die." [14]

U.S. Navy doctor Lieutenant D. O. Bowan and two hospital corpsmen arrived by truck in La Paz at 4:20 AM to give medical aid. Private Jackson died as they entered the house. The medical men attended to the bodies of the captain and the private. They departed La Paz Centro at 5:10 AM to transport CPL Bausch and Private Simon to the closest medical facilities at León Medical University.

Corporal Truesdale and his men went back to camp after the fight. "Somebody'd fixed chipped beef and scrambled eggs for breakfast," he would tell a journalist thirty years later. "We'd seen brains hanging out and everything else. I couldn't eat for three days." [15]

Fourteen rebels were reported killed in the engagement. At dawn, the bodies of Captain Buchanan and Private Jackson were carried to the railroad station. Village natives informed the Marines that the retreating bandits had carried away several killed and wounded. The two Marine dead were loaded into the noon train baggage car and began the trip to León.

Corporal Truesdale learned something more about revolutions, war, and the reactions of hostile natives in a land occupied by a foreign military force. The León detachment formed to meet the train and escort the bodies to the University. As the boxes were lowered from the train and placed into the ambulance, the large crowd that had gathered in the open square surrounding the railroad station began to cheer and jeer and taunt and boo. Catcalls resounded. The ambulance moved through the crowd of natives and "the frenzy of the mob took on diabolical proportions."

It was an experience that CPL Truesdale would remember one day when he later shook hands with a vice president in Washington, D.C.

Captain Richard Buchanan and Private Marvin Jackson were both interred in Arlington National Cemetery, Virginia.

When headlines in the May 17, 1927, *New York Times* reported "Two Marines Slain in Nicaragua Fight," the Truesdales waited anxiously in Lugoff for news of their boy.

Corporal Truesdale was mentioned in 2dLt Chappell's detailed report of the engagement at La Paz Centro forwarded to the Commanding Officer, Landing Forces, León Medical University, on May 18, 1927. [16]

In Managua, Brigadier General Feland, commanding officer of the expeditionary force, sent a report to Marine Corps Commandant John E. Lejeune. "I am glad to state this Marine Detachment, under most difficult circumstances and although outnumbered ten to one, has upheld the reputation of the Marine Corps. Captain Buchanan and his detachment showed bravery of the highest order."

The 11th Marines and VO-4M landed at Corinto between May 17 and 22. Joining the 5th Marines, the two regiments became the 2d Brigade. Two thousand plus Marines were in Nicaragua, and the Second Nicaraguan Campaign, known as "the dirty little war," was underway.

Corporal Truesdale remained with the detachment responsible for patrolling the railroad line. When in Managua, he also participated with the "home guard." During the week before the La Paz battle, the Marines had begun organizing and training the non-partisan, native constabulary. Since Marine non-commissioned officers commonly did all the training for the Guardia Nacional, they were commissioned to serve as officers in the Guard. A Marine, serving as a Guardia Nacional officer made a little extra money—a stipend paid by the NNG.

First Sergeant Thomas G. Bruce, 30 years old, from Hopkinton, New York, serving with the 5th Marine Regiment, 2d Marine Brigade, was one of the original Nacional Guardia officers leading patrols. He was commissioned a first lieutenant in the NNG to lead the recruits he had trained. He and CPL Truesdale were on good terms.

Nicaragua had three distinct geographical regions: the Pacific Lowlands, the North-Central Highlands, and the Atlantic Lowlands. The country was divided into sixteen administrative departamentos, subdivided into 153 municipalities (municipios). Each department had its own capital city. In the next several months, CPL Truesdale would become familiar with place names and outposts and reports of engagements at Matagalpa, Jinotega, Ocotal, Río Coco, San Fernando, Zapotillo Ridge, El Chipote, Telpaneca, Jícaro, San Albino Minas, Las Cruces, and Quilalí in the northern area.

Before the year ended, eleven officers and enlisted infantry men of 8th, 16th, 17th, 23rd, 49th, 16th companies, 5th Marines would be killed in action or die of wounds: most of them near Quilalí. Three Marines would die at Managua: one 77th Company PFC of an accidental gunshot wound (friendly fire recorded as GSW), a 2nd Brigade HQ Company PFC of drowning, and a 5th Marines HQ corporal of suicide. One 20th Company private would fall of a cerebral hemorrhage and a 16th Company PFC of malaria.

Among the wounded in action in the months following the La Paz fight would be three officers and twenty-two enlisted Marines, the clear majority of them from the 8th Company near Quilalí in the last three months of the year.

The 1927 political situation in Nicaragua seemed as unpredictable as its volcanoes and earthquakes. Augusto Calderón Sandino, 32, was equally displeased with the standing government, the prospects of disarmament, wealth and capitalism, and the Marine presence in his native country. He aspired to be his own "Generalissimo," which made other military leaders suspicious of him. Sandino recruited his own band of fighters and marched them into the mountains. They became the first generation of Sandinistas and the annoying gnats in the Marine efforts to be peacekeepers. Sandino earned a reputation as a "notorious prevaricator" to Marine officers. To natives he had earned the nickname Bestia de las Montañas—*Beast of the Mountains*.

For six years, Marines occupying the outposts went in pursuit of the Sandinistas, and the vast terrain favored the guerillas. The Marine pilots and their backseat observers provided aerial reconnaissance reports. Marines on the ground patrolled in regions of dense tropical jungle and nearly unbroken mountain chains. The rugged peaks provided the bad guys excellent vantage points to watch out for the advance columns of government forces. The densely-forested mountain slopes and secluded valleys gave them ample places to hide their camps. The border with Honduras was indistinct and appeared to provide easily crossed supply routes for the insurrectionists' arms and ammunition. [17]

Small, isolated villages in clearings were scattered about the countryside, seeming to be connected only by trails. Roads were nonexistent. Abundant rivers and streams provided irrigation for patches of corn, beans, rice, and sugarcane. Coffee plantations closer to the larger towns gave way to the jungles. Ranchers had grabbed enough land to turn out their cattle into the portreros (pastures) to graze and roam freely.

The Guardsmen familiar with the comarcas (rural districts) added to the intelligence reports. Much of the northern and central areas would prove to be inaccessible to heavily equipped ground troops. The rain forests and jungles were impenetrable except by the few narrow trails cut out by the natives. Horses without riders could barely travel along the trails, and even the pack mules would halt at points congested by vegetation. The system of streams and tributaries of the bigger rivers became impassable for nearly six months during the rainy seasons.

The rebels easily foraged for enough food to feed their camps. They could raid and ambush in the regions they were so familiar with and could retreat into the mountains if it seemed prudent to their survival. The rural campesinos (peasants), often sharing extended bloodlines, tended to be friendly toward the insurrectos and antagonistic toward government authority. Gaining their cooperation and gathering reliable, tactical information from them demanded patient diplomacy. The efforts failed anyway.

In the presence of American invaders, peasant loyalty would go to the home team, and General Sandino and his selected jefes (chiefs) were provided reliable information and advance notice of every government patrol. The Marines were hard pressed to tell amigo from enemigo with the people they encountered.

"This is all part of a Marine's life. He is trained not to expect luxuries and he takes things as they come. A foxhole in the jungle is as good as a cot in the barracks." [18]

The Northern Area of operations was comprised of the Departments of Nueva Segovia and Esteli. Honduras was across the border. The Marines were sent into the Northern Area in June 1927 to escort Señor Arnoldo Ramírez Abaunza, the Liberal appointee for governor, and to establish enough control in the region that fair elections could proceed. The Marine troops in the column moving north had minimal knowledge about the mission ahead.

"Nueva Segovia, now that was like a county. Ocotal was the capital of it." That is what CPL Truesdale knew. Until sixty years had passed, he did not know that Ocotal was twelve miles from the Hondoranian border. What he did know was that the Marines were not going north to save any towns. "We didn't take the money with us. We didn't have no maps, nothing, see? Ya just went."

The Marines established headquarters in the "Pink House" at Ocotal, in the shadow of Cerro Mogoton, a 6,913-foot-high mountain. From the north, the Río Dipilto cut a valley almost from Honduras. The wide, shallow Río Macuelizo, an east-west arm of the Río Coco, was just south of the small town. To the west, the Marines constructed an auxiliary airfield with fuel and ammunition supplies for the aircraft bringing supplies, mail, and payroll from Managua. It was operational in three days.

"Scant Group of American Marines Hold Ocotal Field"

At 1:00 AM on July 16, between 300 and 500 Sandinistas attacked the Ocotal outpost. The forty-one 16th Company, 3rd Battalion, 5th Regiment Marines, under command of Captain Gilbert Durnell Hatfield, aged 35, from Aztec, New Mexico, and forty-eight Guardia, put up a desperate defense, mindful that General Sandino had threatened to wipe out the entire garrison and "drink yankee blood."

For his "extraordinary heroism, coolness and excellent judgment in performance of duty on the occasion of an attack by a vastly superior force on the Marine detachment of which he was a member at Ocotal," First Sergeant Thomas Bruce was presented a Navy Cross.

After a 15-hour battle, more than fifty bandits had been killed. Private Michael Aloysius Obleski Jr., 18 years old, of R.F.D.-2, Roulette, Pennsylvania, 16th Company, 3rd Battalion, 5th Marines, was the one Marine KIA—killed by a sniper. Machine-gun fire wounded Private Charles Sidney Garrison, 19, of 35 West Street, Asheville, North Carolina, through the cheek and left shoulder in the horrific battle. He survived. [19]

General Sandino escaped to his hilltop hideout in San Fernando. The Marines mounted their horses in pursuit. The General kept escaping along hidden trails, learning that his men, fighting with small-arms weapons, could not match the better-equipped and trained fighters from the "Barbaric Colossus of the North." The dispatches and reports of Marine Corps commanders seemed insightful, actually prophetic.

The people of the Northern Area unquestionably stood behind Sandino and were willing to shoot it out and die with their small arms. Putting down the rebellion would take "a real blood and thunder campaign" and would evolve into "a real small war" and the natives would gradually arm themselves with the weapons of government casualties.

Hit-and-run guerilla warfare was evolving in Nicaragua's highest elevation.

Newspaper accounts of Sandino and Ocotal at home triggered protests of America's involvement in the foreign land and demands to bring the Marines home. The Marines stayed. Much later, when CPL Truesdale had had time to contemplate the politics of things, he had a perspective on the protests and outcries.

"But, the American people, they get all excited. . . . that's what determines everything is. . . . the big people in the United States, they're the ones who run everything. Money rules everything."

On August 3, Private Rafael Toro, 17th Company, 5th Marines, from Puerto Rico, died at San Fernando, ten miles east of Ocotal, from wounds received in a sharp engagement with armed bandits on July 25.

It was important for the Marines to clear their thoughts of wounded and killed comrades. When he had a chance for furloughs, CPL Truesdale could get into town with his friends. Since a Marine corporal (E4) only earned active duty basic pay of $13 a month, money was tight—a never-ending issue for enlisted men. He was also entitled to 50¢ per diem when on orders away from the States. Significant fines for various infractions might be as much as 25¢ or 50¢. Of his $13 pay, CPL Truesdale kept $3 for himself and sent $10 home for family. Cash was still hard to come by in Lugoff.

If the cultural differences in Nicaragua had not been apparent when the young man from Lugoff landed in Corinto, there could be no mistaking them during the first week of August when crowds of merrymakers filled the parks and the principal avenues and streets all day and night. The 50,000 residents of Managua filled the Central Park plaza for the traditional Patron Saint fiesta, celebrating Santo Domingo (Saint Dominic) de Guzmán. The Nicaraguan natives called it the time for *Minguito*–their nickname for Domingo.

On September 1, Sergeant Paul C. Splittgerber, 32, of Vallejo City, California, 8th Company, 5th Regiment, was depleted of all resilience. He could take no more of the civil disturbances and took his own life at the Matagalpa outpost. [20]

Second Lieutenant C. J. Chappell's company of Marines was relocated to the outpost at Somoto, fourteen miles southwest of Ocotal and eleven miles from Honduras. The lieutenant received several reports on Tuesday, September 6, that bandits affiliated with Abraham Gutiérrez Lobo and Don Pedro Lobo were roaming in the towns southwest of Somoto. [21]

At 11:15 AM the next day, he took a mounted patrol of nineteen Marines down the dirt road to investigate the situation at Mr. Mosier's ranch. The patrol passed thru Santa Isabel, crossed the streams in the Isabel and Unile ravines, and rode through San Lucas. They encountered no armed bands on the roads or in either town and reached Mosier's ranch at 6:00 PM, where they stayed for four hours. The patrol then set out in the dark, crossed the Río Inali, and proceeded in the direction of Mal Paso and Lobo's headquarters. [22]

Lieutenant Chappell's patrol arrived near Mal Paso (Ciudad Darío), at 7:00 AM, on Thursday, and took fire from a bandit band hiding in a house. After an exchange of four or five rounds, the band retreated to the rear of the building and fled into a ravine, thick in brush. No Marines suffered casualties. The patrol searched the town carefully. They found three men dead and two seriously wounded. It was suspected that more had been wounded and escaped. The two wounded bandits were left with the town's people.

The patrol captured four bandit horses, two saddles, three rifles, and Lobo's red and black banner, and departed Mal Paso. They arrived back at Somoto at 1:35 PM.

Following his report, 2dLt Chappell's company was moved east, traveling through Ocotal, San Fernando, Santa Clara, and posting at Jícaro. Airdrops from the Brigade air squadrons delivered orders, maps, payroll, mail, supplies, and combat support to the remote outposts and patrols.

Corporal Truesdale patrolled in the area around San Albino where Charles Butters had a gold mine. The remote area was in many ways inaccessible on horseback. The Jicaro road was dammed in one location. "They put up poles this-a-way and . . . braced 'em, and cut a tunnel down there. And they got everything but water, that was their power, to, to run that gold mine . . . and run some great big generators, that they—But, it's a miracle how they got 'em in there. But, when they got 'em there, you couldn't, there wasn't no more roads back there. There was a trail, a man trail. There was trails running off to houses and the little villages all around there, and that's where the people were."

Corporal Truesdale had believed his family in Lugoff was poor—until he encountered some of the native tribes and witnessed their maladies. [23] "Just Indians, you know, having a sugar cane patch, a little bit of a banana patch, and ah, little, some coffee, a little bit of stuff they're madin' up, see? But, they're pretty smart."

He watched indigenous women and medicine men treat skin rashes and fungal sores with poultices made of juices from fresh leaves, flowers, and plant roots. Although the Marines were poorly equipped medically, CPL Truesdale tried to help where he could. He put sulfur powder on their skin lesions.

The situation seemed secure and well under control. Washington, D.C., decided to bring some of the Marines home. The 11th Marines headquarters had been disbanded on July 31, and the two battalions departed from Nicaragua on September 6. The 5th Marines remained in country, with 1,415 Marines on duty. Their mission was to search out Sandino on his heavily forested, 5,000-foot-high mountain fortress—El Chipote, northeast of Quilalí in the eastern Segovias.

Two VO 7-M aviators took to the air on Saturday, October 8, 1927. At 10:00 AM, bandit ground fire hit the aircraft near Chipote. Trailing smoke, 2dLt Earl A. Thomas, from Richmond, Indiana, and Sergeant Frank E. Dowdell, formerly of Carbondale, Illinois, made a crash landing on 4,367-foot-high Zapotillo Ridge (Sapotillal in reports). They took the machine gun from the aircraft, set fire to the plane, and escaped unhurt down into the valley.

Stateside newspaper headlines would describe their machine being forced down in impenetrable forest. A patrol was dispatched to rescue them, but had to turn back from El Zapotillo due to the overwhelming guerrilla force they encountered. The State Department listed the two aviators as Missing In Action.

A week later, the story was told in columns beneath headlines: Fear Aviators Held Hostage. [24] No trace of the two fliers had been found, reports of their having reached Jícaro after the crash were erroneous, and Marine headquarters feared that bandits held them as hostages. Joint patrols were organized to go in search of the missing Marines.

On October 18, 2dLt Chappell received his orders via an airdrop. [25] He led a patrol of Marines and Guardsmen from Jícaro to find the downed aviators. A second patrol of twenty-four 8th Company, 5th Marines, and forty Nicaraguan Guardsmen moved northeast from Matagalpa to get to the airplane crash site.

The next day, home newspapers began providing reports of the attempts to recover the lost fliers. Private Harry M. Blanchard wrote a first-hand account of the twelve-day patrol in a letter home to his parents in New Orleans. He described what 2dLt Truesdale and any Marine patrolling in the Northern Area would remember of their time in Nicaragua. [26]

The patrol marched through thick jungle growth and swamps, making between six to eight miles a day, having to cut their own roads with machetes and axes, with mud up to the bellies of their mules, swimming across rivers, climbing high, steep mountains of naked rock, sometimes having to drag the mules up the inclines by their lead ropes.

Lieutenant Chappell moved south, parallel to the Jícaro River, into humid and reeking jungle wilderness. There were few trails to follow. The vegetation on the steep mountain slopes was thick, opening to banana groves here and there. The nearby mile-high plateaus were often hidden in fog and clouds. In addition to the Sandinistas, the native Indians were unfriendly to the Marines.

On October 26, Lt Chappell's patrol reached the plane wreckage. The motor and all metal parts were intact. There was no sign of the two aviators. First Lieutenant M. J. Gould's patrol from Matagalpa was at the site on October 28. For several days, the combined patrol searched the area, harassed and attacked by a larger guerilla force.

Lieutenant Chappell's patrol began operating from Quilalí. Lieutenant Gould began a march north to Jícaro. Near Espino, six miles southeast of Jícaro, a dynamite bomb fragment slightly wounded Private Gilbert M. Fultz, 23rd, 5th Marines, on his left elbow during a thirty-five-minute fight on November 1. Private Blanchard was also hit, but did not report his wound to the commander.

Nicaraguan natives living in Ocotal began talking about the events on Zapotillo Ridge. "Advices from the interior" believed to be authoritative reached Campo de Marte, and Associated Press dispatches were wired to the States on Tuesday, November 8.

Lieutenant Thomas and Sergeant Dowdell had died heroically and with unflinching courage on October 8, against overwhelming odds. Making their way toward Jícaro, one of the Marines was reported to have been assaulted by a machete-bearing outlaw and was slashed on the neck and shoulder. The other flier killed the assailant with his revolver, then, dragged the wounded Marine to temporary safety in a cave. A band of thirty to forty outlaws ambushed them there. Both Marines made "a last stand" with their revolvers, putting up a desperate resistance until the outlaws definitely killed them both in the crossfire. [27]

A First Christmas

Two days after CPL Truesdale's first Christmas in Nicaragua, CPL John Silvernail, Headquarters Company, 5th Marines, killed himself near Managua.

In December 1927, Captain Merritt "Red Mike" Edson disembarked from ship in the Eastern Area of operations at Cabo Gracias á Dios, the mouth of the Río Coco on the Caribbean coast of northern Nicaragua. In command of an infantry company, he immediately began leading patrols into the interior. He contracted malaria. He also developed guerilla and riverine tactics to counter an enemy that hid, ambushed, and fled back into hiding.

The Marines trekked toward the headwaters of the Coco River in the central highlands, patrolling through rural towns, small villages, and remote indigenous communities. Roads did not exist. Travel was by foot or mule or log dugouts (*pitpans*) and riverboats. Captain Edson was in Nicaragua until March 1929. He and CPL Truesdale would get to know each other well after the next World War.

Corporal Truesdale, serving with the 2d Brigade, was a non-commissioned officer training men of the Nicaraguan Nacional Guard. As such, he was a second lieutenant in the Guard. "Well we trained 'em, had a little academy down there to train officers. And then, we worked with the enlisted. . . . had the sergeants and all the way down. . . . made them do the work. . . . drill the men. . . . but you couldn't teach 'em to shoot none. They shot differently, I mean, they shot from the hip mostly. But, they did some pretty good hittin.'"

Having grown up in rural Lugoff, 2dLt Truesdale had a deep understanding of the kind of stubbornness necessary to exist and survive in harsh conditions. Training Nicaraguan troops, accustomed to living poor, required a certain kind of wisdom—an honest finesse.

"But, don't try to change nobody," he would counsel. "When you go into an outfit. . . . go in there and be one of 'em. . . . grow with 'em. And, then teach them after . . . they get used to ya. But, don't come in there and try to change 'em overnight. They'll hate cha. And, you be tryin' to be a big shot . . . that's what gets to them. . . . just be one of 'em."

He ate and laughed with his men. He acknowledged, too, that he might tell a little lie from time to time. When he ate the beans and bread the natives or his troops prepared, he would nod appreciably and say "El mejor que he tenido" in his best Spanish. That the native beans were the best he had ever had might not have been true, "but, that'd get along."

Second Lieutenant Truesdale led his men through the old towns "and just moved out of the main drag." They patrolled the elongated valleys on trails in the Isabelia Mountain Range in the Department of Jinotega region, looking for roving bands of outlaws. The mountains naturally divided the Bocay and Coco rivers from the Tuma River, and Jinotega from the Department of Matagalpa. The mountainous territory was sparsely populated and covered by rain forest and cloud forest. The humid Peñas Blancas Massif, with steep cliff-like walls, was south of their travels. Reaching any plateau, the patrol would rest in the cooler, dry weather.

The farms, coffee plantations, and ranches in the region might have reminded him of rural Kershaw County, except in the Jinotega Department agricultural land gradually rose into sunlit slopes covered in deep rain forest where even the hardy, local mules refused to travel. Trails could narrow to less than the width of his shoulders. Running down the bad guys got tough.

"I mean, a trail that wide, and they're so steep that you couldn't take a mule. He couldn't get up it. He couldn't come down. And, that's why they'd [the bandits] run into a ravine. And, they'd have a tree 'cross it, see, and walk—a man could walk across. The mules couldn't. You'd have to go way around, and that fella would be outta sight before you could get, even get near him, see?

"And now, they could move, there's no gettin' around that. When they're—went down the mountain, they went down there pretty fast. But, then, they trottin' a bit on the level, gettin' up like that. Gettin' away at six miles an hour. But, you couldn't do that. And, you can't take American people in some places like that, and let 'em do a thing. . . . They're not adapted to it."

There was no doubt when they were on the trails that the rebels shadowed the patrols. The men could sense movement in close on their flanks and behind them, but could not determine if an animal with antlers caused the movement or a bandit with a rifle. Seldom were the natives unaware of the approach of a patrol.

"But, a man don't have a chance in someone else's home. You know where nothin' is, and the jungle up there. And you followin' the road. And, he can set out there, and he's twenty feet away from you and ya never see him. And they'd fire at you whenever they wanna. . . . And, then you get wounded, they in one bad shape. Dere's no way to get down. And, and the hills, some of 'em are just that steep." Steep could be a sixty-degree slope.

It did not help that Marines traveled with a lot of gear—not exactly light. "And, then the Marine went along with pots and pans on the dadburned Real Cantrail. . . . you can hear 'em comin' half a—well, two miles. They didn't have a chance, see?"

Leading Guard patrols required tactics contrary to his early training in conventional warfare in the Marines. Lieutenant Truesdale understood that the elusive insurrectos would not openly attack unless they outnumbered and out armed the patrols led by Americans. It was impossible in the terrain to keep contact with the rebels who would fire on a patrol for a few minutes, then disperse into the jungles.

Any encounter, no matter how brief, was tallied as a success if the casualties were inflicted on the bandits, but not on the patrol.

Lieutenant Truesdale was not a proponent of setting up his Guardsmen in ambush sites waiting for the Sandinistas to venture down a trail. He would admit to being too nervous.

"One of those fellows [guerillas] could lie in ambush for a week, where you couldn't do it for two hours. You'd get to worrying why nobody came along."

Lying in wait in the sweltering jungle humidity, in the chill of a night in mountain heights, or drenched under a tropical rainfall; fighting off the mosquitoes, ticks, and fleas; and, watching out for the venomous *fer-de-lance*, with the reputation of being "the ultimate pit viper," added to the challenges.

Savvy about jungle fighting, 2dLt Truesdale conducted his patrols vigilantly. He understood the relationship existing between the villagers and the "bandits." The Sandinistas always knew where the patrols were located, or at least the vicinity of their operations. When 2dLt Truesdale decided on a night bivouac site, he had an initial and a secondary spot picked out. The patrol first set up camp and ate supper at dark. Once dark had settled over the trails, they moved individually to the secondary site and established a defensive perimeter. [28]

Second Lieutenant Truesdale directed his soldiers to lie down and never show a profile at night. "If you have to pee, do it laying down. If I see a profile, it must be a bandit, and I'm going to shoot."

Many times, bandits crawled within feet of the lieutenant's position, but he did not engage them. Without knowing the number or distribution of the bandits, his muzzle flash would only reveal his position. He did not want the bandits to know the patrol's position, so a night firefight in the jungle was to be avoided if possible.

"When the sun comes up and you find out you have shot several of your own men, it's sickening."

There were also times that 2dLt Truesdale had his daytime patrols hide from the overhead aircraft trying to re-supply them or drop messages. An airdrop was a sure signal to the bandits that a La Guardia patrol was on a trail. The exception to that was if they had been out in the field for long days and the men were waiting for their pay. For morale purposes, pay was delivered by airdrop.

On December 30, 1927, Captain Richard Livingston led a column of 200 8th Company 5th Marines from the Jinotega outpost onto the Ocotal–Telpaneca–Quilalí Trail. Second Lieutenant (First Sergeant) Johnny Frank Hemphill, Chicago, commanded a company of 200 Guardia troops. The combined patrol's mission, with its 200 pack mules, was to capture Quilalí, General Sandino's remote war base.

Captain Livingston led the column toward Quilalí on the east side of Río Jícaro. Stretched along the Camino Real in single file, the noisy patrol slowly neared a banana grove 1,500 yards south of their objective. The native guide, Ramon Salini, called the place Trincheras. From the narrow trail in the mountain defile, the 200-foot-wide river was 100 feet down the mountain side at a 45-degree slope.

At 9:05 AM with little warning, hundreds of Sandino's Matagalpa bandits wearing smart khaki uniforms suddenly ambushed from commanding heights. Machine guns, automatic rifles, rifles, pistols, mortars, dynamite bombs, and mountain batter guns opened up on the column.

Private Blanchard found whatever cover he could and dodged dozens of "bombs loaded with broken glass, nails and scraps of all kinds of metal."

Flying chunks of metal from a bursting bomb wounded Private Blanchard and PFC Raleigh R. Brandenburg. Hit in the chin and shoulder, the private summed up his wounding. "It was not bad, but it was enough." He was young and still possessed some Corps' bravado. "That hour of fighting in the jungle was the best excitement I ever had in my life. You know that if you get to be a pretty fair shot yourself you get the idea, somehow, that anybody shooting at you is just as good and is sure to hit you. But almost always when they shot they missed, and almost always when we shot, one of them fell."

The Marines displayed courage "at a time when bullets were piercing flesh and death seemed just around the corner." The patrol inflicted severe casualties upon the rebels and drove them from the field after an eighty-minute battle. Lieutenant Hemphill, four enlisted Marines, and two Guardsmen were killed in the engagement. Captain Livingston and twenty-one others were seriously wounded. Headquarters at Managua issued twenty-one citations for the day's extraordinary heroism. [29]

While Private Blanchard made light of his wounds, he took the tropical rainfall quite seriously. "And talk about rain! It poured every day. You may think you have seen some rain in Louisiana. You want to see it rain in Nicaragua before you ever say you know anything about what rain can do. It drives down in solid masses of water. The force of it on your shoulders is like someone hitting you."

It rained like that in Nicaragua from April to October. Those were the same months the "pickers" would be out in their fields harvesting crops if CPL Truesdale was at home in Lugoff. Those "ol' Northern Area rivers" became dangerous in the rainy season. Shallow in the dry season, between November and April, the waters surged and overflowed the banks when the rains fell. The natives needed no warnings, but the young Marines had to learn their own lessons.

When the rivers "was aboilin,'" CPL Truesdale took caution. "They'd drown you down there."

The Marines were in the middle of a national revolution, serving on the side of the standing government. The revolutionaries used fear and intimidation as tactics in their efforts to unsettle the Marines and pressure them to leave Nicaragua. As is common in guerrilla warfare, rumors of enemy atrocities passed among the outposts and reached the Marine and Guardia headquarters in Managua.

General Sandino took exception to the newspaper accounts of the Marine aviators heroic last stand on Zapotillo Ridge. He dispatched his own report. The Sandinistas, under the command of Captain Abram Centeno, had captured the two airmen, tried them as perpetrators and assassins, and executed them. As proof, he dispatched a photograph to the Marines in Ocotal: 2dLt Thomas hanging from a tree, his hands tied in front of him. The photo was later published in Mexican and Honduran newspapers. [30] The opinion circulated that both Marine flyers had been tortured before being put to death. Their bodies were not recovered.

An incident on Sunday, New Year's Day, 1928, touched CPL Truesdale more closely.

1928

On January 1, 1928, Lieutenant Thomas Bruce commanded the advancing point of a sixty-man La Guardia patrol moving north toward Guanacastillo. First Lieutenant Merton A. Richal commanded a single-file column of 16th Company, 5th Marines, in the rear. The combined column was ambushed at the base of Las Cruces Hill, six miles northwest of Quilalí and west of Zapotillal. [31]

Bullets and bombs showered down from the rebel pine tree entrenchments on the hill. The fight went on for an hour. First Lieutenant Bruce died instantly in the sudden ambush. The Sandinistas had been in the habit of splitting the skulls of fallen Marines with their machetes, and, shaken by their commander's death, the Guardsmen abandoned his body. The rebels gathered Lieutenant Bruce's two pistols, field glasses, map case, compass, and American flag, stripped him, and then brutally mutilated his lifeless body with machetes. Four Marines were wounded in the contact. Reports sent to headquarters numbered the enemy dead to be fifty.

While efforts centered on ending the rebellion, General Sandino would not capitulate, even after the Marines took El Chipote from him in January. He expressed his determination in a letter he provided to a journalist.

"The only way to put an end to this struggle is the immediate withdrawal of the invading forces from our territory . . ." [32]

The official PATRIA Y LIBERTAD seal (Fatherland and Freedom) on General Sandino's letterhead was a daring taunt and an added affront. A U.S. Marine was depicted lying on his back on the ground in front of mountains. A campesino poised with a machete held the American by the hair, about to behead him.

The bleak reports and wild rumors about the guerillas capturing, torturing, and displaying mutilated bodies and the stories of other atrocities infuriated the Marines rather than terrifying them. The 1907 Hague Convention rules regarding the treatment of enemy belligerents and combatants went buried with First Sergeant Bruce. The Sandinista rebels were outlaws, brutal barbarians who deserved no mercy.

The Marines took an especially hard approach toward the peasants in Sandino's home turf. Reports began describing wounded bandits being interrogated and left where they fell, peasant houses being burned down, and prisoners being shot during "escape attempts."

Going Above and Beyond From Above

Corporal Truesdale was in Nicaragua during the days when newspaper reporters filed their stories about Colonel Charles Lindbergh being received in Latin American countries with tumultuous honors—"if he did not land safely somewhere, that would be news." The nation was yet unfamiliar with swaggering Leatherneck aviators; but, there were people in South Weymouth, Massachusetts, who had known one.

Second Lieutenant Ralph Talbot, 21 years old, had flown his De Havilland-4 over the WWI front lines. He became a flying ace and was the first Marine aviator to receive the Medal of Honor. On October 14, 1918, he and his back-seat observer, Gunnery Sergeant Robert Guy Robinson, 22, distinguished themselves against hostile German planes over Pittham, Belgium, and became the last two Marines to earn the Medal of Honor in WWI.

The Gunny came home after the war; Lieutenant Talbot did not. He was killed during a test flight on October 25, when his aircraft motor failed on takeoff. The plane crashed into a high embankment near the airfield and exploded into flames. Lieutenant Talbot was buried in the Les Barracques military cemetery near Calais, France, and his Medal was awarded posthumously.

January 6–8, 1928. On the Río Jicaro, Department of Nuevo Segovia, thirty-three miles southeast of Ocotal, Sandino's rebels had encircled remote Quilalí. The beleaguered Marines turned the grassy main street into a runway.

Second Brigade Marine aviator, First Lieutenant Christian Frank Schilt, 32, from Richland County, Illinois, and his observer, Sergeant Hubert H. Dogan, volunteered for an almost impossible mission. Skimming close over the fighting, he saw wounded Marines lying under "a deadly hail of rifle and machine-gun fire." He landed his Vought Corsair biplane, piled two of the wounded Devil Dogs inside, and flew them to the American hospital in Managua. For three days, flying ten missions, 1stLt Schilt evacuated eighteen wounded, flew in Captain Roger W. Peard, a relief commanding officer, to assume charge of a very serious situation, and brought in supplies and aid to others in desperate need. [33] He landed each time in Quilalí without a scratch.

Lieutenant Schilt had more reason to swagger, and family at home had more headlines to read, before another week passed. From above, the aviator discovered 200 bandits lying in ambush awaiting a column of Marines marching north on the Quilalí–Jicaro trail. He routed the bandits with his bombs and machine-gun runs, killing fourteen and wounding others. [34] In addition to the MOH for his earlier humanitarian flights at Quilalí, 1stLt Schilt was also awarded the Distinguished Flying Cross with one gold star. [35]

Up to that date, beginning with the American Civil War through the 1919–1920 Haiti Campaign, 2,409 Medals of Honor had been awarded. Marines had earned 109 of those. Lieutenant Schilt's was the first of two MOH awards presented to Marines in this Second Nicaraguan Campaign. [36]

The 11th Marine Regiment was reactivated on January 9, 1928, and, with 1,148 Marines, sailed under orders to Nicaragua. They moved into the northern and northwest areas where most of the fighting with the Sandinistas was to occur. They began taking losses in February.

A 52nd Company private died of an accidental gunshot wound at San Rafael del Norte on February 9. The regiment began taking KIAs on February 27, during the engagement at El Bramadero, near Condega, in which four Marines were killed, and nine were wounded. Four days later, a private in the 14th Company died of an accidental gunshot wound at El Gallo. A third 11th Regiment battalion was organized on the east coast on March 21. One 47th Company corporal died of combat wounds in May, and a 52nd Company gunny died of wounds in December. Three more 11th Marines had wounds serious enough to be listed among the 1928 casualties.

Death by other means claimed as many 11th Regiment men in 1928, as combat did. On May 8, another private in the 14th Company died of an accidental gunshot wound at San Rafael del Norte. [37] The death, the rains, and the mountain jungles proved too much a burden to 2nd Company Private James G. Hartley. He died by suicide the next day at Jinotega. On June 8, a 59th Company private drowned near Asang, as far north as Marines were permitted to patrol, and a 46th private drowned at Guacamte on September 19. Two 11th Marine enlisted men died of illness: one with malaria and one with pneumonia.

Second Lieutenant Truesdale and the NNG spent most of the year in the eastern and southern areas with the 5th Marines. The indigenous people were hunters and gatherers and farmers. They lived in round, thatched huts and navigated the region in canoes. In late April and early May, 2dLt Truesdale led his men in a three-column advance into the Pis Pis mining region near the Caribbean coast and chased the rebels from the La Luz mine. Much of the travel was in boats along the rivers swollen by the spring rains.

The Division of the Guardia Nacional Hospital was established at Managua in October. The Marine Hospital was one of the wooden barracks buildings under the shade of coconut palm trees.

In November, the Marines sent out scattered patrols to protect the people going to the polling places to cast their votes for the new presidente. After the election, General Sandino still would not lay down his arms and abandon his revolution.

Corporal Truesdale's first four-year enlistment ended in November 1928. He was 22 years old and signed up for another four-year commitment.

December held grim reminders for the Marines that they were in a foreign and unfriendly land. The month also brought telegrams to families at home and worries to those who read the newspaper headlines.

On December 1, Private Garnett Preston Starnes, 19, from Chattanooga, Tennessee, 51st Company, 5th Regiment, drowned in the Río Cape Gracias, where the Río Coco flows into the Caribbean. On December 6, "attempting to suppress banditry in northern Nicaragua," Gunnery Sergeant Charles Enos Williams of Astoria, New York, with the 52nd Company, 11th Regiment, was on a patrol between Ocotal and Telepacha. The Marines intercepted a band of marauders that had killed a defenseless peasant. The patrol routed the bandits, but a stray bullet, just a chance shot, hit the Gunny in the head. He died of his wound an hour later. [38] Two weeks later, Sergeant Major William L. McKenzie, Port Orchard, Washington, died of malaria at the Ocotal outpost. Four days before Christmas, Private Harry George Schnepp, 22, of Jones County, Iowa, serving with VJ6-M on board the USS *Saratoga*, died of septicemia in Managua.

1929

At the New Year, the 2d Marine Brigade was anticipating a major Sandinista offensive. Throughout 1929, the combat outposts and the mission to put an end to the Sandinistas were gradually turned over to the Nicaraguan Nacional Guard. The Marines remained in the country primarily to train the Guardsmen. Second Lieutenant Truesdale continued leading his Guardsmen searching for Generalissimo Sandino and General Miguel Angel Ortez's camps in the northern area under Honduras.

The only combat-related death for the 11th Marines in the early months of 1929 was Private Elmer Black, 57th Company, who died of wounds at Jocote on March 26. Other fatal causes prevailed. In January, a 60th Company private on the east coast drowned in the Río Prinzapolka. In March, a 57th Company private died of meningitis. On April 30, a 60th Company private was a homicide victim near Danlí, in the east under the Bosawás region.

Summer proved tragic for the next of kin of four 11th Marines at the Ocotal outpost. On June 30, 61st Company 1stSgt Robert R. Stock, 32, from Canton, Ohio, killed himself. Two weeks later, Service Company 1stSgt John G. O'Loughlin, Massachusetts, killed himself at Apalí. The telegram went to his cousin, James F. Gardner, on 118 North La Salle Street in Chicago. [39] The death of his two senior staff non-commissioned officers impacted Service Company Corporal John W. Smith, from St. Bernard Parish, Louisiana. He died of suicide on July 18 at Ocotal.

The last 11th Marine death in Nicaragua occurred on July 22 when 57th Company 1stLt Clarence Mearie Knight, 39, from Oshwa, Ontario, Canada, died in a plane crash near Ocotal.

The 11th Marine Regiment's second deployment to Nicaragua was again brief. The third battalion was disbanded on June 15, and the remainder of the regiment departed on August 31, 1929. Fewer than 1,500 Marines remained in the country. The 5th Regiment garrisoned the towns and the coasts, and the NNG conducted most patrols from the outposts.

Initially, only Marines were officers in the NNG. Some recruits resented that their commanders were not nationals. Second Lieutenant Truesdale and the Marines serving in the

Guardia recognized that men deserting the ranks or mutinying posed an insidious menace. Six American officers died in mutinies. The first was at Telpaneca on October 6.

Disenchanted Guard Sergeant Fernando Larios led mutineers and machine-gunned down 2dLt (Corporal) Lewis Harold Trogler, Haines City, Florida. Second Lieutenant (Sergeant) Charles J. Levonski succeeded the murdered Marine and would later meet a similar fate.

Eighth Company, 5th Regiment, Private Jesse Dean Martin, 19 years old, born in Missouri, went east of Matagalpa into La Rosa. On November 11, he took a .45cal Colt pistol to his head and ended his own life. His body was brought back to the States and interred in Modesto Citizens Cemetery, California.

Lieutenant Truesdale had a grasp of the situation, and there was some irony in it. He was a South Carolinian leading Guardia troops who railed against commands given by the *maltidos yankis*. How often his mother's remarks about *damned Yankees* must have come to mind. He reached a conclusion that took account of local culture.

"And, ah, so, the only way, the only way you could control the people is with the natives." The way to train and lead the native troops was to put one of their own in charge. "He'll train 'em, that can stand what they can stand."

The murders and mutinies against Marines continued into the next year, even after the first Nicaraguan officers were commissioned.

1930

Captain (First Lieutenant) Edward Selby, 35, born in Chicago, Illinois, had just pitched camp for the night at Pisal Seal, a few miles north of Jinotega on March 9, 1930. He posted two sentries, then, went outside the lines to reconnoiter. The sentry reported later that Captain Selby, returning alone in the dark, neglected to answer the challenge. Not recognizing the patrol leader and mistaking him as an insurgent, the sentry shot and killed him. Following an investigation, Captain Selby's death was listed as a homicide, even though his death did not result from a mutiny. [40]

The April headlines told the entire story: Two American Marine Officers Slain By Demoted Nicaraguan Sergeant—Machine Gun Rakes Officers' Beds. A disgruntled Sergeant Morales of the NNG was demoted to corporal because of drunkenness at the Jicaro outpost. At 1:30 AM on April 18, he fired fifty-two bullets into the officers' quarters, killing Captain (Sergeant) Veryl H. Dartt, Nashville, and Second Lieutenant (Sergeant) James Otis Young, 25, of Toledo, Ohio, as they slept. The Guardsmen killed Sergeant Morales. [41]

Beginning in the summer, the Marines ended their active operations against the armed rebel forces—except for CPL Truesdale and the Marines serving as NNG officers. They continued to command Guardia patrols from isolated outposts.

On Wednesday night, June 18, in Matagalpa, a Guardsman fatally stabbed Lieutenant (Sergeant) Albert Andrew Budai of Waseon, Ohio. [42]

The Guardia troops expected effective leadership and a forceful personality from their Marine leaders and could become aggressively intolerant of anything less. To have led and survived as many patrols over the years as he did, Lieutenant Truesdale must have demonstrated a good amount of fearlessness, common sense, enduring patience, good humor, understanding of the Nicaraguan ideals of masculinity, and at least a minimal fluency in Spanish. [43]

Second Lieutenant Truesdale came to believe that he remained alive in Nicaragua only because he maintained the respect and support of his troops. He thought of them as "his soldiers," and they were his responsibility. He shared his food and bought chickens and fruit from the locals for his men, understanding that the Marines who confiscated resources for themselves predictably turned the locals' allegiance to the rebels. [44]

His familiarity with Southern "backwoods" realities served him well in Nueva Segovia, and he did not take native hospitality for granted. "But, but those people'd, they'd kill ya. We was up there with 'em—But, they were the best friends you'd ever had, if they liked ya. If they didn't like you, buddy, you was dead. And, they'd bury you, you know what I mean?"

His continued existence on jungle trails could depend on a single "Tru-ism."

"So, I don't want nobody dislikin' me."

When he had his men on the trail, he would give them short breaks "in one of those little towns." He knew well enough that locals might also be family to some insurrectos, and he stayed watchful of movements around the buildings and houses. The patrol would leave on the trail in about two hours or a little more. The men invariably would seek out the cantina.

"I would always buy 'em two quarts of whiskey, that Casuasa aguara (meaning "watered down"). Casuasa was contraband." He would give the two quarts to the sergeant and have him go down the lines of troops, giving each one a single glass of whiskey. "Don't drink no more while we're here," the lieutenant ordered the men. The leftover whiskey went into his pack for later, not because the liquor was his, but because he wanted to see how disciplined his men were.

His young soldiers were predominantly adherents to the Catholic faith, and 2dLt Truesdale attended many weddings. He learned that padres charged a sum of cash to conduct the ceremony, often beyond the soldier's pay grade. To tell a man he was living in sin, and that babies born out of wedlock would go to hell, then, refuse to marry the couple wishing to live righteously was unfair in the lieutenant's view, not right in any way. Sometimes, he would have a talk with the padre and, then, attend the wedding carrying his '03 rifle. He would later recall with a laugh that the padre "was a little bruised up but appeared eager to conduct the ceremony." [45]

His Guardia troops learned to trust him. "You got, you got them people your friend," he'd say, "they'll go to hell for you." Loyal to their leader, the men checked with him if one of the other Marine officers, whether a lieutenant or captain, gave them an order. They would not do it.

"I'll ask my boss," the troop would defer.

"See? He wouldn't do nothin'. He thought he belonged to me. I just have to—see? That's why I come to believe, I'd tell him to go ahead and do something, and he would do it, see? But those, those people, they got, they got a lot of good sense. They're not all dummies. Naw . . ."

In the months between February and August 1930, Captain Lewis Burwell Puller, an expert in bush warfare who gave commands to his thirty Guardsmen at Jinotega with a Virginia drawl, was tracking and running to ground the Sandinistas in the valley around the Ciudad de Jinotega (13°09'17"N, 86° 00'17"W), south of Lago de Apanás and west of the Isabelia Mountains. He was particularly interested in the San Rafael Del Norte municipality (13°13'0" N, 86°7'0"W) twelve miles to the northwest. Captain Puller's roving, footloose "M" Company NNG troops affectionately called him *El Tigre del Norte—The Tiger of the North*. The Marines who followed him into combat in WWII and Korea would call him "Chesty" Puller.

Lieutenant Truesdale did not personally know or serve with "Chesty" Puller. He did hear the rumors. There was a contest to "compete for a head count and trophies" going on in the northern municipality, with body parts included in the trophy count.

In June, when Lieutenant Truesdale was in the Ocotal area, he met the son of a New England minister, Captain Evans Fordyce Carlson. The NNG captain was assigned to the northern area and was establishing a garrison at Jalapa and patrolling north in the remote villages of Portillo and Pasmate. Captain Carlson understood guerilla tactics and would make a name for himself in WWII when he and Captain "Red Mike" Edson each formed Marine Raider battalions to fight on Pacific islands.

The insurrectos watched for opportunities to ambush patrols moving from one outpost to another along the thirty-four miles of road between Ocotal and Jalapa.

Before the tropical rain season ended, a tragedy occurred in Matagalpa that received little attention in the State Department dispatches and in the stateside news reports. The Marines and Guardsmen were in place to supervise the November congressional elections and watch over the voter registrations scheduled for late September. The political persuasions and propaganda, of course, circulated throughout the rural areas. Whatever pressures burdened Sergeant John Damron Jr., serving with the NNG, he died of suicide on September 14, 1930.

The men talked about death around their campfires. While killing the enemy can turn a person cold, to go on after companions die in combat, hearts must harden against the reality that people die around them. Suicides, self-inflicted deaths, accidents, and fatal diseases were merely another fact of life.

Although it had not often been a topic of discussion at home, 2dLt Truesdale had learned that, fifteen years before he was born, his Grandpa Zachariah had killed himself. Whenever the topic of death, no matter its mode, came up among his soldiers, the Marine from Lugoff had a ready answer. Life is just what it is. You get up and do what you must do to keep going for as long as you can. A person's strength can hold out for only so long. The worst thing is to become a burden on others.

The number of Marine casualties had declined. Only one 5th Marine had been killed in action in 1930, at San Antonio, and two had died of their wounds while leading NNG patrols at Las Cruces and Guapotal. In December, the Guardia patrols had contacts with small groups of armed bandits at Telpaneca and La Constancia. Casualties were light and the bandits suffered the most fatalities.

Details of the death of Second Lieutenant (Sergeant) Charles O'Neill Owen, 25, of Boreing, Kentucky, on Sunday, December 21, were scant the next day. A gunshot had wounded him at Ocotal, and he died in the aircraft transporting him to the Marine hospital at Managua. [46] His death was later reported as a homicide. The news of his killing and the insurrecto attack on the Quilalí garrison late on the night of December 30, when two bandits died, were overshadowed by a massacre.

"They'll kill ya, they'll kill ya."

"It was Christmas of '30." Second Lieutenant Truesdale was present at Ocotal and would remember what happened for the rest of his days. The 2nd Brigade Marines, part of the Electoral Detachment "D" (NNG), waited to toast each other a Happy New Year.

Communication among the outposts was a constant frustration during bandit raids. The telephone lines were in plain sight when riding on the main roads, "from one side to the other hangin' on a tree." As Lieutenant Truesdale saw it, the telephone line was simple. "Ya take a piece of wire, on account of this wire, and take an ol' coka cola bottle, you know, and, for an insulator, and run the wire through the front. Then, their'd people come along and cut 'em. We couldn't talk to the next town."

After Christmas, the telegraph line from Ocotal east to San Fernando was down. Somebody sent word. At 8:00 AM, on Wednesday, December 31, New Year's Eve, Sergeant Arthur Michael Palrang, of Port Lyons, Colorado, one day before his 28th birthday, led nine mounted, heavily-armed, 43rd and 51st, 5th Marines, under orders to repair the line near Achuapa, eight miles northeast of the outpost. They had eight fully equipped mules in their column.

Private Joseph Arthur McCarty, 22 years old, Chillicothe, Missouri, was riding in an exposed position at the point when the wiring party found the downed wire in a densely-wooded area. He climbed up the pole to fix the wire. The others got busy beneath the line.

At 10:30 AM, rifle fire cracked out from the woods all around the patrol. Chief Miguel Angel Ortez commanded the armed bandits. Outnumbered, the Marines could not see from where the shots were coming. Private McCarty was wounded in the first burst, hit in the head when the bandits opened fire, and fell to the ground. [47]

Sergeant Palrang directed the patrol members to take up positions alongside the trail and to immediately return fire in the face of great odds. Without regard for his personal safety and despite his wound, Private McCarty continued to assist in the defense until he was killed.

Private Frank Austin Jackson, 24, from Lawrenceville, Georgia, took a position, returning fire with his rifle. Never thinking of his own safety, he gathered what ammunition he could and kept fighting.

Private Lambert Bush, 25, Bay Minette, Alabama, returned fire with a rifle and grenade discharger. Private Richard James Litz, 20, of 1937 Park Avenue, Indianapolis, took up a position alongside the trail and returned fire with a Thompson submachine gun.

Private Frank Kosieradzki, 19, of 249 Boll Street, Cheektowaga (Buffalo), New York, returned fire with his Browning Automatic Rifle for about half an hour, when he was severely wounded. He continued to operate the Browning until he was killed.

Private Mack Hutcherson, 22, from Zwolle, Louisiana, was armed with a Browning. He was severely wounded in the shoulder during the fighting and was unable to support the weight of the Browning. Private Litz saw his comrade's condition, moved over to him in the face of heavy fire, and gave Pvt Hutcherson the Thompson. Despite his wound, Pvt Hutcherson continued to operate the submachine gun. Having exchanged places, Private Litz continued to fire the Browning until he was killed.

Sergeant Palrang counted the dead. He ordered Pvt Hutcherson to crawl through the outlaw lines, get to Ocotal, and call for help. The private fell wounded again before he could get far.

In addition to their rifle and machine-gun fire, the bandits were freely tossing bombs into the Marine positions. Sergeant Palrang moved coolly about, steadying his patrol's fire, keeping a well-directed and energetic defense. A half an hour into the engagement, one of the bombs was thrown into the group in his immediate vicinity.

He had short seconds to decide what he would do. Protect himself and jump away before deadly shrapnel blew in all directions? Order a private to deal with the bomb? He considered the presence of his men—comrades and Marine brothers likely to be injured or killed by the impending detonation.

Sergeant Palrang shouted a warning, and at the same instant, without thought for his personal safety, picked up the bomb and attempted to hurl it away from the group. The detonation knocked him prone on the ground and seriously wounded him. In the face of heavy fire, Private Bush crawled over to the patrol leader and rendered first aid.

Private Joseph Albert Harbaugh Jr, 21, of 395 Malden Street, Washington, Pennsylvania, was seriously wounded at his position beside the trail. He continued to return fire with his BAR despite his wounds until he was killed. Private Edward Everett Elliott, 40, Des Moines,

Iowa, armed with a rifle, crawled over to Pvt Harbaugh's position, recovered the automatic weapon and continued firing. He was wounded shortly thereafter, but kept on firing until he was killed.

When Sergeant Palrang died, Private Bush returned to his own position, firing away until he was killed.

Private First Class Irving W. Aron, of 141 East 21st Street, Brooklyn, New York, a young man of the Jewish faith, was second-in-command of the patrol. He was one of the last to take a casualty, seriously wounded in the right arm after maintaining his position for about an hour. Ignoring his wound, he continued firing his pistol with his left hand, directing the defense until he was killed.

Lieutenant Truesdale and the Ocotal outpost were unaware of the battle until it was almost over. "But, they wind was blowin' wrong. You couldn't hear 'em shootin'."

Just before noon, a badly frightened native boy burst into town and blathered out that trapped Marines were being annihilated. The alarm was sounded at Ocotal. Lieutenant Joseph John Tavern, 28 years old, an Italian from Sault St. Marie, Chippewa County, Michigan, immediately rushed from the outpost with twenty-five Marines. Lieutenant Truesdale was at the lead of the relief column.

"But, anyway, we heard there was a battle out there. And, I had a big ol' horse, and I was way ahead of the rest of them."

Of the wiring party near Achuapa, Private Jackson, the last to be struck, wounded twice, crawled unseen into a nearby cornfield when everyone else was dead. The echoes of shooting stopped after two-and-half hours.

Lieutenant Truesdale got up to the battle site, and the guide behind him hollered. "Get off!" Pointing ahead off to the left, the civilian guide warned him. "That's where the battle was goin' on."

Lieutenant Truesdale got off his mount and tied the horse to a tree limb on the right side of the road. By that time, some of the Marines had caught up with him. In front of him, the hill sloped slightly from the right to his left. "And, I saw one native runnin' across the road that-a-way [up the slope] with a machete." Lieutenant Truesdale started toward the hill.

"Who's that out there?" somebody called from the tangled undergrowth on the left side of the road. Not quite a sentry's challenge demanding a password, but 2dLt Truesdale recognized a Southerner's voice.

"This is Tru," he replied, "come on out." Private Hutcherson and Private Jackson, both wounded, finally came out of hiding. Lieutenant Truesdale continued ahead, toward where the native had disappeared into the bush. The battle had just ended, and Chief Ortez's men remained nearby.

"Don't go up there, don't go up there," the two wounded Marines protested. "They'll kill ya, they'll kill ya!"

The lieutenant kept going on by himself anyway. "And, there was eight of them dead right down the road, there." Looking down on the bloodied, mutilated dead lying on the ground, he went past them. "Goin'. Just went on slow up the hill so I could get above them, you know."

He walked on that ridge, made the crest of the hill, sat down, and just stayed up there. From his vantage point, he could watch over the bodies of the men and be on the lookout for Ortez's men. The outlaws had captured the Thompson submachine gun, two Browning Automatic Rifles, three Springfield rifles, and the eight mules.

"But, there wasn't no mules, wasn't no matter, wasn't no saddles, well, everything was gone before the mules, and they took their cartridge belts, their ammunition, they took their rifles, and took their shoes. They didn't have very good shoes, their hats, and ah . . . if they had a ring on, they'd cut their finger off."

One Marine sergeant and seven privates had been killed. Lieutenant Truesdale recognized and understood the evident mutilations. A bandit had stood over one of the wounded Marines, his machete raised "gonna hit him, like on the head, see?" The Marine had thrown his arm up in a defensive posture, and the machete had cut his left arm off at the forearm. "Then, they hit him upside the head and killed him." Some of the men had their fingers sliced off. "Like they had a ring on, you know, and they cut the finger."

Once the telephone line was repaired, Lieutenant Tavern called for transportation. The poor roads in the Northern Area made supply trucks almost useless. An airplane could not have landed near Achuapa. Only two vehicles were available at the outpost. "We had two cars. We had a FWD, you know, the four-wheel truck, solid-tire four-wheel one. Well, we had one of those and one car the 'colonel' drove in, like an ol' Dodge without a cab on it."

Colonel Robert L. Denig, the Northern Area Commander in Ocotal, used that one to go out to the airfield and to move around the area. Their International FWD Truck served well in extraordinary situations, but would be slow getting up the road, if it could make it at all. Supply sent the ol' Dodge out to the massacre site to carry back the bodies.

Private Hutcherson and Private Jackson, witnesses to the entire fight, survived their wounds. Each of the ten Marines who participated in the Battle of Achuapa earned a Navy Cross for distinguished service in the line duty. [48]

At the Ocotal garrison, when they told the heroic tales of Achuapa, more than one Marine wondered what they might have done if they had been in Sergeant Arthur Palrang's place and seen that bomb land in their midst.

Whatever 2dLt Truesdale's attitude about Christmas and New Year had been prior to being deployed to Nicaragua, afterwards, wisps of Achuapa could intrude on his mind when others were decorating their trees with tinsel. And ring fingers—seeing a ring on a finger could bring the unwelcome recollection of mutilations of young comrades. For him, it might be better to never wear a ring.

1931

At the start of 1931, Lieutenant Truesdale was one of 160 officers leading the 1,650 NNG troops. [49] Patrols began combing the hills and jungles for the rebels who had ambushed the Marines near Achuapa.

"The Marines, now, we didn't go down to hurt nobody." In 2dLt Truesdale's view, the Marines were in Nicaragua to supervise the elections there in 1928, and the one coming in 1932, to see that the people got a fair election. He also believed it was only the natives who could control the countryside. Train a few of them, and let them train the others. The natives understood best what sort of behavior the rural people could tolerate. But, murder? Lieutenant Truesdale could not stand for that.

"Anyway, then we'd go down in there. We'd go on a patrol, after they got scared of the Marines. . . . They would have little camps on these, um, little ol' trails. Didn't have no cars, but the people would have a lean-to, like a building, take a, dig a hole and put a pole in with a fork in the top, and, you know, make a rail, and they had beds in there, maybe twenty-five or six, under the back in the bush where there was water. In fact, there generally was a banana patch and a cane and sugar cane field, like that. And, they put bridges every—certain natives move to 'em. And they would—just every so often you'd find one. And they'd come in and cook and travel off to the country, see? That's people providin' for. But if you could find 'em, that's what you want."

News reached the Ocotal outpost on Saturday, January 3, that Captain Ernest Russell was bringing a patrol of twenty Marine sharpshooters up from Totogalpa to look for the insurrectos. Just over a six-mile ride, they would have to cross over the Río Macuelizo south of the town's pastures. Word also reached the guerillas. Under cover of nighttime darkness, they attacked the patrol in a thickly-wooded ravine. Private James Robert Earnhardt, 19, of Concord, North Carolina, suffered a serious wound in the spine. [50]

For Southtown, Chicago, native Private David Monroe Kirkendall, 20 years old, 43rd Company, 5th Marines, the campaign was over. According to his hometown newspaper, he had sought adventure and found it. He had enlisted in the Marines in summer 1930, and was at the Ocotal garrison when his companions were killed in the bandit raid at Achuapa. He was riding with Captain Russell's Saturday patrol.

A jungle sniper's machine-gun bullet wounded him slightly, and the flash of his return fire as he fell to the ground revealed his position on the trail. Machine-gun bullets cut into him again and again. The patrol pushed forward.

Lieutenant Truesdale left the outpost with a Marine contingent to reinforce the Totogalpa patrol and aid in the pursuit of the bandits.

The wounded Marines were evacuated from Ocotal by airplane in the morning and flown to Managua. Per the initial USMC Communiqué, Private Kirkendall was expected to "probably recover." He died of his wounds in the Managua hospital on January 19. [51] Private Earnhardt survived his "adventure."

The Service of Farewell for the eight Marines killed in action at Achuapa was conducted in the Campo De Marte Post Chapel on Thursday morning, January 8. A Marine quartette and the Post Band filled the chapel with renderings of *Under His Wings*, *Near to the Heart of God*, *Nearer My God to Thee*, and *Abide With Me*. The services ended with the sounding of *Taps*. Major Joseph D. Murray, second in command of the Marine forces, formed up the funeral cortege at the chapel and led the mounted police detachment, 5th Marines band, four squads of escorts of the 23rd Company, color guard, the Brigade Chaplain C. H. Mansfield, and trucks bearing the remains to the train depot. [52]

Newspaper reports of plans to significantly reduce the Marine presence in Nicaragua by June 1, 1931, encouraged families at home in the States. In February, Washington, D.C., decided to begin the immediate withdrawal of 1,000 Marines. The remainder, including 2dLt Truesdale and all Marines attached to the NNG, would be brought home after the 1932 Nicaraguan elections. The folks in South Carolina would see his name in the big city newspapers in May.

Operating in pro-Sandinista territory in the early 1930s, the Marines in the Nueva Segovia region had tried to force villagers to resettle into secured zones to ferret out the bandits. The refugees flooded Matagalpa and Jinotega. The practice was called off.

Lieutenant Colonel Calvin B. Matthews, USMC, was appointed Jefe Director on February 6, 1931, and assumed command of the NNG.

Guardia patrols commanded by Marines continued to have small-scale engagements with armed bandits around Somoto, El Tule, Zapotillal, and Chipote. Lieutenant Colonel Matthews read the patrol reports daily.

The first dispatches he received regarding Lieutenant Truesdale were on March 2 and March 11. The lieutenant's Guardia patrols had made contact with bandits on trails around Condega, apparently without casualties on either side. Later in the month, Lieutenant

Truesdale was at the Ocotal garrison. He departed from there by airplane on March 23 with Lieutenant Rodriguez and arrived at Condega.

El Terrible Terremoto

Spring came, Palm Sunday passed, and the Holy Week holiday had begun. Christians looked forward to Easter, which was on April 5. The Tuesday evening, March 31, 1931, headlines sent shockwaves across America. Notre Dame's beloved football coach had perished in an aircraft crash in Kansas that morning. That stunning news shared headlines with events in Nicaragua that would unnerve Lieutenant Truesdale's family in Lugoff.

A few minutes after 10:00 AM on Tuesday, the Marines at Campo De Marte experienced an explosive devastation that had nothing to do with artillery, dynamite bombs, or grenades. A magnitude 6.0 earthquake, with its epicenter at the stadium, shattered Managua's downtown area and sent shivers throughout Nicaragua. [53] Eleven shock waves hit in the space of several minutes.

Not a stone was left standing in the business center of the city. A major fire broke out, swept into the west side of town by winds, burning into Wednesday, destroying thousands of structures. The America Legation building in the center of the capital was in ruins. Marine guards stood watch over the Legation rubble and watched over the Campo De Marte arsenal. If the fires swept into the camp, the detonations and explosions would be catastrophic. [54] People scrambled through neighborhoods, searching for loved ones and the remnants of their belongings.

By noon, Tuesday, telegrams were arriving in Washington, D.C. Tropical Radio reported at 2:05 PM that Managua had been destroyed by an earthquake and was burning. USS *Rochester* was dispatched from Panama for Corinto, and the USS *Sacramento* was standing by. Navy planes were dispatched from the Canal to investigate the reports. The aircraft carrier USS *Lexington* in Cuba and the Hospital Ship *Relief* were steaming for Managua, a humanitarian relief effort bringing personnel and supplies.

The nearly 1,000 Marines in the Managua vicinity were poised to assist the capital city in any way command directed. The Marines took over the city by evening and Martial Law was declared. Lieutenant Truesdale and the 430 Marines scattered in the northern district outposts would stay in place to continue dealing with the insurgents.

Tremors of considerable intensity continued into Wednesday. The earthquake crippled the entire nation. The hospital across the railroad tracks from Dario Park was overwhelmed with the injured and dying. The number of people killed tallied 2,000 souls. More than 45,000 Nicaraguans were left homeless. The Marines dug in the ruins beside the civilian volunteers looking for survivors, bringing out bodies that had been buried since the quake started. Eight Marines were seriously injured in the quake and others suffered minor injuries during their relief efforts into the night.

The Nicaraguan Nacional Penitentiary sat on the west side of the city, ten blocks from the camp. The prison came down, killing 150 prisoners, all except the few that had been out in the yard. Lieutenant Commander Hugo Fredrick August Baske, 41, Medical Corps USN, from Wisner, Nebraska, had been attached to Marine Corps units throughout his entire career. He was the Northern Area surgeon and held the rank of major with the Guardia. He was assigned as Medical Officer in charge at the prison. Falling walls crushed and killed him instantly.

Major Joseph Daniel Murray had been at the Boston recruiting station in 1930, before his assignment to the 2d Brigade in Nicaragua. His wife, Lillian, and nine-year-old daughter, Eileen, (born August 19, 1922) were with him in Managua. Colonel Frederic L. Bradman, brigade commander, sent a dispatch that Mrs. J. D. Murray, from Concord, Massachusetts, had died in the devastated city. She had been in the market place when it collapsed on hundreds of women and children and erupted into flames. Her death, along with Lt Commander Baske, was confirmed officially by 2:00 AM, April 1. On Thursday night, the major and his daughter accompanied the remains of Mrs. Lillian B. Murray to Corinto where the transport *Chaumont* was going to berth to take them back to America. She was buried in Arlington National Cemetery. [55]

Chief Quarter Master Clerk James Franklin Dickey, 46, from Venango, Pennsylvania, was reported as missing in a telegram to the Secretary of State at 2:47 AM on Wednesday. He had served with the 50th Company at Marine Barracks, Charleston, and was serving as a first lieutenant with the Guardia Detachment. He, his wife, and their two children had arrived in Nicaragua in October. By 3:25 PM, the evacuation of all American family members to the United States was planned. Lieutenant Dickey's lifeless body was recovered from beneath the penitentiary debris.

The Marines set up hospital tents and tent kitchens at La Loma Field. The now homeless came, nearly 20,000 in the first few days, and the military doctors cared for the injured and ill. The Marines provided meals for the many thousands of refugees.

Mixed in with news columns about Easter Sunday parades and special programs and the Red Cross relief efforts in Nicaragua, the bulletin in West Virginia was that Second Lieutenant (Gunnery Sergeant) William Hutcherson Pigg, 36, first listed as injured in the earthquake, had been slain by a Nacional Guardsman in Managua. The telegram was sent late Saturday night to his mother, who could not be located. She had recently relocated from Eckman. "Deeply regret to inform you radiogram Nicaragua National Guard detachment states your son Sergeant William H. Pigg died April 4 from gunshot wounds." [56]

A military board of inquiry convened immediately and concluded that Sergeant Pigg had suffered a "mind break" under the strain of rescue work, had become demented, and threatened the guard on police duty who shot him.

Will Rogers, American humorist and Ambassador of Good Will, hopped on a United Air Lines flight to Managua to see for himself the aftermath of the seismic nightmare. On Thursday, April 9, he wrote a letter from Managua *To the Editor of the New York Times.* Drawing attention to the plight of the residents and the need for financial and material aid to make its way from the States, he made special mention of the Marines.

In the eleventh year of America's ban on the public sale of alcohol, he had some interesting news for the anti-prohibitionists, known as the *Wets.* "Everything in town—churches, schools, banks, stores—was destroyed but the brewery. But it was an act of providence at that, for the water-works were destroyed and all they had to drink was beer. The commandant sent twenty marines to protect it and with the 100 that was already there, why, they were able to hold it."

Will's cables were not all in jest. He had gone for a reconnaissance flight that day with Major Ralph J. Mitchell, Commander Aircraft Squadron, 2d Marine Brigade. "Went all over the bandit country they patrol. You have to see this terrible mountainous country to see what these aviators have been up against. I could tell you for a week some of the things these aviators have done in this country." [57]

The relief work was conducted in such a way as to not affect the normal operations of headquarters "with respect to the control of forces operating against bandits." That meant that during the earthquake and its aftermath, Lieutenant D. L. Truesdale was leading Guardia patrols 105 miles east of the epicenter, in small, populated places around Ocotal. At times his position was better determined by latitude and longitude on maps than by the place names reported by locals.

The plan to withdraw the Marines from Nicaragua was proceeding on schedule, and the Guardia Nacional of Nicaragua had recruited more than 450 men in the northwestern area. Lieutenant Truesdale was one of only twenty Marines remaining near the Ocotal combat outpost where contacts with the principal outlaw bands were most likely. [58]

Captain Harlen Pefley, 36, of Boise, Idaho, NNG, was killed in a clash with fifty insurgents on April 11 in the eastern area near the Logtown outpost, twelve miles west of Puerta Cabezas. [59]

Front Page News

The Navy reported to Washington, D.C., that, on Monday, April 27, a group of armed bandits had attacked a farm near Las Torres, twelve miles south of Ocotal. Overhead aircraft radioed a report that a Guardia patrol was in pursuit—bandit contact #241. Washington sent a special report to *The New York Times* on April 30. The next day, Friday, May 1, 1931, Donald Truesdale was on the front page of a newspaper. [60]

"Lieutenant D. L. Truesdale, of Lugoff, S.C., a corporal in the Marine Corps, was in command." His patrol caught the outlaws at Aguacatel, eighteen miles southwest of Ocotal, above the Río Pueblo Nuevo, west of Condega. Under intense fire, the bandits escaped in the brush. The Guardia suffered no casualties. The patrol captured eleven animals, clothes, and blankets and reported killing two bandits.

A second skirmish with the outlaws took place on Tuesday and was more newsworthy to the Guard headquarters—bandit contact #242. Seventeen miles south of Ocotal, Lieutenant Truesdale's patrol made contact with another insurgent band near Las Oucillas. Chief Lieutenant Chavarria, one of General Sandino's commanders, was killed, and ten in his company were wounded. The patrol captured hats, clothing, flashlights, hatbands, and two bombs. The patrol returned to Quilalí.

The Arts of Patrolling

Verbal orders were passed on June 11, 1931. Bandits had fired on Lieutenant Ross' patrol. Lieutenant Truesdale took a Guardia patrol from Quilalí into the El Golfo vicinity to reconnoiter the scene. No contact was made. He returned to the garrison and reported that the bandits were likely headed west towards Telpaneca. Four days later, he led a Guardia patrol to San Juan de Telpaneca. "No Contact."

The Quilalí garrison was on the Río Jicaro, north of where the river ran into the Río Coco. That was thirty-two air miles southeast of the Ocotal outpost. "Issued a gun and 100 rounds of ammunition," 2dLt Truesdale and two other Marine officers watched over a district of about forty square miles. They encamped with twenty Marines and twenty-five Guardia men "on a hill over a town of maybe thirteen houses."

By the time they manned the Quilalí garrison, the lieutenants grasped the dangers of leading patrols out of town on the trails along the Río Jicaro and the risks of evacuating casualties. "Ya couldn't go out, you couldn't go out, you weren't supposed to leave there with less than eighteen men, you know? Yer goin'—you get somebody wounded and you done play the devil getting 'em outta there. And, ah, we, we always, dey always had an order, don't go, don't leave with less than that many men."

Even so, managing a column of eighteen men on a trail posed the patrol leader more than one challenge. In the vegetation, a rider might be able to see the mule in front of him and the one immediately behind. Eighteen riders on mules typically stretched out of Lieutenant Truesdale's line of sight. "But, you can't see 'em in the bush, that many. See?"

He came to trust the Guard troops on the trail; even preferred to patrol with them instead of the Americans with whom he had come ashore. "And the one thing about it, those people there were shrewd. . . . They could see something comin', might near smell it. Which Americans couldn't do it. I had these two good point men. . . . And they'd see something like a deer, want to kill some deer on the road. There was one of them standing out in front, one of them in front of me would fall this way and the other would fall this-a-away. And I knew something was happenin'.

"They'd do like this, a little sign language, without talkin'. Didn't make no noise, 'cause they didn't have nothin' to make noise with. But the Marines comin' in, like with sidearms, ridin' a mule and all like that, makin' all kinda noise."

Supplies could run short in a week's time, so the Quilalí garrison dispatched patrols north to Apalí, where the Quartermaster maintained stocks of necessities. There were two primary routes, both of which passed through Jicaro. The slower, more precarious trails followed the Río Jicaro, risking encounters with the Sandinistas in the vicinities of the Zapotillo Ridge, the mouth of the Río Murra stream, and the San Albino mines.

The preferred route was along the main road to the northeast for five miles until it branched due north at Las Cruces. After another fifteen-or-so-winding miles, the trail crossed the Río Susucayán stream, on its way southeast to empty into the Río Jicaro. Four more miles northeast, and the patrol could bivouac at Jicaro. Apalí was another fifteen-mile ride. This more-traveled route provided the bandits plenty of opportune ambush sites.

Lieutenant Truesdale did not dally along the way. "It was forty miles to Apalí, where we would, ah, go to get provisions. But Jicaro was off to one side, which was about twenty-five miles. And some of those people would go there and get the—go to Jicaro, that's twenty-five miles, and camp overnight. Next mornin', get up early and go over to Apalí, and get the provisions, which was about twelve, fifteen mile, and bring it back to Jicaro that night. And keep wa—goin', and then come on back there to Quilalí the next day. But, I wouldn't do that. I'd just take me a straight trip forty miles and camp all day there, and draw it in the mornin', early, come on back. It didn't take me long to make forty miles. But, there wasn't but one stream between the whole thing, to get water. And, uh, I never would drink. Them other two would (referring to two Marine officers), ah, but I'd say, 'Uh uh, not me.' But, you know, you couldn't stand it."

Frugal with his pennies, Lieutenant Truesdale provided more than casuasa for his Guardia troops. "And I think we got about 12¢ a day to feed 'em (equivalent to $1.90 in 2016). I'd say we got about 20¢ ($3.17) a day in the Marine Corps. That was our food allowance, see? Nobody was goin' hungry. Neighbors, neighbors, friends. Yeah. They'd let us get, like, so much pepper, you got it every once, every week, you know, you got your provisions. You couldn't trade it for something else. They had to figure out how much you needed. It's funny to live that-a-way, but—"

On more tactical missions, the troops endured long patrols, measured not in hours or miles, but in days. "Sometimes we spent twenty-five nights out in the bushes." Since the Marines were not issued machetes, the Guard troops hacked their way along the thick, tropical jungle trails with their blades. And the rebels always knew where the hacking was taking place. And, as is true of most combat veterans who experienced events they would like to forget, Lieutenant Truesdale's recollections of the longer patrols could seem to be of inconsequential things.

"And then, just like we'd get on a trail, there, and didn't, didn't have nothin' to—what we had hangin' on us. We would chew sugar cane. I would, could chew two stalks that long, and, you know, some good sugar cane outta, that bigga around. You gotta' lot a juice in 'em. You know, I'd chew it and get—feel it, right quick. And eat a couple more tall tea. There're even some bananas, green, you take a green banana, get down by a road bed or a stream and peel the peelin' off it, open it up and wash the ol' sticky stuff off it, and they go up there where you had a fire built and coals. And, then you lay it in the fire there, and it would get, uh, we'd cook it, rub a little salt on it, and you'd get filled up, and then make no more.

"And then we'd see a deer once in a while, and I could shoot good. Now, I used to shoot a lot of deer. And, we'd eat a little meat. Anything left over, they had a gorge about that long, and they'd cut the top half, you know, clean it out, and put what was left in it, and stick it in yer haversack where it wouldn't turn over, and have something to eat a little later. But, people just eat too much. But, but then, if didn't eat too much, go across the stream, just throw a little water in my mouth, and wash it out, and take my tooth brush and wash my teeth a little bit.

"But, we uh, we fed good. We got it the only way ya can get it, from them people."

The tropical climate in Nicaragua, amounting to only two long seasons, the dry and the wet, also had to be factored in on patrols. Lieutenant Truesdale was at the Quilalí garrison during the summer dry season, what the locals called "verano." The hottest and driest days extended from March to mid-May.

". . . it would get hot, and they would drink water out of a daggoned hoof print. There wasn't no water in the dry season. It was just in the streams, and they had to live somewhere near there to get their water. See? And that was dryin' their land out. But now, it was pretty warm—"

There was almost no rain in the summer months of December to June. In the higher altitudes of hilly and mountainous Nueva Segovia the daytime temperatures averaged around 74°F, and temps seldom dropped below 61°F at night.

Patrols were shorter in the rainy season. For each of as many as twenty days in July, nearly two or more inches of rain fell on the trails night and day. Prudence dictated that eighteen-man columns not go far from the garrison.

That summer, Lieutenant Truesdale made the acquaintance of 2dLt Granville Kimball Frisbie, 27, from Equinunk, Pennsylvania, assigned to the Guardia Nacional detachment as a captain. Second Lieutenant Frisbie had interrupted his graduation plans from Hartford, Connecticut, Trinity College Class of 1926, when he enlisted in the Marines in 1923. While stationed at the Philadelphia Naval Yard, he had married Lycoming College graduate Miss Muriel Cole Teeple on August 26, 1926. [61] They went together to Norfolk, Virginia, while he served at the Marine Barracks, Navy Yard. The couple had a son they named Franklin Cole. They were apart when Granville was assigned to the 2d Brigade in January 1929. That was when he first became familiar with bandits and bad guys. He had sailed home with the USS *Tennessee* Marine Detachment in April 1930. He and Muriel then enjoyed time at Parris Island while he served at the Marine Barracks, Naval Prison—more "bad guys" experience.

Second Lieutenant Frisbie had returned to Nicaragua. [62] Lieutenant Truesdale was his second in command.

On Tuesday, July 28, 1931, Lieutenant Truesdale commanded a Guardia patrol that contacted a group of armed bandits at Chamaste, a populated place near Quilalí. The Guardia reported no known casualties. Three bandits took wounds. The patrol captured four shotguns, shells, cartridges, and miscellaneous articles.

A month later, on August 28 at noon, Captain Frisbie and 2dLt Truesdale led fifteen enlisted men on foot from Quilalí headed for San Juan De Telpaneca, where they linked with Guard 2dLt Lisandro Delgadillo and spent the night. Awake early, Lieutenant Tru took stock of their arms and supplies: four Thompson machine guns, two BARs, two Springfield rifles with grenade dischargers, fifty hand grenades, balance of regular issue rifles and ammunition. Food stuff was loaded on four pack animals.

The combined patrol of three officers and twenty-nine troops set out on the combat mission entirely on foot on the San Juan-Quilalí trail at 8:00 AM. They proceeded to San Lucas, then turned southeast toward the El Ojoche area, arriving at "Loma Chata" at 3:00 PM. The Guardia scoffed at the place as "a boring knoll." It was a rest stop.

Having enlisted a guía civico (civilian guide), the train of men, clearing the trails by hand, made for "Cerro Blanco," three miles northeast of Chamaste, where the guide believed either General Pedro A. Irias or Gregoria Colindres had a camp. The notorious Colindres was one of the first men to join Generalissimo Sandino. On the southern side of the white hill, the patrol found traces of bandit activity and investigated four bandit houses.

Moving on through dense undergrowth, the patrol spotted the bandit headquarters (position 363–236 on 2d Brigade tactical maps) at the head of a cornfield in a most inaccessible position on the hillside. One shack was large enough for thirty men. The roofs of seven smaller shacks were plainly in sight. The bandits had just killed a cow and were preparing it for their supper. "A favorable rain" concealed the patrol's approach as they surrounded the camp.

At 5:30 PM, the Guardia surprised the bandit force of seventy men. The rebels were not able to man their rifles and machine guns effectively, but fire from a Lewis machine gun kept Captain Frisbie pinned to the ground for half the engagement. The men under Lieutenant Tru's leadership "showed every inclination to carry the fire fight to a successful termination." The well-known Chief Agapito Altamirano and two unidentified bandits, including the Lewis gunner, were killed outright and two were wounded.

When their leader was killed, the surviving occupants hastily evacuated the camp, shouting, "Viva Colindres." Prisoners reported that General Gregorio had been present at the fight, but had escaped from the field. The hillside was quiet by 6:00 PM.

The patrol captured one Smith & Wesson .38cal pistol, three Lewis Drums, three BAR magazines, one Krag rifle, eight dynamite sticks, ten yards of fuse, three dry bombs, 210 rounds of ammunition, one bugle, two bayonets, five haversacks, a bandit guard book, bandit correspondence, flags, insignia, and clothing. Some of the gear was USMC issue. The patrol burned the camp and destroyed all bandit articles of value except serviceable items, the ammunition, and correspondence, which they loaded onto the pack animals.

The patrol moved a half league from the hill and made night camp in a favorable defensive location at 7:30 PM. In the morning, the men showed signs of sickness from exposure, and the officers turned the patrol toward Quilalí. They were at the outpost at 12:30 PM.

In his August 31 patrol report to the Octocal Area Commander, Captain Frisbie commended his two lieutenants and the troops for their fighting qualities and for exemplifying the best traditions of the Guardia Nacional in every respect.

Lieutenant Truesdale made sure that his Guardia men enthusiastically celebrated the September 14 and 15 Nicaragua national holidays of the Battle of San Jacinto and the Declaration of Independence.

He and Lieutenant Collins took a Guardia patrol from Quilalí to Jicaro on Wednesday, October 7, and stayed for six days. The patrol departed on Tuesday and returned to Quilalí.

The weather turned inclement in the Central Area in mid-October and communications could go a week without reports arriving at headquarters. For the next two months, Captain Frisbie, 2dLt Truesdale, and 2dLt W. C. Smith manned the garrison at Quilalí. They led patrols along the Río Coco valley between the garrison and Telepaneca and up the Río Jicaro and Río Murra. Reports went to headquarters of Guardia patrols attacking armed bandits at San Benito, at Regadillo near Limay (Department of Esteli), and between Ojoche and El Silencio.

On Friday, October 23, Captain Frisbie and Lieutenant Truesdale led a Quilalí Guardia patrol toward Zapotillo on a combat mission through Tecosintal and La Reforma into the Las Cruces district. On Saturday, they ran into twenty-five armed bandits near Las Cruces under the command of Jefe (Chief) Roque Vargas, armed mostly with cutachas (machetes) and pistols. The Guardia patrol suffered no casualties. Four outlaws died in the skirmish and several were wounded. The patrol returned to Quilalí with one captured pistol, a bandit letter, and other miscellaneous articles.

On October 27, 2dLt Truesdale and 2dLt Smith led a Guardia patrol from Quilalí to Jicaro. The patrol returned to the garrison the next day.

On Monday, November 16, at 1:30 PM in heavy fog, 100 bandits attacked the town of Quilalí (position 235–358) with rifles, two automatic weapons, and dynamite bombs. Captain Frisbie and Lieutenant Smith were in command of the cuartel (barracks) at the time. The insurrectos were driven from the fight after an hour, taking their unknown number of casualties with them. The barracks guard had no casualties.

Lieutenant Truesdale led a police mission patrol from Quilalí into the area of Pamali and La Gloria on November 26. He reported the area quiet when he returned. He went out again with his men on December 1 for a reconnaissance patrol.

Four years had gone by since CPL Truesdale had first landed in Nicaragua. When 1931 neared its end, his fourth Christmas in Central America was approaching. The Marines had been searching out Sandinistas in western Matagalpa, well south of Ocotal, and forcing them to vacate north from the area of La Trinidad and San Isidro. That made contacts between Lieutenant Truesdale's Guardia company and the bandits more likely.

Captain Frisbie was missing his wife and son and planning a mission. On December 22, he and Lieutenant Truesdale took a patrol from Quilalí on a reconnaissance mission. Captured information suggested that either Jefe Rafael Altamirano or Julian Gutierrez were encamped with General Sandino.

On Friday, Christmas Day, the Marines thought about families back home, imagining how their loved ones were spending the day. Many were naturally homesick and hoped at least for a mail drop from a VO-7 airplane. The officers did what they could to keep up the cheer, and kept their own longing for home to themselves.

Generals Sandino and Gregorio Colindres, anticipating a yankee incursión, celebrated the Feast of the Savior's Nativity by clearing out of the mountain fortress (257–379) at daybreak and leading most of their men to Jinotega.

On December 26, the Frisbie–Truesdale patrol found a secret trail in the jungles northeast of El Chipote and nine miles from Quilalí. The patrol advanced into a guerilla camp, an outpost of General Sandino's main camp. Rebel sentries spotted their approach, and the patrol immediately fired on the camp. They killed two Sandinistas and likely mortally wounded another. Most in the camp escaped.

Second Lieutenant Truesdale had to deal with another reality of a guerilla war. The Sandinistas commonly had señoras and señoritas living in the camps with them. "One of the two killed outright proved to be a woman, dressed with clothing trimmed at the neck and sleeves with red and black."

The patrol captured Señora Altamirano, the wife of Sandinista Major Rafeal Altamirano. For two days, the señora prisoner led the patrol to several unoccupied rebel camps. The camps had been constructed near fields of corn, sugar cane, and tobacco. The Guard found stocks of ammunition and bushels of corn. The patrol destroyed everything they discovered, including six camps.

Finding their way back to Quilalí, the patrol was lost for four hours. They finally arrived at the garrison on December 29, exhausted.

Captain Frisbie's January 5, 1932, Report to the Area Commander gave the details of the week-long patrol.

1932 Going Home Soon

As more Guardsmen took over the Marine outposts and positions, Second Lieutenant D. L. Truesdale remained in the Northern Area of Jinotega Department. He and Lieutenant Bilbrey returned from a short patrol on January 4, 1932. "Nothing to report" was the dispatch from Quilalí. Lieutenant Bilbrey took sick and was evacuated to the Managua Hospital by airplane on Saturday, January 9.

Lieutenant Truesdale "cleared" (departed) San Juan with a patrol on February 11 to obtain provisions at Quilalí. Nearing Buena Vista (230–370), they contacted bandits. The patrol killed well-known bandit Filipe Diaz and continued to Quilalí, having captured the bandit's .38 pistol, ammunition, cutacha, and miscellaneous articles. Lieutenant Truesdale took the patrol safely back to San Juan on February 14. Two days later, he took his men out on a combat mission.

The Guardia patrol was in the El Silencio area, west of Quilalí, on Friday, February 19 and made contact with armed bandits at Ojoche. The jefe of the group was unknown. The engagement lasted five minutes. Four bandits were killed in action. Lieutenant Tru's patrol had no casualties. They captured one shotgun, one cutacha, two dynamite bombs, and miscellaneous articles.

On February 28, lieutenants Truesdale and R.A. Trosper took a fifteen-man patrol and one bandit prisoner on a combat mission from Apalí. Being a leap year, when they returned to the outpost, the date was February 29. "Nothing to report." Lieutenant Tru departed with a fifteen-man patrol the next morning, March 1—destination San Juan de Tel.

On the morning of March 2, newspapers reported what became one of the most highly publicized crimes of the 20th century. Twenty-month-old Charles Augustus Lindbergh Jr., was kidnapped the previous night from the home of famous aviator Charles Lindbergh and Anne Morrow Lindbergh in East Amwell, New Jersey.

While the nation waited for news, and before the toddler's body was discovered on May 12, a telegram would go to the home of Earl and Maggie Truesdale in Lugoff.

Second Lieutenant Truesdale was on the front page of a newspaper again on March 16. The *New York Times* headline was "12 Slain in Nicaragua in Three Skirmishes." [63] The news had first been reported from Marine headquarters, dispatched to the Navy Department in Washington and broadcast over Tropical Radio in Managua. The report was a testimony to the lieutenant's leadership skills.

On Friday, March 11, Second Lieutenant Donald Leroy Truesdale commanded a Quilalí Guardia patrol twenty-four miles east of Jinotega, near San Benito in the Province of Nueva Segovia. At 8:00 PM, a sharp skirmish erupted when the patrol encountered a bandit band under the command of Jefe Filiberto Reyes. The patrol surrounded the bandit camp and attacked. Eight insurgents were killed and an unknown number wounded in the battle. There were no Guard casualties. In his Patrol Report of the action from San Benito, 2dLt Truesdale informed headquarters that the insurgent bandit camp was destroyed and considerable supplies and ammunition were captured: one rifle, one pistol, 112 rounds of ammunition, cutachas, and a quantity of Sandino correspondence and propaganda pamphlets. The wounded bandits were not provided any first aid. [64]

On Saturday, a Jicaro Guardia patrol led by Lieutenant Zamora had a running fight with fifty insurgents near the Honduras border. After a ten-minute fight at Rico Montana, the bandits scattered into Honduras. The dispatches reported no known NNG casualties in this contact. Of the bandits: "Many blood trails were found." On Sunday, four insurgents in the Province of León were killed and several wounded. There were no Guard casualties in the third engagement.

Abril 1932—a *Muy Mal* Month for the Guardia

At the start of April, no one suspected the month would go on record as a bad month for the Guardia. "It was by far the worst since the Guardia was organized." [65]

It began quietly for Lieutenant Truesdale. On April 2, he cleared San Juan with a patrol of ten enlisted Guardia and arrived safely at Quilalí. He took an eleven-man patrol back to San Juan on Wednesday, April 6. Once in the station, he learned how badly Abril was going. "An unfortunate occurrence had happened."

First Lieutenant (Sergeant) Charles J. Levonski of New York had been in Nicaragua for more than four years. He had succeeded Lieutenant Lewis Trogler after his murder in 1929, and had an excellent record for gallantry. Lieutenant Levonski was popular with the native soldiers and was considered one of the most efficient officers in the republic. He was with the Guard detachment on the Río Coco, just under the Honduras border in the eastern Autonomous Region of the North Atlantic. His second in command was 2dLt Carlos Reyes, a national.

Discontented native sergeants at the Kisalaya Guardia garrison mutinied early on Monday morning, April 4, 1932, because 1stLt Levonski refused to turn over a prisoner and betray 2dLt Reyes. Lieutenant Levonski was killed in the attack and 2dLt Reyes was wounded.

Ten loyal Guardsmen made for the nearest garrison, while the fifteen fully armed mutineers escaped into the jungle and made their way up the river for the Department of Jinotega. Every effort with aeroplanes and ground patrols were dispatched to capture the murderers. [66] A Guardia patrol tracked down and killed the traitor who had murdered Lieutenant Levonski.

If necessary, and if the weather allowed, the Marines could hope for some air support from the Marine DH-4s and Vought Corsair O2U-1s. Marine aeroplane radio dispatches indicated that bandit activity was escalating in the extensive La Constancia Locality, Departamento de Jinotega. The San Rafael patrols were reporting bandit contacts in the Pantasma Valley and El Tule.

On Friday, April 8, Captain (First Lieutenant) Arthur C. Small and Lieutenant G. D. Snyder led thirty enlisted Guardsmen in the La Constancia Area. The San Rafael Guardia patrol located a bandit outpost and observed an armed patrol of forty bandits. The patrol routed the bandits, killing two and wounding several. No Guardia took casualties. Captain Small pursued more bandits east of Lake Apanas, past the Río Pantasma, a tributary of the Río Coco, and into the Valle de Pantasma, an eight-mile circular crater. The residents of Santa Maria de Pantasma proved to be of no help in the search.

The mutinies and desertions raised tensions at every outpost in the Northern Area. On Monday, April 11, a sergeant and two Guardsmen at Quilalí, men 2dLt Truesdale had trained, each grabbed an automatic weapon and deserted to the guerrillas.

On Tuesday, Lieutenant Truesdale led a Guardia patrol of thirteen enlisted men off the Quilalí trail and north into the Las Cruces ridges. Mensia Vilchez, civico (civilian) guide, rode along with him. When he and his Guardia interpreter tried to get information about "los bandoleros" from the indigenous Miskitos, Mayagnas, and Sumos, the natives seemed to have more to say about "los marinos yankis."

Lieutenant Truesdale could speak Spanish and could understand the language fairly well. He did not let on, though, instead having his native troops negotiate with the locals. "El teniente es estúpido y no entiende," the Guardia soldiers would say to them. The lieutenant took no offense to being called stupid. He learned more when the locals figured he did not understand what they were saying. [67]

The patrol located a group of bandits of an unknown jefe armed with rifles, pistols, and shotguns and exchanged fire for five minutes. A large amount of blood was found at the scene after the outlaws fled in all directions. No bandit bodies were discovered, and whether any had died was unknown. The patrol returned to San Juan on Thursday, and Lieutenant Truesdale regretted to report that Señor Vilchez had been killed in the fight.

On Friday, April 15, 2dLt Fred Dale Beans, 26, U.S. Naval Academy grad, led a Quilalí Guardia patrol west along the Quilalí trail toward San Juan del Río Coco. [68] Just six miles from San Juan, the patrol ran into thirty of Heriberto Reyes' armed bandits and fought for fifteen minutes, killing one bandit. The victorious Guardia patrol reported no casualties among its men.

On Sunday, 2dLt Truesdale cleared San Juan for the Apalí outpost with lieutenants Roberts, Rutledge, and Saenz, and twenty enlisted troops. Lieutenant Roberts took sick south of the station. The officers split the patrol. Lieutenant Truesdale hurried to Apalí with eight men. Lieutenants Rutledge and Saenz put twelve men into defensive positions and held until Lieutenant Roberts could ride. They made Apalí in the evening.

The stay at Apalí was brief. Lieutenants Beans and Truesdale left on April 19 with twelve troops and arrived at Jicaro. The two lieutenants were back on the trail the next day with nineteen enlisted men, headed for Estacion De Quilalí.

Second Lieutenant (Corporal) Laurin T. Covington, from Spartanburg, South Carolina, had been in the field against the Nicaraguan rebels since May 1931. On Thursday, April 21, he was at the Apalí outpost, thirteen miles east of Ocotal. He led a thirteen-man Jalapa Guardia patrol northeast toward the Jalapa outpost. Two hundred well-armed bandits ambushed the patrol as it crossed a small stream near Las Puertas. Four of Lieutenant Covington's men were killed in the intense fighting before he could break contact with the "Nicaraguan irregulars."

Second Lieutenant Lawrence Collins Brunton, 24, a recently married Naval Academy graduate in country for less than a month, led an Apalí Guardia relief column to the ambush site and joined Lieutenant Covington's patrol.

The combined column traveled along the Camino Real trail, the main highroad to Cifuentes on the Honduras border. Moving toward Los Leones, they entered another kill zone the evasive bandits had set up. The column was routed in the second ambush. Both Marine officers, Pharmacist Mate Finnis H. Whitehead, of Grosse Point, Michigan, and six more Guardia troops were killed. Four survived their wounds. The insurgents retired from the ambush site with their dead and wounded. [69]

Hometown newspaper editorials mourned the loss of three more brave young Americans—"three of our defenders with the colors." Familiar protests about the administration in Washington circulated across the country. Either not enough Marines had been sent into Nicaragua to do the job that was promised, or withdrawing the Marine regiments was akin to abandoning allies. Politicians made passionate speeches. The protestors answered. "We now invite assassination of innocent Americans and others by Nicaraguan bandits and take the humiliating position of saying we cannot protect the lives of our citizens." [70]

As April neared its end, the rainy season downpours turned the trails into deep quagmires. Swelled rivers ran high and rapidly, adding to the hardships of patrolling in the bush. Malaria, bad feet, skin ulcers and infections, and sagging morale plagued many of the *Río Coco Marines.*

On Thursday, April 21, Lieutenant Truesdale's sergeant passed along reliable bandit information that Jose Leon Diaz was camped south of the Coco River with 150 of his bandits. As second in command of the patrol, Lieutenant Tru and Lieutenant Beans cleared Quilalí at 8:00 AM on a police mission into the Bujona Area with ten Guardia enlisted men. No bandits or prisoners were located and the patrol returned to the outpost.

On Friday, lieutenants Beans and Truesdale left the Quilalí garrison again with sixteen Guardia Nacional troops, proceeding to Pamali on a combat mission to investigate. The "dos marinos yankis" were easily recognizable to the insurrectos. They wore broad-brimmed field hats, khakis, dusty field shoes, and non-standard-issue bandanas around their necks. They had minimal 782-gear on their belts.

Planning for four days in the field, the two commanders each departed with a rifle, pack, poncho, shelter half, mosquito net, an extra uniform, four extra pairs of socks, and four days of rations of fermented rice and beans, canned corned beef, salmon, and sardines. They planned to keep themselves to two meals a day and would drink muddy river water when their canteens were empty, although Lieutenant Tru rationed his own drinking to ensure there was some water in his canteen.

The patrol captured two civilians, runners for the bandits. One of them, Abraham Garcia, then guided them to Ciudad Viejo and, from there, down the Jicaro to the Río Coco. Heading south to Bilan and Pacayal, they found two bandit camps, each recently vacated by thirty men. Continuing west, the patrol surprised ten men at a large camp in Rica. The men ran, but one was killed and others were wounded. The patrol captured a shotgun, a pistol, a Victrola, correspondence, much food, and other loot. As dark descended, they stayed in the camp that night.

Lieutenant Truesdale rousted the men early, and they destroyed 300 pounds of tobacco, the food supplies, and the camp. The patrol left at 6:00 AM and searched the area and houses around Constance. There were no men in the neighborhood. Women reported that 150 Jose Diaz men had been camped there, but had left on April 20 for Las Naranjas to join Pedron Altamirano in Jinotega.

Lieutenant Beans had the patrol in night defensive positions north of Constance. This contact with an armed Sandinista bandit raiding party did not find its way into the Official Guardia Nacional de Nicaragua Contact Files of the GN-2, GN-3 Section, Headquarters, in Managua.

Patrols had also been looking for bandits further north all day. Gunnery Sergeant John Hamas from Philadelphia led a Guardia Detachment patrol of four officers and forty enlisted nationals from Ocotal on Saturday to avenge the deaths of their comrades. At 3:30 PM, they attacked 100 rebels in Jefe Carlos Salgado's entrenched headquarters camp near Guambuco Mountain in the mountainous jungles on the Honduras border. Under a scathing 25-minute fight, the rebels vacated the camp, leaving three of their dead behind. The wounded escaped with the others. One Guardsman was wounded. Gunny Hamas reorganized his men to hold the position.

When the NNG patrol secured the camp, in addition to bandit food stocks, weapons, munitions, and correspondence, they found clothing and equipment belonging to the three

Americans killed in the Thursday ambush. The bandits continued determined counter-attacks and skirmishes into the evening. At 5:30 AM on the 24th, the rebels again tried to retake their camp in a fifteen-minute engagement. They were driven off and scattered in all directions.

Second Lieutenant George R. Weeks and 2dLt C. L. Ashbrook took a San Rafael Guardia patrol into the hills on Saturday, and found seventy of Juan Altamirano's men at Sacaste. The rebels dispersed after a brief, ten-minute fight. The patrol caught up with the bandits on Sunday at 9:50 AM on a ridge at Loma del Nancia. In this fifteen-minute clash, the patrol captured twelve horses and saddles, twelve hand grenades, and Guardia clothing. For a second time, there were no known casualties reported on either side.

At 11:00 AM, an Algovia Guardia patrol of four enlisted men near El Horno had a two-minute skirmish west of Telpaneca in the Department of Matagalpa with a small bandit group commanded by Alfredo Rizo. There were no casualties, but the contact was fruitful. The patrol captured two civil prisoners, two mules, saddles, and bandit equipment.

One Final Patrol

At daylight on Sunday, April 24, the Beans–Truesdale patrol secretly followed a trail north-west away from Constancia moving toward the Río Coco. The terrain was rugged jungle rain forest and echoed with the chatter of birds and white face, howler and spider monkeys. The Guardsmen chatted about jaguar and puma sightings, and told tales of the giant anteaters, crocodiles, and toucans. Lieutenant Truesdale moved along in the formation, alert and ready for a hostile encounter. He was indifferent to his men's banter that the bandits referred to him as "Felipon," as the name meant nothing to him. [71]

Private (Raso) Jose Cordova was at the point of the patrol. He ran into a bandit carrying a shotgun, fired immediately, but missed. The bandit returned fire, hitting the point man in the heart, killing him instantly. The bandit slipped into the brush under intense fire, was wounded based on the blood trail, but escaped.

Lieutenant Beans figured that the patrol was eight or more leagues (about 28 miles) from Quilalí. With no available mule, it was impossible to get Private Cordova's body back to the garrison. They buried him on the trail, marked the spot with a cross, and continued to the Coco River.

During the patrol's advance at the river, a rifle grenade slipped from its carrier on the grenadier's belt and hit a rock, igniting the detonator. Several patrol members were within five feet of the grenade, putting them in danger of the imminent explosion.

Lieutenant Truesdale saw what happened and understood that the grenade would either kill or grievously wound anyone within the blast radius of roughly seven to eight feet. He had short seconds to decide what he would do. He was yards away from the grenade and had time to protect himself and take cover.

Looking out only for his own interests, it would have been best for him to drop everything from his grasp, put his hands over his ears, and haul ass down the trail away from the grenade. Instead, he hastened to the explosive, picked it up, and tried to hurl it away from the patrol "knowing full well the grenade would explode within two or three seconds, and with utter disregard for his own personal safety, and at the risk of his own life."

With an explosion capable of rupturing lungs, puncturing eardrums, compressing blood vessels, squeezing the stomach, and causing brain hemorrhaging, the grenade detonated before he could dispose of it. The metal debris radiated outward in all directions. So did the flash, the blast wave lasting a few milliseconds and traveling faster than the speed of sound, the sound itself, and the smell. The confined space of the Nicaraguan jungle trail, like a chamber, amplified the impact of the shock (pressure) wave.

The blunt-force trauma ripped Lieutenant Truesdale's right hand to pieces and caused multiple serious fragmentation wounds to his body. His firm grasp of the grenade had restricted the full shock of the explosion to himself, thereby protecting the lives of the others close by. As he would report the event, the noise and shock wave did not render him unconsciousness, even for a few seconds.

Ignoring the effects of the explosive concussion, 2dLt Truesdale sat down, unlaced one of his boots, and made a tourniquet. Gritty, single-minded, he told his soldiers to bring his mule. Lieutenant Beans gave first aid, commanding Sergeant Pedro Flores to make a stretcher and get 2dLt Tru to Quilalí as quickly as possible.

Lieutenant Beans rode for Quilalí with two men to request an immediate evacuation by air. As 2dLt Truesdale regained his bearings, he wanted to mount a mule and ignore the stretcher, then thought better of it. His men picked him up and headed for the aid station.

Lieutenant Beans was at Quilalí by noon. He dispatched a runner to San Juan to request plane transportation for an immediate air evacuation, then organized another patrol, bringing a practicante (medic) and all available medicine back on the trail. They located Lieutenant Truesdale's patrol, and all were back in the garrison at 3:30 PM. The practicante provided medical attention, waiting for an aeroplane to land at the little airfield the Marines had laid out. Twenty-four hours after the grenade detonation, the plane arrived at Quilalí. Lieutenant Tru was put in the rear cockpit and removed to the hospital in Managua.

Rebel correspondences proved that the bandits showed "great elation" when they heard that "Felipon" had been wounded and evacuated from the area.

The savage fighting in the Northern Area went on. On Tuesday, April 26, Gunnery Sergeant Hamas commanded a patrol of five officers and forty-five enlisted men. He led his patrol to what was believed to be General Sandino's main camp and entrenched stronghold manned by approximately 250 bandits. The bandit leader was in the camp. Again greatly outnumbered, Gunny Hamas personally led the assault "with utter disregard for his personal safety." The patrol captured the stronghold in three hours of fighting, leaving ten bandits killed and twenty-one wounded. Gunny Hamas reported the loss of one wounded Guardsman. The patrol also secured large quantities of food supplies, clothing, and ammunition.

In a few months, Gunny Hamas and 2dLt Truesdale would share their tales of leading NNG patrols and stand beside each other on a grassy Campo de Marte parade deck.

A Couple of Months to Heal Up

Gangrene infection had set in. Three days after the detonation, 2dLt Truesdale's arm was amputated just below the elbow. Most of his USMC tattoo was gone. The larger shrapnel pieces were extracted from open wounds. The smaller ones that had peppered his body were left in place, much of it in his left leg, leaving his arms and legs looking pockmarked, with something blue behind the indentations. [72]

On April 29, word was circulating around Guardia Nacional Headquarters in Managua that the Jefe Director was preparing a Congressional Medal of Honor award recommendation for Lieutenant Truesdale.

When the news reached Lugoff that her son's right hand had been blown off in Nicaragua, Margaret Truesdell sat down and cried. It was only the second time in the family's memory that she had cried openly, the first time having been when her first baby died. Eighteen years passed before she cried a third time. [73]

Lieutenant Truesdale survived his encounter with the grenade. When he was presented discharge papers in the hospital, he objected to the "handicapped" designation and saw no reason to be released from the service.

"Give me a couple of months to heal up, and I can whip any Marine in Nicaragua." Regarding the pain, his fortitude was evident. "What difference does that make? Can't do anything about it. Crying won't make it any better."

His commanders and witnesses were impressed by his "extraordinary heroism in the line of his profession above and beyond the call of duty at the risk of his life." A report and recommendation went up to Washington. "His actions were worthy of the highest traditions of the profession of arms."

As Lieutenant Truesdale recuperated, 5th Marine Regiment Sergeant Anton S. Clausen of New York, with twenty-four years of USMC service, serving with the NNGD, died of dementia paralytica at the hospital in Managua on June 4.

Lieutenant (Gunnery Sergeant) Edward Hall Schmierer from Philadelphia, expert in rifle and pistol use, commanding a NNG detachment in San Isidro, west of Matagalpa, was murdered while he slept on Thursday, June 30. Authorities accused Nicaraguan Lieutenant Robert Gonzalez of committing the crime. He had deserted with four native Guardsmen. [74]

Lieutenant Donald L. Truesdale was released from the hospital in Managua on July 22, after more than three months on the casualty roster. He returned to "partial duty." He was a corporal again, no longer a lieutenant in command of a NNG unit.

Had it not been for the loss of his arm, the official telegrams to Lugoff, and the newspaper reports, he might not have informed his family of his wounding. What purpose would there have been in burdening the family with worry? Yet, he could not escape the reality that he had come to the attention of the 31st U.S. President. On the day he was released from the hospital, stateside newspapers reported that he had been recommended for the Congressional Medal of Honor. [75]

President Herbert Hoover had opinions about Lieutenant Truesdale and the Medal of Honor. He had expressed his views when he presented the Medal to Eddie Rickenbacker in a ceremony broadcast by radio on November 6, 1930. "I hope that your gratification in receiving this Medal of Honor will be as keen as mine in bestowing it," the president had said over the airways. "May you wear it during many years of happiness and continued usefulness to your country." [76]

President Hoover had read the recommendation wired from Nicaragua and all the endorsements. On July 28, 1932, he signed a Citation authorized by Act of Congress.

As CPL Truesdale waited for the Electoral Mission Detachment to complete its duties, communiqués circulated around Managua about Marines killed in combat operations. On August 24, 1932, VO 7-M pilot 2dLt Raymond P. Rutledge, 26, from Fetus, Missouri, and Sergeant Orville B. Simmons, 23, his VJ 6-M mechanic and machine gunner, flew into the skies to provide support for a patrol that was searching for another downed aircraft in the jungles near Rama, inland from Bluefields on the east coast. Both died when their aeroplane crashed. The patrol recovered their bodies and carried them to Rama.

Telegraph word reached Mr. and Mrs. Roy Simmons at their 1209 Vine Street home in Hamilton, Ohio, late Wednesday night. The next day, Orville's name was in bold headlines across the top of Page Fourteen in the town's evening paper. One of fourteen children, the former Troop 11 Scout was exceptionally popular no matter where he went. Articles about him would be in the paper until the Marines escorted his body home for burial in October. [77]

On Saturday, September 3, in Managua, LtCol Calvin B. Matthews, Marine brigade commander and brigadier general in the Guardia Nacional, held a quiet ceremony at Campo de Marte to decorate CPL Truesdale and Gunnery Sergeant John Hamas, 35, for their heroism. Sergeant Hamas had earned the Navy Cross Medal for leading the attacks to capture two important Sandinisto rebel camps. Numerous high officials attended. [78]

Corporal Truesdale was surprised when LtCol Matthews presented him with the nation's highest award for heroism. He had done what had to be done, without question and without hesitation. He certainly had no thought for recognition or medals when he rushed to remove danger from his men. His casualty was not incurred under fire or in combat. In his opinion, it seemed little more than an accidental wounding.

LtCol Matthews clasped a bright blue ribbon about CPL Truesdale's neck, over his uniform. At his throat, the ribbon was spangled with a cluster of thirteen white stars representing the original States. Directly beneath the stars was a bronze anchor. The shiny bronze Medal of Honor was fixed to the anchor and suspended below it.

The Medal is a five-pointed star. Each point contains sprays of laurel and oak with a trefoil at the tip. A bas-relief of Minerva, personifying the Union, is depicted within the star's central circle. She holds a fasces in her left hand—an ax bound in staves of wood, the ancient Roman symbol of authority. With the shield in her right hand, she confidently repulses the serpents held by the cowering figure of Discord. Thirty-four smaller stars, representing the thirty-four States in existence in 1861, circle the two combatants.

President Hoover had a greeting inscribed on the back of the Medal with the date of CPL Truesdale's valorous action.

THE PRESIDENT
OF THE
UNITED STATES
TO
CORPORAL DONALD L. TRUESDALE,
U.S.M.C.
FOR EXTRAORDINARY HEROISM
ABOVE AND BEYOND THE CALL OF DUTY

CITATION

28 JULY 1932

LtCol Matthews expressed his pride in CPL Truesdale, and the two exchanged a left-armed handshake, for lack of the hero's right hand. Then, President Moncado, the Chief Executive of Nicaragua, pinned a Cross of Valor upon Second Lieutenant of the Guardia Truesdale's chest.

The Marines would be in Nicaragua for only four more months, time enough for telegrams to go to two more families.

Two days before CPL Truesdale had received his Medal, Captain (First Lieutenant) "Chesty" Puller and 1stLt (Gunnery Sergeant) William A. "Ironman" Lee, 32, departed from Jinotega and led a mounted, forty-man Nacional Guard patrol north toward Mount Kilambe and the Río Agua Carta. On September 26, 150 Sandinistas, armed with automatic weapons and bolt-action rifles ambushed the patrol as they crossed the river about 100 miles from Jinotega. Despite two bullet wounds, 1stLt Lee freed his jammed Lewis machine gun and charged the rebel positions on a ridge. The bandits were forced to withdraw after a long fight, taking ten wounded companions with them. They left ten bandit bodies on the field. Two Guardsmen were killed and four were wounded. First Lieutenant Lee survived the battle. He and Captain Puller both received Navy Cross Medals.

Private John B. West, 28, from Texas, 5th Marine Regiment, with seven years of service, was the last Marine to die in the Second Nicaraguan Intervention. He was with the Electoral Mission Detachment and was little more than a week away from leaving Nicaragua. His death was recorded as Non-Hostile Misadventure. He was shot resisting arrest in Chinandega on Christmas Eve 1932.

Over the years, thousands of Marines had served, most of who had no encounters with bandits. Having been dedicated to "restoring peace to the inhabitants of a troubled nation," the final Marine withdrawal was on January 2, 1933. Corporal Truesdale was among the men who came home with vivid memories of battles and of Marines who had been carried home and interred in hometown cemeteries. Twenty-three Marine officers and enlisted men had lost their lives while serving with the Guardia Nacional de Nicaragua.

A total of 136 Marines gave their lives between 1927 and 1932. Thirty-two were Killed in Action, fifteen Died of Wounds, and forty-one Died of Accident in drownings, plane crashes, shootings, and falls. Six died of Accidental Gun Shot Wounds (friendly fire), and one died of an Accidental Self Inflicted Gun Shot Wound. Twenty-four Marines Died of Diseases, and twenty-four officers and enlisted men Died of Other Causes: including eleven by homicide, twelve by suicide, and one by misadventure. Sixty-seven Marines were wounded in action; many more had injuries or wounds not incurred in combat and not recorded in casualty rosters. [79]

Back in the States

Corporal Truesdale had not been away from Nicaragua for long when he took leave from his duties to attend a funeral. Grandma Mittie E. Truesdale, 84, Zachariah's widow, died at home on January 13, 1933, after a long illness. Reverend W. V. Jermain of Bethune, friend of her son Dr. Ernest Z. Truesdale, conducted the funeral services at Saint John's Methodist Church. She was buried in the church cemetery in Lugoff. [80]

Every now and then, CPL Truesdale would get news of Gunnery Sergeant John Hamas, who went on to be a Marine Corps Rifle team member once back in the States. He was assigned to the Marine Barracks, Portsmouth Navy Yard, and met Miss Edna L. Fox, who was working with the Tariff Commission in Washington, D.C. Gunny and Edna married on Wednesday morning, November 8, at eleven o'clock at the home of friends on Washington Road in Rye, New Hampshire. [81]

The rebel uprising in Nicaragua ended in 1934 when a Guardia commander assassinated General Sandino.

CHAPTER 5

Life Following Combat

✳✳✳

"Adapt thyself to the things among which your lot has been cast." [1]

—MARCUS AURELIUS

DESPITE LOSING HIS RIGHT HAND and forearm, Corporal Truesdale remained in the Marine Corps. That was a good place for him, in part because Marines show special deference to those who wear a blue ribbon with five stars at the top of their decorations. Perhaps more importantly, his greatest comforts were being among military men and knowing what was expected of him. He continued to move up in ranks. In the years ahead, one particular MOH recipient was going to have an influence on his attitude about the government and war: Major General Smedley Darlington Butler.

Following his stint in Philadelphia "cleaning up" police corruption and trying to close the city's protection rackets and profiteering, the general had returned to Marine Corps assignments in early 1926. First, he had assumed command of the San Diego Marine Base; then, in 1927, he took command of the Marine Expeditionary Force in Shanghai, China. The Marines were there to protect American business interests during the conflicts erupting between Chiang Kai-shek's Nationalists and the rising Communists. General Butler remained in China until 1929.

When he returned to the States, he was promoted to major general and given command of Marine Corps Base Quantico. He was a different man. Events in China had caused him to rethink the Banana Wars and America's penchant for sending Marines into foreign countries to intervene in civil conflicts. Who benefited? Major General Butler became a very straight-talking critic of Washington, D.C.'s foreign and military policies.

The general understood the American public's attitude about having its Marines on foreign shores: ". . . but as soon as our losses begin to grow there is a big 'hubbub' . . . and the Corps comes in for unfavorable criticism."

General Butler left the Marines in October 1931. He involved himself in speeches and writings and radio broadcasts. He had come to think that he had taken part in "a series of cynical overseas adventures." His insights troubled him, and he was not shy about saying so. "And during that period I spent most of my time being a high-class muscle man for Big Business, for Wall Street and for the bankers. In short, I was a racketeer for capitalism."

General Butler watched "the international war clouds gathering," predicted war sooner or later, and wrote *War Is a Racket.* [2] In 1935, he made a series of radio speeches over Philadelphia's WCAU, a Columbia network affiliate. He warned America to look back to the "war to end all wars." America's boys had been sent out to die having been fed a smoke screen of beautiful ideals. They went to war to make the world safe for democracy, never told that their dying would mean huge war profits for business and politicians. "They were just told it was to be a glorious adventure." [3]

As years passed, Sergeant Truesdale gave much thought to General Butler's perspective on things. He would also come to understand better that America viewed his Medal to symbolize his bravery—not an accidental wounding.

Union Army soldier Sergeant William H. Sickles, 93 years old, died on September 26, 1938. He had earned a Medal of Honor on March 31, 1865, for rescuing a Union officer who had been taken prisoner by the Confederates at Gravelly Run, Virginia. At the time of his death, he was the last living Civil War recipient. By 1940, the number of living Medal recipients was 279, and most of them were getting on in age.

A Trial Run At It

Sergeant Truesdale was assigned duties in the New Orleans Navy and USMC recruiting office. While he was stationed there, he broke with a family tradition. He married a woman not from Kershaw County. [4] The marital match was a poor one for the Marine. He had survived a grenade blast, but his Cajun neighbors might have wondered if he would survive his betrothal.

"Margret" Truesdale was a domineering woman who was verbally and physically explosive. Donald's description of his bride was that she could be "frantic." On one occasion, he came home to find her in an agitated state of mind. "Margret" was a Catholic, and a priest had told her that her father was in Purgatory. The priest needed $50 to pray him out of his predicament. Apparently, her father had not earned enough plenary indulgences to go straight to heaven. Still, during the Great Depression, $50 was a lot of money, like $862 in 2017.

It cannot be known today if "Margret's" father ever got out of Purgatory. Sergeant Truesdale chose to go straight to an attorney in the Commonwealth of Pennsylvania and pay to get out of his marriage.

As the 1940s neared, Sergeant Truesdale was assigned to Marine Corps Base Quantico in Virginia. He had various reasons to travel the 182 miles between the Quantico railroad station and South Philadelphia, a four-hour trip by bus or train. There was a recruiting post in Philadelphia. Marines stationed at the Marine Barracks on South Broad Street served at the Philadelphia Naval Shipyard at the end of South Broad Street on the Delaware River. Officers' training was conducted at the Marine Corps Station. The half-mile-long parade grounds in front of the Barracks building had once served as a runway for the first Marine aviators. And, Philadelphia residents supported a multitude of attorneys.

James H. Molloy, esquire, was a civil lawyer in Philadelphia who preferred to represent Libellants. Sergeant Truesdale hired him. The attorney gathered the information and submitted the motion to the Court of Common Pleas No. 2 of Philadelphia County on Chestnut Street in March 1939. He petitioned for a Divorce A Vinculo Matrimonii (A.V.M.). Sergeant Truesdale wanted an absolute divorce. His attorney was certain that Margaret's conduct had furnished him a valid ground for divorce.

Judge Theodore Rosen read the Master's Report in the case, made his final absolute ruling, and submitted proof of notices to the parties on June 19, 1939. Donald LeRoy Truesdale, Libellant, and Margaret Truesdale, Respondent, were divorced from the bonds of matrimony. The Cause was made clear: CRUEL AND BARBAROUS TREATMENT and Indignities to the Person. All matters related to the marriage ceased, and Sergeant Truesdale was "at liberty to marry again in like manner as if [he] never had been married." [5]

He stored C. P. Form 18, No. 12683, the divorce papers, and the lawyers' depositions in a trunk. He likely decided then that he would not let such treatment happen to him again.

For his physical check-ups, Sergeant Truesdale went to the Philadelphia Naval Hospital located on 22-acre grounds off Pattison Avenue, a mile up Broad Street from the Marine Barracks. Major General Smedley Butler, 58, two-time MOH recipient who had led troops in three expeditions to Nicaragua during the First Banana Wars, died at the Naval Hospital on June 21, 1940. Sergeant Truesdale spoke of "Ol' Smedley Butler" with a Marine's special regard.

By the time of General Butler's death, Sergeant Truesdale was considering a proposal to a girl from a "well to do" Philadelphia family. Well, anyway, much better off than his South Carolina family.

An Gorta Mór

The Great Hunger of Ireland, known as The Great Famine, occurred when potato crops failed between 1845 and 1850. In their Gaelic tongue, the Irish referred to their anguish as *an Gorta Mór*. Mass starvation and disease claimed the lives of 1.5 million men, women, and children. Nearly a million poor, Irish peasants from rural counties immigrated to the United States during those five years. They had a struggle in the new land, as if *an Gorta Mór* had pursued the Irish descendants to America.

Thousands of the hopeful transplants found their way to low-income, working-class neighborhoods throughout Philadelphia. They rented rooms in the rowhomes southwest of Center City as they found jobs in the mills, foundries, and refineries. Eventually, the Irish-Catholics filled three square blocks bordered by the Schuylkill River, Taney Street, Grays Ferry Avenue, and Christian Street. By the turn of the century, the neighborhood had earned the nickname *Devil's Pocket*. The local tradition handed down by word of mouth was that a priest once claimed that the neighborhood boys were so tough they would steal a chain out of the devil's pocket when they reached hell.

The more "genteel" Irish preferred the refined Pennsport neighborhood in South Philly's First Ward section, bordered by East Passyunk Avenue on the west, Warton Street to the north, the Delaware River on the east, and Mifflin Street to the south.

Wendell Phillips and Elizabeth Smith were first generation Irish-Americans. They married, and a son, William St. Clair Phillips, was born to them on May 16, 1880. [6] His friends called him "Clare" or *Chláir* with a nice Irish brogue. That was pronounced "Klar" and not to be confused with the girl's name.

Chláir married Anna E. Werb of Maryland. She was two years older than he and probably more mature. They began their married life in Oxford, Chester County. Their daughter, Gladys May, was born in 1904. Of Anna's children, Gladys was the only one to survive. [7]

World War I "across the pond" erupted on July 28, 1914. On May 18, 1917, the Selective Service Act made draft registration mandatory for all men living in the United States, ages 21–31, regardless of citizenship status. Chláir had turned 37 years old two days earlier and was not eligible to be drafted. A second draft registration was held on August 24, 1918. The third draft three weeks later lowered the age of registration to men aged 18 years and included all men up to age 45 years.

On September 12, 1918, William St. Clair Phillips went to the Philadelphia City Draft Board Office #41 (of 52) and filled out WWI Draft Registration form # 37–6–15, Serial # 2702. He was of medium height and build and had grey eyes and black hair. [8] Since the war ended two months later, he was not called to report for military duty.

By the 1920 U.S. Census, William was the head of the household in Philadelphia's Ward 40, across the Schuylkill and northwest of the Grays Ferry Avenue neighborhood. The family rented an 870-square-foot, two-bedroom townhome at 720 South Conestoga Street between

South 55th and 54th streets (on the corner of what became West Catherine Street), a few blocks north of the Philadelphia–Baltimore–Washington and Ohio railroads crossing. Anna's mother, Ella Reynolds, 62, had moved in with them.

The residences in the neighborhood were similar in appearance to the ones the Truesdales lived in on West Saratoga Street in Baltimore before WWI.

William worked as a cabinetmaker for the N. Snellenberg & Company, a middle-class clothing department store on Market and South 11th streets. He counted on the Philadelphia Rapid Transit Company branches to get back and forth to his job. That meant paying fares on the P.R.T. Subway-Elevated, double-decked buses, and trackless trolley coaches. He liked to meet up with his chums at the local pubs. Often "in his cups," Chláir was not always welcome at home. He went on days-long benders a couple times a year, and Anna would lock him out of the house until he sobered up.

Anna was the dependable wage earner in the family, working closer to home than her husband. She waitressed long hours at the Grand Crystal Tea Room on the ninth floor of Wannamaker's Department Store in Center City on Market and South 13th streets.

The family obviously was not affluent, but did what they could. William and Anna moved the family west from the "inner city" to a two-story row home at 61 Sunshine Road in Upper Darby, a block from State Road. The four bedrooms in the 1,481-square-foot home was a better fit for a family with a teenager, even if it accommodated only one bathroom. Cobbs Creek was several doors down the street from their front door. A public golf course first established in 1916, and expanded to offer two 18-hole layouts, was right across the creek. Thick woods stretched for miles.

In 1920, Gladys May Phillips, 16 years old, ran off and married Edwin Raymond Garrity, 17 years old. Gladys Claire Garrity was born to them in Ocean City, New Jersey, on July 31, 1921. Edwin had suffered rheumatic fever as a boy and lived with a weakened heart. He had no prospects for work. This dismayed Gladys Claire's two grandmothers, both of whom were having difficulty enough supporting themselves and families. They decided to split the young couple up before any more children came along.

Edwin was sent to New York to live with a sister. Gladys May and the baby returned to live with Anna and Chláir. Big Gladys eventually moved out, leaving Young Gladys in Anna's care. Gladys May visited, acting more like a big sister to Gladys Claire than like a Mama.

In the 1930 U.S. Census, William was the head of the Upper Darby household, and nine-year-old granddaughter, Gladys Garrity, was living with the family. No other children were listed in the household. Anna worked hard to support a family, even through the Depression. If the women were left on their own, the family's existence could be in peril. Ella Reynolds remained in the household and cared for Gladys when the parents were working in Philly. [9]

Big Gladys would meet Young Gladys after school on Fridays to go to a restaurant for dinner and then to a movie or a play. The family went to Ocean City in the summers. Gladys once saw the famed diving horse jump off the Atlantic City Steel Pier. One summer highlight for her was seeing actress Betty Grable in person.

Upper Darby was a "hotbed of crime" in the 1930's. Police logs, snitches tales, and newspaper reporter blurbs generated leads on poison rings, counterfeit rings, bootleggers, and murder-for-hire contracts. Men with the Phillips surname found themselves on both sides of the law.

Chláir was a kind and loving presence in Gladys Claire's early life, and she loved him. She was 14 years old when she came home after school and got the news.

Grandpa Chláir, 55 years 9 months 17 days into his existence, met misfortune on Tuesday, March 3, 1936, when he was murdered during a bender. Anna contracted for the services of the Oliver H. Bair Company undertaker at 18 West Chestnut. The coroner recorded the Determination of death as INQUEST PENDING on Certificate (or File) # 22254. [10] On Friday, the funeral procession took Chláir to Arlington Cemetery in Drexel Hill, a half-mile from Sunshine Road. He was buried in the Grove Section, behind the townhomes on the corner of Fairfax Road and Highland Avenue.

As long as she was in school, Young Gladys would have frequent memories of her grandpa. Upper Darby High School was across North Landsdowne Avenue from the tree-lined cemetery.

Sergeant Truesdale was not one to pay for a bus fare to get around town, preferring to walk. If he ever wanted to tour the sights, Independence Hall and the Liberty Bell were four miles up South 6th Street from the Barracks. From there, Wannamaker's Department Store was a seven-block hike west on Chestnut Street. More to a Marine's liking, historic Tun Alley was four blocks east of Independence Hall, on the east side of South Front Street between Chestnut and Walnut Streets. The legendary Tun Tavern had served hearty beer and cheesesteak to the first Marine recruits in 1775 at the start of the Revolutionary War.

Whenever Sergeant Truesdale went north in Philadelphia, he passed through or near the Pennsport neighborhood. He must have been near a trolley stop on Market or Chestnut one evening when Anna Phillips finished work.

On her way home from her shift at the Wannamaker's restaurant, Anna saw a fine looking, one-armed Marine standing on the street corner. He looked confused. Good-hearted Anna went over to the Marine, who spoke with a strong, southern accent. She invited him home for dinner.

Gladys Claire was a pretty teenager in high school at the time. When she came down the stairs, she was surprised to see a very strange looking man, big with a broad face, in the house. The Marine was very close to her mother's age. Maybe her patriotic grandmother brought him home to meet Gladys May?

The economic disaster of the Great Depression continued relentlessly. Finishing up his fourth enlistment, with more than ten years of service already, the Marine had a secure job. He would also have a pension when he finished out his career. Anna might have seen security for her daughter and granddaughter. She invited Sergeant Truesdale to return for another dinner.

Sergeant Truesdale's younger brother Ebin Trantham married Mary Lou Tomb in 1940, and they had a daughter, Mary Lou "Suzie" Truesdell. Ebin enlisted in the Army Air Corps and would find his way into newspapers from time to time. Already a master sergeant by mid-1942, he departed the Keesler Aircraft Maintenance School to establish the AAFTS Aircraft Electrical Systems section at Gulfport. [11] He would eventually retire from the U. S. Air Force as a Lieutenant Colonel. [12] While Ebin was much more genteel, smooth, educated, and articulate than his older brother, he was also competitive with and jealous of him. He was quite unhappy about all the attention that Don got because of his Medal. [13]

Lieutenant Colonel Red Mike Edson arrived in Quantico, 5th Marines Headquarters, in June 1941 to help organize an amphibious battalion, train with the relatively new Higgins landing craft, and prepare for the war the Marines knew was coming. The pace of duties and training at Quantico and New River was becoming more frantic. Rooted deeply in his experiences in Nicaragua, LtCol Edson went about creating a mobile Raider Battalion capable of quick strikes on enemy positions from the sea. The amphibious force made stops in the Charleston

Navy Yard. For a week in mid-October 1941, LtCol Edson was in Camden, South Carolina, to observe the annual Army tank and air infantry maneuver exercises.

Whether it was the Philadelphia teenager or the Marine sergeant, one or the other or both were smitten. The visits at the Phillips' home continued. Despite his being fifteen years older, Anna considered that Sergeant Truesdale's pension would keep her granddaughter from the poor house in her old age. She urged young Gladys to marry the Marine.

Sergeant Truesdale returned to the Philadelphia Courthouse to get a marriage license. On October 20, 1941, a chief clerk, Prothonotary James M. Scott, certified that the Marine held a true and correct copy of a Final Decree of Divorce. Sergeant Truesdale, 35, married 20-year-old Gladys Claire Garrity on November 1, 1941, at Quantico, Virginia.

A month after their wedding, the United States was at war again.

World War II Years

Sergeant Donald L. Truesdale and Colonel Christian Frank Schilt, the only living MOH recipients remaining on active duty at the start of WWII, were both stationed at Quantico. Reporters sought them out. Three days after the attack at Pearl Harbor, when the nation's attention focused on tiny Wake Island, a mid-point between Hawaii and Guam, Sergeant Truesdale was quoted briefly in newspaper "So They Say" columns.

"We have to be tough in our business," he told a reporter at Quantico. [14] Sergeant Truesdale was concerned about the rush of young men to Army and Navy recruiting stations and all the attention they were getting from the women. It was turning the men's hair "a little bit curly." He thought differently about his three nephews. They would serve in the USMC, and their hair would be "high and tight."

As the Marine Legation was being withdrawn from Nicaragua in August 1925, Sergeant Truesdale's older sister, Edna, had married Robert Marion Edens, moved to Florence, and lived well by Kershaw County standards. The early years of their marriage, and the birth of their three sons and two daughters, had coincided with the second Banana War.

Robert Earl Edens was born in December 1926 when the Marine expeditionary force landed on Nicaragua's east coast and started taking over major port towns. Billy Truesdell Edens was born when his uncle was patrolling trails and rivers in the eastern and southern areas of Nicaragua with the 5th Marines in 1928. When Benny Maxwell Edens was born, 2dLt Truesdale was leading NNG patrols in the hostile Ocotal area. Edna Eugenia "Gene," the first girl, was born a month after Lieutenant Truesdale was mentioned in the special report to *The New York Times* newspaper on May 1, 1931. Edna gave birth to her last child, Margarie Lee "Margie" Edens on September 23, 1932, twenty days after her brother had been presented his Medal in Managua.

Edna was proud of Sergeant Truesdale's Marine Corps service, and her three boys were reared on tales of her brother's glory. As is often true in the lives of Medal recipients' extended families, the Edens boys admired their uncle. Bobby would be the first to enlist when he was old enough, having listened to the accounts of Marines taking Tarawa, Peleliu, and Guam in 1944. He reached a PFC rank during WWII and would retire as a U.S. Air Force Master Sergeant. Billy and Benny had to wait until the Korean Conflict to serve in the USMC.

The island fighting in the Pacific, memories of Nicaragua, and links to Philadelphia seem to have merged for Sergeant Truesdale in the early months of the war.

He closely followed the dispatches about the fifteen officers and 373 enlisted men of the 1st Marine Defense Battalion gallantly defending the Wake Island outpost against superior enemy numbers. He knew that Marine Gunner, 2dLt John Hamas, formerly of Philadelphia, was the Wake Detachment's munitions officer. Wake Island fell to the enemy forces on December 23, and the fate of the defenders was not immediately known. Marine Gunner Hamas had not been listed among the Marine casualties.

The Saturday Morning *Philadelphia Inquirer* printed a relevant obituary on Page 16. Corporal Anthony J. Rausch, 38, a member of the USS *Florida* detachment badly wounded in the La Paz Centro fighting, had been the Rising Sun Post, Veterans of Foreign Wars, commander. He had died on Friday, January 30, 1942, in Philadelphia's Jewish Hospital after a long illness. Only an aunt and a sister survived to attend the Tuesday services at his home. Corporal Rausch was buried with full military honors in Section M, Site 357 at the Philadelphia Soldiers' National Cemetery on Limekiln Pike.

Thursday, February 19, 1942, was an emotional day in the Truesdale household. The Navy Department released the names of 2,210 civilian workers, sailors, and Marines presumed held by the Japanese. Marine Gunner John Hamas was on the list. American diplomats insisted that the Nippon government adhere to the 1929 Geneva Pact provisions for the treatment of prisoners-of-war. It was not confirmed until mid-October that 2dLt Hamas was in a Japanese internment camp in Shanghai with thirteen other 1st Defense Battalion officers. He would remain in captivity until the POW camps were liberated in 1945. [15]

Fewer than four months a bride, Gladys was contacted by her mother. Her father, Edwin Garrity, aged 38 years, in poor health since childhood, had died on February 19. He was buried under trees in the Silverbrook Section in Arlington, a short walk east of "Clare" Phillips. His grave shares the same stone with his Grandfather George W. Redden.

Sergeant Truesdale was promoted to Platoon Sergeant (E-6) at Quantico in early 1942. [16] The happy newlyweds stood for a photo on the walk in front of the Phillips' back porch in Philadelphia. He wore his dress blue uniform with the distinctive three chevrons over an inverted "rocker" rank insignia. The four diagonal, gold service stripes (hash marks) on his left forearm show he had more than sixteen years of service. [17] On his chest was the MOH ribbon over a row of his Second Nicaraguan Campaign, Nicaraguan Cross of Valor, and Purple Heart ribbons. Below the ribbon rack were pinned the awards that gave Sergeant Truesdale his greatest pride: his silver Rifle Expert and Pistol Expert badges.

Smiling radiantly, standing about 5 feet 6 inches tall, Gladys was beside him. She was dressed head to toe in the fashionable style of the WWII era: a wide brimmed hat, dark dress suit with a brooch on the left lapel, a corsage on her overcoat lapel, leather purse under her arm, and white dress gloves folded in her hands.

Sergeant Truesdale officially changed his name from Truesdale to Truesdell on July 25, 1942. The spelling did not always show up in print. When the new M1941 Johnson Semi-Automatic Rifle & Light Machine Gun was being introduced to the USMC paratroopers at Quantico, Platoon Sergeant Truesdale found the new equipment interesting. He appeared in a photo in the Marine Corps' magazine inspecting the weapon. [18]

In 1943, he joined the James Leroy Belk Post 17, American Legion. The post had been established in Camden, South Carolina in 1920. It was the kind of organization that suited his view of the world.

In early 1919, a group of patriotic, "war-weary" veterans of World War I, the sons and grandsons of Civil War-era veterans, had gathered to discuss the impact of war on combat veterans, service members, their families, and the communities to which they returned after the war. Their objective was to be of service, and their determination was unwavering. Congress chartered and incorporated the American Legion on September 16, 1919. The Legion members were committed to continued mutual helpfulness and devotion to their fellow service members and veterans, as well as to mentoring youth, sponsoring wholesome programs in local communities, advocating patriotism and honor, and promoting strong national security. The Legion developed into the largest war-time veterans' service organization in the world. [19]

The American Legion became family to Don Truesdell, and he recruited for the organization wherever he went. He would be a member for fifty years.

Sergeant Truesdale maintained a strong allegiance to his original regiment. The 5th Marines, assigned to the 1st Marine Brigade, had been at Quantico from 1934 through 1940. For a year, they were deployed to Guantánamo Bay, a base of operations familiar to him. In February 1941, the regiment returned from Cuba and was garrisoned at New River, North Carolina, as part of the 1st Marine Division. During the war years, he read the battle reports and watched over the casualty rosters as the *Fighting 5th* fought on Guadalcanal, New Britain, Eastern New Guinea, Peleliu, and Okinawa.

Many of the Marines who had served in Nicaragua with P/Sgt Truesdell would drop in and say hello to him wherever he was stationed. One of those was Brigadier General C. J. Chappell, who had been second in command during the fight at La Paz Centro. He had earned a Navy Cross for his "skill and devotion to duty of a high order" for his service as a Marine aviator for a year in Nicaragua, six months after he had conducted patrols with CPL Truesdale. The general served throughout WWII and did not retire from the Marine Corps until 1949.

Another ol' visitor was Lieutenant Colonel Joseph Tavern, who had rushed from the Ocotal outpost with Lieutenant Truesdale on New Year's Eve 1930, to the massacre site near Achuapa. Joe died on December 2, 1942, and was buried with full military honors at Arlington National Cemetery.

War correspondents and the Washington War Department telegrams to the next of kin reported the facts of Marines killed in action in the South Pacific Solomon Islands. Death of Marines by friendly fire, malfeasance, and misadventure were seldom reported in the newspapers. When reports of suicides during the 1942–1943 Guadalcanal and Tarawa campaigns appeared in print, the correspondents were generally informing readers that the Japanese had been trained to fight, annihilate Marines, or commit suicide. Japanese soldiers and civilians killed themselves in appalling numbers on the islands. Headquarters Marines Corps was also aware that Marines occasionally killed themselves in the jungles.

At Quantico, that fact was not a surprise to P/Sgt Truesdell, having learned of the self-inflicted deaths of Marines at war in Nicaragua. News of one death hit him more closely than the deaths in the Solomons.

Chief Marine Gunner Calvin Arthur Lloyd was a renowned Marine marksman, one of their best "straight shooters." He had been a member of the national championship rifle team in the early 1920s and had helped coach the team when the Second Banana

Wars had concluded. He had been central in the design of the Quantico Marine Base rifle range. Few Marine marksmen ever enjoyed the level of high esteem he attained. Christmas was five days away when the news quickly spread around Quantico and Camp Lejeune.

On December 20, 1943, Gunner Cal Lloyd, aged 55, walked into the woods above Quantico's football stadium with a .45 caliber pistol. He shot himself through the heart, leaving behind a widow, and eleven sons and daughters. Some suggested that the cause of his suicide was that he had "lost his mind." His closest friends and Marines like P/Sgt Truesdell held a different view. His decision to end his life was in keeping with his character. When circumstances are such that there is no longer any reason to continue living, or that one is becoming a burden on family or friends, there is no dishonor in leaving life behind.

The Marine Corps named the Quantico rifle and pistol range complex and an annual shooting trophy in tribute to the marksman.

On the Domestic Front

Donald and Gladys began their family during WWII. Donna Diane "Dee Dee" Truesdell, their first, was born at Camp Lejeune, North Carolina, on July 9, 1944. He was promoted again to a chief warrant officer rank.

Over the World War II years, movies, newspapers, magazines, and radio broadcasts introduced many young war heroes to the nation. Among them, 472 men had received Medals of Honor. Eighty-two of them were U.S. Marines. More than half of all the Medal recipients did not come home to live out their lives with families—273 died during their valorous actions and earned posthumous awards. Of the 199 living heroes added to the MOH rolls in WWII, thirty-one wore Marine uniforms.

At the close of the war, 226,000 Marines were on active duty. President Truman addressed Congress on December 19, 1945. He favored unification of the Armed Forces, merging the military into a single Department of Defense. The Corps was to reduce it size to 100,000 men by the end of 1946. The "Old Order" was coming to an end, and the Corps was in a fight for its own existence. The "Old Breed" began its departure from the ranks and their return to civilian occupations.

On top of all that, the Marine Corps was under pressure to integrate the races into its forces. That alone, did not sit well with CWO Truesdell. Any discussion about Negroes in the Corps stuck in his craw. For the loyal Southerner, integration was wrong. [20]

Eight months after the Japanese surrendered and WWII ended, Donald Douglas Truesdell was born on April 20, 1946, in a hallway at the Camp Lejeune Hospital. After his birth, the umbilical cord grew inside him and wrapped around his intestine. He was anemic, pale and sickly. Medical care was limited at the time, and no one knew what was wrong with the infant. [21]

Chief Warrant Officer Truesdell decided it was time to return to his birthplace to raise his family. He retired from the Marines on May 1, 1946, after 21.5 years of service. Upon his "relief from Active Duty," Four-Star General Alexander Archer Vandegrift, 18th Commandant of the Marine Corps and MOH recipient, put his signature at the bottom of CWO Truesdell's Certificate of Honorable and Satisfactory Service in World War II. [22]

Don returned to Lugoff. Uncomfortable with salutes, accolades, and the spotlight, he intended to live quietly, out of the limelight, and farm in Kershaw County.

CHAPTER 6

The Quiet Life in Kershaw County

✳✳✳

"And it could be that the qualities that make men go into
combat make them tough to live with." [1]

— DONNA DIANE TRUESDELL

WHEN DONALD TRUESDELL WAS HONORABLY discharged, the military and medical establishments had a reasonable understanding of the long-term effects of limb amputations and shrapnel wounds. The concussive impact of a close-in grenade detonation on a person's brain had not been widely covered in medical journals. One 1916 study identified severe headaches, ringing in the ear, hypersensitivity to noise, and tremors following blast events. That remained the extent of general knowledge through 1947.

Don, 39 years old, departed the Marine base with pains he kept to himself. He also took along the unrecognized, undiagnosed, and untreated physical, psychological, and emotional effects of the grenade blast he had suffered thirteen years earlier on the trail at the Coco River. Even today, while he might be considered to have experienced a traumatic brain injury (TBI), without any external, visible skull injury, whether blast forces directly injured his organic brain would be debated.

Many families of veterans returning from the recent Iraq and Afghanistan wars are familiar with blast and concussion head injuries. Common long-term effects of severe and untreated TBI include cognitive, behavioral, and social deficits. Biological and neurological impacts are evident. Headaches persist. A constant ringing in the ears and changes in the taste of food can occur. Problems with impulsiveness, sustaining attention, making decisions, dealing with changes, and identifying, understanding, and expressing emotions are frequent. The strain of acting "appropriate" often results in episodes of social withdrawal, silence, or "cold" staring.

Most troubling to a family are the apparent changes in personality, problems with frustration tolerance, and the inability to control anger. Veterans with a TBI are often described as generally less patient and always irritable, as short tempered, and as quick to get frustrated or angry. Most notable, seemingly uncontrolled outbursts of anger can quickly escalate into frightening verbal or physical aggression when the veteran finds himself in an unexpected or new situation, or is stressed and tired. Over time, those closest to the veteran are left with the impression that he always looks and/or acts "mean."

Beyond war injuries, Don dealt with another reality. Combat veterans and career military men have adjustments to make when returning to civilian life. Day-to-day concerns, seemingly inconsequential, can become irritants. Newly-discharged veterans who have children must manage the ever-occurring changes in routine normal to a child's natural development. Don and Gladys had a two-year-old daughter and an infant. They would have four more children in the next eight years.

It is safe to imagine that Don and Gladys Truesdell were not well prepared for the domestic and family life ahead.

While Don tried to figure out the living arrangements in Lugoff, Gladys and the two children lived in Upper Darby with Anna Phillips. [2] Gladys was back in her old bedroom on the second floor. Anna stretched a gate across the top of the stairs to prevent the children from falling or coming downstairs. Douglas had progressed from rolling across the floor and was learning to crawl. Dee had taken her first steps at Camp Lejeune more than a year earlier and was already looking out for her baby brother.

In the winter of 1946–1947, Don came for a short visit. Among the various matters he and Gladys talked about, several events stood out. One day the gate at the top of the stairs was left open and Doug was crawling down the hall, headed to the stairs. Dee spotted him, determined his locomotion's destination, and alerted one of the adults. "Saving the day" earned her a lot of praise and attention.

Gladys knew all about snow and shoveling sidewalks and ice on Cobbs Creek and wind chill. She remembered how every winter Grandpa Clare would compare any snowstorm to "the worst blizzard ever of 1888" when he was a boy. Philadelphia had stood immobilized. He insisted that several feet of snow dropped on him for four days, and that the family had no way out of their house for a week. The railroads had to tunnel through snowdrifts higher than fifty feet. But then, Clare had been known to exaggerate at times.

The snow did fall and the winds did whirl while the Truesdells were in Upper Darby. Most memorable was when it started on Thursday, February 20. Eleven inches of snow had dropped in the yards by Friday morning. Gladys was relieved that they were not trapped indoors for a week.

A wood fence separated Anna's and the neighbors' yards. The snow had drifted up so high against the fence that it looked like a hill a person could walk up and over. Dee wanted to go over to visit the next-door neighbors. Gladys answered with an immediate NO! Neighbors or not, Northerners were not as friendly as Southerners.

Then, Dee caught a cold. Already worried about her baby boy, Gladys would not let her daughter go outside to play in the snow. Instead, she sat Dee by the window to watch and went out and built a snowman. Confined to the house, missing out on the fun, Dee brooded.

Gladys must have believed that life would be brighter and warmer down south.

If You Believe in Ghosts

Don purchased a tract of land for 50¢ an acre and sold $10,000 of lumber from the parcels. He started to build a homestead at 1084 Ridgeway Road in the Twenty-Five Mile Creek Watershed. The property, thickly forested with pine trees and Turkey Oaks, was near a branch of the creek flowing into a lake behind the house. [3] Cotton fields stretched around the property as far as the eye could see. Highway-34 in front of the house was a dirt road intersecting with paved US-1. Due to building supply shortages after WWII, it took a year to finish the house.

During the spring of 1947, Don brought his family to rural South Carolina, into a region struggling still to recover from the Civil War. They moved in with Earl and Margaret, his parents, in isolated country without streetlights or outdoor lights of any kind.

An incident that became family lore occurred that summer. Don's 17-year-old nephew, Benny Edens, enjoyed staying on his grandparents' farm in the summers, so he was there. He slept up on the second floor.

One dark night, while Dee and Douglas slept, Gladys stood ironing clothes, listening to her mother-in-law, while the men prepared to go to bed. The adults heard footsteps walking across the wooden front porch floor and, then, a knock on the door. Either Don or his father went to see who had knocked. No one was at the door. Strange enough, but it happened a second time. They heard the footsteps across the porch and a knock on the door. The men answered and again found no one.

There was no sense in calling for the county sheriff. Don and Granddaddy Earl loaded their shotguns, went outside, and searched around the house. No shots rang out. There was no trace of anyone to be found. The men went back inside. The footsteps and knock happened a third time. No one went to the door.

Earl simply said, "It's just a Truesdell ghost."

The men went to bed. As brave as Benny could be, he chose not to stay on the second floor that night. Instead, he slept on Granddaddy and Granny's bedroom floor. It was a night Don, Gladys, and Earl long remembered and passed along in tales to the children. [4]

Don and Gladys moved into their new home in spring 1948. The granite, ranch style home had an appearance like some of the stone houses of wealthy Nicaraguans, except that it did not have a red tile roof. The final cost was $17,000. In addition to the money from the lumber sale, Don and Gladys paid off the remainder as quickly as they could while the children were young, so they would be unaware of the family's financial deprivations.

Dee and Douglas sat in an old wagon, sharing space with Dee's stuffed animals, for a photograph in front of their new home.

As far as Gladys believed, even Quantico and Camp Lejeune had more amenities to offer families than did Lugoff, which is not saying much. There was a gas station at the US-1 and Fort Jackson Road intersection and a very small general store on the southeast corner of US-1 and HW-34. St. John's Methodist Church was just south of the store.

For the first time, Gladys, ever responsible for her children, experienced a "strange" and isolated life. She was a Yankee from Philadelphia and had no idea how to make conversation with farm wives. She had no way to keep up with the outside news. In the early years back in Lugoff, they listened to a radio that worked sometimes and subscribed to no newspapers or magazines. She missed the theaters and museums and conversations about the wider world beyond cows and crops. Early on, she did not drive.

Men ran things, and Don believed "the man of the house" was in charge. Gladys was supposed to stay home and take care of the babies and be grateful. According to Don, the Bible said he should be the head of the household, and she should obey her husband. Eventually, she told him what he could do with the Bible.

Douglas was not thriving and remained ill. Don and Gladys took him to Don's uncle in Bethune to find out what was wrong. Doctor Ernest referred them to a doctor in Camden. The baby was obviously weak with anemia, possibly in need of more Vitamin A. The doctor prescribed a remedy.

"Feed him calf's liver to build him up."

What child enjoys the taste of liver? Douglas certainly did not want to eat it, no matter how Gladys coaxed him to swallow the iron-rich helpings. Tensions permeated the Truesdell mealtimes.

Gladys was soon watching what she ate as months seemed to grind along, expecting another baby very soon. She found Don's younger sister to be a caring support.

Lois Lee was married to Stephen Craig "S.C." Clyburn and had two girls and a boy at home between the ages of 6 and 12 years. Their second child, named after Lois, had died in 1939 at age 7 months. "S.C." was a nice man, and, in the eyes of the Truesdells, he was well-to-do. The Clyburns lived in a fine house on Polo Lane, off North Broad Street in Camden, with a barn, a stable for polo and hunting horses, and a pasture in back. They also had a place on the Wateree River. In his free time, "S.C." played polo with the rich folks and rode "to the hounds" in fox hunts. Well known in Kershaw County, he was active in the Rotary Club and served terms as the School Board president.

"S.C." leased and ran a gas and auto repair station in Camden and always drove a new Chrysler. One of his brothers, Frank Clyburn, worked at the station. Twice each year, Frank drove the station's big truck over to the Truesdell's house to deliver fuel oil for their furnace. Two tanks a year were what Don and Gladys could afford to get through the cold spells.

Lois stopped by when she could. She liked to drop off turkeys and hams at holiday times. And, when her children outgrew their clothes, she brought the clothing to Gladys. Such kindness had a lasting impact. Gladys was so grateful to Lois and "S.C." that she would name two of her children after her in-laws.

Granny Margaret was asked to come over to watch the two children, and Don drove his wife to the Kershaw County Memorial Hospital. When he came home, he let Granny know that he was a daddy for the third time.

Stephen Craig Truesdell was born on March 30, 1948.

"Mama Had Eaten Some Peas." [5]

Gladys was pregnant for the fourth time during the summer heat and humidity of 1949. Despite having no air conditioning in the home, she baked a cake for Dee's 5th birthday on July 9. Gladys did her best to have a pleasant day when she turned 28 years old three weeks later, remembering that her husband would be 43 on August 26.

Dee helped her Mama care for Douglas and Stephen. Don's older sister, Edna, had a suggestion. Her daughter, Gene, 18 years old and getting ready to leave home, thought it would be fun to have her younger cousins come over to Florence for a visit. Stephen Craig Clyburn, 9, and Judy Clyburn, 7, were going to come over from Camden. Gladys agreed to let Dee spend a week in Florence with her Aunt Edna. [6]

Dee came home with lots to chat about. The Eden's house was in town. Her cousin Gene had more shoes than she had ever seen, all neatly lined up in a row under her bed from headboard to footboard. There was a sidewalk and places to walk to and the first swimming pool she had ever seen. The older cousins took the younger ones to the pool almost every day. Benny Edens, 19, was especially nice to the cousins. He threw Dee up into the air and caught her on the way down, a whole new experience for a child with a one-armed father. It made her giggle and laugh, and she pestered Benny a lot. Benny took it in stride and would toss her into the air again.

On a Friday, the family of five piled into the car they called "The Old Gray Ghost." Don drove them into Camden and pulled up at the hospital entrance. Gladys climbed from the small coupe, and Don drove out to the street and parked the car.

"Mama ate some peas that didn't agree with her," he told Dee.

She was to be in charge of Douglas and Stephen, all in the back seat. He told them to behave and left for the hospital. Dee was unafraid and took charge. Her brothers behaved as the three waited. How long they were out in the car is not certain, but Don returned at least twice to check on them. At another time, a man dressed in a hat and suit, stopped, looked in on the children, and asked if they were all right. Dee answered confidently.

"Our Mama ate some peas that didn't agree," she explained. "I'm in charge of the boys."

Linda Gayle was born that day, September 2, 1949. She was a happy, laughing baby. Soon the family took to calling her "Gay," and her laughter brightened the family home for almost a year.

Gladys and Don had four youngsters at home. Mama was pleased with the help Dee gave her in the household chores. Yet, as the next summer progressed, the parents knew that their first-born was going to start first grade in the fall. Gladys was left to figure out school clothes, transportation, lunches, and all the variety of needs a child has when they first leave home for five days a week. For Gladys, a year of time was about to escape her awareness.

Donald Douglas was four years old when the doctors finally decided that surgery might reveal why he was sick. Don and Gladys took him to the hospital at the end of July 1950. The intestinal blockage that had plagued his health was discovered and corrected. Administered penicillin shots to prevent infection from spreading, he recovered and went home. He could play again.

Then, war broke out in Korea. Don had reasons to follow the battle news. On August 5, 1950, his old regiment, the 5th Marines, was deployed to the Pusan Perimeter as part of the Provisional Marine Brigade. From there, they would participate in the Inchon Landing, the Battle of the Chosin Reservoir, the Punchbowl on the East-Central Front, and in the Bunker Battles on the hills of the Western Front. For nearly three years, the 5th Marines, 7th Marines, and 11th Marines, 1st Marine Division, pushed back the North Korean Army and the Chinese divisions in Korea.

Don's nephews, Billy and Benny Edens, were in their early twenties during the Korean War years, and both were Marine Corps infantrymen. When the Marines landed at Inchon, Benny was the same age as Private Marvin Jackson—the boy who had died with his brains sticking out at the May 1927 battle in La Paz Centro. Don could only hope that his sister Edna would not receive the same kind of telegram that was delivered to Mrs. Nellie Everett in Chicago.

A few weeks after Douglas came home from the hospital, he caught a mild cold. He might have recovered from the cold, except that his appendix ruptured. It was an emergency.

Don rushed Gladys and Douglas to the hospital. The doctors had to operate even though the boy had a cold. Douglas' coughing grew worse, and he began having breathing difficulty and pains in his chest. He developed pneumonia, and his symptoms would not resolve. He struggled for days. Double pneumonia set in and made his condition worse as fluid filled his lungs. Penicillin injections failed to help. He had developed immunity to the antibiotic during his earlier recovery from surgery. Don took the three children to stay with Granny Margaret. Lois Clyburn went to be with Gladys at the hospital.

Tragedy shook the family on Thursday, August 24, two days before Don's birthday. Dee was on Granny's back porch when Lois arrived with the news. Douglas had died at Kershaw County Memorial. Granny sat down, pulled her apron up over her face, and for the third time that anyone would remember, she cried.

Donald Douglas Truesdell was buried in the family plot at St. John's Methodist Cemetery on Ridgeway Road (SC-34-West), a half-mile walk from home, just past Pine Grove Road (SR S-28-36), and one-point-seven miles north of the US-1 South intersection. The cemetery is in a heavily wooded property between two homes on the east side of Ridgeway. [9] Don and Gladys' faith is reflected in the inscription they had engraved on their son's flat gravestone

"Weep not, he is not dead, but sleepeth."

Gladys planted a small tree near her boy's headstone. Every Christmas, the family visited the cemetery and decorated the tree, watching it grow into a large tree. Today, the family keeps a pinwheel, a mobile, or a toy a child would enjoy near their brother's tree.

Gladys, overwhelmed by grief, still got up in the mornings and kept the children fed and clean. She got Dee off to first grade. Where and what her thoughts were, she kept to herself. Don did the same.

"Now I realize that the Legion was family to him." [7]

Don felt strongly about the military and service organizations. The commitments to his family, to the Society, to fellow veterans, and to the Marine Corps often tugged his loyalties in different directions.

He and the American Legion Post #17 members maintained an affiliation and allegiance to each other across the years. Don traveled from home at times on behalf of the Legion. He established a rose garden in front of the Post and participated in a variety of annual events. One fundraising campaign in the 1950s put him on the front page of *The State* newspaper holding up a South Carolina furbearing marsupial sporting a white pointed snout.

The "Marines Marching for Dollars" set up a moving roadblock along U.S.-1. Drivers were not asked for donations, but were free to contribute in some way to the effort. One man explained to Don that he had no money, only a "possum in a sack." A photographer caught the moment as Don accepted the donation of an opossum. [8]

Another esteemed organization also shined a light on his heroism and invited him to travel from Lugoff. The Medal of Honor Legion was formed on April 23, 1890. The living recipients had banded together to protect the integrity of the Medal. From their example and model, the Congressional Medal of Honor Society (CMOHS) was organized in 1946. Much like the founders of the American Legion, the living recipients intended to perpetuate the ideals that the Medal symbolized, promote patriotism, and foster a love of country in the aftermath of World War II. Their membership began to expand four years later.

The Society members viewed the distinction of wearing the Medal to represent a commitment to service. They would not "rest on their laurels." The Society was vibrant, and Donald Truesdell was an active participant, fully committed to the traditions embodied in the Medal of Honor and in the purposes of the organization.

One winter Sunday in January 1951, five months after they had buried their child, Don and Gladys decided to do something rare. [10] After church, they went with the children to visit another family. The drive home from there started out quietly. Don was driving. Gladys, wearing high heels, was in the front passenger seat holding 16-month-old Gay.

The day was cold. Stephen sat behind his mother, all bundled up in a heavy jacket. His little hat had earflaps, which were pulled down, held by a strap under his chin. Dee was at his side, and the two began to bicker about something.

Mama was out of patience. She turned around and yelled. She told Dee to sit over on her own side, behind her daddy. Stephen was to sit on his side, right behind her. Before Gladys returned her attention out the windshield, she gave the command that every child has heard from a parent. "I do not want to hear another word out of you!"

Heating up in all his winter attire, Stephen tried to roll down his window, but reached for the door handle instead. The door opened, and he fell out of the car. His sister was in a most perplexing dilemma: not say a word or disobey and say something? The car continued on its way. Dee finally spoke up on behalf of her brother.

"Stephen fell out of the car."

By the time Don stopped the car and looked back, the lump on the side of the road was very small. Instead of backing up, he turned off the ignition, and three doors swung open as the alarmed family exited the car and ran back to Stephen. Hurrying in high heels, carrying Gay, Gladys was last to reach him. Stephen was unconscious.

The drive to the hospital was all too familiar to the parents. Don ignored the speed limits. Gladys had passed Gay to Dee in the back seat, and cradled Stephen in her arms. Pulling up to the hospital entrance, Don took his still unconscious son in his arms and rushed inside. Someone stopped him before any aid was proffered and asked if he had insurance. Had Don not had his arms full carrying Stephen, he would have punched out the person right on the spot.

Fortunately, Stephen's bulky jacket and hat with earflaps had protected him from any serious injury. He regained consciousness and the family went home. His parents made him comfortable in their bed and made a phone call. Granny and Granddaddy came quickly. Reasonably, everyone fussed over the boy. Except his sister, who had her own thoughts. For her, the drama was overdone. How dumb could he be to fall out of the car?

Don decided the family needed some changes. He bought a used car from the family just down the road. The "new," shiny, black car was larger than the Old Gray Ghost. Don thought it was also time that Gladys learned to drive. He took the family out for a ride. Having gone a distance, he turned the beautiful car over to Gladys. She tried to turn the vehicle around, messed up on the clutch, and rolled into a tree. The fender of their new car was dented and pushed in against the tire.

Don was well aware of his wife's state of mind. He stayed calm and quiet as he left the passenger seat to survey the damage. He hammered the dented fender away from the tire enough to drive home. He had done what needed to be done—no yelling, no cursing.

Gladys would remember little of the first year following Douglas' death. The anniversary of his funeral passed, and she readied Dee for the second grade. Looking back, it would seem to her that she had lost a year of her life. Yet, family took center stage again. Gladys was four months pregnant.

After the New Year, she let Dee in on the secret that another baby was going to be arriving soon. Dee remembered the fun she had experienced overseeing the boys when Gay was born. She looked forward to going into Camden to the hospital. It did not happen that way; in fact, she slept through her chance to be in charge again.

Dee, Stephen, and Gay were all asleep on the night of January 31, 1952, when Gladys woke Don up. "It's time."

Considering the logistics of waking up the children and packing them into the car, Don instead drove to Granny Margaret's and brought her to the house to stay with the sleeping children. Then, he took Gladys to the hospital. She had been right about the time.

When Don returned home, he wanted to share the good news with his daughter. He woke up Dee to tell her that she had a new sister and was baffled that he had made her cry. Dee was not crying because Lois Lee Truesdell had joined the family, but because she had missed out on the trip to town. Her daddy would make up for that.

On an early-February day, Dee looked up from her second grade desk and was surprised to see her father in the classroom. He was smiling and talking to her teacher, Mrs. O'Caine. Don looked huge to her, and she would always remember his face. How young and handsome he looked that day!

Don had come to get her out of school. They drove together to the hospital to bring her mother and Lois home. Gladys and Dee sat in the backseat of the black car, holding Lois. They would have different memories of the drive: which one of them held the baby's head, and which one held her feet. In time, it would seem to the family that Lois was born to be a horsewoman. She could handle horses as a child and was her happiest self when around one. Any trip to Camden to visit Aunt Lois and Uncle "S.C." and the horse stable would be a treat for her.

The war in Korea was arbitrated to an end on July 27, 1953. During the conflict, 146 Medals of Honor had been earned. Thirty-eight recipients survived their actions in Korean battles and joined the CMOH Society. Marines had earned forty-two Medals. Two of them had grown up in Don's home state, and both had covered grenades to protect others. Fourteen of the Marine recipients returned home. One was Robert Sidney Kennemore from Greenville.

When the hostilities ended, his old regiment participated in the defense of the Korean Demilitarized Zone from July 1953 until February 1955. The 5th Marines returned to the U.S. in March 1955. A shadow seemed to fall over the combat veterans in the war's aftermath.

Sergeant Benny M. Edens was honorably discharged. Dee had celebrated her 9th birthday by the time he returned home. She was at her Granny Margaret's when her cousin stepped into the yard. He did not look like the teenager who had thrown her up into the air at the Florence town pool four summers ago. She would retain a clear mental picture of that moment. When Gladys greeted him, she made a comment that puzzled Dee. [11]

"You look like you have been on a vacation," she heard her mother say.

Over and around Dee, the grown-ups talked in serious tones about Benny and the war. She understood that he was having problems, but no one ever told her what they might be. She came to the conclusions that Benny had been a prisoner of war in Korea. Maybe he had been on a death march; or maybe her mother's remark was because he had spent time at a recovery facility for mental problems before he returned home. What nine-year-old understands the impact of war on a loved one?

On a Tight String

Don's $2000-annual pension did not go far trying to raise the children, and he held tight control of the money. There was almost none, and he seemed to know little about money and budgets. He knew how to shoot and find his way around in the woods. He thought of himself as a businessman, but made poor decisions. Sometimes he threatened to withhold grocery money if Gladys did not agree with him and do as he wanted.

Years passed, and he pressured her into signing loans so he could raise cows down on the 500 acres the family called "The Creek." The trouble was that Don was neither a farmer nor a rancher. Something always happened, and he never made any money doing anything. He dipped into his pension to support what was more hobby than profitable enterprise.

There was a time that Gladys feared she would have to give one or more of the little children away, because she did not think she could feed all five of them. Fortunately, she could do more with a dollar than anyone else in Kershaw County.

Nothing fun went on in the children's lives. They had no television. The radio worked sometimes. They went to school and came home. They went nowhere else but Sunday school and grocery shopping once a week. Their biggest treat was going into Camden.

Gladys did a lot of sewing and made most of the children's clothes as they grew up. If Don or Earl were going to the Camden feed and seed store, Gladys or Dee or another female went along to pick out the sacks of feed and seed. The cotton sacks were finer than burlap and printed in a variety of patterns. The men planted the seeds and doled out the feed to the animals. The women washed the empty sacks and divided the material for clothes. For the girls, one sack was sufficient for a blouse or skirt. A dress called for two sacks.

Providing food for the family entailed both a grocery budget and homegrown chow. The latter could be "one nasty business!" Sunday dinners were usually fried chicken. Don would go out, catch a chicken with his left hand, hold it down with a foot, step on its head, and give a good yank. The chicken would run around the yard without a head, spouting blood. When the fowl flopped over, he retrieved it, hung it by its feet upside down in the fork of a tree, and waited for it to bleed out. Then, Gladys would clean it, pluck the feathers off, singe off the small pin feathers, and cook the chicken for dinner. If she was rushed and did not singe the pin feathers, the skin, a really tasty part of the chicken, had to be discarded.

As she plucked the chicken, Gladys would tell Dee that she never wanted her daughter to have to deal with chickens. Anything having to do with chickens is a nasty business. Gladys would go on about Philadelphia restaurants, theaters, and museums. The only way for Dee to get away from a Lugoff kitchen was to get an education and "Get the hell out of South Carolina!" Dee listened.

Don's idea of cooking was quite narrow, and his favorite meal was rooted in his early family life. He wanted Gladys to bake corn bread every day. She had no idea about corn bread and had to learn the recipe from the Truesdells. She baked the bread in a round frying pan. Don would take the round loaf, break it up in a big bowl, pour buttermilk over it, and eat it with a spoon. The meal was made even better with a side bowl of grits. Cheese on the grits was "getting close to heaven." All he needed for the perfect meal was a big bowl of collard greens with fat back and vinegar on the side.

In his efforts to keep control over the household, Don did his best to run it as if they were all Marines: "Yes sir, no sir, no excuse sir." He did not participate in family activities and was not present for the children's birthday parties or Christmas. No photos of him doing things with the children went into scrapbooks, because he did not do much with them.

He got up early each morning, put on his khaki work pants, work shirt, and high-topped, leather work shoes, and went down to the Five and Twenty Creek to check on his cows. The family had felled trees at intervals across the creek, and he could go from one side to the other across the trees and walk along the trails. The trees and vegetation were thick, not quite like the Nicaraguan jungle trails, but with proper camouflage, a person could effectively move about concealed from view. Familiar with every acre of his property, if anyone invaded Kershaw County, he would track them down and kill them. The creek was one of Don's favorite places. [12]

Once he had reconnoitered the creek, he would tend his acres. More of a hobby for him, farming was never very productive. Since he loved peaches, and there was no space for a peach orchard, he dedicated a lot of space for peach trees. They bloomed beautifully in the spring. He took afternoon naps and went to bed early each night.

The children all knew to leave their daddy alone. Maybe he did not feel well, but they understood that he did not want them to start any conversations with him. He would do the talking. Left with the strong impression that he did not want to interact in their lives, it seemed normal in the family that Daddy did not want to be part of a family or to know and enjoy his children. Passing their father in the narrow hallway in the bedroom–bathroom area of the home without speaking to each other did not seem unusual.

A great part of Don's frustration was doing everything with just one hand. Determined to never be a burden, he disliked asking for any help, trying always to rely on himself. He would hold a knife under his knee to untie a simple knot in a rope or to remove a splinter from his finger. Bleeding from a significant wound was a common result. [13]

Gladys might have been shorter in stature than her husband, but she had Irish blood in her and enough Upper Darby pluck to stand up to him when she believed he had crossed a line. Once Don, in a fit of anger, pushed her up against the refrigerator, held her against it, and reared back with his left arm. [14]

"If you hit me," Gladys warned him, "you better kill me, because once I get up off the floor, I will kill you." That was the end of physical confrontations between them.

Only Dee would be old enough to remember another altercation, having witnessed it as it happened. Stephen and Gay were both toddlers. Don was taking off his belt, preparing to punish Stephen in the bathroom. Beatings with a belt were the common form of discipline in Don's boyhood. It would not be so in Gladys' home. She placed herself between Don and her son.

"Anytime you think you are going to lay a hand on any of the children," she said, "you have to get past me first." Don backed down and never tried that again. Over time, Gladys stepped in enough that none of the children experienced a beating.

"There are wars that are fought without bullets and they can be pretty deadly." [15] Don learned to contain his anger, restricting it to words. When he got mad about something, there were lots of verbal assaults and some days of silence. If displeased with his wife, he could go days without speaking to her.

1954—A Year of Awakenings

Don kept his Marine memorabilia in a trunk stored in the attic. He told his children—better, he ordered them—to stay out of it. No photographs of him in uniform were on display in the house, and he never had an "I love me wall" to draw attention to his service. [16] He kept such a low profile about his Medal, that Dee and Stephen had no idea that their daddy was a South Carolina hero.

Don finally provided the family a television in 1954.

In summer 1954, "Dee Dee" had her 10th birthday. The Korean War had not yet been over for a year, and at the time, she knew nothing at all about the Medal of Honor. She began fifth grade in the fall and was excelling in her studies. One day in class, someone mentioned that her dad had the Congressional Medal of Honor for bravery.

Dee had no idea what people were talking about. Always an advocate for Truth, she responded. "NO, he doesn't." [17]

"YES, he does," answered her classmate Jane McMurdo. The argument persisted, but Jane would not relent. Dee decided that if others thought her father had a medal for being a hero, she would let Jane win. The surprise came when she got home and told her Mama about the argument.

"Jane McMurdo was right," Gladys said.

Learning that her daddy was a local hero was a good thing. The Truesdells were poor in the status-conscious South, and the Medal lifted the family into a much higher status bracket. Additionally, whenever his actions for earning the Medal were brought up, the explanation was that he was "defending our country." That was big in South Carolina.

Don did not talk about his Medal or his heroism or the loss of his arm. The children did not know the details about his actions in Nicaragua. What they knew as they grew up was that their father was missing a limb and had two prosthetic arms that they seldom saw him wear. One of the prosthetics had a hand with fingers and thumb that opened and closed when the elbow flexed. The other had just a hook that opened and closed. The children had permission to play with them like toys. For amusement, one of the kids would sneak up on another and flex the prosthetic arm to give them a pinch. [18]

Thanksgiving was a week away when Gladys had a talk with Dee. She was big enough now to stay home and take care of the family. That was better than the four children going to stay with a relative or having Granny come to watch over them. On Saturday, November 20, 1954, Gladys was sweeping the front porch and told her daughter her plans.

"When I get finished, I am going to make jello, take a bath, and go to the hospital."

The time was coming again. Don waited to start the car. Just as Gladys was getting ready to leave for the hospital, Lois and her daughter, Patricia, 18, stopped at the house on their way to visit Granny. The grown-ups all departed for their destinations. Gladys gave birth to David Jeffrey Truesdell twenty minutes after she arrived at the hospital. Don looked in on her and his baby boy. Told that he was not needed there anymore, he returned home.

Lois and Pat stopped by again after visiting Granny. Finding her brother back from the hospital, Lois gave Don a piece of her mind for being inconsiderate, not waiting until his child was born. Having been through labor and birth four times, she was quite surprised to hear that Don had barely gotten Gladys to the delivery room on time and that Jeff had already arrived.

Dee was commended for doing a good job being in charge. Everyone was fed at the proper meal times. School lunches were packed. She and Stephen did not miss a day in school. She even baked her Mama a cake to celebrate her return home. That year, the Truesdells had a good Thanksgiving. Before the next Thanksgiving, the presence of the television in his home and a presidential campaign brought changes to Don's life.

Gathering in Large Numbers

By a custom beginning in 1955, U.S. presidents invited living MOH recipients and guests to attend inauguration festivities. Following Don's discharge from the USMC, the invitations arrived at the Truesdell residence after the November election results were tabulated. Every four years Don would have to decide on traveling to Washington in January to attend inaugurations: Dwight D. Eisenhower, John F. Kennedy, Lyndon B. Johnson, Richard M. Nixon (twice), Gerald Ford, Jimmy Carter, Ronald Reagan (twice), and George H. W. Bush. Accepting an invitation would mean that Don would find himself in the presence of other living MOH recipients and dignitaries like former presidents, Members of Congress, Supreme Court justices, and high-ranking military officers.

Granny Margaret always took responsibility for organizing family reunions. She made sure that her son showed up with his family on Sunday, August 12, 1956. Granny gathered sixty family members together for their reunion photo. Three generations of Lees and Truesdells knelt, squatted, and stood in a great pyramid of family. [19]

Lee Family Reunion - August 12, 1956

With his Sunday necktie lose at the collar, Don knelt front and center: broad shouldered, square faced, black hair, hardly smiling, seeming the largest of the men in the family. Against his right leg, he propped up David Jeffrey, three months from his second birthday. His big left hand stretched across his youngest son's chest, his right stump under the boy's right elbow. Granny stood behind Don. Stephen stood to the far left of the line of grown-ups, peeping around the side of an aunt or cousin. Gladys stood on a bench at the top center of the pyramid, with a big smile, dressed in her Sunday best. Beside her was 12-year-old Dee, waiting patiently for her chance "to leave South Carolina in the dust." Gayle "Gay" stood in front of her mother, and Lois, the youngest girl, stood in the shadow, slightly behind Gay's right shoulder.

Granny Margaret took pride in her family. Whenever an article about Don appeared in a newspaper, she cut it out to save—loose between the pages of a big scrapbook she kept among her cherished belongings. Dee learned of the scrapbook many years after the family reunions.

A reporter contacted Don early in November 1957. Noting that the former Marine was one of six Medal recipients living in South Carolina, the reporter wondered what plans Don had for the November 11th Veterans Day. Don was leading a quiet life as a farmer in Kershaw County. He had no special plans for the holiday. [20]

Having a Medal of Honor brings with it some responsibility and commitments to the nation. Don accepted a good number of invitations to appear at public tributes, especially for Memorial Day. Larger events gave him pause to consider whether to attend or not.

On Wednesday, May 28, 1958, caskets arrived in Washington, D.C., with the remains of two Unknown servicemen killed in WWII and Korean War combat. The caskets lay in the Capitol Rotunda until Memorial Day, May 30.

That Friday morning at 9:30 AM, Don joined "216 Honor Medal Winners" in the White House Rose Garden to pay their respects. Thirty-three Marine recipients attended. Richard E. Bush, Sergeant William G. Harrell, Jacklyn H. Lucas, and Richard K. Sorenson were among them. President Eisenhower extended his tribute to the gathered heroes, and a brunch was served. [21]

Vice President Richard Nixon stood with the president and shook hands with the Medal recipients. Two weeks before, during a goodwill trip through Latin America, an angry mob had attacked the vice president's car while traveling through Caracas, Venezuela, and had nearly overturned the vehicle. When they shook hands, Don, the retired Marine chief warrant officer, remembered the events in León after the battle at La Paz in Nicaragua and commiserated with Vice President Nixon.

"I'd be willing to give you my Medal of Honor for what you went through," he said sympathetically. [22]

At 2:45 PM, President Eisenhower and his honored guests motored to Arlington National Cemetery. The two caskets were carried on caissons to the plaza in Arlington. The cortege arrived at 3:02, and moved into the Apse. The Marine Corps band played *The Star-Spangled Banner*, followed by an Invocation, a trumpet call, two minutes of silence, singing of *America the Beautiful*, and the presentation at 3:20 PM. The president solemnly conferred the Medal of Honor on each of the Unknowns, and the two were interred beside their World War I comrade.

Known as Don Roy to his friends, he and Gladys taught the children to be respectful, kind, and thoughtful. Not just patriotic, they were deeply religious and civil minded. They had to learn to have a good laugh on their own. Don encouraged outdoor activity beyond walking to school. The kids went fishing and shrimping, swam at Drakeford Park once it had been developed, and played ball in the park. The almost mile of wooded land owned by the family behind their home was an exciting place to give the kids rides on a car hood pulled behind a tractor. And, the woods made for a good rifle range. A sand bank served for a berm.

Don was very proud of his skill with weapons and seemed to treasure his Expert Marksmanship Badge more than his Medal of Honor. His skill was reminiscent of his days on the Parris Island rifle range when he was drilled to maintain and accurately fire the M1903 Springfield. A five-round magazine fed the '03 bolt-action, repeating rifle. Having excellent reflexes, he could shoot extremely well even after losing his right arm. He could just "point and shoot" and hit his target. [23]

Don took young Stephen into the back yard and taught him to shoot, going through the full training exercise: steady hold on the weapon, aim, inhale, exhale, hold, squeeze, clear the weapon, maintain muzzle discipline. Second Lieutenant Truesdell remembered patrolling Nicaraguan jungle trails. He constantly reminded his son that the person holding the weapon was responsible for everything that happened after the trigger was pulled.

Stephen, aged 10 years, had his own .22 rifle and pistol. He was allowed to shoot them only when supervised. Provided five cartridges a day, he could choose rifle or pistol for target practice. Like any boy would, he just wanted to shoot, but his dad insisted on gun discipline. Stephen could shoot all five rounds, or until he missed the target. His father remained frugal in all matters. If Stephen missed, he was to go back to the house and put any remaining cartridges back in the box. The message was drilled into his head as they walked from the woods.

"Don't waste ammo," Don would say, "if you're not going to hit the target."

His father did not waste ammunition. When he took Stephen hunting, his precision was astounding to his son. "I would be mentally processing a movement, and my father had already fired and hit the game."

Don had come to believe that, when Washington, D.C., sent the Marines to Nicaragua, Americans had become unwelcome intruders in someone else's land. In his view, the natives were defending their homes against invaders financed by a corrupt local government. The Sandinistas were shrewd and knew how to use their own terrain to their advantage. He felt the same about his property on the Twenty-Five Mile Creek. He did not like anyone hunting on the family land.

He had once seen a local man hunting on the Truesdell property and told him to leave and not trespass again. One day, he saw the man's pickup parked in the woods on the farm again. He told Stephen that he knew the owner and explained the situation. [24]

His dad was steadfast. "Let's go get him."

They followed the creek that ran through the property and spotted the man on the other side. He saw them and dashed off in the direction of his truck. He would have to cross the creek to get back to his vehicle. At low flows, a person could wade across the creek. But, the water was high and the trespasser would have to traverse the creek using a fallen tree. That posed him a problem. Don knew where the man was going to have to cross to reach his truck, so he and Stephen ran and waited, concealed at the end of the log. Young Stephen was about to witness a thirty-second confrontation and learn a lesson.

The man tried to cross the log. Don stepped in front of him and quickly snatched the shotgun from his hands, startling the man and Stephen. The retired Marine broke open the shotgun, ejecting the shells over his shoulder. The ammo sank into the water. The trespasser was infuriated—and maybe oblivious to who was holding his shotgun.

"You son of a bitch," he spat out, "you threw my shells in the creek."

Stephen was old enough to know that that comment was at least the second mistake the man had made that day.

"Watch this," Don said to the man. He threw the shotgun into the creek.

The man again cussed at Don, demanding to know who was going to get his gun. Don threw a left hook that knocked the man into the creek.

"Get your own gun," he advised, as he and his son watched the trespasser float downstream. He added a warning. "Don't come back, or you'll get your ass beat the next time."

The lesson Stephen had learned: When you disarm someone, unload the weapon just in case you lose control of the situation.

Stephen liked to learn masculine kinds of things. Besides marksmanship, combat, and flying, he had a fascination with welding and anything that made sparks. A couple of Camden inventors indulged his curiosity.

James L. Anderson and Lewis F. Anderson were the proprietors of the Anderson Bros. Machine Shop. On December 19, 1958, they had filed a patent claim for a one-operator, wheeled vehicle for manipulating and transporting a pallet/container holding wood or small logs (US2925186A). Lewis had been a glider pilot in WWII and was married to Lottie (Smyrl), a schoolteacher. Their daughter, Joan, was a schoolmate of Dee's. [25]

Steve enjoyed going along with Don on trips to the shop if equipment needed fixing. Lewis was happy to give him tips about welding and putting machinery together.

The time came when Don had fallen into enough debt that he had to sell off half of the land. The sale involved the property on the far side of The Creek. The business lesson did not sink in. Although he had always promised Gladys that he had not put the house up as collateral when she signed loans, it turned out later that he had. When she discovered that the house was tied into a loan, Gladys "nearly had a nervous breakdown."

Don's dealings had put the roof over the children's heads at risk. So, he was forced to sell the rest of the creek property to pay off the loan and free the house of any liens. Charles Hurst, a neighbor, bought those acres. [26]

Dee was learning to keep her nervous system calm during her daddy's business dealings and the domestic squabbles. "What is done is done," she would tell herself. "No need to waste time pondering it. If you make a mistake, learn from it and do not repeat it. Make all your mistakes original ones!" [27] Dee believed that life was going to work out.

Neither Don nor Gladys sugar-coated their comments to each other. They did not mince words. While their bickering might have been unpleasant, the children all learned to be straightforward, plain spoken, even blunt, in expressing their thoughts and opinions. Young Jeff was no exception.

In summer 1960, he was swimming at the lake. There were no adults around, and Dee sat on the beach watching him. Billy, the Lugoff bully, was near her. Jeff's facemask was on the beach between them. Not yet six years old, Jeff wanted his mask.

"Hey Ugly, throw me that mask!" he yelled from the water to the bully.

Dee's heart raced, sure that the bully would try to drown her little brother and that she was going to have to fight him off. The bully knew enough about the Truesdells. He threw Jeff the mask. That was the end of it.

All the Truesdell children could get a driver's license, restricted to daylight hours, at age 14 years. They got their regular licenses at age 16 years and, then, were eligible to take the commercial license test.

Able to afford only two tanks of gas monthly, Don was very vigilant about how the family car was used. Dee got her driver's license in 1958, when she was 14 years old. Since she had high school activities, she got to use the car a bit. Whenever she did, Don subjected her to the same grilling when she got home as he gave to Gladys when she returned from grocery shopping.

"How much mileage did you put on the car? . . . Where did you go? . . . Who did you see? . . . Did they know who you were?" To Dee, that last question was always strange.

All the rural school bus drivers were 16- to 18-year-old students, earning $1 a day. The district preferred students who lived the farthest away from the school. They could pick up the students, drop them off at school, and bring them back home after hours. The drivers kept the buses overnight. A bus was in the Truesdell yard for several years. Lois began her bus route in 1968 and drove until she graduated. There were no school bus dings, dents, or wrecks in all the years the Truesdells attended school. [28]

Dee got her "permanent" driver's license in 1960. Since she had high school activities, she was permitted to use the car a bit. She would also drive Granny Margaret to visit friends and relatives. Besides the guidance on how to live like a Southern Lady, her grandmother was also the source of Kershaw County Civil War lore, of the days before the family had indoor plumbing, and of the mixing of the family bloodlines. Dee held her own memories of the days when not everyone in Lugoff had in-door plumbing and when she went over to see the Watts family's first indoor bathroom.

Regarding the South Carolina wars, the history lessons were easy to teach in the Camden schools, without the need for textbooks. Students read from the diaries of Revolutionary and Civil War soldiers who had written about how poor the land and people in the center of the state were compared to other regions. They handled weapons used in the Civil War, passed down through family generations. Outside of school, Revolutionary War and Civil War memorials were prominent on about every third city block. [29]

Students walked to the ridge crossing north Broad Street, near the Kirkwood Lane intersection. On that site, General Nathaniel Greene's Continental American Army forces besieged the British garrison forces on April 25, 1781. The Battle of Hobkirk Hill resulted in the withdrawal of the British to Charleston. Classes made field trips over to Ridgeway, twenty-nine miles north of Columbia, where Commanding General Pierre Beauregard, CSA, briefly established his headquarters in the Century House, just across the street from the telegraph office and the Charleston and Southern Railway depot. The students saw the railroad rails that despised General Sherman's right flank left bent around oak trees on their way through the Carolinas in February 1865. There was no doubt that Kershaw County people were still mad about the Union's invasion.

An accident made driving more of a challenge for Don. He was supervising a hired hand cut down a tree on the property with a chain saw. The saw slipped and cut into Don's left foot. Had it not been for the sturdy work boot he was wearing, the saw would have severed his foot in half.

Congress sent legislation to President Dwight Eisenhower. He signed it on August 5, 1958, chartering the CMOHS. Within the charter, the Society outlined the purposes of the organization. [30]

The members intended to create a bond of brotherhood and comradeship among all living MOH recipients. They would maintain the memory and respect for those who had earned the Medal posthumously, and for those recipients who had returned from war and since died. They would protect and preserve the dignity and honor of the Medal at all times and on all occasions and protect the name of the Medal as well as individual recipients from exploitation. Remaining alert to how their comrades were fairing, they would provide assistance and aid to needy recipients, their spouses or widows, and their children. In terms of enduring service, Society members would promote patriotism and allegiance to the Government and Constitution of the United States, serve the United States in peace or war, promote and perpetuate the principles upon which the nation was founded, and foster patriotism, inspiring and stimulating youth to become worthy citizens of the country.

Cotton Farming

In 1961, South Carolina was segregated. White children and African American children attended separate schools and worshiped at separate churches. Black adults could not vote. Constrained by custom and law, the races did not socialize. Black families in Kershaw County lived in unpainted, wooden, ramshackle houses, depending on their fireplaces to heat their homes.

Indicative of prevailing social attitudes, the preachers at the church the Truesdale family attended did not believe that Negroes were on any equal social or mental level with Whites. They spewed their interpretation of the Hebrew Bible Genesis story from the pulpit, informing the congregation of the disembarking from the ark after the flood and how Noah's sons had peopled the earth. Ham, one of the sons, had offended his father, and Noah cursed him. Ham's offspring would be the slaves of Noah's two greater sons. Ham's descendants populated Africa, and God turned them black to punish them for the sins of their father. Don Truesdale had no dispute with the pastors about this lesson. [31]

The Peay family lived less than two miles from the Truesdells. At the time that Don had been a second lieutenant manning the Quilalí garrison and leading patrols along the Río Coco valley, Mrs. Peay gave birth to a son in September 1931 and named him Benjamin Franklin Peay. He went by "Franklin." The white folks around Lugoff did not know much about the

Peays, who knew a lot about hardships and cotton farming. During Franklin's childhood, the cotton industry experienced severe devastations. The family attended a Black Methodist Church in Camden, where Willie Peay, the man of the house, was the choirmaster. Franklin grew up singing gospel music in the church.

As the Truesdells had moved into their new house on Ridgeway Road in 1948, Franklin Peay, 17 years old, had gone to New York, seeking a music career. He performed with gospel groups. One group switched into rhythm and blues and began recording in 1955. That was the year an executive suggested a name change and a solo career.

Franklin began a popular singing and successful songwriting career as Brook Benton. His first solo recording was played on radios in 1956. He appeared as Brook Benton in a 1957 Paramount Pictures musical film, and then, two of his songs climbed into Billboard's Top 10 hits in 1959. He sang duets with Dinah Washington in 1960. Franklin Peay prospered. [32]

Brook Benton's highest-charting single was number two on the Billboard Hot 100 chart for three weeks in the summer of 1961, and was the first Number One song on the Billboard Easy Listening chart. The song reflected his early experiences with boll weevils, an insect that had come from Mexico and infested all U.S. cotton-growing regions by the 1920s. If boll weevils got into a farmer's cash crop of cotton, a year's worth of work could be destroyed.

A farmer in *The Boll Weevil Song* had a conversation with the insect that everyone in Lugoff could understand. The farmer asked why the weevil picked his farm to make a home, and the insect laughed. The boll weevil called the farmer one day and said, "You'd better sell your old machines, 'cause when I'm through with your cotton, heh, you can't even buy gasoline."

Brook came home to Lugoff for a visit that summer.

Sometimes, Don did "business" with the Peay family, letting them chop firewood from some of his land. Apparently, they owed him money for something. Brook called the Truesdell home to tell Don he wanted to stop by to set things right. The call sent a ripple of excitement through the house. [33]

Dee had recently celebrated her 17th birthday. She understood that Mr. Benton, celebrity or not, would not be invited into the house. She asked if she could go out to meet the singer. The resounding NO was very firm. It was completely NOT acceptable. In fact, no one in the family except Don could go out to meet him. So, the family watched the encounter from inside at windows.

A grand car drove up, and out stepped a man dressed in the nicest clothes any of the Truesdells had ever seen. Mr. Benton wore a light, camel colored, cashmere suit. A long, light colored coat was draped over his shoulders. He and Don talked civilly, without any yelling, cursing, or threatening. Whatever the reason for Mr. Benton's visit, the matter seemed to have been settled.

Getting a Proper Education

Gladys and Donald intended to teach their children to live by moral and ethical standards. They were pleased that South Carolina had historically had a strong bond with religion going back to colonial days.

Don had been a daddy for almost twelve years when a church and state issue emerged in the family. He could have traced it all the way to the days when he was 10 years old. It involved temperance and whether his children would accept teetotalism.

Around the time of the Civil War, preachers bellowed that all brews, not just the strong distilled liquors (ardent spirits) like whiskey, gin, and brandy, but also beer, ale, and wine, were abominations. The 1895 South Carolina Constitution later included a liquor law that allowed beer, but not liquor, to be sold in taverns. The Confederate veterans had a part in this. The Revenue taxes were transferring Southern money to the North. Unacceptable. So, in 1916, three years before the 18th Amendment to the U.S. Constitution was passed, the South Carolina counties went completely "dry" when a statewide prohibition took effect—except for the clandestine homemade brews.

The national Prohibition Amendment, activated on January 16, 1920, outlawed the manufacture and sale of alcoholic beverages in the United States. Distillers went underground, into the hills and swamps. Bootlegging, rum running, and official corruption turned as rampant in South Carolina as in any other city or state in America.

One hundred prohibition agents moved silently in the outskirts of Charleston on Saturday night, September 3, 1926, and seized seventeen illicit stills. Thirty-three people were arrested in the Berkeley County liquor raid, including state and local officials. [34] Animosities rose, and things did not settle down.

Don was in the Marines and away from home when the encounters between the distillers and federal agents grew more violent. The Marines had deployed to Bluefields in Nicaragua in 1926, and, then, CPL Truesdale went ashore with the Marine detachments in late May 1927. During those same months, events in South Carolina had been newsworthy to the nation.

Seven weeks after CPL Truesdale had fought in La Paz Centro, State Constable John Bunon "Bunk" Amaker, 39, drove east from his home in Columbia, passed through Lugoff, Camden, and Florence, and met up with other state constables in Horry County on the coast. He and State Officers T. J. Cunningham, B. V. Lightsey, J. M. Pearman, T. W. Blease, Federal Prohibition Officer J. E. Davis, and Horry County Deputy Sheriff Ayers were on a liquor raiding mission. They merged in Floyds Township in the northwest corner of the county near the Little Pee Dee River.

On Wednesday morning, July 6, 1927, ten days before General Sandino's men attacked the Ocotal outpost, the liquor raiding party located the Granger home eight miles from Nichols, near the Marion County line. The officers started down a trail toward the site of a still and came upon men who fired upon them. It was like an ambush. Officers Amaker and Cunningham rushed toward a high bank from where the shots had come. Officer Amaker engaged in a hand-to-hand encounter with Emerson Granger. Granger fired twice in the scuffle, but was quickly disarmed.

That was when Officer Cunningham came up and saw Harvey Granger, a young, unmarried, white man, with his shotgun leveled at Officer Amaker.

"Drop that gun," Officer Cunningham ordered. While Granger lowered his shotgun, he fired, and Constable Amaker fell with a load of buckshot through his shoulder. He never moved again. "He must have died instantly."

As Granger tried to reload, Officer Cunningham shot him twice, once in the side and once in the arm. Other armed white men came up to the still. "We stood them all off," Officer Cunningham reported.

Emerson Granger and another unnamed man were arrested and held in the Mullins city jail, awaiting transportation to the Horry County Jail. At 1:30 PM, Harvey Granger was admitted to the Mullins hospital with gunshot wounds in the back and in the abdomen. His arm had been nearly shot off. He died at 3:00 PM. The Marion County coroner ruled over the body that he had come to his death at the hands of an officer while in the discharge of his duty. During the inquest, a Horry County magistrate placed the responsibility of State Constable Amaker's death upon the young Granger. Constable Amaker was buried on Friday in the Chestnut Hill Baptist Church Cemetery on the Saluda River in Chappells. [35]

The violence, deaths, and loss of federal tax went on. Sergeant Truesdell had been serving back in the U.S. for a year when voters were asked to decide about ending the Prohibition Amendment. In his home state, South Carolinians were overwhelmingly against its repeal; in fact, South Carolina was the only state to vote against repealing Prohibition.

The 21st Amendment was ratified and went into effect in December 1933. Americans were free again to drink intoxicating liquors, whether ardent spirits, beer, or wine. And, to pay the sales tax. Most Southern churches continued to preach against the public consumption of alcohol.

Once Don had moved his family to Kershaw County, he and Gladys, like all good Methodists, favored abstinence, even at wedding receptions held in the Saint John's Methodist Church social hall. The receptions were simple affairs with a long refreshments table for food and drinks: sandwiches with crusts cut off, cookies, and punch. The *Methodist punch* at the end of the table was just punch. In consideration of non-Methodists, or non-abstinent Methodists, at some weddings a second punch bowl at the other end of the table provided punch spiced with a little liquor. [36.]

The Christian Church has traditionally held that a child must attain the age of seven years to begin to reasonably distinguish right from wrong, to make choices requiring moral discernment. That is the point at which a child reaches *the age of reason*. The church also decides *age of consent*, the minimum age at which a person might consciously decide to participate in an act. On this point the church and state can be at odds. At the time the Truesdell children were growing up, South Carolina recognized individuals of 14 years to have reached the age of legal adulthood. By law, a 14-year-old could take an oath, enter a contract, or take a vow without the consent of a parent. Outside of a church marriage, there are few vows that entail "for the rest of my life."

The Truesdell children were each asked to make one of those decisions after they had reached the age of reason, but before reaching the legal age of consent. Dee was the first to encounter a life-long vow—the *Methodist pledge* to never drink alcohol. She was 11 or 12 years old when asked to sign the pledge. The oldest of the siblings, responsible and compliant, she stunned the adults and stood up against some peer pressure. She refused to sign the pledge, recognizing that she could not know what she was going to do later.

"Maybe I'll drink," she said. "And if I do, I do not want to feel bad because I broke this pledge." Giving their word of honor, being honest, was important to the Truesdells. They would be satisfied later that they did not "just sign the pledge and forget it."

Prayer and Bible were as much a facet of public education in South Carolina as were reading, writing, and arithmetic. Classroom prayer, classroom scripture readings, and Bible instruction were included in the curriculum of many schools. There seemed no argument against it. The Bill of Rights had been ratified in 1791. The First Amendment promised religious liberty. "Congress shall make no law respecting an establishment of religion, or prohibiting the free exercise thereof . . ."

Starting in the 1920s, social movements had triggered a legal movement to eliminate overtly Christian religious policies and practices from public schools, calling for a strict separation of religion from public schools. [37]

Then, in 1948, the Illinois Court found in McCollum v. Board of Education District 71 that public schools could not allow religious groups to use tax-supported schools to provide religious instruction to children. The separation of church and state was the heart of the debate. Into the early 1960s, the American Civil Liberties Union (ACLU) backed the campaign against any state using its public system to aid religious instruction.

The Supreme Court began making decisions between 1962 and 1963, ruling that, as schools were publicly funded institutions, the mandate to recite any prayer violated the "strict separationist" reading of the First Amendment's Establishment Clause. In other words, devotional Bible reading, the recitation of the Lord's Prayer, or a state-sanctioned, non-denominational prayer in public schools was a violation of the "no establishment clause" of the First Amendment.

After the announcement of the 1962 verdict, South Carolinians began a letter-writing campaign to U.S. Senator Olin D. Johnston (senior Democrat, 1945–1965) appealing for a Constitutional amendment to nullify the Supreme Court's decision. The senator responded in his June 29, 1962, newsletter—A Washington Letter—and in his July 26 radio show, encouraging his constituents that he would seek to pass a declaration asserting the right of prayer in the public schools of the United States of America.

His opinions did not placate Gladys Truesdell of Lugoff. She was angry about the decision to take prayer out of the schools. When she wrote to Senator Johnston, she demanded, as did many others, that the Supreme Court justices be impeached. The letter he wrote back on July 20, 1962, proved to be dissatisfying in the Truesdell home. [38]

Apart from the prayers in school, the family prayed at home for Don's father. Earl Trantham Truesdell, 80, was in the care of the South Carolina Medical College Hospital in Charleston. He died on Friday, November 16, 1962, four days after that year's Veterans Day celebrations. His funeral services were held on Sunday afternoon, and he was buried in Saint John's Methodist Cemetery beside Donald Douglas' grave.

Don called his eldest daughter into the living room to have a talk about her college education. Dee was a high school senior and would graduate with her Class of 1963. She had plans to attend the University of South Carolina in Columbia. Don told her that he would pay for USC, if she would pay him back by covering the college expenses for her four younger siblings.

Dee had been saving her life-guarding and baby-sitting earnings. She was getting scholarships and would take out loans for any uncovered expenses. She was not sure what she wanted to do with her life, but knew that she was not going to spend it paying for HIS children's education. For maybe the first time, Don heard a resounding NO from one of his children.

Despite that encounter, Don did attend Dee's high school graduation. Granny Maggie was also there, very proud of her granddaughter.

A Dinner With President Kennedy

In the spring of 1963, President John F. Kennedy's staff planned a celebration for the 100th anniversary of the Congressional Medal of Honor on May 2, to coincide with the Annual Military Reception at the White House to honor U.S. military forces. Invitations went to 293 living Medal recipients for their acts of heroism during military encounters. The four invitations dispatched to South Carolina represented four different eras in America's military history.

Army Second Lieutenant John Thomas Kennedy (retired brigadier general) earned his Medal during the Philippine Insurrection of 1909. Army First Lieutenant James Cordie Dozier Kennedy (retired lieutenant general) earned his in WWI. Don Truesdell earned his between the two Great Wars, and Army Private Thomas Eugene Atkins, living near Campobello in the northwest corner of the state under the North Carolina border, earned his award in WWII. [39]

President Kennedy and a line of dignitaries, and some of their wives, waited to greet the arrivals. United Press International notices appeared in Friday's newspaper headlines. JFK personally greeted the MOH recipients. Don Roy Truesdell also shook hands with Attorney General Robert F. Kennedy; Secretary of Defense Robert S. McNamara; Deputy Secretary of Defense Roswell L. Gilpatric; Secretary of the Navy Fred Korth; Military Aide to the President General Chester V. Clifton; Naval Aide to the President Captain Tazewell Shepard; Associate Press Secretary Andrew T. Hatcher; and the First Lady's Social Secretary Letitia Baldrige. Win Lawson and Sam Sulliman, White House Secret Service agents, proudly welcomed the recipients.

After going through the receiving line in proper alphabetical order, the 234 recipients who attended mingled for an hour or more in the late Thursday afternoon sunshine on the White House lawn in the Rose Garden in front of the Oval Office. They were served champagne, plain punch, and a buffet under the red, candy-striped tents. Old friends embraced and recounted old tales. One journalist was impressed that many of the Medal recipients were "just ordinary appearing souls like the man next door, who rose to heights of unbelievable valor in moments of incredible strain." [40]

Not so ordinary Gregory "Pappy" Boyington, the legendary Marine flying ace and POW of the WWII South Pacific theater, always gregarious, entertained others recounting his celebrity television experience in 1957, as a guest contestant on the *To Tell The Truth* panel show.

At 6:00 PM, the guests were called to the steps of the White House, "forming a semi-circle of massive human courage" on the White House lawn. One observer commented, "There are more square yards of courage here than you'll ever again see in your lifetime." Caroline Kennedy, aged 5, and John Jr., 2, watched the proceedings from the second-floor balcony.

President Kennedy saluted the recipients. "Ladies and Gentlemen," he began, "I want to express my great pleasure at welcoming our most distinguished American citizens to the White House. The Medal of Honor represents the strong feeling, admiration for your service to your country." He acknowledged that many of them had been to the White House before to receive their awards from earlier presidents. "We are delighted to have you here again, and in coming here today, you honor us."

The Medal recipients appeared pleased to be honored by the president.

"In honoring you," the president continued, "we honor all those who bear arms in the service of their country. And we are particularly glad that so many of your wives came, because we honor them also."

He described the difficult task and responsibility of sending letters to the next-of-kin of those who had lost their lives in South Viet Nam in the last year. Then, the president concluded his presentation.

"So, gentlemen," he said, "we are delighted to have you here today, and we are very proud of you and, most of all, we are proud of what you represent which is the strong courage of Americans and their determination to defend their country. While all Americans can't win the Medal of Honor, and while all of them can't fight in far-off places, I hope that all are big enough and strong enough and courageous enough to support them."

The Marine band in their scarlet tunics played the background music, while the 1,000 guests enjoyed the outstanding reception supper on the South Lawn.

When Don was meeting President Kennedy, Dr. William W. Savage was the Dean of the College of Education at the University of South Carolina in Columbia. His son was a student of journalism and history at the university, and a staff member of the school newspaper on his way to becoming an academic historian and author of books about cowboys and Indians. Heroes and cultural myths and the tributes to the MOH recipient intrigued William W. Jr., and he wanted to learn more about the events in Nicaragua more than thirty years past.

In September, William Jr., arranged an interview with Don Roy and wrote an article for Columbia's *The State*. "They Were Called 'Banana Wars'" was printed on Section C Page 1 in the Sunday, September 8, 1963, newspaper. [41]

Donald L. Truesdell

Don had many things in common with Merritt "Red Mike" Edson. Both had led patrols in Nicaraguan jungles and along rivers. Both had experienced small war tactics, understood raiding parties, and had learned much about guerilla warfare. LtCol Edson had earned a MOH on Guadalcanal in WWII. Both were involved in training Marines for amphibious warfare duties. Both had knowledge of Ho Chi Minh in 1945 and his insurgent Vietminh. Both had thoughts about the impact of sending thirty-five American military advisors and U.S. weapons to Saigon in August 1950.

When military forces are dispatched to a foreign country to deal with rebels, much of the native population will believe their land has been occupied. "Winning the hearts and minds of locals" by men in uniform and carrying weapons is likely to fail. If America was to send a force into a country, it should send enough to completely obliterate the rebels in short order, or not send any at all. Gradually escalating the numbers of deployed military in a prolonged conflict works in favor of the home-grown insurgents, and the number of nationals recruited or constricted into the rebel forces grows larger.

Don could have advised the president or warned the nation about what was ahead.

"Guerilla warfare, that's the best kind of warfare there is," he said. "You can take five or ten men and ruin things."

Guerrillas had struck the mess hall in the American Biên Hòa compound, twenty miles northeast of Saigon, on July 8, 1959. Army Major Dale Richard Buis, 37, and Master Sergeant Chester Melvin "Charles" Ovnand, 44, were the first American military men killed in combat in Viet Nam. [42] By September 1963, approximately 11,000 U.S. advisory and support personnel were stationed in Viet Nam. Telegrams had been delivered to 142 families to report a son, husband, or brother killed in action.

Two months after his interview with Mr. Savage, Don and Gladys, their five children, and the nation mourned the president's death in Dallas. President Lyndon B. Johnson was faced with decisions about the 16,500 U.S. servicemen in South Viet Nam.

U.S. Army Captain Roger Donlon, Special Forces Team A-726 commander, earned the first Medal of Honor in Viet Nam on the night of July 5, 1964, and joined the fewer than 270 living members of the CMOH Society. The president announced that he was sending 5,000 more troops to the beleaguered South.

The summer of 1965 brought a dramatic change in Don's family life when his eldest daughter enjoyed the taste of real freedom. Dee had graduated in three years from USC with her BA degree. A Baltimore County, Maryland, recruiter interviewed her, and she told him she wanted to teach in an underprivileged area. She was hired right away to teach second grade. [43]

Don's daughter was going to be 500 miles away from home, driving on streets that he could picture in his memory. He talked about living on Saratoga Street and taking his siblings up to Druid Hill Park. Whenever Dee passed that street or the park, she always thought of her daddy.

Dee began paying back her National Defense Student Loans. One day, she caught sight of a sleek Plymouth Barracuda, copper in color, and thought it was the most beautiful car she had ever seen. She needed money for a down payment and knew who to go to for a loan. She borrowed the money from her brother Stephen. On her 21st birthday, Dee became the proud owner of her first car.

For a couple of days, she drove around the area in her Barracuda, showing it off. Don noticed and finally asked how much mileage she had put on her car. Dee told him. The number came as a shock. The "where did you go . . . who did you see" interrogation began. Suddenly a new dynamic emerged.

"I don't have to explain myself to you!" Dee challenged her dad. "It's MY car. I'm paying for the gas!"

Don had to accept that one of his children had grown up and was no longer under his control.

Don and Gladys had another reminder that year that Christmas was not always a happy day. Granny called them. Lois' husband had fallen off a horse, hit his head, and was unconscious in the hospital. He died on December 25, 1965. The Truesdells drove in the funeral procession to Quaker Cemetery in Camden. They walked from Wyly Avenue into Section 15 and stood with Lois as S.C. Clyburn, 62, was laid to rest in the family lot beside his baby daughter.

Don could not miss the dramatic cultural changes that were occurring in 1965, as the United States' involvement in Viet Nam escalated.

On Tuesday morning, August 3, 1965, Delta Company, 1st Battalion, 9th Marines, was sent on a patrol to the south side of the Song Cau Do, three miles southwest of Da Nang. Their mission was to sweep Cam Ne Village and run the VC out of the area. The CBS broadcast of the village sweep portrayed American Marines and the conduct of the war in a distasteful manner, introducing the impression of "atrocity." The news segment about the nastiness of the war troubled a large portion of the TV viewers, adding to the protests over American troops fighting in Viet Nam. [44]

Newspapers printed headlines about the growing war protests, questions about the American presence in Southeast Asia, drug busts, and crime. Protestors made antiwar banners, marched, and gave the peace sign to photographers during sit-ins. A few young men burned their draft cards, the "beatniks" wrote antiwar stanzas in coffee houses, and some college students burned the flag during demonstrations. Servicemen returning from Viet Nam encountered both blame and derision for having answered the call to arms. Most of the criticism came from their own generation.

The South Carolina Federation of Women's Clubs answered. The Southern Ladies planned to honor the state's Medal recipients at a luncheon. [45]

Don Roy went to Columbia on Thursday, January 20, 1966. He was one of the five surviving holders from around the state who attended. Another traveled from Texas, and Robert S. Kennemore arrived from Oakland, California. Guest speaker Governor Robert Evander McNair addressed those at the tables.

"I am pleased to honor these men," he said, "especially when we are involved in a conflict that could explode. I know of no other group that could be honored more than recipients of the Medal of Honor."

A photographer snapped a shot of Donald at the podium, standing between the two retired generals living in Columbia. The Medal recipient never used his time in the Corps or his service in Nicaragua as a point of discussion. It was not so much that he was hesitant to bring the events up, but more that they were just things in the past. [46] What point could there be in bringing them up?

Gradually as he aged and attended more military events, Don went from never mentioning the combat in Nicaragua to talking more and more about it—not so much to Gladys or his daughters, as to Stephen and newspaper reporters. He never spoke about specific operations or patrols, about how long he was in country, or of his travels when on furlough. Occasionally, he did talk to Stephen about how they conducted operations, usually after watching news clips of troops in Viet Nam. He talked about how he treated "his soldiers," the mistreatment of prisoners by both sides, how he could speak Spanish and understand it fairly well, and about getting his hand blown off. [47]

On one occasion, outside with Stephen and his friends, Don demonstrated how to tie up someone with a couple of feet of hay twine and a pine limb. The technique was a common practice with captured rebels in Nicaragua. Sometimes, he said, some patrols left the prisoners that way for days. Don did not agree with that kind of action. He made the message clear to his son. "Don't mistreat people."

"You can't say anything bad about a Marine." [48]

On Monday evening, August 1, 1966, Don and Stephen watched the news together. Footage of Charles Whitman shooting from the University of Texas Tower 28th-floor observation deck in Austin flashed on the screen. Before police killed the sniper in his perch, ending a ninety-minute massacre, he had randomly taken the lives of ten students and civilians and a yet unborn 8-month-old baby. He had wounded thirty-four others: two died later of their wounds. [49]

When the reporter said the sniper was a former Marine, Don had only one comment about the shooting.

"I knew that boy had gotten some good training somewhere." [50]

The MOH recipients gathered for a reunion at the Los Angeles Hilton Hotel, October 13–16, 1966. Bob Hope was master of ceremonies at the Saturday night banquet. The Society was honoring Bob for all he did for the troops over the years. The comedian tried to make light of the strange times. The Beau Brummels and Daily Flash were playing folk-rock revolution music over at the Whisky A-Go-Go on the Sunset Strip, and hippies were outside the hotel with protest signs. The older recipients were getting a sense of what the Viet Nam veterans were dealing with. Some of those signs exclaimed "'YOU'RE KILLERS!"

Although a confrontation at the Hilton's front doors likely would have been an uncontested victory for the recipients and an astounding defeat for the hippies, discretion had won the day. The banquet hosts and escorts brought the veterans and their wives in through the side door.

Recognition of Don's combat experiences in Nicaragua and his knowledge of guerilla warfare went beyond William W. Savage Jr. and South Carolina. Neill Macaulay was considered an expert on Latin American guerillas. He had fought as an officer under Fidel Castro in Cuba, then, began studies as a historian. He published *The Sandino Affair* on March 3, 1967. Reviewers called his writing incisive and first-rate. So absorbing in its facts, the interesting book would have four printings over the next thirty years. Second Lieutenant Truesdale's participation in the fight in La Paz Centro and the patrol in the jungle near El Chipote are described in the book. That he had earned a Medal of Honor is mentioned in two sentences about how "accidents took their toll."

Don was aware that his old regiment, the 5th Marines, was deployed to Viet Nam and in the fight. War news was broadcast as much into the Truesdell living room as in other American homes. The North Vietnam Army's Tet offensive, one of the major battles of the long war, was given much broadcast time. The NVA and Viet Cong attacked every major city south of the DMZ on January 30, 1968, the night of their Lunar New Year.

On February 4, the Sunday night news footage showed a 2d Battalion, 5th Marine company fighting at the wall of Modern Hue's Treasury Building on the south side of the Perfume River. One Marine held his M-16 above his head, pointed over the wall, firing a whole clip of suppressing fire, while he kept himself ducked down.

Don and Stephen watched the broadcast at home. Don's critique of the Marine's actions was typical.

"If that was my soldier, I'd kick his ass and make him pay for the ammo." [51]

More than once, news of sons, grenades, and Medals circulated around South Carolina. **Private First Class Ralph Henry Johnson**, an African American, was born on January 11, 1949, in Charleston. He had attended Courtenay Elementary School and Simonton Junior High before leaving high school and enlisting in the Corps in Oakland, California. He arrived in Viet Nam in January and was assigned duties as a scout with Company A, 1st Reconnaissance Battalion, 1st Marine Division, just before the enemy's Tet Offensive.

PFC Johnson went deep into enemy territory with a team of fourteen other Marines to watch for hostile troop movements as part of the Tet counteroffensives. The team established an observation post on Hill 146, overlooking the Quan Duc Valley. Bomb craters and punji pits pockmarked the hill. PFC Johnson and two Recon Marines dug themselves a fighting hole and settled in for a tense night.

Just after midnight, in the early darkness of March 5, 1968, a platoon-size enemy unit launched an attack against the recon position, charging up the hill and assaulting the Marines with automatic weapons, satchel charges, and hand grenades. The attack continued until the Marines were out of ammunition and had to fight off the enemy force hand-to-hand.

PFC Johnson and his two companions countered the assault on Hill 146 from their fighting hole. During the ferocious engagement, an enemy hand grenade was lobbed into their midst. Seeing the grenade land, PFC Johnson, aged 19 years, shouted a warning and instantly jumped on the projectile to protect the other two from the explosion. He was killed instantly.

President Richard M. Nixon signed the Citation. Vice President Spiro T. Agnew presented the posthumous Medal of Honor to his mother, Mrs. Rebecca Johnson of Charleston, at a White House ceremony on Monday, April 20, 1970. [52] On September 5, 1991, twenty-three years after his heroic act, the VA Medical Center in Charleston would be named in Private First Class Ralph Johnson's honor. The Navy launched DDG-114 from Ingalls Shipbuilding of Pascagoula, Mississippi, on December 12, 2015. The Arleigh Burke-class guided missile destroyer was named the USS *Ralph Johnson*.

Funerals, Weddings, and Invitations

As much as anyone, Don's Aunt Leila was an example of the blood ties among the Truesdale, Lee, and Rosborough families. The proof was in Granny Margaret's photograph collection. In one 1956 photo, Margaret's older brother, T. Orren Lee Sr, veteran of the Spanish-American War, and his wife, Leila, sit in chairs on the farm. Behind them stand their three sons, Karl T. Rosborough, James Rosborough, and Thomas Orren Lee Jr., dressed in their Sunday best. Only Tom Jr. has what might be a detectable smile. At the time, Karl T., WWI veteran, was married to Beulah Mary Hammond and had two children: Leila Grace (1938) and Karl Trevelyn Jr. (1941). Granny Leila was not well.

Leila Brewer Truesdale Rosborough Lee died at home at 4:00 AM on April 2, 1957. The reverends Neil Truesdell and Douglas McArn conducted her graveside services in Saint John's Methodist Cemetery. Karl T. Sr., aged 61, died five months after his mother, when his two children were both teenagers. [53] He was buried near Leila.

Karl Jr. preferred the name Trevelyn. The extended family experienced him to be a brilliant, but strange kind of person. He had graduated very early from Camden High School with honors and went on to the University of South Carolina. Fall semester was starting when Karl T. Sr. died. Just weeks past his 16th birthday, Trevelyn was quite troubled by his father's death, but emersed himself in his chemistry books. He was on campus during the years when school labs had cyanide salts and pills on hand for agriculture and insecticide research, and newspapers frequently reported the deaths of university students by cyanide poisoning—accidental and intentional.

Trevelyn was friendly with an exceptional high school student, Michael Lee Register. His step-father, Sergeant Robert Warren Register, USMC, of Hendersonville, was connected to the university ROTC program. Early on Thursday morning, October 1, 1959, Michael, 14, was found dead on campus between the South Caroliniana Library and a brick wall facing Sumter Street. A match box containing a trace of potassium cyanide was found beside the boy's body. County Coroner Cecil Wiles ruled the death a suicide, but the police were investigating the circumstances.

Trevelyn fell into a depression over the death. Early on Saturday, he went to the library, stood where Michael was found, and attempted to end his own life by swallowing potassium cyanide. Quickly, painfully sick, he scrambled to the university infirmary on Devine Street, reported what he had done, and was administered emergency treatment. From there, he was taken to Columbia Hospital for further stomach washings and observation. USC's resident physician reported the matter to the police.

Trevelyn graduated from USC, aged 19, and went on to earn a PhD in chemistry a few years later. He studied at the University of Texas in San Antonio. While in Bexar County, he married Barbara Marie Haigell, one of Dee Truesdell's friends, on June 9, 1966. [54] The death of his young friend remained in his troubled mind.

Trevelyn was not a first cousin and did not attend the family gatherings. In one of Granny Margaret's photos, Dr. Karl Trevelyn Rosborough stands behind an old 1950s car on the farm with two cousins; to his right is Thomas Orren Lee III and to his left is Raymond Joseph Lee. The boys were so young that Trevelyn, arms down at his sides, could have rested his hands on both of their heads.

Grandma Anna Phillips, aged 70, the woman who had seemed more like Gladys' mother as she grew up in Philadelphia, died on June 4, 1968, and was buried with "Clare" in Arlington Cemetery in Drexel Hill.

Dr. Trevelyn teamed up with Professor Leo H. Sommer of the University of California at Davis and published research studies. He made his way into the pages of the esteemed *Journal of the American Chemical Society* (*JACS*), Volumes 89 and 91, in 1967 and 1969. He and Barbara had a son, Kirk James. Trevelyn's mother married Arthur Green in 1971 and moved from Lugoff to South Daytona, Florida.

In May, before Memorial Day 1969, Don received his invitation to attend the four-day, seventh biennial CMOHS Convention. [55] One of the largest group of recipients ever together at one time, 225, was expected to attend in Houston, Texas, on October 8–11.

Once assembled, the recipients talked over Society business, had bull sessions when they talked about lesser things and happier moments than their battle experiences, and enjoyed other leisure activities. An afternoon parade and Americanism program Friday night was televised locally. Army Deputy Chief of Staff Lieutenant General Richard G. Stilwell spoke to the recipients at their banquet. Outgoing Society President Thomas J. Kelly contrasted the selfless acts of the Medal recipients with the selfish acts of persons who would participate in a national day of protest against the Vietnam War on October 15. The members participated in a Texas-big "Spirit of America" parade on Sunday. [56]

✱✱✱

Four recipients would have to wait for later opportunities to attend the CMOHS reunions. On Thursday, October 9, 1969, at the White House, President Nixon presented one Army enlisted soldier and three Army officers Medals of Honor for their bravery in the Vietnam War.

The last Marine to be awarded the Medal of Honor in Viet Nam for smothering a grenade to save comrades was from a little Blue Ridge Mountain county town—like Lugoff—in the northwestern tip of South Carolina.

James Donnie "Jimmie" Howe was born in Six Mile on December 17, 1948. The one-street town, stretching out to about one square mile, was without a stoplight. The main occupation of its residents was cotton and corn farming. One of the favored childhood recreations was a swim in the Six Mile Creek. He spent his school years in Six Mile, in Cateechee Mill Village, and in Liberty. Jimmie did not appear to be much interested in academia. After his first year of junior high school, he set out to make his way in the world in June 1961. He worked for a painting contractor in Easley, five miles east of home.

Seven years after Jimmy left junior high, one month from his 20th birthday, he went down to Fort Jackson and enlisted in the Marines on October 31, 1968. Time has obscured how the heroism and legacies of fellow Blue Ridge Carolinians might have influenced Jimmie, but there were tales often told around small towns about three Marine MOH recipients from those parts.

Greenville is about a twenty-minute drive east of Six Mile on Highway 123. That is where Sergeant Robert Allen Owens, 23 years old, had been born. On his first day in combat, he had died within less than an hour of going ashore on the northwest corner of Cape Torokina on November 1, 1943. Robert Sidney Kennemore had also been born in Greenville. A WWII veteran, he earned a Medal saving his fellow machine gunners from an enemy grenade in late November 1950, during the brutal Chosin Reservoir campaign in North Korea.

Fifteen miles to the southwest of Six Mile, **Lewis George Watkins** had called Seneca his home for part of his childhood. One day, the Watkins family took a short thirty-minute drive up Route 123, relocating to Greenville. Lewis graduated from high school there. He worked within the local police department for a year. When he was 25 years old, he enlisted in the Marines in September 1950, on the same day the Marines assaulted the beaches at Inchon, Korea.

On the night of October 6, 1952, the enemy overran Outpost Frisco and established themselves in defensive positions in trenches along the crest of the hill. Staff Sergeant Watkins' platoon was tasked to counterattack and retake the hill. In the darkness of the following morning, he led his unit in the assault against grenades and rifle fire. Wounded himself in the charge up the hill, his men pinned down by intense fire, he took an automatic rifle from a wounded Marine and directed its fire against an enemy machine-gun emplacement. His supportive fire allowed the advance to continue as he directed his unit forward. He and several platoon members reached the crest and worked their way along the trench.

An enemy hand grenade landed in their midst. Staff Sergeant Watkins reacted immediately. He pushed the others out of the way, put himself between them and the grenade, picked it up from the trench bottom, and poised to throw it out of their proximity. The grenade detonated while he held it, killing him instantly.

Robert Owens had been dead for five years when Jimmie was born. When Lewis Watkins was killed in action, Jimmie was almost four years old; and, when Robert Kennemore met President Truman at the White House to receive his Medal, Jimmie had celebrated his 4th birthday the month before. Jimmie's heroism was going to link his life to these three legends and, in many ways, to Don Truesdell.

Lance Corporal Howe, a rifleman, was assigned radio operator duties with Company I, 3d Battalion, 7th Marines, in operations against insurgents in Quảng Nam Province. That was the same company in which Lewis Watkins had served in Korea. Called "Mouse" by his friends, he was proficient with radio equipment and liked to entertain the men in his platoon, bringing the sounds of country music to them while in bivouac areas.

On May 6, 1970, India Company was in defensive positions south of Marble Mountain, near the village of Viem Dong, 800 meters from the South China Sea. Lance Corporal Howe and two other riflemen were positioned behind a thicket of bamboo in a sandy beach area. The enemy launched an attack in the early morning darkness.

Under grenade attack, the three Marines moved across sand dunes to give themselves a better position to bring suppressive fire against the enemy. As the assault continued, a grenade landed among the three comrades. With no hesitation, Lance Corporal Howe yelled a warning to the others and dived on the grenade, sacrificing his own life to protect them from the explosion.

Lance Corporal James Donnie "Mouse" Howe's remains were returned home and buried in Liberty Memorial Gardens Cemetery. When he died near the bamboo thickets, he was 21 years old. Seventeen months had passed since he had left Liberty to train to be a Marine. His tour of duty in Viet Nam would have ended two months later. His battalion was withdrawn from the country in October.

✳✳✳

In some Truesdell homes it might have been challenging to say which brought more sadness, funerals or marriages. Neither Don nor Gladys could say that they had seen many resplendent or happy marriages in their families. Well into their own marital life, neither believed that marriage could result in satisfying or prosperous outcomes, and when it came to their children marrying, neither parent pretended to be enthusiastic. Don's attitude was plain.

"Don't be flattered because you found someone to marry you," he chided his girls. "Anyone can get married." [57]

The five Truesdell children took the lessons they had learned, and began to leave home, living as responsible adults. They did not give up on marriage. All five married. Don did not attend all the weddings.

Lois Lee married Otis Bradley in 1970, and discovered that "wedded bliss" was not in store for her. She gave birth to Paul Anthony Bradley on May 11, 1971. Don and Gladys were grandparents for the first time. There would only be a second grandchild for them.

Don and the Truesdell family were reminded on visits to Saint John's Methodist Cemetery in May 1972, that death often arrives unexpectedly. Trevelyn Rosborough, aged 30 years, had coauthored an article about asymmetric silicon and aberrant cotton effect behavior. One month before *JACS* published the article, Trevelyn killed himself at home on May 3, 1972. He had requested to be buried at his father's feet in the Truesdell cemetery in Lugoff. [58] He was brought home and buried in the family cemetery.

Granny Margaret Lee Truesdell lived to be 91 years old. She died on May 29, 1972, after a short illness and was buried in Saint John's Methodist Cemetery next to her husband and grandson, Douglas.

In 1971, Stephen Truesdell followed the examples his father and uncle had set and joined the active Armed Forces, beginning a four-year commitment in the Army. That same year, the CMOHS held its national convention in Birmingham, Alabama, October 23–26.

"Wear whatever you like."

In late 1959, John F. Kennedy's presidential inauguration committee had sent an invitation to Don to attend the ceremony. Lyndon B. Johnson's committee had sent one in 1964, and Richard M. Nixon's did the same in 1968 after his first election. Don chose not to attend.

After the 1954 classroom discussion about her father's Medal, Dee gradually grew more interested in her father's military experiences. As an adult, she wondered what in his history had made him the person with whom she had grown up. Granny Margaret, Don's mother, gave her the scrapbook of newspaper articles about her daddy. Dee arranged all the articles into a nice collection. Don seemed genuinely touched when she showed it to him. [59]

Dee was home from her graduate studies for Christmas 1972 in Lugoff. Her father had received an invitation from the Inaugural Committee and Congress to attend President Richard Nixon's second inauguration to be held on Saturday, January 20, 1973. The president-elect was a "damned Republican." The invitation, on heavy ivory-tinted stock, was left opened, and Dee and her mother read about all the events that the weekend covered. Dee saw an opportunity: it was FREE for the MOH recipient and included a GUEST. She had a suggestion for her daddy. [60]

"I've never asked you for much, but I really would like for you to go to this and take me as your guest."

Don first tried not to answer, then, knowing his confident daughter could be persistent, gave a familiar answer. "I'll think about it and let you know."

Gladys stepped in. "She needs to know now so she can get her clothes ready."

Don gave in to the two women. "Okay. But I am not buying new clothes. I am going to come in the clothes I have."

Don had a Sunday suit, a dress shirt and tie, and one pair of low cut shoes that he wore to church year-round. He noticed that one event was a black-tie dinner, so he asked Dee to buy him a black tie. Happy to just be going along, she did.

Before Dee returned to Baltimore, Don mailed in an acceptance RSVP to attend the forty-second inaugural ceremonies. She was in for a surprisingly good, and memorable, time with her father.

The CMOHS had arranged for lodging in a downtown D.C. hotel for the recipients attending the inaugural weekend. About 170 members and their guests attended. Don flew first class to the Capital City on Wednesday. Dee drove down from Baltimore and met him at his hotel in the morning. Handed a 33-page booklet with instructions on what to wear to receptions and balls and the many weekend events, they would be treated royally at various affairs—a string of breakfasts, brunches, luncheons, dinners, cocktail parties, and receptions. [61]

Anti-Vietnam War protesters were in the area, and someone had made threats to the Medal recipients. All travel from the hotel to the events was on nice buses. Veterans of Foreign Wars representatives attended the buses and police escorted. District police were out in force.

That first night they had drinks and a buffet at an American Legion in downtown D.C. with recipients from all the wars as far back as WWI. Dee, 28 years old, young, pretty and dressed for the gala occasion, had expected to "blend in to the background" and was caught off guard by the interest the recipients—the younger ones from Vietnam and the older men—had in talking to her.

That was pleasant, of course, but many things about that night left their mark on her memory. Having grown up with a one-armed father, the number of men she met who were physically whole surprised her. Of course, there were men attending who had visible wounds. Webster Anderson was a one-armed African American man in a wheel chair from South Carolina. He had lost both his legs and an arm fighting in Viet Nam. She also saw a Native American veteran with most of his face gone.

Seeing them made her wonder why they would have fought so hard for a country that had not treated them well—before or after their valorous service. She did ask someone else in the military why such men would fight at a level to earn a Medal. The man's response could have come from any one of the men at the buffet.

"We weren't defending our country. We fought for our buddies."

For those who have never been in combat and for family members of the veterans, his answer is difficult to grasp.

There are not words in any language to adequately describe the reality of combat. Those who were there do not need words; they know. James Webb was a Marine platoon commander in Viet Nam in 1968–1969. He came home with a Navy Cross, a Silver Star, two Bronze Stars, and two Purple Hearts. The former Secretary of the Navy and Virginia Senator understands a veteran's life after coming home.

"I and my fellow combat veterans stand on one side of a great impassable divide, with the rest of the world on the other." He explained that further during an interview. "There's a great Marine Corps saying. 'If you were there, I don't need to explain it to you, and if you weren't there, I can't explain it to you.' That's the divide." [62]

Dee felt the privilege of "moving among them." The greatest impression left with her was the camaraderie among a group of men who had come from all backgrounds and all socio-economic groups. She saw an acceptance that spoke of having shared an experience of violence and horror that was faced honorably. The Medal recipients were a select group of men deserving great respect, as well as the best health care, and adequate financial compensation to support their families. They were all very, very impressive men.

After the festivities, Dee drove home to Baltimore, looking forward to returning the next day.

Thursday was the official start of the inaugural festivities. The recipients had a luncheon with the Joint Chief of Staffs. A crack military drill unit performed colors at the luncheon, hosted by the VFW. A high-ranking female general was assigned to the table with Don and Dee. There was a tour of the Senate floor and offices and a banquet. In the evening, there was a reception for Vice President and Mrs. Spiro T. Agnew held at the Smithsonian Museum of History and Technology, where they met General Jimmy and Mrs. Josephine Doolittle. After that, the recipients were shuttled to the new John F. Kennedy Center for the Performing Arts Building for a salute to the states.

On Friday night, after a long day, Don walked Dee to the elevator to head back to Baltimore. The elevator doors opened and off stepped Bob Hope. He was in D.C. to emcee the Saturday banquet. There they were, just the three of them; unmistakably, it was Bob Hope.

"Well hey!" exclaimed Dee in a very familiar way.

Don froze in his tracks and pointed. "You are Bob Hope!" is all he could say.

Mr. Hope looked startled and scurried along by the wall, passing the Truesdells without speaking. Dee decided in favor of the celebrity. "I guess it had been a long day for Mr. Hope."

A breakfast was provided at a VFW near the Capitol Building on Saturday. Dee had borrowed an overcoat for her dad. They had good seats outside with the other recipients. Next on the itinerary was the parade. The weather was cold. Don decided to skip the parade and went back to the hotel. Dee had made enough friends in the group that she had fun sitting with them for the parade. Don caught up with the group later to sit about 300 feet from the president at noon as he took the Oath of Office in front of the Capitol.

The black tie inaugural ball was the crowning moment of the weekend. Don wore his church suit and the black bow tie Dee had bought him. Around his neck was the blue ribbon holding his Medal just below his throat. He did not seem to notice that everyone else was in either dress uniform or tuxedo, and he showed no sign of self-consciousness.

One of the other recipients commented to Dee: "Your father is not dressed for a black-tie dinner."

Dee, in her very polite manner, answered in her father's defense. "When you are wearing the Congressional Medal of Honor, you can wear whatever you like."

The Marine Corps band played as the quests entered the hall. There were no table assignments, so everyone chose their own seats. Don sat across from his daughter. Harrison "Jack" Schimtt, a NASA Apollo program astronaut, took a place on one side of Dee.

Before the table filled up, a young man dressed in a tux with a blue ribbon around his neck came over and sat down on Dee's other side, with empty chairs on either side of him.

She very politely said to him, "Either move to the left to sit beside someone or move to the right."

John Phillip Baca moved over and sat beside Dee. He was a U.S. Army veteran from San Diego and had celebrated his 24th birthday ten days earlier. Two years before that, a fragmentation grenade had landed near him when he and his team were on a night ambush mission in Viet Nam. He had grabbed the steel helmet from his head, dropped it over the grenade, and thrown himself on top of the helmet as the grenade exploded. A year of surgeries had put him back together. His experience brought to mind for Dee other soldiers who had been blown to bits and died jumping on grenades to save companions.

There would be others in the future. More than thirty years after her conversations with John Baca, Corporal Jason Lee Dunham, 22, served with Kilo Company, 3rd Battalion, 7th Marines, in Iraq near the Syrian border. On April 14, 2004, he covered an insurgent's grenade with his Kevlar helmet and body, saving the lives of two of his men. Corporal Dunham died of his wounds at Bethesda National Naval Medical Center, Maryland, a week later.

The inaugural dinner was fancier than any the Truesdells would ever sit down to again. Each table place was set with three wine glasses and silverware right, left, and above the plate. That was new for them. They were served chilled white wine with the appetizer, room temperature, red with the entree, and champagne with the flaming dessert. Dee was convinced that she had found the secret to world peace.

"Just give everyone three wines at dinner, and they'd be too happy to fight."

The inaugural weekend turned out to be a fabulous experience for both Don and Dee. Three years later there would be another trip and another opportunity for them to bond and enjoy each other's company. Dee could not say the same thing about a wedding two months after the inauguration.

On March 17, 1973, Don walked Gayle down the aisle at the new St. John's United Methodist Church on Roseborough Road. [63] Lee "Butch" Lilly, the groom, was waiting at the altar to make his lifelong promise to his bride as determined by the Methodist Church's *Book of Discipline*. "Butch" was a veteran and an active American Legion Post 17 member. He admired his soon-to-be father-in-law.

The minister greeted the couple, family, and friends; reminding all that the sacred rite of marriage was a joyous occasion. He led the congregation through the Scripture readings, sermon, prayers, and songs. Gayle and Butch said their vows, acknowledging that they were entering their union through the grace of Jesus Christ.

Gladys was obviously piqued about her daughter's marriage and was uncomfortable when the minister asked the gathering to bless and offer support to the bride and groom. Dee sobbed all through the solemn ceremony.

Gladys did find some comfort in the fact that her two married daughters lived within an easy drive or walk to the home in Lugoff.

Jeff Truesdell, the youngest of the five siblings, married Kay and told the family about it later. He lived within a two-hour drive of Lugoff. When he married a second time, he and Betsy had a small wedding. Gladys was there on her son's behalf, but his dad did not attend.

Stephen finished his active duty commitment in 1975 and lived in Roseburg, Oregon. He went home on a visit and told Don that he had joined the Oregon National Guard as a company commander. That disclosure began a conversation. [64]

"I was in the National Guard once," his father said.

That was a new piece of information, the first Stephen had heard of such. "Which state?" he asked.

"Nicaragua."

"What was your position and rank?"

"Second lieutenant and patrol leader." End of conversation.

Stephen stayed in the Oregon National Guard. When he married Ginger on the west coast, he waited until later to tell his family. He trained as a civilian pilot. Among his memorable flights were those into Kona Airport, above Kailua, on the west side of Hawaii's Big Island. The runway was not yet paved—"Nothing but lava and no beach." He could not imagine the sleepy fishing village to be a sound investment for a resort. Flying also gave him something in common with his next-door neighbor.

Major General Marion Eugene Carl (retired) was a Marine Corps ACE aviator who had shot down enemy planes during the WWII battles over Midway and Guadalcanal. [65] Marion had spent his career on the aviation side of the Corps and told Stephen that he did not know his father. Marion was a close friend of Brigadier General Joseph Jacob Foss (ret), who was the leading WWII Marine ACE and a MOH recipient for his air combat over Guadalcanal. Stephen had the opportunity to meet Joe several times at dinners the Carls hosted. Marion was quiet and reserved at the meals, while Joe easily retold very entertaining stories. Joe once said he had seen Don at a MOH function, but Stephen thought that maybe Joe was just being polite.

General Carl remained heroic to his last breath. At 10:35 PM on Sunday, June 28, 1998, a 19-year-old man with an arrest record for drunken driving, burglary, and criminal trespass broke into the Carl's home carrying a sawed-off shotgun. Mrs. Edna Carl was reading a newspaper. The robber, aiming the shotgun at her head, demanded cash and car keys. Marion emerged from the bedroom and lunged at the gunman.

A glancing shotgun burst hit Edna in the head. The home invader then shot Marion, took $200 to $400 from their wallets, and drove off in the couple's car. Marion was pronounced dead at Mercy Medical Center in Roseburg. His wife was treated at the hospital and released. [66] Authorities arrested the robber, he went to trial, was found guilty of aggravated murder, and is serving a life sentence in prison without the possibility of parole. The airfield at Marine Corps Air Station Kaneohe Bay, Hawaii, and the Roseburg Airport were named in General Carl's honor.

Steven will always remember his friendship with, and admiration of, the WWII ACE. He continued in the Guard after that horrible night. Between 2003 and 2006, he coordinated all the site support resources and training areas for units being deployed to Afghanistan and Iraq. Stephen "spent a lot of time in a hole at the Pinyon Canyon Training Site in Colorado." He retired as Director of the Office of Emergency Management at the rank of colonel in 2006. He continues to teach a class on terrorism at Umpqua Community College in Roseburg.

A Reunion in New Orleans

The CMOHS planned to hold its national convention in New Orleans, September 25–28, 1975. Don thought he would attend, having once been in the New Orleans recruiting office.

Dee was on sabbatical from teaching to finish her PhD and had the time to travel to South Carolina. [67] A neighbor at her apartment development had told her about a multi-course breakfast dining at the Court of the Two Sisters, and it was one stop she intended to make while in the "Big Easy." She drove from Baltimore to Lugoff and flew to New Orleans with her daddy for another four days of festivities. By the time she returned home, she would have a deeper understanding of her father.

Dee told Don that she planned to go to the Court of Two Sisters. He did not say NO outright to the idea; rather, he made sure that each morning they were out and about, walking all over to see all the old places. Typical reluctance. As he showed his daughter the various places he remembered, he made no mention of his marriage to "Margret." That was also typical of Don, not talking about the fighting in Nicaragua or in New Orleans.

Dee was fine with the sightseeing, except that by the time they were hungry and ready to eat, they had gone in a different direction from the Two Sisters. Breakfast ended up being in some drugstore or little café—one course of toast and coffee.

Dee listened to an informal discussion about a Vietnam Medal recipient. Army Sergeant First Class Louis Richard Rocco had been on his second tour in South Viet Nam when he volunteered on May 24, 1970, to go on a helicopter medical evacuation mission. The helicopter was hit by enemy fire and crashed. Seriously injured and under fire, Sergeant Rocco saved three fellow soldiers from burning to death in the helicopter. The Award recommendation stalled. Lieutenant Lee Caubarreaux, the medically retired co-pilot Sergeant Rocco had saved, appealed and lobbied on the hero's behalf. Senator Russell Long of Louisiana got involved. President Gerald Ford formally presented Warrant Officer Rocco the Medal of Honor on December 12, 1974. [68]

Richard was a Barelas-neighborhood native of Albuquerque, New Mexico. He had been a barrio gang member after his family moved to the San Fernando Valley in 1948. When he was 16 years old, he was arrested and jailed for armed robbery. During a break in his sentencing hearing in 1954, he walked to a Los Angeles Army recruiting office and enlisted. The judge passed down a suspended sentence, and Private Rocco began his basic training in 1955. [69]

The discussion in New Orleans was about whether an active duty military man with a history of armed robbery should be wearing the Medal of Honor. Some recipients had the opinion that Warrant Officer Rocco should be stripped of his Medal. That was just an opinion and never happened. Most recipients understand that flaws of character do not diminish acts of valor and a willingness to put one's own life on the line to preserve the lives of others. Warrant Officer Rocco finished a distinguished Army career and went on to be of service to Vietnam veterans and to school youths at risk of drug use.

Dee was forming her opinions about bravery and heroism that most in the CMOHS would share and support. Combat is a most awful experience with lifelong effects. Young people from all kinds of backgrounds who go off to war have it within themselves to demonstrate extraordinary courage and selflessness when a situation calls for it. The Medal recipients represent them all, and while it is important to honor heroic acts, superior lifetime behavior should not be expected of the surviving recipients. The lives of those returning from combat have been changed, whether or not their heroism rose to the level of MOH valor.

The main event of the convention was Saturday night's National Patriots Award Presentation and Banquet. Begun in 1968, the National Patriots Award is the highest award the CMOHS bestows on a distinguished American who exemplifies the ideals that make the United States strong. Individuals are chosen for the award based on their dedication to freedom, their love for fellow man, and their loyalty to the nation's flag and a readiness to take on responsibility for its continued waving. The award was presented at the banquet to former House Armed Forces Committee Chairman, the Honorable Representative F. Edward Herbert, D-Louisiana.

During the banquet, there was a discussion about whether recipients should ever be allowed to return to the battle scenes where they had earned their Medals.

Down to the last morning in New Orleans, Dee finally told her father she was going to the French Quarter restaurant on Royal Street, and would be quite comfortable walking there alone. Not wanting her going down Bourbon Street unaccompanied, he relented and went along.

"But," he insisted, "all I'm having is toast and coffee."

The weather was lovely as they were seated in the beautiful, old courtyard under huge, old trees. Musicians strolled past and a fountain tinkled nearby. According to the menu, breakfast was five, maybe seven, courses. The first course was fruit, then fish, then soup, then an entree of meat kabob with eggs, and then bananas foster for dessert. Despite the seemingly steep cost, Dee ordered the full breakfast with champagne. It was Don's turn to order.

"I want the same thing," he told the waitress.

For two-and-a-half hours, father and daughter sat eating and drinking, talking nicely and acting "like regular human beings." Dee had never been alone with her dad for that length of time. Whatever it was they talked about, their conversation was relaxed and normal. When the check came, things returned to the familiar for Dee. Her father insisted that they split it. "Some stripes you just cannot change."

Having breakfast at the Court of the Two Sisters meant something to Don. He asked to buy a menu to take with him. Back home, he kept the memento in his pickup. When he drove around in Lugoff and Camden, he showed it to people, bragging about his good meal in New Orleans.

Dee came to understand something about her father. Her daddy was frightened of new experiences. The unfamiliar seemed to intimidate him. He knew toast and coffee. That was what he went for when ordering breakfast in a restaurant. He would never have ordered a multi-course meal, if she had not insisted on going to the fancy restaurant and ordering it first. She had witnessed the same at President Nixon's 1973 inauguration. It was easier for him to skip the inaugural fun than to go into unfamiliar territory. She attributed his discomfort to his lack of education and limited social experience.

Official invitations continued to arrive in Lugoff after the New Orleans trip. In 1975, South Carolina was busy conducting statewide *Spirit of '76* fundraising events to commemorate the American Revolution Bicentennial the next year. Don was invited to attend a small, dinner in Columbia. Gladys was not going to accompany him, so he invited his three daughters. Don dressed in his Sunday suit. Dee, Gay, and Lois dressed up in their finest evening attire.

Participants and administrators from all over the state attended on Monday night, October 20, 1975. General William C. Westmoreland introduced the featured speaker.

The memorable highlight for the three attractive young women was not the evening out with Daddy. They enjoyed more the attention the men at the function paid them. The men must have been as glad as Don's daughters were that the girls had not taken the Methodist pledge to be teetotalers. The waiters seemed especially available at their table, ready to pour wine in Lois' glass, obviously appreciating her revealing, low cut dress. Many people around them had fun with the girls, and there was much laughter at the table. Don might have disapproved, but at his public best, he did nothing to disrupt the night's gaiety.

Jimmy Carter sent an invitation to Lugoff in 1976. After Dee had pressured him to go to the 1972 D.C. festivities, Don was more comfortable with the idea. He had survived the unfamiliar waters. He accepted President Carter's invitation and attended both of Ronald Reagan's inauguration ceremonies in 1981 and 1985.

Empty Nest

Once Dee had relocated to Baltimore, she never lived in South Carolina again. She taught, made friends, continued her graduate studies, and created a life for herself. She was living and teaching in Baltimore County when she met Fred Schindler, a U.S. Navy and Vietnam War veteran. He had served two years, providing dental care for sailors and Marines in the Caribbean on USS *Boxer* (LPH-4), a helicopter carrier. He and one of his buddies from dental school could banter humorously about their military experiences, as his friend had spent the same two years working in a tent in Viet Nam.

Fred had a house and his orthodontic practice in LaVale, Maryland, outside of his Cumberland hometown. That was 150 miles west of Dee's two-bedroom apartment. During the summer of 1982, they began to plan their future together. They spent her weekend visits clearing out his furnished, four-level house, making room for her and the belongings she wanted to bring with her, and making renovations so the house would feel as much hers as his.

Gladys' attitude toward marriage persisted, and she had some misperceptions about life in Maryland. "I can't understand why Dee would marry Fred," she said to Gayle, "and spend her life peeling peaches." Gay told her mother that she did not think that her sister's life with Fred would have anything to do with peeling peaches.

Although Gladys had wanted Dee away from South Carolina, she had held on to hopes for her daughter other than a wedding. Through the 1950s and 1960s, the Yankee from Philadelphia had taken a liking to a "Deep South congressman" by the name of Albert William Watson. Congressman Watson was a strict Baptist, a mentoree of U.S. Senator Strom Thurmond, an open segregationist, and an outspoken opponent of President Lyndon B. Johnson's Civil Rights Act. In physical appearance, he had a slight resemblance to Don, except that the politician smiled more than the former Marine.

Gladys imagined that Dee would one day be governor of Maryland. Then she could leave Don and Lugoff, move to Baltimore to live with Governor Dee, and commute to Washington every day to work for Congressman Watson. Of course, she had to change her imaginings when Albert Watson was defeated in his 1970 bid for South Carolina governor.

None-the-less, Gladys could bring her smile to Baltimore on New Year's Day, 1983.

Stephen flew into South Carolina to pick up his mother for the drive up to Baltimore. [70] One of his legs began to swell with blood pooling during the long flights on the airliners, but he said nothing. He rented a moving van and got busy organizing the logistics of moving furniture. Gay, Lois, and 12-year-old Paul left Lugoff on December 30. Dee gave them lodging in her apartment. The next day, the family joined Fred and Dee for a pleasant dinner at the Hyatt Regency on Light Street, overlooking Baltimore's Inner Harbor off the Patapsco River. Smiles all around.

Stephen and Gladys climbed into the van on Saturday morning, January 1, picked up I-95-North, and enjoyed an eight-hour drive together. They stayed with the others in Dee's apartment. Jeff and Kay also drove up on Saturday, but they decided to stay in a hotel. Dee treated everyone to a big dinner at the apartment before she and Fred left for the Hyatt.

The family had become so accustomed to Don not participating in gala ceremonies and family celebrations that no one mentioned his absence at the wedding on Sunday. Dee kept her name, and, after the nuptials, the Truesdells gathered around the bride and groom for a photograph. Everyone was smiling, including Gladys. Someone unfamiliar with the family dynamics might reasonably have asked, "Where's Don?"

Despite the pain and swelling in his leg, Stephen "soldiered on" without a word to anyone that his leg was bothering him. It was one of the early lessons he had learned from his father. Back at Dee's apartment, he led his siblings in loading her spare furniture into the moving van—packing up anything Dee was not moving to LaVale. They finished up on Monday and drove back south.

Stephen flew back to Oregon after helping in Lugoff for a couple of days. The flight home made his leg worse, and he went to a doctor. The family history of circulation problems had reemerged in the seventh generation. The massive clotting so alarmed the doctor, he immediately took Stephen to the hospital himself and had him hooked up to an IV. He was released after ten days of care and monitoring. The family did not learn of his hospitalization until he was back at home and work.

Don and Gladys were going to be grandparents for a second time.

Dee moved into the mountains of western Maryland. William Blane Schindler was born on August 9, 1983. For a time, Dee was a stay-at-home mother. She made up for all the winter fun she had missed out on when she was at her grandmother's in Upper Darby. She took the neighborhood boys sledding on the enormous hill close to their house on National Highway. Even keeping the stairs and cars clean of snow was an enjoyment. Once Billy was in elementary school, she started teaching again and ended up elected to the Board of Education. Fred was avid about Baltimore sports, and young Bill grew up to be a sports broadcaster.

Getting Old

Gladys might have thought her job as Mama and caretaker was done, until she and Don took over rearing their first grandson while Lois went to school to become a registered nurse. Following her training, Lois first worked as a licensed practical nurse, then became a nurse, then a horse farrier, then a midwife, and then a nurse practitioner.

Paul listened to a lot of yelling between Don and Gladys, but his Granddaddy was more involved with him than he had ever been with any of his children, who were amazed that their dad took Paul to the movies! Not surprisingly, Don bought his grandson only popcorn OR a drink—never both. Paul, well-adjusted in life, moved to Austin, to attend the University of Texas, and married Sally Kodros. According to Dee, "they are a well-suited and happy couple."

Autumn 1985 arrived. Don, 79 years old, was among 249 living Medal recipients, down from the more than 300 at the end of the Vietnam War. [71] Organizers had been busy planning the five-day CMOHS National Convention for September 4–8, to be held at the Myrtle Beach Convention Center. In addition to America's bravest men, several dignitaries and high-ranking U.S. officials had been invited. Vice President George Bush hoped to attend the banquet. [72]

They began gathering for their convention on Tuesday: 160 recipients, some going back to WWI. Photographs of smiling men appeared in newspaper articles, joking with each other, making light of getting old. There was little talk among the recipients about the feats that had earned them the nation's top recognition for battlefield bravery and the privilege of attending the convention. They all shared one thing in common—the five-pointed star held by a blue sash around their necks.

They also shared beliefs about going to war. One of the Vietnam recipients said. "If we never got any more members, it would be the greatest thing in the world." Another said, "I think I would smile in my grave if there never were any more members."

Recognizing that the Medal is "easier to win than to wear," a Vietnam recipient explained, "people tend to expect you to be something special. You're just yourself trying to face life daily like anyone else. I'm proud and honored my country bestowed the Medal. But, people view some of the Medal of Honor recipients as supermen, and we're not."

A friend of Don Roy's from Columbia, South Carolina, Army Colonel Charles Patrick Murray, aged 64, WWII recipient who retired after thirty years of military service, expressed his view. "Without exception, every person here would say they did the job they saw that had to be done. You set a person on a pedestal and some people can take that, but the average American can't. You just don't like to talk about yourself. When you start talking about old conflicts and the battles you've been in it brings back old memories that really hurt." Both of his sons had served in Viet Nam.

At the Saturday night banquet, the Honorable Judge Robert F. Chapman, Fourth Circuit Court of Appeals, South Carolina, was the 1985 recipient of the National Patriots Award.

Lieutenant Burton Barr, World War II veteran, Republican, and Arizona House of Representatives majority leader, was master of ceremonies and emcee of the banquet. Secretary of the Army John Marsh presented the keynote address. The Naval Air Training Command Flag Pageant was also featured at the banquet. Performed by officer candidates from the Naval

Aviation Schools Command, Naval Air Station, Pensacola, Florida, the pageant depicted the evolution of the U.S. flag.

The Myrtle Beach convention was the last one Don attended on both legs. The toes on his left foot turned painful and black in 1986. Doctors informed him that he had a serious underlying vascular problem. The toes would fall off, or he could have them amputated.

Gayle and Lois sat in the waiting room during the surgery. One of the surgeons came out to tell them there was a complication. Scar tissue had formed around all the grenade shrapnel left in Don's left leg fifty-four years earlier. The circulation was blocked in his left leg. They would have to amputate the leg below the knee. [73]

A tough and determined Truesdell, having long adjusted to using a prosthesis for the arm he had lost in battle, Don learned to walk on a prosthetic leg—first with a cane, and then free standing, months after the surgeries.

Nicaragua Again in the News

By 1987, Don and two veterans from WWI had worn the Medal of Honor the longest among the living recipients. The two WWI veterans were into their mid-90s. As Veterans Day neared, Don traveled to Irvine, California, for a meeting of the CMOHS. About 150 of the 231 living recipients attended. Only one of the WWI recipients was healthy enough to be there.

Charles Murray was then the president of the Society and led the meeting. He spoke about the meaning of the decoration, and what living with the Medal was like. "The Medal of Honor shows our history in terms of conflicts," he said. "Awards like Truesdell's tie into the growth of the United States (as a world power). When [Donald] accepted the Medal . . . the nation's highest award for heroism not only had memorialized an act of great bravery and selflessness, it also documents one of U.S. history's more obscure moments."

One journalist made a headline out of the very thing Don Roy found uncomfortable. "The Decoration Puts Spotlight on Honorees."

Starting on the Front Page of the Sunday, November 8 issue, the *Santa Ana Orange County Register* presented a long, multi-page article about the lives of the recipients after the award of the Medal and a biographical paragraph for each surviving recipient. The caption under his photograph provided a detail: "Donald L. Truesdell displays his Medal of Honor, awarded for action in Nicaragua in 1932." [74]

Going to California meant that Don was not going to spend his Veterans Day in Mobile, Alabama.

Captain Wade Hampton Trepagnier Jr., decorated Marine, was Adjutant at the summer 1951 Officer Candidates Course and Platoon Leaders Course at Parris Island. He had the privilege of personally knowing some of the notable Banana Wars veterans. Others who had already passed on, he certainly knew by fame and reputation, including: Smedley Butler (MOH), Evans Fordyce Carlson, Louis Cukela (MOH), Alfred Austell Cunningham, Daniel Daly (MOH), Merritt A. Edson (MOH), Logan Feland, Roy Stanley Geiger, Joseph Anthony Glowin (MOH), Frank Bryon Goettge, Henry Louis Larsen (MOH), John Archer Lejeune, Homer Laurence Litzenberg, Harry Bluett Liversedge, William Kirk MacNulty (Navy Cross), Joseph Henry Pendleton, John Henry Quick (MOH), William Henry Rupertus, Holland McTyeire "Howlin' Mad" Smith, and William Peterkin Upshur (MOH).

When Captain Trepagnier retired, he moved to Mandeville in St. Tammany Parish, Louisiana, on the North Shore of Lake Pontchartrain. He became the contact person for the Banana Fleet Marines Association. Barney Daehler, in San Lorenzo, California, was scribe for *The Fleet Banana* newsletter published four times a year. Wade and Barney were determined to get the newsletter to all surviving Banana Fleet Marines. Donald L. Truesdale (MOH) was on their mailing roster along with James Patrick Devereux, Herman Henry Hanneken (MOH), Lewis Burwell "Chesty" Puller, Christian Frank Schilt (MOH), Oliver Prince Smith, and Alexander Archer Vandegrift (MOH).

Notices went out in the newsletter that the 10th annual reunion for Veterans of Central American Operations Association (prior to WWII) was to be held in Mobile. [75]

If Don tried to keep Nicaraguan revolutions and battles from intruding into his thoughts, news events again made the effort impossible. The 38-year dictatorship of the Somoza family ended in bloodshed in 1978–1979. The Cuban-backed, socialist Sandinista National Liberation Front (FSLN) seized the oppressive government in 1979. Honduran-based Contra militants, with U.S. government assistance, began a guerrilla war to take the power from the revolutionaries. For more than six years, direct and secret funding and military aid went to the insurgent Contras during President Reagan's two terms in office. In November 1986, U.S. involvement erupted into a scandal and investigation that went into history annals as the *Iran-Contra Affair*.

Late in December 1987, the family was together in Lugoff for the holiday season, and Nicaragua was in the night's news. When the broadcast was over, Don expressed his opinion about the guerrilla war against the Sandinistas. [76]

"I feel sorry for the people," he said. "All they ever wanted was a government that wouldn't steal all their stuff." Then, he had a moment's reflection. "I still remember my way around, and probably wouldn't come back, but I would go if they needed me."

All the Truesdells were patriots with a deep love for their country. None of them listening to the news about the Contras would hesitate to step up to defend the United States. Dee had come to the realization after years of thinking about the Second Nicaraguan Campaign that the Banana Wars were not about defending the U.S. against an enemy threat, despite the war propaganda system. Dee believes very strongly in the bravery her daddy had exhibited on the Nicaraguan trail. But, she would argue that his heroic act was not in defense of the United States. Her father had been sent to Nicaragua and loyally given his right hand to protect American companies growing bananas.

"Which side would you fight with this time?" she asked him.

In His Own Words

During that December visit, Dee and Fred Schindler's fifth wedding anniversary was approaching. Fred had been in the family long enough to feel comfortable around his father-in-law. While family visited nearby, he and Don, 80 years old, "talked military" for a while. Don, dressed in a red, short-sleeved polo shirt sat in a wheel chair. Fred talked about serving on the USS *Boxer* during the Vietnam War. Don recalled having spent some time on a ship like the helicopter carrier.

As Don talked a little about Nicaragua, Fred had an idea. In the mid-1980s, colleges and communities had begun recording the memories of veterans from WWII, Korea, and Vietnam for posterity sake. Fred had questions about the Banana Wars and his father-in-law's experiences in Nicaragua and wanted to record his conversation with Don on videotape. [77]

Scratching the stump of his right arm with his left hand, Don asked Fred for some clarification about what he wanted him to talk about. His eyes closed; he listened.

Fred: "Well, you know, just when you were down there, how life was down in Nicaragua at that time."

For the next nineteen minutes, Don recalled his years in Nicaragua. He spoke in his South Carolinian rhythms, running words and sentences together, getting his thoughts out quickly. One thought sometimes intruded or interrupted another thought. At points, he closed his eyes, seeming to envision the scenes he recalled. Some memories appeared to spark a nerve, as he scratched the stump of his right arm with his left hand at points in the conversation. And, once he started talking, Fred just listened. He asked Don only two more questions sixteen minutes into the taped conversation.

Don described the roads and trails, the Nicaraguan people and their food, and the climate. He talked about the detachment's mission, leadership, and training methods. He expressed his opinion of the American people. He mentioned Ol' Smedley Butler in there with them the first time the Marines went down in 1912. At five different points, taking up three-and-a-half minutes of his recollections, he described going on patrols. For three uninterrupted minutes, he detailed the Battle of Achuapa. Nicaraguan politics, the elections, and Sandino took up almost another four minutes. When Fred asked about his Medal, Don described the incident with the grenade in fifty-one seconds, then, talked more about the Nicaraguan troops he had led.

Don: "Well, it wasn't no pea rally. We go through these old places and just moved out of the main drag, it wasn't nothin' (leaning forward, looking to his left as if envisioning what he was describing) but, ah, in the Northern Area alone, you know?" (sat back, gesturing with both arms)

Fred: "Hm, hmm."

Don: "—and, and like sand—uh, Charles Butters had a gold mine down there, and I just heard on television a while ago where they're raisin' sand now around San Albino—on this Jicaro road, they dammed it. They put up poles this-a-way and, you know, (gesturing with both arms) brace 'em, and cut a tunnel down there. And they got everything but water, that was da power, that, to run that gold mine, you know, and run some great big generators, that they—But, it's a miracle how they got 'em in there. But, when they got 'em there, you couldn't, there wasn't no more roads back there. There was a trail, a man trail, there was trails running off to houses and the little villages all around there, and that's where the people were. See?" (scratching his stump)

Fred: "Hm, hmm."

Don: "Just Indians, you know, having a sugar cane patch, a little bit of a banana patch, and ah, little, some coffee, and a little bit of stuff they're madin' up, see, but they're pretty smart, you know. And now—they could move, there's no gettin' around that. When they're—went down the mountain, they went down there pretty fast. But, then they trottin' a bit on the level, gettin' up like that (gesturing and envisioning). Gettin' away at six miles an hour . . . But you couldn't do that. And, you can't take American people in some places like that, and let 'em do a thing. You understand? They're not adapted to it."

Fred: "Yeah."

Don: "See? And, they, just like I told you about, ah, it would get hot, and they would drink water out of a daggoned hoof print. There wasn't no water in the dry season. It was just in the streams, and they had to live somewhere near there to get their water. See? And that was dryin' their land out. But now, it was pretty warm—the rainy season? That water, you see, that ol' river was boilin' (gestures as if showing water overflowing banks) they'd drown you down there . . . in the place (closed his eyes and put his finger tips to his lips).

"And then we, ah—The only ones I got—I never did, ah. It was in Quilalí, there. It was forty miles to Apalí, (gesturing to his right) where we would, ah, go to get provisions. But Jicaro was off to one side, which was about twenty-five miles. And some of those people would go there—(coughing, cleared his throat) Excuse me. And get the—go to Jicaro, that's twenty-five miles, and camp overnight. Next morning, get up early and go over to Apalí, and get the provisions, which was about twelve, fifteen mile, and bring it back to Jicaro that night. And keep wa—goin', and then come on back there to Quilalí the next day. But, I wouldn't do that. I'd just take me a straight trip forty miles and camp all day there, and draw it in the mornin', early, come on back. It didn't take me long to make forty miles. But there wasn't but one stream between the whole thing, to get water. And, uh, I never would drink. Them other two would (referring to two Marine officers), ah, but I'd say, 'Uh uh, not me.' But, you know, you couldn't stand it.

"Yeah, when the—the men drank. But just like (scratched his head and looked over to the others talking in the room) when we was on the trail in one of those, ah, little towns . . . I would always buy 'em two quarts of whiskey, that, uh, casuasa—aguara (meaning "watered down"). It was bar, ah, I think . . . casuasa was contraband. And I would give 'em to the sergeant, ah, let 'em, go down each line, give 'em a glass, each one. I said 'Don't drink no more while we're here. When we leave here,' I said, 'in two hours, or a little later.' It's 'cause I want to see who the boys, the men were, not because they're mine.

"And I think we got about 12¢ a day to feed 'em (equivalent to $1.90 in 2016). I'd say we got about 20¢ ($3.17)—We used to get 28¢ ($4.43 in 2016) a day in the Marine Corps. That was our food allowance, see? Nobody was goin' hungry. Neighbors, neighbors, friends. Yeah. They'd let us get, like, so much pepper, you got it every once, every week, you know, you got your provisions. You couldn't trade it for something else. They had to figure out how much you needed (smiling and laughing). It's funny to live that-a-way, but—"

Fred: Laughed with him.

Don: "Anyway, then we'd go down in there. We'd go on a patrol, after they got scared of the Marines. Now we didn't go down to hurt nobody. They would have little camps on these, um, little ol' trails. Didn't have no cars, but the people would have a lean-to, like a building, take a, dig a hole and put a pole in with a fork in the top (gestured), and, you know, make a rail, and they had beds in there, maybe twenty-five or six, under the back in the bush where there was water. In fact, there generally was a (counting on his fingers) banana patch and a cane and sugar cane field, like that. And, they put bridges every—certain natives move to 'em. And they would—just every so often you'd find one. And they'd come in and cook and travel off to the country, see? That's people providin' for.

"But if you could find 'em, that's what you want. But, they'd go out—I mean, a trail that wide (less than his shoulder width) and they're so steep (gestured up), that you couldn't take a mule. He couldn't get up it. He couldn't come down. And, that's why they'd run into a ravine. And, they'd have a tree 'cross it, see? And walk—a man could walk across. The mules couldn't. You'd have to go way around, and that fella would be outta sight before you could get, even get near him, see?

"And, then the Marine went along with pots and pans on the dadburned Real Cantrail. Now we, you can hear 'em comin' half a—well, two miles. They didn't have a chance, see? And, uh, so, the only way, the only way you could control the people is with the natives. Now, you could put a few, in the, he'll train 'em, that can stand what they can stand. But they have—murder—couldn't stand what them two was doin'.

"And then, just like we'd get on a trail, there, and didn't, didn't have nothin' to—what we had hangin' on us. We would chew sugar cane. I would, could chew two stalks (reached above his head) that long, and, you know, some good sugar cane outta, that bigga around. You gotta' lot a juice in 'em. You know, I'd chew it and get—feel it, right quick. And eat a couple more tall tea. There're even some bananas, green, you take a green banana, get down by a road bed or a stream (gestured) and peel the peelin' off it, open it up and wash the ol' sticky stuff off it, and they go up there where you had a fire built and coals, understand?"

Fred: "Mm, mm."

Don: "And, then you lay it in the fire there, and it would get, uh, we'd cook it, rub a little salt on it, and you'd get filled up, and then make no more. And then we'd see a deer once in a while, and I could shoot good. Now, I used to shoot a lot of deer. And, we'd eat a little meat. Anything left over, they had a gorge about that long, and they'd cut the top half, you know, clean it out, and put what was left in it, and stick it in yer haversack (gestured behind him at lower back) where it wouldn't turn over, and have something to eat it a little later. But, people just eat too much. But, but then, if didn't eat too much, go across the stream, just throw a little water in my mouth, and wash it out, and take my tooth brush and wash my teeth a little bit. But, we uh, we fed good . . . (distracted a bit by laughter in the background, unrelated to what he was saying, and scratched at his stump.) We got it the only way ya can get it, from them people.

"And there's like, what they called the Sandinistas. Now, they got that word from Sandino. Now once he at—"

Fred: "Mm, hmm."

Don: "Nueva Segovia, now that was like a county. Ocotal was the capital of it. But, I saw on television, now, they said that Ocotal was twelve miles from the Hondoranian border. Well hell, I never knew that. We didn't go there to save no town. We didn't take the money with us. We didn't have no maps, nothing, see?"

Fred: "Mm, hmm."

Don: "Ya just went, and had, we'd take America high and proper—which it was always that way."

Fred: "Mm, hmm."

Don: "They must'ta got it—We would, uh, went on them trails, and them people would kill ya." (Closed his eyes, scratching his right ear as he remembered facts.)

Fred: "Yeah."

Don: "Now you take, I was, eh, raid in '30, spring of '31, Christmas of '30. It was Christmas of '30. We sent these people out there to fix this telephone line. The way to put the telephone line then, trail with, from one side to the other hangin' on a tree (showed with his hand). Ya take a piece of wire, on account of this wire, and take an ol' coka cola bottle, you know, and, for an insulator, and run the wire through the front.

"Then, their'd people come along and cut 'em. We couldn't talk to the next town. So, they sent word that that kid, somebody, that the line was down (scratched at his stump). So, about Christmas, they said uh, like she'd set the power right (scratched his stump). Our sergeant and nine men went out to fix it. But, they wind was blowin' wrong, you couldn't hear 'em shootin'. But, anyway, they ah, we heard there was a battle out there. And I had a big ol' horse, and I was way ahead of the rest of them, and they all ridin' along, but.

"I got up there, and the guide behind me hollered, "Get off," you know, pointing, "That's where the battle was goin' on (gestured to his left, then scratched at his stump). I got off and tied the horse to a tree limb (on his right), and, ah, I went on up there. By that time, some of the Marines had caught up with me, and they said— And, I saw one native runnin' across the road that-a-way with a machete (pointed from left to his right).

"And ah, somebody said, 'Who's that out there?'

"I said, 'This is Tru. Come on out.'

"One of 'em was named Jackson and the other was named Hutcherson. That was the two, they finally came out, they was on the left side of the road. The hill was sorta like that (indicated sloping down out in front of him from right to left).

"And ah, they said "Don't go up there, don't go up there, they'll kill ya, they'll kill ya.'

"But, I just kept goin' on anyway, goin' just went on slow up the hill (moving up to the left) so I could get above them, you know? And, ah, I sat on the crest of the hill. And, there was eight of them dead right down the road, there (on the left). (scratched his stump) And some of them had their fingers cut off, like they had a ring on, you know? (indicated with his stump, the ring finger of the left hand) And, they cut the finger.

"But, there wasn't no mules, wasn't no matter, wasn't no saddles, well, everything was gone before the mules, and they took their cartridge belts, their ammunition, they took their rifles, and took their shoes. They didn't have very good shoes, their hats, and ah . . . if they had a ring on, they'd cut their finger off (showed the slicing movement).

"But, if one of them was wounded, he would be gonna hit him like on the head, see? With a machete (lifted his left arm up in a defensive posture) and he'd throw his arm up, cut his arm off (at the elbow), you know? Then they hit him upside the head and kill him. And, ah, but, I went right on past 'em. I just looked down on the ground by myself (looking down), walked on that ridge, and just stayed up there, until they, the others joined me. See?

"Then they brought—you could drive up there a little further with a—We had two cars. We had a FWD, you know, the four-wheel truck, solid tire four wheel one. Well, we had one of those and one car the 'colonel' drove in—" (scratched his stump)

Fred: "Mm, hmm."

Don: "—like an ol' Dodge without a cab on it. He'd go da airfield in it, and movin' around there for him, see? They sent that ol', uh, Dodge out there. That's what they brought the dead back in (scratched his stump). But, but those people'd, they'd kill ya. But, we was up there with 'em—But, they were the best friends you'd ever had, if they liked ya. If they didn't like you, buddy, you was dead. And, they'd bury you, you know what I mean?

"You see they had these—President Coolridge loaned 300 of us (scratched his right shoulder) to the president of Nicaragua to train his troops, see? Well we trained 'em, had a little academy down there to train officers. And then, we worked with the enlisted and we get them, you know, the enlisted peop—men around there, had the sergeants and all the way down, and you know, made them do the work. And see, drill the men, and—but you couldn't teach 'em to shoot none. They shot differently, I mean, they shot from the hip mostly."

Fred: "Mm, hmm."

Don: "But, they did some pretty good hittin', see?"

Fred: "Mm, hmm."

Don: "And uh, that's, ah, the way we trained 'em. And we stayed down there. But the American people, they get all excited. Ya understand? And that's what determines everything is. See, the Marines went down in 1912, (scratched his stump) and they came out of there in '25. And then, they went back down there the second time they been in there. Ol' Smedley Butler was in there with them the first time. The second time we went down there was in '27. See? They stayed there until '33."

Fred: "Mmm."

Don: "But, the big hole is, that the big people in the United States, they're the ones who run everything. Money rules everything. And we supervised elections down there (scratched his stump) in '28 and also in '32, to see that they got a fair election. They had two factions. The Liberals and the Conservatives, um, saying that, that . . . And they were always at it. The

Liberals were the strongest of the two. But, they got a better deal outta da Conservatives than outta da Liberals. But, when they, when they left there in '25, they had a Li—a Conservative in there. I forget what his name was, it's in the book there (pointed to his left). But, ah, it's been a long time (shook his head). But, Juan Carlo was a general that wanted to overthrow him. And Sandino was one of his generals. And that's who took off and went to the Northern Area. Up there, where he'd work in the gold—up at the gold mine (scratched his stump), and was sorta smart. He had an Indian mama and some ol' half-breed white fella I think was his daddy. I don't know (scratched his head and pointed to the left)."

Twelve minutes into his memories, Don pointed to his left again. "It's all in the book there. That's the reason I was tellin' ya go to the library and look it up. That gentleman did a better job writin' it, than I could tell it, see? (paused)

"So, then . . . uh . . . oh, after ol' watch-a-call-it went up there, went up there and said, 'Make a circle', tryin' to circle 'em. But, you know, a man don't have a chance in someone else's home. You know where nothin' is, and the jungle up there. And you followin' the road. And, he can set out there, and he's twenty feet away from you and ya never see him. And they'd fire at you whenever they wanna. See? And, then you get wounded, they in one bad shape. Dere's no way to get down. And, and the hills, some of 'em are just that steep (raised his hand to show about a sixty-degree slope).

"But anyway, there, ah, we supervised the elections in '28 and also in, uh—" (paused, distracted by conversation in the background)

Fred: "Okay, go ahead."

Don: "—in, ah, and also in '32. Then, an airplane carrier—I think the *Lexington* come down there. They had a lot of 'em off it, and the Navy and the Marine Corps, so—But if they had a Liberal, he would sit over there (gestured to his left), and the Conservative, he would sit over there (gestured to his right), pickin' the people out of the neighborhood to keep it straight. And, the, the language barrier. So, the Marines, they had two, three Marines—electoral commission they called it, then when—They had two kinds of ballots, some of the people couldn't read nor write. They had a green one fer the Liberals, I mean Conservatives, a red one for the Liberals. They'd pick up a ballot, and 'come here, boy' and tick 'em off right through it dis-a-way (demonstrated that the ballot was pinched). See? Pass through it.

"But, that Liberal and that Conservative, they had to nod (nodded) that they knew him. And the Marine let him come on by. And the next one, he put it in the ballot box, and they'd grab him by the right hand and take the two index fingers and stick it down in dye. They pull it out, and it just dry that quick. And you couldn't get it off that well, took two or three days. You could wash it in gasoline, and it wouldn't come off. They'd take leaves and everything and get mad at us, and said we were crooked up there.

"But, see, them head lead people, they educate their kids in the United States, France, and England. They know how crooked we are. Ol', Ol' Somoza he, he turned arm—the army, the army was turned over to him. He spoke pretty good English. See? Was from around Philadelphia for a time, he had a little money, see? Then, he had two sons who went to that, uh, ah . . . uh, West Point."

Fred: "Mm hmm."

Don: "And, then when they graduated, they come down, and he made one of 'em, his fella in charge of the . . . of the army. When they had 'em, then—once you got in the army, and the head man, you got the whole works, see? 'Cause the fella with the guns, you control everything.

"But, the second election was down there in '32 . . . um, yeah . . . the fella that was elected, and they did, was a fella by the name of Sacasa. See?" (scratched his stump)

Fred: "Mm hmm."

Don: "Ol', ah, Moncada, he, he done run, he got elected the first time, between '28 and '32. So, they had another re-, a re-election in '32, when there were—the second one. And, that's when Somoza, I never did see—I mean, uh, Sacasa, I never did see him. But then, a little later, him and Ol', uh, Sacasa didn't get along with Somoza. Somoza was in charge of the Army. So, he told Sacasa to get goin'—go to Costa Rica, either Honduras, you know what I mean? Run him off."

Fred: "Mm."

Don: "And that's when—after his boy graduated, he made him, eh, he took over as the president for about 30 years down there."

Fred: "Mm hmm."

Don: "And, then the young one, he was his vice-president. Then, the other one graduated, and he come out and gave him the army. Why, they had it sowed up, see? And they, and they had three ships down there. The Somoza family owned them all. That's when they'd import the stuff from the United States, come through the Canal, brought it down there to port of entry."

Sixteen minutes into the videotaping, Fred asked a pertinent question.

Fred: "What happened, what happened down there when you won the Medal? As far as, uh, that story goes."

Don answered in thirty-one seconds. "Well, we was on a combat mission down there, you know what I mean? Just got in a battle down there, and one of the people dropped a grenade and, you know, hit a rock down there, and got all excited, and I picked it up and throw'd it out of the way—attempted to do it, and it blow'd my hand off. We was way back there in the jungle. And then, uh, they brought me out of there, picked me up and brought me out to the little airfield, there. Twenty-four hours later, (scratched his stump) the little plane come in there, and landed on the little field that they put in there. And they, um, they picked me up, put me in one of the cockpits and took me on back down then."

Fred: "How many men then did you save then, in that—when you got that grenade?"

Don answered that question in twenty seconds. "Oh, I don't know. We got fifteen or sixteen with us, maybe eighteen with us. Ya couldn't go out, you couldn't go out, (scratched his stump) you weren't supposed to leave there with less than eighteen men, you know? Yer goin'—you get somebody wounded and you done play the devil getting 'em outta there."

Fred: "Mmm."

Don: "And, ah, we, we always, dey always had an order, don't go, don't leave with less than that many men. But you can't see 'em in the bush, that many. See?"

Fred: "Mm hum."

Don: "And the one thing about it, those people there were shrewd. You could, you know what I mean? They could see something comin', might near smell it. Which Americans couldn't do it. I had these two good point men, you know what I mean? And they'd see something like a deer, want to kill some deer on the road. There was one of them standing out in front, one of them in front of me would fall this way and the other would fall this-a-away (gestured in both directions)."

Fred: "Mm hum."

Don: "And I knew something was happenin'."

Fred: "Mm hum."

Don: "They'd do like this (gestured), a little sign language, without talkin'. Didn't make no noise, 'cause they didn't have nothin' to make noise with. But the Marines comin' in, like with sidearms, ridin' a mule and all like that, makin' all kinda noise. See, the American people are not, uh, are not like other people. We had it easy too long. And they think we're big shots, and they do. If something was 10¢, then the daggum Marine wants to give 'em a 10¢ tip, next time it's 20¢, then next time, daggum give 'em twenty— oh, you got to have a little more, and give them a little more, like that. Ruin the whole thing. But don't try to change nobody. When you go into an outfit, I don't care if they're poor people, what they are. You go in there and be one of 'em. And, then don't, then, then grow with 'em. And, then teach them after you get, they get used to ya. But don't come in there and try to change 'em overnight. They'll hate cha. And, you be tryin' to be a big shot, that's, you know, that's what gets to them. But, just be one of 'em. I've eaten beans and bread, like that, and laughin' with—'The best I ever had.' I had to tell a little lie, ya know, you know what I mean, but that'd get along."

Fred: "Mm hmm."

Don: "So, I don't want nobody dislikin' me (scratched his head)."

Fred: "Until they, 'til they learned to trust you, and—"

Don: "Oh, yeah, yeah. You got, you got them people your friend, they'll go to hell for you. But, like the troops that I had, they wouldn't do—he was also an officer. I was a second lieutenant. He was a second lieutenant or a captain, and he wouldn't do it, unless he said, 'I'll ask my boss.' See? He wouldn't do nothin'. He thought he belonged to me. I just have to—see? That's why I come to believe, I'd tell him to go ahead and do something, and he would do it, see? But those, those people, (scratched his stump) they got, they got a lot of good sense. They're not all dummies. Naw, it's like I told ya. That little ol' piece of poultice says it matters little where you were born, whether your parents were rich or poor, and some of 'em were brilliant, if you just would take—bring 'em and take advantage of it. See?"

The conversation likely went on beyond this point, but, the videotaping ended. Fred and Dee kept the small cassette stored away as they moved from one residence to another. Nearly thirty years passed. Dee would have the videotape transferred to a DVD disc in 2016 and provide a copy to The Camden Archives & Museum.

Before the Joint Assembly

The 2nd Regular Session of the South Carolina 107th General Assembly convened on Tuesday, January 12, 1988, at the State Capitol Building in the City of Columbia. Deliberations opened with a chaplain's prayer and the Pledge of Allegiance to the Flag of the United States of America. Don was going to be invited to attend the session. Two weeks before he knew about that, he attended a funeral. How he felt about the events likely went unspoken. Stoically is the best word to describe how Don and the Truesdells manage situations.

Following his USMC service in Korea, Benny Maxwell Edens had lived in Florida. He married Dorothy Larie Hill in Polk County, and they resided in St. Croix, U.S. Virgin Islands, where he owned his own successful service company. He and Dorothy had two daughters. He was in St. Croix when his father died in 1974. The Edens divorced later in Tampa, Hillsborough County. When his mother, Edna Truesdell Edens, 81, died in August 1986, Benny came to Florence for the funeral. Then, in 1987, he lost significant assets in a small stock market crash. He came back home and lived in his Granddaddy and Granny Truesdell's house. He did not overstay.

Don received the news on Thursday, January 21. His nephew, aged 58, had run out of resilience. Like his Great-granddaddy Truesdale, Benny had killed himself on the back porch of the grandparent's house, right near Granny's pantry. [78] He was buried with his parents in Mount Hope Cemetery in Florence.

A week after the funeral, Don was in Columbia, but not yet before the General Assembly. His children had gathered in Lugoff for a visit.

Stephen and Ginger flew in from Oregon. Dee and Fred and Billy loaded up their motor home to escape the Maryland cold and snow, with plans to vacation in Disney World, Davie, and St. Augustine, Florida. [79] On their way south, they stopped first in Lugoff.

Dee invited everyone to go out for a meal. On Saturday, January 30, the family drove over to the California Dreaming Restaurant on Main Street in Columbia, a favorite eating place on the University of South Carolina campus, known for its giant-sized portions. Even Don's younger brother, E.T., went along. The dinner was the last time the two would be photographed together, sitting beside each other, hardly talking, at the long table.

True to his character, Don walked from the parking lot along the red brick driveway to the front portico on his own. His left leg might have been amputated, but he was determined to walk unaided, even without a cane. To his left, always ready to lend his father support, Stephen walked closely beside him into the restaurant. Dee kept a photo of her dad walking into a restaurant on his own.

Once the family had been seated, Stephen looked over his dad's left shoulder, helping him select from the large menu of American classics.

Don was seldom captured smiling in photographs; but, Lois was. Her 36th birthday was on Sunday, and the family celebrated with her at the restaurant. After everyone had finished eating, out of a box came a big white cake. Under the gay script *Happy Birthday Lois Lee*, a horse and rider jumping a railing decorated the icing—a fitting cake for a born horsewoman.

Conversations over a meal with Lois often turned to horsey subjects. She enjoyed participating in endurance horseback racing. The courses could stretch one hundred or more miles, with stations along the way for health checks for both horse and rider. One race started with her horses' hooves in one Great Lake and ended with the hooves in another Great Lake. When the route went uphill, Lois hopped off and ran alongside the horse to give her mount a break. At one point, she was thrown as she crossed a road, and the horse spooked.

Lois had broken a leg. She might have cursed a little, a talent she had acquired that could put any Marine to shame. She did not "suffer fools gladly," and she did not quit. Reminiscent of her father "staying the course" after protecting his soldiers from a grenade in Nicaragua, Lois got back on her horse, finished the race, packed up her gear, and drove back to Lugoff. Then, she got her leg set and cast and got back to life as normal. The cast on her leg did not dishearten her. One day a tire on her pickup went flat, and she changed it. Maybe it was Lois who inspired Don to hobble into the restaurant without help.

The State House is located seven blocks north of the California Dreaming Restaurant. The Assembly was in recess over the weekend. A State Representative might have been enjoying an American classic meal while the Truesdells laughed together and sang *Happy Birthday* to Lois. At any rate, during the next week, the representatives took up immediate consideration on a motion that was introduced and adopted in the House on February 3.

Donald Harry Holland, 60, of Camden, was a member of James Leroy Belk Post 17 and the VFW. He had enlisted in the U.S. Army after graduating from high school in 1945, at the conclusion of World War II. Following his enlistment, he went to law school and was elected to the House of Representatives from Kershaw County in 1950. In 1968, he was elected to serve as Democratic State Senator from District No. 27, representing Kershaw and Lancaster counties. He remained in office until his death in 2003. The senator understood the significance of the Medal of Honor and admired Don Roy.

On February 4, with unanimous consent, the South Carolina House, the Senate concurring, adopted H*3679 Concurrent Resolution, inviting Colonel Charles P. Murray

(USA-Retired), President of the CMOHS, to address the General Assembly, and inviting the state's MOH recipients to be guests of the joint assembly for the occasion. It was further resolved that a copy of the resolution was to be forwarded to Colonel Murray and each invitee.

Don Truesdell was on the grounds of the South Carolina State House complex on Thursday morning, February 11, 1988, with five of the eight Medal recipients living in the state: three from WWII, one from Korea, and one from Vietnam. Mrs. Truesdell, keeping to her pledge not to be seen in public with him, was unable to attend the event. He went to the Hall of the House at 1100 Gervais Street just before noon.

At 12:00 PM, the Senate appeared in the Hall. Lieutenant Governor Nick Theodore, the President of the Senate, opened the forty-minute ceremony, calling the Joint Assembly to order and announcing that it had convened under the terms of a Concurrent Resolution adopted by both Houses. The Reading Clerk of the Senate read the resolution to the assemblage, then, Colonel Murray, the guest speaker, and the distinguished parties were escorted to the rostrum. [80]

Representative Samuel R. Foster made brief introductory remarks and introduced the honored guests. He asked the recipients to please raise their hand as each was recognized so that the Assembly would know who they were.

"Ladies and gentlemen of the Joint Assembly," he opened, "it's a high honor and privilege today for us to recognize the special guests of South Carolina." Then, he read a brief statement about each of them.

"First of all, the Honorable Donald L. Truesdell, United States Marine Corps, Retired. Awarded the Medal of Honor for action while serving in the grade of corporal in the vicinity of Constancia, near Coco River, Nicaragua, on April 24, 1932. Then CPL Truesdell was serving as second-in-command of a Guardia Nacional Patrol in active operations against armed bandits. Born and now lives in Lugoff, South Carolina, the Honorable Donald Truesdell." Don Roy raised his hand to the applause.

After introducing the others and calling attention to the two native South Carolinian MOH recipients living out of state, Representative Foster called the name of each person who was to make an individual presentation to the recipient. Senator Donald H. Holland made the Honorable Donald Truesdell's presentation, acknowledging that the State Commander of the American Legion was present.

"This is Don Roy Truesdale, who I've known, he's in my American Legion Post . . . I know of no greater privilege in my life, or pleasure, Don, than to present you this."

Following the eight presentations (two made in absentia), Lieutenant Governor Theodore introduced Colonel Murray. "We're delighted on behalf of the Joint Assembly to have so many distinguished South Carolinians in our Chambers today. I know you're all courageous men. . . . We're delighted to have each one of you here, and it's my privilege to have this opportunity to introduce to the members of the Joint Assembly and the guests assembled here an outstanding individual."

Charles Murray spoke for the recipients. "We thank you from the bottom of our hearts for permitting us and inviting us to be here today. . . . It is our great honor and privilege to be in this historic hall. In recognizing those of us here today, those six of us, you honor all recipients of the Medal of Honor, and I bring you their greetings. You honor in a very special way the twenty-eight MOH recipients who are accredited to the State of South Carolina, those whose names are memorialized in bronze and stone on the walls of this great building. More than that, you bring honor to the uncounted thousands who have served so bravely here and around the world, those who have fought and suffered and died in the name of South Carolina. . . . In honoring us, you honor them all."

Upon the conclusion of his address, Colonel Murray and his escort party retired from the Chamber.

Don Truesdell's wall plaque with his portrait, accompanied by the citation describing the heroic actions that merited him "this most elite decoration," was on display with thirty-four other South Carolina recipients of this prestigious award. The South Carolina Medal of Honor Recipients Room is at the South Carolina Military Museum, 1225 Bluff Road in Columbia.

The wall plaque was opportune. Time was running short for those wanting to extend a tribute to Don.

World War One recipient, U.S. Army Corporal Thomas A. Pope, aged 95, of Alhambra, California, died on June 14, 1989. U.S. Navy Lieutenant Edouard Victor Izac, 99, of Bethesda, Maryland, died on January 18, 1990. Don Truesdell was then the oldest recipient wearing the Medal.

The Last Thanksgivings

On September 22, 1989, Hurricane Hugo hit Charleston and ripped through South Carolina. The major storm might have served as a symbol in the Truesdell household. Don suffered the first of many mini strokes. He fought back, but never recovered the balance to walk unaided. Requiring more and more help, he demanded that Gladys care for him. That he was less and less able to do things for himself rankled them both. So much shorter than her husband, Gladys was not really up to moving a large man around. He swore that if she hired someone, he would be so nasty they would leave. Gladys gave in, but not quietly. [81]

Don continued to decline, and the decibel levels rose in the home. Gladys apparently had much more to yell about than he did. She had been free from child rearing only to find herself tied down again. The battles continued, and the adult Truesdell children took note of their Mama's persistent crankiness.

The Truesdells gathered in Lugoff every year after Thanksgiving. Dee celebrated the holiday in Maryland with her husband and son. Stephen and Ginger would fly from Oregon to meet her, and the two families would drive to South Carolina the day after Thanksgiving. Jeff drove in from Charleston. "Gay" and Lois met them at the family home. [82]

Each year photos were snapped outside the house, some with spouses and significant others and others of just the blood relatives. The last family group with Don on his feet was Thanksgiving 1991. His hair was white and his skin was pale. Jeff held his father by the stump of his right arm, and Stephen's hand rested on Don's shoulder as his dad leaned on Ginger. Paul Bradley and Bill Schindler represented the eighth generation of Truesdell descendants in America.

Thanksgiving 1992 was the last time Don was in the family photo. He sat in a chair on the front porch, surrounded by his five children, two grandsons, and Gladys, cradling her one-year-old black puppy in her arms.

Dee served on an elected school board in Allegany County, Maryland, for eight years. During her two terms, there were lots of crazy newspaper articles. She had learned from her mother to write a letter if something was important to her. In February 1993, she wrote a letter to the *Cumberland Sunday Times* Editor in response to a "rash of arrogant letters expressing the writers' intolerance of opinions or beliefs different than their own." [83] She implored Americans to remember their immigrant ancestors and to honor and respect diversity.

Dee recalled that her ancestors had come to the American colonies and fought against England during the Revolutionary War. She was proud of her family lineage. Her father was among the many Truesdells still living in South Carolina, and he had worn the Congressional Medal of Honor longer than anyone alive at that time. He had served in the Marine Corps and given an arm and a leg in military service to this country.

Like her siblings, Dee is "honest to a fault" and does not abide a lie. With no tolerance for people who could look her in the eye and lie, being on the school board gradually turned her into a cynic.

In mid-May 1993, the CMOHS's headquarters moved from New York. The Society planned to dedicate its new memorial and headquarters in October on the hangar deck of the USS *Yorktown*. The old aircraft carrier was docked at the Patriots Point Naval and Maritime Museum in Mount Pleasant, across the Cooper River from Charleston and in sight of Fort Sumter. Don's name was on the 100-foot-long silver wall listing the names of all the men to have earned the nation's highest honor for bravery. The Society was also planning to hold its convention in Charleston.

Before Memorial Day, Don was one of the 203 Society members to receive invitations. Even though the USS *Yorktown* was berthed just a little over two hours from Lugoff, Don was not going to attend either event. Instead, a memorial wreath was going to be hung for him on the Museum wall.

Gladys injured her back trying to move Don. He was finally taken to Columbia and admitted into the VA hospital in early September. The situation was detestable for the Medal recipient. He refused to eat. The medical staff suggested a feeding tube. Don would have no part of that. If he could not do things his way, he had no reason to live. Totally dependent on the care of others, having become a burden in his view, he wanted to die. Gladys and his five children stood behind his decision. It took three weeks. [84]

Before he departed this life, he had a request of his eldest child. He asked Dee to make sure Jeff did not starve.

Don lived out his long life as fulfilling as his background, combat wounds, and cultural limitations made possible. He was fortunate to see five of his children grow to adulthood and watch them live as decent people who valued being of service to others and contributing to society. They are honest, hard working, dependable, and faithful friends. They each possess the capacity to see the funny side of things and can tell stories that fill rooms with fits of laughter. Don's children and two grandsons are a great portion of his legacy.

Donald Truesdell, aged 87, died on September 21, 1993, seven months after his daughter had written her letter to the Editor. Looking back across the five generations of fathers from whom he had descended, only James Rembert Truesdale, the five-year-old boy who had im-migrated from Kinghill, Ireland, in 1772 had lived more years—92.

As he had wished, Don was cremated. He had asked that his ashes be sprinkled into Five and Twenty Creek. American Legion Post 17 renamed the garden in front of the facility the Donald Truesdell Memorial Rose Garden, and asked the family to bury their father's ashes in the garden. [85] The family did both.

Gladys had her husband's flat stone, military marker placed in the Truesdell family plot at Saint John's Methodist Cemetery. An American flag and a blue MOH flag are often placed to mark his grave. Most of the fifty-four markers at the cemetery belong to Jordan, Lee, Rosborough, Truesdell, and Watt family members. Don Roy is considered the one "fa-mous interment" at the cemetery, although his remains are not under his marker.

Posthumous Tributes

Don had driven across the Wateree River Bridge on U.S.-1 into Camden hundreds of times. One of his destinations was located on the southwest edge of town, where U.S.-1 intersects Chestnut Ferry Road and SR S-28-592. The Legion Post was a comfortable place for him. He was a distinguished member there for fifty years, and the members who knew him often talked about what a wonderful man he was. They made sure that their friend would be remembered.

Gay's husband, "Butch" Lilly, is an active Post 17 member. Gay knows well that her daddy is a big deal there, as people are always coming up to her, talking about how wonderful Don was. She restrains herself, just smiling and saying nothing. [86]

A brick walkway leads from the front door of Post 17 to the Memorial Post Garden. Nine flags stand as sentinels along the walkway. Old Glory stands at the end, sometimes casting a shadow over a tiered water fountain. The stone marker stands at the base of the American flagpole. [87] Sitting on one of the stone benches on either side of the walk, it is easy to read the tribute etched into the buffed stone face.

U.S. Marine
Donald LeRoy Truesdell
Memorial Post Garden
Medal of Honor Recipient
Nicaragua, April 24, 1932

James Leroy Belk Post 17
The American Legion
Workman——Hordsby Memorial.

A portion of Don's remains was laid to rest in the garden. On a sunny November day, the family gathered in Lugoff for Thanksgiving, and the American Legion held a goodbye ceremony for their MOH recipient. Two Legion commanders flanked Gay, Lois, Jeff, Steve, Dee, and Gladys when they stood behind the monument and under the American flag for photographs.

The Post did some reconstruction at the garden years later. The family took possession of Don's ashes and sprinkled them into Five and Twenty Creek as he had wanted.

Gladys was very aware that Don had an important part in Kershaw County's rich history. She donated his original Medal of Honor to the Camden Archives & Museum in 1993. The blue ribbon was in good condition, but not as bright as it had once been. The bronze Medal was not as shiny as it was when LtCol Matthews presented it to Don in 1932, but Minerva plainly still kept Discord at bay.

The curator was honored to accept the Medal. The Truesdells represented the third family from the county to give a Medal into the care of the museum. The other two Medals had been earned in WWI.

John Canty Villepigue spent his entire life in Camden, until he enlisted in the South Carolina National Guard. Richmond Hobson Hilton hailed from tiny Westville, an unincorporated community fifteen miles north of Camden, with a population one-third the size of Lugoff. Both men were assigned to Company M, 118th Infantry, 30th "Old Hickory" Division, as Washington, D.C., deployed troops to Europe. Sergeant Hilton, 20, earned his Medal in France on October 11, 1918. Corporal Villepigue, 22, earned his on October 15, and died of wounds on April 18, 1919. R. H. Hilton died on August 13, 1933; a year after LtCol Matthews had put the blue ribbon around CPL Truesdale's collar.

The Camden Archives & Museum established a permanent, "official" display for the three Kershaw County men. The exhibit was maintained in the gallery until 2013. The Medals of Honor were displayed several times in temporary exhibits in the years since, but are not currently kept on display. Members of the public have at times requested to view CPL Truesdale's Medal. [88]

Gladys' mother, "Big Gladys" Garrity, died on June 20, 1994. She was buried in Arlington's Grove Plot with her parents. The death might have made Gladys wish that she could have a conversation with her grandmother. Anna (Werb) Phillips, during the Depression years, had convinced Gladys that marrying a career Marine would grant her later pension security. It did not.

An officer at the MCB Quantico Disbursing Office/Finance Office called Gladys with an apology. Don had not indicated that any portion of his retirement pension should go to her upon his death. Instead, he had bequeathed his pension to his five children. They had each inherited $10,000. The Corps could not override Don's stipulations. Gladys received a small provision from a Corps' widows' fund. [89]

South Carolina's "elective share" law did help a little. Gladys, as the surviving widow, had the right to inherit at least one-third of her deceased spouse's estate. The estate included all property Don had acquired during his lifetime. Don left his wife of fifty-two years the absolute minimum that the law forced him to bequeath. He left the Truesdell land to be divided between the two boys.

The children thought that their daddy's final financial arrangements were thoughtless and selfish toward their Mama. They each generously turned over their share of Don's pension to her. Gladys was finally free to do whatever she wanted, although she held on to her habit of pinching pennies.

Traveling was a dream and highlight for her, and she did get to take some memorable trips. Once Dee's son, Bill, was old enough to come home to an empty house after school, annual mother-daughter trips began. Gladys chose the destinations. Their travels would provide good memories for Dee later.

Initially they took fun trips to Europe. Then, Gladys preferred cruises, so she could see different places without packing and unpacking. In 2000, Paul Bradley had an idea. He told his grandma about the attractions in Las Vegas. She could see Paris, Rome, and Venice all in one place, plus shows and the Grand Canyon. That is where she wanted to go. She and Dee booked Las Vegas for October 2001. It almost did not happen.

Instead, 9/11 happened. Gladys called Dee and told her to cancel their travels. Dee refused right away. Canceling would damage the airline and hotel industry, and that would be unpatriotic unless there was another attack. Gladys accepted. A couple of weeks passed. She called Dee again. She was worried. She had heard that attendance was down in Las Vegas and shows were being cancelled. Aged 80 years, she worried that they would not see enough action!

Yet, Gladys did not live out her years in peace and happiness.

The esteem in which the South Carolina representatives in the state capital held Don remains evident to this day.

On February 24, 1994, in their General Assembly 110th Session, the South Carolina Senate introduced and adopted SJ-4, expressing the sympathy of the members of the Senate to the family and friends of Donald L. Truesdell of Lugoff, a recipient of the Congressional Medal of Honor.

Senate Resolution S*1218 read: Whereas, the members of the Senate were saddened to note the death on September 21, 1993, of Mr. Donald L. Truesdell of Lugoff; and, Whereas, Mr. Truesdell was one of that extraordinary group of American servicemen who were recipients of the Congressional Medal of Honor; and, Be it resolved by the Senate: That the members of the Senate express sympathy to the family and friends of Donald L. Truesdell of Lugoff, a recipient of the Congressional Medal of Honor, and, Be it further resolved that a copy of this resolution be forwarded to his widow, Mrs. Gladys Truesdell, at her home address.

The South Carolina Legislature returned to using the Truesdale surname in reference to Don Roy, in part, because that was the name on his Medal Citation when it was awarded to him in 1932. On May 19, 2004, the House introduced, adopted, and sent HJ-33 to the Senate, which returned SJ-31 with concurrence. H*5314, a concurrent resolution and posthumous memorial, went into the General Assembly 115th Session record.

"Be it resolved by the House of Representatives, the Senate concurring: That the members of the General Assembly commend the extraordinary heroism of the late Donald Leroy Truesdale who was awarded the Medal of Honor for his valor, which is the highest award that can be bestowed upon a member of the Armed Forces of the United States. Be it further resolved that a copy of this resolution be forwarded to the family of the late Donald Leroy Truesdale."

In the General Assembly 117th Session on June 21, 2007, The House introduced, adopted, and sent HJ-59 to the Senate, which concurred and referred SJ-79 on to the Committee on Transportation on January 8, 2008. H*4304 read as follows: "A concurrent resolution to request that the department of transportation name the Twenty-Five Mile Creek Bridge situated along South Carolina Highway 34 in Kershaw County the "Donald L. Truesdale Congressional Medal of Honor Recipient Bridge," and erect appropriate markers or signs at this bridge which contain the words "Donald L. Truesdale Congressional Medal of Honor Recipient Bridge." That bridge is located north of Lugoff on the edge of the 9-hole Green Hill Golf Club, where the Flat Branch and Cook Run creeks run into the Twenty-Five Mile Creek. The resolution included a complimentary conjunction: "Whereas, he was married to Mrs. Gladys Truesdale, and together they raised six wonderful children."

The City of Lugoff named a half-mile-long section of State Road S-28-356 in his honor. Roy Truesdell Road starts at Main Street and ends at Ridgeway Road SR 34 in front of the elementary school.

An Egregious Crime

Sometime between 7:30 PM Sunday, June 27, 2004, and 7:30 AM Monday, someone broke into the Patriots Point Naval and Maritime Museum aboard the dry-docked aircraft carrier

Yorktown. The thief, or thieves, went to the MOH exhibit in the museum maintained by the CMOHS, broke the display case, and stole seven original Medals, leaving other Medals untouched. Medals from the Civil War up through the Vietnam War were stolen. Corporal Truesdell's was one of the display Medals taken. Police and the FBI investigated. The FBI was involved because selling a Medal of Honor is a federal offense. Investigators were not able to identify suspects or recover the stolen Medals. [90]

The FBI was experienced in these matters. The Medal's value brings a presumption of interstate transportation. A year earlier, in May 2003, the agency had identified a Mississauga, Ontario, Canada, resident auctioning stolen Medals of Honor on ebay.com. The man was apprehended in July and arrested, pled guilty, and was sentenced to prison in 2004. The FBI took possession of the Medals from the Civil War, the Spanish-American War, and World War II in March 2004. The three precious, recovered Medals were presented to President of the CMOHS Gary Littrell on May 27, 2004. [91] The theft at the museum a month later had to have been more than provoking.

To enhance protections relating to the reputation and meaning of the Medal of Honor, Congress passed the Stolen Valor Act in 2005. President George W. Bush signed the Act into law on December 20, 2006, making it illegal for unauthorized persons to wear, buy, sell, barter, trade, or manufacture any decoration or medal authorized for the U.S. Armed Forces. Anyone falsely claiming to have been awarded a Medal of Honor for personal gain could be charged with a crime and faced a year in a federal prison.

Prosecutions, convictions, and courtroom arguments followed. The U.S. Supreme Court finally ruled that the Stolen Valor Act was an unconstitutional abridgment of the First Amendment's freedom of speech and struck down the law on June 28, 2012. The Act was revised and rewritten. President Barack Obama signed H.R. 258, the Stolen Valor Act of 2013, on June 3, 2013, making it a federal crime to fraudulently claim to be a recipient of certain military decorations or medals to obtain money, property, or other tangible benefit.

While Supreme Court Justices wrote arguments about the Stolen Valor Act, Tom Morris Jr. began his own investigation into the 2004 MOH thefts, the black market financed by shady collectors, and the despicable trend of men fraudulently claiming to be Medal recipients. Tom was a senior correspondent and a segment producer for the Fox TV Network, and his work was featured on *America's Most Wanted*. He considered the theft to be a "different sort of crime, an egregious one against the people who bled and died for their country."

In early February 2007, radio shows and newspaper staff writers called attention to a TV broadcast intended to assist America's most honored. The top crime fighting show was going to put a national spotlight on the thefts featuring Correspondent Morris' discoveries. [92]

On Saturday evening, February 17, Fox TV Network aired "The Medal of Honor Heist" on Season 20, Episode 18 of *America's Most Wanted* show. John Walsh wished to crack the case that endangered "the honor and integrity of U.S. service members who have received the nation's highest award for valor." The segment included a re-enactment of the theft. John asked for tips that could help recover the Medals.

On Friday, August 21, 2009, five "dark-suited FBI agents" returned two stolen Civil War Medals of Honor to the museum at Patriots Point. Major General James Livingston, USMC (ret), Vietnam MOH recipient, accepted the confiscated Medals from the agents on behalf of the CMOHS. Since the open, pending investigation into the Medals stolen from the museum was still ongoing, no details were released on the recovery of the Civil War Medals. The agents were keeping their fingers crossed that CPL Truesdell's Medal would "show up one day." [93]

A Part of Camden's Proud History

The American Legion Post believed that Don Roy's memory should go beyond the Post. He belonged to Camden, as much as to Lugoff.

At the start of the Revolutionary War, the British had their headquarters on the south side of Camden. They erected a palisade around the town and built several small forts around the perimeter to defend against any Colonial attack. The fortified west redoubt was positioned where Campbell Street ended on Meeting Street at the east edge of the Quaker Cemetery.

The first burials in the cemetery, a four-acre tract, dated back to 1759. Over many years, long after the British had evacuated their stronghold over the Wateree River Ferry, the cemetery was enlarged to about fifty acres. Today, Meeting Street runs east-west through the center of the cemetery. The Cemetery Association and the United Daughters Of The Confederacy (U.D.C.), John D. Kennedy Chapter #308, both tend Section 14—called *Little Arlington*. Annual Memorial Day services center around the stand that is erected under the Memorial Oak.

Confederate Sergeant Richard Rowland Kirkland is buried on Memorial Avenue in *Little Arlington*, and has a tall, distinctive monument where he is laid to rest. Renowned as the "Angel of Marye's Heights," he carried water to wounded comrades and Yankees for an hour-and-a-half at the battle of Fredericksburg, Virginia, on the night of December 13, 1862. Two World War I MOH recipients are buried on either side of Sergeant Kirkland. Sergeant Richmond Hobson Hilton lies to his south. In addition to his Medal of Honor and Purple Heart, the stone lying over his grave records his service and medal awards from five other nations. On the other side, Corporal John Canty Villepigue has a tall, distinctive stone monument over his grave with a Medal insignia at the top.

In 2001, the American Legion was granted permission to enclose the portion of *Little Arlington* lots with a handsome stone coping.

The Legion Post returned to *Little Arlington* on Monday morning, September 2, 2002, to hold a ceremony honoring "the quiet hero" who had so often recruited on its behalf. [94] On Memorial Avenue, a short walk off Meeting Street and 700 feet from the Revolutionary War West Redoubt, they had erected a memorial monument to Donald Leroy Truesdell with permission from the UDC. The standing granite stone is similar in appearance to Corporal Villepigue's, except that Don Roy's stone has the Marine Corps emblem engraved at the top. [95]

Gladys Truesdell, 81, was present, and Jeffrey Truesdell, 47, had arrived from Charleston. Post 17 Second Vice Commander D. Carlyle Baxley acted as speaker and master of ceremonies. Marine Captain Matthew Youngblood was the keynote speaker. Post Commander Perry McCoy opened the ceremony, saying, "We pause today to remember Donald Leroy Truesdell." Carlyle Baxley read a letter from then Senate Armed Services Committee Senator Strom Thurmond.

"Corporal Truesdell went above and beyond the call of duty. This demonstration of courage is what brought you all here today. This monument will communicate his example for generations to come. We must never forget."

Legionnaire Baxley asked Gladys and Jeffrey to come forward. They stood where the monument honoring the Kershaw County hero was unveiled. The photograph printed in the *Chronicle–Independent* showed that the marker stood as tall as Jeffrey. Carlyle read the monument's inscription.

DONALD LEROY
TRUESDELL
AUG. 26. 1906
SEPT. 21. 1993
MEDAL OF HONOR RECIPIENT
PLACE/CITATION: COSTANCIA, [96]
NORTHERN NICARAGUA 1932

TRUESDELL, SERVING IN NICARAGUA AS SECOND IN COMMAND OF
A GUARDIA NATIONAL PATROL, WAS SENT OUT ON A MISSION WITH
ORDERS TO MAKE CONTACT WITH A PREVIOUSLY DISCOVERED GROUP
OF OUTLAWS ON THE 24TH OF APRIL 1932. DURING THE SEARCH A
RIFLE GRENADE FELL FROM ITS CARRIER, STRUCK A NEARBY ROCK,
AND IGNITED. SEEING THAT SEVERAL PATROL MEMBERS WERE IN
DANGER, TRUESDELL RUSHED FORWARD, GRASPED THE GRENADE AND
ATTEMPTED TO HURL IT AWAY. THE GRENADE EXPLODED BLOWING OFF
TRUESDELL'S HAND, PART OF HIS ARM, AND INFLICTING SEVERAL OTHER
MAJOR INJURIES ON HIS BODY; HOWEVER BY TAKING THE BRUNT OF
THE EXPLOSION HE SAVED THE OTHER MEMBERS OF HIS PATROL FROM
SERIOUS INJURY OR LOSS OF LIFE.

Jeffrey then spoke on behalf of the family. He recalled how his dad had never complained about his time in the service. His dad was made uncomfortable later in life when he met with dignitaries and with active military men on aircraft carriers, and they would salute him. "He didn't like the spotlight."

John D. Kennedy Chapter of the UDC President Ann Morgan Martin stepped to the podium after the unveiling. "It is a very great privilege and pleasure to have this marker placed here," she said. "This area was specially designated to honor Kershaw County's honored soldiers. We hope visitors who come here will reflect on his sacrifice to his country and fellow soldiers."

Captain Youngblood then spoke to the crowd about the meaning of the monument and Don's USMC service. He believed that CPL Truesdell epitomized what the Marine Corps aspired to embody. "What I say today won't do justice to what Corporal Truesdell did," he said, "but we must do as he did or else lose what he sacrificed for. . . . This is Corporal Truesdell's legacy. May his actions never be forgotten for all of us to emulate."

Perry McCoy closed the ceremony, reminding those present that the event was special. "Marker dedications aren't common anymore, but they are a reminder of our history."

Gladys had gotten into the habit of fighting during her long marriage to Don. She could not stop, aggravated in conversations with her children. Dee talked to her about it. Stephen pointed out that she had only so many years left in life. "Why not be happy during them?" Lois Lee showed her mother the 1956 Lee family photo. "Look at how happy you looked. Why don't you try to look that happy again?" It was to no avail.

Gladys was likely depressed, but refused to see a doctor. She had spent her entire adult life with a man proud to have been a Marine. She often said things like a Marine would say. "I'll just kick myself in the butt and get going," she would insist.

Her mini strokes had begun in 1982. By 2008, she had lost both her speech and the ability to swallow anything more than ice cream. She asked Dee to keep the family together. Then, she did what Don had done fifteen years before. "She turned her face to the wall and starved herself to death." [97]

Gladys Claire Garrity Truesdell, 86, died on June 11, 2008. She was the third burial at St. John's Methodist Cemetery since Donald's funeral. She is the last of twelve Truesdells buried with the family.

There was that attic trunk where Don had stored his Marine memorabilia. [98] After the funeral, when they cleaned out the house, the siblings felt safe to inventory the contents. The divorce papers and lawyers' depositions from their father's first marriage to "Margret" were in the trunk.

Don's children had never asked about the details and knew very little about that marriage. Don had talked a little to Stephen about it, but never to his daughters. Gladys knew some of the "dirt" about the other woman. At one point, just before or after Don had died, she had mailed a package of information to her children with a cover letter in which she detailed the first marriage.

Dee, for one, would later remember opening the package, reading the first part of the letter, and throwing it all away without reading further. [99] As the oldest of six children in a turbulent household, she had enough information rattling around in her brain and did not need any more. She saw no purpose in reading through the materials and did not care to demean her daddy. Gayle and Lois would not recall ever receiving the package from their Mama, but Gay did keep her father's divorce papers in a "lock box" at home.

Stephen retrieved the *Book of Contacts* that logged the many patrols and engagements his father had participated in during the Banana Wars. He also kept photographs of him in uniform—some in his Marine uniform, but wearing the Guardia Nacional second lieutenant rank and insignia. Jeff took some of the items in the trunk, which have since disappeared. Some items were donated to Post 17. The Military Museum in Columbia was also interested in some of the memorabilia to keep on display.

"And, now we are four."

Gladys' youngest child followed her in death. Outdoorsman David Jeffrey Truesdell, 57, did not make it to the New Year. He died on Saturday, December 31, 2011. According to his obituary, he was survived by his wife, Betsy, Dede Truesdell and Fred Schindler, Stephen and Ginger Truesdell, Gay and Butch Lilly, and Lois Bradley. The family requested that memorials be made to the Intrepid Fallen Heroes Fund, New York, New York. [100]

His siblings understood that Jeff wanted his ashes sprinkled on an island in the Five and Twenty Creek—his father's beloved land. Their brother had been a very colorful character, marching through life to his own music. In the spring, family and friends gathered on the island "down at the creek." They toasted Jeff with leis and Margaritas, honored his wishes, and sent him off.

Dee found comfort in the tributes. "So, Daddy and Jeff are really part of the Creek now." [101]

Lois, closest in age to Jeff, said to her siblings, "And, now we are four."

On Saturday morning, August 23, 2014, local KOOL 102.7 FM radio reported in its local news that a gathering was occurring at the James Leroy Belk American Legion Post No. 17. Military veterans, interested residents, and family members of Kershaw County's three MOH recipients were there for the start of a ceremony. The I-20 Bridge between Lugoff and Camden, east of the Wateree Farm Ponds and over the place where Buck Creek empties into the Wateree River, was officially re-named in honor of Richmond Hobson Hilton, John C. Villepigue, and Donald Leroy Truesdell. [102]

Newly-installed Legion Post 17 Commander Clay Carruth spoke about the importance of remembering the deeds of Kershaw county's heroes. The bridge is a little more than a mile-and-a-half across woodlands and agricultural fields southwest of the three recipients' memorial monuments in *Little Arlington*.

On March 18, 2010, the U.S. Department of Defense Budget for 2010 was reported to include a super-expensive Zumwalt-class 'stealth' guided missile destroyer to be named the USS *Donald L. Truesdale*, Hull Code, DDG-1003. The fourth ship in its class, it was planned to be laid down in 2011, launched in 2014, and commissioned for service in 2016. [103]

The USS *Zumwalt*, DDG 1000, built at Bath Iron Works in Maine, was launched on October 29, 2013. She headed out to sea for the first time on Monday, December 8, 2015. The USS *Michael Monsoor*, DDG 1001, was christened and launched on June 21, 2016. The USS *Lyndon B. Johnson*, DDG-1002, encountered budget conflicts, was still under construction at the end of 2016, and planned for a 2018 commissioning date. Dealing with the budget pressures, Department of Defense officials considered terminating funding for Zumwalt-class destroyers and pushed the Navy to chop DDG-1003 from its plans. The debate for the USS *Donald L. Truesdale* continues.

Twelve days after Donald Truesdell's death, two U.S. Army soldiers, Master Sergeant Gary I. Gordon and Sergeant First Class Randall D. Shughart, earned posthumous Medals demonstrating exceptional valor in combat engagements in Mogadishu, Somalia, on October 3, 1993. Since 2002, during the ongoing War on Terror, the Medal of Honor has been awarded to sixteen soldiers and Marines in Iraq and Afghanistan. Eleven survived to have President Barack Obama present the Medal to them at White House ceremonies. [104] Two of the three Marines saved companions from a grenade blast.

Across those same years, the recipients from WWII, Korea, and Vietnam continued to greet each other on *Heaven's Scenes*.

The CMOHS's annual convention convened in Boston on Wednesday, September 16, 2015, two years after the marathon bombings killed three spectators and wounded 260 others. Invitations went to the seventy-eight living MOH recipients from World War II, Korea, Vietnam, and Afghanistan. [105] The six oldest were WWII veterans. Six had survived Korea. Forty-two attended the reunion.

Blessed to live long lives, they might be idealistic and wish for "the greatest thing in the world," that no new members be added to the MOH muster roll; but they are also pragmatists. There will always be "wars and rumors of wars." [106]

The number of living Medal recipients is the lowest it has ever been since the Medal of Honor Legion was formed in 1890.

Don's influence on his descendants comes to mind at times. On Tuesday, July 12, 2016, the first of his two grandsons were in Navarra, Spain, attending the San Fermin Festival. Paul Bradley, aged 45, dressed in traditional white pants and t-shirt, with a red bandana around his neck, "Ran with the Bulls" down the center of a narrow, cobbled thoroughfare in the old quarter of Pamplona. Spectators watched from balconies and cheered on the multitude of mozos (runners) trying to outrun the beasts. Two of the six black, 1,600-pound fighting bulls charged behind Paul on their way to the bullring. The pointed curve of one toro bravo's long horn nearly grazed his back, but he veered aside and avoided being gored. Paul had never shown any inclination to be reckless, so his Pamplona escapade generated a little contemplation in the family. Dee Truesdell had her opinion.

"I think Daddy would point to the family gene pool." [107]

✳✳✳

Corporal Donald Truesdell took an action inconsistent with the nervous system's instinctive reactions. He could have sheltered himself away from the imminent blast of a grenade, wholly consistent with survival instincts. Instead, he tried to get the dangerous explosive away from himself and others. Many more Marines have followed, acting completely contrary to what their own nervous systems would dictate. Few survived.

Remembering those who have passed on, like Don Roy Truesdell, is now more important so that the images and representations of genuine bravery and valor do not vanish into dusty histories.

CHAPTER 7

Dynamic Upheavals

✳✳✳

"May you have a strong foundation when the winds of change shift." [1]

— BOB DYLAN, DULUTH, MINNESOTA

ONLY NINE YEARS HAD PASSED from the time of Corporal Donald Truesdale's September 3, 1932 award ceremony in Managua until another Marine, First Lieutenant George Ham Cannon, earned a posthumous Medal of Honor on Midway Island: December 7, 1941.

Eighty-two Marines earned Medals of Honor during WWII, six in somewhat isolated engagements: on Engebi Island; off the Eniwetok Atoll of the Marshall Islands; on Makin Atoll in the Gilbert (now Tungaru) Islands. Marines earned the other seventy-six Medals in clusters during well-known operations: Guadalcanal and Bougainville in the Solomon Islands; Tarawa, the low-lying, coral atoll in the Gilbert Islands; Roi-Namur of the Kwajalein Atoll in the Marshall Islands; Guam, Tinian, and Saipan in the Marianas; Peleliu in the Palau group; Iwo Jima in the Izu Shoto Islands; and Okinawa Shima in the Ryukyu Islands. Twenty-two Marines, the greatest number of Medals of Honor awarded in Marine Corps history during a single operation, earned the valor distinction in thirty-six days of fighting on Iwo Jima.

Marines began having close-hand encounters with enemy grenades on Makin Atoll and Guadalcanal Island in August and September 1942. Two acting against natural instincts to survive and willing to offer their lives that companions might live sacrificed themselves on grenades on Bougainville in November 1943. The toll for those cradling grenades began rising on February 1, 1944, when three earned Medals of Honor on the Marshall Islands atolls. Two followed on Saipan, two on Tinian, six on Peleliu, eight on Iwo Jima, and five on Okinawa. Of the twenty-seven Marines who earned Medals for saving fellows from grenades in WWII, twenty-three were killed in action. Four Marines dived onto grenades in battle and survived the horrible blasts.

Descendants of Norsemen

Sorenson is the kind of last name that brings to mind regions in Iowa and Minnesota. Families sharing this name also share Norwegian ancestors. The earliest "Norskie" arrivals to America's shores were agriculturalists with given names like Nels, Jens, Olaf, Ole, Otto, Soren, and Swen. They had an affinity for Norse lore and sailing on ships. Many could still read and interpret rune stones.

Soren and Jensina Sorenson-Lah brought their family to America from Gaupne, Sogn og Fjordane fylke, Norway, in 1854. The eldest of their children, 19-year-old Frederik Lah, remained in Norway. [2] The family homesteaded in Silver Lake, Worth County, north central

Iowa, above Mason City, just under the Minnesota border and due south of Albert Lea. The region supported the summer home lodgings of the Sioux and Winnebago native tribes.

Just before the start of the American Civil War, Nels Christian Sorenson-Lah was born in November 1859. Nels was the seventh and last child of the newly arrived immigrants. He lived with three brothers and three sisters, all born in their native land. Before his death in 1912, Nels would have children, grandchildren, siblings, uncles and aunts, cousins, and nieces and nephews throughout Worth County and stretching north into Albert Lea, Minnesota, and beyond.

Jens Sorenson Lah was his second-oldest brother. Jens was proud to be a veteran of the Grand Army of the Republic after the Civil War. He married Marit Olsdatter Sorbo, a Norwegian immigrant from Vang, Oppland fylke, Norway. They lived in Emmons, Minnesota, and had twelve children.

Nels' third brother also fought during the Civil War upheavals. Soren Sorenson, 21 years old, enlisted in Company K, 27th Iowa Volunteer Infantry, on August 8, 1862, and served for three years. In 1868, he married 19-year-old Jorgine Knutson, born in Oslo, Norway. They moved up to Freeborn County, Minnesota, and over many years farmed near Austin, Hayward, and, finally, Albert Lea. They had twelve children together, and were blessed by seventeen grandchildren and four great grandchildren.

The Sorenson girls lived out their lives in Worth County. Metta married Torkel Torkelson Brua and they had two children. Anna Sophia married Asgrim G. Dahl, and they had six children. Marie Kristense, youngest of the girls, married John Anderson. They farmed the Lah homestead and had three children.

Nels Sorenson married Mary Anderson from Forest City, and they had six children before the start of the First World War. Carl Siren Sorenson was their first boy, born on February 7, 1896. His older sister, Jeanette Sorenson-Lah, married Oscar Eckland and raised two children in Freeborn County. Carl was also brother to one younger sister and three brothers—Alvin, Mabel, Raymond K., and Morris N. [3] Family was dear to the Sorensons, and the siblings would have close ties.

Carl was 16 years old when his father, aged 53, died on May 3, 1912. Nels was buried in plot 63 at the Emmons' Oak Lawn Cemetery on the Minnesota-Iowa State Line Road.

Five years after the funeral, America entered WW I on April 6, 1917. Sorensons answered the call. Carl joined the Navy and served as a gunner on a tanker in the North Atlantic. He also served on the USS *New Mexico* battleship. [4]

In early July 1918, Private Fred Sorenson, of Benson, in west central Minnesota, went by train down to Camp Wadsworth in Spartanburg, South Carolina, and joined Company "G", 54th Pioneer Infantry. Private Herdum Sorenson left 3326 Minnehaha Avenue S, Minneapolis, and joined Company "L". [5]

The companies left Virginia on August 30, 1918, on the *Caserta* transport, to battle the Hun, debarking at Brest on September 12. The Sorensons fought through the Clermont Woods, Bourieulles, Varennes, Avocourt, Malancourt, and Montfaucon. After victory was declared in Europe on November 11, 1918, they moved through Vauchreville, Verdun, Dun-sur-Meuse, Consenvove, and various villages and towns in Germany, joining the Army of Occupation, Third U.S. Army, on December 24, 1918. The 54th was garrisoned near the German towns of Wittlich and Coblenz, where the Rhine and Moselle rivers joined, until ordered home on December 30. The companies began returning home in January 1919.

Carl Siren Sorenson was discharged from the Navy after the November 11th Armistice and returned to Minnesota. His next younger brother, Alvin was the head of the household in

Shell Rock Township, Freeborn County. His mother and two youngest brothers lived there. Carl resided with them and worked as a farm laborer for a wage.

Meeting Brides in Duluth

The veteran had extended family living up in the region around Duluth, Minnesota. On a visit north, he met Virginia A. Mox. She was a first-generation American, two years younger than he, working as a cashier at the Duluth theater. Her sister Jean, a telephone operator, was also adding earnings to the Mox family nest egg. Both young women lived with their parents at 918 8th Avenue East, on the north side of town between Central and East hillsides. The spelling of their parent's surnames had been abbreviated once they had come to America. Facts about how their father had arrived in the new land, as told to later generations, were a little vague and shrouded in mystery.

Frank William Wachasovich Mox was born on May 2, 1866, in Prussia when people of Polish descent were struggling to regain their independence from Russia, Germany, and Austria. Poland had been divided into four sections at the time of his birth. Census records give his birthplace as Leipzig, Germany, in the Zaxony region. Frank's "mother tongue" was Polish. His grandparents had been landowners during the Prussian Revolution of 1848. His father was later involved in the uprising of 1863–1864, after which Russia enacted reforms that disempowered the landed gentry and allowed peasants to stake claims on confiscated lands.

When Frank was an adolescent, his father was executed, apparently for his part in the earlier uprising. [6] Mox families had departed for a better life in America and were putting down roots in Maryland, New York, Pennsylvania, Ohio, Indiana, and Michigan. Fearing reprisals against her son, or conscription into the Russian Army, Frank's mother sent him to live with monks for safety. They eventually got him to the Port of Bremen, Germany. In 1884, a monk went to the Norddeutscher Lloyd Steamship Company and walked from the office with a Prepaid Passage Receipt, Good For One Year from the Date of Issue.

"Received from (said Monk) the sum of Twenty-two Dollars for the passage of Frank William Wachasovich Moxhe, as one in steerage of one of the Steamers of the North German Lloyd from Bremen to New York, district of the United States."

Over the age of 12 years, Frank was considered an adult passenger, and his steerage ticket was without a space reservation. He boarded the SS *Hermann* for his transatlantic journey, leaving behind his brother, Bruno Mox, and looked for any place he might recline in the ship's lower, converted cargo deck. He hoped for a short trip, as the compartments were notoriously crowded, dark, unsanitary, and foul smelling. Depending on the sea conditions, he spent as much time as possible on the benches along the upper deck.

Once disembarking in America, he boarded a train to Duluth to join a few relatives who had already emigrated from Europe. His brother, Bruno, also came to Duluth at some point.

How and when Frank met his bride is not clear. Mary Jaski was born on March 6, 1873, in Germany. Her family had immigrated to America in 1881, when she was eight years old, and settled in Duluth. Her parents spoke in the Polish tongue and had shortened their name from Jaździewski (or Jaszczerski) when they emigrated. She was only 12 years old when Frank found lodging in Duluth.

Frank married 16-year-old Mary on May 2, 1889. She delivered eight children by the time she was age 36. Frank Jr., their first child, was born three years after their wedding vows. [7] The couple became naturalized citizens in 1895. The next year, their first daughter, Marion, was born. Every couple of years thereafter, another child joined them: Virginia A., Genevieve, Martha, Leo, Raymond, and Rose.

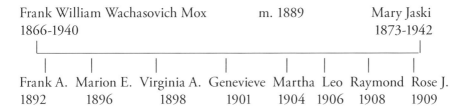

Frank William Wachasovich Mox	m. 1889	Mary Jaski
1866-1940		1873-1942

Frank A.	Marion E.	Virginia A.	Genevieve	Martha	Leo	Raymond	Rose J.
1892	1896	1898	1901	1904	1906	1908	1909

Frank Sr. worked as a packer at a wholesale hardware. To support his growing family and put some savings away, he was always on the lookout for another job. He got to know the foreman in the Northern Pacific Railroad Company warehouse, Robert Duncan "R.D." McKercher. "R.D." was eight years younger than Frank and was going to become prominent in Duluth civic affairs, eventually being appointed Chief of Police.

Having been on good terms for many years, Chief McKercher guided Frank into fulfilling the department's hiring requirements. Once he passed muster to enter upon "public duties as a humane agent" for the City of Duluth, Frank served on the police and fire departments, which took him out into the various communities. The two men maintained a friendship when Chief McKercher entered the automobile business with the Oldsmobile Sales Company in Duluth.

Frank would be pleased that all his children followed his example. They grew into responsible and hard-working citizens, and found life partners, just as he had.

Marriages occurred in proper birth order for the elder Mox children. In 1918, Frank Jr. was the first to marry. Employed as a plumber, he and his wife, Mary B., the daughter of a German immigrant, resided at 108½ East 8th Street in Duluth. However Frank Jr. got along with his German in-laws, he and Carl Sorenson had war stories to tell each other. Frank had joined the 54th Pioneer Infantry with 2,031 other Minnesota men in August 1918. [8] He left the States aboard the *Duca d'Aosta* transport, debarked with the Supply Company at Brest, and fought in the Clermont Woods. In the last six weeks of the Meuse-Argonne offensive, he was at Bourieulles and Aubreville, and after the Armistice, he moved through Varennes, Montfaucon, Dun-sur-Meuse, Verdun, and Longuyon. On December 3, he joined the Army of Occupation, and stayed in German towns until coming home to Duluth in 1919. [9]

Marion Mox married in 1919, after her older brother and her fiancé were back from the war. Leonard P. "L.P." Gagnon had served as a PFC in the Army Medical Department. The couple lived in an apartment on 52nd Avenue West, close to his family. "L.P." worked as a truck driver at a foundry, then as a machinist in the shipyards. Grandchildren soon added joy to the lives of Frank Sr. and Mary Mox.

Carl Sorenson took Virginia Mox to be his bride in 1920. Their marriage proved to be a lasting bond. Rather than return to the Shell Rock farm, the young couple decided to live with the Mox family in Duluth, while Carl looked for employment. Relocations and changing addresses would seem routine over the next years.

Settling in Anoka and Flint

In 1922, Frank Sr. moved his family to Anoka, eighteen miles from central Minneapolis. He had enough in savings to put a deposit down on a two-story, white frame house at 444 Benton

Street, the second house from the corner of Green Avenue. At the time, the three bedrooms and two bathrooms could accommodate more than a single family. Built in 1900, mature lawns and trees surrounded the home on three sides. For anyone wanting to go fishing, two rivers flowed nearby. The family lived blocks north of the Mississippi River and west of the Rum River. Grandpa Mox opened Franks Mobile Gas Station and Confectionery on the corner of Benton Street and South Ferry.

The Village of Anoka is the county seat and a northwest suburb of Minneapolis. It was a patriotic community of about 4,300 residents. Twenty-eight of the east-west streets had been named for the first thirty two U.S. presidents. Not that it had anything to do with patriotism or with the Mox's settling there, Anoka had earned a title after WWI. In 1920, the village hosted one of the first Halloween parades in the U.S. Ever afterwards, the annual event captured the nation's curiosity, and Anoka became the *Halloween Capital of the World*.

Life in Anoka reflected how close-nit was the family. Frank Jr. and Mary Mox lived on Fremont Street, one block north of Frank Sr. "L.P." and Marion Gagnon lived on the next block on Park Street. Their children, gregarious cousins, would be able to walk back and forth through back yards to play together.

Carl and Virginia resided in the two-story at 444 Benton Street. So, they did not have far to go when Virginia's time arrived. Three blocks east, at 1841 South Ferry Street, Gates Hospital (today an apartment building) overlooked the Rum River. The hospital was a one-block walk north of Frank's gas station.

Richard Keith "Ricky" Sorenson was born at Gates on August 28, 1924.

That was the same year Grandpa Frank Mox had an idea. He had not forgotten his love of the land. Getting his hands into soil and growing things was a reminder of his Prussian homeland. From the east bank of the Foster farm in Ramsey County, north of Anoka, he looked at twenty-two acres of woodland across a narrow, 200-foot channel of the Mississippi. Undeveloped Foster Island was the fifth island upriver from the mouth of the Rum: seven miles upriver to be exact. Nearby Cloquet was the fourth upriver island and was more than twice the size of Foster. [10]

Grandpa Frank leased Foster Island from the Miss & RR Boom Company for $10 a year (buying power of $137 in 2016). His two youngest sons, Ray and Lee, still single teenagers, got busy and erected a small, temporary building to live in. That made them the first white people to inhabit the island. Ray hauled the lumber up river from Anoka in a rowboat, making one trip a day. The prevailing winds in the spring made navigating the river a challenge. The brothers tapped maple trees for syrup in the spring, raised tomatoes and strawberries in the summer, and cut firewood in the winter. They brought boatloads of firewood and produce downriver, which was a more pleasant trip. [11]

Frank Sr. had watched the ferry carry autos from Itasca Station across to Dayton and taught the boys the proper technique to navigate a boat line. They stretched a cable from Foster's farm across to the tiny beach landing on the island's east side and used a large boat for a ferry. In winter, they could drive automobiles back and forth on the ice.

Genevieve (Jean) Mox married Ralph McLaughlin in Anoka in 1925 and moved into an apartment on Wingfield Avenue, north of Main and close to the elementary school. They would move to Fremont Street later, a block from Benton, when Ralph started working as a machine adjuster in an ammunition factory.

Running a service station, Grandpa Frank maintained his many connections to people in the automobile and truck industry. He was also familiar with Michigan, because many extended Mox families farmed around Grand Traverse Bay in Michigan's northwestern Lower Peninsula.

Carl Sorenson found employment with the Buick Corporation, "the maker of premium automobiles" and General Motors Corporation's financial pillar. He and others in the family moved to Flint, Genesee County, Michigan, in 1926. Raymond and Rose Mox moved with them. Carl rented a house at 816 Mary Street on the west side of the Flint River. Employed as a machinist at the auto manufacturing factory, on his days off he liked to fiddle with his radio set at home or fish on the river. The young family's prospects seemed good for the next three years.

Ricky Sorenson was too young to remember the family festivities leading up to his Aunt Rose, the youngest Mox sibling, being the first to live a great distance from the family. She had met a man in Flint. When she was old enough to marry—that was in 1927 when she turned 18 years—she married Walter H. Brog. They moved to Seattle, Washington, and lived for years in an apartment at 6002 East Lee Street in the Madison Park neighborhood. Rose was a short walk from Lake Washington and was often reminded of her early life living on the shores of Lake Superior. Walt started out as a collection agent for a credit union.

One of Ricky's earliest memories was that his little brother, William, was born in Flint on November 24, 1927. That was Thanksgiving Day. Between the two brothers, Bill's birth would be a great source of bantering about Sorenson turkeys. Apart from his birthday and the national holiday, one future Thanksgiving would have great significance for Bill and the Marine Corps.

Ricky's next "big memory" happened a year later, in the months before and after his 5th birthday party.

In 1929, Grandpa Frank, Ray, and Lee cut logs and built a cabin with a cellar on Foster Island. Grandpa built a wood saw and a fireplace. There was an abundance of firewood for fuel. In addition to having excellent drinking water eight feet away, they dug a well with a pump inside the cabin. They put in a crystal radio set with two sets of headphones. Ray and Lee lived in the cabin for three consecutive years. Young Ray trapped muskrat, mink, and weasel depending on the season, and watched the hunting methods of the large owls that habited the island. The Mox "wilderness men" ate rabbits all winter.

Sometimes, the locals made mention of the log cabin on *Mox Island*. Ray and Lee would agree that some of their happiest days were on their island.

Ricky spent some of his summer vacations on the island, where he had many fond, childhood memories of times with his grandparents. [12] Mostly, his greatest pleasure on the island was fishing with his grandpa, dad, and uncles. The latter days of October 1929 were not counted among the happy ones.

October 29, 1929, the infamous *Black Tuesday*, was the day the stock market crashed and lost fourteen billion dollars. Individual market investors, businesses, and bank customers lost their money. Businesses and banks declared bankruptcy and closed. Ten years of economic hard times were ahead for all of America. As bank failures continued, the decline of the money supply had far-ranging impact. The biggest was unemployment.

On average, 12,000 people lost jobs every day. In three-years time, 20,000 companies and 1,616 banks went bankrupt, and twelve million people were out of work—one of every four American workers. Some of General Motors' competitors went under, but GM managed to stay afloat by consolidating its operations, closing plants, and laying off employees. Consumers across the country were left with no money, and the demand for premium automobiles went into a serious slump. Buick was hit hard.

Vera McFarland worked her way along Mary Street and found the Sorensons home on April 31, 1930, to take census information. Carl was still employed as a machinist.

Back in Anoka City's First Ward on April 3, 1930, the 29th dwelling George D. Goodrich, enumerator, visited was the household of Frank Jr. and Mary Mox on Fremont Street. Ricky's cousins, Francis, 10, and Clifford, 4, were at home. Two doors later to the north, George sat down with L.P. and Marion Gagnon on Park Street. Kenneth James, 9, and Virginia May, 8, were somewhere in the house "doing homework."

Soon after the Flint enumeration was completed, Carl and other family members lost their jobs at the auto plants. The family returned to Anoka and moved back into the Mox home on Benton Street. An implement company hired Carl as a machinist. With so many children and grandchildren living in the home, the grandparents relocated to the "cottage" on Mox Island. Ricky looked forward to visiting the retreat on weekends.

Another cousin joined the family. Beatrice Mox was born in 1931. Frank Jr. worked as a plumber in building construction, supporting a wife, two sons, and a daughter. He and Mary moved from Fremont Street to 602 Benton Street on the corner of Levee Avenue, a block away from his parents. "L.P." was earning a living as a deliveryman and clerk at the nearby grocery store. With a son and daughter to get to school, he and Marion moved to 624 Benton Street, three houses west of the Mox home.

It must have seemed that the Mox, Gagnon, McLaughlin, and Sorenson kids filled the neighborhood—Francis, Clifford, and Beatrice Mox, Kenneth and Virginia Gagnon, Robert and William McLaughlin, Ricky and William. No matter in what direction Ricky would walk from home, he might encounter an uncle, aunt, or a cousin. The older cousins often included the younger boys in their river adventures. The boys were all childhood companions.

Ricky enjoyed close relationships with his three grandparents. His Grandmother Mary Sorenson eventually moved from Shell Rock to Albert Lea to be nearer her adult children and her grandchildren. Everyone looked forward to weekend visits to the island cottage.

Franklin Elementary School at 215 West Main Street was a six-block walk north from home. [13] The primary school did not have a kindergarten at the time, so Ricky's education began in first grade a week after his 7th birthday in 1931. He passed by his grandpa's Mobile Gas Station and Confectionery every school day. Due to a series of illnesses, Ricky missed much of the school year. Carl and Virginia accepted the teacher's recommendation that he repeat first grade. [14] He began catching up in fall 1932, and trekked to Franklin until he finished sixth grade. He was going to grow taller than his classmates and would impress school coaches with his athleticism.

1934 Celebrations

Ricky was in second grade. The New Year started out promising for his Aunt Martha. Clarence C. Hall had proposed. The last of Frank's daughters to marry, Martha said her vows in January and promised to visit home as often as she could after moving to Miami Beach, Florida. The sisters began planning. Before the year ended, the Anoka *Union* society pages informed readers that the Mox family had enjoyed at least one happy month in 1934.

Rose came from Seattle with her two-year-old son, Bobbie Lee, to spend the summer with her parents at the island cottage. Martha arrived in August. The entire Mox family was all together in Anoka for the first time in 10 years. [15] The family celebrated Ricky's 10th birthday on August 28.

Mary Mox invited her daughters' high school friends for an afternoon tea on what the newspaper columnist liked to call "Languor Island." Marion had the family over for dinner. Lee Mox was host for an outdoor supper on the island, and Miss Alice Baldwin, his fiancée from a Swedish family in North Dakota, gave an afternoon party. Rose left the island on September 13. Martha left on September 26.

Carl and his boys enjoyed the outdoors, hunting and fishing whenever there was time.

Since Ricky repeated first grade, Bill was only two grades behind him in school, rather than three years as their age difference might have determined. That changed in the 1936–1937 school year when Ricky was in fifth grade and Bill was in third. An incident involving the boys' love of football occurred during one recess. [16]

Mr. Wes Mason, the Anoka football coach, brought a ball over to Franklin Elementary for recess and got a game together. Just as the bell rang for the kids to come in, Bill, 9 years old, was carrying the ball. He was tackled, and everybody piled on top of him. He felt the middle of his right shin break. He tried to get up, but couldn't. He told the coach he thought his leg was broken.

"You got a Charlie horse. Get up and walk on it."

Bill tried and fell again. Ricky and one of the Spurzem twins, either Robert or Richard, from Benton Street, helped him up and into the classroom. Mrs. Dempsey wanted to know what was going on, and the coach told her about the Charlie horse.

"Make him walk on it," he advised.

The teacher tried, and Bill fell flat on his face. She was sure he was faking, dragged him to his desk, and had him sit for the rest of the day. At 5:00 o'clock, she packed up her things. "I'm leaving," she said. "You can go anytime you want."

Abandoned in a seemingly empty school, Bill hoped a janitor would come down the hall. Another Benton Street neighbor had been made to stay after school. When he came downstairs from Mrs. Smith's room, Bill got on his back. He was able to carry him down the steps and out the door, but no farther. He put the third grader down. "When I go by your house," he promised, "I'll tell your mother."

Virginia did not drive, so she rushed from the house and kitty-corner over to Mrs. Esther Weaver's for help. Esther did drive a car and happened to be on the school board. Bill was sitting outside the school when they pulled up. The two women examined his leg. It *was* broken. They carried him in their arms to the car and hurried to Gates Hospital. An x-ray showed the break. An intern put a tongue suppressor in Bill's mouth, had the women hold him down, and set the leg with a swift jerk. On went a cast, and Bill was out of school for six weeks. The Sorensons lived upstairs, and when the cast came off, Bill had to learn to walk all over again.

Mrs. Dempsey flunked him, and he had to repeat the third grade, putting him a year behind the Spurzems and three grades behind his big brother.

Twists and Turns of Junior High

Beginning in fall 1938, Ricky walked east, crossed the Rum River Bridge, and began seventh grade at the junior high on the corner of 2nd Avenue and Monroe Street. The junior high shared the same building with Anoka High School. Ricky walked the hallways with 699 junior and high school students. The school had no cafeteria, so, like many students, he planned to either take the short walk home for lunch or carry his lunch with him. [17]

At the end of April 1939, he said a goodbye to his maternal grandparents. Grandpa Frank was retiring from working at his service station, and he and Grandma Mox took a trip to visit

Aunt Rose. Uncle Walter was doing well as a bakery salesman and had bought a nice home for his wife and son at 10726 Palatine Avenue in North Seattle.

Walt drove his in-laws a little over a mile west of the house for a scenic ride along the Puget Sound. The number of overcast spring days was a usual mealtime conversation. For those with rain gauges, precipitation had almost reached the three-inch mark by April's end. One afternoon when the temperature got above 50°F, Billie Lee walked his grandpa over to Pipers Creek in Carkeek Park. The unquestionable highlight of the visit was the 50th Mox-Jaski Wedding Anniversary on May 2.

Ricky readied himself for eighth grade that summer. A second addition was under construction on the west end of the school building, and extensive repairs on the older part of the school were almost completed. Before the doors opened for the start of the school year, a true dynamic upheaval almost blew the doors from their frames.

Besides looking out for his little brother, Ricky experienced the endangerment of neighbors' lives and volunteering to render aid to those in dire need. When people around the nation paid 3¢ for their newspapers, if they did not already know, the headlines alerted them to the disaster in Anoka.

Nine Dead: 220 Injured. Sunday, June 18, 1939, was not the most pleasant of summer days in Anoka. The heat was "sultry," drizzling rain fell intermittently, and hail chased many children and grownups into shelters. Many attending a carnival midway on the outskirts of the town had gone home. Picnics and trips to lakes had been postponed for a better day, which ultimately turned out to be a good thing.

A towering, black, funnel-shaped cloud touched down near Corcoran Village, ten miles southwest of Anoka, demolished four dwellings, and struck a car on rural State Highway 101, tossing it 200 yards into a field, smashing the vehicle to pieces, and killing all four occupants—the Minneapolis man behind the wheel and three women passengers.

Travelling to the northeast for five minutes, destroying farm houses in its path, the twister hit Champlin, killing one man, injuring thirty, and wrecking several homes and buildings. Then, it crossed over the Mississippi at the mouth of the Rum River, lifting the waters until the river bottom was in view and stopping the current's flow until the funnel hit the river's north bank on the south side of Anoka.

The funnel blasted into Washington Street and 2d Avenue on the east side of Rum at 3:28 PM, and cut a path two-to-three-blocks wide diagonally to 3rd Avenue across the town, moving with terrific speed through fifty square blocks of the "little Mississippi river town"— hitting Adams, Jefferson, Madison, skimming past the high school at Monroe, crossing Main, then Jackson, Van Buren, and kept going until the storm hit Roosevelt and passed from town.

The twister swept through the carnival grounds, wrecked the Ferris wheel, and damaged the merry-go-round. The armory was wrecked, one wall completely gone. Buildings fell, trees were uprooted, dropped onto houses and into yards, and timbers were thrown as high as 300 feet into the air. Small articles of furniture, personal belongings, clothing, and papers were carried fifty to seventy miles into the next counties.

The sudden fury levelled or damaged as many as 250 private homes, demolished two churches, wrecked the Masonic Temple, destroyed much of Main Street, and obliterated normal water, electric, and telephone services. The tornado just missed Anoka High School. A violent rain and hailstorm followed. Storm debris covered the streets. It was difficult to estimate the number of residents who had so quickly been rendered homeless.

The injured jammed Gates Hospital, lying in hallways and on the floors of rooms. The high school served as an emergency hospital. Kerosene lamps and candles initially gave physicians flickering light to administer first aid. Emergency gasoline generators later provided glaring lights. Many of the seriously injured were transported to Minneapolis hospitals.

Newly elected Governor Harold Edward Strassen arrived within hours to personally direct relief. Three hundred 2d Battalion, 151st Field Artillery, Minnesota National Guardsmen patrolled the streets, maintaining order and directing rescue efforts, putting the town under martial law. The 300 American Legionnaires attending a district convention at the city hall volunteered for police duty. Roads into the village were blocked to all but official traffic. A drastic 9:00 PM curfew was put into effect to keep the streets clear during the night. Large utility crews rushed in and began the work of restoring the infrastructure, a task that would take weeks. The state militia remained on duty until June 26, when traffic was permitted back into the city. [18]

The death toll in the wake of the storm did not reach the numbers initially feared. The *Anoka Union* newspaper surveyed the devastation and reported that 240 families and 1,450 persons were affected by the disaster. Property loss was estimated at $500,000 ($8,447,321 in 2016).

Later, a newspaper reporter nicknamed one of the school teams the *Tornadoes*, and the name resonated with the community. Anoka High School became the *Home of the Tornadoes*.

More than the summer tornado, events in September 1939, altered the course Ricky's life otherwise might have taken. In March, Nazi Germany had taken Czechoslovakia. On a Friday, three days after Ricky's 15th birthday and days before the Labor Day holiday, the Nazis invaded Poland on September 1. The war in Europe had started. Grandpa Mox had his thoughts about the invasion.

Another Move

Carl rented a home at 4500 South Blaisdell Avenue, on the corner of West 45th Street in Minneapolis, and moved the family for a short time. There were lakes and parks within an easy bicycle ride, but Anoka, eighteen miles up the Mississippi, remained central in Ricky's life.

Ricky's maternal grandparents were members of the Church of St. Stephen Catholic parish. Grandma Mary was a devout member of the Holy Rosary Society. Both had a close relationship with Father E. S. de Courcy. Frank suffered an unexpected stroke at home on Benton Street on Thursday night, July 4, 1940, and never regained consciousness. He died on Sunday night, aged 74. Ricky attended the funeral services and followed the hearse to Calvary Cemetery on the south side of town, just outside of downtown.

Grandma Mary was not left on her own. Lee and Alice and their five-month-old daughter, Patricia, lived with her. Ray also resided with them. The 30-year-old bachelor was thinking that he would one day marry Minnie Philibina Pomraning from Ramsey Township.

By the time of Grandpa Mox's funeral, the Soviet Union had allied itself with Germany, split Poland with the Nazis, and invaded Finland. Hitler's forces had invaded Denmark, Norway, France, Belgium, Luxembourg, and the Netherlands. Europe appeared to be surrendering one country after another to the Nazis. Allied troops had evacuated from Dunkirk. Italy had declared war on Britain and France, and the Germans had occupied Paris. German U-boats were attacking merchant ships in the Atlantic, and Hitler was planning the Battle of Britain.

In the week before Ricky's 16th birthday, newspaper headlines continued to cast doubt on U.S. neutrality. The Italians were occupying lands in East Africa, and the German bombing of England's airfields and factories had begun. Hitler ordered a blockade of the British Isles and air raids on London. In September 1940, as Ricky started ninth grade with the Class of 1944, the Germans were expected to begin an invasion of Britain.

High school football rivalries were a welcome diversion from the escalation of war in Europe for teens and families in schools and homes. Fifty-three sophomores, juniors, and seniors put on *Tornadoes* uniforms for the 1940 season. As a freshman, Ricky would not be on the varsity football team roster. He would be inspired, however.

In five of their victories, the *Tornadoes* defense shut out St. Louis Park, Princeton, Elk River, Milaca, and Osseo. The offense carried the day in two wins against St. Cloud Cathedral and Cambridge. The one game that would "live long in the memory of Anoka sport fans as the hardest-fought high school game they [had] ever seen" was against the Hastings *Raiders*. The final score was 13–12. The *Tornadoes* only loss of the season was that one-point margin. [19]

After the loss to Hastings, something remarkable happened. The *Tornadoes* won their last four games and went on record as the 1940 District Champions. Seven outstanding players earned All-District honors.

Alert to vacancies left by the graduating seniors, Coach G. Nash and his assistant coaches, Arch G. Pease and E. R. Larson, watched for more potential talent in the school hallways. They had their eye on Ricky, taller and heavier than most of his classmates. He was going to experience the exhilaration of playing on a winning team. The *Tornadoes* went on an 18-game winning streak for the remainder of his high school days.

Richard had his photograph in the spring 1941 *Anokan* yearbook; smiling brightly in the second photo in the fourth row down from the page top among his ninth grade classmates. What activities he might have participated in that first high school year would be difficult to determine. The yearbook focused on the senior class without much mention of what the underclassmen were doing. Some activities were described in a paragraph without a photo and a list of the participants' last names. He had cousins in the school, and the participation of a Sorenson did not mean it was Ricky or a relative. [20]

In the fall, he began his sophomore year and his first season on the *Tornadoes* football team. He was big and strong enough to play tackle on the line. The team finished the 1941 season undefeated, with a 7–0 record. Richard Sorenson's name is listed under the team picture. He is standing in Row 2 and wearing #71. [21]

Tuesday, December 2, 1941, was a school day. The football season was over. Christmas was too many weeks ahead to give it much thought. The family had some news. Ricky learned that his cousin, Kenneth James Gagnon, 21 years old, had gone to an office and enlisted in the U.S. Army. Five days later, enlisting would be on Ricky's mind also.

Upheaval on a Striking Scale

On Sunday, December 7, 1941, the Sorensons returned home after attending church. Snow was falling in Anoka. Virginia had some of her relatives visiting from Duluth, celebrating the birth of her baby, Mary Carol. Ricky, 17 years old, joked a little with his 13-year-old brother. The family was sitting in the living room and turned on the radio. In Ricky's words, "And, there it was."

"This battle has been going on for nearly three hours. . . . It's no joke, it's a real war!" The first wave of Japanese aircraft arrived over their Pearl Harbor targets shortly before 7:55 AM, Honolulu time. The three major stateside radio networks began interrupting regular programming at 2:30 PM, bringing news of the attack that was still in progress in a harbor unknown to most Americans. NBC radio reporter Hans von "H.V." Kaltenborn broadcast the news from the Pacific to the stunned nation.

No one listening to the broadcast in the Sorenson living room could have guessed that one day before WWII ended, they would be listening to Ricky on the radio.

Patriotism and a sense of service to the country were in his blood. His father had been a sailor and his uncle had been a soldier in World War I. Rick Sorenson decided to quit Anoka High School. On Monday, December 8, he did not go to school. Instead, he went downtown to the Navy Recruiting office and made out the enlistment papers for the Navy. When he went home to get his parents' signatures, they thought otherwise.

"No," Carl said, "I'm not gonna sign." Virginia agreed. She would not let her first child go to war.

Rick stayed aware of the war news as he finished out his school year. The Sorensons followed the war news as most others on "the home front" did—they read newspapers and listened to radio broadcasts. Television had not yet found its way into American homes.

Like many teenage boys, he hoped it would last long enough for him to get in the fight. It did. Ten years later, he would tell a *Minneapolis Star Tribune* reporter that he understood what Civil War General William Tecumseh Sherman had said. His enthusiasm for war was no more.

"What a chump," he would say. "If you're a kid, don't ever wish anything like that for yourself—or anybody else. There are some things worth fighting for, but war is pretty much as General Sherman said it was—hell." [22]

The family returned to Calvary Cemetery in the summer of 1942, while Ricky waited for the start of his junior year at Anoka High and his chance to play on the varsity football team. On Thursday, June 25, 1942, Mary Mox, aged 69, died at 7:35 AM at home on Benton Street. Ricky had eleven first cousins by then. He and three of his cousins and two of their friends served as the pallbearers at her funeral services. Mary was buried with her husband. [23]

At the outbreak of WWII, Ricky's Uncle Lee Mox was assistant supervisor at the Anoka State Hospital. He and Alice stayed in Anoka. Raymond and Minnie P. left Anoka and Mox Island for the west coast to work in the Bremerton, Washington, ship yards. Frank Jr. and Mary also moved their family to Bremerton when the war started. The family stopped leasing the island acres. Gradually over decades, the cottage would fall into disrepair until only the remnants of the wood saw and fireplace were evident. Sometimes, locals unfamiliar with the Mox occupation of the little isle called it Mystery Island.

Grandma Mary Sorenson worried about the number of Sorenson boys from Albert Lea and Freeborn County who were going to the recruiting offices. Her two youngest boys, Rick's uncles, would serve honorably. Raymond K. Sorenson had been inducted in the Army on October 21, 1941, before the attack on Pearl Harbor. His younger brother, Morris N. "Porky" Sorenson, would not leave for Army service until October 18, 1943.

Brothers Russell N. and Harold W. Sorenson, from Albert Lea, joined the Army on February 12, 1942. Kermit C. Sorenson also left in February to join the Army Air Corps. He would make sixty-eight missions as a B-26 Gunner. Robert L. Sorenson left for flight training. Frank P. Sorenson left for training in aircraft maintenance. Melvin B. "Monk" Sorenson left town in May for the Army. Richard H. Sorenson, Evarts Sorenson, and Edwin T. Sorenson all departed for overseas duty in the South Pacific, England, and Europe.

United Newsreel, the U.S. Office of War Information (OWI), began disseminating war news in June 1942, via radio broadcasts, newspapers, posters, photographs, 8.5-minute newsreels, and feature films. [24] Teenagers like Rick, and adults as well, could follow war news at local theaters, watching the motion picture newsreels before the feature films were projected onto screens. Five major American newsreel companies (Fox Movietone News, Universal News, Hearst News of the Day, Paramount News, and Pathé News) released two 8–10-minute newsreels per week. Each newsreel contained six or seven short stories: not just "News of the Day," but clips of people, events, and topics meant to entertain the movie audience. Newsreels began presenting actual combat footage and morale-building stories about the war in the South Pacific.

All summer, Rick "waited around until that fall," anticipating his 18th birthday in August. America's first major offensive of the war began three weeks before his birthday. The 1st Marine and 2d Marine divisions began landings on August 7, 1942, in the Solomons on Guadalcanal, Tulagi, Savo, and Florida islands to take them back from the Japanese invaders. The campaign went on for six months before the Marines could claim America's first victory in the Pacific.

In his junior year, in a school where state-wide wrestling dominance was the big thing, Rick put on the maroon and white colors of the Anoka High *Tornadoes* football team. The team duplicated the previous season's record, winning all seven games. The season ended in October 1942. He had played well and earned the distinction of wearing the letter "A" for the rest of his high school days. Likely, he could have expected a starting spot on the *Tornadoes* line and another letter in his senior year football season.

Rick *was* destined to gain *Tornadoes* notoriety later as a Notable Alumni, but not for athletics and not with the Class of 1944. He had little chance to wear a letter sweater. He did buy an Anoka High School class ring and was proud to wear it.

United Newsreel released US MARINES STORM GUADALCANAL on October 21, 1942, as the lead story of four news events to be shown in movie theaters.

On Guadalcanal Island, 25-year-old Sergeant John Basilone was in charge of two heavy machine gun sections. During a savage and determined enemy nighttime assault on October 24–25, he fought valiantly to maintain the tenuous Marine defensive line.

Two nights later, on October 26, Sergeant Mitchell Paige, 24, commanding a machine-gun section with fearless determination, manned his gun alone, in a deadly hail of Japanese shells, and, "moving from gun to gun, never ceasing his withering fire against the advancing hordes until reinforcements finally arrived." Then, he dauntlessly and aggressively led a bayonet charge that drove the enemy back and prevented a breach through the Marine lines.

The tales of Sergeant Basilone and Sergeant Paige quickly became the stuff of legends.

Official Films Inc. of New York City began including war news in each volume of its *News Thrills of 1942* releases. Volume 3 was out in October, including a one-minute segment: U.S. Marines Capture Solomon Islands. *News Thrills* advertisements appeared in magazines. Creative teenagers who paid 25¢ for a *Popular Photography* magazine could imagine making their own movies after reading about Amateur Movie Making and New Home Movies. One ad might also entice them to buy an 8mm Short for $1.75 or a 16mm Short for $2.75. "Brings the War's Most Sensational News to Your Home Movie Screen. *All these exciting events complete in one reel!*" [25]

Coach Arch Pease, 34, left Anoka to serve with the U.S. Army in the Philippines. He would retire at a colonel's rank.

Many young men felt the call to arms before finishing high school, fearing that the war was going to end before they had a chance to be tested in battles. After the football season in October 1942, months before the battle on Guadalcanal ended, when Rick Sorenson did not need his parents' signed consent, he went back to the recruiting office and enlisted. In the USMC, not in the Navy. The lines of young men wanting to enlist were long. So many young men were applying at that time. Some birth certificate problems further delayed Rick's entry into the service. Two months passed before he was called in.

"Why do you want to be a Marine?" Carl asked his son. He told Rick about the bad experiences he had had with the Jarheads onboard ship—the drunks, their scavenging, and all their crass talking. [26] Rick was undeterred.

In November 1942, U.S. Marines On Guadalcanal Push Back Jap Troops was the lead 3.5-minute story in the U.S. OWI 8.5-minute newsreel. Sergeant Basilone was promoted to Platoon Sergeant on November 23, 1942. Moviegoers learned all about his heroics in the newsreels. Rick was not a Marine private yet, and had no idea that he would shake hands with the Marine legend one day. By the time the two met, Sergeant Basilone had been a gunnery sergeant for four months (promoted on March 8, 1944) and was training Marines for the fight on Iwo Jima.

A year after he had listened to the radio broadcast from Honolulu, Rick reported for swearing in on December 13, 1942. He was officially in the Marine Corps. As he waited for his own departure date from Anoka, other Sorenson servicemen were finishing Army training.

On January 3, 1943, half way through his third year of high school, Private Richard K. Sorenson boarded a train for the first time in his life in Minneapolis, the only recruit from Anoka. At first, he knew none of the others he travelled with as the train chugged to Kansas City, Missouri, and on to Tijuana. He had made friends before they reached their destination at the Receiving Station, San Diego Marine Corps Recruit Depot. He would be in combat training for all of 1943.

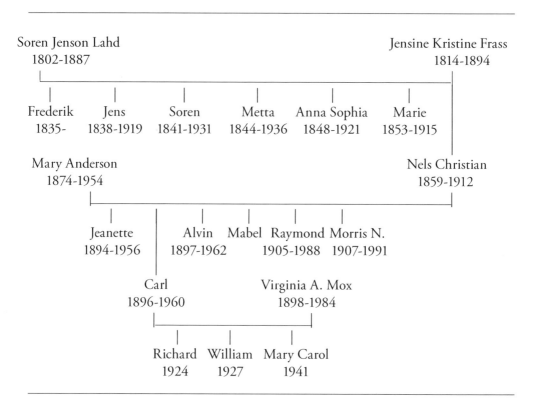

Four generations of Sorensons in America.

CHAPTER 8

Proud to Serve

✳✳✳

"An Act of Bravery That Makes Even Brave Men Shudder" [1]

"WE HAD FIFTEEN MINUTES TO shower and shave and then given four shots each. We received our boondockers (boots), dungarees, piss cutter (cap). We stenciled everything. We had sixty Marines on one clothes iron." [2]

Private Sorenson was out of bed at 4:30 in the morning. The recruits broke out of their huts, had inspection, and then, the drill instructors ran them to chow at 5:30 AM. Everyone took seriously the sign over the mess hall door: "Take all you want . . . but eat all you take." They went through breakfast line and ate fast—"on the double, cuz we only had about fifteen minutes to eat." He thought the Marine Corps food was good. "Yeah, no problem there."

As he would remember the repetitive routine of those days, after chow the recruits fell back out and were run back over to their huts. They would go in, get their weapon, and fall out at 6:00 AM for morning formation and inspection, followed by calisthenics and close order drill for an hour or so. They would have some lectures, then, fall into formation again. They went for chow at noon, with the same routine coming back again—close order drill, more lectures, and then on it went every day.

The marching commenced and another drill began, demonstrating the Corps reliance on learning by repetition, over and over again. Each time the recruits responded a little quicker and more uniformly. One boot camp drill was so etched into Private Sorenson's memory that, like any private graduating from the recruit depot, he could recite it for the rest of his life.

"They taught us to never call our rifle a gun." Anyone who made that mistake had a drill sergeant shouting in his face, making the recruit yell out loudly: "This is my rifle (holding on to his issued weapon), this is my gun (grabbing his own groin)—this is for shooting and this is for fun."

Once a week, Pvt Sorenson had two hours to do laundry. He scrubbed his own clothes with the scrub brush, then, fell out for inspection. If anything were deemed dirty by the DI's standards, the sergeant would throw the article on the ground, stomp on it, and give the recruit ten minutes to go back to the tubs and get it clean. That was one of the things Pvt Sorenson found to be humorous about recruit training.

Training at San Diego went on for seven weeks, while news of the capture and defense of Guadalcanal continued into early February 1943.

Having completed boot camp, Pvt Sorenson was transferred up the coast to Camp Pendleton. The amphibious training base had first been plotted on the expansive Santa Margarita y Las Flores cattle ranch in March 1942, and the conditions for the Marines a year later were austere and primitive.

Three Marine regiments were deployed in large tent camps in the sprawling hills: Tent Camp 1 in Las Pulgas Canyon, Tent Camp 2 at San Onofre, and Tent Camp 3 at Cristianitos Canyon, in the northernmost reaches of the base near Talega, twenty-five miles from Camp

Pendleton's main gate. Situated to conduct training in small arms combat, infantry tactics, and grenades and bayonet use, each tent camp had combat and qualification ranges. The ranges were laid out for rifle, machine gun, moving-target, and mortar firing. There was a range dedicated to tank, anti-aircraft, and artillery training.

The troops training in these areas carried their tents and other equipment with them and lived under combat field conditions. Going days and nights sleeping on the ground without a tent was a common experience. Only a few dusty, unpaved roads had been laid down and transportation was limited. Hiking was a constant. Private Sorenson would hump the miles to Chappo Flats, Las Pulgas Canyon, Windmill Canyon, San Onofre, and Aliso Beach.

He joined the 3d Separate Infantry Battalion (reinforced) at San Onofre Tent Camp 2. For the next ten months, he washed and shaved in cold water and slept and ate meals "under canvas." The summer heat at Tent Camp was described as broiling and oppressive in letters home. Then, in contrast when the sun went down, no matter how many blankets he might gather, fending off the cold in Las Pulgas Canyon at night was impossible. That made the night attacks near the swift waters of the Santa Margarita River in the Chappo Area, rubber-boat landings at the Del Mar boat basin, and the combat swimming seem to be preferable exercises.

Camp Pendleton was becoming the staging area for the Fighting Fourth Marine Division, first organized in February 1943, when operations in the Central Pacific area were accelerating. The 24th Marine Regiment was organized on March 26 at Pendleton from the three Separate Infantry Battalions (reinforced) and assigned to the 4th MARDIV. The 3d Separate Battalion became part of the 3d Battalion, 24th Marines.

One time, Pvt Sorenson's sergeant pulled him out of a formation and sent him over to the mess hall—not for chow, but for a work detail. He was assigned temporary duties as a night cook, preparing meals until 4:00 AM for the truck drivers. He did such a good job cooking that the mess sergeant considered sending him to Cook and Bakers School. Private Sorenson wanted no part in that and requested assignment to the infantry. He was selected for machine guns and went to a special service unit. [3]

"We were a team and all buddies. There were five to nine in a squad." Private Sorenson was assigned to "M" Company (Weapons Company) and introduced to the "Machine Guns Have *No* Conscience" instruction. The weapons company was comprised of a heavy machine-gun platoon, a mortar platoon, and an assault platoon. He trained with the machine-gun platoon, learning to take the weapons down and put them back together—repeatedly, over and over and over, until he knew every part by heart. Then, doing it blindfolded, again and again. Expecting night operations, he had to know by feel where every part of the heavy machine gun fit together.

"In the face of obstacles ~ COURAGE." For anyone in Anoka who had a question about Pvt Sorenson's training and duties, one popular 1943 OWI color poster promoting the U.S. Army Infantry provided a visual. The poster depicted a three-man machine-gun team firing a Browning M1917A1 .30 caliber, water-cooled, heavy machine gun in battle.

Some wartime events are easier to remember afterwards than the clamor of combat. The rattlesnakes and tarantulas at Camp Pendleton always proved memorable: as much, maybe, as encounters with celebrities.

Tyrone Power, American film, stage, and radio actor had been a great screen presence since before 1936. He starred in the Technicolor movie, *Crash Dive*, which was released in theaters on April 22, 1943. Private Sorenson had already met the actor by then. Private Power, 28, had enlisted in the Marine Corps in August 1942 and went through boot camp at the San Diego Recruit Depot at the same time as Pvt Sorenson. [4] Private Power trained briefly at

Camp Pendleton, before he went on to Quantico to be commissioned a second lieutenant and train as a Marine aviator.

The Marine/actor left an impression on Pvt Sorenson. "Tyrone Power was a really nice guy."

On Saturday, May 8, 1943, both Lieutenant Robert Sorenson and Private James Sorenson arrived home in Minnesota from Army Air Corps training for a fifteen-days furlough.

In a Balcombe, Australia, stadium on May 21, 1943, while the 1st Marine Division recuperated from Pacific Island battles, Colonel Merritt Austin "Red Mike" Edson, 46, Platoon Sergeant John Basilone, Platoon Sergeant Mitchell Paige, and Major General Alexander Archer Vandegrift standing in front of a formation of Marine battalions, received Medals of Honor for their actions on Guadalcanal.

Platoon Sergeant Basilone was sent back to the States in July, to help raise money during the Third War Loan Drive. Appearing in newsreels and gathering much media attention, "Manila" John Basilone was becoming a Marine Corps legend and an uncomfortable celebrity.

The 23d Marines arrived at Pendleton by train from Camp Lejeune during the first week of July. Other units transferred by ship and train until the 4th Marine Division was officially activated on August 16 with orders to get ready for Pacific combat duty. The division's T/O would be up to full strength—17,831 Marines—by September 30.

Private Sorenson celebrated the last birthday of his adolescent years on August 28, a Saturday. He was 19 years old and had earned a promotion to private first class. After training he had a chance for some liberty, usually entailing a hike over to the Del Mar or Oceanside slop chutes and honky-tonks. His other choices were to make his way to the Post Exchange at Mainside for a milkshake or to join friends that night at the slop chute (the base tavern) where beer was abundantly stocked.

The bantering and tales about the "Peaches" and "Fi-Fi girls" off base served as an amusing diversion for the vigorous Marines. The Women Marine Reservists over at Mainside's Base Administration also enlivened a good share of conversations and daydreams.

Liberty was regular free time, usually weekends and holidays, unless the Marine was on a duty detail. Marines on liberty were supposed to remain in the "immediate area" in case there was reason to call them back to their unit. In wartime, training often stretched into Saturdays and Sundays and liberty was minimal. Extended liberty opportunities were scarce.

To go out beyond the bounds of the local area required a "liberty pass" and, typically, a bus ride. The ride down to Redondo Beach and Hermosa Beach was four hours, to Long Beach or downtown Los Angeles was three hours. Young men did not want to sleep away their liberty time, so the long rides to and from liberty destinations provided off-duty Marines and sailors time to catch up on sleep. "Sleeping it off" for some.

A "liberty pass" was earned and could be lost. Once granted, any revocation of the time off could generate a very strong agitation. It was as if Congress had ratified a Marine's liberty on December 15, 1791, and it "shall not be infringed." PFC Sorenson learned a lesson at Pendleton during an inspection, when a platoon member tried to pull a fast one, and the men convened an unofficial tribunal to deal with the guilty party.

"The Platoon had a 72-hour pass one weekend, but an officer doing inspections found clothes stuffed away in a place where they should not have been. So, the entire platoon lost the weekend pass, and at that point the officers and sergeants disappeared. The men of the platoon held a Kangaroo Court and took him into the showers and scrubbed him down with sand soap. He screamed and cried in anguish. He later left and was not seen again." [5]

The 4th MarDiv trained as a complete unit on the Camp Pendleton beaches and canyons for the remainder of 1943. PFC Sorenson gained a sense of what Pacific combat would be like as veterans of the Guadalcanal battles conducted the intense training. The rifle companies were subjected to agonizingly realistic exercises—combat drills, ship-to-shore movement, demolitions, pillbox clearing, employing tank groups, coordination of supporting arms—to prepare them for what was ahead. Special weapons teams practiced destroying concrete pillboxes with plastic explosives and using bazookas and flamethrowers. The assault elements of the regiments went into the Windmill Canyon hills to practice assaults on exact replicas of the pillboxes the Japanese manned in the Pacific.

On Sunday, September 19, Platoon Sergeant John Basilone got a mammoth welcome in his Raritan, New Jersey, hometown. The parade made its way to the Doris Duke Cromwell estate where a huge crowd of 30,000 people gathered to see him, including beautiful movie stars and numerous celebrities. Former governors, senators and mayors gave flattering speeches. The national press was on hand to report on the hero's homecoming.

"Manila" John was gracious, but humble. "Only part of this Medal belongs to me," he said. "Pieces of it belong to the boys who fought by my side on Guadalcanal."

After the parade, he toured the country raising money for the war effort. For Americans and military servicemen overseas who could not attend, *Life* magazine reported on the gala events with words and pictures in back pages of its October 11 issue—Life Goes to a Hero's Homecoming. [6]

Readers first glancing at the *Life* cover, a close-up profile of a lady looking into the camera, might have thought it were Veronica Lake. Mrs. Betty (Riddle) Cross, wife of Lieutenant John Cross in Australia, was modelling the new style of headwear for the HALF-HAT cover story. While hats were not particularly interesting to teenage boys when a war was on, the articles and photographs inside the magazine reported on the military hospitals in Australia and New Zealand, the Navy landing at Lae in New Guinea, the Raid at Stuttgart, the use of models at Camp Lee, Virginia, to put on mock theater of operations trials, and Attu in the Aleutians. Full-page merchandise advertisements included drawings of military themes and encouragements to *Back the Attack*, *Buy More War Savings Bonds and Stamps*, *Save GAS for WAR!*, *Progress through Victory*, and *Ration Materials and Ensure Our Boys Have Ammo.*

Listerine insisted that a tube of brushless shaving cream was "Guaranteed not to contain any secret WEAPONS! Why try to blitz your beard . . ." In its half-page advertisement of seven frames, Colgate toothpaste depicted Marine Sergeant Joe and Corporal Mac in their dress blue uniforms reaching the conclusion that Mac was not getting a girl, because he was an "Eight Ball" with bad breath.

While popular magazines conducted their advertising campaigns, the Marine Corps began its island-hopping campaign. The WWII legends of Marines "hopping" onto grenades began in November.

***

The Bougainville Campaign

The 3rd Marine Raider Battalion, 3rd Marine Division, was tasked to take Bougainville Island from Japanese control in November 1943. The enemy knew that the Allies would do everything possible to interrupt their wartime shipping and aviation activity. Islands on which airfields were constructed were especially likely to be attacked by the Americans. The earlier loss of the airfield on Guadalcanal increased the importance of Bougainville to the Japanese, and they readied the island to repulse any Allied attempts to invade it.

The 3d Marine Division participated in the occupation and defense of Cape Torokina from November 1 to December 15, and in the consolidation of Northern Solomons in December 15–21.

During the Bougainville operation on November 7, 1943, Sergeant Herbert Joseph Thomas was the first Marine in WWII to give his life diving onto a grenade for the sake of comrades. Two days later, a second Marine made the same decision. Their actions had an influence on the Bougainville veterans who were assigned duties to train the new Marines readying themselves to go to war. The stories of the two who died doing the unthinkable kept their sacrifices very alive in the Pendleton tent camps.

Herbert Joseph Thomas Jr. was born in Columbus, Ohio, on February 8, 1918. When he was seven years old, the family relocated to South Charleston, West Virginia. His mother died when he was 13 years old and on his way to South Charleston High School.

A parent's death is a disruptive event in a child or adolescent's life. While making necessary adjustments, the surviving parent reasonably becomes less available. The child's sense of stability, safety, and predictability are undermined. Relationships, educational pursuits, and recreational activities are altered. Parental death can stall, retard, or accelerate a child's personal development.

Of the eighty-two Marines awarded Medals of Honor during the four years of fighting in WWII, at least twenty had experienced the death of a parent while growing up. George Phillips had lost both his father and mother. Most of the recorded deaths were of fathers. Of the working class, these fathers had often died in accidents: for example, two were firemen, one a police officer, one a miner, and one a farmer.

Herb Jr. managed his grief as well as an adolescent can do. He was known to be of strong character as well as outgoing. He devoted himself to football. Leadership seemed to come naturally to him. The other players not only admired him, they formed lasting bonds of friendship with him.

Herb starred as a *Black Eagles* halfback and earned scholarships to Greenbrier Military School and Virginia Polytechincal Institute. After playing for Greenbrier, he transferred to Virginia Polytech in the fall of 1937, joining the freshman class of 1941. He played three years of varsity for VPI and became legendary in Virginia football history. In his senior year, he led the team in pass receptions and scoring and was leading scorer in Virginia and second in the Southern Conference. He earned places on the Virginia All-State College eleven, in the Virginia Tech Sports Hall of Fame, and a mention on the All-American football team.

In late October 1943, Sergeant Thomas, a squad leader with Company B, 1st Battalion, 3rd Marines, 3rd Marine Division, boarded the USS *President Adams* and set sail for an undisclosed location. On November 1, D-Day, the troops lined the railings of ships at 6:14 AM, looking out at a clear sunrise. Ahead of them was Empress Bay, Cape Torokina, the mountain range of Bougainville, and Mount Bagana, a smoking volcano. The smoke rising from the explosions of naval gunfire gave the men a good idea of where the landing sites were on the island.

At 6:45 AM, Sgt Thomas led his squad of Marines down the cargo nets into their landing craft. They were part of the first assault wave, assigned to land on the right flank on Blue Beach 1, Cape Torokina. Once loaded into the assault boat, they had 5,000 yards to think about what was ahead of them. Baker Company joined the departure line and headed for the beach at 7:10 AM. The enemy artillery, mortar, and machine-gun fire started before the landing ramps dropped.

Sergeant Thomas' skill at running with a football and leadership of team members served him well on Bougainville. Baker Company reached Blue Beach at 7:30 AM and engaged the 300 Japanese defenders positioned on the Cape. High dense underbrush near the water's edge slowed the advance and kept the landing force vulnerable to the crossfire of machine-gun positions in pillboxes and in sand and log bunkers. Sergeant Thomas led his squad in the fight against one bunker after another.

The lines were finally consolidated by evening, and Baker Company had advanced 1,000 yards away from the beach. More than 50% of the first wave of Marines was either killed or wounded before the beachhead was established.

Pitch-black jungle nights spent in foxholes, half-asleep, fending off periodic, frenzied enemy counter attacks followed. The jungle undergrowth was dense and movement was slow and dangerous. The enemy used the jungle well to cover and conceal their locations.

By November 7, Baker Company had been repositioned east of the Koromokina River. At 6:00 AM, just before dawn, the enemy unleashed a major attack into the Koromokina Lagoon area. Having been held in reserve, Company B entered the fight at 1:15 PM, advancing with hand-to-hand fighting and grenade exchanges.

Across the Koromokina River, a hidden machine-gun emplacement opened up, inflicting several casualties on Sgt Thomas' squad members. He directed his men forward against the machine guns, skillfully destroying two positions and their crews. Despite being under heavy fire and taking casualties, he spotted a third machine gun. Sergeant Thomas positioned his men close about him and quickly prepared them to assault. They should charge the position after he suppressed the enemy fire with the Mk-2 hand grenade he was holding.

He pulled the pin from the fragmentation grenade, released the pressure off the handle, and heard the fuse ignite. The detonation was four to five seconds away. He lobbed the one-pound grenade toward the machine-gun crew.

Jungle vines deflected the device, and it bounced back into the Marines gathered for the assault. Without hesitation, the squad leader demonstrated a Marine's willingness to take on a responsibility rather than shirking from it, and a personal characteristic common among Marine MOH recipients—the tendency to accept accountability for their own actions.

Sergeant Herbert Thomas, aged 25, immediately threw himself onto the grenade, fully absorbing the explosion. The flash lifted his body and dropped it to the jungle floor. Protected from injury, his men charged the enemy machine gun crew, destroyed the position, and pressed their attack to other hostiles. In the evening, they reported what they had observed to their platoon sergeant. The Navy would launch a destroyer, DD-833, in Sergeant Thomas' name on March 25, 1945. [7]

Private First Class Henry Gurke was also on the west side of Bougainville. Isolation was not new to the 6-foot-1-inch, 180-pound Marine from Neche, North Dakota. His small hometown sits on the Pembina River, two miles down Route 18 from the Canadian border. Neche, much like a small island in the middle of prairie, farmland, and forested hills, had maybe 400 inhabitants, far fewer than the thousands of Japanese defenders on Bougainville Island.

A month after graduating from high school, Henry had joined the Civilian Conservation Corps and helped build a dam in Larimore, eighty-five miles from home. He was promoted inside the CCC to an Assistant Leader's position. The Japanese attack on Pearl Harbor was the kind of thing the North Dakotan could not ignore, and he enlisted in the Marines the following April. His sojourn away from the Pembina had begun.

In Neche on November 6, 1943, his parents, Julius and Hulda Gurke, and his two sisters, Elsie and Ella, remembered that the day was Henry's 21st birthday. They knew from letters that he had been on a lot of islands: the tropical islands northeast of Figi, British Samoa, the Wallis Islands, American Samoa, the New Hebrides, Guadalcanal, and New Caledonia. In February and March, he had participated in the four-week-long uncontested invasion and occupation of Pavuvu Island in the Russell Group. The family wondered what he was doing on his birthday. PFC Gurke was making an assault landing on Bougainville with Company M, 3rd Raider Battalion, 2nd Raider Regiment.

His platoon took control of a road near Empress Augusta Bay. Serving as a rifleman at a roadblock, PFC Gurke shared a shallow foxhole with another Marine manning a Browning automatic weapon. The enemy's main force attacked just before dawn on November 9, attempting to break through the blocked road and push the Marines back to the beaches. PFC Gurke and the BAR-man tenaciously poured as much firepower available to them into the hostile vanguard. Explosions from enemy grenades intensified and closed in on the foxhole. The noise of the battle was deafening. The two Marines kept up their fire.

As the enemy ferociously pressed forward, a grenade landed in PFC Gurke's foxhole. There was no time even to yell a warning. Intending to protect his fellow Marine Raider and the much-needed BAR automatic rifle, he aggressively pushed his companion aside and hurled himself onto the grenade. His body smothered the explosion and saved the BAR-man's life. PFC Gurke was killed instantly.

When the grenade exploded, PFC Philip G. Irvine was in a foxhole yards away from his good friend. He and the BAR-man would write witness statements and talk about PFC Gurke's valor. Whenever the story was told among the brave Marines from Bougainville, a natural thought would arise for anyone aware of the destructive force of a grenade.

"Could *I* do *that?*"

Defense of the Torokina perimeter passed to the Army's Americal Infantry Division, and the Marine force began to leave Bougainville on December 15, 1943. Most Marines were off the island by December 28. PFC Irvine would survive the war and have a long life afterwards in Santa Rosa, California. Nearly thirty-four years after the roadblock, the November 9 enemy attack, and PFC Gurke's death, he wrote a succinct line.

"It was a night no one is likely to forget!!" [8]

The destroyer USS *Gurke* (DD-783) was launched in Tacoma, Washington, on February 15, 1945.

Holidays Spent Away From Home

Wednesday, November 10, a date celebrated by Marine units worldwide, was the 168th USMC birthday. Lieutenant Colonel Alexander A. Vandegrift Jr. directed his companies to report to an open field for a 3d Battalion formation.

Private Sorenson watched the commander cut the birthday cake with his Mameluke sword. The battalion sergeant major assisted. In customary fashion, the first piece of cake was presented to the battalion's guest of honor. The oldest Marine present at the formation received the second piece of cake. Then, symbolically, the oldest Marine passed a piece of cake to the youngest Marine on the field. After the traditional celebration, the companies returned to their training schedules.

In two weeks, American families would wish their husbands and sons could be at home to make a painting come to life on November 25, Thanksgiving Day.

Norman Rockwell, a popular artist, had finished *Freedom from Want* in 1942. The *Saturday Evening Post* published the painting of a large family gathered around a dinner table for a holiday meal in its March 6, 1943 issue. The magazine made "feast of plenty" reproductions available, and the OWI contracted for posters of the painting. By Thanksgiving, *Freedom from Want* was displayed in homes across the States.

The Marines had their minds elsewhere—capturing the Gilbert Islands. Operation *Galvanic*, the amphibious assault of the Tarawa Atoll, began at 9:00 on Saturday morning, November 20. The battle was over in 76 hours. The Marines declared Tarawa secure at 1:30 PM on Tuesday. The toll on both sides was heavy. The Marines reported 1,009 killed in action and 2,101 wounded. The enemy lost 4,690 troops and construction laborers killed. Only 146 were captured.

After Operation *Galvanic*, training in amphibious operations became a top priority for the 4th Division. The tactical lessons of Bougainville and Tarawa would be taught to Marines readying themselves for island battles. One reality that trainers drilled into the minds of the Leathernecks was that they could expect to have U.S. "pineapples"—the standard issue anti-personnel Mk-2 hand grenades—tossed at them. The Japanese had captured tons of U.S. munitions during the four-month, 1942 Battle of Bataan and were using them against American forces on the Pacific Islands.

Repeatedly, the veterans at Pendleton hammered home another lesson to the inexperienced combat Marines like PFC Sorenson. "Cover the grenade! Don't let everybody get it just to save your own hide." [9] It was an action hard to imagine. Better not to think too much about *that* possibility.

Private First Class Sorenson's Anoka High School classmates would remember him if they paged through their copies of the 1941 *Anokan* yearbook. His friends from the weapons company would also be able to look him up in a book later. When the 24th Regiment was formed at Camp Pendleton in 1943, the famous *Red Book* was issued to the officers and troops. The sailors called it a *Cruise Book*. The book contained a short history of the regiment, pictures of the regiment around Pendleton, and rosters with photos of each man in the regiment by battalion and company.

Operation *FLINTLOCK*

At the Washington Conference in May 1943, the CCS had recommended to the Allied heads of state that an offensive into the Marshalls Islands should be launched. At the August 1943 Quebec Conference, Allied leaders agreed that an effort against the Marshalls should follow the successful conquest of the Gilberts. Accordingly, the JCS issued Fleet Admiral Chester William Nimitz a directive on September 1 to undertake the operations he had recently proposed. On September 22, Admiral Nimitz directed Rear Admiral Raymond Ames Spruance to prepare to assault the Marshalls on January 1, 1944. Admiral Nimitz issued the FLINTLOCK operation plan on October 12. The 4th Marine Division was going to cross the Pacific.

Most 4th MarDiv men had never been under enemy fire. The Marines needed to hold rehearsals. Admiral Nimitz tried to be patient.

The 4th Division planned in conjunction with Admiral Richard Lansing Conolly's Task Force 53 support ships and transports. On December 14–15, before either the admiral or

General Harry Schmidt were certain what course FLINTLOCK would follow, the first division-level amphibious landing exercise was held on the Aliso Canyon beaches.

On December 20, Admiral Nimitz ordered the operation to get under way "not later than 31 January 1944."

Saturday, Christmas morning came with bright sunlight. Camp Pendleton was "quiet" and little moved. It was one of the last days PFC Sorenson and his friends would be granted liberty to savor a turkey meal, maybe stand under some mistletoe, and find their own enjoyments. He would not wear his PFC insignia again for a while. Private Sorenson had lost his PFC rank, demoted for returning late from liberty. [10]

On December 27, 1943, word spread around the tent camps that Platoon Sergeant "Manila John" Basilone was assigned to Camp Pendleton's training base.

Following the New Year, the 4th Division boarded ship and sailed to San Clemente Island, off the Southern California coast. This second landing rehearsal included amphibious shipping, warships and carriers, and live fire support.

Private Sorenson and the Marines stormed the beaches on Sunday, January 2. They "captured" the island, re-embarked aboard their ships, and repeated the entire exercise on Monday. Although the San Clemente landing was staged to promote close cooperation between the LSTs and LVTs, the sailors and Marines gained little confidence in one another. The "snafus" on both sides generated much grumbling among the "squids" and "jarheads."

After training off San Clemente Island, the battalions landed on Onslow Beach and hiked twenty-three miles over mountains back to Camp Pendleton. It took almost twelve hours to return to the tent camps.

There was no doubt that the division was preparing to move out. The months of training had been geared toward a specific amphibious operation. The grunts bantered and guessed at what objective awaited them in the Pacific. Despite all the scuttlebutt, their destination remained TOP SECRET. Training at Pendleton ended.

Old AP *Liberty Ships*, serving as troop transports, docked at San Diego as part of Rear Admiral Marc A. Mitscher's Task Force 58. The Liberty ship, the "ugly duckling workhorse" of the maritime fleet, was primarily a cargo ship with five cargo holds. The ship drew forty feet of water and was armed with 3-inch, 5-inch, and 20mm AA guns at the bow and stern, and 20mm AA guns at midships above the bridge deck. The ships were pressed into emergency use and converted into *limited capacity troopships* to carry no more than 550 troops. Landing Craft, Medium (LCMs) were stacked on top of the #2 hold, and the Higgins boats (Landing craft, Vehicle, Personnel, LCVPs) were loaded on top of the #4 hold.

The 'tween deck (under the upper main deck and above the much deeper lower holds) held the administrative office, electrician and machinist workshops, crew storage areas, potable water tanks, officers' quarters and mess room, showers, latrines, a bake shop, dry stores, pantry, troop galley and mess hall, sick bay, surgery suite, medical stores, pharmacy, an isolation ward, and two cells for "mental cases." The Navy had installed the bunks and increased the troop capacities: 348 bunks stacked on the forward 'tween deck spaces and another 436 bunks in the lower hold. The embarked 'tween deck passengers rode just above the water line when the ship sailed fully loaded with cargo.

Just after daybreak on January 13, 1944, Pvt Sorenson and the 3rd Battalion (Reinforced), 24th Marines, combat loaded onto 469-feet-long USS *Wayne* (APA-54). The *Wayne* was relatively new, having first launched on December 6, 1942. She held 1,300 tons of cargo in her 170,000 cubic feet of holds. Her complement of fifty-seven naval officers and 478 enlisted sailors was ready to berth ninety-three Marine officers and 1,340 enlisted troops on their way to island battles.

The Marine companies berthed below decks were stacked in bunks five and six deep, held by metal chains from the deck to the overhead bulkhead. Each bunk was 24 inches wide, with two feet strung between each one.

As the hundreds of men filed into the hold, the platoon sergeants barked out their orders. "Everything you grunts call your own goes with you in your bunk space! Nothin' is on the deck!"

"There was hardly room to crawl into it." Private Sorenson's rack was down at the very lowest level of the troop ship, thirty feet below the water line. He stored his pack, helmet, rifle, cartridge belt, canteen, gas mask, and other sorts of stuff with him in the bunk, slinging the heavy stuff from the metal piping above his bunk. He would see for himself if there was any drunkenness, scavenging, and crass talking in the holds like that which had so rankled his father in WWI.

The *Wayne* pulled anchor and steamed from San Diego in convoy. Men of the 24th Marines stood on the decks and watched the coastline become a haze in the ship's wake. The troops had to decide if they should sleep on deck or go below.

The troop ship had an old ventilation system and was non-air-conditioned. The troop quarters turned stifling hot. The air was quickly stagnant, and clothes were constantly drenched in sweat. The smells of sweat-soaked shorts and t-shirts, and of hundreds of armpits and feet, mixed with the odor of oil and cleaning fluids drifting in from the passageways. Cigarette and cigar smoke took the place of more fragrant "air fresheners." Damp clothes and towels hung everywhere. Some Marines slept on the ship's deck, because it was too hot in the troop compartment. Having been on the upper deck, they checked a gagging reflex upon re-entry to the lower holds.

For eighteen tedious shipboard days, across 4,400 sea miles, the Leathernecks spent most of their time sitting below decks belting ammunition, cleaning weapons, writing letters, and playing cards all day long. As part of the machine-gun crew, Pvt Sorenson spent long hours in the ship's holds, linking up the ammunition onto belts. Each day, he went up to the main deck for an hour of physical training (PT).

He was hungry most of the time. Fortunately, as the machine-gun crew descended the bulkhead ladders back down to the bowels of hold #1, they passed the *Wayne's* galley. If Pvt Sorenson had a thought about his father's disdain for shipboard Jarheads and their scavenging, it did not matter. Posting a lookout, they slipped unnoticed into the kitchen and stole from sacks, filling their pockets with onions. They munched joyfully, a little tearfully, as they belted their ammo. [11] Onion breath did not enhance the hold's odors.

The typical Marine propensity for light-hearted jaw-jacking in the face of adversity relieved a good amount of the tensions. When not declaring what they intended to bring down on "the Japs," conversations about girls, cars, *Popular Mechanics* magazines, pin up photos, letters from home, and football increased the noise level in the troop compartments.

The NFL season had ended the day after Christmas. Coach Curly Lambeau had led the Green Bay *Packers* to a 7–2–1 record, but finished second-place in the Western Conference. The NFL championship game had been played at Wrigley Field in Chicago two weeks before the 4th Division departed San Diego. On Sunday, December 26, 1943, the favored *Bears* defeated the Washington *Redskins* 41–21.

The real champions were not necessarily on the gridirons. No matter the hometown team, just about every young Marine knew about, had even been in boot camp with, a star NFL player who had left a football jersey in the locker room to serve in the Corps.

Jack Lummus, son of a Texas cotton farmer, was one of the earliest. He had been a walk-on for the 1941 New York *Giants* team and, at 6 feet 3 inches, 194 pounds, played in nine games as a rookie end. He was on the Polo Grounds field wearing #29 against the Brooklyn *Dodgers* on December 7, when the Associated Press ticker messages sent word about Japanese airplanes attacking the Pearl Harbor Naval Base. The *Giants* took the East Conference title with an 8–3 record. Four days before Christmas, Jack was at Wrigley Field playing in the NFL championship game. The *Giants* lost to the *Bears* 37–9.

On January 30, 1942, Jack enlisted in the Marine Corps Reserve as a private. [12] He was commissioned as a second lieutenant on December 18, 1943, and assigned to the elite 2d Marine Raiders at Camp Pendleton. The Raiders were disbanded on January 8, 1944, a week after the 4th Division's amphibious landing rehearsals on San Clemente Island. Second Lieutenant Lummus' new assignment was as executive officer, Company F, 2nd Battalion, 27th Marines, 5th Marine Division.

Another NFL player familiar to Pvt Sorenson was 5 feet 10 inches, 195 pounds, Green Bay *Packers* guard and backup linebacker Howard "Smiley" Johnson, who had made a name for himself during the 1940 and 1941 seasons. In Smiley's second season, when Pvt Sorenson was in his sophomore year at Anoka High playing tackle on the undefeated *Tornadoes* team, the *Packers* had a 10–1 record and looked to take the division title. They lost to the *Bears* in a division playoff game. "Smiley" and Jack Lummus had that, and more, in common.

"Smiley" Johnson enlisted in the Marine Corps in January 1942. By May, he was training in Hawaii. [13] First Lieutenant Johnson arrived in Camp Pendleton in July 1943, assigned to I Company, 3rd Battalion, 23rd Marines, 4th Marine Division. He was on a Task Force 58 *Liberty* ship.

The Jarheads from Detroit had their own football star to chitchat about, but had to accept some witty remarks when they mentioned him and the *Lions*. Second Lieutenant Charlie Edwin Behan was a carpenter's son from Crystal Lake, Illinois. Suiting up at 6 feet 3 inches, 195 pounds, he was a rookie end on the 1941 Detroit team. Despite the *Lions'* disastrous 0–11 season, finishing last in the NFL West, he was off to a sound start for a professional career. Instead, he enlisted in the Marines in 1942. Months after the Task Force sailed from San Diego, Second Lieutenant Behan was assigned platoon leader duties in Company F, 2nd Battalion, 29th Marines, 6th Marine Division.

The boys from Hammond, Indiana, could boast about a real legend without any concerns for joking. Second Lieutenant Jack Chevigny had coached the Chicago *Cardinals* in 1932. He was already famous by then. Jack, 5 feet 7 inches, 170 pounds, had entered football history as one of the best running and blocking halfbacks for Knute Rockne's 1926–1928 Notre Dame football teams. On November 10, 1928, he scored the tying touchdown against Army at Yankee Stadium. As he plunged into the end zone, he yelled out, "That one was for the Gipper." [14] The *Fighting Irish* went home with a 12–6 victory and a catchphrase that found its way into later politics.

After graduating, Jack had stayed in South Bend for three years as Knute's assistant coach. He enlisted in the Corps in 1943 and coached Camp Lejeune's football team. He requested to join a combat outfit and was assigned duties as a liaison officer with the 27th Marines, 5th Marine Division. First Lieutenant Chevigny and First Lieutenant Jack Lummus talked football together at Pendleton and, later, on the deck of the USS *Rutland* as they steamed to Iwo Jima Island in February 1945. [15]

Private Sorenson would read newspaper articles about all four of these NFL Marines in 1945, when the divisions stormed onto the beaches of Iwo Jima and Okinawa. [16]

The Often Short Life of a *Liberty* Ship

The Fifth Fleet Amphibious Force, Task Force 58, was made up of four separate fast-carrier task groups, each one built around three large fleet aircraft carriers and light carriers, three newly built fast battleships, several cruisers, nine screening destroyers, and six to eight support vessels. The ships of each task group sailed in a circle formation centered on the large carriers: USS *Yorktown* (CV10), USS *Enterprise* (CV6), USS *Intrepid* (CV11), USS *Essex* (CV9), USS *Saratoga*, and the USS *Bunker Hill* (CV17). Altogether, TF 58 could launch 700 aircraft against the enemy.

Despite the impressive and reassuring spectacle of carriers, battleships, cruisers, and destroyers escorting the convoy of transports, when Pvt Sorenson had a chance to line the rails with his comrades after PT sessions, he joined in with the joking about periscope sightings and whether they would actually reach their Pacific destination.

Day and night, Marines took every opportunity for "grab assing" and joking. Being so far beneath the ocean water line made the ship's hull seem awfully thin. Calling their ship a "sailing troop coffin" took some of the edge off.

"Did you know about?" There were plenty of stories to recount as the Task Force made its way. Choppy seas seemed to bring out various renditions with a similar theme. "Torpedoed and lost" had become a common newspaper headline.

The families at home reading about Liberty ship travel in newspapers, letters, and telegrams probably did not share in the humor.

In the months of 1942, while Rick Sorenson waited to leave Anoka High, enlist, and depart for San Diego, German wolf-packs *U-66, U-103, U-106, U-123, U-130, U-160, U-172, U-173, U-177, U-201, U-215, U-255, U-129, U-408, U-432, U-444, U-505, U-510* were all active. Enemy submarines sank fifteen troop and cargo ships. Newspapers reported sinkings off Brazil; in the North Atlantic, the Caribbean, the Virgin Islands, the Arctic, and the Kara Sea; off West Africa, three off Trinidad, off South Africa, off New Caledonia; and in the Indian Ocean.

At 7:08 PM on May 20, 1942, *U-173* hit the unescorted, armed SS *George Calvert* on her maiden voyage in the Gulf of Mexico, fifty miles off Cuba's northwest coast. The first torpedo struck the #3 hold six feet below the waterline. The second torpedo hit twenty feet forward of the stern, exploding the magazine. A third torpedo hit amidships at 10:03 PM, broke the ship in half, and sank her. [17]

A German torpedo bomber sank a Liberty ship in the Barents Sea; another ship was torpedoed from the air and scuttled. One ship was sunk by gunfire in the South Atlantic, and two were lost to mines: in the Denmark Strait and off Bizerta, Tunisia.

Three torpedoed ships did not sink outright, but were scuttled off Greenland. Other torpedoed Liberty ships were repaired or scrapped: off New Caledonia and off Sydney. Four ships went into logs as wrecked and lost, scrapped, or scuttled: near Cape Town, off Ascension, off Moreton Island, and on Okinawa.

While Pvt Sorenson was in training in 1943, the tonnage of Liberty ships entered in the *Register of Ships* torpedoed and lost was more alarming than in the previous first year of the war. One went down in the Gulf of Mexico, one in the Atlantic, ten in the North Atlantic, one off Greenland, two off Ascension Island in the South Atlantic, two off Cuba, two off Brazil, and one off Paranagua.

Enemy torpedoes sank troop ships off Ireland, two off the Azores, one off France west of Lisbon, two off Sardinia, one off Sicily and another off Salerno. Around the African continent, ships were lost off Algeria, off Oran, two off Bizerta, off Sierra Leone, off Sassandra,

West Africa, off South Africa, two off Mozambique, five in the Gulf of Aden, and one in the Arabian Sea. Five troop ships were sunk in the Indian Ocean, three off Durban, one off Newcastle, New South Wales, one off Sydney, Australia, two off Guadalcanal, one off New Caledonia, off the Canary Islands, off the Maldives, and one near Fiji.

Two troop ships were bombed and lost off Salerno, one in Sicily, another four in Bari; one off Gibraltar, Tunisia, and Belgian Ostend of West Flanders; one wrecked and lost in the Aleutians, another wrecked and abandoned off Mexico, two wrecked and lost off Panama; and one exploded and lost in a collision off Cape Henry, Virginia.

Traveling in a convoy from New York heading to Liverpool, the SS *Henry Wynkoop* was damaged, but still afloat, after hitting a U-boat in 30-foot-high North Atlantic waves on March 11, 1943.

Torpedoed ships that did not sink, but were damaged beyond repairs in 1943, were scuttled or scrapped: one in the North Atlantic, one off Brazil, off Dutch Guiana, off South Africa, and one off Guadalcanal.

Other troop ships reported to be torpedoed, bombed, mined, or wrecked, were then salvaged and returned to service: off Cuba, in the North Atlantic, in the South Atlantic, off Dutch Guiana, off Paramaibo in the Caribbean, in the Hebrides, off Bizerta, four off Algeria, in Gibraltar, off Sicily, off Palermo, off Salerno, in Naples from the air in the Mediterranean, off Casablanca, in Bari, in the Arabian Sea, three in the Pacific, two off Guadalcanal, and one near the Cook Islands.

The SS *Albert Gallatin* seemed to be sailing with the thrust of a *windfall*. At 5:10 PM on August 28, 1943, off Savannah, Georgia, *U-107* fired three torpedoes at the ship. Two missed, and the third hit the ship, but failed to detonate, leaving the steam merchant unharmed. Four months later, her luck ran out. On Sunday, January 2, as Private Sorenson and the Marines readied to capture San Clemente Island, the *Albert Gallatin* departed from Aden, sailing unescorted for Bandar Shahpur, Iran. The Imperial Japanese submarine *I-26* torpedoed and sank her in the Arabian Sea at 4:52 AM.

The Liberty ship SS *Sambridge* was also lost in the Arabian Sea, torpedoed by the Japanese submarine *I-27* on November 8, 1943.

As the 24th Marines crossed the Pacific, strange rumors about the mass-produced Liberty ships jostled about in the lower holds of the ships. Some of the stories were not fabrications. The early Liberty ships suffered hull and deck cracks, and many ships' logs recorded significant brittle fractures. In 1943, newspaper headlines informed readers of three *Liberties* breaking in half without warning. Invariably when Marines bantered about submarines and torpedoes, high seas, and steel coffins, someone made mention of the *Curry*, *Hooker*, or *Gaines*—names that could raise suspicion and apprehension among troops and families at home.

During the night of March 5–6, 1943, convoy ON-168 encountered nearly hurricane winds in the North Atlantic, off Nova Scotia. The SS *Thomas Hooker* began developing structural damages, and a two-foot crack opened across the main deck forward of the #3 hatch, down the side, and from the same hatch to the storeroom deck, causing flooding. At dawn, the forty-five crewmembers and seventeen armed guards abandoned ship in lifeboats before the ship could break in two.

The *Thomas Hooker* drifted for six days. *U-653* spotted her in the morning of March 12, and hit her with a torpedo at 2:09 AM. The German sub unleashed a second torpedo at 4:33 AM, and the wreck sank by the stern at 4:35 AM.

The SS *J. L. M. Curry* encountered heavy weather in enemy water in the North Atlantic, en route from Murmansk, Oblast, Russia, sailing for Loch Ewe, Scotland. Her hull cracked on March 7, and she was scuttled and sank on March 8. [18]

The SS *John P. Gaines* was the most recent Liberty ship to break in two. She suffered a hull fracture a third of the way back from the bow section in heavy seas off the Aleutians. The *Gaines* sank in the icy waters at 2:41 AM on November 24, 1943, the day before Thanksgiving. Ten lives were lost. [19]

Realistically, the threat of Japanese submarine attacks on troop ships in the Pacific was mostly scuttlebutt. The enemy's I-class submarines *had* sent the carrier USS *Saratoga* to dry dock for repairs in January 1942 after Wake Island and had helped sink the USS *Yorktown* at Midway in June. In September at Guadalcanal, *I-19* sank the carrier USS *Wasp*, and damaged the battleship USS *North Carolina* and the destroyer USS *O'Brien* (DD-415). However, by the time Pvt Sorenson sailed from San Diego, Japanese submarines, lacking radar technology and losing boats to the American anti-submarine warfare (ASW) efforts, had been consigned primarily to ferrying supplies to isolated island outposts waiting for the Marines to make amphibious assaults.

Spending weeks on a "sailing troop coffin" could put Marines in a frame of mind to look forward to charging an island beach and facing enemy crossfire, rather than spending one more day in the confines of a converted cargo hold. In the quiet moments, when rack chains rattled slightly and snoring was low, the men did not think so much about submarines, periscope sightings, and silent torpedoes. They tried, instead, to tuck away thoughts of how they would perform under fire, meeting an enemy known to be fanatical and tenacious.

Like most of the men, this was Pvt Sorenson's first time at sea. He summarized his impression of his first ocean trip, crammed in with men and equipment, in one word.

"Crowded." [20]

Operation *Flintlock*

The large convoy passed through staging points in the Hawaiian Islands late on the night of January 20 and early morning of January 21, 1944, to refuel before sailing again. The transports anchored near Lahaini Roads off the coast of Maui. The USS *Wayne* took on fuel from oiler USS *Tallulah* (AO-50) and stocks and supplies from store ship USS *Pastores* (AF-16). The weather was delightful and warm. From the ship's railing, Pvt Sorenson could see the beautiful island in the distance. It was an alluring sight, but no one was permitted to go ashore. The senior officers gathered for a final briefing.

The 24th Marines left the islands behind on Saturday, January 22, as part of a huge armada of three hundred ships. Across the horizon, Pvt Sorenson saw battleships, cruisers, aircraft carriers, destroyers, oil tankers, cargo ships, troop transports, and LSTs (Landing Ship, Tanks). The Marines had their own name for the LSTs, preferring to call them *Large Slow Targets*. More than 53,000 assault troops were underway.

That the Liberty ship SS *Samuel Dexter* had broken up in the North Atlantic due to a hull fracture the day before, sinking with no lives lost, was of little concern. The Marines knew they were going into battle as part of Operation *Flintlock*. Familiar with the code name, they did not know on which Pacific Island they would be landing until word of the 4th Division's destination passed down to all hands when they were southwest of the Hawaiian Islands.

The ships had shoved off to "capture and hold Kwajalein Atoll in the Ralik Chain (western), in the Marshalls," a place easier to pronounce than to spell in letters home. The atoll was 2,100 nautical miles (3,900 km) southwest of Honolulu, 600 nautical miles south of Wake Island, and 2,200 nautical miles east of the Philippines. Steaming into the Central Pacific waters at 11 knots (12.5 mph), the amphibious forces planned to arrive off the atoll early on Monday morning, January 31. [21]

The Marshalls consist of two island chains and are comprised of thirty-four scattered, low coral atolls with sandy beaches and impressive lagoons. Aerial reconnaissance estimated that 130 Japanese aircraft were dispensed among the bases in the Marshalls. A massive U.S. air and naval bombardment had been ongoing for some two months on selected islands. The Marines were sailing to the Marshall Islands to make amphibious landings and seize enemy airfields.

Kwajalein Atoll was recognized as the enemy's pivotal point in its defense of the Marshalls. Admiral Michiyuki Yamada exercised command of the whole area from there. The atoll's ninety-seven islands and islets, with an average height above sea level of 5 feet 11 inches, surrounded the world's largest landlocked lagoon. The lagoon opened to the Pacific on its southwest and provided harbor for a naval base with fueling and repair facilities. Kwajalein also served as the distribution center where enemy reinforcements were gathered and dispatched to other atolls. That Kwajalein was a submarine base, garnered a good amount of Leatherneck amusement about the sluggish speed of their "sailing troop coffins."

The Army Seventh Division was tasked to capture Kwajalein Island, the southernmost and largest of the islands.

Roi and Namur were the large islands in the north end of the atoll, with a total area of one square mile. A spit of land on the lagoon side and a 450-yards-long concrete causeway connected the twin islands. Triangular-shaped Roi measured 1,200 by 1,250 yards at its widest points and was relatively bare of any vegetation. The Japanese had constructed an airfield across the island that looked like a giant 4 on the reconnaissance photographs. The principal airfield in the Marshalls, it was the headquarters of the enemy's 24th Air Flotilla.

All the airfield support facilities, the shops, and barracks were on smaller Namur, 800 by 900 yards. The undergrowth on Namur was dense, providing the enemy cover and concealment and devastating interlocking fields of fire.

The 4th MarDiv was assigned to take the twin islands. The landing was to be made from the lagoon side on the islands' four beaches. The 23rd Regimental Combat Team's 1st and 2d Battalions, landing abreast on Beaches Red 2 and 3, would strike Roi airfield. At the same time, the 24th RCT's 2d and 3rd Battalions would attack Beaches Green 1 and 2 on Namur.

As the USS *Wayne* sailed toward the Kwajalein Atoll, tactical maps were drawn and unfolded. A "Restricted Not To Be Taken Ashore On D-Day" directive was stamped or penned across the operation maps. [22] The code name for Roi was BURLESQUE Island. Namur was CAMOUFLAGE. Private Sorenson listened to the explanation for the names. Approaching their respective beaches, the assault forces facing Roi would see bare white and gray coral rock. The 24th RCT battalions would see green and brown vegetation and would not recognize the enemy positions in front of them until they moved off the beaches toward Objective Line-1.

Between 1,500–2,000 enemy pilots, mechanics, sailors, and aviation support troops manned the Roi–Namur garrison. Security was in the hands of 300 to 600 men of the 61st Naval Guard Force and more than 1,000 Korean laborers, naval service troops, and "stragglers." The guard force men were the only ones on the two islands fully ground-combat trained. Most of the approximately 3,500 Japanese defenders were expected to be in the installations on CAMOUFLAGE.

The maps showed numerous coastal defense guns, heavy and medium antiaircraft guns, machine-gun emplacements, blockhouses, concrete shelters, fifty-two pillboxes, numerous antitank trenches, lines of barbed wire, and storage buildings. The enemy had positioned their weapons to cover the likely landing areas in order to annihilate the Marines in the water and on the beaches. Two pairs of twin-mounted 127mm guns covered the ocean approaches to the island, so the landing forces would not have to worry about those weapons.

The 3rd Battalion was going to attack the left third of Namur, where most the buildings and defensive installations were most densely concentrated. The 2d Battalion would take the right two-thirds.

H-Hour (W-Hour in some references) was set for 10:00 AM, Tuesday, February 1, 1944.

The pre-landing naval shelling started in the morning of January 31, the day before the assault. The hangars, pilot shack, and maintenance shops on Roi were destroyed, making the airfield useless to the enemy. The bombardment avoided damaging the airfield runways. Many hundreds of the atoll's defenders had been killed or wounded. Anticipating the amphibious assault, a small force defended BURLESQUE while the enemy abandoned the island and fled to CAMOUFLAGE.

Commanders briefed their men in front of a very detailed model/diorama of the Roi–Namur complex, pointing out the defenses and installations on the islands. Private Sorenson and the machine-gun team had a good idea of what they would be up against once their boondockers hit the coral sands on CAMOUFLAGE. [23]

Private Sorenson's squad was attached to 1st Platoon, Item Company, 3d Battalion, 24th Marines, to provide automatic fire support with their .30 caliber machine guns. He was ready to carry ammunition and fill in the firing line whenever he was needed.

Captain Albert Arsenault commanded the infantry company, and 1stLt Wray C. Lewis from Fallston, North Carolina, was his XO. [24] The platoon commanders set about briefing their troops: 1stLt Anthony T. Moore from Delaware County, New York; [25] 1stLt Benjamin S. Preston Jr. from Charleston, West Virginia; 1stLt Ralph E. Reiss from 1652 Edenside Avenue, Louisville, Kentucky; and 2dLt Lyman E. Reifsnyder of Altoona, Pennsylvania. [26]

As fire teams and squads and machine-gun crews drilled, the thought of an enemy grenade landing in a foxhole reasonably came to mind. The lesson had been drummed into them at Camp Pendleton, and men wondered if they could cover a live grenade or if they would save their own hide.

When the troop transports arrived, Pvt Sorenson could see the islands in the distance the Marines were supposed to take from the Japanese. The coral atoll islands were beautiful. Any large palm trees remaining swayed slightly in the breeze and bright sun light. The USS *Wayne* dropped anchor before going through the passage into the lagoon. The LSTs (Landing Ship–Tanks) waited far out in the lagoon. Word spread. The water depth was too shallow for the Liberty ships to enter the sixty-mile-long lagoon.

The operation planners had also learned that the Higgins landing craft (LCVP) could get hung up getting over the barely submerged coral reefs. If the front ramp were lowered, thirty-six grunts with eighty pounds of gear on them would step into twenty feet of water and go right to the bottom of the lagoon. The open Amtrac (Landing Vehicle, Tracked, LVT) only carried eighteen assault troops, but had treads and could chug over the reefs and deposit the men on the shore. The infantry battalions readied to disembark from the troop ships.

In the dark night, the LCVPs were swung over the sides of the transports. Private Sorenson climbed down the rope ladder hanging from the *Wayne's* deck and gained his balance in the bobbing boat. The Higgins boats carried the landing force through the atoll passes to the LSTs.

Once aboard the LST, the men were briefed that they would climb into Amtracs in the morning at 6:30 and track toward the designated beaches at 10:00 AM. The atmosphere in the troop quarters and on the LST's deck was charged with adrenaline and excitement as the non-stop pounding of the naval guns went on. Those who had not previously encountered the enemy's tenacity in surviving shellings and bombings did not believe there could be anything left of the defenders. The mood changed overnight.

Private Sorenson and his team were sitting out on the LST weather deck, eating K-rations. Three months had not passed since the 2d Marine Division had taken Tarawa Atoll in the Gilbert Islands from the Japanese. The bloodied beaches and the horrible cost of that three-day amphibious attack wrestled in the back of everyone's mind. More than one Marine had grenades on their minds.

"One of the fellows brought up the subject—and I don't know why—of what to do if a grenade comes into our position. We were heavy water-cooled machine gunners, and it's important to keep the gun in action."

Private Sorenson's answer was matter of fact and straight to the point. "Well, the best thing to do is either throw it out or fall on it," he said. "Whoever is closest should smother the grenade with his body." [27]

That thought made one of his buddies uncomfortable. "Jeez," he said, "you shouldn't have said that, Rick . . . because saying that, it'll probably happen."

All within hearing of the conversation would have to decide later if it was irony or fate's mockery they had overheard.

The Navy cooks below decks began preparing the assault day breakfast for the troops a little past midnight. They changed the usual menu the Marines had become accustomed to during the voyage from California. Marines who had any appetite stepped through the serving line and watched the cooks pile sizzling steaks and mounds of eggs onto their trays. Reminiscent of the final meal offered to those on death row headed for the electric chair, the Leathernecks referred to the delicious spread as "the condemned man's breakfast."

"Get off the beach!"

At dawn, 6:50 AM, the support ships began their initial salvos on CAMOUFLAGE—the 24th Marines' objective. Around 8:00 AM, the Marines entered their LVTs. The tank-like amphibian tractors rumbled down the LST ramps, dropped into the water, circled about in the lagoon, rendezvoused, and puttered to the Line of Departure. Item Company was on the very left flank of the 3rd Battalion's line of Amtracs. Private Sorenson was 4,000 yards from the shore.

At 9:35 AM, the cruisers, destroyers, and LCI(G)s began to hurl salvos into the assault beaches. The explosions were distributed throughout the area 100 yards seaward from the edge of the water, 200 yards inland, and 300 yards beyond both flanks. To the men in the landing craft, the smoking island was nothing more than a streak of sand in front of an obscure haze. The Navy was demolishing the twin islands into pieces.

On the ships, some troops waited for landing boats to pull aside to get them into the lagoon. The assault lines were not full. Orders went out over the radios to the wave commanders. "Delay the landing!" Men in the circling Amtracs waited nervously. The assault units were finally waved over the departure line a little past 11:00 AM. The run to the beach was expected to take thirty-three minutes.

The cruisers ceased their bombardment when the landing craft were 1,000 yards from shore. The destroyers kept up the barrage until the leading assault waves were 500 yards or less from the beaches. The LCI(G)s waited until the Amtracs were near the shores before they stopped their shelling. Marine and Navy dive-bombers streaked down, dropping 1,000-pound bombs on the installations still standing. In the coordinated pre-landing attacks, fighter planes continued strafing runs as the treads of the amphibian tractors chewed into the beach and the troops jumped over the sides.

To the defenders on the twin islands, the shelling barrage had seemed non-stop. Navy ships had delivered 2,655 tons of ammunition, and the Marine 75mm and 105mm howitzer platoons had bombarded them from five nearby islands. Only three battered buildings—a large administrative building, a concrete radio station, and an ammunition storage building—had survived the shelling. Nearly all the senior officers, including Vice Admiral Yamada, were dead on Namur.

Instinctively ducking his head to the rapid pinging of enemy bullets hitting the Amtrac, Pvt Sorenson landed with the first assault wave of Landing Team 3 at 12:00 noon, four hours after the landing craft had dropped into the lagoon waters. He was fifty to seventy-five yards to the left of Yokohama Pier and, for the first time, under enemy fire. The machine guns had to get forward.

Private Sorenson was under fire, although he did not know it at the time.

"The problem is that when you are under fire you really don't know it," he would tell a correspondent later. "With the noise, you don't hear the bullets, and you see a guy go down to the right and the left of you. You know you're under fire, but you think 'they can't be firing at me, because I'm not hit yet.' There's too much noise to hear the bullets." [28]

The division training exercises had drilled it into the assault force: boat teams should drive straight for Phase Line O-1 upon landing and not delay for reorganization into their normal squad, platoon, and company formations until reaching that line. The O-1 line, usually an easily identified feature in the objective area, was utilized for control and coordination of military operations. On CAMOUFLAGE, Sycamore Boulevard served as Phase Line O-1.

The vegetation and shrubs above the beaches, in many places more than six feet high, gave the defenders excellent concealment. Many enemy emplacements were out of sight until their Nambu bursts clattered into the charging Marines. Also, although the enemy beach and antitank obstacles were comparatively few in number, a series of antitank ditches and trenches extended across the island.

On the left, the 3rd Battalion ran into trouble immediately from several undamaged pillboxes. Scattered along the beaches, enemy gunners in ten pillboxes connected by trenches, mounted 7.7mm machine guns, a 37mm rapid-fire gun, a pair of 13mm machine guns, and two 20mm cannons. Marines were hit as soon as they jumped from the landing boats. Before midnight on this first day of the assault, the 3rd Battalion would lose thirty-four men killed in action. Company I would lose the greatest number.

When Pvt Sorenson saw Marines fall on the beach, he did not stop. "You just move like a robot and do the job you're supposed to do, and watch your NCO."

Navy Corpsmen attended to the wounded and the dying on the beach. The regiment's first dead were carefully and respectfully covered with ponchos. Pharmacist's Mate Second Class James V. Kirby, of Pontiac, Michigan, was on the beach with the 3rd Battalion's aid station treating the wounded and tagging the dead.

First Lieutenant Ralph Edward Reiss, 25, died early in the assault. The later After Action reports presented some conflicts among his Item Company platoon troops. The company commander reported that enemy fire had killed the lieutenant. Rumors among the grunts had it that one of his men had deliberately killed him. One handwritten notation in the regiment's *Red Book* points out that "dirty enlisted men" killed him. Why that might be so, or who among his men might have been so hostile toward the Kentucky schoolteacher, did not go into logbooks. The cryptic telegram that went to his father, Mr. George F. Reiss in Louisville, was that his son was KIA on February 1, 1944.

Squads took cover behind the seawall. The beach masters yelled above the clamor of the fighting. "Get off the beach! Keep moving!"

Many of the concrete pillboxes were still operating. Rather than charging them, the assault companies were ordered to by-pass them where possible. The medium tanks and demolition teams could take them out with armor piercing shells and high explosive rounds and satchel charges.

Moving beyond the seawall, Pvt Sorenson and several Marines encountered a small bunker—a moment that would become a life-long memory.

"We hadn't gone ten feet off the beach, and we heard something. We lifted up this piece of tin and packed in there were . . . I'm not sure if they were Korean or Japanese . . . one of the guys threw in a grenade and we shut the cover. That was the end of that."

Private Sorenson had moved a short distance inland. He figured that the breezes off the beaches made a gas attack on the island unlikely, since any gas cloud would descend back on enemy positions. He got rid of his gas mask and machete. He kept his shovel on his pack. [29]

Private Sorenson and Item Company moved off Green Beach 1 and fought for a foothold throughout the day. Thousands of shell craters pitted the island. Clusters of shattered coconut palms and breadfruit trees were down or left bent in odd angles. Hundreds of Japanese dead sprawled in the ditches and shell holes, most of them mutilated beyond recognition. Body parts were all over the island. Still, unless a body was in parts, the advancing line of Marines could not be certain that a dead Japanese was really dead. Some of the enemy guard waited until the Marines were close enough, then jumped up and charged in a suicidal dash to kill Americans in honor of the Empire.

"They were great at hiding and they would crawl under debris and so forth. And, then, when we passed through, they'd come up behind us, and start shooting at the reserve. We just kept moving ahead as fast as we could to keep the enemy unsettled."

A half hour after grinding ashore, Pvt Sorenson crossed over east-west Succotash Boulevard and moved about 100—150 yards onto Namur. The rubble and debris had made the streets impossible to tell apart from the yards of littered ground they crossed. In front of him, empty rows of concrete pilings that had supported the barracks stuck out of the ground. Twisted, torn, perforated sheets of corrugated iron provided possible enemy hiding places.

Resistance stiffened as he neared the ruins of buildings. Within one hour of Item Company reaching the beach, the enemy launched a mortar attack.

"Our heavy gun was hit and put out of action by a mortar round that put a hole in the water jacket." Private Sorenson's gunner and assistant gunner, men he had trained with at Pendleton, were killed. The crew's water-cooled heavy machine gun was knocked out.

His squad continued forward, giving support with a spare "light" machine gun, the same .30 caliber as the heavy machine gun. The light gun did not fire as rapidly, "but you could still give them fire support." Item Company, under the leadership of individual boat team commanders, fought through the rubble of a dozen or so destroyed concrete buildings.

At 1:05 PM, the advance halted as every square inch of Namur heaved. Private Sorenson felt the shudder. From out in the lagoon and looking across from Roi, it appeared that all of CAMOUFLAGE had blown up.

Company F, 2d Battalion, had landed on the right flank of Green 2 near Sally Point and advanced straight toward Nadine Point. The company ran into a heavily reinforced blockhouse a couple of hundred yards inland. After blowing a hole into the side of the building, First Lieutenant Saul Stein's team threw satchel charges inside. The blockhouse was more than a defense installation; it also held a stockpile of bombs and torpedoes. The massive explosion obliterated the building. A concussion of white smoke and vapor more than 100 feet high pushed the air away from the center of the explosion in all directions. A cloud of black smoke and rubble rose 1,000 feet into the air. [The moment is captured in the Back Cover image.]

For a time, thick black ash, dust, and smoke obscured Pvt Sorenson's vision. Concrete chunks, wood, shrapnel, and torpedo warheads rained down on the whole right half of the island.

"We suffered a lot of casualties."

Twenty Marines were killed, including 1stLt Stein and Platoon Sgt Charles Lada. One hundred Marines were wounded. Private Paul Richard Wreede died of his wounds shortly after.

The explosion was a lasting memory for everyone who survived the Kwajalein Atoll battle. As Pvt Sorenson would recount decades later, it also had an immediate impact on the landing forces.

"Everyone scrambled to find a gas mask when the torpedo warhead bunker blew up and covered most of the island with smoke." [30]

Pushing forward when the dust settled, Pvt Sorenson reached Sycamore Boulevard by 2:00 PM. Peter Road over the inlet to Pauline Point (between Roi and Namur) and the Roi airfield were to the left. Item Company paused to reorganize. Japanese defenders in formidable concrete blockhouses forward of the O-1 Line made sure the Marines kept their heads down. Tanks and halftracks came up from the beach to put the troublesome blockhouses out of commission.

Private First Class James Rocco "Jimmy" Zarillo, 20, from 192 South Center Street in Orange, New Jersey, was another light machine gunner. He had trained and drilled with Pvt Sorenson in M/3/24 at Pendleton. A hostile pillbox had his assault team pinned down in an exposed position in front of the lines. He daringly launched a lone attack against the Japanese fortification, destroying it with his machine gun. PFC Zarillo was killed in the charge and was awarded a posthumous Navy Cross. [31]

There was little enemy resistance on BURLESQUE, but opportunities for individual heroism occurred. One mortarman of Company E, 2d Battalion, 23rd Marines found himself in a position to save several comrades from death or injury—from a "friendly" grenade, not one tossed by the enemy.

✳✳✳

Private First Class Richard Beatty Anderson, 22, was from Port Angeles, Washington, on the Strait of Juan De Fuca, in the shadows of the Olympic Mountains. Standing 5 feet 6 inches, the skilled mortarman landed with the first assault wave to the left of Tokyo Pier on Red Beach 3, in front of the Bruce Blockhouse. Three hours later, Easy Company was at the center of Roi airfield, two-thirds of the way across the island.

PFC Anderson moved well ahead of his mortar team to search out the positions of enemy snipers firing on the Marines. He jumped into a bomb crater 300 yards in front of the enemy position. Lieutenant Joseph Salome, Sergeant Joseph Kennedy, and Private Harry Pearce had already taken cover in the fifteen-foot-deep hollow.

PFC Anderson, in his first day of combat, pulled a grenade from a canister. The grenade should not have been armed as it came out of the container. The safety pin had somehow been dislodged and the grenade was live. PFC Anderson attempted to throw the armed device out of the crater over his shoulder. The explosive rolled back towards him.

Instead of vacating the hole or yelling at the others to do so, putting them at risk of enemy fire, he threw his body over the grenade just like Sergeant Herb Thomas had done on Bougainville. He cradled it in his groin, curled around it, absorbed the full charge of the blast, and shielded the others from the explosion.

The detonation was contained, but PFC Anderson was grievously wounded. Both of his hands were blown off, as were parts of his abdomen, chest, and face. He clung to life long enough for a corpsman to administer morphine and plasma. He was evacuated to the beach and treated by surgeons who would remember the tattoo on his arm declaring *Death Before Dishonor*. PFC Anderson was taken aboard the USS *Callaway*. He died of his wounds.

The three Marines with whom he had briefly shared a shell crater were uninjured in the grenade blast and would remember his actions for the rest of their lives. The Navy would launch the destroyer USS *Richard B. Anderson*, DD-786, in his honor on July 7, 1945. The Marines would establish Camp Anderson in Diwaniya, south of Baghdad, in his honor during Operation *Iraqi Freedom* (2003–2010).

By 6:00 PM, six hours after the landing and with less than three hours of actual offensive assault, Roi was declared secured.

✳✳✳

Private Sorenson's crew found some cases loaded with Japanese Nambu Type 14, 8mm semi-automatic pistols in a damaged warehouse. The handgun was similar in appearance to the German Army Luger pistol and was considered a superlative war trophy. Private Sorenson tucked one into his dungarees, along with a holster and an 8-round magazine to slip into the pistol grip. Moving beyond the building, he also picked up an M1 Garand .30 caliber semi-automatic rifle from a wounded Marine. Trained in weaponry at Camp Pendleton, Pvt Sorenson did not think much of the lightweight .30 caliber M1 carbine he had been issued. "It lacked the knockdown power of the Garand." [32]

For two-and-a-half hours, Pvt Sorenson waited for the order to advance. "Doc" Kirby was sent up to the front during the late afternoon to assist company corpsmen.

Once the beachhead and front line had been consolidated, Landing Team 3 with tanks in support assaulted forward at 4:30 in the afternoon, pushing the Japanese into the small northwest sector of the island at Nura Point. The Japanese rifle and machine-gun fire only slowed Pvt Sorenson's movement along Nipp Street. He was about three quarters of the way across the island, 175 yards north of Sycamore and south of Nectar Street as dusk started to descend.

"Didn't Get the Word"

At 7:30 PM, RCT 24 was directed to dig into night defensive positions and hold the ground gained. Private Sorenson inched forward, "settling in for the night" in a shallow depression with five other Marines from I, K, and L companies. They were in the ten-foot-by-twenty-foot basement remains of a building, with footings all around them—500 yards from the lagoon and about 100 yards from the northeast coast of the island. They were also facing Japanese pillboxes and batteries of 20mm AA guns and 13mm single mount dual-purpose machine guns. They set up a perimeter and watched. There would be no rest throughout the night.

In the night, small groups of Japanese hit Landing Team 3's positions. Fires burned and rain fell. Tracer rounds crisscrossed the lines. Grenade and mortar bursts gave deadly illumination to the dark. All night long the Navy fired starburst shells that dimly lit the sky over the island.

"So, nobody was getting any sleep. The Star Shells gave the sky an eerie color. Nobody got up for fear of being hit."

The overhead flares made everybody freeze motionless. At 6 feet 3 inches tall and 175 pounds, Pvt Sorenson made for a good target. He lay on his back looking up into the sky, seeing tracers going every which way over his head.

"The sky above was a maze of red, with tracers going in every direction you can think of. . . . If you'd lifted up, it would have torn your head right off. We all lay there and said, 'Look at that!'"

Between the overhead illumination bursts, a lot of shooting echoed across the lines.

"When they would go out, it was an eerie feeling, because then the firing would start. The Japanese had spotted us or we'd spotted them. There would be a mass of firing, then the next flare would go up and everything would go quiet."

Rather than waiting for the inevitable Marine charge in the morning, several hundred enemy soldiers staged a Banzai assault under cover of the rain and dark. Companies I and L took the brunt of the attack. Over the next several hours, the opposition pushed the forward companies backwards, making it necessary for the entire line to pull back to stronger defensive positions. Poor communications had troubled the assault, especially following the early afternoon blockhouse explosion. The assault units relied on runners to pass along the situation updates and command directives. The nighttime enemy actions only increased the confusion.

Mingling Among the 10 Percent

"What's the word?" The Marines have long had an accepted adage about communication and the passing along of "the word." No matter how information was transmitted or disseminated, and no matter how important or mundane was the announcement, a statistically certain number of Marines would remain uninformed. NCOs and commanders might try to beat the odds, but usually had to report at the end of any day: "Sir, 10 percent of the men did not get the word."

Colonel Franklin Augustus Hart, 24th Marines commander, realized that a pocket of his men was ahead of the troops on the regiment's right flank. Wanting to straighten up the lines, he sent the runners forward with "the word" to drop back.

"And so, they ordered a withdrawal back to what they called the phase line. Well, we didn't get the word—there's always that 10 percent. The next morning, we found ourselves caught up there when the Japanese counterattacked. We were completely surrounded."

The night Main Line of Resistance was 200 yards back from Nora Point. Private Sorenson and thirty-five others ended up 100 yards ahead of the main body of Marines. In shell holes and an open basement in an extremely hazardous sector of the enemy's defenses, they were unaware that they were too far forward and cut off from the main body. The Marines behind them did not know that a platoon was in a pocket in front of them.

"And we were caught up there at night. We thought we had our own people all around us."

"Friendly" rifle, machine-gun, and mortar fire from the rear harassed them as much as the enemy probes did. Fortunately, the Japanese did not recognize the gap that made the isolated pocket vulnerable to encirclement. The enemy soldiers did sneak and crawl about in the night, probing for Marine positions. Private Sorenson would find out how close the prowlers came to his shell hole.

"During the night four Marines in a nearby hole had their throats slit."

"Doc" Kirby had collected a group of wounded Marines into a large bomb crater adjoining Pvt Sorenson's and a short distance behind the isolated unit to await litter bearers. Orders passed throughout the regiment to fire on anyone moving about at night. The litter teams stayed on the beach. "Doc" and the wounded hunkered down between the enemy and the phase line.

Whenever he heard the newly wounded groan and cry for "Sailor" in the darkness, "Doc" Kirby crawled out and found them, brought them to the crater, settled them down, and dressed their wounds. After administering first aid, "Doc" cheered them up with his good-natured optimism, put a blackout poncho over them, and gave them cigarettes to smoke. He knew that going back to find the phase line for help would have endangered his own life as well as the lives of the wounded. "Doc" Kirby stayed with the casualties through the night.

When the casualty reports for February 1 were finally sorted out, twelve Item Company, eleven Company K, ten Company L, and one M Company Marines had been killed in the day's actions. [33]

In addition to First Lieutenant Reiss, the Item Company KIA roster included:

Sergeant Bert Thomas Foley, 25, 687 E. 49th Street, Brooklyn, New York.
Corporal Francis Michael Gill, 24, Middle Island, New York.
PFC Milton Broadbent Jr., 18, 2140 Pond Avenue, Scranton, Pennsylvania.
PFC Herbert Spencer Carpenter Jr., 30, 2 North Main Street, Monroe, New York.
PFC Frederick Anthony Didier Jr., 19, 211 W. Thomas Street, Tampa, Florida.
PFC Carl Clarence Lucas, 21, 4223 Auburn Road, Huntington, West Virginia.
PFC Clyde Wesley Piatt, 25, 3347 Franklin Street, Bellaire, Ohio.
Private Charles Newton King, 19, 1003 Walnut Avenue, Baltimore.
Private Wiley Ray Routt, four days past his 18th birthday, 4900 10th Avenue, Sacramento, California.
Private Carlton Lloyd Satterfield, 20, Chattanooga, Tennessee.
Private John Burton Underhill, 19, Brockton, Massachusetts.

"Kind of a Hairy Situation for a While"

"The next morning, as the sun started rising, the Japanese attacked suddenly, and then they found that we were there, and tried to annihilate us." Company I was hit by a Japanese assault of approximately company strength just at dawn, between 6:00 and 6:30 AM. The four available tanks immediately rushed to provide support. "We were completely surrounded. We felt like General Custer."

The Marine line charged forward to retake the ground they had claimed the day before. The small, isolated pocket holding its position and "Doc" Kirby's first aid crater were in the crossfire of the battle. Private Sorenson remained at his machine gun.

"There were Japs all around us. But, we were holding our position." [34] He picked off "18 or 19 Japs" from his position in the basement.

Company I lost another officer in the morning. First Lieutenant Benjamin Spottsworth Preston Jr., 30, from Rt. 1, Concord, Tennessee, had skillfully and daringly led his assault platoon from Green Beach 1, taken fortified pillboxes and blockhouses, and engaged the enemy throughout the night. On Wednesday morning when his platoon "was subjected to withering fire from a heavily entrenched Japanese machine-gun position, he launched a lone attack, throwing grenades with deadly accuracy and engaging the enemy in hand-to-hand combat until the emplacement was destroyed. Boldly continuing the assault into a trench system behind the gun position, he was attacked by seventeen Japanese and, fighting desperately against this overwhelming force, succeeded in destroying several of the enemy before he himself was killed." He was awarded a posthumous Navy Cross for his extraordinary heroism. [35]

An hour into the morning fight, Pvt Sorenson noted the casualties around him. "Well, we were busy defending ourselves, and there was about 15–14 or 15 guys that had already been wounded and were laying in the hole."

An enemy soldier crawled in the darkness close enough to Private Sorenson's machine-gun position to toss a hand grenade into the hole. Private Sorenson's back was turned. His buddy gave a shout.

"Grenade!"

Private Sorenson turned and saw the explosive rolling toward him. It was not the standard Imperial Japanese Army Type 97 fragmentation hand grenade. The hostile explosive had either been taken from a dead Marine in the assault or was one of the U.S.-manufactured grenades the enemy had captured during the Battle of Bataan. Private Sorenson understood the enemy's preference to toss American grenades.

"It was not completely unheard of for the Japanese to use our grenades, since theirs were not all that reliable compared to ours." [36] Cast in iron to enhance fragmentation, the low explosive Mk II "Pineapple" landed three feet from his boondocks.

"And that's when that grenade came in. I looked down and it was sputtering . . . I didn't have time—" The 19-year-old Marine in his first battle had short seconds to decide what he would do.

"It came right next to our gun, there, where I was, and of course, it was closest to me, so I took it."

That live grenade had a blast radius of roughly seven feet, and enough iron to kill or grievously wound them all. Private Sorenson was going to over-ride his own nervous system. Like any human, he possessed an instinct to escape from adverse situations and to survive an impending danger. And, like any Marine experienced when a grenade landed within a close radius, those natural instincts drove his nervous system. Sheltering himself away from the blast would have been wholly consistent with survival instincts. His nervous system had generated enough adrenaline in that moment to either vacate the position by diving out of the crater or to desperately grab the grenade and throw it back in the direction of the enemy.

A panicked nervous system can render even a strong person immobilized, freezing every muscle into inaction while awaiting the outcome of the present danger. Sergeant Herb Thomas, PFC Henry Gurke, and PFC Richard Anderson had all felt the surge of adrenaline and did not panic. Private Sorenson was not in a panic, and he was not alone in the crater.

Marines do not jump on grenades when alone. The indomitable resolve to jump on a grenade can only come from within the individual, and the sole motivation to cover a grenade before it sends deadly shrapnel in all directions is to protect comrades from injury and death. He considered the presence of other men—comrades and Marine brothers likely to be injured or killed by the impending detonation.

"There wasn't time to think." There was no time, either, to pick up the deadly projectile and throw it from the crater. No time for anyone to vacate the hole. In that instant in time when all other alternatives seemed without merit or without the necessary time to accomplish, Pvt Sorenson overrode his own nervous system instinct for self-preservation and quickly decided to cover the explosive device with his body. Acting against natural survival instincts and overcoming powerful fear to save others from explosive projectiles is heroically brave in the extreme.

"Cover the grenade!" had resonated through the training tempo at Pendleton. Private Sorenson unhesitatingly hurled himself face down on the grenade, absorbing the full impact of the explosion.

"I no more got down and she went, Boom."

He was blown into the air, and his pack was ripped off his back. His arm had protected his face and head from flying shrapnel. The explosive force blew off the butt stock of his rifle.

"I remember going up in the air. I thought I was up about twenty feet . . . but I wasn't. It was a funny feeling. I was just floating, you know, like on a cloud, then, boom, I hit [the ground]."

No one else was wounded.

"I knew I'd been hit bad. I knew I was bleeding. Something told me I was going to live."

CHAPTER 9

Fragments Forever

✳✳✳

"Be aforehand warned
And plan it well,
If you intend my doom to spell,
For I intend to fight." [1]

—Corporal Vincent H. D. Cassidy Jr.

"I just threw myself on the grenade," he said. "There was nothing else to do." [2] There was a sense of prevailing Devil Dog duty to save the weapon and the lives of others that he would describe over the years. "Somebody had to do it. And, ah, it just happened to be me." That is what he said.

"After it exploded, I then crawled to the side of the hole."

He would quietly talk about that moment with some emotion much later in his life. "It wasn't something that was planned," he would say. "It just, it just happened. And, I could have avoided it. But, you got very close to the fellas . . . and, ah, a lot of comradeship there. And it was . . . it, it bothers you when the fellas got killed. You don't pay any attention to the gunfire or anything. You just, you know what you got to do and you're gonna do it." [3]

Fragments of the grenade severed an artery and pierced his thighs, hips, right leg, and right arm. Although the shrapnel had ripped into him, no one else in the crater was hurt. He had saved the lives of at least five fellow Marines. He would never know how he had escaped death—except that it was a miracle.

"The good Lord must have been guiding every piece." [4]

He took stock of his situation and looked for his comrades. He was quite thirsty.

"I had some live grenades on my belt. I took those off and gave them to my buddies. Then I just lay down and asked them to give me a drink, but they wouldn't give me a drink."

All the grunts had listened to first aid lectures from their platoon corpsmen. Private Sorenson's abdominal wounds were obvious and severe. Giving him water would have been dangerous.

Initially, he experienced only shock and numbness in the stomach, legs, and arms. Then, sickness and nausea and vomiting hit him.

"Doc" Kirby crawled over to him, tied the completely severed artery in a knot, covered the severe wounds to stop the bleeding, and gave him a "couple shots of morphine" to kill the pain. He dragged Pvt Sorenson into the crater with the other casualties. He lay in the hole for about an hour after the explosion blasted him into the air.

He knew that his wounds were serious and he was out of action. He offered his rifle to one of his buddies in the hole with him. The Marine looked at the weapon with no butt stock and replied simply. "What am I going to do with this?" [5]

The fighting went on for an hour. Private Sorenson and the other casualties could not be evacuated from the forward positions. His blood was seeping through his bandages and uniform into the Namur soil. Friendly mortar and artillery shells dropped on them.

"Cuz they didn't know we were there either, see, and they were trying to stop the Japanese. It was kind of a hairy situation for a while."

When daybreak February 2 came, and the Marines finally broke through the enemy attack, a crew of corpsmen advanced from the beach to find "Doc" Kirby and the wounded. Seventeen of the thirty-five Marines cut off during that night were wounded. There were no officers among the survivors, only two corporals.

Private Sorenson was carried to the beach and set down, waiting for the Higgins boats to cross the lagoon. He had no pulse for some time. The wounded were separated from those killed in action. The KIAs were set aside for graves registration personnel to manage. "But my problem was, I almost bled to death while I was laying there on the beach."

After Pvt Sorenson had been evacuated from the front line, his buddies gathered up the bloodied, outer shell fragments of the Mk II grenade that he had covered. Eventually, three of those fragments would be returned to the man who had saved their lives.

For his meritorious service on Namur, Pharmacist's Mate Second Class James V. Kirby was later awarded the Bronze Star. The medal reflected the high regard Pvt Sorenson would hold for "Doc" Kirby and the corpsmen that served and died in the Pacific Island battles.

Private Sorenson was loaded onto a Higgins boat with other wounded and taken out to a transport in the lagoon. As they carried him to the ship, his helmet fell off into the water. Item Company PFC Russell John McDonnell, 20, Millersville, Pennsylvania, was in the LCVP. He died of his wounds aboard the transport and was buried at sea.

Once Pvt Sorenson was on the ship, a Chaplain recognized his condition and gave him his last rites. [6] Orderlies took off his watch and Anoka High School *Tornadoes* ring. Private Sorenson protested, afraid his possessions would be lost. He was able to hold onto the 8mm Nambu pistol. The Chaplain talked him out of holding the Nambu, convincing the bleeding Marine that he would secure the pistol and other keepsakes for him in the Officers Mess.

"This man should be in the hospital ship. Not here." When the litter bearers got Pvt Sorenson to the medical ward, the doctors recognized the severity of his wounds from his waist to his knees. He was in such bad shape that one surgeon doubted his survival. "I wouldn't give a wooden nickel for his life."

Without time to transfer him to the USS *Relief* or the USS *Solace* hospital ships, the surgeons started working on him right there. They did not have much hope for him as they collected eleven bits of the fragmentation grenade from his body, ranging from his arms to his bladder and down his legs. They gave him three O or B+ blood transfusions—five pints in all.

Private Sorenson would not remember much after that and "was out for a couple of days." The ship remained at anchor in the lagoon. Despite the medical pessimism, Pvt Sorenson never really thought that he would die. His wry sense of humor certainly survived.

"When I woke up, I told the doctor, 'Thanks for saving my life, but I never planned to die anyway.'" [7]

CAMOUFLAGE Taken

Landing Team 3 jumped off at 9:00 AM on Wednesday, advancing into the last few hundred yards of Namur's thick, tangled foliage, downed trees, damaged buildings, and scattered debris. The 2d and 1st Battalions moved up at 10:00 AM.

The fight on CAMOUFLAGE progressed steadily. The medium tanks incapacitated one concrete pillbox after another with armor piercing and high explosive rounds. Item and King companies sent their runners back to the beach at 11:00 AM to report to headquarters that they had overrun Nora Point and linked up with the lead elements of the 1st Battalion on their right flank. Love Company moved forward, fought to the northern shore, and secured Natalie Point at 12:15 PM.

Other than mopping up the few defenders who had found hiding places behind the Marine lines, the battle for Roi–Namur was over: 24 hours and 15 minutes after Pvt Sorenson had landed on Green 1. The determined defense left only fifty-one enemy survivors of the original 3,563 in the garrison.

Military historians would come to consider the capture of the atoll and Roi–Namur as the key to subsequent successful amphibious assaults on Guam, the Northern Marianas, Iwo Jima, and Okinawa.

The 24th Marines re-embarked on the transports while the final mopping-up patrols continued down the atoll for several days to root out the last of the islets' defenders. Two incidents significant enough for Pvt Sorenson to recall later, took place before the 4th MarDiv departed Kwajalein—one involving the chaplain on board ship and the other on Roi.

Into his recovery, Pvt Sorenson asked the chaplain about his Nambu pistol and personal items. The Chaplain was saddened to report that someone had taken all his things from the Officer's Mess. This was not a matter worthy of chuckling. As any grunt might do talking to a clergyman or not, Pvt Sorenson added some expletives to his retort, reminding the Chaplain about his reassurances that he would keep the war trophy and his belongings safe. [8]

The other unforgettable incident occurred on February 12.

"I was on the ship in the lagoon when the bombing took place. The bombers only made one pass through."

For five minutes, twelve enemy twin-engine Mitsubishi (G4M) "Betty" Bombers from the Japanese airfield on Truk Atoll attacked. Flying high, the bombers dropped incendiary bombs on Roi Island. Suddenly, the dump was an inferno, and BURLESQUE was covered in sheets of flame. Tracer rounds illuminated the sky, and red-hot fragments fell from the sky onto the Marines rushing to extinguish the blaze. The explosions and fires went on for four hours. Casualties were numerous. Marines on the ships still in the lagoon rushed topside to watch what was happening.

"The trip by the ship from Kwajalein took six days to reach Hawaii." The 24th Marines sailed for Maui on February 13. Private Sorenson was dropped off at Pearl Harbor. He was back on friendly soil.

"They'd taken all the stretcher cases, and they took us to Base Eight, which was right on the water there on the bay." Only afterwards when the Naval hospital patched him up did he feel the searing pain of his eleven shrapnel wounds.

The news that Pvt Sorenson had survived a grenade detonation and was in the hospital on Hawaii reached the family and circulated through the Anoka, Hennepin, Wasaca, and Freeborn counties. The Albert Lea family wing was grateful, sharing the reports with their own boys back at home getting a feel for snow again and enjoying their ma's cooking.

That February, 1stLt Robert Sorenson was home on furlough. Staff Sergeant Franklin Sorenson, Army Air Forces liaison pilot, had graduated from a training school and was planning to get home. Army Sergeant Frank P. Sorenson had been promoted to S/Sergeant. Aviation Cadet Arthur L. Sorenson was in U.S. Navy pre-flight training. Letters informed family that Sergeant Richard Sorenson would be home in March for a twenty-day furlough, and 1stLt Clayton A. Sorenson, Army Air Force, Sergeant 1c Herbert Robert Sorenson, Pvt James H. Sorenson, Army Air Force, and Army PFC Donald F. Sorenson were all doing fine. Army Pvt Morris N. "Porky" Sorenson got a phone call late on Tuesday night, February 22. His wife, Helen (nee French), had given birth to their first boy, eight pounds, in Naeve Hospital in Albert Lea.

Even though he was overseas in the European Theater of Operations, reports of his cousin's WIA status did not take long to reach Ken Gagnon. Like his father before him, Ken was serving in the Army Medical Department. He was a Supply Sergeant with the 100th Evacuation Hospital, Third U. S. Army. He had arrived in England on February 11, 1944, and was busy preparing to sail over to France. He was a friend of Master Sergeant Joseph Michel and liked to tease "Joe" about his infatuation with a nurse they called "First Lieutenant Catherine." Always outgoing, Sergeant Gagnon found time to brag to the officers, surgeons, nurses, and enlisted men of the Surgical Division about his younger Marine cousin.

✳✳✳

Another Atoll, Another Grenade, Another Family

Prepare the beds. Three weeks had not yet passed from the time Pvt Ricky Sorenson had been evacuated from Green Beach 1. While he struggled to recover from his wounds in Hawaii, dispatches of another amphibious assault on a Marshall Island atoll reached the hospitals.

Thirty small sand and coral islands, encircling a large lagoon, make up Eniwetok Atoll. None of the islands has an elevation higher than fifteen feet. Engebi Island, triangular, forms the northern tip of the atoll. Each side of the island is about a mile long, and much of the lagoon shoreline is beach. The strategic importance of Engebi was that the Japanese had built an airstrip on its coral surface. The 22d Marines launched an assault against five of the Eniwetok islands on February 17, 1944, and had them all secured in six days. The assault on Engebi began the morning of February 19.

Anthony Peter "Tony" Damato, born on March 28, 1922, had grown up in Shenandoah, Schuylkill County, Pennsylvania, in the eastern Appalachian Mountains. The one-square-mile town, once known as "little New York" because of its cultural diversity, sat in a basin surrounded by mountains. Along the ridges of Spring Mountain, with its scrubby trees, the sky seems to stretch forever. The headwaters of both the Schuylkill River and the Swatara Creek are a valley or two over, southeast and southwest of the town. It was a remote and desolate place, hardly settled even by the time of the Civil War. The census of 1870 had registered only 2,951 inhabitants.

The region sits upon fields of mid-Anthracite coal, and the discovery of coal brought people to the land. Irish, German, Italian, Hungarian, Russian, Lithuanian, Slovakian, and Ukrainian immigrants had poured into the town by the end of the 19th century. Those of Polish descent comprised 25% of the overcrowded population.

Shenandoah could be a wild town and had the early reputation for spawning rough and resilient people. In the late 1800's it was the site of labor movements, striking coal miners, and the violent Irish Molly Maguires. By the time Anthony was born, nearly 30,000 people were crammed into the congested borough, far more than the 4,854 inhabitants who would be living there in 2016. Wild or not, the hard-working immigrants were intent on providing for their large families.

Tony, one of eight children, grew up watching his father, John Damato, don miner's clothes, go off to work wearing a cap with a small lamp attached, and coming home blackened by anthracite dust. The young Italian American finished elementary school and went on to J.W. Cooper High School. Afterwards, he went to work as a truck driver.

As was true for so many young men of the time, 1941 was a turning point in his life. He was 19 years old. His father had died that year, leaving his mother, Frances, to tend to the children still at home on West Penn Street. His older brother, Neil, had already joined the service, was working his way up in the officer's ranks, and was sending money home. And, Pearl Harbor was attacked.

On Sunday of the attack, the Philadelphia *Eagles* were in Washington, D.C., playing the *Redskins* at Griffith Stadium: game time at 2:00 PM. The 27,102 fans were alerted that something was happening when the public-address messages began midway through the first quarter and continued throughout the game. Without explanations, military officers, government officials, and diplomats were urged to leave the game and report to their Washington offices. By halftime's end when the players returned to the field, thousands of spectators had left the stadium, as had the news reporters and photographers. The final score was *Redskins* 20, the *Eagles* 14. The season was over for both teams. It was the last NFL game for Michael Martin "Nick" Basca.

"Nick" Basca, 5 feet 8 inches, 170 pounds, was a rooky halfback for Philadelphia. He enlisted in the U. S. Army on December 10, 1941.[9] The sense of patriotic duty to leave whatever occupation a football fan might have had and defend the country spread quickly.

Tony Damato enlisted in the Marines on January 8, 1942, and received meritorious promotions in the two years after his initial training. His mother sent him the news in a letter. She had received a Western Union telegram from the War Department. REGRET TO INFORM YOU YOUR SON FIRST LIEUTENANT NEIL DAMATO IS MISSING IN ACTION NEAR HOLLAND PERIOD YOU WILL BE ADVISED AS REPORTS ARE RECEIVED. Corporal Damato would never learn all the details about his brother's fate.

His brother, 332nd Bomber Squadron, 94th Heavy Bomber Group, 8th Air Force, bombardier, departed RAF Station Rougham, England, on November 5, 1943, in aircraft no. 42-31066. The B-17F was on a bombing mission to Gelsenkirchen, Germany. After the raid, enemy fighters intercepted the bomber flying at an altitude of 27,000 feet. The aircraft was hit, exploded, and crashed into the North Sea at 1:53 PM, 300 yards west of Holland. First Lieutenant Neil Damato's body was not recovered, and he was classified as MIA.

Corporal Damato, assistant squad leader, made the assault on Engebi Island with the 2d Battalion, 22d Marines, 5th Amphibious Corps. His assault company advanced inland rapidly. By late afternoon, within six hours, the island had been largely cleared of hostile combatants. By evening, a forced withdrawal of nearly half the invasion force for the assault on Eniwetok Island the next morning had depleted the Marine lines. Because small pockets of enemy forces remained on Engebi, the Marines in night defensive perimeters on February 19–20, remained alert for counterattacks. Night fighting was the worst, and no one slept a wink.

Corporal Damato, one month from his 22nd birthday, shared a foxhole in the company perimeter with Corporal Herman F. Dohms Jr. and PFC George W. Gale. A Japanese soldier stealthily slipped through the thinned line to the foxhole and dropped in a grenade.

Corporal Damato heard the grenade land and reached for it in the dark, but could not clutch it. Instead, in a split-second decision, he hurled his body onto the ground where it had landed. The blast killed him instantly. His watch stopped at 4:07 AM when the grenade exploded. Corporal Dohms and PFC Gale both survived the explosion.

"That took a lot of guts," their commanding officer, 2dLt Richard M. Pfuhl, told a correspondent. He would remember Corporal Damato for his actions on Engebi. "He was one of the best men I had. I took him with me wherever I went." [10]

Mrs. Frances Damato, 54 years old, was presented his Medal of Honor at a ceremony in Shenandoah on April 9, 1945. Then, she and her surviving children were brought to Staten Island, New York, to christen the destroyer USS *Damato* on Tuesday, November 20, 1945, in honor of her son. Photographs circulated on the AP wire of Tony's mother and sister Mary breaking into tears. Public school children in Shenandoah stood at attention at 9:25 AM in commemoration of the launching. Mrs. Damato's adult children had not yet informed her that Captain Neil Damato's status had been updated to Killed-In-Action. [11]

✳✳✳

The Lord's Sustenance

"The Navy doctors did a fantastic job on me." In Hawaii, Pvt Sorenson endured six major surgeries. The doctors rebuilt his severely damaged urethra. Early in his hospital stay, he received a Purple Heart medal. "A two-star admiral came to my bed and presented it to me. I never got the case. . . . The aide kept the box. I guess they figured I was going to die anyway." [12]

Private Sorenson knew that his Item Company companions were at Camp Maui, Hawaii, taking on replacement troops and training for another amphibious assault—Operation *Forager*. In mid-May, the regiment was again living in troop transports. The USS *Calvert* carried them to Oahu, and moored at Hickam Field. Friends visited Pvt Sorenson when they were granted some liberty. First Lieutenant John C. Chapin, 23, King Company, 3/24, sent his greetings.

Private Sorenson was out of the wheelchair and on crutches. The surgeons felt he was well enough to be put aboard a ship and transferred to the Seattle Naval Hospital. He left Hawaii on Sunday, May 21. He had departed the islands before the disaster.

Thirty-four ships were docked in West Loch, off Waipio Peninsula across the channel from the USS *Calvert*, to load ammunition, supplies, and high-octane aviation fuel for amphibian tractors in preparation for Operation *Forager*. At 3:08 PM that Sunday, a series of explosions sank *LST 353* and tore through seven other LSTs—five of those sank, and two others were too damaged to participate in the planned operation. The raging fires and smoke rising over the harbor were reminiscent of the December 7, 1941 loss of ships and men. It took 24 hours to extinguish the inferno.

The Navy "hushed up" the incident and misreported some details to not jeopardize *Forager*. Waiting four days, Admiral Chester W. Nimitz reported from U.S. Pacific Fleet Headquarters, Pearl Harbor, that "several small vessels" had been destroyed in an explosion that occurred while ammunition was being unloaded from one of the small landing craft. There was "some loss of life, and a number of injuries." Further information would be announced later. A month later, the public report was that twenty-seven men were killed in the explosion, 100 were missing, and 380 were wounded. The final casualty list included 163 dead and 396 wounded. [13]

The 24th Marines departed Hawaii for Saipan on May 29.

Before July ended, it would seem that news of Pvt Sorenson's medals was bracketed by news of sensational ship explosions.

He convalesced at the Seattle Hospital, expecting to be returned to general duty. He was still pretty weak and still getting a lot of treatment. In his opinion, the Lord sustained and strengthened him to go on. He was promoted back up to Private First Class in June. In late June, he had the chance to meet Captain Joel T. Boone, the medical officer-in-command of the facility. The Navy captain had earned a Medal of Honor on July 19, 1918, while serving as a surgeon with the Marines in Vierzy, France, in WWI. He had been physician to three presidents while serving in D.C. The doctor's appearance made an impression on PFC Sorenson.

"He was a very distinguished looking man with a white mustache."

Captain Boone informed PFC Sorenson that his wounds were such that he would not be returning to a combat unit. In fact, he had so much shrapnel imbedded in his body that doctors would be picking it out of him for the rest of his life. Shrapnel in his arms, especially, would occasionally trouble him. It was the physician's pleasure, however, to officially inform the Marine that his valor was to be recognized in a ceremony.

"He took me aside and informed me that in a few days I would receive the Medal of Honor, and not to tell anyone about it." [14]

Private First Class Sorenson had seen plenty of bravery in the less than 24 hours he had fought on Namur Island. He had witnessed men die and casualties quietly wait for evacuation. He knew that the 24th Marines had again embarked on a Liberty ship for an enemy-occupied island. He prayed for them. The news that any medal would be pinned to his chest was humbling.

That the award recommendation made it to President Franklin D. Roosevelt's desk for his signature in five months illustrates how incredible commanders viewed PFC Sorenson's valor to have been. Never mind that the Democrats were planning to hold their National Convention at the Chicago Stadium, July 19–21, to nominate the president for an unprecedented fourth term.

✳✳✳

The Marines assaulted the beaches of Saipan in the Mariana Island chain at first light on June 15, 1944. The 24th Marine Regiment, held in reserve until afternoon, was called ashore into heavy fighting, charging inland past mangled bodies, burning LVTs, shell holes, destroyed enemy pillboxes, scattered debris, and shattered trees. In the next seven weeks, four Marines would earn posthumous Medals of Honor for jumping on grenades on Saipan and Tinian.

Harold Glenn Epperson was a year older than Private Sorenson. Born in Akron, Ohio, on July 14, 1923, he had spent his youth and school years in nearby Massillon in the midst of two brothers and three sisters. Massillon was a steel town, and most of its inhabitants were hard-working and sometimes hard-fighting, blue-collar laborers. Most Ohioans knew about Massillon, primarily because of its high school *Tiger* football teams. The *Tigers* had started playing in 1894 and had won more state and national championships than just about every other high school in America.

After graduating from Massillon Washington High School in 1941, Harold went to work at Goodyear Aircraft Company in Akron. He enlisted in the Marine Reserves on December 12, 1942, and waited to be called to service. Once activated, he was trained in special weapons and assigned duties as a machine gunner. He sailed to New Zealand as a replacement troop for the casualties the 1st Battalion, 6th Marines, 2nd Marine Division, had suffered on Guadalcanal. He earned his first promotion.

Private First Class Epperson landed on Tarawa Atoll's Green Beach at dusk on November 21, 1943, the second day of the assault. He fought with distinction during two attacks on the next day and remained on Tarawa until the Marines had secured it. Afterwards, he was in Hawaii while the regiment reequipped and trained replacement troops at Camp Tarawa. He prepared to depart Pearl Harbor in the days prior to Private Sorenson's transfer to the Seattle Hospital.

Into the tenth day of fighting on Saipan, PFC Epperson was on post, manning his machine gun in the predawn morning of June 25. The Japanese launched an attack in hopes of infiltrating the defensive line. PFC Epperson's machine gun position was the point of their attack. He and his companions quickly put the gun into action with a steady rate of fire, causing the Japanese many casualties. When the assault appeared to have been repulsed, an enemy soldier thought to have been killed tossed a grenade into the machine-gun emplacement.

Private First Class Epperson, three weeks shy of his 21st birthday, instantly hurled himself on top of the grenade, absorbing the full impact of the explosion and saving the lives of his comrades.

Grant Frederick Timmerman was born on February 19, 1919, in Americus, a small town of fewer than 700 hundred people in the tallgrass country of east central Kansas. He had attended public schools in Emporia, ten miles down the road. Both towns sit off the main route between Wichita and Topeka.

Grant's parents, Fred and Esther, were "down-to-earth" folks, not taken to fan-fare. They had recognized that their son was studious and smart and allowed him his various boyhood interests. Grant learned to speak, read, and write French and Russian. He played saxophone for two years in the high school band. For enjoyment, he went small game hunting. He wondered what he would do after high school; employment opportunities being somewhat limited for multi-lingual musicians in Depression-era Americus.

After graduating with the Class of 1936, Grant studied pre-engineering at the State College in Emporia for a year. The next summer, 1937, he decided to leave his hometown to search for a meaningful vocation and travelled west to San Mateo, California. He found a job as an electric welder. Rather than returning to Kansas, he enlisted in the Marines that October and served for four years. Fourteen weeks after his discharge, two months after the attack on Pearl Harbor, he reenlisted and rose in rank to sergeant over eight-months' time.

Sergeant Timmerman was assigned to tank commander duties with Company B, 2d Battalion, 6th Marines. He went ashore with the tanks on Tarawa Atoll and helped finish up the seizure of that island. He retrained in Hawaii, then, sailed for the Mariana Islands.

Sergeant Timmerman spent his first night on Saipan without sleep or rest. He directed his tank guns, protecting the Marine line during Japanese counterattacks. He manned his gun in such a vigorous and accurate manner, that he was awarded a Bronze Star for heroic achievement. Three weeks of fighting followed. He sustained a minor shrapnel wound to his right forearm during a last-ditch banzai attack on June 28. Enemy resistance on Saipan seemed nearly at the end.

On the morning of July 8, 1944, Baker Company tanks advanced against hostile emplacements, trenches, and pillboxes. Sergeant Timmerman maintained fire upon the enemy with the antiaircraft sky mount machine gun. Ordering the tank to stop, he stood exposed in the turret and swung the 75mm gun to open fire on a critical target. There were Marines around his tank.

"Get down!" he ordered them to the ground to avoid the expected muzzle blast.

An enemy grenade came at the turret, headed for the hatch, endangering his tank crew. Sergeant Timmerman, 25 years old, intercepted the grenade with his body and held it to his chest, preventing its blast from killing any of his crew or the Marines near his tank. He died instantly.

The Marines declared Saipan "secured" the next afternoon at 4:15 PM.

Family News and Newspaper Headlines, July 1944

At the time Captain Boone talked to him in Seattle, Private First Class Sorenson did not look like a serviceman. His "digs" were part Navy, part Army, and part Marine Corps uniform. In July, a Marine major sent him down to San Diego by train to get fitted out for all the uniforms he needed.

On Sunday, July 16, a Sorenson extended family reunion was held in Albert Lea's Tourist Park. About 100 attended. Much of the catching up was about the many Sorenson boys from Minnesota and Iowa who were off to war. Ricky's uncles, Morris and Raymond Sorenson, were serving in the Army and Marine Corps, respectively. Grandma Sorenson moved from 120 South Broadway in Albert Lea to live with Ricky's family in Anoka. She expected to move back as soon as the war was over. [15]

She cut out newspaper articles about her Grandson Ricky to save for when he came home. There might have been more attention paid to his Medal ceremony, except for a violent event near San Francisco—more ship explosions—two days before PFC Sorenson's "great personal valor and exceptional spirit of self-sacrifice" were celebrated. The disaster took more lives and captured more newspaper print than the blockhouse detonation on Namur.

Late on Monday night, July 17, two ammunition ships exploded at Port Chicago: a mystery explosion that was the largest U.S. home-front loss of life during WWII. It dominated headlines for weeks. The calamity sent the $2 million *Quinault Victory* and $1.6 million Liberty ship *E. A. Bryan* skyrocketing into the air in a sheet of white flame and nearly demolished the small town of Port Chicago. The packed town theater was wrecked while a movie played, but only two patrons were injured. The blast was felt in fourteen counties within a radius of fifty miles, was heard 200 miles away, killed an estimated 377 people, and injured between 500 and 1,000 more. The few survivors on the docks had no details.

The Navy had no explanation for the newspapers. [16] Investigations and ramifications—issues of race and segregation, mutinies, and court-martials—extended well into 1946. Front-page news columns about PFC Sorenson's Medal award appeared beside columns about the rising death toll in the munitions blast. By Wednesday, only four bodies had been recovered from the explosion's debris. President Roosevelt was attending the Yalta conference overseas at the time.

"They turned out the whole hospital." The ceremony was conducted at the Seattle Naval Hospital on July 19, 1944. In front of other patients, doctors, and nurses, Major General Joseph C. Fegan, USMC, commanding the Department of the Pacific, presented the Medal of Honor to PFC Sorenson. It was the only time General Fegan presented a Medal of Honor to a recipient. Seattle's CBS Network KIRO Radio broadcast the ceremony. [17]

"That was quite a thrill." Reading of his Citation went over the radio frequency. "The President of the United States takes pride in presenting the MEDAL OF HONOR to PRIVATE RICHARD K. SORENSON . . ." He became the second living enlisted Marine in WWII to wear the Medal.

Private First Class Sorenson thought the service ribbon he received for the Medal looked rather odd. When he thought about it, he wondered if the nurses had manufactured it spur-of-the-moment for the presentation. The WWI-style box the ribbon and Medal came in also seemed somewhat beat up. That would always give him a chuckle. He suspected that maybe Captain Boone switched the boxes for the presentation and, then, kept the newer box for his own Medal. Even if that conjecture were true, it did not tarnish his view of the Navy surgeon. [18]

A/P and UPI reporters found the words in PFC Sorenson's Citation to be inspiring, recapping them for headlines. The Minnesota newspapers made note of the fact that, after the Marine Corps checked its records, PFC Sorenson was the first enlisted Minnesota serviceman of all service branches to have received the award in either WWI or the ongoing war. [19]

After being decorated, he was placed in charge of work details at the hospital. First, he was given liberty and ordered to get PFC chevrons on his uniform. While he was busy with that, news about his uncle reached the home front.

On Friday, July 21, Helen Sorenson received a telegram in Austin. Private Morris "Porky" Sorenson, her husband, had been seriously wounded in action in France on July 6, 1944, during the Normandy invasion. He was hospitalized somewhere in England. Helen received his Purple Heart later in August.

The Gagnon and Mox families tried not to worry that a telegram might be delivered to them as well. Sergeant Ken Gagnon had arrived in France on July 18, with the field and evacuation hospitals assigned for medical service with the 1st U.S. Army. His unit would revert back to the 3rd U.S. Army control on August 1, as one of General Patton's tank columns advanced rapidly up the Brest Peninsula, while another of his columns moved into the heart of France.

In three-and-a-half months, the 100th Evac Hosp doctors performed more than 6,000 operations; treating gunshot, machine-gun, grenade, and artillery shell wounds, as well as mine, booby-trap, and self-inflicted injuries. Combat exhaustion and psychological injury cases outnumbered the bloody wounds by five times.

✳✳✳

One devastating telegram was delivered to a young widow in West Frankfort, Illinois. The newspaper accounts about that telegram and stories about Marines who did not survive grenade blasts on Pacific islands added a modest dimension to PFC Sorenson's own Medal award and would always be a reminder to him that the Lord had watched out for him.

Joseph William Ozbourn was from Herrin, Williamson County, southern Illinois. He came from a family line of hard-working Scot ancestors who had immigrated west out of Baltimore and through Philadelphia. The Ozbourn family crest has as its motto *Pax in bello*, translated to mean, *Peace in war.*

Herrin sits among rolling green hills and lies on a rich vein of accessible coal. The United Mine Workers of America Local Union was strong in the area, because so many husbands and fathers were employed in the coal mines. Tuberculosis, pneumonia, suicide, and gunshot wounds were often the reported cause on death certificates.

Joe's parents had married as teenagers in 1912. Thomas Ozbourn was a coal miner. Eva Ozbourn was a stay-at-home housewife. Their first baby, Ina, died on October 27, 1915, and was buried in Herrin City Cemetery. James was their first son, born in 1918.

Born on October 24, 1919, Joe was 29 months old when a nationwide strike began on April 1, 1922. After two months without work, at least fifty men in Herrin, "strike breakers," decided to go back to work. On June 21–22 an angry mob of striking miners chased "the scabs" from the strip mine, murdering twenty-two of them. National news agencies referred to the events as the "Herrin Massacre."

After the strike ended, Tom moved the family up to Buckner Village in Franklin County and rented a house on East 3rd Street. The Ozbourn boys went to grammar school in the village. Benton was a five-mile walk, and Logan was another five miles east. West Frankfort was not so close—six miles south on the railroad tracks from Benton. The three towns offered the boys opportunities Buckner did not.

James and Joe finished their schooling at eighth grade and began looking for jobs. The residents living along East 2nd and 3rd Streets were mostly mining families. In 1935, Tom, Eva, and Joe moved up to East 2nd Street. Walking to work on the street, Joe met immigrant neighbors from Austria, Italy, Poland, and England. James moved down the street to live on his own on Burleston Street. He married Pearl from West Frankfort.

The Great Depression was in its ninth year at the start of 1939. The war in Europe dominated national headlines as significant changes occurred in the Ozbourn family.

Joe was 19 years old when Eva, aged 43, died on March 11, 1939, in West Frankfort. In June, he was an uncle for the first time. James and Pearl had a daughter, and named her Eva, after his mother. James was a physical recreation worker for the Works Progress Administration (WPA), helping to conduct leisure time activities like athletics, sports, swimming, and other types of physical recreation. Joe had gotten to know the Meacham family and thought it was time for him to start his own family.

Walter Scott Meacham was a coal miner. In 1900, when he was 20 years old, he married Jane "Jannie" Barnard, who was 16 years old. By the 1930 Franklin County Census, they had three sons and four daughters, and lived on Franc Street, off Jackson Street, in the center of Benton. [20] Helen Bernice was their sixth child, born in 1921.

Joe married 18-year-old Helen from Logan/Hanaford Village, and the couple lived with his father on East 2nd Street. [21] Tom was doing roadwork for the WPA, and Joe, a rugged young man, strong and mechanically inclined, was a WPA laborer.

Following the Sixteenth Census of the United States in April 1940, Joe went to work in the Old Ben Coal Corporation coal mines down in West Frankfort. He and Helen lived on 1911 East Oak Street and had a son, Ronald Dale. Joe was a trip rider—hard labor and sometimes dangerous. He worked with and around underground locomotives and was responsible for lifting and hauling fifty to one hundred pound sacks, operating and repairing equipment, switching cars, and maintaining engines. Much of his work required that he move about in a crouched position. It was good preparation for the Marine Corps. He enlisted on October 30, 1943, just as the Marines approached Bougainville.

After boot camp, Private Ozbourn was sent to special weapons training and was designated a Browning Automatic Rifleman. On January 8, 1944, he was assigned to the 2d Squad, 3rd Platoon, Baker Company, 1st Battalion, 23d Marines, 4th Marine Division. The company's *Red Book* had already been compiled, so, his comrades would not have a photo of him later when they looked back to their service time. They would never forget their image of him. PFC Herman Schwab saw him "as a steady performer and someone you would want on your side when the chips were down". [22]

Private Ozbourn sailed to the Central Pacific with Task Force 58 in a troop ship much like the one Private Sorenson was berthed in. He made the February 1, amphibious landing on Roi with the first assault wave, crossing Red Beach 2 in front of a pillbox and Bernie Blockhouse. The squad moved beyond Runway Able, reaching Runway Baker. He was to the left of the crater when PFC Richard Anderson, Company E, 2d Battalion, saved comrades by covering a "friendly" grenade. Private Ozbourn would deal with a "friendly" grenade five months later.

After Roi–Namur was secured, the 23d Marines returned to Hawaii for further training. Private Ozbourn then participated in the fight on Saipan in June, and survived twenty-four more days of fighting. Next was Tinian Island, a few miles south. He landed on Tinian late in the afternoon of July 24, 1944.

The mission was to remove a garrison of 9,000 Japanese. Over the next several days, the forces rapidly surged south across open plains towards the oblong Masalog Hill at the southern tip of the island. The 23d encountered a complex of well-camouflaged cave fortifications and mine fields along the coast near Sunharon Bay and slowed to clear them. Crouching along in some of the caves was a reminder of trip rider work in the Illinois coal strip mines.

On July 30, 3d Platoon was tasked to clear out the remnants of enemy soldiers resisting in pillboxes and dugouts on the right flank. Private Ozbourn advanced in the middle of a five-man, line-abreast fire team. Squad Leader Eddie Newman, PFC Herman Schwab, PFC Otto B. "Tex" Freeman, and Private Delbert Wayne Fliear moved with him to the opening of one of the enemy dugouts. PFC Clarence M. Harron was nearby. [23]

The BAR-man pulled the pin from a grenade and let the spoon fly. The sound was recognizable to the team. "Pop." He started to throw the explosive inside the fortification. Before he could toss the activated grenade, an explosion at the entrance wounded all five men and temporarily stunned them. Seconds passed.

Private Ozbourn, 24 years old, was unable to toss the grenade into the dugout or throw it beyond the proximity of the other four wounded Marines. He clutched the grenade to his body and fell on it. Although the explosion took his life, his four companions were spared from the blast and survived the war. Tinian was declared secured for American use by 6:30 PM two days later.

The telegram was delivered to his wife, and she returned to Logan with her boy to live with her family. Helen would receive official notifications for two years. Marine Headquarters in D.C. notified her in May 1945 that the Medal of Honor with Citation, signed by President Roosevelt, was to be awarded posthumously to her husband. Arrangements for a formal presentation were pending. She was invited to Washington to receive the Medal from the Secretary of the Navy.

On the first day of winter, just before Christmas 1945, Helen was in Bath, Maine, to christen DD-846, the USS *Ozbourn*. [24] She was brought to the Boston Naval Shipyard on March 5, 1946, to commission her husband's namesake.

Joe's widow remarried in 1946 to Raymond J. Bandy. Ronald would be a half-brother to two sisters and two brothers. Helen seldom talked to her first boy about his father. She did keep his posthumous Medal of Honor and the ceremonial champagne bottle used to christen the destroyer.

Those keepsakes would pass down to Joe's three grandchildren: Ronald, Timothy, and Lynn Ann Ozbourn. [25]

Tinian had been secured for use after Private Ozbourn's heroic action, but the sacrifices and dying were not over on the little island.

Robert Lee Wilson grew up thirty-five miles northwest of Joe Ozbourn's family. Joe E. and Annie Wilson had married in 1911. They owned a house at 408 North Davis Street in Centralia, Illinois, while they raised their children and farmed. They already had two sons and three daughters when Robert was born on May 24, 1921. [26] They added two more boys to the family by the time Bob went off to grammar school.

Bob's hard work and diligence earned his father's respect. In his dad's opinion, "He was one of the best workers I ever saw." He was engaging and personable and made friends easily. One good friend was Lucille Patton, an attractive young woman who would have a long career as a Broadway stage actress. When Bob decided to enlist in the Marines three months before the attack on Pearl Harbor, his eldest brother, Walter, and an uncle lived down in Herrin. Walter was with the WPA.

Bob boarded a train in August 1941 and waved goodbye to his parents. That would be the last time Joe and Anna saw their son. [27] The war was a major topic of conversation in the Wilson household for the next four years. One of Bob's older brothers volunteered for service in the Navy, and his two younger brothers enlisted in the Army.

Private Wilson "fought in practically every major engagement in the Pacific" prior to Tinian. He had participated in the campaigns for Tulagi, Gavutu, Tanambogo, Florida, and Guadalcanal in late 1942, and the four bloody days of fighting on Tarawa Atoll in November 1943 with the 1st Marine Division. He earned a promotion to private first class, was assigned to the 2d Battalion, 6th Marines, 2d Marine Division and, then, fought for the capture of Saipan with his company. He was still on Tinian, assigned to Company D, 2d Pioneer Battalion, 18th Engineers Regiment, when the forty square miles of island was secured on August 1.

Company commanders reported isolated pockets of well-concealed Japanese in caves and ravines on the southeastern ridge. Lieutenant Colonel Edmund B. Games, 2d Battalion, 6th Marines, ordered his officers to either capture or silence the remaining enemy defenders still resisting the Marine presence on the island.

As had happened on Saipan, enemy soldiers and civilians acted out mass suicides, some parents throwing their children over cliffs into the ocean. Japanese soldiers pushed civilians over cliffs and even forced civilians into groups of fifteen to twenty frightened individuals, attached explosive charges to them, and blew them into eternity.

On August 3, PFC Wilson advanced with a squad searching out secluded and camouflaged enemy positions in heavy underbrush. They believed that enemy soldiers had concealed themselves behind a pile of rocks. "Fully aware of the danger," PFC Wilson moved to the lead, while his companions formed into a covering group behind him with their automatic weapons. Before reaching the suspected hiding place, a grenade landed among the squad members.

Private First Class Wilson, 23 years old, reacted immediately. Shouting a warning to the others, he hurled his body onto the grenade. Having sacrificed his own life, his comrades survived the explosion.

✳✳✳

A Salute from the Hero of Guadalcanal

Minnesota to Fete Its Greatest Hero. [28] USMC divisional headquarters in Chicago sent the first definite word to the Minneapolis Marine Recruiting Office on Wednesday, August 2. Private First Class Sorenson had been transferred from Seattle to San Diego Marine Base. His furlough would be granted from San Diego, and he would have his homecoming in Anoka within a week to ten days. Plans neared completion for the "Ricky Sorenson Day" welcome in the Cities to honor "Minnesota's greatest living hero of this war," sponsored by the Minneapolis Recruiting Office and the Junior Association of Commerce. A luncheon was to be open to the public.

Two weeks after his Medal presentation, PFC Sorenson was released from the hospital, given a thirty-day furlough and sent home on convalescent leave. He made a quick trip to Los Angeles and had a chance to visit an aunt living there. Then he went to Camp Pendleton. [29] Wearing the nation's "highest token of esteem," he was promptly handled in the Reclassification and Redistribution Center.

Gunnery Sergeant John Basilone and his wife, Sergeant Lena Mae Riggi, were not long back from their honeymoon in Portland. The Gunny, the other living WWII enlisted Marine holding the MOH, was training with Charlie Company, 1st Battalion, 27th Marine Regiment, 5th Marine Division, preparing to go to Iwo Jima. He strode across the

Navy Photo, NEA Telephoto

training area to greet PFC Sorenson heartily. Photos of the two smiling heroes went out on the newspaper wires.

Gunny Basilone, aged 27, was a Marine Corps legend. Shorter than the PFC, he looked obviously the older of the two. "Congratulations, kid," he said. "We've heard all about what you did. I am really very happy to know you."

The UP correspondent asked the young recipient some questions about covering a grenade. Described as "an ammunition carrier," PFC Sorenson quipped a little.

"I sat on it for a minute and then it went off." He admitted to being surprised to receive the Medal, and thought that he must be the first man to win a Medal of Honor by just "sitting." On a serious note, he said what most grunts would say. "Any good Marine would have done what I did. Lots of other fellows are doing the same thing—only most of them aren't living." [30]

Meeting Gunny Basilone before the Guadalcanal hero returned to the Pacific would carry more memories for PFC Sorenson than his Medal ceremony in Seattle. Later, knowing that an enemy mortar obliterated Manila John Basilone's life on the Iwo Jima beachhead on February 19, 1945, he thought that the Corps' decision to return the gunny to the war was most regrettable.

"I think it changed everybody's life." [31]

As PFC Sorenson waited to leave Pendleton to board a plane in San Diego, "he was as calm as the day he raised his right hand and was sworn into the Marines." His every minute was spent thinking of his family, their house on Benton Street, and his homecoming in Anoka. His father and mother, his brother, William, 16, and Mary Carol, three years old, and 7,000 hometown residents prepared to welcome their boy home. Of his father, he recalled, "Dad kind of expected me to go into the Navy. . . . But, I guess he is pretty well satisfied about the way things turned out."

After the photos were taken, PFC Sorenson was put on an airplane and told he would be going home, with brief stops in Kansas, Chicago, and Minneapolis. When the plane taxied to a stop in Kansas, he had a thought.

"I don't want to go to Chicago. I can just get off here, take the bus, and go into the train depot."

He grabbed his sea bag, got off the plane, caught a bus, went into Kansas City, and bought his ticket to Anoka at the depot. Waiting to board the train, he sent a wire to his mother, letting her know that he would be on the train and home in about seven to eight hours.

The flight from Kansas landed on schedule at Chicago. Unbeknownst to PFC Sorenson, a full colonel and a Marine Honor Guard were waiting on the tarmac to receive him. A parade and reception had been organized for his welcome and, then, a train ride to Minneapolis. When he did not disembark from the plane, "the Marine Corps came unglued." The colonel was standing out there when he was informed that Mrs. Sorenson had received the telegram about her son's itinerary change. PFC Sorenson found great humor in the Chicago events when his mother told him.

As the train arrived at the Anoka depot on Friday night, August 4, PFC "Ricky" Sorenson was having a conversation with a fellow passenger. "I suppose everybody's waiting for you," the man said.

"No," replied the young Marine. "My parents will be there, but that's about all."

The homecoming crowds who swarmed the train depot surprised him. His mother, tears of joy streaming down her cheeks, was the first to greet him as he stepped from the train. All his schoolmates, his entire family, and the whole town cheered him. Some admiring girls from Anoka gave him invigorating hugs, and Carl explained to a reporter, "There isn't any special one."

PFC Sorenson appreciated the hero's welcome, but preferred time with his family. "Gee," he gasped, "I haven't been so happy in a long time—but, I hope we can be left alone pretty soon." [32]

Under the caption, Marine Hero Comes Home, a photo of the family at home was front-page news. Standing in the center in his uniform, his father to his right holding Mary Carol in his arms, his mother and brother on his left, all looking proudly at him. He was inches taller than them all. [33]

On Saturday morning, he "quietly partook of the first of his mother's home cooking" he'd had since he left home ten months earlier. He held a press conference that morning, and, while newspaper reporters, photographers, and officials of the Junior Chamber of Commerce asked him questions and tried to plan a "Sorenson Day" to honor him, he savored his mother's home-baked cinnamon-pecan rolls. On Sunday, he spent what must have seemed like his last quiet day at home with his family. Radio broadcasts and daily newspaper headlines for "the first Minnesota enlisted man to win the Congressional Medal of Honor in two wars" kept readers apprised of his whereabouts.

Minneapolis designated Wednesday, August 9, as "Ricky Sorenson Day." On Monday, PFC Sorenson privately expressed the hope that public acclaim and homage would have run its course after the festivities so he could get on with the fishing trip that had been thus far delayed. In deference to his wishes, Tuesday was a day of privacy and rest for him. [34]

The next day in Minneapolis was in no way quiet. In the morning, "he was called on to exhibit himself at a parade through the loop and a noon luncheon." The temperature got up to about 80°F, the wind blew gently, and the sky was cloudy enough that the sun did not beat down on him. At the Nicollet Hotel, he was told that he would have to make a short speech. The combat veteran was so nervous he could not eat. Food would not get past his throat.

"They had this beautiful steak in front of me, I couldn't even take a bite. It was right up in here."

After the meal and accolades, the parade traveled up to Anoka, where Sorenson family relatives from Duluth, Albert Lea, and Austin had gathered to visit with Ricky. The city had closed the stores, and all of Anoka was out for the hometown parade that ended up at the bandstand on City Square. As the crowd thronged all around, Rick and the prominent guests took the pavilion stage under the sign stretched across the roof proclaiming Welcome Home "Ricky".[35] It seemed odd that Anoka Mayor Robert B. Ehlen, Republican, so effusively shook the hand of "a high school dropout."

"And it was awful nice." The Anoka homefolk had a fitting gift ready for him and telephotos went out on the news wires. Sitting beside his young brother Bill and surrounded by a group of children, PFC Sorenson, wearing his Medal of Honor around his neck, tried out his new fishing rod and reel with the help of the other "enthusiasts." [36] The hero worship with which kids greeted him when he returned to Anoka always drew an uncomfortable chuckle. What he looked forward to most was a fishing trip to Detroit Lakes.

On a deeper level, reporters' questions and comments about his being the "first enlisted man from Minnesota to win the *coveted* Medal of Honor" demonstrated little understanding of the meaning of the nation's highest award for bravery in combat upon the recipients.

On a later occasion, "after coming home from fighting in the Pacific," he treated his brother and sister at the Anoka soda fountain. In his Marine dress greens, sitting between two children on either side of him, he sipped a half-finished soda, frosty with a scoop of vanilla ice cream, from two straws. Over his left breast pocket, his blue MOH ribbon was pinned above his Purple Heart, American Campaign, and Asiatic-Pacific Area Campaign ribbons. [37]

Bob Paulson, commentator at radio station KATE, "serving Albert Lea 18 hours daily at 1450 Kilocycles," invited PFC Sorenson down to the studio. The folks in the Albert Lea–Austin area tuned in at 6:30 PM on Thursday to hear Minnesota's foremost war hero on the air. [38] That was just the first of his radio broadcasts.

That same day during the state American Legion tournament on August 10, St. Paul sports columnists informed readers that Anoka's relief pitcher Richard Sorenson was no relation to the Marine hero of the same name.

Not entirely convalescence or a furlough, the Marine Corps was out at his house at 7:00 AM to take him to one function after another, going all over. They sent him to the parade grounds—not to do any parading, but to make speeches. PFC Sorenson became a member of the Junior Association of Commerce, the Marine Corps League (Life Member and later Chapter Commander), and the Anoka Veterans of Foreign Wars Post. [39]

The next Wednesday morning he left with his family for Chicago. On Thursday, August 17, he participated in a re-enactment of his MOH "adventure" broadcast on the 9:00 PM, CBS "First Line" national radio program. [40]

On Sunday night, August 20, when the telephone rang back at home, he learned one of the unexpected actualities of wearing the Medal.

In Mankato on Sunday, American Legionnaires at their state convention "thought they were having a genuine treat Sunday when a soldier was introduced as 'PFC Richard Sorenson, Anoka, one of two living enlisted marines to wear the congressional medal of honor.'" A "gullible visitor" had met the serviceman on the street and, after he had introduced himself as Sorenson, invited him to speak at the convention. Apparently, the Legionnaires had not yet seen an official photograph of the Medal holder.

The unknown soldier accepted the honor, spoke briefly, and quickly left the Legion hall. Some more astute and skeptical Legionnaires wondered why the speaker wore corporal stripes when Sorenson was a PFC. They checked and discovered that the genuine Medal recipient was spending a quiet Sunday at home with his family. The police were on the lookout for the imposter. [41]

Family in Albert Lea was notified that Sunday that Sergeant Russell N. Sorenson had been seriously wounded in the back in action against the enemy on July 31, earning his second Purple Heart. He was recuperating in an England hospital. [42]

Rick's uncle Private Morris Sorenson, wounded in France in July, was still in the hospital "somewhere in England" when Ricky had his homecoming parade. Morris would be transferred to the El Paso military hospital in September for convalescence, then, would be home with family and friends for a twenty-two-day furlough. He was home again in December for Christmas on a thirty-day leave with his wife, 10-month-old son, and his mother, who was residing on Bridge Avenue. Private Sorenson was a special guest at an American Legion Post dinner on Tuesday night, June 12, 1945, to honor seven local men leaving for the Armed Services.

Rick's furlough was almost over when he finally had some real R & R. Aware of his love for fishing, the Detroit Lakes Junior Chamber of Commerce had PFC Sorenson and his family as guests from Monday until Friday, August 21–26. [43] The family was back in Anoka to celebrate his 20th birthday on Sunday.

At the end of August, PFC Sorenson reported for duty to the Marine Air Detachment at the Minneapolis Naval Air Station. He was there long enough to be promoted. 18th Commandant of the Marine Corps General A. A. Vandegrift, MOH recipient for actions on Guadalcanal, ordered his promotion to permanent corporal, effective on September 1. In September, he was assigned to the Central Recruiting Division headquarters in Chicago and promoted to sergeant on October 1. His job was to help keep the Marine ranks full of inspired young men.

As he learned of the expectations and obligations associated to wearing a Medal of Honor, Sergeant Sorenson read official dispatches and newspaper accounts of Marine campaigns in the Pacific.

Bloody Nose Ridge

On September 15, 1944, the 1st Marines, 5th Marines, and 7th Marines of the 1st Marine Division climbed into LVTs and charged onto the beaches of Peleliu Island in the South Pacific Palau Island Group to battle more than 11,000 enemy occupiers. The small island sits in an archipelago abreast the Philippine Sea. Low-lying coral foundation and impregnable vegetation, hiding numerous lakes and lagoons, rendered most of the archipelago uninhabitable. Humans could be found on only eight of the two hundred Palau Islands.

Coral-decked, shadeless Peleliu was a place where Marines sacrificed their blood and lives in large numbers, as they had on Guam, the Atolls, and the Solomons. The Japanese poured fire into the Marines from their fortified positions, established in caves and caverns within the dozens of coral ridgelines. The slow advance required the assault of one cave and fortification after another. The fighting went on for seventy-three days.

Eight Marines earned Medals of Honor on the island in twenty days of battle during September and October. Six hurled themselves on top of grenades to protect comrades from injury and death. Two of the actions occurred on the first day of battle. One of those recipients survived the blast and came home. Sergeant Sorenson would meet up with him from time to time in the years after the war. Another of the Peleliu recipients had gone to school miles from Anoka, linking his valor to Sergeant Sorenson's.

✳✳✳

Lewis Kenneth Bausell was the first of the six. Born on April 17, 1924, in Pulaski, Virginia, he lived there for only a few years. His family relocated to Washington, D.C., where he did all his public schooling until he was 17 years old. After leaving school he worked with a local printing firm as a bookbinder. One week after the attack on Pearl Harbor, he left behind his parents, two sisters, and brother and enlisted in the Marines.

Corporal Bausell had fought at Guadalcanal and Tulagi and at Cape Gloucester and the Willaumez Peninsula on New Britain. He went ashore with Company C, 1st Battalion, 5th Marines on September 15, and moved with them to the left flank of the front line, in front of the Umurbrogos Ridge. An enemy pillbox kept a vital sector of the beach pinned down under fire. Corporal Bausell, 20, placed himself at the head of his squad and led a charge against the cave fortification.

First to reach the emplacement, he fired his automatic rifle into the opening. As his men closed in on the position, a Japanese grenade was tossed into their midst. Corporal Bausell, first to act again, swiftly threw himself on the deadly weapon, taking the full blast of the explosion to save his men. He was evacuated from Peleliu with serious wounds and died aboard a hospital ship on September 18. Umurbrogos Ridge became known as Bloody Nose Ridge.

Carlton Robert Rouh was a 25-year-old first lieutenant from Lindenwold, New Jersey. The war came to an end for him later in the afternoon of September 15. He led his mortar platoon across Orange Beach 2 in the advance for the airfield on Peleliu, with the mission to cut the island in two. Wounded in front of an enemy pillbox, he saw an enemy grenade land in his team's midst. He lifted himself into a crouching position, pushed men away from the grenade, and put himself between them and the detonation, taking the brunt of the grenade blast. He was evacuated to one of the hospital ships off shore and was at home for Christmas.

Charles Howard Roan was born in Claude, Texas, on August 16, 1923, the middle son of three boys. The small town rests on Route 287, near the Mulberry Creek and on the high plains of the panhandle. His father was an automobile mechanic. When not at Guydell Woodburn's Corner Drug buying soda pops and sipping malts, Charley's friends could find him after school and on weekends working as a mechanic and truck driver at a local service station and garage. In 1941, he left the Roan home on Richmond Street in North Claude and went to California to live with his older brother. He enlisted in the Marines in 1942, and was sent to the Pacific in June 1943, serving with the 2d Battalion, 7th Marines. Both his brothers enlisted: Henry Jr. in the Army, and younger Joe in the Navy.

On September 18, Private First Class Roan, 21 years old, was wounded by a grenade blast. The exchange of grenades continued before a medic could reach him. He and four squad members huddled together in a foxhole, fighting off the barrage. A grenade landed among them. PFC Roan did not hesitate when he saw the sputtering grenade. Without saying a word, he dived on it immediately. His action spared his four buddies from the explosion, which instantly took his life. [44]

John Dury New made a quick decision to save two other Marines in a similar circumstance a week after PFC Roan's death. John had been born on August 12, 1924, in Mobile, Alabama.

193

His mother died before he had finished St. Joseph's Parochial Grade School. Known to be decisive and quick to act, he was the first man in Mobile to enlist after Pearl Harbor was attacked, walking into a Marine recruiting center on December 8, 1941. He was 17 years old, and the Marines were under assault on Wake Island.

Private First Class New landed on Peleliu with the 2d Battalion, 7th Marines. When the assault force had advanced against the Umurbrogol Massif, with its jumble of sharp coral ridges, sheer cliffs, knobs, hollows, caves, tunnels, and sinkholes, the battalion moved inside the West Road to attack Umurbrogol from the south.

On September 25, PFC New's unit had set up a mortar observation post on a ridge to bring fire to bear on enemy positions ahead of and above them. Unseen on the cliff below them, an enemy soldier stepped from a cave, and threw a grenade into the observation post. Private First Class New, 20 years old for a month, threw himself onto the grenade before it detonated, ensuring that he alone would take the impact of its explosion. At the cost of his own life, he had protected two forward observers from certain injury and possible death.

Another week of fighting passed. Reports of the youngest Marine to be killed saving others from a grenade on coral Peleliu started up the chain of command. He was a year younger than Sergeant Sorenson, and their two names would become linked in Anoka County with a third young Marine hero.

Richard Edward Kraus had just started grade school when his parents moved to northeast Minneapolis. He did not have much opportunity to learn about his family history.

Hazel M. (Peters) Kraus, a housewife, was an 18-year-old teenager from Bowbells, northwest North Dakota: a very remote, small town under the Canadian border. She and August N. Kraus, 21, lived in an apartment at 6926 North Clark Street in Chicago, six blocks west of Columbia Beach Park and Lake Michigan. August, born in St. Bonifacius, west of Minneapolis, was earning a living as a laborer. On the Monday before Thanksgiving Day 1925, a cold, partly cloudy day when temps averaged around 26.5 °F and the wind was a Canadian Northwester, August took Hazel a block up North Clark to Rogers Park Hospital.

A boy was born to them on Tuesday, November 24, at 3:25 AM. Richard's name was recorded on his Certificate of Birth. [45] August found work as a janitor, and moved the family up to 7326 Clayton Court in Chicago's Ward 49. Their daughter, Yvonne Mae Kraus, was born on August 28, 1928.

In 1932, August relocated the family to fifteen miles down the Mississippi River from Anoka and rented a house in Ward 5, on the west side of the river. By the time of the 1940 U.S. Census, the family circumstances had changed. The couple had divorced.

August was living with 11-year-old Yvonne. Hazel had married Edwin Olsen, 38, and had two daughters, Gail (1935) and Marlys (1940). The Olsens resided at 1827 Johnson Street NE, Ward 9, on the east side of the Mississippi. Richard K. "Olsen" was listed as a member of the household. To see his father and sister, young Rich had to cross the Mississippi at the Lowry Avenue Bridge. That meant that he often passed by the corner where another boy his age, Jim LaBelle, was living. For a brief time, Ricky Sorenson was also living on the west side of the river, five-and-a-half miles south of the Kraus residence.

Rich had only a few blocks to walk up to Pillsbury Elementary School. The later walk over to Edison High School on Monroe Street and 22nd Avenue was less than a mile. That is where he was attending when Pearl Harbor was attacked. There was not much time for him to have a photo taken for the *Wizard* yearbook. [46] Not wanting to wait until he finished school, 16-year-old Rich tried to enlist in the Marines to come to the defense of his country.

Records are contradictory about what happened next. His mother apparently would not give her permission for him to enlist. Rich appears to have left Edison High, then was drafted into service on his 18th birthday in 1943. He went to the Minneapolis recruiting station on Christmas Eve and, this time, successfully enlisted in the Marines. Before leaving for the Pacific, he was proud to wear his Rifle Expert and Pistol Sharpshooter marksmanship badges on his chest for his official USMC photograph.

Private First Class Kraus had been a Marine for six months when he departed the States in June 1944 for overseas. He wrote home while he participated in amphibious landing exercises with the 1st Division, training to provide amphibious fire support during the final approach to the enemy beaches. He drove a Mark I armored amphibious landing tractor onto Peleliu with the 8th Amphibian Tractor Battalion, 3d Amphibious Corps, under mortar and machine-gun fire on the assault's first day. In nearly three weeks of combat, he had advanced to the northern portion of the island. The Marines had secured most of Peleliu, but they were taking casualties as they advanced upon Radar Hill, a phosphate plant, and the caves overlooking the area. PFC Kraus was in the forward lines.

On October 3, D-Day-plus-18, a comrade fell under the blazing Japanese defense. Private First Class Kraus quickly volunteered to join a stretcher party to help evacuate the Marine, an action as hazardous in battle conditions as attacking enemy fortifications. He and three others advanced beyond the front lines to retrieve the wounded man. Before the stretcher-bearers could reach the casualty, the enemy opened up with a blistering rate of fire and an intense hand grenade attack.

The stretcher party was forced to withdraw back toward their lines, unable to close the distance to their wounded comrade. Two soldiers approached, appearing to wear Marine uniforms. The stretcher-bearers demanded the day's password. Rather than answer, one of the disguised Japanese soldiers hurled a hand grenade into the group.

With no hesitation to act on behalf of others, PFC Kraus dived onto the explosive and was killed instantly when it detonated. The three others in the stretcher party were uninjured.

Hazel wondered what must have happened when her son's letters stopped arriving. On November 7, the Navy Department announced a list of casualties "not heretofore released," including 53 dead, 192 wounded, and 6 missing on Peleliu. Mr. & Mrs. Edwin Olsen received a telegram. [47] Private First Class Kraus was among the 1,121 killed, 5,142 wounded, and 73 missing Marines of the 1st Division on Peleliu.

Richard Kraus' mother and step-father went to Bath, Maine, for the launching of the USS *Richard Edward Kraus*, DD-849, on March 2, 1946.

The Last on Peleliu

On the day after PFC Kraus was killed, the last of the six Marines to cradle a grenade on Peleliu protected the lives of fellow Marines. His heroically brave actions would be the last to earn a Marine a Medal of Honor on an island in 1944.

Wesley Phelps was born on June 12, 1923, in Neafus, a populated place in northwestern Kentucky too small to be located on maps or to have its own schools. Butler County is a rolling region rich in bluegrass, farmland for tobacco and other crops, horse farms, and coal reserves. His parents owned a 70-acre farm near Rosine, on which he helped out.

Wes went to the Ohio County schools and graduated from Horse Branch High School in 1942. Less than a year after he finished high school, the Marines drafted him on April 9, 1943, and trained him to use the Browning 30-caliber Heavy Machine Gun to be a light machine gunner. He had joined the 3d Battalion, 7th Marines in December, and a few days later departed with Company M for the landing on Cape Gloucester, New Britain. Combat tested, nine months later, reassigned as a light machine gunner with Company K, 3d Battalion, he crossed the coral reef ringing Peleliu.

Private First Class Phelps battled his way ashore on the right flank of Orange Beach 2. King Company fought inland on September 15, sustaining numerous casualties. By dusk, two platoons of the company, cut off from adjacent units, held *The Point*. The 21-year-old experienced enough combat in the next nineteen days that further promotions would have been certain.

The 7th Marines captured the lower third of the island, having destroyed an elite enemy infantry battalion in fortified defensive positions in three days of brutal battle. After "mopping up," the regiment was turned north to engage in the encirclement of the Umurbrogol Pocket.

Private First Class Phelps moved up the West Road with King Company, establishing a road to the northern sector of Peleliu and providing a communication line around *The Pocket*. On October 3, four battalions of Marines attacked the ridges. On the next day, after two weeks of fighting for Umurbrogol, King Company advanced along Boyd and toward Hill 120. Meeting fierce resistance, unable to hold the hill, the Marines withdrew and took up defensive positions.

That night, Company K dug into a line across one slope of a coral ridge, within hand grenade range of the Japanese on the opposite slope. Private First Class Phelps was in a forward defensive machine-gun position on the crest with his foxhole buddy, PFC Richard Shipley.

The Marines had had enough encounters with the Japanese on the islands to expect a night of aggressive counterattacks on their line. The men in forward positions, especially those in listening and observation posts, were the first defense against enemy infiltration. The attack was ferocious when it came.

"Look out, Shipley!" Private First Class Phelps and PFC Shipley had prepared themselves for the onslaught, and the two of them fought off the aggressors. When an enemy grenade landed in their foxhole, PFC Phelps saw it first. He shouted a warning to his companion and immediately rolled on top of the grenade. The explosion shattered his body, killing him instantly. So completely had he smothered the projectile, PFC Shipley received only a small shrapnel scratch and survived to bear witness to the Kentuckian's bravery.

The Marines declared the dozens of coral ridgelines on Peleliu secure on November 27. Four of the Marines KIA saving others from grenades on Peleliu had ships commissioned in their names. A ship with PFC Wesley Phelps' name on the hull was never launched.

Four months passed before the Marines moved on to the next island, and men again would make decisions about their own lives and those of comrades. One of those Marines had grown up just to the north of PFC Kraus' neighborhood.

✳✳✳

For Marines who did not already know of his Medal award for heroic actions on Namur, the *Leatherneck* Magazine made first mention of PFC Sorenson in the November 1944 issue. All in all, the Corps' 169th year had been action packed, and he was one of ten Marines to receive the high honor in the past year. [48]

Bill Sorenson did not need that issue of the *Magazine Of The Marines* to inspire him. He had always wanted to join the Marines, even when he was "a little tyke," before his big brother went to war and came home a hero. He was only in his sophomore year at Anoka High and wanted to get into the war like so many underage kids did. On his 17th birthday, November 24,

1944, he quit school, went down to the draft office, and tried to join. Virginia would not sign a waiver for her younger boy, but Carl did, having changed the stance he had taken with Ricky. [49]

"As long as you want to go," he said, knowing that his wife was going to have some words for him.

Bill only weighed 115 pounds, and the Marines sent him home until he could fatten up a little. Those platters of his mom's home-baked cinnamon-pecan rolls fit the bill.

Sergeant Sorenson continued to experience the commitments and responsibilities associated to wearing the Medal of Honor. He was in the Duluth Warlet Butler shipbuilding yards when America marked the third anniversary of the December 7 enemy attack on Pearl Harbor. He and Army PFC Lloyd Hawks, a Medal recipient from Park Rapids, were the principle speakers at the launching of two ocean-going cargo vessels. The two ships were christened in honor of two Army men awarded posthumous Medals of Honor for heroism in the Pacific. [50]

After New Year's Day, weighing 117 pounds, Bill returned to try again. The Marines took him for the duration of the war and one year. His brother, still at home, filled him in on what to expect.

The news of Marines earning Medals of Honor and diving on top of grenades continued to reach Sergeant Sorenson as American forces closed in on mainland Japan. More Medals were awarded in five months on two islands in 1945, than in any other full year in the Corps' history. Thirteen of those involved men and grenades. Sergeant Sorenson would meet three of them in the years following the war; but, one of the recipients who did not come home from the Pacific would often enter conversations in Anoka when Rick Sorenson was mentioned.

✳✳✳

James Dennis "Jim" Labelle, born on November 22, 1925, two days before Rich Kraus, was the third youngest of Wilfred Cyril and Theresa Gertrude (Murphy) Labelle's eight living children. He had two older brothers and three older sisters, all a year or two apart in age. Although he would hear his mother speak of them, Jim had two brothers he had never had a chance to know.

Wilfred was three years younger than Theresa when they married in 1913. Their first boy, Kenneth, was born in January 1914. Robert was next, born in August 1916, and lived for only eleven days. Children continued to arrive. Then, Kenny died eight days after his 6th birthday in 1920. Life went on, and two more daughters and a son joined the family before Jim was born. His two younger sisters, arrived years later—Mary Lou in 1929, and Elaine in 1931. [51]

Wilfred owned a little house at 2323 NE Taylor Street, valued at $6,000 ($82,500 in 2016) on the northeast side of Minneapolis. Rich Kraus would live with his mother and step-father just a few blocks to the southeast at 1827 Johnson Street.

Jim went to grammar school in his own neighborhood. Before he started second grade in the fall of 1933, he faced one of life's greatest challenges. On Sunday, August 27, Wilfred Labelle, 42 years old, was killed in a head-on automobile collision. [52]

At the time of the 1940 U.S. Census, Theresa Labelle, aged 53, was widowed and the head of the household. She had been unable to carry the mortgage on their home and was renting a second-floor apartment at the corner of 2503 Central Avenue Northeast and Lowry Avenue. Jim's eldest sister, Virginia, "Virgie," had married Earl J. Carpentier and moved from home. They rented an apartment at 2201 NE Marshall Street on the Mississippi River with three other young couples starting out. Jim was close to Virgie and visited when he could. He was an uncle to one-year-old David.

Howard, 22, still lived with the family, helping their mother. Marcella and Evelyn were both in high school, and Norman and Jim were in the eighth grade. Jim was going to have to decide about high school. Edison High School was only a five-block walk away. Had he chosen to attend there, he and Rich Kraus would have been classmates.

Jim Labelle chose to take the trolley car up Central Avenue and go to Columbia Heights High School. Though he was a very humble kid, he excelled in sports and was known to be a "wiry scrapper." At 5 feet 7 inches, 130 pounds, he starred on the high school *Hylanders* basketball, baseball, and boxing teams. He went to work at a hamburger joint to help Theresa pay household bills. Jim intended to finish school and work at a trade. He was learning wood and metalworking and apprenticing as an acetylene welder.

His plans changed when Pearl Harbor was attacked. He wanted to drop out of tenth grade and join the service. Not just patriotic, enlisting would allow him to send money home and help support the family. His mother insisted that he finish high school.

Both of Jim's younger sisters, Mary Lou and Elaine, would attend Edison High School after Rich Kraus had left the hallways.

On November 18, 1943, four days before his 18th birthday, with his mother's permission, Jim enlisted in the Marine Corps. Six days later, Rich Kraus enlisted.

Private LaBelle took a train to San Diego for his recruit training and wrote his first letter to "Virgie" Carpentier on January 21, 1944. [53] At Camp Pendleton, he was assigned to Weapons Company, 27th Marines, 5th Marine Division, and sailed from the States in August 1944, on board the USS *George F. Elliott* troop carrier.

While PFC Labelle was in amphibious combat training at Camp Tarawa near Hilo, Hawaii, PFC Kraus died on Peleliu. Although PFC Labelle would live a life five months longer than PFC Kraus', the two lived through nearly the same number of days in combat.

In December, PFC Labelle heard that a fleet of transports had arrived at Hilo. The division began loading on ships on December 16. He pulled out of Camp Tarawa on January 4, 1945, and the 5th Marine Division departed from Hawaii. PFC Labelle wrote his last letter to "Virgie" on January 25. His destination was Iwo Jima.

Private First Class Labelle went ashore at Iwo Jima's Red Beach 2 on February 19, 1945. Fighting on the 5th Division's right flank, he experienced the daily grueling fights for yards of black volcanic terrain, the nights without sleep wracked with artillery and mortar explosions and enemy attacks, and the meals of cold K-rations and water. The Weapons Company destroyed pillboxes, mortar and machine-gun emplacements, and caves as the 27th Regiment took Airfield No. 1, Airfield No. 2, Hill 362-A, Nishi Ridge, Kita Village, and Hill 362-B. Then, the Marine advance stalled as the forward units encountered an overwhelming barrage of mortars and machine-gun fire in the approach to Kitano Point and Hill 165.

Eighteen days of combat, and PFC Labelle no longer looked like a bright-eyed teenager.

On March 8, the forward assault units advanced only a few yards as the Japanese desperately held on to the northern remnant of their fortress island. The Marines dug in for the night, prepared to jump off again at dawn's light across the ravines and ridges toward Hill 165.

That night, PFC Labelle, 19 years old, stood the watch in a foxhole shared with two other Marines. A Japanese hand grenade landed in their shelter, just out of his reach. He yelled a warning to his companions and immediately jumped onto the grenade, sacrificing his life and shielding the others from harm.

The battle for Iwo Jima ended on March 26. No letters or telegrams reached the Labelle family in Columbia Heights. Their apprehensions were confirmed when the official Navy Department notification of his death arrived in June. Another year passed. Jim's mother remarried. She was never invited to Bath, Maine, because a ship was not launched in her son's honor.

✳✳✳

Recruiting Duties

"They put me on limited duty and sent me on a war bond drive. I was very lucky."

President Roosevelt died on April 12, 1945. While the nation mourned, and the Marines continued to fight on Pacific islands, Sergeant Sorenson was sent to Fargo, North Dakota, to stake out a recruiting substation. Humble about his valor on Namur, he did not use his Medal to win over others or to entice men to enlist. Anyone who met him could attest to that.

Robert "Bob" Thompson, 22, a veteran of three combat landings in the Pacific, was home on furlough in Fargo. Neighbors recalled that he had left Texas A&M in 1943 to enlist in the Marine Corps. He looked up friends from his Central High School Class of 1941, and gathered the scuttlebutt about Phil Swanson, a friend since kindergarten, and Ralph "Tod" Gunkelman Jr. and Donald M. Sorlie, fellow classmates. Bob knew that a number of the 1941 class member families had received notifications that their sons had been killed in action or had died of wounds. [54]

In his Marine uniform, he joined family members at a tavern. [55] A young man tapped him on the shoulder, quietly greeting him.

"Hi, Marine. Nice to see you."

The stranger was not a FCHS classmate. Bob did not give the greeting much thought, and the man walked away. His brother had recognized him.

"Do you know who that is?" Bob's brother asked. "His name is Rick Sorenson. He has a Medal of Honor."

Sergeant Sorenson had his own brother in mind. Private William P. "Bill" Sorenson was sworn in to the Corps on April 23, 1945, as the Marines secured Motobu Peninsula on Okinawa.

Sergeant Sorenson had been in Fargo for only a couple of weeks when headquarters called him. "You're going on the Seventh War Bond Drive."

For several months, he was taken all over to promote the bond drive—going to Indianapolis, St. Louis, Kansas City, and Chicago. Seven days a week. "I hardly had time to get my clean laundry."

In Minneapolis, Colonel Norman E. Ture, Ninth Naval District Marine office, contacted Hazel Olsen in early September to discuss her son's posthumous Medal of Honor. They decided to make the presentation a local event to be broadcast at 710 AM on radio dials. On August 2, 1945, Richard Kraus' father, mother, step-father, and three sisters met at the Elks Club building at 625 Second Avenue South and went up to the CBS WCCO radio station auditorium on the fourth floor. Colonel Ture presented the award to Mrs. Edwin Olsen. [56]

Two weeks before Sergeant Sorenson's 21st birthday, President Harry S. Truman convened a White House press conference on August 15. The Allies had been victorious in the Pacific, and World War II had reached an end. He declared *Victory over Japan Day*. Worldwide celebrations began. The Japanese signed the formal surrender on September 2, 1945.

Having survived the war without a Purple Heart, Corporal James Sorenson of Albert Lea received a skull fracture in a head-on collision twelve miles south of Minneapolis on Highway 65, on Saturday night, September 22, 1945.

After VJ Day, Sgt Sorenson decided to make the Marine Corps a career. [57] He was next transferred from Chicago in September 1945, and attached to the St. Louis Midwestern Recruiting Division, Missouri. The division sent him back to the Fargo Marine Corps Recruiting Station.

He stuck around a while, and then, just after Christmas, decided to get out. A job was waiting for him. He had received a letter from the White House. President Truman had signed Executive Order 9628 on September 25, establishing a contact representative position, GS7, with the federal government and Veterans Administration for every MOH recipient. [58]

Sergeant Sorenson called down to Minneapolis to tell them he would be getting out of the Marines and would like the contact representative position. They said, "As soon as you get out, you report here."

"And boy, I was happy, 'cuz jobs were kind of scarce." He was transferred back to Great Lakes Hospital, Illinois, for forty more days of treatment, then, sent over to the Separation Center. He signed his discharge papers on February 23, 1946.

By the time his brother completed recruit training at San Diego and Combat Training at Camp Pendleton, the war had been over. Private William P. Sorenson was discharged in April 1946, disappointed that he did not get over to the Pacific. He returned to Anoka. The brothers were civilians again.

Newspaper articles periodically highlighted the relationship Rick Sorenson shared with Rich Kraus and James Labelle.

Hazel Olsen felt a sense of prominence for a time, as her son's honor was passed along to her. The U.S. Navy chose her to sponsor one of its newest and largest destroyers. Edwin and Hazel traveled to the Bath Iron Works in Maine, to attend a christening ceremony. On Friday, March 2, 1946, the new ship towering above her awed Hazel as she broke a champagne bottle over the gleaming bow. The 2,200-ton USS *Richard E. Kraus*, DD-849, was launched.

As the ship's sponsor, Hazel remained in contact with the ship's crew and was involved in special events involving DD-849. She went to the Boston Naval Shipyard in mid-May 1946 for the ship's commissioning. USS *Richard E. Kraus* had completed her sea trials. The crew reported for duty aboard the ship on Thursday, May 23. VIPs and an audience gathered at the dock. Commander R. J. Oliver, in command, read the orders given for the ship and its personnel. Hazel was introduced as the sponsor and the ship was placed into active service. [59]

Minneapolis residents celebrated the 1946 Fourth of July with picnics and fireworks at South Minneapolis' Powderhorn Park. Then, the Director of Marine Corps Public Information in Minneapolis contacted Jim LaBelle's mother. Her son had been awarded the Congressional Medal of Honor. Brigadier General William Edward Riley presented the Medal to Mrs. Theresa Hodge in a ceremony at Powderhorn Park on July 21.

At the end of World War II, thousands of American servicemen remained temporarily interred in military cemeteries in North Africa, France, Italy, Belgium, Germany, and the Pacific Islands. The U.S. began to return the remains for permanent burial back home in 1947. The transport USS *Honda Knot* arrived at San Francisco on October 10, 1947, carrying the first American war dead returned from the South Pacific. The USS *Joseph V. Connolly*, USS *Carrol Victory* (VC2-S-AP3), USS *Greenville Victory* (T-AK-237), and the USS *Lawrence Victory*, began bringing honored remains home.

The remains of both PFC Kraus and PFC Labelle were returned to the States in late 1948. Both were buried in Fort Snelling National Cemetery in Minneapolis. Each had an avenue dedicated in his name.

Richard's little sister, Yvonne Mae Kraus, married a Mr. Blanton and had two daughters and two sons. In 1973, she married a second time to John Theodore "Ted" Jansen Jr., a WWII U.S. Navy veteran and St. Paul firefighter. [60] Ted had had a daughter, Delores Ann, with Lucille Ann Facklam and, then, married Lucille. The couple had three more girls and three sons. Jean M, born on April 8, 1958, was one of their younger daughters. Delores died before her time, and Ted and Lucille divorced. He and his children were in for some sad days. Jean died on October 11, 1972, and Lucille, 51, died on March 30, 1979.

Yvonne and Ted lived in the W. 7th area for thirty years. Yvonne, aged 75, died May 15, 2003. The first line of her obituary read: "Preceded in death by brother, Medal of Honor recipient, Richard E. Kraus." She was buried with Ted's 14-year-old daughter in Fort Snelling National Cemetery's Section N—not far from her brother's avenue. Ted joined his "Beloved Wife" the next year. [61]

People in Columbia Heights might think of James Labelle when they walk on the trail circling LaBelle Pond in Labelle Park. A memorial plaque honors him at the park entrance on 42nd Avenue NE. In John P. Murzyn Hall, the city community room on the grounds of Huset Park, the LaBelle Lounge/Bar is on the backside of the brick wall and fireplace. Jim's picture, Medal Citation, and memorabilia are displayed in glass cases. He is also recognized on a plaque outside the Columbia Heights City Hall that memorializes all servicemen from the city who have died serving their country. [62] La Belle Street is a short road in a townhouse development a block south of Murzyn Hall.

CHAPTER 10

Return to Civilian Life

***

"And honor's thought Reigns solely in the breast of every man." [1]

— WILLIAM SHAKESPEARE

RICKY SORENSON WAS A YOUNG man who had felt the call to go to war when Pearl Harbor was attacked. He did not seek honor, but had hoped he would dutifully support Marine infantrymen under enemy fire. He had acted honorably and performed his duty. He wore a Medal around his neck as a testimony to that fact. Now his thoughts of honor were not about war, but of living responsibly in civilian attire.

Rick got home to Anoka on Friday, March 1, 1946, reported to the Minneapolis VA on Monday, and was put right to work. He was advised to finish his high school diploma in a special program to enhance his employment opportunities. The VA sent him to two weeks of school. He and Bill and thirty-five other men who had quit high school to enlist for war got their GEDs at the same time. Rick was assigned to the VA Mankato Office as a contact representative. His civilian career of thirty-five years began.

He enlisted in the Fourth Infantry Reserve Marine Battalion, USMCR, on July 10, 1947. Most of the men were from Minneapolis, St. Paul, and the surrounding counties. The part-time Marines held weekly evening drills at the local Naval Air Station in Minneapolis and went to various east coast bases for two weeks of training in the summers.

Rick brought his brother into the battalion. Bill, who worked for Bob Ehlen at Federal Premium Ammunition, and at the Anoka Post Office during Christmas holidays, got several of his good school buddies to join. Two were brothers—Leon and Loren L. Patchen, twins. They lived at 1733 S. 3d Avenue, blocks from the high school, and had been a grade behind Bill. Robert Richard "Dick" Runquist, a close Benton Street neighbor, also joined the unit. He was several months younger than the Patchen twins. They called him "Runkie." Sergeant Rick did what he could to keep the "grab assing" among the Anoka High alumni to a minimum at the evening drills.

The Fourth Marine Division, headquartered in Washington, D.C., set out to compile statistics and write a history. The division had been on the active duty rolls for just over twenty-seven months during the war. In the thirteen months the Fighting Fourth had been committed to combat campaigns, the division had made four amphibious assault landings: Roi–Namur, Saipan, Tinian, and Iwo Jima. Engagements with the enemy amounted to sixty-three days under fire. The division took 81,000 Marines into combat. Battle casualties totaled 17,722—3,298 killed in action or died of wounds and 14,424 suffering wounds. Thirteen officers and 177 enlisted Marines had died on Roi–Namur, and another 547 Marines were wounded.

While all had fought bravely, the chroniclers considered the twelve Medal holders to represent the bravest of them—their place was among the "Giants of the Corps." Rick was one of the youngest of the twelve. Of the five who had survived the war, Justice Chambers, born in 1908, and Joe McCarthy, 1911, were the "old salts." Pharmacist's Mate First Class Francis Pierce, three months younger than Rick, had just been celebrating his 17th birthday on December 7 when Pearl Harbor was attacked. Doug Jacobson was the youngest of them: 16 years old when President Roosevelt asked Congress for a Declaration of War with Japan. Having any of the five "Giants" at an official function was important.

The first postwar reunion of the Fighting Fourth was held in Kansas City, Missouri. Rick joined 500 members of the former outfit who got together to renew friendships on Friday, June 4, 1948. The city was proud to host them, making sure there were plenty of thick steaks and liquid refreshments for the weekend. Since so many of the men were single and without wives or girlfriends, the flirtations and wedding proposals flattered an unrecorded number of pretty K.C. girls. [2]

The first order of business was the election of officers. Former Sergeant R. K. Sorenson was elected master-at-arms. The highlights of the convention were on Saturday. Rick was in a parade downtown, led by the Quantico band, the Washington Marine Barracks Drum and Bugle Corps, and the Marine Reserve band. Commandant of the Marine Corps General Clifton B. Cates was emotional as his old command marched past the reviewing stand. Thousands of spectators lined the streets, cheering and clapping enthusiastically. A steak banquet capped the night.

The reunion was such a success that the members decided it should be planned every year. A committee was formed to decide on the place and date for the 1949 reunion. Whether he would attend a Fighting Fourth convention would become an annual summer discussion over the family dinner table for Rick.

He was getting accustomed to being recognized as a MOH winner. When the Twin Cities Marines conducted their summer training at Camp Lejeune, North Carolina, in July 1948, a FOR IMMEDIATE RELEASE dispatch went to the newspapers with a photograph. Kneeling over CPL Sorenson's shoulder, Sergeant Sorenson was passing "on a few machine gun tips to his younger brother." In the prone position, finger on the trigger mechanism, Bill aimed down the long barrel of a Browning .30 cal machine gun. [3]

Life was full for Rick. In addition to his duties at the VA and in the Reserves, he entered St. John's University at Collegeville (St. Cloud) in 1948 to study business. His roommate's girlfriend had a girlfriend from St. Paul. One night in the fall, Rick and Mildred (Milli) Virginia Snow, 19 years old, went on a blind date. They seemed made for each other.

Milli was the second daughter of James H. and Edith A. Snow. Her sister, Eleanor, was three years older. The family lived in Ward 11, at 1650 Hartford Avenue, a very short drive from Anoka.

During a holiday break, Rick took Milli to an Anoka restaurant. As they entered to find a table, other patrons stood, first clapping politely, and then applauding boisterously. Strangers lined up. It seemed as if everyone wanted an introduction to Rick Sorenson. Milli wondered what it was all about. That was how she found out her boyfriend had earned a Medal of Honor.

"He'd never mentioned it before that." [4]

The young couple celebrated her birthday in March, married in 1949, and became lifetime companions. Looking back across the years of their long marriage, his beloved wife would recall: "He never talked much about the war, not even through 55 years of marriage."

Rick and Milli bought a wooded lot on Silver Lake in Saint Anthony Village from Kenny Lee, a prosperous farmer who owned most of the property in the northern part of the village at that time. East of the Mississippi River, their home address was 2933 Silver Lake Drive. [5] Their home was built step-by-step, with Rick doing a lot of the work himself. The newlyweds lived in the basement as the house went up. The incentive to complete the building was strong.

Two newsworthy events marked 1950 for them. The first was joyous and happened on Flag Day, the 173rd anniversary of the day the Continental Congress had adopted the flag as the emblem of the United States. Robert, their first child, was born, on June 14.

The second event burst into news broadcasts eleven days later and was alarming. The North Korean People's Army charged across the 38th Parallel. Five years after most WWII veterans had returned home, the Korean War commenced on June 25, 1950.

Rick was going to experience what families back home deal with when a loved one must face a hostile enemy away from home. His "little brother" was going to war. Rick would be reading headlines, scanning newspaper columns, calling VA colleagues, and watching for General Douglas MacArthur's press releases.

A Brother's War

News cables, letters, and telegrams began arriving in Minnesota homes from Korea. Private First Class George A. Sorenson had grown up in Blue Earth, above the Iowa border, west of Albert Lea. He was a runner in 1st Platoon, Headquarters Section, Company K, 3d Battalion, 5th Cavalry Regiment, 1st Cavalry Division, U.S. Army, garrisoned in Japan. He deployed to Korea on July 18, landing in the middle of a typhoon, twenty-three days into the North Korean invasion. He would have very few opportunities to write letters home.

The Regiment marched four days toward Taejon and encountered the North Koreans on July 23, suffering severe losses over the next days. The 5th Regiment withdrew to defensive lines at Hwanggan, and then moved back near Kumchon, taking defensive positions along the Pusan Perimeter's western line.

Army Corporal Marvin Lyle Whitehead, 18, had grown up at 1535 6th Avenue in Anoka. He was killed on July 30, 1950. His remains were not recovered.

Rumors that the Marine Reserves would be activated started at the Minneapolis Naval Air Station. Sergeant Rick passed the word at a drill meeting. Reserve Marines were being called to active duty on August 1, 1950. He would stay behind because of his administrative duties at the VA.

On August 9, five enemy divisions attacked, pushing toward Taegu. The 5th Cavalry pulled back, and PFC George Sorenson dug in with King Company. His mother hoped that the card for his 20th birthday had reached him by August 12.

The Fourth Infantry Battalion was called up on Saturday, August 19. The whole battalion boarded trains and left Minneapolis on August 21, arriving at Camp Pendleton on Thursday at midnight. Corporal Sorenson and Leon Patchen went together. Private Loren Patchen belonged to the inactive Reserves and did not get called up right away. Sending twin brothers into battle was avoided in most circumstances. [6]

The Minnesota men marched about, drawing rifles, packs, 782 gear, and cleaning stuff. The M-1 rifles were full of brown-colored, wax-like cosmoline, with its petroleum-like smell. Corporal Sorenson and Pvt Patchen tore their rifles apart, soaked them clean in kerosene, and reassembled the weapons. There was little time for any training.

"They were in such a hurry to get us over there," CPL Sorenson had to say. The battalion boarded ship for Korea on Tuesday, August 29. They had yet to fire their rifles. Once afloat, they began live-fire exercises off the ship's fantail. Hope that there would be a stop in Hawaii was dashed when the ships passed the islands.

Despite two more ferocious assaults over four weeks, the North Koreans could not break through to Taegu. By September 8, it appeared that the enemy had been stopped.

A firefight erupted on September 12, when King Company attacked the North Koreans on Hill 174. The fight was "just short of chaos." PFC George Sorenson and the soldier beside him, PFC William R. Geraghty, were killed on the hill, but their bodies could not be recovered before the company pulled back from the assault. The enemy took their dog tags and left the bodies on the hill for days, making the identification of the casualties difficult when the 5th Cavalry took Hill 174. [7]

On Friday September 15, the 1st and 5th Marines landed at Inchon and began to battle toward Seoul. The Fourth Battalion landed at Kobe, Japan, to link up with the 7th Marines, 1st MARDIV. The Minnesota battalion was going to be distributed to fill gaps in the 1st and 2d battalions. Some of the activated Reservists would go to the 5th Marines.

Corporal Sorenson had been in the Corps before and was to be assigned to a rifle platoon. He boarded a transport again on Saturday. Private Patchen had not had enough training at drills, so he stayed at Kobe and would not get to Korea until October. The two friends never saw each other again.

Corporal Sorenson was at Inchon on September 16, and helped unload ammo, supplies, and equipment. The 7th Marines, under command of Colonel Homer L. Litzenberg Jr. of Philadelphia, shipped out from Japan and entered Inchon Harbor on Thursday afternoon. The regiment unloaded on Saturday, D-Day+8.

Corporal Sorenson was assigned to lead a fireteam in Company B, 1st Battalion. The Baker-One-Seven officers he would get to know best were Captain Myron E. Wilcox, the company commander, 1stLt John Weaver (1st Platoon), 1stLt Bill Graeber (2d Platoon), 1stLt Hank Kiser (3d Platoon), and 1stLt Chew Een Lee (machine-gun platoon). Baker-One-Seven joined in the battle to capture Seoul.

The 7th Marines crossed the Han River at noon with orders to seize a mountain pass north of the city. The battalions crossed the Kaesong–Seoul highway, passed through Hoengjeoe-ri, west of Seoul's Sodaemun Prison, and set up in the ridges of Hills 338 and 342. First Battalion was held in reserve with Seoul in their rear. The regiment cut off enemy escape routes from the city. Engagements intensified on September 26–27. Seoul was secured on September 29.

Baker-One-Seven pursued the fleeing North Korean People's Army up the northern highway. Second Lieutenant Hugh Donald Adair, Jr., a Charlie-One-Seven platoon commander, died on the crest of a hill south of Uijongbu on the day before the hostilities at Seoul ended. After two days of heavy resistance and endless mortar fire, the 7th Marines routed the enemy from the ruined town of Uijongbu on October 3.

General MacArthur's confidence was buoyed. The North Koreans could not stand up to the Marines. His press releases suggested that the conflict would have a quick conclusion. All the Fourth Infantry Battalion families around the Twin Cities hoped their boys might be back home for Christmas.

The 7th Marines moved into staging areas back near Inchon on Saturday, October 7, and began preparing for another amphibious assault. Corporal Sorenson boarded LST *Q010* on Tuesday and waited five days for anchors to be raised. On Sunday, October 15, the entire 1st Marine Division embarked in a convoy of seventy-one ships and entered the Yellow Sea. Task Force 77 was underway to Kalma Peninsula, Yonghung Bay, and the oil port of Wonsan on Korea's east side. Corporal Sorenson was sailing with 1,119 Marine officers and 20,597 enlisted Marines—many of them would never see another Christmas.

Two aircraft carriers, a light cruiser, twenty-four destroyers, minesweepers, and supply ships surrounded the troop ships. Before the assault forces reached Yonghung Bay, the Task Force would become an armada of 250 ships. The convoy circled to the east side of the Korean peninsula into the Sea of Japan, bypassed the 38th Parallel, sailed along another eighty miles of North Korean coastline, and readied itself to land the Marines at Wonsan.

On Thursday, at 5:00 PM, the ships reversed course for twelve hours, seeming to steam back to Pusan, then turned north again toward Wonsan. Rumors and griping escalated in the ship's compartments. Damned higher command could not decide if the war was over or not. The troops dubbed their mission *Operation Yo–Yo*.

Higher Marine Command, as frustrated as the Marines in the holds of ships, had a better grasp of the situation. For one thing, the rapidly developing mission orders went through a series of mutations, changing the anticipated ground-level operations of the infantry units. For another thing, the situation at Wonsan was far from constant and predictable—never a good thing for an amphibious assault on beaches.

Three days before Task Force 77 had departed Inchon, five U.S. Navy minesweepers entered Yonghung Bay to clear a channel to the beaches for the assault forces and to give the U.N. ships better access to Wonsan Harbor. The USS *Pirate*, AM 275, and the USS *Pledge*, AM 277, struck mines and sank that first afternoon. The same fate befell Japanese Minesweeper 14, JMS 14, and Republic of Korea Minesweeper 516, YMS-516, near the harbor in the next days.

What had been expected to be a four-day sail turned into a nearly two-week cruise. The ships' mess facilities virtually ran out of food. Water was rationed. The assault forces were served one cup of black coffee three times a day. Dysentery, gastro-enteritis, and an outbreak of smallpox swept through the troop ships.

On Monday, October 23, the Department of Defense notified Mrs. Reaka Sorenson in Lake Crystal, southwest of Mankato, that her son was missing in action in South Korea. Another telegram arrived later, regretfully informing her that PFC George A. Sorenson had been killed in action while fighting the enemy on September 23, 1950. Her son's remains were returned to Minnesota and buried in Fort Snelling National Cemetery.

The LSTs finally entered Yonghung Bay early in the morning on October 26. The ships' crews were ordered to battle stations, and the convoy set a zig zagging course toward the harbor, hoping to miss any undetected and submerged enemy magnetic mines. Four destroyers, four cruisers, two aircraft carriers, five minesweepers, and the USS *Missouri*, the only WWII American battleship still afloat, blasted enemy positions in preparation for the amphibious landing.

The landing at Wonsan had turned into an "administrative landing." The ROK had taken Wonsan from the communists and secured the town on October 11. By October 17, a ROK regiment had occupied Hamhung and Hungnam on the road to a major reservoir. Replacing the ROK forces at the reservoir had become the Marines' mission. The Corps considered the Wonsan landing to be "the most embarrassing moment in Marine history." Instead of enemy forces on Blue Beach, Bob Hope and actress Marilyn Maxwell and their USO show were already there to greet the disgruntled Leathernecks. Other than that, the beach landing and establishing the beachhead turned uneventful.

The Frozen Chosin Campaign

Corporal Sorenson and his fireteam trucked five miles north of Wonsan and set up bivouac in a church and school at Munpyong-ni, awaiting orders. They talked over the mission. The 1st MarDiv was to take a big hydro-electric plant about forty air miles south of the Manchurian border. The plant was an important objective, because it supplied the bulk of North Korea's vital hydro-electric power, as well as supplying electric power to Manchuria. The plant sat under the Changjin Reservoir, which correspondents and legends would memorialize as *The Chosin Reservoir*.

For the next forty-eight days, CPL Sorenson marched and trucked his team along the Main Supply Route (MSR) through places called Hamhung, Majon-dong, Chinhung-ni, Sudong Gorge, Funchilin Pass, Koto-ri, Hagaru-ri, the Toktong Pass, and a war-deserted town called Yudam-ni—and, then, Hungnam Harbor. The 1st Marine Division had not trained for mountain warfare or cold winter fighting, and two terrible forces awaited the regiments—the Chinese Communists and the Siberian winter.

The 7th Marines, with the 1st Battalion at the head of the assault column, left Wonsan by foot, truck, and rail on Tuesday, October 31, making fifty-three uncontested miles to Hamhung, where the rail stopped. Baker-One-Seven made the last few miles in the back of 6x6 trucks. The battalions spread out establishing defensive perimeters along the high ground on both flanks.

Baker-One-Seven settled into a dirty, rat-infested warehouse. A sergeant ordered CPL Sorenson to report to the platoon commander, who introduced him to LtCol Raymond G. Davis, 1st Battalion commander.

"I want you to take this jeep, take your fire team," the commander told him, "and go down and report in to Colonel Litzenberg. Tell him we've made it up here without enemy incident. We didn't run into any guerillas."

"Sir, I don't know the way down there." Corporal Sorenson was thinking that he did not even know where they were situated themselves.

"Never mind. The driver knows the way."

So, the fireteam drove in the dark of night, past a Y-fork in the road, to 7th Marine headquarters. After reporting, Colonel Litzenberg had a job for CPL Sorenson to do.

"I'm sending you over to the OMS (Office of Mission Support) Marines. That's our artillery outfit, Third Battalion, Eleventh Marines. And I want you to guide them up there."

Corporal Sorenson knew better than to tell a colonel that he did not know the way back to Hamhung. "I didn't ever tell 'em that." He went over to OMS, and, with two majors in the jeep with him, he guessed his way back.

While he was away, the Quartermaster had issued the regiment extra layers of winter clothing, including cotton long johns, green sateen winter trousers, extra socks, pile-lined hooded parkas, wool caps, alpaca vests, woolen mufflers, leather gloves with wool mitten inserts, maybe pile-lined hats with earflaps, leather laced boots with rubber soles ("shoe-pacs"), and heavy liners for their sleeping bags. The winter gear would make marching with a haversack, knapsack, and bedding roll more cumbersome, but the Marines would be glad they had the extra gear in just a few days.

Back at Baker Company, CPL Sorenson asked where all the winter gear—the parkas and stuff—had come from. He learned that "out of sight, out of mind" could apply to corporals running errands for commanders.

"Well, where's mine?"

"You didn't get any. They wouldn't give us, uh, let us have any extra. So, you'll have to wait until somebody gets wounded before you get a parka."

From Hamhung, the forty-three miles north to Chinhung-ni followed a two-lane highway and somewhat flat terrain. The next day, Wednesday morning, November 1, the Marines put Hamhung behind them, traveling about twenty-seven miles by motor lift to the Majon-dong village area. Another twenty-nine road miles climbed to the southern foot of the reservoir.

The North Korean People's Army (NKPA) had prepared fortified defenses along the main routes of advance. Holding the high ground on strategic hills, well armed in trenches and dugouts, Communist China's People's Liberation Army (CCF) divisions reinforced them. The Marine infantry battalions had to secure the high ground along the MSR to allow men, equipment, and supplies to "safely" maneuver along it.

On Thursday, light and scattered enemy resistance put the battalions on alert and slowed the advance toward Sudong-ni village. At 10:30 AM, CPL Sorenson and the Marine column moved forward, advancing 1,300-yards into a small, narrow valley, the Sudong Gorge, situated between Hungnam and the Taebaek Plateau. A dry riverbed bordered the gorge on the west, and hills, steep and high, some rising taller than 1,500 feet, encircled the valley. Rocks were everywhere.

Anticipating greater resistance, the column halted at 4:30 PM and bivouacked for the night, south of Sudong-ni. The regiment tightened its perimeter and dug in along a two- to four-mile stretch of the MSR. The fireteam pulled C-rations from their haversacks and ate. Dark was fast descending on the hills around them, and the air in the valley turned crisp with a sharp chill. They needed little encouragement to pile into their warm sleeping bags.

Shortly after midnight, the blaring sound of bugles and whistles rousted any Marines able to sleep. The 124th Division, CCF, launched a surprise assault. A multitude of soldiers shouting in the dark charged down the hills and up from the riverbed. Parachute flares exploded in the starless skies above the valley. Rifle and machine-gun fire shattered the silence as Marines reacted from defensive positions on the flanks. The Chinese, wearing their quilted cotton jackets, had the 7th Marines surrounded on three sides. The agonizing cries for "Corpsman!" soon began. CCF forces infiltrated to the road and surged between the 2d and 3d battalions. The first confrontation between the Marines and CCF fighters had begun.

The fighting went on all day. Airdrops provided resupply to the regiment. The CCF pulled back at dusk, the firing ceased, and the 7th Marine battalions found the night quiet. Corporal Sorenson and his team remained in their positions through the night and into the next morning. Rifle shots sounded sporadically as sentries fired at shadows. The badly mangled CCF army division did not attempt another major counterassault. Chinese snipers became the only menace on the road. The 7th Marines entered Sudong on Saturday.

Sixty-one Marines died in the three-day fight at Sudong. Nine more died of battle wounds, and another 162 were wounded. The bodies of the dead were brought to the road, identified, covered with ponchos and shelter halves, and "awaited further disposition" by the Graves Registration Sections. The numbers circulated.

Another realization struck at the minds of the young men. A staff sergeant from Charlie Company was missing in action. Staff Sergeant Ward Oliver Bard, 46, was found KIA in a railroad tunnel near hill 985. Marines sharing foxholes began wondering and whispering about what they would do if ever captured by Chinese fighters.

Marine patrols reconnoitered north of Sudong-ni, looking for enemy positions as the road climbed six miles to Chinhung-ni, a wretched mountain hamlet. CCF forces held commanding positions in the high ground around the hamlet. On Sunday morning at 8:00 AM, the 3d Battalion passed through the 1st and took over as lead guard in the column.

The assault toward Chinhung-ni began at mid-afternoon and progressed slowly. The enemy defenders poured automatic, mortar, and artillery fire down from prepared positions on the hills bracketing the road. The 7th Marines halted after advancing little more than three miles. The battalions dug in on high ground for the night. On Monday, the Marines pressed forward, gaining another 1,000 yards and repulsing CCF counterattacks.

At 4:15 PM, second lieutenants Newton and Reem, How Company, 3d Battalion, led their platoons in an assault against enemy trenches and foxholes on the southern tip of Hill 891 northeast of the hamlet. Near the crest, **Second Lieutenant Robert Dale Reem**, 25, of Lancaster, Pennsylvania, threw himself on a live enemy grenade to save his squad leaders gathered around him. His actions earned him a posthumous Medal of Honor. The Chinese held back the Marines, and the two platoons disengaged in a fighting withdrawal at 6:10 PM as dark fell. The company returned to the battalion lines at 10:00 PM. Tenth Corps commanders began referring to Hill 891 as "How Hill."

That night, the CCF forces quietly withdrew from Chinhung-ni.

Days behind the events on the northeast front, hometown papers reported the news from Sudong on Monday. According to the frontline dispatches, the Marines had attacked a fresh Chinese battalion at Sudong and run into "a stonewall communist defense." The enemy counter-attacked. Despite heavy hand-to-hand fighting, neither side gained any ground. The Marines were a dozen miles south of the Chosin Reservoir. On Tuesday, newspapers reported briefly that the 7th Marines had "slugged forward a mile against light resistance to a point five miles north of Su on the main road to the Chosin Reservoir."

Carl and Virginia Sorenson had been through this before when Rick went to the Pacific. Now they waited for news from Bill. Naturally, Milli wondered what her brother-in-law was going through. Rick tried to be reassuring. Milli then tried to be reassuring to Virginia.

The 7th Marines moved through Chinhung-ni on Tuesday, November 7. The sight was one that would become a lasting image for CPL Sorenson. Enemy bodies littered the ground.

The road out of the hamlet narrowed to one dirt and gravel lane as it left the low country. The 3d Battalion advanced two miles north of the abandoned town, establishing positions along the road, and moved up the massive slopes of Hills 891 and 987, on either side of the road. The regiment was stretched from 1,000 yards north of the hamlet to the two hills.

Having patrolled all day, CPL Sorenson dug in on what would be the last of the flat ground as the column waited to continue north to the Changjin Reservoir. The companies searched for the vanished enemy 124th Division forces until Friday.

On the morning of November 10, the regiment motor lifted another eight miles. The twisting road without shoulders entered the Funchilin Pass, described as "a cliff on one side and a chasm on the other." Climbing 2,500 feet above the valley floor, at times seeming to go straight up, the column clung to the side of mountains to avoid slipping down cliffs. At the top of Funchilin, crossing a bridge spanning a 1,500-foot-deep gorge, the column emerged onto an open plateau. The road leveled and continued two miles to Koto-ri—another hapless, tiny hamlet of mud-wattle huts with thatched-roofs.

The 3d Battalion maintained security on the road as the 1st Battalion passed through their perimeter. After an hour-and-a-half march, Baker Company entered Kotori. The regiment was now eleven miles from Hagaru-ri village and Changjin Lake: the Chosin Reservoir. At the higher elevation in the mountains the temperatures began to drop. The platoon set up warming tents, heated by camp stoves. Little of this was familiar to CPL Sorenson—except one thing.

"It's something like Minnesota weather." Even that would soon not be true.

November 10 was the Marine Corps Birthday. An evening hot meal was prepared for the battalions and punch and cake were served party-style. For the grunts in foxholes on the plateau, the party ended after the cake. The temperatures dropped to -8°F that night, and winds of 30 to 40 mph swept the plateau. Then, it began to snow.

Over the next forty-eight hours, patrols went forward from Kotori to scout the road north. The men managed the intense cold as best they could; wearing cold weather clothing, maintaining adequate movement, trying to heat up C-rations, and, most importantly, keeping their carbines oiled to ensure they fired properly as the wind chill dropped to well below -40°F.

"The cold was the worst, you know," said CPL Sorenson. "I'm from Minnesota, but I've never had cold like that."

The 7th Marines began a slow advance to Hagaru-ri over icy mountain trails on Monday, November 13. As if the temperatures on the plateau had not turned cold enough, an unexpected and unusual Siberian cold front moved over the Chosin Reservoir on Tuesday. The Marines reached Hagaru, flattened by bombing, on Wednesday. They had destroyed the better part of a Chinese division, some 10,000 men, in their move toward the reservoir.

War correspondents sent dispatches that Colonel Litzenberg was at the southern tip of the Chosin with a motorized patrol at 4:00 PM. A half hour later, "troops began scrambling onto ground commanding the lower tip of the artificial lake." Mess wagons moved about the companies with welcome hot chow and fresh bread.

Yudam-ni, the regiment's planned staging area on the west side of the Chosin, was fourteen miles ahead. Marines from Chinhung-ni, Koto-ri, and Hagaru-ri to Yudam-ni would be in mutual support of each other across the thirty-five miles of narrow, winding, climbing, tortuous road they had covered. Engineers constructed an airfield, supply dump, and ammunition dump in the flattened area southeast of Hagaru to ensure adequate support for the extended regiments.

Corporal Sorenson remained at Hagaru for another five days.

Sergeant Rick Sorenson was ordered back to active duty on November 17, and was stationed at the Twin Cities Marine Corps Recruiting Station. He reassured Milli that he would not be called to Korea.

On Monday, November 20, the 7th Marines departed Hagaru-ri and began the climb up the steep, winding, gravel road to the sheer mountain peaks above the 4,000-foot-high Toktong Pass. Reaching the end of the three-mile-long pass, the 1st Battalion looked down on the Yudam-ni Valley. As they descended, it could seem like they were marching straight down. Along the way, they were slowed, but not stopped, by company-strength enemy forces and undefended roadblocks. Pushing through snowdrifts, careful of ice, they reached a small village, the halfway point seven miles southeast from Yudam-ni. The CCF appeared to be retreating from the advance.

Wednesday afternoon, the 1st Battalion established defensive positions 2,500 yards beyond the village. Baker-One-Seven moved up Hill 1276 on the left side of the road, below the Chosin power plant, while the 3d Battalion continued ahead. The Marines were in positions on the plain south of Yudam-ni, where the ground was covered in snow and ice. The 5th Marines took the ground east of the reservoir.

Corporal Sorenson would turn 23 years old on Friday. Thursday was Thanksgiving Day, and the hill he was on was going to be given an ironic nickname.

Colonel Litzenberg received orders to seize Yudam-ni at once with one battalion. The push north had gone so well, the Marines were tasked to drive westward out of Yudam-ni in four days, across the Taebaek Mountains, closing the gap with the Eighth Army's right flank and cutting off the CCF at Mupyong-ni.

The chow trucks came down the road to serve the companies roasted turkey dinner with the traditional trimmings of cranberry sauce and candied sweet potatoes, fresh oranges and apples, fruit cake, and mince and pumpkin pies for dessert.

At 11:00 PM, Captain Wilcox ordered his Baker Company platoons to come down the hill, one at a time, for their hot Thanksgiving dinners at a galley trailer that had pulled into the valley. As the grunts found places to sit in the snow and on boulders, they found that forks could not penetrate the mashed potatoes covered in congealed giblet gravy. The cranberry sauce turned into sherbet, and the oranges were as hard as baseballs. The headless turkeys froze. Corporal Sorenson and his men went back up to their places as hungry as they had been when they had walked down to the galley.

The first aid tent began treating Marines with dysentery and other intestinal problems from eating frozen chow. That dinner turned out to be the last meal the Marines had at the Chosin Reservoir. Later, when B-1-7 had to fight through the same valley, there were so many turkey carcasses discarded everywhere that they renamed Hill 1276—"Turkey Hill."

All the units at Yudam-ni had two days' supply of rations, ammunition, and fuel. At the time, that seemed enough, since the vital MSR was open to the stockpiles at Hagaru.

Thursday and Friday hometown front-page news columns provided troubling facts, some of which the Marines moving along the MSR did not know. The Allied forces were forging ahead toward the Manchurian border all along the frigid 250-mile North Korean front on Thursday. The Marines had "clashed with a sizable communist force in the mountainous center of the peninsula, advancing as much as three miles along the west side of ice-coated Changjin Reservoir. The 7th Marines, "probing west of the great Changjin reservoir, bumped into a communist force of undetermined size." Two Marine companies had skirmished with the Red outposts. At the engagement's end, a captured communist soldier reported that the Chinese were massing a large force in the mountains west of the reservoir. Although unconfirmed, the entire Chinese 42nd Army was suspected to be in the area.

By Friday, U.N. forces had rolled northward to within twenty-three miles of the Manchurian frontier "in a blazing bid to reach the border" before the weekend passed. The Marines continued to probe the mountains around Changjin Reservoir. Along most of the front the communists were avoiding any major engagements, but they were building up forces in the mountains. A spokesman estimated that 100,000 Chinese were available in the northwest, and that their armies were equipped with American artillery captured by Chinese communists from Chiang Kai-Shek's Nationalists.

Meeting only light Chinese resistance as they advanced, the Marines had the battered village of Yudam-ni occupied by Saturday afternoon. The frozen Taebaek Mountains, the spine down the center of the Korean Peninsula, rose to their west. Roads led into three valleys to the west, southwest, and northwest. Having pushed the North Koreans to the Yalu River, the 3d Battalion dug in on the hills and high ground commanding the road into the southwest valley. The 2d Battalion moved to the north, except F-2-7, which stayed on Hill 1653, behind B-1-7 and overlooking the Toktong Pass.

On Sunday at noon, the 5th Marines began to move from east of the reservoir into Yudam-ni. Corporal Sorenson did not know that Private Patchen had come over from Japan and was with the 5th, passing through the 7th Marines' lines. Had he known that at the time, CPL Sorenson would have looked for his buddy. PFC Dick Runquist, who would be promoted to sergeant, was also with the 5th Marines.

The 2d Battalion, 5th Marines, moved into a gap between the 7th's forward companies. Dog-Two-Five stretched across the road leading into the Taebaeck, placing them closest to the rugged, snow covered, and thickly wooded mountains. The terrain was thick with more than trees.

The Chinese had been "secretly" massing forces across the Yalu River into Korea for over a month, and the CCF had entrenched themselves in the high ground on the ridges around Yudam-ni. Four Chinese armies with ten divisions waited on the east and west sides of the Chosin Reservoir, planning to tighten a circle around the Marine regiments.

The divisions had been divided to make nearly simultaneous attacks at Yudam-ni, the Toktong Pass, Hagaru-ri, and Koto-ri. The commanders had orders from Chairman Mao Tse-Tung. Block the MSR out of the Chosin, annihilate all the Marines between Yudam-ni and Chinhung-ni, and wipe clean the Marine command post from Hagaru.

Monday, November 27, proved to be unforgettable. The Marines prepared to "jump off" into the Taebaek Mountains. The battalions sent company-sized patrols out to probe the enemy defenses and gather information about the ridges ahead. At 8:30 AM, the 7th Marines sent patrols west and north in support of the 5th Marines, and ran into the Chinese troops controlling the surrounding ridgelines southwest and northwest of the village. Advancing two-and-a-half miles in heavy fighting, they seized Hills 1403 and 1426 from the entrenched enemy.

The grunts would remember those patrols for all the shooting—and for the cold. Nearly everyone who came home had an opinion about footwear. Their boots were made of rubber with a half-inch-thick, felt insole to absorb perspiration. Totally inadequate for Siberian cold, the insoles froze.

"We had the shoe-pacs," recalled CPL Sorenson, "but they were bad 'cuz when we'd go on a patrol, your feet would sweat. You know, in these shoe-pacs. And then, when you stopped at night—you stopped, they'd get cold, you know, and they'd start—your feet would start freezing. And what are you gonna do? You just—all night long we were trying to keep warm."

The extreme pain of frozen feet prevented the grunts from getting any sleep.

The elements were just as dire on the Chinese in their cotton uniforms and tennis shoes.

"In fact, you know, they were freezing up there. They would—we'd find them sometime on the patrols where they were froze right in their foxhole."

The CCF waited for darkness. By then, Colonel Litzenberg's battalions were stretched out along six-and-a-quarter miles of the MSR—from Hill 1403 on the Northwest Ridge, across the Southwest and South Ridges, all the way to Fox Hill (Hill 1653) overlooking the Toktong Pass.

The "quiet" was broken at 9:00 PM. The CCF launched the first probing, heavy attack from the north ridge above Yudam-ni, putting the Marine regiments on 100% alert. Thirty-five minutes later, they attacked from the Northwest Ridge, striking H-3-7 from three sides on Hill 1403. Within thirty minutes, the Marines were pushed back from the hill.

At each of their objectives, the Chinese came in furious, human wave assaults. The crushing numbers of enemy fighters, employing small arms, automatic weapons, and concussion hand grenades, charged in endless waves of hundreds of soldiers and overran the Marine positions. More than 20,000 Chinese regulars attacked at Hagaru, threatening to overrun the Marine command post.

The CCF penetrated the defenses along all the ridges surrounding Yudam-ni. Individual companies, platoons, squads, and men were surrounded and cut off from others. On the MSR south of the village, C-1-7 was surrounded and isolated on the slopes of Hill 1419. The enemy attacks continued into the early morning hours. and the encirclement of the regiments was becoming obvious.

Captain Wilcox was wounded and out of action. 1stLt Joseph Richard "Joe" Kurcaba, 33, his executive officer from New York City, took command of Baker.

"Oh, I was scared." Corporal Sorenson could have been speaking for every Marine on the hills. His thoughts echoed those his big brother had on the Namur Island beach. "Plenty scared that I would be wounded or killed, because when you see kids right alongside you get killed, you wonder how come I'm still here and he's gone. So, yeah. I was scared."

Staff Sergeant Robert Sidney Kennemore, 30, from Greenville, South Carolina, was a career Marine, having fought on Guadalcanal and Tulagi in WWII. He had left his wife, Mary Jo, with their five boys to go to war a second time. He was a machine-gun squad leader in E-2-7 in place northwest of Yudam-ni.

A large enemy force overran Easy Company's defensive perimeter in the night assaults. When his commander was seriously injured in the attack, SSgt Kennemore took over lead of the platoon. He quickly reorganized the defensive line and consolidated the men into effective tactical positions. Two machine gun positions provided the platoon its strongest defense. The assaulting force overran one of the emplacements. Easy Company's situation was suddenly more desperate.

Commanding the platoon from the remaining machine gun position, SSgt Kennemore directed the fire of his squad into the charging hostile force. Two enemy grenades landed among his machine gunners. He spotted them, immediately stomped the explosive devices into the snow and mud, and kept his feet pressed down. The blasts propelled his body into the air, taking both legs, but not his life.

Easy Company rallied and eventually repulsed the enemy attack, holding on through the night attack. SSgt Kennemore was found in the morning light, his legs just frozen stumps partly encased in blood-soaked snow. The freezing nighttime temperatures at Yudam-ni had saved him from bleeding to death. The oldest Marine to muffle a grenade's explosion in Korea was evacuated from the Chosin.

Rick Sorenson later met Bob Kennemore at Medal of Honor conventions and funerals, and might have learned more about events at the Chosin from him than he did from his brother.

Colonel Litzenberg ordered LtCol Davis to pull the 1st Battalion into Yudam. Able, Baker, and Charlie companies had fought their way to the village by 9:10 PM on Tuesday. A perimeter was reestablished a thousand yards nearer the village by 10:00 PM. On a map, CPL Sorenson was digging in at 40°28'56" North latitude, 127°6'46" East longitude, at an elevation of 3,500 feet above sea level. The CCF had cut the MSR from Hagaru and isolated the regiments at the Chosin from the rest of the 1st Division.

Another image was etched into CPL Sorenson's life-long memory. "And some of the kids—when we were up and fighting in the hills, we had to leave the kids that were killed. We took the wounded with us. We got the wounded out, but the other kids that we knew were dead, why, we just left them there in the snow."

Baker Company lost CPL Frank Carl Hoffman Jr., 22, from Houston. KIA on Monday, his body was not recovered. Corporals Gene Alfred Turgeon of Connersville, Indiana, and Frank Earl Yeager, 22, from Murrysville, Pennsylvania, were KIA on Tuesday, neither body recovered. Corporal William Karl Grauman, 20, from Chicago, and PFC Warren Sheldon Rosenberger, 19, from San Antonio, were both MIA on Tuesday, neither ever seen again.

The first reports of Marine casualties for November 27–28, numbered 136 killed, 60 missing, 675 wounded, and 355 non-battle casualties, most of which were by frostbite. The 7th Marines' rolls at Yudam-ni reported 22 killed, 4 missing, and 160 wounded in action for November 28.

Tuesday night was bitterly cold as temperatures dropped below -20°F. Well-tended weapons became inoperable. Digging a foxhole took as long as six to eight hours.

"You could have a little foxhole, but it wasn't protection, you know, because it was all snow and stuff, and you couldn't dig any further. You just couldn't dig a foxhole or anything, so you just, uh, snow . . . and you kept down in the snow."

It was evident to all, including correspondents, that the Marines were in a fight for survival. Days and nights of sleeplessness were ahead.

In addition to the enemy assaults, the casualties, the cold and frostbite, being cut off from the logistics supply line, there was hunger. The C-rations froze and became inedible.

"And there's no place to cook or anything," CPL Sorenson described it. "All we had was snow. Thirty-five degrees below zero. So, the only thing they could do is, they supplied us by air with Tootsie Rolls. That was what we ate. It's the only thing we had was Tootsie Rolls. And no water. We used the snow like we would do when we were kids, sledding. You know, where you used to take a scoop of snow, and used that for water.

"You know, there's no place to warm up. No place. So, day after day after day, that cold weather, you know, kids got frostbite. They—if they were wounded, that helped a little bit because the blood froze." Helicopters evacuated the badly wounded kids to the airfield at Hagaru, so they could get them out of the encirclement. "Thank God for that."

The Eighth U.S. Army in the west was in full retreat. The Marines were clearly not going to push through the Taebaek Mountains. On Wednesday evening, Major General O. P. Smith was ordered to withdraw the two depleted regiments from the Chosin and return his Marines to Tongjoson Bay for evacuation from North Korea. The commanders at Yudam-ni began reorganizing composite units up to battalion level.

By dawn on Thursday, the battalions were ready to displace from the Reservoir, leapfrog the companies through the Toktong Pass, down the road toward Hagaru-ri, and fight all the way to Hungman Harbor. Unable to withdraw and carry out all their dead and wounded, most of the Marines killed in action were buried in field cemeteries—mass graves—along the perimeters before the battalions pulled back to the outskirts of Yudam-ni. The 7th Marines buried eighty-five comrades at the Reservoir.

Helicopters evacuated 109 of the wounded before the column began its move south.

Private Leon Ernest Patchen was seriously wounded, shot in the head, at Yudam-ni. He was flown out and evacuated to Japan. Corporal Sorenson learned later that his friend died of his wounds on December 12. His remains were brought home and buried at Fort Snelling National Cemetery. Leon's twin brother, Private Loren L. Patchen was getting ready to deploy to Korea at the time. The Marines did not send him over. Corporal Sorenson understood.

"But, they didn't want to do that to the family."

On CPL Sorenson's last night at the Chosin, he and two other kids were up a hill, out in front of the Baker line, trying to dig a row of foxholes. One of the guys shot himself in the foot and was taken to the medical tent. The other went down the hill to get a case of grenades, slipped and fell on the way back up, and cracked three ribs. Corporal Sorenson was alone with his M-1 and a clip with eight shots.

"So, then there was just me! I don't know why they left me out there. I think it was suicide, but they left me out there all alone. Nobody on the right—the right or the left. And the machine gun—they put the machine gun up on the hill in back of me. So, I think they did it so I would let them know the Chinese were coming, but, I'd probably make it back up that hill."

"A Tactical Redeployment of Forces"

The battalions, unshaven, beards and mustaches frigid with mucous icicles, dirty, bloodied, and wrapped in parkas, began pulling back from the ridgelines around Yudam-ni at 8:00 AM on Friday, December 1, taking what dead and wounded they could carry. Some 1,500 casualties moved from the Chosin. No one had changed clothing for weeks and, if anyone had slept at all at the Reservoir, it had been in very short intervals.

The 7th Marines moved overland climbing over boulders, trudging through knee-deep snowdrifts, and crossing a jumble of ridges, meadows, mountain crests and slopes on both sides of the MSR. They put themselves between the Chinese and the convoy to cover the column flanks. The 1st Battalion began the breakout toward Toktong Pass, displacing one company at a time, joining the column as the day pressed on, moving to the east flank.

The air temperatures dropped to -15°F. The wind stirred the snow pack. The going was slow and arduous. CCF machine guns, rifle fire, and grenades slowed the companies, but did not stop them. The under-strength rifle companies held against the Chinese counterattacks. Some men felt compelled to lie down on the frozen ground and go to sleep, despite the reality that sleeping would mean capture or freezing to death. Comrades pushed, shoved, and carried them, rather than leaving them behind in the dark. Plodding along in parkas, mittens, and shoe-pacs, with Three-Seven covering the west flank of the breakout and "no time to lose," One-Seven established a new consolidated perimeter south of the village. The CCF Divisions struck en masse at midnight and kept coming until 6:00 AM on Saturday.

Fox-Two-Seven, depleted of riflemen, was desperately holding Fox Hill at the Toktong Pass. Baker Company was ordered forward to relieve them in place. First, Baker retook "Turkey Hill." Other hills rose in front of them for miles. CCF companies held positions in the crests, waiting for the column to come down the road. With the Chinese above and the road below, Baker made its own trail.

"So, we had to be real quiet. No talking. No nothing. Just walkin' . . . It was hard, 'cuz the snow was up to our knees, and we had to make a path, you know. We'd slip and slide and everything else. You could hear the Chinese up above. I don't know why they didn't hear us, but, uh, they never opened up on us or shot at us until we got just about to the pass, and then we had to fight for that one hill, that they were overlooking the pass, and once we took that hill, then we went down and we relieved Fox Company."

Baker Company privates first class Albert Wendell Hazelton Jr, 19, from Richfield Springs, New York, and Edward Cozed Leneve, 21, from Berkeley, California, were both KIA on Saturday, bodies not recovered.

Consolidated, the two companies tenuously held the Toktong Pass open for the column. Corporal Sorenson and PFC John J. "Jack" Gallapo Jr., from Chicago, got to know each other well. The PFC was 1stLt Kiser's platoon runner. He was seriously wounded on Fox Hill and carried into Hagaru. [8]

The fighting along fourteen miles of narrow road from Yudam-ni to Hagaru-ri lasted seventy-nine hours. The lead Marine company reached the Hagaru perimeter at 7:00 PM, on Sunday. The cooks provided the weary Marines hot pancakes and hot coffee around the clock—their first taste of hot food since the chow trucks had arrived at the Reservoir on Thanksgiving.

Corporal Sorenson and the last of the Chosin Few entered the 1st Division's perimeter on December 4. PFC Bernardo Ramos Ayala, 20, of Corpus Christi, Texas, was MIA.

If PFC Milton Eugene Lawson, 18, of Aberdeen, Washington, had a hot meal in Hagaru, it was his last. He was MIA on Tuesday.

A flotilla of 109 U.S. Navy ships waited for the Marines and soldiers at Hungnam Harbor. The Marines refused to talk about escape, evacuation, capture, or annihilation. Unfortunately for the Chinese and North Koreans, the Leathernecks had merely changed their direction of attack and were "advancing in a different direction" to conduct an organized "tactical redeployment of forces" to another area in the theater of war. The Marines intended to take every living, breathing grunt in their lines aboard the waiting ships.

The breakout to the Hamhung–Hungnam Harbor continued Tuesday, and the rear guard departed during the night of December 6–7. The seriously wounded, unable to walk out, found room in trucks. The frozen bodies of the dead were piled deeply into the backs of trucks and on the fenders of jeeps.

The Marine column marched in the furious cold, crossed the wintry landscape, tried to warm themselves at fires, crouched behind jeeps while under fire from the hills on either side of them, and pushed wrecked vehicles off the road. Under constant attack in the snow-covered mountains, the regiments fought their way through a valley of fire to the plateau at Koto-ri. Men died in action there on Friday.

Charging an enemy position on a hill in blinding snow during B-1-7's last big firefight, 1stLt Joe Kurcaba was killed. Second Platoon BARman PFC Attilio Michele Lupacchini, 20, of Yardley, Pennsylvania, charged an enemy machine-gun position and was killed. His body was not recovered. On the same hill, PFC Conrad Kowalski was the last B-1-7 KIA in the days of the breakout. His body was not recovered.

The trucks carrying the deceased could hold no more. The men somberly watched as dog tags were retrieved from the dead, and the still-frozen bodies of 117 Marines were buried. The location of the Koto-ri burial site was recorded "in hope that someday their remains would be retrieved." [9]

The column of totally exhausted Marines reached the port of Hungnam on December 11, having walked seventy-five miles, surviving most days virtually without food, water, or sleep. The last Marines reached the outskirts of Hungnam two days later. All the Marines had "walking pneumonia" and stood in line to get a penicillin shot.

Counting replacement troops, B-1-7 had landed at Wonsan with about 300 officers and men. Twenty-seven walked into Hungnam. All the company officers except, 1stLt Hank Kiser, had been wounded. Of the original fifty in CPL Sorenson's whole platoon, only four got back. The rest? "They were either wounded, killed, or had frostbite."

In official reports, the Marines counted 4,418 battle casualties from the Chosin Reservoir Campaign, October 26–December 15. Of these, 718 were KIA or DOW. The 3,508 wounded did not include the 7,313 non-battle casualties. An additional 192 were missing in action. [10]

Before he boarded a ship, CPL Sorenson was witness to an event that remained vivid in his mind fifty years later. More than 400 wooden crosses stood over the graves of First Division Marines killed in the heavy fighting between the Chosin Reservoir and the fight to Hungnam. "They dug a big trench and buried all these kids there. They left 'em. They're still there. . . . Hundreds of 'em. That's where they dumped 'em. They used a bulldozer and, uh, buried them there."

General Smith paid a final tribute to his dead Marines during a memorial service at the cemetery on Wednesday, December 13. Then, embarkation of the 5th and 7th Marines began.

The majority of the X Corps Marines were on their way to Pusan by Friday. The last of the Marines departed from Hungnam at 2:36 PM on Christmas Eve, December 24, 1950.

For the Sorenson families back in Minnesota, there was no greater yuletide gift than to learn that Bill had survived the Breakout.

Still in the Fight

The 1st MarDiv regiments redeployed to Pusan. The Marines climbed into trucks and took a forty-mile "motor march" to their assembly area at Masan. Baker-One-Seven, absorbing replacements, went on daily patrols to the Naktong River.

Corporal Sorenson was back onboard LST *Q0l0* on January 16, 1951, and disembarked the next day up near Pohang-dong, on Korea's east coast. [11] Among the grunts, place names predictably led to joking. The 1/7 Command Post was at Ijon-dong. During the *Pohang Guerrilla Hunt*, the companies patrolled near Topyong-dong and captured Hapton-ni, Chiso-dong, and Kawa-dong.

The treacherous hills, on the other hand, were nothing to laugh about. At 3:45 PM, January 25, Baker Company was in a firefight on Hill 400. From there, they patrolled to Kodusan and took Hill 531. Of the twenty-nine casualties Marine rosters reported in January, fifteen were listed during the last three days of the month.

In his four months on foreign soil, CPL Sorenson had developed a seasoned Marine's sense of combat. "You've got a sense that when you're going up a hill, you're lookin' for a place to go if they start shooting. You look for anyplace that you can dive to—this side, that side, behind a rock, a tree, or anything."

In early February, 1/7 moved into the Myong-dang-dong and Kusan-dong areas. Then, on February 22, CPL Sorenson took a motor convoy 270 miles up to Chungju in central Korea, then to the front lines at Wonju, southeast of Seoul and southwest of Hoeng-song. Baker Company patrolled at the airfield. Thirty-four Marine casualties were reported in February. Operation *Ripper* was planned for the Marines to advance north into the Chunchon Corridor at the 38° Parallel.

Corporal Sorenson found out in a letter that Dick Runquist was with the 5th Marines—on 1/7's right flank. Rather than carry his M-1, he borrowed a pistol from a kid, and walked over by the road separating the two regiments. Asking after his Anoka neighbor, he was told that he was up the hill having chow. When PFC Runquist spotted his friend, he threw his chow gear all the way down the hill, ran, and gave CPL Sorenson a bear hug. Moments like that in war are both funny and memorable.

"After that," Bill would recall, "I never seen him again."

Baker Company was in reserve at the start of March, then took Hill 481 from the enemy and stayed near Hongchon at Phase Line Albany, east of Seoul. Contact with the enemy and combat engagements intensified. The Marines advanced on bunkers, working in close range, taking enemy soldiers out with grenades and bayonets. For the last week of the month, 1/7 withdrew to the base area for extensive training seven hours daily. The Marines incurred forty-three casualties in March.

The 7th Marines crossed the Soyang River and seized Phase Line Kansas above the 38° Parallel, near the Hwachon Reservoir. In the evening of April 14, while patrolling, B-1-7 was under small arms and machine-gun fire, and took six mortar rounds. The regiment then moved over the Pukhan River to the Pendleton Line.

On Sunday, April 22, at 7:00 PM, 1/7 was ordered to advance 5,000 yards and consolidate on Phase Line Quantico and be prepared to destroy the enemy south of Phase Line Wyoming. The CCF Spring Offensive kicked off at 10:45 PM.

At 1:25 AM on Monday, a large enemy force attacked the line with small arms, machine guns, grenades, and 60mm and 120mm mortar rounds. Able Company's left flank broke at 4:00 AM, and an hour passed before the platoons could seal the penetration. The Battle of Kapyong continued throughout the day and evening. At 6:00 PM, 1/7 disengaged and withdrew to secure positions.

In the dark of Tuesday morning, a mortar round hit near CPL Sorenson's position. A piece of shrapnel struck the boy beside him under the chin and killed him instantly. Shrapnel pierced the soft tissue of CPL Sorenson's right side.

Native civilian Koreans acted as litter bearers, getting wounded grunts to the casualty aid station. Helicopters brought in bandages, plasma, and other medical supplies during the day and shuttled casualties out. The battalions pulled back on Tuesday, and 1/7 was in the base area by Thursday.

The Marines reported 128 casualties in April; 84 of those were logged on April 22–24. Corporal Anthony Frank DeMeo, 20, of Brooklyn, New York, was among the casualties B-1-7 reported. He was KIA on April 23. PFC Harold Edward Ellison, 22, of San Antonio, was KIA on April 24. His remains were not recovered.

Baker went back into reserves for two weeks. Corporal Sorenson went to the hospital, and the mortar shrapnel was removed. After a week's stay, he returned to the company and did not have to make up for any lost time. He was flown down to Pusan on May 10. He and others departed Korea on a ship, sailed to Japan and then home to the States.

The Sorenson family was relieved to know that Bill had landed at Treasure Island. He was granted thirty days of leave and given orders to proceed to MCB Quantico, Virginia, at the finish of his leave to train new officers on the ins and outs of combat in Korea. When the Administration Section realized he did not have enough time left until his expiration of enlistment date, he was put in charge of a platoon of guys in the separation battalion who did not have regular jobs. During the day, he marched them out of the barracks and found work jobs for them.

Rick Sorenson was promoted to staff sergeant in May 1951. He could serve the country and remain close to his family—a happy state of affairs for him.

Bill was discharged from the active Marine Corps on August 17, 1951. He returned to Anoka and to work at Federal Premium Ammunition.

Before the year ended, Anoka learned that, in addition to Marvin Whitehead and Leon Patchen, three U.S. Army soldiers, *Tornado* alumni, had been KIA in 1951: 1st Lieutenant Harold Glenn Hippie, 26, Lieutenant Keith Anders Jensen, 30, and Corporal Gerald Randall Emmans, 18.

Rick and Milli managed his family, military, and VA responsibilities. Their first daughter, Wendy, was born in 1952.

He was promoted to master sergeant in June 1953, a month before the Korean War was arbitrated to an armistice at Panmunjom on July 27. As veterans came home, he helped men like his brother apply for their benefits. Returning to employments they had left to be of service to the country was a priority. Families also inquired about back pay and burial rights and assistance for the remains of husbands, sons, and brothers being repatriated. Most heart rendering were inquiries about the servicemen missing or believed to be held in captivity in North Korea.

Across all the armed services, 188 men from the Twin Cities gave their lives during the war. Fifty-four were Marines, and twenty-three of them had been in the 7th Marines.

Rick and Milli were soon uncle and aunt to a nephew. Bill married his girlfriend, Shirley Lou Johnson, in 1953. Mark was born to them, the first of four boys. Bill was hired by the post office again for the holidays, then, quit Federal and worked full time as a city carrier in Anoka. He would eventually get the postmaster job at Champlin. Milli would tender her support and consolation when Bill and Shirley's only daughter died at birth.

Master Sergeant Sorenson accepted a second lieutenant's commission in November 1953 and was ordered to the Marine Corps Schools at Camp Barrett, Quantico, Virginia. He completed the Officers' Basic School (TBS) in April 1954 and went back to Camp Pendleton to serve as 7th Engineer Battalion's Assistant Supply Officer. Eleven years had passed since he had been there to train for war on Pacific islands, and ten years since he had met Gunny John Basilone on the training grounds. This time, he returned to Pendleton with Milli, a young son, and a daughter.

Grandma Mary Anderson Sorenson-Lah lived to age 79 years. She died on June 18, 1954, and was buried beside Nels in the Emmons' Oak Lawn Cemetery.

Second Lieutenant Sorenson was appointed to first lieutenant in September 1954, and transferred to the 2nd Replacement Battalion in January 1955. In March, he was ordered overseas for duty with the 3rd Engineer Battalion, 3rd Marine Division, on Okinawa, Japan. That meant he missed the first Fleet Marine Force Concurrent Reunions when all six World War II divisions met at the Hotel Roosevelt in New York City, June 24–26, 1955.

As had been true in his childhood, family was at the center of his concerns. Being away from his growing family for six months was an experience he did not wish to repeat. First Lieutenant Sorenson returned to the States in November 1955, ready to re-enter civilian life again. He resigned his commission, voluntarily reverted to a master sergeant's rank, and was discharged from the active Marines. When he looked back thirty-six years later, he would say his years of military service had many long-term good effects on his life.

Settling Down Involved Some Moving About

The family returned to Minnesota, and Rick resumed his work with the VA for two years. Debby Sorenson was born in 1956. Looking ahead to having more children, Rick and Milli talked about his government salary. His valor medals did not figure much into their considerations. It had been ten years since the Congressional Medal of Honor Society had been formed, and the members had very few legislated privileges and special benefits.

Rick would have to wait until he turned age 65, in 1989, to be eligible for the $10 monthly pension that Congress authorized for Medal recipients in 1916. That would not change until 1964, when a $100 monthly MOH pension was legislated for recipients over the age of 50. Then, Rick would be eligible for the special pension in 1974. [12]

He was offered an opportunity in 1957 and took employment as an insurance underwriter for Equitable Life Insurance. The following May, he accepted an invitation from President Eisenhower.

On Wednesday, May 28, 1958, the remains of two Unknown servicemen killed in WWII and Korean War combat arrived in Washington, D.C. The caskets lay in the Capitol Rotunda until Memorial Day, May 30. Over 200 MOH recipients came to pay their respects. On Friday morning, Rick shook hands with the president and vice president in the White House Rose Garden. He mingled with thirty-two other Marine Medal recipients and greeted Don Truesdell, Richard Bush, and Jacklyn Lucas. After brunch, he attended the solemn interment ceremony at Arlington National Cemetery when the president conferred the Medal of Honor on each of the Unknowns.

With Robert, Wendy, and Debby at home, Milli counted on the sitting services of her sister, Eleanor, or the kids' Grandma Edith Snow if she was to travel with Rick. Not too bad in 1958, but the arrangements would get a little more complicated in a couple of years.

Back from Washington, Rick packed for the June 27–29 weekend in Philadelphia, where Marine Corps history began. More than 500 veterans of the Roi–Namur, Saipan, Tinian, and Iwo Jima battles showed up for the eleventh Fourth Marine Division Association (FMDA) re-union. He checked into the Sheraton Hotel on Friday. At the Saturday meeting, members voted to establish a Scholarship Fund for children of deceased or disabled division members to attend a college or trade school of their choice that would otherwise have been beyond their means. Over the next five decades, the fund would provide financial support to thousands of children and grandchildren. Across those same years, after the quarterly FIGHTING FOURTH MARINE DIVISION OF WWII Volume 1 newsletter went to the printers in 1963, stories about Rick and the eleven other 4th MarDiv Medal holders would delight the readership.

Tours of Independence Hall, the Liberty Bell, the Marine Barracks, Tun Alley, and the site of Tun Tavern filled the reunion itinerary. Philadelphia's Mayor Richardson Dilworth declared Saturday "Marine Corps Day" and the City of Brotherly Love provided the ovations along the Division's parade route.

Rick and Milli celebrated the birth of their fourth child when James was born in February 1959. Two boys and two girls in the family might have seemed like a good balance. It lasted for eleven months. [13]

For most of his adult life, as it does for Medal recipients, Memorial Day weekends presented Rick with choices between family obligations and civic commitments. Few holidays passed without official invitations and requests—some close to home, others requiring travel.

On May 25, 1959, Rick and Milli and many of the family went to John Ward Park for a Memorial Day celebration. American Legion Edward B. Cutler Post 102 was dedicating the post-WWII Anoka Veterans Memorial, across Church Street and overlooking Forest Hill Cemetery to the west. A granite monument inscribed with IN MEMORY OF ANOKA'S DEAD OF ALL WARS stood upright about fifteen feet from the curb. A monument dedicated IN MEMORY OF THOSE FROM ANOKA WHO SERVED sat at the base of the American flagpole, twenty-five yards in from the street. Six flagpoles of the armed services flanked either side of the American flag. A full sized, green 105mm howitzer directed its muzzle toward Church Street, symbolizing the ready defense of the flag.

Rick was one of six World War I and World War II MOH recipients accredited to Minnesota who had survived their combat actions: two Marines and four Army soldiers. By the time he started his career as an underwriter, he was one of three still surviving. [14]

Army Sergeant Michael "Mike" Colalillo was born in 1925 in Hibbing, Minnesota, a town in the center of the Mesabi Iron Range, a good 190 miles north of Anoka. His family had moved to Duluth in 1928. He entered the U.S. Army from there, was trained as a Browning machine gunner like Rick, and earned a Medal of Honor in action on April 7, 1945, near Untergriesheim, Germany. Mike was down-to-earth and surprisingly shy. Humble, even uncomfortable, about being called a hero, he never looked forward to giving a speech. The impression he left on one reporter was that Mike treated fame like perfume. "It's great to be around and wonderful to smell, but he wouldn't want to swallow it."

Mike and Rick became close friends flying with Medal recipients aboard military transports to military funerals at national cemeteries, presidential inaugurations, and other national events. The American Legion's 41st National Convention in August 1959 was an opportunity to catch up on family news.

On November 11, 1919, the first anniversary of WWI Armistice Day, the new American Legion organization had gathered in Minneapolis–St. Paul and marched in their First National Convention Parade. The Legionnaires dedicated themselves to veterans' welfare, education, youth work, health activities, and patriotism. Forty years had passed, and they returned to the Twin Cities.

On Friday, August 21, 1959, all the standing commissions and committees held meetings to plan the weeklong convention of meetings, selection of new officers, reunions, parades, contests, dinners, concerts and dances. At 9:00 AM on Saturday, the Legionnaires began registering in large numbers at the Lowry Hotel and St. Paul Hotel and the Leamington, Radisson, Dyckman, Nicollet, and Curtis hotels in the heart of downtown Minneapolis. Hotel registrations were organized according to states. Delegates from the Forty & Eight organization (40 infantrymen or 8 horses in a WWI train boxcar headed to the front lines) and the ladies of the American Legion's Auxiliary, celebrating their 39th National Convention, were welcomed. The distinguished guests were shown to their rooms in the Leamington headquarters on 10th Street and 3rd Avenue South.

Milli had been married to Rick for thirteen years and had grown accustomed to the invitations he received to attend functions as an honored or distinguished guest. This convention was special, and he was counted among more than 220 invited guests: a former United States President, the vice president, U.S. senators, governors, congressmen, mayors, generals, admirals, ambassadors from other countries, chiefs of police, school superintendents, national newspaper managing editors, and MOH recipients.

Throughout the days ahead, former President of the United States Harry S. Truman, Vice President Richard M. Nixon, Democratic Senate Majority Leader Lyndon B. Johnson, Minnesota U.S. Senator Hubert H. Humphrey and Eugene J. McCarthy, Minnesota Governor Orville L. Freeman, Minneapolis Mayor P. Kenneth Peterson, St. Paul Mayor Joseph E. Dillon, American Federation of Labor and Congress of Industrial Organizations President George Meany, and Dr. Charles W. Mayo all shook hands with the MOH recipients.

Two days of Junior Drum and Bugle Corps, Band, Junior Band, Color Guard, Motorcycle Drill Team, and Firing Squad contests kicked off at the University of Minnesota Stadium on Saturday morning. Mary Ann Mobley of Brandon, Mississippi, 1959 Miss America, was an honored guest at the Senior Drum and Bugle Corps Finals on Sunday morning.

At 3:30 PM, Rick was at the Minneapolis City Hall as the Patriotic and Memorial Parade assembled on 3rd Avenue South and 5th Street. The small column moved solemnly along the half-mile route, south on 3rd Avenue to Grant Street and the Minneapolis Municipal Auditorium. The Memorial Program began at 4:30 PM, presided over by Right Reverend Monsignor John J. Twiss, National Chaplain from Massachusetts. The packed auditorium was asked to maintain a reverent silence during the program in respect to the memory of those who had died at war. "Please do not applaud."

The program started with a Gold Star Mothers' processional, an invocation, and the combined Sioux Falls, Milwaukee, Indianapolis, and Millville, New Jersey, Legion Post Choruses singing the *Lord's Prayer*. Following the Reverend's Memorial Address, the combined choruses sang the fitting verses P.W. Dykema had adapted from I Corinthians 16:13 in 1951.

> "There's a voice comes ringing o'er the world today,
> Quit you like men, be strong;
> 'Tis the Master calleth, now the voice obey,
> Quit you like men, be strong."

The placing of memorial flowers, *Taps*, and a moment of silent prayer brought many in the auditorium to tears as fallen sons, fathers, brothers, uncles, and comrades came to mind. Rabbi Morris Cwiel Katz of St. Paul provided the Benediction after the combined choruses sang *The Battle Hymn of the Republic*. The Memorial Program ended with the Gold Star Mothers' recessional.

Rick had scheduled time off from his usual Equitable Life Insurance work to participate in as many convention events as he could. The grand and mammoth American Legion Parade was on Monday. His morning started early as a guest at the 7:30 AM National Chaplain's Breakfast. An aerial bomb was fired at 8:30 AM to signal that the parade would start in thirty minutes. Another aerial bomb was fired at 8:45 AM.

Rick made his way to the chartered buses and the assembly area on downtown's far west side at Wayzata Boulevard and Linden Avenue. He did not have to rush. The planners had organized the parade into ten divisions, each assembling a half hour behind the preceding one. Rick found the Tenth Division placards.

All the elements had been assigned to specific divisions, each under the direction of a Marshal and a Parade Coordinator. Anticipating the Legionnaires' tendencies to entertain each other, they also readied the marshals and coordinators to enforce various bans in the line of march, insisting that anyone caught should be summarily dismissed from the parade. Prohibitions included: the drinking of or simulated drinking of intoxicants; being under the influence of intoxicating liquors; water pistols and electric shocking devices; firecrackers; female impersonators; any immoral or bad taste presentations or representations; tossing of souvenirs, treats, promotional or advertising material from floats or marching units; rear movements during the march; and locomotives or box cars with women passengers.

The First Division, some 3,000 Armed Forces members, marched east on Wayzata when a third aerial bomb was fired at 9:00 AM. Miss Mary Ann Mobley and a host of marshals and dignitaries led the way under sunny skies. The air temperature was 75°F, perfect for a march. The American Legion leadership and members and the uniformed American Legion Auxiliary women, assembled in order of states, comprised the other nine divisions. The marshals, intent on maintaining proper distances between the elements and divisions, kept the other 17,000 waiting marchers corralled.

The Second Division marched onto Wayzata from east of Penn Avenue North at 9:30 AM and turned toward downtown. Joseph Jacob "Joe" Foss, leading World War II USMC fighter "Ace of Aces" and MOH recipient for his air combat during the Guadalcanal Campaign, waved from the dignitary's car at the lead of the South Dakota Legionnaires.

The Tenth Division, comprised of thousands of Minnesota Legionnaires, was assembled on Wayzata Boulevard, extending west to Cedar Lake Road. The Massed Colors, eight (8) abreast, followed by the Band & Drum Corps stepped off at 1:00 PM. Wearing their blue Legionnaire caps and Medals of Honor, Rick, Mike Colalillo, and S/Sgt. Donald Eugene Rudolph Sr., 38, recipient from Minneapolis, rode in a single column of cars behind the line of authorized floats.

The weather had changed. Temperatures were climbing toward 95°F, the dew point was 68°F, humidity was high at 97, and the winds averaged about 12 mph. Scattered rain and thunderstorms began dropping .03 inches of precipitation. The Division Marshal maintained the pace regardless of the weather conditions.

The tail end of the parade moved east on Wayzata Boulevard, through Parade Stadium, back to Wayzata, continued east to Lyndale Avenue, then one block right (south) to Huron, left (east) on Huron to Harmon, east on Harmon to 12th Street, right (south) on 12th Street to Nicollet Avenue, left (east) on Nicollet to the City Central Library, and finally south on

4th Street to 3rd Avenue. The line of march covered miles into the city center. Rick did not reach the dispersal point at City Hall until twilight. The American Legion Parade had treated Minneapolis to a ten-hour pageant.

The opening session of the National Convention on Tuesday was covered by radio, television, and newspaper reporters—another long day "packed with drama." Rick took his seat among the dignitaries in the Minneapolis Municipal Auditorium at 8:30 AM. At 9:00 AM, the Call to Order began. Advancement of Colors, solo singing of *The Star-Spangled Banner*, the Invocation, the Chaplain's Memorial Address, lighting of the Convention Peace Candle, the Benediction, and *Taps* followed. The National Commander asked Rick and the others to stand at 10:45 for the Presentation of Recipients of Congressional Medals of Honor.

President Dwight D. Eisenhower's message was read at 11:00 AM, starting the series of brief welcome addresses. The award ceremonies began at noon. Vice President Richard M. Nixon, wearing a Legion cap, stepped to the podium at 1:45 PM and addressed the auditorium for thirty minutes. He offered assurances to the Legionnaires that there need be no concern about Premier Nikita Khrushchev's upcoming visit. The president would not be taken in or bluffed by the Soviet leader. Yet, condemning the visit, or any other misunderstanding between the two world powers, could provoke a war. The visit was an opportunity to settle international differences peacefully, though neither the president or vice president believed it would change Communist goals for world domination.

When Mr. Nixon finished speaking, the Legionnaires stood for the Salute to Colors and adjourned for the afternoon recess. The break presented an opportunity to newspapermen.

Medal recipients get used to the approach of reporters and questions about the details described in their Award Citations. They expect it whenever they wear their Medal in a public setting. No matter how much time passes, the questions probe and pierce a discomfort familiar to all recipients. Memories tucked tightly away, the images that visit frequently during sleep, emerge during interviews. Thirty-six years after the 1959 convention, Mike Colalillo explained it.

"I don't like to remember it to tell you the truth," he told a journalist. "I was scared. Very scared. The feeling I had was to shoot or they'd shoot me. It was something you had to do. I think of how your friends got killed alongside you. That comes back to you once in a while." [15]

Early Tuesday evening, Rick and Milli stood in a line outside the Hall of States in Hotel Leamington. Ahead was the kind of event, familiar as it was, to which they never completely felt comfortable—the National Commander's Dinner to Distinguished Guests. At 7:00 PM, the hall was called to order. When it was their turn, they stood in the doorway.

"Please rise for the entrance of Richard K. Sorenson, Medal of Honor winner, and his wife, Mrs. Mildred Sorenson." The guests were escorted to their reserved table.

Dinner was served after the Salute to Colors, Invocation, Pledge of Allegiance, singing of the *Star-Spangled Banner*, and brief welcoming remarks. Table conversation was light-hearted for the most part. The late 1950s were relatively peaceful years for Americans. The antagonism between the U.S. and the Soviet Union was ongoing, but there had been no direct military campaign in the Cold War. The longer National Football League rivalries had begun in 1920, a year after the First National Convention Parade. So, mention of football was unavoidable.

The Legionnaires exchanged gibes depending on their favored teams. The preseason exhibition games had begun on Tuesday night, August 11, when the Pittsburgh *Steelers* had toppled the Cleveland *Browns*, 34–20. On Friday, as the Twin Cities prepared for the convention, the Baltimore *Colts* had trounced the New York *Giants* in one-sided play, 28–3, and the Washington *Redskins* had beaten the Los Angeles *Rams*, 23–21. On Saturday, Cleveland lost another one to the Detroit *Lions*, 9–3, the Chicago *Bears* edged out the Philadelphia *Eagles*,

24–21, and the Chicago *Cardinals* took out the *Steelers*, 21–10. Mike Colalillo was pleased that the Green Bay *Packers* had given their new coach—Vince Lombardi—his first win on Sunday over the San Francisco *Forty Niners*, 24–17.

Old and new rivalries came up during the dinner. Joe Foss had been elected to his first term as governor of South Dakota in 1954, and was re-elected in 1956. His second term ended in defeat in January. He was nonplused about that, since he was going to be the first commissioner of the newly created American Football League in November. Always gregarious and outspoken, he shared his opinions about the chances of the *Vikings* joining the NFL in 1960 and having any success as an expansion team.

For any Legionnaires "on the wagon," there might have been lively discussions about the legendary rivalry between Coca-Cola and Pepsi that had been going on for sixty years. Everyone was familiar with the jingles and ads.

"Be really refreshed . . . have a Coke!"

"Be sociable, have a Pepsi refreshment, preferred by today's trim, active people."

Milli and the wives talked about family life and their children. Donald and Helen (Furberg) had married in November 1942 and had a teenage son, Don Jr. Mike and Lina Colalillo had married in 1945 and had Albert, 12, and two daughters, Joanne, 10, and "Shelly," 6 years old. The ladies asked Milli about having a six-month-old baby at home again. The questions earned a smile and a whisper. Milli was four months pregnant.

Joe was the oldest of the Medal holders at the table. He had married June Ethel Shakstad in August 1942. She was in Sioux Falls with Cheryl, 15, Mary Joe, 13, and Joseph Frank "Frankie," 8 years old. The women understood that Cheryl was born with cerebral palsy and that June usually remained at home as Cheryl attended the Crippled Children's Hospital School. At the time of the convention, Joe was president of the National Society of Crippled Children and Adults.

One of the wives remembered the touching moment three years earlier (March 7, 1956) when Joe was starting his second term as South Dakota governor, and Ralph Edwards honored him on the NBC-TV program *This is Your Life*. Joe had daubed at his eyes with his handkerchief as Cheryl walked across the stage. [16]

The friends at the table knew about some of Joe's misfortunes, and would not have inquired much during a social event. Joe, on the other hand, tended to be blunt and straight-talking, hardly ever mincing words. He recalled the days leading up to his departure from the governor's mansion. On Saturday evening, January 3, 1959, June had gone into premature labor. She gave caesarean birth to Eric Peter Foss at the Sioux Falls Hospital at 6:30 AM, Sunday morning. The baby lived for only five hours, expiring of a lung complication. June was temporarily on the critical list. Joe's various commitments meant that he had been an absentee husband and father a good part of the time across their marriage. Whereas June recovered bravely from their son's death, the couple's marriage did not. Joe had separated from his wife of 17 years.

Laughter returned to the table while desert was being served. Joe took some ribbing about Legionnaires approaching him to autograph the 10 Cents, June 7, 1943, *LIFE* Magazine with his picture on the cover.

Almost an inch of rain fell on Wednesday, so it was good that most of the day was spent in the Municipal Auditorium. Former President of the United States, the Honorable Harry S. Truman, addressed the convention at 1:15 PM, leading to some good-natured joking among the Medal recipients. Mike Colalillo and Don Rudolph had both received their Medals from President Truman in 1945. President Franklin D. Roosevelt had presented Joe Foss his Medal at the White House in 1943. From one Marine to another, Joe looked to Rick.

"Major General Fegan? Not the president? Wasn't he "just" Camp Pendleton's first commanding general?"

"Yeah, sure. And, he was the commanding general of the Department of the Pacific, too."

There was no mention of the general dying of injuries at Pendleton's hospital on Thursday, May 26, 1949, after a car accident on the previous Saturday.

A more serious matter than who had suspended the Medal around their necks was decided before the afternoon adjournment. Rick and Mike and most Legionnaires agreed on one side of a national debate, advocating a tougher stand against the Soviets in the Cold War. Despite President Eisenhower's expressed belief that Premier Khrushchev's visit to the U.S. in September served the nation's best interests, the Legionnaires remained critical of the tour. The war veterans continued to note the colossal Soviet military machine being built and Mr. Khrushchev's rabid protests against world disarmament and international inspections. The Legionnaires had passed a resolution in 1958 opposing all visits to the U.S. by Communist leaders. On Wednesday, a resolution opposing any cultural exchanges between the U.S. and the Soviet Union was approved. Politicians took notice.

That evening proved to be a gala highlight for the wives. The guest cars pulled up to the Prom Ballroom on 1190 University Avenue in St. Paul's Midway neighborhood for the Convention Ball, sponsored by the United States Brewers Foundation. The ballroom was impressive—well known to Twin Cities' locals who celebrated many a New Year's Eve there. The Medal recipients found their reserved tables inside the sprawling venue. At 8:30 PM, Jules Herman took the stage at the head of the 9,000-square-foot, hard maple dance floor to welcome the Legionnaires and introduce his eleven-piece orchestra.

Anyone with teenagers at home might have remarked that the big band music was not much favored by their kids who danced to Bop and swing and cha-cha music. Parents in millions of households had learned that watching Dick Clark's *American Bandstand* weekdays at 4:00 PM EST took precedence over chores and homework. The tunes of teen idols like Elvis, Chuck Berry, Ray Charles, Ricky Nelson, Paul Anka, and the Everly Brothers had been blaring from Twin Cities' jukeboxes for years. In fact, Buddy Holly, Ritchie Valens, and the Big Bopper had performed before a swarm of teens at the Prom Ballroom on Tuesday, January 27, 1959, seven days before the three musicians perished in a plane crash in an Iowa snow storm. There was no Twisting at the Convention Ball, but the "old timers" had a *Hot Time in the Old Town* that night anyway.

The convention reconvened in the Municipal Auditorium on Thursday morning. The Legion delegates prepared to vote on foreign relations resolutions. Texas Senator Johnson read from his prepared text at 10:00 AM. "Americans must and will stand behind President Eisenhower in making the visit of Soviet Premier Nikita Khrushchev serve the nation's best interest." He urged the Legion to support Mr. Khrushchev's visit, saying that the country could gain by opening the premier's eyes to America's progress. "I have no fears that Mr. Khrushchev can contaminate the American people." [17]

AFL-CIO President George Meany addressed the convention next. He echoed Mr. Johnson's points, but added cautionary warnings about sweet words and jovial manners and Mr. Khrushchev's declarations to defeat the U.S. in peaceful competition. He was certain that the military strength of the Western free nations had been all that had so far deterred the Kremlin from engaging in a war aimed at world domination.

The Legion's Foreign Relations Committee took a vote and submitted a surprising, last-minute resolution, accepting "with dignity" Mr. Khrushchev's visit.

The convention's Final Adjournment was at 2:00 PM. Looking ahead, Rick let Milli know about probable future Legion invitations. The National Executive Committee had selected Miami Beach for the October 1960 convention, Denver for September 1961, and Detroit for August 1962.

Milli's travels would be curtailed after the 1959 Christmas and New Year's holidays. Another boy joined the family. Thomas' birth in January 1960 completed the Sorenson family. Five children were at home.

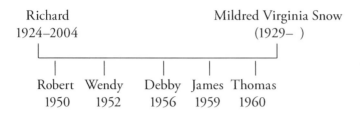

The World War II Marine Division Associations met in Washington, D.C., June 24–26, 1960, for the second massed Fleet Marine Force Concurrent Reunions. [18] Reporters described it as "the largest group of Marine veterans ever to ascend on the nation's capital." More than 5,000 Marine veterans, wives, and guests attended. Registrations filled the Mayflower Hotel and Sheraton Park Hotel. The 4th Division occupied the Shoreham Hotel for the weekend.

As customs dictated, Saturday was busy. After individual morning meetings, the divisions united for a thirty-mile trip south to Quantico for a special military demonstration. Returning to their D.C. headquarters, each division held its own cocktail party, then rejoined on buses for an evening parade—guests of the Marine Band and Drum and Bugle Corps and the men of 8th & I. Afterwards, the social highlight for the Fighting Fourth was its own traditional banquet and dinner dance.

Friendships were always renewed at the reunions. So were memories of fallen comrades. On Sunday afternoon before departures began, the combined associations gathered at the Marine Memorial, the Iwo Jima Monument in Arlington, for memorial services.

A few days before the Labor Day holiday, Rick attended a funeral in another National Cemetery. Robert, Wendy, and Debby would remember times with their Grandpa Sorenson, but the two youngest boys would only hear stories of him.

Carl Siren Sorenson, 64, WWI Navy veteran, died on August 29, 1960. He was buried in Fort Snelling National Cemetery, Plot: Section D Site 3150, on the west side of the cemetery, close to the funeral cortege entry Gate 2.

Ordinary Life

All the Silver Lake lots had been purchased by 1960, and a dozen or so neighbors joined the Sorensons on the lane. Kenny Lee sold the farm across from them in 1961. From their back yard, the Sorenson kids could see, maybe boat out to, wooded islands in the lake. The Salvation Army Fresh Air Camp for Children was on the north shore. In front, the kids could cross the street, walk through a tree line into a large open field, and watch urban development in action. The Apache Plaza shopping center, one of the first malls in the Minneapolis area, opened around 1964. (Today, the site of the Silver Lake Village Shopping Center.)

The Sorenson home was about two-and-a-half miles northeast of the house and neighborhood where James Labelle had lived. Rick knew that, but the children never learned of it as they grew up in St. Anthony Village. [19]

The family was active in the village. Robert and Wendy were in elementary school. Rick participated in the community activities. An Honorary Lifetime Member of the Minneapolis

Jaycees, he was elected to the St. Anthony City Council in 1964. Regarding that effort, he gave his view to a *Minneapolis Star Tribune* reporter.

"You can't complain too much if you don't take an active part."

He was a member at the rifle range. Keeping his rifle and pistol marksman skill remained very important to him his entire life. He had no respect for hunters or anyone else who used automatic weapons. When he took time to spend with Robert, it was off to the rifle range. Rick was keen about teaching gun safety, and father and son would spend the whole day carefully shooting at targets. [20]

From the children's perspective, their dad was always a hard worker, often coming home from his insurance agency, having dinner, and working again late into the evening. He wanted his children to learn to be responsible and to work hard. He did not give the kids an allowance, even when they were teenagers.

"If you want money, you must work for it."

In 1963, Robert started working odd jobs at age 13, shoveling snow, mowing lawns, and delivering newspapers. He was working regular jobs by age 16.

The City of Anoka was proud to claim a MOH recipient as a hometown son. Twenty years had passed since the city had closed its stores and the crowd had welcomed Ricky home at the City Square bandstand. In 1965, the Council began discussions about a tribute, turning their attention to the park in the triangle formed by Rick's boyhood home, the Mississippi and Rum rivers, and the American Legion Post. Rick attended the dedication ceremony on the grounds that he, his cousins, and friends would hardly have recognized.

Mayor Donald K. Elvig read the inscription on the plaque. "RICK SORENSON PARK. NAMED IN HONOR OF RICHARD K. SORENSON, AN ANOKA MARINE WHO WAS AWARDED THE UNITED STATES CONGRESSIONAL MEDAL OF HONOR DURING WORLD WAR II. RICK PLAYED HERE AS A BOY."

The park on 2015 State Avenue is open year-round and has baseball and softball fields, tennis courts, a basketball court, a playground, picnic area and grills, all-season activity building and warming house, and winter skating rinks.

The 4th Marine Division held its annual reunion June 23–26, 1965, at Philadelphia's Warwick Hotel.

On January 8, 1966, Senate Majority Leader Mike Mansfield (D-MT) reported his findings to the Senate Foreign Relations Committee following his tour of Viet Nam. His assessment was gloomy. The war had expanded into Laos and Cambodia. The military situation had not improved since America's initial involvement. He was pessimistic about truces and peace negotiations and predicted that the entire Southeast Asia peninsula was going to become a battlefield.

Invitations, notifications, and birthdays constantly overlapped for the Sorensons. After young Tom's 6th birthday and around Jim's 7th birthday in February, Rick was notified that the 4th Division was reactivated as the Marine Forces Reserve's only division. His presence was requested—nine days after Bob's 16th birthday. The FMDA was going to have its meeting at Camp Pendleton in June. On Thursday, June 23, 1966, the Association presented their World War II Division Colors to Major General Robert E. Cushman Jr., Camp Pendleton's commanding general.

When the Anoka park was dedicated in his name with a plaque mentioning his Medal award, it was inevitable that, if they were not already aware of his heroic actions in WWII, people in St. Anthony Village would talk about Rick. One of them was an elementary school teacher.

Debby had no idea that her dad was a hero. [21] One day in 1966, she went off to school just like any other day. She was 10 years old, and the day turned memorable. In addition to the usual reading, grammar, spelling, and arithmetic lessons, the teacher told a story during history class. It was about what Rick Sorenson had done in WWII. Debby was shocked that her dad had never said anything about heroism and the Medal to his children. That night at home, she asked him about what the teacher had said in class.

Her father looked embarrassed and answered in a soft voice. "You just don't talk about those kinds of things."

Talking about "those kinds of things" was one thing, thinking about them was something else. Thoughts about the war could intrude at any time; not talking about them was one way to tuck them back in their place. Such memories can make a man humble, even feel guilty, about having another day, another birthday.

Rick and Bill Sorenson had seen brave teenagers die in wars—friends who did not come back home and live out their lives. From time to time would come another realization—surviving a war did not grant any veteran a long life.

"It was horrible." By Wednesday, September 14, 1966, Minnesota's traffic death toll had risen to 615, compared with 560 on that date the previous year. On Thursday, Rick and Bill read the newspaper about one of those deaths and got on the phone to each other.

Dick Runquist, their old Benton Street neighbor and friend, had come home from Korea with a Purple Heart. After his Marine Corps service, he was employed as an over-the-road truck driver, hauling cars and trucks. He had a house with his wife and two little kids near Detroit Lakes. After a delivery on Wednesday, he had jumped into his pickup and headed home. "Runkie," two weeks from his 37th birthday, was known to have a hard time staying awake after being on the road. Four miles east of Detroit Lakes, he fell asleep, ran off the road, and hit an embankment. The truck flipped over in a ditch, and gasoline from the full tank began leaking into the cab. He could not open the door and drowned in the gasoline. [22]

Dick's remains were brought home to Anoka and buried in Section 5, Block 4 at Forest Hill Cemetery. The monuments in memory of Anoka's war dead and of those who had served were in the park, a short walk from his grave. Rick and Bill had seen comrades die in combat and had stood at the side of many graves. This was a sad funeral.

Six months after "Runkie" was buried, the names of two young men fighting in Viet Nam were added to the IN MEMORY OF ANOKA'S DEAD OF ALL WARS' roster. Army Staff Sergeant Bradley Eugene Peterson, 23 years old, was KIA on March 11, 1967. Corporal Bruce Vernon LeNoue, 20, USMC, Anoka High Class of 1965, Honor Society graduate and athlete, died on March 30, four days after he was wounded in Quảng Nam Province. His remains were interred in Section 5, Block 2 at Forest Hill Cemetery. Before spring of 1970 ended, six more names had been added to the local roster.

Drafts Turn into Whirl Winds

Veterans of WWII and Korea, American Legionnaires, and MOH recipients had strong opinions about U.S. involvement in Viet Nam. They also had sons old enough to enlist in the Armed Forces or who were eligible for the draft. All 18-year-old men were required to register at their local Selective Service (Draft Board) Office, making them eligible to be called for, or inducted into, military service. Any male between ages 19 and 26, fit for service and classified 1-A, was subject to the draft.

Before President Kennedy was killed in Dallas on November 22, 1963, he had planned to withdraw 1,000 of the 16,500 U.S. troops deployed in South Viet Nam on December 3. By year's end, President Johnson clearly intended to continue U.S. involvement as he considered raising the number of servicemen in Southeast Asia to 100,000. In 1964, he had 23,310 troops deployed. The "peacetime" draft had become more of a wartime draft, and the number of men called for service began increasing appreciably—by 40%.

The idea of *conscription*, compulsory enlistment into the Armed Forces, held a foul and bitter tinge for many young Americans. The civil disquiet and draft protests spread.

It was uncertain and seemingly random who might be drafted for military service; yet, by the mid-1960s, adolescents in high school, from sophomore year on, and their parents, had Viet Nam on their minds. In every high school across America, there was a good chance that students knew someone from their school, neighborhood, or town who had been "called up" to go to war.

The casualty counts increased—6,350 deaths in 1966. At the beginning of 1967, there were 385,300 American troops in South Viet Nam. Year-end reports estimated 485,600 troops deployed. Telegrams, letters, and newspaper columns could not be denied. In 1967, combat, wounds, malfeasance (homicides), accidents, illness, presumed fatalities, and suicide had claimed 11,363 American lives, in addition to the 99,742 WIA. The greatest number of telegrams went to families the next year when 536,100 troops were deployed, and 16,899 deaths were recorded.

Rick's cousin, Ken Gagnon, had married Doris Mason, from Fleetwood, Lancashire, England, above Wales, in October 1945 and was discharged from the Army two months later, on December 31. The couple resided in Southern California and had a daughter, Cynthia. Ken worked for the VA Regional Office in Los Angeles, as well as for the Aero Space industry. [23] His enthusiasm for West Coast life was infectious.

Moving from one household to another had been imprinted in Rick's consciousness before he left Anoka for WWII. He had been married to Milli for eighteen years in 1967, and living on Silver Lake Drive had been the longest he had ever resided in one place. They had talked about it at times and finally decided to relocate to California. All five children were in school, so Milli planned around the St. Anthony Village school calendar.

The University of Minnesota was also planning the end of a school year. The 1966 *Golden Gophers* football team had compiled a 4–5–1 record and finished fifth in the Big Ten Conference. The highlight of the season had been beating Ohio State at home in front of 49,500 fans. Eighteen of the players readied for graduation and the end of their college draft deferments. If any of them had been involved in the University's Army, Navy, or Air Force Reserve Officers Training Corps (ROTC) programs, they knew where they would be going in the summer.

It had been twenty-three years since Rick had earned the MOH, and Captain J. M. Marshall, USN, Head of Department and Professor of Naval Science at the university, had him in mind. He contacted Rick and the Marine Corps Association (MCA). Midshipman Grant P. Gustafson, Excelsior, NROTC Company "B" Commander, had opted for a commission in the Marine Corps. He was going to accept the silver Gymkhana trophy on behalf of Company "B" for scoring the highest points in military skills and was to receive an honorary membership in the United States Naval Institute.

The MCA annually recognized the high endeavor of "embryo Marine officers." According to a University Press Release, former Marine and MOH winner Mr. Richard Sorenson was on Northrop Field for the Annual Naval Awards Day ceremonies, Thursday, May 11, 1967, at 11:15 AM. He presented Grant a handsome, MCA "Certificate of Achievement" inscribed with the midshipman's name. He was also pleased to tell the young man that the award included an initial membership in the MCA. [24]

That summer, weeks after Bob Sorenson, their eldest child, had finished his junior year with the St. Anthony Village High School Class of 1968, and Wendy had completed her freshman year, the family relocated to Westlake Village, a western suburb of Los Angeles. Keeping in mind that a person must be actively involved if he wants to have a say, Rick joined the Westlake Village home-owners board.

He returned to working as an assistant contact officer with the Veterans Administration in L.A., eventually advancing to division chief of the Veterans Service Department. Over the next eleven years, the shrapnel in his arms occasionally troubled him, but did not interfere with his dedication to veterans, or with his travels.

Rick and Ken Gagnon had remained quite close, as much friends as cousins. The two families had many reunions in California. [25] Ken was known to love good cigars, Crown Royal Whiskey, poker games, and golf. The two WWII veterans seldom exchanged war stories in the presence of their children. Only later did Jim and Tom learn that Ken had participated in the liberation of the German submarine pens in France.

The WWII Nazi U-boat bases in France were located at Brest, Lorient, Saint Nazaire, La Pallice, and Bordeaux. As the U.S. Army had swept towards Germany, one pen after another was surrendered. At one of them, Sergeant Gagnon had also liberated a brand new, unissued German Luger (P08) that he brought home as a souvenir. There were many other war memories Ken would rather have forgotten—he certainly seldom mentioned them.

After bottling up the enemy garrisons at the pens in May 1945, the U.S. Army's 66th Division learned of Nazi atrocities. The Germans had used forced labor when they built their thick-walled fortresses at the pens. The outraged townspeople cried over hundreds of French men and women who had been mixed into the concrete alive. The American liberators forced German prisoners to break up the concrete and remove the bodies. Captain Jack G. Garrison of Richmond Heights, Montana, was the Division's public relations officer. He released a statement to the Associated Press in October 1945, when Sergeant Gagnon was back in England marrying a pretty Brit.

"We recovered 43 bodies the first day." [26]

A swig or two of Crown Royal Whiskey had understandably made a difference for any number of WWII veterans seeking services at the VA.

Rick and Mike Colalillo were among the 271 living members of the CMOHS to receive invitations to attend a dinner at New York City's Waldorf-Astoria on Monday night, December 11, 1967. Newspapers reported that the event was the first time that chairmen of the Joint Chiefs of Staff had ever been honored as a group at a public function. Reporters also surmised that the largest group of MOH winners ever assembled attended. Honored at the dinner were present chairmen of the Joint Chiefs of Staff General Earle G. Wheeler and former chairmen, General of the Army Omar N. Bradley, Admiral Arthur W. Radford, General Nathan F. Twining, General Lyman L. Lemnixter and General Maxwell D. Taylor. Honorary chairman Dwight D. Eisenhower, Harry S. Truman, and New York Governor Nelson A. Rockefeller attended.

The weekend was another chance for Rick and Mike to talk about family, "hanging out with the generals," and the war. Minnesotans have a reputation for keeping their feelings buried and enduring pain or hardship without complaining. Even so, dads worry about their sons, and Medal holders are no exceptions. Mike's son, Albert "Butch," aged 20, had graduated from the UofM in Duluth, and was drafted by the Army. He would serve two tours in Viet Nam. That he encountered Agent Orange while in-country would be a later conversation.

Rick's Marine Corps experiences at times filtered into his parenting. He often told the boys to eat all the food on their plates, quoting the Mess Hall dictum: "Take all you want . . . but eat all you take."

Learning of his father's actions on Namur Island, Jim developed a great interest in WWII, the Pacific theater of operations, and collecting Japanese WWII militaria. He loved hearing war stories, especially about his father's experiences. Some of the stories he read seemed to conflict with each other, and he tried to separate fact from fiction. Over the years in their conversations, he asked his dad about certain facts.

"Was the grenade really an American Mk II fragmentation grenade?"

Rick had kept the three grenade fragments that had nearly taken his life on Namur. He showed them to his son. The fragments were definitely not from a Japanese Type 97 Nambu, but indeed American *Pineapple* grenade fragments. On occasion, Jim would ask his father to pass on one of the fragments to him. Rick promised that he would one day have a fragment to keep.

As is the nature of boys to wonder, and sometimes to inquire, Jim once asked about a specific detail.

"How many Japanese did you kill?" [27]

And, as fathers who have seen combat tend to do, Rick gave a brief answer. "I'm not sure. I probably killed a couple in all the fighting."

Jim recognized that his dad "certainly did not glory in the thought of it."

While she was growing up, Wendy preferred listening to her dad's stories about his childhood. Those were interesting. Rick never really talked about anything to do with the war or the Medal when she was young. She thinks she would not have understood it all anyway. When her dad and Jim talked about wars and battles, she would get uncomfortable. Not interested in the war stories, Wendy often left the room during those conversations. [28]

Bob Sorenson graduated from Agoura High School, *Home of the Chargers*, on West Driver Avenue in Agoura. He was 18 years old. Like all male high school graduates, he had to wonder if a letter was going to be delivered to the Sorenson home.

In his travels, Rick began collecting spiked military helmets, some from the USMC, some from Germany, others from France and Russia. In a passion that would cross thirty-five years, his favorite would be the World War I, copper and zinc helmet worn by the Prussian Gardes du Corps, the personal escort of the Kaiser. [29]

In May 1969, Rick received his invitation to attend the four-day, seventh biennial CMOHS convention. [30] He sent in his RSVP. He remained modestly quiet about the blue ribbon with five stars that he was entitled to wear around his neck at public functions. Yet, his patriotism often was reported in the L.A. newspapers.

Readers who paid 10¢ for a copy of the *Valley News* learned of his valor, because of the annual Westlake Village Special Memorial Day Services. At 10:00 AM Friday morning on May 30, 1969, Rick was at the Valley Oaks Memorial Park to oversee the laying of the wreaths, the Thousand Oaks Boy Scouts placing of American flags, and the Westminster Presbyterian Church reverend's invocation. The paper reported that he had earned the Medal for "conspicuous gallantry and intrepidity at the risk of his life" hurling himself on an active Japanese grenade. [31]

In August, Rick attended the Marine Corps League's Midwest Division's three-day, annual fall conference in St. Louis, Missouri. All the Corps' recipients had been invited. The convention's theme and slogan was *With Respect and Honor*. The League and the city treated the conference as an opportunity to honor MOH recipients. Rick was among the thirteen recipients able to attend, representing veterans of WWII, Korea, and Viet Nam. [32]

The event opened with a downtown parade and ceremony to honor the Medal recipients and to pay recognition to the League. Rick Sorenson, Dick Bush, Hector A. Cafferata Jr., and Robert E. Simanek all rode in the vehicles, bearing the shrapnel they had endured since protecting comrades from enemy grenades. Justice M. Chambers, Raymond G. Murphy, Mitchell Paige, Richard A. Pittman, Carl L. Sitter, Luther Skaggs, Jr., Albert J. Smith, Kenneth A. Walsh, and Harold E. Wilson also waved to the crowds. Their friendships deepened.

The parade ended in front of the Soldiers Memorial at 1315 Chestnut Street. The Medal holders presided over a wreath-laying ceremony and the dedication of a permanent plaque inside the memorial to commemorate the occasion. St. Louis Mayor Alfonso J. Cervantes (R) proclaimed the day *Medal of Honor Day.*

The Medal recipients enjoyed many social events, especially the brewery tours and sampling of their generous libations. A banquet attended by 400 guests capped the conference. Following the keynote speeches, the League and the City of St. Louis presented Rick and the other recipients each a replica of the St. Louis Arch to take home with them.

Rick agreed with a comment one Leaguer said as the conference closed. "Not that we needed to be made aware of our loyalty to America, but it sure doesn't hurt to take a little time out to talk about all the good things this country's done for us, and to realize that we all owe it a fair shake."

Rick traveled from home again in October. He was among "the largest group of recipients ever together at one time" meeting in Houston on October 8–11, 1969. Rick, like most of the 225 recipients present, had a sense of what it meant to wear the blue ribbon around his neck.

"You become conscious of what you do and how you do it, because you're living in a glass bowl. You have to be careful that what you do won't tarnish your name or the Medal of Honor Society." [33]

His VA position kept him apprised of military matters, often before the public was informed. Rick and the Medal holders kept some information restrained to quiet hospitality room conversations in Houston. The nation would be informed in due time.

When Numbers Mattered

Before Rick and Milli sat in front of the television at 6:00 PM, on Monday, December 1, 1969, they reminisced a little about an old NBC Radio broadcast. Milli's recollections were not quite as strong, since she was only 13 years old at the time and not yet in high school.

On March 17, 1942, at 5:00 PM in Anoka, America's wartime selective service lottery arrived on the airwaves from Washington, D.C. Well into the night, thousands of numbers were drawn from a giant fishbowl. The draft lottery had not directly affected Rick. Each shell drawn corresponded to a birthdate for men between the ages of 20 and 45. He did not turn 18 until August 28, five months after the broadcast. Then, on November 11, 1942, the draft age was lowered to 18 years. That did not matter either, as he had made his decision a year earlier. Rick raised his hand on December 13 to swear an oath of allegiance to the U.S. Marine Corps.

Rick and Milli's lives had certainly changed in the twenty-seven years since the radio broadcast.

The Selective Service System had announced it would call 850,000 men of military age into the service in 1970. President Nixon altered the mood in American households the day before Thanksgiving 1969. On Wednesday, November 26, he signed an amendment to the

1967 Military Selective Service Act. A lottery was to be conducted in five days to determine the order of call to military service for men born from January 1, 1944 to December 31, 1950.

Bob was 19 years old and had returned to St. Paul, living with his Grandmother Snow and Aunt Eleanor. He was experiencing an aspect of the times familiar to male high school graduates and often ignored by social gurus. Not only was "the heavy cloud of the draft" hanging over him, his draft status made employers hesitant to hire him. Turned down dozens of times, he started to work for himself. Just a week before Thanksgiving, he had been called in for his draft physical. Designated 1-A, Bob believed he did not have much time before he would be drafted. He shouldered the mantle of the first-born son. His parents' stance on the issue was clear.

Before calendars turned to December, Rick and Milli let him know that they expected him to serve if his number was called. "Don't embarrass us" was the moral point. They reminded him that his birthday was Flag Day. The lottery would answer any questions about his being drafted.

CBS had pre-empted its regularly scheduled broadcast for a live News Special Report—The Draft Lottery—held at Selective Service headquarters in D.C. at 9:00 PM EST. Reporter Roger Mudd sat up front, turned to the camera, whispering during the ceremony. He thought the event was "a very systematic, almost mechanical, lottery." The dozen demonstrators picketing outside, denouncing the draft, the lottery, and the war, did not interfere.

A large glass jar sat on a table, holding 366 blue plastic lottery capsules, each one with a birthdate inside. New York Republican Congressman Alexander Pirnie drew the first capsule and handed it to Mrs. Sadie Peters. She opened the capsule, unrolled the small slip of paper, and announced "September 14 . . . September 14 is 001." The date was assigned Lottery Number 001. She handed the slip to a man who fastened it in the 001 slot on a large board listing numbers from 001 to 366 in rows and columns. The lowest numbers on the board would be first to get Selective Service notifications. Draft-eligible men between ages 19 and 26 years born on September 14 would be receiving letters immediately.

A line of young, college student delegates, Youth Advisory Council members, participated in pulling capsules from the glass jar. Several read objections to the draft and the war and refused to reach into the jar. The lottery proceeded for a half-hour. The numbers up through 150 were expected to be called to service by May. Bob's birthdate had not been announced by then. Men with numbers up to 195 could anticipate being drafted before 1970 ended. Statisticians had calculated that the odds of being drafted were slim with a number after 200. Bob's birthdate still had not been pulled from the jar—and it was not announced until only eleven capsules remained.

"June 14 . . . June 14 is 356."

Not even a small likelihood existed that Bob would be summoned for induction into the military. It was a solemn relief for Rick and Milli. Both felt compassion for the parents of men with low numbers on that board.

Bob had been in Minneapolis with a group of friends when the lottery was broadcast. He did not know two of the boys very well, but they already knew their lottery numbers. One mentioned that his was #1 and the other was #7 (October 26). As any group of young men would that night, their discussion turned to whether they wanted to hurry and enlist in the military branch of their choosing or wait to be drafted. Bob never saw either of those two boys again. When he got home, his grandmother and aunt told him that his birthdate was the 356th number drawn. What a relief. He could look into a future that held some promise.

"I was happy my number did not come up."

Wendy was in her senior year at Agoura High School and was the next Sorenson ready to graduate. Her history teacher approached her to talk about her dad's actions on Namur and his being awarded the Medal. Wendy was proud of her dad, but had to admit that she really knew very little about his war experiences. When people spoke of his heroism, the idea was always a little abstract and intangible to her. Her dad's heroism was a personal matter to her. Rick was *her* hero for all the many loving things he did for her just being her father.

The teacher contacted Rick and asked permission to use his Medal as an artifact for a history lesson he was giving to his students. Rick agreed, and Wendy was in charge of bringing the Medal to and from the school.

"I remember my dad being a little nervous about the Medal being out of his possession." [34]

That the larger community considered her father a war hero was no surprise to Wendy. From the time when she was a little girl, and all her life, she would think of her dad as her personal hero, because "he was always there for me." [35] Her understanding of the impact of his bravery would deepen when she went off to college.

Wendy, 18, was in the newspaper weeks before she walked on stage in cap and gown with the Class of 1970.

On Saturday, May 16, *Chargers* began arriving at the Odyssey Restaurant in Granada Hills for the fourth annual junior-senior prom. The revelers enjoyed an 8:00–9:00 PM banquet with a punch bar in the lobby. Dancing to music by the twelve-piece *Blue Notes* orchestra started at 9:00 PM and was to go on until 12:00 midnight. The orchestra took a break at 11:00 PM for a ceremony. Wendy was crowned Senior Prom Queen. Barbara Briethaupt, Barbara Edlund, Sally Keown, and Valerie Whittle were the other nominees in her court. [36]

The lives of Medal recipients remain newsworthy locally and nationally, particularly around holiday times. As time passed, Americans were reminded of Private Sorenson's heroism, despite his modesty about it.

Two weeks after the prom, Wendy and Rick were together in a Front-Page newspaper photo over the caption WORLD WAR II HERO. Smiling, he cracked jokes with his daughter on the patio of their Westlake home as she scrutinized the official book about MOH winners. [37]

The father-daughter photograph was accompanied by headlines. War Hero Will Place Wreath During Rites: Former Marine Got Citation for Throwing Self on Hand Grenade. This long, two-column article was much more detailed than the 1969 story.

Decoration Day, Saturday, May 30, was going to bring "a quiet, reflective moment, saturated with memories of a bigger war of another day, of another era" for the Westlake war hero. Rick had been "awarded the nation's highest military accolade for an act of bravery which makes even brave men shudder" and had "carved a niche in the legends of war heroes the world over." The reporter described his actions, intensive hospital care, and federal and civic service over the years. According to military records, Rick was among seventy-seven Allied servicemen who "had thrown themselves on enemy grenades during WWII and in the Korean War in order to save comrades."

Conejo Valley Boy Scouts arrived early in Westlake's Valley Oaks Memorial Park on Memorial Day and stood at more than sixty veterans' graves with U.S. flags. Rick walked about, commending and encouraging the boys.

The community ceremony began at 10:00 AM when James E. Rodgers, American Legion, escorted the distinguished guests forward and introduced them. A USMC four-man Color Guard and eight-man rifle team presented colors. Donald E. Locke Jr, Order of the Purple Heart Chapter 83 Commander, led the Pledge of Allegiance and the national anthem was sung. Reverend Guy S. Morrison, Westlake United Methodist Church, shared in the

Invocations. Rick placed a wreath after the speeches. The rifle squad fired a three-volley salute. The bugler sounded *Taps*.

Five Marines had had a close brush with death in a shell hole on Namur Island when the Mk II grenade landed at their feet. But for Private Sorenson's valor, each might have died or been severely wounded. The fighting went on after Private Sorenson was evacuated, and two more 3rd Battalion, 24th Marines were KIA on Namur. One more died of his wounds.

The Mariana Island Campaign was next for the 24th Marines. The 3d Battalion fought on Saipan in June–July 1944, and then in the toughest battle for the Marines in WWII—Iwo Jima in February–March 1945. In those two battles, seventy-eight (78) Company I men were KIA or died of their wounds; sixty-three (63) in Company K died; and eighty (80) Company L men were KIA/DOW. Those numbers increase the possibility that some of the Marines in the crater with Private Sorenson did not survive the war. At least one of them did and never forgot the young machine gunner who was willing to sacrifice his life for him.

That Marine told his daughter what Rick had done in the foxhole on Namur. She wrote to Rick. He did not know the girl nor recognize her name. With the letter, she had enclosed a paper she had written for a college course about "the most important thing in my life." She concluded her essay with a touching sentence.

"Richard Sorenson is a man I held in awe even before I learned his name, because one of the men he saved is my dad." [38]

Rick shared the letter and paper with Wendy.

"I remember finally realizing how significant his sacrifice on the grenade had been," Wendy has said, "because it had impacted so many lives, even those of the next generation."

Jim found that letter to be a very touching tribute to his father. He also understood the appreciation in the heart of the Marine's daughter. Jim and his siblings had many thoughts about the Marines who had looked out for their dad: "Doc" Kirby, the litter bearers, the surgeons, and nurses.

"I too hold gratitude to the many men and women who saved my father's life. I and my brothers and sisters owe our very lives to their efforts to save my father. We cannot put into mere words our gratitude! Bless them!!" [39]

The Sorensons understood that the corpsman who had initially tied their father's completely-severed artery into a knot after the explosion had saved his life. Across his adult years, Jim has tried to learn what became of Pharmacist Mate 2d Class James V. Kirby. Did *he* have any descendants to thank for saving his father's life? To this day, his search has been unsuccessful.

Rick kept the correspondence from the grateful daughter in his file cabinet.

He continued to work for the VA through the 1970s and into the 1980s. His position allowed him to search for the surgeon who had worked on him on the transport in Roi–Namur Lagoon. He tracked down the doctor's son and expressed his gratitude to the man for his father's life-saving care.

As he had grown up, the doctor's son heard all about Rick. His father had told him about what bad condition the Marine was in when he had arrived in the ship's Medical Ward. He was the surgeon who, at that time, "would not have given a wooden nickel" for the life of the young Marine awarded a Medal of Honor the next July. [40]

For Rick, "living in a glass bowl" could mean the L.A. Coliseum. On Thursday afternoon, July 27, 1972, he was in a parade, exhibition, and huge, one-hour pageant in Los Angeles. He and three other Medal recipients represented WWI, WWII, Korean War, and Vietnam War veterans. The Marine Corps Mounted Color Guard—the only equestrian outfit of its type in the nation—spearheaded the tail end of the parade.

Then, at 7:30 PM, the four heroes took their special guest seats at the Coliseum for the 21st annual North–South Shrine football classic. The fans had paid $5, $3, or $1.50 for tickets. By halftime, it was clear that quarterback Vince Ferragamo was leading South's pre-college all-stars to victory. The award-winning 160-piece Torrance Youth Band put on a halftime routine, after which Rick and the three others stepped onto the field. Their entrance roused the 35,957 fans to stand and pay them tribute. [41]

The South finished in a "stunning rout." Vince went on to quarterback the Los Angeles *Rams*, and led them to a National Football Conference championship and the 1979 Super Bowl XIV in Pasadena. The Pittsburgh *Steelers* took the victory from them in the fourth quarter.

"This Type of Thing"

Tributes and parades came and went, but Rick's commitment to veterans, especially Marines, was constant. Some days, it was somber and dark work. The POW experience was an example, in part because it was in the news and people asked for his views.

From February through March 1973, North Vietnam released 566 military prisoners of war. The VA took them under its care to assist them in adjusting to *Operation Homecoming* freedom. Doctors reported that all of them were in worse mental and physical shape than had appeared when they stepped off the planes. Many were having serious post-imprisonment problems, including widespread marital disruptions, schizophrenic reactions, flights of euphoria, bouts of depression, and seemingly unjustifiable fright. Some came home to chastisement. [42]

Sergeant Abel Larry Kavanaugh, 24, had disembarked from a plane at 2:20 PM on March 18, having been released from the plantation prison camp near Hanoi. His story caught the attention of news reporters. He and a fellow Marine had been in a defensive position at an LZ near Phu Bai, South Viet Nam. When their unit was extracted, they were accidentally left behind and captured on April 24, 1968. After five years in enemy hands, he was one of ten POWs charged with aiding the enemy while in prison. He went home to his Denver apartment for sixty days' convalescent leave with his 22-year-old wife and five-year-old daughter and was scheduled to return to Camp Pendleton on July 6 for reassignment. He insisted to his wife, then pregnant with their second child, that the accusations were fictions. If he was innocent, the charges that he had made anti-war statements to hasten his release from the POW camps drove him over the edge.

On Wednesday, June 27, Sergeant Kavanaugh put a .25-caliber handgun to his left temple and shot himself. The one bullet ended his turmoil and life. That was twenty-four days after the first suicide was reported.

Air Force Captain Edward Alan Brudno, F-4C *Phantom* fighter bomber pilot from Quincy, Massachusetts, had been shot down deep in North Viet Nam territory and captured on October 18, 1965. He and his backseater, separated two days after ejecting, were shuffled through different prison camps for 7.5 years. He was released from Hanoi on February 12 and was in the first group of returning prisoners.

He was not happy to be home, in fact shunned all welcome, obviously despondent. He wrote a *Last Will and Testament* dated May 22. On June 3, Alan was at his in-law's home in Harrison, New York. His wife, Deborah (Gitenstein) Brudno, was at his parents' home. He penned nine sealed letters to Debra, his parents, his father-in-law, his brother Bob, and several others, the contents of which were not disclosed. His last correspondence was a note, written in French, explaining his despair.

"My life no longer has any meaning." [43]

On June 3, the night before his 33rd birthday, he took an overdose of phenobarbital sedatives and placed a plastic bag over his head. Following an autopsy, Dr. Henry Ryan, Westchester County deputy chief medical examiner, initially determined the exact cause of death to be "inconclusive." The collective evidence finally pointed to suicide.

In Washington, the two suicides worried the Pentagon and the VA. Dr. Richard S. Wilbur, chief health officer, released an announcement. "This is the type of thing we were hoping we'd be able to prevent or hold to a minimum." Fearing an epidemic of self-inflicted deaths, the Pentagon planned to keep a medical watch on the returned POWs.

Veteran Administration representatives and contact officers were on alert. Rick counseled his supervisees to be watchful for signs of despondency.

Invitations for Rick to travel as an honored guest continued. He was selective, even to events that were close to home. Camp Pendleton was 130 miles south of Westlake Village, which amounted to a three-hour highway drive on a good day. Two days after Sergeant Larry Kavanaugh had taken his own life, the 4th Marine Division's WWII veterans assembled at Camp Pendleton for their 30th anniversary celebration. Rick, former Marine and MOH holder, was on hand. [44] The situations facing the returned POWs was talked about quietly in the Oceanside hotel hospitality room.

The FMDA met in Kissimmee, Florida, for the June 23–30, 1974 weekend.

More than being seated at a head table, Rick enjoyed organizing tributes to others. He was chairman of the May 7, 1976, CMOHS Patriot Award Dinner in Los Angeles. Bob Hope was awarded the tribute for his thirty-five years of enthusiastic dedication and personal effort in entertaining more than twelve million American Armed Forces personnel in three wars. More than fifty Medal recipients and many celebrities attended the dinner. [45]

Then, as he did every summer, like the 5,000 association members, Rick had to decide if he was going to be absent from home for another weekend and attend the 29th FMDA reunion. The June 23–26 convention was held at the Sheraton Boston Hotel. The Sunday memorial service was conducted at St. Cecilia's Church, 18 Belvidere Street.

James "Jim" Sorenson graduated with the Agoura High School Class of 1977. The 30th FMDA reunion was in Houston during late June. The next month, on July 4th, the family's attention turned to Anoka.

In 1963, when Rick, Milli, and their children lived in St. Anthony, Anoka County had claimed 1,600 acres of sandy soils, tall grass prairies, and oak forest between Coon Rapids and Andover to create Bunker Hills Regional Park. Within the boundaries, family picnic pavilions, a playground, hiking and horse trails, an archery range, camping sites, a water park and beaches, and a public golf club were developed. The park is a great place to celebrate Memorial Day, Independence Day, Labor Day, Veterans Day, and the October Nordic Festival.

At the foot of one hill, a Korean War-era tank stands sentinel. Up the trail is the impressive square, 20-meter-by-20-meter, Anoka County Veteran's Memorial, set off by seventeen American flag poles. On July 4, 1977, fourteen years after the county had acquired the park, the Mighty Seven V.F.W. Posts and Auxiliaries of Anoka County dedicated a tall, engraved granite monument in the center of the memorial. [46]

Under the MOH emblem, Minnesota's three Northeast Twin Cities WWII MOH recipients are named.

P.F.C. U.S.M.C Richard E. Kraus
P.F.C. U.S.M.C James D. La Belle
PVT U.S.M.C Richard K. Sorenson

Thomas "Tom" Sorenson, Rick and Milli's last child, graduated from Agoura High with the Class of 1978. The "old" veteran and his spouse were going to be "empty nesters" after twenty-nine years of marriage. Changes were ahead.

Following Tom's graduation march, Rick had some thoughts about his own childhood. He was planning to go back east in early September for migratory waterfowl hunting in Canada. Regretting that he had never gone hunting with his father, he realized that his kids had never had the opportunity to go out with him.

First, the FMDA gathered at the Opry Land Hotel in Nashville, July 21–24.

Rick understood that Bob was a vegetarian and was genuinely against shooting any animals, but he wanted his two youngest to have a chance for a special hunt. So, he invited Jim and Tom to go up to Manitoba for a Goose and Duck hunt. The young men were thrilled to spend time with their dad. [47]

The Sorenson hunters first went for a visit to Anoka to see Rick's mother, Virginia. He drove his sons around the area where he had grown up. He showed them the island in the Mississippi River that they had heard so much about as kids. He also took them to see the monument at Bunker Hill Park. Jim and Tom were very impressed with that wonderful tribute, but at the time, did not yet know the full extent of the sacrifices the three Marines had made. Then, early in the morning, they set out on an eight-hour drive to Manitoba. Once back in California after the hunting, all three men agreed.

"This was a fabulous trip."

Considerations for other trips, like attending the June 27–30, 1979, FMDA reunion at the New Orleans Marriott Hotel and the June 25–29, 1980, reunion at the Disneyland Hotel in Anaheim, California, gradually held fewer complications for the Sorensons.

Rick transferred to Reno, Washoe County, Nevada, as Director of Veterans Affairs for the state and nine counties in California. As always, he stayed active in community affairs and organizations, serving on the United Way Board of Directors, the Northern Nevada Boy Scout Council Board of Directors, and the Reno Rotary Club. These were in addition to his loyal memberships in many organizations, including the CMOHS (Regional Director), the Military Order of the Purple Heart (Chapter Commander), the Navy League Board of Directors, the American Legion, the VFW, the Marine Corps League, the FMDA (Life Member), and the Knights of Malta (Life Member).

Rick and Milli enjoyed many conversations with Robert and Mary Jo Kennemore at CMOHS reunions. Robert lived quietly and privately in Oakland. The two "Southerners" were raising a large family. They had married in May 1942, just before Corporal Kennemore left for the Solomon Islands and a month before Mary Jo Smith turned 18 years old.

Robert was a dad for the first time before he fought on Guadalcanal. Eight years later, he was ashore at Wonsan, Korea, when his third son, David Lee, turned three years old. Once recovered from his Chosin Reservoir wounds, Robert and Mary Jo had a daughter and three more sons, similar in age to the five Sorenson kids.

Besides chats about how their children were doing in school, Milli and Mary Jo shared a belief in miracles—their husbands had survived grenade explosions. Mary Jo's faith was put to the test in 1980.

James A. Kennemore, 38, an Oakland Police Officer, was first to get the call from Officer Sharon Jones about his younger brother. David Lee, 32, was the night supervisor for the Quarter Pound Giant Burger drive-in restaurant chain in Oakland. He was a big man, 6 feet 1 inch tall and 200 pounds. In the early morning hours of Monday, July 28, 1980, he returned to the drive-in (Ben's Burgers today) at Durant Avenue and MacArthur Boulevard. Two of his employees were in the middle of a burglary attempt.

At about 4:45 AM, David took a blunt trauma blow to his head, numerous contusions and abrasions, and twenty-nine stab wounds to his face, neck, chest, arms, and hands. His body was found in the back of a company van at 8:30 AM. He had died from shock and hemorrhage. He was survived by his wife, Patricia, and their daughter, Jennifer.

Rick and Milli offered as much solace and support as they could as the extended Kennemore family resolutely sustained themselves through David's funeral, two first degree murder trials, and conviction appeals that continued through 1983.

Rick had provided services for Marines who had survived the January 21–July 9, 1968, Siege of Khe Sanh, in Quảng Trị Province, South Viet Nam: a battle as epic as Iwo Jima and the Chosin Reservoir. Army veterans were also familiar with the remote outpost.

In the early 1980s, Rick recruited Michael John "Mike" Fitzmaurice, from Jamestown, North Dakota, for a contact representative job in Reno. Army Specialist Fourth Class Fitzmaurice was in a bunker at Khe Sanh, fourteen miles below the DMZ and six miles from the Laotian border. On March 23, 1971, he threw himself on an enemy sapper charge, saved the lives of three soldiers, and earned a Medal of Honor. He and Rick became long-time friends and travelled often with Mike Colalillo as representatives of the CMOHS.

"Those guys [in World War II] had it rougher than we did," Mike told a reporter. "They stayed for the duration. We were over there but a year." [48]

Rick's fellow recipients considered him to be "a humble, gentle man" and "a good fella" and "a straight shooter" who would not lie about anything.

Jerry Yocum, who would take the position of the public-contact team supervisor at the VA office, thought as much. "Even though he was the big boss Monday through Friday, he was just a normal guy at Friday night bowling."

"Nobody goes to Kwajalein"

As Vietnam War veterans struggled to make their adjustments to post-war life, WWII veterans considered going back—in time and place. Beginning in late 1981, newspapers began writing stories about the 40th Anniversary of the Pearl Harbor attack. Then, in 1982, it was Guadalcanal. Thus it continued into 1985, when the Marine Corps took men in their early- and mid-60s back to Iwo Jima and Okinawa. So, it was only natural that family and friends of the 4th Marine Division veterans wondered and asked.

"Would you ever want to go back to Kwajalein? To Roi–Namur?"

Kwajalein Atoll was often in Rick's thoughts; it would have been impossible otherwise. Any serious reader of newspapers had some familiarity with concerns and debates about the Marshall Islands. After WWII, Washington had negotiated with the natives on Bikini Atoll and Eniwetok Atoll to vacate their homes during years of atomic weapons testing. Hundreds of Bikinians were moved to Kwajalein, 220 miles southeast of home, then to Kili Island, another 180 miles southeast. The islanders and their grown-up children wanted to go home, and they were lobbying for the U.S. government to remove three feet of topsoil on Bikini and decontaminate their atoll.

There was also the Pentagon's ongoing development of a "Star Wars" defense system against nuclear weapons. Kwajalein was a nerve center of U.S. missile tracking and testing. The U.S. Army's Ronald Reagan Ballistic Missile Defense Test Site was on Kwajalein Atoll, and the atoll was one of five monitoring stations used for operation of the Department of Defense NAVSTAR GPS system.

Vandenberg Air Force Base, California, routinely launched Minuteman I Intercontinental Ballistic Missiles (ICBMs) 4,835 miles down the Pacific Missile Test Range to pre-determined targets near Kwajalein. Sometimes, testing was doubled up—missiles launched hours apart—for cost management to save money. Landowners on the South Pacific atoll were filing a federal lawsuit to halt the testing and close the long-range missile test site.

In addition to the *Star Wars* controversies, every now and then a newspaper columnist would take an interest in Kwajalein and mention that the *Enola Gay* had landed on the island on April 29, 1946, during "Operation Crossroads" nuclear tests. Another interesting moment in the atoll's history occurred on December 22, 1946, when Nazi Germany's *Prinz Eugen* capsized and sank on the edge of Enubuj, two miles northwest of Bucholz Army Airfield, KWA, after the heavy cruiser had survived the Bikini Atoll nuclear weapons tests.

The entire Kwajalein Island is a U.S. military base and security was tight. No one could book passage on Air Micronesia to the atoll without official orders from the commanding officer allowing them to disembark on the island. Commercial flights could stop at Bucholz Army Airfield for refueling during trans-Pacific flights, but, non-military passengers were prohibited from exiting the airport. Occasionally, arrangements could be made to catch a boat ride north to and from neighboring Ebeye Island. The idea of a 40th Anniversary Battle of Kwajalein Atoll Commemoration seemed improbable. More than one Marine gave it a try.

Hilliard Eve Miller Jr. (1921–1993) had served as a forward observer, spotting artillery fire for the Fighting Fourth Marine Division, and had been awarded the Distinguished Flying Cross for actions against enemy forces in the Pacific Theater of Operations. He was residing in Colorado Springs with his wife, Zoya, and two grown sons. In July 1983, he looked into a flight on Air Micronesia and was told "Nobody goes to Kwajalein." [49]

So, he wrote to General Paul Xavier Kelley, newly assigned as the 28th Commandant of the Marine Corps, and explained that he wanted to take a "sentimental journey." The general made his own inquiries and wrote back. Regulations barred Hilliard going to Kwajalein or Iwo Jim on his own. He wished the veteran luck and suggested he contact Valor Tours, a military history tour operator that was putting together a trip for the FMDA.

Valor Tours *was* organizing a March trip that included Kwajalein Atoll. Plans were supposed to be finalized by December. Unfortunately, the trip package was expensive and many veterans pulled out. Valor Tours cancelled the trip in January. Hilliard, determined *Devil Dog*, did not give up. With the help of the friend of a friend, the USAF Military Airlift Command, General Kelley's aides, and the USAF Chief of Staff, he was ordered to duty as part of a C-130 aircrew for a day. He and Zoya made the sentimental journey together.

There were no automobiles on Kwajalein—"just bicycles and a few official pickup trucks and vans which served as free 'taxis' for all." The morning after arriving, a *Caribou* aircraft took them for a fifty-mile flight to the Roi–Namur Airport. Delighted for the flight, he was unprepared for what he saw. He was not expecting unspoiled beauty and impossible grandeur with the beautiful lagoon water on one side and the pounding ocean surf on the other side.

"Our *Caribou* landed at Roi–Namur . . . I had remembered it as a mass of stinking devastation and here was a small island paradise. Coconut and flowering trees were everywhere. I walked alone along the landing beaches and dropped to one knee for a moment thinking back

40 years. Again I found tears sliding down the cheek. It had been costly to do what the Fourth Marine Division had done. I took the last souvenir of sand."

Rick Sorenson did not return to Roi–Namur for a 40th Anniversary, but he would stand again near the crater where he had once protected friends from an enemy grenade. When Hilliard Miller was getting ready for his return visit to the Pacific Islands, Rick made a sad trip to Minnesota.

The day in Reno was cold, gusty, and overcast on Monday, February 13, 1984, the day before Valentine gifts were exchanged. With the wind chill, it felt like the temperatures stayed in the low 30°s. In Anoka in early February, the daytime temperatures had been rising above -0°F toward the 32°F mark. The seventeen consecutive days of strictly below freezing temperatures had ended in late January. The winter had so far been somewhat mild. Four inches of snow had fallen in the last two weeks, bringing the average depth of snow in the front yards and outdoor parks to six inches. Light snow or flurries were expected throughout the day and night.

Virginia A. Mox Sorenson, 85, died that Monday. Rick and Milli and the family returned to Minnesota. When his mother was buried with her husband at Fort Snelling in Section D, Site 3151, Rick's uncles, aunts, and cousins were among the sixty-one other Sorensons interred in the national cemetery.

A year after his mother's death and a month before Rick entered a new phase of his life, Roi–Namur was in the headlines. The National Park Service had concluded a national historic landmark theme study of WWII in the Pacific, determining that the islands possessed "sites that were of national significance and sufficient integrity to warrant being nominated for designation as national historic landmarks." The Roi–Namur battlefield was added to the National Register of Historic Places on February 4, 1985. [50]

Rick retired from the VA on March 2.

Above and Beyond was published, providing a history of the Medal of Honor from the Civil War up to Vietnam. There was not much about Rick; in fact, there was one paragraph concerning him, about a college girl who had written a letter to him years before the book was in print.

On August 18, 1986, the Secretary of the Interior dedicated Roi–Namur as a National Historic Landmark. Lieutenant General D'Wayne Gray, commanding general, Fleet Marine Force Pacific, flew to Kwaj for the official October 20, 1986 battleground dedication ceremonies. Representatives of the 4th MarDiv attended. Connor Cleckley Dyess Smith, daughter of Medal recipient Lieutenant Colonel Aquilla J. "Jimmie" Dyess, participated in the ceremony. She saw for the first time the crumbling WWII ruins of Japanese blockhouses, pillboxes, concrete building remains, blasted out bunkers and arsenals, five-inch gun positions, rusty hunks of cannons, and tank-stopper seawalls. On the back walls of some remnants, the visitors could still see Japanese writing. Scarred coconut palms and a corkscrew tree hinted at the utter devastation the battle had dealt the enemy forces.

General Gray paid tribute to the Marines who had captured Roi–Namur. "One can unhesitatingly include the battles of Roi and Namur among the list of island victories that ultimately led to the defeat of the Japanese Imperial Forces."

The battlefield tour, including seventeen STOPs with plaques and narratives, circled the then-joined islands. Before the guests set out from the Beach Pavilion (Building 8270) to STOP #1 under the runway, the Roi Invasion Beaches, the guide read a sobering warning associated to the Historic Landmarks.

"The highly corrosive atmosphere has seriously deteriorated the WWII fortifications; therefore, it is important that you not go inside any of the bunkers. Falling concrete and exposed sharp and rusty rebar present a hazard to those who enter. . . . Also, be aware that removal of any battle artifacts or human remains, from the structures, the ground, or the reef is prohibited. There is also the danger of encountering unexploded ordnance (UXO). Do not disturb any cartridges, projectiles, shells, fuses or bombs."

The first seven STOPs circle Roi. The site of PFC Richard B. Anderson's heroism is near STOP #6, where his photograph and Medal of Honor Citation stand on a concrete pedestal. Green Beach 1, STOP #8, is the start of the Namur tour. STOP #10 is the location of the explosion that halted the Marine advance and obliterated the armory blockhouse. Large blocks of burned and blackened blocks of rubble are scattered about. The place Lieutenant John V. Power earned his Medal is at STOP #14. PVT Richard Sorensen's photograph and Citation are at STOP #15. Lieutenant Colonel Dyess bravery is described at STOP #16. The battleground tour ends at STOP #17, the concrete remains of the Japanese support building complex. [51]

The FMDA erected a plaque at STOP #17, listing the names of the 190 Marines killed in action or died from wounds during the two-and-a-half days of fighting.

Over the next six years, Rick gradually retired from his board of director responsibilities, but remained active in the Rotary and appeared at a lot of functions when called. He remained a member of volunteer and non-profit groups. He travelled to many parts of the country and around the world. His loyalty to his fellow recipients and the CMOHS stayed strong.

Robert once had a conversation with his father about his absences from home. In addition to his various community responsibilities and veteran conventions, Rick explained a sense of obligation attached to his valor award. Medal recipients always try to attend another recipient's funeral. A CMOHS member is designated to attend funerals in several surrounding states near his own state and, when possible, travel to a distant state. Rick fulfilled this duty for several years. [52]

He was among the 231 living holders of the Medal from WWI to Vietnam, across all the services, invited to gather in Irvine, California, for the Society's 15th Biennial Convention, November 12–15, 1987. Rick was one of the 150 recipients who attended, including nineteen USMC recipients from WWII. A short, one-paragraph summary of his Medal actions was printed in column five of six columns across entire pages in a list of all recipients in the Sunday, November 8, 1987, Santa Ana, *Orange County Register*. [53]

Rick and Harvey Curtiss "Barney" Barnum Jr., Marine Medal recipient from the Vietnam War, became close friends. Smoking cigars together always punctuated the enjoyment of seeing each other. [54]

One unfortunate event took place in 1988. Ken and Doris Gagnon did not have the luck in their marriage that Rick and Milli had found. They ended their 42-year bond. That changed the attendance at the Sorenson and Gagnon family reunions for a few years.

As the CMOHS arranged for recipients to attend May 29, 1989, Memorial Day events, sad news circulated about a funeral. Robert Kennemore, 68, hero of the Guadalcanal Campaign and the Chosin Reservoir, had died on Wednesday, April 26, 1989, in Oakland. Medal recipients were asked to attend the funeral service at St. Cuthbert's Episcopal Church and the burial with full military honors at Presidio San Francisco National Cemetery.

Mary Jo, her children, and many grandchildren, sat beside the grave at Plot H, CA-404. James and Susan Kennemore, Scott and Kelly, Clinton and Lamis, Phillip and Hana, Jeffrey and Melinda, and Paul Kennemore all lived in the greater Oakland area. Jon and Linda came from Indianapolis. Gail Lynne Kennemore (Blaser) came from Waukegan, Illinois. Medal recipients and friends surrounded the family during the interment.

Milli planned for a short trip after Memorial Day. The FMDA annual summer convention was to be held in Las Vegas, a seven-hour drive down US-95.

The next CMOHS Biennial Convention was held in Albuquerque, New Mexico, November 9–12, 1989. Looking ahead, the Society officers and members began considering bids for the 1991 National Convention site, eventually selecting the City of Vancouver, Washington. Representative Rod Chandler (R), 8th Congressional District, had a lot to do with that decision. The Medal holders began arranging their schedules and making travel plans—until their attention was directed to another war and combat veterans coming home.

As in most American households, Rick and Milli watched the daily news broadcasts on their television set.

On August 2, 1990, an international crisis erupted when Saddam Hussein's Iraqi military forces invaded Kuwait. The largest Marine deployment since the Vietnam War began. By late August, Leathernecks were massing in Saudi Arabia. The 1st Marine Division departed from Camp Pendleton, joined by units from 2d Marine Division, 2d Marine Air Wing, 3d Marine Air Wing, 4th Marine Division, and 4th Marine Air Wing. Before the ground war began, half of the Corps' active-duty forces were in the Middle East.

War was much on Rick's mind. New Year 1991 for hundreds of thousands of America's veterans meant the 50th Anniversary of the beginning of their service during World War II was approaching.

Operation *Desert Storm* kicked off on January 16, 1991, with massive air strikes by the coalition forces over Iraq and Kuwait. On Saturday, January 26, when more than 75,000 protesters marched in Washington, D.C., MOH holders were reminded of the wounds America felt over the nation's involvement in Viet Nam.

On Sunday, Rick marched with flag-waving Americans to demonstrate his support for the U.S. troops in the Persian Gulf going to war against Saddam Hussein's forces.

Twenty-three teams of University of Nevada students stretched a twenty-three-mile yellow ribbon of support around the Reno area, each team stretching out a mile of ribbon on the ground. Rick tied the final two ends together. He acknowledged that anti-war protestors had marched around the White House the day before.

"We have been divided before," he said, "but now is the time to stand behind our men 100 percent and hope they can come home safely." [55]

Two days later, on January 29, the first major ground combat action took place at the Battle of Khafji, a Saudi town.

On February 24, the Marines and coalition forces began a ground assault on Iraqi defenses just south of the Kuwaiti border along the Persian Gulf. What became known as the First Gulf War was over in 100 hours in an astounding and decisive coalition victory. President George Herbert Walker Bush declared a cease-fire on February 28. Gradually, the attention of news and media outlets moved away from *Desert Storm's* success.

Resolutions

The 101st Congress had been in session during Operation *Desert Storm*. Representative Rod Chandler, the State of Washington, wanted the federal government to set aside a day to honor men like Rick Sorenson. On September 24, 1990, Mr. Chandler introduced a bill that he was sponsoring. He had convinced eighty-two Democrats and sixty-two Republicans from the House and Senate to co-sponsor House Joint Resolution 652.

The resolution was "An Act to designate March 25, 1991, as 'National Medal of Honor Day.' Whereas the Medal of Honor is the highest distinction that can be awarded by the President . . . Whereas the 1st Medal of Honor awards were presented to 6 men on March 25, 1863, by the Secretary of War . . . the President is authorized and requested to issue a proclamation calling on the people of the United States to observe the day with appropriate ceremonies and activities." [56]

The Senate signed the measure on November 9. President Bush signed Public Law 101–564 on November 15. The first annual National Medal of Honor Day was celebrated on Monday, March 25, 1991.

That he had been retired from the VA for six years did not mean that Rick stopped looking out for veterans and their families.

In 1991, a veteran from Bishop, California, was in the intensive care unit at the VA Sierra Nevada Health Care System Medical Center in Reno. He and his wife did not have money enough for her to stay in a local motel and did not know anyone in the Reno/Sparks area who could help with lodging. The woman and her children spent the night sleeping in their car.

Local Reno veterans discovered this and realized that other veterans and their families were doing the same thing, because they lacked a place to stay while the veteran received medical treatment. The veterans established the non-profit Veterans Hospital Foundation.

Rick was one of the twenty-eight founders who shared an "unwavering commitment and loyalty to providing our service members, veterans, and their families" a safe, warm, and clean place to stay while dealing with their health care needs at medical facilities throughout northern Nevada. [57]

A small home called the "Spouse House" was opened in 1994, at 880 Locust Street, Reno. By 1998, the home provided five beds for veterans and their families. The facility would be officially named the Veterans Guest House in 2002. Rick would not be present on Veterans Day 2004, when the organization, with only private donations, purchased and renovated a three-story home able to accommodate up to seventeen long-term and short-term guests across the street from the VA Medical Center.

Rick enjoyed his roles as dad and grandpa. All five children married, and three raised their families near their parents' home in Reno. Robert, their eldest, had returned to his birthplace and lived in St. Anthony Village, a few blocks from where the children had grown up in the 1960s. He was the last of the five to marry.

Rick had more time for his hobbies and pastimes, including hunting, boating, and fishing. He was a patriot, an avid reader, historian, artist, craftsman, woodworker, and dancer. He took pleasure in games of strategy and was a skilled chess and Monopoly player. His children and grandchildren inherited his passions for all these things. Rick and Milli enjoyed having times with their seven grandchildren

Their middle son traveled from home. James joined the Air Force in 1988 and served six years as an officer, living on various air bases with his wife and daughter. Naturally, he was the recipient of much good-humored ribbing from his dad for not serving in the "real" Armed Forces—the Marine Corps. Jim always took it well, understanding interservice rivalries and his father's sense of *Semper Fidelis*.

"My Dad loved serving in the Marines." [58]

In 1991, Rick was asked more than once what his son was doing in the Air Force. Depending on who asked, he might have answered that Jim was a Missile Launch Officer with the 509th Strategic Missile Squadron (SMS), 351st Missile Group, 351st Strategic Missile Wing—the *Sentinels of Peace*. That's a lot of numbers and might have been an end to a conversation. Given the times, more questions about missiles might have come to a curious civilian's mind. The USAF unit designations would have made sense to a military-minded person.

The landowners in sixteen counties east to south of Kansas City, Missouri, had a good idea of what Jim was doing at Whiteman. And, anyone traveling south on State Hwy 13 into the Garden City area could see where he was working.

The 509th Missile Squadron was one of three the Strategic Air Command (SAC) had activated in 1962 at Whiteman, each of which was operational in early 1964. A USAF squadron is comprised of five flights. The fifteen flights at Whiteman each controlled ten operational LGM-30 Minuteman ICBMs in hardened, unmanned Launch Facilities (LFs).

First Lieutenant Sorenson was serving at a Launch Control Facility (LCF) in the fifth flight. [59] He and a dozen or so airmen and officers were assigned to the facility. Rick's son spent a lot of time underground.

In sight at the LCF was a "soft," above-ground Launch Control Support Building (LCSB), referred to as the "Farmhouse," for security police, cooks, and facility personnel: a large radio tower; a tall "top hat" HF antenna; and some recreational facilities—all secured within a fence and patrolled by security personnel. A helicopter landing pad and sewage lagoons were situated outside the fence.

First Lieutenant Sorenson's greatest responsibilities took place in a buried and hardened Launch Control Center (LCC) inside the fence where the command and control equipment for ICBM operations were located. He and another launch officer staffed the LCC, sharing the primary control and responsibility for the flight's ten underground missiles. He served crew duty for some time at L-01 (Lima-Zero-One), situated forty-one miles outside of Whiteman. Because he was also periodically on duty in the LCFs at the other four flights, he was in command of all fifty missiles within the 509th SMS at one time or another. When necessary, First Lieutenant Sorenson also "pulled alert" at thirteen of the fifteen LCFs within the 351st Wing.

During times of quiet reflection in the LCC, 1stLt Sorenson could feel a meaningful bond to his father's service. [60] America's nuclear mission was impossible to conduct without Kwajalein. The atoll was absolutely vital for the U.S. to prove to its allies and adversaries alike that its ICBMs were accurate and reliable. His connection to Kwajalein and to his father's sacrifices remained a source of pride for him—and for Rick.

Speaking of connections—and coincidences—they could seem countless to MOH recipients and their families. Rick had a conversation with at least one man who did not need an explanation of 1stLt Sorenson's duties. Dad gladly repeated that chat later to Jim.

Rick was the Army's guest at the Kwajalein Atoll at the same time that Brigadier General Thomas E. Kuenning Jr., Commander of the Strategic Missile Center at Vandenberg AFB, was inspecting the Kwajalein missile range. The two boarded a helicopter with several other passengers for a tour of the range tracking facilities and the lagoon at the Reagan Test site. Rick recognized that the general was in a USAF uniform, not Army. Almost in passing, he mentioned Jim to him

"I have a son in the Air Force, stationed at Whiteman AFB in Missouri serving as a Missile Launch Officer."

Caught off guard, the general's eyebrows raised. Hard to believe. He told Rick that he had not too long ago been a colonel and had been the Wing Commander at that missile base.

"Who's your son?"

"Jim Sorenson."

"I knew Lieutenant Sorenson," answered General Kuennin. "He was one of my select and upcoming officers."

When his father told him about the helicopter ride and the general's comment, Jim had to chuckle. He figured that the general was just being polite to a Medal recipient. Lieutenant Sorenson considered himself to be a very unknown and average, even ordinary, officer.

"I was just proud to serve, even in an unglamorous job as a missile jockey."

Rick and Milli celebrated glad festivities in May 1991. Ken Gagnon and Penny Jones had fallen for each other in Southern California. Ken was close to his 71st birthday when they wed in Carson City, Nevada. Penny's daughter, Lisa Dickerson, was welcomed to the family reunions.

Ken appreciated his cousin's love of marksmanship. He gave Rick the pristine WWII German Luger that he had brought home from the submarine pens in France. Rick used it regularly for target shooting. He later passed it on to one of his boys as a gift. [61]

Away From Home

The City of Anoka asked Rick to come home for the May 27, 1991, Memorial Day. He was American Legion Edward B. Cutler Post 102's guest. He spoke humbly to the crowd from the surrounding region at the Anoka Veterans Memorial on Monday.

Legion Post 102 unveiled a memorial bronze statue of a Marine with a heavy machine gun slung over his right shoulder. [62] The statue was dedicated to honor Rick and WWII veterans. A plaque at the feet of the statue records his Medal Citation in embossed text and has a bas-relief image of his MOH ribbon and Medal. [63] Channels 4, 9, and 11 covered the day's events and featured Rick on the 10:00 evening news broadcasts. His statue is considered "the most distinctive feature" of the Memorial.

On Tuesday morning, Rick talked on KTSP radio in St. Paul about the outstanding tribute. Then, he went to the Anoka County Historical Society on 3rd Avenue. The ACHS was specializing in the 50th Anniversary of WWII. Pat Schwappach interviewed him for the Oral History Collection, put on tape to eventually be transcribed for future generations. [64] Rick signed the wonderful lithograph of him that Legion Post 102 had donated to the Historical Society.

He answered questions about his childhood, December 7, 1941, his Marine Corps experience, his grenade injuries, medical care and recuperation, his life after receiving the Medal of Honor, meeting Milli on a blind date, his children and grandchildren, and his retirement. At the time Pat talked with him, Jim was up for a promotion to captain the next month at Whiteman AFB.

As the interview concluded, Pat asked the MOH recipient if he had any special words of wisdom that might be recorded for posterity. Caught off guard and laughing, Rick took a moment to think, then answered.

"Well, I think that really what we have to do in future generations, we have to be concerned about our freedom. We won our freedom in just one generation, and in one generation, we could lose it. That freedom is a very dear and precious thing, and I really don't think people understand how valuable it is until they lose it." [65]

Vickie Wendel was a young staff member with less than a year at the historical society. About covering that grenade on Namur Island, he told her his thoughts at the time he protected his fellow Marines from the blast.

"If I don't do this, it's going to hurt all these other guys around me. I have to protect them."

Rick left a lasting impression on her. "He gave off the kind of aura that said this was a special person," she would remember twenty years later. "He never bragged. But sometimes you just know." [66]

Evident in his love for history, Rick and Milli supported the ACHS's efforts to preserve the legacies of the region. In 2001, ten years after his jovial conversations with Pat Schwappach and Vickie Wendel, Rick donated a huge Revolutionary War drum to the society.

Jim Sorenson shared his parents' love of history. When his father gave him the Purple Heart medal the two-star admiral had presented to him in the Hawaii hospital, the medal obviously had had more wear and tear than Rick's other medals. "It was in really rough condition with a lot of scratches."

Jim asked about it. "Why is it in such poor condition compared to the others?"

"It's because I never received a case for it," was his father's reply.

Vancouver, Washington, hosted the November 7–12, 1991, 17th Biennial Convention of the CMOHS in recognition of the spirit and sacrifice of the valiant Medal recipients. The theme was Celebrate Freedom: America Honors its Heroes. An event was held at Vancouver Landing. A tribute was paid to four recipients at rest in Vancouver Barracks Cemetery, established inland from the Columbia River at Fort Vancouver in the 1850s. On November 8, the Society presented the CMOHS Monument to the city at the corner of East Evergreen Boulevard and Fort Vancouver Way—now a roundabout with Officer's Row. Major General Patrick H. Brady, CMOHS president, and General Colin Powell, Chairman of the Joint Chiefs of Staff, spoke at the dedication ceremony.

At its general meeting, the Society decided to plan annual conventions rather than every other year. Plans were already in motion for some international relationship mending. Rick was going to participate in "perestroika" and "glasnost."

President Reagan and Mikhail Gorbachev had negotiated through the geopolitical tensions of the Cold War. The Soviets had pulled out of Afghanistan in February 1989 after nine years of war with the insurgent mujahideen. That June, Poland declared itself independent of Soviet dominance. The destruction of the Berlin Wall began in November, and the communist government started dismantling it in June 1990. President George H. Bush and Boris Yeltsin, first President of the Russian Federation, picked up the discussions of their predecessors in July 1991. Another fourteen Eastern Europe republics had declared independence by late 1991, and the Soviet Union dissolved. The Cold War had presumably ended.

Milli had been at Rick's side in many patriotic parades across their years together, traveling with him in and out of the country. Their trip to western Norway was more personal than patriotic—a visit to the homeland fjords of his ancestors, Soren and Jensina Sorenson-Lah. Their May 1992 venture into Communist Russia was unquestionably patriotic.

The MOH recipients were invited to Russia to march with other World War II veterans across Moscow's Red Square for the May 9 Victory-in-Europe Anniversary Parade. [67] The annual (military) parade commemorates the Allied WWII victory at the Eastern Front and Nazi Germany's capitulation in 1945. The Medal holders travelled with a congressional group and joined the "Heroes of the Soviet Union," men who held the highest honorary title in the Soviet Union, awarded for heroic feats in service to the Soviet state and society. The great majority of the Heroes had received the title during World War II. The U.S. MOH recipients and Soviet Heroes were honored in the huge Red Square ceremony.

The 50th Anniversary Commemoration of the invasion and capture of the Kwajalein Atoll was in the works for 1994. The islanders pitched in to help the base prepare for the anniversary.

Smiling school children helped clean up the entire island. Local clubs and organizations made parade floats and concession booths. The occasion proved more meaningful to Rick and Milli than a parade in Red Square.

They departed Honolulu on Saturday, February 5, 1994, for a five-hour flight to the atoll. The veterans and their wives were transported around the island on the seven new airport shuttle buses that had replaced the old step vans. Each air-conditioned bus was christened with a Marshallese name the drivers had chosen.

On Sunday, the couples shuttled back to Bucholz Airfield, elevation ten feet, and boarded a commuter plane. With an east-north-east wind, the aircraft taxied to Runway 6/24 and took off on a 240° heading. Climbing in a turn to the north, Rick and Milli looked from the window over tiny Enubuj and saw the submerged hull of the *Prinz Eugen* with her stern and two of her three propeller assemblies sticking above the lagoon's surface.

The pilot made the fifteen-minute flight interesting, pointing out sights of other wrecks, telling the passengers that military divers had mapped out more than forty WWII ships, planes, and landing craft wrecks lying in the lagoon. At least eleven Japanese merchant ships had been dispatched to the bottom prior to the 1944 amphibious assaults on Kwajalein and Roi–Namur. [68]

Approaching the north end of the atoll from the air, the Yokohama Pier on Namur's south side plainly jutted out into the lagoon, still seventy-five yards from Rick and Item Company's landing site on Green Beach 1. Green jungle growth, a reminder why the island was called CAMOUFLAGE for the amphibious landings, dominated the several radar tracking stations and the big satellite dishes. Roi looked a little more developed, less green, with a small housing area, a nine-hole golf course beside the runway, a swimming pool, and various recreation facilities and courts. Little evidence remained of the shell craters that had pitted the islands long ago.

The commuter touched down on the Roi Namur (KMR) Dyess Army Airfield. Outside the terminal, a demonstration U.S. Army Nike missile supported on a pedestal welcomed the visitors to the small, remote launch facility, the domicile of short-range rockets that climb into the atmosphere to interrupt the target run of bigger missiles. The Marines had returned.

Brigadier General C.D. Kuhn Jr., Deputy Commander, Marine Forces Pacific, spoke to Marine veterans on Roi–Namur. He introduced Rick as the 4th Marine Division guest of honor. Rick wore the Medal around his neck and his white CMOHS Valor baseball cap with the round, blue emblem fringed in gold. Ever respectful, many in attendance, wearing their red 4th Marines and the "Kwajalein Atoll WWII 50th Anniversary 1994" baseball caps, asked for photographs with him.

Some walked along the paths, avoiding the waist-high growth, others rode in golf carts, following the map of the battle landmarks. In a direct line from STOP #8, Green Beach 1, north along what had been drawn on the battle maps as Nipp Street, past the large satellite dish, the veterans reached STOP #15, where Rick had cradled a grenade to protect others.

Sixteen members of Marine Bombing Squadron Six-Thirteen (VMB-613) were at the anniversary observance, grateful for the opportunity to meet Rick and other 4th MarDiv veterans. Charles F. "Charlie" Knapp, VMB-613 Association President was acting photographer. Rick, in the center, stood for a photo in the coconut tree grove with Frank L. Pokrop

(G/2/24), James Dee Garls (VMB-613), and Chester Dunham (Hq/2/23). The day was Frank's first return to the atoll. He had been wounded multiple times on Namur and spent six months recuperating at Pearl Harbor and in California. Apart from that, he preferred to talk about writing to Connor Dyess Smith in February 1988 and the Smith's family visit in Kohler, Wisconsin, that same May.

Foster K. Cummings, VMB-613 veteran, had his photo taken with the guest of honor and had it framed to hang on a wall at home in Wakefield, Massachusetts. He was proud of the friendship that deepened over the next years. He pointed out the photo to his two sons and daughter, and to his three grandchildren. Rick would keep in contact with him and visited with Foster and Doris on his trips to the northeast.

Captain Phillip Thompson, USMC, had a chance to interview the MOH recipient. [69] Rick recounted the actions that had earned him the Medal fifty years earlier, recalling his Marine service with pride tinged with sadness. He softly admitted to the emotions he felt during the commemoration ceremonies held on the serene, green grasses of Roi–Namur.

"It choked me up some. That was because of the thoughts that were running through my mind of some of the good friends that I lost. I lost more friends, not only in this battle, but in Saipan, Tinian, and Iwo Jima."

Standing on the spot where he had fought gallantly and protected friends, he spoke wryly, regaining his steadiness with humor, as Medal recipients tend to do. "There's a story that some people don't know."

He told Captain Thompson all about the night aboard the LST before the landing, when the fellow brought up grenades, and he had answered, "the best thing to do is either throw it out or fall on it."

"Jeez, you shouldn't have said that, Rick," the buddy had said, "because saying that, it'll probably happen."

With his characteristic poise, Rick ended the story. "And it did."

Of his many hours touring, Frank Pokrop reached a conclusion like Rick's.

"It was a deeply moving experience," he said, "interspersed with prayers for those that did not survive."

The anniversary tour included dining at the Roi Café. The wives scrutinized the menu for wholesome food. Salad was a favorite selection. Husbands joked about the meaning of "hole some." Maxine Pokrop admonished Frank that it did not mean the half-pound Missile Burger and fries. One wife, whispering, asked why a server referred to the cooks back in the kitchen as "Roi Rats." It was probably in jest. Yet, recalling that the large rats seemed more numerous on the island in 1944 than the enemy shooting at them was not pleasant meal-time bantering.

The blueberry ice cream was the dining highlight for Rick and Milli.

On Monday, the 2,881 Kwaj residents gathered to commemorate the 1944 battles and pay tribute to the men who had liberated the islands from an enemy occupier. The veterans rode on the floats in the parade and stopped at the many booths for food and memorabilia. They visited the Island Memorial Chapel dedicated to the soldiers and Marines who had fought on the atoll.

The veterans stood silently during the unveiling of a tall, stained glass window funded through voluntary donations from residents. In a circle near the top of the window, as if viewed through a large magnifying glass, a serviceman dressed in combat greens, his helmet chinstrap unbuckled, rests with one knee to the ground. He grips the butt of a carbine with his right hand, barrel down to the ground. Dog tags dangle from his left hand. It is a pose common after battles that all the veterans would recognize.

Symbols and flags representing the 7th Infantry Division, the 4th Marine Division, the United States, and the Republic of the Marshall Islands surround the soldier/Marine. The green, flowering blossoms in the lower panels of the window represent the restoration of a war-devastated land. The text inscribed across the bottom of the window states, "In memorial to those gallant men who paid the supreme sacrifice for freedom at Kwajalein, 50th Anniversary, February 1944."

The *Kwajalein Hourglass* printed a special edition newsletter to commemorate the 50th anniversary of the Battle for Kwajalein and Roi–Namur. The *Hourglass* would have more to tell about Rick and his family after another ten years passed.

Rick and Milli thought Jim's leaving the Air Force in 1994 was good news. His knowledge of ICBMs served him well. After his service, he moved near Hill AFB, between Ogden and Salt Lake City, Utah, only 543 miles from Reno—a day trip for family visits—and went to work in the aerospace, defense, security, and advanced technologies field. [70]

Another family move added some delight to Rick's retirement. Ken and Penny Gagnon moved to Reno in 1997, so Ken could enjoy his own peaceful retirement. He puttered in his yard and visited the Nevada casinos.

Neither Rick or Milli kept a journal of their travels, but their passport pages filled to a point that new visas were necessary. After Memorial Day, May 29, 1995, they took a trip to the United Kingdom. Immigration Officer (48) greeted them at the Gatwick (London) North terminal. The 31 May 1995 *Leave to Enter Stamp*, noting their Visas were good for six months, along with the corresponding *Entry Stamp*, prohibited employment and recourse to public funds. Their 17 June 1995 stamp indicated departure for home from the same terminal. [71]

Ordinary men doing what they were trained to do.

"Ordinary" is a word often used to describe a Medal holder. It seems like a misnomer. Are men who jump on grenades commonplace or normal with no special or distinctive characteristics? Every one of the recipients would say so. The Medal holders view themselves as just "regular guys." Maybe before the battle—maybe after, when they came home. Or maybe their "ordinary" can be applied only to men and women willing to go into combat with comrades.

In 1995, the CMOHS kept 186 living MOH recipients on the rolls. They all held strong to their ideals to put service before self, to inspire patriotism, to be spokesmen for those who did not come home from their battles, and to remember the veterans in VA hospitals. Proud to be grand marshals, keynote speakers, and honored guests, they were humble in the face of praise, each believing they were no braver than the men who had fought to their right and left.

Before Independence Day 1995, Rick went over to Colorado Springs on Monday, July 3, and toured the Air Force Academy and the Cheyenne Air Force Base. Jack Lucas was there. In the afternoon, the two Marines stood in front of the Academy Chapel shoulder to shoulder with Jack Montgomery, Walter Ehlers, Silvestre Herrera, Ernest Chief Childers, John Baker, Don Doc Ballard, Eugene Fluckey, and Joe Rodriguez to watch an overhead, fly-by salute.

The FMDA extended its own salute. Entitled *Valor*, the September 1996 *49th Annual Reunion Publication* was dedicated to the twelve Medal holders of the 4th MarDiv.

Retired USMC Colonel Barney Barnum, 59, bantered and smoked cigars with Rick at CMOHS functions. One chance was at their week-long 1999 annual convention in Riverside, California. Invitations had gone out to 154 men. Those who would attend began to arrive on Tuesday, October 30. Reporters mingled among them, hoping for a welcome to the hospitality room and an interview with men they believed to be in "one of the most exclusive groups in the world." [72]

The camaraderie among the men was evident. They gathered to renew their commitments, reflect on the purpose of service, and to remember the sacrifices of others. And, they talked about fear and duty and their "unwavering love and devotion to their country" more than they did about honor. Society President Paul "Buddy" Bucha, 56, explained the purpose of wearing the award over civilian clothes.

"When someone sees the Medal, we hope it reminds them of the absolute potential that exists within each and every person."

Retired USMC Major General James E. Livingston, 59, who had earned his Medal for actions in Viet Nam, attended reunions "to remind ourselves of our great responsibilities to this nation and the cost to live as a free people." He believed the CMOHS's purpose was "to focus our country on patriotism, commitment, love and brotherhood, to challenge the spirit of a free society."

At each reunion, Barney Barnum dedicates his Medal "to those who did not make it off the battlefield" on the day he earned his highest award.

Former Army 1st Lieutenant Brian Miles Thacker, 54, also earned his Medal in Viet Nam in 1971. He explained why all eighty-five recipients at the reunion had received their Citations.

"We were ordinary men doing what we were trained to do."

On Friday, November 5, the ordinary men went to Riverside National Cemetery to participate in the dedication of a memorial still under construction.

On September 22, 1999, the House of Representatives in the 1st Session of the 106th Congress had adopted a bill, H.R. 1663, to be called the National Medal of Honor Memorial Act. Three locations to honor recipients of the Medal were thereby recognized as National Medal of Honor sites: Riverside National Cemetery Medal of Honor Memorial, the memorial at the White River State Park in Indianapolis, dedicated on May 28, 1999, and the Congressional Medal of Honor Museum at Patriots Point in Mount Pleasant, South Carolina. The fourth recognized Medal of Honor Memorial national site in Pueblo, Colorado, would be dedicated on September 21, 2001.

Saturday night was the Patriots Award Dinner. Over cocktails, the men talked about where each would be on Wednesday night to attend a Marine Corps Birthday Ball. Had anyone accepted President Bill Clinton's invitation to be in Arlington National Cemetery on Thursday for the Veterans Day wreath laying ceremony at the Tomb of the Unknowns? NBC News Anchor Tom Brokaw, biographer Stephen E. Ambrose, and former California Governor Pete Wilson were honored at the dinner. The recipients would meet with Tom and Stephen again in three months.

The Society held its memorial service on Sunday morning. It was the biggest event at the reunions for Barney Barnum—the time for the men to "pause to honor those we have lost since our last gathering. We pay tribute in our own way." Ten Medal holders had died in 1999.

The January 1, 1951 *TIME* Magazine cover had declared the American Fighting-man to be Man of the Year. In June 1999, *TIME* looked back across the 20th century and compiled a list of the 100 most influential people: scientists, politicians, heroes, entertainers, sports figures, musicians, artists, and industrialists. General Colin Powell, former Chairman of the Joint Chiefs of Staff, and Stephen Ambrose nominated G.I. Joe for an upgrade. The nomination provided Rick and Milli an opportunity to return to Washington, D.C.

Secretary of Defense William S. Cohen and his wife, Janet, invited all the Medal recipients to the second annual *Pentagon Pops* concert at the Daughters of the American Revolution Constitution Hall in the nation's capital. The audience was to enjoy a musical salute to "America's Hero of the Century." More than sixty recipients attended. Some news releases put the number closer to 100. [73]

The Cohens hosted the Monday, February 21, 2000, President's Day ceremony. Tom Brokaw was the Master of Ceremonies. Military bands played and choruses sang. Service members in historical uniforms from WWII up through the Persian Gulf War served as a rear guard when Stephen Ambrose, keynote speaker, stepped to the podium. Keeping to the theme, he proclaimed that everyone in Constitution Hall and millions of people owed their freedom to America's G.I. Joe, Hero of the Century.

Several Tuskegee Airman were special guests. Representing the 300 surviving Airmen, Wilie W. Selden Jr., WWII fighter pilot from D.C., led Clevelanders Joseph Burrucker, Clarence C. "Jamie" Jamison, Edward Lunda (Akron), Arthur Saunders, and Roy Richardson onto the stage, all in their formal Red Tail blazers.

Senator John Glenn, D-Ohio, greeted the Medal recipients when they were welcomed to march across the stage. They stood in a grand formation to a standing ovation. The military chiefs, government officials, and many celebrities who attended the tribute waited for a chance to shake hands with the heroes, have a photo taken, and maybe get an autograph.

A Sense of Urgency

When Barney Barnum attended the next CMOHS memorial service, ten members would be toasted. Three were Marines. Robert Hugo Dunlap, WWII, died on March 15, and Carl Leonard Sitter, Korea, died on April 4. The third Marine died shortly after the FMDA's 53rd annual reunion.

The phone rang at the Sorenson residence on Monday, August 21, 2000. Two of Rick's good friends thought it was urgent that they speak with him. William L. "Bill" More, FMDA president, and Barney Barnum, CMOHS president, wanted to let him know that another friend had passed on.

Douglas T. Jacobson, aged 74, had died of congestive heart failure and pneumonia on Sunday in Port Charlotte, Florida. One of Doug's three daughters also called. Doug's wife Joan wanted her husband's remains taken to the Arlington National Cemetery Columbarium, as were his wishes. With the old golfer's death, Rick was the only surviving Fighting Fourth Division Medal holder.

Milli thought it would be nice to get all the children home for a visit.

In December 2000, the Sorensons were all together and had a chance for a family photograph. [74] It was a happy time.

Not that they needed reminders, but five months after the family photo, Rick and Milli had reason to be grateful for their five children as they extended sympathy and comfort to dear friends. Mike and Lina's daughter, Joanne Lee Colalillo, 51, had died on May 6, 2001, in Duluth. Parents were not supposed to outlive their children. The impermanence of life more frequently came to mind.

Front row (L-R): Rick, Debby, Milli
Standing: Tom, Jim, Wendy, Bob

No matter how much or little Rick and his cousin might have talked about their WWII years, reminders of that "Day of Infamy" when an enemy attacked Pearl Harbor resurfaced in news broadcasts.

Terrorists attacked the World Trade Center and the Pentagon from the air on September 11, 2001, killing 2,996 Americans and wounding more than 6,000 others. News outlets immediately began comparing the events to the surprise attack at Pearl Harbor when 2,403 Americans were killed and 1,178 others were wounded.

Four weeks later, on October 7, 2001, President George W. Bush sent American forces into Afghanistan, launching *Operation Enduring Freedom (OEF-A)*. Another generation of Marines and soldiers went to war. Rick was sure the young men would be brave in combat, and that some would go above and beyond what was expected of them, even sacrificing their own lives so their companions could return home. It turned into a very long war.

On Monday, December 2, 2002, Kenneth James Gagnon, 82, died in Reno—sixty-one years to the day after he had enlisted in the Army just before the attack on Pearl Harbor. Rick lost a dear cousin and friend.

In just a few weeks, he would turn his attention to what another friend, a Marine Corps general, was doing.

"I know one thing," Major General James Mattis briefed his commanders on December 17, 2002. "The president, the National Command Authority, and the American people need speed. The sooner we get it over with, the better. Our overriding principle will be speed, speed, speed." [75]

Operation Enduring Freedom (OEF-I) in Iraq was near its end. On Thursday, March 20, 2003, as part of the 1st Marine Expeditionary Force (I MEF) ground forces, the 1st Marine Division under command of Major General Mattis invaded Iraq, fighting through the Rumaila oil fields. *Operation Iraqi Freedom (OIF)* had begun.

For six weeks, embedded correspondents, noting the speed of the American advance, made their reports about Basrah, Iraq Highway 1, An Nasariyah, Talil Airfield, Fallujah, and Baghdad.

Coalition forces took Baghdad on April 9. On Saturday, April 12, the I MEF left Baghdad and set out for Tikrit, Saddam Hussein's hometown in north-central Iraq. The mission was short and to the point: "Attack and destroy any type of regime forces in the area." Having traveled ninety miles, the Marines occupied Tikrit on Sunday.

On May 1, President Bush stood on the flight deck of the USS *Abraham Lincoln* and, in a televised address, declared "major combat operations" of the Iraq War over. From May to October, the 1st Marine Division conducted operations in Baghdad and Tikrit and south-central Iraq.

Having Time to Think

The Congressional Medal of Honor Foundation interviewed Rick as part of their Oral History Project. [76] His Profile of Valor is included in Peter Collier and Nick Del Calzo's 2003 book, pages 242–44 and 257. He is quoted in the Front Matter.

"I believe in liberty and justice and will fight to defend the dignity of man."

Rick was the only Medal recipient living in Nevada in 2003, and at age 79, he was still called upon for honorary duties. The Nevada Day Committee members were planning the Nevada Day Parade in Carson City for the state holiday first designated by the state legislature in 1933. The first parade was held in 1937. The committee approached Rick to be Grand Marshal for the Saturday, November 1, 2003. His reply was characteristic of him.

"I'm pretty proud that they would select me." [77]

Two weeks later, the theme of the 2003 Reno Veterans Day Parade was "Marching for Freedom Past, Present and Future Veterans." In addition to the veterans from all wars, Reno conducted a ceremony at 10:45 AM on the corner of Fourth and Virginia streets honoring Nevadans who had lost their lives in the Iraq conflict. More than sixty marching units started along Virginia Street in downtown Reno at 11:00 AM on Tuesday. The Sparks Elks Lodge No. 2397 and Sparks Elks Ladies made presentations to veterans in the medical facility. Veterans were honored from 1:00-4:00 PM at the Veterans Guest House. Reno Mayor Bob Cashell, Sparks Mayor Tony Armstrong, and Washoe County Commissioner David Humke presented awards to three local veterans.

Rick was asked about his own war experiences with the 4th MarDiv on Namur Island in the Marshall chain. He succinctly recalled the two days of February 1 and 2, 1944.

"You're moving from one hole to another. You can't sit there, because they're shooting at you." On the second day of fighting, he was with five other Marines, cut off and surrounded. "We didn't know it until the morning, when the Japanese launched a counterattack. We were fighting them off as best we could." When the grenade landed in their midst, he was closest to it. "I fell on it. You don't have time to think. You know what has to be done." After the grenade exploded under him, bleeding badly, he crawled into a nearby foxhole. "I never thought I would die."

Rick was thinking not only of his war and about veterans, but also about the young soldiers fighting in Iraq.

It had been seven months since 20-year-old, former Army supply clerk Jessica Lynch had been rescued from her POW ordeal in Iraq. Reluctantly struggling with her national hero status, she considered the soldiers who had liberated her on April 1 to be the heroes.

A young woman from rural West Virginia had carried a rifle in combat that had jammed— she did not get off a shot—and was an ex-POW. That was not an American experience in WWII. Nevada's only living MOH recipient understood that his war was different from the current conflict; but some things about war had not changed. For one thing, young men and women were willing to fight for many of the same basic reasons Rick had—for their buddies to their left and right, their families, their country, and for freedom.

"It's a nasty situation over there," was Rick's perspective. Despite the successful invasion, Marines and soldiers continued to face sniper attacks. "It's tough. You can't see the enemy."

He also knew other significant unchanging aspects of war that the young soldiers were facing. "Anybody who's been in combat knows what they're going through. What they're going through is fear. You don't know what the next hour or day is going to bring." Yet, he also guessed that any teenage soldier in Iraq was too busy to dwell on his fears for long. "You don't have time to think about whether you are going to be hit or not. You never really think that it's going to be you that's going to be hit." [78]

✳✳✳

A Marine from small town Scio, on the Genesee River in the Allegheny Mountains of western New York, might have agreed with Rick—except that he had a chance to think about it. This young man had had a conversation with his lieutenant about what he might do if there was ever a grenade endangering his friends.

News spread in the small communities south of Buffalo, Rochester, and Syracuse before CMOHS members read the accounts in the Syracuse *Post-Standard* and *The Wall Street Journal*. [79] Gary Burnell Beikirch, 56, a former U.S. Army sergeant from Rochester who had earned a Medal of Honor in Viet Nam, learned of it before the nation did. Friends called Rick in Reno and asked if he had read the newspaper story.

The 1st Marine Division had taken control of the Al Anbar province in western Iraq in February 2004. On his second tour, **Corporal Jason Lee Dunham**, 22 years old, was a rifle squad leader in 4th Platoon, Company K, 3d Battalion, 7th Marines, serving near the Syrian border. A little after noon on Wednesday, April 14, 2004, a convoy was attacked in the town of Husaybah. Corporal Dunham rushed with his 14-man team to reinforce the patrol under fire.

At the town gates, an Iraqi insurgent jumped from a parked car with a charged grenade in his grasp and assaulted CPL Dunham. The squad leader fought to wrestle the grenade from the insurgent. Staff Sergeant John Ferguson crossed the street to help. The grenade dropped to the dirt alleyway. Corporal Dunham yelled a warning, covered the explosive with his Kevlar helmet, and fell on it. The blast wounded Lance Corporal William B. Hampton and PFC Kelly Miller, but they survived. Near enough to the explosion, Lance Corporal Jason Sanders was momentarily deafened.

Corporal Dunham was alive, having sustained shrapnel wounds to his skull. He was evacuated to a field hospital at Al Qa'im, then to Al Asad, then to a surgical hospital in Baghdad. From there, he was transferred to Germany, then to Bethesda Hospital, Maryland, arriving in the States on April 21. The Marines made sure that his parents were at the hospital that Wednesday. General Michael W. Hagee, 33rd Commandant of the Marine Corps, was with Dan and Deb Dunham as they made medical decisions.

Corporal Dunham died of his wounds at 4:43 PM on April 22.

Second Lieutenant Brian "Bull" Robinson, Staff Sergeant Ferguson, Sergeant Major Dan Huff, and Lieutenant Colonel Matthew Lopez, 3/7 battalion commander, had already talked over the facts with the three witnesses. A Medal of Honor award nomination was on its way to Washington by May 13.

"I deeply believe that given the facts and evidence presented, he clearly understood the situation and attempted to block the blast of the grenade from his squad members," LtCol

Lopez stated. "His personal action was far beyond the call of duty and saved the lives of his fellow Marines."

Corporal Dunham's family would meet President Bush at a private White House ceremony in the East Room. The president attended the Marine Corps 2006 Birthday in Quantico. He took the occasion to announce the award. [80] The MOH was presented to Mr. and Mrs. Dunham on January 11, 2007.

Eternal Vigilance and Sacrifice

Showing his MOH case in his den at home. On the wall behind his right shoulder is an artist's rendition of him as a young Marine in uniform wearing the Medal. In the drawing, the triangular *Fighting 4th Marine Division* patch is on his left shoulder and behind him. The drawing was on its way to the Missile Defense Test Site on Kwajalein Atoll.

Veterans Day, with the dedications, commemorations, parades, and gatherings of old friends was always a special day for Rick. The promise of the 2004 holiday was singularly special. The people of the Marshall Islands certainly thought so. Rick had been invited to be their guest of honor.

"He was looking forward to that trip," Milli Sorenson would tell a reporter when the day came. "He said he was determined he was going to go, but we didn't know if he was going to make it." [81]

As a member of the CMOHS, Rick did more than attend meetings, conventions, and reunions. When he was able and not prevented by other obligations, he also attended the funerals of fellow Marine WWII recipients. As Veterans Day 2004 approached, Rick knew that friends he had marched with in parades and joked with at reunions were already guarding the streets on Heaven's scenes.

Of the five 4th MarDiv recipients who had survived WWII, Rick had lived the longest. Justice Marion "Jumping Joe" Chambers had died on July 29, 1982, in Bethesda; Francis Junior Pierce died of cancer on December 21, 1986, in Grand Rapids, Michigan; Joseph Jeremiah McCarthy died in Palm Beach, Florida, on June 15, 1996; and Doug Jacobson had died in Port Charlotte.

Of the thirty Marine Medal recipients who had survived WWII, funerals had been conducted for eighteen others. William George Harrell had died on August 9, 1964, in San Antonio; Carlton Robert Rouh had died on December 8, 1977, in Lindenwold, New Jersey; Anthony Casamento died on July 18, 1987, in Northport, New York; Wilson Douglas Watson died on December 19, 1994, in Russellville, Arkansas; Franklin Earl Sigler died on January 20, 1995, in Montclair, New Jersey; James Lewis Day died on October 28, 1998, in Cathedral City, California; Robert Hugo Dunlap died on March 24, 2000, in Monmouth, Illinois; Joseph Jacob Foss died on January 1, 2003, in Scottsdale, Arizona; Mitchell "Mitch" Paige died on November 15, 2003, in La Quinta, California; and Richard Earl Bush, died on June 7, 2004, in Waukegan, Illinois.

Ten funerals had been conducted at Arlington National Cemetery. Merritt Austin "Red Mike" Edson had died on August 14, 1955, in Washington, D.C.; John Lucian Smith had died on June 10, 1972, in Encino, Los Angeles; Alexander Archer Vandegrift died on May 8, 1973, in Bethesda, Maryland; Luther Skaggs Jr. died on April 6, 1976, in Henderson, Kentucky; Justice Chambers; David Monroe Shoup died on January 13, 1983, in Arlington; John Harold Leims died on June 28, 1985, in Conroe, Texas; Gregory Boyington died on January 11, 1988, in Fresno; and Kenneth Ambrose Walsh died on July 30, 1998, in Santa Ana. Doug Jacobson was the most recent to have full military rites at Arlington.

Each death, eulogy, funeral dirge, and echo of *Taps* was a reminder. Liberty demands eternal vigilance and sacrifice.

His Final Cortege

Nearly sixty years had passed since a newspaper photographer had taken a shot of smiling PFC Sorenson enjoying an ice cream float at the Anoka soda fountain with his brother and sister. Aged 80 years, Rick's mind "was sharp as a tack," and a scoop of ice cream could still brighten his smile.

On Saturday, October 9, 2004, he sat at the table eating ice cream with Milli in Reno. He suddenly collapsed and was gone that fast. He died of a heart attack.

Richard Keith "Rick" Sorenson's obituary was published in the Thursday, October 14, 2004, *Reno Gazette–Journal*. Rick was described as a "loved man, a respected man, a dedicated man, a good man . . . he will be greatly missed." Regarded as a "60-year miracle," having not been expected to survive his MOH actions, his survivors included Mildred; his five children, Robert, Wendy Thorson, Debby Hanaway, James, and Thomas; his seven grandchildren, Joseph, Megan, Brock, Karen, Elizabeth, Bryan and Luke; his brother, William Sorenson of Zimmerman, Minnesota; his sister, M. Carol Atkins of Dassel, Minnesota; his cousin, Virginia Ridge; and numerous other cousins. The old warrior had died before having a chance to know one of his grandsons. Richard "Ricky" Sorenson was born on July 21, 2012. He would hear stories about his grandpa and meet men who had prized his friendship. [82]

There was no doubt in the minds of any in Rick's family that he had led "a successful life as a loving husband, father and grandfather, while also attaining admirable professional achievements."

Unknown to most outside his immediate family, his cremains gave testimony to the blast that had almost killed him in 1944, and to the pains he kept to himself for sixty years. Several pieces of shrapnel emerged in his ashes. [83]

An 11:30 AM memorial service was held for him on Monday, October 18, at Mountain View Mortuary on 425 Stoker Avenue in Reno. A reception followed. His ashes were then flown to Minneapolis for a memorial service at Fort Snelling National Cemetery.

The long funeral cortege turned off 34th Avenue at 12:45 PM on October 26, and entered the cemetery grounds through Gate 2. Section D to the left, where Rick's parents were buried, was familiar to Milli. The cars halted briefly at the assigned Assembly Area, until a cemetery representative led the funeral procession to the Committal Shelter for the 1:00 PM Committal Service.

Richard Allen "Rick" Pittman, 59, introduced himself to the family before the funeral ceremony. He had traveled from Stockton, California, and was wearing a Medal of Honor. "Rick" explained it was his position to be sure to attend funerals of other recipients, just as their father had years before. [84] Of course, he did not talk about his own Medal.

Rick was born in the fertile San Joaquin Valley, at the French Camp county hospital just months before WWII was ended. Military service was part of his heritage. His father had served in the Navy during the war, and several of his uncles were in other branches of the wartime services, including the Marines. Rick was the oldest of five children growing up in Stockton. Both he and a younger brother enlisted in the Marines and fought in Viet Nam.

Despite the childhood blindness in his right eye that had prevented him from enlisting in 1963, Rick enlisted in September 1965. Promoted up to lance corporal, he was a squad leader with India Company, 3d Battalion, 5th Marines. He led his men in various operations near Quảng Nai in Phu Yen Province and in the Song Cau District.

On July 19, 1966, during Operation *Hastings*, a very bloody campaign, Company I left Dong Ha Combat Base on the eastern end of Route 9 and disembarked from helicopters near Cam Lộ. They moved into the region north of the Cua Viet River searching out enemy positions. On July 24, moving along a narrow jungle trail close to the DMZ, the leading platoon walked into an ambush.

Lance Corporal Pittman, 21, immediately put himself in harm's way, disregarding danger, to rescue others. He dropped his rifle, picked up a machine gun and belts of ammunition, left his own platoon in the middle of the advancing column, and rushed forward into a gauntlet of mortar explosions, sniper fire, automatic weapons, and small-arms fire, silencing one position after another with the machine gun. He calmly established an exposed position in the middle of the trail ahead of the dead and wounded Marines. As he assisted the wounded, a platoon-size force of thirty to forty NVA rushed out of the jungle toward him.

He poured out a blistering cover of machine-gun fire into the advancing enemy. His machine gun jammed, and he grabbed an enemy submachine gun from the trail and a pistol from a fallen Marine. He continued firing until he had expended every round of ammunition he had. The enemy withdrew from his relentless defense of comrades as he threw his last grenade in their direction. Having ensured the safe evacuation of wounded comrades, Lance Corporal Pittman returned to his platoon and took up his own rifle again.

He was proud to look out for the family of a fallen fellow Medal holder during the funeral.

✳✳✳

Rick Sorenson was rendered full military honors. After the service his remains were interred in Section B, Grave 149-1, a short walk from the American Flag Pole circle on the west side of Mallon Road and the Avenue of Flags.

Milli understood better than anyone that her husband, like all recipients, seldom talked about the war and his MOH actions. She also was certain how he would like to be remembered. "Once a Marine, always a Marine," she said of him. "People can remember him any way they'd like. I think he just wanted to be remembered as a Marine." [85]

And, a true reflection of both Rick and Milli, the family requested that, in lieu of flowers, donations and memorials could be contributed to the CMOHS Scholarship Fund or the Anoka County Historical Society. Bill and Shirley Sorenson regularly make general donations to the Historical Society.

At the time of Rick's funeral, there were 112 Sorensons buried in Fort Snelling. [86] One reporter believed, because of the single act of bravery he had demonstrated nearly sixty years before, Richard had become the best-known Minnesotan with the Sorenson surname. [87] Listed among the Notable Persons buried in Fort Snelling, he was the second-from-last of nine USMC, Army, and Navy MOH recipients located in the cemetery, five of who had earned their Medals posthumously.

Captain Richard Eugene Fleming, 24, USMC aviator born in St. Paul, is not buried in Fort Snelling. He died on June 5, 1942, during the WWII Battle for Midway when he flew his Vought SB2U-3 *Vindicator* bomber in a screaming dive directly into the enemy cruiser *Mikuma's* after-turret. His remains were not recovered, assumed to have gone down with the *Mikuma* when it sank the next afternoon. Captain Fleming has a memorial grave in Assembly Area 3 (F-1).

Eight Marines from WWII continued to wear the Medal of Honor. Jefferson Joseph Deblanc residing in Lafayette, Louisiana, Robert Edward Galer in Dallas, Arthur J. Jackson in Boise, Idaho, Jacklyn Harrell Lucas in Hattiesburg, Mississippi, Everett Parker Pope in Bath, Maine, James Elms Swett, in Redding, California, Hershel Woodrow Williams in Fairmont, West Virginia, and Louis Hugh Wilson Jr. in Birmingham, Alabama, said their prayers and goodbyes for Rick. Today, Arthur J. Jackson, 92, and Hershel "Woody" Williams, 93, remain alive.

Enduring Tributes

Thursday, November 11, 2004 was Veterans Day. U.S. Army Lieutenant Colonel Anne Daugherty was in command at the Ronald Reagan Ballistic Missile Defense Test Site on Kwajalein Atoll. She had for months been planning a Veterans Day parade and a special ceremony in honor of Rick Sorenson, hoping to have him present for the christening of a boat. When LtCol Daugherty learned of his death, she arranged for his widow and five children to attend in his place. The invitation was an unexpected honor.

Milli and her children were flown to Kwajalein on November 10, the day Marines across the world gathered to celebrate the Corps' gallant history and its 229th birthday. When the plane landed at Bucholz Army Airfield and pulled into the chocks, the other 100 plus passengers were asked to stay seated while the "Honored Guests" departed. That was only one of the many surprises and unimagined honors extended to the family. As they departed the plane a band played, and a U.S. Marine Honor Guard waited to welcome them. [88]

"The kindness and honor bestowed on us was a very emotional experience!" That is how Jim Sorenson would remember the days on the atoll. "It was an incredible honor. . . . That privileged visit remains one of the highlights of my life!"

On Thursday, the Sorensons were escorted to a vehicle. The Marine Color Guard led the parade down Lagoon Road to the Marine Department where the dedication took place. Crowds lined the streets cheering as the procession made its way to the Kwajalein boat dock. Like their father, and like so many adult children of Medal recipients, the five were humble—ordinary people, nothing overly special about them, connected only by their father. The cheering and being honored by so many was embarrassing.

"We felt guilty to even be there without our father."

Ronald "Bull" Hall, commander of the Kwajalein American Legion Post 44, was the keynote speaker at the ceremony. [89] The WWII veteran understood the importance of the day and the tribute to follow. "Our freedom did not come easy," he said. "We shall never take our veterans for granted and are forever thankful to them and to those who serve today."

Then, Milli, with LtCol Daugherty's assistance, smashed a champagne bottle against a ceremonial boat bow, thus christening the Pvt. Richard K. Sorenson Catamaran (FB 224). A tribute to the hero who risked his life in 1944 on Namur Island, hurling himself onto a live grenade and saving his fellow Marines, is displayed inside the actual catamaran.

"The christening was overwhelming," Milli acknowledged. "It's the nicest thing that's ever happened to me and my family."

Rick and Milli's daughter agreed. "Kwajalein was so special to him—not so much because of what he did—but the sacrifices of everyone else," Wendy Thorson said. "He'd be very honored. It's sad that he's not here, but he's always here in spirit."

On Friday, Rick's widow and five children took the fifty-mile flight to the other end of the atoll and walked on the soil where he had shed his blood and so many Marines had given their lives.

"We were flown north to Roi–Namur where we landed and were given a VIP tour of the islands," Jim recalled. "We marveled at the many remaining structures that were to be seen there. All four recipients have memorials on the island. The most touching for us was when we were shown where the event actually took place for my father—a small green grassy area that appeared so peaceful. One could never imagine the horror of war that existed there so many years before. Now it appeared to just be another pretty view on a paradise island. We were actually able to see and stand where he smothered the grenade those many years ago! It was an incredibly emotional and heart stirring event. How we wished that we could have shared that moment with our father, but I did feel his spirit there with us and thanked him for what he did. . . . for what all of our servicemen did for us, not only at Kwajalein, but throughout the war."

Jim asked his mother about the three grenade fragments that had nearly taken his father's life on Namur. Rick had promised one to him. Along with his father's Purple Heart, Jim keeps the fragment as a much-cherished memento. [90]

"Word has been received that Richard passed away on October 9, 2004." As news of Rick's death spread, Milli received condolences from friends around the nation. Veteran newsletters continued to print columns. For the surviving members of Marine Bombing Squadron Six-Thirteen Association who had met him in 1994 at the 50th Anniversary of the Kwajalein Atoll invasion, his passing was announced in their January 4, 2005, monthly newsletter. [91]

The public was invited to attend a special ceremony at 10:00 AM on Veterans Day, November 11, 2006, at the Medal of Honor monument in Fort Snelling National Cemetery. Reverend Dr. Kenneth Beale Jr., Chaplain of the Fort Snelling Memorial Chapel was the speaker. The Memorial Rifle Squad and Bugles Across America members performed Honors and *Taps* in recognition of the last two MOH recipients to be buried in the cemetery—Rick Sorenson and Army Second Lieutenant Donald Eugene Rudolph Sr., who had passed away on May 25, 2006. Both had their names inscribed on the Medal of Honor monument.

Today, each of the nine recipients has a plaque at the Medal of Honor Memorial Circle in the center of the cemetery on Kraus Avenue describing the gallantry and service that earned the Medal. Seven cemetery avenues are named for recipients. Sorenson Drive is on the cemetery's south side looking over Interstate Highway 494.

Milli Sorenson understood how the VA system operated and how veterans with war injuries often resist applying for benefits, compensation, or pensions due them for their service. One of those was her brother-in-law, who had been having trouble with his feet for quite a while—he had no feeling in his feet, all the time. They started swelling. In fact, he had no feeling in his legs up to mid-thigh. Sometimes he would stumble or lose his balance.

"Cuz you don't have any feeling down there," Bill Sorenson would say. "You don't know where you are." [92]

Milli was sure it went back to the Chosin Reservoir. She kept after him, as she knew Rick would have been doing.

"Get in there," she would insist. "Go in there."

"By the time they give me something," Bill would protest, "I'll be dead."

Bill was a member of the Chosin Few Association and read *The Chosin News*. The newsletter listed things that were going on with the guys that had been up there in the Reservoir. The Association was advising Chosin survivors with any of the conditions noted to go in to the VA and make a claim. Bill started thinking about his feet, but was not inclined to go to the VA. It was not so bad, not like the survivors who had been terribly wounded. He did have to admit that Milli and *The Chosin News* agreed that he was entitled to compensation for a combat-related disability.

Finally, in 2007, he went down to the VA hospital and filed a claim for having no feeling in his feet. He was 80 years old and could not remember when it started, but it had been a while back. Bill returned for a physical.

The nurse examined his legs. He did not know that the girl had a big pin. She was sticking him all the time during the exam, and he never felt it. "You know," she said, "you really don't have any feeling in those legs, do you?"

"No, I don't," he answered. So, the VA gave him compensation for the health impairments incurred because he fought at *The Chosin*.

On Thursday night before the September 8, 2011 *Tornadoes* home-opening football game against Andover, Anoka area residents began to assemble at the high school auditorium on 3939 7th Avenue North. [93] The school had established a Hall of Fame and, at 6:00 PM inducted the inaugural class of twenty-four illustrious alumni. A reception followed in the cafeteria. Tables dedicated to each inductee were on display, decorated in a way to represent the individual. The event was free and open to the public.

There was no table dedicated to Rick Sorenson, because he was not one of the alumni selected, but the weeks of publicity about the Hall of Fame had rekindled interest in his remarkable heroics. Milli was staying with Robert in the Cities and was out to visit Richard's grave at Fort Snelling. Paul Levy of the *Star Tribune* talked to her about Anoka's MOH son. [94]

Rick's memory reverberated in the community. Three years later, on September 11, 2014, four more distinguished athletes and one coach were inducted into the Anoka High School Hall of Fame. Medal of Honor recipient Richard K. Sorenson was one of the inductees in this second class of alumni to be recognized. The formal ceremony repeated the events of the 2011 induction. [95]

On Thursday, November 10, 2011, the Marines celebrated their 236th year. The next day was the national celebration of Veterans Day. Both days were just two of many days when Rick is in the thoughts of the Sorenson generations. Karen Rosemary Sorenson would say so.

Rick's granddaughter is an illustrator who loves life and art. Early on Friday morning, she posted a tribute to her Grandpa on her blogspot, including photos, his Medal Citation, and links to more information about him. "Today I wanted to thank and honor my Grandpa. . . . Thank you, Grandpa! I love and miss you." Karen. [96]

Cousin Jennifer, "The Alchemist," added her comment hours later. "That is a great story, and a great legacy to have in your family. Thanks so much for sharing."

Milli continued her dedication to the Anoka County Historical Society, sending a generous donation to the ACHS in early 2013. The Society printed a Thank You to her in its spring newsletter. [97]

2015

Beginning on February 7, 2015, the first Saturday of the month, members of the North Mankato American Legion Post 518 gathered at 10:00 AM for a Flag ceremony to pay a month-long tribute to Marine Master Sergeant Richard Keith Sorenson, a deceased veteran, as their new Veteran of the Month honoree. The Flag already flying was retired and the honoree's new flag was unfolded, raised in MSG Sorenson's honor, and flown for the next month. A short biographical tribute was read, then, placed in a display stand in front of the flagpole.

"The Flag flying from this site is flown in honor of USMC MSG Richard Keith Sorenson from February 7, 2015 to March 7, 2015, by North Mankato American Legion Post 518." At the March 7 ceremony, the colors were lowered, folded, and retained for the Sorenson family. [98]

In April 2015, Lisa LaCasse, City of Anoka Parks Recreation Supervisor, on behalf of the Park Board, sent a request to the Heritage Preservation Commission (HPC) for input about possibly replacing the plaque at Rick Sorenson Park. The HPC met at Anoka City Hall on Tuesday, May 12 to consider this New Business. The proposal was discussed at several meetings.

The commissioners recognized that not every city has a MOH recipient like Rick Sorenson and agreed that the current plaque at the park two blocks from the home in which he had grown up was not noticeable. First, they decided to replace the "very generic" plaque with a new 16"x20" cast bronze plaque with text and photo of Rick. The new plaque was to be a replica of the one at the foot of his statue in the Veterans Memorial Park, was to stand upright on a post, and was to be placed in a prominent place at the park. [99]

Drawing Inspiration From Incredible Stories

In 2009, Minnesota Statutes, Chapter 10, Section 1, 10.575, passed into law. March 25 would thereafter be observed as *Medal of Honor Day* in honor of the seventy-two Minnesotans who had received the Medal. The day was designated to reflect that March 25, 1863, was the first date the Medal was presented. Since that date up to December 20, 2016, a total of 3,498 Medals had been awarded. Each year, beginning in 2010, the Minnesota governor was to issue a proclamation to honor the observance. The day would be a statewide opportunity to remember inspiring heroism.

The words ordinary and extraordinary and incredible often come naturally to mind when telling any story of a Medal recipient. Thomas Jerome Hudner Jr., U.S. Navy MOH recipient, Korea, expressed his own thoughts about this. "The Medal of Honor is proof that ordinary men and women have within them the potential to challenge fate and literally change the course of history. It only requires the courage to try." [100]

When Thomas Gunning Kelley, USN MOH recipient, Republic of Vietnam, took the CMOHS president's position in early 2015, he wanted young people to share the bond and patriotism that the Medal represents. "They need to know that ordinary people are capable of extraordinary things," he has said. "Part of our mission is to foster patriotism and to inspire our youth to be better citizens of our country."

The CMOHS Foundation, building on these principles, established a legacy project—the Character Development Program—with a curriculum promoting the ideology that "everyone has the capacity to be a hero and the courage to do the right thing."

At least eighteen Minnesota recipients entered the service at Minneapolis, Fort Snelling, or St. Paul. Eleven recipients were either born or raised in Minneapolis–St. Paul. It is incredible that Rick Sorenson, Rich Kraus, and Jim LaBelle, teenage Marines, earned Medals saving others from grenades in WWII. Just as extraordinary is that four U.S. Army enlisted men who had either been born in or entered the service at Minneapolis also threw themselves on grenades, absorbing the full and fatal impact of the explosions to protect the lives of soldiers in Viet Nam: Specialist Fourth Class Michael Blanchfield, 19, Specialist Fourth Class Kenneth Olson, 22, Staff Sergeant Laszlo Rabel, 29, and Specialist Fourth Class Dale Wayrynen, 20 years old.

The CMOHS holds its annual, multi-day convention and general meeting to strengthen the bond of brotherhood and camaraderie among the living recipients. Additionally, the members meet to reverently and respectfully remember the men whose awards were posthumous and the recipients, like Rick Sorenson, who are now deceased. At their convention, the Society endeavors to inspire school students and to recognize patriotic citizens whose lives have promoted and perpetuated American principles.

One focus of their meeting agenda is the selection of the host communities for future conventions.

The Twin Cities submitted a bid to be the 2016 Convention site. Liz Dapp was the chairwoman of the MOH Twin Cities Executive Committee. Representative Bob Dettmer, Chairman of the Minnesota House of Representatives Veterans Committee, and Larry Shellito, Commissioner of the Minnesota Department of Veterans Affairs, assisted in the efforts. On March 26, 2015, the Minnesota House of Representatives GOP Communications section began circulating the News Release that the CMOHS had selected Minneapolis–St. Paul to host the 2016 CMOH Convention for the first time. Thomas Kelley officially announced the selection on February 17, 2016, for the October 4–8 gathering.

Liz Dapp spoke for all Minneapolis–St. Paul citizens. "Hosting the Medal of Honor Convention in the Twin Cities is a once-in-a-lifetime opportunity for our community to recognize our nation's greatest heroes and draw inspiration from their incredible stories." [101]

Various Twin Cities committees got busy raising sponsorship funds and planning a wide range of public and private events, including fourteen school visits, memorial services, meet-and-greets, and concerts.

June R. Anderson, Laura Gallup, and Cindy Jorgenrud, of the Anoka Chapter of the Daughters of the American Revolution (DAR), decided to write biographies of the local Minnesota MOH recipients. When they had completed nine biographies, June suggested that they collect biographies of all seventy-two state recipients and collect them in a book for the October CMOHS convention. The finished book, *Minnesota Medal of Honor Recipients From the Civil War to Vietnam*, was published in September in time for the memorial dedication and convention. [102]

Coinciding with the convention, Governor Mark Dayton officially proclaimed Thursday, October 6, as Private First Class James D. LaBelle Day.

Of the seventy-seven living recipients, forty-one could attend the convention. The events began on Monday, October 3, with aircraft flyovers, reenactors, and music during a ceremony at the main entrance of the State Capitol Mall. Since the main CMOHS convention was several days away, only a percentage of Medal recipients were at the dedication.

The recipients attended the dedication and groundbreaking of the new Minnesota Medal of Honor Memorial to be incorporated into the 1958 Promise of Youth bronze sculpture and reflecting pool at the St. Paul Veteran's Services Building. The memorial is one more location for Americans to remember the service and sacrifices of Richard K. Sorenson, Richard E. Kraus, and James D. LaBelle.

Robert Sorenson understands the impact his father has had on his life. Rick had taught him about responsibility and hard work and devoting a part of his life to his community. Following the example of his father, Bob has found being on boards and being involved in the community to be rewarding in his own life. He was pleased to be invited to the dedication ceremony at the State Capitol. Channel 5 interviewed him in great detail just before the ceremony. [103]

Across the years, Bob had met many of his father's comrades at conventions, reunions, and funerals. He had met Rick Pittman at his father's funeral ceremony and looked forward to meeting him again. He was also looking forward to seeing some of the recipients who had become his personal friends. Sadly for Bob, most of those had passed away in the few years leading up to the Minneapolis–St. Paul convention.

When he looked about the VIP section, he was the only son or daughter of a recipient to attend. The other people were more distant relatives of recipients. Bob was surprised that his uncle, Bill Sorenson, had not received an invitation. He did recognize a few of the recipients. One had been his father's very close friend.

After the ceremony, Bob and Barney Barnum renewed their friendship. Naturally, Barney reminded him how he and his father had always enjoyed smoking cigars together. Bob introduced Barney to his wife, Dewi, and their four-year-old son, Richard "Ricky" Sorenson. Talking for a while, the adults had a good laugh caught on camera by two television stations.

"Call me Uncle Barney," said the Medal recipient to Rick's grandson.

"You're not, Barney," the astute young boy corrected the old guy. Ricky knew full well that Barney was the purple dinosaur on television, and Barney Barnum was in no way purple.

The moment sealed a new friendship between Ricky and Barney. Unknown to the Sorensons, the television stations filmed Barney holding the boy, and the two of them playing together. Channel 5 had a special segment on the evening news about the ceremony and Richard Sorenson, MOH recipient. The piece included Robert's interview, old photos, the bronze memorial statue, facts about Richard, a view of his Fort Snelling National Cemetery gravesite, and footage of his grandson frolicking with Barney Barnum.

The entire day serves as an example of how one man's bravery can have an influence on his family, the greater community, the nation, and the generations that will never have a chance to know him personally. Having seen a friendship begin between a Medal holder and his son, the day left its impression on Robert.

"This was a special day in my life to attend the ceremony at the capitol!"

A ceremony was held on Wednesday at the new U.S. Bank Stadium. Patriot Guard Riders held flags providing a path for the recipients to take the stage. Governor Dayton welcomed the heroes to Minnesota. An autograph session followed.

On Thursday morning, Columbia Heights Public Schools dedicated a memorial plaque and flagpole to James D. LaBelle in front of the Columbia Heights *Hylander* Center. Thomas Kelley and Hal Fritz, Medal recipients, attended the unveiling and visited with students at Highland Elementary School and Columbia Heights High School. U.S. Senator Amy Klobuchar, CMOHS Foundation President Ron Rand, and Vice President of Education Cathy Metcalf also attended the ceremony.

Jim's two younger sisters, Mary Lou Steiner and Elaine Lauer, were pleased with the monument honoring their late brother. Mary Lou acknowledged that a lot of recognition had been extended to her brother over the years. She thought the new memorial was the family's favorite. "After all these years, we were surprised," she said. "LaBelle Park and all those other things, but this is really something."

Like their brother, the sisters were humble about adulation. "I don't know if he would've liked all this attention," Mary Lou guessed. "That's just the way he was—that's how we all are."

Columbia Heights City held a flagpole rededication ceremony at LaBelle Park on Friday.

The CMOHS Convention concluded with the Patriot Awards Gala at the Minneapolis Convention Center: a black-tie affair that upwards of 2,000 guests attended on Saturday evening.

The Sorenson generations, Anoka, and Minneapolis–St. Paul have every reason to be proud. They have provided examples of bravery's legacies and how important it is to remember and honor heroism. Any community that can claim just one Medal recipient as one of their own has a native model for what "ordinary" men and women can achieve.

On Thursday evening, October 13, 2016, five days after most had departed from Minneapolis–St. Paul, the Medal recipients began receiving phone calls. Their comrade and brother-in arms, Richard Allan Pittman, aged 71, from Stockton, San Joaquin County, California—an ordinary and brave man who had earned a Medal of Honor as a Marine Lance Corporal serving near the Demilitarized Zone in the Republic of Vietnam—had passed away.

Seventy-six Medal of Honor recipients remained alive.

CHAPTER 11

The Hero Of Peleliu

✳✳✳

"For war is man's matter, and mine above all others
of them that have been born in Ilium." [1]

— HOMER, *THE ILIAD*

THE HIGHEST CASUALTY RATE OF any American amphibious invasion during the Pacific War, in terms of men and material, took place on Peleliu. Although it was a Marine victory, historians continue to debate its strategic purpose. Like the dispute about America's use of atomic bombs over Japan, some commentators insist that the assault on Peleliu was unnecessary and highest command's tragic, if not arrogant, blunder. Other historians argue that the capture of the island, while unquestionably terrible, was an unavoidable inevitability in the destruction of the Empire's military might.

Eight Marines earned Medals of Honor on Peleliu. Corporal Lewis Kenneth Bausell, 1st Battalion, 5th Marines, was the first on September 15, 1944. He died on top of a grenade on Beach Orange 1. First Lieutenant Carlton Robert Rouh, 1st Battalion, 5th Marines, smothered a grenade blast before evening on the same day. Three days into the battle, on September 18, the valorous actions of Private First Class Arthur J. Jackson, 3d Battalion, 7th Marines, and Captain Everett Parker Pope, Company C, 1st Battalion, 1st Marines, earned them Medals. Private First Class Charles Howard Roan, 2d Battalion, 7th Marines, earned his posthumous Medal saving others from a grenade. The last three Medals were awarded posthumously to privates first class for absorbing the full blast of hand grenades to ensure the survival of comrades: John Dury New, 2d Battalion, 7th Marines, on September 25; Wesley Phelps, 3d Battalion, 7th Marines, on October 4; and Richard Edward Kraus, 8th Amphibious Tractor Battalion, on October 5.

The Battle of Peleliu was fought more than seventy years ago. Most Americans today would not relate mention of the island to a bloody WWII confrontation. Anyone reading a book about the battle will learn much about heroism, and might or might not be introduced to First Lieutenant Rouh.

Eugene Bondurant "Sledgehammer" Sledge was a private first class when he fought on the coral island with Company K, 3d Battalion, 5th Marines. He survived the battle and wrote a memoir of the events involving King Company and *the Old Breed*. His only reference to a Medal of Honor was his view that 3d Battalion Commander Lieutenant Colonel Lewis Walt should have been presented that Award for his actions on the night of D-Day, September 15. [2] More recently, Bill Sloan wrote about the *Marines at Peleliu*. He mentioned that 1stLt Rouh was one of the six Marines on Peleliu to throw "himself on top of an exploding grenade to save the lives of his comrades." [3]

When James H. Hallas introduced his readers to 1stLt Rouh in his account of the assault on Peleliu, he elaborated on the details described in the lieutenant's Medal Citation. [4]

One thing about Carlton Rouh is that he was a pragmatist. He solved problems as situations presented themselves. When the country called for men, he enlisted. When it rained, he slogged through the mud. When he was responsible for men, he protected them. He had been that way since boyhood. He was probably an apple that did not fall far from the family tree.

The Middle Boy

Charles Francois Rouh (1875) was a boy from Delaware. [5] His ancestors were French, and the spelling of his family name had changed from Roux to Rauh and, finally, to Rouh. In 1899, he married Amelia Charlotte Heine (May 1877) and relocated to Precinct 2, City Ward 8, Camden County, New Jersey. By the time of the 1900 U.S. Census, the couple had one baby girl, Etta B., born in March. Over the next eight years they added two more girls and two boys to the family: Charles S. "Chas" (1903), Anna H. "Anny" (1904), Florence A. (1905), and Ellwood P. (1908).

The growing family lived on the corner of Broadway and Ferry Avenue, a half mile from the Delaware River and a few blocks up from James P. Croker's Tammany House, a social club. Amelia enjoyed a pleasant Thanksgiving Day with the family on November 24, 1910, but began feeling a discomfort late into the evening. She died suddenly of acute indigestion on Friday. Her funeral was held in the family home on Tuesday, and she was buried in Evergreen Cemetery. [6] Charles was a widower with five children between 2 and 10 years old.

Charles married Adelheith Muller (1885), and they had three sons. Carlton Robert Rouh, born on May 11, 1919, was in the middle of the boys, between Howard (1913) and Russell H. (1922). [7] At the time of the 1920 U.S. Census, Adele was caring for five step children and two of her own boys.

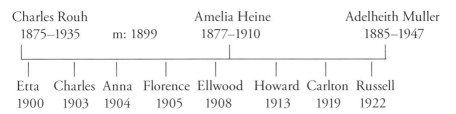

A month before Carlton's 10th birthday, the Borough of Lindenwold was created from Clementon Township, Camden County, First Congressional District, 4th Legislative District. The borough would have a place in his heart for his entire lifetime. Later, so would the politics of the municipality.

The Rouh family resided at Maple and Carlton Avenue, on the east side of the railroad line. Carlton could look through the tree line on Berlin Road and see Fire Hall No. 1 a block away.

When the 1930 Census takers knocked on Charles and Adele's front door, only the three younger boys resided with them. Etta had married one of the Dawson boys. Anny had married Henry Gerbing and lived with his mother in Oaklyn. Florence had married John Graham, and Ellwood was living with them.

Carlton was an outgoing boy, made friends easily, and acquired nicknames. His school friends called him "Rouby." Later friends liked to call him "Cobber." Phyllis Lorraine Rowand was one of his grammar school playmates—a pretty girl who happened to be three months older than he. [8] The Rouhs and Rowands spent a lot of time together. One branch of the extended Rowand family operated a prosperous charcoal mill and grocery store in Clementon.

Phyllis was born on February 23, 1919, the daughter and eighth child of Wallace Pratt and Hannah (Shearwood) Rowand. Hannah had many sorrows, and Phyllis did not get to know all her older siblings. Two had died in childhood before Phyllis was born. John Albert lived only four months in 1912–1913. Alice Irwin died on March 6, 1918, one day after her birth. By the time Phyllis was forming recollections of family life, her two older sisters, Florence May and Eleanor Ida, were already teenagers. When Phyllis started off to grammar school, Florence had married Edward Thompson. Eleanor, W. Grant, Ernest, and LeRoy were all in grades ahead of Phyllis.

After six years of being the baby of the family, Phyllis became an older sister to Herbert Murray, born in 1925. The next year, Hannah and the family were rocked with anguish before the school year ended. Eleanor Ida, 18 years old, died on Thursday, May 6, 1926. Phyllis was then the only girl in the house with her mother, and she would develop a keen sense of taking care of others.

Carlton and Phyllis often found time to play outdoors, ice-skating at Pine Lake and roller-skating outside Fire Hall No. 1, up at East Linden Avenue and Berlin Road. On summer evenings, they gathered with other kids at the corner of Chestnut Avenue and Hawthorne Street—an intersection of four tree-lined blocks of homes—and played outdoor games like hide-and-seek and lie low sheepie (another variation of hiding and seeking which involved captains and teams) until 9:00 PM. Then the parents stepped out onto front porches and blew whistles to signal the time for the neighborhood kids to come home. [9]

Carlton was bigger than the others his age and would grow to be 6 feet 4 inches and 260 pounds. In fall 1933, he started attending Haddon Heights High School with the Class of 1937. Football was his activity, and he played all four years.

In his second season with the *Garnet* gridmen, he was one of twenty-nine players. The team faced eight opponents and "had a most successful season on the gridiron." All but two of the games were close matches, including victories over Mt. Holly, Palmyra, and Audubon. The "big thrill" of the season was ending Audubon's twenty-four-game winning streak, defeating the Group Three Conference champions. There was a scoreless tie to Camden County Vocational and losses to Cape May and Haddonfield. Mooreston and Woodbury gave them shellackings. Despite the 3–4–1 record, the team had not had such success since 1927. [10]

Charles F. Rouh, aged 60, died in 1935. Phyllis stood beside Carlton at the gravesite as his father was lowered into the ground at Berlin Cemetery. After the service, the two teenage friends went to the Rowand plot in the cemetery to visit Eleanor, John, and Alice's graves.

Legendary Coach George "Cap" Baker took over the football team in Carlton's junior year and the team's fortunes changed. [11] A fighting spirit and teamwork became evident among the forty-nine teammates. "Rouhey," wearing #85, and Tim Gerngross began sharing duties at left end. The days of shellackings had ended.

Going into the last game against Haddonfield, played at home on Thanksgiving Day, the *Garnets* had a chance for the Group Three championship. They had defeated Mt. Holly, Palmyra, Mooreston, Camden Vocational, Woodrow Wilson, and Audubon. Only Woodbury had been able to stand up to their fury and beat them at home, 20–0. The final game was a slugfest to the end. The *Bulldawgs* eked out a victory, 6–2, cheating the Heights of their conference championship run.

The summer before his senior year, rather than taking things easy, Carlton did what he could to get himself in shape for his last football season. He took a seventy-five-mile ride up to the National Guard camp at Sea Girt on New Jersey's coast. [12] The extra efforts paid off. "Rouhey" was the starting left end for the season opener against Mt. Holly on Saturday afternoon, September 26, 1936. One of the finest football records ever made by a Heights grid team was ahead. Phyllis cheered him on.

Only four of the starters had lettered in the previous season. Coach Baker schooled forty inexperienced players, and the team went out onto the gridirons and shut out five opposing offences. Only four touchdowns were scored against the *Garnets'* defense. The record crowds that witnessed the contests would long remember the team's victories over two of their annual rivals, Audubon and Haddonfield. Their only loss was a close one, 0–14, to Woodbury, the 1936 Group Three champs. The Heights team tied for second place in the conference. [13]

Letterman Rouh is on the left end, second row, facing the photographer.

Carlton earned a *Garnets* sweater and letter. Having gone above and beyond to ready himself to capture a starting position and learning team play, an instinct for protecting quarterbacks, blocking for running backs, and knocking opponents to the ground had emerged.

Along with his senior year photo in the *1937 The Garneteer Yearbook*, "Rouhey" was described as "A laughing, happy-go-lucky slave to football (and women)." Various classmates looked forward to attending Penn State, Virginia State, and Dexel Institute. He was undecided about his post-graduation plans. [14]

"There's a Small Hotel" [15]

Richard Rodgers had composed a melody and Lorenz Hart had written the lyrics about a get-away place where a person might go if he needed a laugh or two, where funny people could have fun, and where a couple could share one bright and neat room together. Doris Carson and Ray Bolger were the first to perform the popular verses. The chatter on Broadway was that Richard had been inspired to write the song while visiting the Stockton Borough Inn on the Delaware River in northwest New Jersey.

When Carlton's friends dropped in for a little camaraderie, they might have toasted "Rouhey" with a nice rendition of "'Good night, sleep well,' We'll thank the small hotel together."

Howard, Carlton's next older brother, had completed four years of college and was starting out in the hotel and restaurant management profession. [16] After graduating from high school, Carlton, 18, went to work at the Hotel Linden, on the edge of town. With twenty-one rooms and a bar-and-sandwich counter, it was not a luxury place, but it provided earnings for all four of the Rouh boys to help support their widowed mother. [17]

Carlton worked as a manager at the hotel. Those in authority recognized that he could be put in charge, and things would get done. He was big, serious-minded, soft talking, and practical. His brothers would add that he could be hard headed. He wore an apron, handy man's overalls, bookkeeper's green eyeshade that did little to conceal the black, shining eyes of his French ancestors, a manager's felt hat over his black hair, and a worried look when he took money to the bank. He developed a keen and deep sense of responsibility for the job, the place, and for the employees.

Careful with his money, Carlton looked to have a bright future. He imagined that in the years ahead, he would have a family to scratch up food for, a house and icebox, and an automobile pretty nearly paid off. [18]

He and Phyllis returned to Berlin Cemetery in the winter of 1940. Hannah Rowand died on February 18, 1940, and was buried with three of her children. Phyllis celebrated her 21st birthday five days later. She had almost completed her nurse training.

Carlton had to postpone decisions about marriage and family. President Roosevelt, with his eye on the war in Europe, knew that America's military forces were undermanned. Anticipating what was ahead, he signed the first peacetime selective service draft in U.S. history. Notices went out to municipal Draft Board offices on October 16, 1940. All men between 21 to 31 years residing in the United States were to report to pick up a draft registration card for possible selection into the armed service. That meant "Rouhey," who had had his 21st birthday in May.

Carlton's younger brother, Russell, had finished four years of high school and briefly went to work. He went over to Fort Dix four months after his 19th birthday and finished the paper work for voluntary enlistment in the U.S. Army Infantry on June 18, 1941. He would rise in rank to Staff Sergeant.

Brotherhood and joining in the fraternity of like-minded men were big parts of Carlton's life. On April 28, 1941, he joined Carpenters Local 8 of Philadelphia. He had enjoyed his initiation into this Brotherhood for eight months when he considered joining another one.

"When the war came on December 7, 1941, it was a game where everybody in the country was dealt a hand, and from then on you play your hand." That was Carlton's view. The hand dealt to many was enlisting in the Armed Forces rather than waiting for a draft notice.

From a strategy point of view, the Japanese attack at Pearl Harbor served as a diversion. Tokyo had ordered an invasion fleet to attack and seize Wake Island in the western Pacific Ocean, 2,000 miles southeast of the Empire's mainland. Wake was a coral atoll consisting of three small islets east of Guam and west of Honolulu. Two hundred and forty Marines were garrisoned on the island to provide security for Wake's military base and the Pan Am air facility.

The Wake attack began on December 8, and the outnumbered, besieged Marines fought from bunkers, trenches, foxholes, and sandbagged machine-gun and artillery emplacements. For fifteen days, Carlton listened to dismal news broadcasts about Wake. News correspondents began referring to the heroic defense of the island garrison as the *Alamo of the South Pacific.* [19]

Overwhelmed by enemy forces, the defenders of Wake surrendered on December 23, 1941. Forty-seven Marines had been killed in action, and two were missing in action. Twenty-three of the dead were aviation personnel. All twelve VMF-211's F4F-3 *Wildcat* planes had been destroyed. At least 433 servicemen were captured and taken to POW camps. The invaders executed five prisoners on the island. Another fifteen died in the camps.

With one son already in the military ranks, Adelheith Rouh, 56, fretted about the war. All three of her boys would leave home to serve. Carlton enlisted in the Marine Corps (Service No. 351122) in January 1942, one month after Pearl Harbor and Wake. Howard, her eldest son, would enlist on September 3, 1943.

Phyllis Rowand went to the closest American Red Cross station responsible for recruiting nurses for the Army Nurse Corps and joined up. She was commissioned as a second lieutenant. Six months after the Japanese bombed Pearl Harbor, she was one of the 12,000 nurses on duty in the Nurse Corps. Most of the ladies had no previous military experience. Phyllis' younger brother, Herbert Murray Rowand, went into the U.S. Navy and reached a rank of Motor Machinist's Mate 3rd Class Petty Officer.

Another draft registration was ordered after the Pearl Harbor and Wake Island attacks. All men ages 20–21 and 35–44 were called to report to their draft boards on February 16, 1942. WWII ration stamps became a form of subsistence for American families.

CHAPTER 12

Joining the Leathernecks

***

"For after all, the best thing one can do
When it is raining is to let it rain." [1]

— HENRY WADSWORTH LONGFELLOW

HE WAS A BUCK PRIVATE, at the bottom. All the ranks above him made it clear, "many times in a nasty way," that his job was to worry about what was between his shoelaces and his hair comb, and they would worry about all the rest. He had been a manager, the boss, for too many years not to make problems and solutions his business. He adjusted to taking orders, but his propensity for leadership was going to become evident. [2]

After his training, Private Rouh departed the States in late May 1942, assigned to Company M, 3d Battalion, Fifth Marine Regiment, 1st Marine Division. He left with a gift knife Russell had given him. It had a walnut handle and was the most beautiful knife he had ever seen in his life. He carried it everywhere.

The convoy of ships was sailing to the South Pacific for what historians would call the First American Offensive against Imperial Japan's forces. Most of the embarked 1st Division, including Pvt Rouh, were inexperienced infantrymen.

The news that the U.S. Navy had scored a crucial and decisive victory at the Battle of Midway in the Pacific, June 3–7, signaled that the Japanese forces were not invincible.

The 5th Marines reached Wellington, New Zealand, in mid-June. Having sailed from California with a stop in Hawaii, the June weather on the lower tip of the North Island came as a surprise to the arriving troops. June is autumn and typically brings more rain and the hint of snow. Temperatures ranged between 46°F and 54°F, and the chance of rain was 58% on any day. Wind and gales were a constant from either the Tasman Sea or the South Pacific Ocean.

The invasion date was set, and the pace of operations on Wellington's docks intensified. The combat troops, tasked to unload, then, reload the cargo ships, replaced civilian stevedores. Private Rouh joined in the round-the-clock working parties. The rainstorms slowed the momentum, but never stopped the work. The convoy pulled up anchor, and Pvt Rouh readied himself for another eleven-day cruise.

In his mind, he had made the war his business for the time being. If he made good at it, he would get what he wanted, which was to return home with as little time wasted out of his life as possible. [3]

The armada, with its screen of carriers, sailed 1,400 nautical miles north, reaching tiny Koro Island amid the Fiji Islands on July 26. The amphibious forces practiced landings for two days. Actually, they exercised riding in the landing craft, since the reefs around Koro prevented actual beach landing trials.

The Operation *Watchtower* invasion force sailed from the Fijis on July 28, making a nine-day feint, as if headed for Australia. B-17s began a bombardment of their intended destination on August 1. From the railings of their troop ships, the 1st Division Marines bantered among themselves as the convoy turned north at 12:00 PM on August 5, headed for the Solomon Islands and the sizeable forward enemy outposts on Tulagi and Guadalcanal. They were determined to avenge the fates of their brothers at Pearl Harbor, on Wake Island, and at Midway.

During the night of August 6–7, the assault force, under cover of heavy clouds and dense rain, slipped from the west into the channel between Cape Esperance and Savo Island. When the moon came out later, the Marines could see the silhouettes of the islands. The Japanese had not detected the convoy's approach.

Private Rouh was up well before dawn and on deck of the assault ship on Friday morning, D-Day, August 7, waiting to climb down the rope ladders to the bobbing landing craft. At 6:13 AM, the heavy cruiser USS *Quincy* (CA-39) began shelling the northern landing beaches on Guadalcanal. The signal to "land the landing force" went out to the ships at 6:41 AM. The sun came up nine minutes later. Colonel LeRoy P. Hunt's 5th Marines chugged into their formations. Private Rouh was on the left flank in front of Red Beach with the 3d Battalion.

The pre-assault naval gunfire shelling and the sight of the ships offshore left no doubt in the minds of the unprepared Japanese defenders what was being unleashed upon them. They fled west into the island's interior jungles.

Before the landing craft lurched forward from the line of departure, Pvt Rouh convinced his lieutenant, a Harvard graduate, that the men could clear the beach with the ammunition in their belts and come back to the boats to get the spare ammunition cases, rather than chance each man carrying a case on his shoulder as he waded to the beach. [4]

The old-style landing craft did not have the hinged front ramps that dropped forward, so the Marines would have to climb over the sides and jump down into the surf. They did not know what opposition they would meet; so, going over the sides under fire was a precarious possibility. Private Rouh and the squads in the first wave planned to jump from the boats, race across the beach, and melt into the thick jungle tree line to regroup before taking on the waiting enemy.

The first assault troops stormed ashore between the Ilu and the Tenaru rivers at 9:09 AM. The beaches were silent. There were no enemy defenses established and no resistance to the landings along the beaches. The 5th Marines prepared to attack inland to seize the airfield. The plan was to set up a defensive perimeter from the Tenaru west to the ridges below the airfield, up to Lunga Point and over to Kukum Village. The Lunga River served somewhat as a barrier on the west side of the airstrip. The Matanikau River was 8,000 yards further west from Lunga Point. [5]

Two Navy medical officers and twenty hospital corpsmen accompanied each assault battalion and established aid stations on the beach. Medical companies, consisting of six medical officers and eighty corpsmen landed later to set up field hospitals.

Once the battalions were all on land, the assault troops moved off Red Beach into the jungle, reached the steep banks of the Ilu, waded across the sluggish, fifty-foot-wide river, and headed for the enemy airfield. Landing craft began the ship-to-shore delivery of ammunition, rations, tents, aviation gas, and vehicles.

The Marines consolidated their positions ashore on Saturday and seized the airfield. They dug in along the beaches between the Tenaru and the ridges west of Kukum. Inland, they busied themselves digging defensive gun pits and foxholes along the west bank of the Tenaru. They set up outposts in the densely jungled ridges and ravines south of the airfield.

The 5th Marines took responsibility for the beach defense area "on the west" above the airfield from Lunga Point to Kukum. Private Rouh dug his foxhole on a ridge position covering the coastal road. The Matanikau River and Point Cruz were to the west of the 3d Battalion. The 1st Battalion took the hills along the east bank of the Matanikau. Kokumbona Village was seven miles west of the river. The beachhead was established.

Private Rouh and every Marine on Guadalcanal stood night defensive duty. An enemy attack, infiltration, or counter-landing was anticipated somewhere, anywhere, everywhere along the Marine perimeter.

That night Japanese bombers began targeting the beaches and the Allied ships in the channel. The Imperial Japanese Navy advanced into the channel at Savo Island, and the 5th Marines listened to the shelling and watched explosions light up the sky during the naval battle. The enemy sank the USS *Quincy* and three other heavy cruisers without losing a single vessel. With Allied ships at the bottom of Sealark Channel, Americans took to calling the waters "Iron Bottom Sound."

At dawn, landing boats circled and searched for survivors. Approximately 1,300 sailors died in the night volleys. Another 700 suffered wounds or burns.

A Propensity for Problem Solving

Private Rouh worried about any and every problem his Mike Company platoon encountered, like it was his business to solve. He would measure his solution against the one his squad or platoon leader came up with and let them know if he thought his was better. [6]

When he was "hanging around the platoon command post doing nothing" on August 8, he heard about wounded Marines on a trail. His ingrained attitude that he was not doing enough if he was not up doing something kicked in. He ignored the long-standing Marine rule to "never volunteer for nothing."

"I'll get them out," he offered.

The lieutenant assigned a patrol of Marines to him, advising him that no enemy soldiers were located near the casualties. Private Rouh led them from the CP.

"But, the Japs were there all right, firing a machine gun across the path we were on."

Private Rouh motioned the patrol down, held a grenade in his hand, and went by himself to have a look. The noise and the arc of machine-gun fire let him know where the enemy position was concealed. He walked to the edge of their position, pulled the pin from his grenade, and prepared to toss it. In the confusion of the fight, one of the wounded Marines on the trail took aim on the patrol leader.

"Don't shoot!" Pvt Rouh yelled at him.

The Japanese turned their machine gun on him and fired eight rounds through his pants leg. One of the bullets hit his leg and knocked him to the ground, the grenade still in his hand. Rather than chance a bad toss, in what he would later think was "a kind of cowardly thing," he put the pin back in the grenade, hung it on his belt, laid behind a tree for a time, and gave the impression that he was dead. He wished he had taken a bayonet along with him.

In the night, four hours later, Pvt Rouh was pulled from the trail. A corpsman administered plasma and applied a dressing and splint. He recuperated in the hospital 200 yards behind front lines. He had earned his first Purple Heart.

On August 9, unloading of supplies abruptly ended as the U.S. attack vessels and transports withdrew from Guadalcanal. Some of the cargo ships were half-full when they steamed away, and Marines were still embarked on the departing ships. That left the Marine forces ashore with enough ammunition for only four days, and rations that could be stretched across seventeen days. The Marines rummaged what they could from captured Japanese food, whiskey, gear and equipment stocks.

Ashore in the Marine beachheads, General Alexander Archer Vandegrift ordered rations reduced to two meals a day. The reduced food intake would last for six weeks, and the Marines would become very familiar with Japanese canned fish and rice. Private Rouh had lost some weight during his training at Parris Island. More pounds dropped from his frame.

As one night followed another, Pvt Rouh learned to distinguish the sounds of approaching enemy aircraft. The twin-engine night bomber flew from the enemy airfield on Rabaul and harassed the Marines, erratically dropping bombs and flares along the beachhead and on the airfield. The Marines began referring to those planes as "Bedcheck Charlie" and "Washing Machine Charlie." "Louie the Louse" was a different plane: a single engine, reconnaissance floatplane launched from a cruiser. A Louse overhead signaled Pvt Rouh to hunker down in his foxhole. Japanese cruisers and destroyers were about to let loose a shelling on the ridgelines.

The Marine's engineers completed the airfield runway and officially named it Henderson Field in tribute to Marine Aviator Major Lofton R. Henderson, who had died in action at Midway. The first PBY-5 *Catalina* flying boat landed on August 12 to bring in supplies and evacuate a load of wounded. The first Marine Corps VMF-223 F4F Grumman *Wildcats* landed on Henderson Field on August 20, to begin air missions against the Japanese.

The enemy had been reconnoitering and probing the Marine lines for thirteen days. The arrival of the Marine fighter squadron alerted them to action. Having bombed and shelled the ridge southeast of the airfield for two nights, screaming and frenzied enemy troops stormed the 1st Marines' lines on the Ilu River sand bar at 1:30 AM on August 21.

At daybreak, the 1st Battalion moved upstream and surprised the enemy on their flank. *Wildcats* made strafing passes, and five light tanks blasted the enemy force. The first defeat of an enemy force in the war was concluded before dusk. More than 800 Japanese had been killed in their failed assault. They would have to rebuild before attacking again.

The Japanese took refuge in the ridges and ravines stretching inland from the coast to the west of the 5th Marines' positions. They regrouped in the Matanikau River and Point Cruz peninsula area. Enemy troop ships continued attempts to land reinforcements.

On August 27, the 1st Battalion, 5th Marines, went in search of the enemy beyond the Matanikau, making a shore-to-shore landing near Kokumbona Village. They marched back east toward the beachhead, as the 3d Battalion waited to trap any retreating enemy forces. Not much happened.

The enemy withdrew into the jungle, choosing to pick their own time to engage the Marines. That time came two weeks later. The Marine commanders correctly anticipated the enemy plans. The 2d Battalion, 5th Marines, was moved into position to reinforce the Raider Battalions holding the line south of the airfield.

For two nights, September 12 and 13, a brigade of 2,000 Japanese made one thrust after another on the ridge at the center of the Marine line. The fighting was intense and evolved into hand-to-hand engagements in the foxholes and gun pits. The enemy filtered past the forward positions and attacked the Marines from the rear.

At the same time, enemy troops attacked the 3d Battalion, 1st Marines lines on the east flank. At least 200 enemy soldiers died there. They attacked the ridge over the coastal road on the west perimeter that Pvt Rouh and the 3d Battalion, 5th Marines, held. The determined enemy force reached the battalion's front lines, but could not penetrate the perimeter.

The Marines were proving themselves to be able jungle fighters.

At dawn on September 14, the Marines scouted forward from Henderson airfield. They counted more than 600 enemy bodies left on the bloodied ridge slopes and in the surrounding jungle. Another 600 enemy troops withdrew from the ridge with wounds. The vanquished enemy remnant retreated west through the jungles as far from the Marine regiments as they could march, hoping for an evacuation from the island.

With his own force decimated on what became known as "Edson's Ridge," Colonel Merritt A. Edson was given command of the 5th Marines.

Finally, on September 18, reinforcements and supplies for the Marines on Guadalcanal began.

"Fighting Turns Boyish Marines Into Very Tough Men."

The weeks in the tropical heat took a toll on the Marines. Their clothing and bedding were constantly damp, due either to sweating or drenching rain downpours. More than eight inches of rain could fall during a 24-hour period, and camp walkways turned into meandering streams. In their foxholes, the men endured rashes that turned into tropical skin infections and fungal disorders on their feet, armpits, elbows, and crotches. Exhausting illness, as much as wounds and injuries, sent men to Battalion Medical. Mosquito-borne malaria proved to be a scourge, and malaria attacks were pervasive; cases numbered into the hundreds.

No less than C-rations, quinine sulfate, Plasmochin, and Atabrine were in short supply on the island. Daily doses had to be doled out carefully. Marines might grumble about their skin turning yellow, but bantering about the side effects of their Atabrine tablets was preferred over the fatigue, fever, chills, sweats, headaches, nausea, and vomiting a mosquito bite could bring. Stomach cramps plagued many. Gastroenteritis sapped the strength of some to the point they could not raise their carbines.

The Marines turned their attention again to the enemy positions in the Matanikau River area. On Wednesday, October 7, five infantry battalions organized a thrust inland to clear the Japanese along the Matanikau up to the coast. The 3d Battalion, 2d Marines, and the 1st and 2d battalions, 7th Marines, marched into the jungle and made 2,000 yards upstream on the Matanikau, meeting light enemy resistance. The 2d and 3d battalions, 5th Marines, moved from the perimeter and advanced west toward the river. The 2d Battalion pushed through slight, harassing opposition and made it to the Matanikau's riverbank.

Private Rouh did not reach the river. Four hundred yards from the Matanikau, the 3d Battalion ran headlong into the advance units of the enemy's 4th Regiment, which had crossed the river to establish a forward artillery base. The intense fighting stalled the battalion's progress. Turning north to hit the inland flank of the enemy troops, forcing the Japanese into a pocket, 3/5 took a holding position on the right, facing the beach.

The Marine battalions dug in for the night and prepared to attack the Japanese lines.

All day Thursday rain poured down, halting any forward movement. The close-in fighting around the 3d Battalion's lines continued as the Marines gradually encircled the enemy positions. A savage hand-to-hand battle erupted as the Japanese attempted to escape. While the enemy troops smashed through to the river, Mike Company stayed in the fight well past midnight.

In the dark of Friday morning, October 9, a feeling came over Pvt Rouh. He had to do something. He unhesitatingly volunteered again, this time to journey to the jungle river line still held by the enemy and retrieve wounded Marines. The hostile fire was tremendous.

"With cool courage and utter disregard for his own personal safety," he helped carry injured Marines on stretchers to the company aid station. To those who observed him, he seemed fearless and persistent, keeping up his assistance until enemy fire wounded him. The company commander sent up a recommendation to Colonel Edson. Private Rouh's "heroic conduct, maintained at great risk in the face of grave danger, was in keeping with the highest traditions of the United States Naval Service." [7] President Roosevelt would take pleasure in presenting him a medal.

By Monday night the Marines counted 65 of their own killed in action on the Matanikau and another 125 wounded.

Every night, enemy ships and planes shelled and bombed the Marine perimeter and airfield. Thousands of enemy troops were landing to the west and making their way on jungle trails towards the Marines. Their probing attacks began on October 20. The main attack struck both flanks of the Marine perimeter in driving rain just before midnight on October 24.

The line held secure, and the enemy pulled back at dawn. They attacked again the next night with the same results. When they withdrew from the Matanikau and Tenaru area before morning, the enemy left an estimated 3,500 dead troops behind. The American casualties were reported to be about 300 killed and wounded.

Colonel Edson was determined to clear out the sizeable enemy pockets from the Matanikau area. In the dark of Saturday night, October 31, under the protective watch of the 5th Marines, engineers laid bridges over the Matanikau. The 1st and 2d battalions, backed up by the newly arrived 2d Marine Regiment, attacked across the river on Sunday morning. The reserve 3d Battalion joined in the fight on Monday. The 5th Marines surrounded the enemy defenders west of their base at Point Cruz. By day's end, the Japanese force had been eliminated; more than 300 enemy had been killed.

Into November, while bold newspaper headlines declared that General Rommel's Axis army was in a desperate plight in the Egyptian desert, shorter front-page columns informed readers of the daily aerial engagements, naval clashes, enemy troop landings, and "soul-wrenching battles" on Guadalcanal as the Marines held the airfield and the Japanese attempted to recapture the island. The need to get reinforcements to Guadalcanal was evident. Another Thanksgiving passed at home. Dispatches from the "Cactus" Marines described their turkeys reaching the occupied island two days late, the roaming, routine ground patrols, and the isolated, local skirmishes. Into early December, correspondents reported about the surrounded and beleaguered Marines.

The communiqué reached General Vandegrift on November 29, but was censored for release to newspapers. The 1st Marine Division was to be relieved without delay and sail to Australia for rehabilitation and employment.

In its casualty rolls, the 1st MarDiv listed 954 officers and enlisted men Killed in Action, 103 Died of Wounds, 145 Missing, Presumed Dead, and 3,070 Wounded in Action. Another 8,580 casualties had contracted malaria, jungle rot, and various other tropical ailments. [8]

On to Camp in Australia

At 2:00 PM on December 9, the first elements of the 5th Marines, worn out by four months of fighting and ravaged by wounds, malaria and malnutrition, and the death of comrades, began boarding the USS *President Adams* (AP-38) to sail to Australia. News correspondents described them all as "young men grown old."

Private Rouh took a 1,150-nautical-mile (1,324 miles), four-day voyage. The regiment arrived at Brett's Wharf in Brisbane on December 13, 1942. The 1st Division Marines briefly went into garrison at Camp Brisbane, then, relocated to Camp Balcombe on the

Mornington Peninsula—guests of the Australian Army—to rest, rebuild its strength, and refit for future combat.

Although not exactly "pampered," the Marines found themselves well provided and cared for over the next nine months. The friendship and cordial hospitality the Marines encountered was the substance of thousands of letters home.

The finance office disbursed payroll in Australian currency, and the men had no trouble finding ways to spend their pay. Having subsisted for so many months on C-rations, canned fish and rice, and ship chow, the Australian food and diet was forever like a sumptuous banquet. The life style and night bustle was a perfect antidote for the nightmares of menacing enemy shrieks and jungle perils. Driving on the left side of roads spawned bantering about close calls. Snappy Aussie words and phrases gradually stumbled into the men's vernacular: G'Day, bonzer, gone walkabout, gettin' on the turps, chuck a wobbly, pig's arse!, crack a fat, no worries!, bull dust, dinky-di, and havin' a middy, half pint, or schooner of beer soon needed no native interpreter.

Private Rouh picked up the "Cobber" nickname, the Aussie word meaning "our pal."

The Japanese accomplished their final evacuation from Guadalcanal on February 7. The "total and complete defeat of Japanese forces on Guadalcanal" was wired to Washington on February 8, 1943. America had achieved its first ground victory of the war.

The Marines experienced a few of the accolades and thrills that epic victories bring. On Washington's Birthday, February 22, the 1st MarDiv participated in a grand parade. Thousands of cheering spectators lined Swanton Street in Melbourne as the division band marched past and important dignitaries stood in front of the magnificent Melbourne City Town Hall to review the troops.

While the Marine veterans of Guadalcanal fell in love with Australian ladies, Pvt Rouh was among the many thousands of Marines requiring first aid and medical care. His good fortune was that his sweetheart was already in Australia.

There was a great need for nurses in Australia to care for the wounded and ill. Five general military hospitals had been established on the continent in the early days of the war. The U.S. Army 42nd General Hospital unit took over Stuartholme girls school in Brisbane, and the U.S. Army 4th General Hospital unit was in Melbourne. There were also six evacuation hospitals and one field hospital in Australia.

Lieutenant Phyllis Rowand was stationed at the U.S. Army 4th General Hospital.

Regimental "light training" began with disciplinary and small unit drills as new replacement troops filled the depleted ranks.

On March 29, whispers about an offensive—"hot dope" about code name CARTWHEEL—spread among the regiments. The Allies had their Bismarck Archipelago maps out, looking to the east of Papua New Guinea. Aiming to take back the New Britain and New Ireland islands from the Japanese and secure New Guinea, commanders planned a campaign to isolate and capture the major Japanese base at Rabaul on the northeast tip of New Britain. The capture of two enemy airfields at Cape Gloucester in the northwestern regions of the island would come first.

Rehabilitation and recovery in Australia returned the 1st MarDiv to a combat ready, amphibious-capable infantry force. The troops were in better physical condition and the training intensified and expanded. Long forced marches with full pack and weapons and overnight bivouacs around Mount Martha kept them from town. From April to June, the tactical training and field exercises gradually built up to large-scale amphibious landing team and combat team exercises near the Dromana cliffs, employing live ammunition for all weapons.

The 1st MarDiv held a parade and MOH ceremony at Camp Balcombe on May 21. MajGen Vandegrift, Colonel Merritt A. Edson, 2dLt Mitchell Paige, and PltSgt John Basilone received Medals for their valorous actions on Guadalcanal.

In July, Carlton Rouh was promoted on paper to PFC. He was awarded the Silver Star medal, the third highest award for valor in combat, for his October 9, 1942, actions against enemy Japanese forces on Guadalcanal.

Later, he would try to explain his conspicuous gallantry and intrepidity. "You get this feeling that it's your turn and you move along with it . . . Then the people back home read about it in the newspapers and say 'For God's sakes!' and wonder what kind of a guy that is, when he is just the same guy he always was, only the feeling came into him that it was his turn." [9]

Private First Class Rouh was given a field promotion to second lieutenant. Besides surviving his wounds, he had beaten some other odds.

Professor Robert J. Havighurst, University of Chicago's Committee on Human Development, and Mary Russell, Walgreen Foundation researcher, had just completed a study of the role education had in attaining an officer's rank in the military. A typical mid-westerner with a college degree had a 50-50 chance. A high school graduate like PFC Rouh had those same odds to reach a sergeant's pay grade, but only a one in four chance of becoming a commissioned officer. [10]

When he got a platoon of his own, he experienced butterflies in his stomach realizing the responsibility he had been given. [11] "It wasn't the work I was afraid of, but just the idea of giving men jobs to do that might kill them."

Second Lieutenant Rouh was assigned to an 81mm mortar platoon in Major William H. Barba's 1st Battalion, 5th Marines. [12] He reported to the battalion's headquarters company, was put in command of a mortar section, and assigned a jeep and trailer. Under his charge were a sergeant, a section leader, ten men performing observer, ammunition carrier, or telephone lineman duties, and two mortar squads, each comprised of a corporal, a squad leader, and six men crewing one 81mm mortar. The three Marines with him in platoon headquarters carried two 60mm mortars as alternate weapons.

The M1 81mm mortar was the largest weapon in the infantry battalion's arsenal. The mortar provided an indirect fire capability out to 3,290 yards, could hit within a range of 100 yards at high angles, and could strike sheltered targets in defilade. Second Lieutenant Rouh could get mortar shells on targets using map coordinates or radio directives to his section from a forward observer's position.

The news reached Washington on July 3 and was picked up by the Associated Press and *The New York Times*. A Jersey Marine had been honored. C.R. Rouh of Lindenwold was a hero at Guadalcanal and had been awarded the Silver Star Medal, "because he '"unhesitatingly volunteered time after time to act as stretcher bearer with cool courage and utter disregard of his personal safety during the Guadalcanal battle.'" [13]

Family, friends, neighbors, and former Heights football teammates took cookies and casseroles over to Mrs. Adelheith Rouh's home to hear more about her son's heroics.

On Saturday, September 4, 1943, Carlton told Phyllis that the 5th had been issued a Warning Order to prepare for deployment. The Operation Order was issued two days later. He was going back into the tropics. The two second lieutenants talked about the future and took some furlough from their duties. They went to Sandringham, a small neighborhood in South Melbourne, and took a walk along the beaches of Half Moon Bay. Then on Thursday, September 9, the couple who had been childhood friends in Lindenwold went to the Church of England and said their vows before the pastor, pledging to be man and wife until death due them part.

The 5th Marines, Colonel John T. Selden commanding, began movement to Melbourne's docks on September 14, finding uncomfortable quarters in newly converted Liberty troop ships. The reinforced regiment was designated Combat Team A and was assigned to serve as the division reserve to either reinforce the Cape Gloucester landings or conduct operations against the offshore islands west of New Britain.

Second Lieutenant Rouh said "hooroo" (Australian way of saying goodbye) to his bride on September 26, and embarked from Port Phillip, sailing north for New Guinea to join the BACKHANDER Task Force.

Tolerating 1,701 nm (1,957 miles) of passage in inadequate births, the 5th Marines arrived at their advanced staging area at Milne Bay on the eastern tip of New Guinea for final training and rehearsals. The date was October 8, 1943. The amphibious training went on until just before Christmas. The 5th Marines moved to Cape Sudest on Ordo Bay, northeast New Guinea, on December 25, and waited at anchor in four troop transports.

At 7:46 AM on Sunday, December 26, Colonel Julian N. Frisbie, 7th Marines commander, and Lieutenant Colonel Lewis B. "Chesty" Puller, the executive officer, both of whom had honed their combat know-how during the Banana Wars in Nicaragua, led the assault battalions onto the Yellow Beaches near Cape Gloucester. They encountered sporadic enemy opposition until nighttime. [14]

Tropical forest bordered the landing area. Inland, the undergrowth, swampy lowlands, high ridges, and rugged rain forests with few trails and waterways, awaited the Marines' movement. The assault battalions of the 7th Marines initially pushed ahead, capturing Target Hill on the left flank, and then paused to await reinforcements. During the day, more battalions arrived, including the 1st Marines, landing and wading into the swamp forest.

It started raining D-Day afternoon, heralding the northwest monsoon. The deluge filled front-line fox holes with water. The Marines plunged into muck and mire, slogging through knee-deep mud. Men stepped into holes, only to find themselves up to their necks in a crater. Hurricane-velocity winds, blinding lightning, deafening thunder, and collapsing trees hampered the advance for five days. The storms persisted for two weeks.

Refusing to get bogged down, the reinforced 7th Marines established a beachhead near the principal objective, the Cape Gloucester airfield complex.

Late in the night, General Rupertus, the division commander, requested that his force reserve—Combat Team A—land as soon as it could make the storm-tossed 218 nautical miles from Cape Sudest. Second Lieutenant Rouh, his mortar section, half of 1/5, and most of 2/5, immediately embarked in nine APDs.

The enemy defenders were in bunkers and emplacements on a promontory west of the landing beaches, a position the Marines called Hell's Point. The 1st Marines had obliterated the airdrome's last defense by 5:00 PM on Tuesday. The route to the airfields was just ahead of the Marines' perimeter at Objective Line "0".

In the continuing downpour on Wednesday at 7:30 AM, the 5th Marines began coming ashore, three miles to the right of the Yellow Beaches on newly opened Beach Blue, just behind the 1st Marines vanguard. Close to the Cape Gloucester airfields, all were on the beaches by 9:35 AM. Some units landed down on the Yellow Beaches and had to march or drive to link up with the battalions, delaying the planned advance on the airfield.

Major Barba's 1st Battalion moved out in a column at 3:00 in the afternoon, leading the way for Lieutenant Colonel Lewis H. Walt's 2d Battalion. The 1/5 marched into a swamp, in places as deep as five feet. Standing at 6 feet 2 inches, 2dLt Rouh was in only up to his chest or shoulders, but he had to be concerned for his young mortar men, some no more than 5 feet tall. At dusk, 2/5 reached the center of Airfield No. 2, behind the 1st Marines. Two reinforced 2/5 companies marched across to Airfield No. 1 and established a perimeter running all the way to the beach.

The "lost" 1st Battalion, having made a wide sweep to the left flank in the swamp, moved through the chest-high kunai grass covering the edge of Razorback Hill—the ridge running diagonally across the southwestern approaches to Airfield No. 2 cleared earlier by the 1st Battalion—and took up night defensive positions.

The 3d Battalion, 5th Marines arrived in two echelons on December 30 and 31, and helped the 7th Marines enlarge the beachhead.

At 7:30 AM on Thursday, 1st Battalion moved up Razorback Hill in a column and ran into the sturdy enemy bunkers on the steep slopes under airstrip No. 2. A *banzai* attack slowed the assault, but did not stop the Marines. Second Lieutenant Rouh directed his 81mm mortar section to target enemy positions on the ridge. The fight abruptly ended at 11:30 AM. The 1st Battalion counted six of its own killed and twelve wounded. At 6:00 PM, enemy resistance ceased.

The battalion took a position in the perimeter's center between Razorback and the coast. Second Lieutenant Rouh moved his section into position below the north-south Airstrip No. 1. His men manned their tubes shirtless with their pant legs rolled up above their knees. The 1st and 5th Marines controlled both airfields and all the important high ground overlooking the airdrome.

Tractors carried the dead and wounded to trucks that carried them either to grave registrations or the evacuation hospital on the beach.

On New Year's Eve day, General Rupertus had the engineers drive a slender tree trunk into the ground beside the wreckage of a Japanese bomber at Airfield No. 2. At noon, the American flag was raised thirty-five feet to the top of the trunk.

Combat correspondents described the Marines to be in some of the most rugged terrain and inhospitable conditions anywhere on earth. Everything quickly rotted or fell apart in the intense humidity and heavy rainfall—clothing, paper, leather, jungle hammocks, huts, logs, even trees. Weapons and ammunition corroded. The Japanese defenders could be bivouacked an arm's length away, chatting, yet out of sight in the almost impenetrable jungle.

The Marines quickly determined why village natives built their log and kunai grass huts on stilts four feet above ground. The rains flooded the land and turned volcanic soil into slippery mud.

Constantly wet, unshaven, and dirty, the men contracted fungus infections and endured open sores. Mosquitoes carried malaria, and insects were a constant bother. In the dark,

Marines risked giving their positions away if yelping out from the bite of a little black ant, a little red ant, or a big red ant. Marines writing home insisted that even the caterpillars had teeth.

When he had a chance to take cover from the drenching rain under his own tent and write a letter, 2dLt Rouh, of course told Phyllis about the mud, rampaging streams, wet feet and uniforms that never completely dried, extreme humidity, the 90°F daytime and 72°F night time temperatures, enmired armored vehicles, and LVTs bringing in the supplies and mail. If he did not mention places like Coffin Corner, Suicide Creek, and Aogiri Ridge, the news correspondents did.

Marines moved out from the beachhead into the unforgiving jungle to locate and destroy a determined and resolute enemy. Securing Hill 150, Aogiri Ridge and Hill 660, the Division's infantry regiments secured a foothold around the landing beaches at Borgen Bay.

At 10:00 AM on January 2, 1944, D+8, the 3d Battalion, 5th Marines, attacked to the southeast. On January 7, having crossed through the enemy defenses at Suicide Creek, the battalion advanced rapidly against the strongpoint up on Aogiri Ridge. The 3d Battalion commanding officer and executive officer were both wounded and taken out of the fight. Lieutenant Colonel Puller temporarily assumed responsibility for the battalion. The battalion finally overran the hill.

In the dark at 1:15 AM on January 10, the Japanese charged through a curtain of rain, shouting and firing until repelled. They made four more screaming, furious attempts to dislodge the Marines, each time failing. The enemy had lost its hold on Aogiri Ridge by 8:00 AM.

Reports started going up to General Rupertus that the fighting, terrain, and weather had sapped the men of their physical strength. Morale was low and their endurance had reached their limits. He gave them a day or two to rest and reorganize themselves.

On January 16, the 5th Marines began moving toward Target Hill to relieve the battalions holding the front line. Second Lieutenant Rouh, Weapons/5, and 1/5 moved into the lines on January 18. Intent on seizing control of the Borgen Bay-Itni River line, Major Barba led the 1st Battalion east along the coastal trail for two days.

On January 20, at Natamo Point, a Japanese stronghold, the column collided with an enemy company, dug in and supported by automatic weapons. Two hours into the firefight, 2dLt Rouh's mortar section provided cover to allow the leading patrol to withdraw to the battalion perimeter. Landing craft brought Marine reinforcements on January 23, and the companies overran Natamo Point that afternoon.

Major Barba dispatched patrols inland along the west bank of the Natamo River in chase, trying to outflank the enemy positions near the mouth of the stream. The Japanese retreated eastward, effectively concealing their route of travel and positions. Bad weather continued.

At one point during the pursuit, a bullet hit one of 2dLt Rouh's men just below the ribs. He lay with the wounded man for long hours, comforting him. The fellow did not seem so bad off at all. He just laid there, smoking cigarettes until the litter bearers could get to him. The thought crossed the lieutenant's mind. If he was ever to be wounded again, as he had been on Guadalcanal, rather than get hit in the legs or arms, he wanted to get hit just below the ribs. [15]

The 5th Marines probed the trails leading inland along the coastal track in quest of the enemy. The companies would hike for a day and encamp for three or four days, never making marches on two consecutive days. They might also load into ten LCMs and try to leapfrog ahead of the retreating Japanese. In the final days of January, Major Barba moved his battalion southwest toward Magairapua, Nakarop, and Agulupella villages along an unmapped trail.

The weeks of jungle fighting in monsoon rains were taking a toll. By January's end, more than a thousand Marines impaired by disease or non-battle injuries had been carried to the evacuation hospital and forced to leave New Britain. More than one in ten returned to duty on the island.

In early February, the 5th Marines were again tasked to move west along the northern coast to seize key enemy supply points and trap the elusive Japanese forces. Major Barba planned to conduct coordinated over-land and over-water patrols. High seas delayed the over-water patrols. The 3d Battalion marched over-land and seized the Karai-ai supply point on February 21.

Second Lieutenant Rouh landed with 1/5.

Iboki Point plantation, a main enemy supply point, was a hop and jump ahead to the east. The next day, 1/5 marched along the coastal trail, and 2/5 leapfrogged by water. The 5th Marines occupied Iboki on February 24 and took three days to establish the area as the regimental command post.

Second Lieutenant Rouh and his 81mm mortar section had put sixty miles between themselves and the Cape Gloucester airfields.

The remnants of the main enemy force remained at large. Seeming always to be twenty to thirty miles ahead of the Marine columns, barges had withdrawn most of the enemy forces the day before the Marines occupied Iboki. They moved sixty miles east to Willaumez Peninsula, a mountainous place supporting four extensive coconut plantations. The Japanese had also constructed a grass airstrip at Talasea, on the east side of the peninsula.

Colonel Oliver P. Smith took command of the reinforced 5th Marines on March 1. That same Wednesday orders arrived for another shore-to-shore amphibious assault. On Sunday afternoon at 1:00 PM, 2dLt Rough and the regiment began loading into LCM gunboats and LCT's. They departed Iboki in the night and reached the landing site on Monday as light broke over the mountains on the west coast of Willaumez Peninsula.

The 1st Battalion loaded into LVTs and waited at the line of departure in front of Beach Red and the Volupai coconut plantation. Ordered to advance in lead of the assault at 8:25 AM, the 1st Battalion crossed over the coral reefs. The first amphibian tractors hit the soft sands in front of Little Mount Worri at 8:35 AM. The enemy defenses had been abandoned, and the assault companies initially encountered no serious opposition. They established the beachhead and dug in to protect the perimeter. All of 2/5 was ashore by 12:30 PM. The battalions occupied the coconut plantation by evening and dug their night positions.

On the morning of March 7, 1st Battalion sent Company C to the right of Little Mount Worri on a muddy trail leading to Liappo Village—except that after a short distance, trees and vines hindered their passage. The Marines hacked their way forward through the dense undergrowth until night descended. They were short of Liappo. Companies A and B advanced on parallel paths the next day and ran into the muddy ravines choked with vegetation. The battalion was stretched along the trail at nightfall.

The retreating Japanese did not dig in to defend any of the villages around Little Mount Worri. The 5th Marines resumed their advance east, opening a route across the Willaumez Peninsula. The engineers bulldozed a way through the trails on March 10. The Marines took the Talasea grass airstrip and began dispatching patrols south to the base of the peninsula. They captured an enemy straggler or two and reported the retreat of the main body of the enemy force.

Second Lieutenant Rouh and his platoon enjoyed a respite of sorts for a couple of weeks, providing security patrols while the division captured enemy stocks and equipment and established a comfortable headquarters, training sites, a hospital, and a rest area off the Garua beaches. The Navy built a base on the peninsula for torpedo boats. The hot springs ashore provided the Marines swimming and bathing facilities.

Having accomplished its mission to capture the Cape Gloucester airfields and drive the Japanese from western New Britain, the 1st MarDiv planned its departure from the jungles. The 5th Marines began to deploy aboard ships again on April 6.

Second Lieutenant Rouh was meritoriously promoted to First Lieutenant on Easter Sunday, April 9, 1944.

Operation *Stalemate II*

First Lieutenant Rouh, like all his men, had hoped to return to Australia for R & R. A reunion with Phyllis would have been good for his spirits, but the ships sailed southeast for a 756-nautical-mile voyage to Pavuvu in the Russell Islands, thirty-five nautical miles north of Guadalcanal. Their new home was eight miles wide and nine miles long and covered by coconut plantations. Other than the facts that no one was popping up and shooting at them and mosquitoes did not carry malaria, the Marines considered Pavuvu to be a miserable, tropical hellhole. Sand crabs infested the island and millions of rotting coconuts covered the ground. It was no place to derive great satisfaction for their victorious campaign. For the next four months, 1stLt Rouh was challenged to elevate the morale of his men.

First the battalions cleared out the coconuts to set up a tent city. Then they crushed coral and laid out roads and trails—not high on the list of recommended R & R activities. Next to the island's pier, they created an open, crushed coral parade ground for award ceremonies and training. That area, at least, would provide the Marines one of their most pleasant Pavuvu memories.

Bob Hope, comedian Jerry Colonna, dancer Patty Thomas, singer and film actress Francis Langford, and guitarist Tony Romano landed at the pier. On August 7, 1944, they performed a USO show on an open-air stage on the parade ground. The Marines found it entertaining. After Bob and his retinue departed for other places, the 5th Marines had nineteen more days on Pavuvu to entertain themselves.

The entire 1st Marine Division sailed south from Pavuvu on August 26. Reaching Cape Esperance on Guadalcanal the next day, the division began three days of rehearsing full-scale amphibious landings, August 27–29. The 5th Marines practiced transferring from a troopship to a landing craft, climbing down a hairy rope ladder, then up again, humping fifty or sixty pounds of equipment on their backs—an effort that cost some Marines a broken leg and others their deaths.

First Lieutenant Rouh learned in daily briefings that the Marines were going to sail to two coral-decked islands called Peleliu and Angaur, in the archipelago of Palau, wherever that might have been. Peleliu was a small, six-by-two-mile island abreast the Philippine Sea. The Japanese had built an airfield on the flat southern side of Peleliu and a phosphate refinery on the northern tip. Tiny Angaur was located approximately six miles southeast of Peleliu Island. The 1st Division was given the mission to seize them both and clear the enemy forces from the bigger island.

Codenamed Operation *Stalemate II*, commanders predicted that the Japanese would be off Peleliu in four days. First Lieutenant Rouh listened to briefings of what was ahead, peering at maps, aerial photographs, and a plaster and toy model of the larger island. He passed the word on to his men.

About 11,000 Japanese occupied Peleliu, and their defenses would be formidable. They had learned what to expect of a Marine assault. The landing beaches on the southern tip of the coral island were mined, and enemy artillery and mortars were registered to bring precision shelling along the landing sites. The enemy was in beach fortifications, concrete pillboxes, and in caves and tunnels positioned in limestone ridges above the beaches.

On Monday, September 4, a flotilla of nearly 800 ships sailed from Guadalcanal and Pavuvu. First Lieutenant Rouh was on a ship again. He stood with other Marines lining the rails of an LST (Landing Ship, Tank) as the ship set a zig-zagging course to avoid the threats of Japanese submarine attacks. He travelled another 2,100 miles west across the Pacific, and, no matter in what direction he looked from the ship's railings, more ships were all he saw.

For the many Marines who had fought to take Guadalcanal and Cape Gloucester from the Japanese, this eleven-day trip was a somber journey. First Lieutenant Rouh kept his Marines busy and did all he could to bolster their spirits. The Marines above and below decks filled their free time checking and rechecking gear, maintaining their "spit and polish," and trying to catch some sleep in stagnant quarters or on perching decks in choppy seas. They played cards and had long "bull sessions" about woman, their favorite foods, the approaching start of the NFL season with the Brooklyn *Tigers* playing at Green Bay, the chances of the Major League Baseball World Series in October coming down to the St. Louis *Cardinals* playing the cross-town St. Louis *Browns*, or any other topic that might keep their minds from troublesome thoughts and apprehensions.

The troopships dropped anchor a mile offshore from Peleliu's coast.

According to the D-Day plan of operation for September 15, the 1st Marines would land on the left flank of the beaches. The 5th Marines would be in the center of the advance elements, with 1st Battalion to land on Beach Orange 1 and 2d Battalion onto Beach Orange 2. That meant 1stLt Rouh and his platoon, along with 1/5, and 2/5, would charge onto the island in front of the enemy airfield runways. The 3d Battalion would follow behind 2/5 and link with the 7th Marines on the right flank, to capture the southern portion of the island. Objective Line-1, the beachhead, was several hundred yards into the island just in front of the runways and an airfield road. [16]

The seas were calm as 1stLt Rouh climbed into the LVT-4 (Landing Vehicle, Tracked) before dawn's light on Friday. His platoon rode in four "Alligators," the kind where the back ramp drops down to let the men get out. He stood on the top of one of them: twenty of his fully equipped mortar men crammed into the open compartment behind and below him. [17]

The amphibian tractors transporting five battalions of Marines formed into assault waves, circling 4,000 yards from the island, and waited in lines stretching along a half-mile of sea on the western side of Peleliu. Vomit splashed onto sea-soaked boots. Operation *Stalemate II* had reached the assault phase.

Navy support ships began the direct high explosive shelling on the enemy beach defenses at 8:00 AM, and adrenaline began pumping. White phosphorous shells inland from the beaches formed a smoke screen to cover the approach of the assault force. When the smoke drifted seaward, it also obscured the view the LVT drivers had of the target beaches.

The "amphibian tanks" and personnel assault waves moved from the line of departure toward the shore. Before they reached the coral reef ringing Peleliu, enemy shells began falling among the vehicles. The detonations threw water geysers into the air and hit or rocked the landing craft. As the LVTs crawled over the reef, artillery and mortar fire dropped on them. At least twenty-six LVTs were demolished, left as burning and smoking wrecks on the reef. The leading assault waves raced across a 150-yard-wide lagoon, tracked onto the beaches at 8:32 AM, and slowly advanced inland, assaulting dugouts, caves, and fortified shelters.

The two mounted .50 caliber machine guns at the front of the LVT sprayed bullets into the coconut grove. First Lieutenant Rouh's platoon landed at 8:33 AM, one minute behind the first wave. The beaches were more congested than expected, and the beach master was doing everything possible to establish the units along the proper lines.

As the infantry came ashore, Japanese mortars and cannons swept the beaches, hitting both flanks. Enemy machine-gunners raked the Marines from concealed fortifications at the water's edge and from inland ridges. Fifteen tanks were almost immediately on fire—direct hits of enemy artillery and mortars. Bodies of the dead and wounded began piling up on the landing beaches. Dispatches from war correspondents described the scene on the beaches as "sheer pandemonium."

"The beach was really bad." First Lieutenant Rouh's Alligator tracked onto the shore and slammed to a stop. The ramp dropped in the back. His twenty men ran from the LVT and clustered behind it. In a blast he would forever remember, an enemy shell dropped on his men. [18]

The 1st Battalion met only scattered resistance on Beach Orange 1 and maneuvered through the coconut groves. They reached the O-1 phase line at 9:30 AM. In the initial hour on shore, the 5th Marines had gained a 100-yard advance onto the island. They faced flat, open ground ahead of the woods. Murderous artillery and mortar fire from the high ground to the north swept the open airfield to their front. The companies were ordered to remain on the line until the 1st Marines could advance beyond the daunting coral ridge on the extreme left flank.

Shortly after noon, strong resistance from enemy pillboxes erupted. In the hours ahead, a company of Japanese infantry advanced across the airfield. Enemy tanks formed in defilade east of the ridges a short distance above the airfield. More ground troops emerged from hiding. The enemy advancing across the open ground was 400 yards forward of the Marine line.

Into the afternoon, 1stLt Rouh counted twenty-nine men lost to casualties in his platoon. By 3:00 PM the platoon had worked their way up to the edge of the airfield. They looked across the runways to the ridges where the enemy artillery was positioned.

First Lieutenant Rouh's forward observation post was at the edge of the airfield, on the east side of Umurbrogos, 500 yards forward of his position, locating targets and calling for, adjusting, controlling, and coordinating mortar fire. He wanted to make sure his men would survive the night. Carrying his own radio and rifle, he moved to the 81mm mortar OP to take a look. The enemy had carved a ditch into the coral, at one end tapering down to nothing. At the other end, where it reached the mouth of a dugout entryway to a pillbox, the ditch dropped to eight feet deep.

His men at the OP were lying against the coral deposits left in piles above the ditch, trying to spot the enemy guns in the ridges on the far side of the airfield. The stench in the air, a mixture of smells, was unmistakable—gunpowder, gasoline and napalm, and scorched human flesh.

An M1A1 flamethrower squad had approached the ditch ahead of his mortar team, releasing half a gallon of flame in a one-second burst, and had silenced the pillbox. Two enemy dead lay near the doorway. Wisps of smoke still blew from the mouth of the dugout, which was apparently empty. Artillery and mortar fire from enemy positions on Umurbrogos continued.

The men recognized the difficulty of digging into coral under fire and wanted, instead, to establish their observation post within the dugout. First Lieutenant Rouh agreed that it did not seem safe staying on the coral bank during the night hours when a Japanese attack was likely. He thought the dugout would provide better protection for the men under his command, after it had been investigated.

In all his months on the islands, 1stLt Rouh had resolved to never go into a cave that the enemy had occupied, no matter how much time had passed since they had vacated the enclosure. His men were busy spotting and calling in targets of opportunity for the 81mm mortars. Against his better judgment, he decided to make a personal reconnaissance of the enclosure to ensure its safety for them. He jumped into the ditch and carefully slid along its side, making his way to the entrance.

By dusk on D-Day, the assault forces had established the beachhead, held the left flank, the southern half of the airfield, and about one quarter of Peleliu's southern tip on the right flank. By that time, 1stLt Rouh had been evacuated from the island.

"A lot more than just a bullet in the stomach."

First Lieutenant Rouh entered the darkened emplacement by himself, his carbine at the ready. With his back against a wall, his eyes adjusting to the lack of light within, he could see stacks of ordnance and supplies. He saw a whisky bottle and packages wrapped in cloth on a shelf. He threw a package up to Private Stillwell, telling him to give it to that kid from Intelligence who was looking for souvenirs.

"Then I did a foolish thing. I moved farther inside. I had a quick hunch that I had better be ready for trouble and brought my carbine around to be ready." He made sure the safety catch was off. Too late.

"Then bang!" Concealed behind the supplies, an enemy rifleman fired at him, seriously wounding him in the left side. "There was a shot. I heard it before I felt the bullet. There was an awful sock in my stomach."

Hit just below the ribs, wounded in action for a third time, 1stLt Rouh doubled over, was tempted to fall down, but willed himself to run out doubled over. He ran along the ditch until it was low enough for him to jump out. His boys pulled him forward, and he lay there for a minute until his mind came together and his breathing eased. He remembered the fellow on New Britain who had taken a bullet under his ribs and thought that he would live, too.

Having emerged wounded from the fortification, three of his men immediately assisted him to a less exposed location. They began to take his belt off to administer a first aid pack to the wound. An enemy soldier dashed out of the bunker. One of 1stLt Rouh's men yelled.

"Look out!"

A Japanese grenade landed in the midst of the mortar team assisting their lieutenant. Weakened, but alert, 1stLt Rouh saw the grenade that endangered his team's lives. He again reacted immediately to protect men under his command.

"I got to my feet. I remember that." Beyond that moment, he would "remember things only in patches with blind spaces in between."

He lifted himself into a crouching position, pushed the two men aiding him away from the grenade, and ensured that his body was between them and the explosion. He was down on both elbows and a knee over the grenade when it detonated, taking the full blast of the explosion himself. Although he was riddled with shrapnel, his chest, abdomen, and left side and limbs took the brunt of the blast. One steel fragment punctured his left lung and dug in near his heart. His whole side was torn off.

CHAPTER 13

The Greatest Defiance

✳✳✳

"Does it grieve you, Death,
That I defy you,
That I refuse to be taken by you?" [1]

— CORPORAL VINCENT H. D. CASSIDY JR.

FIRST LIEUTENANT CARLTON ROUH WAS prone on the ground, vulnerable and helpless. Fifteen Japanese soldiers rushed from the darkened pillbox, throwing grenades as they exited. The team protected themselves against the deafening explosions and lethal shrapnel. Private Pruden straddled the lieutenant and opened up on the Japanese in the ditch with his Browning automatic gun.

Still under enemy artillery and mortar fire, 1stLt Rouh lay back against the coral bank. He spotted Doc Edward J. Crain Jr. passing along the ditch. "There's the doc," he said to Private Stillwell. "Get that doc." [2]

Doc Crain administered plasma and gave first aid to 1stLt Rouh's pockmarked body. A mortar shell exploded nearby and took a piece out of the back of 1stLt Rouh's skull. He would not remember that detonation at all. Then a litter team carried him to a casualty evacuation point back on the beach.

"That was a miserable trip back," he would recall. "I thought they would get all the men with me. But somehow we made it."

The hospital ships USS *Bountiful* (AH-9) and USS *Samaritan* (AH-10) were on station. Before lapsing into unconsciousness as he was evacuated to one of the ships off shore, he had one question.

"Are the men all right?"

First Lieutenant Rouh's wounds were too serious for him to return to duty. The surgeons were hard pressed to treat all his wounds, and he was evacuated to the naval medical facilities at Pavuvu for more prolonged care. His left lung was completely collapsed and would recover only half of its effectiveness. The other lung's functioning was also affected. Once 1stLt Rouh was up and about, he would become easily short of breath.

From Pavuvu, he sailed to Honolulu, for more surgeries, and then to San Francisco. The war had come to an end for 25-year-old 1stLt Carlton Rouh.

The expectation that the Marines would have the 4.7-square-mile island secured within four days did not come to fruition. Battle results were far more important than battle reports as the fighting continued. So, the witness reports of the events at the trench did not immediately leave the company's command post. Lieutenant Colonel Robert W. Boyd, commanding officer of the 1st Battalion, read the report and recommendation after the battle for Peleliu ended on November 27, 1944. He had no hesitation to endorse the fact that "His exceptional spirit of loyalty and self-sacrifice in the face of almost certain death reflects the highest credit upon 1stLt Rouh and the U.S. Naval Service." The Medal of Honor recommendation was forwarded to Colonel Harold D. "Bucky" Harris, in command of the 5th Marines, and was on its way up to the president.

In the earliest months of the war, Army Sergeant Bill Mauldin, the 45th Division's "Star-Spangled Banter" cartoonist, was best known in Texas and New Mexico. His dispatches began coming home from Italy in July 1943. Sergeant Mauldin joined the *Stars and Stripes* newspaper staff in February 1944.

By the time 1stLt Rouh saved his men from a grenade, Sergeant Mauldin's cartoon characters of American combat infantrymen Willie and Joe were becoming familiar *Up Front* newspaper features. Before Christmas 1944, 1stLt Rouh's heroics would be pictured in a cartoon format. And, the Marine from Lindenwold would meet President Truman at the White House three days before tired and haggard Willie appeared on the June 18, 1945, *Time* Magazine cover.

Master Technical Sergeant Victor A. Donahue, USMCR, had been on Guadalcanal and Cape Gloucester with the 1st MarDiv. He was an artist, and many of his drawings inspired the troops, as well as officers. Technical Sergeant Ward Walker circulated a Combat Report of the September 15 events on Peleliu to the artist. Vic wired his depiction of 1stLt Rouh's gallantry back to the States. [3]

Hero Of Peleliu appeared in newspapers. Captions under the action cartoon's five panels explained the details. "1—On D-Day at Peleliu. Second Lieutenant Carlton Rouh, 25, of Lindenwold, N.J., led his unit of Marines in an assault of a Jap-infested cave. 2—As Rouh rushed forward, he was shot. His weapon fell from his arms. 3—Two of Rouh's men ran to drag him back, but the young lieutenant began to get up by himself. Just then a grenade came flying from the mouth of the cave. 4—Rouh leaped at the men and knocked them to the ground. 5—Then he threw himself on the grenade, huddling it with his body as it burst. As the heroic Marine Corps officer was evacuated to a hospital ship, his question, before lapsing into unconsciousness, was, 'Are the men alright?'"

After the 1945 New Year, the account of his heroism spread across the United States—he had smothered a grenade to save his men and lived to tell the tale. Many newspaper columns included an AP Wirephoto and caption: SMOTHERS GRENADE AND LIVES. [4]

Cobber visited his widowed mother at home in Lindenwold with Phyllis, "the girl he played with in grammar school." A reporter asked questions while the Marine lieutenant sat together with his wife—both in uniform. The U.S. Army nurse sat on the arm of the chair with her arm around her husband's shoulder. The smiling couple looked lovingly at each other. They recalled getting married in Australia, where she had been serving.

The reporter was curious about how Carlton had been wounded in the stomach. The veteran recounted the September 15, Peleliu invasion events haltingly. Every time his heroism came up in the conversation, he had a lapse of memory. Some of what had taken place was not too clear to him. [5]

"What went on in my mind that I can remember wasn't hero stuff at all."

Like anyone who survived a close encounter with an exploding grenade or mortar shelling, he was experiencing memory gaps. He did not remember pushing the kids out of the way or turning back to the grenade. He did not even remember seeing the grenade. What he did remember was hearing "Look out!" and getting to his feet.

"I just remember getting up, and then my mind skips over things and I can remember being on the ground and rolling toward the bank where the grenade had been. Then, I remember lying there and shooting going on and Pruden coming toward me shooting and stepping over me and straddling me, shooting into the ditch."

When he got to the part where his men were giving him first aid for his stomach wound, he paused.

"I don't remember a lot from there on for a while. They told me that a Jap threw a grenade, and that I pushed our boys out of the way and threw myself on it." He could not say with any certainty. "Maybe I did. All I know about it is that I got a lot more than just a bullet in the stomach. Hell, if I did what they say, I'm glad it wasn't an American grenade, because—I wouldn't be here."

On Easter Sunday, April 1, 1945, the Marines conducted the largest amphibious landing in the Pacific theater, invading Okinawa Island. Carlton paid close attention to the newspaper reports, as many of his battle comrades in the 1st Battalion, 5th Marines fought on the island, engaging the enemy in what would become the longest and bloodiest battle of the Pacific War. Eighty-three days. On May 29, companies of the 1st Battalion, 5th Marines, were ordered to seize Shuri Castle. The fighting went on for another twenty-four days. No one yet knew that Okinawa would be the decisive final battle of WWII.

Carlton was home when newspapers reported that he was to be awarded the Medal of Honor. No one made much of it. The president had to delay the Medal presentation while the doctors finished "recapping and retreading" the lieutenant for limited service. Marine Corps representatives went to Lindenwold and offered to assist in any celebrations the town planned— "throw in a band and a parade and the rest." Nobody in town was interested, and there was no parade. In fact, there wasn't anything. The people thought, "All right, he was a hero, so what?" [6]

Interest in the Marine who had protected comrades from a grenade blast increased as summer neared. *Cavalcade of America*, sponsored by the DuPont Company, presented a real-life love story of the war on Monday night, June 3, 1945. "The 2nd Lieutenants Come Home," starring Bob Bailey and Marjorie Reynolds, was broadcast from Hollywood to NBC radio listeners. The drama was about a wartime service marriage that lasted through long separations and combat. The hero was Lt. Carlton Rouh of the Marine Corps, and the heroine was Lt. Phyllis Rowand Rouh of the Army Nurse Corps. If listeners had not read about it in the newspapers, they learned how Carlton Rouh had earned the Medal of Honor. [7]

Washington, D.C. (AP)—Four War Heroes Awarded Medal of Honor. First Lieutenant Rouh stood with three other recipients under a burning sun for a White House ceremony on Friday, June 15. USMC Major Everett P. Pope, Army PFC Geno J. Merli, and USMC PFC Luther Skaggs chatted with him and waited on the sloping lawn outside the president's office. Marine Corps Commandant General A. A. Vandegrift rendered his salute to the four, demonstrating that all ranks, officers and enlisted alike, salute men who have earned a Medal of Honor. The president came down the portico steps at noon to present the awards.

Sitting with the admiring guests, Lt. Rouh's wife and his mother, Mrs. A. Rouh, beamed with pride. Private Howard Rouh, Mrs. J. Rouh, and his sister-in-law Betty Jane, Russell's wife, also attended the presentation. His three half-sisters, Mrs. Etta B. Dawson, Mrs. "Anny" Gerbing, and Mrs. Florence A. Graham, watched as the president moved from Major Pope to their brother. Miss Floretta Graham stood up from her chair to get a good look at the proceedings as her uncle's name was read. [8]

President Truman had trouble pronouncing Peleliu (Pe-lay'-le-oo) and stumbled on the name when he read Lt. Rouh's Medal Citation. He had to reach up from behind to put the Medal around the tall Marine's neck.

After fastening the fourth Medal, the president turned to the four, congratulated them again, and remarked that he had said time-after-time again that he would rather have that Medal than be the President of the United States. [9]

There was time for photographs on the steps of the west wing, with the group facing the mansion's formal gardens. Newspaper columnists had a favorite. [10] President Truman, standing on the first step of the White House portico, was central in the photo. At either side of the president stood Army Chief of Staff General George C. Marshall, Secretary of the Navy James Forestal, and Deputy Chief of Naval Operations Vice Admiral Richard S. Edwards.

Major Pope and PFC Merli stood on the walk to the president's right. PFC Luther Skaggs, standing on crutches, the pants leg pinned up behind the knee of his missing left leg, and 1stLt Rouh, obviously taller than the rest, stood on the walk to the president's left. Floretta Graham was in front of President Truman, standing between the two sets of recipients. On the second portico step in the background, smiling family and friends gathered behind the president and the dignitaries.

The honorees and guests went to lunch with the president at 1:00 PM. He excused himself at 2:15 PM for a scheduled meeting with three of his generals.

Although details from his Citation were quoted in newspaper columns and magazine stories, the public would never be fully informed about 1stLt Rouh's valor across three battle campaigns. Citations provide a summary based on witness reports. In most cases, there is no need to include gore and in many cases, important details are deliberately censored. "For reasons of security, the deed for which a man receives a decoration often cannot be fully described in the actual citation he receives. There may accordingly be reports which do not tell the whole story." [11]

"Play your cards the way they fell."

A week after 1stLt Rouh's visit to the White House, the Marines declared victory on Okinawa on June 22, and began planning for the invasion of Japan's mainland. On August 6, an American B-29 bomber dropped an atomic bomb over Hiroshima. Three days later, a second atomic bomb was dropped on Nagasaki. That detonation induced the Japanese emperor to accept the terms of an unconditional surrender. His armed forces surrendered to the Allied forces on August 15, 1945. World War II in Asia was over.

On the weekend of September 16, 1945, 1stLt Rouh was invited to New York City to give a talk to men coming home from the war. [12] Introduced as a Marine hero from Guadalcanal and Peleliu, he wanted them to know that he was not bragging or complaining. He was a pragmatist and intended to tell it straight to the returning fellows.

He described the common veteran's experience after finally getting "thru the meat chopper" and getting a foot ashore in the United States of America.

"They all think the same thing," he told them. "'Holy cracking jeepers,' they think, as if the United States was a beautiful girl for them to touch."

Quickly, reality strikes. The same dirty old overalls were still hanging on the peg waiting for them. What a shock to see. "For the returning veteran, it's like being a child and getting a 'sensible' present for your birthday."

Without bragging, he wanted to illustrate the point. "I'm the only fellow in my home town who ever won the Congressional Medal of Honor, and, you can name your own odds, I'm the only one around there who ever will win it. They don't come easy." So, despite newspaper reporters showing up at his mother's door and his Medal and him appearing in photographs with the president and being introduced as a hero, he put it into perspective. "When I got back, I didn't get patted on the back by anybody hard enough to hurt."

Not all the men listening to the first lieutenant wearing the Medal around his neck might have known that the next highest award for combat heroism was the Navy Cross. The Navy and Marine veterans understood why 1stLt Rouh was telling them a story of a Marine hero he knew personally.

"Here's another fellow, out of the Philadelphia area, and he comes home with the Navy Cross—another tough one to win. He can't go nowhere without there's people opening his mouth for him and pouring drinks down. It's all very nice for quite a while. Then, he comes up to District Headquarters and holds out the medal and says, 'Take it back.' That's really what he said. 'Take it back,' he says, 'it made a bum out of me.' [13]

"The reception the soldiers get when they come home is a mixed-up kind of thing."

The essential point 1stLt Rouh had come to tell them was that everybody in the country was dealt a hand when the war came. It was a game where you played your hand, whether you were the fellow back home, on plush, saying the income tax was ruining him, or the fellow shaking up and down on his breaking bones in a foxhole somewhere, or the enlisted fellow who had the break of drawing a defense job—they were all playing the cards they drew.

"The fellows overseas drew the bad cards," he acknowledged. "There's no looking around that one. That's a fact." Then, he added a thought that binds all young men who come home from war. "This way, with the cards I drew, I wind up with empty pockets and a patched-up hole where my side used to be, getting on toward 30 years old, and still 20 years behind the game.

"So what?" he asked them. "That the way things are, and if you take them that way you don't get hurt." First Lieutenant Rouh was pragmatic, not pessimistic. He wanted the veterans to know that, looking ahead, if they played the cards now being dealt to them, the game would turn out all right.

"There's no direct pay-off on a war record, but there are plenty of indirect pay-offs. The country is grateful the best it can be, the way it is geared. A fellow with a war record he has a right to be proud of can find it a useful thing to have for the rest of his life. The other veterans in the town respect him if he proves the same kind of fellow in peace as in war. The government gives him a little, the best of it in their dealings. People generally respect him if he proves to be the same kind of civilian as soldier."

He looked into the future and imagined a conversation he, and they, might have.

"No, you tell me 20 years from now, 'You were a hero—so what?'" His chin jutted out and his head nodded. "And, I think I'll be able to answer, 'Brother, so plenty.'"

The Hero of Peleliu concluded his welcome home and readjustment speech. "The whole thing is to play the cards the way they fell and not cry over them and take the country the way it is geared, and not cry over that either, and just take up where you left off and get going." [14]

First Lieutenant Rouh's prediction would prove to be farsighted: as if he had been able to see the next thirty-two years.

Collier's Weekly Magazine was published the next Tuesday. On the cover was Lieutenant Karl Milroy's drawing of a Navy lieutenant junior grade (O-2), with aviator wings and three service ribbons on his white uniform, hiding a strawberry ice cream cone behind his back as he salutes a Navy Captain (O-6) passing him by. The cover story, in bold print, was Lester Velie's article: UNEMPLOYMENT IS HERE AGAIN. Inside, loyal readers could read six fictional stories, an editorial giving advice to veterans, and ten articles. One of the articles proved to be one of the first biographies written about Carlton Rouh. [15]

Novelist Ira Wolfert entitled his article, THAT'S HOW IT IS, BROTHER. His subtitle summarized the article for the readers: A hero talks, simply and realistically, of heroism and its reward—neither of which are very hard to find once you have learned where to look. [16]

At the top of Page 14, Carlton, dressed in a civilian short-sleeved shirt and tie, smiled from behind a cash register, cigarette in his right hand, and his big left hand resting on the counter top at Hotel Linden. Bob Leavitt had taken the photograph. William Von Riegen drew the story illustrations.

In the four-page article, 1stLt Rouh described how the hardest thing to learn for a combat soldier knocked around by war is to want to take up things where he left off and get going again. He believed that the "very best break a soldier can get is to throw the whole thing over his shoulder, count his life in the war as dead and take up as a civilian where he left off."

Ira was so intrigued about Carlton's "amnesia" for critical events during his combat experiences that he consulted a well-known New York psychiatrist about why the mind would shut out such memories. The doctor explained Carlton's sense that he was dying when he had been seriously wounded and of his love for his brother Russell. Ira might have had a better grasp of the impact of combat casualties if he had consulted with a battle surgeon like Doc Ed Crain.

Carlton's response to the psychiatric interpretation of his actions: "Well, I don't know." He had given the matter some thought. "A fellow looking into his own mind, trying to figure out why he did what he did in the war has got a big mystery on his hands alright."

Ira Wolfert and the psychiatrist were not alone in trying to explain why a man would consciously and deliberately shield others from an armed grenade. The men who Carlton saved on Peleliu, others who served with him, and correspondents who wrote about his actions, would often wonder in quiet moments what they might have done had they found themselves in the lieutenant's position. Would they have been able to unhesitatingly throw themselves on a grenade, covering it with their body, knowing the destructive power of the imminent detonation?

Three years had not passed since Carlton was evacuated from Peleliu when L.R. Alwood asked himself that question and wrote of his belief in miraculous outcomes. [17]

He wondered if an occasional angel wanders down from Paradise to intervene in the affairs of men, discovering a mortal in desperate jeopardy that could have been avoided had the mortal so chosen. The angel, then, would become an actual guardian in that mortal's behalf. On Peleliu, Lieutenant Rouh pulled the one play left open—a typical football tactic. Simultaneously, he blocked the advance of the two rapidly approaching Marines and hurled himself directly on top of the grenade! His recovering was attributed to his youth and a rugged constitution, along with the expert care of Navy medical men. L.R. Alwood insisted on the appropriateness of seeing that Lieutenant Rouh's exploit and sacrificial courage be rewarded.

Back to Lindenwold

First Lieutenant Rouh was honorably retired from active duty on December 1, 1946. Upon his retirement, he was promoted in the Reserves. He wore captain's bars on the shoulders of his dress blue uniform and four rows of medals/ribbons over his heart.

Medal of Honor
Silver Star-Purple Heart w/one gold Star-Combat Action Medal,
Presidential Unit Citation-Good Conduct Medal-Selected Marine Corps Reserve Medal
World War II Victory Medal-National Defense Service Medal-Overseas Service Medal

Carlton and Phyllis returned home to Lindenwold after their service, probably believing their service and the war would gradually fade from the nation's memory. He received medical care in various military and veterans' hospitals for two years. Carlton went back to work at the Hotel Linden. Phyllis worked as a nurse in several local schools. She would have a strong influence on their daughter when it came to providing care to others. They were members of St. John's Episcopal Church in Gibbsboro.

The Lindenwold Woman's Club was one of the first to pay a lasting tribute to their hometown hero. [18] On September 15, 1946, the second anniversary of his valor on Peleliu, the club presented Carlton a tall, engraved, bronze and black plaque. Under the Medal emblem are the words:

"WITH SOLEMN PRIDE AND GRATITUDE
THIS MONUMENT IS DEDICATED
TO THE HONOR OF
LT. CARLTON R. ROUH, U.S.M.C.R.
WHOSE GALLANTRY ABOVE AND
BEYOND THE CALL OF DUTY AGAINST
ENEMY JAPANESE FORCES ON
PELELIU ISLAND, 15 SEP. 1944
EARNED FOR HIM THE HIGHEST AWARD
OUR NATION CAN BESTOW,
THE CONGRESSIONAL MEDAL OF HNONOR."

The plaque would be a long-standing inspiration to Clementon and Lindenwold high school students. The Work Projects Administration (WPA) had erected and opened the Lower Camden County Regional High School at 40 South White Horse Avenue in 1939. A granite stone monument topped by a sundial was erected in front of the high school between two sidewalks where students enter and leave the building. The shiny, black plaque was fastened to the monument's front side facing the avenue. [19]

Carlton demonstrated many of the personal characteristics common among Medal holders: one was keeping a connection, an allegiance, with other men like him. He did not seclude or isolate himself after his combat experiences. He held life memberships in the CMOHS, the First Marine Division Association, the VFW Post 7927 of Blackwood, the American Legion Post 94 of Clementon, and the Army and Navy Union Garrison on the Delaware River waterfront. He was a charter member of the non-profit sportsmen's Square Circle Gun Club in Gibbsboro and joined the Cruiser Olympia Association of Philadelphia. The USS *Olympia* (C-6/CA-15) was a steel U.S. warship commissioned in 1895 and in service until 1922. The Navy ceded title to the cruiser in 1957, and the ship became part of the Independence Seaport Museum. The *Olympia* would be designated a National Historic Landmark in 1966.

As years passed, Cobber socialized with his fellow Medal recipients; attending functions, dinners and fundraisers when he could get away from Lindenwold. His travels from home were not always private affairs, finding space in newspapers from time to time.

He and Phyllis went down to Annapolis in early October 1949, to visit friends. Captain and Mrs. Rouh spent a weekend at Mr. & Mrs. E. R. Flathmanns' home in Bay Ridge. On Saturday, the friends took their seats in the Naval Academy's Thompson Stadium to cheer with 22,000 other fans. The weekend before, the Navy *Midshipmen* football team had finally ended a fifteen-game losing streak and was roaring back along the comeback trail. Their opponents that day, the Duke *Blue Devils*, were enjoying an unbeaten season, and the prognosticators favored them to win. The fans watched the teams take their benches on Farragut Field. Duke's 14–7 half-time lead seemed to have confirmed the odds.

No one in the crowd of spectators knew better than Carlton that being down did not mean that the game was over. The Rouhs and Flathmanns cheered as the hard-striking *Middies* broke the ball game wide open in the second half with three touchdowns. The friends celebrated the 28–14 victory that night, attending the Academy dances. [20]

Public Service

Carlton's USMC service had been an important part of his life, a reflection of his character. He took many opportunities to continue a life of service to the larger civilian community. He stayed active in Republican Party politics for the rest of his life.

In 1948, he made an unsuccessful bid for a Camden County Board of Freeholders office, the County's governing body. Undeterred, he ran again in 1950, was elected to the Board of Freeholders, and served a three-year term.

On Wednesday morning, August 15, 1951, a heavy, wet fog sat over the Delaware River Valley. Seven years after his heroics, Carlton stood beside New Jersey Governor Alfred E. Driscoll in New Castle, Delaware. They discussed how the lack of transportation had long caused the southern parts of their state to remain underdeveloped and that the days ahead would change dramatically. And not just for on-land traffic. The river bottleneck impeding the ferry and ocean-going vessel routes was over.

The Delaware governor greeted the New Jersey contingent and the crowd of 2,000 onlookers.

Carlton stood at the Delaware approach to the sixth longest suspension bridge in the world, and the first land-to-land link between New Castle, Delaware and Deepwater, New Jersey. The 2,150-foot, $44 million Delaware Memorial Bridge, a four-lane roadway spanning a mile of water, with towers rising 437 feet above the river, was opening. The bridge was dedicated in honor of the men and women from both states who had made the supreme sacrifice during WWII. There was a ribbon cutting and brief ceremonies at the tollgates. [21]

Carlton had been invited to attend the ceremonies in New Castle's Veterans Memorial Park. The War Memorial was visible from the northbound-side lanes for drivers and passengers who paid the bridge toll 75¢ for cars and 50¢ per axle for all other vehicles. Cobber and Sergeant James P. Connor, Delaware's only living Medal recipient, placed wreaths at the cast bronze plaque. The War Memorial became a popular site for annual Veterans Day and Memorial Day ceremonies.

In 1956, Carlton took over as Lindenwold mayor when there was a death in the borough. It was a chance for leadership, and he served one term. The Lindenwold government consisted of a mayor and six council members (the Borough Council). In his partial term, he and the council represented the borough as a whole. [22]

More auspicious than being mayor or attending MOH ceremonies that year was the good news that he was going to be a dad. Into their late 30s, Carlton and Phyllis welcomed a daughter into their lives. Jacquelyn "Jackie" Rouh was born in November 1956. When she was a kid, influenced by her dad and mom having been veterans, Jackie helped make floats for parades related to politics. [23]

That same November, Carlton went down to Florida. Newspapers reported that 338 recipients of the "coveted" Medal of Honor lived in communities from coast to coast. Of those, 176 belonged to the CMOHS. All holders of the Medal were invited to the Society's first annual national meeting in Lakeland, Florida. On Veterans Day and the Marine Corps' birthday, Saturday, November 10, citizens lined the streets to welcome and cheer the honor guard and 145 Medal recipients riding in open cars.

Claus Kristian Clausen attended the five-day convention. He had earned his Medal during the Spanish-American War (June 2–3, 1898) and had served in World War I. At age 87, he was the oldest living recipient.

Reporters who had never interviewed a recipient might have anticipated many tales of bravado. Encountering modesty when among heroes came as a surprise. There was little talk of past deeds or swapping of war stories among the battle-scarred heroes of two world wars and the Korean conflict. Rather, they enjoyed passing around photos of their offspring, and talking about their wives, the weather, Marilyn Monroe, and bantering about the New York *Giants*, *Dodgers*, and *Yankees*. They talked politics. Open for discussion was the re-election of popular incumbent Republican President Dwight D. Eisenhower for another term on Tuesday, just before they had started arriving in Florida. [24]

Nicholas "Nick" Oresko of Bayonne, New Jersey, attended the weekend. He had been gravely wounded knocking out two German machine-gun bunkers. Serious and quiet, working as a VA contact man, he did not care to talk about his own valor. One of his biggest goals in life was to find a way to help the children whose fathers had died in the wars.

Richard William O'Neill, WWI U.S. Army recipient from New York City and the Society's executive director, explained why Carlton Rouh might have had "memory lapses" when he came home. "Actually, a Medal of Honor recipient doesn't remember what happened to him on that certain day. Others tell him about it later."

Charles William Shea, WWII U.S. Army recipient, also from New York City, was the Society's secretary and the assistant director of the New York City Veterans Center. He expressed a distinct dislike for the reference to "winners." "You don't win it," he insisted. "It's not like getting something in a contest."

The recipients viewed themselves as no different than other soldiers, sailors, Marines, or airmen. By the fortunes of war on the human side, they had been chosen as shield bearers for the only real heroes of any war—the "ever-to-be-remembered sacred dead who sleep under the white crosses."

The solemn side of the gathering was to give the recipients a chance to rededicate themselves to the service of God and country. One consideration underway was to set up a college scholarship for the recipients' children, especially for the men who had earned the decoration posthumously. The society sent a *thank you* to President Eisenhower and Congress for preserving peace and keeping the nation strong.

Twenty Years Had Passed

Memories of World War II were inescapable for the veterans in 1962. In January, twenty years had passed since Carlton had enlisted in the Marine Corps. The USS *Arizona* Memorial at Pearl Harbor in Honolulu was dedicated on Wednesday, May 30, 1962. August brought the twentieth anniversary of the Marines landing on Guadalcanal.

Luther Skaggs Jr., the Marine from Henderson, Kentucky, who had stood on the White House steps beside Carlton when President Truman put Medals around their necks, was the CMOHS national chairman. [25] He was responsible for planning meetings, conventions, and reunions.

When the newspaper headlines were all about the mysterious death of Hollywood actress Marilyn Monroe on Sunday, August 5, 1962, tucked into short columns in corners of newspapers, the news in communities across the country was about "Vets Of Marine Battles To Meet Wednesday Night." 1st Division Marines began gathering for thankful 20-year reunions.

A 1st MarDiv reunion in San Diego honored famous Leathernecks including the five-time Navy Cross recipient, Lieutenant General Lewis B. "Chesty" Puller.

About 140 members attended the Thursday to Saturday national CMOHS convention in Detroit, October 25–28, 1962. The recipients commemorated the 100th anniversary of President Abraham Lincoln creating the Medal.

Five months after the convention ended, borough residents in Lindenwold had first-hand reports of the tenacity for rescuing others that their former mayor had demonstrated in Pacific Island battles. Carlton was in the headlines again. His heroics might have had more print, except that the worst submarine disaster in peace or war had occurred on Wednesday morning, April 10, 1963. Nuclear-powered attack USS *Thresher*, SSN-593, with 129 men aboard, went to the bottom in the North Atlantic, east of Cape Cod.

Rescuing an Unconscious Boy

Boy Saved By War Hero. [26] The Rouh and Scott families were neighbors. As the U.S. Navy searched for the *Thresher* on Wednesday night, Carlton happened by the Scott house and recognized the two children standing in the front yard. The house was in flames. He realized that others had to be inside.

The Scotts had taken three of their children shopping and left 13-year-old Thomas home to watch after his five-year-old brother and two-year-old sister. The teenager had accidentally started a fire playing with matches in his bedroom. He was able to get his younger siblings out of the blazing house, then, had gone back in to save his father's coin collection. He fell unconscious on the living room floor.

Carlton broke a front window, squeezed into the burning home, found the teenager, and carried him to safety. The boy was taken to Our Lady of Lourdes Hospital and treated for smoke inhalation. The Scott house was destroyed, but Thomas survived the fire.

When a reporter interviewed him about rescuing the unconscious boy, Carlton responded in MOH recipient fashion.

"I didn't do anything special," he said.

If rescuing a boy from a home engulfed in fire was not anything special, qualifying Carlton's community contributions is made difficult. For instance, he had a hand in establishing the Lindenwold Public Library system.

Two Lindenwold teachers had started a book loan program from the Camden County Free Library in the summer of 1952. [27] The Lindenwold Public Library was officially instituted on Monday, February 1, 1965. Carlton was one of the founders of the library located in School #1 in the nurse's office at Linden and White Horse Pike. [28]

The borough purchased a vacant home in 1969, and converted it into the new Lindenwold Library. The mayor and Council of the Borough of Lindenwold officially adopted responsibility on November 17. Thereby was established within the Borough of Lindenwold a library to be known as the "Public Library of the Borough of Lindenwold."

The building proved to be inadequate for the community. Ground breaking for a new library at 310 East Linden Avenue took place in June 1975. The Lindenwold Public Library opened on December 1975, and the old library was demolished.

By the end of 1963, President Johnson had made his decisions to reinforce the 16,500 U.S. servicemen in South Viet Nam with more troops. Carlton watched the political and military developments closely and took an active part in the events on the home front as Marines again faced a determined enemy in the South East Asian theater.

Four years after fire destroyed the Scott home, anti-war protesters in New York City and San Francisco organized marches. As word spread, more communities planned protests and marches against America's Viet Nam policies. Across the nation, a coordinated protest took place on Saturday, April 15, 1967. The orderly marches tended to be non-violent.

Local American Legion and VFW posts assembled to jeer the protestors, and, in many places, hecklers outnumbered the marchers. One sign common in the marches that particularly rankled the WWII veterans declared "We're Sick of War."

Carlton was in Philadelphia that Saturday, attending a pro-U.S. intervention rally behind Independence Hall. Dressed in civilian clothes, he stood on a podium with two other Medal recipients who attended in uniform: Major Douglas P. Jacobson, USMC, Iwo Jima, from Wilmington, North Carolina, and Army Spec-6 Lawrence Joel, the first African American to earn the Medal in Viet Nam. The three recipients addressed the 1,000 persons who had gathered in favor of U.S. Vietnam policy. [29]

Carlton understood better than the protestors what young Marines at war faced. For more than thirty years, he had thought of men who did not come home from the Pacific war. He had counted every day as an unearned piece of good fortune. He had said as much to a Philadelphia columnist.

"I looked into my own grave on September 15, 1944."

Almost annually, Carlton and Phyllis decided what gatherings they would attend. The next year, Thomas J. Kelly, of New York, CMOHS president, invited the Rouhs and all holders of the Medal to attend the October 10–13, 1968, national convention in Seattle, Washington. [30]

Prior to the CMOHS October 9–12, 1969, convention in Houston, Texas, Carlton traveled over to Valley Forge, Pennsylvania, to meet up with other Medal holders and dignitaries.

The Freedoms Foundation at Valley Forge was founded in 1949. South of the Schuylkill River and adjacent to the National Historical Park, the campus—a patriotic land of natural woodland, groves, and gardens, of flags, statues, marble monuments, memorials, pavilions, gazebos, buildings and museums—is on grounds where General George Washington encamped his forces during the Revolutionary War.

The Foundation had developed fifty-two acres of woodland as the Medal of Honor Grove, designed as a living memorial to all the recipients of the nation's highest military decoration and promoted as the first Medal of Honor memorial in the nation. Each of the fifty states, Puerto Rico, and the District of Columbia had a 1-acre plot. Carlton was there on Wednesday, September 17, 1969, for the dedication of New Jersey's acre to memorialize the ninety-two New Jersey recipients. [31] Dressed in his smart civilian clothes, he strolled through the wooded trails with other recipients accredited to the state.

WWI U.S. Army First Sergeant Benjamin Kaufman (1894 –1981), a former executive director and national commander of the Jewish War Veterans of the United States and the manager of Trenton's State Employment Service office attended. WWII U.S. Army Technical Sergeant Stephen Raymond Gregg (1914–2005), from Bayonne, New Jersey, and WWII U.S. Army Staff Sergeant Freeman Victor Horner (1922–2005), from Shamokin, Pennsylvania, walked with them. The men were happy to welcome Mr. Thomas McGuire Sr., 76, from Ridgewood, New Jersey. His son was WWII Army Air Force Ace Major Thomas Buchanan McGuire Jr., posthumous Medal recipient after whom McGuire AFB was named.

Freedoms Foundation trustees, The Legion of Valor officers, NJ Army National Guard officers, and the Hudson County American Legion commander were proud to shake hands with the recipients. The Foundation Drill Team started off the ceremony.

Assistant Secretary of Defense Roger T. Kelley was the keynote speaker. He believed the MOH winners were "men who did not drop out and brought honor to themselves, their states, and their country by their solitary, selfless acts." To the assistant secretary, the military man was "the kind of guy who can look about him, see the needs of some of our citizens and say to them, 'I will give you more than just my physical resources. I will give you of myself, my time, and my attention.'"

For anyone who asked how he could equate a man's courage on the battlefield with his charitable acts at home, he had an answer ready. "I do not equate them," he said. "They are two sides of the whole man. But I do believe that the same quality of selflessness that causes our military man's courage also leads him to serve those less fortunate than himself."

New Jersey Chief of Staff, Major General James F. Cantwell, addressed those in attendance in the grove. Then he unveiled the State Seal on the 7-foot-high, granite obelisk standing on a brick square. The Foundation trustees invited the guests to walk around the monument to view the stainless-steel markers with the name and organization of each recipient, the date, and location of the act of valor. Each marker was mounted near a living tree that family members and service organizations had donated.

After the dedication of New Jersey's Medal of Honor Grove, Carlton gathered for a variety of group photos. In one shot, from left to right, stood Freeman Horner, General Cantwell, Ben Kaufman, Carlton, Stephen Gregg, a Freedoms Foundation trustee, and Mr. Thomas B. McGuire Sr. [32]

In addition to his work as Chief of the Veterans Assistance Section in the VA's Philadelphia office, family life was Carlton's focus in the early 1970s.

Jackie Rouh graduated from high school in 1975. She went off to Eisenhower College in Seneca, New York, that autumn, attending on a Medal of Honor scholarship. She met other children whose dads were Medal recipients and shared stories with them, realizing how much they had in common. The recipients were just dads to them. It would always strike Jackie as surprising whenever she realized "that these men were often viewed differently by others!" [33]

While she was away, Carlton served as a member (commissioner) of The Camden County Board of Freeholders. [34]

Lindenwold continued to extend tributes to her father. In 1976, the city rededicated Lucaston Field in his name. Then, on September 17, 1977, the neglected and vandalized sundial in front of the school, having been cleaned and restored to its original luster, was rededicated. The New Jersey Department of Marine Corps League, Clementon American Legion Post # 94, and the Blackwood Veterans of Foreign Wars Post 7927 sponsored the rededication.

In San Jose, California, 167 Medal recipients gathered for their semi-annual meeting, November 10–13, 1977. During the November 11 Veterans Day parade, the men with blue ribbons around their necks road in convertibles down eight downtown streets. Two jet fighters and a military helicopter flew by in tribute. The next time the CMOHS held its national convention, they would make special remarks in remembrance of Carlton Rouh.

Still Lindenwold's Hometown Hero

Thanksgiving Day was November 24, 1977. Carlton and Phyllis looked forward to the next holiday—Christmas—when Jackie would be home with them. No one had any inkling that Thanksgiving would be their last celebration as a family.

Carlton's 58th birthday was in May. He was a young man, but being over age 40, doctors encouraged him to have his blood pressure checked at least once every year. Phyllis, nurse that she was, concurred with that recommendation. High blood pressure ran in his family and claimed the lives of many in the Rouh blood line. Whenever he went in for a physical checkup, readings of his systolic over diastolic blood pressures tended to be over 140/90 mm Hg. Not good. Notes in his medical chart had "hypertension" underlined. He could predict what his physician was going to say before he went to an appointment.

"Lower your stress, don't drink too much alcohol, don't smoke, and cut down on your salt intake."

Nambu machine-gun bullets and an enemy grenade had been unable to filch the life from him, what could two high numbers on a chart do?

Days after Thanksgiving, Carlton picked up the phone and called a cousin he spoke with from time to time. On Wednesday night, December 7, the day America remembered Pearl Harbor, he went to the VFW to join in the toasts to those who had died in the surprise attack. Fellow members would remember that night as their friend's "final muster."

Phyllis and Jackie would reach the same conclusion.

"He was tying up loose ends!" [35]

Carlton died on Thursday in John F. Kennedy Hospital, Stratford, after suffering a massive heart attack. He had lived an additional thirty-three years after that guardian angel had acted on his behalf on shadeless Peleliu.

The community extended their condolences to Phyllis, Jacquelyn, and Carlton's two brothers and two sisters during the viewing held at the Knight Funeral Home in Berlin on

Sunday, from 6:00 to 10:00 PM. The borough and county communities turned out for the funeral services conducted on Monday at 11:00 AM. [36]

One of the borough's most notable people, celebrated resident, and household name was laid to rest immediately following the service. His interment with full military honors was held at Berlin Cemetery in Track 4, Section 5, Block O, Lot 6. A vast assemblage of family, friends, MOH recipients, 1st Marine Division Association members, and other dignitaries attended.

In the years from WWI to the end of the Vietnam War, 999 Medals of Honor were awarded. Of those, the recipients who survived their actions to wear the Medal numbered 454. [37]

Carlton was the third recipient to die in 1977. Jerry Kirt Crump, 43, U.S. Army Korean War recipient, died on January 10, in Cornelius, North Carolina. Donald Arthur Gary, 75, U.S. Navy World War II recipient, died on April 9, in Garden Grove, California. [38] As Christmas neared, the CMOHS reported that 285 recipients remained living in American communities.

When Carlton's remains were lowered into the grave, the other four Marine Medal recipients who had protected comrades from grenade blasts and survived had years of life ahead of them. Don Roy Truesdell, 71 years old, was considering official invitations and a house empty of children. Richard Sorenson was 53 years old. He had moved to Reno and was working as Nevada's Director of Veterans Affairs. Dick Bush would have his 53rd birthday in two weeks. He was reading in an association newsletter about the death of an old Marine Raider friend after a car accident and was making his plans to attend a July 1978 Raider reunion in San Diego. Jack Lucas, 49, was the youngest of the WWII recipients. He was trying to stabilize his troubled life and decide what to do with his assets following a wife's plot to have him executed. For these four Marines, news of Carlton's death renewed their contemplations about mortality.

At the time of her father's funeral, Jackie was midway through her junior year at Eisenhower College. Carlton missed out on seeing his daughter prosper. In her senior year, she was selected for a nationally recognized award—Who's Who Among Students in American Universities and Colleges. [39] Faculty, administration and student body committees in over 2,300 universities and colleges nominated a select number of outstanding undergraduate seniors for the award. Jackie was selected based on her leadership ability displayed in the areas of scholastic aptitude, community service, and extracurricular activities. Having been named an honoree for this award, she was eligible for special reference services for post-graduate employment or admissions to graduate school.

Jacquelyn married Joseph P. Govan. Phyllis enjoyed her days spent with two granddaughters, Colleen and Carol. The girls had no opportunities to get to know their grandfather. Jackie was granted her Registered Professional Nurse license to practice in New Jersey on September 12, 1990.

The Lindenwold Borough renamed a one-mile section of road running parallel to the railroad tracks between Pinelawn Avenue to Gibbsboro Road, where he once played and skated with Phyllis. Carlton Street ends at Lindenwold High School.

During the 96th Congress (1979–1980), Representative James J. Florio [NJ-1] introduced Bill H.R.2601 on March 5, 1979, in the House. He proposed that the new Veterans Administration Medical Center in Camden, New Jersey, be designated the "*Carlton R. Rouh Memorial Veterans' Medical Center.*" Ten other New Jersey Representatives had agreed on January 3 to cosponsor the Bill. H.R.2601 was referred to the House Committee on Veterans' Affairs. During the 97th

Congress (1981–1982), Representative Florio tried a second time. He introduced H.R.2023 in the House on February 24, 1981. This time twelve representatives cosponsored the Bill. Again, it was referred to the House Committee on Veterans' Affairs. The Bill was set aside.

The Medical Center in Camden was just a "proposal," and the VA decided against the construction. Instead, Camden would have a VA Outpatient Clinic with eight staff members. Veterans were able to receive comprehensive primary care and behavioral health services at the small facility.

"In Every Clime and Place
And Never Lost Our Nerve"

In the fall of 1982, President Ronald Reagan sent Marines to Lebanon on a peacekeeping mission. On August 20, a multi-national force was ordered to Beirut, the war-torn capital, to help coordinate a Palestinian withdrawal from the troubled territory. Eight hundred U.S. Marines manned the U.S. Embassy and the four-story, concrete Marine Barracks. On September 30, Corporal David Lee Reagan, 21, from Virginia Beach, was the first Marine to die—while defusing a bomb. [40] A year later, snipers and suicide bombers killed six more peacekeeping Marines.

Marine veterans of the three previous wars paid attention to newspaper and television broadcast accounts of the Beirut mission and mourned for their young brothers. Then, while the 1st Marine Division Association organized a return to Peleliu, the greatest single-day number of deaths for Marines since the Battle of Iwo Jima occurred on October 23, 1983.

A Lebanese terrorist drove an explosives-packed truck into the Marine Barracks, killing 241 U.S. military personnel: 220 Marines, 18 sailors, and 3 Army soldiers. The main Marine force left Lebanon on February 26, 1984. Of the original 800 Marines, 250 lost their lives during the Beirut mission. The Marines had not departed Lebanon yet when Peleliu was again in the news.

Three retired 1st MarDiv enlisted men, a corpsman, and a retired Army soldier, sailed again into the Palau archipelago embarked on the USS *Peleliu* (LHA-5), a big deck, amphibious assault ship. [41] On February 6, 1984, they looked out from the ship's railings to Peleliu: not barren and burned as they had seen in 1944. Thick green vegetation shaded the white, landing beaches and the entire island.

The veterans visited for three days, attending ceremonies and touring battle sites, rocky caves, and forests. The underwater shipwrecks, derelicts of landing craft, rusting and gutted tanks and Amtracs with foliage in every opening, unexploded ordinance, relic hand grenades in rocky crevices, turned green by time, twisted metal, and bullet-riddled Marine helmets brought back memories.

The tour went beyond the airfield toward Umurbrogol Mount and the island's central ridges. They turned left off Crocodile Road onto a short side road at the base of "Bloody Nose Ridge" and passed the Japanese Shinto Shrine. At the end of the road, on the far side of a grass field, rose a massive, four-sided, concrete stele. Attending the dedication of the monument was a highlight of the visit to Peleliu.

The stele, sponsored by the First Marine Division Association, commemorates the men of the 1st MarDiv for their actions on Peleliu. The large plaque on the face of the monument— "In memory of the Marines who gave their lives in the seizure of Peleliu"—is topped by the Marine Corps emblem. The division emblem is at the bottom of the plaque, beside the words:

YOUR BROTHERS IN ARMS
FIRST MARINE
DIVISION (REINF)
UNITED STATES
MARINE CORPS

The memorial was rededicated on September 15, 1994, the 50th Anniversary of the Peleliu landings. The First Marine Division Association dedicated two smaller bronze plaques. On the left side of the monument is the 1st Division's Presidential Unit Citation. The bronze MEDAL OF HONOR plaque on the right side recognizes eight Marines. Under lines from the Marine Corps Hymn, their names, units, and states are listed in alphabetical order. First Lieutenant Carlton R. Rouh's name is at the bottom of the plaque. The Peleliu Marine Veterans donated a plaque for the backside of the stele in memory of the various units that had contributed to the capture of the island.

Anyone who attends a Lindenwold Day in September on a Saturday can enjoy various amusements and all-day live entertainment. There will be a parade, amusement rides, dozens of vendors, and fireworks to top off the evening. Most of the day takes place on the southeast side of town on the six-acre Carlton Rouh Memorial Ballfield at the intersection of Egg Harbor Road and United States Avenue, adjoining the Lindenwold Police Department building grounds.

Berlin Cemetery, on the White Horse Pike (US Route 30) on the west side of town, is an historic place, founded in 1766. The steel fencing around the entire perimeter of the grounds allows a full view of the cemetery from the street. Whether a visitor enters from the north through the main gate on the White Horse Pike or from the west through the Hayes Avenue gate or through the south entrance on Clementon Road, the driveways lead to a tree-shaded circle at the cemetery's center where Old Glory ripples above the treetops.

On Memorial Day, May 27, 1991, the Berlin Cemetery War Memorial was dedicated within the circle. The memorial comprises a series of monuments honoring the area residents who have died in armed conflict serving their country. The World War II War Memorial, a large, stone monument under the flagpole, is plainly in sight from the White Horse Pike gate. A stanza of a familiar memorial poem is inscribed on the face of the monument.

Nor shall your glory be forgot
While Fame her record keeps,
Or Honor points the hallowed spot
Where Valor proudly sleeps. [42]

On one smaller stone monument dedicated IN REMEMBRANCE OF ALL VETERANS BURIED HERE, Capt. Carlton R. Rouh is mentioned for being awarded the Congressional Medal of Honor during World War II. He is buried a few yards away from this monument.

The Military Order of the Purple Heart Chapter #116 in Gloucester City, New Jersey, is named in honor of Captain Carlton R. Rouh.

The local Veterans Advisory Committee planned to recognize Camden County residents who had been awarded the Congressional Medal of Honor. They selected a site in Cooper River Park in Pennsauken Township, a few dozen feet from the banks of the river. A 40-foot-long concrete pathway leads to the Medal of Honor Memorial, dedicated in 1998. [43] The ornate memorial is a metallic flowing piece of silver and gold attached to a 10-foot-tall brick wall. Carlton R. Rouh is one of eight recipients to have their names scattered throughout the memorial "wreath." In front of the memorial wall, a sundial sits on top of a square brick pillar, acting as a symbol of the monument's theme. The memorial gives tribute to the eight in an inscription.

"The only real wealth is time how much time you have to spend in doing what you prefer doing with your life—This meditation park is dedicated to those who gave all their wealth in time to the citizens of Camden County."

"Who was he?"

Carlton's devoted wife, Phyllis Lorraine Rowand Rouh, 93, went home to be with the Lord and her husband on October 16, 2012. She was survived by her loving daughter Jacquelyn A. (Joseph P.) Govan, two cherished grandchildren and two precious great grandchildren. Her funeral services were held Monday morning, October 22, at St. John in the Wilderness Episcopal Church in Gibbsboro, New Jersey. She was buried with military honors at Berlin Cemetery immediately after the services. [44]

The Haddon Heights High School alumni chose Carlton as the 2013 Alumnus of the Year. That distinction came as no surprise to most people in Lindenwold. That year, 17,501 residents lived in the borough's 7,465 households. For most, Carlton Rouh was a household name, remembered more for his years in public service than for having been the mayor.

Lavinia DeCastro, newspaper staff writer, was certain of the likely answer if anyone in Lindenwold was asked, "Who was he?" [45]

"Carlton Rouh was a hero."

CHAPTER 14

Defend What Is Yours

✳✳✳

"The characteristic of genuine heroism is its persistency." [1]

— RALPH WALDO EMERSON

BOYHOOD EVENTS SET THE PATH toward manhood, and the foundation of heroic bravery is laid down early in life. Any man who is brave in combat situations is likely to have already developed an evident pattern of certain behaviors and characteristics long before he went to war. Another way to say this—the actions of heroically brave individuals demonstrate an early pattern of behavior rather than a single, isolated act.

Marines who earned Medals of Honor provide examples of what was likely true of a great number of their comrades. These men faced early challenges in life, resulting either from life situations in which as boys they had no direct part, or from deliberate choices they made. Routinely in situations in which they would be challenged and tested, they learned to contend with adversity rather than withdraw from or submit to it. And, if they were not challenged by early life experiences, not content to wait and see what fate had in mind for them, they found ways to challenge themselves. Their response to most challenges was to face them directly or to find a way to triumph. Some of their responses would have been immediate and spontaneous, perhaps impulsive. Others were thought out, planned, and rehearsed in their minds.

Men with the capacity to act heroically brave learn from early experiences that their efforts result in achievement. Overcoming early challenges seems to breed an unquestioned confidence. They come to believe that striving leads to positive outcomes.

Known to take risks without undue apprehension, they seemed never to anticipate dire or dreadful outcomes to their actions. That included striving, contending, or vying against rivals and opponents—facing a known enemy was the ultimate competition.

Family and friends remembered many of the recipients as wanting to be "the best at whatever he did." The interests to which they turned their attention triggered the impulse to achieve excellence.

Bravery demands a certain kind of single-mindedness. Many Medal recipients were described as having been a "strong willed," strong-minded, determined, or even a "stubborn" child. "Steadfast" would be a good word. Once set on a course of action, it was difficult to redirect, deter, or talk them out of their plans. With an objective in mind, the boys persisted in efforts to attain their goals. Not easily distracted from something they intended to accomplish, most other things took a place of secondary importance. What emerged was a willingness to do "whatever it takes" to achieve an objective.

Every MOH recipient was ready to volunteer to go into harm's way: even looked forward to the opportunity to do so. Taking on unwelcome or intimidating tasks or responsibilities that others avoided or abandoned presented them special challenges. Risking frustration, fatigue, or failure, sometimes facing ridicule and criticism, did not alter their course. Above all risks, the recipients demonstrated a readiness to encounter injury and pain, as well as threats to life and limb, to accomplish the task—not necessarily a sense of duty; it was the nature of their character. Obvious examples of this tendency are enlisting in the Marines during a time of war or national emergency, persuading a parent to sign an age waiver, or lying about his age to get to boot camp.

This persistent pattern of deliberateness, the willing self-sacrifice evident in genuine bravery, can be no more evident than in the actions of a boy from North Carolina.

The Tar Heels

Stories about soldiers marching through the pine trees of North Carolina woods, getting tar on their heels, go as far back as the American Revolutionary War. The "tar heel" nickname stuck and North Carolinians have worn it with pride ever since.

Jacklyn Harrell Lucas was born in Plymouth, Washington County, North Carolina, on Valentine's Day, February 14, 1928. He would see much irony in his birthdate later in his life. His parents, dyed-in-the wool Tar Heels, instilled patriotism in his upbringing. [2] As far back as Jackie could recall the stories, his ancestors had fought for their liberty and had come to the defense and aid of beleaguered family members and neighbors. He listened and reveled in stories of family members standing up to bad people.

"I always enjoyed hearing the tale of my grandfather's liberation of the young woman (Mae Phelps) and very much admired his role as rescuer." [3]

The town was like that, too. The main streets of Plymouth, the kind of town after which the television series Andy of Mayberry was fashioned, are named after presidents and forts and Civil War legends. Jackie could walk past the big antebellum Windley-Ausbon House at the intersection of Washington and Third streets and look up at a second-floor window. Thirty Union bullet holes fired at a sniper during a failed 1862 Confederate raid are visible around the widow casing. Further south on Washington is the location of the Union earthworks and Fort Williams. One of his best childhood friends lived near there. The USS Southfield still lies east of town at the bottom of the Roanoke River.

Jackie came from strong, Irish stock on both sides of his family. He was proud of his ancestors, spread out in Washington, Hyde, and Brunswick counties. They had fought in the Revolutionary War and in the Confederacy against the Union forces during the Civil War. Two of his ancestors wore a Victoria Cross on their chests, the highest award for gallantry "in the face of the enemy" the British government gives to its armed service members.

From the beginning of the Southern Rebellion, northeastern North Carolina had favored the Union cause. Residents owned few slaves and had close trading ties with the North. Like many large Civil War era families, the Lucas men were not always on the same side. Sixty-eight Lucas Tar Heel farmers fought for the Confederates. Jack's great-great-grandfather, Confederate Private James Harvey Lucas, served with Company C, 1st Battalion, North Carolina Heavy Artillery, and died of malaria. His eldest boy, Jack's great-grandfather, Confederate Private Boyd Lucas, was with Company H, 17th Regiment, North Carolina Infantry (2nd Organization), and was wounded by a miniball to the skull on a Virginia battlefield. He returned to Company H after a four-month convalescence. [4]

Two of Boyd's younger brothers took opposite sides. Union Private Joshua Lucas served with the 1st Regiment, North Carolina Infantry. Confederate Private James Harvey Lucas Jr. was in Company C, 1st Battalion, North Carolina Heavy Artillery, when his father passed away.

The rift in loyalties during the war was evident in Plymouth—the town in which Jackie was raised. The town's original plot of land on the Roanoke River, lot number 48 on the original map, was purchased from Arthur Rhodes in 1789 for five pounds. Across the next seven decades the township grew into a prosperous farming community.

Federal Army and Navy forces occupied Plymouth in 1862 and held it through most of the war. The Confederates raided the town on December 10, 1862, but the attack failed. They burned the buildings along Main Street and most of Plymouth as they withdrew from the raid. The Confederate Army returned in April 1864, and took the town in the Battle of Plymouth. [5]

Union and Confederate gunboats steamed up and down the river. The Ironclad Ram CSS *Albemarle*, a small boat built at Edwards Ferry, harassed Union traffic, sending the USS *Southfield* to the bottom a half-mile east of downtown on April 19, 1864. The *Albemarle* ranged throughout the summer, until fifteen hundred Union troops recaptured Plymouth in October 1864. The two forces exchanged cannon balls, bullets, and hand grenades during the ensuing battle. The Rebel Ram *Albemarle* was sunk in six feet of water at the end of Washington Street on October 27, 1864. The boat was salvaged after the war, and only the smokestack and a cannon remained as relics.

The generations of Lucas sons and daughters married the daughters and sons of Davenport and Swain and Phelps and Moore and Edwards neighbors scattered about the townships. The men were farmers, overseers, and day laborers. The women were weavers and housekeepers. Any daughter unmarried by age 18 years was recorded on census roles as a "spinster."

Washington County Lucas ancestors are buried in small cemeteries surrounding the Plymouth, Lees Mill, Scuppernong, and Skinnersville townships. In southwest Plymouth, the tiny Lucas Cemetery sits between Wilson Street and Hwy 64, behind one of the early family farms. More family members are buried in the larger Windley and Hillside Memorial Gardens Cemeteries. [6]

Jack's paternal grandfather, William Franklin Lucas, was a tobacco and dairy farmer, as was *his* father. He married once and provided for eight children, in an eastern region of farms, lakes, and marshlands below Albemarle Sound. The Roanoke River flowed by his home.

Louis Harold Lucas, born in Plymouth on September 25, 1894, was the fifth of William's children and the fourth son. Two more children followed in the next five years. Around 1900, William purchased the large *Springwood* farm, a former Civil War hospital on NC 90 Highway (before it became U.S. Route 64 in 1934). Besides his family and his prospering farming, he was proud to say that the oldest pecan tree in the state towered more than 100 feet into the sky in his orchard. Before his last child, Avis, was born, Grandpa William was involved in an incident that increased the number of children he provided for. The matter became family lore passed down through the next generations.

In 1903, William learned from a neighbor that his sister's husband was treating his 12-year-old daughter poorly. William and his 16-year-old son, Thomas, rowed down the Roanoke River to the Phelps home. Following an angry confrontation with the father, William returned home with his niece. [7]

When the 1910 U.S. Census District ED 111 enumerator completed Sheet Number 1B, Household 20 included William and "Mazura" Lucas, all eight of their children, Aunt Mary "Molly" Lucas, niece May Lucas, 18, and Annie Lucas, an 18-year-old "border." [8] Louis had stopped attending school the year before and was working as a laborer on the Springwood home farm.

Before the next census, Samuel Boyd Lucas served as a private in the U.S. Army during WWI. James C. Lucas, another of Boyd Lucas' grandsons, was also a WWI veteran.

At the time of the 1920 Census, Louis was 26 years old. He was still living on his parents' farm along with his siblings, Samuel and Pauline, who were both public school teachers, and with Avis, a single 14-year-old girl.

The Edwards family was spread out on farms along the Scuppernong River. Louis met Margaret Edwards, a pretty, honey-blond young woman, who had completed nine grades of schooling. The two decided they were old enough to marry. Margaret was 21 years old when they said their vows in 1924.

Louis and his bride went west to Durham to join his older brother William P. in the dairy business. A few years passed and a dairy business opportunity presented itself. The couple moved to the little town of Washington, on the Pamlico River, thirty-eight road miles southwest of Plymouth. Louis began making milk and ice cream. The business thrived and would grow into the Maola Ice Cream Company.

Louis and Margaret began experiencing extended-family strains that Jackie would hear about as he grew up.

Challenges Had Begun

Grandpa William took ill a month after Jackie was born in 1928. Louis left the ice cream company and returned to Springwood to help manage his father's farm. William Sr., 69, died six months later on September 27, 1928. More sad news followed.

Louis' Great-Aunt Jacqueline had married William Fletcher Gray some six years after the Civil War had ended. The couple resided in Norfolk, Virginia, and had a number of children, who of course had their own children. Louis and Margaret enjoyed visits with the Grays. Jacqueline Lucas Gray died on May 15, 1929. Five months later, the nation plunged into the Depression years.

In April 1930, six months past *Black Tuesday*, October 29, 1929, the day the stock market crashed and lost fourteen billion dollars, two-year-old Jackie was living on the family farm with his parents, Grandma Missouri, and his 60-year-old Great-Aunt Rocksie Swain. Uncle Sam Lucas, a general farmer, was living next door with his wife and five-year-old son, Oliver "Sam." Jackie's cousin Sam was one of his first playmates. They would one day be shipmates on their way to battle on a Pacific island. Uncle Richard Lucas, a preacher and dairy farmer, his wife and 15-year-old son, and his sister Pauline, 30, lived on the other side of Louis and Margaret.

All of America was having economic hard times. Many were left with no money, and credit was nearly impossible to obtain. Bank failures continued despite calling in outstanding mortgages and loans. In three years' time, crop prices plummeted, and five percent of the nation's farmers had been evicted from their lands. Farmers across the nation fell into very dark moods. Louis began to feel pressure from family to leave Springwood.

In 1932, Louis and Margaret took four-year-old Jackie to Virginia to get a break and visit friends. A gunshot was going to ring out for the first time that he would remember. While the kids were supposed to be taking a mid-afternoon nap, an older boy took a .44 caliber gun out of a nightstand drawer. He fired a round that went right over Jackie's head and hit the little girl asleep beside him, wounding her arm. The young girl ran screaming from the house into the yard as blood streamed from her wound. If there were a more frightening experience early in his life, he would not recall it. [9]

Not long after the Virginia trip, another gunshot impacted the family. One day, Jackie's father grabbed a shotgun and ran into a freshly seeded field to scare off blackbirds. Louis lost his footing and the gun accidentally fired, shooting off his hat and blackening his face with powder. The power burns impaired his vision from that day on.

Louis was a sensitive father. He thought that Jackie needed a furry companion, since he was an only son. He gave his boy a Jack Russell terrier puppy. Jackie named the dog Skippy, and the bond was strong. While living in Plymouth, a laundry truck ran over Skippy as he bounded across the street to Jack's call. The dog was killed instantly. Jackie screamed and tried to hide the tears that welled up. He felt guilt for not protecting his little buddy and cried himself to sleep many nights afterwards.

The next year, Jackie was playing in the middle of the meadow down the street from home. The tall grass was dry. Older boys, playing with matches, unintentionally set the field on fire. The smell of smoke and sounds of kindling popping filled the air. Quickly, the blaze surrounded and trapped Jackie as flames leaped higher than his head. No avenue of escape presented itself, and he thought he was going to burn to death. He could not see the others in the field, but could hear their panicky shouts as the flames closed in on him. The older boys tried to beat down the fire and get to him, but the field was being engulfed rapidly. Finally, they were able to open a small path through the fire for Jackie to charge through. He credited them with having "the strength and fortitude to set me free." [10]

In 1933, Louis and Margaret bought a tobacco farm in the country a few miles outside of Plymouth. In Jackie's mind, they had moved to a nice white farmhouse and had fresh fruit, a bountiful garden, a smokehouse full of meat, and a crash crop of tobacco. He felt lucky—even fortunate.

He spent most of his early years with family living and farming around Plymouth, Pine Ridge, Roper, Pea Ridge, Creswell, Skinnersville, and Williamston. He plowed fields and cared for livestock and took a bus to school. He went fishing on the Roanoke and Scuppernong rivers. Much play was on horseback and mules.

Frank Edwards, a favorite uncle, put a Marine dress cover on his head when he was six years old. He felt an instant bond with the Marine Corps that stayed with him all his life.

One Christmas, Jackie was surprised to find a saddle under the tree. Then, Louis surprised him further, giving him a pony and a cart that he had bought from Uncle Frank. Jackie named the horse Charlie and enjoyed taking friends for rides in the cart up and down the dirt roads. [11]

Friendship seemed to come naturally to him. Jackie was gregarious and tended to be constant with anyone he considered a buddy.

Some of his fondest childhood memories included his good buddy Marshall Lafayette Moore, the youngest of the Moore kids. The family lived at the corner of Fort Williams Street and 504 Jefferson Street, an easy walk or horse ride from the Lucas home. Marshall's father, Walter Clarence Moore, farmed and worked at the City Ice and Coal plant.

Young Walter had grown up on a farm on Long Acre Road, south of Plymouth, playing and working with the neighbors, the Batemans and the Satterthwaites. He married Virginia Satterthwaite in 1916. Virginia came from good, strong stock. Her father was an honest man and her mother was a kind, affectionate woman considered to be a friend to all. Walter and Virginia were a good match, and they accepted the ways of the Lord.

Martha Louise was born to them on September 9, 1916 and died on November 4, 1918. Thomas Layne, their first boy, was born on December 9, 1919. He did not survive childhood either, living until March 6, 1920. Their daughter, Myra, was born in 1920, would go on to college, and married a Ward boy. Two boys, Mahlon, born in 1923, and Marshall, born June 24, 1926, stayed closer to home.

Marshall was nearly two years older than Jackie. He had a little trouble in school, though, and was one grade behind his friend. The two enjoyed many days of riding horses together down the sandy, dirt roads and playing cowboys and Indians in the woods with the other neighbor boys. They had a long friendship, but Marshall "never lived to be an old man." [12]

Jackie was an "only child" for seven years. He became a big brother in 1935, when Louis Edwards Lucas was born. That was an event. Bigger ones came the next year.

Jackie was eight years old when his father injured his right foot breaking up a fight between two friends on an Albemarle Sound beach. The injury turned to a bruise, then to bone spurs, then to cancer. Eventually the leg was amputated below the knee. Fitted with a prosthesis, Louis was unable to farm. Health problems developed. It "was an anguished period for all the family." [13]

Jackie had always been most comfortable spending time with older boys. Now, he was helping the man of the family more on the farm. Keen-witted and short-tempered, he enjoyed making others laugh and responded to perceived insults with a sharp punch to any adversary's jaw, believing it was what his dad would do, too. Hostile engagements emerged with the bigger boys on the school bus. Jackie loved collecting newspaper articles, magazines, posters, and photographs about boxing, and imagined one day that he would be a great pugilist. He perfected an explosive right hook.

If there were any chinks in his armor, they would prove to be his love of girls, fistfights, and nice cars.

"My father was gone." Thursday, October 12, 1939, was Columbus Day, a new federal holiday. Jackie, 11 years old, had school anyway and was just home in the afternoon. His father whispered to him from bed to go find his brother. By the time the two boys got home ten minutes later, their mother was sobbing, and friends were gathering. After several years of injuries and illnesses, Louis, 45, was dead. [14] The man that Jackie had admired more than anyone, the only authority figure who could give an order that he would willingly follow, had departed from this life.

Jackie's Uncle Richard Lucas, the reverend, conducted the funeral services, an experience that triggered "a steady stream of tears" rolling down the boy's cheeks. Louis was buried in Windley Cemetery, a large cemetery on the south side of town between Roosevelt Avenue and Washington Street. On a partly cloudy day, when the temperature struggled to get to 60°F, Jackie stood beside the grave with his mother, little brother, Grandma Missouri Lucas, uncles and aunts and cousins. Before leaving the cemetery, they visited Grandpa William's grave. Those were the saddest days Jackie could ever remember.

A Short Time as Man of the Family—But Not Head of the Household

After his father's death, Jackie became resentful and could be belligerent. Maybe his February birthday had a part in that. Those under the Aquarius zodiac sign have a reputation for temper tantrums that can result in violence. Full of bitterness and anger, he would recall being "rambunctious" and "shattered." For a year, he was "a mean kid," and his mother was finding him hard to manage.

"I became kind of a tough kid after that to handle; my mother couldn't handle me."

Margaret was 35 years old when her husband died. Louis had provided well for her, leaving her with the house and farm and enough money to support the boys.

Josephine F. Bryan began her U.S. Census work in Plymouth South District #1 on April 15, 1940. She gathered family data from Linden Street, Golf Road, Pine Street, Maple and Cedar courts, Alden Road, and went further south. When she had finished up her enumerations on

June 13, she had visited 518 homes. The Lucas home was the 195th Plymouth Township location she visited. [15]

Josephine knocked on the door on May 10, 1940. Margaret was a widow in mourning and adjusting to her head-of-household role. She owned the home that Louis had purchased. Josephine valued the residence at $2,500 ($43,000 in 2016 dollars)—one of the more expensive homes in district (ED) 94–5. Margaret had earned no income in the twelve months of 1939. Jackie H., 12, and Louis Ed, 5, were at home. Three sharecroppers lodged at the residence: William Latta, 60, married; Earl McIntyre, 34, divorced; and Hilton Shavender, 33, single.

Josephine probably did not ask, and was not told, that Margaret kept a .38 caliber pistol on hand to add some defense to the farm. She knew how to use it and did not hesitate to put her finger to the trigger. She stopped at least one break-in and assault by sticking the .38 into the ribs of an intruder, scaring the sharecropper to run from the house and not return. [16]

For his next school year, in hopes of providing Jack more discipline, Margaret sent him 136 miles inland to Edwards Military Academy in Salemburg, where "Pistol Pete" Maravich would later become a basketball legend. Jack thrived on the discipline in the swampy, forested region east of Fayetteville. He channeled his anger into competitive sports and excelled. He worked his way up to cadet captain. The urge to be a Marine grew stronger. He was seventy miles northwest of Camp Lejeune.

Jack was an athlete and outdoorsman from the start. He was also a leader and team player. Standing 5 feet 5 inches and weighing 158 pounds, he was the captain of his high school football team his first year at Salemburg High School. He played basketball, baseball, softball and wrestled and boxed. For recreation, he went horseback riding, hunting, and trap and skeet shooting.

While Jack was away, Margaret took Louis Ed down to Lake Landing, Hyde County, on the south shores of Lake Mattamuskeet to visit a branch of the Lucas family. Sometimes she made stops in Swan Quarter and Belhaven. Apparently, that is how the pretty, honey-blond young woman met a man who would cause Jack much dismay.

Radford L. "Rad" Jones had married Mattie Carawan in 1920, and resided in Swan Quarter, a tiny town on the Pamlico Sound. They had a daughter and two sons before their marriage ended. Mattie married again to Don Harris. Radford relocated thirty-nine miles northwest to Belhaven, on the Pungo Inlet, and tried to make his living in automotive sales. His older cousin, Elbert Jones, was a World War I veteran, having been a private in Company M, 120th Army Infantry. Elbert had come home with a Purple Heart. Radford advertised that he always made special arrangements for military veterans.

He proposed special arrangements to Margaret, she accepted, and they married. The Lucas family relocated to East Main Street in Belhaven.

Jack was not happy to have a step-father and admittedly despised Mr. Jones. Rad was a sad man who had trouble with alcohol. He mismanaged Margaret's family money, trying to establish Rad Jones Chevrolet Company in Belhaven. [17] He eventually failed in his car sales business and in his efforts to dominate his older step-son. Tensions flared whenever Jack was home from school, at times leading to threats of mutual violence. The marriage survived for seven years.

Jack found what pleasures he could in Belhaven. He hung out with friends at the soda fountain at the local drug store. The Pungo River beach was a block from the house, and he spent hours there. Wearing his straw hat, he caught fish for crabs off the dock with a string, a twenty-pound nail, and a piece of chicken for bait. Back home with his catch, Margaret greased up her pan and broiled the best, lightly-browned crab cakes in town. [18]

Another good thing, Jack gained a step-brother from Radford's first marriage. Billy Jones (1925), three years older than Jack, was a likeable sort, a kind of big brother to look up to. The two boys had stories about fires in common. Jack had the fire in the field. Billy recalled the fire that destroyed his Grandpa Cale Jones' Swan Quarter home in March 1936. The fire's origin was not known, but suspected to be at a chimney flue. [19]

Billy had attended elementary school in Swan Quarter. He graduated from Belhaven High School in 1941. He did not see much of his older sister before he departed home. She was married to John Moore and lived in Southport, Brunswick County, on the Cape Fear River south of Wilmington. Billy enlisted in the U.S. Navy in August 1941, and named Mrs. Mattie Harris, of Swan Quarter as his sole next of kin. After his training at the Norfolk Navy Yard Mechanic's School, he was ordered to sea duty.

To Jack, Clifton Cason Jones, born on March 24, 1930, was too much like Radford, and the Edwards cadet had little to do with his younger step-brother.

The Japanese attack on Pearl Harbor cut Jack's athletic career and high school education short. The 8th Grader took the bombing personally and was enraged. Living in North Carolina, about as far away from Hawaii as a young American could be, he could not sit still for such a surprise affront as a sneak attack.

"I was kind of devastated when we got the news of what all those people suffered at Pearl Harbor. That very day a cold chill ran down my spine. I just, I just became obsessed that I had to do something."

Jack knew that the standard enlistment age was 18 years of age and no younger than 17 years with a signed waiver from a parent or adult family member. He also knew that many under-aged men were lying to the draft board officers and recruiters to go to war and avenge their country. "They had that good old American spirit. They wanted to stand up for America."

He talked to his Uncle Tom Lucas about enlisting early in the Marine Corps. Forty years earlier, his uncle had rowed down the Roanoke River to help Grandpa William rescue Mae Phelps. Surely he would help and sign his consent. Jack got nowhere. He talked it over with his mother.

Margaret already had things to worry about. Early in the year around Jack's 14th birthday, Louis Ed had been riding his bike down Belhaven's Main Street when a car struck him, knocking his hip out of its socket. He had to wear a full body cast and would lie on his back for eighteen months. After the last of four casts was removed it would take another four months until he could walk on his own. [20]

For months, Margaret refused to lie about Jack's age and would not sign a consent form. Her 14-year-old son finally convinced her that he would resist her every objection. He took the matter of joining the Marines into his own hands.

A Fraudulent Enlistment

Jack got the DD Form allowing 17-year-old boys to enlist if a parent had signed it. He forged his mother's signature. She agreed not to submit an official objection. He said goodbye to Margaret, they hugged, and she wished him well. His destination was the Norfolk, Virginia, recruiting station.

Arriving without a copy of his birth certificate, Jack would need an adult to verify his age to be 17 years. That eliminated boarding a Norfolk Southern Railroad passenger train alone at the Belhaven station. Rad was willing to lie about his step-son's age, happy to see him go. They packed into his car and took the 130-mile drive up to Norfolk. The two-and-a-half-hour drive was quiet. [21]

Jack stood at 5 feet 8 inches and weighed 180 pounds. His muscular build and military bearing seemed to fit the age on the consent form. Radford assured the recruiter that his stepson was seventeen. The recruiter accepted the deception and directed Jack to the line of newly arrived recruits. A Marine colonel would discover his true age fourteen months later. For now, Jack was pleased to be following in the footsteps of his ancestors answering the call to arms.

Jack Lucas raised his hand and swore the oath to defend his nation. As of August 6, 1942, he was a proud USMC private.

The timing was momentous for him. The first American offensive in the South Pacific on Guadalcanal was a day away.

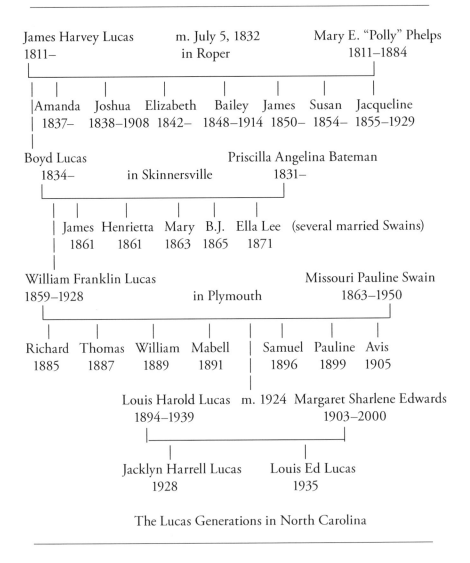

James Harvey Lucas   m. July 5, 1832   Mary E. "Polly" Phelps
1811–   in Roper   1811–1884

Amanda   Joshua   Elizabeth   Bailey   James   Susan   Jacqueline
1837–   1838–1908 1842–   1848–1914 1850–   1854–   1855–1929

Boyd Lucas   Priscilla Angelina Bateman
   1834–   in Skinnersville   1831–

James   Henrietta   Mary   B.J.   Ella Lee   (several married Swains)
1861   1861   1863   1865   1871

William Franklin Lucas   Missouri Pauline Swain
1859–1928   in Plymouth   1863–1950

Richard   Thomas   William   Mabell   Samuel   Pauline   Avis
1885   1887   1889   1891   1896   1899   1905

Louis Harold Lucas   m. 1924   Margaret Sharlene Edwards
   1894–1939   1903–2000

Jacklyn Harrell Lucas   Louis Ed Lucas
       1928   1935

The Lucas Generations in North Carolina

CHAPTER 15

A Place of Grenades, Gore, Guts, and Glory

✳✳✳

"I am tired of the sickening sight of the battlefield with its
mangled corpses & poor suffering wounded." [1]

— General George McClellan to his wife in 1862.

CERTAIN BATTLES RESONATE IN THE annals of American military history. Bunker Hill, Gettysburg, Normandy, Iwo Jima, Heart Break Ridge (Korea), and Khe Sanh (Vietnam) have all been memorialized in books, magazines, and movies.

All Marines remember Iwo Jima, 700 miles southeast of Tokyo, as the volcanic island that forever ensured the Corps' existence. More Medals of Honor were earned in that black ash than in any other single engagement or campaign in which Marines have fought. In fact, more Medals were awarded in five months in 1945, than in any other full year in the Corps' history.

The Pulitzer prize-winning photograph of the flag raising on volcanic Mount Suribachi, the monument at the entrance of Arlington Cemetery, and the movies going back to 1950 have made it difficult for any American to not know about the small pork-chop-shaped island, taking up eight square miles—two-miles wide and five-and-a-half-miles long.

Over 77,000 Marines of the 3rd, 4th, and 5th Divisions landed on the black volcanic ash beaches. Once the battle was engaged on the island, it took the Marines five days to progress 400 yards and capture its most prominent feature—550-foot Mount Suribachi. The American flag was raised over Iwo on Friday, February 23, 1945.

There was no weekend liberty before returning to work. The battle went on for thirty-one more days and nights before Japanese resistance gave way, and the fighting stopped on the island. Marines died every day.

Official casualty reports following the battle gave a sense of how many telegrams were delivered to families at home: 4,554 Marine officers and enlisted men were killed during the hostile action. Another 1,331 died of wounds received in the battle. Forty-six were never found or identified afterwards and were presumed dead. An additional 17,272 Marines were wounded in action. Medical records also reported that 2,648 Marines had been out of the action due to combat stress and fatigue.

Navy officers and sailors among the casualties accounted for 363 who were killed in action, 70 who died of wounds, 448 who were missing and presumed killed, and 1,917 who were wounded in action. Counted among the killed or wounded were 827 corpsmen.

The island defenders died in greater numbers. The Japanese recorded 20,703 on their death rolls. Only 216 survived the battle, having been captured, malnourished and barely conscious, and taken prisoners during the month-long assault.

Those who demonstrate heroic bravery must overcome their own nervous systems, the natural instincts to survive, and then act in unexpected ways that seem humanly unpredictable. While many more likely deserved the honor, twenty-two Marines were awarded the MOH for their actions on the volcanic island. The nature of their gallantry must have been truly conspicuous to stand out from the thousands of courageous acts occurring daily on the island.

Captain James Giffen Headley understood bravery, having witnessed plenty of it. A lawyer from Cincinnati and USMC reserve officer, he was a company commander. He took command of a battalion when his commander was wounded in action and evacuated from the island. Five months after the war ended, Captain Headley summed up his impressions of the battle.

"I saw so many acts of courage and bravery that it's almost impossible to remember them all. They died so fast that the whole business of heroes and death is a little mixed up in my mind. You'd see a man do something almost unbelievable and a minute later you'd see him die. It's pretty hard to pick out any outstanding man or men." [2]

Seven men earned Medals of Honor smothering grenades with their own bodies to save fellow Marines during the first twenty-four days of savage fighting. Only one survived to wear his Medal.

Private Jack Lucas had waited two-and-a-half frustrating years to get into the fight against the nation's enemies. His encounter with lifeless Marines, scattered body parts, and enemy grenades occurred on Iwo Jima.

Harsh Realities

Private Lucas completed basic training at Parris Island with Platoon 603 at the end of September 1942. He anticipated being assigned to an infantry unit and sent into the South Pacific to fight on Guadalcanal. Always an excellent rifleman, he had qualified as a sharpshooter. It did not go his way.

In October, he was first assigned to the Jacksonville Naval Air Station in Florida, then to the Green Cove Springs Naval Air Station on December 31 to guard the gate and the camp perimeter. Liberty in the Navy towns was exhilarating for the teenager. He was introduced to too much corn liquor and dancing with more mature young women in dance clubs.

At the end of March 1943, the reality of the World War hit home. [3] His mother let him know the news about his older step-brother. Mattie Harris had received a telegram on Saturday, March 20, from the Navy Department.

The day after Christmas 1942, Fireman 1st Class William Jay Jones was aboard the USS *Eberle*, DD-430, operating out of Recife, Brazil. On January 4, his fellow sailors toasted him in the South Atlantic on his 18th birthday. On March 10, 1943, the *Eberle* intercepted a German blockade runner flying the Dutch flag, 400 miles west-northwest of Ascension Island. The German crew on the *Karin* (former *Kota Nopan*) readied themselves for the *Eberle's* boarding party. Having planted demolition charges throughout the cargo ship, the Germans set fire to the *Karin* to scuttle her and abandoned the ship. [4]

Fireman 1st Class Jones was the youngest of the *Eberle's* party and among the first to make his way down the gangways into the blockade runner. The first timed explosions killed half of the boarding party outright—he and six fellow sailors died instantly. Two others died before they could gather intelligence materials and escape the demolition explosions. The body of Fireman 1st Class Jones was not recovered from the *Karin* before it sank to the bottom.

In addition to Billy, the Navy Department released the names of the others killed in action on the *Karin*:

Fireman 1st Class Dennis Joseph Buckley Jr. (born 1920);
Fireman 2nd Class Wilbur Gaylord Davis (1923);
Watertender Second Class Alex Maxwell Diachenko (1919);
Coxswain Joseph Erene Henry Metivier (1920);
Machinist's Mate 1st Class Merton Bernell Myers (1912);
Signalman 3rd Class William Joseph Pattison (1921);
Carpenter's Mate 1st Class Robert Merrill Shockley (1917);
Seaman 2nd Class Carl Welby Tinsman (1924).

Billy's obituary was printed in the local papers a week after Mattie received the telegram. In addition to her, survivors included his father, Radford Jones of Belhaven; his sister, Mrs. John Moore of Southport; his brother, Clifton Jones of Swan Quarter; his paternal grandparents, Cale (1875) and Dartha (1881) Jones of Belhaven; his maternal grandfather, George Carawan of Swan Quarter; and one nephew, John Moore Jr. of Southport. The obituary did not include Billy's step-mother or step-brothers. [5]

Billy was awarded a posthumous Silver Star and Purple Heart. In the early months of 1944, the Navy launched a destroyer, two destroyer escorts, and three transports bearing the names of six of the boarding crew. Billy Jones was one of the three who had no ships launched in their honor.

His death was unsettling to the family, Belhaven, and Swan Quarter. The war had become personal. Private Lucas wanted to get into the fray even more.

Doing Whatever It Takes to Get in the Action

On June 22, 1943, Private Lucas was back in North Carolina for machine-gun training at Camp Geiger, near Camp Lejeune. He and some friends took a bus ride to Belhaven for a short period of leave one weekend. Besides entertaining his friends, he helped eight-year-old Louis Ed regain some strength in his legs, holding him up under his arms as his brother relearned to walk.

Private Lucas finished his training at the top of his class on August 20, qualifying as a first gunner with a heavy machine gun. He was the "trigger man" and anxious to go to war. A month passed and again he was in for a disappointment. On September 21,1943, he received orders to remain at Camp Geiger as an instructor. He eked out the days, but the assignment with nine other instructors grated on his nerves.

"It was not my cup of tea."

Disregarding his orders, Private Lucas boarded a train to the west coast with Marines destined for war. That he was going AWOL did not concern him, even if it turned into thirty days in the brig. "I packed my sea bag and got on the back end of that train and went to California."

Next stop, Camp Elliott, a tent city north of San Diego. Administrative logjams worked in his favor.

He trained in the Linda Vista hills, visited a San Diego tattoo parlor, had a Marine Corps emblem with a bulldog tattooed on his right bicep, and took liberty in Tijuana. He boarded his first ship on November 4, and sailed on the USS *Typhoon*. Seven days later he disembarked in Oahu, Territory of Hawaii, and checked in at Camp Catlin, a replacement and refurbishing depot.

The camp was in the cane fields on the east edge of Honolulu and stretched along the island's main highway. With some administrative wangling, his name was added to a roster of troops earmarked for an amphibious assault on another Pacific atoll. His overseas pay went up to $54 monthly.

While at Catlin, Private Lucas wrote a letter to a girlfriend in Swan Quarter. He mentioned that he was 15 years old: a careless mistake for someone who had so strictly kept his age secret. Before stamping and initialing the cover of the U.S. POSTAGE * VIA AIR MAIL envelope, military censors looked inside and caught that detail. His underage status was reported to commanders.

He was immediately removed from the combat unit on its way to Tarawa. Disappointed, he was summoned to Pearl Harbor to have a conversation with a colonel. The letter to his girlfriend was a problem for the Marines. He admitted his age and his intention to go to war. The commander did not have him discharged, but would not send a 15-year-old into combat.

Private Lucas was assigned to trash truck-driving duties at a supply depot. When he had spare time, he stood reverently beside grave mounds at the Oahu and Halawa cemeteries. His resolve to avenge the death of the buried Americans deepened. He managed a promotion to private first class.

One highlight, maybe triumph, of his stay on Hawaii occurred at a road side service station between Honolulu and Pearl Harbor. The allure of chrome pipes off the hood, spare tires in the fenders, the town and country horn, and a $150 ($2,045 in 2016) offer mesmerized him. He persuaded three friends to go in with him to buy and restore a black 1935 Auburn convertible, his first car. [6] The sales staff at Rad Jones Chevrolet might have nodded in approval.

The unlicensed car afforded the four Marines ample liberty escapades around the island. Private Lucas' 16th birthday was like a wild luau party.

When assigned to another tent city between Camp Catlin and Pearl Harbor, with duties again keeping him out of the fight, his hot temper and a combination of adolescent bravado and delinquency merged. Angry about being left behind, he became a discipline problem for the Corps. [7] Drinking too much beer and smoking, he got into fights with other Marines. He went on scavenging raids for loads of beer and ice. He had a court-martial and was in the brig several times, pounding rocks and eating bread and water for a total of five months.

Letters from his mother and friends, sometimes with newspaper articles, kept him updated about life back home. He knew that his cousin and childhood playmate, PFC Oliver "Sam" Lucas, was assigned to the 1st Battalion, 26th Marines, 5th Marine Division. The 26th Marines had been activated at Camp Pendleton on January 19, 1944. PFC Sam Lucas sailed from San Diego on July 22, 1944, as part of the 1st Provisional Marine Brigade area reserve force during the Battle of Guam. What Jack did not know yet, was that his cousin had arrived at Hilo on December 29, and had moved to Camp Tarawa at Kamuela for further combat training.

Other news was that PFC Lucas' buddy, under-aged Marshall Moore, had remained in Plymouth during the early war years. His big brother was writing letters from Europe. Mahlon was serving in the 42nd Cavalry Squadron, 2nd Cavalry Regiment, Patton's Third Army. He had landed in Normandy in July 1944 and, by September, was near the city of Luneville, in northeast France, preparing to drive east into Germany. In October 1944, Marshall, 18, went to the recruiting office and enlisted in the Navy. [8]

One bit of news did not reach him in Hawaii. His 64-year-old step-grandmother, Mrs. Dartha (Overton) Jones had passed away at her Belhaven home on Saturday, January 6.

Margaret helped arrange the funeral services. Mrs. Jones had been a member of the First Christian Church in Swan Quarter and was an active worker as long as her health permitted. Reverend Kenneth Gaskill, Free Will Baptist minister, officiated at the services held from the home on Sunday afternoon. Interment was in the family cemetery near Swan Quarter. Her husband, Cale Jones; one son, R. L. Jones of Belhaven; four sisters; two brothers; and two grandchildren survived her. Margaret, Jack, and Louis Ed were not mentioned in the obituary. [9]

After two years of service, PFC Jack Lucas was not getting close enough to the action. The former football team captain took his own initiative to conclude the issue of being in the rear of the fight. In his eagerness to see action, he walked out of the tent camp on Tuesday, January 9, 1945, with a pair of boots and a set of fatigues, determined to find his way into a combat unit. He was AWOL again, but would be off Oahu soil the next day.

More than two hundred ships were moored at Pearl Harbor. Higgins boats shuttled men and supplies out to the troopships. PFC Lucas casually strolled aboard a Higgins, unconcerned to which ship it would carry him.

The USS *Deuel*, APA-160, was birthed in the Harbor, preparing to transport the 5th Marine Division into combat. PFC Sam Lucas was on that troopship. The Higgins came aside, and PFC Jack Lucas stepped onto the *Deuel*. With the help of happenstance and a 5th Marine, he found his cousin. Sam found him a place to hide on the ship.

USS *Deuel* steamed out of Pearl Harbor on January 10, as part of Transport Division 46. At last, PFC Lucas felt he was a real part of the Pacific war operation—"ready to explode at the first opportunity to draw blood."

On Wednesday, when he could not be located on Oahu, PFC Lucas was first declared absent without leave. That was of little consequence to the young Marine. He was at sea with an assault division.

"I didn't even know where the ships were headed. . . . I knew I was on the way to war. And that's what I wanted. That was my obsession."

At night, the two Lucas cousins slept topside, secreting themselves inside a Higgins boat. During the day, the assault companies studied maps, aerial photographs, and relief models of an island somewhere in the Pacific. The plan-of-attack details were explained to everyone in daily classes. Without his own unit to sit with, PFC Lucas relied on his cousin and his cousin's friends to fill him in on the gouge.

On February 5, the 5th Division reached Eniwetok Atoll for refueling and staff conferences. The USS *Deuel* sat at anchor for two days, until the convoy set sail again on February 7.

With enough sea between the *Deuel* and Hawaii, PFC Lucas decided to surrender himself. At 3:30 PM on Thursday, February 8, he turned himself in to Captain Robert Dunlap, the senior troop officer. The captain and Lieutenant Colonel Daniel Carroll Pollock, 1st Battalion's commanding officer, talked it over. Rather than throwing PFC Lucas in the brig, he was assigned duties with Headquarters Company, 1/26th Marines. Captain Dunlap wished that all his men could have been as gung-ho as this young stowaway.

On Oahu, PFC Lucas was declared a deserter and was reduced back to a private's rank on February 10.

The next day, the *Deuel* joined hundreds of other ships in Magicienne Bay anchored off Saipan to conduct a practice amphibious landing. The assault troops transferred from APAs to LSTs just prior to rehearsals and went down the nets into Higgins boats for the final practice run toward a beach. At dawn on February 14, the armada began weighing anchors.

PFC Lucas celebrated his 17th birthday. He was officially age appropriate to go into battle. In five days, he would finally have the chance to again grapple with an adversary. Six days later he would earn a Medal of Honor.

Once the entire convoy was underway, their destination was passed to all hands—the 3rd, 4th, and 5th Marine Divisions were bound for Iwo Jima, 625 miles north of Saipan. When he learned that, PFC Lucas could have been speaking for most of the 77,000 Marines sailing in the armada.

"Well, I'd never heard of Iwo Jima in my lifetime."

Scars of Black Volcanic Ash

Private First Class Lucas was attached to Company C, 1st Battalion, 26th Marines. PFC Sam Lucas, his cousin, was in the same unit.

At 6:40 AM on Monday, February 19, 1945, the Naval guns began shelling Iwo Jima. The USS *Deuel* lowered the Higgins boats, and the landing craft circled, waiting to receive troops. At 7:45 AM, 482 amphibious tractors (LVTs) carrying eight Marine battalions churned into the water from LSTs and began to circle well off shore from the beaches. As dawn broadened, the sea's surface was calm, the sky clear, and visibility limitless. The Marines could see the smoke rising from the bombardments occurring on Iwo. The sounds of the battle were carried on the light breeze.

At 9:00, the Amtracs lined up along their line of departure 4,000 yards from the beaches and started forward. The first wave of Marines landed on the island at 9:05 AM. The Japanese allowed the arriving waves of American forces to assemble and bunch up on the two-mile stretch of soft black volcanic sand—rock really. Men, tanks, trucks, and artillery pieces sank into the terraced beaches.

The plan was for the 28th Marine Regiment to cut Mount Suribachi off from the larger portion of the island, seize the fortified mountain from the elite 2,000 Japanese soldiers dug into caves and ravines, and hold control of the volcano. The main USMC force was to take the rest of the island and its three airfields. What they would really have to take were 21,000 Japanese soldiers in steel-reinforced concrete fortifications, pillboxes, and blockhouses, and in caves and caverns, underground bunkers, and tunnels.

At 10:15 AM, Lieutenant General Tadamichi Kuribayashi ordered the carnage to be unleashed upon the Marines. His orders to his men were clear. "You will each kill no less than ten Marines before sacrificing your life for the Emperor."

Private First Class Lucas watched from the *Deuel's* deck. "Thank goodness I didn't have to go in the first wave. 'Cause when we went in, it was all hell broke loose, about artillery, it was just tearing people up. And it was just a continuation from night and day for the rest of that battle."

The Lucas cousins climbed down a landing net on the side of the ship and stepped into the same Higgins boat at 11:06 AM. The monotonous circling at the line of departure began. PFC Lucas had waited for years to get into combat, and now he would spend most of D-Day in a landing craft waiting to land on Iwo Jima's beach. [10]

He scrambled from the Higgins boat into deep water and struggled onto Red Beach 1 around 5:30 PM. Lifeless and wounded Marines lay everywhere, along with scattered body parts. Ruined Amtracs and machinery blocked the way. Company C moved through the powder-like sand into an assembly area along the southwest tip of Airfield Number 1 and moved from one foxhole to another, one shell hole after another, to take up defensive positions. Dug in for the night, the 26th Marines experienced a night of mortar barrages.

"I saw a lot of people get killed around me. The only thing you could do to survive was to keep fighting. You were there to stay and that's what we did—we stayed."

Recalling the bloody battle later from a distance of forty years, he would reach a warrior's conclusion. "They paid their price and we paid ours. I hope somebody learned a damn lesson from it." [11]

On the second day of battle, PFC Lucas was on the western front line that stretched across the small neck of the island. In front of his battalion were enemy pillboxes, harrowing ravines, machine-gun emplacements, and land mines. The terrain provided little protective cover from the blistering Japanese fields of fire.

For more than half-an-hour just after dawn, friendly artillery, rockets, mortars, and naval gunfire opened on enemy positions just in front of the Marine line. Fireteam leader PFC Riley Eugene Gilbert, 21, from Plainview, Texas, briefed PFC Lucas, PFC Malvin B. Hagevik, 24, of Milwaukee, and PFC Allan Carl "Al" Crowson, 19, the BAR man of Dierks, Arkansas, on the morning's mission. At 8:30 AM, the Marines pushed off north to take the upper two-thirds of the well-defended island.

The fireteam spotted a Japanese soldier step from behind cover at 10:30 AM, and all fired at him. PFC Lucas searched the dead soldier's pockets for intelligence information and found some personal postcards, pictures, a notebook, and currency. The soldier's handwriting was very convoluted, hard to read even for an intelligence officer able to interpret Japanese. PFC Lucas would bring the postcards home and keep them for the rest of his life. At one time, he would try to get the postcards translated hoping to learn something of the sender's life, but had no luck. Always unsure what to do with them, he would wonder: "Who would I send them to?" [12]

Flamethrowers fired napalm deep into enemy tunnels. As the Japanese fled out into a trench, Pvt Lucas' foursome killed many at point-blank range. It was kill or be killed. The fireteam made their way through a twisting ravine close to the treacherous front lines, intent on destroying a pillbox up near the first airfield.

"We had knocked out this pillbox and this four-man fireteam that I was attached to, we ran down into one of these trenches to take cover from all this direct fire that was coming our way."

Around noon, PFC Gilbert jumped over in the other trench and immediately jumped back, "'cause he had jumped on the back of some Jap. And he stood up and he came back into our trench quick. Well, all hell broke loose then."

A patrol of eleven Japanese in a parallel trench four feet away ambushed them with rifles and grenades. The men sought the protection of two shallow foxholes as the grenade barrage continued. The four Marines opened fire on the Japanese. PFC Lucas shot one of the enemy in the forehead.

"I saw the blood spurt from his head as he stared at me." He shot a second time, killing another enemy soldier. On his second shot, his rifle jammed. Grenades fell directly in front of the four Marines.

"When I reached down to unjam my rifle, I saw two grenades. How long had they been down there? I didn't know . . . two seconds? If my rifle had not jammed, they would have probably wounded all of us—not killed us, but wounded us. And then those Japs we were supposed to be killing in front of us would have finished us off."

He reached a reasonable consideration given the circumstances. "How far could I have gotten if I had tried to run?"

PFC Lucas, six days past his 17th birthday, reacted with no hesitation.

"Grenades!" he hollered to his pals to get them out of the way as he drove one grenade into the volcanic ash with his rifle butt. Then, he "did a Superman dive at the grenades." He pulled the other one under him with his right hand, covered both explosives with his body, and "prayed to God." A third grenade fell at his feet, but did not explode.

Acting as a shield for his companions against the explosive concussion and deadly grenade fragments, he absorbed "the whole blasting force of the explosions" under him.

CHAPTER 16

Blessed, Lucky, or Jinxed?

✳✳✳

"Luck affects everything; let your hook always be cast; in the
stream where you least expect it, there will be a fish." [1]

— Ovid

HURTLING ONESELF ONTO A GRENADE to smother the explosive blast is unquestionably a brave, selfless act. Deliberately diving on top of two grenades to save others at the probable cost of his own life, Private First Class Lucas had demonstrated complete selfless disregard for the outcome of his action. He had been eager to see action and had displayed valor in two days of fighting in one battle. Months would pass before he learned that he had achieved celebrity before his adolescence ended. The war had made him a man and a national hero. The war had not endowed him with super powers.

He let out a scream as the grenade exploded.

"I wasn't a superman after I got hit, when that thing went off. Only one went off, so one tore me up pretty bad."

Remarkably, he remained conscious as the battle on the island went on. "The force of the explosion blew me up into the air and onto my back. Blood poured out of my mouth and I couldn't move. I knew I was dying."

Slices of rifle butt wood had pierced his chest. One lung was punctured. From his head to his thighs, 250 shrapnel pieces had pierced his body. His right eye had been blown out of its socket and dangled on his cheek. His right side was brutally injured, and his right arm was twisted so far underneath him that he thought it had been blown off. There was a terrible ringing in his ears. He could feel warm blood running down his throat and oozing from his head, chest, abdomen, and thighs. Still conscious, he spit out blood in his throat, "clearing the way for life-giving oxygen." His clothing was shredded and tattered and his backpack was gone. First, he felt numbness throughout his entire body. Then, the excruciating pain enveloped him. [2]

Although the soft volcanic rock along the beaches had hampered the invasion forces on D-Day, on this second day, that same soft porous ground absorbed a good amount of the grenade blast. The black volcanic ash deeply imbedded into his wounds stemmed the bleeding. The good Lord and the bandolier of six grenades he wore across his chest had deflected the shrapnel from his heart.

As the battle raged on, the enormous wounds to his right arm, right leg, chest and torso meant that he would not be among the "walking wounded" finding their own way back to the beaches. The urgency of his medical needs and the doctrine of getting wounded Marines back into the action as expeditiously as possible, also meant that he was a low priority for battlefield first aid.

Having witnessed the explosion lift PFC Lucas from the ground and flip him 180 degrees onto his back, blowing off his combat clothing, his three companions thought he was dead. Collecting the dog tags from his body was left for later. They moved forward, continuing the fight and leaving PFC Lucas in the shallow depression.

Except that he was barely alive, PFC Lucas would not have disagreed with their assessment. "Luke, you're gonna die," lingered in his mind. He figured they'd be back to the trench at some point to gather his remains and turn them over to the Grave Registrations people. Unable to move, covered with blood, his clothes in shreds, severely wounded, PFC Lucas waited to die.

"Finally, another outfit moving up saw me."

PFC Lucas kept moving the fingers on his left hand to signal to somebody that he still had life in him. A Marine from another unit approached, recognized that PFC Lucas was an American casualty, and called for a corpsman. The medic decided to provide life-saving first aid. When a Japanese soldier burst from a hole in the trench, the corpsman fired eighteen rounds from his carbine into him. Then, a mortar barrage walked up to the edge of the trench. The stretcher-bearers took cover.

"Then they came in and got me and they started runnin' with me to take me away from the immediate action."

As the litter-bearers hurried off, one stumbled and dropped his end. The back of PFC Lucas' head was split open on a rock. Once on the beach, he was pumped full of brandy, morphine, penicillin, and blood, then covered with a poncho. Once it was dark enough for the landing craft to safely take wounded out to the LSTs, an Amtrac evacuated him from the island.

In and out of consciousness, PFC Lucas was given sixteen pints of blood over several days, until a Higgins boat could transfer him to the hospital ship USS *Samaritan*. His blood and the black volcanic ash had coagulated, acting like a cast and saving his arm from amputation. Over the next few weeks he underwent numerous surgeries. More therapies and convalescence began on Guam. All combined, PFC Lucas underwent twenty-six operations in the following months. He was proud to say that "the only time I was ever knocked out in my life was when they gave me an anesthetic."

On February 26, the Marine Corps removed the deserter classification from his record. The seventeen convictions included in his service record were expunged. His private first class rank was restored.

Two days after the Marines declared Iwo Jima secured, PFC Lucas was returned to the States on March 28, 1945, and treated at the San Francisco Naval Hospital. On April 3, he was carried to a troop train for transfer to the U.S. Naval Hospital in Charleston, South Carolina. He arrived there on April 14.

X-rays detected metal in every major organ, and doctors continued to remove what shrapnel they could. They had to leave eight pieces in his brain—one of those lodged in the left frontal lobe—six in his right lung, two in his heart, and more than 100 in his body. His arms were speckled with grenade fragments that could be seen just under the surface of his skin—battle testimony he would show to the curious.

He learned that a telegram had been delivered to Mr. and Mrs. Samuel Boyd Lucas on Route 1 in Plymouth. His cousin, PFC Sam Lucas, had been wounded in action on Iwo Jima.

A total of thirty-three Washington County men had given their lives in the service of their country before WWII came to an end: among them were Bateman, Davenport, Swain, and Woodley relatives. [3]

PFC Gilbert, PFC Hagevik, and PFC Crowson all came home from Iwo with Purple Hearts. PFC Crowson was so severely injured retaking the airfield that he spent eighteen months in military hospitals. [4]

✳✳✳

Private First Class Lucas would learn that six other Marines had gallantly given their lives that others on Iwo Jima might survive. Two days after Jack had smothered grenades, **Private First Class Donald Jack Ruhl** also overruled the instinct to save himself from a grenade, took initiative "in the face of almost certain death," and demonstrated "the unfaltering spirit of self-sacrifice."

Don Ruhl was born on July 2, 1923, in Columbus, south central Montana, where he completed grade school. The town lies on the main east-west route through the state, where the Yellowstone and Stillwater Rivers meet: an easy drive from mountains and national forests. Granite Peak, at 12,799 feet the highest mountain in Montana, was forty miles south. Spending most of his youth within walking distance of the Yellowstone, he enjoyed the wilderness spaces and hunting for small game.

Don went over to Joliet for high school and grew to be 5 feet 11 inches, and 147 pounds. He worked hard as a farm hand in Joliet. Then, for five months in 1942, he worked as a lab assistant in what became a Cenex refinery in Laurel.

In September 1942, Don went to Butte and enlisted in the Marines. He left Montana for San Diego and in three months he had earned his first promotion to private first class. Athletic, he was a strong swimmer and competed in boxing, baseball, and basketball while in training later with the Marines. Before leaving the States in March 1943, he had also qualified as a sharpshooter, a combat swimmer, a parachutist at Camp Gillespie, and a 60mm mortar crewman.

Private First Class Ruhl experienced his first combat on Bougainville Island with Love Company, 3rd Parachute Battalion, in November, serving with Captain Robert Dunlap, who commanded Bravo Company. After Bougainville, he returned to the States for seven months, was reassigned to Company E, 2nd Battalion, 28th Marines, then, left again for Hilo, Hawaii. By February 1945, he was waiting in Saipan for his next combat operation.

Like so many before and after him, PFC Ruhl's conspicuous bravery was not restricted to a single act. He had already demonstrated heroism on Iwo Jima before hurling himself on a grenade. Tasked to take Mount Suribachi on the first day of the battle, he had single handedly attacked a group of eight Japanese defenders escaping from a blockhouse and killed two of them before the others fled.

Having had little sleep during the night, the 28th Regiment pushed the assault forward against the defenders of Suribachi at 8:30 AM the next morning. Easy Company was on the left flank. Slowly advancing toward the base of Suribachi under relentless mortar explosions and machine-gun fire, of his own volition PFC Ruhl left a protected position and crossed forty yards of exposed terrain to rescue a wounded Marine. Then, "again running the gauntlet of hostile fire," he evacuated the man to an aid station on the beach, over 300 yards distant from his position.

Having returned to the front lines, when the advance stopped at 5:00 PM, he volunteered to crawl seventy-five yards forward of the company's flank to ensure that an enemy gun emplacement had been abandoned. As close as any Marine had yet reached to the base of Suribachi, PFC Ruhl remained at the position throughout the night to ensure the Japanese did not reoccupy it.

At 8:25 AM, February 21, Easy Company assaulted forward again. During the fighting, PFC Ruhl and his platoon guide, a senior noncommissioned officer, crawled to the top of a Japanese bunker to fire upon enemy soldiers on the other side of the bunker. A hostile grenade landed between the two of them. PFC Ruhl could have effortlessly rolled from the edge of the bunker roof and dropped to the ground below to protect himself from the blast of the grenade. Instead, he immediately shouted a warning to the other Marine on the bunker and dived on the grenade.

His Easy Company comrades finally consolidated their positions at 11:00 PM that night. PFC Ruhl was not with them. Nor was he among them two days later when Company E took the crest of Mount Suribachi and raised the American flag over the island. The explosion of the grenade had shattered his body and taken his life.

Those with whom he had advanced across Green Beach to the foot of "Hotrocks" remembered him. The actions of Private First Class Donald Ruhl, 21, were cited as directly responsible for the survival of his fellow Marines and for the placing of the flag atop Suribachi.

William Gary Walsh, born on April 7, 1922 in Roxbury, Massachusetts, came from a long line of Irishmen who were proud to do public service and responded to people in dire need. They embodied the lyrics of a Gaelic lament. "May her sons be true when needed." Arlington National Cemetery records indicate that his father was a Boston fireman, who died during the rescue of people from a burning building. Bill's brother, a Franciscan priest, served in WWII. After the war, he would serve as an Army Chaplain with the 180th Regiment, 45th Infantry Division, in Korea where he earned a series of medals for valor, coming to the aid of wounded soldiers while under enemy fire. A bridge joining Boston and Quincy was later named in the Father's memory. [5]

Bill attended public schools in Boston. He walked into a recruiting station in April 1942 when he was 20 years old and enlisted in the Marines. After boot camp, he was assigned duties as a Marine Scout, then saw duty with Carlson's Raider Battalions. He quickly gained combat experience and rank, participating in the campaigns on Guadalcanal, Bougainville, Tarawa, and the Russell Islands. After two years of fighting, he returned to the States briefly in 1944 and married Mary Louise Ponrod, who had been a member of the USMC Women's Reserve. He then joined the 5th MarDiv as they prepared for their entry into the Pacific Theater.

Gunnery Sergeant Walsh was assigned duties as an infantry platoon leader with Company G, 3d Battalion, 27th Marines. He spent most of the morning of February 19 in an LVT with his platoon, watching the smoke and fires rise from the beaches of Iwo Jima, as the waves of his sister battalions were bunched up and pinned down on Red Beaches 1 and 2. As the Marine line progressed across the narrow portion of the island, George Company came ashore at 11:30 AM and joined the fighting, staying 200 yards behind the lead battalions. Gunny Walsh led his platoon in mopping up enemy positions that had withstood the lead assault. By 3:00 PM, the Marines had reached the west coast and Company G dug in only 200 yards from the cliffs.

Each day George Company took casualties as they advanced north past the western edge of Airfield No. 1, through the hostile bluffs, over jagged ridges, and beyond Airfield No. 2 to the east. Having moved forward about 300 yards on the eighth day of fighting, the company dug into night positions 800 yards south of Hill 362-A. George Company waited for the inevitable enemy incursions and counterattacks.

At 8:00 AM, February 27, Gunny Walsh and his platoon went forward on the right flank towards the base of the barren hill rising sharply from the rocky island floor. They encountered fortified pillboxes, machine-gun bunkers, and static medium tank positions dug into hollows on the hill. The enemy was as much in the hill as on it, and caves and a tunnel complex provided the Japanese significant advantage for fighting, protection, and re-supply.

Artillery and mortar shells from both forces pounded the terrain around the Marines as they pushed forward. By noon, intense enemy machine-gun fire from interlocking positions and mortar fire from adjacent high ground had stalled Company G. The platoons were being pummeled.

Pinned down at the base of a steep ridge, Gunny Walsh charged ahead with his platoon against a machine-gun position dug into the ridge and a trench full of Japanese soldiers. The enemy responded with increased fire and grenades and repelled the attack.

Gunny reorganized his depleted platoon and attacked again, ignoring the steady flow of automatic weapons fire directed at him. This time, the platoon reached the crest of the ridge. Before the remnant of his men could consolidate, they were confronted with a barrage of enemy hand grenades thrown from reverse-slope defensive positions. His men took shelter in whatever depressions and trenches they could reach.

A grenade landed among some of his men sheltered in a low trench. Gunny Walsh did not hesitate. There was time only for him to jump onto the grenade before it exploded. His platoon's assault against the machine-gun emplacement allowed George Company to advance further towards Hill 362 and hold the ground they had won. Although the remnant of his platoon survived, Gunnery Sergeant William Walsh, 22 years old, died in the grenade's blast.

Charles Joseph Berry, was born on July 10, 1923 in Lorain, Ohio. He demonstrated a tough competitive edge playing football at Clearview High School. After graduating in 1941, he went to work as a truck driver. War was looming. Chuck enlisted on October 1, two months before the attack on Pearl Harbor. He saw combat first with the 1st Parachute Battalion on Bougainville in November 1943. By July 1944, he had reached the rank of corporal.

Corporal Berry and the Lucas cousins had trained together on the USS *Deuel* and in the practice landing off Saipan. He served as a machine gunner with the 1st Battalion, 26th Marines. Corporal Berry went ashore on Iwo on D-Day. By March 3, thirteen days into the battle, his unit had fought beyond Hill 362-A, Airfield Number 3, and had reached the upper northwestern quadrant of the volcanic island. That night they tried to find some rest facing Kito Village.

Corporal Berry remained alert in the front lines. Just after midnight, Japanese soldiers initiated a "surprise" attack on their position. He and his fellow team members returned fire and exchanged hand grenades with the enemy. In the pitch of the engagement, a Japanese grenade landed in their foxhole. According to his comrades and the citation that followed, Corporal Charles Berry, 21 years old, "unhesitatingly chose to sacrifice himself and immediately dived on the deadly missile, absorbing the shattering violence of the exploding charge in his own body and protecting the others from serious injury." His body was returned home to Elmwood Cemetery in Lorain in 1948.

Private First Class William Robert Caddy also "boldly defied shattering Japanese machine-gun and small-arms fire to move forward with his platoon leader and another Marine during a determined advance" on March 3.

Bill had been born in Quincy, Massachusetts, on August 8, 1925, the second child of Harold F. and Hattie B. Caddy. His long-distant ancestors had settled in the Boston area. The first James Caddy had come from Wales to Boston in 1635. Bill's dad had come over from Australia to marry a Massachusetts woman.

He was not a great scholar, but loved baseball—often truant from school to practice on his own. At 5 feet 7 inches, 140 pounds, Bill had played on the Montclair High School varsity baseball team. America entered the war when he was 16 years old, and everyone tightened their belts. He quit high school after his second year and went to work delivering milk around town on horseback, giving most of his $25 weekly pay to his mother to help with expenses. He was drafted into the Marines two months after his 18th birthday in 1943.

Following extended special training, PFC Caddy was assigned to Company I, 3d Battalion, 28th Marines, as a rifleman. Five more months of training for an amphibious assault began. More than two years of island victories and legends of heroic bravery had become Corps' history by the time he went into battle on Iwo.

Item Company had fought its way up the western side of the island and past Nishi Village. Private First Class Caddy worked his way forward with his platoon leader and platoon sergeant looking for an advantageous way to silence the machine-gun emplacements holding the company in place. Under intense fire, they moved into an artillery shell hole. Machine guns and sniper fire immediately pinned them down, unable to advance or withdraw.

The Japanese tried to annihilate the three Marines in an exchange of hand grenades. During the fight, an enemy grenade landed in the shell hole. Private First Class Caddy, 19, unhesitatingly threw himself upon the explosive. PFC Ott Farris had no doubt that his friend had "yielded his own life that his fellow Marines might carry on the relentless battle."

After Iwo Jima was secured, telegrams were delivered to the mothers of four young Marines from Quincy who were killed during the battle. Mrs. Hattie B. Caddy's telegram arrived at 252 Holbrook Road. The three others were delivered within a few short blocks of each other. Private Malcolm John MacPherson, 18, of 422 Granite Street, was KIA (C/1/25th Marines) on February 19, the first day of the landings. Private John William Jackson (3rd-MarDiv) had lived up the same street at 280 Granite. He was KIA on March 3, the same day as PFC Caddy. Private John Richard Koski Jr., 22, of 10 Buckley Street, was the last of the four, KIA (G/2/25th Marines) on March 12. His remains were repatriated and buried in Quincy.

Private First Class Caddy was buried at the National Memorial Cemetery of the Pacific in Honolulu. Private Jackson's memorial is at the Courts of the Missing, Honolulu. Private MacPherson was listed in the casualty reports on May 12, 1945. Whether his remains were recovered and repatriated is unknown.

The Marine Corps League Detachment #124 in Quincy was named in PFC Caddy's honor in 1946. The park along Quincy Shore Drive across from Wollaston Beach was renamed "Pfc. William R. Caddy Memorial Park" in 1963. A William R. Caddy Memorial Service is conducted there annually. A short side street several blocks north of the Neponset River in the Lower Dorchester Mills section and two miles across the river from Holbrook Road was named Caddy Road. The twelve homeowners on the street remember to proudly display their flags on Memorial Day holidays.

James Dennis Labelle, 19, was born on November 22, 1925, and grew up in Columbia Heights, on the north side of Minneapolis (see Chapter 9). On the night of March 8, after eighteen days of combat, the "wiry scrapper" stood watch over two other Marines in a fighting hole in front of the ravines and ridges leading toward Hill 165. A Japanese hand grenade was lobbed into their shelter, landing just out of PFC Labelle's reach. He yelled a warning to his companions and immediately jumped on the grenade, sacrificing his life and shielding the others from harm. His remains were returned to the U.S. in late 1948, and buried in Fort Snelling National Cemetery, Minneapolis.

George Phillips was the orphaned kid from Rich Hill, Bates County, Missouri. His childhood was spent in Labadie with the James O'Brien family (see Chapter 1). Three months short of turning 18 years old, George enlisted in the Marines on April 25, 1944. He joined the 2d Battalion, 28th Marines, 5th Division, in Hilo, the same battalion as PFC Don Ruhl. On the night of March 14, Private Phillips shouted a warning to his squad mates and threw himself onto a grenade. He was the last Marine to dive onto a grenade to save other Marines on Iwo Jima.

Private First Class Jack Lucas had witnessed the bravery of a combat corpsman attached to a Marine unit. He understood the bond Marines have with Navy corpsmen, their "Docs." Wherever Marine infantry go into harm's way a corpsman will be close at hand. Marines believe that the corpsmen who serve with them are as much Marines, if not more, as they are seamen.

PFC Lucas asked after the "Doc" who had first provided him aid in the trench and twice saved his life. He learned that his corpsman had not survived the battle. [6]

The Navy Medical Service casualty rolls on Iwo Jima were gradually calculated: 178 combat corpsmen were KIA; 19 Died of Wounds; another 541 were WIA. [7] Five Navy men earned Medals of Honor for their gallantry on Iwo Jima—four of them were corpsmen. Third Battalion, 27th Marines platoon corpsman Pharmacist's Mate 1st Class John Willis, 23, was one of them (see Chapter 1). He died saving a Marine casualty on Hill 362 from nine grenades on February 28, 1945.

✳✳✳

One of the doctors who treated PFC Lucas was quoted in newspaper reports. "Maybe he was too damn young and too damn tough to die."

In early summer 1945, Jack was able to get home to Belhaven for a few days' respite from his medical convalescence and physical therapy. His mother bought him a manual shift, blue 1936 Ford coupe that he quickly learned to drive left-handed.

Margaret was glad that Jack was doing so well, recuperating in Charleston. Yet, her father-in-law was having a hard time. Cale Jones was no stranger to war veterans and sadness. His father, Cason Walter Jones, 84, had been a Confederate private in Captain E. S. Swindell's Company, Partisan Raiders of Hyde County, and had passed away in 1930. His mother, Almeta Jones, 91, had died in April 1941. His grandson, Billy, had died on the German blockade runner in 1943. He was not over the death of his wife, Dartha, in January, when more grief hit.

Cale's brother, Walter Shelton Jones, 77, died on Sunday, July 22, 1945. Margaret and Radford attended the funeral services at Middletown Christian Church in Lake Landing Township on the Pamlico Sound, Monday afternoon at 4:00 PM. Walter was buried in the church cemetery. For a family, Cale was left with his son, two brothers, Preston Mayo Jones (1882–1964) of Swan Quarter and Raleigh Jones of Pantego, and a couple of nephews. [8]

Doors Open for the Tobacco Farmer's Son

Declared physically unfit for military duty due to disability associated to his wounds, PFC Lucas was honorably discharged from the Marine Corps on September 18, 1945, three years after his enlistment. He would turn 18 years old in five more months. He went home to Belhaven to enjoy some of his mother's home cooking. He had another kind of warmth in mind, too.

Jack had known pretty, brown-eyed, Carolyn Brown since they were children. He had been infatuated with her since the first time he had seen her. When he returned to North Carolina, Carolyn was living in Portsmouth, Virginia, 115 miles north of Belhaven, working as a clerk in the Norfolk Navy Shipyard. He considered her to be "the loveliest little dolly in the world."

Completely taken with the 17-year-old, he had proposed to her in June while he was recuperating in Charleston, and she had accepted. Carolyn came down to Plymouth and stayed with friends. Jack went up to meet her, and stayed with his Aunt Mittie Edwards Blackman.

"Of course I had to go home to see my gal friend and get some lip sugar. But, Mr. Truman called me and interrupted my plans there."

He had been back in Plymouth for a week when his mother called. He had received an unexpected phone invitation to be present at the White House in his Marine dress uniform. He thought the call was malarkey. A second call a week later convinced him that the president really wanted to meet with him.

On Tuesday, October 2, Jack took a train to Washington, D.C.—an all-expense-paid trip. The reporters swarmed him after his arrival at the Capital. He had had time enough to think about heroism. "Let's get this straight about my winning the Medal of Honor," he told them. "Those buddies of mine in that trench saved my life just as much as I saved theirs." [9]

His blue eyes sparkled when he grinned. "I'm a hero, I guess. Even the president ought to be proud to meet me. But my buddies got those Japs who threw the grenades that got me. You put that in the paper so everybody will know that."

Jack believed that he had wanted into the action because it was in his Lucas blood. He added, "That's Indian blood—Cherokee Indian—that has made me a scrapper all my life and made me just crazy enough to throw myself on the grenades the Japs tossed."

He told the reporters about two men he admired—his brother, Billy Jones, and his cousin, Sam Oliver Lucas.

Jack did not always make light of heroism. As he matured, so did his thoughts about warriors. "I wasn't even cognizant about medals when I was in the military. I never thought about 'em. That wasn't my thing—to go to war for some medal. It was to fight for my country. I don't feel like I'm some big hero or anything like that. The real heroes are the ones who had to give their all—their life. They are the truest heroes in my book." [10]

Louis Ed drove the car up to D.C. on Wednesday with his mother, Radford, Clifton Jones, and Carolyn, his big brother's sweetheart.

"Still, all the attention was beginning to go to my head a little."

Miss Margaret Kernodle, Associated Press reporter, treated Jack to a morning pancake

breakfast at the swanky Mayflower Hotel. He was surprised when she asked him about the seventeen convictions and brig confinements and his going AWOL logged in his military records. Afterward, the reporter took Jack and Carolyn to the *Washington Post* office. They were both tickled to see the photo of them that was sent out on the national wires.

ALL THIS, AND A MEDAL TOO! WHAT HE WAS FIGHTING FOR! The captions under newspaper photographs of the couple described the young hero as having eyes only for his girl. That was pretty thrilling stuff for two teenage Americans in 1945!

Jack was interviewed again as he, his mother, and his fiancée sat at a dinner table in a D.C. hotel on Thursday night. His best friend, Merchant Seaman Llyod G. McNair, and Carolyn's best friend, Margaret Waltz, both up from Plymouth, had joined the party.

Jack proudly displayed the discharge pin on the lapel of his light tan suit. It seemed that he had things on his mind other than meeting the president to receive a Medal. He ignored the southern fried chicken on the plate in front of him. [11]

"I love that woman," he said of Carolyn Brown. "I's crazy about her."

"Brother, you can say that again," his fiancée agreed.

"She's some jitterbug," he added fondly.

Carolyn caressed the engagement ring with its five diamonds on the third finger of her left hand. "You can say I'm proud of him," she averred, "but please don't say much more."

"Luke," as his friends and Carolyn called him, explained that he wanted to go back to school so he could "really get somewhere in the world." He was considering taking an electrician course at the same time to please his fiancée. About November 1, he planned to go to the rehabilitation center at Fayetteville to see about returning to school under the G.I Bill of Rights. He insisted that he and his sweetheart would be married "long before I finish school, but not soon."

Not one to leave his pretty, young mother out of the flattering comments, the blond ex-Marine, nodded toward Margaret. "Look at her," he said. "Beautiful in any dress she wears."

Miss Kernodle liked to write that PFC Lucas had been promoted from Marine Corps' juvenile delinquent to hero on Iwo Jima. *The Daily Oklahoman* told its readers the story under the headline "Boy Marine Fought MPs, Police, Japs—and Won the Medal of Honor." In Mississippi, the Friday *Hattiesburg American* front-page headline was "Marine Hero All Man at 17." Unbeknownst to the Hattiesburg readers, the town would one day be able to boast that Jack was one of their own.

On Friday morning, October 5, the skies were clear, the sun was bright, and the temperature was climbing up from 44°F to 66°F. Dignitaries, top-ranking military officers, and guests took their seats on three sides of a hollow square on the South Lawn at the White House. Navy and Marine enlisted men stood at ease in lines behind them. The Navy band waited. Mrs. Truman sat in the shade of the south porch. Newsmen and photographers stood along the portico stairs behind the speaker's table.

General George Marshall, commander of the Army, took the seat next to Jack's mother, a lasting source of family pride. Eleven Marines and three Navy men took their seats, chatting affably with each other. Eight of them had been summoned to receive the nation's highest military honor for their actions on Iwo Jima.

The 45-minute ceremony began at 10:30 AM. President Harry S. Truman greeted the assembly. "This is one of the pleasant duties of the President of the United States," he said. "These are the young men who represent us in our fighting forces. . . . we go to war for principles, and we produce young men like these." Like the victories in Europe and Japan, he asked that the Nation win the peace the Japanese dignitaries had signed on September 2, 1945, to prevent other young men from being killed or maimed. [12]

The recipients were called forward individually in order of their rank. Commodore James K. Yardman handed the president each Medal and Vice Admiral Louis E. Denfeld read the citations while the president hung the symbol of valor around each recipient's neck. The top Marine ace of World War II, LtCol Gregory "Pappy" Boyington, released from a Japanese POW camp, was first. PFC Lucas watched and listened as each Citation was read. After Corporal Hershel "Woody" Williams was presented his Medal, a Navy corpsman was next, then PFC Lucas—the twelfth hero to swagger forward. When he raised his right hand to his temple to salute the president, the injuries to his hand and arm were evident.

As he did with each recipient, President Truman made a point to tell PFC Lucas his view of the award. "I would rather have this Medal around my neck, than to be President of the United States."

"Sir, I'll swap ya," the young Marine answered. His remark got a laugh from the president.

The bold print of the newspaper headlines heralded a new life for the teenager and would seem to become fixtures for the rest of his life. The handsome 17-year-old with wavy hair who had cradled two grenades under his body on Iwo Jima was the youngest Marine and the youngest member of the military in any conflict other than the Civil War to receive the Medal of Honor. [13]

And, he had vowed his love for his fiancée.

A parade down Pennsylvania Avenue followed, as well as a standing ovation at the Capital, and sitting in a reviewing stand to watch a parade on the Washington Monument grounds. The evening ended with a gala event at downtown Washington's Mayflower Hotel. Jack was impressed that General Marshall spoke with him and Carolyn for half an hour.

Newsreels and newspapers made much of the nation's Youngest Hero.

14 MARINES AND
SAILORS WIN
HIGHEST AWARD.

Days after the White House presentations, thirteen of the recipients flew up to New York City for a ticker tape parade. Mayor Fiorello La Guardia met them at the airport. Although gray clouds threatened to rain on the parade, four million turned out to cheer along the length of the route during the Admiral Chester W. Nimitz Day celebrations of Tuesday, October 9.

Tuesday was a work day in the Norfolk Navy Shipyard, so Carolyn did not accompany Jack on this trip. He did not seem to notice her absence.

At 12:05 AM, 175 handpicked Marines, veterans of the Pacific action, marched from Battery Park. Six Navy and Coast Guard bands behind them alternated playing martial music. Another 3,800 Navy, Marine, Coast Guard personnel, 600 WAVES (Women Accepted for Volunteer Emergency Service), women Marines, the Coast Guard Women's Reserve SPARS ("Semper Paratus—Always Ready"), and Navy nurses followed. They led the motorcade up Broadway (Avenue of Heroes) and Cedar Street to City Hall in Manhattan, down Fifth Avenue, and then to Queens. Police riding motorcycles and horses flanked the vehicles. Along the East River, watercraft celebrated with whistle blasts, and two fire boats spewed water from every hose nozzle.

Admiral Nimitz and his party of dignitaries rode in convertibles. "Pappy" Boyington, sitting beside Commander Chester W. Nimitz Jr., the admiral's son, waved from the back of the last convertible. Behind them, six jeeps driven by an enlisted sailor carried the others. Two recipients, riding in the order of their rank, sat in the back of each jeep. Corporal Hershel Williams and PFC Jacklyn H. Lucas rode in Jeep No. 5. Privates Franklin E. Sigler and Wilson D. Watson, who had both earned Medals on Iwo Jima, rode in the last jeep.

None of the recipients were quite as exuberant as PFC Lucas. A photographer captured the image of him waving from the Jeep, a moment that newspaper readers enjoyed sending to him once he was home. [14] He stood in the back seat of his Jeep, waving and throwing kisses to the women who had lined the streets. One pretty, young lady even ran from the curb to plant a big kiss on him as his jeep drove past.

"I was gettin' so much attention from the girls," he would recall. "And these women would run out and try to kiss me. New York women just treated me so nice. I had a ball for the next couple of days. I really enjoyed that."

For any young man, such accolades could easily swell a head. Jack would admit that. "I never really thought of myself as a hero, period, but they chose to decorate me," he said. "Then, I was cocky after all that fanfare. It really blew my mind, women jumping on me and kissing me and half-dragging me out of the automobile. I loved it. I was popular. I was really hitting my stride, see."

He would remember that one spontaneous kiss on Fifth Avenue as a turning point in his life. "I would never again be without a woman's companionship. Females would prove to always be my weakness." [15] He could not have known as he rode in parades that he would get engaged three more times in the years ahead as his life played out in newspaper headlines.

The parade ended on the corner of Park Avenue and 56th Street. Mayor La Guardia took them up to the Skylight Room for dinner in a special room on top of the Waldorf Astoria Hotel. More than the room mesmerized Jack.

"They had a delicious looking model escorting me. I didn't know any better." Friends would always chuckle when they told how "Jack had a real eye for the ladies."

Perhaps in an off-handed way, he expressed a desire "to read about myself," asking newspaper readers to send him any clippings portraying his heroic career as a Marine. That remark crisscrossed the nation.

"What did it feel like to get that award?" he was asked. "To parade down Fifth Avenue in New York City with confetti flying, girls blowing you kisses and Harry Truman shaking your hand?" [16]

"It felt terrific."

Jack still had steel in his chest "which must come out when it gets to hurting too bad." He came down with a chest cold after the Admiral Nimitz Day celebration.

The Medal granted him a lifetime membership in an elite club. Doors would be opened for him that might otherwise not have been for "the son of a tobacco farmer." Yet, the Medal proved to be something of a load. While he could bask in glory, he would also learn that with honor came commitment. The Medal would bring him fame, take away his privacy, and keep his triumphs and failures under media scrutiny. He would be friends with other recipients, sharing with them a common pride and sense of obligation. At times, the Medal would stir rivalry and jealousies among higher-ranking officers. They were, after all, competitive warriors. [17]

Still a teenager, he would routinely be asked to appear at civic functions, to preside over July Fourth and Memorial Day ceremonies, to serve as a Grand Marshall at parades, to dedicate monuments and memorials, and to give public speeches, just like the other MOH recipients. Unsolicited job offers gave him choices for financial opportunities. At later reunions, he would hear stories about older recipients having honorary degrees, sitting on corporate boards of directors, advising government committees, and testifying at Senate hearings. His own tales would include sitting on the podium at a president's inauguration and attending a State of the Union Address.

Belhaven's Boy-Hero

Avalanche of Mail Pours into Belhaven For Marine Hero Who Won Medal At 17. For three weeks after the New York parade, letters arrived at the Belhaven Post Office. Jack estimated that he received 10,000 letters from folks who responded to his request for newspaper clippings in which he recited his heroic career as a Marine.

"Plenty came from every state in the Union."

Most clippings came in letters from Texas, next most from Indiana. Many came from Hawaii and some from Canada. Only twelve letters chided him for the way he told the story of winning the Medal. They said he "bragged too much." [18]

His pretty mother, Mrs. Margaret Jones, replied to one resentful mother. In return, Jack immediately received an apology from the other mother's son.

"It took the whole family to help me open all that mail," he reported to Margaret Kernodle in Washington. Jack had returned to the Capitol on Friday, October 19, to share honors with Senator Clyde Roark Hoey (D-NC) at the North Carolina's Society's first gathering of the fall season. "We haven't finished yet, and if I hadn't got a chest cold after attending the New York celebration for Admiral Nimitz and had to stay in bed where I opened letters from morning to night, we never would have opened 'em all."

Jack was a little worried "We can't answer that many letters, but tell the folks we do appreciate them."

Once recovered from his cold, Admiral Nimitz took him all around the country on a War Bond tour.

The letters to Jack from grateful and admiring Americans continued—by the tub full. Eventually, he had more than 50,000 to open, many with money tucked inside the envelopes. The gifts mounted up, and he bought a prime building lot in one of Plymouth's nicest sections. A local car dealer had his eye on the same location and proposed a deal. Jack turned over the title deed and drove off in a brand new, black Chevrolet. [19]

From those days forward, newspaper articles would make a difference for him, as he became a symbol of patriotism in the ensuing decades, meeting presidents and traveling the world to speak with frontline troops and fellow veterans.

Jack's friendships with other Medal recipients were strengthened at gatherings he attended. Sometimes, competitive grappling with one or another in contests to determine the toughest reversed his physical recuperation. Before 1945 ended, the American Legion invited him to join other recipients in Chicago. While there, he accepted a proposal.

Likely the only high school freshman in history to have earned a MOH in combat before attending classes, Jack began the special high school program for veterans at the University of Illinois in Champaign during the winter 1946 term.

Travels between Illinois and North Carolina and Norfolk in his new Chevrolet took their toll. His birthday fell on a Thursday that year, and he headed east to enjoy a Valentine's Day with Carolyn. Love was the conqueror. Despite all the attention of university administrators, faculty, and coeds on campus, Jack transferred his education to Maury High School in Norfolk to be closer to his *one-and-only jitterbug*. Then, only periodic trips associated to MOH and American Legion events interrupted his time with her and his studies.

Having enjoyed conquests of ladies while on liberty forays in Florida and California, some unexpected experiences aggravated the steel pieces left in Jack's heart. His fiancée, influenced by her parents, broke his heart when she left him.

He would have to acknowledge later "nothing has gotten me in more trouble in my life than my pursuit of love." [20]

Jack had overcome serious challenges in his childhood. He had gone to war and, for a time, earned the acclaim of the nation. Carolyn's rebuff brought him back down to earth. Like so many veterans and Medal recipients, he was finding that settling down and keeping things together did not come easily. Life turned tumultuous at times.

Nightmares—images of men dying and bodies mutilated—disrupted his sleep. His arms would flail about in the darkness, and his own incoherent shouts would wake him. And, as outgoing as he was, his penchant for quick jabs to a jaw did not go away. Jack tried counseling until his psychologist died by suicide. What could care providers do for him, if he was sounder of mind than they were? He would deal with his problems on his own. [21]

He had become fixed to Iwo Jima in the minds of Americans. Iwo Jima was fixed in his mind. He was back on the island almost every night. He did not know that he would step on the island again in forty years. By then, much had happened in his life: he had built and lost a fortune, walked away from several serious automobile accidents without a bruise, and survived a murder plot hatched by his wife. He would come to believe that he had always lived two lives.

"Jack Lucas, that lucky dog, and Jack Lucas, the poor guy who can't get a break." [22]

Jack would sum it all up for a reporter during a trip back to Iwo Jima. "I had one outstanding year in my life, and I have been jinxed ever since." [23]

About Those Forty Years

Jack took a position with the Veterans Administration in Winston-Salem as a representative. He enrolled at R. J. Reynolds High and graduated in eighteen months. He would work for the VA on and off throughout the next ten years. He did not have much to do with his step-family, but his mother kept him informed.

Cale Jones remarried for a short time, and Mrs. Jones apparently enjoyed shopping in Washington on Thursday afternoons. [24] Cale eventually died of a self-inflicted gunshot wound. [25]

Relief came Jack's way when Margaret ended her marriage to Radford Jones. Rad struggled on in his car business until he was killed at age 60, in a one-car accident on July 18, 1961. He was buried at Belhaven Community Cemetery on West Main Street. Jack's step-brother would also die at an early age. Clifton Jones, 56, died on August 10, 1986, and was buried beside his father.

Jack took advantage of the G. I. Bill in fall 1948, moved his attention east to Durham, and enrolled in Duke University. Two of his roommates were on the football team. In 1950, after his second college year, one of them convinced him to go down to Birmingham, Alabama, for a summer job. He met Mary Helen (Solley) Russell and fell in love. Helen had two young boys from a previous marriage. Jack transferred his studies to Birmingham Southern University and proposed marriage. Helen would have to make some adjustments in life. She drove up to New York City with Jack to get married on live television.

IWO JIMA HERO SAYS 'I DO'

And, Jack had to make an admission. He had not been nervous as he approached the Iwo Jima beaches, but he was unnerved being in front of television cameras in a New York City studio.

The CBS Network ran a daytime series featuring U.S. servicemen getting legally hitched on television. Unlike current popular TV "Reality Shows," the real couples on *The Bride and Groom Show* were in love and betrothed, and not put together just for the program. They legitimately took their vows live on the air.

A photo accompanied the headlines—Iwo Jima Hero Says "I do." On March 26, 1952, Jack and Helen stood before the Reverend Jesse W. Stitt of the Village Presbyterian Church. Charles "Byrd" Looper, Jack's former roommate and Duke football standout, was best man for the ceremony. The bride and groom were lavished with gifts and prizes, including a beautiful diamond ring to replace the one Jack had purchased. After a paid, week-long trip to the Poconos, Jack and Helen went home with more furniture than an apartment could hold. [26]

Jack adopted Helen's two boys, moved his family to Winston-Salem, and returned to his work with the VA. They lived in an apartment near Baptist Hospital for their first year. In 1953, he bought his first home on Ransom Road. Third son, Louis Harold Lucas, was born on January 14, 1954.

On November 10, 1954, Jack took Helen and the three boys to Washington, D.C., to attend the Marine Corps' 179th birthday celebration and the dedication of the Iwo Jima Memorial at Arlington. He had a chance to shake hands with President Eisenhower, Vice President Nixon, and the three surviving flag raisers.

Jack took a leave from the VA to finish his college studies. With courses at High Point University, a United Methodist Church private liberal arts school in North Carolina, he finished a business degree in 1956. He was 28 years old.

Jack started a new life as a family provider. A year later, an accident reminded him that tomorrows are not promised to all men. He would wonder again why the Lord had not taken him home, when so many good men perish.

"The whole community was saddened by the loss." [27] Jack's buddy, Seaman First Class Marshall Moore, had been discharged from the Navy in June 1946. He returned to Plymouth and remained a single man living on the family farm with his parents. He joined the Williamston Moose Lodge Membership and got a job at the North Carolina Pulp Company mill, a mile-and-a-half from home. The mill had opened in 1937 on a bend in the Roanoke River, where the old Union Fort Gray once fruitlessly fired cannon balls down on the CSS *Albemarle*. Marshall took a job as a machine operator. The first paper machine at NCP started up in 1947.

Following the Korean War, Mahlon Moore was honorably discharged from the 42nd Calvary, and came home to work as a supervisor in the mill's wood yard. Mahlon had married Helen Lewis, and Marshall enjoyed being an uncle to nieces and nephews. He also enjoyed his brother's tales of the April 1945 rescue of several hundred Lipizzaner horses from German captivity near the town of Hostau on the western Czechoslovakia border.

Marshall, 31, had grown into a responsible, fine young man. He was at his machine on Wednesday, September 11, 1957. If he had any thoughts that day about Weyerhaeuser acquiring the mill, he kept them to himself. At 12:45 PM, during a "haying out operation," he was pulled between two industrial rollers into a paper reel core. He suffered traumatic shock, internal injuries, and mangling of his left hand, foot, and ankle. He spoke his last words to a co-worker.

"Tell my mother I'm not coming home."

He was rushed to Washington County Hospital. Mahlon rode with him and provided information to the attending doctor. Marshall hung on for nine hours. He died of Acute Renal Failure at 9 o'clock in the evening. [28]

An Episcopal minister conducted his funeral services at the Veterans Building on Saturday afternoon at 3:00 PM. The procession then drove a mile past the juncture of Roosevelt Avenue, Washington Street, and the Conaby Creek to the Thomas Lafayette Satterthwaite Cemetery. It is a private place at the old Satterthwaite homestead; a mile from the road, behind a field at the edge of deep woods, it is not easy to find.

Williamston Moose Lodge members oversaw the graveside services. Marshall was only the seventh burial as he was laid to his final rest with his maternal grandparents, his sister and brother, an aunt, and an unknown infant. [29]

After five years at the VA and trying various business ventures, Jack returned to active military service on June 5, 1961. He was commissioned as an Army first lieutenant, completed paratrooper training, and served in the 82nd Airborne Division. His active duty status did not interrupt invitations related to his Medal status.

Jack and Helen were invited to sit on the presidential platform when John F. Kennedy took the oath of office on January 20, 1961. "It's one of the greatest thrills I've ever had," he told a reporter. "And my wife—I'm just trailing her around while she shops. She can hardly wait to get there." Jack talked about his wounds and surgeries. His last operation was in 1953. "I get occasional pains from the wounds. But then, doesn't everybody have occasional pains?" [30]

Jack enjoyed attending grand events in D.C. He was invited to be a guest at President Kennedy's spectacular birthday celebration on May 19, 1962. [31] It was memorable for him. Twenty thousand people took seats in New York's Madison Square Garden. He met Frank Sinatra, Dean Martin, Jimmy Duante, Peggy Lee, Ella Fitzgerald, and Lena Horne. Most unforgettable for the son of a tobacco farmer was to be present when the president's brother-in-law, Peter Lawford, introduced the "LATE" Marilyn Monroe to sing "Happy Birthday, Mr. President" on stage.

As the war in Viet Nam was escalating, First Lieutenant Lucas and his family were stationed at Fort Ord, California. His second oldest adopted son, Captain Jimmy Lucas, served two tours in Viet Nam. Jack requested a combat assignment to Southeast Asia, which was denied.

His old habits when bitterly frustrated returned. His drinking and fighting with Army officers escalated. At his request, he received his second honorable discharge on February 21, 1965, a week after his 37th birthday.

An old friend stepped in. Robert Eugene "Bob" Bush, from Tacoma, Washington, had a lot in common with Jack. He had quit high school in 1944 to enlist in the U.S. Navy and served as a Hospital Apprentice First Class. He earned a MOH on Okinawa, for aiding and protecting a wounded Marine officer, despite the serious wounds to his own eyes and shoulders from grenade fragments during a savage enemy counterattack on May 2, 1945. Bob was the youngest World War II Navy man to receive a Medal of Honor. He sat beside Jack on the White House South Lawn on October 5, 1945, as they waited to be called to receive their Medals from President Truman. In the order of the fourteen presentations, Bob Bush was eleventh. Jack was next. Their friendship began that day.

Bob was a successful businessman in Washington State. A friend of his offered Jack a job in the meat business in Fresno. [32] The career opportunity seemed a perfect fit, taking him back to his North Carolina roots in dairy farming. The job required that Jack move frequently from place to place. Helen moved with the boys back to Winston-Salem, waiting for Jack to arrange permanent East Coast employment.

Jack had never intended to be attached to two women at the same time, but it happened. [33] On a business trip to Houston, he met Erlene Muckleroy Alford, a waitress at Gilley's nightspot. She was filling in for a friend who was off for the night. If that was not a coincidence, it had to have been preordained in some mystical way.

Erlene was a divorcee with four children: Becky Arlene, Tena Colene, Deborah Pauline, and David Wayne Alford. Her father, William Butler Muckleroy, was a retired boilermaker and a U.S. Army World War II veteran. Erlene was born in the home of her maternal grandparents, James and Beatrice Crume, and was the oldest of five Muckleroy sisters. At age 28, prosperity seemed only a dream for the Texas damsel. She became the other woman.

The situation was untenable for Helen. She divorced Jack, taking all their belongings and the three boys. Jack married Erlene in 1966. He opened several butcher shops in California and lived in various places in the U.S. with his new family, wherever the meat business took him. A boy, Kelly Swaine Lucas, was born to them in 1968. Peggy Sharlene Lucas was born in 1969.

As often as he had been in Washington, D.C., Jack decided to relocate there. He launched five meat shops in the area. The family resided in a luxurious motor home on a ranch outside of Old Bowie, Maryland, between the Capitol and Annapolis, raising their own beef, processing and selling fresh cuts to order, and raising horses. Jack handled the business end; Erlene managed the company books, and the children worked on the ranch.

The family meat business prospered, grossing $2.5 million in 1973. Jack had five stores and fifty employees. With a great deal of money coming in, Jack drove his powder blue Lincoln Continental, and Erlene drove her dark green Continental. Time had come for a mansion.

Jack and Erlene found the Gardiner House on the south side of 9408 Juliette Drive, Clinton, Prince George's County, Maryland. [34] They liked what they saw, touching the Carolinian's love of antebellum history. The Georgian Revival mansion was south of D.C., east of the Potomac River, and southwest of Andrew's Air Force Base. It had been built in 1922, on a 210-acre working farm. The extensive property was then divided into subdivisions in the mid 1950s.

The 15-room house sat on the 1.18-acre, tree-shaded Lot #12, Block D, in the Surratts Gardens subdivision. Attractive plantings in the surrounding yard added to its allure. The house also held historic significance. The stylish, estate-type building with its large, old chimney stacks, was believed to have incorporated a part of the old, antebellum Robey farmhouse within its walls.

The couple stood in the circular drive looking at the front entrance with its two smooth wooden columns on Doric capitals and lots of windows. They walked around the large, square, two-and-one-half-story, hipped-roof frame structure. The west façade, a two-story enclosed porch of horizontal bands of windows on both floors and a flat roof, enclosed a high-corbelled brick chimney.

Surrattsville High School was just about across the street. The Surrattsville tavern and house was under restoration on a 1-acre plot of land near the intersection of Brandywine and Piscataway roads, a short walk north. A century earlier, Mary Surratt, the co-conspirator hanged at 1:31 PM on July 7, 1865, for her part in the Abraham Lincoln assassination, had once owned that red domicile. The historical site would be open to the public on October 2, 1975.

Jack and Erlene signed the deed to the Gardiner House on June 14, 1973, and moved in with their youngest children and a pet chimpanzee. A decade away, the news of co-conspirators would be more personal in Jack's life than the Mary Surratt story.

Erlene was making lavish purchases without Jack's knowledge. She was also siphoning thousands of dollars in cash and equipment from their prosperous retail business and had $44,000 hidden from him in their home. Jack was working hard and drinking too much. The couple quarreled violently, and their marriage turned tempestuous. Not surprisingly, money was blamed to be the center of the problem. Married for eighteen years, Jack threatened to cut Erlene and her 19-year-old daughter out of his Will. Erlene had a talk with Jerry Ray Morgan.

Jerry Ray, 19, worked for Jack. He also was married to Erlene's daughter, Becky, and lived in the Lucas home with their baby. Erlene had decided to have her husband killed. The conspirators arranged to hire a professional killer. The two plotters reached out to a former employee of Jack's who they believed had the right connections. The murder plot was going to make for sensational television news broadcasts and front-page headlines in major national newspapers.

"Really hit me!"

Jack Lucas and Dennis Kucinich, an Ohio politician, could thank a bogus hit man for living longer lives. Jack's former employee, uneasy about his involvement, had gone to the authorities. The tipster was actually a jailed criminal awaiting sentencing in Delaware for two robbery convictions and looking for a deal. State Prosecutor Charles M. Oberly III met with Larry under a highway motel sign. Mildly skeptical, Mr. Oberly forwarded the information to the Maryland State Police.

They called on "Gene," an undercover D.C. area policeman in his early 40s. [35] Under dark, heavy brows, he had a piercing stare that made people look away. The beard and street hood's strut made him look tough as nails. Gene set out to punch Jack in the face—a prospect that had left many men with bruised jaws. The owner of the Clinton meat cutting business was as tough as he looked: a brawny 5 feet 8 inches, 240 pounds, heavily muscled, 48-year-old man with a bull neck. Knocking Jack out would not be easy.

The State Police called Jack into their station on a Sunday afternoon to warn him that his wife had taken out a contract on his life. Jack, more than stunned, realized how bad his marriage had turned. He figured his Texan bride had planned his murder because he had threatened to change his *Will*. The nastiness was planned for the next day. Jack listened to the details.

Gene had met with the conspirators. He was to be paid several thousand dollars after the job was done. Jerry Ray had cashed his paycheck, earned at the Lucas Beef Retail Packing Company store in Suitland, and made a $137 first installment. Gene insisted on a bigger down payment and $6,000 cash for the finished hit. Erlene gave the "hitman" $350 and a .357 magnum revolver as an additional up-front payment.

Erlene had the plan. Jack would be handed a beer laced with knockout drops at his office. Gene and Larry would drag her unconscious husband into the back seat of his car. Jerry Ray would drive them to the Lucas farm in Bowie. That's where Gene was to execute him. She told Gene to put the barrel of the gun in her husband's mouth and pull the trigger; then, put his finger on the trigger to make it look like a suicide.

Gene changed the plot, explaining that a sedative might show up in an autopsy after Jack was discovered dead. Rather than drug Jack, he would knock him out. The plotters were fooled. The change would allow Gene to carry the plot only halfway and gather enough evidence against Erlene and Jerry Ray without finishing Jack off.

Jack agreed to go along with Gene's "sting." Back home in bed that night, as he was kissing Erlene, he wondered how she could act so loving and carry out her dastardly plot.

The "hitman" showed up at Jack's office before midnight, Monday, June 27, 1977. [36] The informant and accomplice stayed outside: Gene's ally in the back seat of the car and Jerry Ray at the steering wheel. Alone for the knock out clout, they staged it convincingly. Gene punched Jack hard enough to leave a knuckle mark. Not good enough for Jack.

"Really hit me!" he ordered. Jack broke some office furnishings to make the struggle more realistic, then, he played unconscious.

Gene dragged the "victim" outside to the car and put him on the rear floor. He climbed into the back seat and handed his informant a knife. "Cut his throat if he wakes up," he told him.

Gene terrified Jerry Ray. During the twenty-mile drive en route to the farm, the teenager told Gene about his mother-in-law stealing from the firm and hiding cash all over the house. That infuriated Jack, and he tried to get up. Gene pushed him back down.

Arriving at the farm, Jerry Ray jumped from the car and ran. Gene grabbed the long-haired youth by his ponytail and told him he was under arrest. Other officers emerged from hiding. Jack climbed from the car, brushed himself off, and had something to say to Jerry Ray.

"I guess you know, you dumb son-of-a-bitch, you just lost your job, too."

Jack thanked Gene profusely.

Erlene, 38, and Becky Morgan, 19, waiting for a report in front of a convenience store three miles away in Old Bowie, were arrested for the "murder" and held for trial. Charges against Becky were dropped, as it was not clear how she would have benefited from her step-father's murder.

Jack and Erlene made up and reconciled during her six weeks of incarceration. He sat with her at the lawyers' table, holding her hand during her trial. She pleaded guilty to a charge of soliciting to commit murder. He asked the court for mercy, which was granted. Both conspirators drew reduced, 10-year suspended sentences. Although he had found it hard to speak to his wife, Jack explained his change of heart to a reporter.

"Like a nut, I took her back," he said. "It was the only way to save her. I didn't want our own children, ages 11 (Kelly) and 9 (Peggy), to have a mother in prison. That would be worse than anything. It broke my heart, though. It drove me crazy. I'd go outside in the front yard and lay down and scream. I thought, 'What the hell am I driving myself for?'"

Jack tried various methods to calm his nervous system of its agitation. "I tried marijuana once after my wife tried to have me killed, and it made me silly." He was not sure that the illegal drug had any beneficial effects. "Any fool who would sit and laugh at a stereo for four hours—now that's what I did, and that's silly. If you can't control yourself any better than that. . . ." [37]

There was no mending of his life after the murder plot. He was estranged from Erlene, and his marriage was in angry shreds. He had feuds with neighbors. Then, he discovered that

Erlene's financial finaglings had created a debt for which he was going to be held responsible. Jack sold the Gardiner House on June 28, 1978, and moved north up Route 301 to the mobile home on his Bowie property. His teen son lived with him.

Then, on January 13, 1983, the IRS slapped him with a $55,000 claim for unpaid taxes, a fee that more than doubled in penalties, and interest that was compounding rapidly. In total, he owed the IRS $135,360.28.

Jack was feeling hopeless, like he had an IRS noose around him. He lost his business and had little visible income. He depended on his draw of $690 monthly in VA disability checks earned forty years earlier and his $200 monthly federal MOH pension. He despaired of ever working again. "I can never pay it off."

The IRS clamped a levy on his disability checks, blocking all payments. They could not touch his $200 monthly MOH stipend. Congress had passed a law forbidding the IRS to touch the bonus Congress granted to the nation's highest award recipients for extraordinary bravery in combat.

"The IRS stripped me of assets," he claimed. "I'm jobless because the IRS takes every damn thing I earn without letting me keep a cent."

Jack and Erlene finalized their divorce in the summer of 1984.

The 40th Anniversary

"When I think of Iwo Jima, mostly I remember lying on my back trying to keep from choking on the blood in my throat." Jack was going to be 57 years old on February 14, 1985, forty years after he had cheated death on Iwo Jima.

Left almost destitute, his landlady had informed him that the lease on his rural ranch property near Bowie was not going to be renewed. Evicted early in 1985, he was charged with trespassing and carrying a concealed gun in a failed attempt to save many of his dispossessed possessions from destruction. He was scheduled to go to trial in March.

Jack had purchased nearby acreage and moved his mobile home. He had electricity, but no telephone or running water. Neighbors had some grudge against anyone living on that property, and the previous resident had experienced arson damage before selling to Jack. Kelly, 18 years old, moved in with him.

Seth Kantor, Cox News Service, a Washington correspondent for *The Detroit News*, took an interest in him as the anniversary of the amphibious landings approached. Many other correspondents, like J.L. Battenfeld and Mary Boudreaux, wrote lengthy articles about the anniversary. The various headlines on front pages reminded readers of the date's importance— Brutal Iwo Jima Battle Remembered 40 Years Later; Veterans Remember Iwo Jima; Youngest Hero Returns to Bloody Battlefield; Violence Haunting Hero's Life.

Seth went to the mobile home to meet the WWII hero before he left on a flight to Tokyo. Jack told him that he desperately wanted to overcome his problems, but the specter of violence still haunted him. Photojournalist Rick McKay took a shot of Jack at the door in his living room—the last photograph of the home's interior.

Seth's *Return to Iwo* almost filled a page with the flag-raising photo and three columns about brawny Jack Lucas and his downhill slide. It was a "riches to rags saga of wounded World War II hero Jack Lucas"—an American hero on hard times; both the victim and perpetrator of violence throughout his life. Seth described "ups and downs as big as the Alps" in Jack's lifetime. The latest was the deep valley he was in after the IRS made its move on him. [38]

Jack "hitchhiked" on military aircraft to return for the first time to the island where he had earned the Medal for valor under fire, some 10,000 miles from his home. He arrived in

Tokyo on Sunday, February 17, carrying 100 pieces of shrapnel in his right arm, and joined nearly 200 U.S. veterans for the solemn rendezvous. On Monday, the veterans, still haunted by painful memories, had lunch with 100 Japanese veterans of the battle.

On Tuesday, the veterans from both forces flew to Iwo Jima for a Reunion of Honor ceremony and dedication of a monument overlooking the invasion beaches. The gathering stood just a few yards away from the bloodied landing beaches. During the war-memorial service, a four-foot, granite plaque was unveiled. The Japanese Association of Iwo Jima and John Wayne's family had financed the gray marble slab with English and Japanese inscriptions on both sides.

The Marines read the translation facing the beaches. The Japanese read the inscription facing inland, where they had fought to defend their airfields.

"On the 40th anniversary of the battle of Iwo Jima, American and Japanese veterans met again on these same sands, this time in peace and friendship. We commemorate our comrades, living and dead, who fought here with bravery and honor, and we pray together that our sacrifices on Iwo Jima will always be remembered and never be repeated."

Following the dedication, the veterans mingled for "a handshake of peace." Then, the veterans scattered across the island: some somber, others with almost a party spirit. While many rode to Suribachi's summit, Jack and others walked down to the invasion beaches, stooping for handfuls of souvenir black sand.

He led a film crew through some caves and deep subterranean tunnels, getting sweaty and dirty. The atmosphere turned sauna like. Back out on the island's surface, he developed a relentless cough. He was immediately flown to the Naval Hospital on Okinawa where he stayed for eight days. Iwo Jima had failed a second time to take his life.

Then, Hades tried its second claim, having missed its chance when flames had surrounded and trapped young Jackie in a Plymouth meadow.

Once back in Maryland, according to newspaper headlines, Jack had much to deal with. Late at night on March 25, after he and Kelly had gone to bed, Jack was awakened by the smell of smoke inside the mobile home. He saw a line of fire on the ground in front of the home. The "suspicious fire" quickly engulfed the entire residence. He could get Kelly out, but the uninsured trailer was destroyed. Two days later, he recovered only a few belongings from the charred wreckage, including the bronze star-shaped Medal. The pale blue ribbon was gone, but replaceable. Kelly went to live with a friend.

Completely exhausted, Jack was hospitalized for a brief period. When he was discharged, his medical records noted a diagnosis of Post Traumatic Stress Disorder. He was 100% disabled.

All he had left after the fire was an old, abandoned walk-in meat locker in an open shed on his property. The Red Cross furnished him a cot to sleep on in the meat locker. The fire department investigators believed the trailer home Jack shared with his son was burned to the ground by "some type of set blaze."

The national Disabled American Veterans organization came to his aid. Jack was not a member, but the DAV furnished him with money and other essentials and took up his case with the IRS.

In early June 1985, Walter Phillips, associate national DAV service director, arranged for a high-level meeting with the IRS on Jack's behalf. "We stressed the special circumstance involved here, during that meeting with the IRS," said Mr. Phillips. "We emphasized that Jack Lucas has lost all dignity and has no desire to work because of the impossible demands of the IRS."

United States Representative James Jarrell "Jake" Pickle (D-Texas), a WWII Navy veteran with South Pacific service, got involved. Representative Pickle chaired a House subcommittee charged with investigating the IRS. He sent a letter to IRS Commissioner Roscoe Egger on June 24, 1985, insisting the IRS "at once refund the thousands of dollars that apparently have been wrongfully seized from government funds owed Lucas because of his extreme wartime wounds." Representative Pickle intended to introduce legislation barring the agency from seizing combat disability checks from the nation's military veterans who owe back taxes "if steps are not taken to correct the situation involving Jack Lucas."

The IRS agreed to immediately allow Jack to temporarily resume receiving his $690 monthly disability checks, while the federal tax-collecting agency reviewed the case and considered a compromise solution. The Austin, Texas, VA agreed to the arrangements. The disability payments began again, effective Monday, July 1, 1985. The VA also promised to provide him a home in a veterans' facility in the Prince George's County area.

Charles W. Brooks, the IRS chief of collections, Baltimore district, notified the DAV in writing that in "an atmosphere of open communications and earnest efforts in resolving Mr. Lucas' tax problems," he would also allow Jack temporarily to resume work without having any earnings garnished by the IRS.

That was good news. And, as it seemed a constant in Jack's life, "not so good news" soon followed. Another "episode in a life marked by very good luck and very bad luck" was right around the corner. Better said, it was right around the next cornfield. The *New York Times* and *The Washington Post* dispatched reporters. The various headlines read, "War Hero Arrested on Pot Charge" and "War Hero's Hard Luck." [39]

Living in the shed on the mobile home site, at an all-time low in his life, a friend called Jack in August and suggested that he come over to his place. So, he did. Larry Melvin, 31, asked him for help building a patio on the property he rented near Elkton, in northeast Maryland.

Jack decided to camp out, rather than commute between Bowie and the farm. He borrowed a bag for his dirty laundry and a book on how to grow marijuana, "out of curiosity," from Larry. With the landowner's permission to live there, he pitched his tent in a cornfield and spread out his equipment. He also had a shotgun, rifle, and three pistols, all loaded.

"They think I'm a big wheel in a dope racket." Jack was aware that marijuana plants dotted the cornfield. A Department of Natural Resources airplane flying on a routine patrol in the area spotted the marijuana crop and informed the Maryland State Police. The police raided the cornfield on Wednesday, August 28, and found 90 marijuana plants, valued at $90,000. The troopers searched Jack's tent and found the borrowed book, marijuana residue at the bottom of the laundry bag, several marijuana plants in the process of being dried, and his firearms. They arrested Jack and jailed him in the Cecil County Detention Center. He was charged with possession of marijuana, possession with intent to distribute marijuana, and manufacturing marijuana.

He had been in the cornfield for a week.

"I knew the marijuana was out there," he said, "but I didn't plant it. Anybody with any rationale knows they aren't mine. You don't grow plants seven feet tall in such a short time. I don't smoke it or raise it. I don't even smoke cigarettes. I knew the stuff was there on the farm, but I couldn't run up to my friend and tell him not to grow it. He did a lot of things for me."

Jack spent two nights behind bars. He cooperated with the State Police in their investigation. Larry Melvin was also arrested on identical charges a few days after Jack. One of the Lucas boys was able to raise the $5,000 bond, and Jack was released on Friday. A preliminary hearing was on the court docket for September 27.

Jack had no real plans for his future. He could not afford counsel and waited to get a court-appointed attorney. Daniel Saunders, a district public defender from Chestertown, was assigned to represent him. The attorney had the preliminary hearing pushed out to October 24. Mr. Saunders' view of the case was simple.

"Mr. Lucas was just in the wrong place at the wrong time."

Jack was freed in time to consider a weekend trip to Myrtle Beach, South Carolina, on Friday, September 6. The CMOHS was having its biennial meeting at the Myrtle Beach Hilton. At the time, 249 Medal recipients were alive; 160 gathered in Myrtle Beach.

Sue Anne Pressley of *The Washington Post* was there to mix with the elite and dwindling group. She saw Jack, a stocky, balding man with a Medal hanging from his throat, nursing a whiskey in the Hilton lounge while other recipients celebrated around him. There was little mention of battlefield glory. She already knew that the recipients were aware of Jack's recent trouble, but preferred not to make a public issue of it. She watched them treat Jack affectionately and approached the man who had once been the century's youngest Medal recipient.

"At first, I thought I wouldn't come," Jack told her, "and then I figured, why the hell not? I wanted to see them and there are not that many of us anymore. I don't want to embarrass the Medal of Honor. I love these guys. They wear the Medal proudly. When I got my Medal, they didn't say, 'Jack Lucas, you've got to be a saint from now on. You've got to guard every moment.' I'm not sure the other guys are all angels either. I know I've never grown any wings."

Sue Anne asked him about the Maryland situation.

"I don't really have the heart to think about anything," he said. "Seems like my world just keeps falling apart on me."

A Myrtle Beach couple was sitting at the bar. Unaware of Jack's recent troubles, they interrupted the conversation.

"Jack?" said the man. "You don't know us, but we just wanted to shake your hand."

"And say, thank you," the woman added, "for what you did."

Jack solemnly stood up and shook their hands.

Jack's third son, Louis Harold Lucas, had come from Woodbridge, Virginia, with his wife, Georganne, to attend the Medal gathering. Georganne told Sue Anne what she thought of her father-in-law.

"He's like a cat with nine lives."

While Jack was in Myrtle Beach, Daniel Saunders was at work. Obviously, the marijuana plants were already full grown when his client started camping in the cornfield. He also believed that Jack's heroic service to his country deserved merit. He and Cecil County State's Attorney John Scarborough began exchanging phone calls and letters. On October 23, Mr. Scarborough read a prepared statement. Jack would not be prosecuted on drug charges and would be a material witness in further proceedings.

"He couldn't be happier," Mr. Saunders said. "At last, he thinks he may be able to see the light at the end of the tunnel." [40]

Out of the Tunnel

West 57th was a primetime, CBS Tuesday night news magazine series which first aired on August 13, 1985. One of the early segments featured Jack's compelling profile. Nick Kolinsky, 48, a World War II buff and owner of Nick's Ice House, a college bar-lounge, and a moving company, was watching the show in Hattiesburg, Mississippi. He started crying as he watched the program.

"I simply couldn't understand how our nation could let somebody like him—a hero in every sense of the word—get in a situation like that." [41]

Nick was a Pennsylvania native. After an enlistment in the Army, he went to the University of Southern Mississippi on a football scholarship. He played on the 1962 Small College National Championship team and was an All-American lineman in 1964. He is an example of the determination a story about valor can inspire.

Nick called the CBS affiliate in Mobile the next day and was told he should call the national network. He made one call after another to the West 57th CBS building. "All I wanted to know was if someone was going to help this man. If they had said yes, I would've quit pursuing it. But nobody could tell me that. So, I kept talking and getting passed on to someone else."

Finally, producer Beth Flanders gave him a phone number for Jack, and Nick called him. When Jack answered the phone, Nick could not believe it.

"I was like, 'This is the man.' The only thing I asked him was how could I help. I ain't rich. I'm just a family man trying to make a living."

Nick was thinking about his wife, Carol, and their four children. He did not have $100,000 to send Jack. He just wanted to help. He also understood that Jack had been exploited. Even though Jack did not say so, Nick knew the Medal recipient had to be wondering what this stranger's interest was in his plight. Nick said persuasively, "I don't care what situation you're in right now, I can offer you something better here in Mississippi."

"What will your family think?'" Jack asked him.

Nick knew his family would welcome the old hero with open arms. "So, I offered him the best thing I had to offer—a family. People who would love him, care about him."

Jack visited the Kolinsky family in Hattiesburg. Nick visited him at his meat locker in Maryland.

"No running water," Nick recalled, his voice breaking. It turned out that he could barely say a dozen words about Jack without crying. "I remember we shaved outside in a little bowl. It was like being at deer camp. All I ever wanted was for people to respect this man, for this nation to give him his due."

Jack took some time to think about the offer. In 1992, He bought a truck and a new trailer home and drove south to Hattiesburg. He bought a 1,600-square-foot house at 75 Elks Lake Road and knew he would live out the rest of his life there. Kelly also moved down to Hattiesburg and helped his dad clear some virgin pines from the property and remodel the house. Eventually, the home was 4,000 square feet with a guesthouse behind it.

The Kolinsky family and Jack grew close and had a special bond. They referred to him as "Uncle Jack."

Jack's mother was 90 years old in 1993 and living in Washington, North Carolina. She was frail and needed constant looking after. Despite that, she wanted nothing to do with a nursing home. Jack moved her down to his new residence in 1994.

An estimated 15,000 young men had manipulated recruiters, falsified documents, and told lies to serve in the military forces before reaching the legal age to enlist. Many feared that exposure would result in a court martial or loss of their pension, even though policy letters from all military branches clearly stated that the underage veteran and military retirees had nothing to fear. The Veterans of Underage Military Service (VUMS) organization was founded in 1991 to come to the assistance of the aging veterans. Jack was one of 958 members. He contributed his story for the first of the VUMS' *America's Youngest Warriors* three volumes. [42]

In January 1995, President William J. Clinton was preparing his State of the Union speech. First Lady Hillary Rodham Clinton had an idea. Invite the youngest American of the century to receive the Medal of Honor. The president invited Jack, 67, to be his guest on Tuesday night, January 24. He flew in to D.C. on Monday. Before the speech, Jack chatted with the Clintons.

Jack, wearing his Medal of Honor, sat in the gallery next to Hillary during the address before the 104th Congress. His second oldest adopted son, Jimmy Lucas, a Vietnam veteran and Winston-Salem veterinarian, and Matthew Lucas, his grandson and high school student, sat to his right. Jack leaned over and flirted a bit with First Lady Clinton.

"I told her, I said, 'You are a magnificent looking lady. You look a whole lot prettier in person than you do on television.'" A photographer caught that moment for some press coverage. Another photo that appeared on front pages was Hillary standing and waving back to her husband. Jack was to her right happily clapping. [43]

Near the end of his address, President Clinton reintroduced the nation to Jack and his heroics on Iwo Jima fifty years earlier. "The last person I want to introduce is Jack Lucas from Hattiesburg, Mississippi. Jack, would you stand up?"

As Jack stood, the president saluted him, then continued. "Fifty years ago, in the sands of Iwo Jima, Jack Lucas taught and learned the lessons of citizenship. On February 20, 1945, he and three of his buddies encountered the enemy and two grenades at their feet. Jack Lucas threw himself on both. In that moment, he saved the lives of his companions, and miraculously in the next instant, a medic saved his life. He gained a foothold for freedom, and at the age of 17, just a year older than his grandson who is up there with him today—and his son, who is a West Point graduate and a veteran—at 17, Jack Lucas became the youngest Marine in history and the youngest soldier in this century to win the Congressional Medal of Honor. All these years later, yesterday, here's what he said about that day: 'It didn't matter where you were from or who you were, you relied on one another. You did it for your country.'" [44]

Both houses of the U.S. Congress honored the World War II hero with a rousing standing ovation. The assembly clapped for five minutes. It was humbling for the Iwo hero.

One lasting thrill happened to him after the speech when he returned to the Capitol's lower level. He got to hug Mrs. Clinton and Tipper Gore, the vice-president's wife!

"I got so choked up," Jack said when he got home. "I couldn't even smile. Honest to goodness, I had to swallow a hundred times to keep the tears from running down my face. I thought, 'Gosh, here's the son of a tobacco farmer, and all these people, and Mom—she was down here in Mississippi—watching me on TV.'"

He received thousands of letters after his appearance.

"It never really ends," he said.

Getting Older Now

Jack was back in Arlington at the Marine Corps Memorial three weeks after meeting the Clintons. On Sunday, February 19, 1995, he was chauffeured to the commemoration of the 50th anniversary of the pivotal Iwo Jima battle. His sons, veteran Jimmy Lucas and Louis Harold Lucas, with his family, accompanied Jack, along with his daughter Peggy and Jowjie Lucas, a grandson. Jack walked down a red carpet rolled out at the base of the monument. A crowd of 3,000 listened to Medal recipient William E. Barber's introduction.

"I am older now, as are you, but I can still see the colors of that February morning. The sky. The island. And sometimes I think I can still hear the noise of battle."

President Clinton gave the keynote remarks beneath the 78-foot bronze statue. He paid tribute to the memory of all the soldiers who fought on the island. "Our country saw a true definition of courage."

Jack sat directly in front of Mr. Clinton with three other aging heroes; Robert Dunlap, Douglas Jacobson, and Joseph McCarthy, all four of whom the president mentioned. Urging Americans to honor those in uniform who defend our liberty, he closed his talk.

"—the men and women of Iwo Jima will forever stir our hearts, spur our conscience, and summon us to action." [45]

The next week, Harvey Curtiss "Barney" Barnum Jr., Medal recipient from the Vietnam War, wrote a newspaper column to protest the U.S. Supreme Court's decision to allow the physical desecration of the American flag as a form of free speech. He advocated for a Constitutional amendment to protect the flag, to prohibit its desecration, and to overturn the Court's decision. "Barney" recalled the president's recent tribute to a hero named Jack Lucas, how he had asked Mr. Lucas to stand, how the president had saluted the Marine hero. Jack Lucas had made his own indelible mark in military history.

"Our nation's military history is written by individuals like Jack Lucas," Barney wrote, "people transported by patriotism and fate to play their small role in the larger struggle for freedom. One by one, the men and women who have served their country in time of war have added their own distinctive notes to America's military symphony." [46]

For most Medal recipients, giving speeches and attending parades, seminars, and dedications, could become a full-time commitment to American communities. Jack spoke regularly to veterans' groups all over the country and made frequent visits to schools and veterans' organizations to speak to the public about the service and sacrifice required of those who live in a free society. He had to decline many invitations to speak, or he would have been on the road constantly.

When he did speak, he was always moved when young people told him how his story had influenced them to join the Marine Corps. "I try to teach patriotism wherever I go. Love your country, the flag, and what it means to be an American." [47]

Jack believed in education and was well known on the University of Southern Mississippi's campus. The mission at Southern Miss was to teach leadership and engage and empower students to transform lives and communities. Jack was a valued friend of Dr. Andrew Wiest, co-director for the Study of War and Society program, which examines the impact of war and its relationship to society. The program endeavored to link its studies to the community of veterans, military personnel, and interested members of the community in a meaningful way. [48]

Jack served on the program's advisory board, and Dr. Wiest considered him to be "a true hero in so many ways." The Medal recipient possessed a solid grasp of war and understood the need to teach students and the leaders of tomorrow about war's realities.

"It's hard for young people who are enjoying so many good things, our many luxuries, to sit down and assess the price that has been paid." [49]

Jack joined ten of the 186 still living recipients on Monday, July 3, 1995, in Colorado Springs to tour the Air Force Academy and the Cheyenne Air Force Base. They were "older fellows wearing ball caps and windbreakers stitched with military patches or slogans." The single star dangling from a sky-blue ribbon around their necks symbolized a single act that had changed their lives forever. Tourists stopped the recipients in front of the Academy chapel to shake hands or pose for a photograph.

"I don't know what my life would have been like without the Medal of Honor," Jack said to columnist Genevieve Anton. Were there perks to wearing the Medal? A young woman gave Jack a hug as he answered questions. "That was one of many over the years. That's the best part about the Medal of Honor. You can put aside all the accolades. Just give me the hugs." [50]

Jack's mother had a stroke in 1996. Margaret shuffled along slowly on a walker at the Hattiesburg home. Her eyes were infected, and glaucoma was developing. Jack spent his days caring for her, cooking her meals, and making sure she took her medicine on schedule. In time, she would have to be lifted and carried wherever she needed to go. The demands would get physically and emotionally taxing on her son.

That summer, Jack was proud to show his Mama the cover of a magazine that was printed bimonthly. He was a member of the Marine Corps League, an organization that was founded after WWI. The MCL perpetuates the traditions and spirit of the men and women who wear or have worn the Corps' eagle, globe, and anchor. Whenever he was in D.C., Jack would try to swing by the League's Headquarters in Merrifield, Virginia. The summer publication's cover featured a painting of Jack fighting in the trenches on Iwo Jima and a quote.

"It was not in me to turn and run." [51]

A reporter visited the Lucas home one morning in November 1997, to ask if Jack planned to attend a traditional ball and cake-cutting ceremony on the Marine Corps' 200th birthday the next Monday night. [52]

The old Marine would be 70 years old in 3 months. He looked healthy, stocky, and strong as a mule. Jack stirred a bowl of oatmeal for Margaret's breakfast, then, put a spoonful to his lips for a taste test. "Got some goodies in it, Mama," he said. "Bananas. Apples. Honey. Milk."

Jack turned the bowl to line the spoon up conveniently with his mother's right hand. "You go ahead and eat, Mama, and I'll get your coffee."

The reporter did not have to ask.

"It's my duty," Jack told him. "That's my Mama. I give away a lot of my freedom, but I ain't letting her lay there in a nursing home, calling out to strangers for help. I just won't have it. That's my Mama."

The reporter did have a question. "Do you think life has been good to you?"

Jack shrugged. "I've had a wonderful life," he said. "I've experienced things that 98 percent of the people in America never experience. Sure, I've had some ups and downs, but more ups than downs. Heck, I still get fifty to 100 fan letters a month, wanting my autograph or a picture."

Other than his devotion to his Mama, the subject of women in Jack's life did not come up. Maybe it was discretion on the reporter's part not to inquire or write about it. It would have been an interesting conversation.

A delightful and intelligent woman—59-year-old Ruby Catherine Clark—had caught Jack's eye, and he was thrilled to introduce her to Marine traditions. One invitation arrived that he was no way going to decline.

Jack and Ruby took a pleasant 95-mile drive down to the Ingalls Shipyard in Pascagoula, Mississippi, on Friday, December 12, 1997, for a ship's keel laying and "stepping the mast" ceremonies. The tradition was an old maritime custom dating back to the ancient Roman and Greek sailors of placing coins under a ship's mast to guarantee enough money to pay the crew if a ship wrecked at sea.

The structure of the USS *Iwo Jima*, LHD-7, a new amphibious assault ship, was in five sections. A bottle of Iwo Jima sand, various battle memorabilia, and stories about Private First Class Jacklyn H. Lucas were placed in the ship's hull. The 31st Commandant of the Marine Corps, General Charles Chandler Krulak, contributed customary coins. Jack added a copy of his MOH Citation.

It was a glorious day.

In 1998, having lived with her son for four years, Margaret wanted to return to North Carolina, so she could be laid to rest beside her husband when her time came to pass on. Her second boy, Louis Edwards Lucas, was living in Greenville. Her two sons moved Margaret to be near her younger boy for a while. Jack would visit Greenville several times a year.

For a very brief time, there was no woman living with him at home on Elks Lake Road.

Jack, a devoted member of the Dixie Baptist Church on Frye Road, believed his life had turned around in Hattiesburg. His Mama was in good care. He and Ruby joined in wedded bliss in 1998. He would be grateful that she could tolerate most of his faults and for her "unlimited patience."

Ruby did a lot of traveling with Jack. One of her memorable outings was to Texas, where her husband was considered "a true American cowboy."

James Jones had written a novel in 1962, about the WWII Guadalcanal Campaign. For those who had not read the book, *The Thin Red Line* movie was released on Christmas Day 1998. It was a box office hit, reminding Americans of the Marine Corps' South Pacific battles. Letters to Editors described how the movie had helped sons and grandsons better understand how the war had affected their veterans. In February 1999, "This Week in History" newspaper segments further reminded Americans about a particular WWII battle.

The Iwo Jima Survivors Association of Texas, located in Bowie, southeast of Wichita Falls, had held its first annual reunion in 1991. Survivors of the invasion and battle and family members of deceased veterans attended. The Association held the 54th Anniversary National Reunion of the battle, February 20–23, 1999, at the Wichita Falls Holiday Inn. Veterans from the service branches who participated in the land, sea, or air operations before, during, and after the battle attended. Retired Marine Phil Phillips, president of the Iwo Jima Veterans Family Group, came from California to brief the rapidly developing service program. [53]

Of the four Marine MOH recipients from Iwo still alive, Jack and Woody Williams and Douglas Jacobson attended. Robert Dunlap had recently had a stroke and was unable to attend. Jack missed the chance of seeing Bob again. Captain Dunlap was the 1/26th Marines company commander PFC Lucas had surrendered himself to aboard the USS *Deuel* on their way to Iwo.

Army recipient George Wahlen, the only surviving soldier recipient, joined the three Marines at the event. James Bradley, son of one of the flag raisers, was working on a book. He was there to narrate the two flag re-enactments and was the featured speaker at the evening banquet.

Jack and Ruby's next trip was in May.

All 158 living MOH recipients were invited to Indianapolis to attend a special Memorial Day weekend, May 28, 1999, all travel expenses paid. Jack and Ruby made the trip together. On Friday, they attended the gala unveiling of a new Medal of Honor Memorial in downtown with ninety-five other recipients. Twenty-five thousand school children filled the park and surrounding streets. They stood in line for hours waiting for the chance to shake Jack's hand, get an autograph, and hopefully a photo. Ruby stood beside him, and they stayed until the last child walked away. On Saturday, they rode in the Indianapolis 500 Festival Parade. Then, before Sunday's race, Jack completed one lap around the mile-long Indianapolis Motor Speedway track.

After a D.C. meeting with President and Mrs. Clinton in early 2000, Jack stopped in North Carolina to have lunch with his nephew Bill Edwards, a Beaufort County Community College (BCCC) student. Jack had on his USS *IWO JIMA* LHD7 cap. Bill was enrolled in Humanities 120, Cultural Studies. The course published an annual issue of *Life on the Pamlico* written by students—a journal preserving North Carolina's coastal heritage through oral histories. Dr. Dixon Boyles sat with them to interview Jack, who recounted his colorful life experiences. His was one of the three biographies included in the 2001, 68-page journal. [54]

Jack returned to Pascagoula with his lovely wife on Friday, February 4, 2000, and watched the USS *Iwo Jima* launching. He told Ruby how similar in size and appearance the ship was to a World War II aircraft carrier. They were back on Saturday, March 25, to say hello to General Krulak and his wife, Zandra. Fleet Admiral Chester W. Nimitz's words were quoted and became the USS *Iwo Jima's* motto, boldly proclaimed on the sides of the bridge tower.

"UNCOMMON VALOR
WAS A COMMON VIRTUE"

Dozens of veterans watched Mrs. Krulak break the traditional bottle of champagne across the bow of the ship. Once christened by her sponsor, the ship was readied for her maiden voyage a year away. [55]

Jack was back in North Carolina in November to spend his Mama's final days with her. Margaret Sharlene (Edwards) Lucas died on November 7, four days before her 97th birthday. At least Jack had a chance to tell her about the *Iwo Jima*.

Before the ship was commissioned, Jack returned to Iwo Jima in early 2001. Steven Spielberg, historian Stephen E. Ambrose, and film director, James Moll, wanted his assistance in producing *Price for Peace*. The documentary, narrated by Tom Brokaw, chronicled the WWII Pacific Theater events starting with the Pearl Harbor attack and ending with the American occupation of Japan in 1945. Eyewitnesses to the battles from both sides provided their perspectives, sometimes in tears as they recounted memories older than 55 years. The film concentrated especially on the final days of the War in the Pacific.

Ruby accompanied Jack. He showed her the black sands of Red Beach 1 and Mount Suribachi's crater. The trenches near Airfield One in which the Marines had fought and died were covered over in thick undergrowth, so he could not point out the exact place he had covered the two grenades. [56] The word repeated for the documentary segment on the Iwo invasion was "chaos." Jack summarized the first-day landings.

"It was a bloody mess out on that beach—people gettin' blown all to pieces."

The return to Iwo was tough. Jack got ill from lack of water and was hospitalized on Guam until he had had enough intravenous fluids to make the trip home.

Price for Peace aired on the NBC network on Memorial Day Monday, May 27, 2002.

The commissioning crew moved aboard the USS *Iwo Jima* in April 2001. Jack, 73, and Ruby were in Pascagoula one more time on June 23, 2001. They watched in the pouring rain with hundreds of Iwo veterans as the crew of 1,000 men and women in dress white uniforms boarded the gray ship. Then 2,000 World War II veterans joined the crew for the eighty-nautical-mile maiden voyage to Pensacola, Florida. On the wall of the wardroom was a big painting of Jack, copied from the Marine Corps League Magazine cover. Jack, Woody Williams, and Corpsman George Wahlen, residing in Roy, Utah, were the only three living Medal recipients from the battle.

Woody recalled the day he earned his Medal to a reporter. "It was just rat-ta-tat-tat. There are some things about that action that are just like a daydream. They don't even seem real to me."

The USS *Iwo Jima* was commissioned a week later, on Saturday, June 30, 2001. Artist Felix DeWeldon, who had sculpted the Arlington Iwo Memorial, was in attendance. General Michael J. Williams, assistant commandant of the Marine Corps, gave a dedication speech.

"No name is more fitting for a ship that will carry Marines and sailors into combat than *Iwo Jima*. The courage and self-sacrifice of the Marines and sailors who fought on Iwo Jima set a standard for valor and a standard for courage that has never been excelled." [57]

Jack's chest swelled, but not his head. He had become modest about his service. A symbol of patriotism for young men and women, he had met every president since Harry Truman, except Jimmy Carter. He shared tales with the likes of Colin Luther Powell and Norman Schwarzkopf Jr. He traveled the world to speak with front-line servicemen and fellow veterans.

Captain John Nawrocki, commanding officer on the *Iwo Jima*, designated Jack and Ruby as honorary crew and family members of the ship. Jack would sometimes be a special guest on the *Iwo* when she was in homeport at Naval Station Norfolk or docked at New Orleans.

8th & I and Beyond

Marines who had served at the 8th & I Marine Barracks had their own organization—The 8th & I Reunion Association. The 1983 Reunion was their first. Jack liked being on the parade grounds and accepted invitations when other commitments did not interfere. He and Ruby attended the 2001 Reunion among the Marine MOH recipients with wives celebrating the 200th Anniversary of the Barracks. They were also present for the 2003 Reunion, cheering at the Iwo Jima Memorial parade. Jack waved appreciably when he was introduced at the banquet.

Bruce Kauffman is a historian, newspaper columnist, and author. Bruce's History Lessons is a weekly column. Bruce was inspired by Jack Lucas' bravery. After the July 4, 2002 holiday, he wrote America's Most Courageous history lesson. He started by asking, "What does it take to throw yourself on top of a live grenade and then pull a second one under your body so your fellow soldiers would live?"

He went on to point out that all of the MOH winners like Private Jack Lucas—officer and noncom alike—are "ordinary people who, at the moment of truth, performed in an extraordinary fashion. In the vast majority of cases, they made the ultimate sacrifice for their country—they gave up their lives."

Bruce made some good points in his column about there being only 145 recipients surviving, their numbers rapidly shrinking, their average age being 70, and their stories not being given enough media attention. But, he did not have all his history facts correct. Regarding his opening query, he wrote: "Jack Lucas can't answer that question because he died in the act, on the island of Iwo Jima in 1945."

Jack and Ruby might have had a good laugh about that. Jack, an unassuming sort of man, frank about his failings, was still breathing successfully. [58] In fact, "I ain't dead yet!" would be among the last words he spoke as death came to claim him.

Republican Senator Bob Dole from Kansas, a WWII United States Army veteran, was badly wounded by German machine gun fire in April 1945. He was proud to call Jack his brother in arms. That feeling was mutual.

Jack was in Kansas City with ten other Medal recipients for the Senator Bob Dole Institute of Politics dedication on Monday morning, July 22, 2003. The Institute was created as a non-partisan forum to celebrate public service and promote civil discourse. Jack took his seat at the Medal of Honor Memory Tent to participate in a panel discussion with three others. Two brethren Marines were beside him: his friends Robert E. Bush (HA1c Medical Corpsman, Okinawa) and Woody Williams. Seven recipients sat in the audience. When Jack was introduced, the audience erupted with a standing ovation.

The reporters were astonished that Jack had fought on Iwo Jima and considered it "nothing less than a miracle that he survived."

The old Marine took it all in stride. "I did what I had to do on that particular day." [59]

While the "tales of heroism [were] in plentiful supply," so was the good-natured bantering. Woody Williams liked to deny ever having met Jack in the past. He joked that it took him thirty-six days of combat to earn his Medal on Iwo, while Jack had accomplished that feat in just two days.

"There's nothing fair about that!" the West Virginia recipient laughed. For Woody, it was not all bantering. He would not claim ownership of the Medal. As is common among the recipients, he choked up a bit as he spoke of his comrades.

"It doesn't belong to me," he said firmly. "It belongs to those Marines who did not get to come home."

Jack smiled warmly as he signed a lot of autographs at the Memory Tent for young boys whose faces beamed with admiration. After the dedication ceremonies, the former Marine went up north to the Circle S Ranch for a luncheon with former Senator Dole. Jack had made sure to put fresh batteries in his hearing aids. He had become accustomed to the ringing in his ears that never stopped. He joked about the grenade fragments in his brain and lungs setting off metal detectors in airports, and showed the scars on his right arm, with spots of discoloration made by black volcanic ash. About his joint replacements and worries about his lungs, he said little.

Some patriotic American communities fondly remembered Iwo Jima by sponsoring re-enactments of the battle and flag raising. Fredericksburg in Gillespie County, west of Austin, Texas, put one together with a four-day Public Tribute to the Heroes of Iwo Jima on the 60th anniversary in 2005. The tribute began with a parade down Main Street on Saturday morning. Jack and Woody rode in the beds of large WWII trucks, waving to the spectators. [60] Combat-decorated Marine Colonel Oliver North rode in a military jeep. The steady drizzle of rain and overcast skies did not stop spectators from greeting, cheering, and applauding the veterans. Many held up "THANK YOU" signs.

Twice as many spectators than expected, over 10,000, found parking on the Welge Range in Doss, thirty miles north of Fredericksburg, for the Saturday reenactment of the *Battle of Mount Suribachi*. They bunched up in parking lots, and the vehicles trying to get in stretched in a mile-long line. When there was no more room, hundreds were turned away. The event organizers decided to schedule a second show for Sunday.

More than 300 volunteers dressed in WWII gear performed. WWII aircraft, halftracks, fifty Sherman tanks, mock gunfire and explosions, smoke, and flamethrowers lighting up enemy bunkers gave realism to the demonstration. Corpsmen tending to wounded re-enactors and litter bearers carrying others to the rear did as much to trigger memories for Jack and the Iwo veterans as the noise. The battle reenactment finished with the second of the two flag raisings.

Writing it All Down

D. K. Drum was a writer and Jack's friend. Dorea Kuck grew up in Lincolnton, North Carolina, 305 miles west of Jack's hometown. Her family was deeply patriotic. In spring 1970, when her brother, Dennis Franklin Kuck, joined the U.S. Army, she was in the seventh grade.

She was a freshman at Lincolnton High School, Class of 1975, when Dennis completed his tour in Viet Nam and came home after Thanksgiving 1970; honorably discharged, a veteran with a Bronze Star. Dorea married Tommy Dale Drum, a three-times decorated Vietnam veteran. She and Jack Lucas began collaborating on the Medal recipient's memoir, retracing the life events important to him.

Jack took Dorea to the house where he was born and showed her the memorable places in Plymouth. They went together to Washington to research materials. [61] In 2004, Jack, Ruby, and Dorea met at Naval Station Norfolk after the *Iwo Jima* had returned from sea duty.

Captain John W. Snedeker Jr., second CO of the ship, had invited them to stand on the flight deck where the McDonnell Douglas AV-8 *Harrier* vertical/short takeoff and landing (V/STOL) jets operated. In a touching ceremony, Captain Snedeker renamed the flight deck "PFC Jacklyn H. Lucas Airfield." The next trip for Dorea was to Iwo Jima Island.

The Honor Reunion

The Battle of Iwo Jima 60th anniversary brought fifty U.S. veterans with hundreds of family members back to the small Japanese military outpost on the island. The legendary Jacklyn "Jack" Lucas was among the two-dozen distinguished guests. They mixed with a dozen surviving Japanese veterans to remember one of the bloodiest and most symbolic battles of WWII.

The island D. K. Drum saw for the first time was nothing like it was when the young Marines first landed on its shores. It was desolate, covered with rough jungle and pocked with caves. Weeds covered concrete bunker windows. Rusted cannons sat idle. Inside the caves, the visitors saw rifles, hand grenades, and spent shells. Not a person saw souvenirs. They left the relics lay where they had been abandoned sixty years prior. The remnants of vehicles marked the locations where Marines had landed. The once-shelled civilian villages were gone.

Jack's view of the island was grave. "It was still an ugly piece of real estate, seemingly worthless and reeking of sulfur."

Before the ceremony, young and old Marines gathered for lunch. A line of young Leathernecks formed near Jack and quietly waited. When he finished his meal, one by one, they respectfully stepped forward to shake his hand. Despite the neurological damage to his right wrist and fingers that made his autographs shaky, his grip was strong and firm.

After lunch, the aging combat veterans gathered on a hillside over the landing beaches to offer prayers and wreaths for the dead. An A/P photographer snapped Jack's profile standing in line with Marine Corps brass with his hand over his heart.

After the ceremony, the veterans and families split off to find particular battle sites. Jack went to the top of Suribachi again and surveyed the island. Emotions surfaced; grief for the thousands who had been buried in Marine Division cemeteries during the thirty-six days of fighting, and a simmering anger toward an enemy, long gone, that had dared to attack his country. Yet, there was the contentment that the Marines and soldiers had taken the island from the Imperial Japanese defenders. Like many American veterans, he wished that the U.S. had not returned the island to Japanese jurisdiction in 1968.

Visiting Red Beach for the last time, Jack reached down and dug his fingers deep into the warm black ash, holding tightly to the black grains where so much American blood had been absorbed. He snapped a salute and looked forward to his departure from the island.

Newspaper correspondents wrote their articles about the Honor Reunion, filling as much as the entire top half of a page. [62]

Americans who enjoyed reading about war and military history made James Bradley's *Flags of Our Fathers* a *New York Times* bestselling book in 2000. James wrote that some of the fiercest "boys" on Iwo Jima's frontline beaches were "kids barely out of childhood." For any readers unfamiliar with Jacklyn Lucas, James introduced him. The author had asked the old Marine a question in 1998. [63]

"Mr. Lucas, why did you jump on those grenades?"

Jack answered without hesitation. "To save my buddies."

The book, *Medal of Honor: Portraits of Valor Beyond the Call of Duty*, was published on October 1, 2003. Jack's portrait was included in the 144 contemporary Profiles of Valor. He is quoted in the front matter, recalling the familiar New Testament passage often inscribed on the grave markers of men who died in combat—John 15:13 KJV. "Greater love has no one than this, that someone lay down his life for his friends." Jack was resolute. "From the Revolutionary War, forward, our American servicemen and women have done that in the name of the freedom you enjoy today."

He and other Medal recipients visited schools and civic organizations, but the CMOHS believed more had to be done to teach young people about sacrifice and courage. As part of a grass-roots project in South Carolina, Smith Barney's CEO Tom Matthews contributed copies of the book for each Aiken County middle and high school. Tom liked to cite Jack's heroism as something for teenagers to emulate. The American Legion of South Carolina had also provided the book to 400 schools, and Ross Perot had purchased one for every school in Texas. Dr. Linda Eldridge, Aiken school superintendent, was unwavering. "Our children are looking for heroes. But sometimes the images they select are based on what they see on television and movies and in their music. This gives them some true heroes to appreciate." [64]

The *Medal of Honor* books were distributed with a sense of urgency. In the later 1960s, there were 1,800 Medal recipients. As 2003 neared its end, 148 remained alive. Smith Barney also took on an Oral History project, collecting eight-minute excerpts from one-hour interviews with the recipients. Jack's interview was included among those kept in the Smithsonian and the Capital Visitors Center.

As Jack and Dorea reviewed the final draft of his memoir, he received a sad call about a good friend in Tumwater, Washington. Corpsman Robert E. Bush, USN, Medal recipient from the Okinawa campaign who had sat beside Jack on the White House South Lawn and helped him get started in the meat business so long ago, died at age 79 years on November 8, 2005.

Americans who cared to learn more about Jack's life, beyond newspaper articles, had their chance on May 2, 2006, when Da Capo Press published *Indestructible: The Unforgettable Story of a Marine Hero at the Battle of Iwo Jima*. D. K. Drum explained that the book was written for a seventh-grade audience to reach as many people as possible. [65]

"If he has a chance to say one thing to people, it's to never say 'I can't,'" she said. "You don't know what you can do until you try."

Commandant of the Marine Corps General Michael William Hagee invited the sixteen living Marine MOH recipients and families of ten deceased recipients to come to the 8th & I Marine Barracks in D.C. On Thursday evening, August 3, 2006, in front of over 1,000 people,

General Hagee and Sergeant Major John L. Estrada, 15th Sergeant Major of the Marine Corps, presented the twenty-six flags. [66]

In one photo, General Hagee shakes Jack's hand as he presents him his flag during the ceremony. The final flag presentation was to Sergeant Major Allan J. Kellog Jr., a Vietnam War recipient. The crowd of family, friends, and Marines gave the honorees a rousing standing ovation.

The United States Marine Drum and Bugle Corps' played the Marines Hymn to conclude the parade ceremony. The 200 Marines of Alpha and Bravo companies, residents of the Oldest Post in the Corps, passed-in-review and rendered an official salute to the recipients and families. The spectators were on their feet.

"Nobody does it up like the Marine Corps," Jack said of the ceremony. "To have these young men here in our presence—it just rejuvenates this old heart of mine. I love the Corps even more knowing that my country is defended by such fine young people."

Sixteen USMC recipients. On the parade grounds in front of the Commandant's House at the 8th & I evening parade. Jack Lucas, wearing his favorite red Marine blazer and Marine  Corps League "piss cutter," stood between Vietnam recipients, James Everett Livingston and John James McGinty III. Woody Williams is on John McGinty's other side.

Clint Eastwood made James Bradley's book into a movie, released on October 20, 2006. Two months later, Clint followed up that movie with *Letters From Iwo Jima*, released on December 6. Never out of the memory of its veterans, the 1945 battle reemerged in American consciousness.

Louisville Courier–Journal columnist Bob Hill thought the two Clint Eastwood movies about Iwo Jima flags reminded Americans of the stories of brave men, "of a different time, a different, very threatened world—a different sense of commitment." The stories made Bob wonder "what made them do it—and would we do it, as teenagers, today?" He was writing about men like Jack Lucas. He thought that Jack was the youngest Marine in history to win the Medal of Honor, that it took twenty-two operations to restore his body, and that at age 79, he still suffered the effects of his instinctive bravery.

Jack was in Louisville on Saturday, February 24, 2007, at the Ohio Valley Military Society Show of Shows in the South Wing of the Kentucky Exposition Center. While at the fairgrounds, he signed his "aptly named" book. On Sunday, 1:00 to 5:00 PM, he was at the Jefferson Mall food court for a "speak and greet." [67] And as always, he would "scratch out an autograph or two" for any young Marines he met in Louisville.

Word from Tokyo on Monday, June 18, 2007, that Japan was returning to using Iwo To (ee-woh-toh), Iwo Jima's prewar name, rankled most veterans of the battle. "Frankly, I don't like it" was uttered caustically in both languages. Jack would have no part in the name change.

Democratic presidential hopeful Senator Hillary Rodham Clinton stopped in Hattiesburg on March 7, 2008, during a presidential campaign appearance. She greeted her supporters at the train depot and acknowledged Jack. He was wearing his Medal of Honor, USMC jacket, red MCL hat, nasal oxygen tube, and his hearing aids. Carolyn Kaster captured his salute back to the senator in an AP Photo. [68] The photograph pops up in countless places.

Major Wesley T. "Wes" Prater (Ret.) was at Marine Corps Base 29 Palms in California. He was a co-founder/administrator of *Marines: Together We Served*, a military-themed social networking web site. Jack has a gallery of photos across his lifetime on the site. [69] Sixty-eight younger veterans are proud to include a "Jack Lucas and me" photo in their Shadow Box Photo Album.

Major Prater helped organize the first officially sponsored TWS Get Together. "TWS Island Storm 2008" was held in Beaufort, South Carolina, and aboard MCRD Parris Island, April 10–12, 2008. Wesley invited PFC Jack Lucas, Iwo Jima MOH recipient, to be the Guest of Honor. The March TWS Newsletter recognized Jack as one of the finest of American Heroes and informed the members that he had graciously agreed to attend the event and conduct a book signing.

TWS members checked in on Thursday—120 strong, from all ranks and spanning more than eighty years of service from WWII to the current days. They "represented a tremendous amount of living Marine Corps history." The attendees were elated that they each received a copy of *Indestructible* and had the opportunity to have Jack personalize it with his signature. His stories needed no embellishments at the catered registration reception.

Friday events began at 6:00 AM, with the TWS group boarding buses for a ride to the Parris Island Depot. In addition to his Medal and red MCL cap, Jack wore his distinctive red, white, and blue suspenders. The group attended Morning Colors at 8:00 AM sharp, a moving experience for them. The Depot Band paid a special tribute to Jack. He was back to the place where his Marine Corps experience had begun. How many of his fellow P.I. Platoon 603 graduates had survived WWII? How many might still be living in American communities with nightly visits to Pacific islands?

Jack held a book signing at the MCA Book Store for his memoir. The many visitors aboard the Depot for the next day's recruit graduation appreciated the chance to greet him and walk away with his autographed book. Noon meal was served at the Chow Hall. An "all-you-care-to-eat South Carolina style BBQ with music, plenty of books being signed, loads of door prizes and corporate goody bags, and more than a few cold drinks being served" ended Friday's schedules activities.

On Saturday morning, the group donned their matching Green Island Storm polo shirts and went for a semi-formal breakfast. Jack considered the Medal and his association with the Marines as a brotherhood to be the highlight of his entire life. He spoke from his heart to the group, sharing his Iwo Jima story and the life events that followed through the years after he had been presented the Medal at the White House. Getting the story "straight from The Man himself" was considered "a once in a lifetime opportunity" for the TWS group. Known to be rich in his use of language, one of Jack's comments soon became a TWS Quotable Quote.

The group attended the Morning Colors ceremony, then, moved to the parade stands for the graduation ceremonies. Jack was recognized again during the ceremony. For the remainder of the day, the group toured various training areas, the Depot Museum, Gift Shop, ate at the WFTBN chow hall, had a photo-op at the "Yellow Footprints," and enjoyed a guided tour of the crucible training events as recruits were put through their paces.

The Boot, MCRD Parris Island's newspaper covered the TWS Island Storm event in its 18 April 2008 issue.

After everyone had departed the reunion, Major Prater got busy designing a polo shirt. The April 2008 shirt was scarlet red with gold screening. The eagle, globe, and anchor symbol was on the left breast, over the title MARINES. Arching over the image was the web site address—marines.togetherweserved.com. Jack's breakfast speech quote was emblazed in gold on the back of the crimson shirt. [70]

"Marines . . .
We are the Toughest, Meanest Bastards Alive!"

PFC Jack H. Lucas, USMC
Medal of Honor, Iwo Jima, 1945
TWS Island Storm 2008

The shirt was featured for sale in the April MTWS monthly newsletter. Under the column explaining Orders & Payment details, Major Prater also included a ***Special Note.***

"You may have heard that Jack Lucas has been ill lately and since we're quoting him on the shirts, I'm going to send 25% of total proceeds, after printing and shipping costs, to Jack and Ruby Lucas as a Thank You from all of us here at TWS for spending time with us at Island Storm and as encouragement to hopefully lift his spirits. I have no way of knowing what the size of this gift might be, hopefully it will at least be enough for them to enjoy a good Steak Dinner and a movie, on us!"

Jack was diagnosed with a form of leukemia in April. His decline seemed to come on quickly. His family and friends knew he was fighting for his life. It "tore apart his body," Ruby reported. His chemotherapy treatments were proving ineffective. Dialysis was required a minimum of every other day.

Jack had spent long years reflecting on his surviving the blast of grenades. He addressed the questions frankly in the Epilogue of his book. Jack believed and accepted that God had worked in his life and spared him from death many times to allow him to make a difference in the world. He was a spokesman for all the brave men who fought for freedom and died doing it. He recognized that, because of the Medal, the good will of people had bolstered him through hard times. He also acknowledged that he was "as imperfect as they come" and was disappointed in some of the things he had done in his life. [71] Jack was an honest man.

Going back to 1998 on the job, Police Officer John had never seen a Medal of Valor plate on a vehicle. He saw one when he made a routine traffic stop in late May 2008, before Jack went into the hospital. He would never see a plate like that again. Officer John intended to give a verbal warning for a minor offense. He walked back to his patrol car with a signed copy of *Indestructible* that Jack gave him. After reading the book and researching other resources, he reached his professional opinion. "This guy had major brass."

Six years later, Officer John learned what happened shortly after that stop. "I feel blessed to have shook his hand, and I have never said that about anyone else I had ever met." [72]

Mississippi Lieutenant Governor Phil Bryant wrote a Letter To The Editor printed on the Sunday before Memorial Day 2008. He recalled that the holiday was first celebrated in Columbus, Mississippi, in 1866. He urged locals to reflect on the reason for the special day, in the spirit of the sacrifices and contributions of American heroes like Jack Lucas. Mr. Bryant viewed Jack as "a living American legend. . . . Known the world over as a patriot and profiled by media throughout the country". [73]

Teen WWII hero, now 80, gravely ill with cancer.

Jack got weaker by the day and could no longer walk without assistance. He spent his last days in the hospital with Ruby, family and friends, and a lot of company. Dorea and Tommy Drum were among the steady stream of visitors keeping a vigil over Jack with Ruby. Newspaper headlines in the first week of June seemed quite ominous.

Ruby was getting phone calls from all over the country. General James F. Amos was to pin on his fourth star in July and take on duties as the Assistant Commandant of the Marine Corps. He called Ruby on Monday, June 2.

Jack did not have energy for an interview, but D. K. Drum, his biographer, provided information to reporters on behalf of the family. She reported that he was in "grave" condition at Forrest General Hospital in Hattiesburg and was in the fight of his life, battling cancer. Family and friends were staying with him 24 hours a day. [74]

"He is fighting very hard, very hard," she said. "It's probably his hardest fight, but he's not giving up."

Jack was mildly perturbed about his situation. "This is not the way a warrior should go down," he said to Ruby. As stalwart as her husband, Ruby reassured him.

"Baby, you're a warrior no matter how you go down."

Sergeant Mike Fishbaugh served in the Marine Corps from 1967 to 1971. He was with the Force Logistics Command in the Republic of Viet Nam. He had come to be close to Jack and his family. He knew that Jack was ill and dropped by at Forrest General. On one visit, he wore the TWS crimson shirt with Jack's quote on the back. Mike's attire tickled the old warrior. [75]

The dialysis had removed thirty-six pounds of fluid from his body, but he was still really huge. He mostly kept his eyes shut, but was not asleep. Breathing was a struggle, his voice was down to a whisper with no sound coming out at all, and he was unable to speak on the phone. Ruby was taking most of the calls.

Mike was at the hospital to visit Jack and Mrs. Ruby again on Tuesday, June 3, wearing a red Marine Corps ball cap and a red shirt. He talked quietly with Mrs. Ruby when he walked into Jack's room. Jack had had four consecutive days of dialysis, and it was just too much for an 80-year-old in his condition. Jack had requested no dialysis that day, because it drained him so much physically. When Jack heard Mike's voice, he opened his eyes and smiled brightly. He motioned for Mike to come to him, wanting him to turn around, so he could read the back of shirt.

Jack must have been thinking that the red shirt was the one that Major Prater had designed. "It'd go good with your red cap," Jack whispered approvingly. Mike committed to himself to wear the TWS shirt when he went back to the hospital.

In his post to Marines the next afternoon, Mike expressed his concern for Mrs. Ruby. "The reality of losing the person that she has waited on hand and foot and loved all these years is finally becoming a realization to Mrs. Ruby. She is a very, very strong Lady, but she is breaking down just a little more each time I am with her."

The former sergeant wanted to alert the Marines that Jack was still fighting and would not quit, but the inevitable would come soon. Jack would not be able to serve the country much longer. Mike suggested that those who wished to visit or contact Jack or his family should do so as quickly as possible. One woman from North Carolina, who had never met Jack, had called on Monday and was already on her way to Hattiesburg to see him before it was too late.

Mike was finding the posts getting harder to write.

In Jack's final hours, visiting was stopped, and Ruby spent a few quiet moments with her hero.

"Jack, you know you're dying," she whispered. Jack just raised his head off the pillow.

"I ain't dead yet," he said as plain as day.

Ruby was not surprised, and had a loving response. "That's Jack Lucas. He wants to get the last word in."

Late on Wednesday night, Jack asked the doctors to remove the dialysis machine. [76] He died shortly after midnight, Thursday, June 5, 2008.

Jack's survivors included: his wife, Ruby C. Clark Lucas; four sons, William Wayne Lucas of Adel, Georgia, Jimmy Randall Lucas of Lewisville, North Carolina, Louis Harold Lucas II, of Safford, Virginia, and Kelly Swain Lucas of Petal, Mississippi; a daughter, Peggy Charlene Lucas of Petal; three step-daughters, Joan Martin, Debbie Mitchell and Melinda Carroll, all of Petal; a brother, Louis Edwards Lucas of Greenville, North Carolina; fifteen grandchildren and sixteen great-grandchildren.

All three of PFC Lucas' Iwo Jima fireteam buddies had long lives after the war. Jack was the youngest of them when they jumped from the Higgins onto the black beaches; and, he was younger than each of them when he was laid to rest. Malvin Hagevik, 84, had died on April 26, 2004. Riley Gilbert, 84, died five days before Jack, on May 31, 2008. Allan Crowson, 83, died on December 17, 2008.

Day of Mourning

Word of Jack's death traveled quickly through the Corps' ranks. On Friday, Assistant Commandant of the Marine Corps General Robert Magnus released a statement, mourning the loss of a hero. "The Commandant of the Marine Corps and I join Marines of all generations in sending our condolences to his wife Ruby and their family. I knew Jack Lucas, a Marine and true American hero. Jack was a great warrior who epitomized the individual fighting spirit of our Marines." [77]

"I never met anyone like Jack Lucas," Gunnery Sergeant Will Price said. He remembered the response to a rousing speech Jack gave at Marine Corps Headquarters in Washington. "When he came, the Marines just crowded around him. He's the epitome of the values of the Corps. They were just captivated by him. Everything that came out of his mouth was pure gold and pure motivation."

Mary Draughn, Jack's young friend and former Marine, agreed with that view. "He's a hero," she said. "He had a contagious personality and a patriotic drive he inherited from his father as he grew up in Plymouth, North Carolina." [78]

Robert D. "Bob" Ledford, commander of Hattiesburg's Chapter 690 of the Military Order of the Purple Heart was a longtime friend of Jack. Bob was at home when he got the news of his friend's passing. He looked at a photo of a group of World War II veteran friends. Jack was the most recent of the group to die. Tearful emotions surfaced when he thought of Jack's unselfishness during the war.

"We learned to respect one another. And in combat situations, we had the buddy system where one guy would help out the other fellow. . . . It makes me sad. He was well respected by his fellow veterans. He was a veteran. He was a Medal of Honor winner. He served honorably and did what the country asked him to do."

Mississippi Lieutenant Governor Phil Bryant read a prepared statement. "America has lost one of its great heroes with the passing of Jack Lucas."

Words Jack once expressed resonated with Governor Haley Barbour, at the City of Jackson Capitol. "I would not settle for watching from the sidelines," the Medal recipient had said, "when the United States was in such desperate need of support from its citizens."

The governor ordered that the State flag be lowered to half-staff on Monday, June 9, in honor of the World War II hero. "Jack Lucas' life is an inspiration to every American and is an important story of honor, duty and devotion to country," he said. "While we honor his life and heroic service with this gesture of respect and appreciation, we will also keep his family in our thoughts and prayers."

Governor Barbour and Secretary of State C. Delbert Hosemann Jr. composed Executive Order No. 997, including nine WHEREAS, a THEREFORE, and an IN TESTIMONY WHEREOF. "On June 5, 2008, Mississippi lost one of its most valuable citizens with the passing of World War II Veteran and Medal of Honor Recipient Jacklyn "Jack" Lucas . . . a Marine and Soldier, [he] has set an example for all Americans to follow . . . his love for his state and his country will forever be remembered . . . the prayers of this State are with the family and friends of Jack Lucas . . . by the authority vested in me as Governor by the Constitution and laws of the State of Mississippi, [I] do hereby proclaim a period of official mourning in the State of Mississippi and further do hereby order the flag of the State of Mississippi be flown at half-staff on all buildings and grounds of the State of Mississippi and all areas under its jurisdiction beginning at sunrise and ending at sunset on June 9, 2008." [79]

The major newspapers, like the *New York Times*, *The Washington Post*, *The Chicago Tribune*, and the *Los Angeles Times*, and papers across the country printed long obituaries on Friday with similar headlines—Jack Lucas Dies at 80; Earned Medal of Honor at 17.

As per Jack's wishes, the family requested that memorials be directed to the Marine Corps League Commiskey–Wheat Detachment #1073, P.O. Box 18290, Hattiesburg, Mississippi, 39404.

Author and political commentator Debbie Schlussel was concerned about what girls and young and future adults of the nation found important. On June 6, she drew attention to the fact that World War II heroes were dying every day all over America. She guessed their story would die out. "Soon, there will be almost none left. And sadly, many Americans will forget them."

Debbie was not going to forget the contributions of heroes like Jack Lucas, an "amazing American patriot and hero [who] was able to understand the call to duty and sacrifice for his country" when he was 14 years old. "Sadly for us, they don't make 'em like they used to," she wrote. "Jacklyn 'Jack' Lucas, Rest In Peace." [80]

Visitation for Jack was held on Sunday at Moore Funeral Home, Hattiesburg, from 5:00–9:00 PM. His funeral services were at 10:30 AM, Monday, at the Hattiesburg Lake Terrace Convention Center. A memorial service was also conducted on the University of Southern Mississippi campus. His interment followed in Lot 47, Section 32, at Highland Cemetery, 3401 West 7th Street. Legions of Marines and friends attended the funeral services.

On his stone, under the Marine Corps emblem and his image:

"Do not judge me by my beginning,
only by my end, nor by the path
I took, but where it led me."

On the back of his stone, the Medal of Honor emblem is etched under his name. On either side of the emblem are brief portions of his Citation.

Jack is the second famous Marine MOH recipient at the cemetery. Hattiesburg native son, Major Henry Alfred Commiskey Sr., earned his Medal on September 20, 1950, near Yong Dung P'o, Korea. He died on August 16, 1971, and has a small flat stone and a standing MOH marble memorial cenotaph at Highland.

"He was a valued friend." That is how Dr. Andrew Wiest, of the Southern Miss Study of War and Society program, remembered Jack. His friend's contribution had made the program in the study of war one of the best in the nation, making it a success in establishing valuable outreach efforts to the community. Dr. Wiest announced that Richard McCarthy and Craig Howard, both supporters of Southern Miss and the Study of War and Society program, had created an endowment to fund the Jack Lucas Award and numerous outreach efforts, including a successful speaker series and community book club. [81]

"With the support of interested members of the community like Lucas, McCarthy and Howard, our programming will continue to expand, allowing us to better understand war, better serve the community and better honor veterans like Jack Lucas."

The University of Southern Mississippi made an announcement on June 24, 2008. Ruby Lucas had established the Jack Lucas Award for Undergraduate Research in the Field of War and Society to both recognize the excellent work of USM undergraduate students and to honor her late husband. The special academic award in Jack's name would acknowledge the best paper on a topic in warfare history written by a Southern Miss student. Richard McCarthy and Craig Howard, supporters of the Dale Center for the Study of War and Society, created an endowment to help fund the award, which would include a $250 cash contribution. [82]

John Fitzmorris a history doctoral student from New Orleans had an opinion about the news. "To have an award named for someone who set such an example of courage and devotion lends honor to the author of the winning paper and the entire history program."

Ruby would present the inaugural award to Patrick Lofton of Newton, a spring 2009 graduate. Each spring since, the Center has presented Jack's award to a deserving student author.

Wes Prater composed a statement for the TWS members in their June 2008 *The Guidon* Newsletter. "It is with complete sadness that we announce the passing of a Legendary Marine, an American Hero and our friend Jack Lucas on 5 June 2008." He offered a personal *Thank You* to everyone who had responded to the Memorial Forum Thread on MTWS honoring Jack, and extended "a special thanks" to those who had attended the funeral services in Hattiesburg. [83]

Wes described what so many people across Jack's life would say of him—how easily he had an influence on another's life. "I personally developed a friendship with him at the TWS Get Together in April and I can't say how much of an honor it was to spend time with him. Men like him don't come along very often and it is with a heavy heart that I make this announcement, we miss you Jack."

Nine months after Jack's death, the General Assembly of North Carolina in Session 2009, the House of Representatives and the Senate concurring, expressed the appreciation of the State and its citizens for the valiant service he rendered to his country as a member of the Armed Forces. Whereas, Jacklyn "Jack" Harold Lucas spent much of his youth on a farm in Plymouth, North Carolina, the General Assembly extended its condolences to his family and his survivors. The Secretary of State transmitted a certified copy of the resolution to the family, effective upon ratification.

HOUSE JOINT RESOLUTION 562
March 12, 2009
A JOINT RESOLUTION HONORING THE LIFE AND MEMORY OF JACKLYN "JACK" HAROLD LUCAS, ONE OF THE YOUNGEST MEDAL OF HONOR RECIPIENTS OF THE TWENTIETH CENTURY.

Jack Lucas' impact has continued. Retired Army Sergeant First Class Richard Powers and his wife, Josie, of Rineyville, Kentucky, have had a part in that. When Richard was on active duty, he made a point of looking up Medal recipients in every town around the country to where he was sent on orders. Jack was one of the first in Mississippi, and he talked with him for hours about the hero's actions on Iwo Jima. The two became long-time friends. [84]

One day Jack punched him in the stomach. Richard explained the punch was "because he was a Marine, and I was a soldier, and he wanted to see how hard a soldier was." Jack gifted him his blue MOH ribbon, and Richard held on to it for years. "I decided I had to do something with it."

He designed a case to keep it in and hung it in his basement. It has a wooden base with a glass cover housing a display bust with the MOH ribbon. The medal portion of the award is etched into the glass cover and appears to float over the ribbon when viewed from the front. Jack's Citation was etched on one side of the glass, and an image of him was on the other side.

Realizing that the prestigious honor was more than a decoration, Richard dedicated his time and money to research and educate American youth about acts of patriotism, heroism, and bravery. He began donating the display to high schools for a year at a time, with Jack's permission and approval to be displayed in his honor. The tribute was designed as an instructional and an inspirational piece. The case was first displayed at the American Legion in Elizabethtown, Kentucky, then at North Hardin High School in Radcliff, Fort Knox High School, and Central Hardin High School Junior Reserve Officer Training Corps classroom in Elizabethtown.

The tribute grew into a much larger project, and Richard began making tributes to surviving MOH recipients of all the services. He created a Web site to inspire students to do more research. His mission: Knowledge.

"This is a great way to showcase the actions of one of our nation's heroes and to teach students about the military," said Gunnery Sergeant Allen Rosenblatt, staff noncommissioned officer in charge of Recruiting Sub-station Elizabethtown. "Military history isn't always something that a lot of students are taught, so it's always good to see things like these tributes out in the community."

Hattiesburg continues to remember Jack. According to the Mississippi Code, Title 65, Designation § 65-3-71.140 (2013), the portion of U.S. Highway 49 in Forrest County beginning at the intersection of U.S. Highway 49 and Hardy Street in north Hattiesburg and extending southerly to the Forrest/Stone county line (thus, between Hattiesburg and Wiggins) would be known as *Jack Lucas Medal of Honor Memorial Highway*. The Mississippi Department of Transportation erected and maintains appropriate signs along and approaching that portion of highway. [85] The thirty-mile highway spur begins on the eastern edge of the USM campus.

On Friday, May 27, 2016, Memorial Day weekend, *The Clarion–Ledger*, republished Billy Watkins' November 7, 1997, story about Jack's WWII valor and life's grit. [86]

Four months later, Mississippi learned that the Navy and Marine Corps intended to honor Jack with more than a newspaper story.

An Arleigh Burke-class Destroyer

On Saturday, September 17, 2016, Mississippi's favorite college football team, the Ole Miss *Rebels*, at home, took on their rivals, Alabama's *Crimson Tide*. Fans numbering 66,167 filled Vaught Hemingway Stadium in Oxford. Secretary of the Navy Raymond Edwin "Ray" Mabus attended the game. The *Rebels* were ahead, 17–3, when the secretary stepped onto the field during a ceremony in the first quarter of play. In case any of the students did not know, he was introduced as Mississippi native, 60th Governor of Mississippi from 1988 to 1992, and Ole Miss alumnus.

Secretary Mabus made an official announcement. He had decided to name Navy destroyers for two World War II Marine MOH recipients from Mississippi: Jack Lucas of Hattiesburg, for his actions on Iwo Jima, and Louis Hugh Wilson Jr. of Brandon, 26th Commandant of the Marine Corps, for actions during the Battle of Guam. Jack and Louis had received their Medal from President Truman at the White House on the same day. The stadium erupted as fans rose and cheered and gave a long, standing ovation to show their approval.

The *Rebels* held a 24–3 lead at one point in the second quarter and went into the locker room for halftime with the score at 24–17. The *Crimson Tide* came back in the second half to defeat the *Rebels* 48–43. At least the Ole Miss fans could still hold on to their enthusiasm for the tributes to be paid to their two Mississippi heroes.

The new Navy destroyer, DDG-125, will be named in honor of PFC Jacklyn H. Lucas. The 509-foot-long Arleigh Burke-class destroyer will be built at Huntington Ingalls Industries shipyard in Pascagoula. It is expected to enter Navy service in 2023. [87]

CHAPTER 17

Survival Rooted In Resilience

✳✳✳

"Another day!
And here I am,
Alive and well." [1]

— Corporal Vincent H. D. Cassidy Jr.

THE MARINE'S ISLAND CAMPAIGN DID not end in March on Iwo Jima. One more island awaited their beach landing. Before the war ended in the Pacific Theater of Operations, eleven more Marines distinguished themselves and earned Medals of Honor for their valor. The first five did so by hurling themselves upon grenades.

Okinawa Shima was a heavily fortified outpost island of mainland Japan sitting between the East China and the Philippine seas. The steep, green with vegetation, cliffs of the northern coastline presented a formidable sight from the sea. Mount Yonaha-dake on the island's northeast reached to 1,643 feet above the sea. Mount Yae Take on the northwest Motobu Peninsula rose to almost 1,500 feet. The midsection of the island, south of the Ishikawa Isthmus, was most inviting for an amphibious assault. The land there around Hagushi, mostly cultivated by local farmers and sparse of vegetation but for green conifers, sloped gently from the beaches toward inland hills. The strategic Yontan and Kadena airfields sat about a mile inland.

Once inland, the terrain to the north turned from hills into mountainous rises. The roads were primitive, unsurfaced, and narrow. Steep ravines hampered traffic. Partially concealed trails traversed wooded hills and ridges. Caves pitted the coral walls, crags, and cliffs of the mountains.

Far more formidable than the land itself was the fact that Japanese forces numbering about 115,000 men had been deployed to defend the island. Commanders had selected the most advantageous pieces of terrain from which to fight and committed carefully designated units to defend their positions. They had doubled the amount of artillery common in defense networks, even incorporating naval guns. Mutually supporting ridgelines and steep defiles protected their fortified positions.

The battle for Okinawa, entailing eighty-two days of combat, was the longest, most costly engagement in the Marine Corps' history. When it was over, casualty rosters listed 19,500 Marines. Few of those young men had grown up in terrain anything like the island's northwest.

Today, grandparents and great-grandparents who lived through WWII and the Vietnam War might tell a story or two to curious youngsters. When Richard Earl Bush grew up in Barren County, south central Kentucky, grandparents had lived through the Civil War years. There were many a mighty tale to whisper, some fearful, some inspirational, and some that could stir a seething need for vengeance.

Richard was one of the casualties carried off Motobu Peninsula. He had trained for and been at war for two years and three months. His experience provides an example of how childhood tales and the stories that only men in combat have locked away in memories and how witnessing other men's courage inspires valor in a man already prone to heroism.

Born in the Land of Creeks and Caves

Barren County, primarily rural, hilly country, is a watershed area sharing a state line with Macon County, Tennessee. Plentiful rivers and streams make the rolling farmlands and meadowlands perfect for agriculture; except in cave country where poor soil makes for difficult and hardscrabble farming life. Growing burley tobacco and hay, as well as raising dairy and cattle, are predominant occupations.

The Scottish Highlander heritage of the county's pioneers is evident. Glasgow, west of the Appalachian ridgelines and 130 miles from the Cumberland Gap, sits on one of the early trails through south Kentucky. The town is at Barren's center. Hunters with their muzzle-loading Kentucky flintlock longrifles once traipsed in for supplies. No matter from what direction they approached, they had to cross over or through a stream to get to the Mercantile Store. Beaver Creek, Little Beaver Creek, South Fork Beaver Creek, Huggins Branch, Barren Fork, Boyd's Creek, Rose Creek, and Falling Timber Creek all flow around Glasgow.

Glasgow was established as the county seat in 1799. In the 1800 Second Census of Kentucky, Barren County's population included 4,279 whites and 505 slaves. The post office opened in 1803.

Richard Bush's ancestors were among the county's early arrivals, coming primarily through Virginia after the Revolutionary War. The men, who earned their keep as general farmers and farm laborers, tended to marry young women and have many children. Throughout the 1800s, it was common practice for daughters to be housed with other family members, like grandparents and uncles, or neighbors. They helped with household chores and learned the craft of diligent housekeeping. Reaching suitable ages, the children tended to marry and farm close to their birthplace.

Generations of Bush, Wakefield, and Davis descendants intermarried and resided all their lives around Glasgow: in Tracy, Temple Hill, Roseville, Cave City, and Hiseville. The extended Bush family, in large numbers, also farmed in Hart County, especially around Horse Cave. [2]

Marriage records dating as far back as 1803 at the Barren County Court House tell of males with the Bush surname finding suitable brides. Most of the grooms were Caucasians, but some of the Bush males were Black—both slaves and freemen. The common practice of the times was that slaves were given the last name of their owner.

John Bush was wed to Nancy Bass on January 15, 1803; William T. Bush married Sally Matthews on May 23, 1805; James Bush wed Betsy Barlow on March 2, 1811; and Isaac Bush married Catharine Whitney on December 11, 1815.

Property deeds and county census lists also tell of the early presence of Bush ancestors. In 1814, Ambrose Barlow and his wife, Anna, deeded land on Big Barren River to James Bush and to William Bush. Joel Yancy, Jno Gorin, Benj. Harrison, and Newman witnessed the purchases. [3] George Bush, Isaac Bush, James Bush, and Walton Bush all appeared in the 1820 Barren County Census lists.

In 1840, enumerators scoured Kentucky, collecting the Whole Number of Persons living in the state. Only the Heads of Household were named; everyone else was a number in a column, based on age range, gender, and race. Ninety Bush Heads of Household were located throughout Kentucky, most of them in the central regions. Five Bush males and one female were included in the Barren County Census Schedule of the Whole Number of Persons; five were Free White Persons.

John V. Bush lived with his wife, aged 20–30, one boy, and one daughter between the ages of 5–10 years. In Roseville, Josiah F. Bush, 35 years old, resided with his wife, Jane Ann (Button), aged 25, William T., 8, George P., 6, and one daughter, Carthagena, aged 1 year. [4] Before the next census, two more sons and three daughters were born. Thomas A. Bush was born on September 18, 1845. He died at age 17 years on January 26, 1863—weeks after a hostile cavalry had raided through the Barren countryside.

Peter Bush and his wife, Lucy Caroline (Franklin, Bewley), aged 20–30, had two sons under 5 years old and two daughters between 5–15 years. Another white male over 20 lived with them. Thirteen persons lived in Willy A. Bush's Glasgow household: his wife between 30–40, six boys under 15 years, two boys ages 15–20, one girl under 10, and two males between ages 20–30.

Walter Bush had departed the troubles, strife, and suffering of the world. He left his two boys, Walter, 11, and Hezakiah, 7, and four daughters, Kitty, 13, Elizabeth, 9, and two girls aged 15–20 years, in the care of his 40-year-old widow, Cynthia Ann "Cinthy" (Whitney) Bush.

George Bush was a Free Colored Male over the age of 55 years and the head of a Glasgow household.

Holding Slaves

As far back as 1820, party factions in the North endeavored to prohibit slavery. The anti-slavery issue entered the presidential contests of 1852, 1856, and again in 1860. Barren County Vital Statistics records give evidence to slave ownership among Bush families, and the prohibition of slavery principles raised the wrath in more than one Bush household. [5]

Isaac Bush's sons had inherited his property. James Bush, aged eight years, born in Barren County, was a male slave, belonging to Isaac's heirs. He suffered from blackening of feet occasioned from freezing in the late winter of 1852, and then, from inflammation of the bowels. If the family tried to relieve his discomfort with ardent spirits or Pure Jamaica Ginger, it was of no benefit. James died on March 2, 1852.

Barren County folks sought some leisure before the backbreaking cutting and stacking of the tobacco crop began in September. One summer diversion was the arrival of a circus.

Almost twenty circuses travelled the northern and southern American countrysides. In 1853, P. T. Barnum's Grand Colossal Museum and Menagerie travelled through Kentucky. [6] Farmers working their fields along the rural roads watched horse and elephant teams pulling wagons, one of which was a tank carrying a hippopotamus. Those who could afford the price of admission in town—50¢ ($14.29 in 2016) for adults, 15¢ for children—entertained neighbors with their narratives of the many animal species they had seen. The next summer, neighbors would be sharing extracts and hoping that local practitioners of medicine would possess a reliable and efficacious elixir.

A traveling circus came to Glasgow in July 1854. For months, cholera and bloody flux (dysentery) spread through the town and out into the county. Bodies of the dead were hastily buried in the streets and yards, contaminating the water source. Over half of the population died. Armilda Bush, three months old, daughter of Ransom Amos Bush, died on October 26.

Jack Bush, 65, a slave belonging to Josiah Bush, died in September 1858.

The death toll for Bush slaves was particularly high in 1859. Thomas Bush's one-year-old male slave, William Bush, died of cold on January 10. Mary E. Bush, ten months old, died on February 13. Nancy J. Bush, a single 18-year-old slave, died on July 5.

Martha D. Bush, 47, farmed in Glasgow District 2 with her 11-year-old daughter, Mary. Martha owned slaves. Susan Bush, her one-year-old female slave, died of measles in August. America J. Bush, ten months old, died on October 15.

White slave owners had begun to move further into the Deep South. The Black and Mulatto (mixed white and black ancestry) freemen were relocating themselves to the North.

According to the 1860 U.S. Federal Census, the Barren County population had dropped by almost 18% since the 1850 Census. The county population was comprised of 12,548 Whites, 729 of whom were slave owners, and 47 free Blacks and Mulattoes. The number of Black and Mulatto slaves had declined from 4,549 to 4,070 over the 10-year period. The War of Rebellion would erupt a year after this census.

In 1860, George P. and Nancy Bush farmed in Barren County District 1. Their daughter, Lucy C., was six years old, and their son, James T., was four years old. The youngest boy, George Bush, three years old, was living in District 2, Barren County, with W. C. Sewell, 45, his wife Elizth, 48, their six daughters, ages 8–20, and two sons, one and four years old. Mr. Sewell was a farm laborer.

What prompted the Sewells to provide upkeep for George Bush is unknown. Whether George remained with the family during the Civil War years is not known. The Sewells dropped from Kentucky census population schedules after 1860. What is certain is that the realities, tales, and legends of the approaching rebellion would be forever imbedded in young George's memory.

Slaves helped widow Matilda D. Bush, 46, to farm and raise Rebecca J. (1833), Willis (1835), William W. (1837), Martha A. (1839), Nancy I. (1841), and Alice (1848). Matilda had real concerns about holding slaves. George Ann Bush, her 12-year-old female slave, died of consumption in September 1861—at the same time the Kentucky Home Guard clashed with invading forces over near the Cumberland Gap.

"Tramp, tramp, tramp, the boys are marching." [7]

The Bush generations down the line would not have to read history books to learn how Barren County figured in to the *War of the Rebellion*; the stories were told and retold as if they were first-hand accounts. Stories that could rouse little boys to want to be soldiers when they were big, unless of course it was mothers or grandmothers recounting the particulars.

In mid-November 1859, the news of John Brown and the Harper's Ferry Insurrection was in circulation around Barren County. The debates about slavery triggered heated discussions across farmland fences. Finally, Abraham Lincoln's 1860 election pushed South Carolina to be the first to secede from the Union on December 20, 1860.

The Confederate cannons began bombarding U.S. Fort Sumter near Charleston, South Carolina, on April 12, 1861, and continued firing for forty hours. Two days later, the Union forces surrendered the fort. War had begun. People in the South considered it "The Second American Revolution." President Lincoln called for army volunteers, and the federal government requested men.

The divide in loyalties was evident in Kentucky, Tennessee, Missouri, Arkansas, and Louisiana where brothers and cousins joined the ranks of both the Union and Confederate armies. The farmers in Kentucky tried to remain "neutral."

Kentucky was a border state. Not quite equally split on the secession crisis, a greater number of Kentuckians were Union sympathizers. At least 171 Union veterans are buried in Barren County cemeteries; while 104 Confederate veterans found their final resting places in Barren.

George P. Bush, Hezekiah Bush, Josiah Bush Jr, Walter Bush, and William T. Bush, all enlisted in Kentucky Federal Militias. Albert Bush, 19, left the county and went up to Louisville, to enlist in Company A, 115th Infantry Regiment, U.S. Colored Troops, on October 27, 1864. [8] Willis P. Bush (1832) joined the Confederate 6th Kentucky Infantry. [9]

The entire 9th Kentucky Volunteer Cavalry mustered in at Eminence, northeast of Louisville, on August 22, 1862. From Horse Cave in Hart County, brothers Andrew Jackson Bush and Henry B. Bush volunteered in Company B and Company E, 9th Kentucky Cavalry, Union Army, for a one year period. William A. Bush joined Company B, 9th Kentucky Cavalry. Private George Bush enrolled in Company H on August 7, and Edmund Bush enrolled on August 9.

The Confederate States of America did not recognize the state's stance of neutrality and set out on an offensive drive into Eastern Kentucky in the fall.

Before he was old enough to go to school, young George Bush would ask the meaning of words like attack, skirmish, engagement, and siege. Whenever he heard someone speak of such things, he would notice the sense of apprehension and dread that came with the words. During the four years of the war, apart from the major battles in Kentucky, local newspapers would give print to at least 257 skirmishes, seven engagements, eighteen actions, twenty affairs, five attacks on towns and places, and one siege in the state. [10]

On August 22, 1861, the U.S. gunboat *Lexington* captured the Confederate steamboat, *CSS W.B. Terry* on the Ohio River, at Paducah. In reprisal, Rebel forces with the "complicity of a mob of Paducah citizens" captured the mail steamer *Samuel Orr*, running between Evansville and Paducah.

On September 19, 1861, an early skirmish at Barbourville, 138 miles east of Glasgow on the Cumberland Turnpike, resulted in a Confederate victory over the Kentucky Home Guard. Two larger battles, Union victories, broke out at Camp Wildcat near London, October 21, and at Ivy Mountain near Pikeville, on November 8. Sixty Americans died in these first three engagements.

Brownsville, Edmonson County seat on the Green River, west of Mammoth Cave, was a stop on the Louisville and Nashville Railroad. The L&N RR line was a main USA supply route between Louisville and Bowling Green. The Union garrisoned troops at important junctions, and the Confederates attacked the line wherever their commanders could find the advantage. Thirty miles northwest of Glasgow, the Brownsville Ferry and bridge were under the guard of the newly organizing Union 3d Kentucky Volunteer Cavalry.

On November 20, 1861, the Confederate 1st Arkansas Battalion raided the town to get needed medical supplies. They rode into the public square and began firing on the Federal camp in the woods across the river. The Rebel volleys sent the Yankees scattering and fleeing back into the woods. P. H. Solman was the town's merchant, identified as a Unionist who had helped the Union troops. The Rebels took the spirits they had come for from his shelves. News of the skirmish told of the Federal defeat. Eight Union troops died, four more survived their wounds, and two were captured. Only one Confederate was wounded.

Among the first groups of Kentucky men to answer the call to arms was the Union 11th Regiment Kentucky Volunteer Infantry—organized at Camp Calhoun and mustered in on December 9, 1861, for three years of service. The Houchin brothers, G. Alexander, 33, and Woodford Mitchell "Woody", 25, of Brownsville, and three cousins volunteered on September 18, and were assigned to Company E. Woodford, known to be a wild adventurer, was commissioned as a captain. His youngest sister, Nancy Paradine Houchin, 17, had married Jesse C. Kinser, 22, on July 9, 1861. Jesse enlisted as a private in Company E on September 22, at Brownsville. Private Moses Houchin, 28, would enlist in Company E on September 1, 1862. [11]

Captain Houchin lost five of his men to illness at Camp Calhoun: two from typhoid, two from pneumonia, and one of an unspecified disease. Of the ninety-seven Brownsville men who had volunteered, few would return with him after their first battle in April.

John Hunt Morgan and John Breckinridge Castleman, both from Lexington, James W. Bowles of Louisville, Marcellus Jerome Clarke from Franklin, and John "Jack" Allen of Shelby County, each exemplified the rift in Bluegrass State loyalties. To property owners loyal to the Union, they were dangerous and ruthless—notorious enemies, "cruel and bloodthirsty wretches" who evoked fear and outrage. To people sympathetic to the Confederate cause, they were heroic and legendary—mythical figures deserving of tributes, safe passage through the land, and sanctuary if under any duress.

Captain Morgan and his sixty men of the "Lexington Rifles" militia were inducted into Confederate service on October 27. The company rode down to Bowling Green to join forces with the Confederate Army of Kentucky under command of Brigadier General Simon Bolivar Buckner. On November 5, the general consolidated three under-strength companies into Morgan's Cavalry Squadron.

Under orders to patrol throughout the Green River area, Captain Morgan took Company A to Glasgow Junction, at the fork of three roads between Rocky Hill and Cave City. Setting up his squadron headquarters at Bell's Tavern, a stagecoach stop, he began his mounted patrols, raiding against the L&N RR—cutting telegraph lines, destroying stockades and rolling stock, burning railway trestles, and halting food and ammunition deliveries to the Yankees. [12] One of the squadron's first raids that month was the destruction of the railroad bridge over Bacon Creek, seven miles north of Munfordville.

On December 5, Captain Morgan descended on Bacon Creek again with 105 men and burned the railroad bridge a second time. Northern newspaper correspondents picked up on the story, and the daring cavaliers became known as the notorious "Morgan's Raiders."

George Bush was four years old when marching armies in blue and gray uniforms tramped down nearby roads a week before Christmas. Rowlett's Station was a whistle stop on the Green River in Hart County, nine miles north of Cave City. The Union and Rebel forces clashed there at a L&N RR bridge on December 17, 1861, and battled to a draw. More than forty-one soldiers lost their lives. On December 28, the Confederate Offensive reached into western Kentucky at the Battle of Sacramento. Twelve soldiers died in the CSA victory.

On December 31, 1861, Confederate Major General Thomas Carmichael Hindman Jr. had his 9,000 troops of the Arkansas Legion encamped at Cave City. The general was low on coal oil for lamps. He sent Captain Morgan and a squadron of cavalrymen to Brownsville to forage for supplies. Union Captain Baker and his thirty Home Guards had cut down trees on the north side of the Green River and piled up logs in a breastwork. When Captain Morgan reached the Brownsville Ferry, several volleys of Union fire turned his party around. One Rebel was killed in the skirmish. [13]

The Confederate Eastern Kentucky Offensive continued into the New Year, and the battles intensified. Union forces carried the day on January 10, 1862, at Middle Creek west of Prestonburg. The forces suffered ninety-two casualties. The war moved within seventy miles of Glasgow on January 19, when the Union Army was victorious at Mill Springs. The two armies lost 164 killed.

Promoted, Colonel Morgan led his men to southwestern Tennessee to fight in the April 6–7, 1862, Battle of Shiloh. The 11th Kentucky Infantry was at the battle. Although the victory went to the Union, the battle held its torments for the Company E men from Brownsville. Three enlisted men died of wounds after the battle. Six died of typhoid, two of pneumonia, and one of tuberculosis. Disease, wounds, disabilities, desertions, missing or absent without leave, capture, and transfers to other depleted companies decimated the company more than the firefights.

Private Jesse Kinser was slightly wounded at Shiloh on April 7, 1862. He recuperated at Paducah General Hospital and was back in Brownsville on furlough in May and June. As if his strength could not prevail, he took sick at Bowling Green in July–August and was sick at home in September–October.

Privates William Houchin, 44, and James W. Houchin, 23, deserted together from Company E at Shiloh on April 23.

Second Lieutenant Francis Thomas "Frank" Houchin, 25, was sick at Hamburg, Tennessee, in May and June. He returned to Edmonson County in July–August, sick at home. Unable to return to full health, he resigned his commission on December 6, due to ill health. He was discharged at a captain's rank on December 15, at Nashville.

Captain Woodford Houchin had no more than twenty men left in Company E. He and the remnant went home on furlough in May–June. In a letter Captain Houchin dated "28 Jun 62", he requested leave to take his sick brother home.

Private Alexander Houchin was home on furlough in May and June, and again in January–February 1863.

An "affair" meant many things in the war. One occurred at the Cave City L&N RR station on May 11, 1862. Colonel Morgan led 143 cavaliers to the station at noon. He was expecting to capture a train from Nashville carrying 280 Rebel prisoners northward. Instead, he captured two locomotives carrying passengers from Louisville bound for Nashville. He took prisoners of Union Majors Helveti and Coffee, Woodford's 1st Kentucky Cavalry, another unnamed officer, and four privates. The Rebels burned forty-eight freight cars, four passenger cars, and one locomotive.

Colonel Morgan released all the passengers to return to Louisville on two cars behind the second locomotive. H. W. Stager, the Cave City telegraph operator, gave notice of these facts to Bowling Green. The upward train with the Rebel prisoners was stopped and turned back to Nashville. [14]

In the summer, Colonel Morgan began to make swift, daring raids through Kentucky, concentrating on the L&N RR lines in the regions familiar to his men. He set out on July 4, 1862, with 370 soldiers of the 2d Kentucky Calvary. Captain John Allen commanded Company B; Captain James W. Bowles commanded Company C; Captain John B. Castleman commanded Company D. They routed 9th Pennsylvania Cavalrymen garrisoned in Tompkinsville, capturing thirty retreating enemy, destroying tents and stores, and taking twenty wagons, forty horses, fifty mules, and sugar and coffee supplies. The Raiders rode though Glasgow setting fires to Union supplies.

Morgan's Raiders destroyed railroad and telegraph lines, burned down depots, seized Union supplies, and took prisoners in sixteen other towns. They rode through the Lexington area on July 17, and made for the covered bridge into Cynthiana, defended by 345 soldiers of the 7th Kentucky Cavalry, USA Kentucky Home Guards, and 18th Kentucky Volunteers.

Colonel Morgan reached the town at 5:00 PM. Before withdrawing victorious early that night, the Raiders had destroyed the Union commissary, medical stores, tents, guns, and ammunition stocks and captured about 300 Federals, 300 cavalry horses, and a large supply of pistols. The "paroled" Federal prisoners were escorted to Falmouth, taken by train to Cincinnati, and ordered to Camp Chase, in Columbus, Ohio, to await an exchange with the Rebels imprisoned there. Estimates of casualties on both sides included forty-seven Americans killed and sixty-seven wounded. [15]

National newspaper headlines bellowed about the mayhem Colonel Morgan's cavalry wrought—his squadron dashing down mountainsides like a thunderbolt, leaping fences and ditches, galloping furiously headlong with war whoops that filled opposing soldiers with fright and terrorized their sleep. The attention earned him the admired and fearsome name "Thunderbolt of the Confederacy" in the South. The good people of Glasgow had mixed opinions of his raids.

A band of eighty Confederate guerillas from Meade County, on the Ohio River southeast of Louisville, got on the road to join Morgan's Raiders. They headed south from Leitchfield on Sunday, August 17. Word reached Union Captain W. B. Wortham. A company of thirty Rock Creek Home Guards chased the Rebels for forty miles and caught them near Mammoth Cave. One Confederate captain was killed in the skirmish and his entire band was captured. The home guards confiscated all the Rebel horses. [16]

The Confederates prevailed at Richmond during its Heartland Kentucky Offensive on August 29–30. The two forces lost 284 men killed. Then, the Confederates captured Frankfort, Kentucky's capital city, on September 3, and held it for a month.

In late August 1862, Confederate General Braxton Bragg, in command of the Army of Mississippi, crossed the Cumberland River near Gainesboro, Tennessee, with orders to recapture Kentucky. Lexington was his intended destination. His column of 16,000 Rebels crossed the border and marched up the pike through Tompkinsville and Temple Hill toward Glasgow, foraging for plentiful corn, milled grain, hogs, and livestock as the army moved. As the locals would say, anyone with "three ideas above an oyster" could see that the prospects for Unionists were dim.

The 500 Glasgow residents stirred as General Bragg halted for supplies and took over a large brick home on Front and Broadway for his headquarters. His exhausted troops went into camp on the north edge of town, stretching up the hill to the cemetery. Residents experienced some minor looting and break-ins as the Rebels scavenged for brandy, sugar, butter, bacon, and coffee.

General Bragg remained at Glasgow, planning his way to Lexington. His departure was delayed. On Sunday, September 14, a Rebel force moved on Munfordville, a Union garrison town on the Green River, northeast of Rowlett, twenty-three miles north of Glasgow. The stockade fort at Bacon Creek surrendered to the Confederates and was burned.

The 1,800-foot-long L&N RR bridge that rose 125 feet above the Green River south of Munfordville was left intact. The fight began at 3:00 o'clock on the first day and was over by 11:00 AM. The Louisville newspapers reported that the Rebels had been whipped, having sustained heavy losses in their frontal assaults on Union bulwarks. General Bragg sent a column of reinforcements the next day. Rebels pushed captured boxcars onto the Bacon Creek RR bridge, setting fire to both, destroying the bridge for the third time, and stopping the arrival of Union reinforcements.

On Wednesday, the Munfordville defenders came out from behind their extensive fortifications and surrendered. The Rebels added more than 700 soldiers to their casualty rosters. Federal rosters included 4,150 casualties and captured.

General Bragg's forces patrolled mostly in the neighborhood of Glasgow. Union General Buell's army was moving up the lower turnpike from Dripping Spring toward Bowling Green. A conflict was expected in Barren County at any moment. Skirmishes broke out almost daily until the end of September.

On September 17, the Federal cavalry captured 460 Rebels at Glasgow. Skirmishes occurred over the next three days at Glasgow, Cave City, Horse Cave, and Bear Wallow. Three Union cavalry regiments drove the Rebels from Munfordville on September 20–21. The Confederates retreated to Glasgow, where several skirmishes took place on September 30.

General Bragg evacuated Glasgow, and his army passed up the turnpike through Cave City with a train of over 400 supply wagons hauling tents, blankets, clothing, knapsacks, cooking utensils, spare armaments, and ammunition. The Confederates left behind many mementoes of their occupation of the town. One was a story of a dastardly affair to be reported in the North, reminding Kentucky readers that travelling from home could be dangerous. The *Louisville Journal* and *Louisville Daily Democrat*, October 22, printed the story of an "atrocious piece of cruelty." The Cleveland, Ohio, *Daily Leader*, published it on its October 25 Page 1. *The New York Times* followed on October 29.

While General Bragg's army was at Glasgow, Mr. T. T. T. Tabb, of Gallatin, Tennessee, set out from Nashville for Louisville with his wife and "two interesting little girls." The Union army had taken Gallatin in February. The purpose of the family's journey was not reported, but to Mr. Tabb's misfortune, a company of Bragg's assassins caught them near the Kentucky line and brought them to Glasgow. The Rebels reassured Mrs. Tabb that her husband would not be harmed and persuaded her to return to their Tennessee home.

"So soon as the poor distressed mother and daughters started for home, Mr. Tabb was ordered to be shot, and was accordingly led out like a beast, tied to a tree and shot." [17]

From Munfordville, General Bragg pushed his army north, camping at Bacon Creek for three days. Union forces advanced on his rear guard at 12:00 noon on September 22. The engagement ended at dusk.

On September 27, the Union Kentucky Home Guard defeated the Confederates at Augusta on the Ohio River across from Ripley. Thirty-one soldiers died.

Colonel Sanders D. Bruce of the 20th Regiment Kentucky Volunteer Infantry routed a party of Rebels near Glasgow on October 1—ten Confederates of Company A, 2d Georgia Cavalry, were taken prisoners, including Lieutenant Colonel Charles Constantine Crews, Captain Brown, and Lieutenant Thomas.

"Two gentlemen of truth" who had come up from Lexington informed the *Louisville Journal* of more shocking deeds. [18]

James Townsend was a man of 18 years when he went off to soldier in the War of 1812. He saw battle in New Orleans and afterward was granted 10,000 acres at Sand Lick and Upper Mill Creek, near Three Forks Road and Red's Hollow in Estill County, southeast of Lexington. James was pleased living in the wilderness north of the Kentucky River near the Biley Fork stream. There was a huge cave on his property that served as a barn. Neighbors called it Townsend's Cave. Patsey, Cob Hill, and Furnace were the inhabited places closest to his tract of land. [19]

James and Susan (Sookey or Saucie) Robinson, a half-blooded Cherokee or Choctaw Indian, married on January 24, 1815, and started their family, having six children who survived to adulthood. Eda, their first daughter (1833) married William Lemon Bush Jr.

James was a patriot, and the Townsend family favored the Union cause. He took a captain's commission in the Red River Home Guards at the outbreak of the Rebellion and was "very efficient as a commander of Home Guards in protecting the persons and property of his Union neighbors."

His eldest boy, Reuben, mustered into the Union Company K, 8th Kentucky Infantry Regiment, as a private on January 15, 1862, the eve of his 46th birthday. The regiment was "composed of men with unflinching bravery and patriotism." Across ten months, he was in numerous marches and battles, the last one being reconnaissance on Madison Road on October 19, then the march to Nashville. He died in Nashville's Hospital #7 on November 18, apparently one of the regiment's 144 enlisted men who died of disease. He was buried in Nashville's Union cemetery.

James' two youngest sons, William and Robert, also served in the Union Army. Robert, 20, had been killed in a gunfight with H. J. Anderson in September 1861, in Stanton. James knew about Robert being gunned down in the street, but would never learn of Reuben's death.

On October 6, 1862, a party of Colonel Morgan's miscreants surrounded Captain Townsend's cabin, apparently scavenging for money and gold. When the Rebels made their appearance, James was absent from the residence, so they waited. One of the Townsend daughters-in-law ran from the cabin with her children and hid in the woods and bushes. They witnessed what happened.

Upon James' return, the murderous scoundrels began shooting. James, 69, and Susan, 65, returned fire. As she was loading her husband's rifle, a Rebel ball hit Susan. The Rebels "fired Captain Townsend's house, killing his wife, a most estimable lady," and subsequently captured him. They beat him, burned his feet, and hanged him, ruthlessly murdering him. Family buried James and Susan beside each other in a single grave above Townsend's Cave. [20]

On October 7 six miles north of Glasgow, a party of Rebels searching for water sources in the vicinity was caught. A few were killed and several captured. The Federals lost no troops and returned to camp with fifty Confederate horses and some cattle.

The CSA continued to press toward Lexington and Louisville. On October 8, the armies met unexpectedly. The largest battle on Kentucky soil was fought in the Chaplin Hills at Perryville. The forces suffered 1,355 casualties in the Union victory. By October 16, newspapers reported that General Bragg was in rapid retreat. His entire army was marching in two columns toward the Cumberland Mountains.

Rocky Hill was a coal dropoff for the L&N RR near Gardner's Sinking Creek, eleven miles west of Cave City, and thirteen miles southeast of Brownsville. A railroad station, a livery stable, Cowles and Mitchell's general store, and a hotel alerted travelers on the road that they had reached the small town. During the war, Rocky Hill Station was also a dropoff for soldiers coming home on both sides of the conflict. A "trifling" skirmish there had its few citizens hiding on October 17. Brigadier General Joseph Wheeler reported that his Confederate 1st and 3d Alabama Cavalry had defeated Federal troops in skirmishes at Rocky Hill and Valley Woods. Losses on both sides totaled 167.

The skirmish at Burkesville on November 8 did not get much national public attention.

The Raiders continued to harass the Union supply routes around Glasgow in October and December. Colonel Morgan was promoted to brigadier general on December 11, 1862. On December 22, he crossed into Kentucky again and captured a Union supply wagon making for Glasgow. His force camped six miles south of Glasgow.

At twilight on Christmas Eve, Captain Thomas Quirk, in command of Morgan's Scouts, took some Raiders into a Glasgow tavern to celebrate the Good Saviour's birth. Men from the Union 2nd Michigan Cavalry, having marched from Gallatin, Tennessee, had the same idea. A desperate skirmish ruined the holiday for two Union soldiers and three Confederates who were killed. Two of Morgan's men were taken prisoner. The Raiders captured sixteen Federals and dozens of Christmas turkeys.

The Union cavalry retreated to Cave City, and General Morgan held Glasgow. From there on Christmas Day, he started out on a 32-mile ride north through Cave City into Hart County, bound for Bacon Creek Station, the two wooden trestles at Muldraugh's Hill at Elizabethtown, and the L&N bridge span over the Rolling Fork at New Haven.

En route through Glasgow, brief skirmishes took place on the Bear Wallow turnpike, on Burkesville Road, and at Green's Chapel. General Morgan's advance guard encountered a 2d Michigan Calvary company at their massive stockade, within 100 yards of the Bacon Creek Bridge. The next day, December 26, a five-hour engagement ended when the Rebels burned the stockade and the railroad bridge. Two days later, after three hours of bombarding two Union stockades, Morgan's Raiders burned the two Muldraugh's Hill trestles. On December 30, despite ninety minutes of strong Yankee opposition and successful defense of Fort Allen, the Raiders destroyed the bridge at New Haven and damaged several miles of railroad track.

Winter weather, hazardous to troops on the march, hit Kentucky. Freezing rain, ice, and sleet hampered any fire setting. General Morgan reported his Christmas Raid to have been successful. He had only two cavalrymen killed and twenty-four wounded. He had taken 1,887 Union soldiers prisoners and destroyed at least two million dollars' worth of Union property. On New Year's Day, 1863, the Raiders returned to Tennessee well armed and better mounted than when they had entered Kentucky. General Morgan began planning.

For most of the next six months, life was relatively quiet in Glasgow and Barren County.

Union Glasgow Garrison

General Bragg's occupation of Glasgow had been a distasteful affair for the county. The Union constructed Fort Williams in March 1863, on the hillcrest above the town cemetery. Across from the higher Standpipe Hill and overlooking the railroad line, the small fort was named for Union General Thomas Williams, who had been killed during a battle in Baton Rouge on August 5, 1862. Glasgow was then a fortified garrison town providing pickets, armed patrols, and scouting parties for Barren County.

Early on the morning of June 7, 1863, a seventy-man Union 5th Indiana Cavalry scouting party was near Edmonton, nineteen miles east of Glasgow. They had a brief encounter with a detachment of Colonel Richard M. Gano's Texas Cavalry Battalion, took nine Confederate soldiers as prisoners, and turned back toward Glasgow.

Captain William J. Davis, commanding 1st Brigade, Morgan's Cavalry, moving at Button's Cross Road, learned of the attack and rushed his 200 men to Edmonton. The Federals recognized that a large Rebel force was about to intercept them four miles from Edmonton. Mrs. F. E. Wood watched as the 5th Indiana took cover in barns and outbuildings on her farm. Keeping under cover in the woods and creek bed, Captain Davis's party stealthily surrounded the farm. The skirmish ended in eight minutes. Fifty-three men of the 5th Indiana were able to retreat. Captain Davis, six miles from Glasgow, halted the pursuit to overtake them.

The 5th Indiana Cavalry lost two men, had four wounded and fifteen captured. Captain Davis suffered no losses and freed the nine CSA prisoners. The Confederates also captured forty Union horses, thirty guns and accouterments, and twenty pistols. [21]

Brigadier General Morgan gathered 2,460 of his best cavalrymen and rode out of Sparta in central Tennessee on June 11, 1863. Feinting west, he turned north on June 23, heading for Kentucky's Lebanon-Campbellsville-Columbia Turnpike. The Raiders crossed the swollen Cumberland River in the dark of night on July 2 and advanced through Burksville, thirty-eight miles southeast of Glasgow. Making Columbia, they proceeded to Cane Valley, camping south of Campbellsville. Reaching Louisville was General Morgan's ambitious intention.

On July 4, 100 of General Morgan's men cut telegraph wires and burned down the Rocky Hill Depot as the people "stood idle" witnessing the raid. The Confederates attempted to cross the Green River at Tebbs' Bend. The Union force stopped them. Forty-one died. The Raiders withdrew southward, making their crossing at Johnson Ford, then rode to Campbellsville. On July 5, the Raiders tangled again with the U.S. Army at Lebanon and moved on as victors. Forty-one casualties were left behind.

The citizens of Barren County and Glasgow, prepared to deal again with General Morgan's raids and pillaging, felt relief when the Confederates rode north. The infamous general was on his way to Ohio.

Morgan's Raiders advanced beyond Bardstown, crossed the northern turnpike to Louisville, and navigated the Ohio River near Brandenburg into southern Indiana. They rampaged their way through Corydon and entered Ohio above Cincinnati. The 9th Kentucky Volunteer Cavalry was in pursuit for three weeks as the Confederate raid stayed on the north side of the river, pillaging one town after another. Newspaper accounts and military reports added up the toll. The Raiders disrupted the railroads at more than sixty places, destroyed thirty-four crucial bridges, burned to the ground military and public buildings and supplies, inflicted 600 casualties on Union forces, and captured and paroled about 6,000 prisoners.

On July 12, the Union caught the Raiders at Buffington Island and overwhelmed them, capturing 750 Rebels. About 300 Raiders reached safety in West Virginia. General Morgan escaped north with 400 of his cavaliers. Finally on July 26, 1863, General Edward Henry Hobson's Union cavalry and the 9th Kentucky Regiment captured General Morgan and the remnant of his cavalry at Salineville, Ohio. The Rebels had suffered twenty-eight officers killed, thirty-five wounded, 250 enlisted men killed or wounded, and 2,000 captured.

General Morgan and several of his officers were imprisoned at the Ohio State Penitentiary in Columbus. Kentucky would have more encounters with him in less than a year.

Captain Woodford Houchin was at Glasgow from July to September 1863, with the 11th Kentucky Infantry.

The 9th Kentucky Cavalry returned to Eminence and mustered out of service on September 11, 1863. Private Henry B. Bush, 25, died in 1863. He was buried in a grove of trees on the Green River at Bush Cemetery at the end of Poteet Road on the Old Ransom Amos Bush Farm, about eight miles northwest of Horse Cave.

Confederate forces surrendered the Cumberland Gap to the Yankees on September 7–9, 1863.

Having its own fort, Glasgow began recruiting and organizing its own Union regiment on September 17, 1863. The inexperienced boys enlisted from Barren, Monroe, and Cumberland counties. Colonel Charles S. Hanson commanded the 37th Kentucky Regiment Mounted Infantry. Major Samuel Martin, Headquarters, and Lieutenant Isaac Chenoweth, Company A commander, were the veterans. The regiment's mission was to operate against guerrillas and protect public property. It was not fully organized and mustered in with 1,219 men on its roster until December 22.

By early October, George Bush was six years old. Going to town and seeing 420 soldiers in the tent camp outside the fort must have been a thrill. With a fort and a regiment, citizens likely felt more secure going to church, the train depot, liveries, the bank, the merchants, and the Union hospital that had been converted from the Urania College building. Their assurance was soon shaken.

Before dawn on October 6, 1863, Confederate Colonel John M. Hughes led 120 Rebels of the 25th Tennessee Infantry into Glasgow, headed in the direction of Fort Williams. Fifty Union men of Captain J. O. Nelson's company, acting as Provost Guard, were camped in the Court House square. Thirty soldiers were out on patrol. The Rebel horses charged into town at dawn. Gunfire broke out in the square, waking the 37th Kentucky from sleep. Then, Colonel Hughes sacked the camp, routing the defenders in the early morning light, and attacked the fort.

Major Sam Martin was not at the fort during the attack. He later reported to Colonel Hanson that one of the three casualties died of wounds. Of his officers and men, 142 had been captured, taken to the Tennessee border, and paroled. The enemy commandeered wagons and buggies from the citizens to carry their eleven wounded Rebels from Glasgow. Four died. The Confederates had also carried off 100 carbines, 200 horses and equipment, two wagons of clothes and goods, $9,000 taken from the bank, and goods worth $400 robbed from one store. [22]

Colonel Hughes' report to his Confederate commander varied in its details. "We killed 9, wounded 26 and captured 226, together with quartermaster's stores in the amount of $250,000.00. My loss was 1 killed and 4 wounded."

On November 26, General Morgan and six of his officers escaped from the Ohio prison. Captains John B. Castleman and T. Henry Hines are known to have been with him. Captains Jacob J. Cassell (Company A) and James W. Bowles are also believed to have made their escape. Major Thomas Binton Webber (Company F) had spent a portion of October in solitary confinement and remained at the penitentiary as of December 1, 1863. Major John Allen, Captain John B. Hutchinson (Company E), and Captain Robert McFarland, (Company G) are not known to have been at the prison. General Morgan made his way back to Tennessee. He was given command of another cavalry regiment and set up a base in southwestern Virginia.

In spring 1864, Confederate Major General Nathan Bedford Forrest launched his expedition into West Tennessee and Kentucky, fighting toward the Ohio River. On March 25, he raided Paducah. The Rebels were victorious. The two sides suffered 140 casualties.

The 37th Kentucky Regiment Mounted Infantry departed from Glasgow in March 1864, and moved east to Columbia. The boys joined in operations against General Morgan from May 31 to June 20, engaging the Confederates at Mount Sterling on June 9, and at Cynthiana on June 12. The 37th Kentucky would muster out of service on December 29, 1864. Eight enlisted men killed or mortally wounded and ninety-eight dead of disease were lost from the company rosters during the regiment's service.

In Eastern Kentucky, the Confederates pushed north along the turnpike toward Lexington and met the Union skirmishers at Paintsville and Salyersville on April 13–14, 1864. More than twenty-four soldiers died. The battle went to the Union.

Desperate and Marauding Bushwhackers

Captain Marcellus Jerome Clarke, 20, joined Brigadier General Morgan's command that summer for another raid into Kentucky. He had enlisted as a Confederate soldier in 1861, and served in the 4th Kentucky Infantry. He had received his officer's commission from Lieutenant Colonel John "Jack" Allen, Shelby County, of the 3d Kentucky Cavalry Regiment and formerly in command of Morgan's Company B.

General Morgan led the 600 cavalrymen of 2nd Brigade up Pine Mountain and slipped back into Kentucky through Pound Gap at Jenkins. They rode 133 miles to attack the Union supply depot at Mount Sterling. They captured the town on June 8, 1864, taking 380 prisoners, burning buildings and material, looting stores, robbing citizens, and pilfering $59,000 from Farmers' Bank. In the evening, General Morgan split his command and returned to Lexington for the final time.

Early in the morning of June 9, Union forces recaptured the town and beat back the outnumbered Confederates General Morgan had left behind. Although the Union considered the battle at Mount Sterling to be a Rebel defeat, losses were sustained on both sides. The Union reported eleven killed and 150 wounded.

General Morgan rode into Lexington on June 10. The brigade captured horses and badly needed provisions and organized a large raid. At dawn on June 11, his command of 1,200 men surrounded Cynthiana and launched an attack at Keller's covered bridge over the Licking River. The Union pickets fell, and the Rebels set fire to the town, destroying many buildings. Two more separate engagements spilled into the next morning. The Union forces counterattacked at dawn on June 12, causing the Confederates to flee deeper into Cynthiana. Many were killed or captured. The two forces suffered 2,092 casualties, and the Union held the town. General Morgan and his remaining cavalrymen retreated from Kentucky on June 12.

Captain Woodford Houchin had been promoted to major on January 27, 1864. While on leave, he married Mary R. Fox, 19, on April 14, 1864. Private Kinser, his brother-in-law, was sick at Marietta, Georgia, in July–August. Major Houchin made sure the private got home. He would be discharged from the 11th Kentucky Regiment on December 16, at Bowling Green.

While newspapers printed stories of desperate bushwhackers and spies infesting the Paducah area and a little boy who drowned himself in New Haven to escape the cruel whippings of his father, the brisk, little skirmish near New Haven, on August 2, did not get much attention. [23] General Morgan was going to get a lot of attention a month later.

A Union attack surprised the "Thunderbolt of the Confederacy" during his raid on Greeneville in northeast Tennessee on September 4, 1864. He was shot in the back while trying to escape.

George Bush was by then old enough to labor in the county fields and better understand conversations about outlaws.

General Morgan's death launched Captain Clarke's six-month life leading his own guerrilla band. Captain Clarke, the grandson of ex-Governor Clarke, returned to Kentucky on October 4, making hit-and-run raids throughout the state, killing Union soldiers, and destroying supplies. The gang concentrated their operations between Lexington and Louisville and along the Bardstown Turnpike.

George Prentice, editor of the *Louisville Daily Journal*, introduced readers to Sue Mundy's "band of cutthroats" in the October 11, 1864, issue. Sue Mundy had murdered Hugh Wilson in cold blood, shooting him five times and stabbing him twice with a dagger. Mr. Prentice did not yet know that the notorious woman leading the gang of desperadoes, committing the most inhuman, "diabolical outrages," and perpetrating "some of the most cruel atrocities we ever heard of" was Captain Clarke. [24]

The guerrilla party came within one mile of Louisville, went back up the Bardstown Turnpike, and robbed every one they met. They captured a soldier with the Totten Hospital Mail, took him captive, murdered him, and left his body on the spot in the vicinity of Jeffersontown. In retaliation, four Rebel prisoners of war were executed in the same spot on October 31. [25]

Raiders quickly struck on the lower Kentucky border, southwest of Bowling Green. "On the night of Oct. 31 another raid was made on the little village of Allensville, on the Memar's branch, between Russellville and Starkville. The guerrilla band numbered 50 men, and the several stores of the place were robbed of goods valued at $12,000."

Captain Clarke was evading Union patrols between Lexington and Frankfort. On Tuesday night, November 1, his gang surrounded Mr. Adam Harper Jr.'s house two miles south of Midway to get horses, made the 64-year-old Union man a prisoner, "and without the slightest provocation murdered their victim in the most cowardly and brutal manner." [26]

Barren County was not spared the outrages. Corporal William Charles Fox, 21, had been born in the county. After enlisting in the Confederate Army, he had deserted and joined the Union Army. On Wednesday afternoon, November 2, he was aboard a train on the Nashville Railroad to pay a brief visit to his parents, Charles and Emma. At the time, his mother was stricken with grief that her baby boy, Joey D., had died on April 21, after living for forty-seven days. Joey was the first interment in the Fox Family Graveyard. When the train pulled into Rocky Hill Station, Corporal Fox was five miles from the family farm, in Pig, Edmonton County.

Twenty-five guerrillas dashed into the station. "There were two sleeping cars on the track. In one of them was an old negro man with both legs broken. They ordered him to get out. He could not move quick enough for them, and they shot him. They then set fire to the cars and burned them, with the old negro. They met William Fox, private in the 6th Kentucky regiment, and after robbing him, shot him."

Major Houchin was at the Rocky Hill depot as the guerrilla band attacked. He hid in a barrel under some quilts to escape the tragedy that befell his wife's older brother. Word quickly reached Brownsville that the major had seen Sue Mundy and his brother-in-law had been murdered at Rocky Hill.

Emma Fox was inconsolable hearing the news that Sue Mundy and Henry Magruder had killed her eldest child. William was buried beside the baby brother he had never known.

Major Houchin was discharged from service on December 17, at Bowling Green. His tales of war would be well known after the war when he returned to farming in Edmonson County District 8. A fervent Republican, he was elected Edmonson County judge in 1866. At the time of the 1880 U.S. Census, he and his wife had in their household Mary's brother, John Sibley Fox, 25, who worked on the farm, Nerila Fox, 4, a niece, and Mary Houchin, 8, a niece. Another of Mary's younger brothers, Elisha, farmed next door, with his 15-year-old bride, Rebecia, and their one-year-old daughter, Leora. [27]

On December 24, 1864, Confederate Brigadier General Hylan B. Lyon with 800 men raided the Bacon Creek Station for the fifth and final time and withdrew with the L&N RR bridge burning. The person who passed for Sue Mundy was spotted at Bardstown on Thursday, December 29.

Mr. Prentice wrote frequent press columns about the woman guerrilla with the wholly-corrupted heart and fiendish nature. Late in December, the *Louisville Daily Journal* editor disclosed some speculations, and Northern editors informed readers that, on good authority, Mundy were in reality Jerome Clarke. [28] The truth would soon be told. William Clarke Quantrill, a former schoolteacher and infamous Confederate partisan, had some inside information.

"Despicable Raiders" and Their Women

Familiar with General Morgan and Mundy raiders, Barren County gave cursory notice to the raiding along the Missouri–Kansas border in the early war years. Dispatches to Fort Williams in Glasgow, 525 miles east of Lawrence, Kansas, would alert the garrison to a new threat's arrival in early 1865.

Quantrill's Raiders, a band of several hundred men, had begun attacking Unionists in late 1861. Portrayed as savage desperadoes in Northern newspapers, they financed their raids, in part, by such despicable means as robbing citizens and capturing escaped slaves in exchange for reward money.

William T. "Bloody Bill" Anderson had lived at various places in Kansas with his three sisters, Josephine, Mary, and Jennie. In summer 1863, he removed his sisters to the Missouri side of the line near Blue Springs and stayed with the Mundy/Munday family in Sni-a-Bar Township. James Mundy, 17, was then the head of the household and a Confederate partisan guerrilla. His father, Robert Munday, had left Catharine (Stanley) Munday a widow in 1847, and James had recently buried his mother beside him. At home with James were his three older sisters, Martha "Mattie" Mundy (1849), Lucinda "Lou" Mundy Gray (1838), whose husband were a guerrilla, and Susan Anne Mundy (1843). [29]

During a Union sweep on Tuesday, August 11, the Mundy and Anderson sisters were arrested as spies and held on charges for giving aid to the Quantrill Raiders. Susan, described as a young woman of indomitable will, was charged with aiding the Confederates, having furnished food for her brother. Other wives and sisters arrested were Susan Crawford Vandever and Armina "Mina" Crawford Selvey, sisters of William, Marshall, Marion, and Riley Crawford.

The women were eventually confined in a three-story, brick building serving as a makeshift Yankee jail in Kansas City, Missouri. At least fourteen women and girls were incarcerated there. Charity McCorkle Kerr, guerrilla Nathan Kerr's wife, John McCorkle's sister, and cousin of the Younger brothers was in the jail, as were the Younger sisters, Josie, Caroline, and Sally. Also jailed were guerrilla Thomas Harris's sister, widow Nancy "Nannie" McCorkle, William Grindstaff's sister, Mollie, Alice Van Ness, a Miss Hall, and a Mrs. Wilson. [30]

The next evening, guerrilla bands struck in retaliation. George Todd and thirty-three of his men raided the Kansas City outskirts. He left a note behind for the authorities, threatening to burn down Kansas City unless the girls were freed. [31]

On Thursday, the Kansas City jail building collapsed. Charity Kerr, 27, Susan Vandever, 28, and Armenia Selvey, 25, were killed instantly. Josephine Anderson, 15 years old, died buried in the ruins. The mysterious Mrs. Wilson, mangled in the collapse, died from her wounds a few days later. According to family lore, Jennie Anderson, 13, had been shackled to a ball-and-chain for unruly behavior. She suffered two broken legs and other injuries. Mary Anderson, 18, was crippled for the rest of her life. Mollie Grindstaff had broken bones and an injured back. Nannie McCorkle, 19, survived with a broken ankle. Sue Mundy and her sisters were among the survivors.

William Quantrill's guerillas, suspecting that Union guards under orders deliberately caused the jail's collapse, harbored a righteous sense of vengeance. In early morning, August 21, 1863, Quantrill headed out with 450 Confederate raiders made almost rabid with rage over the deaths and injuries of the Southern women. "Bloody Bill" Anderson and James E. Mundy rode with the raiders into the Unionist and anti-slavery stronghold of Lawrence, Kansas.

During the four-hour massacre, one-fourth of Lawrence was set afire. The raiders pillaged and looted banks and businesses. Nearly 200 Unionist men and boy Jayhawkers were killed. When news of the upheaval reached Henry Raymond, owner and editor of *The New York Times*, he summed up his view.

"It is a calamity of the most heartrending kind—an atrocity of unspeakable character." [32]

Newspapers described guerrilla raids as atrocities and calamities. Northern papers tended to downplay the murderous actions of Union soldiers and partisan guerrillas. The "achievements" of Rebel guerrillas in Missouri and Kentucky served as comparisons for any "gratuitous wickedness" a family or community might experience. The outcry for punishment of the guilty parties was frequent.

Pursued by Federal regiments, Quantrill's Raiders gradually broke up into smaller groups and escaped from Missouri. The real Sue Mundy entered Kentucky around April or May 1864. As happens, a legend rooted in misinformation, more fabrication than truth, smoldered.

As it was told, Sue Mundy was a handsome and accomplished young maiden, engaged to be married to Marcellus Jerome Clarke. She was living with her mother in Kentucky when federal soldiers marched through, pillaged the house, and burned it to the ground. The troops treated the mother and daughter disrespectfully, and Sue died. [Jerome] Clark swore to revenge her death. He gathered a band of desperadoes around him, told them the tale, and "perpetrated deeds of blood which put to blush the Indian cruelties of former days" with *Sue Mundy* as their battle-cry of vengeance. Thus did Captain Clarke come to be called everywhere as Sue Mundy. [33]

If Susan Anne Mundy was ever betrothed to Captain Clarke, the wedding obviously did not happen. By March 1865, she was alive and well living with her married sister Lucinda in Kansas. Sue married Michael Napoleon Womacks in Blue Springs.

William Quantrill made his way to Kentucky in January 1865 wanting to join Sue Mundy's band. Uniting with him, dressed in stolen Union uniforms, were Bill Anderson, James Mundy, Oscar "One Arm" Sam Berry, Frank and Jesse James, Thomas Coleman "Cole" Younger and his brothers, and the "gallant, soldierly, and deadly Confederate Raider," Captain William "Bill" Marion. Captain Henry Clay "Billy" Magruder joined at some point. Captain Clarke knew Henry, as he had been a private with John Hunt Morgan when they made the Great Raid through Ohio.

Captain Marion and Sue Mundy led the Raiders on a trial operation. The band roamed in the region long familiar to Clarke, staying east of Frankfort and following along the Kentucky River. The weeklong raid concentrated on the forty-five miles between Midway and Danville.

Henry Magruder and four other men set out on their own operation. On Thursday, January 5, 1865, they entered the home of Benjamin Franklin Caldwell in Clermont, Bullitt County, on the turnpike twenty-seven miles south of Louisville. Benjamin, 54, had died on July 22, 1863, but the home was not vacant. His son was there. Sergeant Edward Curtis Caldwell, 28, Company D, 15th Kentucky Volunteer Infantry, USA, had taken leave—purportedly to go home and bury his father. Magruder gunned down the unarmed soldier.

Afterwards, Captain Clarke, Captain Marion, Quantrill, Magruder, Berry, and the others banded together to participate in "military" engagements.

The public outcry that marauding bushwhackers be hunted down and strung up intensified. Captain Clarke likely had an idea what would be his fate should he be captured consorting with these insurrectionaries.

Nathaniel Marks had served in Company A, 4th Kentucky Volunteers, CSA, formed at Salyersville in October 1862. He also roamed through Northeastern Kentucky with two Rebel partisan bands: Field's Rangers, organized by a Carter County sheriff, and Sid and Dave Cook's Guerrillas of Boyd County. Guerrilla Marks was captured and imprisoned in Louisville. Having been tried and convicted of being a guerrilla and a robber in a court martial, he was led beside a chaplain to the Broadway and Eighteenth Street gallows on Friday, January 20, 1865. He spoke his last words to the gathering crowd at 3:45 P.M. [34]

"The charges which are against me are untrue. Lord, forgive us all our sins! Let the Lord be blessed. I don't fear to meet my God. I love every man and child and I do not feel any guilt on my mind. I would to God that everybody felt as happy as I do now. I wish all the heathens in this world could die as happy and were as prepared to die as I am. Oh God, take me in thy care. Amen."

He choked in the noose for eighteen minutes before life left his body, and he was cut down from the rope. Five days later, a massacre further enraged Kentucky Unionists against all guerrilla bands.

In Louisville on January 25, "Official authorities are advised that Munday's gang this evening killed at Simpsonville thirty negroes." Thirty men of Company E, 5th United States Colored Cavalry, veterans of Virginia battles, and most of them former slaves, transported 900 head of government cattle toward Louisville. East of their destination and one mile from Simpsonville, twenty-six Confederate guerrillas (partisan rangers) "came upon the rear guard of the negroes, and at once opened fire upon them." Twenty-two Company E men died in the ambush. Six more died of wounds afterward. [35]

That evening, the *Louisville Daily Journal* wrote of the ambush, calling the massacre "a horrible butchery." Northern newspapers quoted a local resident who thought the event was "one of the bloodiest tragedies." Captain Clarke would enjoy fewer than two months more of freedom.

A Union bullet wounded Henry Magruder in the right lung while the guerrillas were on the run. He, Captain Clarke, and Lieutenant Henry Metcalfe, from Ohio County, looked for a safe haven. Lieutenant Metcalfe was not a guerrilla. He had been captured on Morgan's Great Raid, was imprisoned in Louisville, then at Camp Chase, then at Camp Douglas from whence he escaped. He had made his way to Tennessee and joined General Hylon Lyons' army. Under orders from the general, he was riding with the guerrillas to bring them south out of Kentucky.

The three Confederates hid for days in John Cox's tobacco barn ten miles south of Brandenberg. They were captured there on Sunday, March 12, 1865, and held in the Louisville military prison, "having at last come to grief." On Wednesday, Captain Jerome Clarke, nom-de-guerre Sue Munday, faced a Court Martial.

At 3:00 PM, he declared he had no malice against anyone and loved everybody. He was not guilty of one-tenth of the outrages he was charged with, and the *Louisville Journal* had done him great injustice. He positively declared that he was not present when the Negro soldiers were killed near Simpsonville, but was far from the scene and wounded at the time. He also denied being present when Kalfus and Roberts were killed. For those murders, he blamed Captain Marion. His spiritual adviser, the Reverend Mr. Talbot, of St. John's Episcopal Church, wrote four letters on his behalf, one expressing his love for a young Kentucky woman.

Provost Marshall, Captain George Swope, 5th Indiana Calvary, led a handsome, cultured, refined gentleman from the military prison on the north side of Broadway at 10th Street. He was taken by wagon to a field at 18th Street and Broadway, where the scaffold, "a hastily constructed affar," waited. He spoke his last words to Mr. Talbot. "I hope in and die for the Confederate cause."

"Thus ended the career of the notorious Sue Mundy." The Confederate soldier was hanged at 4:00 o'clock and took twenty minutes to expire. He would have turned 21 years old on August 25. The gory details of his execution, his hard struggles and convulsions, were printed in the Thursday, March 16, *Louisville Journal*.

Henry Magruder remained in prison recovering from his wounds.

The End Comes

Companies D and E, 39th Regiment, Missouri Infantry, were at Glasgow for scouting duty and operations against guerrillas. Company D went on a weeklong scout patrol to Perche Hills of

West-Central Boone County, Missouri, on March 7. Company E remained at Fort Williams. One of the last skirmishes in Kentucky took place near Glasgow on March 25, 1865.

General Robert E. Lee surrendered his Army of Northern Virginia at Appomattox, Virginia, on April 9, 1865. Slavery would be ended legally when the Thirteenth Amendment went into effect on December 18, 1865.

Justice, perhaps retribution, was demanded against Confederate Raiders still at large. Quantrill's Raiders were caught in a Union ambush at Wakefield Farm near Taylorsville, southeast of Louisville, on May 10, 1865. The Rebel chieftain was seriously wounded by a gunshot. William Quantrill died in Louisville on June 6.

Federals took Samuel "Champ" Ferguson, a legendary and notorious Confederate partisan ranger and guerrilla, into custody in Sparta, Tennessee, on May 26, 1865. When the war began, he had sided with the Rebels, although his entire family supported the Union. His brother James, for whom he held a hostile attitude, was a Union soldier in Company C, 1st Kentucky Cavalry, and was killed by an angry citizen near Stanford, Kentucky, southeast of Danville, on December 18, 1861. Champ's perspective at the time was that the region was having a miscellaneous war. "Every man was in danger of his life—if I hadn't killed my neighbor, he would have killed me."

The people of Glasgow might not have heard of Champ's first killings in 1861–1862, which began in Clinton County on the Tennessee border, east of the Cumberland River, but accounts of his ill repute appeared in newspapers across the war years. His supporters circulated a justification for his killing Unionists.

The tale was that, while the former Kentuckian and scout for General John Morgan was away from Sparta, eleven Union men had come to his home and dishonored his wife, Martha, and young daughter. The intruders forced the woman and girl to disrobe and marched them down the street. Although Champ said the story was "absurd," his sympathizers held on to it.

He insisted to his captors that his band of men were not assassins, but a company of Confederate soldiers, and he expected to be paroled. Known to have perpetrated massacres of wounded and imprisoned Union officers and soldiers, he admitted only that he had killed enemies to the Confederacy in self-defense, but had never murdered or tortured anyone. He denied that he had been present when his men hanged nineteen 5th Tennessee cavalrymen during the skirmishes around Sparta at Johnson's Mills and Calf Killer River on February 22, 1864.

The military court charged and tried him for fifty-three murders. His followers boasted that he had killed over 100 Union soldiers and pro-Union civilians. His trial before a military tribunal began in Nashville on July 14, progressed slowly, and concluded on October 18. He was found guilty of twenty-one of twenty-three specifications. He exhibited no emotion hearing his death warrant; not a muscle moved.

In his final statement, Mr. Ferguson declared: "I was a Southern man at the start. I am yet, and will die a Rebel. I believe I was right in all I did."

The execution was to be strictly private, and there was no hope of a presidential reprieve. His wife and 15-year-old daughter, Ann Elizabeth, arrived in Nashville that evening. On Friday, October 20, Reverend Mr. Bunting, of the First Presbyterian Church, walked with him to the scaffold. Champ Ferguson, 43, was hanged at seventeen minutes before noon. His wife and tearful daughter watched his lifeless body dangle at the end of the rope.

The *Nashville Times* printed a long account of Mr. Ferguson's hanging and a long list of the killings. [36] Northern newspapers, like the Monday, October 23, 1865, *Boston Post*, described the execution of the "cold blooded murderer" with no sympathy. "Champ Ferguson fell from a high platform last week into eternity."

While Champ dangled from a rope that Friday, Union authorities hanged Henry Magruder in the courtyard of the military prison in Louisville. Only his mother, sister, relatives, and friends were permitted to be present. He was the fourth Rebel guerrilla to be hanged in Louisville since the outbreak of the war.

Such were the sorts of recollections citizens held in their memories of the tramp, tramp, tramping of armies through Barren County. George Bush would grow up and have children and grandchildren. He could not have known that one of his grandsons would change the meaning of *Raiders* for the citizens of Glasgow.

"No more shall the war cry sever, Or the winding rivers be red." [37]

George Bush's boyhood obviously spanned the Civil War years. He had learned the labors of a farm hand during the turmoils and would work in the fields his entire life. As was common for laborers, every now and then he would find a musket ball, saber, buckle, and all sorts of discarded military equipment buried in the dirt. Whatever he had learned about war's travails and tragedies, one of his sons would have opinions about such matters, and he would pass them down to his own sons.

George married the first time in 1877, in Glasgow Junction (Three Forks Hamlet), ten miles from Glasgow, apparently to a woman five years older. He was a farm laborer and his wife, Jessie, kept house. They had three children.

George Bush 1857- Jessie A. 1852-

William D. 1878 Lou Ada 1880 Eugene 1884

Family events are surmised to have occurred following Eugene's birth. At the time of the 1890 Kentucky Census, Jessie was no longer in the household, nor did she appear in the 1900 Census or any records afterward. [38] If George was widowed, he had married a second time in 1889. He and Margret E., aged 23, resided on a farm near Hiseville, in the Corrill Hill (Coral Hill) area. [39] Before Margret gave birth to a child who survived, she and George were grandparents.

George's first son, William, married Fannie B., 21 years old, in 1895. They farmed in Temple Hill. Bessie G. Bush was born to them in September 1895. A son, Robert, was born in April 1899. When the enumerator collected 1900 household information, Eugene Bush, 16, had left his parents' home and was living with William's family in Temple Hill. Lou Ada Bush was not listed in that census and had likely married. William and Fannie had two more daughters, Beatrice and Elbie, and eventually relocated to Vienna Township, Indiana, to farm.

George and Margret's marriage lasted. Five daughters would have to find husbands. Their oldest did so before the start of WWI. Only two sons, Clarence and Hugh, were born to help with the farming. Clarence, the older of the boys, was born on June 26, 1897. He found a bride before the Great War ended. One of the Wakefield girls working a patch of ground caught his eye.

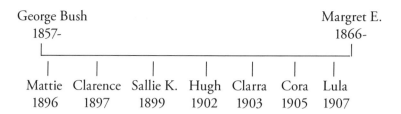

George Bush
1857-

Margret E.
1866-

Mattie	Clarence	Sallie K.	Hugh	Clarra	Cora	Lula
1896	1897	1899	1902	1903	1905	1907

Elmer Morris Wakefield, aged 30 (May 29, 1869), was farming near Red Boiling Springs, Macon County, Tennessee. The nineteenth century had almost ended when he and Clarrenda Ella Meador, aged 24 (June 16, 1874), decided to marry in 1899. Their first baby, Eloise O., was born on August 11, 1899. A son they named Clinton was born in 1903. Clarrenda died on January 26, 1904.

Elmer watched his wife lowered into her grave at Irving Meador Cemetery, near the west end of Sunrise Road, four miles northwest of Red Boiling Springs. The first burial at the small cemetery had been 13-year-old Hugh B. Meador on June 29, 1843. Clarrenda was the twelfth internment.

Elmer moved north from Macon County, crossed the state border, and found farm work thirty-seven miles from home in Magisterial District 4, near Hiseville, in the northeast corner of Barren County. Eloise and Clinton were with him. After discussing the matter with his neighbor, Jeff Davis, Elmer married 16-year-old Nettie Lena Davis in 1908.

Eloise, known affectionately as "Lois," adjusted to being only eight years younger than her step-mother and finished eight grades of grammar school. She was close to her own marrying age when two half-sisters came along: Nettie L. in 1914 and Eunice in 1917. National news had turned to the global war in Europe.

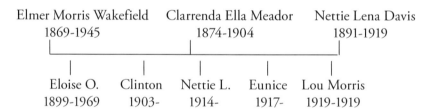

Elmer Morris Wakefield
1869-1945

Clarrenda Ella Meador
1874-1904

Nettie Lena Davis
1891-1919

Eloise O.	Clinton	Nettie L.	Eunice	Lou Morris
1899-1969	1903-	1914-	1917-	1919-1919

Clarence Bush ended his education after completing six grades. At age 13 years, he was farming on the home property. He seemed much like a big brother to the Wakefield children, except to Lois.

Having turned age 21 years, Clarence married Eloise "Lois" Wakefield, 18, in July 1918. They made their home on a Hiseville farm. The happy news was that Lois was soon pregnant. So was her step-mother.

Elmer and Nettie Wakefield had a third daughter, Lou Morris, on March 15, 1919. Their last baby did not prosper, and Nettie, 27, became ill from the childbirth. She had a burning fever, racing heart rate, troubled breathing, and fell into a state of confusion. She died of septicemia on March 22, a frightening death to observe.

Hatcher and Saddler Funeral Home in Glasgow handled all the arrangements. Elmer, 46, and the family gathered on the right side of Tick Ridge Road just past the Hutcherson Road intersection, northeast of Glasgow. Clarence and Lois, nearing the end of her third trimester, attended. They walked 500 feet to the Defevers Grave Yard to witness Nettie's burial. [40] They returned to the cemetery days after the funeral. Lou Morris Wakefield, 11 days old, died on March 26, and was buried with her mother.

The death of his second wife and infant daughter was a hardship for Elmer. He left his children behind with family and moved to Goshen in Warren County, between Glasgow and Bowling Green. For a time, he lodged with Forest and Hallie Hardcastle, a young couple just starting a family, and worked as a farm laborer with Forest.

Clinton Wakefield was just a baby when his birth mother had died. Nettie had been his step-mother for 11 years before she died. He was 16 years old when the family buried her and his half-sister. Clinton went to live on Rusford and Minnie Camthon's Hiseville farm with their five children. He had two titles: orphan and farm laborer. Still unmarried in 1930, he was a hired hand on Charles and Minnie Gautier's farm in Hickory Flat, Warren County, south of Bowling Green—four miles from the Tennessee border.

Lois Bush gave birth to Velma M. Bush in April 1919, shortly after her step-mother was buried. Lois' half-sister Nettie L. Wakefield, six years old, came to live with them for a time in Hiseville. It is how families provided for each other.

Elmer Wakefield would eventually return to Glasgow. Six months after the Wall Street crash, as the Great Depression era gathered steam, he had a house in Magisterial District 1. Aged 60, he was working as a salesman for a nursery. Eunice, his 13-year-old daughter, resided with him.

Between the World Wars

Clarence and Lois Bush had started their family at the end of WWI and would have eight children before WWII began: three sons and five daughters. Clarence Morris, their first son, was born on July 4, 1921. Not to be confused with Clarence Sr., the boy was called Morris. Lois remained mindful of how death could come unexpectedly and tear at a family's fabric. She was a busy farm wife and mother, and she intended to see all her children into their adult years. She had no time to keep a diary of family life, and little is written about the children's early lives.

The Bush family was of the protestant faith and would not have given much thought to the Zen Buddhism principle that "physical man walks in the element of time even as he walks in mud." [41] The Bush children would all know what it was like to walk in mud, to drag themselves along as their lives unfolded, to keep going without marking time's passage. Lois' second son would outlive both his brothers, plumbing an inner core of resilience to keep on through 79 years. Most of his walk in time, his many days, cannot be recovered here, yet important dates marked his life. For ease of transmission, the life of Lois' second boy is described ahead as if borrowed from a Battalion Log Book.

December 23, 1924. Richard Earl "Dick" Bush was born in Glasgow, the third child of Clarence and Lois. Clarence moved the family from Hiseville to live on a rented farm on Cave City Road. All their neighbors either farmed or worked in the oil fields. The highest grade most of the husbands and wives had completed was eighth.

South in Glasgow, the Lyon Opera House had been renovated and reopened as the Trigg Theater in 1917. Then, in 1934, the Plaza Theater was opened in downtown. Pinching their pennies, getting tobacco to the nearby warehouses, Banner County farmers tended not to frequent the theaters. When work was finished, the many streams provided a respite for those who enjoyed fishing for smallmouth bass. The cave systems of the Green River Valley and other nearby regions offered exploring adventures for young people.

The Sink Hole Spring Creek had carved out a cave within Cave City's town limits. Up the road on East Main Street in Horse Cave, Hart County, the Hidden River Cave had opened for commercial tours in 1916. As the Bush children grew up, raw sewage from the town seeped into the river water. The stench within the cave eventually forced the town to close the cave in 1943. By then, two of the Bush sons had gone to war. [42]

The greatest of all attractions in the region was Mammoth Cave and the extensive park miles north of the Bush farm. When Dick was 10 years old, the cave made national headlines.

June 7, 1935. Two cave guides discovered the skeletal remains of an adult male lying face down under a large boulder in the far depths of a cavern in Mammoth, a half mile from Violet City. Apparently the 5-foot-3-inch man had been digging for something and disturbed the rubble supporting the seven-ton rock. The boulder had shifted and settled onto the victim. It all might have been just of local interest for speculation over dinner tables and farm fences, except for what the guides reported finding.

The man's prehistoric remains were mummified. He was wearing a woven fiber loincloth and a shell necklace with a fiber cord. Woven sandals and crude tools were found nearby. Archaeologists determined that the ancient victim was a pre-Columbian, Native American miner who had met his fate over 500 years earlier. The newspaper reporters took to calling the remains "Lost John of Mummy Ledge." The cave mummy was put on public exhibition in Mammoth, and out-of-state visitors stopping to ask for directions at the Bush farm increased. [43]

During the days when Lost John's remains were newsworthy, Dick Bush was a big brother to two sisters and a brother. A baby girl joined the family that same year. Dick would be a big brother to one more sister four years after that.

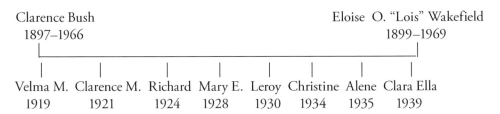

Clarence Bush 1897–1966							Eloise O. "Lois" Wakefield 1899–1969
Velma M. 1919	Clarence M. 1921	Richard 1924	Mary E. 1928	Leroy 1930	Christine 1934	Alene 1935	Clara Ella 1939

Velma, the oldest of the siblings, was first to leave home. She married C. I. Edmunson before 1940. At that time, Grandpa Elmer Wakefield was living alone in a boarding house at 400 Broadway in Glasgow.

As quiet and humble as Dick was by nature, he showed an early propensity for volunteering. When Velma left home, Clarence and Lois had seven children to provide for, and the economy was tough. Dick helped on the family tobacco farm in 1937. He completed 8th grade in 1939. His greatest summer enjoyment was playing sandlot baseball. Before going on to public high school, he decided that farming was more important than returning to school.

Buford Wood, enumerator of the 1940 census, wrote on May 13, 1940, that Richard was 15 years old, had completed seven years of schooling, and was no longer in school. He was driving a tractor for his father on Old Cave City Road. Morris was still at home, laboring on the farm. Dick began attending Glasgow High School in September 1941.

December 7, 1941. Dick was 16 years old when the Japanese struck at Pearl Harbor. His older brother, Morris, was already draft eligible. Morris might have been waiting for the notice to arrive, but as the eldest boy helping on the family farm, he might not have been concerned about being called up.

On January 11, 1942, a Japanese submarine surfaced in the Samoan archipelago off quiet Fagasa Village, on Tutuila Island's west central side, and fired fifteen 84-pound shells over a mountain. The Utulei fuel tank farm on the other side of the island was the target. Most of the rounds landed harmlessly in Pago Pago inlet. One shell wounded a Navy radioman and an island guardsman. Another destroyed Shimasaki's store, the only Japanese-owned building and business in the Tutuila territory. [44]

Reinforcements were dispatched from the States. The tropical climate and the terrain, hills with steep and rugged peaks, made the volcanic island an ideal "stop-over" for Marines on their way to amphibious offensives in the Solomons. Tutuila became a vast advanced Marine combat training camp and staging area in the Pacific before 1942 ended. Following their stay on Samoa, the grunts were better prepared for jungle combat.

August 7, 1942. WWII had been underway for ten months. The U.S. Marines and Allied forces launched surprise attacks on Tulagi and Guadalcanal in the Solomon Islands. Operation *Watchtower*, the first American offensive of the war, stirred young men across the States to stand in enlistment lines.

September 1942. Dick had been employed for five years as a general farm hand helping to cultivate and harvest tobacco, corn, and grain crops on his father's 260-acre farm. He had completed one-and-a-half years of high school, with Math as his subject of greatest interest. His brother, Morris, had an idea.

Veterans of the Civil War, Indian Wars, and WWI resided in Barren County. The outbreak of WWII rekindled the tales about their fights with hostiles. Clarence Bush had heard the Civil War and Indian Wars stories while growing up. The tales had become as much remnants of old county legends as they were factual accounts. Clarence also knew that descendants of William Day's relatives lived and farmed around Cave City and Hiseville.

A Medal's Legacy

William Day (1784) had resided in the Rocky Station District, Lee County—the westernmost corner of Virginia. He married Sophia W. Strange (1798) and began his family: Robert (1818), Frances Ann (1820), Martha Virginia (1824), and Caroline Matilda (1826). William packed up the family, crossed over Cumberland Mountain, and settled on a farmstead on the west side of Boyd's Creek, three miles southeast of Glasgow. Owen and Hayden and Willie Groce were not yet farming acres near the creek.

Emily Day was born on the rural farm in 1832.

William Logan Day was born on his parent's farm on September 21, 1836. Before William Jr. had any chance to get to know his eldest sister, Frances married Matthew N. Lasley and lived in Green County District No. 2. Matthew made a living as a merchant until they relocated to Louisville, where he served as a reverend. William Jr. was old enough to remember when Martha said her vows to become Thomas Childs Dickinson's second wife.

William Day Sr. died on October 9, 1848, and was buried in the Day Family Cemetery on the farm property. According to Assistant Marshal H. Eubank, William Jr. was a 14-year-old Free Inhabitant of the Barren County First Division at the time of the 1850 Census. His mother was the head of the household, and his brother, Robert, had assumed the running of the farm. More family deaths were ahead before the nation faced its calamity.

Sophia Day died on May 4, 1854, and was buried beside her husband. They are the only two internments in the family graveyard. Four years passed, and Caroline, aged 31, married

Frederick T. Miller on January 4, 1858. She gave birth to a son in September and died on April 21, 1859. At the time of her burial in Glasgow Cemetery on Knob Road, across from the Cumberland Presbyterian Church, Robert and William had left the family farm. Robert, 41, was living and working as a laborer on the Burks' farm; William, 22, was living and working as a hired laborer on Jas and Lorian Barrick's farm.

That November 1859, the Harper's Ferry Insurrection was all the news. Seventeen months later, the War of the Rebellion began.

William moved up to Louisville to reside with Frances and Matthew. The city had been a hub of slave trading and a stop on the way to freedom across the Ohio River for fugitive slaves. Slave owners waited for the hoped-for outcome of the war.

Four months after the Confederate surrender at Appomattox, William enlisted in the U.S. Army in August 1865, rising in the ranks. He was assigned to the 5th U.S. Cavalry Regiment, the Union Honor Guard at Appomattox Courthouse. Kentucky's slaves were legally emancipated that December. The Indian Wars were escalating as European Americans migrated into the western plains en masse.

First Sergeant Day led patrols against hostile Natives in Kansas, Nebraska, and Arizona. In 1871, the regiment, under the command of Brigadier General George Crook, was dispatched to Camp McDowell, on the west bank of the Verde River in Arizona. Sergeant Day was in Company E. The 5th Cavalry soldiers who could best attest to his gallant service included Captains Emil Adam, John Gregory Bourke, William H. Brown, James Burns, J. W. Mason, and R. H. Montgomery; Lieutenants John B. Babcock, William Preble Hall, Frank Michier, George Frederick Price, W. F. Rice, William J. Ross, W. S. Schuyler, R. T. Stewart; Sergeants James E. Bailey, Clay Beauford, Daniel Bishop, James Brown, Frank E. Hill, James M. Hill, Patrick Martin, Henry Newman, Rudolph Stauffer, G. Stewart, and Rudolph von Medern; Privates Michael Glynn, George Hooker (KIA), James Lenihan, John Nihill, and Ebin Stanley.

Captain Price commanded E Troop. Sergeants Bailey and Frank Hill were First Sergeant Day's close friends in the company. Already familiar with ambushes and raids, mutilations and massacres, they familiarized their men with Squaw Peak, Mazatzal Mountains, the Four Peaks, the deep Salt River Canyon, and the Tonto Basin.

The 1872–1873 winter was a particularly perilous season for warriors on both sides of the skirmishes. General Crook dispatched nine detachments, using Apache scouts recruited from the reservations, into the snow-covered mountains of the Salt River Canyon. The soldiers crisscrossed the Tonto Basin for weeks in constant pursuit of the Apaches.

On December 14, 1872, Captain Price led E Troop into "Indian Run" and captured nine Natives. [45]

On December 28, Captain Brown's company caught a band of Yavapai warriors and their families hiding in a cave. The shooting stopped four hours later. Seventy-five Yavapai warriors and family members were killed and about twenty mortally wounded. Fewer than twenty women, girls, and boys were captured and survived. Newspaper accounts soon called the battle the *Apache Cave Massacre.*

First Sergeant Day was well north of Camp McDowell and moving toward Camp Verde on December 30. He led his E Troop detachment through the deep and rugged Bishop Creek Canyon, carrying bacon, bread, a little coffee, Springfield Army rifles, and ammunition. Silently reaching remote Baby Canyon, the patrol found a hostile campsite. A scathing engagement erupted. Six Natives were killed, one was wounded, and two were captured. Many in the Apache band escaped east.

After resupplying at Camp Verde, First Sergeant Day and a detachment of Scouts followed trails leading into the eastern wilderness. On January 19, 1873, they tracked down their quarry on the East Fork of Verde River and killed five Natives. On April 27, the last of the Apaches surrendered at Camp Verde.

Eighteen Medals of Honor, including eight to Native Scouts, were awarded for the 1872–1873 winter Tonto Basin Campaign. First Sergeant Day's Medal for gallant conduct during campaigns and engagements with Apaches, signed by President Ulysses S. Grant, was issued on April 12, 1875.

First Sergeant Day, 42, was honorably discharged from the Army on November 10, 1878, at Fort McKinney, Wyoming Territory, after the Great Sioux War. At that time, he was not married and had no children. He did not return to Kentucky, but is believed perhaps to have settled in Arizona or California. Medal of Honor historians have found it difficult to locate his burial place, as the date and place of his death remain unknown. [46]

The Marine Corps Readied to Bring Retribution

Lieutenant Colonel Merritt A. "Red Mike" Edson had been inspired by guerrilla fighting during his Banana War experience and by the tactics of the British Commandos. His First Marine Raider Battalion was formed within months of the Pearl Harbor attack and activated on February 16, 1942. Lieutenant Colonel Evans F. Carlson organized the Second Marine Raider Battalion, activated on February 19. He had fought against the Japanese with the 8th Chinese Route Army and learned many of their guerrilla tactics. He adopted their slogan "Kung Ho" which meant "Work in Cooperation" or "Work in Harmony." In English, the motto became "Gung Ho."

The Raiders would be involved in almost every major Pacific campaign from August 1942 to January 1944. There were going to be many stories and newspaper accounts of bravery. Before the war was over, seven would earn Medals of Honor, 141 would earn Navy Crosses, and 330 would earn Silver Star Medals for combat operations. [47] Dick Bush would be privy to details of Raider exploits not disclosed in the newspapers.

August 7, 1942. Edson's 1st Raider Battalion, assigned to the 1st Marine Division in the British Solomon Islands, landed on Tulagi in support of the Guadalcanal Campaign. Major Kenneth Dillon Bailey was Company C commander. During the initial landing on Tulagi, he earned a Silver Star, the third-highest military decoration for valor awarded to members of the U.S. Armed Forces. Although wounded through the fleshy part of his thigh after taking an enemy fortification, he led another assault, wiping out an enemy machine-gun nest. He was seriously wounded a second time and forcibly evacuated and transported to New Caledonia. Captain Robert "Bob" Thomas took command of Charlie Company.

Major Bailey lost five of his Marines on D-Day. Private Robert I. Paine was ordered to envelop a hostile machine gun position. Although exposed to severe small arms fire, he had persisted in his advance against the enemy until he was killed. His grim determination and great personal valor contributed to the final destruction of the hostile machine gun unit. Private Paine was awarded a posthumous Silver Star. [48]

Corporal Walter J. Rozga, 22, from Grafton, Ohio, had advanced under heavy hostile fire and destroyed a group of entrenched enemies who were in a well-concealed position, enabling his platoon to move forward and complete the destruction of the Japanese fortification. Corporal Rozga was awarded a posthumous Silver Star.

PFC Woodrow Wilson Barr, 29, PFC Lois J. Carpellotti, 24, and Private William A. Strandvold, 19, were also KIA. [49]

Except for mopping up, the battle on Tulagi was over in three days. Private Patrick Joseph Walsh, 30, was killed on August 8, Private John W. Allan, 20, on August 9, and Private Jack Clarke on August 10. Major Bailey had eight letters to write to families.

At the end of August, Edson's Raiders were brought over to Guadalcanal from Tulagi to reinforce the perimeter defense of Henderson Airfield at Lunga Point. A high, grass-covered, 2,000-yard-long ridge of coral rock rose above the jungle canopy and protected the airfield's south perimeter. About 1,000 yards from the runway, the ridge radiated a mile south away from the airfield.

Marine patrols had spotted a Japanese force advancing from the west. On Thursday, September 10, Edson's combined unit of 840 men moved on to the forward slopes a mile south of Henderson's runway. Two hills were prominent features: Hill 100 (Hill #1) was the forward elevation at the edge of the jungle. A dirt trail connected that hill to Hill 123 (Hill #2), 700 yards to the north. A lagoon paralleled the base of the ridge for more than 500 yards on the west side.

Company B, 1st Raiders stretched its line down from the top of Hill 80 into the kunai grass and jungle to the west. Company C moved into the jungle and "dug in" on the right flank, "tied" to B on the left and extending 800 yards to the Lunga River on their right. First Lieutenant John Pomeroy "Black Jack" Salmon's platoon was on the flank. The three rifle platoons fortified their positions as well as they were able with a little barbed wire and without construction materials. Once they dug a little below the dirt for a foxhole, they struck an impenetrable coral layer.

September 11. Enemy planes began bombing runs along the ridge.

On Saturday morning, Major Bailey returned to the Raiders and stayed on The Ridge with the battalion CP. Daytime patrols ran into enemy patrols. Charlie Company spent most of the hot day fortifying their foxholes. Third Platoon dug in on a knoll overlooking the Lunga River. Once night fell over the ridge at 6:16 PM, enemy ships began shelling the area. Then, at 9:00 PM, 2,000 enemy soldiers charged out of the jungle against Colonel Edson's left flank, closing to bayonet range.

Driven back by Marine rifle and machine-gun fire, they attacked again in three prongs against the right flank, penetrating gaps in Company C's positions. At midnight, Major Bailey's line was collapsing back toward the ridge. Lieutenant Salmon's platoon, farthest to the right, was overrun. Nearly surrounded, they fell back under the overhanging rainforest along the river. The platoon had to cut their way through the jungle and left several men behind who had been cut off during the withdrawal. To escape and evade the Japanese, those men would have had to find a fallen tree to cross a stream in the dark.

Private Malcolm John Hogan, 22, was one of the first believed to have been killed in C Company during the first enemy wave. What happened to him is unknown, as he was never seen again. PFC Salvatore A. Cracco, 25, was defending an advanced position when the company was overrun in the night battle. Eyewitness accounts of his actions and last moments do not exist. His remains were never located. PFC Francis Calvin Potter, 21, an expert rifleman, was trained as a Raider sniper and was probably killed before the company withdrew from the flank. His remains were never identified. Private Francis L. Roberts, 20, was either left behind or was cut off by the enemy during the withdrawal. His body was never identified.

Accounts of the fight for the ridge state that 1stLt Salmon "was extremely upset, visibly shaken, and in a bad way about leaving men behind." In reorganizing, Company C repulsed a second attack. The enemy came at the flank again at 2:30 AM, but the line held, and the enemy force was thrown back a third time.

On Sunday morning, Colonel Edson called Major Bailey and his company commanders to Hill 123. He was certain that the night's attack was a probe to test the Marine defenses. "They'll be back," he told them.

The colonel pulled his lines in to Hill 123. Consolidating the defenses, he moved Company A to the Lunga to re-take Charlie Company's abandoned positions on the forward line's right flank. Company C was to pull back after dark to new positions farther up the ridge. Once repositioned on the right flank of the hill, Major Bailey's company would be the battalion reserve.

Privates Paul P. Ratcliffe, 20, and Joseph M. Rushton were best of friends from northwest Philadelphia. They had attended St. Athanasius school, enlisted in the Corps, gone to Parris Island, and joined the Raiders together. They were both in 2d Platoon, Charlie Company. Private Rushton, a BAR man, had taken some shrapnel in his backside and upper legs during the Friday afternoon enemy bombing runs, but refused evacuation.

In the afternoon, the two friends were part of the squad Lieutenant Salmon ordered to establish a defensive position in the jungle, a good distance from the main line. They had to file over a slippery, fallen tree trunk to get across a lagoon to take up the position. As evening approached, reality was dawning on the men. If they could not hold the position during a nighttime attack, they would have to withdraw back across that log. They rolled out a telephone wire to guide them back to the fallen tree. [50]

PFC Kenneth Earl Ritter, 20, was managing a bad case of dysentery and debilitating exhaustion. At points on the trail to their night positions, he collapsed and had to catch up with the squad.

In the evening, Private Ratcliffe found his friend for a chat while they shared a smoke. Private Ratcliffe's voice sounded flat and apathetic, and his eyes had the "thousand-yard stare." The two agreed that, by all appearances, they were expendable. As darkness was falling, the friends shook hands, and Private Ratcliffe went back to his spot on the line. Private Rushton looked out for his assistant BAR man.

Company C was finally in its assigned position at 9:00 PM. Lieutenant Salmon sent four Marines to establish a listening post in advance of his platoon's new position. Sergeant John "Squeaky" Morrell, PFC James V. Mallamas Jr., Private John J. Redden, and Private John Michael "Boondocks" Langdon moved down the ridge finger to their left front with a field telephone. They set up along the trail without foxholes and almost instantly heard the enemy approaching.

The furious, battalion-size attack came at 10:00 PM, and, it seemed, the enemy was everywhere. For the next ten hours, they came in ceaseless waves to be mowed down. The Marines fought them hand-to-hand in the foxholes and gun pits. The Japanese surged through gaps in the main line.

Platoon Sergeant Stanley D. "Ed" Kops, a tough old Marine, commanded a platoon in the center of Company C's position. Ordered to move during an enemy attack of overwhelming odds, he redeployed the platoon to positions farther to the rear. Several Raiders from other units straggled into his platoon's position, and he quickly organized them into a provisional platoon. Sergeant Kops then led a charge on the enemy position. He killed the enemy soldiers and seized their positions in desperate hand-to-hand fighting. Platoon Sergeant Kops gave his life, but his actions inspired his men to repulse the enemy off the ridge. He was awarded a posthumous Navy Cross.

Lieutenant Salmon's platoon held on until the machine gun on their flank was lost. In danger of being surrounded, the platoon was ordered to fall back. Crawling on their hands and knees the men looked for ways back across the lagoon. The Japanese were all over the trails. The screams of wounded Raiders being bayoneted and hacked with sabers could be heard above the gunfire and the explosions of mortars and grenades.

PFC Roger Albert Sramkoski, 20, from Saginaw, Michigan, charged toward the top of the knoll. He "was heaving grenades as fast as [he] could pull the pins" when he was hit by enemy fire as 3d Platoon recaptured a gun position. [51]

An artillery blast seriously wounded Private Rushton and PFC Ritter, and they tried to crawl quietly away. PFC Ritter was in great pain and unable to move on his own. Private Rushton dragged him with one arm, carrying the BAR with the other, inching along, looking for some shallow part of the lagoon to cross. Several enemy soldiers discovered them, and Private Rushton killed them.

Hiding in the swamp, PFC Ritter died of his wounds just before dawn. Private Rushton hid the body under some brush to avoid its discovery and defacement by the enemy and made his way back to the ridge. He was immediately evacuated from the Marine lines after reporting PFC Ritter's death and location.

"Friendly fire isn't friendly." Sergeant Morrell's listening post was trapped on the trail in both directions. "Friendly" mortar artillery shells burst in the trees and flung shrapnel all over the area. Private Langdon took a huge chunk of steel in his right thigh above his knee. PFC Mallamas tended to the wound, taping two field dressings around the protruding shrapnel and over the wound. The four-man team concealed themselves from the roving enemy.

At 3:00 AM, some of the attackers broke through the main line on the right flank and attacked Hill 123 from the rear. First Sergeant Jerome J. Stark, 27, repeatedly led men against the enemy assault "with relentless fighting spirit and utter disregard for his own personal safety," fighting in violent hand-to-hand combat. When he was severely wounded, he was forcibly evacuated from the lines to a dressing station. Major Bailey's company finally repulsed the attackers as he moved about the men directing them to better positions.

The Raider companies on the right flank were getting hammered and began to pull back to the ridge. Major Bailey called for every weapon he could to cover the forced withdrawal. He assisted in slowing the retreat, reorganizing the troops, and extending the reverse position to the left side of the hill. The Raiders had formed into a horseshoe-shaped line around Hill 123. The situation was desperate.

In a series of frontal assaults, the enemy charged from Hill 80 and from below the ridge's east side. Overhead flares illuminated the swarm of enemy surging up the saddle of Hill 123. The fighting turned hand-to-hand. The Marines around the hill were receiving severe sniper fire from all sides and running critically low of firepower. Major Bailey, under fire and having sustained a severe head wound, rushed about the horseshoe, replenishing ammunition and grenade supplies. The Marines withstood several more assaults.

Teamed up in Company C's mortar section, PFC William Barnes, gunner, and Private Nicholas J. Willox, assistant gunner, had kept up an accurate and almost continuous fire against the advancing enemy assaults, even as the platoons withdrew to other positions. They helped evacuate the wounded and carried ammunition to the men at the front line. When the fighting got so close that firing mortar rounds was untenable, the two voluntarily joined the squads withstanding the assaults. Enemy grenades killed them both during the closing hours of the battle, and each was awarded a Navy Cross.

Reinforcements joined Colonel Edson's men at 4:00 AM, and helped repulse two more enemy attacks.

The Japanese attempted to set up advantageous positions on the ridge along Charlie Company's sector. Sergeant Daniel Wayne Hudspeth, 29, repeatedly led his squad directly into devastating fire, inspiring his men to take the hostile positions. Fighting relentlessly, he was killed in action and awarded a Navy Cross for his courage.

Private First Class Jimmy Wilson Corzine, 22, worked his way forward under the intense hostile fire. He encountered an enemy machine-gun team setting up and charged their position alone. He bayoneted the leader and routed three others. Having captured the machine gun, PFC Corzine turned it against the fleeing enemy soldiers. Other squad members came forward to join him as he effectively kept the machine-gun in action. When the ammunition ran out, he disabled the weapon and held stubbornly to his advanced position. The enemy persisted in their attacks until PFC Corzine was killed, and the squad withdrew back to the platoon's line. Private First Class Corzine was awarded a posthumous Navy Cross.

In the thick morning smoke and fog, Sergeant Morrell tried to get his team around the enemy blocking the trail to the ridge. They slipped into the lagoon at the bottom of the hill. He and Private Redden went to the south, and PFC Mallamas and Private Langdon went down to the left of the pathway to the northern part of the lagoon. Thirty feet of lagoon separated them from Company C's perimeter. They went into the swamp but could not cross the open area, because the Japanese had set up in machine-gun positions directly above them. They stayed motionless in the water for an hour, weapons over their heads, curious crocodiles circling around them, until grenades began landing around them.

Private Langdon darted from hiding, swimming and wading to the mud bank across from him. The machine guns opened up, firing full bore and blowing apart his entire chest area at the water's edge. PFC Mallamas grabbed him, pulled him up out of the water onto his back, and saw that his friend was dead. Still under heavy fire, he slipped into the jungle and made his way to Hill 123 on his own. Private "Boondocks" Langdon's remains were never recovered from the lagoon.

As dawn approached on September 14, the enemy survivors pulled back from the ridge to regroup west of the Matanikau River.

At sunrise, 6:15 AM, the assault on the ridge was nearly over. Scattered pockets of Japanese troops continued to fight along both sides of the ridge. About 100 Japanese soldiers stayed in the open on the south slope of Hill 100.

Major Bailey called for an airstrike. Three U.S. Army 67th Fighter Squadron aircraft took off from Henderson Airfield, strafed the Japanese, and killed most of them. The few survivors retreated into the jungle. More than 600 enemy bodies were strewn over the slopes and in the surrounding jungle. Battle estimates reported another 600 Japanese wounded. The Marines held Henderson.

In the four days and nights of fighting, Colonel Edson's force suffered 163 casualties: Twenty-two KIA, twelve missing in action, and 129 wounded. Counted among Company C Raiders killed on the morning of September 14 were: Corporal William A. "Bill" Keblish, 20; PFC William E. Matthews, 18; PFC Charles W. Roberts, 20; Private Ludger A. Maynard, 22; and Private Albert Metras, 19. Platoon Sergeant John J. Quigley, 26, and Private John C. Rock, 19, were reported missing. Sergeant Quigley would be reported KIA on October 9, 1942. [52] Private Rock would be declared KIA on March 26, 1943.

September 14, 1942. On Monday, the day the battle on Edson's Ridge ended, Morris Bush convinced Dick to take a 48-mile ride with him to Bowling Green, where they visited the recruiting officer at the Sub-District Headquarters Station (SDHS). Dick was more than three months from his 18th birthday. Staff Sergeant Lawrence H. McCullough, USMCR, sent him back home with USMC Form N.M.C. 523—A&I.

Clarence Bush had his opinions about wars and heroics and medals and sons leaving farms to be buried far away from family cemeteries. Without saying, he and Lois worried about their boys' welfare and safety. Yet, in the presence of a county Notary Public, they signed their consent as parents for Richard, a Minor, to enlist as a PRIVATE in the Marine Corps and to serve four years, unless sooner discharged.

Dick took a week to think it over.

About enlisting, Clarence laid down the law to Morris and Dick. "Let me tell you something," he said to them. "If either one of you comes home with a medal, I'm going to beat you to death."

His sons reassured Clarence that they would not be volunteering for anything hazardous nor would they be earning medals. In fact, Dick did not really want to go. For the remainder of his life, he would repeat two thoughts that he had when he and his brother left to go into the service: one with humor, the other more seriously.

"I still have all the splinters in my fingernails from where they came and pulled me off the porch." About medals, he was certain. "I didn't want to get any medals." [53]

Clarence had taught the boys a lesson about fighting, and he repeated it before they left the farm for the Cave City train station. "He who fights and runs away lives to run away another day."

Dick was going to be hearing a lot of memorable sayings in the months ahead. And later, 100 years to the day after William Day Jr. was discharged from service, Glasgow citizens would be reminded of the Barren County first sergeant and the connection Dick had with the old soldier.

September 15. Charlie Company's wounded first sergeant was listed as missing. The family in Altoona, Pennsylvania, was notified in November and assumed that either the crude field hospital was destroyed or it was overrun and captured by the enemy. First Sergeant Stark's fate was never determined. His Silver Star award was held in case it could be presented to him in the future. Two of his fellow Marines wrote to the family in June 1943 to report that they had seen him fall, that he was dead, and that his body was not recovered from the sea. First Sergeant Stark was declared KIA in September 1944. [54]

Several days after the battle on the ridge, Lieutenant Salmon led a Charlie Company patrol back over the field. Crossing the old position his platoon had abandoned on September 13, the putrid odor of death hit them. They found three badly decomposed and defiled bodies near what had been Private Malcolm Hogan's position. The flies and ants had carried on after the enemy had been forced back into the jungle. Certain that the unrecognizable bodies were those of his Marines, Lieutenant Salmon reported that positive, personal identification of the remains was impossible. The bodies were buried as Unknowns on the battlefield.

No one who survived the night attacks ever saw Private Paul Ratcliffe alive again after his smoke with Private Rushton. Search parties did not locate PFC Ken Ritter's remains.

The official date of loss for most of those missing on the ridge, but determined to be killed in action, was reported as September 15, 1942.

September 22, 1942. Dick went back to SDHS Bowling Green on Tuesday with his bag packed. A U.S. Navy doctor gave him a medical once over. He had blue eyes, medium brown hair, and a ruddy complexion. He stood at 72 inches, weighed 158 pounds, and had a 32-inch waist. He had 20/20 vision in both eyes. His hearing was 15/15 in both ears. His pulse was 72 before exercise, 100 after exercise, and 76 after rest. His blood pressure was 120/80. He had a permanent mark on his left collarbone, permanent scars on both knees, a half-inch scar on his left scapula, and one-inch scar on the back of his left hand—all within regulations and common for a young man off the farm. He had all his fingers and both thumbs. He was sober when medically surveyed. There was no evidence of disease, mental defects, or physical disability.

His first dental exam looked like many of the men entering the services from family farms. He had adjoining chips in his upper right incisor and right front (central) tooth and chips on both sides of his left front tooth. He had cavities in his left 2nd Bicuspid (molar 13) and his 1st molar (14). On his lower mandibular, he was missing his right 1st molar (19) and his left 1st molar (30). There was one cavity on his left 2nd molar (31).

In all regards, his examination was NORMAL. Lieutenant Commander John J. Eberhart, Senior Medical Examiner, concluded that Dick was medically qualified for enlistment. [55]

Dick signed a variety of forms. He obliged and subjected himself to serve until the end of the war and to voluntarily reenlist or extend his enlistment if so required. He affirmed that he was by present occupation a farmer, was not married, had no dependents, and had not graduated from high school. He had never been rejected for enlistment; never been in jail, reform school, or prison; never been arrested or convicted of a crime or sentenced by a court; he was not then, nor ever had been, on probation. At war, should he be missing, interred, or captured by the enemy, he wished that his father would be allotted 50 per cent of his base pay plus longevity. Clarence (no middle initial) Bush was to be notified in case of an emergency. He was given Service ID No. 449381, Reserve Class III c.

Major F. S. Kieren, USMC, ret, certified that he had minutely inspected Richard previous to enlistment and gave him a train ticket to the DHS Louisville. He was to be transferred to his final destination, Recruit Depot San Diego, on September 23.

CHAPTER 18

Want *ACTION?*
Join the U*S*MARINE CORPS!

✳✳✳

"We salute you, as Raiders, as Marines, as Americans, as Men.
God bless you." [1]

— COLONEL EVANS FORDYCE CARLSON.

THE JAPANESE TROOPS WERE STILL on Guadalcanal and the fighting for Henderson Field along the Matanikau River continued. The Marines first moved against the enemy forces west of the river on Wednesday, September 23. Major Bailey, 31, was killed instantly during an intense battle to repulse the enemy on Saturday: shot between the eyes by a machine-gun bullet. Baker Company Raider Clifford James Fitzpatrick, 32, expressed the common opinion about Major "Ken Dill."

"I never saw any Marine braver or more dedicated." [2]

PFC Julian Knight Dobson, 18, died of his wounds on September 28.

The 1st Raiders safeguarding of Henderson Field was to become legendary and remembered as the "Edson's Ridge" or "Bloody Ridge" Battle. Colonel Edson and Major Bailey were both awarded Medals of Honor for their heroic actions and inspirational leadership. President Franklin D. Roosevelt presented the posthumous award to Major Bailey's wife on March 24, 1943, during a special ceremony at the White House. [3]

When Guadalcanal was finally secured, the 1st Raiders needed trained replacement troops. The Corps was mobilizing and deploying large numbers of fighting men into the Pacific to fill gaps and stop enemy occupation of islands that did not belong to them. Stories of Raider bravado drifted around the USMC Recruit Depot battalions.

Training Replacements

September 27, 1942. Private Bush, Richard E., arrived at the San Diego Marine Corps Recruit Depot, 2d Recruit Battalion. At six feet tall, he stood out as soon as he stepped off the train.

One event, a memory all the Marine hopefuls arriving at the receiving barracks shared, was the first night march to the barbershop. "Next." Private Bush's head of hair was shorn to the floor in less than twenty seconds. "Next."

The DIs bursting through doors at 5:00 AM, banging on garbage cans, screaming, and cursing relentlessly was an awakening unlike any he had experienced in his seventeen years on the family farm. The sergeants reveled in telling him and the other recruits the many reasons they would be sending them back to their mommas on a train. The privates discovered that the drill instructors had humorous, mostly derogatory, names for them. Once having arrived at the Depot, the recruits' first names dropped out of popular use. By tradition, Marines call those below the non-commissioned officer (NCO) ranks—privates, privates first class and lance corporals—only by their last names. To the DIs and commanders and fellow recruits, Dick was now just "Bush."

September 28. The photoflouroscopic examination of his chest was NEGATIVE. He stood in line for a Tet Tox (tetanus vaccine) inoculation and a Cowpox vaccination, the first of three Typhoid and Paratyphoid Prophylaxis.

After surviving the receiving barracks, haircut, medical checks, administrative humdrum, clothing and gear issue, Marine chow, and much marching about, he waited with the "crapheads" to meet their assigned DIs.

September 29. The 884th Platoon, 1942, First To Fight, was formed and ready to begin training. Private Bush, wearing a service tie, collar tight around his neck, holding a board across his chest with his service number, stood for his first official Marine Corps photograph.

Captain E. R. Ames and the DIs had seven weeks to turn the raw recruits into basically trained Leathernecks. Four to six hours became the norm for a "full night's sleep."

September 29. Lieutenant Colonel Harry Bluett Liversedge had been ordered to Tutuila, American Samoa. He began organizing the 3d Marine Raider Battalion, the only Raider battalion to be organized and trained overseas. The 4th Raider Battalion was cre-

BUSH, Richard E.
Enl 22Sep42
Taken 29Sep42

ated at the same time at Camp Pendleton, under the command of Lieutenant Colonel James R. Roosevelt, the president's son. He had earned a Navy Cross medal serving with the 2d Marine Raiders during the Makin Atoll raid.

Following their battles on Tulagi and Guadalcanal, the 1st Raider Battalion embarked to New Caledonia in October 1942. The Free French territory's location in the South Pacific made it a usual stop for ships bound for the Pacific Islands. Dozens of islands comprised the archipelago. Grand Terre, the main island, is a cigar-shaped coral mass, 240 miles long and about 30 miles wide. Noumea, the capital city on the southwest coast, sits on a peninsula jutting west into the Coral Sea. It was not much of a town.

The Raiders established a tent bivouac overlooking a river at St. Louis Mission, ten miles northeast of Noumea. The camp and the chow were Spartan, befitting the Raider ethos. The mess tent dished out "C" rations and Spam for meals.

October 3. Private Bush was called back to the medical ward for another photoflouroscopic examination of his chest. NEGATIVE was the report.

For three weeks, Private Bush underwent grueling hours of drill, field training, and physical training in his winter service "B" uniform, with tie, web belt, backpack, and campaign helmet. Some hours of training were given to rote attention to detail, interior guard duties, and various garrison subjects. If anything were out of proper order during inspections, he would have to walk around with a bucket over his head. He experienced the pounding, rhythmic cadence of hundreds of combat shoes on the Depot grounds.

Private Bush also experienced the very real tremors of the Depot grounds that would prove to be a portent to the reverberations of grenade, mortar, and artillery explosions on battlegrounds.

October 21. At 9:30 AM, a magnitude 6.5 earthquake struck at a depth of 35km along the southernmost section of the San Jacinto fault zone, sixty miles east of San Diego. Rockslides blocked roads, Highway 80, and a railroad line. The quake caused minor damage in San Diego. Recruits writing letters home in the following eight days reported feeling at least forty aftershocks.

November 1. Private Bush met with 1stLt S. F. Elliot to complete his optional Application For National Service Life Insurance (NSLI). He answered "no" to every question on Veterans Administration Insurance Form 16-18722-1 about his health. His parents, brothers, and sisters had never been afflicted with tuberculosis, paralysis, insanity, epilepsy, or apoplexy. He had never been hospitalized or attended to by a physician for an illness, surgical operation, or an accident or injury. He had never had any of the thirty-seven serious illnesses listed, starting with appendicitis up to varicose veins. He did not use alcohol or habit-forming drugs and had never been treated for alcoholism or drug addiction. He had not consulted with a doctor for any reason concerning his health in the previous five years.

He elected the five-year level premium term plan in the amount of $5000, to be paid by a $3.20 monthly allotment, a deduction beginning with his $50.00 November base pay. The policy went into effect on December 1. Lois Bush was the primary beneficiary.

More to his liking regarding recruit training, Private Bush traveled to the Camp Matthews rifle range near the Depot for weapons training. During those two weeks, he became proficient in weapons handling, sight alignment, trigger manipulation, and firing of the service rifle, pistols, the Browning Automatic Rifle, and other infantry weapons in the Corps' inventory.

November 12. Private Bush scored a 306 on the Rifle Qualification Course. He was designated Expert in Rifle. Then, he spent one more week back at the recruit depot.

November 16. He qualified in Bayonet Handling with a score of 60. On his Professional and Conduct Record, Private Bush was rated on a six-point scale: 0, Bad; 1, Indifferent; 2, Fair; 3, Good; 4, Very Good; 5, Excellent. He was given the highest marks, 4.5s and 5s, to indicate his character for Military Efficiency, Neatness and Military Bearing, Intelligence, Obedience, and Sobriety.

November 18. Private Bush was examined by the MCBSD Medical Department and found physically qualified for transfer.

November 19. Sixty-three privates graduated with the 884th Platoon. Five rows of trim, smartly dressed men posed for a platoon photograph. Captain E. R. Ames and the two drill instructors sat center in the first row of bleacher seats.

One of the taller Marines in the platoon, Private Bush was third from the right end of the top row in the photo. Private WRIGHT JR, Clyde J., from Blanding, Utah, was the first Marine on the other flank of the top row. Private ELA, Wendell Phillips, 20, from Grand Junction, Colorado, was on the right end of the second row from the top. Private CROSS, Irvin L., 19, stood in the second row, fifth from the right. All four of these Marines would serve with highly decorated Marine Raider battalions. Three of them would survive the war, and the platoon photograph would circulate among old friends in 1978.

As has been true for Marines who successfully transfer into the Fleet Marine Force after recruit training, Private Bush would long remember the great influence his DIs had in his life.

"I remember how mean my D.I. was to me when I was there in BOOT CAMP in 1942 . . . They made me wear those BIG SHOES." [4]

Private Bush was transferred to a replacement battalion at Camp Elliott, fifteen miles northeast of San Diego (on the site of today's Marine Corps Air Station Miramar). The camp was used for small unit training, replacement battalions, and specialist schools. He joined H&S Artillery, 2d Artillery Battalion, under command of 2dLt Arthur O. Maller, for further training as an armorer to eventually fill a gap in a deployed unit in the South Pacific.

Training with the .30 caliber Browning Light Machine Gun was on the itinerary. His principal duty was Cannoneer. Field Artillery Crewman (603) was added to his primary Rifleman (745) military specialty. He completed the Communication Personnel Course and the Field Artillery School.

December 7. Private Bush joined Casual Company, Fleet Marine Force, Training Corps (TC), Camp Elliot. For two months, he was under the watchful eyes of Gunnery Sergeant Louis Lawrence Gorski. On his Semi-Annual fitness report, Private Bush continued to earn 4.5 and 5 marks.

December 8. The MCBSD Medical Department examined Private Bush. Assigned temporarily to the 2d Anti-Tank Battalion, he was physically qualified for transfer.

December 23. Private Bush was a Marine, and he turned 18 years old.

January 1943. The 1st Raiders' New Caledonia hillside campsite was renamed *Camp Bailey*—a tribute to Major Kenneth Dillon Bailey. Everyone in the unit knew that he had been Charlie Company's commanding officer, had earned a Medal of Honor during the battle on Edson's Bloody Ridge, and had been killed in action two weeks later at the Matanikau River.

February 1. Private Bush was transferred to Camp Pendleton and joined H&S Battery, Artillery Battalion, TC, for a month.

February 25. He sat through three-and-a-half hours of Chemical Warfare Instruction and qualified as a 2nd Class Swimmer. His Gas Mask was measured to be Size 3.

February 28. The legend of a Navy chaplain began to circulate. Father Paul Redmond, Order of Saint Dominic, was born on March 27, 1899, in New Haven, Connecticut. He wore a Marine uniform with the Raider Patch on his left shoulder. Few chaplains were more revered by their men than was this padre. He referred to the Marines as his children.

The 4th Raiders were in the New Hebrides getting ready to take an island from the Japanese. Father Redmond prayed for a piano for onshore services. The Raiders heard his prayer, knowing there was an upright in the recreation room aboard the USS *President Polk* docked at Espiritu Santo. On their last dark night of off-loading, while the good Father kept the *Polk's* officers and men distracted with entertaining stories, a carefully selected detachment covered the piano in shelter halves and ponchos and secreted the "cargo" off the ship, manhandling it into a landing boat. The piano was lugged ashore to the makeshift Native Church.

The Padre gave it a look over. "Hide it where I won't know where it is," he told the Raiders.

The piano became the chapel's altar. John P. Zeller served Mass for Father and kept silent about what was under the alter cloth. [5]

The *Polk's* irate, sputtering captain sent out search parties and threatened brig time over the bullhorn for those responsible. The Raiders on shore denied all knowledge of the filching. Father Redmond finally returned the ship's piano after services on March 26, 1943.

March 11. On Thursday, from the epicenter 218 miles east, a 6.6-magnitude earthquake hit Le Mont-Dore on the southern tip of New Caledonia at 9:34 AM. The shaking did not quite reach Noumea, thirty-one miles west. Then, a 6.8-magnitude quake hit the island on Sunday at 5:11 PM. The Marines sleeping in their tents felt the rumble when the Monday, 6.9-magnitude quake reached Noumea and Camp Bailey at 2:24 AM.

March 15. The Marine Corps created the 1st Raider Regiment and gave Colonel Harry B. Liversedge control of all four Raider Battalions. The 1st Raider Battalion stayed on New Caledonia, conducting training exercises while the battalion was brought back to full strength. Replacement troops arrived two and three times each week. Captain "Black Jack" Salmon commanded Company C.

April 1. Private Bush joined "E" Battery, 2d Battalion, 14th Marines, at Pendleton, continuing his duties as a cannoneer.

April 27. The 2d Raider Battalion completed construction of Camp Allard on New Caledonia, three miles from a Marine replacement camp. Sergeant Robert V. Allard, Company B, had been captured during the Makin raid when he and four others attempted a rescue effort from the submarine back to the island. All five were awarded the Navy Cross posthumously. [6] Camp Allard became the 4th Raider Battalion's home.

June 2. Private Bush joined 1st PA Battery, Artillery Battalion, TC, Pendleton.

Intelligence gatherers estimated that 15,000 Japanese troops were positioned in the Central Solomons and that 90,000 were 400 miles further north at Rabaul.

June 7. On Monday, the 1st Raider Battalion sailed from New Caledonia aboard the USS *President Hayes* (APA-20) and debarked at Tetere Point on Guadalcanal on June 11. The Raiders had three weeks of planning ahead.

Guadalcanal was becoming a major and secure supply base and a major U.S. military staging area and rear base in the Solomons. The facilities made life at the camp reasonably comfortable for a Pacific Island stay. A screened-in galley and mess hall provided the battalion good food. There were screened latrines and fresh water showers. There was a post office, a Red Cross unit, an outdoor theater with log seats, and a major medical "sick bay."

Jungle training on Guadalcanal was in no way comfortable. Letters home described the tropical terrain to be "a solid wall of vegetable growth" reaching as tall as 100 feet. Huge palm leaves, taro elephant-ear leaves, ferns, and banana tree leaves obstructed the views of advancing patrols in all directions. The tangled jungles were dark even at midday. Marines constantly brushed ants, spiders, praying mantises, and other strange insects from their leggings and packs.

Returning to this island, where companions had died was sobering for the original Raiders who had fought on Tulagi, Tasimboko, and Guadalcanal.

June 11. Private Bush was issued his two I.D. Tags at Camp Pendleton.

New Georgia

New Georgia was a large island in the Central Solomons, halfway up the island chain and on the southern flank of *The Slot*. The Japanese had completed an airstrip on New Georgia's southwestern Munda Point by December 1942. Their barge bases at Enogai and Bairoko on the northern coast served as supply depots. Seizure of the island was planned under Operation TOENAILS. The Northern Landing Group (the 1st Raider Regiment headquarters, the 1st Raider Battalion, and two army battalions) would simultaneously go ashore at Rice Anchorage, then attack overland to take enemy garrisons at Enogai Inlet and Bairoko Harbor.

June 21. Consolidated PBY *Catalinas*, the flying boat airplanes, landed four 4th Raider patrols at New Georgia's Segi Point on the southeastern tip of the island to reconnoiter and gather intelligence. The actual D-day was June 30, with simultaneous landings in four places. The Raider battalions anticipated losses on New Georgia. Scouts searched throughout the Marine Corps for Raider volunteers.

Marines had to volunteer to join the Raiders and be individually hand-selected by the commanders to start training. Being selected was an achievement. Higher risks of combat casualties were anticipated, so higher standards for entry had been implemented. These included to be strong and exceptionally physically fit, to be durable and able to make long marches at a fast pace, and to be a strong swimmer. The inflatable boats they used did not always make it to and from the beaches, and the Raiders might have to be their own means of transportation on and off islands. Raiders were expected to do more than the average grunt, to work longer and harder, to endure great hardships, and to in no way accept defeat as an option. Individual performance was a given; the real question was whether the Marine volunteer could bond with a team and fight for its survival over his own.

June 25, 1943. The reassurances Private Bush had given his father when he enlisted had apparently slipped his mind. He shared the experience common to the original Raider volunteers, men like Kenneth H. "Mudhole" Merrill, the youngest of Carlson's Raiders during the August 17–18, 1942, Makin Island Raid.

"I was in boot camp and heard about them forming a catch-me-kill-me outfit," Ken explained the start of his Raider adventure, "so, I volunteered. There were eleven of us, and we were interviewed by Jimmy Roosevelt, the president's son, and out of the eleven I was the only one who was picked." [7]

Thirty to forty prospective Raider candidates at a time trucked into Camp Pendleton for the commanders to screen. Private Bush decided to join them. He reported to Captain Rex H. Crockett and was assigned to H&S Company, 2d Raider Battalion, TC.

Private Bush "didn't know nothin' from sour apples" about Raider tactics, but was a quick learner. Each Raider battalion had a weapons company and four rifle companies composed of three rifle platoons and a weapons platoon. These platoons consisted of ten-man squads comprised of three-man fireteams. Each platoon was a lightly equipped force using conventional tactics to accomplish special missions. Every squad and fireteam boasted "the roughest, toughest, meanest bastards from all sides of hell." [8]

The Raider mission was to operate as amphibious light infantry, landing on enemy-held islands in ten-man rubber boats, BAR man at the bow to provide covering fire, and penetrating behind enemy lines. Envisioned as "commandos" who would make quick, "hit and run" strikes behind Japanese lines from submarines and then disappear, the Raiders took on the aura of an "elite" force. Marine Corps historians cite the Raiders as the first special operations force in the United States—the "crème de la crème" in USMC history.

Private Bush was selected to stay with the Raiders, while many more left the camp. Even those selected did not always make the grade. Raider training involved extensive weapons familiarization, bayonet fighting, judo, hand-to-hand combat, stalking, killing with a stiletto and K-Bar, demolitions, mountain climbing, toggle rope use, communication skills, and first aid. Falling out during a hike or staggering during physical training meant the Marine would be transferred out of the Raider battalion. Over the next two months, 4 and 5 marks went into Private Bush's Record Book.

New Georgia went into the Raider's book of legendary battles.

July 4. On Independence Day, Pvt Bush wondered where his brother, Morris, was spending his 22nd birthday.

The 1st Raiders embarked at Tetere Point aboard four destroyer transports for the fast run to Rice Anchorage: the USS *Schley,* APD-14, *Kilty,* APD-15, *Crosby,* APD-17, and the USS *McCallan*, DD-488. The other assault units loaded aboard the USS *Dent, Talbot, Waters,* and *McKean.* Their destination was the "backdoor to Munda Airfield" ten miles due north of the facility. Their mission was to block the trail connecting Enogai–Bairoko with Munda.

Radiomen Charles Y. Begay, Wilsey H. Bitsie, Eugene Roanhorse Crawford, Carl Csinnijinni, Edmund John, Alfred Leonard, Joe A. Quintana, and Felix Yazzie, all Navajo Code Talkers, were among the Raiders. Gene Crawford was assigned to Company C, 1/4. This would be the first use of the Navajo language code in the Pacific. [9]

July 5. Task Force 18, USS *Strong* (DD-467), a Fletcher-class destroyer, was on a bombardment mission to Kula Gulf. An enemy submarine-launched torpedo hit her at 12:46 AM, Monday, and she sank quickly on the way in. [10] Her depth charges had all been set and began detonating under the approaching APDs.

The 1st Raider Battalion replacements had their first taste of combat in the dark, at 1:30 AM. They climbed down the side of the APD into a ten-man rubber raft towed in the rough sea by a landing craft as enemy artillery shells splashed among the ships in Kula Gulf. The USS *Waters* suffered a minor hit when four enemy 140mm guns at the inlet opened fire on the heavily laden ships.

The 1st Raider Battalion spearheaded the night landing of the Northern Group at Rice Anchorage in a driving, torrential rain. They stepped out of their rubber boats into knee-deep mud 600 yards inland from the mouth of the Pundakona River and mucked ahead for 300 yards into the jungle darkness.

Private First Class George Richard McGraw Jr., aged 28, of Altoona, Pennsylvania, was a D Company Number-2 man on a mortar gun. The rubber boat he was riding in overturned. Encumbered by his pack and mortar shells, he drowned. He was first reported missing in action off New Georgia Island and later officially listed as "Died in Action."

The Raider regimental headquarters and all assault forces were ashore by first light of day at 6:59 AM, five miles north of their objective. The loyal natives had cut fresh trails leading to the Giza Giza River south of Enogai Inlet. The canopies of trees, thirty to forty feet tall, hid the trails from enemy aerial observation.

The battalion advance overland began at 7:00 AM from Rice Anchorage to capture the enemy's barge bases and seize Dragons Peninsula, between Enogai Inlet and Bairoko Harbor. Company D was in the lead, with C behind them. The Giza Giza River, a swamp, the Tamakau (Tamoko) River, and 500 Japanese defenders were ahead.

As the days played out, the Raiders ate canned rations and huddled in wet ponchos, seeking cover under banyan roots. Feet turned purple from the water in their boots. Moving along tortuous trails at the base of a coral ridge, many men tripped over roots and fell, ripping open hands and knees on the sharp coral.

July 7. Each platoon had a corpsman. Company C, 3d Platoon, had Corpsman Byron H. Eller. He administered the daily doses of salt and atabrine to stave off malaria. He warned the Raiders of the risks of fatal cerebral malaria or Blackwater Fever if they refused the medicine. He squelched the unmanly tale of atabrine causing sterility as just an unbecoming rumor. Doc Eller was also responsible for the "unfit for duty" company roster. He recorded in the morning log that Pvt Walter B. Scott had sprained his ankle very badly and was able to walk only with great difficulty. After taping it as best he could, Doc Eller sent him to the rear. [11]

Other Raiders were falling ill, unfit for duty with malaria, dysentery, piles and boils, foot fungus and rash, and kidney infections. Later in the day, Doc Eller found Private Scott again, not in the rear as advised, but back with 3d Squad, barely able to keep up on the trail. "HE WAS DETERMINED TO STAY THERE!!"

The Raiders occupied Triri Village, at the western end of the ridge leading to Enogai Inlet, set up a perimeter for the night, and arranged ambushes along the trails entering the village. They augmented their canned food with wormy rice uncovered in Triri. The wounded were given aid in a large grass shack.

Father Paul Redmond first saw combat on New Georgia. He would earn a Legion of Merit award. He wore a baseball cap and carried a carbine. Along with his Bible and extreme unction and Last Rites pouch, he also carried a .45 pistol whenever he was moving among the Marines on the front lines. A man-of-God Marine, the Raiders gave him several nicknames: "Jungle Padre," "Father Two Gun," "The Pistol Packing Padre," and "Cuss-em, Kill-em, Bless-em Redmond."

Father Redmond and Father Murphy presided over a dignified service, and the Raiders buried their dead under a big banyan tree.

July 8. On Thursday, Company C moved to relieve Company D under fire. Utilizing a 60mm mortar barrage and deadly machine-gun fire, Company C forced the Japanese to break off contact, leaving behind fifty dead. The Raiders reported casualties, but no deaths.

In the afternoon, the 1st Raider Battalion moved from Triri, covered 1,500 yards, ran into an impassible mangrove swamp, and had to back up to Triri for the night, until scouts could find a better trail. Another brief firefight broke out with an enemy company of 400 men late in the afternoon. The Raiders counterattacked and drove the enemy back, killing twenty.

Company C Private James Hortin Roosevelt, 20, impressed comrades as a happy, carefree grunt, smart as a tack and mischievous. When asked, he could be vague about whether he was any relation to LtCol Roosevelt or the president. Private Roosevelt was killed in action. In his personal effects sent home to Albion, Illinois, were his Raider stiletto knife, a Zippo lighter, and his ID card, stained in dried blood. Company D's Pharmacist's Mate Third Class James Jasper Corbett, Distinguished Service Cross recipient, was also listed as dead on Thursday.

July 9. The Raiders headed out on the new trail toward Enogai at 7:30 on Friday morning. Captain Salmon's Company C platoons were in the center of the advance, with 1st Squad, 1st Platoon in the lead. Scout Bombing Squadron-132 began dropping 1,000-pound bombs on their targets. The trail led onto the high ground that dominated their objective. With Leland

Lagoon in sight by 11:00 AM, the Raiders cautiously turned north along the ridge toward Enogai.

Second Lieutenant Philip A. Oldham, 29, and Sergeant Lawrence Holmes Flynn, 22, led 3d Platoon in the advancing column. Private First Class Martin Flaum, 20, Syracuse native, was close to them. He had enlisted on December 8, 1941. Company C was 750 yards from Enogai Point at 3:00 PM and nearly through the enemy's Main Line of Resistance (MLR). The platoon was in a rain forest of giant trees with thick jungle canopy and little undergrowth.

The company encountered a Japanese outpost of at least platoon strength as two Nambu .25 caliber machine guns, the "Widow Makers," opened up. Corporal Charles H. Craig, 2d Squad Leader, was the first 3d Platoon Raider hit in the initial burst of fire. His wounds were serious enough that Doc Eller later believed he ended up KIA. He survived and went home to Fairfield, Illinois. Private First Class Flaum was killed outright. [12] First Squad Leader Corporal Ersel Theodore Patrick, 25, 1st Squad PFC Alfred John Booth, PFC George C. Bubelnick, 3d Squad, and Sergeant Flynn all fell wounded. PFC Booth was dead on the field.

Moments into the engagement, 2dLt Oldham rose up behind a tree to survey the dug-in enemy position. Doc Eller saw him get hit and fall mortally wounded.

Third Platoon had lost their commander, platoon sergeant, and two squad leaders. The squads quickly deployed to the point squad flanks, answering the enemy with rifle and BAR fire. Both forces had good fields of small-arms fire, but the Raiders could not fire mortars, because of the overhead canopy. Grenade explosions punctuated the machine-gun chatter. Corpsman Eller was awarded a Silver Star for aggressively rushing to the aid of five wounded Marines under intense enemy fire and evacuating them to safety.

The Japanese fired their mortars from prearranged clearings, delivering accurate rounds that exploded in the treetops and on the ground. Tree limbs made a terrible clatter, crashing down through the timber above the Raider positions. "It was as if the world was falling apart." [13]

Second Lieutenant Alec Monroe Sim, 24, skillfully led his Company C platoon in two successive attacks against the superior enemy forces. Private Burrell D. Hodges was killed. Despite the stiff resistance, the platoon drove the enemy from their fortifications.

Company A moved into line to Company C's left, anchoring its own left flank on Leland Lagoon. Company B took the right flank, and Company D was in reserve, guarding the rear. Companies C and A charged with grenades and machine guns, but were pinned in place. Company C Private Elmo LeBleu was killed in the action. When he was interred at home in Lake Charles, Calcasieu Parish, Louisiana, his parents, three sisters, and four brothers would remember that Private LeBleu had died on his 20th birthday.

Company B reported no contact to its front.

At 3:40 PM, a Marine Douglas R4D *Gooneybird* transport airdropped rations at Triri, but the supplies could not be brought to the forward forces.

PFC Barney Zinkevich, 26, was one of the "Gramps" among the Company C, 1st Raiders. Born in Inkerman, Pennsylvania, on January 23, 1916, he had grown up on the Susquehanna River, north of Wilkes Barre. Little is known about his family. His father, Mr. George Zinkevich, was not in census records as a head of household. Barney went down to Philadelphia and enlisted in the Marines on May 21, 1942. Before he went overseas, he took out his government insurance policy, listing his mother as Next of Kin. Mrs. Victoria Zinkevich was living at 103 Wickham Terrace, Columbia, South Carolina.

PFC Zinkevich was killed in the fighting near Enogai, dead of a fracture compound of the frontal lobe. He was temporarily buried 150 yards south by southwest of the Enogai Outpost. The 1st MAC message, RAD #262145, would be forwarded to the Secretary of the Navy (SECNAV) on July 26 and Certificate of Death #24936 would be received the next day. [14]

As dusk came, the firing slacked off. The Raiders had gone without food since morning chow, and they were out of food. Water and ammunition had to be carefully rationed. The companies dug in. The rain fell hard all night. Casualties could not be evacuated from the forest. [15]

An enemy mortar hit near the LtCol Samuel Griffith's 1st Battalion command post. PFC Robert W. Johnson was knocked out by the blast, but not evacuated. SSGT Joseph Andrew Szakovics, 25, of Steubenville, Ohio, was the Radio Chief. A giant tree limb fell on him and Private Harry Reinhold R. Seymer, 22 years old. SSGT Szakovics died of his wounds the next morning. The doctors had to amputate Private Seymer's arm at the shoulder.

Corporal Ersel Patrick died of his wounds in the aid station that night. Sergeant Flynn passed away the next morning.

July 10. Early Saturday morning, the squads drank the water from the jungle leaves for their breakfast, then, continued their staggering jungle march. Company B patrols moved forward on the right. Companies C and A renewed the attack on the center, hardly moving, but gradually scattering the defenders. By early afternoon, the Raiders had taken the village of Enogai, destroyed the Japanese garrison, and surrounded two small pockets of enemy holdouts. The supplies air-dropped to Triri finally reached the Raiders in the evening. After thirty hours of going without food, it was like a banquet.

The day had been bloody. Company C lost Platoon Sergeant John G. Combs, 26, PFC Jerry W. Visco Jr., 18, Private Harvey John Medicis, 18, and Private Harley Bennett Seaton, 18, all killed in action. Private Walt Scott, 3d Squad, 3d Platoon, fighting with his badly sprained ankle, was also killed.

Dying For Things That Make Life Worth Living

July 11. The Company C officer in charge of a mopping up patrol was wounded in an engagement against one of the small enemy pockets. PFC Robert M. Snider, 20, took a gunshot wound to the chest. He later lost his right leg when evacuated to Guadalcanal. Platoon Sergeant John G. Combs, 26, assumed command and continued a skillful attack on the Japanese holdouts without interruption. He crawled close enough to throw a hand grenade and silenced that position. Sergeant Combs immediately drew fire from another enemy gun and was killed in action. He was awarded a posthumous Silver Star.

An enemy grenade landed at the feet of one boy. He reacted in a reasonable way. He picked it up and tried to throw it back. He was not fast enough and his hand was blown to shreds. He walked in to the field aid station and asked easily, "Can you fix me up, Doc?" [16]

Able Company Private William G. Bovenschulte, 19, a star football and basketball player at Garfield High School, in Terre Haute, Indiana, was killed. Private Reinhard J. Sauer, Company A, 1st Raiders, from Morgan Avenue in Brooklyn was also KIA. Father Redmond held a Memorial Mass for them. The Padre was crying as he gave Communion to Sauer's buddy. The Raider said something that the priest would never forget. [17]

"No man is too young to die for the things that make life worth living."

Tropical diseases kept Doc Eller as busy as did wounds. Malaria, dengue, dysentery, fungi infections, rashes, sinus, stomach, and kidney problems, trench foot, and piles took a toll on Company C. PFC Alton Leonard Glenn, 22, from Rt. 1, McLean, Texas, was evacuated from Enogai "ineffective" for a horrendous case of boils, an illness that took him to Tulagi, then back to New Caledonia.

The 1st Raiders began planning for the seizure of the Bairoko Harbor garrison, two miles away, sending out patrols to reconnoiter the existing trails. Company C had lost so many

Raiders, it became a skeleton unit, defending Enogai and serving as part of the reserve during the next phase of the assault.

July 20. The attack on the Bairoko garrison commenced at 7:30 on Tuesday morning. The Raiders were in a pitched battle by 10:45 AM, taking one yard after another from the enemy. Company C Second Lieutenant Alec Sim had effectively led his platoon against superior odds eleven days earlier and carried the day. Again, he displayed inspiring combat leadership, driving his composite platoon through well-entrenched, hostile outpost positions. He was killed in the afternoon attacks and was awarded a posthumous Army Distinguished Service Cross for his conspicuous bravery at Enogai and Bairoko.

By 4:00 PM, the 1st and 4th Raiders had lost thirty percent of their men—244 casualties—and another 150 to litter bearers and evacuation teams. The 1st Battalion companies lost seventeen Raiders killed and sixty-three wounded. The assault force made an orderly withdrawal back east to the lagoon to set up in a defensive perimeter. The "walking wounded" struggled back to Enogai through the jungle darkness.

July 21. Bairoko battle casualties began arriving at Enogai at 11:00 AM. Three PBYs landed at 3:00 PM to fly them out to Tulagi, a ninety-minute flight. Two had departed full by 4:00 PM. At 4:30 PM, as the third plane lifted airborne with twenty-six wounded Raiders aboard, two enemy *Zeros* attacked. The PBY's port engine was damaged, and the fuselage was riddled with bullet holes. Two crewmen and a Raider casualty were hit. The *Catalina* was forced to land back at Enogai.

The wounded were removed and carried to a protected cove in Higgins boats until they could be safely evacuated. The boats were covered with canopies to protect the casualties from the rain and conceal their positions. Flies and mosquitoes swarmed the stuffy little boats. The steamy heat and stench of wet blood and putrefying blood turned the air stale. They waited thirty hours.

Doc Eller tended the wounded in one of the boats. His inability to provide adequate care for two men accentuated the horror, frustration, and sadness of that night—PFC Stevo Popovich, 4th Raiders, and PFC Davis. PFC Popovich had a gunshot wound to the chest, and all Doc could do was apply layers of bandages to the sucking chest wound trying to make an airtight seal. For the rest of his life, Doc Eller would hear those sounds: the cries, those moans. APDs finally evacuated the casualties on July 23. [18]

The two Raider battalions settled into defensive positions for the rest of July. The sole action during the "stalemate" consisted of patrols toward Bairoko and nuisance raids from Japanese aircraft.

August 10. The enemy was clearly evacuating its units from Bairoko Harbor. The depleted Raider battalions held on.

August 17. Private Bush reported to the Pendleton Training Center Dispensary. His Medical History was stamped: "This man has been examined and found physically qualified for transfer."

August 18. On Wednesday, Private Bush was back at Camp Elliot, joined to the 28th Replacement Battalion, TC, living in "a big barn" with fifty other men. His friends knew they would be leaving the States for the Pacific soon. They talked about taking a bus over to Yuma, Arizona, to sit in some bars; or, they could go into the wilds of the Chocolate Mountains or the dunes of the Colorado Desert or seek out the seamy side under the Salton Sea in the dim taverns in Brawley and El Centro. For some Raiders, the days ahead would be their last ever to have a night of liberty in the States.

August 20. On Friday night, Private Bush left camp with some comrades for a short liberty. At 6:45 AM on Saturday, he was reported AWOL. He returned on Monday morning. The duty officer logged him in at 5:00 AM. Major W. D. Masters, his commanding officer, referred to the Marine Corps Manual and subjected Pvt Bush to an Article 10–99 (1) disciplinary action. The major awarded him ten days' confinement to quarters for the offense. Time lost for pay was two days. Of the two punishments, the $3.33 deducted from his August pay was the greater loss.

August 28. On New Georgia, the Raider headquarters and both Marine battalions boarded APDs on Saturday night and into the morning of the 29th. The 1st Raider Battalion sailed from Enogai aboard the USS *Talbot* (APD-7) and the USS *Crosby* (APD-17). The 4th Raider Battalion departed on the USS *Kilty*, *Schley*, and *McCallan*. [19]

The campaign had been a costly one. Both Raider battalions had suffered battle casualties of more than twenty-five percent. In addition, sickness had claimed an even greater number. Company C's roster listed PFC Norton V. Retzsch as MIA. His remains were never recovered. PFC Francis C. Potter, 22, was MIA and would be classified as KIA on September 15, 1943. His remains were never recovered or identified. A gravestone would mark empty ground in the Memorial Section of the NH Veterans Cemetery in Boscawen, Merrimack County, New Hampshire, to memorialize his sacrifice. [20] PFC William A. Pelkey was also MIA. [21] PFC George R. McGraw, 28, Company D, was listed as MIA on July 5.

August 30. The 1st Raider Battalion arrived back on Tetere, Guadalcanal, at 11:30 AM on Monday. The men filed ashore, dirty, ragged, and haggard. A slight wind whipped the flag on its pole. A band greeted the returning gallant men and played the Marine Corps Hymn. The battalion had just 245 "effectives" on its roster.

August 31. The final entry in the 1st Raider Regiment Journal was made at midnight: "1st Marine Raider Regiment relaxes (bunks, movies, beer, chow)." [22]

Doc Eller had his own perspective of the Raiders: "That's what the RAIDERS were like . . . A magnificent bunch of men . . . I was proud to be with them. The RAIDERS accepted their corpsmen whole heartedly and saw to it that we were well taken care of." [23]

New Georgia was added to Raider battle history with Makin, Tulagi, Tasimboko, and Guadalcanal. Due to the casualty losses, Company C, 1st Raider Battalion, badly needed replacement infantrymen. The growing collection of legendary tales provided tools for absorbing and training new troops.

September 1, 1943. Sergeants talked matter-of-factly about the odds of a Raider dying or losing limbs in Pacific Island combat. Private Bush took out a second NSLI policy in the amount of $5000, to be paid in a $3.25 monthly allotment beginning with his August pay. The policy went into effect that day. Lois Wakefield Bush was the primary beneficiary. His life was then insured for a total of $10,000. He also elected to have a $25 monthly allotment sent by government check to his mother, for the purpose of savings, beginning on the last day of October. He was found to be in good health by the Medical Examiner. Major Masters approved the payments and entered the allotments into Pvt Bush's Service Record Book.

September 4. The 1st Raider Battalion embarked aboard the USS *Fuller*, APA-7, and sailed from Guadalcanal for their return to New Caledonia.

September 14. The battalion was back in Camp Bailey in time for the biggest earthquake to hit New Caledonia that year. On Tuesday, at 2:01 AM, a magnitude 7.2 quake started at the epicenter, 243 miles to the east. The earthquake reached Noumea at 3:47 AM, with a 7.1 magnitude.

Introduction to Nautical Miles

September 22, 1943. On Wednesday morning, Private Bush departed San Diego with the 28th Replacement Battalion. Once a serviceman sailed into international waters for overseas duty, his base pay was increased twenty percent. Private Bush's monthly pay went up to $60.

He adjusted to the Pacific Ocean's huge, rolling swells, and occasional rainsqualls. Most Marines aboard ship overcame any seasickness within a few days. They cleaned weapons, exercised, played cards, shot dice, taunted each other, and read letters. The chaplain held church services topside every day. Eight days and 2,925 nautical miles later, Marines on the upper deck sighted land as they passed Christmas Island (today Kiritimati).

More than nine hours later at 154.017°W longitude, the ships crossed the equator. Watching the Navy's nautical ritual of veteran "Shellbacks" initiating the greenhorn "Pollywogs," dressed in shorts and socks, to their first journey into the southern hemisphere, amused the young man from Kentucky.

For another five days (1,250 nm), the troop ships with their escorts sailed southwest, reaching Pago Pago Harbor on the south-central side of tiny Tutuila in the American Samoa archipelago. Up until the day Pearl Harbor was attacked, a tiny garrison of Marines had protected the U.S. Naval Station in Pago Pago Harbor. The garrison served as the southern anchor of the Hawaii–Samoa defense line.

Private Bush was one of the tens of thousands of replacements and reinforcements who trained on Tutuila during the war. He hiked up Taro Patch to the range above Pua Pua Village. He took care on night maneuvers over the mountains to not take a wrong turn and step off a cliff. Diarrhea plagued the men.

October 7. Private Bush was assigned to the 1st Raider Battalion. Before his transfer, Major Masters crossed out Military Efficiency, Neatness and Military Bearing, and Intelligence in his Service Record Book, and gave Pvt Bush 5s for Obedience and Sobriety. The next three entries spanning fourteen months would be semi-annual reports, all with high marks across all five characteristics.

Private Bush boarded a troop ship again and departed Tutuila. A day and a half out to sea (392 nm), the ships passed the Tonga Islands. The next day the ship's speakers broadcast: Position, 180°W longitude, the International Date Line, reset all clocks and calendars. Another four days and 1,075 nm passed before Pvt Bush looked from the deck railing and saw the mountain peaks of New Caledonia appearing on the horizon.

The ships finally dropped anchor in Noumea Harbor. Private Bush was 794 nm northeast of Brisbane, Australia; 846 nm north of Auckland, New Zealand; 839 nm south of Guadalcanal; and 992 nm south of New Georgia in the Solomons. The island boasted of fabulous coral reefs, beautiful beaches, starfish, and a vibrant European atmosphere. French inhabitants, with a mix of Melanesians and Polynesians, populated New Caledonia. The maidens were memorable. Private Bush climbed down a cargo net to the waiting transports.

French gendarmes and security forces in their shorts and short sleeve uniforms greeted the new arrivals on the Grand Quai dock. The Marines dressed for combat, carrying their weapons and gear, climbed into the back of 6x6 cargo trucks and rode through Noumea. They whistled and called out to the bare-footed, dark-skinned Melanesian women walking along the streets, dressed in bright-colored, ankle-length dresses and carrying baskets on their heads filled with food or laundry. Arriving at Camp Bailey, the trucks drove past a few corrugated-steel Quonset huts.

Private Bush was a replacement Raider, filling an empty place in 3d Platoon, Company C, 1st Raider Battalion. He and three others organized their gear in a pyramidal tent on a wooden floor, each taking a canvas folding cot and blanket. Sergeants Raymond F. Greenwood, Albert J. Shaheen, and Walter F. Hannon Jr. led 3d Squad at different points in time.

The company took forced marches in full equipment miles up the road to fire their carbines in the hills. Night operations were frequent. Rubber boat training in the lagoon included paddling ashore, deflating and folding the boats, dragging them into the vegetation and hiding them, and camouflaging them with jungle cover. The rubber boat allowed the Raiders to secretly and safely land in areas the enemy would have considered otherwise inaccessible.

Private Bush endured.

He was advised to clean his weapon daily. Jungle rain and mud could make an '03 Springfield inoperative when he might want it to fire. Stretching a prophylactic "rubber" down the rifle barrel end was recommended. He was assigned working details. He played poker and waited for mail call and pay roll and went to the club tent. He watched movies, shot the bull with the chaplain, and listened to wise cracks about earthquake drill. The southern half of New Caledonia had been shaken in March and September, and the Raiders liked joking about the earth getting a cavity at any time and ruining their tropical holiday.

The men were discouraged from fraternizing and consorting with the native women, the "Tonkineese Belles," especially at night in the Kanak villages. Instead, for those who were bored or missing sweethearts at home, there were legal brothels in town for those so inclined. The Pink House was described in tent camp variously as the "famous haven for lost souls" and the "Parisian house of instant happiness." The Marines better knew Bonita House as "No Lick-Lick."

The Raiders who had friends among the Headquarters troops or business with Headquarters Fleet Marine Force went to Camp Goettge on Noumea's outskirts. The campsite was about 100 yards from an excellent beach for relaxing and swimming. When able to get into town, the Raiders socialized in the restaurants, hotels, taverns, and the Red Cross Service Club. The finer old buildings in Centre Ville, like the Hotel de Ville on the Avenue Paul Doumer, seemed a little "off limits," except maybe for field grade officers and above. A favorite site for homebound photos was in front of the Le Monument aux Morts—a war memorial at de la Place Bir Hakeim on Rue Olry.

The French waitresses took a lot of orders for ham sandwiches and the passion fruit juice, the contents of which no one was sure. Record players stood in for "juke boxes." Private Bush's buddies joked that the pidgin English accents of the waitresses outdid his Kentucky accent.

The grunts mixed with the British troops in the soldiers' pubs and joined in with some of their drinking songs. The sentimental favorite might have been "We'll Meet Again/Don't know where/Don't know when," but, the grunts preferred the lewd lyrics of "I don't want to be a soldier/I don't want to go to war. . . . Don't want a bullet up my arsehole/Don't want my bollocks shot away."

Song lyrics, beer, a march back to camp, or a dark night outside the tents could trigger memories of battles and comrades who had taken a real bullet. PFC Charles Paul "Gabby" Gannon, 2d Raiders, would always remember the fighting on Guadalcanal. Sitting in his tent, telling stories among squad members, after a couple of beers a young friend would come to mind.

Private Owen Merton "Little Chick" Barber, 19, a farmer's son from Pana, Illinois, was in Company C. Private Barber was killed in action on November 11, 1942. PFC Gannon could not have known that his friend's death would never leave his memory—even after 35 years had passed.

"He was wounded, captured, castrated, tortured and mutilated . . . I can still hear his screams" [24]

Censored Letters Home

Recovering from wounds, illnesses, and the rigors of combat, writing reports, and attending services for dead and missing comrades, the Raiders wrote letters to family in the States. Most tended to keep the graphic details to a minimal. Anyway, there were things other than combat to write about.

Some 1st Battalion letters spoke of squads adopting mongrel dogs. Other letters included photos of the battalion mascot/pet—a local goat. A corpsman had confiscated some purple dye and painted RAIDER on the animal's side. The goat ate well around the tent camp, fed by any and all passers-by.

Between September 29 and November 20, the two echelons of the 1st Battalion, exchanged places, sailing, to Auckland, New Zealand, for three weeks each of rest and rehabilitation. The smaller 1st echelon embarked aboard the auxiliary personnel assault transport USS *Mormac Port* and arrived at Auckland on October 3. The companies returned to Camp Bailey on October 22.

Private Bush was with the 1st Raiders' 2d echelon embarked aboard the USS *Rixey*, APH-3, on October 18 and arrived back at Noumea on November 20. The R&R had been memorable, quiet and peaceful at times, rip-roaring, wild and woolly at other times; the nights full of dancing, singing, girls, chugging litres of pungent hops, slurping ice cream, and confronting Shore Patrol. It seemed that the smiles might never fade.

While on New Caledonia, Pvt Bush ran into one of his MCRD 884th Platoon boot camp buddies. PFC Clyde J. "Boondocker" Wright Jr. had landed on New Georgia with Company D, 4th Raider Battalion. At Enogai, he had plucked up a Japanese souvenir—an automobile horn that sounded a lot like Donald Duck. [25] The last time the two saw each other, PFC "Boondocker" was "tootin' his own horn."

November 1. Monday, All Saints Day events made it into letters and correspondents' wires to the States. In many combat journals, the day was noted as a "Hectic Day!" The Marines on New Caledonia woke up early and waited for news. At dawn, the 3d Marine Division invaded Empress Augusta Bay on Bougainville Island. Training duties occupied Camp Goettge and Camp Bailey troops.

Noumea Harbor was crowded with ships. Four cargo ships unloaded ammunition and explosives at the Nickel Docks piers located at the southern end of the harbor: SS *Juan Cabrillo*, USS *Cassiopeia* (AK-75), SS *James Buchanan*, and SS *Cape Breton*. At 2:10 PM, a tremendous explosion in the harbor brought all training to a halt and everyone to their battle stations. Was it another Pearl Harbor attack? There were no enemy airplanes over the harbor. Had submarines slipped past the destroyer escorts anchored outside Noumea?

Bright red tongues of flame from the original blast at the Nickel Docks leaped over large parts of the piers. Huge billowing clouds of smoke climbed into the sky, and flying debris hailed down. Hundreds of smaller explosions began. The inferno went on until after 6:30 PM. The ships were moved from their moorings without having sustained serious damage, but the loss of life was staggering. Accounts varied due to the wartime "classified" status of the destruction, but handling of munitions had caused the explosion. About 100 men were either killed or missing and another 100 were wounded. [26]

All Saints Day had turned into a demon of a day.

Christmas 1943. This was the second Christmas Pvt Bush celebrated as a Marine—his first away from the States. Just after the holiday, Lieutenant Colonel Samuel Duncan Puller took command of the 1st Raider Regiment. The competitive nature of the Raiders spread from tent to tent. Their commander was the younger brother of LtCol Lewis "Chesty" Puller, then the 7th Marine Regiment executive officer. "Chesty" was leading Marines at Cape Gloucester, New Britain, and would earn his fourth Navy Cross. The Raiders planned to outfight the 7th Marines and earn honor for their own LtCol Puller.

January 21, 1944. The battalion left New Caledonia aboard the MS *Bloemfontein*. Three days later the companies disembarked at Tassafaronga, on the north side of Guadalcanal. Point Cruz was to the southeast, astride the mouth of the Matanikau River. The tent camp was situated under neat rows of tall, coconut palms, spread along the Iron Bottom Sound on the south side of the channel across from Savo Island. The streets, comprised of sand and gravel, were raised on berms in case of heavy rains. Miles of supply dumps stretched along the coastal road.

The rusting hulks of beached and burned Japanese troop transports and wrecked enemy barges destroyed during the November 30, 1942, naval battle littered the shores near Tassafaronga. When the winds were from the west, the Raiders could hear the artillery battalions training at Cape Esperance on the northwest coast of the island.

The rain fell in torrents. On Guadalcanal, the average annual rainfall was 160 inches. Twenty inches of that average fell in January.

Raider Private Marvin Dean Butterfield, 18, from Glendale, Colorado, joined the same squad with Pvt Bush at Tassafaronga Point, just in time for rain gauge repartee. Private Butterfield had arrived at Camp Geottge in Noumea in September. Private Bush took the "youngster" under his tutelage.

January 30. The Raiders had Sundays off from training. Father Redmond went up and down the rows of tents with a baseball bat, thumping on tent poles, calling out the hour for services. It was best to get out of tent camp early.

Sunday was a time for souvenir expeditions into the bows of the ship relics or along the small tributaries flowing into the Bonegi River or inland on the back-country trails. The swift currents, ear fungus infections, and shark-infested waters ("pagoa, pagoa" to the natives) discouraged casual swimming in the Sound, but shark fins made fine targets for rifle marksmanship drills. When the Raiders were bored, they might also toss some hand grenades into the surf and collect the fish that floated to the top—"lazy man's fishing."

The march of millions of land crabs abandoning their burrows, each with a huge claw held menacingly into the air and scurrying through the tent camps to spawn in the surf, also discouraged any lounging on the beaches during the weeks of their terrestrial migrations.

Far more sobering on clear mid-noon rides on APDs, when the waters were still, was the sight of outlines and hulks of large U.S. Navy ships lying on their sides at the bottom of the Sound with holes in the hulls.

February 1. Once in camp on Guadalcanal, the 1st Raider Battalion was "disbanded" and converted back into an infantry unit. The four battalions of the 1st Raider Regiment were merged and re-designated the 4th Marine Infantry Regiment. The 4th Marines had a proud history. The regiment had garrisoned Shanghai in-between the two World Wars and had gallantly fought on Bataan and Corregidor in the early months of 1942.

Edson's 1st Raiders became the 1st Battalion, with Companies A, B, and C. The 4th Raiders became the 2d Battalion, with Companies E, F, G, and H. The 3d Raiders became the 3d Battalion, with Companies I, K, L, and M. On the Table of Organization, Carlson's 2d Raiders underwent the greatest changes. Their battalion was designated the regimental weapons company. What had been Company D in each of the four battalions now went into the first company in each battalion.

The battalions were no longer considered to be Raiders, but veteran Raiders filled the ranks. Lieutenant Colonel Alan A. Shapley took command of the regiment and shuffled his battalions around. Lieutenant Colonel Samuel Puller served as executive officer. The regiment trained on Guadalcanal.

Private Bush walked past the 1st Battalion, 4th Marine Regiment, area sign every day. The blazing unit motto was HOLD HIGH THE TORCH. Not much changed for him, except that he would meet new friends.

Nicknames Tell a Story

First Lieutenant Lawrence S. Bangser, 22, was assigned as Charlie Company's C.O. He had earned "Bang Away At" Bangser as a nickname. He enjoyed retelling the escapades of playing right guard on the 1st Raider Battalion officer football team. His sergeants liked to tell the details of a six-day patrol on Bougainville, Solomon Islands, November 21–26, 1943.

Attached to Company E, 2d Raider Battalion, 1stLt Bangser volunteered to lead three Marines and three natives on a perilous mission deep into the heart of enemy-held territory. Disembarking fifty miles in the rear of the hostile line, he led the patrol five miles inland through dense jungle and enemy positions and established an observation post twenty-five feet from the main supply road. For more than 24 hours, he collected information about the comings and goings of a large hostile force. Without losing a man, he led his patrol out of the jungle and back to the Raider's base. His men looked up to him as daring, courageous, and unselfish. His commanders made sure he was awarded a Silver Star *For Gallantry in Action*.

Corporal Joseph B. Clark, of Boonville, Indiana, had also picked up a nickname. The men of 3d Platoon called him "Pappy," in part because he smoked a pipe, but more because he had fought in Company C, 4th Marines, on Guadalcanal. Wounded at Enogai Inlet, "Pappy" had been assigned to Company A when he recuperated. On Guadalcanal, he was back with Company C. He and Pvt Bush became good friends. [27]

Private Bush and PFC Hubert Junior Brewington, born in Muncie, Indiana, also became close buddies while on Guadalcanal. PFC Brewington was a year older than Private Bush, but their birthdays were only six days apart. Private Bush celebrated his 19th birthday two days before Christmas 1943. PFC Brewington's 20th birthday was after the holiday, on December 29. One bond the two felt was having that innate character of American men at war to appreciate the ridiculous.

"Advance at your own peril." The Japanese did not always retrieve the bodies of their soldiers from the beaches, fields, craters, and caves where they had died in battles with the Marines. Grunts commonly came upon partially or fully skeletonized Japanese bodies: a reminder of the harsh, cruel, and dehumanizing realities of war. Enemy skulls seemed to be plentiful. As early as September 1942, Marines hung Japanese skulls on tree branches and posts along trails and in bivouac areas with signs underneath. "Danger! Marines ahead. Move Fast!"

During the Pacific War years, newspaper and magazine articles sometimes included photographs of mutilated corpses of Imperial Japanese troops. Ralph Morse, *Life* Magazine war correspondent, was with the Marines on Guadalcanal and had been witness to the destruction and burning of an enemy tank during the fifteen-day Battle of Grassy Knoll, December 18, 1942–January 2, 1943.

When the fire went out, Marines propped up a severed Japanese head, still wearing its helmet, below the tank's gun turret and gun barrel. Ralph's photograph of that event was among those he sent back to Chicago. For 10¢, *Life* readers got a seven-page, pictorial update on the fighting around Henderson Airfield. His article concluded with a stark, full-page image of the skull. The caption: "A Japanese soldier's skull is propped up on a burned-out Jap tank by U.S. troops. Fire destroyed the rest of the corpse." [28]

Although American servicemen faced "stern disciplinary action" if they took the skulls of dead Japanese soldiers as wartime keepsakes, trophies, or souvenirs, the practice was well known in the Pacific theater. It was a familiar sight to any Marine on Guadalcanal.

The fact that the patch on their left shoulder, having evolved from Carlson's Raiders insignia, was a skull in a red diamond bordered by the five white Southern Cross constellation stars on a midnight blue background contributed to their tendency to flaunt and parade enemy skulls.

PFC Brewington was a thin young man when he arrived in the islands, and Raider training had given him an even thinner appearance. One day, he held two enemy skulls up on either side of his head. All present staring at him had to agree that no one could tell Brewington apart from the skulls. From that day forward, he was known as "Skull." [29]

PFC Ken "Mudhole" Merrill got his nickname bantering with the president's son. He was stretched out, taking cover in a depression filled with water. Ol' Jimmy Roosevelt came along checking the lines.

"Merrill what the hell are you doing?" he wanted to know.

"I'm getting a drink, sir."

"Get out of that mudhole!" the commander ordered. That was all PFC Merrill's friends had to hear. The "Mudhole" name never went away.

PFC Howard J. Mann, C/2, had a nickname, too. He carried a "BOYS Rifle," a .55 caliber anti-tank rifle with a five-round magazine of armor piercing shells and a muzzle velocity of 3,000 feet per second. He was deadly accurate out to 200 yards. PFC Mann was known as "Pigiron" on Guadalcanal, maybe because he was crude or because he had a lot of iron in his teeth. He would later serve long-term as Morgan County Sheriff in Colorado.

The Art of Scavenging: Doing More With Less. Generally during the WWII years, the Corps was the last branch considered in budget planning and supply runs. When they did not have what they needed to accomplish a mission, Marines found supplies, or, they charged ahead to their objective doing without. While the Marines have a long history of "doing more than others would, with less," they also have a reputation with the Army and Navy services for getting away with things that had not been issued to them. In fact, sailors thought Marines had some sort of "looting instinct."

The Raiders were particularly adept in nighttime mess hall raids to capture pork chops and steaks and in Slop Chute raids to build up stocks of wine and Ballantine's Scotch Whiskey. Private Bush put some officer insignia on his collars, a court martial offense if caught, "borrowed" a JEEP, and he, PFC Brewington, and a fireteam drove into an Army camp and absconded with some essentials. [30]

Radio Broadcasts

Loud speakers had been installed high in the palm trees around camp to better disseminate daily information and broadcast air raid signals. Notice of some aircraft arrivals expected at Henderson Field brought a sense of home to the island. United Services Organization (USO) shows often traveled to Guadalcanal. Ray Milland and three Hollywood actresses visited in February 1944.

Whenever American forces captured an island, the radiomen arrived. A network of Armed Forces Radio Services (AFRS) stations eventually broadcast in the South Pacific. WVUS Noumea, New Caledonia, was the first.

February 1, 1944. WVUS Noumea began transmitting regular programs. The next month, the American Expeditionary Station AES-Guadalcanal (WVUQ) set up its studio in a plywood structure, a Dallas hut, in a coconut grove a mile from Henderson Field, near the Lunga River, a half-mile from Lunga Beach.

March 13. The radio station first announced itself as AES-Guadalcanal at 5:30 AM, when regular broadcasts started. Other broadcasts travelled the short air waves from AES-Auckland, New Zealand; WVUR Espiritu Santo, New Hebrides; WVUT Nandi, Fiji; WVUV Pago Pago, American Samoa; Navy Radio Tutuila; AES-Munda, New Georgia; AES Bougainville, New Guinea; and WVTI Cebu City and WVTM Manila from the Philippines. [31]

Staff Sergeant George Dvorak operated the AES-Guadalcanal daily morning shift from 5:30 AM to 8:05 AM, and is credited with proclaiming that the station was part of *The Mosquito Network* rather than the American Expeditionary Stations. The name caught on. Technician Fifth Grade-1 (Corporal) Hyman Jack "Hy" Averback had the next shift and handled the 11:00 AM to 1:00 PM programs. Corporal Allen Botzer came on the air at 1:30 PM to broadcast the afternoon's prepared programs, and then announced the evening transmission from 5:00 PM to sign-off at 10:00 PM.

AES-Guadalcanal was on the air 85 hours each week. Fourteen of those hours comprised U.S.-made AFRS transcriptions. Decommercialized U.S. network shows like the *Bob Hope Show, Bing Crosby's Music Hall, Jack Benny, Radio Theater, The Boston* and *NBC Symphonies, Command Performance,* and others flown in from the States took up 28 hours. The weekly *Command Performance* program was especially dedicated to AES-Guadalcanal. Stars like Kate Smith, Randolph Scott, Billy Gilbert, and Jimmy Wakely sent their greetings and encouragements. When Kate sang Irving Berlin's patriotic song *God Bless America*, morale boomed and hearts quickened in time to her stirring rendition. The other half of the station's output was local material—base news and announcements, war correspondence readings, and music.

The entire broadcast staff operated shifts on Sundays during a 12-hour workday when religious programming aired from the Chapel beside the military cemetery near the Tenaru River. Catholic and Protestant church services were rebroadcast later in the day.

"From the fungus-festooned Fern Room, high atop the elegant Hotel DeGink in downtown Guadalcanal, we bring you the dance music of the Quinine Quartet." Some of the programming was innovative and suited Pvt Bush's sense of amusement. Corporal Averback's comedy and music program was particularly entertaining for the troops. He created the character of Tokyo Mose and invented make-believe locations and situations for his show. Background sound effects of a murmuring crowd, women's laughter, and ice tumbling into cocktail glasses accompanied his *Atabrine Cocktail Hour* program—all to encourage the men to take their anti-malarials, even if it turned their skin yellow and their reproductive plumbing sterile.

The loudspeakers brought much laughter around the tents during *McGoo's Booze Hour*. "Next time you visit your PX take home a handy family-size container of *McGoo's Old Man* in the convenient 60-gallon drum."

Armed Forces Radio provided background music as Marines went about their daily routines. By late 1943, many Marines preferred that the broadcasts be switched over to Radio Tokyo (NHK) during the English-language, 75-minute *The Zero Hour* program. The sultry-voiced D.J. gave herself the "Orphan Ann" handle, but U.S. troops in the Pacific Theater preferred to call her "Tokyo Rose." Despite her slanted battle reports, taunting banter, and "sweet propaganda," she liked to play the popular American "big band" sounds of the Shep Fields, Tommy Dorsey, and Glenn Miller orchestras. While she tried to turn young men homesick, spinning song lyrics like "I'll never smile again/Until I smile at you/I'll never laugh again/What good would it do?" into flirtatious rhetoric, the Raiders made light of her persuasions.

Tommy Dorsey and his Orchestra's version of Ruth Lowe's 1939 song, *I'll Never Smile Again*, and *In the Chapel in the Moonlight* and *Twilight Time*, once released, could turn brave men sentimental.

March 8. On Wednesday, Pvt Bush whistled to more than the background music. Lieutenant Colonel Charles L. Banks promoted him to private first class. For pay purposes, his monthly base pay increased to $54: $64.80 for duty outside the States. His new rank would last only two months.

The Battle that Turned Out to be a Drill

Allied forces were closing in around the Japanese base at Rabaul. Commanders drew circles around a chain of islands surrounding the enemy outpost. Emirau was one of the St. Matthias Islands, located 100 miles northwest of Kavieng, New Ireland, in the seas west of New Ireland. It seemed a suitable site for an airstrip to block enemy supplies going to Rabaul.

Emirau was a tiny ribbon of coral island, relatively level and densely wooded, eight miles across east to west. A fringe of mangrove swamp covered the south coast. Surrounded by many small islets and reefs, the highest elevation on the island was 120 feet. Elomusao Islet was 1,500 feet off the eastern tip of the island. Larger Mussau Island was thirteen miles northwest across a channel.

The four 4th Marines battalions had been organizing in the New Guinea province, preparing for the Kavieng campaign as part of a general movement west. Ready for a battle, they were directed to "seize and occupy Emirau at the earliest practicable date, not later than 20 March." Emirau would be the reformed regiment's first combat operation. [32]

March 14. Brigadier General Alfred Houston Noble, 3d Marine Division, commanded the invasion force carried on ten fast transports, protected by nine destroyers. The assault force of nearly 4,000 Marines left in two echelons. Private First Class Bush and the Marines of the two assault battalions, the 1st and 2d Battalions, 4th Marines, travelled on nine high speed transports (APDs) while the remainder of the force sailed on the dock landing ships (LSDs) *Epping Forest*, *Gunston Hall*, and *Lindenwald*, and the attack transport (APA) *Callaway*. One LSD carried the sixty-six LVTs for crossing Emirau's fringing reef, one carried three LCTs, two of them loaded with tanks, and the third carried three LCTs with radar sets and anti-aircraft guns.

Early in the morning, four battleships, two escort carriers, fifteen destroyers, and two small aircraft carriers of the Task Force began a diversionary shelling and bombing of Kavieng.

The attack group arrived in Emirau's transport area at 6:05 AM. The LVTs were launched, and the assault troops transferred to the amphibious tractors using the APDs' boats, supplemented by those from *Callaway*. VMF-218 flew their Vought F4U *Corsairs* overhead to watch for signs of the Japanese on the island.

The assault waves touched ground on schedule. PFC Bush came ashore on the left flank of the southeast beaches with the 1st Battalion. The 2d Battalion was on the right. In reserve, 3rd Battalion's boats grounded on the reef, and the companies waded ashore through knee-deep water.

A small detachment was sent to occupy Elomusao Islet to cover the right flank approaches to Emirau. As the detachment neared the beach, someone reported being under fire. The amphibious tractors and a destroyer opened fire. The islet was silent. The Japanese did not occupy the islet, and there was no fighting.

A "friendly" shell fragment wounded one Marine—PFC Edward Clemens Krisha, 19, Company F, 2d Battalion, from New London, Ohio. His death on Emirau Island was "accidental and did not occur in action against the enemy."

The Marines' landing on Emirau was unopposed. Captain Thomas D. Pollard, in command of Company A, 1st Battalion, wore a distinctive red bandana instead of a helmet once ashore. He had earned a Distinguished Service Cross at Enogai. Lieutenant Joseph L. Deal led one of Company A's platoons. They found no Japanese on the island. "Native Willie #1 Boy" reported that the occupiers had vacated Emirau in January. He believed that a small enemy detachment might remain on Mussau Island.

The APDs and the USS *Callaway* began landing supplies at 11:00 AM. By nightfall, 3,727 Marines and 844 tons of cargo were on the island.

March 21. The hike along the road from the landing beaches to the northern peninsula was a little more than five miles. U.S. Navy Seabees began construction of a fighter and bomber airfield immediately, simply clearing away the topsoil to expose the coral base below for two parallel runways on the Emirau plateau.

March 22. The 1st Provisional Marine Brigade was activated on Guadalcanal with its skeleton headquarters located at Pearl Harbor. The troop strength of the brigade was not immediately available, because the 4th Marine Regiment was occupying Emirau.

March 23. PFC Bush and the Marines patrolled the island confirming that no Japanese remained on Emirau. Marines and Seabees occupied the undefended island. The battalions began to turn the island into a powerful base.

Intelligence reports indicated that an enemy detachment defended fuel and ration dumps on Mussau and a radio station on a nearby island. Destroyers shelled the installations and suspected fortifications. When the assault detachment landed, there were no enemy soldiers ashore. Natives again informed them that the Japanese garrison had days before evacuated in an outrigger canoe and paddled south.

March 27. The USS *Hoel*, DD 533, intercepted Japanese soldiers in a large canoe forty miles south of Mussau. The enemy troops fired on the destroyer with rifles and machine guns. The *Hoel* returned fire. The canoe was destroyed and all occupants killed. The only fighting in the St. Matthias Island Group was over.

The Emirau airfields took shape. The smaller Fighter Strip, called the Inshore Airfield, was on the lower part of the peninsula. The nearby parallel Bomber Strip ran all the way to the end of the upper part of the peninsula, ending at a high cliff jutting out from the island. The bomber strip was designated the Northern Cape Aerodrome.

The two airfields would be operational by May. Captain Joe Foss, Marine Ace from Guadalcanal and MOH recipient, and VMF-115 would fly missions in their F4U *Corsairs* from the smaller airfield to support operations over New Ireland, helping to neutralize Kavieng. The bomber base sent squadrons against long-range targets as distant as the Truk Islands, 600 miles to the north. By the time the fighters and bombers were using the fields, PFC Bush and the 4th Marines were back at Guadalcanal training for an operation that would test their mettle.

April 11. Nearly 18,000 men and 44,000 tons of supplies had been landed on Emirau. The Army's 147th Infantry Regiment relieved the 4th Marines as the garrison's defense force.

April 12. PFC Bush missed it, but the 1st Provisional Marine Brigade troops camped at Tassafaronga wrote home about it. *The Mosquito Network* airtime musical program featured indigenous Solomon Islander choral groups singing their most-liked Anglican hymns and popular non-secular songs. Anyone from Kentucky and Tennessee could appreciate their versions of "Humonderange" and "Cummin round the montan."

April 18. The final echelons of the 4th Marines arrived at Guadalcanal from Emirau. The 22d Marines arrived from Kwajalein. The regiments became part of the 1st Provisional Marine Brigade and began the training cycle for the brigade's assigned mission. For an amphibious assault, the training was significantly shortened.

Retaking Guam

Raider veterans and Pacific islanders had witnessed enough to tell the stories. Private First Class Bush and the 4th Marines battalions readied themselves to avenge their brethren; those who had been captured at the start of the Pacific War; the mistreated and tortured, the executed and beheaded; the servicemen and civilians starving away in enemy POW camps.

West of the International Date Line, the fifteen Mariana Islands form a crescent-shaped archipelago of dormant and active volcanic mountains south-southeast of Japan in the North Pacific Ocean. The islands sit in a central position that dominated the Western Pacific. Saipan in the Northern Marianas was the second largest of the islands and had been a possession of Japan since the end of WWI. Active volcanoes on the ten small islands north of Saipan made them largely uninhabitable. By the start of WWII, Japan had airfields on Saipan and Tinian. These islands were part of the inner defense perimeter guarding the sea routes to Japan.

Guam, largest of the Marianas and the southern-most island of the chain, was a U.S. territory. Thirty miles long and seven to eight miles wide, the island is surrounded by a coral reef, 20 to 500 yards wide. Narrow at the waist, equal northern and southern halves divide the island. The southern half is an 8x16-mile oval, running south to north. The 7x14-mile northern half, projecting to the northeast, is rugged and mountainous. The inland mountains rise to elevations of 600 to 1,200 feet.

The island, a focal point of the Pacific communication network, held strategic importance for the U.S. in 1941. Ships making long trips to the Orient stopped there for fuel. The trans-Pacific cable had a station there. The U.S. Navy operated a radio station at Agana, on the west-central side of the island. Pan American World Airways' clippers on the San Francisco–Manila–Hong Kong flights landed in Apra Harbor, on the southwest, for stopovers. The Standard Oil Company had two oil storage tanks on the island. Surveys and construction plans for airfields on Guam had been ongoing through 1941.

The Marines maintained a small garrison at Sumay Town on Orote Peninsula, between Agana and Agat Town. The situation in the Pacific was obviously volatile, and Washington, D.C., ordered U.S. Naval Captain George Johnson McMillin, the Guam Governor headquartered in Agana, to evacuate all dependents. The last U.S. civilians departed Guam on October 17, 1941.

Lieutenant Colonel William K. MacNulty stayed with five other officers, one warrant officer, and 118 enlisted Marines. Lieutenant Colonel MacNulty had earned a Silver Star for gallantry during the WWI Battle of the Argonne Forest in France, and a Navy Cross on February 27, 1928, commanding a 57th Company, Second Battalion, 11th Regiment, patrol against bandits in Nicaragua.

On Sunday, December 7, the Christian people of Guam prepared for a holy day of obligation. The next day was the Feast of the Immaculate Conception and a big holiday for the whole island. Monday, at 4:45 AM, Captain McMillin received a cable alerting him to the Pearl Harbor attack.

Japanese planes flying in formation of threes departed Saipan and began dropping bombs on Sumay at 8:27 AM on December 8. The USS *Penguin*, Minesweeper #33, the largest U.S. Navy vessel at the island, steamed out of Apra Harbor, was bombed and strafed off Orote Point, and then scuttled. Air attacks all over the island went on until 5:00 PM.

The bombers returned at daylight on Tuesday. The Marines left their barracks with '03 Springfield rifles and mounted .30 caliber machine guns. They fortified positions in the rifle range butts on the Marine Reservation, waiting for the anticipated assault. The Japanese forces came on Wednesday.

An enemy heavy cruiser, four destroyers, twelve troop transports, four gunboats, five sub chasers, a minesweeper squadron, and auxiliary ships surrounded Guam in the dark of morning on December 10. Flares illuminated the skies over Dungcas Beach, at Tumon Bay above Agana, at 4:00 AM. A 400-man landing party from Saipan came ashore and engaged in a firefight with the eighty men of the Insular Force Guard (native police) in the Agana plaza. Twenty-one Native Chamorros and military personnel were killed and many others wounded.

A reinforced enemy brigade of 5,500 men landed on the beaches below Agat and moved north to take on the Marines on Orote. The Marines valiantly resisted the invasion force, but Captain McMillin measured the odds of battling the enemy's superior numbers. Rather than endanger the native civilian lives by holding out, he ordered the garrison to surrender at 5:45 AM and surrendered Guam to the Japanese naval commander just after 6:00 AM.

Thirteen Marines were killed in the attack and thirty-seven were wounded. The well-armed enemy force quickly spread out and had control over the entire island.

The enemy evacuated the Marines and Navy members from the garrison on January 10, 1942, sending them to mainland Japan prison camps, an oppressive three-day journey in the holds of the *Argentina Maru*.

One official listing of 486 Guam POWs included: LtCol MacNulty, six of his officers and 112 enlisted men (four died as prisoners) from the Marine Barracks, Sumay Detachment;

one Marine officer and twenty-eight enlisted men from the Insular Guard Patrol (two died in prisoner camps); 131 Navy officers and enlisted sailors (seven died in prisoner camps), nine Navy doctors, five female nurses, and fifty-five enlisted pharmacist mates; thirty-one civilian employees (one died a prisoner), seventy contractors (three died in prisoner camps); twenty-two local Guam civilians (two died as prisoners); thirteen clergy; and one civilian wife, her newborn daughter, and a civilian dentist. [33]

Guam and the Southern Marianas became part of the outer zone of the Japanese homeland defense.

May 9, 1944. Promotions served as an indication of "time in grade," solid field performance, and proven leadership. Promotions also served as a reminder of men who had held the rank before. And, as all things in the Corps, promotions could be gist for rancor or humor. On Pacific islands, rising in rank was due to another reality: "not due to my ability, but those other fellows kept knocking off people above me." [34]

Private First Class Bush was told to sew another stripe on his uniform. He was promoted to corporal by order of LtCol John T. Rooney. One good thing was that his monthly base pay went to $66.00: increased to $79.20, because he was overseas. This "time in grade" would be the longest of his career.

For reasons now forgotten, CPL "Pappy" Clark took to calling CPL Bush the "Sheriff of Tassafaronga Creek." One rendition was that Pappy's friend was good about "policing up" the squad's area and bringing the men to order. Another version might have derived from an adolescent's tale CPL Bush had told comrades. There was no question that he was a high-spirited young man. Scuttlebutt was that he had been grabbed up by a Kentucky sheriff for some indiscretion back home and was given the choice to enlist in the service or go to jail. [35] Corporal Bush called CPL Clark the "Mayor of Tassafaronga."

May 12. The Commanding General, Forward Areas South Pacific, allotted an area near Cape Esperance on Guadalcanal to TF-53. Final pre-rehearsal training of the attack force sea and land elements commenced. Each combat team and its supporting transport division had three days of ship-to-shore exercises and landing techniques practice.

May 19. On Friday, air support activities in combination with more regimental landings began and continued into Saturday. Two more days of combined air and NGF operations, using live bombs and ammunition, followed. The preliminary exercises for the two attack groups were completed on Monday. [36]

May 22. In the evening, TG 53.1 sortied from Guadalcanal and Tulagi with the 3d Division (the Northern Attack Group) embarked and travelled all night in the approach formations planned for Guam. The group arrived off the Cape Esperance practice-landing beach at 6:00 AM, and the troops started to disembark. LVTs loaded with men and assault equipment crawled down LST ramps into the water and started toward the beach. NGF and air began firing on the landing area. The first waves moved ashore, and the tractors returned to a predetermined point to transfer troops and equipment from landing boats. Once ashore, the regiments completed the operation plan maneuvers.

May 25. The second phase of the rehearsal started. The Southern Attack Group, following the Agat landing plan with the brigade and corps artillery embarked, made a "dry run" assaulting the Esperance beach. Corporal Bush led his team ashore. The ships returned to Tassafaronga, and the brigade shore party rehearsed unloading supplies and setting up dumps just as they would on Guam.

W-Day for STEVEDORE was confirmed as June 18. Phonetically, June 18 was William-Day—easier to radio and write in log entries as W-Day

Operation STEVEDORE

June 4. The faster transport and support groups departed and joined the LST group at Kwajalein on June 8.

June 15. As Task Force-53 sailed toward Guam, progress of the Pacific War was broadcast over ship radios. The assault divisions of VAC landed on Saipan, the northern-most big Mariana Island. The 2d Marine Division and 4th Marine Division assault waves hit the southwestern beaches near Charan Kanoa.

June 16–25. The ferocity of the Saipan battle was evident in the casualty reports being wired. W-Day for the Guam assault was cancelled, and TF-53 was directed to steam toward Saipan. For a week, CPL Bush and the Marines of Operation STEVEDORE advanced and retired 150 to 300 miles eastward of Saipan and Guam, acting as a floating reserve in case the Marines and soldiers battling on Saipan needed to be reinforced. Enemy bombers attacked several LSTs in the convoy.

The shipboard grunts reasonably wanted the gouge about the monotonous delay. Word reached them about the initial three brutal days of the Charan Kanoa beaches assault. More than 5,000 casualties had been suffered. Sixty-eight Marines were on the MIA rosters, fifty-nine of them lost on the first day. Two men from Kentucky, CPL Andrew E. Kearney Jr. of Rt. 6 in Lexington, Fayette County, and PFC Bernard D. Sloan from 1605 13th Street in Ashland, Boyd County, were both on the missing rolls.

June 30. The situation on Saipan was more in hand, and the Southern Attack Group was released from the floating reserve. The troops had spent a month at sea. They were not "fresh" for an amphibious beach assault. The ships proceeded east to Eniwetok Atoll. The grunts struggled to fight off the lethargy that builds in extended ship-board voyages.

Once the transports anchored in Eniwetok's lagoon, commanders set up a regular schedule of landings, which enabled troops to move ashore and regain their land legs. Some units employed debarkation arrangements that would be used at Guam. The men always disembarked and came back on board over cargo nets. On the many sand spits in the lagoon, troops participated in small-unit tactics and engaged in various forms of daily calisthenics and athletics. In the evening, back on board the ships, boxing matches and movies helped the Marines to relax. The rest, exercise, and training had them in good physical condition for an island assault.

Corporal Bush found sleep to be evasive. All day long, the tropical sun turned the steel ship decks into convection plates. The lower troop compartments broiled. Doc Eller was busy treating heat rash and skin infections. He advised the men of 3d Platoon to bed down "topside" under the night sky. Corporal Bush did his best to keep his team motivated for an amphibious assault.

Admiral Richard Lansing Conolly ordered some briefings. Intelligence reported on the enemy situation on Guam. The Japanese were waiting in force and their defenses were formidable. The weathermen recounted that the Guam climate tended to be pleasant, with a high temperature that varied little from a constant 87°F. The prevailing trade winds kept the southern beaches awash in surf. The average annual rainfall on Guam was a total of 90 inches; two-thirds of that falling from July to November, when it rained twenty to twenty-five days every month. A greater concern was that they were already at the start of typhoon season. The southern and westward storms could produce swells that made for rough landing conditions on the western beaches. Roads would become quagmires hampering military operations.

Forecasters predicted favorable weather for July 21. Admiral Conolly confirmed that date as W-Day. He set H-Hour for 8:30 AM.

July 9. The Marines reported Saipan secured. The inner defensive ring of the Japanese homeland had been penetrated. The long, prelanding bombardment started on Guam in the outer zone of the enemy's defense.

July 15. The transport and tractor groups of TF 53 made ready to depart from Eniwetok. Screened by a host of destroyers, gunboats, mine sweepers, patrol craft, and submarine chasers, the LST's left the anchorage. Two days later, CPL Bush got under way. The escort carrier group covering units accompanied the attack force transports.

First Lieutenant William Howard Carlson, 29, Company C, 1st Battalion, was an ordained Methodist minister in civilian life. He found a tight space on his crowded LST deck to conduct an informal church service en route to Guam.

July 20. By afternoon, W-minus-1, all *Stevedore* forces were either in position or approaching on schedule. The assault forces had been on the convoy LSTs for sixty days. For CPL Bush and all the Marines who had joined as replacement troops yet tested in battle, this would be very different from the landing on Emirau.

The Southern Assault

July 21. The TF 53 troop ships moved into their positions in the transport area under cover of darkness on Friday. Astute war correspondents wrote about an American characteristic that emerged in hard times. Scripps-Howard newspaper writer Ernie Pyle witnessed it and experienced it himself no matter where he traveled among American servicemen in combat circumstances.

"You laugh at some very sad things in wartime." [37]

Father Paul Redmond held a service on the deck of the 1st Battalion's LST. PFCs Kenneth Fried, Harold P. Loeffel, and Howard R. Schultz had never attended a service, but thought it might be a good way to start out an invasion day. The Padre was known to give his Catholics their last rites before an assault. The three men were unsure whether they should take that as an act of humor or a serious premonition. The good Father did not answer their question and sent them on their way.

All assault units were in their assigned areas by 6:00 AM. LSTs carrying the assault LVTs and DUKWs (amphibious trucks) moved into launching areas and lowered their ramps. Naval gunfire and bomber and fighter plane strikes commenced. The LVTs went waterborne, rendezvoused, and circled. The morning sky turned clear and bright.

Merging with the rumbling bombardment sounds as the Leathernecks lumbered over the side, down the cargo nets, and into landing vehicles, the *Marines Corps Hymn* played over ship loudspeakers.

The assault waves formed behind LCI(G)s and LVT(A)s and started toward the shore at 7:40 AM. The naval gunfire increased, sending a steady stream of shells screaming overhead the landing craft. A tremendous rocket barrage erupted on all the beaches. The gunboats opened fire with 20mm and 40mm guns as they neared the reef. Smoke and dust turned the sky hazy.

The assault waves moved across the line of departure. Ahead, a black pall obliterated all views of the landing beaches. The pre-assault shelling had obliterated Agat Village in front of the 22d Marines on the left flank of YELLOW 1.

At 8:22 AM, eight minutes before the assault troops were to land, the Task Force ships unleashed a devastating barrage of naval gunfire on the immediate beach areas. The large caliber shelling continued until the landing waves were 1,200 yards from shore, then lifted and moved inland. The 5-inch shelling continued until the LVT(A)s started across the reef.

The well-organized enemy shore defenses consisted of numerous pillboxes built in coral outcroppings and large, concrete blockhouses covered in mounds of sand and concealed in palm tree groves. The Japanese began hitting the approaching assault waves with brutal mortar and artillery fire as the LVTs crawled across the reef.

In the south, LtCol Shapley's 4th Marines were to establish a beachhead and protect the brigade's right flank. The LVTs passed beside Alutom Island and crossed lines of reefs all the way to Beach WHITE 2. Enemy opposition increased immediately after they crossed the reef. Enemy 75mm field pieces and a 37mm gun enfiladed the beaches. Mortars, antiboat guns, and artillery scored direct hits on LVTs.

The scheme of maneuver called for the 1st and 2d Battalion to land and drive inland, while the 3d Battalion waited in reserve. As the advance moved ahead, extending the zone of action, the 3d Battalion (less one company) would work in on the right, next to the beach.

Plans calling for LVTs to move 1,000 yards inland before discharging troops were abandoned. The two assault battalions landed abreast, and the platoons scrambled ashore on all beaches one minute later.

Two of Major Bernard W. Green's 1st Battalion assault companies came ashore in front of Mount Alifan at 8:33 AM. Corporal Bush with Company C, initially in reserve, stayed afloat.

Enemy small-arms fire intensified, and casualties were heavy on the beaches. Bodies of the dead and wounded began piling up. Company A, on the right, had to overtake pillboxes before starting across the open fields at the foot of Mount Alifan. Company B advanced rapidly inland against light resistance moving 1,000–2,000 yards by 10:30 AM.

Company A, PFC Paul M. Carroll had flamethrower tanks on his back, and a sniper quickly took aim on him. He heard and felt the slug go past him, and he dove to the deck. He got up and charged ahead again. Another "zing" sent him to the deck. He finally dove into a shell crater, soon joined by PFC Duane R. "Oscar" Overass, a 60mm mortarman. An enemy machine gun held them both under fire. Neither was hit. "But we sure were petrified!" [38]

When the attack had progressed 700 yards, Company C transferred from the Higgins boats into the Amphibious Tractors at the reef line and landed on White Beach. Corporal Bush rolled over the side of the Amtrac, watching out for shell craters. At the water's edge and up the beach, he could see Amtracs that had been blown apart by mines. Marine corpses floated in the surf and littered the beach. Third Platoon passed the bodies drifting in the water and the ones in parts on the beach—some torsos without heads or limbs.

Nambu machine-gun rounds glanced off the disabled Amtracs. The ground was all cratered and minced up. Mines on top of 500-pound bombs were scattered about the beach. The shredded stumps of coconut trees provided some cover if a grunt crawled flat on the ground. There was no shade. Ahead was a half-mile of low brush and a few coconut trees. Then, the coral began the incline up Mount Alifan.

Sergeant Albert Shaheen, a 3d squad leader, led the point of his platoon along the beach. PFC Robert M. Snider and PFC John A. Shelton were in the same fireteam and behind him. The heavy enemy mortar and rifle fire stopped the platoon's advance. Sergeant Shaheen crawled within hand grenade range of a hostile emplacement. He rushed forward firing his automatic rifle and silenced the position. Having watched his inspiring actions, his squad continued to lead the platoon in the advance.

The company moved inland into the sword grass plain, swung right, and crossed a defile where a small stream emptied into the ocean. Enemy 90mm mortar crews on Mount Alifan fired barrage rounds. Moving up the incline, the Marines ran into enemy trenches and pillboxes between Bangi Point and Hill 40. The hill dominated the road paralleling the beach north into Agat.

The Japanese strongly defended the prominent terrain feature. They had a trench system dug into the coral from the hill to the beaches. The positions on the hill gave the enemy clear lines of fire to enfilade the beaches.

Company C crept ahead under fire. A deadly stream of fire from the well-concealed machine guns halted their advance. Platoon Sergeant John O. Casdorph Jr., 22, and PFC Morton Gottlieb, 20, were killed. [39]

Major Green called for two Company A tanks. The Marine Shermans closed in and fired point blank into the positions. The attack advanced and Company C captured Hill 40.

Charlie Company Sergeant Francis S. Scheffer, 25, from South Lyon, Michigan, was KIA on the casualty roster. First Squad, 3d Platoon, PFC Francis J. Maloughney, 21, and PFC Merton Clyde Revak, 18, were both KIA. Father Redmond prayed over the burial plots.

Second Battalion PFC Allen Eugene Rolette from Blue Island, Iowa, had starred on his high school football squad his junior year and had been sports editor of the school newspaper. He had enlisted on March 31, 1943, right after graduating with his class and had joined the Raiders. PFC Rolette, 20, was missing.

First Lieutenant Larry Bangser was wounded in the fighting, hit in the chest—"got his tit shot off"—and he was sure mad about it. He returned to duty. PFC Robert C. Upham was also WIA.

As planned, the 4th Marines had established a beachhead on the brigade's right flank. The reserve 3d Battalion arrived ashore, and relieved the 1st Battalion. Company K took over Hill 40 and Bangi Point. All the units were in position to resume the attack to seize O-1. The assault elements jumped off at 1:45 PM, making satisfactory progress against scattered resistance.

Company B, 1/4, established a roadblock on Harmon Road on the regiment's left flank by 5:30 PM. The 2d Battalion, 22d Marines was in sight across a deep gully on their left, but not physically tied in. From Harmon Road, the regiment's lines bent back around Alifan's lower slopes to Hill 40 and on to the beach.

Nightfall on Objective Line-1

Company C went into reserve near the regimental CP with orders to be prepared to move out during what was to be a sleepless night.

Before nightfall, CPL Bush dug a foxhole deep enough to be able to comfortably lay on his back without his knees sticking up above the protective bank he had built with the excavated soil and coral.

When they moved about in the dark, the squad fastened ropes to each man so as not to get lost. The squad shared whatever pogie bait each had left over from home. It was too early in the campaign for a canteen cup of "raisinjack." The brew was made from fermented dried fruits and sugar, a collection of C-, J-, and K-rations, with yeast added to the mix. Percolating under a poncho, it turned into an alcoholic beverage with a strong kick. The suggested ration was half a canteen cup, always before 3:00 PM.

A check of the 1st Provisional Marine Brigade lines at 6:30 PM identified the situation inland of the Yellow and White beaches: 350 casualties, critical fuel and ammunition shortages. The bodies of seventy-five 22d Marines had been counted on YELLOW Beach 2 alone.

The combat-experienced Marines, anticipating violent Japanese counterattacks, prepared night defenses. Front line observers requested illumination throughout the harrowing first night. Artillery registered in normal barrages.

Enemy grenades did not always land by surprise. The Japanese armed their grenades by striking the arming button against their helmets. Ten seconds passed from click, "pop" of the activated fuse, to detonation. Never knowing where the explosive might be tossed, Marines watched for their glint in the dim light of the night flares.

At 11:30 PM, the Japanese probed all along the front. At midnight, an intense mortar barrage came down on the 4th Marines right flank as the enemy made a first attempt to penetrate the brigade lines. A battalion of Japanese, 750 men, charged against the front lines in waves, hooting and hollering, tossing demolition charges and small land mines. Six Marines died—bayoneted in their foxholes—before the attack was repulsed.

Streaks of red flew over CPL Bush's foxhole as the ships fired Naval Gun support. Smoke billowed into the night sky. Enemy tanks in flames added light around the mountain. He fixed his bayonet to his rifle. The air wafting toward him had the smell of cordite and sulphur. Soon would come the scent of burning flesh and bloodied soil.

PFC Harry L. Forbes, Company C, was seriously wounded on Mount Alifan near Harmon Road. He lay in the dark until Saturday morning when the corpsmen picked him up. He was evacuated and would spend fourteen months in hospitals. [40]

The USS *Indianapolis* fired up flares and star shells close to the beach until radioing at 1:00 AM that she was out of flares. The Marines called from one foxhole to the next, accounting for each other. Casualties were left where they lay, waiting for sunup evacuations.

The next attack hit 1stLt Martin J. "Stormy" Sexton and his Company K, 3/4, platoon on Hill 40 at 1:00 AM. The situation became tenuous. The enemy rolled grenades into the trenches. A Japanese officer killed a corpsman and a Marine with his sword, then, was killed with his sword when a Marine took it from him. The Company K platoon was forced to withdraw. The men reorganized at the foot of the hill, counterattacked, recaptured the lost ground, and were driven back a second time. First Lieutenant Marvin C. Plock led two Headquarters Company squads of reinforcements, and the determined Marines took back the hill.

At 2:30 AM, Marines holding the line near a reservoir northwest of Mount Alifan readied themselves. The rumble of truck motors and tank treads grinding the limestone shale preceded the Banzai screams. Enemy mortars and artillery hit. Under the light of flares, tanks and truck-mounted guns and shadowy troops charged ahead. The Marine line held. Small enemy groups infiltrated at various points, accomplishing little more than harassment.

A coordinated counterattack hit both 1st Battalion flanks at 2:30 AM. On the left, four enemy tanks lumbered up Harmon Road toward Company B's roadblock at 2:30 AM, followed by guns mounted on trucks and infantry. Private First Class Bruno Oribiletti, 23, a bazooka man, met the column head-on, took out two Japanese tanks, and stopped the breakthrough before enemy fire from a third tank killed him.

On the right flank, under cover of a heavy mortar barrage and supported by machine guns, the enemy surged through a draw toward the Company A lines. The fighting was fierce. An officer carrying a flag on a bamboo pole led shouting men swinging Samurai swords and throwing hand grenades. Some of the enemy closed within 400 yards of the beach, almost to the artillery positions. The Marine artillerymen halted the attack.

Company K took the brunt of a third assault on Hill 40 at 3:30 AM when its position was overrun in a banzai attack. Private First Class Rudolph G. "Rudy" Rosenquist, 19, was bayoneted in the left side, abdomen, and lower chest. He was hit in the head and took a gunshot wound in his right leg. His right hand was injured, and he took multiple shrapnel wounds in both legs. [41]

The Navajo Code Talkers bravely handled the stretcher details. Private Rosenquist was evacuated to Base 8 Hospital, Honolulu, and weighed only 98 pounds when he could finally stand without help.

The enemy could not dislodge Company K from Hill 40.

In the morning, CPL Bush moved about his men's positions to account for their whereabouts. They watched as squads along the line did the same thing.

Marines were found dead, their lives ended by grenades that had been rolled into their foxholes. The Imperial soldiers who had crawled to the foxholes were also there, usually with fatal rifle shots to the head. Forty-five enemy soldiers were dead on the hill. Another 345 Japanese bodies littered the ground and ditches around the base of the hill; more than 200 of those were in front of the right flank lines.

Casualties reduced the roster of one Company A platoon to four men. Second Lieutenant Lee Neil Minier, 27, was dead. Since the regiment had no replacements available, Company A continued the Guam campaign with only two platoons.

W-Day proved fatal for several 1/4 lieutenants who had been gridiron stars. Three were KIA on the next morning's rosters. Company A had lost two. Second Lieutenant Max Belko, 30, had been an All-American center and tackle for the University of Southern California *Trojans* and was designated right halfback for the Guam football team. Second Lieutenant Charles R. McAllister, 24, Princeton Class of 1942, had been the left guard on the *Tigers'* team and relished in recounting the standout play of his teammates Dave Allerdice and Bob Peters during the four-year winning streak over their rival Yale *Bulldogs*. [42] Company B lost 1stLt Roger Eastman Smith, 23 years old, a former Middle Tennessee State University student body Class of 1942 president and a football standout.

Before departing to Guam, 2dLt Belko had laughed with friends "Our football days are behind us," he said. "Of course, we could take our scrapbooks to Guam with us, but I don't think the Japanese would be impressed." He had led 3d Platoon up a hill, 100 yards inland from the landing beaches. Tall grass and vegetation covered the area around the hill, and the enemy kept popping up from their hiding places. A sniper fired up the hill, hitting 2dLt Belko. He fell onto his back, instantly dead.

Corporal William "Chief" Dae (Native American) killed the sniper and his spotter. Corporal John Loomis, 27, was nearby. His admiration for the lieutenant had begun before they landed together on Guam. Max had been his football coach at Arroyo High School in California, and they had often enjoyed lunch together at John's home.

The Navy Department did its best to notify the families of Marines killed on W-day before the War Department released Casualty Lists of KIAs to newspapers. Included among the 4th Marines initially buried in Cemetery Guam #2 near Agat were: Corporal Niels Peter "Pete" Nielsen, 19; PFC Clyde Alva Campbell, 22; PFC Robert Fred Engel, 20, 2d Battalion; PFC John W. Holley Jr., 20; PFC Philip Wilfred Jones, 29; PFC Edward T. Luedtke, 20; PFC Theodore V. Lyons, 19, from Cleveland, Ohio; PFC Francis T. Maloughney, 21; PFC Rolland Eugene Pryor, 19, E Company, 2nd Battalion; PFC Paul E. Reiber, 20; PFC Charles Irvin Simmers, 20; PFC Alvin Fredric Wachlin, 22, Company A, 1st Battalion; PFC Robert Conrad Wallis, 19; PFC Ray Wilson, 21; and Pharmacist's Mate Third Class Oscar Klause.

Muster rosters listed other Marines who were not interred in the Guam cemetery.

Before he had enlisted, PFC James Howard Batts, 21, lived at 204 Elm Street in Eminence, Henry County, east of Louisville, with his father, Raymond Batts. Life had had its challenges. His mother died when he was a boy, his father had troubles with alcohol, and James had lived a good part of his boyhood with his grandparents, Ben and Joanna Batts. When his father died at home on May 7, 1943, PFC Batts was stationed in San Diego waiting to join M Company, 3d Raider Battalion. He went to war an orphan without siblings and was last seen near Agat Village on Guam. His body was never recovered or identified. The notifications went to his Uncle Carlisle Batts, in Eminence. His one cousin, Marian, a couple of years older than he was, would always believe that James was buried somewhere on Guam.

In addition to PFC Rolette and PFC Batts, also missing from the 4th Marines on the first day of the assault, bodies not recovered, were: Corporal David W. Lewis, 29; Corporal Joe Stepan; PFC Russell W. Brubaker, 22; PFC Leonard J. Gorzalski, Company H, 2d Battalion; PFC Robert E. Swanson; PFC Robert Conrad Wallis, 18.

Missing from the 22d Marines: Corporal Edward L. Boozer; Corporal Evert L. Finlay; PFC Albert J. Bouckart; PFC Roy E. Gross.

Missing from the 1st Provisional Marine Brigade troops: PFC William S. McNary; PFC James H. Ramsey; PFC Nelson C. Tudor.

From the 3d Marine Division landing in the north, one second lieutenant, a master gunny sergeant, a sergeant, two corporals, seven PFCs, and two privates, most of them from the 3d Marine Regiment, were missing in action.

✳✳✳

In the north, CPL Bush's fellow Kentuckian earned a Medal of Honor dealing with an enemy grenade during the first day and night ashore on Guam. His actions provide an example of what a Marine might do when finding himself alone in the proximity of a grenade.

Private Luther Skaggs Jr., 21, from Henderson, on the Ohio River, in the northwest corner of the state, served as a section squad leader with King Company, 3d Battalion, 3d Marines. His section leader was taken out of action by mortar fire shortly after landing under the Chonito Cliffs. Private Skaggs took command of the 81mm mortar section, supporting his unit's attack. He led them across 200 yards of beach scathed by machine-gun fire. Into the night, he effectively directed the fire of the mortar section. Despite critical wounds, he led his men in repulsing several strong enemy counterattacks.

During one of the engagements, an enemy hand grenade was hurled into his fox-hole and exploded. With the lower part of one of his legs shattered, PFC Skaggs quickly fashioned a tourniquet and applied it to the injury. He then propped himself up in his foxhole and for the next eight hours fought off the enemy incursions with his rifle and hand grenades.

PFC Skaggs did not call out for assistance, nor hamper the defense of the beachhead by taking others away from their positions. Instead, in the light of the morning on July 22, he crawled to the rear himself to continue the fight from there until the Asan-Adelup beachhead was secure.

✳✳✳

July 22. On Saturday, W-Day+1, the brigade in the south prepared to forge ahead to the Final Beach Line (FBL), as swarms of big, green blow flies fed on enemy carcasses. Corporal Bush joined his fireteam around a small fire to drink coffee and eat his C-ration breakfast.

The 4th Marines had orders to advance and seize the Mount Alifan massif, then extend along the top of the ridge south toward Mount Taene rising east of Mango Point. The regiment started across the foothills toward Alifan's steep slopes at 9:00 AM, immediately encountering a well-entrenched enemy in coconut log bunkers.

Numerous little rounded hills rose from the northern side of the ridge, offering the enemy effective positions for enfilade fire from the reverse slopes. Caves honeycombing the hills provided shelter for machine-gun teams. Marine demolition teams sealed the caves, and hand grenades took out the log bunkers. After that, only scattered resistance met the forward elements moving up the narrow trails.

Having helped secure the Agat Beachhead, Company C was tasked to take the high ground on Mount Alifan. From the beach, their destination was a one-mile, straight-line distance. First Lieutenant Bangser led the company up the mountain in a single file column, zig zagging through the dense brush, repulsing direct enemy attacks and sniper fire. The Marines trudged slowly upward.

The terrain grew worse when the advance neared the mountaintop. The undergrowth covering the almost vertical cliff sides was snarled and thorny. The thick roots of pandanus trees sprawled across the paths and hampered all upward progress. Large, entwined vines grabbed at the men's equipment. Packs and any excess gear were soon shed along the trail. Fortunately, the Japanese had not been able to prepare adequate defenses.

Second Lieutenant William A. Kerr led an 81mm mortar platoon from the 1st Battalion Weapons Company to the summit of Alifan and found no enemy. Since the position was indefensible, he returned the patrol to the foothills.

Company C reached the top at 2:00 PM, having taken a three-mile hike up the mountain path. Corporal Bush dug in. Chow and nightfall were not far off.

Besides fighting off the enemy, the grunts and the corpsmen dealt with the unbearable jungle heat, the stench of decomposing enemy bodies, swarms of flies, food shortages, explosions of all sorts, disfigured and mutilated bodies of comrades, and skin yellowed by atabrine tablets to prevent malaria.

The brigade defensive line stretched from north of the Ayuja River, along the high ground northeast of Harmon Road to Alifan, continuing southwest along the ridgeline toward Mount Taene, and curving to the sea until anchored on Magpo Point. The enemy tried to infiltrate at various points along the lines during the night, but no penetration occurred. The large-scale counterattacks expected from Harmon Road and Orote Peninsula did not happen.

The 4th Marines reported only a few casualties on the second night ashore. One of those was PFC Harry A. Vittori, 21, Company A, 1st Battalion, who died from wounds received in the day's action. [43]

July 23. At daybreak, Sunday morning, the 4th Marines advanced rapidly and completely occupied the O-2 line by 10:20 AM. During the morning, the 22d Marines found the enemy falling back and putting up only scattered resistance. In the afternoon, the 4th Marines continued advancing north, and the front lines tried to swing across the neck of Orote Peninsula.

Some sights on Guam would never be forgotten, never erased from recollection. The men stopped the remembering when they could, admitting, "I will stop remembering now, as it hurts TOO MUCH." [44]

PFC Donald B. Heffron, PFC Robert W. "Bobby" Ball, and PFC Frank T. Fash were close buddies in Company A, 1/4. PFC Ball was a company runner. PFC Heffron found him on Sunday, pinned to the ground with a 2x2 stake driven through his chest and into two feet of soil. His arms and legs were twisted grotesquely and his eyeballs were lying out on his cheeks. PFC

Heffron, himself wounded, would never forget the sight of how his friend had died and would never let himself stop hating the enemy he had faced on Guam.

Intense enfilade fire from a series of small hills surrounded by rice paddies hit the assault units. The enemy had organized each hill as an excellently defended strong point providing mutual support to each other.

Troops sank hip-deep in the mushy ground as they tried to attack the hills. Making matters worse, enemy observers in the Northern Landing Force objectives area along the Mount Chachao, Mount Alutom, and Mount Tenjo chain and in the smaller Cotal and Inalas hills called in reports of the Marine movements. Mortars and artillery rounds from Orote and the Mount Tenjo area pounded the assault companies.

Marine tanks moved forward through levelled Agat Village to knock out the enemy hill positions. The soft rice fields hindered their maneuvering, so they tried the road approaches. Enemy antitank weapons knocked one tank out of action for the day. Another tank tracked over a mine, sustaining only minor damage.

It was hot. Mosquitos overran the dense, brushy swamp between Agat and the peninsula. Enemy machine-gun positions, hidden in the thick brush that covered the hills, waited for the advancing Marines and fired with random.

Company A, 1st Battalion, lost PFC Thomas H. Priest, 25, killed in action. Private Ervin Walter Harmer, 21, H&S Company, was KIA. PFC Harry L. Forbes, Company C, was seriously wounded. He and radioman Charles Y. Begay, Navajo Code Talker, returned to the States on the same hospital ship. [45]

At nightfall, the Southern Landing Force units reported that all the dominating terrain overlooking Orote Peninsula in its area of responsibility was in hand. After Marines had liberated an enemy Sake cache, they shared swigs from bottles of rice beer. To break up the monotony of C-rations, they passed around cans of mandarin oranges and canned fish.

The order for Monday's assault on Orote went to the 4th Marines after midnight. The brigade's W+3 attack was set to jump-off from the rice paddy edges at 9:00 AM.

July 24. The grunts slept fitfully under the swaying light of illumination rounds. In the morning at 8:30 AM, commanders ordered the attack delayed to extend the naval gunfire barrage on Orote for a half hour. Another delay was ordered at 9:30 AM to allow an additional thirty-minute barrage. The regiments started the simultaneous assault at 10:00 AM.

PFC Merle John Stowe, 20, and PFC James E. Hart, a machine gunner, were killed in action.

Relief of the 4th Marines was completed at 3:00 PM. The southern beachhead was firmly established. Four days and nights of continuous fighting had greatly fatigued the troops, but the brigade had the enemy bottled-up on Orote Peninsula.

The operation plan for July 25 ordered the brigade to assault Orote Peninsula and move to Objective Line-3. The brigade commander requested a day's delay for the assault to give his two regiments a day's rest. Authorization to delay the attack until Wednesday at 7:00 AM was radioed early in the evening.

During the enemy's first attempt to penetrate 2d Battalion's lines that night, PFC Charles F. Ringgold, 19, was seriously wounded while countering the attack with his machine-gun squad. In the quiet afterwards, he crawled to the rear for medical treatment. Sufficiently bandaged in his opinion, he voluntarily returned to the flank position to rejoin his squad.

Japanese troops persisted in their efforts to infiltrate the machine-gun position, but PFC Ringgold, determined to remain at his post throughout the night, repeatedly fought off the incursions. He killed two enemy soldiers who got close to his position. Largely responsible for the successful defense of the company's flank, PFC Ringgold died of his wounds at his gun in the morning, July 25. He was awarded a posthumous Navy Cross.

July 25. A fifteen-minute air and artillery preparation began at 8:15 AM. The brigade battalions began moving at 8:30 AM, with the 22d Marines leading along the Agat–Sumay coast road into the neck of the peninsula. The 4th Marines moved to the assembly areas. Enemy opposition was immediate.

To protect their strong points in the Dadi Beach area, Japanese artillerymen around the airfield and near Neye Island began a barrage on 1/22. Well-entrenched enemy, camouflaged emplacements, machine-gun nests, and concrete pillboxes poured withering fire on 3/22 as it drove, with little cover or concealment, across the lowlands toward Apra Harbor and the Piti–Sumay Road. Enemy tanks led counterattacks on both assault battalions. Marine bazooka teams slowed the enemy armor, while Marine Sherman tanks rushed into the front. Eight Japanese tanks were destroyed and four others were on fire.

All day Tuesday, intermittent rain showers dampened Guam. Having postponed 1/4's attack on Orote gave the assault units time to reorganize, assemble into the best possible positions, re-supply and equip, and repair worn gear.

So heavy were the 1/22 casualties, that 1/4 came through its lines at 12:00 PM to replace the depleted assault battalion. Moving past the aid stations, the men of 1/4 got a sense of what the morning had been like. Company A, 1/22, was in bad shape, but better off than Companies B and C, that had no officers. The six officers who had landed on the YELLOW beaches with each of the companies had been lost to casualties. Both companies were below 50% enlisted strength. The battalion had also lost both medical officers, over 50% of the corpsmen, and many headquarters personnel.

Corporal Bush was back on the front line by late Tuesday afternoon. Company C dug in on the left, from Dadi Beach on Agat Bay to across the Agat–Sumay Road. The airfield, old Marine rifle range, and former barracks were up the road.

PFC Karl Clayton Hutchings, 18, from Spokane, was killed in action. PFC Gerald Steward, 20, Company G, 2/4, had graduated from Thomas Jefferson High School in Council Bluffs, Iowa, in 1942, and turned his attention to enlisting to defend his country. He was also killed on Tuesday. [46]

With 3/22 halted just short of the extensive mangrove swamp bordering Apra Harbor, the brigade held the area at the base of Orote Peninsula.

The main body of Japanese in the south, a force of 2,500 troops, was now confined in the peninsula's eight square miles. Enemy barges were spotted moving out into Apra Harbor at 5:00 PM. Their attempt to evacuate parts of the Orote garrison force was unsuccessful, stopped by air and artillery fire. Rather than hold the airfield, now useless to them, the enemy planned to break through the Marine lines and join the defenders in the northern areas.

Rain showers became more frequent after dusk and turned the roads into bogs. The night was pitch black and a torrential downpour, as well as the expected enemy counterattacks, made any sleep in foxholes unlikely.

Corporal Bush and the Marines along the night perimeter listened to the Imperial soldiers scream, yell, laugh hysterically, and break bottles. Their shouts and bugles sounded as they made their first banzai charge at midnight, coming out of the swamp to hit 3/22 with samurai swords, infantry weapons, grenades, pitchforks, sticks, ball bats, and pieces of broken bottles. Waiting until the enemy was within range, the Marines fired Howitzers, 37mm guns, 81mm and 60mm mortars, machine guns, rifles, and grenades, repulsing the attack.

A second counterattack came at 2:00 AM. The fighting was savage and close-in. Wave after wave came out of the swamps in the dark of morning, each eliminated in deadly Marine cross-fire. The break-through attacks finally faded at dawn. The Japanese remained trapped on Orote Peninsula, and the end of enemy resistance on Guam was just days away.

At home, family and friends read the newspaper accounts and listened to radio broadcasts about the American amphibious assault on the Island of Guam. War correspondents sent dispatches detailing the 1st Provisional Marine Brigade's fighting "yard by yard over cliffs and through mangrove swamps and dense jungles."

July 26. Naval gunfire and Marine aviation and artillery unleashed a softening-up preparation at dawn. The 4th Marines in a column on the left began the assault into the peninsula at 7:00 AM. The 1st Battalion spearheaded the advance along the Agat–Sumay Road, followed by the 2d, with the 3d mopping up behind. The regiment encountered only light opposition and moved so rapidly that, at 11:45 AM, the commander requested that they continue past Objective-3 Line and continue the advance to the old Marine rifle range (O-4 Line).

On the right, the 22d Marines were under an enemy artillery shelling and could not cross the line of departure until 8:00 AM, leaving the right flank of the 4th Marines column exposed for several hours. Slowed by mud and waist-deep water in the mangrove swamps on the right of the road and by enemy snipers, the 22d did not clear the area and contact the 4th Marines until 12:45 PM.

At the junction (RJ15) with the Piti–Sumay Road, 1/4 ran into a marsh on the left of the intersection. The 200-yard corridor between the marsh and mangroves on the right was mined with aerial bombs. The Japanese opened fire with automatic weapons from well-concealed pillboxes and brush-hidden mounds. Artillery and mortar fire fell on the infantrymen from the cliffs behind Neye Island. Marine tanks came forward, setting up a base of fire, while the riflemen maneuvered to silence the strong point. The advance halted as the men pulled back.

Along Company C's line, fighting step by step, the platoons ran headlong into enemy pillboxes and fortified positions. The fighting was intense. Private Marvin Butterfield was the Company C runner for 1stLt Bangser. Corporal Bush saw his friend and squadmate get hit. The wounds appeared fatal to their corpsman, and Private Butterfield was later reported KIA on July 26. Nearly forty years passed before CPL Bush learned the fate of his young friend. [47]

A withering barrage from an enemy pillbox kept 1st Platoon pinned down as the squads advanced across an open field. Corporal Herbert Helpingstine, 24, a bazooka man, unhesitatingly left his place of comparative safety and fearlessly proceeded to a position on the firing line. Moving even closer to a Japanese emplacement, he knelt exposed to intense hostile fire and coolly sighted on the pillbox. Before he could fire his weapon, a sudden volley from enemy guns struck him down. Mortally wounded, fighting with determined aggressiveness to stay alive, he resumed his position and destroyed the pillbox with a well-aimed burst of fire before he died.

Private First Class James M. Branch, 18, a Charlie Company BAR infantryman, advanced across a clearing with his squad and ran into a well-concealed pillbox. Intense automatic fire pinned them down. Inching forward on his own flank, his squad leader moving on the other flank, they attempted to close on the enemy emplacement. A furious barrage of interlocking fire forced them to take cover. The squad was in a precarious situation, unable to maneuver in any direction.

Private First Class Branch stood upright, advancing on the pillbox with his own automatic weapon. He moved steadily forward, fiercely returning the enemy's persistent fire.

Unhesitatingly risking his life under fire, he killed two Imperial Empire soldiers in the pillbox. His squad was able, then, to flank and destroy the hostile position. Private First Class Branch had sustained a fatal wound.

The daring initiatives and great personal courage of CPL Helpingstine and PFC Branch in the face of grave peril contributed materially to saving many Marine lives. Both received posthumous Navy Cross awards for their actions. [48]

Private First Class John Milburn Doss Jr., 18, a Texan with H&S Company, 1/4, had talked his mother into giving him permission to enlist in the Corps when he was 15 years old. His father had been killed in a hunting accident ten months before he enlisted. Homefolks took to calling him Colorado City's "Baby Marine." He shot expert with whatever weapon was issued to him. Persisting in his efforts to volunteer for overseas duty, he was finally sent to the South Pacific and joined the 1st Marine Raiders in December 1942. In his most recent letter home, he wrote that he was the acting company runner for his commanding officer carrying messages from headquarters to the front and back. PFC Doss was killed in the day's fighting. [49]

Corporal Bush had gotten to know PFC Jack R. Chuda, 23, the company runner for Lieutenant Bangser. The former Raiders did not have to read the dispatches that had been sent to Omaha in winter '42–43; the story had been circulated as soon as PFC Chuda had volunteered for the Marine Raiders.

He had enlisted in May 1942, and eight months later he was assigned to a gun crew aboard the USS *Chicago*, CL 29, sailing as part of a task force roughly 200 miles straight south of Guadalcanal. Japanese Betty torpedo bombers hit her with two torpedoes at 7:40 PM, January 29, 1943, just before sunset. PFC Chuda and members of the gun crew stayed with their guns, warding off the enemy planes. The *Chicago's* engines were killed, and she was listing and dead in the water. The USS *Louisville* took her sister ship under tow after midnight and steamed for safe harbor.

PFC Chuda was back on the guns at 4:25 PM when enemy torpedo planes returned and hit *Chicago* with four more torpedoes. Not until the "Abandon Ship" command was broadcast, did the gun crew leave their post. The heavy cruiser rolled over and sank off Rennell Island at 4:43 PM. Already "famous," PFC Chuda joined the 1st Raiders on Guadalcanal on February 10.

The news from Guam did not reach Mr. and Mrs. William Chuda on 3318 Dodge Street in Omaha until the first week of October. First, one of Jack's buddies sent them a note with $30, saying that he owned their son the money, so he was sending it to them. That letter left them "in an agony of dread." On Sunday, October 8, they received a War Department notice that PFC Chuda had been killed; date and place not disclosed. Lieutenant Bangser wrote a letter too. They received it on Wednesday, after the War Department notice. Newspaper columns put it in headlines: Captain Tells His Death on Errand of Mercy.

"Jack was killed in the evening of July 26 while his company was attacking the enemy airfield. At that time he was my runner, and so we were together all the way. That evening we hit very heavy enemy resistance and suffered many casualties. It was going to the aid of a wounded man that Jack was hit in the chest. He died almost at once and while I was holding him. He is buried in a beautiful little cemetery overlooking the airfield he had given his life to secure, and below a mountain which his outfit had fought for and captured earlier in the campaign." [50]

Company C lost other men to casualties. During the company's advance, a Japanese officer attacked Sergeant Shaheen from behind, severely wounding his shoulder twice with a saber. The squad leader spun around and killed the officer with his rifle. He continued to lead his squad in the attack, despite his wounds. Sergeant Shaheen personally ended seven enemy lives before a litter team evacuated him to the beach. For his leadership and valor in the first six days of the battle, he earned a Navy Cross.

By evening, the 4th Marines on the left had moved 1,500 yards since "jump off." Corporal Bush and the forward companies prepared night positions along the O-3 line, from the west beach to the road. The 22d Marines' line was bent back to the east along the lower edge of the thick mangrove.

Progress of the advance onto Orote was reported as "satisfactory."

"Satisfactory" is not the word Mrs. Marcella "Minnie" Phemister would ever give to that day. She was at home at 203 South Marion Street in Carbondale, in Southern Illinois, between the Mississippi and Ohio rivers. She looked forward to letters from the two men she loved who were serving in the Pacific Theater—both on Guam. She did not want telegrams.

Her husband, Faunt Dillon Phemister, aged 51, was with the 25th Special (Naval Construction) Battalion SeaBees. Attached to the 3d Marine Division, he had been on Bougainville building bridges and clearing jungle to construct the Tokokina Fighter Strip. SeaBee Phemister had landed on the Red Beaches and was carving out roads and tank paths in Guam's Northern Area. Minnie's son, Private Edward Eugene "Gene" Phemister, 17, was with Company C, 1/4, in the Southern Area.

She just knew when she received a telegram from the Navy Department that the news was about her son. Private Phemister was MIA on Guam.

July 27. The 4th Marines jumped off at 7:15 AM, with the 1st Battalion moving forward on the left and the 3d Battalion on the right, next to the road. The rolling terrain was covered with heavy undergrowth and interspersed with swamps—and one line after another of enemy bunkers. The advance to the Sumay Road, a narrow dirt road, was restricted to the narrow strip of land in front of the 4th Marines. Mine fields had to be cleared before tanks could progress. Company C and CPL Bush were on the right flank of the 1st Battalion's forward position.

The fighting was more severe than the previous day as the battalions closed in on the Japanese garrison. Intense and withering automatic-weapons fire from a ridge 300 yards to the front stopped the Marines after they had moved only 100 yards. Beyond the ridge, a coconut grove extended 500 yards on gently sloping ground. Past that, another higher, brush-covered ridge hid the Orote airfield from view.

The heavy and light machine guns in well-camouflaged dugouts and mutually-supporting positions along the base of the first ridge made it impossible for the 3d Battalion assault companies to advance further. Marine tanks fired at point-blank range and silenced the enemy positions. The battalion took the ridge.

Sergeant Nicholas John Pappajohn, Company L, 3d Battalion, was thirty feet away from PFC George "Chuckie" Garcia and PFC Louis N. Beaudry. PFC Garcia, 20, was a former Golden Gloves and professional boxer. He had saved Sergeant Pappajohn's life five days earlier. Private Beaudry, 20, had been mentioned in January 1944 dispatches from the South Pacific for charging a Japanese machine-gun nest alone and wiping out the gun crew with grenades. [51]

Sergeant Pappajohn witnessed what happened. "One lone shell whistled in" and blew the two Marines to pieces. The image of the Marine who had saved his life was printed in his memory. "I shall always remember Garcia who got no glory or won no battles." [52]

Corporal Joseph W. McCracken, 34, K/3, a Texan, and PFC Robert E. Nowakowski, L/3, from Cook County, Illinois, both died on the ridges before seeing the airfield.

On Wednesday, September 6, 1944, the War Department would release a list of 309 men killed or wounded at war. Three Marines from Kansas had been KIA on Guam. The families of PFC Clarence Eugene Cole, 22d Marines, Wichita, KIA on July 25 and CPL Irwin Earl Axline,

19th Marines, Medicine Lodge, KIA on July 26, would receive telegrams. Herbert Barr in Dodge City would read a telegram that his son, PFC Leroy Barr, 19, L/3, had died on July 27. [53]

The report that PFC Harold E. Lowry, 23, was KIA would reach his parents and five brothers in Madera, California, on Saturday, August 19. Four weeks later, newspapers would print the family's "most sincere thanks . . . for the nice letters and cards of consoling words and sympathy during our bereavement in the loss of our son. . . . We ask God to comfort each and every family during the loss of a loved one as he has us." [54]

In late afternoon, a Company C platoon reached the unpaved road that intersected Sumay Road. Abandoned and ruined concrete buildings were on the north side of the road. Private First Class Francis E. Roberts, 21, from Kelso, Washington, moved with the platoon to extend the flanks along the road. Heavy enemy rifle and machine-gun fire hit them from across an open field.

Private First Class Roberts and five others rushed to one of the concrete buildings for cover. Two concealed pillboxes in the rear fired upon them as they moved into the building. PFC Roberts spotted one of the emplacements, fearlessly charged outside the house alone with his rifle, and effectively silenced the hostile weapon's fire. He then took a dangerously prominent vantage point and shouted aggravating remarks at the enemy to draw their fire. When they revealed their position, PFC Roberts answered with devastating counter-fire against the emplacement.

As he took a more favorable firing position, a machine gun across the field again opened fire. The odds of progressing forward were obviously tremendously slim. He remained behind, covering his five companions as they withdrew back across the road. Then, he boldly pressed forward against the remaining pillbox and destroyed the machine-gun position. An enemy sniper fatally struck him down. He received a Navy Cross for his intrepid and courageous actions.

Private First Class Raymond J. Powers, Company C, was the son of a WWI Marine Corps private. He liked to make comparisons of South Pacific island terrain with that of lakes country around Minnetonka, eight miles west of Minneapolis. He was seriously wounded and evacuated from Orote. Twenty-six "glorious months" in the hospital would elapse before he would fish again in Minnesota.

The afternoon advance through the coconut grove was a yard-by-yard contest. The road congestion prevented tanks from getting forward to support the assault units.

On the right flank, the rapid advance of the 22d Marines toward the old Marine Barracks opened a 500-yard gap with the 4th's right flank. The regiment faced enemy fortifications on the rising ground near the barracks. Pillboxes, dugouts, mortar and automatic-weapons fire, and mines stopped the attack within 200 yards of O-4 and 300 yards short of the barracks.

The 4th Marines fought out of the grove at 3:30 PM. The enemy defenses on the next hill in front of the old rifle range, half way up the peninsula, were strong enough to halt forward progress along an unimproved road 300 yards short of the rifle range road. The next hours were spent softening up the ridge with tank and artillery fire and mopping up the area taken during the day.

A Japanese sniper killed Lieutenant Colonel Sam Puller, 38, the 4th Regiment's executive officer.

Mrs. Leta Jordan Selby had been a widow since before Christmas 1928. She had two boys to raise, her only children, on 211 McKee Street in Burr Oak, Michigan. The boys had gone through high school, one grade apart, and both were attending Michigan colleges when Pearl Harbor was attacked. They left their studies to enlist in the Marine Corps, and both went to the South Pacific as machine gunners. Leta received the telegrams weeks apart in August 1944.

Private First Class Ralph W. Selby Jr., 22, manned his gun flying fighter sweeps and bombing runs over New Ireland and New Britain in a MAG-24 Douglas SBD-5 (Scout Bomber Douglas) *Dauntless*, always in the face of heavy AA. Flying from Emirau Airfield on May 30, 1944, enemy anti-aircraft fire shot down the plane one mile due west of North

Cape, New Ireland. He and the pilot were officially declared dead, Bodies Not Recovered, the day of the mission. [55] His brother was finishing up the assault exercises on Guadalcanal and remained unaware of Ralph's death.

A man among men, PFC Robert B. "Bob" Selby, 21, had joined the 4th Marine Raiders Battalion. He had received a Purple Heart medal for wounds received in the Bairoko battle on July 20, 1943, but had never mentioned that in letters to his mother, not wanting her to worry about her younger son "over a little thing like that." He had also participated in the capture of Emirau. Thought of as one of the best Marines anyone would want to fight beside, he probably had more buddies in the machine gun company than anyone.

Private First Class Selby landed on Guam with the 2d Battalion. On July 27, he was leading a machine gun squad down a trail through extremely hazardous and densely wooded terrain on the peninsula when a concealed enemy machine gun on their flank opened fire and knocked him to the ground. Seriously wounded, he daringly struggled back to his feet, deliberately exposing himself to more enemy fire. His action gave five fellow machine gunners a chance to locate the hostile weapon, deploy and take cover, and wipe out the enemy machine-gun nest. The eight Imperial soldiers who had fired on PFC Selby and killed him were dead.

Within the hour, his body was carried away to the slopes of Mount Alifan, given a military funeral with a 12-rifle salute, and buried in the 1st Brigade Cemetery, overlooking Orote Peninsula and the sea.

Mrs. Leta Selby was proud to receive her son's Navy Cross. She cherished the letter from the men who had fought beside him, former 4th Marine Raiders. Gunnery Sergeant John P. McGinty, Sergeant Henry A. Bauer, CPL Roy P. Grenier Jr., CPL William J. Van Velzen, PFC R. O. Campbell, PFC Joseph S. Flanagan, and PFC Haywood C. Martin all signed the tribute.

"The company as a whole wants to extend their deepest sympathy. We know there is nothing we can say to lighten your burden, but Bob died like a true Marine, and that in our opinion is a man among men."

The 4th prepared its night lines from Haputo Point to Sumay Road, having progressed 500 yards during the day's fighting. The casualties in both regiments had been heavy. Based on their situation reports, the operation order for the next day was sent in the evening. The regiment was to take the rifle range and airfield. The 22d was to occupy what was left of the barracks site and Sumay village.

The enemy still held the high ground surrounding the airfield and controlled Apra Harbor.

Fortunately, the night was "quiet" along the entire front. Rather than "crazy" night charges, the enemy soldiers prepared in their strong line of bunkers for the attack they knew would come in the morning. In front of them, they had cut fire lanes through the dense underbrush, anticipating the attackers' lines of approach. Japanese command had ordered them to hold the positions until killed.

July 28. Corporal Bush was up at dawn's light. The pounding noise began in front of the regiment. Marine air dropped bombs on the enemy defenses in front of the airfield for forty-five minutes. Naval gunfire added a thirty-minute barrage. Then, multiple 155mm and 105mm howitzer batteries and 90mm gun batteries laid down a final preparation artillery barrage for thirty minutes. The regiments started forward at 8:30 AM, advancing slowly through the dense scrub growth. The 4th Marines were in a line: 1/4 on the left, 2/4 in the center, and the 3/4 on the right. Ahead was one of the most formidable enemy positions the brigade would encounter in the entire Guam operation.

The 1st Battalion advanced through the heavy vegetation, but progress was slow along the line. Corporal Bush's friend, PFC Brewington walked point for his squad. Having reached an enemy fortification, he was first to jump over the wall. Before the others in his fireteam joined him, an enemy mortar/artillery shell fell directly on them. PFC Brewington was the sole survivor at the wall. [56]

Private First Class Donald Leon "Don" Wellbaum, 20, H/2/4, of Illinois, did not find the "humping" at all physically challenging. He had been in athletics before graduating from Decatur High School. After leaving home on 1741 East Hickory Street and enlisting in the Marines on August 25, 1942, he had taken radar training, then, volunteered to join the 4th Raider Battalion. An enemy machine-gun burst killed him instantly, putting a third star on his Purple Heart ribbon. [57]

News of his death reached his parents in August. His younger brother, John, was just getting ready for his senior year at Decatur High. Having always looked up to his big brother, John enlisted in the Marines in November, went through training, and would leave for overseas in April, intent to get to Guam and visit his brother's resting place. He was there in May and found the grave in the Army-Navy-Marine cemetery on the Orote Peninsula. Private Wellbaum wrote home.

"Don's grave is in a pretty spot and the cemetery is well-cared for."

The dug-in enemy's resistance was intense, especially in the center and on the right of the 4th's area, where two strong points held up the advance. Heavy automatic-weapons fire kept 2/4 from moving. Even tanks could not lay down fire in the thick foliage in front of the battalion. The Shermans did help 3/4 break through the coconut log pillboxes on the right at 2:30 PM and advance to the O-4 line.

All four tank platoons were organized for a massed tank-infantry assault along the regiment's front. The tanks ripped the rifle range defense line at 3:30 PM, allowing infantry units to follow closely behind, destroying more than 250 pillboxes and emplacements at the enemy strong point. The 4th Marines set up for the night at the rifle range, short of O-4 and 150 yards from the airfield.

The 22d Marines had spent their day sweeping across the O-4 Line and through the rubble and fractured frames of the former barracks. They recovered a tattered "Old Glory" and the original barracks plaque from the rubble. Their right flank was established on the outskirts of Sumay.

Most of the enemy garrison had been wiped off the peninsula. The Marines had a quiet night readying themselves for the morning's assault. The 1st Provisional Marine Brigade intended to conclude the Orote campaign the next day—their fourth on the peninsula.

Corporal Melvin Ralph White, 19, was good about writing letters home. He'd had enough combat to view his situation pragmatically. His religious upbringing, the state of the world at war, and his belief in the devil might have mixed to darken his outlook. His letter reached his parents, W. H. "Doc" and Dorothy White, and his brother, William Hanford Jr., before the telegram arrived.

"Dear Family: Well we're off again," he had written as G/2/4 departed Guadalcanal. "I don't know just where but we all think it is Guam. If so, a lot of us aren't coming back. If you get this I'll be one of them. We always write a last letter just to let the folks know how we feel. I'll probably be scared all the way thru it; you always are.

"But if I do get mine, don't worry Mom, I'll be in safe hands. The Lord said He would take all the men who fought for him. I do believe in the Lord and when we go into battle, we ask the Lord to forgive us and make us Christians. I'll be with uncle Melvin and I've always wanted to see him. I don't want to die any more than anybody else. I don't want to kill the Japs, either, because they are human just like us.

"Don't believe it about Japs wanting to die because when you kill them they scream and beg for mercy, but you can't give them mercy because they are part of the devil and it has to be killed so the rest of us can live the clean lives we want to. Some day the devil may rule this world and in a way I kind of hope I do get mine, then I won't ever have to go thru all this again.

"Take care of yourself and may you always have the best of luck because you certainly deserve it. God bless and keep you forever.

"Always your loving son, MELVIN WHITE." [58]

Mr. and Mrs. Hanford White found comfort in knowing that Melvin had expressed his faith before he was killed on Guam on July 28, 1944.

Company G/2/4 platoon leader 1stLt Julian E. Leonard was KIA before the night defenses were completed.

July 29. Saturday morning might have been the loudest day in CPL Bush's life. Marine aircraft carried out the heaviest air strike since W-Day. Eight Task Force ships and six artillery battalions bombarded the enemy fortifications near the airfield in preparation for the planned assault. The 4th and 22d Marines moved out from their departure lines at 8:00 AM and met only meager resistance.

Meager did not mean absent. The readers of the *Oakland Tribune* had long been familiar with CPL Max L. Evans, 28, G/2/4. He had been a standout athlete at Roosevelt High School and at San Francisco Junior College. He played on the San Francisco Olympic Club soccer and basketball teams and had competed in the Denver basketball tournaments from 1938 through 1941. He was a member of the Oakland Order of DeMolay, an organization dedicated to preparing young men to lead successful, happy, and productive lives. Max enlisted in September 1942, volunteered for the 4th Marine Raiders, and had been overseas for eighteen months. He was killed on Saturday. [59]

When the War Department released the July 29 casualty notification on Saturday, September 9, PFC Mike Emil Sergo, 19, A/1/4, appeared on the Official Report of Wisconsin Casualties simply as "Dead." Second Lieutenant Thad Nelson Dodds, 29, B/1/4, was wounded in action.

The regiments had passed the O-5 Line and advanced half the length of the airstrip in two hours. They kept up the attack to the O-6 Line. Orote Airfield belonged to the Marines just after 2:00 PM. The regiments established a defensive line 150 yards past the west end of the landing strip.

The 4th Marines took over the entire front line, stretching from the south to north peninsula coast. The 22d began mopping-up details behind the 4th at 3:00 PM. Tanks led the 1st Battalion on a patrol to the lighthouse on Orote Point at the tip of the peninsula. Only two Japanese soldiers emerged. The patrol reported its findings and the brigade commander radioed that Orote Peninsula was secured at 4:00 PM. The Marines and Army had possession of the entire southern half of Guam.

July 30. All that was left to do was mopping up. Father Redmond held Sunday Mass services on the airfield. Corporal Bush, a Protestant, had a passing acquaintance with the priest. Their relationship would be closer after thirty years passed.

The 4th Marines, responsible for the entire peninsula except Sumay, conducted extensive patrolling from one end to the other end. The 22d Marines secured the village, and thus, Apra Harbor was once more an American forward fleet anchorage. The Marines efficiently got the airfield into operational condition for light planes. Marine Aircraft Group-21 (MAG-21) squadrons soon flew close support strikes from Orote over the front lines in the Northern Area. Marine Night Fighter Squadron [VMF(N)]-534 was at the field.

"Mopping up" and "cleaning up" meant that enemy combatants still held positions around the airfield after it had been captured. Company L, 3/4, patrolled up Sumay Road toward the lighthouse. Corporal Derrol Dean Hubbard, 19, one week from his next birthday, had been a football, basketball, and track standout at Smith Center High School in Kansas. He was killed in action leading his squad near the airfield. [60]

Private First Class Sterling H. Parks, 21, from Lebanon County, Pennsylvania, was also killed in the engagement with Japanese holdouts. In the H&S/2/4 area, a sniper killed Private First Class George Warren Small, 19, from Marlin, Texas.

In addition to Private Phemister and the fifteen 1st Provisional Marine Brigade Marines missing on W-Day, MIA reports listed nine more Marines before Orote Peninsula was secured.

Missing 4th Marines: PFC George Kostic, Company C; PFC William Edgar Mitchell, Company Q, of Rt. 4, Highland Avenue in Versailles, Woodford County, Kentucky; and PFC Leonard Robert Sliva, HQ Company. [61]

Missing 22d Marines: Sergeant Darrel F. Hartman, Sergeant Garrett G. Hope Jr., Sergeant Arnold O. Powell, PFC John W. Ant, PFC Claude O. Ellis Jr., and PFC George L. Morrison.

For a week, the 1st Provisional Brigade reorganized, cleaned themselves up, searched for the missing, tended to graves, and listened to reports of the 3d Marine Division fighting to the north of Orote along the Piti–Sumay Road and on the Chachao–Alutom–Tenjo ridgeline.

Father Redmond, the Raiders' Padre, presided over the graves of the Marines. He earned a Bronze Star on Guam.

August 2, 1944. At some point in the fight, CPL Bush had been wounded in his left shoulder. His uniform bloodied, he had stayed in the front of the fight and did not seek a corpsman's aid or go to the field medical tent. On Wednesday morning, he became nauseated and vomited several times. Diarrhea hit. The next day, he reported to the Company "A" III Corps Medical Battalion Field Hospital tent.

Lieutenant T. A. Glass and Lieutenant H. V. Weatherman examined him. Corporal Bush was dehydrated and was diagnosed with acute Gastro-Enteritis. DNEPTE, meaning "did not exist prior to entry." Origin was not misconduct. His abdomen was essentially negative. He was put on 2,000cc 5% Glucose by IV and restricted from any oral ingestion for 12 hours. The doctors also noted: "Has small healing wound on left shoulder." That entry would be missed in an investigation three years later.

August 3. What happened to PFC Alton Glenn, a former Company C, 1st Battalion Raider, proved to be a wartime mystery. After his evacuation from Enogai to Tulagi, then to Guadalcanal, he recuperated from the jungle boils and was returned to the "effective" ranks. Rather than rejoining the 4th Marines, he was assigned to the 9th Marines, 3d Marine Division. On Sundays, he would meet up with friends in the HOLD HIGH THE TORCH area and tell small-town, Panhandle Texas tall tales.

The 9th Marines had made landing on Blue Beach in front of Chonito Cliff, on the right flank of the Asan Point assault. The regiment pushed rapidly south along the Piti–Sumay Road toward Orote Peninsula to seize the Piti Navy Yard. In the first days of August, the battalions advanced north on the Agana–Yigo Road (RJ 177) toward Finegayan Village. Private First Class Frank Peter Witek, 1/9, earned a posthumous Medal of Honor for his actions on August 3, during the fight for Finegayan. Private First Class Glenn was listed among the wounded.

Mr. and Mrs. Dexter Glenn would receive a telegram that their son had been wounded in action during the retaking of Guam. He had been awarded a Purple Heart. The Navy made the announcement on October 13. The parents, their four daughters, and their other four sons wondered for three weeks when they would hear from Alton. The Glenn's had already received another telegram when the Navy Department announced casualties on Friday, November 3.

PFC Glenn had died on October 8, "at an island in the Coral Sea as a result of his wounds." He had been interred in a military cemetery. [62]

August 6. Bob Hope arrived down at the Tassafaronga dock on Sunday at 9:00 AM with Betty Hutton and Greer Garson, diminutive singer Frances Langford, curvaceous dancer Patty Thomas, movie comedian Jerry Colonna, and guitar player Tony Romano. The Bob Hope Special USO show was on Guadalcanal for the two-year anniversary of the August 7, 1942, Canal assault. Captain Spencer Allen interviewed Bob for AES-Guadalcanal. The show, held at the outside theater, was attended by "to put it mildly, an enthusiastic crowd."

August 7. Corporal Bush was returned to duty. The Form H-S notation in his medical records about his shoulder wound on Guam was added to his Health Record and Medical History.

He was up early and ready to depart from the peninsula. On Monday at 7:30 AM with 1/4 leading on the left and 3/4 following, the 4th Marines started its advance along Guam's west coast, passing through the 3d Marines' 1st and 2d Battalions. The 22d Marines, the reserve regiment, moved into the line on the 4th Marines' left. The two regiments began the coordinated attack planned for the drive to the end of the island. Meeting only moderate resistance, 1/4 pitched ahead toward the O-4 Line anchored at Haputo Point. Due to the rapid progress of the final drive, 1/4 was directed at 9:10 AM to continue the attack to 1,000 yards beyond the unpaved road at O-4. The 22d Marines were ordered to move forward to a new assembly area in the Ague vicinity near the western cliffs.

The 1st Battalion was at the new objective just after 10:00 AM and began preparations to rapidly push ahead. The operation order to seize the O-5 Line came just after noon. The battalion lurched forward another 2,000 yards, holding a line at 4:00 PM, with 3/4 on the right and tied to the junction of several roads at RJ 460. The paved road led north to the tip of Guam.

Captain Paul Hills Todd flew from Orote Field in a Grumman F6F-3N, *Hellcat*, BuNo 41157. The VMF(N)-534 Operations Officer got on the radio when the *Hellcat* was overdue back at the squadron's flight line. Captain Todd never replied. The CONFIDENTIAL cause of his disappearance was cabled: "UNKNOWN." A telegram that he was MIA went to Mr. and Mrs. Arch G. Todd, his parents, living at 1216 E. 41st Street, Kansas City, Missouri. Promoted in absentia, Major Todd was declared KIA on August 8, 1945.

The enemy withdrew into the extreme northeastern part of the island. The rest was up to the 1st Provisional Brigade. The 3d MarDiv units stayed anchored to the brigade's right flank and the Tarague Cliffs on the east coast on the right.

August 8. The day's fighting on the front was not intense, and Japanese resistance in the Yigo area in the east was quickly reduced. The III Amphibious Corps' lines had moved ahead 6,000 yards in some zones. First Battalion, 4th Marines, was east of Uruno Point. They took up their night defensive positions 5,000 yards in front of Mount Machanao and the Ritidian Point Light House. That evening, the assault units received orders for the following morning's attack—the capture of the remaining corner of Guam.

The plan directed the 22d Marines to pass through the left battalion of the 4th Marines, coordinating the morning attack with LtCol Shapley's unit. The 4th had secured the O-5 in its zone and had linked up with the 22d along that line at RJ 470 by 4:00 PM. The regiment sent units along the road toward Tarague to tie in with 3d Battalion, 3d Marines. Once the 3/3 was located, 2/4 set up 700 to 800 yards east of RJ 462 for the night. Along the trail 800–1,000 yards to the north, 3/4 prepared a perimeter defense, strongly oriented to the northeast sector.

Company A, 1/4, Private John L. Luger, 19, was wounded and evacuated from Guam.

August 9. The regiments executed the passage of lines maneuver at 7:30 AM as the attack began. As had been the case on the Orote Peninsula, 1/4 was first to reach the northernmost tip of Guam. One unit after another gained the northern beaches. Patrols from the 22d Marines descended the cliffs near Ritidian Point, while those from the 4th reached the coastal plain just south of Mergagan Point. The mopping-up details met only scattered opposition. At 6:00 PM, General Shepherd announced that all organized resistance had ceased in the brigade zone. The end of the Guam campaign was in sight by nightfall.

August 10. The announcement was made at 11:31 AM. Organized enemy resistance had ended on Guam. The liberation of the island was complete, and clean-up and mopping-up activities finished the campaign. As IIIAC organized the departure of the assault units, regiments continued to conduct strong patrols and reinforced ambushes, hunting for hidden Japanese holdouts and stragglers. Over the next week, hundreds of starved and emaciated enemy combatants were either killed or captured.

Company and battalion commanders began to submit their muster rolls and rosters. The 1st Battalion, 4th Marines, had suffered 236 casualties: 58 KIA, 6 DOW, and 172 WIA. The 2d Battalion reported 207 casualties: 29 KIA, 5 DOW, and 186 WIA. The 3d Battalion had 268 casualties: 51 KIA, 13 DOW, and 213 WIA. Counting the casualties among the non-assault and support companies, the 4th Marines suffered another 24 KIA, 4 DOW, and 157 WIA. Eighteen 4th Marines enlisted men were listed as missing in action, presumed dead.

In addition to the W-Day missing from the 3d Marine Division: one first lieutenant, a sergeant, a corporal, eighteen PFCs, and one private were missing in action, most of them from the 3d Marine and the 21st Marine regiments. Sergeant Arthur "Duck" Vanmeter, 21, A/1/21, was reported missing on July 27. That was going to be devastating news to Walter Valentine and Rose Nell Vanmeter in Louisville, Kentucky. Weeks before the telegram arrived, they had been notified about "Duck's" older brother. U.S. Army 82nd Airborne Division Corporal Walter E. "Junior" Vanmeter was reported missing in action at Normandy on July 4, 1944. [63]

The 9th Marines reported that PFC Argus Emerson Cain, 22, from Rineyville, Hardin, Kentucky, was missing on July 28. PFC Walter Coble, 21st Marines, was the last Marine to be reported missing during the 18-day second battle for Guam: August 11, 1944.

The Marines missing on Guam who had no known grave would eventually be listed as Personnel Not Recovered and Presumed Killed in Action. After the war, they would have memorials at the Courts of the Missing, Honolulu Memorial National Memorial Cemetery of the Pacific in Hawaii. Approximately seventy U.S. service members remained unaccounted for on Guam. Some of the men were lost to the sea as they fell wounded or dead from the landing craft near the beaches.

The effort to recover MIA remains lying in unmarked graves on Guam would continue. In May 2012, a seven-person JPAC research and investigative team spent two weeks on the island. They interviewed eyewitnesses to the battle and burials and attempted to locate wreckage, equipment, or personal effects to specifically correlate sites to missing Americans. As late as August 2015, JPAC sent teams of POW/MIA investigators to the island to search for information on Americans who have remained missing. [64]

Like all the Marines who survived the battle, CPL Bush was grateful to have lived through it, but had somber thoughts of the friends who did not make it. The men paid their respects at the crosses in the graveyards. Father Redmond, 45, walked with them. He understood and would remember for the rest of his life what the facial expressions of the survivors in his extended "congregation" told him.

"Men tried in the cauldron of adversity. A family so knit that when one died, some part of each one died." [65]

A Little Bit of Hope on Guam

Comedian Bob Hope understood that the Leathernecks and GIs had endured a bloody battle and recaptured another island from the Imperial Empire. He packed his entourage of show-biz personalities onboard a *Catalina* flying boat and flew to Guam to lighten the mood and lift the spirits of American troops. He arrived with Francis Langford, Patty Thomas, Jerry Colonna, Tony Romano, and a bevy of singers and dancers.

August 12. On Saturday, the Bob Hope Special "coming from somewhere in the South West Pacific" was broadcast over NBC affiliates in the United States. Even though the "USO gypsies" were on Guam at the time, his mention of the Mosquito Network suggested that the show had been recorded in the Solomon Islands.

Bob put on an absolutely hilarious show. His brand of humor was the kind that CPL Bush appreciated. He wanted the Marines on Guam to know that none of the males in his troupe were draft dodgers. Jerry Colonna went to the draft board and was classified 5-X, meaning "too fat to fight." "Tony Romano has the distinction of being one of the few able bodied American men to be classified Double-S Double-F—meaning he's a single man with children." That was Bob's play on the Double-4 Double-F classification for physically unqualified for induction into military service. Bob's biggest laugh came when he revealed his own classification. He was 4-Z, a classified "Coward."

Bob referred to the steaming Pacific jungle islands as *Loew's Malaria Circuit* and the *Pineapple Circuit*. He introduced Francis Langford, and when she walked onto the stage, the battle-worn crowd went into a frenzy. Bob did little to settle them down with his one-liner.

"You grunts'd start howling at just the sight of two coconuts close together."

Francis sealed the hearts of many when she sang her rendition of *I'm in the Mood for Love*.

On Monday, the entertainment departed Guam for a return flight to Sydney, Australia. Bob and his troupe would have more memories to be thankful for. Over the Tasman Sea, off the Mid North Coast of New South Wales, nineteen miles SSW of Port Macquarie, the *Catalina* developed mechanical problems. The pilot ordered the startled entertainers to jettison their luggage out of the open hatches. Baggage, wardrobes, and several crates of whisky went into the sea, 242 miles north of Sydney, as the pilot looked for a place to safely put the aircraft down. Shortly afterwards, the residents of small town Laurieton were surprised to see a *Catalina* skimming down on the Camden Haven River.

August 15. Washington, D.C., received the wire that the combat phase on Guam was over. Patrolling would continue. The 4th Marines were embarked on ship, returning to Guadalcanal.

CHAPTER 19

The Space Between Battles

✳✳✳

"Then what should war be?" [1]

— WILLIAM SHAKESPEARE

WAR IS A LARGE ENTERPRISE. Never comprised of a single clash of armed forces, to the men in the field war is a protracted mix of skirmishes, contacts, engagements, battles, raids, ambushes, actions, affairs, attacks and counterattacks, marches and movements, strategies and tactics, and terrible sights, sounds, and silences. Corporal Bush's grandfather had learned this as a boy while armies brought havoc to Barren County. Even in the Civil War the armed lines made hellish and frenzied charges into each other's perimeters. On the Pacific Islands, such frightening charges were called *banzai* attacks.

Commanders know that, while victorious in a battle, an army can be defeated in a war. Fatigue and exhaustion, as much as casualties, weaken the might and will of a fighting force. The remedy is respite and recovery. A carefully measured rest can replenish a warrior's spirit. On the other hand, the rest—the lull—between battles can give him too much time to think, thus germinating a hesitation or resistance to fighting, DNEPTE (did not exist prior to entry), and a terrible apprehension about what might happen to him and his comrades in the next battle.

William Sorenson, brother of a MOH recipient and himself a veteran of the Chosin Reservoir campaign in the Korean War, understood the space between battles and how hard it is for even brave men to return to the Main Line of Resistance. He never wanted *leave* from the field and would not have liked it had it been ordered.

"Because once you get out of combat, you lose your sense of it. . . . It's sort of a knowledge or sense. . . . If you go back and you're out of combat, you lose that, because you come back, and boy, that's even worse trying to get back into the sense of combat again."

Corporal Richard Bush had readied himself to go into his first battle with veterans and raw replacement troops like himself. Emirau had turned into an amphibious training exercise; it was not a battle, not even a light skirmish. Guam was a battle, and it had been grim. The war had not ended on that island, and other Pacific battles would rage. He had Marines to lead. His body and mind needed rest. His spirit was intact.

Back on Guadalcanal

The 4th Marines began preparations for their next amphibious landing as the advance toward mainland Japan and the assaults on Iwo Jima and Okinawa Shima were sketched out. Both enemy outpost islands were heavily fortified to defend strategic airfields. Due to their proximity to their homeland, the Japanese would give up neither island without a bare-knuckle scrap.

Allied planners had already designated Okinawa, sitting between the East China and the Philippine seas, as a staging base for an invasion of Japan. The island was smaller than Guadalcanal in area—66x19 miles (485 square miles)—and the Marines would have to seize every square mile of it. The "green" 6th Marine Division, having not yet operated as an entire unit in combat, got the call. Comprised of the 4th, 22d, and 29th Marines infantry regiments, the veteran troops readied themselves for another assault.

Corporal Bush's attention was not yet on an island 3,362 miles to the northwest of Guadalcanal. He reported to the 6th Marine Division Hospital with severe pain in his left jaw that he had been tolerating for some time. The dentists performed a root canal to his lower left 2nd molar (31). The pain was gone in a couple of days.

October 23, 1944. Word came down that the 6th Division was to be the core for Operation ICEBERG. Large numbers of replacements reported in to the regiments. After convalescing and recovering, many of the wounded from Guam returned to their units on Guadalcanal, determined to "get ready for the next one." The training intensified.

Pre-invasion intelligence gathering provided some sense of what awaited the assault forces. Japanese forces numbering about 115,000 men had been deployed to defend the island. Their commanders had selected the most advantageous pieces of terrain from which to fight and committed carefully designated units to defend their positions. They had doubled the amount of artillery common in defense networks, even incorporating naval guns. Impressive howitzers, mortars, and antitank guns were readied with ample munitions stockpiled. The enemy, occupying thousands of fortified caves, had positioned themselves to be protected by mutually supporting ridgelines and steep defiles. Snipers had had more than enough time to pick advantageous hiding places.

The 6th Marine Division was tasked to seize Yontan and Kadena airfields about a mile inland from the landing beaches and, then, to take the northern half of the island from the Japanese. Casualties were expected to be high.

December 1. Corporal Bush had been in two combat operations. He had over twenty-six months in the Corps and almost eight months in his present rank. Promotions up to a corporal's rank were almost automatic, based simply on time-in-service and time-in-grade. A promotion to sergeant, a "rated" rank, was more competitive and tended to rely on a vacancy within the Marine's MOS. An extra stripe overseas with less than three years of service would make his overseas monthly pay $93.60.

His company commander gave him the highest marks as to character for a promotion to sergeant. First Sergeant C. O. Wilibert, 1/4/6, reviewed his qualifications and Record Book. On the 5-point scale, CPL Bush had averaged 4.3. He lost a point for his AWOL offense and got only two points for schools. His weapons qualifications helped. The battalion first sergeant called CPL Bush in for an oral examination and a field examination. He gave him high marks for tactics, weapons, and being an NCO-in-Charge of his squad in attack and defense. His overall score was 72.5 out of 100. The recommendation for promotion to sergeant went forward.

In early December, CPL Bush was reminded of a former Raider. Men from Illinois in Company C and in the 1st Battalion were passing around newspaper articles sent to them from home about the friend they had called "Phemister." Commandant of the Marine Corps Lieutenant General A. A. Vandegrift had sent another telegram to "Minnie" Phemister in Carbondale. The message was printed in short columns at the bottom of local newspaper front pages.

"Deeply regret to inform you report just received states your son, Private First Class Edward E. Phemister, U.S.M.C.R., previously reported missing in action, was killed in action on 26 July 1944 at Guam Island, Mariana Islands in the performance of his duty and service of his country. Report states remains interred in grave 16, row 7, plot C, Army, Navy and Marine Corps Cemetery, Guam Island, Mariana Islands. To prevent possible aid to our enemies do not divulge the name of his ship or station. Please accept my heartfelt sympathy. Letter follows." [2]

His friends would not forget PFC "Gene" Phemister. Few of them would be alive when Carbondale residents remembered him more than six decades after the war. Then, PFC Phemister's parents would not be home to get the phone call. Dillon Phemister died in 1949 and Minnie Phemister in 1983. In 2011, an Australian army reservist on a peacekeeping and security deployment in the Solomon Islands found a box of old dog tags belonging to nine Marines, six Army soldiers, and one sailor. [3] He thought the tags deserved to get home to the rightful owners or families, rather than rust away in a box. Six of the tags belonged to 1/4 Raiders. One belonged to PFC Phemister. Another belonged to Corporal Eugene Sheffield, a C/1/4 comrade of CPL Bush. In August 2012, PFC Phemister's dog tags were returned to his cousin, Morris L. Phemister, in Southern Illinois.

December 23. Corporal Bush celebrated his 20th birthday. PFC Hubert Junior "Skull" Brewington celebrated his 21st birthday after Christmas.

The New Year came and went and the 4th Marine Regiment continued training on Guadalcanal, the site of most of the III Amphibious Corps (IIIAC) combined arms training and field maneuvers. Some of the bloodiest fighting for the Marines in the Pacific was months away.

January 11–13, 1945. All Marine artillery in the Solomons assigned to ICEBERG conducted a combined firing exercise on Guadalcanal, simulating the conditions at the target. As their training cycle reached the large unit stage, the 1st Marine Division's RCTs (Regimental Combat Teams) were rotated from Pavuvu Island in the Russells to Guadalcanal. The special emphasis was night operations training.

Corporal Bush knew that the amphibious operation was a major affair. He readied his squad. No one had any idea, yet, that they were going to enter the longest and most costly single engagement in Marine Corps history. In eighty-two days of combat, 19,500 Marine casualties would be recorded. Eleven Marines would earn Medals of Honor—five would be awarded for protecting others from grenades.

Operation *Iceberg*

January 22. American fighters and bombers began conducting air attacks on Okinawa.

February 19. The Marines of IIIAC in their final days on Guadalcanal listened to sobering news and scuttlebutt about the invasion of Iwo Jima. In the first two days of that amphibious landing, the Marines counted 3,650 dead, wounded, or missing.

February 23. Mount Suribachi was taken in the morning. By that time, casualties on Iwo had risen to 5,372. The toll of crosses being erected in the Divisions' cemeteries was a number only whispered among the 4th Marine grunts—and thought about silently when alone.

February 25. Joe Rosenthal's inspiring photograph of the flag raising went into circulation, time enough for the newspapers to reach Guadalcanal and for Marines to stuff copies into their packs.

March 12. The LSTs and LSMs of the Northern Tractor Flotilla, fully loaded with amphibious vehicles, tanks, artillery, and combat equipment, had limited berthing space for passengers. To avoid exposing assault troops to the crowded conditions and prolonged shipboard confinement, most of the 4th Marines were embarked on the faster attack cargo transports (AKAs). The slower landing ships got under way on Monday morning for movement to the IIIAC's staging area at the Ulithi Atoll lagoon on the western edge of the Caroline Islands, well southwest of Saipan. Corporal Bush and the amphibious landing forces waited for their own departure. Operation *Iceberg* was afloat.

March 15. Three days after the tractor flotilla departed, CPL Bush left Guadalcanal. The APAs and AKAs fully loaded with men and equipment departed for Ulithi. The ships maneuvered across Iron Bottom Sound, gathering near Tulagi as the armada formed. The embarked Marines were about 1,962 miles and six long days away from the staging area. They were sailing toward the largest and costliest single operation of the Pacific War. The Japanese defenders anticipating another Marine assault did not know their desperate days of island combat would be the last in the Pacific war.

As the ships plowed through rough seas, 3d Platoon Sergeant James Wallace Woodruff, 23, talked over operation plans with his squad leaders. Corporal Bush briefed his men and talked about enemy tactics. Corpsmen moved about the squads, briefing the men to avoid eating fresh fruits and vegetables grown on the island destination. The scuttlebutt was that Okinawan natives used their own human waste as fertilizer.

Estimates suggested that 250,000 civilians inhabited Okinawa. The "little brown natives" worked in their fields, sustained themselves, clung to their ancient ways, and shied away when foreigners spoke to them. The Japanese occupiers were going to force the local males into fragile militias just days before the Task Force arrived off the coast.

The shipboard Marines followed the slow progress of their brothers' advance toward the final Japanese stronghold on Iwo Jima.

March 21. Both elements of TF-53 arrived at Ulithi on Wednesday, rendezvousing with the 647 ships already at anchor in the lagoon.

March 22. The APA-borne assault troops transferred to landing ships. Some of the companies were put ashore on the tiny islets for brief physical conditioning and recreation programs. At the railing of his transport, CPL Bush watched the impressive maneuvering of battleships, aircraft carriers, cruisers, destroyers, and an endless haze of smaller ships.

Each day more ships anchored in the harbor prepared for the invasion of Okinawa. Some ships departed for preliminary strikes and bombardment, and others arrived with the scattered elements of the Joint Expeditionary Force troops. Task Force-58 carriers, battered by enemy suicide air attacks, hobbled into the vast anchorage. The nightly alarms on the troop ships, alerting the embarked force to the arrival of Japanese snooper planes, interrupted already-disturbed sleep cycles.

March 25. On Sunday, 722 ships began to lift anchors. Their departure from Ulithi continued until Wednesday. The IIIAC had begun the remaining 1,400-mile-leg of its journey.

All the decks of the troop "buckets" were jammed with men, howitzers, ammunition crates, equipment and supplies, jeeps and trucks. Corporal Bush spent his days under the top deck or talking quietly with the squad on the upper deck. The pontoons tied along either side of the LST hull provided restful spots, as long as the ocean swells were slight.

As the task force sailed north, more ships joined the armada. Forty aircraft carriers, eighteen battleships, and 1,200 transports assembled into the largest amphibious invasion force in naval and land warfare history. No matter in what direction CPL Bush gazed, there were only ships on the horizon—almost 1,500 in total.

March 26. Families in the States watched and listened for any news about the Marine's Pacific Island Campaign. So did the embarked forces. Five days from reaching their own destination, the ships' loud speakers announced that enemy resistance on Iwo Jima had ended. The Marines had completely secured the island. The jubilation stirred excitement among the landing forces, relieving some of their mounting tension. Another island awaited their beach landing.

March 31. The Japanese expected the invasion force to arrive off Okinawa and believed that they could win a victory by destroying the Allied Fifth Fleet. They had prepared to crash massed flights of aircraft into the ships. The Marines on LSTs presented the enemy pilots targets of opportunity. Before sunset, Mitsubishi *Zeros* began strafing assaults against the troop ships. These were not kamikazes—those strikes began the next day and would ultimately sacrifice 1,465 enemy pilots and planes during the long days of the impending battle.

April 1. In the dark before dawn on Sunday, the flotilla silently began dropping anchors off the west coast of Okinawa and the surrounding Ryukyu Islands. It was Love Day, and CPL Bush, a rifle squad leader, was only 350 miles from southern Japan. He had been awake and briefing his men long before dawn.

At 4:06 AM, Admiral Turner made the traditional signal: "Land the Landing Force." Reveille was at 5:30 AM, and CPL Bush stirred as the assault forces awakened. The men shaved, dressed, and made sure their dog tags were securely fixed in place. The Navy cooks served the amphibious force steak and eggs for breakfast. The wardroom was unusually quiet as the men ate.

There were some prayers—not just because of the day's plans, but because it was Easter Sunday 1945. Father Redmond had already conducted Easter Mass services. There might also have been some jokes or pranks, because it was April Fool's Day.

The Marines' task was to seize Yontan Airfield, a mile inland from the beaches. The south end of Yontan's runway served as the dividing line between the 6th and 1st Marine Divisions. According to the Landing Plan, 1/4 was to land on the 6th Division's right flank on Red Beach 2 and 3, just to the north of Sobe Town and 1,400 yards in front of the airfield. The 3d Battalion would land to their left on Red Beach 1. The 2d Battalion was the division reserve and would stay afloat. The 22d Marines would take the left flank and land on Green Beaches 1 and 2, in front of Takashippo and Hanza villages. The 1st Division regiments would assault the beaches to the right of 1/4. [4]

Third Platoon Sergeant Woodruff again briefed and encouraged his combat veteran squad leaders. The men cleaned and re-checked rifles. Ammunition was distributed. Backpacks were securely tightened. Medics surveyed their "unit one" pouches, especially for morphine capsules. The assault companies with rifles and packs began forming in their designated spots topside and below deck in the troop and equipment staging areas, ready and waiting for the order to embark onto chugging amphibious landing tractors.

Corporal Bush and his squad waited for what was to be the largest amphibious assault of the island campaigns.

Chaplains intoned their prayers.

Twenty minutes before dawn, ten battleships, nine cruisers, twenty-three destroyers, and 177 gunboats in the East China Sea unleashed the vicious and deafening naval bombardment of the landing areas on Okinawa's west side. Standing along the ship's railings, the Marines could see their objective, although the coast was soon obscured by smoke and dust.

The shape of the island's northern part was similar in ways to Guam. Motobu Peninsula poked out on the west coast. The steep cliffs of Okinawa's northern coastline, green with vegetation, presented a formidable sight from the sea. Mount Yonaha-dake on the island's northeast reached to 1,643 feet above the sea. Mount Yae Take on the northwest Motobu Peninsula rose to almost 1,500 feet. The midsection of the island, south of the Ishikawa Isthmus, was most inviting for an amphibious assault. There, the land around Hagushi, mostly cultivated by local farmers and sparse of vegetation but for green conifers, sloped gently from the beaches toward inland hills.

Air support arrived in force at 6:50 AM; 138 planes began orbiting over both flanks of the beaches.

The assault troops commenced debarkation at 7:00 AM. The troops in APAs transferred to landing craft. Landing ships disgorged armored amphibians and amphibian tractors pre-loaded with troops and equipment. Simultaneously, mechanized landing craft (LCMs) carrying tanks floated from the flooded well-decks of landing ships, dock (LSDs), and tanks rigged with T-6 flotation equipment debarked from LSTs.

Landing vehicles formed into five to seven waves behind the line of departure, marked by control vessels lying off each landing beach. A line of landing craft nearly eight miles long waited two miles out from land.

At 8:00 AM, the sky was bright with sunshine, and the air was a cool 75°F. Visibility was good and the sea was calm, disturbed only slightly by a mild breeze. The surf along the shoreline amounted to only ripples. There was no significant enemy response to the bombardment or to the amphibious assault. The control craft hauled down the pennants fluttering from their masts.

A line of support craft crossed the line of departure and began the 4,000-yard run to the beaches. The first wave of troop-carrying LVTs followed. Hundreds of LVTs then swept toward the shore at regular intervals. Scattered hostile artillery and mortar fire fell ineffectively into the approach assault waves.

Corporal Bush and his men felt the adrenalin flood their blood stream. Their neck muscles tightened.

Naval gunfire lifted as the landing force neared the beaches. The LVTs fired on suspected enemy positions. Aircraft swooped down, blasting the landing area with bullets, bombs, and incendiaries. The first landing craft arrived at their designated landing sites at 8:30 AM against practically no opposition. Enemy resistance to the landing consisted of sporadic mortar and small-arms fire. All the LVT(A)s spearheading the IIIAC attack reached the beach by 8:40 AM. The eight assault BLTs had all stormed ashore within a half hour.

With the 4th Marines in the middle of the line, the assault forces surged up the terraced slopes behind the beaches and drove northeastward, inland toward Yontan Airfield. First Lieutenant James G. Washburn, commanding Company C, moved his platoons forward.

The 4th Marines on the 6th Division's right encountered only isolated enemy pockets built around light machine guns. The regiment swiftly penetrated several hundred yards inland and linked with the 7th Marines on their right. Continuing the advance, the 4th Marines' skirmishers walked slowly upright fifteen feet apart, reaching the airfield at midmorning. The field was essentially intact, but all buildings had been stripped, and the anti-aircraft emplacements contained only dummy guns. The airfield was reported secured at 11:30 AM.

The Army XXIV Corps had captured Kadena airfield by 10:00 AM.

Unopposed, except for occasional sniper fire, the 4th Marines swept ahead of adjacent units and secured their objective to the east of Yontan by 1:00 PM. The 22d Marines on the left flank had only reached the vicinity of Hanza. An appreciable gap in depth had formed between the regiments. The 4th Marines advanced again at 1:30 PM, meeting scattered resistance on its left.

The narrowness of the roads and trails made it impracticable for the LVTs to go very far inland. To avoid traffic congestion, jeeps, jeep trailers, weasels, and carrying parties transported needed supplies to the front. Nearly three miles inland, the advance halted between 4:00 and 5:00 PM.

Corporal Bush was near China Village.

The attacking infantry dug in, and units established contact with each other all along the IIIAC line. The companies patrolled extensively to their front. Throughout the night, the 4th Marines experienced intermittent mortar and machine-gun fire. The enemy made unsuccessful attempts to infiltrate the night defenses.

The 6th MarDiv planned the move into northern Okinawa. The 4th Marines were going to meet steadily mounting enemy resistance.

April 2. The morning started quietly, without air strikes or artillery preparation. Colonel Shapley's regiment resumed the attack at 7:30 AM. The 1st Battalion was still on the division boundary, with the 3d Battalion to their left. Caves honeycombed the difficult and heavily broken terrain in front of them. These were not like Kentucky caves; there was no mummy under a boulder, just enemy soldiers with rifles, Nambu machine guns, and grenades.

At 11:00 AM, a 3/4 platoon entered the mouth of a steep ravine formed by two noses of a ridge. The defenders watched from a series of mutually supporting caves on both sides of the draw. They opened up with small-arms fire. Twelve Marines were quickly wounded and isolated in the firefight. The enemy strongpoint held on until the platoon charged into the draw and another platoon came down one side of the pocket. The casualties were finally recovered at 3:00 PM.

During that time, the 1st Battalion reported a significant 1,000-yard gap to its right flank. The 7th Marines were ordered to move over to its own left boundary, a movement that placed 1/4 behind them. The 1st Battalion side-slipped back to its own zone and ran into strong enemy positions in caves. A tank platoon helped destroy the stiff opposition, and 1/4 advanced farther northeast.

The island inhabitants had fled the aerial and naval bombardments with their belongings and cowered in caves near their homes. The Marine squads encountered hundreds of dazed civilians. Cautious because enemy snipers masqueraded in civilian clothes, the Marines interrogated locals and sent them to the Division Intelligence section.

Orders came at 6:30 PM for the 4th Marines to cease their attack.

Corporal Bush had his squad dig their night foxholes 1,000 yards forward of what had been designated the L-plus 3 line. The assault was ahead of the operational plan. The 6th MarDiv had captured 3,500–7,000 yards of enemy ground. A VMO-2 observation plane landed at Yontan late in the day—the first American aircraft on Okinawa.

Evening musters counted the day's casualties. Company C Platoon Sergeant Richard A. Hays, Mount Vernon, Illinois, and Corporal Stephen Edward Advent, Gray's Landing, Pennsylvania, were KIA. [5]

Company B reported to 1/4 Headquarters. First Lieutenant Thad Nelson Dodds, 30, previously wounded on Guam, had been killed in action. First Lieutenant Charles E. James took command of the company.

Besides the notification of their son's death and his Purple Heart and Silver Star medals, Nelson and Iona Dodds received a communiqué in Langeloth, Pennsylvania, from the American Red Cross at the end of May. Three buildings at Yontan Airfield were named the Thad N. Dodds Recreation Center. [6]

Gains Measured in Yards, Not Miles

April 3. At daybreak, Japanese troops in the formidable hill mass behind Yontan and southwest of Ishikawa offered light and sporadic resistance to the 4th Marines' advance. The hilly terrain was a challenge to navigate, made more difficult by the absence of roads. The regiment secured the hills and ended its attack at 4:30 PM. The 6th Division held its left flank at the base of the Ishikawa Isthmus. Commanders radioed that operations in IIIAC's area were almost twelve days ahead of the planned schedule.

Corporal Bush was 3,000 yards from the east coast and three miles southwest of Ishikawa Town.

April 4. The attack resumed at 7:30 AM. On the left, the 22d Marines drove toward the Ishikawa Peninsula: 2/22 forced its way up the west coast road using a mobile tank-infantry column; 1/22 moved into the interior; 3/22 took the regiment's right flank and drove across the base of the peninsula to hit Ishikawa.

The 4th Marines struggled over steep ridges against moderate resistance and fell behind. By midday, CPL Bush had reached the east coast. The regiment had crossed the entire island—twelve miles—but was out of the line of advance due to the 22d Marines reaching Ishikawa.

Orders came: shift 90 degrees as had been planned during the previous four months of training, and sweep north, up the Ishikawa Isthmus. What might have been considered "hospitable" terrain for maneuvering ground forces was going to be behind them. Once inland, the Okinawa terrain to the north turned from hills into mountainous rises. The roads were primitive, unsurfaced, and narrow. Steep ravines hampered traffic. Partially concealed trails traversed wooded hills and ridges. Caves were concealed in coral walls, crags, and cliffs of the mountains.

The 22d Marines, reinforced by 1/29, were now responsible for covering the entire 6th Division front from one coast to the other.

The enemy seemed to be making their way towards Motobu Peninsula, blowing road bridges as they moved.

As CPL Bush pushed the squad forward, they encountered small Japanese units and stragglers who had been forced north. In the afternoon, a major rainstorm that lasted into the next day turned the roads and trails into muddy bogs and slowed them down further.

After clearing its zone, the 4th Marines assembled in division reserve at 4:00 PM, as ordered. The attack continued against scattered resistance. By nightfall, the assault forces had advanced up Ishikawa Isthmus and established their lines from Yakada on the west to five miles north of Ishikawa Town on the east. The advance through the mountain range had gained 7,500 yards, but had strained supply lines.

Corporal Bush bivouacked with 1/4 at Ishikawa.

April 5. H-Hour was delayed so that supplies could reach the forward assault force. While they waited, the battalions patrolled 500 yards to their front. At 9:00 AM, the 6th Reconnaissance Company moved up the west coastal road in an armored column toward Chuda and the Motobu Peninsula, searching for the enemy and routes of advance.

The 4th Marines sent Company F, 2d Battalion, reinforced with a tank platoon and tank dozer, to conduct reconnaissance up the east coast road. Charlie Company remained as rear guard with 1/4 at Ishikawa.

Meeting little to no organized opposition, only undefended roadblocks delayed Company F's reconnaissance. The assault battalions progressed rapidly behind the mobile reconnaissance forces. Tanks engaged a small number of Japanese at Chimu Town without taking casualties. In late afternoon, having advanced twelve miles, Company F turned back and linked up with the battalion eight miles to the south. Scattered rains fell in the early evening.

At the end of the day, the 22d Marines held a line from Atsutabaru to Chimu. The 6th MarDiv had gained another 7,000 yards.

Small, scattered, well-armed enemy groups attempted to penetrate the Marine defenses from behind the lines through the night.

Third Platoon Sergeant Woodruff gathered CPL Bush and the squad leaders for a briefing. Colonel Shapley's plan was to rapidly advance the regiment up the main east coastal road fourteen miles north to Ora Village. The 2d and 3d battalions had assembled just behind the 22d Marines' lines and prepared to pass through the regiment in a column in the morning. The 1st Battalion would follow from Ishikawa, and the 22d Marines would revert to division reserve.

Corporal Bush passed the word and let his squad know that enemy activity was increasing.

April 6. The 4th passed through the 22d Marines. The 2d Battalion reinforced by a platoon of tanks led as the advance guard. The regimental CP moved out in a jeep convoy at the head of the main body, moving along the shore in a "contact imminent" formation.

Corporal Bush, with 1/4, was at the rear of the column, behind the 3/4. The column slowed whenever encountering the few roads leading west, inland into the mountainous and generally uninhabited interior. Patrols from the advance guard detached to investigate all roads and trails to their end. Ahead, friendly air had destroyed three bridges, further slowing progress and hampering supply operations.

The 22d Marines began active patrolling back to the reconnaissance company's Area of Responsibility, mopping up enemy remnants to that boundary, then, began patrolling up the Ishikawa Isthmus to the Yakada-Yaka Line. The 29th Marines drove up the west coast in a column of battalions behind an armored spearhead, sending patrols to the east to probe inland. The regiment reached its objective at Chuda by noon.

On the east road, the detachment of small patrols had depleted 2/4 by 1:00 PM. The 3d Battalion passed through, and the 2d Battalion reassembled at the rear of the column behind the 1st Battalion. Charlie Company passed beyond 781-foot Ishikawa Take and 1,184-foot Onna Take in the spinous mountain range to their west.

Word from the Hagushi beaches would not catch up with the advancing battalions until the evening supply run. At 3:00 PM, 200 kamikazes began a carefully planned attack at the Hagushi anchorage. The suicide attack went on for five hours. At 3:30 PM, a kamikaze crashed into the USS *Bush*, DD-529, a Fletcher Class destroyer on picket patrol. Two more suicide planes followed. USS *Bush* went under at 7:50 PM.

Having advanced seven miles, the 4th Marines' column halted at 4:00 PM. Corporal Bush and his squad dug in south of Madaira.

The Japanese continued their retreat north during the night, destroying highway facilities behind them. At intervals, they built obstacles with logs and tree branches, laid in rows across the roads. The sense of urgency in which they were retreating from the Marines was evident in that they did not take time to mine or booby-trap or wire the fortifications in place.

April 7. The 4th Marines resumed their advance in the morning, planning to repeat Friday's operations. They would advance another seven miles through enemy territory. The battalions moved out in the same formation in which they had halted the evening before. Tank dozers and bulldozers easily pushed aside the passive defense abatis left by the enemy, and forward progress was hardly slowed, except by the poor condition of the road. The 3d Battalion committed security detachments to the flanks. The extensive patrolling through enemy territory and the rugged terrain proved physically exhausting to the footsore grunts.

On the western flank, the 29th Marines continued the drive to the base of the Motobu Peninsula, seizing the bomb- and shell-flattened town of Nago at noon. Enemy resistance began to stiffen on the peninsula. The Marines swung up the west coast road to Awa and Taira villages and established a line across the base of Motobu to Nakaoshi.

The 1st Battalion, 4th Marines, began passing through the 3d Battalion to take the advance guard position on the east at 12:00 PM. The mountains closed in on the sea, and the coastal road narrowed to the point that armor and trucks could not penetrate. The engineers scraped along the trails, widening the "thoroughfares." By late afternoon on Love Day-plus-six, 1/4 had reached their assigned objective to the north of Ora Village. The companies set up a perimeter defense. Once their flanks were secured on the coast, the regimental CP and Weapons Company took position in Ora. At 1,000-yard intervals on the road west of the village, 3/4 and 2/4 established defensive perimeters.

Five miles of mountains separated CPL Bush from Motobu Peninsula to his west.

The 22d Marines dug in between the peninsula and the 4th Marines. Their regimental CP was near Taira. The regiments had taken the Ishikawa Isthmus, and the enemy remnants made their way towards Motobu Peninsula.

Commanders began planning to seize the area up to Hedo Misake at the northernmost tip of Okinawa, Motobu to the west, and the several small Shimas (islands) around the peninsula. Aerial observation and reconnaissance photos made it clear that the enemy garrison fortified in the rugged Motobu mountains was preparing for a fight. In six square miles, the Japanese had established defensive outposts and the commander's fortress on Mount Yae Take.

April 8. On Sunday, CPL Bush briefed his squad near Ora. The 1st Battalion companies would remain in position to support and reinforce either the 29th Marines advancing on Motobu or the 22d Marines moving north. No significant encounters were reported as companies of the 4th and 22d Marines spent the day searching out the enemy in the rugged interior and patrolling to the north.

By day's end, the 29th Marines had progressed into the narrow neck of Motobu. The forward line stretched across the peninsula. Dark descended on the heavily wooded ravines and the twisting rocky ridges of Yae Take's sprawling, steep slopes.

April 9. The 29th Marines moved out in three columns in search of the enemy's main force. The 3d Battalion took the south coast road from Nago, through Awa, toward Toguchi. On the north coast road, the 2d Battalion set out for Nakasoni Village and the submarine and torpedo boat base at Unten Ko. The 1st Battalion's objective was Itomi, up the peninsula's center.

The 4th Marines continued patrolling north on the east side of the island as the 22d Marines patrolled up the west side.

On Motobu, the 29th Marines ran into a heavily defended enemy experienced in mountain combat. A considerable enemy force confronted all three advancing columns from Toguchi east to Itomi, and the opposition was stiff. Field artillery batteries, light mortars, 25mm naval guns, and 20mm dual-purpose cannons fired from fixed hill emplacements around the Yae Take fortress. The rising terrain provided the Japanese abundant ambush sites around their defensive perimeter. Vegetation and short trees concealed cave openings. Roadblocks, mines, and demolitions made the roads practically impassable. Machine-gun outposts kept fire on the Marines. Enemy resistance was most stubborn in the center. The advance halted.

The 3d Battalion was near its objective at Toguchi. On the right, 2/29 had patrolled to Nakasoni. In the center, 1/29 dug in for the night 600 yards short of Itomi.

April 10. The operational plan for Motobu was to patrol around the mountain to determine enemy positions and hold them in place. Gray storm clouds cloaked the peninsula in the morning. Another tropical storm unleashed a torrent on the island, and rain fell all day Tuesday. CPL Bush and his men covered themselves with ponchos and watched their foxholes fill with muddy water.

The 29th Marines did much of the day's fighting. The Japanese had established a submarine and torpedo boat base at Unten Ko. The 2d Battalion seized the base, finding large amounts of abandoned equipment and supplies. The peninsula civilians reported that 150 naval personnel had fled into the inland mountains.

On the other side of Motobu, 3/29 captured Toguchi, and then, sent patrols into the interior. The 1st Battalion pushed forward through Itomi and encountered well-prepared positions on the high ground north of the village. The terrain was difficult, and enemy ambushes and artillery fire increased northwest and southwest of Itomi. When 1/29 set up in its night defensive perimeter, enemy counterattacks intensified. One attack came late in the night and lasted into the morning, supported by artillery, mortars, machine guns, and 20mm dual-purpose cannon fire.

April 11. The rain continued unabated on Wednesday. Patrols in the high ground all around Yae Taki pinpointed the Japanese battle position between Itomi and Toguchi. The Marines had the mountain surrounded and waited for orders to assault the fortress heights that commanded the outlying islands and all Nago Wan. For two days, they reconnoitered and probed the enemy defenses.

On the north side of the island, the 4th and 22d Marine patrols linked together eight miles north of Ora, establishing an east-to-west line across Okinawa in the "gentle terrain" between Kawada Wan and Shanna Wan.

April 12. The tropical storm had passed over Okinawa, and the Marine lines on Motobu took intense mortar, light machine-gun, and sniper fire from all directions early in the afternoon. The Japanese had organized their defenses, anticipating the directions from which the Marines would attack. All avenues of approach, nearly impassable, had been heavily mined and covered by fire. The steep, broken terrain would deny tank assaults and slow the infantry. Intelligence estimated that 1,500 enemy troops, firmly fixed in the surrounding 6x8-mile area, defended the fortress.

Company I, 3/29, moved forward into the high ground dominating the western coastal road south of the Manna–Toguchi road and immediately ran into the bulk of the enemy force waiting behind the ridges. Nearly 1,000 Japanese ambushed the company, cut off the platoons, and badly mauled them.

Radio traffic made it clear that one reinforced battalion would not be able to take the stronghold. Machine-gun units, light and medium artillery, 75mm and 150mm artillery, and two 6-inch naval guns capable of putting shells on the coastal road for ten miles south of Motobu supported the infantry inside the enemy garrison. The regiments reconsolidated their positions, and, with the afternoon's reports, division command concluded the plans for the Mount Yae Take assault.

That night, operational plans passed to the regiments. In the morning, commanders were to hold and defend the Bise Sake area on the northwestern tip of Motobu; secure the Kawada Wan–Shana Wan Line to prevent enemy movement toward Motobu; seize, occupy, and defend Hedo Misaki in the north; and destroy the enemy forces on the peninsula.

April 13. On Friday morning at dawn, as the squads ate K-rations for breakfast, word began to spread over ship bullhorns off the coast. Runners carried word to the commanders. "Attention, attention, all hands! President Roosevelt is dead. Repeat, our supreme commander, President Roosevelt, is dead."

President Franklin Delano Roosevelt had suffered a fatal brain hemorrhage on the afternoon of April 12. Ship flags went to half-mast. The vice-president was sworn in as the 33rd President. While Harry S. Truman might have been largely unknown to the servicemen at war, he was a man CPL Bush would admire.

Airstrikes and artillery bombardments punctuated the day.

Colonel Shapley sent the 4th Marines battalions in different directions. The 3d Battalion rode tanks and trucks and dashed northward to Kawada on the east coast. The 2d Battalion moved out on foot across the island, with the 1st Battalion behind them, passing west through the 22d Marines and onto Motobu. Once reaching Yofuke, just south of Nago, 2/4 was directed to march to a point on the southwest corner of the peninsula. The battalion reached its destination just below Toguchi at 5:00 PM, having covered eighteen miles of rugged terrain since morning.

Corporal Bush had his squad digging in at Yofuke at 4:30 PM, when 1/4 was ordered to move to a new position three miles west of Awa. The platoons loaded into trucks and shuttled past Awa one company at a time. The regimental headquarters stayed with the Weapons Company at Yofuke. Corporal Bush was digging in again before dark.

The 1st and 2d Battalions faced Yae Take in separate defensive perimeters three miles apart on the southwest coast of Motobu. Corporal Bush and his men were on the right flank. The 3d Battalion was twenty miles away protecting the rear on the east coast of Okinawa.

By evening, Marines held Hedo Point secure. On Motobu, supply trucks provided CPL Bush and his squad large Baby Ruth candy bars. He made sure his squad stripped down their M1 rifles and cleaned them to prevent any jamming or misfires. He waited for 3d Platoon Sergeant Woodruff to pass along word about what to expect in the morning.

A coordinated attack to destroy the Japanese garrison from two opposing directions was planned for the next day. The 1st and 2d battalions, 29th Marines, would drive west and southwest from the peninsula's center. From the west coastal road, 3/29 would take the left flank attached to the 4th Marines.

Corporal Bush was on the right flank again with 1/4, and 2/4 was in the center. The three battalions were to attack easterly 1,200 yards inland from the coast and seize the 700-foot ridge where Company I had been ambushed two days earlier. Yae Take would sit between the two assault regiments, blocking most overlapping artillery, air, and naval gunfire support. There would be no more reports of the assault force making "giant strides."

April 14. L+13 marked two weeks of battling on Okinawa. Before dawn, the Japanese ambushed a 1/4 security patrol in regimental reserve. The patrol took eight casualties, but drove the enemy group back into the crevices of the hill mass. At dawn, the artillery, aerial, and naval bombardment of the inland ridge began. The assault jumped off at 8:00 AM. Protecting what had been the open right flank, 1/4 moved up the coast to an assembly area on 2/4's right rear.

First Lieutenant Washburn received the order at 11:00 AM. Company C was to seize the high ridge to 2/4's right front. Scattered enemy mortar and light artillery fire hit the advancing line. Small enemy groups opposed Charlie Company, but could not stop the assault. Both 1/4 and 2/4 were on the ridge within the hour. Company A was on the left of Company C, and Company B was on the right.

Corporal Bush looked to his front at another ridge 1,000 yards away. The broken terrain and low ground between the two ridges was covered in scrub conifers and tangled underbrush. As he moved about the squad, sharing rations and canteens, the enemy mortar and machine-gun fire intensified.

The three battalions were ordered to take the next high ground. Naval gunfire and artillery barrages pounded the ridge, followed by two air strikes. The advance toward Yae Take continued.

Company C moved down from the ridge and crossed through the hills and steep ravines. The enemy waited in fortified and concealed positions in the dense vegetation. Small groups fired on the advance with heavy Hotchkiss machine guns and Nambus, then, relocated to other well-prepared positions. Responding with rapid bursts of gunfire, the Marines would find the enemy nest empty, with only blood trails to testify to Japanese casualties.

Reaching the ridge, narrow trails served as the avenues of approach to the enemy garrison. The advancing platoons and companies moved warily. The concealed enemy had prepared fields of fire on portions of trails and planned to inflict casualties on the assault's commanding officers.

The enemy watched the lead Marines pass. Major Bernard W. Green and his 1/4 headquarters section reached a designated point. The hidden machine-gun team hit him with a burst of fire, killing the commander instantly. Lieutenant Colonel Fred D. Beans, Regimental Executive Officer, took charge of the 1st Battalion.

Brutal enemy rifle, machine-gun, mortar, and artillery fire hit Company G and Company E, 2/4, just before 2:00 PM. Company G suffered many casualties, and Company F moved in for support. The Marines spotted the artillery piece and called for naval gunfire and artillery support. The enemy position was destroyed.

During the day, 3/4 moved across the island by motor march, passed Awa, and relieved 3/22 in division reserve.

With Company C fighting in the center, 1/4 took the high ground on the right of the ridge. The 2d Battalion made a final frontal assault and envelopment from the right, cresting the ridge and contacting 1/4 on the flank. By 4:30 PM, all three battalions were digging their night defensive positions on the objective. The two assault regiments held the lower ridgelines around Yae Take. The enemy defenders had been pushed farther up the mountain slopes.

Commanders studied the operational plans for the next day. The 4th Marines would advance in the same formation in which they had taken the high ground and halted for the night. The 22d Marines were tasked to make an uphill assault from the lower eastern ridge they had seized. The 4th Artillery Battalion, 15th Marines, in support, was to destroy any fortified enemy positions preventing the advance on the Yae Take stronghold.

The nation's attention was not on Yae Take that Saturday. At 10:05 AM, President Roosevelt's body arrived at Union Station in Washington. A military procession led his coffin to the White House. Watching silently, 500,000 people, mourned as his caisson passed by in the hot April sun. The president lay in state in the East Room for five hours. Thousands of citizens lined the iron fences outside. Hundreds attended his simple funeral service. Afterwards, the caisson carried his coffin back to Union Station. His funeral train departed at 10:00 PM for Hyde Park, New York, where the president was buried.

April 15. Company C jumped off at 7:00 AM on Sunday. Only small, scattered enemy groups slowed the attack. The morning seemed to be going like the previous day. Corporal Bush was halfway to the objective, and his squad started to climb the steep mountainside.

At noon, from caves and pillboxes situated in dominating terrain, the enemy laid down heavy and effective fire on the assault units.

Father Redmond looked about at the troops. He did not see the shining, heroic figures that might be the images in song and poetry. "But the reality was a dirty young man with tired eyes, muddy and bloody, ready to throw himself on a live grenade to save his fellow Marine." [7]

✶✶✶

Private First Class Harold Gonsalves had moved onto Motobu with the 4/15, in support of the 22d Marines. Standing at 5 feet 9 inches, weighing 178 pounds, what he would do on this day would not have been a surprise to his classmates in Alameda, California. He had been an active, athletic, and talented boy. In high school, he participated in football, baseball, track, and swimming. He also liked to sing and write and had been a member of the glee club. He had quit high school halfway through his junior year to go to work, and, at age 17, walked into the Oakland Recruiting Office on Thursday, May 27, 1943, to enlist in the Marines. He had already participated in the combat on Engebi and Parry Islands and in the recapture of Guam before landing on Okinawa, his final battle.

Private First Class Gonsalves was part of an eight-man forward observation party. His duties involved coordinating supporting artillery fire for the advancing battalion. Acting as Scout Sergeant of the team, he and another Marine laid telephone lines for communication with the artillery battalion. During the fighting, he had repeatedly risked injury making his way to the observation post to more accurately direct the artillery.

His commanding officer wanted a more advantageous position to better place fire on the enemy stronghold and decided to move further ahead into the front lines. Despite the heavy enemy rifle, grenade, and mortar fire directed against them, the commander led PFC Gonsalves and another Marine uphill to a forward position.

An enemy grenade landed amongst the three Marines, within a foot of the commander. With no hesitation, PFC Gonsalves hurled himself onto the grenade before it detonated. His body absorbed the blast entirely and protected the other two Marines from even small grenade fragments. Private First Class Harold Gonsalves, 19, was the first Marine on Okinawa to earn a Medal of Honor for covering a grenade to protect comrades.

The enemy, at least two companies in depth, had correctly anticipated the direction from which the Marines would attack the stronghold. They had prepared and organized defensive fortifications in the difficult terrain to their greatest advantage. The emplacements within the mountain fortress let loose a barrage of artillery, mortars, and rifle fire at the advancing force.

Charlie Company's PFC Leonard Daniel Bartczak, 21, from Cleveland, Ohio, was KIA. First Lieutenant Washburn was WIA, and evacuated. First Lieutenant William H. Carlson took command of the company. He would be WIA in May, returned to duty four days later, and then KIA on June 5.

The supply situation became acute, casualties mounted, and fatigue weighed on the troops. The forward companies sealed one cave after another. The count of enemy dead climbed to 1,120 defenders.

The 4th Marines reached the stronghold's forward position and halted on the objective at 4:30 PM. The two battalions dug in again. On the left flank, 3/29 stopped slightly short of the ridge, but formed its night perimeter in a favorable position.

The battalions reconsidered the merits of a frontal assault. Commanders decided to contain and envelop the enemy garrison by flanking it from the right and shifting the direction of the main assault from east to the north. That put Charlie Company and CPL Bush's squad at the forefront of the morning's attack on the right. The 3d Battalion returned to the 4th Marines' control, and 1/22 was ordered into division reserve back at Awa.

April 16. On Monday, CPL Bush was in the vanguard of the final assault on the Mount Yae Take fortress. As the enemy artillery concentrated its fire on the advance, he directed his squad of thirteen Marines up the precipice, over the ridge, and into the enemy trenches. Their assault drove the Japanese out of their fiercely defended positions.

Charlie Company Corporal Augustine John Rodzinka, 19, and PFC Thomas John Smith, 20, were killed in action. Company A, on the left, lost CPL Chester L. Smith. Corporal "Pappy" Clark, squad leader in Company A, earned his second Purple Heart.

Corporal Forrest H. Miller, a 20-year-old machine-gun squad leader from Chicago, was with Company C on Emirau and had fought on Guam. He was wounded three times on Okinawa, the first time on Monday. When his gunner was wounded during an enemy counterattack, CPL Miller unhesitatingly manned the weapon. His machine gun was hit through the receiver and put out of action. Painfully wounded, he refused to be evacuated. He picked up his rifle and some grenades, crawled forward to a firing position, and aggressively engaged the enemy until hostile fire damaged the rifle. Boldly remaining in his position, CPL Miller continued to engage the enemy by throwing hand grenades. He was awarded a Silver Star for his conspicuous gallantry and intrepidity. [8]

Corporal Bush's squad was on the right flank of the three-battalion line. He pressed his men forward on the eastern mass of Yae Take. The enemy fired from concealed nests with their Nambu .25 caliber machine guns. Enemy artillery drilled into the rocky precipice the men were climbing.

In the Face of Trepidation

Words do not adequately depict their experience. Yet, every Marine who survived the fighting on Okinawa returned home with stories they would tell only to each other. The squad kept climbing. They did not stop to think about fear or bravery.

Private First Class William C. Council was WIA on Okinawa. "A Nip mortar shell exploded eight feet in front of me, spun me around and caused some minor injuries . . . It smashed hell out of a kid from Alabama" and another from Vermont. Later, on another night at 1:00 AM near Naha, one of his squad mates lost his legs near him.

Acting bravely means perceiving a danger or threat, real or imagined, and, then demonstrating an admirable human action, an indifference to fear, and a disregard for personal danger. This indifference to fear is not the absence of it. Bravery is about managing fear, not being without it. A brave person consciously rises to meet a challenge that triggers fear, draws upon a personal strength, and takes an initiative few might endeavor. Again, a brave person does not act without fear. Corporal Bush was aware of that reality.

"I was scared most of the time," he would admit later. "Some of the guys I fought with seemed fearless and crazy, and I guess at the time they felt the same about me." [9]

Marines who had fought in the earlier Pacific Island battles, along with MOH recipients who had demonstrated heroic bravery in obviously dangerous and life-threatening situations, also experienced natural fear. Corporal Bush would share "sea stories" with many of these men in the future.

Famed 1st Battalion Raider "Red Mike" Edson, reputed to have willingly and coldly looked death in the eye, wrote of his extensive combat experiences: "I have been scared half to death more than once, more often than anyone realizes." [10]

Major Justice M. Chambers, commanding Company D, 1st Raiders, had a surprise encounter with a Japanese soldier in a clearing during the first day of fighting on Tulagi, August 7, 1942. [11] He dove to his left while firing his Reising submachine gun. His summation of that moment: "It was just a question of who was the most scared." [12]

Captain John Lucian Smith, Marine Ace pilot who was in command of VMF-223 flying from Henderson Airfield on Guadalcanal during the Battle of Bloody Ridge, willingly admitted to being afraid during the early days of the first American offensive: "They were just as scared of us as we were of them." [13]

First Lieutenant James Elms Swett, who had also flown over Guadalcanal, said: "I was, number one, scared—number two, frightened—number three, ready to bail out of that darned thing . . . you couldn't believe how nervous I was." [14]

Of his heroic actions on Hill 100, Peleliu Island, Captain Everett Parker Pope said: "We were all scared but able to overcome our fears and do what was expected of us." [15]

Captain Joseph Jeremiah McCarthy had earned a Medal during the approach to Motoyama Airfield No. 2, during the first days of fighting on Iwo Jima. He said: "I was scared all the time. Any man tells you he wasn't scared was an imbecile. But you dealt with it." [16]

Ernie Pyle, combat correspondent, wrote about ordinary soldiers and Marines in foxholes in the front lines, first covering combat in North Africa, Italy, and France, then, landing with the Marines on Okinawa. He wrote personally about fear. "I don't believe one of us was afraid of the physical part of dying. That isn't the way it is. The emotion is rather one of almost desperate reluctance to give up the future." [17]

Corporal Bush and his squad were in the presence of threat and danger. They were not feeling *brave*—they were feeling fear, and it had put them in a heightened state of agitation in which their attention was concentrated and focused on overtaking the objective realistically perceived as a threat to their survival.

On the other hand, the men were confident in their squad leader. Corporal Bush did not make much about it, but he had been wounded in action on Guam and had avoided treatment by medical personnel. He had once been ill and out of the fight, then insisted on returning to his unit. He would see them through this fight, but he had to admit to being afraid.

"I was afraid to die, but didn't want to die afraid." [18]

Corporal Bush led his squad over a ridge, the first to penetrate the inner defensive perimeter on top of 1,200-foot Mount Yae Take. About 100 enemy soldiers fired on them and wildly threw grenades. The squad drove the Japanese out of their entrenched fortification, killing about seventy-five, but taking casualties.

Charlie Company 2dLt Eugene Pierre Cyprien Constantin, III, 22, of Dallas, Texas, was killed in the assault. Corporal Augustine John Rodzinka, 19, Perth Amboy, New Jersey, and PFC Thomas John Smith, 20, Oak Park, Illinois, both died of their wounds. Platoon Sergeant Woodruff was wounded in the right leg.

Corporal Bush was among the serious casualties. Enemy bullets hit both of his thighs. The bullet to his left thigh, missed bone, and exited the back of his thigh. Initially ignoring the bullet wounds, he was ordered to a makeshift field medical station and was evacuated to a "protected" place with a rocky outcrop above.

The enemy fought to hold on to the ridge. Corporal Bush lay prone among injured Marines as the doctors administered treatment. He was as "alert and courageous in extremity as in battle."

An enemy hand grenade landed near him, endangering medical staff and wounded Marines.

Corporal Bush, 20 years old, instantly reached out, grabbed the grenade with his right hand, and pulled it into his body, cradling the projectile into his abdomen with his left leg and arm, smothering the shattering explosion and containing its violent impact to himself.

CHAPTER 20

Setting a Good Example

✳✳✳

"The boundaries which divide Life from Death are at best shadowy and vague." [1]

— EDGAR ALLAN POE

CORPORAL BUSH'S BLOOD PRESSURE INDICATED that he was alive. He had hundreds of holes in his body from grenade shrapnel and Japanese bullets. To stop his bleeding, a corpsman patched him up as best as he was able, gave him a shot of morphine, and went on tending to the others.

A truck took the wounded down the road, back to the beach. He had multiple shell fragments in his face, chest, and stomach. His right hand was a mangled mess and parts of three fingers were missing. A Navy doctor came by and administered more morphine. Medics scribbled on his casualty card—"not due to his own conduct . . . Negligence not apparent . . . Wounded in action against an organized enemy."

"And not being able to get up again at the time, that is where the war ended for me." Corporal Bush wrote that in a letter years later.

The events of April 16 would forever remain somewhat unclear in his mind. He would never be able to recall the reason a recommendation had been sent up the chain of command to the president. He would remember leading his thirteen men up the hill and the wild scuffle that ensued. ". . . but I can't figure out exactly what I personally did to rout them."

The one thing he would remember clearly was picking up one of their grenades. "I figured I could throw it back at them before it went off, but my missing right eye shows I figured wrong."

April 16, 1945. His stretcher was strapped onto a pallet in the bottom of an amphibious tractor, and he was transferred to the USS *Arcturus*—LST(H) 951. Corporal Bush had a noticeable bullet wound to his left leg and multiple small shrapnel and powder wounds to the right side of his face, behind his right ear, on his left shoulder, chest, trunk, abdomen, and anus. He was in a state of concussion. That night, a laparotomy through the left upper quadrant of the abdominal wall gave access into the abdominal cavity. The 8-inch incision allowed shrapnel to be removed from his stomach.

Following required sanitary duties, the fleet surgeon noted in "this 20-year-old man's" health record a diagnosis and the cause under which his injuries were incurred. Notations of CPL Bush's #2564 (multiple wounds) diagnosis included "Key letter K," indicating "wound, gunshot received in action" and "DNEPTE."

April 17. On a whole-blood-plasma IV, CPL Bush was taken up on the USS *Samaritan*, AH-10, to be treated by a variety of doctors and surgeons. The hospital ship pulled up anchors and sailed for USAH Saipan, 1,207 nm south. His long voyage home had begun.

Physical and X-Ray examinations located the damages—primarily to his left side. Most of his bones were intact without fractures. His most obvious wounds were to both hands and both legs above the knees.

There was an abrasion of cornea-conjunctival hemorrhage of his left eye. The anterior eye chamber was well formed, his pupil reacted, the media was clear, and the fundus normal. There was no apparent vision impairment and no neurological signs. His right eye appeared normal. The injuries to his eyes were not as urgent as his more obvious wounds.

An X-Ray showed a linear skull fracture, running transversely across the right temporal and parietal bones, terminating in the anterior fossa at the base of his skull.

His abdomen showed no evidence of intra-pathology, but many minute metallic foreign bodies appeared in the right upper quadrant and throughout the left side. The X-Ray did not determine if the metal was intra-abdominal or in the abdominal wall.

There was no evidence of fracture of the right knee, but several minute metallic foreign bodies were noted. The lower half of his left thigh, including the knee joint, showed no evidence of fracture, but numerous minute metallic foreign bodies were noted throughout the soft tissue.

His left wrist and hand showed no evidence of fracture. Many minute metallic foreign bodies were noted. The left hand was scrubbed and dressed.

His right forearm and wrist showed no evidence of fracture. Many minute metallic foreign bodies were noted in the forearm and hand. To promote healing, Doctor H. Lohnaas first removed (debridement) the unhealthy and dead tissue from the wounds to CPL Bush's hands and thighs.

The two bones of his right 5th (little) finger were separated (disarticulated) at their joint. The metacarpal head was cut (rongeured) off. The doctors trimmed back the metacarpal until bone was covered by soft tissue. The upper half of his finger was gone. The lower bone (proximal phalanx) of his ring finger remained, but had been fractured into numerous fragments. Doctor Lohnaas decided to leave this, since the skin circulation was good. The tips (distal phalanges) of his index and middle finger were missing. His thumb was intact. "This hand was trimmed up and repaired."

Corporal Bush had numerous wounds on his left thigh. The wounds were left open with a clamp, front and back, to permit drainage. All his wounds were left open with sulfa and Vaseline gauze dressings.

The Marines finally swept over Yae Take on April 17.

April 18. Motobu Peninsula was cleared of all significant resistance. Before a telegram reached Glasgow that CPL Bush had been wounded in action, newspapers at home printed bold headlines of a grim death on Okinawa that took place two days after CPL Bush had saved others from an enemy grenade. It was gloomy news he would learn about in California. Ernie Pyle, 44, had joined the thousands of men who would never come home to sing and dance again.

A Japanese sniper fired from a hidden machine-gun pit on the Isle of Ie Shima off the northwest coast of Okinawa. A bullet struck Ernie in the left temple just under his helmet, set him back on his heels, and instantly killed him. Shortly after he died on the ridge, a combat photographer took a shot of the old correspondent dressed in Army fatigues and boots, his helmet slightly ajar. Stretched out peacefully on his back still wearing his glasses, a thin trail of blood trickling from the right corner of his mouth, he appeared to be asleep. His hands, holding a military cap, were folded across his waist. [2]

April 20. USS *Samaritan* arrived at Saipan. The doctors began digging out and removing what shrapnel they could. Corporal Bush had about twenty small shrapnel wounds on his anterior chest and upper abdomen, about forty in his right forearm, and about 120 in his right arm and hand. The greatest damage was to his left lateral thigh and leg and to his right hand. He had approximately 300 small shrapnel wounds in his left leg. He had lost a portion of his right middle finger and most of his ring and little finger. His right index finger was also injured. The operations were painstaking and his convalescence slow. His body temperature was gradually trending down toward normal. He was at the USAH for two weeks.

April 21. Headquarters Marine Corps, Washington, D.C. received a MAILBRIEF reporting that CPL Bush was a battle casualty: nature of his wound was shell fragments to the face and chest.

April 22. Marine command declared Motobu Peninsula secured on Okinawa. The 6th Marine Division lost 207 Marines killed in the battle. Corporal Bush was counted among the 757 wounded, although his Company C comrades did not know his condition. Over 2,500 enemy soldiers were killed. Only forty-six were captured and taken prisoners.

After the enemy's Motobu defense had crumbled and the Marines had captured Mount Yae Take, firefights continued with small groups of Motobu battle survivors and stragglers trying to make their way from the peninsula to the island's mountainous interior. The 4th Marines moved up the west coast of the main island to the small village of Genka, five miles from the peninsula.

April 27. Scattered rains curtailed supply operations and tank support. Then, during the afternoon, a reconnaissance patrol sighted a column of 200 hostiles infiltrating from the Taira area and moving in the direction of the east coast through the regiment's northeast corner. The fighting was bitter, bloody, close-quarter infantry combat. Charlie Company Second Lieutenant John F. Sudro, 27, Woodhaven, New York, died in the fighting. He and his close friend, 2dLt Michael Dunbar, had served together in various places as corporals since before 1942, and had earned field promotions. Lieutenant Dunbar was with the 2/4 and would always remember that day when he was told his friend was KIA. Forty-five years later, he recalled in an interview. "I cried when he was killed on Okinawa." [3]

Private First Class "Skull" Brewington was wounded in the fighting. He came home with a Purple Heart medal and a Japanese officer's saber. He would later describe to family that he had earned the medal, because he got "poked in the butt." He kept the details to himself. [4]

April 30. Lieutenant Colonel Fred D. Beans, Commanding Officer, Forward Echelon, 1/4, collected the witness statements from 1stLt William H. Carlson and 2dLt Corbin B. Bryan III, included a sample Medal of Honor Citation, signed the award recommendation, and forwarded it up the chain to the Secretary of the Navy via Colonel Alan Shapley, the 4th Marines commander.

May 4. Corporal Bush was transferred to a U.S. Government Transport and flown to the USNH Aieah Heights overlooking Pearl Harbor on Oahu, Territory of Hawaii. Most of his small shrapnel wounds had healed nicely. The long incision across his abdomen was healed. Two large wounds on his right forearm were still open. For the next many months, he was going to listen to many conversations about phalanxes and metacarpals, interphalangeal and metacarpal joints, metacarpal-phalangeal joints, distal and proximal, flexion and extension.

The large wounds on his right ring finger and 5th finger were infected, and his entire right hand was markedly swollen, especially his index and ring finger. New connective tissue and microscopic blood vessels were forming on the surfaces of six dime-sized wounds on his left thigh. The granulation tissue was good evidence of healing.

May 5. First Lieutenant John W. Barr, 148th General Hospital, San Francisco, sent a notice of present casualty status, written in nontechnical language, to Mrs. Bush. Her son was "making normal improvement" with his diagnosed "slight fracture of temporal region of head."

May 7. After the fighting near Genka on Okinawa, the 6th Division assembled near Chibana to take over the zone the 1st MarDiv was holding. In places unfamiliar to CPL Bush, three men of the 1st Marines had died protecting comrades from grenades in that first week of May.

✳✳✳

William Adelbert Foster was born in Garfield Heights, Ohio, on February 17, 1915. Growing up to be just under 6 feet tall, weighing 170 pounds, he graduated from a vocational high school and went right to work as a machinist in a machine and tool company. He joined the Ohio National Guard, serving with them for six years. Although he might have remained out of combat circumstances by maintaining his Guard status when WWII began, Bill enlisted in the Marines on April 1, 1944, and left Ohio behind.

On Easter Sunday, exactly one year after joining the Marines, PFC Foster, a rifleman with K/3/1, had waited on the transfer line for available landing craft to take him ashore. The 1st and 2d battalions made landings at 6:00 PM. It was too late to transfer to LVTs, and the 3d Battalion was ordered to remain in the boats on the transfer line all night. Private First Class Foster landed with King Company on Monday morning and entered combat for the first time. The battalion was assigned as the 1st Division reserve ashore behind the assaulting 5th and 7th Marines. He then turned south with them in their sector of operation.

One month later, having fought his way across the island and north in the conquest of the upper island, PFC Foster redeployed south to relieve the Army units who had encountered bitter Japanese resistance. The objective was to press the defenders along the western coastal flank in the southern sectors. The enemy was putting up a desperate defense at the Shuri perimeter, trying to hold on to the little bit of island left to them. The Japanese were also planning offensive actions in hopes of repulsing the American advance.

By midnight on Tuesday, May 1, PFC Foster had passed through Yafusu Village, on the east side of Machinato Airfield.

At 4:20 PM on Wednesday, in a gloomy, driving rain, he watched a Marine artillery barrage hit a series of small hills 300 yards south of Miyagusuku Village. Ten minutes later, Company K led a ferocious assault against a strong enemy hill fortification. Continuous enemy machine-gun fire and knee mortar shells fell on the forward elements as they fought through the broken ground southeast of the airfield.

The 3rd Battalion was ordered to hold its present position at 10:00 PM. Private First Class Foster dug in, sharing a foxhole with another Marine at the point of the perimeter defense line. He was one year, one month, and one day into his enlistment.

Japanese soldiers did not give up ground easily and typically counterattacked "fanatically." Some penetrated the defensive perimeter and engaged the Marines in close proximity. The hand-to-hand clashes on the hill were violent. Company K struggled to keep the high ground.

Private First Class Foster and his companion fought to maintain their position, exchanging hand grenades with the closing enemy soldiers. A grenade landed in their foxhole, just beyond their reach. Private First Class Foster dived upon it, smothering the explosion with his body.

Stunned and terribly wounded, his life seeping into the Okinawa ground, he had time enough to consider himself, his injuries, his fate; to think of his homeland, his family who would receive a telegram about him; to recite a prayer. Instead, PFC Foster's thoughts were of the fight and his duty. He concentrated his remaining strength for one last heroically brave action.

He had two grenades left with him in the foxhole. Without the strength to throw them himself in the ongoing fight, he handed them to his fellow Marine. Before dying from his wounds, PFC William Foster, 30 years old, spoke his last words to his comrade.

"Make them count." [5]

Elbert Luther Kinser was born in eastern Tennessee on October 21, 1922, in the foothills of the Appalachian Mountain range near the border with North Carolina. His boyhood was spent in a scenic land of long valleys and rolling hills, forests, creeks, still-water lakes, and tree-stump backwaters. Elbert lived, went to school, and worked on his father's farm in rural Greenville until he was 20 years old. In December 1942, he enlisted in the Marines.

By the time he was assigned to Company I, 3d Battalion, 1st Marines, in Melbourne, Australia, Elbert had demonstrated his proficiencies as a rifleman in practice landings. The Tennessean had a steadiness, a groundedness about him; perhaps grown out of helping his father labor to preserve a Depression-era family farm. At the end of 1943, he had fought with his company at Cape Gloucester on the northwestern tip of volcanic New Britain Island, a place the Marines remembered as *The Green Inferno*. Promotions in rank followed. He went ashore with Item Company again on Peleliu Island in September 1944. Before the end of the year, Corporal Kinser was promoted to sergeant and assigned duties as a platoon leader.

On Easter Sunday, just as PFC Foster had, Sergeant Kinser and I Company waited all night on the transfer line to land on Okinawa. He landed with his platoon on Monday morning. At the end of April, he redeployed south with the battalion in the same column as PFC Foster.

On Friday morning, May 4, his platoon advanced at 10:00 AM, driving 350 yards to the heights overlooking a defile on their right flank. Uchima Village and the north bank of the Asa Kawa were to their front. The company immediately encountered heavy fire from well-integrated defensive positions on three sides of their advance, but took the ridge.

Intent on holding the position, Sgt Kinser moved up the ridge among his men to survey the situation and place them in effective fighting positions. Enemy soldiers, dug into trenches on the reverse slope, opened on the platoon with vicious fire. Sergeant Kinser was in close to the entrenched enemy and immediately engaged them in an exchange of hand grenades. One enemy grenade landed in the proximity of several of his men.

Sergeant Elbert Kinser, 22 years old, dived onto the grenade before it exploded. His action protected his men from the blast at the cost of his own life.

John Peter Fardy was born in Chicago on August 15, 1922, two months before Elbert Kinser was born in Tennessee. [6] John had grown up in the windy city when gangland battles added to the noise and notoriety of Chicago. He was drafted into the Marines on May 8, 1943, said goodbye to his parents and sisters on South Calumet Avenue, and left for the San Diego Recruit Depot.

Private First Class Fardy served as an automatic rifleman with C/1/1. He had first stood up to the rigors of combat at Cape Gloucester, landing there on the day after Christmas 1943. He next waded through the surf and struck the beaches during the amphibious assault of Peleliu on September 15. Private First Class Fardy fought in the capture of the airfield on the island and in the routing of the Japanese from caves in the coral hills inland from the airfield. He departed from Peleliu with his regiment in early October when the island had been secured. He was promoted to corporal in December and assigned duties as a squad leader.

Corporal Fardy had participated in the Easter Sunday landing, stepping onto the beaches at 6:00 PM. On May 6, after five weeks on Okinawa, C/1/1 engaged a well-defended, heavily fortified Japanese emplacement near Uchima Village. His squad was moving along a drainage ditch when a force of concealed defenders opened fire upon them with rifles and other small arms. The enemy soldiers kept the squad pinned down with relentless fire.

The ditch accorded the Marines some protection against the small arms, so the Japanese attacked with grenades. One of the explosive devices rolled into the ditch. Corporal Fardy, 22, immediately jumped on it, taking the full force of the detonation himself. He survived the blast and was evacuated to a field hospital, but died of his wounds on May 7. He was the last Marine in WWII to earn a Medal of Honor for sacrificing his life on top of a grenade.

✳✳✳

May 10. Colonel Alan Shapley, 4th Marines commander in the field, signed and forwarded the 1st Endorsement of CPL Bush's MOH award package, recommending approval. From that point on, the recommendation was to be reviewed by Marine generals, all of them combat veterans, and Navy admirals.

May 11. Lieutenant Commander P. C. Guzzetta Jr. predicted prolonged convalescence for CPL Bush and recommended evacuation to the mainland for further treatment and disposition. Corporal Bush would not have a single dance with hula girls while on Oahu. All movement was on a hospital litter.

May 14. Major D. Routh, USMC, Casualty branch, Adjutant General's Office, War Department, sent a notice to Mr. and Mrs. Clarence Bush in Glasgow. A brief report had just been received that their son had sustained a shrapnel wound of the head and chest in action against an enemy on Okinawa Island. "Your anxiety is realized, and you may be sure that any additional details or information received will be forwarded to you at the earliest possible moment."

May 17. The Navy Dentist noted damage to his upper right canine, upper left front tooth, and a second cavity on his upper left molar 14—all DNEPTE.

May 18. A month had passed since a corpsman had first written "multiple wounds" on a field casualty card. From Hawaii, CPL Bush was flown to USNH Oakland in California. Most of his shrapnel wounds had healed well, and his physical exam was "essentially negative" for symptoms. His right hand and amputated fingers where there was still some drainage remained the chief medical concern. His temperature was normal; his pulse was 80/min; his blood pressure was 116/74. He was to continue receiving penicillin until May 22.

"Mugsy took one in the chest, but made it back." A month into his recuperation, naturally, CPL Bush was relieved to be away from the dangers of combat. But, he had been a squad leader and wondered about his men. Had he been physically capable, he would have requested to return to the Pacific Islands. He learned gradually of the 6th Division's attacks on the enemy defenses in the Shuri Heights, on Sugar Loaf and Half Moon hills, and on the Oroku Peninsula. When comrades visited with him at the hospital, he heard all about the unrelenting Okinawa rains and the slick and deep mud. More difficult for him was learning of the men he had known from Company C who were killed in action as the battles continued. He would not learn of some of the names until the former Raiders began searching for each other decades later.

Private First Class William M. Jaspers, 20, died on May 15. Privates first class Alvin Roy Ahlgrim, 21, and Billie Bryant Fornof, 19, both died on May 20. Private First Class Wendell Phillips Ela, 23, Company G, 2d Battalion, who stood below CPL Bush in the 884th Platoon MCRD San Diego photo, was KIA on May 21.

May 23. The day was one of the worst on Okinawa for Charlie Company. The 4th Marines intensified its early morning patrol activities south of the Asato Gawa. The companies began wading across the stream at 10:30 AM, moving toward Machisi and Naha City. Resistance intensified as the assault troops approached a ridge 500 yards south of the Asato. The enemy had fortified many of the Okinawan tombs on the forward face of the ridge. Mortar positions studded the reverse slopes. Under heavy fire, the advance slowed to a crawl.

First Lieutenant Jack Willard, 26, Binghamton, New York, 2d Lieutenant Corbin Braxton Bryan, III, 26, Falls Church, Virginia, Sergeant Santos Domingo Rodriguez, 21, Sterling, Illinois, and Corporal Samuel Eyewind Mundell, 20, Wichita, Kansas, died before darkness fell on the ridge. Privates First Class Glen Sherlie Stout, 22, Wilmar, California, and 3d Squad, 3d Platoon Private First Class Albert Martin Wood, Greensboro, North Carolina, both died in the approach to the ridge. Staff Sergeant Thomas Joseph Allen, 23, Catasauqua, Pennsylvania, was also on the KIA rolls.

May 23. "Patient is now up and about and feeling well." Corporal Bush, a stretcher patient, was fit for travel and transfer.

At the ridge near Asato, Private Calvin Coldren Gingrich, 19, Mifflintown, Pennsylvania, was killed the next day, and PFC Gene Edward Crawford, 19, Alliance, Nebraska, was KIA on May 25.

May 29. Corporal Bush was fit and feeling well enough to want to have some cash to spend. His April and May checks had not reached him at USNH Oakland or at Marine Barracks, Navy Operating Base, Terminal Island, San Pedro (MBNOB, TI). Adjustments had to be made to his pay since he was no longer overseas. So, LtCol Erwin Mehlinger, Paymaster, cut him an emergency payment check of $20. The TI Paymaster continued to provide him emergency payments: $40 on July 6; $20 on July 20; $20 on August 7; and $15 on August 22. Lois Bush was still receiving the $25 allotment her son had arranged before he left for the Pacific Islands.

June 1. General Lemuel C. Shepherd Jr., 6th Marine Division Commander in the field, signed the 2d Endorsement to the MOH award, "heartily concurring" with the recommendation. From General Shepherd, the Recommendation would have to pass muster with three others before it went to the Secretary of the Navy.

June 1945. Company C lost more combat veterans during the battle for Oroku Peninsula. Private Hershell Paul McMillan, 27, Athens, Tennessee, was KIA on June 3, 1945. Corporal Robert Earl Grant, 20, Janesville, Wisconsin, PFC Milton Joseph Smith, 19, Chipley, Georgia, and Private Chester Arthur Hyche, 20, Searles, Alabama, were killed on June 4. First Lieutenant William Howard Carlson, 30, Company C's ordained Methodist minister from Cohoes, New York, Corporal Calvin Verne Sarchet, 20, Laramie, Wyoming, and PFC Richard Lee Yaeger, 19, Gallipolis, Ohio, were KIA the next day. Corporal Murray Bruce "Mugsy" Arnold Jr., 19, was seriously wounded in the chest and evacuated from the peninsula on June 5. PFC Frank Jay Nist Jr., 19, Dallas, Oregon, died of wounds on June 8, and Corporal Merrill Craig Rannells, 20, Lower Lake, California, died on June 10.

June 8. General Roy S. Geiger, III Amphibious Corps Commander, signed the 3d Endorsement and forwarded it recommending approval.

Captain L. B. Brooks, USMC, Casualty Branch, Adjutant General's Office, War Department, sent additional information to Mr. and Mrs. Bush. The office had been informed that, on May 22, CPL Bush had been transferred to an undesignated hospital in the United States. "It is hoped that he has communicated with you since that time and that you are fully informed of his welfare."

June 13. Corporal Bush was issued emergency clothing—complete Winter Service uniform—from Casualty Company #1 at USNH Oakland. He was transferred to Casualty Company #2, MBNOB, TI, for further treatment at USNH Long Beach.

Most of the small wounds to his face, shoulder, chest, abdomen, forearm, and legs were healed scars. The bullet wound on his left thigh was still draining on front and back, and the wound on his right leg was quite tender. There was 1x1 cm of granulating tissue on his forearm, palm side, at the junction of the middle and upper thirds. The 1 cm shrapnel wound on his right chest at the 7th rib level was granulating.

Corporal Bush's right hand got most of the attention. His fingers, in semi-flexed position and with very slight movement, were swollen. The flexion and extension of his shortened index finger were very slight. A 2x2 cm area of granulating tissue was on the outside (dorsum) stump of his middle finger. The two fingers were held in the flexion position. The open wound on the remaining portion of his ring finger was still draining. There was good motion in his wrist.

June 15–17. Corporal Bush had strength enough on Friday to go on weekend liberty. He went to visit his sister, Velma Edmunson, and stayed at her home ambulating with difficulty on crutches. He was a slender teenager the last time Velma had seen him. Now, he was a well-developed and well-nourished man with fresh scars on his face and bandages on his right hand and forearm. He had grown an inch to 6'1" and weighed 172 pounds.

On Saturday night, he had no appetite for supper, but retired to bed feeling pretty good. He woke up on Sunday morning at 8 o'clock, feeling okay. He had a glass of milk at 10:00 o'clock, vomited, and began to have a chill, aches in his legs, and a headache. Velma applied ice packs to his forehead for an hour, until the spell passed. Then, he became hot and feverish. He could not retain water and vomited five or six times. Velma called for an ambulance at 5:00 o'clock, and CPL Bush was returned to the Long Beach Naval Hospital.

His temperature had risen to 104.6, pulse was 104, respiration 20, and blood pressure 115/50. His skin was hot and moist. His pharynx was moderately injected; he was quite restless and in obvious discomfort. A malaria smear showed positive, and treatment was started immediately.

Private First Class William Henry Ehlen Jr., 20, from Bloomfield, New Jersey, had earned a Purple Heart on Guam. That Sunday, he died of wounds on Oroku Peninsula, five days before the fighting for Okinawa ended.

June 18. Although CPL Bush had full range of motion in his left knee, considerable atrophy of the quadriceps muscle group impaired his movements. Physical exercises for his leg muscles continued.

June 19. Corporal Frank Eugene Wood, 20, Goldsmith, Indiana, 3d Squad, 3d Platoon, Company C, PFC Linus Noal Holland, 21, Rising Sun, Indiana, and PFC Robert Charles Wright, 19, Los Angeles, were all KIA on Tuesday.

June 20. X-Rays taken through the bandages of CPL Bush's right hand and forearm showed innumerable small shrapnel pieces in the soft tissues about the fingers and thumb. The largest was 3mm in diameter. A few pieces were evident in his lower forearm. Moderate decalcification of the bones was present. Whirlpool baths to the right hand began.

Corporal Bush met Raider comrades in Ward C-3. Corporal Raymond John Powers, 20, from Minnetonka, Minnesota, a C/1/4 grunt wounded on Guam on July 27, 1944, was eleven months into his twenty-six "glorious months" in the hospital. Private First Class George Alexander MacRae, 27, of Halifax, Nova Scotia, K/3/4, had stories to tell of his Olympic hopes when he was setting track records at LSU before the war broke out. He had lost the use of his right arm and would spend more than two years in and out of hospitals recovering from his wounds. Arnold Miller supported himself on crutches when his photo was taken with the three Raiders outside on the hospital grounds.

Corporal Bush, Ray, and George listened to the war news on the ward radio. While they talked about their medical care in Long Beach, about the war, and about whether they would return to units fighting their way to mainland Japan, casualties from the islands joined them with battle updates.

June 20. They would be remembered side by side. First Lieutenant David Nathan "Big Dave" Schreiner, 24, had been named to the 1941 All-Big 10 college football team and was a unanimous All-American in 1942. The glue-fingered right end was co-captain of the 1942 University of Wisconsin *Badgers*. Stocky, big grinning, good-natured Bob Baumann played left tackle with him for four years and was an honorable mention All-American. Coach Harry Augustus "Stuly" Stuhldreherof would remember them both when the news reached the States.

A sports writer told his readers: "You can't write about Dave Schreiner without dealing in superlatives. He was that kind of boy, that kind of an athlete." [7]

Lieutenant Schreiner's A/1/4, platoon had moved into the front lines for the final assault in the Shuri Castle and Meat Loaf Hill region. On June 6, his men were pinned down while fighting toward the ridgeline summit of the Japanese defenses. Lieutenant Baumann, commanding another platoon, worked his way through a gully to let his teammate know tanks were on the way. He was killed on the trail. Lieutenant Schreiner ran up the trail and discovered his friend's body.

Fourteen days later, Lieutenant Schreiner went on a nighttime, pre-attack patrol up 300-foot Kiyama Gusuku hill mass. A Nambu machine gun fired from a cave, hitting him in the chest. A bullet lodged in his spine. As he was loaded onto a jeep to carry him to a field hospital, his men heard his last words. "If any of you think I'm crying, I'll get out of here and kick the shit out of you!"

First Lieutenant Schreiner died of his wounds in the early hours of June 21. [8]

Company C lost two men on June 20. PFC Paul Daniel Curtin, 23, New Castle, Pennsylvania, and Private Trent Earl Brady, 20, Statesville, North Carolina, were both reported killed in action.

Private Napoleon Ephrem LeDoux, 27, Portsmouth, New Hampshire, was killed on June 21. Sergeant Charles Amons Laucks, 29, Red Lion, Pennsylvania, was KIA on Friday, June 22, the same day American forces declared Okinawa secured.

June 25. Commanding General, FMF, Pacific, Holland M. Smith signed the 4th Endorsement recommending CPL Bush's Medal of Honor "as a suitable decoration for the act cited."

June 28. Corporal Bush's physiotherapy was progressing. He was carrying his full weight on both legs, and his left leg was strengthening. There was some improvement in the appearance and condition of his right hand, but little motion in his fingers.

July 4, 1945. Father Redmond was with the Marines during the final terrible battle on Okinawa. He was 46 years old when CPL Bush pulled a grenade to his own body to protect wounded companions. The average age of the Marines buried at the Sixth Marine Division Cemetery on Okinawa was 19 years. The padre intoned a heart-felt eulogy over 1,697 graves at the cemetery dedication.

"This is not a bivouac of the dead. It is a colony of heaven. And some part of us all is buried here." [9]

More than twice their age when most of them went to war, Father Redmond had buried 3,000 of his kids on Pacific islands. He was tough and firm and, at the same time, kind and sensitive toward humankind in a way that the young Raiders had found hard to understand. His cussing vocabulary, sending damnations from on high while under fire, would make for favorite tales at later Raider reunions. He and CPL Bush would form a friendship more than thirty years after the last Marine was buried on Okinawa.

July 6. The MOH recommendation arrived at the office of the Commander in Chief, U.S. Pacific Fleet and Pacific Ocean Areas for the 5th Endorsement. By Direction of the commander, O. L. Thorne, Flag Secretary, forwarded the package to Vice Admiral Walden Lee "Pug" Ainsworth, President, Pacific Fleet Board of Awards, for consideration. The Board held an expedited meeting on that date, reviewed the package, and returned it, recommending the award (intra-office 6th Endorsement).

July 7. Corporal Bush was making "slow but steady gain" with his right hand. There was good motion of his thumb, but none in his index finger. The fingertip was fully healed, but the bone remained "somewhat prominent" and would need some surgical repair. The ring finger stump had very little motion and was still granulating. The little finger stump was well healed. The exit wound on his left thigh was still forming new tissue. He would continue physical therapy over the next two weeks, showing gradual improvements.

July 9. Corporal Bush's maternal grandfather in Kentucky, Elmer Wakefield, died in Bowling Green, Warren County. He was buried in Defevers Grave Yard with Nettie and their infant daughter, Lou Morris. Corporal Bush was unable to leave USNH Long Beach to attend the services.

July 18. Fleet Admiral Chester William Nimitz signed the 5th Endorsement recommending that the Medal be awarded to CPL Bush.

July 21. All CPL Bush's wounds were noted as healed. He had little motion in his fingers "as yet," but the skin condition was improved. Plans began for a six-week transfer to the Special Hospital at San Bernardino, after which he was to return to Long Beach.

July 27. Corporal Bush was transferred to USNSH Arrowhead Springs and joined Casualty Company #2. The chief medical complaint was that his left thigh was still draining and his right thigh, although healed, was tender. Examination under the bandages showed multiple black spots of powder burns and grenade shrapnel on his right hand. The wounds to his fingertips were still healing. The next morning, because the multiple wounds above his left knee had healed, he was assigned to the Class I road gang, Whirlpool and exercise treatments were prescribed for his hand.

August 1. General Alexander Archer Vandegrift, Commandant of the Marine Corps and a Battle of Guadalcanal MOH recipient, signed the 6th Endorsement and forwarded his recommendation, "Concurred in by all," for CPL Bush's Medal award.

August 9. On official records as Endorsement-8, Rear Admiral Robert Ward Hayler, Navy Department Board of Decorations and Medals, concurred with the previous endorsements and recommended that the Medal of Honor be awarded to CPL Bush "in recognition of his extraordinary heroism in action." His endorsement went to the Secretary of the Navy, via the Commander in Chief, United States Fleet, Admiral C. W. Nimitz.

August 14. All his wounds were healed and asymptomatic. Treatments had resulted in only a slight increase in the motion of CPL Bush's right hand. Vision in his right eye was 13/20; in his left 20/20. His color perception was normal.

War Plans Continue for the 4th Marines

The success of Operation ICEBERG had not ended the war. The Allies had Operation DOWNFALL on the planning tables, and the capture of Okinawa's airfields established the island as a staging and supporting base for the invasion of Japan. The IIIAC Headquarters and the 6th MarDiv readied themselves in the Marianas.

Operation OLYMPIC, the first phase of the invasion, was to be an amphibious landing on Kyushu, the farthest main island in the south, on November 1. The Marines studied the beaches at Miyazaki, Ariake, and Kushikino. Operation CORONET was the second phase planned for early spring 1946, to strike the Japanese on the Tokyo Plain.

The atomic bomb detonations over Hiroshima and Nagasaki on August 6 and August 9 ended the preparations for Operation DOWNFALL.

August 15, 1945. The end of the Pacific War was cabled from Japan early Wednesday morning.

August 23. Fleet Admiral Ernest Joseph King, Commander in Chief, U.S. United States Fleet and Chief of Navy Operations, concurred with the recommendation for CPL Bush's Medal of Honor. The Ninth Endorsement went to the Secretary of the Navy for action.

August 25. Acting Secretary of the Navy Artemus Lamb Gates, former WWI Navy lieutenant commander, signed his approval of the Medal award.

August 30. The 4th Marines went ashore at Yokosuka Naval Base three days before the formal surrender ceremony, which took place aboard the USS *Missouri*, BB-63, on September 2.

September 8. Corporal Bush returned to Long Beach Naval Hospital without any open wounds on his hand, which was peppered throughout with small dark areas from the grenade explosion. The amputation sites had healed with heavy scars. His right wrist could move about half its normal flexion, but all his fingers were greatly restricted and held in inward flexion. The doctors concluded that no further surgery was indicated, but the hand needed more physiotherapy.

September 13. At 6:12 PM, the Administrative Division, Headquarters Marine Corps, transmitted a *Priority Precedence* dispatch to Casualty Company #3, MBNOB, Terminal Island. CPL Bush was to be transferred to Company "C", First Headquarters Battalion, Headquarters Troops, Marine Corps, Washington, D.C., for duty.

"Stop. ESSENTIAL ARRIVE PRIOR FOUR OCTOBER NINETEEN FORTY FIVE. Stop. TO BE AWARDED CONGRESSIONAL MEDAL OF HONOR AT WHITE HOUSE FIVE OCT NINETEEN FORTY FIVE. Stop."

Corporal Bush was to be advised that he may invite any friends and/or relatives he so desired at the White House for the presentation of the award—not at government expense.

Upon arrival at USMC Pacific Headquarters in San Francisco, L. J. Gelinas immediately typed up the transfer request and forwarded it on to San Pedro, adding a paragraph. "Please inform these Headquarters immediately in the event that Corporal Bush is not physically fit for this transfer."

September 20. The therapy brought no change to CPL Bush's hand. He was informed that he would be transferred to Casual Company #2, MB NOB, Washington, D.C., to receive the Medal of Honor on October 5.

September 22. Saturday would have been the end of CPL Bush's three-year enlistment. He was at MBNOB, D.C., and his discharge was postponed until medical review terminated his convalescence.

September 24. Headquarters Marine Corps Paymaster dispersed an emergency $50 payment, Check No. 82395, to him.

September 27. It was all formal, by regulations. Corporal Bush submitted his request to Company "C", First Headquarters Battalion, that he be transferred back to Casualty Company #2, NBTI, on or about October 6, for continued treatment at USNH Long Beach, after the October 5 Medal presentation. Major Thomas P. Jackson recommended approval of the request.

September 29. General A. A. Vandegrift, Headquarters Marine Corps, wired a message to Mr. and Mrs. Clarence Bush at 8:54 PM, informing them that the president would award their son the Medal of Honor at the White House at 10:00 AM on October 5. They were asked to notify Headquarters if they were going to attend the ceremony and if hotel accommodations should be made for them. "IT IS REGRETTED THERE ARE NO GOVERNMENT FUNDS TO DEFRAY EXPENSES." [10]

October 1. Charles Ross, White House press secretary, announced from Washington that a Marine corporal who had absorbed the force of a Japanese hand grenade explosion to save his comrades would receive the Congressional Medal of Honor from President Truman at a White House ceremony. [11]

October 2. The 48th United States Secretary of the Navy James Vincent Forrestal sent a memorandum to the Naval Aide to the President, requesting that President Truman sign the enclosed nine Medal Citations. Corporal Bush's Citation was submitted with Citation's for Captain Joseph J. McCarthy, Captain Louis H. Wilson Jr., Platoon Sergeant Joseph R. Julian, deceased, Sergeant William G. Harrell, Corporal Herchel W. Williams, Private First Class Douglas T. Jacobson, Private First Class Jacklyn H. Lucas, and Private Wilson D. Watson.

October 2. Barren County was rightfully proud of CPL Bush. Adjutant William H. Jones Jr., Glasgow American Legion Post, wired General A. A. Vandegrift. Mrs. Clarence Bush was going to attend the White House Medal presentation to her son as a guest of the Legion Post. She would arrive in D.C. on Thursday morning, 8:30 AM. William W. Vaughan, White House Press Gallery, would be in touch with the Commandant about hotel reservations.

"IT IS PRESUMED YOUR OFFICE WILL PROVIDE NECESSARY ESCORT FOR CEREMONIES WHICH WE WILL APPRECIATE."

It appears from the exchange of telegrams, that Clarence Bush decided not to travel to the Medal ceremony at his own expense or anyone else's.

October 3. *Deferred Precedence* Naval messages were transmitted from Headquarters Marine Corps at 8:43 PM to Glasgow and Company "C". Corporal Bush was to meet his mother in the morning. Reservations had been made for the two of them at 1308 Massachusetts Avenue NW—a hotel down the street from the National City Christian Church and a few blocks northwest of the White House. Headquarters would provide the necessary escort for the ceremonies.

October 5. Corporal Bush's admiration of President Truman grew stronger on Friday. Fleet Admiral Chester Nimitz returned from overseas and landed at the Bethesda, Maryland, Naval Air Station to take part in the MOH presentation ceremony scheduled for 10:30 AM. The Washington parade in his honor was to follow the presentations. Corporal Bush was with the president, looking forward to meeting the admiral before the ceremony.

"I was waiting for him at the White House. He was due at the White House at 10:00 AM. I wanted to go meet Nimitz when he landed, but Truman said, 'No, let him come to us.'"

Corporal Bush met eight other Marine recipients at the White House. Sergeant William George Harrell, 23, and PFC Jacklyn H. Lucas joked with him about shaking hands with each other. Sergeant Harrell, a Texan, had lost both hands to grenades on Iwo Jima. [12]

The president presented fourteen Medals at the ceremony on the South Lawn. Vice Admiral Louis Emil Denfeld read the Citations. Corporal Bush was the eighth presentation, after Sergeant Harrell. He resisted wincing when the president shook his deformed and flexed right hand and held him by the forearm.

Corporal Bush hardly envisioned himself to be a war hero. Still recovering from the severe wounds he had sustained in the April assault on Mount Yae Take, he was not interested in giving interviews to reporters.

October 7. Corporal Bush lost his Marine Corps Identification Card around Massachusetts Avenue N.W. and 14th Street. If someone recognized the Marine's name from the newspapers, the person disregarded directions on the card that it belonged to the Government and should be dropped into a U.S. Mail box or brought to a Federal Office, instead keeping the ID card as a souvenir. Corporal Bush submitted a request to be issued a new card the next day. Company "C" endorsed his request and forwarded it to the USMC Director of Personnel.

October 8. Major Jackson, Company "C", 1st Headquarters Battalion, wrote up the orders. Corporal Bush was to be transferred to San Pedro and report to the MBNOB, Terminal Island, on October 11, for treatment. The USMC Quartermaster General would furnish the necessary transportation and travel subsistence. His travel was necessary in the public service. Corporal Bush was "directed to maintain proper decorum while traveling on trains or other conveniences and [was] warned not to discuss matters pertaining to the Naval Service." Violations of his orders would result in disciplinary action.

October 9. Corporal Bush was in New York City for the Nimitz Day Parade. More than four million spectators turned out along the ticker-tape parade route to cheer. Ahead of him in a column marched hundreds and thousands of Marine veterans of the Pacific, Navy and Coast Guard bands, Navy, Marine, Coast Guard members, women of the WAVES, Coast Guard Women's Reserve, and Navy nurses. Behind the limousines carrying Admiral Nimitz and his party, CPL Bush rode in Jeep No. 7 with CPL Douglas T. Jacobson, 20 years old. [13]

October 11. From Washington, CPL Bush returned to Casual Company #2, Roosevelt Base, at NBTI. He reported to USNH Long Beach on October 15. At the end of the month, the Chief of Orthopedics reported that, while all wounds had healed, CPL Bush had limited motion in his right hand. The flexion of his finger stumps was almost complete and extension was limited. His case was going to be referred for Disability, Pension and Medical Survey—discharge from the service.

November 9. There was very little soreness or tenderness in his right hand. Corporal Bush stated to Lieutenant Commander C. E. Easley that he did not desire a survey from the service. The doctor surmised that the corporal might require surgery at a later date.

November 16. Determined to be medically fit, he was returned to duty.

November 27. Corporal Bush was discovering the special recognition and high regard extended to Medal recipients. Mr. Eugene S. Duffield, Special Assistant to the Secretary of the Navy, telephoned the Commandant's office and asked for names of Marines who could be considered for the U.S. Junior Chamber of Commerce recognition, "The Outstanding Young Man of 1945."

General A. A. Vandegrift sent a memorandum two days later, enclosing biographical sketches of Captain Joseph J. McCarthy, 34, First Lieutenant Melvin L. "Mel" Jarvis, 24, Navy Cross recipient, Corporal Bush, and Corporal Doug Jacobson.

November 28. Corporal Bush submitted a request for a transfer to a Marine Corps activity near his home address, Route #4, Glasgow. The Terminal Island Base Medical Officer had advised him that he was unqualified for sea or foreign shores duty without further hospitalization for treatment of his right hand. Casual Company #2 Commander, acknowledging that the corporal's Service Record Book showed he had served twenty (20) months overseas and had been awarded the Medal of Honor, forwarded the 1st Endorsement recommending approval. The 2d Endorsement went forward on December 6, and the 3d Endorsement on December 10.

December 20. Three days before CPL Bush's birthday, the Commandant forwarded the transfer order. He was to report to the Marine Barracks, Naval Ammunition Depot (MBNAD), in Crane, Indiana. The MBNAD Paymaster was alerted.

Corporal Bush was glad that he would be stationed 195 miles from Glasgow, but, he was unfamiliar with MBNAD and had to ask around. It turned out to be an interesting place for a man recovering from a grenade explosion.

At the beginning of 1942, the Navy was provided with a 98-square-mile site of what had been agricultural land to develop an inland depot. By the time CPL Bush was on his way east, MBNAD, with its administration and shop buildings, personnel facilities, production facilities, minor industrial buildings, 138 miles of railroad, 226 miles of roads, and 65 miles of water line, was gigantic. The Indiana depot supported 1,054 earth-covered, arch-type magazines, 510 inflammable materials magazines, 167 inert storehouses with humidity and temperature control, five torpedo storehouses, a case-ammunition filling house, a bag-charge filling house, an Explosive-D loading house, and production lines for small projectile and flare loading, mine and bomb filling, case preparation, rocket motor assembly, and 20mm and 40mm ammunition manufacture and cartridge filling.

Civilians Again

After the parades, America turned its attention to economic recovery, prosperity, and entertainment in the aftermath of the Depression years and World War II. More than 8,000 men had worn the Marine Raider patch on their shoulders during the war. The fate of hundreds of them was lost to history, because they were transferred to Marine organizations outside of the six infantry divisions. Records include 892 known Raiders, 11%, who were KIA (795), DOW (69), or MIA (28). The number of Raiders who were wounded in battle is understated, because those bleeding did not always go to an aid tent or field hospital. Based on the 2,406 Purple Hearts awarded, at least 27% were WIA—281 had two or three awards.

The Raiders came home and lost touch with each other for decades. They did not always know what happened to comrades who were evacuated from the Pacific Islands and often were unaware of medal awards and citations for men with whom they had served.

They had come from all walks of life before the war. Once home, most tried to leave their combat experiences to the past. They found employment or went to school. They married and started families, proud to have children. Their children often thought their fathers found jobs, careers, and professions more important than family.

Raiders had resumes that included: an advertising production manager, Alaska pipeline worker, artists and cartoonists, barbers, bartenders, beer distributor, boilermaker, book authors, bus driver, carpenters, casino slot manager, cattle foremen, coal miners, Columbia Pictures cameraman, commercial artist, commercial fisherman, construction workers, choral arranger and singer, dairymen, diamond minor and jeweler, director of purchasing, draftsman, 18-wheeler truck drivers, electricians, electric company lineman, farmers, floor covering worker, gas station owners, golf pro and owner/operator of a golf course, Goodyear Tire and Rubber Company employees, grocer, historians, home builder, house painter, Indianapolis Speedway official, Lake Superior charter fishing boat skipper, livestock buyer, locomotive engineer, loggingman, machinists, master watch and clock maker, Miami yacht club chef, meat cutter, milkman, movie and theater actor, National Geographic Society photographer, newspaper publisher, oil driller, plumbing supplies salesman, private detective, professional auto racer, public relations directors, radio personalities, railroad conductor, railroad yardmaster, ranchers, refinery tester, sales representatives and real estate developers, a sculptor, security supervisor, self-employed businessmen, shipyard worker, spray painter, steel company foreman, structural iron worker, tavern owners, telephone repairman, toolmaker, TV broadcaster, United Mine Workers of America National Representative, welders, and a woodsman.

Raiders entered the sports world. One was a Cincinnati Reds Player Personnel Chief, and another was a Cincinnati Reds scout. Roger C. Spaulding, C/1/4, played semi-professional football. New York *Yankee* outfielder Henry A. "Hank" Bauer and Houston *Oilers* head coach Oail A. "Bum" Phillips Jr. had both been 4th Battalion Raiders. Hank shared an apartment with Mickey Mantle in the 1950s. "Bum" had been a runner and bodyguard for Father Redmond.

The aircraft and auto industries offered jobs to the veterans. Among the rank and file were an industrial engineer for the Boeing Corporation, a missile engineer for Douglas Aircraft, an engineer at Lockheed Aircraft, another at Northrop Aircraft, and a Hughes Aircraft administrator. An American Motors Corporation forklift operator, a Chevy salesman, Chrysler assembly line worker, a Dodge dealer sales manager, a Ford Motor Company press operator, and a General Motors engineer had long careers.

Former Raiders put their uniforms away, graduated from universities, and wore the outfits of: accountants, architects, attorneys, bank presidents, a Baptist missionary, clergymen and pastors, college professors, counselors, dentists, funeral director, high school teachers, coaches, and principals, a gynecologist, hospital laboratory supervisor, Mansfield Training School retardation aide, medical doctors, museum directors, newspaper editor, obstetrician, psychiatrist, school superintendent, university athletic director, university dean, and veterinarians.

John J. Flynn, for one, was a former Company C, 1st Battalion Raider. He made a name for himself as a Phoenix criminal defense attorney, best known for successfully arguing a case before the U.S. Supreme Court in 1966. Due to his appeal argument, the Court concluded that Ernesto Miranda's rights against self-incrimination had been violated and that he had the right to remain silent during a police interrogation. The original conviction was reversed on June 13, 1966. [14]

Government hired the veterans, and citizens voted them into office. Raiders went to work as: an air traffic controller, ambulance service director, Arkansas Circuit Judge, captains of detectives, CIA operatives, city aldermen, city councilmen, city mayors, congressmen, Director of Agriculture, elected state legislators, FBI agents, federal civil service worker, firefighters, foreign servicemen, L.A. Police Force officers, mail carriers, Memphis Police Commissioner, National Association of Letter Carriers President, National Institute of Allergy and Infectious Diseases scientist-director, National Parks ranger, parole officers, Peace Corps mentors, Police and Fire Commissioner, police sergeants and captains, post masters, public utilities foreman, state game warden, state highway patrolmen, state motor vehicle license agent, U.S. Congressman, U.S. Customs Chief, U.S. Special Intelligence Agent, Veterans Administration workers, Youth Authority workers, and a Wyoming governor.

After the war, officers and enlisted men of the Raider battalions also stayed in the Corps or transferred into the Army until their military retirements. Several fought in both the later Korean and Vietnam wars. Assistant Commandant General Lewis William Walt became the highest-ranking former Raider—four-stars. Had Corporal Bush had his way, he would have stayed.

January 7, 1946. Lieutenant Colonel A. G. McCormick, Commanding Officer, Marine Barracks, NBTI, signed the Post Transfer Order, sending CPL Bush to MBNAD. The NBTI Post Quartermaster was to make the travel arrangements.

January 12. Corporal Bush joined MBNAD, at Crane. The Depot was equidistant from Louisville and Indianapolis. He was initially assigned Guard Duty. These regular duties would pertain until April.

January 16. The Chicago Jaycees hosted a banquet and ceremonies during the 25th anniversary Junior Chamber of Commerce week. Approximately 1,000 Jaycees Foundation participants and guests attended the banquet. The Outstanding Young Man of 1945 was not Corporal Bush, Corporal Doug Jacobson, "Mel" Jarvis, or Joe McCarthy. The distinction went to former Navy Lieutenant Henry Ford II, Ford Motor Company President.

January 17. Corporal Bush reported to the USNH Great Lakes and joined 4th Casualty Company. Plastic surgery was applied to his right hand. His physical defects made him unqualified for full Marine duties and his wish to re-enlist was doubtful. There would be months of letters exchanged with commanders, the Bureau of Medicine (BUMED) and Surgery in Washington, D.C., and Headquarters Marine Corps.

Discharged from the hospital, it would take him five more months "of hard trying, begging and ear banging to get them to let me stay in. I almost stopped trying several times and would have, if I hadn't been a refugee from insecurity. Except that I have the Congressional Medal of Honor, I never would have been able to have stayed in; or perhaps some of those involved were angry because I happened to get one and they didn't. I have a good pair of eyes, most of my right hand, and a good digesting system."

February 1. Doctors noted that whirlpool baths, massage, and active and passive motion had not improved the function of his hand. Corporal Bush applied for enlistment and requested a waiver for his deformity.

February 4. Although CPL Bush had been under constant suppressive atabrine therapy while overseas, the grenade blast had evidently compromised his immune system. He had been in sick bay six times since his first malaria attack in June 1945. On Monday at 2:00 PM, another attack of marked chills occurred. Acutely ill, he went to sick bay immediately.

Laboratory results were positive for the parasite Plasmodium Vivax, the most frequent cause of recurring Benign Tertian Malaria. He was prescribed atabrine and hot blankets. He felt better on Tuesday and had no complaints on Wednesday. The atabrine was continued for another week.

February 13. Corporal Bush was discharged from the hospital and returned to duties.

February 17. He was transferred to Great Lakes to determine if additional plastic surgery could be obtained or if reexamination should be initiated.

February 21. The MBNAD commander wired BuMed requesting a waiver for his physical defects to allow him to re-enlist for a period of two full years. Flexion and extension of his surviving fingers were seriously impaired. According to the Depot's Senior Medical Officer, physiotherapy and reconstructive surgery should give 90 percent function of his right index and middle fingers. The Chief of BuMed agreed that CPL Bush needed further treatment. On February 28, he forwarded "Request waiver for enlistment" to the Commandant.

March 4–28. Corporal Bush took twenty-five days of furlough while the members of the Medical Survey Board at USNH Great Lakes reviewed his medical/health history to determine if the acquired deformity of his right hand should exclude him from re-enlisting.

March 11. The Director of Personnel, Headquarters Marine Corps, replied to the MBNAD commander's dispatch. "The reenlistment of [Corporal Bush], waiving disability, is not authorized at this time. He will be retained in the service for further treatment, at the end of such treatment you will direct his re-examination to determine his physical fitness for the services and forward the results of this examination to this Headquarters."

March 27. Corporal Bush was admitted to USNH Great Lakes for re-examination to determine his physical fitness for service and for plastic surgery. His hand was studied and evaluated. Navy doctors, Lt C. E. Lockart, Lt (jg) Max E. Dodds, and Lt (jg) H. Vonleden forwarded their findings and conclusions to the Commanding Officer.

Corporal Bush's right index and middle fingers were frozen in a claw position, the joints fixed in 30 degrees of flexion. The tip of his middle finger was missing down to the base of his nail, leaving a small portion of good nail. He had full range of motion at the knuckles and sensation was normal over the entire hand. Bluish splotches of powder burns covered the backs (dorsum) of his fingers. His grip was good for large objects, but poor for tiny ones. He could fire a pistol with his right hand and had displayed marksmanship with either hand. The multiple physical scars over his trunk, abdomen, and lower extremities were nonimpairing.

The doctors suggested that his future medical care would be minimal. "No further surgical procedures [plastic or orthopedic] can be utilized to improve the functional value of the right hand." They went on with more encouraging words. "However, the hand in its present state offers a large degree of usefulness."

The Board acknowledged the patient's view that he was "still able to perform the same duties required of him in the Marine Corps, as before his injury, whether of a combat or peacetime nature," and that he desired to remain in the Corps. The Board's opinion was that CPL Bush was physically fit and recommended that he be returned to full duty status in the Marines.

Was the war ever really over?

Correspondent Ernie Pyle had been in the front lines of the war in Africa and Europe for years. He was in Paris on August 24, 1944, when the U.S. 4th Infantry Division joined the liberation of the city. After a couple of days of exuberant local welcome, applause and kisses, gaiety, and comfort, he found himself becoming irritable, like celebration and peacefulness were getting on his nerves. He wrote about it before he died on Okinawa.

"I guess it indicates that all of us will have to make our return to normal life gradually and in small doses." [15]

Hilliard Miller Jr., the forward artillery fire observer for the 4th Marine Division in the Pacific Islands, would also write about returning to normal life after extended combat. He saw battle experience to be like an athlete who had trained tirelessly for each contest, experiencing a "high" in the competition; and then, afterwards, feeling the pride of winning and the hurt of bruising, with time to reflect on the experience before the next competition. Each successive contest becomes more important, and each "high" is higher than the last. When his career abruptly ends, the athlete never again feels the strain of every nerve or ascends to such a high.

"Nothing in life will again so stir and stress the psyche.

"So it was with combat. Each time, one reached a "high" in horror and fear, then went to a rest camp with time to reflect, count one's blessings and to re-examine the odds of surviving the next one. Each time it was harder to go. Each time the 'high' was higher and more intense. You mumbled to yourself, 'I'm safe until one has my name on it. But, where is it? I'm scared, but I wouldn't leave this unit if I had the chance. If they go, I go too. I despise combat. I'm terrified, but it is good to kill the enemy. The more you kill the sooner this thing is over and we go home. Besides, I should destroy those who killed my friends. How come my buddies die on both sides of me, but I live? Should I feel guilty for being lucky? Perhaps I could have done more. But I gave it all I had. Four personal decorations and three unit citations attest to that.'"

Forty years after he had come home from the war, his experiences lingered in his mind. "But like the ghost in a haunted house, it never totally went away. The United States Marine Corps and the 'experience' left an indelible mark that I carry with sorrow, but with pride." [16]

Looking back, veterans like CPL Bush sometimes expressed the sense that the Marine Corps, and especially the Raiders, had trained and conditioned them to face life and reality. That was good, because adjusting to peacetime civilian life, settling down adrenaline-altered nervous systems, and recovering from wartime injuries, required determination and resilience. Most of the brave men returning had enough "grit" to get started and see it through.

Once home, many died young and unexpectedly of natural causes: so many heart attacks and complications from wartime injuries. Cancer deaths were numerous. Some died at home with family or alone, some on operating tables during surgeries, and many died in VA hospitals. Some deaths were peaceful, perhaps fortified with the Sacraments of Holy Mother Church, others not so peaceful. Many were reported with "details unknown." [17]

In truth, for many Raiders and other war veterans, no matter how brave they had been under fire, the close calls, the might-have-beens, and the awful realities followed them home. Year after year, reports of tragedies appeared in newspapers, often in front-page headlines. Accidents, homicides, and self-inflicted ends occurred in greater numbers among the veteran Raiders than the rates among the general population would have predicted. The post-war death toll was already evident in 1946.

Local comrades would recollect when reading newspapers. "I served with him in the Pacific."

✳✳✳

First Lieutenant Richard Rhea Patton "Dick" Goheen had been born in Venguria, India, where his father was serving as a Medical Missionary. He graduated with the Princeton University Class of 1936. He had led a Raider platoon in the assault on Emirau and earned a Silver Star on Guam. Serving as a E/2/4 platoon leader on Okinawa, he was wounded by a mortar fragment on May 19, 1945, and by an enemy hand grenade two days later. Both times, he refused to be evacuated, continuing to lead his platoon in the assault.

Lieutenant Goheen was among the first of the battle-hardened Marines to land on Futtsu Peninsula at 5:58 AM on August 30, 1945, to begin the disarmament of Fort Okahodai, Mainland Japan. He was awarded a Navy Cross medal on June 3, 1948, but never read the citation.

"Clinton, NY (UP)—Dick Goheen, 32, suffering from a deep combat fatigue and under medical care in New York, died by his own hand on March 17, 1946."

Dick's younger brother, Robert Francis Goheen, also a veteran of the war, would go on to be the president of Princeton University. He was described as "bristling-mad" on Tuesday night, May 7, 1963, when two-thirds of the undergraduate student body, almost 2,000, went on a destructive springtime rampage through the campus and university town. He called it "a shocking display of individual and collective hooliganism."

It was not clear who had been in the driver's seat early on Saturday, August 3, 1946, in Canaan, Somerset County, Maine. Former 3d Battalion Raider Lawrence M. Chisholm, 24, of Newport, was in the automobile with Richard Flynn, 20, a WWII Apprentice Seaman Navy veteran, and his wife, Louise (Morton) Flynn, 18, of Pittsfield. The car crashed into a cement bridge over the Carrabassett Stream on the town's main street (U.S. Hwy 2). Lawrence and Mrs. Flynn died at the scene. Critically injured Richard was taken to Skowhegan's Redington Memorial Hospital in serious condition. [18] He died on Wednesday.

Joseph S. Royal Jr., 2d Battalion Raider, was born in New Jersey and lived for a time in Brownsville, Texas. His bride, Ruth, was from Ohio. They were starting out their lives together, living in Winnetka, Illinois, on Lake Michigan, east of Naval Air Station Glenview, near Joe Sr.'s home. On a trip to Ohio to visit Ruth's family, Joe, 25, died on Wednesday, September 18, 1946, in an auto accident near Cleveland. His funeral was on Saturday in Winnetka, and his remains were interred at Memorial Park Cemetery, between Skokie Boulevard and Gross Point Road in Willmette. [19] His grave is in the Evergreen Section, Lot 27, Block 5, Grave 3.

George A. Crawley, 22, of Rolling Prairie, Indiana, took a Sunday motorcycle ride on September 29, 1946. Three miles north of LaPorte on State Hwy 35, he was killed when he was thrown from his skidding motorcycle into the path of an automobile. Walter A. Leahker, 25, of LaPorte, was driving the car and was uninjured.

Roger Schacht, 25, lived at 1514 Algonquin Road in Des Plaines, Illinois, a few blocks from the Des Plaines River and the woods. Those close to him recognized that he was not the same young man who had joined the Marines. He suffered some tropical illness because of his war service. On Monday morning, December 9, 1946, he parked his '34 Pontiac on River Road near Lions Woods, a quarter mile north of Rand Road and a quarter mile south of All Saints Cemetery. He raised a government .45 caliber Colt to his head and fired a round.

A passer-by notified the Cook County Sheriff's office at 10:45 AM that a man was slumped over the steering wheel of a parked car. Roger was alive, but unconscious when the police arrived. They rushed him to Northwestern Hospital. He did not regain consciousness, and died at 4:20 PM. The Tuesday inquest provided evidence that the death was self-inflicted. [20]

✳✳✳

Stories of Raider bravery on Tulagi and Guadalcanal had inspired Dick Bush. Stories of post-war tragedies would be printed in veteran association newsletters and be retold at reunions years down the road. They would serve as reminders to Dick that, despite disabilities and pain, he was fortunate to wake up in the mornings with breath in his lungs and a will to go on. He endured.

April 17, 1946. Lieutenant Colonel H. R. Huff ordered CPL Bush to be transferred back to MBNTC at Great Lakes for treatment at the hospital. A USMC vehicle transported him to the train station in Bloomington. First Lieutenant Marton G. Truesdale, Post Quartermaster, had furnished him $1.00, cash, for necessary subsistence in travel, that being "one supper enlisted man." With his Coach Class ticket, CPL Bush boarded the 1:50 PM train to Chicago, arriving there at 8:30 PM. He had a half hour before boarding the 9:00 PM train to Great Lakes, arriving at the base at 9:56 PM.

Corporal Bush continued to receive medical care at the Great Lakes Hospital, thirty-five miles north of Chicago's center. He was 446 miles away from Glasgow according to the Pay Branch. He got to know life at Naval Station Great Lakes, spread out over 1,649 acres on the western shore of Lake Michigan. There was Hospitalside, Mainside to the north and east, and the Naval Reserve Center, located on Green Bay Road and Cavin Drive.

A good portion of his days was spent south of Buckley Road and Downey Road. He lived in the barracks, ate in the messes, and shopped at the commissary and Post Exchange. He listened to the married people talk about family housing conditions in Halsey Village and Nimitz Village and Forrestal Village. And, while he was a patient at Great Lakes, he met a Navy WAVE who was his surgeon's secretary.

"Give Me Five Minutes More"

Corporal Bush was hoping the Corps would extend his time, but, in terms of minutes, he had his "good eye" on the secretary. While Perry Como's *Prisoner of Love* hit climbed to Number 1 on the 1946 Billboard Charts, Frank Sinatra's *Five Minutes More* was more apropos. "Ol' Blue Eyes" was crooning about having so much fun, looking forward to a kiss, dreaming about a Saturday date, and begging for a little more. All things to which CPL Bush could relate.

Stella Mae Ramsden had her stories, too. She had known some disruptions in her early life. Her father, David A. Ramsden, a Canadian, had immigrated in 1900 and married Sarah Langely from Michigan in 1905. When they married, David was 25, and Sarah was 16 years old. Both had eighth grade educations. All Stella's grandparents were Canadian.

What brought David down to the States was the growth of the coal mining industry. The married couple spent their early years in Duluth, Minnesota. When Stella was born on March

30, 1925, she already had two teenage brothers and a sister four years older than her. All four children were Minnesotans.

According to the 1930 Federal Census, when Stella Mae was five years old, the family was living in St. Charles Village, southwest of Saginaw, Michigan, where the Bad River and its South Fork cut through the countryside. It was coal country, and the Somer Brothers, among the chief suppliers of Michigan coal, had three successful mines in operation south of the village. Stella's father was working as a blacksmith in one of the nearby mines, and her eldest brother, Adrian, 19, was employed as a "puller" in the mine. Edwin, 16, was finished with schooling, but not yet working.

David was renting a house for $25 monthly on the small town's south edge. The house sat in a triangle formed by Clifford, Sanderson, and Chesaning streets. There were agricultural fields as far as Stella could see.

She had started school, walking there with her closest neighbor, 11-year-old Wilma Boswill. Wilma's mother, Ida Boswill, 52, owned the only other house in the triangle. Her 16-year-old daughter, Gertrude, had just married Melvin Brocket, 20, who was a digger in the mine, and the newlyweds lived with her. Ida also rented rooms to boarders. At the time, Fred Beng, 34, lived at Ida's and made his way to the mine with the Ramsdens.

Stella overheard many conversations the big men around her had about black dust, black damp, black powder kegs, seams and veins of deposits, bituminous, whatever that big word meant, ventilation shafts, punching machines, and wash houses. Fred Beng from time to time talked of a steam boiler explosion that killed miners east of St. Charles in 1903. That was a long time ago, but Stella could not help herself from wondering if some disaster might happen to her father and brother. She was 10 years old when a death did dramatically change her life. Stella would spend her teen years back in Duluth.

After several years in St. Charles, David had relocated the family to Bay City, near the base of the Saginaw Bay on Lake Huron, where there were many mines in operation around Salzburg. He was still employed as a coal miner. His wife was not enumerated in the next census.

Sarah Ramsden, 49, died in 1935.

Stella's sister, Helen Louise, 14, was sent to live with Carmelite nuns from England at the Corpus Christi House on what was the north end of 12th Avenue East in Duluth. [21] The home was a Catholic institution for unwed mothers, delinquent teen girls, and young women with various sorts of problems.

Stella went to live with her maternal aunt and uncle, Margaret and Hugh N. Shannon, renting at 429 North 59th Avenue West in Duluth. The house was a few blocks from Grand Avenue and a ways from the ship docks on the St. Louis River, the dividing line between Minnesota and Wisconsin. [22] She was a good distance from the Corpus Christi House on the other side of town. Hugh was working as a stationary engineer for the iron industry, then as an engine operator for a gas manufacturer. Stella's cousin Thomas P. Shannon was already out on his own and married.

In June 1939, Stella learned that she was an aunt. Besides Reverend Patrick O'Riordan, the Chaplain, and seven nuns, Helen Ramsden remained at the Corpus Christi House with thirty other women between the ages 14 and 26 years. She had completed eight grades of school and had with her a daughter, 10-month-old Janice M. Ramsden. Each girl's Relationship to Head of Household in the 1940 Census was listed as "Inmate."

By the time of the census, Stella's father, 60, was a widower, still working in the mines and boarding with Joe and Elvira Brustmaker in Akron Township, Tuscola, Michigan, under Saginaw Bay. What became of Stella's older brothers is unknown. Neither Adrian, 29, nor Edwin, 26, showed up in the 1940 enumeration results.

Stella attended Denfeld High School, about a mile walk east to 401 North 44th Avenue West. She had 420 classmates—Class of 1943. She was nine months older than Mike Colalillo, a future WWII MOH recipient and later good friend of Rick Sorenson. She did not know him until they were both at Denfeld High. Mike was living down at 332 S. 57th Avenue, at the end of the street, right beside the railroad tracks—a tough neighborhood. He was quite shy, but Stella learned that they had some things in common.

Mike was not originally from Duluth. He had been born up in Hibbing. He was third from the bottom of nine children, and eighteen years separated him from his eldest sister. His parents were Italian immigrants. The four oldest Colalillos had been born in San Paulo, Brazil, then lived two years in Italy. Papa Carlo and Victoria (Gianovi) Colalillo moved the family to Hibbing, where Jennie, Albert, Mike, and Carmella were born. In 1928, the close-nit family relocated to Duluth and stretched out along Raleigh Street, between S. 56th and W. 57th. Mike's youngest sister, Grace, was born two years later. All the Colalillos were hard working laborers. Papa Carlo worked at Zenith Furnace Company and eventually rented the home on S. 57th.

At the time Mike entered Denfeld High, all five of his older siblings had married Italians and moved from home. Concetta was married to John Cucinelli. Patrick and Lorraine Colalillo lived at 515 N. 58th Avenue West, not far from Stella and the Shannons. Pat owned his own auto body and fender shop. Nicoletta Colalillo was married to Mathew Di Nicola. Alex and Elizabeth Sisto were also Italian immigrants and had started their family in Duluth. They lived a block away from Carlo and Victoria. Alex worked as a laborer at an iron blast furnace. Mary Colalillo married one of the Sisto boys, Patrick, and lived on Raleigh Street. Jennie Colalillo married Patrick's younger brother, Anthony, and lived a block east on Raleigh. Mike had a very short walk to enjoy being an uncle.

The 1941 school year began with much promise and excitement. The Denfeld *Hunter* football team took the city championship. Mike's closest brother, Albert, was contributing to the family budget, coming home with tales of tonnage, storms, ports and maritime adventures on the Great Lakes. Then life changed, and Stella and Mike shared in another experience. His mother died at age 55 years.

Mike turned 16 years old on December 2, and the Japanese attacked Pearl Harbor five days later. Albert signed on as a Merchant Marine, a branch of the Coast Guard. To help Papa Carlo take care of the kids still at home, Mike quit school and took a job as a baker's helper at Grand Bakery on the corner of N. 57th Avenue West and Grand Avenue. He did everything from cleaning pans to filling Bismarck pastries with jelly. It was a short walk for Stella to pop in to the bakery and say hi to him.

As a Denfeld *Hunter*, Stella most enjoyed participating in groups. In the 1942 *Oracle* yearbook, she appeared in photographs of two clubs on pages 49 and 51.

Mr. Earl Peterson and Mr. Glen Card might have described her as an enthusiastic member of the Camera Club, learning the art of taking pictures using correct lighting and effective background. The thirty-three budding photographers studied various types of cameras. Stella participated in a close-of-the-year contest when the members displayed their achievements and best photographs. [23]

More to her liking, she represented her homeroom as one of the forty-two members of the Pyramid Club. Miss Louise Hall, the faculty advisor, would have fond memories of Stella's dedication. The club focused on safety hints and proper social behavior. A week every year was dedicated to student discussions in homerooms and general assemblies about the paramount importance of courtesy, high ideals, and firm standards. The members raised funds by sponsoring Tag Day and the popular Sun Light Dances and by collecting donations and student pledges.

Weeks after the attack on Pearl Harbor, the Pyramid contributed thirty-nine Christmas baskets to needy families. In the spring, Stella had a chance to attend a formal Pyramid dance, climaxing the club's busy and successful year of work.

After her 18th birthday, March 20, 1942, before her junior school year ended, she went to the Duluth Social Security Office to get her Social Security number. [24]

Mike Colalillo joined the Army in February 1944 when he was 18 years old. He went overseas that October. In late April 1945, Stella heard from folks at the Grand Bakery that he was a private first class with the 100th Infantry Division and was in action somewhere near Untergriesheim, Germany.

Two years after her graduation, feeling serious, noble, feminine, and patriotic, Stella enlisted in the Navy WAVES (Women Accepted for Volunteer Emergency Service) program on May 31, 1945. That women were receiving equal pay, rank, and the promise of promotions as the sailors was an incentive. She reported to Great Lakes Recruit Training Command for boot camp at Camp Porter. The U.S. Navy then regulated all aspects of her physical appearance. She was given four uniforms: summer greys, summer dress whites, working blues, and dress blues. Navy regulations specified that she should wear her hair short, and she was encouraged to wear feminine hairdos, skirts, and gloves. Yeomanette Ramsden endured eight-hour days of classroom study for 12 weeks, training to perform secretarial and clerical functions.

After basic training, she was assigned administrative duties and worked as a secretary for a surgeon at USNH Great Lakes. Her Denfeld High friends and her Aunt Margaret kept her updated about Duluth events.

Sergeant Mike Colalillo was home on leave. He married Lina Nissila, 20, from Cedar Valley, in November 1945. The more exciting news Stella could read for herself in the newspapers. Mike, Papa Carlo, and several family members were in Washington on December 18 to meet President Truman in the Oval Office at the White House. The president placed a Medal of Honor around Sergeant Colalillo's neck for his heroic actions on April 7. She knew a Medal winner!

Yeomanette Ramsden was no stranger to quirks of fate. A month after Mike Colalillo had been awarded a Medal, Corporal Bush arrived at Great Lakes. In short order, the Marine recipient had fallen for the Navy WAVE. The Medal of Honor was going to be an enduring influence in her life.

May 2. Corporal Bush received a letter citing his impending discharge from service on May 18. He submitted a Request for Waiver. He wanted to stay in the Marines.

May 9. Chief of BuMed and Surgery endorsed the request for waiver and his transfer to MBNTC, Great Lakes.

May 15. Corporal Bush was returned to full duty, awaiting BuPers action on the Board's recommendation. He joined Operation Battalion, Great Lakes Separation Center, the next day, unsure if his re-enlistment was going to be authorized.

May 17. He was given his discharge physical examination. The rolled ink imprints of his left thumb and four fingers were complete and matched his 1942 enlistment record. The DNEPTE change to his right hand was apparent. His 1942 enlistment record included ink imprints of his right thumb and four fingers and an individual ink fingerprint of his right index finger. His discharge P.E. had a rolled imprint of his right thumb. All four fingerprints were missing—marked "Amputation."

The Commandant forwarded the 3d Endorsement for waiver to the Medical Officer in Command at USNH Great Lakes. The Endorsement was followed by a dispatch to the Commanding Officer, MBNTC. Corporal Bush was to be assigned to full duty upon the recommendation of the Board of Medical Survey. The commander was directed to make an appropriate entry in his Service Record Book to the effect that he was physically qualified for all duties at sea or in the field.

At Great Lakes, 35mm film indicated calcified hilar lymph nodes, indicating a high probability that he had benign lesions in his lung. Termination of his Health Record was ordered due to expiration of his enlistment.

May 18. Corporal Bush was honorably discharged, by reason of physical disability. He was paid $23.30 in full at discharge. In the case of his discharge, complying with instructions, the USMC Separation Center Paymaster, NTC, made a $300 lump sum Mustering Out payment to Richard E. BUSH. At discharge, his two NSLI policies were discontinued. Monthly $25 allotment payments to his mother, in effect since August 1943, were stopped.

May 19. On active duty at MBNAD, CPL Bush re-enlisted in the regular Marine Corps for two years. He was to be "given extremely light duty during times between periods of hospitalization, since in fact his physical condition did preclude performance of general duty." Since he was not married and had no children, he again designated his mother or his father as beneficiaries for his Death Gratuity payment. He renewed his two allotments for his NSLI policies, which were reactivated on June 1.

Major Francis J. O'Connor Jr., Separation Center Recruiting Officer, reappointed him a corporal (temporary line), a rank effective back to May 9, 1944.

Based on the Armed Forces Voluntary Recruitment Act 1 of 1945, he received mustering out pay and a $50 re-enlistment bonus for each year of his active service. He was granted a 60-day re-enlistment paid furlough with travel paid to home and return. Following his leave of absence, he was to return to MBNAD no later than 8:00 AM, July 18. His furlough address was with his family on Rural Route #4 in Glasgow. Although he had no dependents, he became eligible for family allowances for the two-year term of enlistment and for benefits under the GI Bill of Rights. [25]

Eligible for Family Housing

Corporal Bush had some ideas about what he would do with his time off from duties. His furlough was going to be more than a vacation. He would need a license to say the vows he planned to keep longer than his two-year re-enlistment. Yeoman Ramsden had promised to give him more than five minutes.

May 29. Five months after President Truman had put a MOH ribbon around CPL Bush's neck, he and Stella Mae drove up to Waukegan in Lake County on Wednesday, filled out some paper work for County Clerk Jay B. Morse, and accepted Marriage License No. 43150, valid for thirty days after issuance. Then, the two 21-year-olds stood before Justice of the Peace Emil W. Lindvahl, who was legally authorized to solemnize marriage. Betty Jean Richel and Earl A. Thompson witnessed the ceremony. Justice Lindvahl provided them a nice certificate validating that he had united them in marriage. Mr. Morse filed the event in Marriage Register 195 on May 31.

June 28. Corporal Bush submitted a family allowance application to the Commandant of the Marine Corps, on behalf of his first dependent. He and Stella were living on RR #4. LtCol H. R. Huff witnessed CPL Bush's signature. Despite injuries from a grenade blast, his signature had changed very little since he had signed his name to an enlistment form. Stella appended a photostatic copy of Justice Lindvahl's marriage certificate to the application, which was received at Personnel, Headquarters Marine Corps, Washington, D.C., on July 8.

June 30. A Family Allotment "Class A" withdrawal began from Corporal Bush's monthly pay.

July 9. Yeoman Ramsden was released from the WAVES. [26]

July 13. Captain G. E. Allison wrote to Mrs. Stella Bush informing her that the marriage certificate copy was not acceptable. A certified copy of the public record of her marriage "prepared and certified under seal by the custodian in charge of the records in the office where the marriage was recorded" was necessary. Only then could a permanent authorization of a family allowance be made for her.

Stella went up to Waukegan. On July 23, Mr. Morse notarized true, perfect, and complete copies of the marriage license and certificate of marriage. Stella mailed them off. Her response was received in D.C. on July 29. As of August 7, 1946, for purposes of being a dependent and pertaining to her name change, she was officially Mrs. Bush, and her family allowance was approved.

The couple's home address was no longer in Glasgow. The newlyweds lived in base housing adjacent to MBNAD, Crane, Indiana; residing at 201 Earle Street, a single-family home with three bedrooms and one bath—surrounded by forest at the end of the street.

August 3. On Saturday night, CPL Bush began to feel sick to his stomach. He thought he would feel better after some sleep. In the morning, when the pain persisted, he thought it was because he had not eaten for quite some time. Immediately after eating some chow, he felt nauseous and began vomiting the food. The abdominal pain in the region of his umbilicus grew more severe.

He reported to the USNAD hospital. The abdominal pain was no longer present by 5:30 PM, and he was feeling much better. By Monday morning his temperature was normal. On Tuesday, he was hit with chills. The lab smear for Plasmodium Vivax came back positive, and atabrine therapy was started for Benign Tertian Malaria. Corporal Bush was unable to hold down the medication due to gastric upset.

On Wednesday, he was tolerating the atabrine and feeling much better. His temperature was normal, but he had a slight headache. By the following Tuesday, the smear for the parasite was negative, the atabrine therapy was concluded, and he was released from the hospital, fit for duty.

He returned to the MBNAD dispensary with a nagging pain in his left jaw. After examination, he was sent to the dentist, who performed a root canal to his lower left wisdom tooth (3rd molar, 32) and filled a cavity on his upper left 1st molar (14).

September 19. He had been a corporal for eighteen months. More than nine months had passed since the battalion first sergeant had examined him overseas for a promotion to sergeant. Whenever CPL Bush inquired about the promotion, he got nowhere. Such "monkeying around" could make a combat veteran impatient. He had a few Army friends who had been in the service for a short time and had so many rates, that they wondered why he had never made a rate. They acted as if they were a lot smarter than CPL Bush.

"Maybe I am pretty dumb or I wouldn't be in the shape I am in today."

He decided on another approach. He was a regular reader of the *Leatherneck* Magazine. He typed a letter to the editor–publisher, wondering if there was room in his next issue to find someone that could answer his question. He described his service time and the events of April 16, 1945. "I was wounded three times and I have so many holes in me I whistle when I ride fast. I have three bullet holes and one hundred shrapnel holes."

Corporal Bush related that he had a bad knee, not speaking of several other things, and had lost sight in one of his eyes, a part of his right hand, and one good digestive system. "And I must have been doing a pretty good job, part of the time anyway," he concluded, since he had gone on to win a Congressional Medal of Honor as a squad leader.

He described the "three months of hard trying, begging and ear banging" that followed his hospital discharge to get them to let him ship over. He was in the fifth month of his second cruise, and was still only a corporal. He closed the letter to the publisher, repeating the purpose of his writing. "And I am wondering what else I can do to make my friends happy and prove to them that I am responsible."

September 25. Major R. A. Campbell, Office of the *Leatherneck* Magazine might have recognized that some of CPL Bush's comments were tongue-in-cheek, but, he also thought the Marine's plight had some merit. "It does seem that the corporal has some grounds for complaint." He wrote a memorandum, attached the letter, and forwarded it to the Enlisted Promotion section, Room 1425, at Marine Corps Headquarters, Washington.

October 1. Colonel Archie E. O'Neil's office investigated the case and requested that the colonel give special consideration to authorizing the promotion to the rank of sergeant, citing three facts. CPL Bush had been awarded the Congressional Medal of Honor, he had re-enlisted even though medically qualified for permanent discharge and, eighty of the July authorizations to sergeant had been returned cancelled. One of the openings could be used for CPL Bush's promotion.

October 2. Colonel O'Neil, Director of Personnel, dispatched authority for the commanding officer, Marine Barracks, Crane, Indiana, to promote CPL Bush to sergeant, Line Duty, temporary. For purposes of seniority only, his date of rank would be this date. His promotion date for pay would be the date the letter was marked received at the Naval Ammunition Depot. His monthly pay for over three years of service would be $105, plus the extra $2 per month for his Medal award. Regarding the letter to the magazine publisher, Colonel O'Neil made no reply to either CPL Bush or *Leatherneck* Magazine.

Dick requested that the allotments for his two NSLI policies with his mother as beneficiary be discontinued. His medical charts recorded that he had grown to 73 inches and weighed in at a healthy 180 pounds.

December 5. As he completed a Special Noncommissioned Officers Fitness Report for the period August 1–October 31, Lieutenant Colonel Huff had to decide in his own mind how Sergeant Bush was to be rated on performance of duties and qualifications when compared to "the ideal sergeant." He put checks in the Very Good and Excellent blocks. Regarding "the quality of rendering faithful and willing service, and unswerving allegiance under any and all circumstances," the commander rated Sgt Bush as Outstanding. He particularly desired to have him under his command and estimated his "General Value to the Service" as "very good to excellent."

January 11, 1947. Sergeant Bush submitted a request that he be awarded a Purple Heart Medal, citing his wounds during the battles on Guam and Okinawa. The MBNAD endorsed the request and forwarded it on to the USMC Director of Personnel. The Senior Medical Officer added his endorsement, stating that medical records verified the Marine's claims and recommended approval.

January 30. Headquarters Marine Corps had no record of Sergeant Bush receiving a wound at Guam and requested that the BuMed Chief War Casualty Unit verify that he had been wounded in action on Guam.

February 5. Lieutenant Colonel C. L. Jordan completed Sergeant Bush's Semi-Annual Fitness Report, repeating the rankings on his previous report, adding his opinion that the sergeant was "capable and dependable."

February 11. BuMed requested by Air Mail that the Senior Medical Officer, USNAD, immediately forward via Air Mail, Sergeant Bush's entire original health record. Headquarters was holding correspondence in this matter in abeyance pending receipt and review of the records. The USMC Health Record was forwarded from Crane the next day.

February 12. On Wednesday, Sergeant Bush was admitted to the USNAD dispensary with complaints of upset stomach, aching joints, headache, and general malaise. He was put on atabrine therapy. By Friday, he was feeling much improved. He was "up and about" on Sunday, and atabrine was stopped. Sergeant Bush was discharged from the hospital on Monday, fit for duty.

February 19. Leo J. Gallenstein checked through the 1944 records, noting that the Company A, III Corps Medical BN on Guam included care for GASTRO-ENTERITIS, ACUTE for dates August 3–7, 1944. He so informed Lt (jg) O. S. Abernathy, BuMed: "No record can be found of other wound." Leo had missed MC-USNR Lieutenant T. A. Glass' August 3, 1944 Physical Examination entry on Page 3 of Sergeant Bush's Medical History: "Has small healing wound on left shoulder."

February 24. Mr. Abernathy reported to the Commandant that Sergeant Bush's record on file showed no record of being wounded in action, other than the shell fragment wound incurred on April 16, 1945. The BuMed Chief did not acknowledge the field report of Sergeant Bush's bullet wounds to his two thighs, received prior to the grenade casualty. Headquarters requested "certified copies of any health record entries pertaining to the wound allegedly received at Guam."

February 28. Lieutenant Colonel C. L. Jordan, in command at MBNAD, signed off on Sgt. Bush's Enlisted Data Sheet, noting that the sergeant's regular duties at Crane since June 1946 had been Mail Orderly.

March 4. Sergeant Bush's Health record did not include an entry for hospitalization of any wounding on Guam. The investigation had missed the left shoulder wound. Headquarters also seemed to miss the facts cited in his Medal of Honor Citation that he had been wounded twice on Okinawa. Shedding blood in two different combat events entitled him to a Purple Heart medal and a Gold Star.

March 26. The Commandant wrote that all records reviewed failed to show any wounds other than those Sergeant Bush incurred on Okinawa, for which he would be awarded a Purple Heart. The award of a Gold Star (in lieu of a second Purple Heart medal) was denied him at that time.

Sergeant Bush had to have been put off by the third paragraph of the Commandant's letter. "If Bush can furnish this office with a statement from the Medical Officer or hospital corpsman who treated him for the wound in question, or with statements from eye-witnesses who were present at the time the wound was received, further consideration will be given relative to the award of a Purple Heart in his case. Such information should contain the time, place and type of wound."

He, like most men returning from combat, especially those recovering from disabling wounds and injuries, had more adjustments to make than noncombat veterans who had served in the rear areas. Marriage and financial hardships could seem to be weighty burdens. "Small matters" could be quite agitating. And, any sense of unfairness after serving the country could escalate into a fight of some sort.

Sergeant Bush had other concerns than a second Purple Heart. Adding to his circumstances, he was looking ahead to becoming a father. Stella was five-months pregnant, and she was in an annoying clash with the Post Exchange Laundry that had started while Sgt Bush was doing all he could to re-enlist. To make matters more troublesome, he was noticing a little bit of trouble reading letters and documents.

May 15. On his Relief of Reporting Officer report covering February and April, LtCol Jordan lowered Sgt Bush's ratings to good and very good (average and above average), noting that a service-connected disability had adversely affected his efficiency. He also lowered his opinion to "be glad to have him" and value to the service as good.

That's No Way to Treat a Lady's Coat

June 13. Dick respectfully penned his signature above "Sgt. Richard E. Bush, CMH" and mailed an undated, typed letter to the Legal Assistance Branch, Office of the Judge Advocate General, Washington, D.C. The ramifications of his letter extended into early August.

Colonel William P. Connally Jr., Chief, Military Affairs Division, received the correspondence on June 20, signed the 1st Endorsement, and forwarded it on to the JAGO. On June 25, "as a matter under the cognizance of the U.S. Marine Corps," E. I. Snyder, Chief of the Legal Assistance Office, forwarded Endorsement-2 to the USMC Headquarters Exchange Officer, with the Subject Line: *Claim against Post Exchange Laundry*. In his 3rd Endorsement forwarded on June 30, Lieutenant General Pedro A. Del Valle, Director of Personnel, recommended that the matter be referred to the Inspector General. On July 2, W. F. Brown, by direction of the Inspector General, acknowledged receipt of the Claim in his 4th Endorsement and sent it on for Action. On July 3, the 5th Endorsement went to the Commandant of the Marine Corps for consideration.

The matter had been researched. It appeared that the exchange council had given no consideration or taken no action, and the Inspector General assumed that Sgt Bush had not submitted a proper claim to the council. The I.G. recommended that Sgt Bush's letter and endorsement be forwarded to the Commanding Officer MBNAD. The Base Exchange Council should review the situation and make a recommendation.

July 7. General Lemuel C. Shepherd Jr. signed approval and penned his request to be advised of the action taken. The matter went back to the Director of Personnel. Lieutenant General Del Valle read again the contents of Sgt Bush's letter.

Stella had several times taken her favorite coat to the Post Exchange laundry with other articles of uniform and civilian clothing for cleaning with satisfactory results. According to the letter, the last time the laundry cleaned the coat they had ruined it beyond any use. Sergeant Bush valued the *Season Skipper* lady's wool, gabardine sport coat with detachable lining—"the best on the market"—to be of $51 value ($561 in 2016). Stella had been informed that the laundry would not be responsible or pay for the coat. Since his monthly pay only came to $105, Sergeant Bush could not afford to pay $50 every time a coat needed cleaning. He did not feel that the PX laundry, like any other business, should be freed of paying for such losses. He realized that "in the book it states that the PX will not accept responsibility but there is no sign to effect posted in the laundry, and the only persons in possession of the book are the Commanding Officer, the Executive Officer and the First Sergeant." Stella had called Captain Milton B. Rogers, senior member of the Post Exchange Council. He treated her inconsiderately "and stated that his time was fully occupied with things less trivial." As a veteran herself, Stella deserved "a little more courtesy."

Sergeant Bush did not "mean to be getting smart or anything," but he wrote what he felt when the laundry could "take expensive clothing and ruin it, and then tell you that, 'that's tough, you shouldn't have brought it here.'" Anyway, what kind of American business puts out a sign warning customers to "You do business here at your own risk?"

He added an opinion of the Government's handling of his wife's complaint. "This is as bad a situation as I had when trying to re-enlist in the Marine Corps. . . . If the Government is going to treat me like this, I think it is a mighty poor Democracy. If a Medal of Honor doesn't rate any more consideration than that, then I would like to give the medal to someone else, or maybe trade it for something I could eat, like two hamburgers and a chocolate malt."

Sergeant Bush had been advised by Mr. Brewster, from Bloomington, a WWI veteran and reputedly a former VA employee, to write directly to the JAGO. He wanted to explain how he felt; expressing great appreciation if the JAGO could help him in any way.

General Del Valle might have been getting annoyed when he drafted his follow-up letter to MBNAD.

July 14. Having proofed the general's letter, Mr. Carley at the Special Services Office sent a memo to Major General Robert H. Pepper, Assistant Director of Personnel, informing him that there was no regulation requiring or permitting the use of the letters "CMH" after a person's name in official correspondence, as Sgt Bush had signed on the letter he had mailed on June 13. Mr. Carley suggested retyping the official letter to MBNAD to avoid the appearance that HQMC had sanctioned the use of CMH as a title. General Pepper agreed and sent a Memorandum back to Special Services, requesting that "CMH" after the name in General Del Valle's Subject line be omitted.

July 18. General Del Valle signed the letter and forwarded it to Crane, Indiana. He requested that the commander "investigate the actions of Sergeant Richard E. Bush in regard to the subject matter, ascertain why a non-commissioned officer of his length of service and experience knows so little of Marine Corps procedure as to write directly to the office of the Judge Advocate General of the

Navy and take such action as you may deem appropriate." He asked also that the Post Exchange Council look into the matter and that the return of all papers with a report of action taken be expedited to his office.

July 28. On Monday, Captain Rogers, 1stLt Edward D. Murray, and 2dLt George C. McNaughton of the Post Exchange convened in a special meeting at 1:30 PM to reconsider the issue they thought had been resolved in earlier conversations with Sergeant and Mrs. Bush. The Council adjourned at 2:40 PM, a letter of proceedings was typed, and the three officers affixed their signatures and forwarded their conclusions to the MBNAD commander.

July 29. On Tuesday, Major Tom R. Watts read the proceedings letter. Upon investigation, it had been determined that the wool fibers in Mrs. Bush's coat had contracted to an excessive degree during the cleaning process. The civilian women employees at the laundry had unsuccessfully tried to stretch the coat to its original shape. Such shrinkage was not considered to be the responsibility of the laundry employees or the dry-cleaning solvent. The Council agreed "that the incident is regrettable and while every effort is made to prevent loss or damage to clothing laundered or dry cleaned at the Post Laundry, all patrons are aware that such laundering and cleaning is done at the owner's risk and such has been the generally accepted policy hereat." The Council went on describing the sign over the laundry counter and prohibitive insurance rates. They viewed the cleaning of civilian and officer's clothing "as a convenience only as much as there are other civilian dry cleaning establishments in the vicinity whose services may be utilized." The Council recommended that Sergeant Bush <u>not</u> be reimbursed for the damaged coat.

Major Watts called Sgt Bush into his office and had a chat with the Medal recipient. After their meeting, the base commander wrote up his endorsement of the Post Exchange Council's conclusions. The Subject block was "Claim against Post Laundry, case of Sergeant Richard E. Bush." The major knew that the endorsement would be going up the chain to Headquarters Marine Corps, Washington. He might have been writing with a commander's sense of exaggeration.

"While Sergeant Bush's actions in this matter have been entirely reprehensible and deserving of disapprobation it is the opinion of the undersigned that Sergeant Bush was motivated by misinformation." Major Watts did not believe that the sergeant actually wrote the letter, but had "received considerable assistance from a party as yet unidentified." He believed this, because Sergeant Bush did "not have the necessary use of his right hand to accomplish such a task."

Upon his questioning, Sergeant Bush had admitted writing the letter and assumed full responsibility. He also revised some of his earlier statements. Captain Rogers had not been abrupt or inconsiderate to his wife, nor say that this was a trivial matter. Rather, he had devoted considerable time and effort in investigating the damaged coat situation, had spoken at length with Sergeant Bush on two occasions, and once with Mrs. Bush.

Major Watts concluded his endorsement. "Sergeant Bush has been severely reprimanded by the undersigned for his actions in this matter. Further disciplinary action was withheld in view of his previous good record and his outstanding war service. He was further advised of the correct procedure to be followed in all future cases of a like nature."

Major Watts approved the Council's report and forwarded all papers to HqUSMC, inviting attention to the Council's proceedings. Headquarters accepted the invitation.

July 31. On Thursday, Dick drove thirty-five minutes southwest of Crane to celebrate the birth of his first child. Judith Carol Bush was born at Daviess Community Hospital, in

Washington, Indiana. When he returned to MBNAD that afternoon, Sgt Bush completed a required beneficiary slip noting the birth of his daughter. In the case of his death while on active duty, not the result of his own misconduct, Stella would be entitled to six months of his pay. The family was going to move to Larrimer Street, still on the north side of Crane.

August 1. Major Watts was the reporting officer for Sgt Bush's April 29–July 31 Semi-Annual Fitness report. He rated him as Very Good in his regular duties as Mail Orderly and in his handling of enlisted men. For most of his qualifications, Major Watts lowered his rankings to Good, and stated that Sgt Bush had been the subject of disciplinary action during the reporting period. He would "be willing to have him" in his command and did not consider him fully qualified for a promotion. Sergeant Bush's value to the service had declined to "Good."

August 7. Major General Pepper, Assistant Director of Personnel, sent a memorandum to his boss. He summarized the situation at the MBNAD laundry in three long paragraphs and made clear his recommendation. "No further disciplinary action against Sgt. Bush. The Post Exchange cannot legally divest itself of responsibility for damage to a patron's property which has been entrusted to its care. Although Sgt. Bush displayed bad judgement in writing the letter in question, he still has legitimate cause of action against the PE which the PX should not be permitted to ignore by stating that such cause of action is non-existent. Recommend all papers and memo be forwarded to Special Services for such action as may be deemed appropriate." Lieutenant General Del Valle initialed his approval to the recommendation.

Before the officers and enlisted men celebrated the Marine Corps birthday in Crane, Indiana, the PX would reimburse Mrs. Bush $50 for her damaged *Season Skipper* lady's coat.

August 11. In his own handwriting, Sgt. R. E. Bush applied for a family savings allotment for Judith. He included a certified copy of his daughter's birth certificate.

October 1. Sergeant Bush went over to the Admin Building to have an official photo taken for his Service Record Book. The Mobile Dental Unit, Hqs 9th Naval District, filled some cavities for him at MBNAD. The base dental department would finish his dental care in February 1948 with more fillings.

BUSH, Richard
Earl (449381)
Enl 19May46
Photo 1Oct47

November 4. Sergeant Bush filled out VA Form 9-1575, requesting allotment information. Deductions from his pay had continued after he had discontinued his NSLI policies, and he was requesting a refund of said allotments. The Officer In Charge, USMC Claims Division, acknowledged receipt of his letter. It was necessary to examine the pay account for the entire period of his active service, and his refund was "Pending." A great volume of claims had been submitted since the beginning of demobilization. Regrettably, settlement of his claim was estimated to be eighteen to twenty-four months in the future.

Sergeant Bush also completed an Application for a Victory Medal World War II, for which he was entitled for his service beginning on September 22, 1942. The medal was to be awarded to all persons serving between December 7, 1941 and December 31, 1946. His present address was 110 Larrimer Street, Crane, Indiana.

November 6. Finances remained a concern for Sgt Bush as he provided for his young family. He filed a claim for an insurance waiver via the Disability Insurance Claims Services, Central Office.

December 5. Captain M. B. Rogers, USMC delivered the Victory Medal World War II and insignia to Sgt Bush.

December 14. Major Watts had changed his opinion of Sgt Bush when he completed his Relief of Reporting Officer report covering the period August 1–December 14. He raised most ratings to Excellent (highly efficient; qualified to a high degree). The sergeant's Loyalty was Outstanding. While he would be glad to have him in his command, Sgt Bush was not qualified for promotion, because he would have difficulty serving in a line organization.

"Sergeant Bush while an excellent man is in poor physical condition due to combat injuries, for which he received the CONGRESSIONAL MEDAL OF HONOR."

Still, Major Watts believed the sergeant's value to the service was Excellent.

Although Sgt Bush did not like that his future MBNAD reporting officers would note that he was "considerably handicapped in sight as a result of battle injuries," he had to admit that much of his time was spent at USNH Great Lakes. His Semi-annual Reports were completely marked Not Observed. The end of his second enlistment was five months away and his separation from the service seemed likely.

February 13–15, 1948. Most 1st Battalion Raiders lived on the East Coast after the war. Those who were members of "Red Mike" Edson's Raiders Association gathered for their "first annual reunion" at Quantico. Captain Frank J. Guidone would remind the Raiders later that the first reunion had actually been in 1944 at Montford Point, Camp Lejeune, at an old crab shack near the base. He and at least thirty-two other 1st Raiders got together there to drink beer and toast their comrades who were buried on Pacific islands.

March 3. Sergeant Bush received a letter from the Commandant informing him that he would receive a yearly Aviation Transportation Card. As a holder of the Medal of Honor, he was provided an Authorization Card permitting him to ride as a passenger on Armed Service Aircraft to cover the period July 1, 1948–June 30, 1949. If he wanted to renew the authorization, he should furnish his address to the Commandant's office on or before May 1, 1949. General C. R. Cates concluded his letter.

"I hope that this privilege may be of value to you and that you will accept it as a further token of appreciation of your country for the outstanding service you have rendered the Nation."

April 27. Sergeant Bush was admitted to the USNAD hospital with a diagnosis of Foreign Body, Trauma to Eyes. His vision had been steadily decreasing in his right eye since the exploding enemy hand grenade injury. With his right eye vision at 13/20, he was unable to read print. He thought his right eye vision was getting worse. He was having frequent headaches. He was transferred to Great Lakes for treatment.

April 28. Commander E. J. Olenick recognized that, while shell fragments had pierced both of his eyes, no treatment had been given to either eye when he was cared for on the Okinawa beach or on the USS *Samaritan*. X-Ray examination showed fine metallic foreign body shadows scattered around both orbital regions, as well as over the maxillary soft tissues. The shadows were the same as those appearing scattered through his hand and up his forearm to his elbow. Intraorbital localization would have to be made to determine the position of the fragments to the eyeballs.

Examination of Sgt Bush's left hip showed no bone changes. There was one, small 1x3mm fragment projected into the greater tuberosity and several smaller foreign body shadows in the soft tissue above the wing of the left ilium.

The sergeant's major injuries were to his hand. In the surgeon's opinion, "He is most fortunate that what contractures he has have occurred in a position of function." The only operative interventions the doctor would dare undertake were to excise some small, needle-like bone fragments (spicule) and possibly a tendon graft to Sgt Bush's third finger extensor.

Treatment to his eye was to be principal.

May 5. The ophthalmologist, using subjective endoscopy, a nonsurgical procedure with a light, determined that foreign bodies were present in the vitreous of both eyes.

May 12. No essential dental treatment was required at this time for Sgt Bush. He was given an oral prophylaxis.

May 18. Sergeant Bush had reached the end of his second enlistment. Colonel Martyr referred to the Marine Corps Manual for guidance on separation of men in hospital from the service. He cited Article 3-13(2)g—"Discharge of enlisted men upon report of medical survey for disability will not be effected until the man has been discharged from treatment in the hospital, except in cases of mental or incurable diseases." Since Sgt Bush was under medical care for injuries incurred in combat, not for either a mental or incurable disease, Colonel Martyr endorsed the Chief Medical Officer's recommendation that he be retained in the service post end of his enlistment time.

May 25. Dr. J. P. Cowen, a civilian specialist, considered Sgt Bush's condition to be "calavacta complicata"—a medical term borrowed from Latin that the military doctors took to mean "complicated actions to the skull." Dr. Cowen considered surgery to be disadvantageous, because of adhesions that might be induced in so young a patient. It was advisable to wait, reexamine in fifteen days, and see if opacification (the eye becoming cloudy or opaque) progressed at an appreciable rate.

May 28. Sergeant Bush had been minimizing his vision problems. He was put on fifteen days of Convalescent Leave.

June 15. Examination revealed that the lens in both eyes were cataractous with metallic bodies lodged in each lens. Sergeant Bush was unable to read newspaper print. He could see letters at an angle if he moved his eyes. Visual acuity in his right eye was 1/40; in his left it was 3/20. Dental plates of the anterior segment of each eye showed small pinhead shadow, likely in the lens. His diagnosis was changed to Foreign Bodies Traumatic Eyes.

The war years slowly drifted into the past. Deaths of "old" friends who had survived battles, some without a scratch, provided a paradox for the former Raiders.

After the war, Charles J. Quade, 24, of Elizabeth, New Jersey, had the kind of job that found its way into Hollywood movie scenes. He was employed at Galen Hall, the red-roofed, seven-story resort hotel and the most famous resort on South Mountain in Wernersville, Pennsylvania, west of Reading. On Sunday, August 3, 1947, he and two friends were driving on a rural Berks County road near Wernersville, and the car overturned. State Police blamed the motor crash on a tire blowout. Charles died in a Reading hospital two hours later. The other two in the car received cuts and bruises. [27]

Patrick D. Fleming, 22, had earned a Silver Star for gallantry in action with Dog Company, 1st Raider Battalion, at New Georgia on July 10, 1943, for "killing an enemy machine-gunner, and assisting in the safe evacuation of two wounded comrades from a position well within the enemy's lines." The Marine combat veteran was considered a war hero around the small towns between Butte and Missoula, Montana. On Saturday, August 16, 1947, he was working in a farm field near Deer Lodge. His crushed body was found under a tractor. The death was ruled accidental. [28]

Charles Konopka, 28, had grown up at 21 Second Street, Larksville Township, Pennsylvania, two miles west of Wilkes Barre. The youngest of nine born to Polish immigrants, he had three sisters and five brothers. He had served with the 1st Raiders, was wounded on Guadalcanal and Iwo Jima, and was a member of the Military Order of the Purple Hearts. He lived briefly with his sister, Bernadine, in their childhood home, then resided with his older brother, Benny, in Collinsville, Connecticut. He died at 11:30 AM on Sunday, November 23, 1947, at his brother's home. Funeral services were held in Collinsville. His body was returned to Plymouth on Friday for an 8:30 morning Requiem Mass at St. Mary's Church and burial in the family plot in the parish cemetery, 1594 S. Main Street. The cause of his death was not disclosed. [29]

On Thursday night, June 17, 1948, Britton Lyman "Jack" Ellis, 26, of Edgerton was giving four teenage girls a lift home from Kaycee, Wyoming. Virginia Hackworth, 16, and Oma Jean Creek, 14, were from small town Midwest. Barbara Tyler, 15, and Yvonne Endersby, 13, were both from Edgerton, a mile further east on Route 387.

Travelling south for over eight miles on Old Hwy 87 (Route 196), they approached the bridge on the South Fork of the Powder River. Rising on the southern slopes of the Bighorn Mountains, west of Casper, the South Fork is a tributary of the Yellowstone River. Jack's car failed to make the curve and left the highway. Highway Patrolman Art Wilson of Buffalo reported that Jack was killed instantly. The four teen passengers were shaken up, but escaped the crash with slight injuries. [30]

Dale Cecil Carlyle, 24, was shot five times on Thursday night, July 22, 1948, in Kirksville, Missouri. He was in the local hospital with critical wounds: three in the chest, one in his heart, and one in his right leg. The shooter turned himself in at police headquarters and was charged with felonious assault. [31] Dale died in the VA Hospital at Haynes, Illinois, on October 13, 1949.

The newspapers made it clear that Michael Megura, 24, of 104 Howard Avenue, Ansonia, Connecticut, was a Marine veteran who had been decorated for wounds in the Pacific Theater. Michael tried to attend regular services at Three Saints Russian Orthodox Church, but was having trouble with alcohol. After midnight, on Thursday morning, June 3, 1948, he was on Hull Street in Shelton, just south of the Route-8 bridge over the Housatonic River.

In an intoxicated state, attempting to enter a home for reasons unknown, Michael broke a small window in the rear door of a house occupied by two men. The two went outside to investigate, and a fight ensued in the back yard. Shelton Patrolmen Frederick Zalmer and Herman Pastore arrived. Michael struggled with them when they intervened. He resisted their attempts to get him into their patrol car. At 2:15 AM, he was booked at Shelton police headquarters on charges of intoxication and resisting arrest and was moved to "the tank cell to dry out."

Police Lieutenant Emil Fortier went to check on him at 2:30 AM. He found Michael dead, hanging by his belt in the cell. Dr. Edward J. Flynn, medical examiner, pronounced the death a suicide. [32]

Stanley Debosik, 27, of Oglesby, Illinois, was killed near Wenona on Thursday night, July 8, 1948, when his motorcycle ran into the side of a truck at an intersection on Route 51. Charles Sullivan, 22, the truck driver, was not injured. [33]

PFC Walter Joseph Paczkoski Jr., 25, from Glen Lyon on the Susquehanna River, nine miles west of Charles Konopka's Larksville home, was a Polish-born young man with an excellent war record. Son of a coal miner, he had served with the 1st Raider Battalion and had earned Purple Hearts on Bougainville and Saipan. He was later hospitalized several months for treatment of malaria. He returned to the family home at 190 East Main Street on a disability pension, suffering the ruins of shell shock. His death was reported on Wednesday, July 21, 1948. Walt was buried in Corpus Christi Parish's Saint Adalbert's Cemetery. The cause of his death was undisclosed. [34]

✱✱✱

August 4, 1948. Sergeant Bush was given procaine retrobulbar analgesia. A simple extracapsular cataract extraction was performed on his right eye to remove the cloudy lens inside the capsule. A plastic lens was implanted in front of the capsule. A clean sclera-corneal suture was used. No complications occurred. Postoperative, he was administered cocaine, atropine, and adrenalin injections under his eyelid (subconjunctival).

August 5. Mrs. Stella M. Bush wrote to the Paymaster Dept, Allotment Office, HqUSMC, requesting a change of her address from 201 Earl Street, Crane, to Route 2, Box 236, Waukegan, IL, c/o Earl Snyder.

August 11. "The light seems to bother my eyes." Sergeant Bush's right eye was showing sustained, forced, involuntary closing of the eyelids (Blepharospasm) and photophobia. There were corneal striae and a deep rim of blood stained cortex in the anterior chamber. His left eye pupil was well dilated.

August 20. Colonel C. W. Martyr, Casual Company Commander, MBNTC, Great Lakes, promoted him to permanent rank of Staff Sergeant. His base monthly pay for service over three years was increased to $120.75, plus his Family Allowance. Staff Sergeant Bush figured that his base pay would go up to $126.50 on September 23, when his service period was over six years. The pay increase did not go into effect until January 1, resulting in a "shortpaid" situation.

September 2. Staff Sergeant Bush noticed a slow decrease in his vision, problems with glare, and objects looking slightly hazy. The capsule in his right eye had become thickened and cloudy and was dense in the center.

While a cocaine topical and procaine infiltration analgesia were applied, the ophthalmologist explained that he was going to open the eye capsule and break up the lens' cortex with a needle knife. Discission of the secondary membrane [after cataract] was performed without apparent complications.

The operative wound healed normally, and SSgt Bush's vision was brought to 20/20 with corrective lens. Penicillin eye baths, sulfonamide, and calcium gluconate were started.

November 10. His vision difficulties grew worse. A vitreous hernia was observed in the right eye anterior chamber. The pupil opening was good and the interior well seen. There were vitreous opacities.

November 17. Staff Sergeant Bush could not say his vision was better. "It's like there's a shade from above over my right eye. It's cloudy when I look up. . . . Colors show up in the eye, and they change from dark to purple." He also complained of having persistent nasal bleeding.

The clouding in his upper visual field and the appearance of colors concerned the medical staff. The inside of his right eye was not visible through the cloudy lens. A right detachment was evident.

December 3. It had been more than three years since SSgt Bush had met President Truman at the White House. His 24th birthday was weeks away. He was still learning what a Medal of Honor meant to the Marine Corps and to families around the nation.

The MBNTC commander received a communiqué inquiring about SSgt Bush's availability to serve as a Medal of Honor escort. Two Marine Medal recipients were being repatriated on the SS *Dalton Victory*, AP3. The temporary duty would involve seven days in Columbus, Ohio, around December 18, and seven days in New York in early January.

The remains of Corporal Tony Stein, initially buried on Iwo Jima, were coming home for reinternment in his native Dayton, Ohio. His funeral at Our Lady of the Rosary Church and burial with full military honors were planned for December 17.

The identity of the second recipient was not disclosed.

December 4. USNH Great Lakes wired Casualty Company, Personnel Division, Headquarters Marine Corps, at 12:03 PM. SSgt Bush's availability was uncertain, due to scheduled eye operations.

December 7. The ophthalmologist was concerned about the right eye. Little light reflected off the back of his eye. The floating opacities in the vitreous were accumulating. A "marked reduction in vision" was noted. The doctor prescribed omnadin intramuscularly to alternate daily with the calcium gluconate.

Omnadin was a non-specific immune stimulant, comprised of lipids and proteins; and, it had a dubious reputation after the war. One of Stella's friends at the Great Lakes hospital told her that doctors sometimes called it a *snake oil*.

New Year's Eve traditionally holds its many traditional festivities and sometimes-tragic anguishes. Chief Warrant Officer Everett Wesley Davis, 47, had counted his war service in the 1st and 2d Raider battalions to be the highlight of his Marine Corps career. He died in a Camp Pendleton car accident on Friday night, December 31, 1948.

$$***$$

January 1, 1949. New Year was a Saturday, and SSgt Bush was at USNH Great Lakes. From his view, "It didn't look good."

The diagnosis of his poor vision was changed to Cataract, Traumatic, Right Eye, caused by foreign bodies, DNEPTE. He was essentially healthy except for his eyes. During treatment on January 10, the diagnosis was changed to Uveitis, Right Eye, a complication of the cataract condition.

January 11. Staff Sergeant Bush was "6 years 3 months 24 days" into his Marine Corps service. The Medical Survey Board convened to review his medical history. He had foreign bodies in each eye. His right eye was not improving. There was an eye inflammation (uveitis), characterized by floating opacities in vitreous, and impairment of vision caused by numerous spots and thread-like strands in his view. The absence of fundus details alerted the ophthalmologist to an apparent vitreous hemorrhage that could not be observed at the interior surface of the eye opposite the lens. The Board concluded that SSgt Bush was unfit for duty, probably for an indefinite future duration, recommending that he be retained for further treatment. Staff Sergeant Bush was informed of the findings. He did not desire to submit a rebuttal.

January 31. Captain A. N. Fassino, commanding officer, Casualty Company, Marine Barracks, Great Lakes, completed a Semi-Annual Fitness Report for August 1, 1948–January 31, 1949. He checked all the Not Observed blocks, except for SSgt Bush's dignity of demeanor, neat and smart appearance, which he rated as Excellent. He recommended a promotion to Technical Sergeant.

February 1. The Commanding Officer, MBNTC, awarded Staff Sergeant Bush with a second Good Conduct Medal. He had met the requirements and had completed three years of continuous active service on September 20, 1948. Headquarters Marine Corps provided him a Good Conduct Medal Bar (Second Award Bar) on April 14.

April 1. The diagnosis regarding his right eye was changed again—this time to Opacity, Vitreous Humor.

April 5. The Medical Survey Board met again. The numerous floating opacities in vitreous were obvious in his right eye. He had good light reflex and a bit of his inner eye was visible. Subjective endoscopy was positive, and his vision was limited to light perception. On examination, his left eye revealed a traumatic cataract with deposits of foreign particles in the lens. Visual acuity in his left eye was 10/200. Given what happened after the cataract extraction of his right eye, the surgeons were concerned about an intraocular complication and reduction of vision in his left eye. They found it inadvisable to operate on his left eye, for fear of a further reduction of vision.

Based on the Military Physical Profile Serial System (PULHES) used to qualify an enlistee's physical abilities, the Board determined him to be Serial 343141—permanently unfit for duty—and recommended that he be discharged from the Marine Corps. There was no disciplinary action pending in his case. Staff Sergeant Bush did not submit a rebuttal.

April 20. Chief of BuMed approved the discharge by reason of medical survey. Colonel Martyr wrote out the Honorable Discharge Order, noting that Technical Sergeant Bush had been retained in the service 340 days post end of his enlistment time under provisions in Article 3–13(2)g, Marine Corps Manual.

April 22. Colonel Martyr promoted SSgt Bush to the permanent rank of Technical Sergeant (Master Gunnery Sergeant) at the time of his Honorable Discharge. The Senior Medical Officer forwarded on his closed Health Record and Pension Claim, noting "Terminated by reason of Medical Survey."

Lieutenant Junior Grade J. J. Carroll, MCR USNR, closed out TSgt Bush's Medical History Record—"Invalided from the service."

Technical Sergeant Bush submitted an Application For Arrears of Pay, claiming that his staff sergeant pay had been short credited $21.65 in the period 23Sept48–31Dec48. He requested that the settlement amount be sent to his father in Glasgow. The claim was forwarded to the Claims Division, then the Legal Division, Headquarter Marine Corps, for investigation. A memorandum was sent to the Quartermaster General. It was determined that TSGT Bush had been SHORTPAID.

Warrant Officer C. L. Craig sent the completed NAVMC 78-PD, Report of Separation, to Headquarters. Technical Sergeant Bush had filed his pension claim, was provided an Honorable Discharge Certificate, and was returning home to Kentucky with his two dependents. The Dischargee's last civilian employment as a general farm hand, employed by his father, was in September 1942. Technical Sergeant Bush desired job aid. In Block 40, Preference For Additional Training, WO Craig entered: "This man will have to take some sort of training but at the present time he is undecided about it. He is a total disabled Medal of Honor man and will probably receive training from the Vet. Administration."

On his uniform, he was authorized to wear medals or ribbons for: his Medal of Honor, Purple Heart with gold 5/16-inch star (two awards), Combat Action Ribbon, Presidential Unit Citation for Okinawa, Navy Unit Commendation for combat on Guam, Good Conduct Medal with one bronze star (1942–1948), American Campaign Medal (1942–1953), Asiatic–Pacific Campaign Medal with three bronze stars (Bismarck Archipelago Operation, Marianas Operation, Okinawa Gunta Operation), and the World War II Victory Medal. [35]

Technical Sergeant Bush departed MBNTC with his Promotion and Discharge Certificates and his Honorable Service and Honorable Discharge lapel buttons.

***

Technical Sergeant William K. Robinson, 26, of Martins Ferry, Belmont County, Ohio, across the Ohio River from Wheeling, West Virginia, was the Marine Corps recruiter in Steubenville. His station was an easy 24-mile drive north from his family home. One night, Sergeant Robinson took a 21-mile drive further north. At 2:25 AM on Friday morning, May 27, 1949, alone in the car, he was killed when his auto struck an abutment at a Wellsville street intersection. Columbiana County Coroner Ernest Sturgis said the former Marine Raider had died instantly of a broken neck.

✳✳✳

May 31, 1949. The Paymaster mailed Gov't Check No. 274827 to c/o Clarence Bush. The amount of the Supplemental Final Settlement was $18.59.

CHAPTER 21

A Normal Life

✳✳✳

"He is most powerful who has power over himself." [1]

— Lucius Annaeus Seneca (4 BC-65 AD)

AFTER HIS DISCHARGE, OFFICAL CORRESPONDENCES were addressed to Mr. Richard E. Bush. He and Stella moved from Indiana to Rural Route #4, Glasgow, Kentucky. Judith would be two years old on July 31, so the couple had time to plan their future before their daughter started off for school. As a Marine Corps veteran and a MOH holder, Dick had some things to work out.

His life serves as an example of the responsibilities and commitments placed upon MOH recipients. In addition to his family, many other affiliations claimed his time over the years: the Veterans Administration; Glasgow, his home town; Kentucky, the state to which his Medal of Honor was accredited; Waukegan, Illinois, his long-time place of residence; the Congressional Medal of Honor Society (CMOHS); the Marine Corps; the 6th Marine Division; the 1st Raider Battalion; and the 4th Marine Regiment.

In total, Dick figured he had spent four years in Navy hospitals. Almost totally blind, he retained a little sight in his left eye. Eventually, he would lose his right eye and be fitted for a glass replacement. He had no use of his right arm and only partial use of one leg. He was often in pain. Grenade shrapnel would work its way out of his body for the rest of his life. Yet, he was determined. He had an answer for those who might say he was totally handicapped.

"I try to lead a normal life."

June 30, 1949. He missed the May 1 deadline for requesting his yearly Aviation Transportation Card, but mailed it two months late anyway. Commandant General Cates mailed his authorization to ride as a passenger on Armed Service Aircraft on August 4, covering the July 1, 1949–June 30, 1950 period. Dick and Hqs Marine Corps would continue this annual exchange of correspondences until 1959.

Stella did not care to live in Kentucky. Since he was so familiar with the Chicago area, Dick gave serious consideration to President Truman's offer. As a MOH recipient, he could accept a contact representative position, GS7, with the Veterans Administration. Coming to the aid of other veterans would be a good fit, but he did not want a disability to be a factor considered in his hiring. The VA had some questions about his discharge.

Dick wrote to the VA Central Office in Washington, D.C. He argued that his return to duty in May 1946 upon the Board of Medical Survey recommendation was ordered, because he did not wish to be discharged from the Marines by reason of disability. He had waived the disability status. He stated that, since the disabling conditions had been caused by action for which he was awarded the Congressional Medal of Honor, his return to duty was ordered. Thereafter, he was given extremely light duty during times between periods of hospitalization, since in fact his physical condition did preclude performance of general duty.

Four years had passed since the conclusion of WWII, but news of Raider deaths continued.

✳✳✳

Around Lenoir City, Tennessee, folks knew that Lloyd C. Hickman, 26, and Nettie Katheryn Bright, 21, were sweethearts. Lloyd was the associate publisher of the *Lenoir City News*, and the couple had been dating for some time. On Friday evening, August 27, 1949, the two went motor boating with Thomas Allen Milligan, 23, and Betty Ann Brown, 17, on nearby Fort Loudoun Lake.

Their outboard motor stalled, then started again with a roar. The boat upended, and all four were pitched into the deep water. Lloyd was an excellent swimmer and likely could have made it to shore after the accident. All four bodies were recovered by midnight. As his friends imagined, and Raider comrades would surely attest, Lloyd had sacrificed his life in an attempt to rescue Miss Bright instead of saving himself. His arms were tightly locked around Nettie when they were pulled from the waters. [2]

✳✳✳

August 30. Mr. O. E. Carlton, Records Service, VA Records Verification Division, wrote to Hqs Marine Corps forwarding Dick's letter, requesting a statement regarding the veteran's allegation. His office was also requesting copies of any regulations or other instructions relating to Richard's contention about his return to duty being unrelated to a disability. Mr. Carlton referenced the matter as Claim # 6 125 609.

September 22. The Director of Personnel, Hqs Marine Corps, responded to the request for information, sending photostat copies of Richard's Assignment to duty and Waiver for Reenlistment documents.

October 5. Miss Burnstead made a telephonic request to the Director of Personnel Office asking for more specific information. The Director sent a letter to her attention. Records showed that CPL Bush was honorably discharged on May 18, 1946, by special order of the Commandant for the convenience of the government. He enlisted in the regular Marine Corps the next day. On April 22, 1949, he was honorably discharged upon report of medical survey for disability. That was all the VA needed to know.

Before his birthday and a new year began, despite constant problems with his one functioning eye, managing without fingers, and dealing with twenty-seven large pieces of shrapnel embedded in his body, Dick began handling claims work for the VA in the Chicago area and working as a counselor at Downey VA Hospital, adjoining the Great Lakes facility in North Chicago. [3]

Stella was pregnant with their second child, so Dick looked for a house for the growing family nearer to his work. He purchased a two-story single-family home, with two baths, 1,728 square feet of living space, and an unfinished, 594-square-foot basement at 2407 Galilee Street, Zion, Illinois. The home was between Waukegan and the Wisconsin border, west of the nature and beach preserves on Lake Michigan, and within walking distance of

West Elementary School and Shiloh Park Elementary. Judith, not yet three years old, became a big sister when Richard Jr., was born.

The family would reside on Galilee until late in 1957. For the latter part of the year, Dick's mail went to P.O. Box 545, Waukegan.

✳✳✳

Robert Edward Gores, of Burlington, Wisconsin, went for a motorcycle ride on his 28th birthday—Sunday afternoon, October 23, 1949. His ride was going to be front-page news, accompanied by a photograph of his battered cycle. Fred Peterson was driving north on County Trunk U with a passenger one mile west of Hwy 41. He looked both ways as he approached the County Trunk V intersection, but saw no traffic near the crossroads.

Robert was speeding west on County Trunk V, three miles south of Kenosha, and was ten feet away when Fred's car reached the middle of the intersection. At 4:11 PM, the motorcycle rammed into the passenger side of the big, black, four-door sedan, buckling in the front fender. Robert was hurled against the car, striking the passenger's window, suffering a basal skull fracture, fractured neck, wrist, and leg.

Fulmer Towing Service arrived before the sheriff's ambulance. Robert died en route to Kenosha Hospital. Neither occupant in the sedan was hurt seriously. [4]

✳✳✳

March 8, 1950. Dick was experiencing dental problems and submitted a claim to the VA. He was alleging service related disease or injury. The Claims Division sent VA Form 3102 to HqUSMC requesting T/Sgt Bush's entrance and discharge examinations and all available treatment records. The VA received the information on March 23, confirming the dental treatments Dick had been provided while on active duty.

June 14. He mailed his request for an Authorization Card permitting him to ride as a passenger on Government service planes when space was available. Then, he wrote again on June 21, requesting two duplicate Medal of Honor Rosettes to be worn on civilian clothes.

June 25. Although medically unlikely, Dick considered the possibilities of returning to active duty. At 4:00 AM on Sunday, the dogged North Korean People's Army (NKPA), with Soviet support, crossed the 38th Parallel and pushed south past Seoul. The communists intended to drive American and South Korean forces off the peninsula and unify the two halves of the peninsula. By July 13, they had advanced to the major town of Taejon, a strategic road hub in the southern peninsula along the Kongju-Taep'yong-ni line on the Kum River, in the western foothills of the Sobaek Mountains. By mid-August, the NKPA had over-run two-thirds of South Korea's territory and had pushed the defenders back into a corner of the peninsula.

The Marines, "woefully" equipped and understrength, held the Pusan Perimeter, hard-pressed to keep the invaders from taking the vital supply port in the southeast. President Truman ordered Army and Marine forces back to full wartime strength.

Dick would learn that former Raider "brothers" died during the Korean War years—some on battlefields, some at home. One death on a Korean hill called "Old Baldy" would cut him more deeply than even the deaths of friends on Okinawa had.

July 12. The Decorations and Medals Branch sent him one duplicate MOH Rosette. Headquarters could not provide him two, as per his request, because of the limited supply of rosettes. His travel card was issued to him on July 26.

✳✳✳

Sergeant James J. "J.J." Starr, 31, a Boston native, had received a battlefield commission to first lieutenant on Guam. He stayed in the Corps after the war and was stationed at Camp Lejeune. According to a note written in his own hand over the weekend, he was having domestic troubles. He went into an abandoned barracks at Onslow Beach. He was discovered hanging there on Monday, July 17, 1950.

Korean casualty list No. 152 was released on November 15. The Marine Corps reported that Sergeant William Russell Moore, 29, was among the first to have been killed in Yongsan, Korea, at the Naktong Bulge on September 3, 1950—serving with the 5th Marine Regiment, 1st Provisional Marine Brigade. New Hampshire claimed him as a son. His Home of Record, where he enlisted, was Canyonville, Oregon. He is buried at Beverly National Cemetery, New Jersey.

Staff Sergeant Clayton Leroy Roberts, 26, from Oklahoma City, died while leading a B/1/1 light machine-gun squad in action against the enemy on Hill 109 near Kojo, North Korea, on the night of October 27. His widow, Opal, would be twice invited to ceremonies to receive her husband's medals, awards he never wore.

As a private first class, SSgt Roberts had fought across the Guam beachhead on D-Day, July 21, 1944, with a mortar platoon in Major John S. Messers' 2d Battalion, 4th Marines. When his section was being harassed by a group of hostile snipers, he volunteered to search them out. He was wounded, refused to stay in the rear aid station, and returned to his duties until ordered to be evacuated.

At a Dallas Naval Air Station ceremony on July 13, 1951, Opal received his posthumous Silver Star for heroism against the Japanese forces on Guam. On Friday morning, November 30, 1951, at the Baptist Church in Rattan, Oklahoma, she was presented his posthumous Navy Cross award for his daring actions in Korea. Sergeant Roberts also was credited with a Purple Heart medal with two oak leaf clusters. [5]

Corporal Mitchell Red Cloud Jr., 24, from Merrillan, Wisconsin, was a Ho-Chunk (Winnebago) Nation member and had lived at the Tomah Indian School Reservation before he was a member of Carlson's 2d Raiders in WWII. He fought on Midway Island, the Makin Atoll, and Guadalcanal and contracted malaria. A bullet in his left shoulder earned him a Purple Heart and evacuation from Okinawa on May 17, 1945. He enlisted in the U.S. Army in 1948, and went to Korea with Company E, 2d Battalion, 19th Infantry Regiment, 24th Infantry Division.

On November 5, 1950, Corporal Red Cloud was dug in on Hill 123, northeast of Anju–Chongyon on the Chongchon River Line when the Chinese attacked E Company. He left his position, was wounded, and braced himself against a tree to deliver devastating fire on the enemy, allowing his unit to consolidate and evacuate casualties. Severely wounded a second time, he kept up his fire until he was overrun by the rushing hordes of communists and killed. Corporal Red Cloud earned a posthumous Medal of Honor for his actions. [6]

His remains were returned to the Winnebago Mission and buried in Decorah Cemetery.

Two A/1/5 Marines were killed in action in North Korea on December 7, 1950, during the Chosin Reservoir Breakout, from Hagaru-ri to Koto-Ri. Master Sergeant Daniel Joseph Carroll, 30, of Newark, New Jersey, had earned a Silver Star on New Georgia in WWII. His wife received word on Wednesday, December 20, 1950, that her husband had been KIA. [7] Master Sergeant Franklin Joe Lawson, 28, of Maysville, Oklahoma, was also KIA near Hagaru-ri. He left a wife and four-year-old daughter.

Staff Sergeant Oscar Bradford Terry, 32, of Austin, had been a Texas news service reporter after WWII. He returned to active duty in August 1950, and was stationed at Oceanside, California, awaiting overseas orders. His wife, Alice, and daughter, Iris, 7, remained in Austin. A shot rang out in a company storeroom on Wednesday, April 25, 1951. Sergeant Terry was found dead, shot in the head with his own carbine. The Marine Corps board of investigation could not immediately determine whether the shooting was accidental, but it was apparent that the fatal bullet was self-inflicted.

"Let me talk with him, I know him." Pikeville is a legendary town in east Kentucky, most famous for the 30-year grudge carried on by the Hatfield and McCoy families after the Civil War. Sergeant Augustus Borden Justice, 29, a Company C, 1st Battalion Raider, had enlisted from there. He stayed in the Marines after the war, stationed at Camp Lejeune.

Home for some leave in May 1951, Sergeant Justice, two of his brothers, Bennie and Elmer, and three friends, Charles Lee Sawyer, Elmo Webb, and Paul Short, camped out for some R & R at Card Mountain Gap on Lick Creek, eighteen miles from town.

At midnight on Saturday, May 19, Mallard Williams, 32, drove up in a Jeep with his .22 caliber rifle and accused Paul Short of disturbing his home. Sergeant Justice recognized the irate man and said he would talk with him. Mallard shot the sergeant to death. The Kentucky State Police arrested him on Sunday and held him in the Pikeville Jail.

The five men present at Card Gap testified at a Monday inquest that Mallard had shot Augustus. Mr. Williams claimed that he was not there and knew nothing about the shooting. He was charged with murder on Tuesday. Sergeant Justice was buried at Hackney Creek Cemetery in Pike County, where Hackney Creek and Levisa Fork meet on the Kentucky border. [8]

Mr. Williams realized the stakes were against him. In 1950, two men had been electrocuted in "Old Sparky" in Eddyville for murder. Then, on June 8, only three weeks after Mallard had slain Sergeant Justice, the 410th man executed in Kentucky died in the electric chair for a murder-robbery. Mr. Williams decided to plead guilty. On August 20, Circuit Judge E. D. Stephenson sentenced him to life in prison.

Lieutenant Colonel Robert Harry Thomas had been aide-de-camp to Commandant of the Marine Corps General Clifton B. Cates in 1951. He was three days from his 35th birthday when he "died of other causes" in the Western Outposts in Korea on October 13, 1952. He was awarded the Legion of Merit for exceptionally meritorious conduct in the performance of outstanding services starting on August 21, 1952, until his death. He was buried in Section 3 at Arlington National Cemetery.

November 22, 1950. Dick received his Good Conduct Medal for service 1942–1945.

January 17, 1951. Registered mail arrived on Galelee Avenue for Dick. The Commandant sent him a commemorative copy of *Medal of Honor, The Navy*. The book depicted the valor of men awarded the Medal through Wars and Campaigns since 1861. "It pays tribute to you and other heroic men of the Naval Service and I am sure you will find it interesting and valuable."

"Beat Them or Get Out"

The debates in Washington, D.C., about U.S. involvement in Korea shared the newspaper front-page headlines with columns about the apparent stalemate in the foreign land. Obviously, not all the senators favored keeping up the peace talks or the fighting. Maps showed the battle line to start at the Kimpo Peninsula on the Yellow Sea coast, north of Panmunjom, stretching in an arch thirty-five miles northeast from the Imjin River near Munsan-ni to a point east of Kumhwa in the central regions.

Dick's older brother heard the call to arms again. Clarence Morris Bush enlisted in the Army in January 1951, and was first in Europe, then was dispatched to Korea. He was assigned duties as a light weapons infantryman with the 23d Infantry Regiment, 2d Infantry Division, and spent many of his days fighting the Chinese and NKPA in the hills of North Korea, a few miles above the 38th Parallel. He wrote letters home about the weather and the rugged ridges and deeply eroded terrain of Yokkok-Chon Valley.

April 25. Colonel R. E. Dingeman, State Project Officer, State of Nevada, 25 East Taylor Street, Reno, wrote to the Commandant. Dick's Medal was to be on display in Reno for Armed Forces Day, May 20, 1951. He requested a new Medal of Honor Neckband, because the present ribbon was badly soiled and worn. On May 8, the Decorations and Medals Branch, handling the request with speed, sent the colonel a new neckband, with the guidance, "may be delivered to Mr. Bush at the time the Medal of Honor is returned to him."

Dick read *Chicago Tribune* accounts of the outpost battles along the *Jamestown Line* and tried to determine his brother's location.

From the Marines Who Were There

September 15, 1951. The Raiders might have been disbanded after New Georgia and the Enogai Inlet battle, but the veterans counted those days to have been the most important of their Corps' service. The Marine Raider Association (USMRA) held its first organizational and incorporation meeting. Sixteen former Raiders living in the Los Angeles area, representing the 1st, 2d, and 4th Raider Battalions, had contacted all the known Raiders in California. Most of the initial members hailed from Carlson's 2d Raider Battalion.

They established their founding principle. "The Marine Raider Association was founded to expound the special Esprit de Corps we shared in the Marine Raiders and perform a few worthy charitable acts as we go through our twilight years into obscurity." The photographer assembled the thirty-four members in three rows for their incorporation photo.

The Association set out to track down or account for every man who had served even a day in the Raider battalions. [9] They put ads in newspapers and magazines about conventions and reunions. Eventually, the Association would compile a complete Master Raider File with name, rank, serial number, Units, campaigns, wounds, decorations, and current status, including those who had "washed out" from training. Early investigations listed 889 Raiders killed in action.

Thousands of the Raiders, including Dick Bush, did not learn about the organization in its early years of existence. Many died before the Association was able to locate addresses for them. More than twenty years passed before Dick became a Life Member.

In order to reunite old friends and help them stay in contact, the organization began publishing *The Raider Patch* and mailing it to the members. [10] The earliest newsletters amounted to a few pages with notices about meetings, conventions, reunions, dues, and scholarship drives. Articles provided advice about the GI Loan Program, National Cemetery guidelines, life insurance planning, writing a Living Will, and health tips. Books written about the Raiders were reviewed. Raider mementoes could be purchased at the Gift Store. The Bullsheet section printed letters to the editor. The short correspondences typically described what the members and family were doing, anniversaries, whom they were in contact with, which old buddies they were searching for, vacation destinations, and holiday party news. Compliments about the newsletter were frequent.

The Patch was serving its purpose. "Lost Raiders" would be located well into the 1990s. "Always a pleasure to see Old Buddies' names in the Bullsheet."

Early "austere" reunions had small turnouts. One of the first was held in Washington, D.C.. Raider Chapters formed in various regions and held their own small parties and get-togethers. As more Raiders learned of the Association and applied for memberships, the Bullsheet pages expanded. News included marriage announcements, births, divorces, hospitalizations, illnesses, and deaths. Sometimes, wives or sons or daughters wrote to inform the membership that a Raider had died. *The Patch* began compiling a list of deceased Raiders for the Honor Roll. Each issue began including a memorial and obituary column.

By 1980, the newsletters stretched out to four to nine pages. Histories of the Raider battles and biographies of admired men filled the pages. The men reconnected with former commanders. Chartered trips to former battle sites were organized and featured in issues afterwards. In addition to searching for Raiders and new members, the editor requested first-hand accounts and vignettes of personal experiences while a Raider. Each Raider had experienced "some very special and unique adventures while in the Pacific" and was in a position to write a personal account of missions, colorful incidents, and some historical event.

Gradually, the former Raiders wrote memorable recollections revealing the human side of the missions. They added eyewitness details to the official accounts of crucial battles. Readers acknowledged that the stories brought back vivid memories—some fond, some horrible. For many, the writing and the reading proved cathartic, even therapeutic. The letters and articles were ". . . authored by the men who were in the thick of it and told it like it was, the fear, the hatred, the horror and the pride—yes and the humor." [11]

The Patch grew to average 24 quality pages of history and personal disclosures, like an early form of social media, well before FaceBook. The Raiders wrote about what it was like to be widowed, divorced, to have second and multiple marriages, and to struggle back from financial woes and hardships.

September–October 1951. Army Private Clarence Bush fought in the battle of heavily fortified Heartbreak Ridge near Ch'orwon. Companies of the 23d Infantry scrambled up the rocky slopes of the seven-mile-long hill mass, assaulting enemy bunkers one after another. They took the crest, only to be driven back down the hill in counter-attacks by Chinese reinforcements. Before Heartbreak was finally encircled and secured, the Army lost over 3,700 men to casualties. Sometimes, entire platoons and companies were almost entirely wiped out on the slopes and in the bunkers. The 2d Infantry Division was relieved and placed in reserve until December. Private Morris Bush, and his family back home, had a respite from the battles. Then, the regiments returned to the front outposts to replace the 25th Infantry Division.

✳✳✳

Sergeant Thomas Richard Bodell, 26, former Company B, 1st Raider, from Salt Lake City, had been at the Chosin Reservoir and was killed at the Punchbowl with E/2/1 on June 10, 1951. Corporal Lloyd Raymond Lusher, 29, former 3d Raider from Kansas City, Missouri, was KIA in Korea on September 11, 1951.

Gillis Barnes "Chick" Naylor Jr., 27, wore three Purple Hearts. He was WIA on Iwo Jima and twice in Korea. He died in a motorcycle accident in Oceanside on September 18, 1951.

Winifred Cornish had accompanied her husband to an appointment to see a psychiatrist earlier in the evening on Thursday, December 6, 1951. Albert B. Cornish Jr., 26, was despondent and in ill health. Later, at 10:15 PM, in the den of his Syracuse home at 406 Willis Avenue, he shot himself with a .22 rifle. Winifred was able to drive him to the Onondaga General Hospital. He died early Friday morning. [12]

Ralph Milton Wilson, 27, was living at 100 Craighill Avenue, Richland, very near the confluence of the Columbia and Yakima rivers, just northwest of Kennewick in the southeastern corner of Washington State. He was employed as a railroad brakeman at Hanford. Local servicemen were being brought home for burial from Korea. On Wednesday, January 23, 1952, 480 AFL Iron Workers walked off their jobs at the Hanford Atomic Plant. On Thursday, 1,500 other AFL craftsmen were laid off. The situation seemed bleak for many Richland families.

Police were called to the scene on Saturday night, January 26, 1952. They reported one male dead of a self-inflicted gunshot wound. Mueller Funeral Home in Kennewick conducted Ralph's funeral services on Tuesday, and he was buried in Grandview Cemetery in the heart of the Yakima Valley.

First Lieutenant Harold William Emree, 29, had been in the 1st Raider Battalion. He joined the Army to go to Korea. Assigned to Sandia Army Base, the principal Department of Defense nuclear weapons installation, located on the southeastern edge of Albuquerque, he lived with his wife at 2445 North Palomas Drive. On Friday night, February 29, 1952, he, Sergeant William Mick, and Master Sergeant Alvin Showalter were passengers in a car driven by CPL Robert G. Ballard, aged 30.

Near Encino, sixteen miles west of Vaughn on Hwy 60, a car driven by Kenneth May, collided with CPL Ballard's vehicle at 8:40 PM. Lieutenant Emree was killed in the two-car collision, and his date of death was recorded as March 1, 1952. Everyone else survived with minor injuries, not considered in serious condition. According to the Sunday Morning *Albuquerque Journal*, Page 1 column, State Police charged Mr. May with drunk driving.

Major Wilfred S. LeFrancois, 51, of Carlsbad, California, formerly of Watertown and Syracuse, had been a Marine for twenty-three years and was serving on combat duty in Korea. He was wounded by small-arms fire, evacuated, and died in a military hospital in Japan on June 9, 1952.

✳✳✳

June 6, 1952. UN forces began to battle for three critical outposts in west-central North Korea that dominated the western approaches to Ch'orwon—Old Baldy (Hill 266), Pork Chop Hill, and T-Bone Ridge.

For the first two weeks of July 1952, the 23d Infantry pulled back from the *Jamestown Line* to replenish the companies and train in the Kap'yong Valley, north of Kap'yong Village on the Pukhan River.

July 4. Private Bush's family in Glasgow, and Dick living in Waukegan, wondered how Private Bush was spending his 31st birthday—in Korea.

July 16. The 179th Infantry Regiment, 45th Division, troops occupied the right portion of Old Baldy. Companies E and F, 2nd Battalion, 23rd Infantry, came forward from the left into the Yokkok'chon Valley to relieve elements on Wednesday night. Private Morris Bush was killed in action on Old Baldy that night.

Funerals, Weddings, and Baptisms

Funerals and weddings brought Dick home to Kentucky. His brother's remains were repatriated and interred in Glasgow Municipal Cemetery. Velma and C. I. Edmunson came from Los Angeles. Mary was at the graveside. She had married Robert M. Tansey, a U.S. Navy WWII veteran, and had moved to Vermilion, Ohio. Dick had three Tansey nephews: David, Edward, and Thomas. Leroy, Christine, Alene, and Clara Ella Bush still lived in their parent's home on Rural Route 4 in Glasgow.

Tom Ray Daniels, 33, former 1st Raider, left his home in LaBarge, Wyoming, in his pickup truck on Sunday morning, July 27, 1952. Driving at a high rate of speed, the pickup left the highway just inside the Sublette County line near LaBarge and overturned several times. Several people witnessed the accident and rushed to the scene. The truck was demolished. Tom Daniels was dead.

Floyd Lanter, 30, former Echo Company, 1st Raider, had been working on his brother-in-law's farm near Cynthiana, Kentucky, for the past year. He was an avid hunter and enjoyed trekking about in woodlands where General John Hunt Morgan and his Confederate cavalry once rummaged.

On Sunday, January 4, 1953, he went the forty-six miles north to Walton, apparently to visit his mother and step-father. How he arrived there was not reported, but he stopped at Guy St. Clair's service station just east of a Louisville and Nashville railroad crossing that evening.

Floyd went to the rear of the station and sat down on one of the rails. M. C. Gordon, engineer of the splendid *Hummingbird*, saw him sitting there as the southbound passenger train approached. The train struck Floyd, knocked him between the rails, and ran over him. His badly mangled body was removed to a Walton funeral home. Coroner Robert Brugh identified the victim from a hunting license found in his pocket. Mr. Brugh gave a verdict of accidental death. [13]

***

Dick Bush got used to receiving letters, requests, and invitations. *Daily Mail* Columnist Walter Winchell mailed a letter to him in early 1953, inviting him to attend the annual "Stars Salute to the Bravest and Finest" in New York City, all travel expenses paid, with the 285 Medal recipients alive at that time. Mr. Winchell was treasurer of the organization that sponsored the event.

March 14–16, 1953. For three days, from every state in the Union, ninety-four MOH holders with their families were guests of New York City. They stayed in donated suites at the Hotel Statler, across the street from Pennsylvania Station and Madison Square Garden, and at the Astor, the Essex House, the Park Sheraton, and the Waldorf Astoria.

The recipients had accepted Mr. Winchell's invitation with purpose. The first national meeting of the newly formed CMOHS was held on Sunday. The recipients told reporters their objectives: comradeship and worthy causes, but no political pressuring. They attended the big Madison Square Garden benefit show to help raise funds for the widows and orphans of New York City firemen and policemen killed in the line of duty. [14] Visits to the Stork Club triggered standing ovations from other patrons.

The days were reminders of USO shows on Pacific Islands, as a cavalcade of entertainers greeted them: like Nat "King" Cole, Jackie Gleason, Les Paul & Mary Ford, Arthur Godfrey and the McGuire Sisters, Milton Berle, Johnnie Ray, Perry Como, Danny Thomas, Rex Harrison, Danny Kaye, Veronica Lake, Rosalind Russell and Gloria De Haven, Sugar Ray Robinson and Joe Louis, Eddie Fisher, and Yul Brynner. Tyrone Power looked for the Medal holders he had trained with at Camp Pendleton and Quantico.

✶✶✶

Before the year ended, more former Raiders would also leave behind widows and orphans. One decided not to leave a widow behind, one was killed in the line of duty, and another died crossing a street.

Murle Burnem Jones, 33, a Company C, 1st Battalion Raider from Oklahoma, had a hard time settling down. He worked as a guard at the Walla Walla Prison, Washington, for a few months in the winter of 1948–1949. Keeping his prison-issued .32 caliber pistol and badge, he moved back to Phoenix, Arizona, from where he had enlisted for WWII. His 26-year-old wife, Barbara, was from there. In 1953, they relocated to Denver, Colorado.

On Monday, September 21, 1953, they drove to the east edge of the city and parked their car on a back road. Whether they went for a walk or Barbara exited the auto, they apparently got into an argument. When authorities arrived, it looked as if Murle had dragged Barbara back to the car, leaving tracks in the dirt road. Both were dead, found slumped in the car. Murle had the .32 automatic in his hand.

The deaths went on record as a murder-suicide. [15] Murle Jones was interred at Fort Logan National Cemetery in Denver. Although Barbara was entitled to be buried with him, she was laid to rest in Wheat Ridge, Jefferson County, twelve miles apart from her husband.

Flora Bradley of Black, Alabama, suffered a respiratory attack on Saturday night, October 3, 1953. Her brother, Rueben Hughes of Geneva, Alabama, rushed her to a hospital. He stopped two Highway Patrolman and asked for an escort into Dothan.

Patrolman Julian Fred Draughon, 29, former 1st Raider from Dothan, and Patrolman E. H. Jones activated their sirens to speed the woman to the hospital. Eddie Hallford of Dothan, driving his truck, claimed to not hear the motorcycle officers' sirens. Patrolman Draughon's motorcycle collided with the pickup truck at a Dothan Rt. 1 intersection. He was catapulted over the truck and landed in the street. His motorcycle skidded into Patrolman Jones' and injured him. Fred Draughon was the third highway patrolman in eighteen months to be killed in traffic accidents while on duty. [16]

His friends in Company D, 3d Marine Raiders, had much fun with his *Loving* surname. Knowing his hometown was Corrigan, Polk County, Texas, a tiny town surrounded by extensive national forests northeast of Houston, most did not know that Charlie Thomas Loving was his name on record. Both his parents had died in 1934 and were buried in Corrigan's Damascus Cemetery, where many of the Loving extended family members lay in peace. After his WWII service, he had returned to Corrigan. His friends did not know much about his life for the next eight years, until a single sentence appeared in Texas newspapers.

Tom Loving, 43, was a pedestrian in Houston late on Friday night, November 6, 1953. An auto struck and killed him as he crossed a street. Police Officer Fred McGee was on the scene to investigate. [17]

The Marine Raider Association was searching and sending out postcard inquiries in 1954. At least five Raiders that year missed their greetings.

Warren S. Dowson, 32, a 2d Raider corpsman from Columbus Junction, Iowa, was an experienced Navy diver. Having been in the Navy for fourteen years, he was participating in "free ascent" training at the Pearl Harbor submarine base on Tuesday, April 20, 1954. After having been subjected to high pressures in a dive, air bubbles entered his blood circulation. The Navy said that he died as the result of a diving accident—a victim of air embolism. He left behind his widow and four children. [18]

Mrs. Rosa B. Evans never really got used to telegrams about her son arriving at 477 Lena Street in Cumberland, Maryland. Commandant of the Marine Corps Samuel C. Shepherd Jr. wired the last one on Monday, May 15, 1954. "Please accept my heartfelt sympathy in your bereavement."

Master Sergeant William Seymour "Bull" Evans, 33, had been a Cresaptown hero since WWII. He had left home at 17 to enlist and joined the legendary Carlson's 2nd Battalion Raiders. He fought on Midway and was temporarily attached to the Company C, 1st Raiders, on Tulagi, where he witnessed his older hometown friend, PFC Woodrow Wilson Barr, killed on August 7, 1942.

On Guadalcanal, he was hit by shrapnel during the Asamana Ambush on November 11. He recovered, returned to the Raiders, and fought on Bougainville. There, he was awarded the Bronze Star for heroism in the Battle of Piva Forks when he was separated from his patrol and trapped behind enemy lines for ten hours. He earned the nickname "Bull" for going on rampages in the jungles and killing great numbers of enemy. Enemy gun fire hit his right thigh on Guam on July 22, 1944.

Sergeant Evans was with the occupation forces in Japan after the war and met his wife, Chiyoka. They had two children. He remained in the Marines, was attached to the 3rd Battalion, 1st Marine Regiment, 1st Marine Division, and fought along the Korean front during the Second Korean Winter Campaign and the Summer-Fall Campaign of 1952. He was twice wounded. Shrapnel and machine gun fire in the stomach, chest and arm caused the second, more serious injury. His stomach wound required sixty-six stitches.

The Tuesday, May 18, 1954, *Cumberland Evening Times* (Page 1, Section 2) reported that he had planned to be at the U.S. Naval Base Hospital in Yokosuka, Japan, for more treatments. Bill had died suddenly of a massive heart attack on Sunday, May 16.

Ralph Lewis Kauffman, 31, had decided in his late 20s to get a business administration degree and had completed two years at Humboldt State College in California. He was a member of the Accounting Club. His wife and a son were proud of him. He thought he'd get some R & R on Saturday afternoon, June 19, 1954. He and Robert Mecham left Indianola and drove up Route 101 to do some fishing on the Smith River near the Jedediah State Park in the very northwest border of California. At 2:00 PM, their outboard motor developed trouble. Ralph tried to fix it, and the motor fell into the river. He reached into the water, trying to retrieve the motor. He fell in and drowned. [19]

When Ralph Rue Whalin from Atoka, Oklahoma, was five years old, his 45-day-old baby brother died. His mother, Daisy, died in 1942. Ralph married Miss Dale Harris, also from Atoka, and they began their family during the war years, before Ralph left for the Pacific. He earned a Purple Heart before returning home. Ralph moved the family up to La Suer, Minnesota, where he wanted to raise his one son and two daughters. The city lies along the Minnesota River between Mankato and Minneapolis.

On Thursday, June 23, 1954, Ralph, 29, and Joie, his nine-year-old son, took a drive on Route 60, near Heron Lake, and were in an automobile accident. Ralph clung to his life for more than a month in a Heron Lake hospital, but died on Tuesday, July 27, 1954. When his father died, Joie was still in the hospital and not yet out of mortal danger. Ralph's remains were returned to Oklahoma for services and burial in Atoka Cemetery with his mother and brother. [20]

William Lee "Billie" Hankins was born in Coffeyville, Kansas. After the war, he lived in California, worked for the Post Office Department, married, and had a daughter. Just back from a job in Saudi Arabia, he was killed in a traffic accident in Sunset Beach on Sunday, August 1, 1954. [21]

✳✳✳

November 10, 1954. Marines everywhere celebrated the 179th Birthday of the Marine Corps with special flair and turned their attention to Arlington. The day before the national Armistice Day holiday became Veterans Day, special guest President Dwight D. Eisenhower led a procession to the northern border of the national cemetery to witness Commandant of the Marine Corps General Lemuel C. Shepherd Jr. dedicate the Iwo Jima Memorial. A crowd of over 10,000 people was assembled for the first glimpse of the massive, 100-ton bronze statue memorializing the historic flag raising on Iwo Jima's Mount Suribachi.

Those attending the ceremony included members of "The President's Own" United States Marine Band; Vice President Richard M. Nixon; the three surviving flag raisers and the mothers of the three men who had died on the island after the large flag was unfurled; James R. Michels from Chicago and Charles W. Lindberg, two Marines in the patrol that raised the first small flag over the island; sculptor Felix de Weldon; photographer Joe Rosenthal; Marine MOH recipients; military personnel and dignitaries; and veterans and friends of the Corps. [22]

In the years after his brother's funeral, a brother-in-law, a sister-in-law, and two nieces joined Dick's extended family. He was home in Kentucky for a wedding in 1955. Alene Bush married Willie Dee Ritter, of Glasgow, a Korean War Veteran who had served with the U.S. Army's 1st Armored Division. [23] The couple moved to Marion, Indiana, where Willie Dee worked for RCA for thirty years of service. Kimberly Gaye Ritter was their daughter. The Ritters eventually returned to Glasgow.

June 26, 1955. "Story of Kentucky Marine Hero To Be Related" was a Sunday morning headline in Louisville, and the Bluegrass Region took notice of *The Courier-Journal* Radio and TV Section 5. Dick shared print space with Patti Page, Jack Benny, Arthur Godfrey, Dave Garroway, Sid Caesar, Bing and Bob Crosby's kids, and Ronald Reagan introducing television receivers and appliances. As readers readied themselves for church, they planned their afternoons. WKLO recognized that Marines held a special place in the city's heart and had started airing *Marines In Review* weekly news in the early 1950's, featuring stories of local Leathernecks. This Sunday was sunny and warm without any rain, perfect for families to have radios tuned in as they sat and played in back yards. "The story of Glasgow's Marine CPL Richard Earl Bush, who won the Medal of Honor for heroic action on Okinawa, will be dramatized today at 1:05 PM on WKLO . . ."

July 9. On Saturday, Dick received a letter from the Commandant informing him that the Marine Corps had established a policy to forward two Medal of Honor Rosettes to accompany the yearly Aviation Transportation Card. The rosettes were enclosed with Dick's card and letter.

$$*\ *\ *$$

Galen A. Brehm, 32, who had loved the Marines, started an appliance business in the small village of Fayette, forty-three miles west of Toledo, Ohio. He was killed in an automobile accident on August 10, 1955. Galen left behind a widow and five little boys.

On Saturday night, August 13, 1955, Merritt "Red Mike" Edson, aged 58, beloved and admired Marine Raider leader and MOH recipient for his actions on the ridge above Henderson Field on Guadalcanal, pulled his car into the family garage, closed the door, and let the engine run. His wife discovered him dead the next morning. He was buried in Arlington National Cemetery, Section 2, Site 4960-2. The USS *Edson*, DD-946, was launched on January 4, 1958. [24]

Cleatus Leroy and Myrtle (nee McNutt) Stanfill lived with their four young children in Campbell, California, in the San Francisco Bay Area. They could look from their corner house and see the San Tomas Aquinas Creek and Smith Creek join 150 feet from their front door. Cleatus, a 2d Marine Raider and Tennessee boy, worked hard as a machinist's assistant. Early on Monday morning, November 15, 1955, he took North 101 through Sunnyvale and Palo Alto and clocked in at the Schick Products plant on 591 Quarry Road in Belmont. He had just started working at the plant as a forge press trainee.

That morning, he assisted John Schultz to remove dies from a hydraulic forge press. They used a piece of scrap metal to give the press he was helping operate more leverage. Under strain of terrific pressure, the fragment flew out of the press and struck him in the left chest, piercing the lower edge of his heart. He lay beside the press bleeding profusely from the wound.

Belmont Police Sergeant George Dipaola was first at the scene, followed by an ambulance a few minutes later. Cleatus, aged 34, was pronounced dead on arrival at Community Hospital. [25]

John J. Callahan, was a PFC in 2d Squad, 3d Platoon, C/1, who Dick Bush knew well. His squad mates did not know much about him and lost all track of his whereabouts after the war. He was killed in an automobile accident in Hialeah, Florida, on July 13, 1956.

Master Sergeant William J. McDonald, 32, 1st Raider from Danville, Pennsylvania, was attached to a helicopter transport squadron in Yokohama, Japan. The fourteen-year Marine veteran was killed in a car accident when his car overturned on Monday night, October 1, 1956. His body was flown to Danville, arriving on Friday with his widow, two young sons, 6 and 1, and daughter, 4, on board. He was buried in Saint Joseph Cemetery.

After their service and before the State of Alaska entered the Union in 1959, many Raiders found the wild territories of Alaska preferable to the louder and "civilized" lower Forty-Eight. Former Able Company, 1st Raiders, John (Zigmund) Tadzik from Dupont, Pennsylvania, went north in 1952, to Fairbanks, into the traditional lands of the Tanana Tribe. He married Gail McMullen and became step-father to Ricky Lee. The family lived in the Golden Heart Trailer Court at 1916 S. Cushman Street. They attended Immaculate Conception Catholic Church. Gail worked at Tok Lodge, a three-and-a-half-hour drive to the southeast of town.

As Christmas 1956 neared, John was unemployed. He was last seen alive Thursday afternoon, December 13, when the temperatures varied between -38 °F and -45 °F, and the visibility was about two miles with some fog during the day. Gail was working out of town. At some point, John fell in front of the trailer and crawled inside, collapsing on the floor. The trailer door was left open. Thinking the family was out of town, Frank Sexton, a friend, went to check on the trailer on Saturday morning. He found John lying face down on the floor.

The police investigation and the U.S. Commissioner's Court inquest determined that John Tadzik, 34, had frozen to death. [26]

✷✷✷

August 24–26, 1956. A precedent was being established. Forty-four Raiders met at the Congressional Hotel in Washington, D.C., and put on nametags for the start of a "bang-up time" and the "most memorable" reunion in the Raider Association's short history. Friday evening started at the 8th & I Marine Barracks where they watched the very impressive Sunset Parade. Then, the Raiders returned to the hotel for a reception and cocktail party in the Presidential Room to renew "old acquaintances," introduce their wives, and to share in "a little smoke-stacking"—that is, story telling. The Raiders still had their love of life, good food, good drink, and good company.

On Saturday, buses carried them down to Quantico Marine Corps Base for a tour of the installations, a stop at the NCO Club (the Slop Shute), and an astounding demonstration of "modern-day warfare" on the Potomac River: including a new type of landing craft, helicopters, and jeeps with 75mm howitzers. That night, the annual dinner included music by seven members of the President's Own USMC Marine Band, entertainment, and dancing.

Sunday was dedicated to farewells. The Raiders visited Arlington National Cemetery to lay wreaths on the graves of their former commanders. They visited the Tomb of the Unknown Soldier and stopped at the Iwo Jima Memorial for services and *Taps*. [27]

The Association planned to hold its 1957 convention/reunion, a much bigger affair, in Chicago. The planning committee readied to welcome 500 Raiders and wives.

"Because of the Medal, I always try to set a good example for the community." [28]

In civilian life, Dick held true to the CMOHS's principles: heroes make sacrifices and service over self. Invitations to speak to or be honored by different veterans or community groups came frequently. "Naturally I can't attend them all," he would acknowledge, "but I answer every one personally."

January 21, 1957. The inaugural committee sent invitations for President Eisenhower's second inauguration, and 120 Medal recipients accepted. Dick was one of the five from Illinois to return to the Capital. The skies were overcast and occasional spatters of rain fell as he rode in the long parade down Pennsylvania Avenue. He watched solemnly while Chief Justice Warren administered the oaths to Vice President Nixon and the president. The Medal recipients participated in the various inaugural activities, including the President's Ball. [29]

August 9–11. City Fathers called the weekend the *Marine Raider Days*. The Raiders met in the lobby of the Shoreland Hotel on 55th and South Shore Drive. An invitation letter to Raider wives had helped bolster registrations. [30]

"Dear Mrs. Raider, I married a Raider too. It was really quite romantic when he was introduced by friends 'Romulus was a Raider, you know.' Oh yes, then there were all those wonderful "sea stories." For eleven years I heard them about one hundred and one times; I can recite them without a miss."

The Association had not yet located Dick, though he was living very close to all the Raider events, so Stella did not receive the invitation to wives. Dick likely was aware of the gala. There was plenty of television and newspaper coverage of the Raiders going to the U.S. Naval Training Station Rifle Range to fire rifles, of their ride on the USS *Silversides* submarine to take the 57th Street Beach, the moonlight cruises on Lake Michigan, the two cocktail parties, the banquet dinner in the Crystal Room, and their attendance at the famed *Tribune* All-Star football game. The 257 Raiders, wives, and guests especially enjoyed the dancing that followed the banquet.

There was much talking over the weekend about the Association's Merit Scholarship—a four-year college scholarship the members had established on January 26, 1957.

Late 1957. Dick put his GI Bill mortgage loan to use and purchased a home in Waukegan's southwest. The 840-square-foot, single-family home at 2200 Marshall Street, built in 1952, was on a 7,842-square-foot lot. It had three bedrooms and one bath on a single floor and a full basement. The family lived a block north of the Greenbelt Forest Preserve and Dugdale Lake. Dick could travel less than three miles down either Lewis Avenue or Green Bay Road to get to work.

Some of the boys from his squad would drop by his house. They did much of their chatting downstairs in the basement where Dick kept a small bar. They would enjoy some gin and martinis together. Photographs of Dick with a variety of presidents and politicians adorned the wall. It made for an impressive background to their reminiscences. The stories would get to what Dick had done on Yae Take. He had been wounded and sedated, barely survived, and long afterwards, his mind was fuzzy about what had happened to him. [31] When they talked about the dead enemy soldiers left on the ridge, Dick had reached his own opinion about heroism.

"I hope I didn't kill any of them, because I believe whenever one human kills another he really kills part of himself." [32]

For a number of decades, Victor A. Sneller, a first-generation Yugoslavian American, lived two houses east of the Bush family. [33] Victor had been the youngest of eight children. Six years older than Dick, he had been an Army sergeant in World War II; left the States for England in late 1943, and was in Europe for a year and a half. [34] He had landed at Normandy and moved through France and into Germany to the Czech border with General Patton's Third Army. After the war, he married his girlfriend, had a daughter, Carol (Foltz), and worked as a mechanic for Johns–Manville and Chevrolet in Waukegan. On occasion, he and Dick shared some war memories.

Victor thought that Dick was always friendly. In private moments, Dick would often confide to his neighbor about the hardships he had faced in the war. Victor had earned his own Purple Heart, but expressed a clear opinion of his neighbor. "He had it much rougher than I did."

December 31. Joining the Los Angeles West Coast Chapter, the Mid-West Raiders Chapter was established with five officers and sixteen members. [35] Its headquarters was at 307 N. Michigan Avenue in Chicago. Primo A. Tanaglia, Company C, was the only 1st Battalion member. Second Raiders' Aldo J. Cason was the contact person. "If you know of any other Raiders . . . drop us a line so that we can give them personal contact."

The chapter held a meeting in the Clayton Hotel's Manhattan Lounge in Waukegan on Sunday, April 13, 1958, at 12:00 PM. Four new members from the Mid-West had joined. Corporal Richard T. "Dick" Vana, from Des Plains, had been a 2d Squad, 3d Platoon, Company B, 1st Battalion, squad leader on Okinawa.

Dick, 19 years old, had enlisted in January 1943, and followed Dick Bush's path by a few months: he and his brother, Jack, enlisted at the same time, he took a train to San Diego Recruit Depot, joined the Raiders, left for overseas in September 1943, and trained as a replacement on New Caledonia while the New Georgia operation was conducted. He was there for Thanksgiving and Christmas. He was at Emirau; evacuated after a medial dislocation of his right ankle jumping into a Higgins boat. He was evacuated from Guam with a serious head wound, then returned to the front lines on Orote Peninsula in mid-July. There, his memory faded in and out for a week, possibly due to a severe concussion from howitzer 155mm shell explosions. The next thing he remembered was that the Marines had captured the enemy barracks near Sumay, but he had no recollection about getting there. Dick Vana was to be an active Raider Association member.

Dick Bush had not yet been identified as a former Raider eligible for membership in the growing national association. Later, the two veterans would become close friends.

The North California Chapter, Galveston South Central Chapter, Memphis, Milwaukee (Brewery), and New Hampshire East Coast chapters would be organized by 1965.

✳✳✳

Questions arise when a young person dies at home and the cause of death is not reported: no mention of illness, natural cause, accident, or murder. This was the case for many former Raiders.

Glenn Harold Garland, 36, is one example. His childhood had been spent on a Montana ranch. After his discharge in 1946, he returned home and resumed his work as a machine operator for the Great Northern Railway. He, his wife, and daughter lived nine miles west of Whitefish, Flathead County. He died at their home on Saturday, August 17, 1957. His obituary and funeral notice made no mention of his having been ill and did not mention the cause of death. [36]

Lyle K. Hubler married Madeline Crandall on August 3, 1939, at Watseka, Illinois. They moved to Paxton, shortly after their marriage. He was a private in the Raiders during the war. He was employed at the Central Soya Plant of Gibson City for eleven years. He and Madeline had three sons and a daughter. Lyle was a proud veteran and was a member of Chicago's Marine Raider Association, the American Legion, and the Veterans of Foreign Wars.

Lyle was five minutes north of home at 11:45 PM, Wednesday, November 6, 1957. He approached a car stopped at the Illinois Central Railroad crossing, a block south of the Loda depot. A freight train approached. The flasher signals at the crossing were operating and the trainmen had blown their whistle. Lyle, 36, wanting to get home, drove his car around the stopped auto. His car apparently stalled on the tracks. He abandoned the vehicle just before the collision, but was unable to get out of the way. He was killed in the train-car crash. [37]

Maybe because it was peacetime on Marine Corps bases and hostile combatants were not involved, no posthumous award recommendation made its way to the president. When he learned the details later, Dick Bush would believe that a Medal had been warranted.

Staff Sergeant Gilbert L. Brown Jr., of 870 Belmont Street, Watertown, Massachusetts, had been with the 1st Raiders and had stayed in the Corps. Serving as an Explosive Ordnance Disposal technician at Camp Lejeune on Wednesday, September 26, 1956, he was in a grenade practice area with fifty Marines. A "dud" grenade tossed from another pit landed yards from the Marines. Staff Sergeant Brown threw himself over the grenade just before it detonated. He survived the blast, in critical condition and unconscious with a compound skull fracture and penetrating head wounds. Eleven occupants in the pit had only minor injuries from the freak explosion.

Unconscious since the accident, promoted, 1st Lieutenant Brown, 36, died in Portsmouth Naval Hospital, Virginia, on Tuesday, November 26, 1957. His wife and two daughters survived him. [38] His daughter, Patricia E. Brown, would be awarded the Navy's first EOD Memorial Scholarship in 1972.

Miles Chester Henley, 34, resided in Walters, Cotton County, Oklahoma, north of the Red River and the Texas border. On March 16, 1958, he took Chester Lee Garrison, 20, for a Sunday evening drive in his new 1957 Chevrolet. Traveling south on SH 5, they reached the 90-degree turn five miles from Walters at 8:00 PM.

Chester Lee, in serious condition, told Trooper Herbert Barber what had happened. The Chevy failed to make the curve, left the roadway, skidded out of control for 360 feet, struck a culvert, and overturned several times. Chester was hospitalized at Walters for treatment of facial and head lacerations. Miles Henley died of internal injuries and facial injuries at 12:45 AM on Monday.

The Wednesday, April 9, 1958, Chillicothe *Constitution Tribune* printed the stark photograph on Page 4, over the caption, PRELUDE TO DEATH. On Saturday afternoon, William John "Bill" Wehner, 36, dangled from his safety belt, stunned, at the top of a power line pole, appearing as if he was in an arched, backward high dive. He had been accidentally shocked repairing tornado-damaged electric lines near his Sainte Genevieve, Missouri, home. He was lowered from the pole and rushed to a hospital where he died three hours later. Bill left behind a widow and two young sons.

✳✳✳

May 28–30, 1958. Dick Bush was in Washington, D.C., with thirty-three Marine Medal recipients for the Memorial Day events. Visiting the Capitol Rotunda, he stood in front of two caskets and payed regard to the Unknown servicemen killed in WWII and Korean War combat. On Friday morning, he was in the White House Rose Garden with Don Truesdell, Jack Lucas, and Rick Sorenson. President Eisenhower and Vice President Nixon said hello. After brunch, he stood among the honored guests at Arlington National Cemetery as the remains of the Unknowns were ceremoniously interred.

August 1–3. The Raiders Association Convention was headquartered in the Washington Hotel, in Indianapolis. Seventy-six Raiders and wives attended. They nicknamed the hotel's hospitality room *The Raider Fox Hole.*

The war had not yet been over for fifteen years, and the former Raiders, still young, getting well into their 30s, wondered about comrades they had not seen since returning home. Many of the combat veterans had this "weird sense" of a foreshortened future, as if they would not live out long lives. It was hard to explain, but at every convention and reunion, Raiders saluted recently deceased brothers with a fare-thee-well.

Dick Bush would be 34 years old in December.

✳✳✳

Harold F. Hoose, 35, died of a fractured skull and crushed chest in a Labor Day racing accident on the Port Royal Speedway in Pennsylvania on September 1, 1958. His auto turned over on a curve during the 104th annual Juniata County Fair.

Herbert R. Schuster, 36, was a Philadelphia machinist. He went down to Hudson, Maryland, on the Delmarva Peninsula, near Cooks Point, to spend the 1958 Thanksgiving weekend with his family. His brother, Rudolph, and sister, Lorraine, also spent the holiday with Mr. and Mrs. Oscar Schuster.

On Sunday, November 30, the police were called to the home. Herb was found shot in the temple, with a rifle next to his body. Rushed to Cambridge Maryland Hospital, he died without regaining consciousness. Dorchester County Deputy Medical Examiner Dr. Elridge Wolfe returned a verdict of suicide for the death. Herbert had taken his own life, but the Schusters had no reason for the act.

In another of life's ironies, Everett I. "Moe" Willhauck had survived WWII battles only to be gunned down by an Oklahoma City teenager in a jealous "feud" over a woman. Everett, 34, and Mrs. Connie Logan, 37, owned an advertising firm together. Detective E. B. "Salty" Meals investigated the Sunday night climax. The tale could have been a stanza right out of the *Cowboy's Lament* ballad. "For I'm shot in the chest, and today I must die."

Delano Fite, an 18-year-old employee, was having a relationship with Mrs. Logan. Everett demanded that it stop. The two men squared off in the office on February 22, 1959. Delano pumped two pistol shots into "Moe," declaring self-defense.

Former 1st Raider Arthur C. Levi, from Saginaw, Michigan, learned of the death. "A tragic end for one of the gutsiest RAIDERS I ever knew." Arthur would have similar thoughts about another of his buddies, Frank L. Walsh, in 1977. [39]

On Saturday, June 6, 1959, William Charles Hoover, 38, of Niles, Michigan, took his family and friends boating on Christiana Lake, near Edwardsburg. The boat overturned, tossing him, his four-year-old son, Jimmy, his wife, and two others into the water. Bill was struggling to save his son, and both went under. A nearby boat picked up the other adults. Delbert Cleghorn, 34, dove into the water and rescued Jimmy. Bill had not resurfaced and had apparently drowned. The Cass County Sheriff's Department recovered his body later. [40]

***

June 22, 1959. Dick had met the deadline for mailing in his Aviation Transportation Card request and received his authorization to ride as a passenger on Armed Service Aircraft. The Decorations and Medals Branch had updated their policy. From this point forward, the card would be good for a two-year period; this one was until June 30, 1961. As a holder of the Medal of Honor, he was also provided two rosettes. A booklet—*The Unknowns of World War II and Korea*—was also enclosed with this delivery.

***

From one holiday to another, vacation times could prove to be more tragedy than recreation for former Raiders.

A family fishing trip ended in a tragic mishap. Harold Joseph Raplee, 34, 3rd Raider Battalion, had found a job at the Ideal Cement Company in Ada, Pontotoc County, Oklahoma, as soon as he was back from the Pacific in 1945. He started working as a driller at the plant's Lawrence Quarry in 1952. He and his wife, Addie, resided with their two daughters at 416 West Seventh in Ada. As his wife knew, and the Raiders who had served with him would recall, he was an expert swimmer.

Harold and his friend, Bill Steele, planned a family fishing trip to coincide with a July 4th vacation in 1959. They could pick up the Mill Creek just twelve miles south of Ada and fish for bream, bluegill, largemouth bass, or smallmouth bass anywhere along its course, until the stream emptied into the Washita River. They wanted to snare the bottom dwellers that liked to feed in deep water channels and settled on a campsite near Ravia.

On Saturday, July 11, Harold and Bill asked two men fishing if it would bother them if a trotline were let out nearby. All right, they said. Addie, Cathy, 12 years old, and Amelia Lynn, 5, were out of sight at the camp near the creek. Several other families were also enjoying outings nearby.

The two Adans began wading in shallow water to set out the heavy fishing line with the attached snoods and baited hooks across the creek. They got near the stepoff, and Harold, wearing overalls and a tee shirt, "kinda stepped back." Suddenly, he stepped into deeper water. He grabbed Bill's foot, trying to stay above water, but went under. Harold began to thrash about, and some women, witnessing his efforts, screamed that the man was drowning.

Richard Don Ray, 31, one of the other fishermen, jumped in and grabbed Harold. It appeared that the former Raider "panicked or something" and grabbed on to Richard. Fearful that he would get pulled under and drown, Richard had to let him go. Harold's body was finally recovered thirty minutes later. The fishermen tried to get a resuscitator unit to the scene, but it was too late.

A man ran up to tell the Raplees and Steeles that a man had drowned in Mill Creek. The fishermen put Harold's body into their car and took him to a funeral home in Tishomingo, east of Ravia. Later, he was transported to an Ada funeral home. [41]

Later stories of fishing trips with Dick Bush would bring Harold to mind.

August 7–9. Seventy-two Raiders and wives registered at Hotel Claridge in Memphis for the Raiders Association Convention. The membership looked ahead to reunions at the Tariff Sheet Hotel in Santa Monica, California on August 11–14, 1960, the Buccaneer Hotel in Galveston, August 10–13, 1961, and August 2–5, 1962, in Chicago. As the Raiders looked around the country for old companions, they continued to discover that they had "just missed" reconnecting with an old buddy.

Lebanon Junction, Kentucky, is a small town south of Louisville on the eastern edge of Fort Knox. William C. and Laverne (Collings) Fiedler lived there. Post-war, the couple soon began having daughters. Susan, born March 2, 1946, and Pamela Jean, born on Sunday, December 21, 1947, were the older two. Penelope Jane "Penny" Fiedler was born on November 25, 1949. The four grandparents all lived in town and helped out. The family attended services at Lebanon Junction Methodist Church.

At age 21-months, Penny was taken to General Hospital where she passed away at 5:00 AM, on Thursday, August 16, 1951. Her funeral was at 3:00 PM on Saturday. William and Laverne stood at the side of the grave as their baby was buried in Lebanon Junction Cemetery. [42] The anniversaries of those days proved difficult for the family.

Eight years later, on Tuesday, August 18, 1959, at noon, Police Chief Delmar Eskridge had an occasion to jail William on a charge of public drunkenness. He told the former Raider to sleep it off on his City Jail cell bunk. Chief Eskridge went to check on him at 6:00 PM and found William dead.

Bullitt County Coroner Walter Keith was required to write an autopsy report, but did not think the final verdict in the death would be complicated. William Fiedler, 37, had one end of a sheet knotted around his throat and the other end knotted around a bar above his cell bunk. His death was ruled a suicide. [43] He was buried beside his baby daughter Penny.

September 1959. Stella Ramsden finally made an application to the Social Security Office for a name change. The name Stella Mae Bush would be associated with her SSN until April 1971.

∗∗∗

Robert Lee "Bob" Wilson, 35, former 1st Marine Raider resided at 846 W. Ventura Street in Altadena, California, directly north of Pasadena. He had married an older woman with two children—Marilyn and William. Bob was employed as an electronic technician at the Jet Propulsion Laboratory. He had trouble managing rage. Many times he had hit Bessie Fay Wilson, 40, with a flashlight. Young Bill, 18, was scared of him, fearing for his life. His step-father had beaten him numerous occasions.

"My husband was not only the kind that had to beat you," Bessie would testify to a jury. "He was the kind that couldn't stop. He had to beat you into unconsciousness."

On Tuesday, September 22, 1959, Bob came home from work "like a mad dog." An argument started at 5:00 PM about Bill being unemployed. It was the sort of family quarrel that claimed more than one victim. Bob struck Bessie Fay in the face and tried to choke her.

Bill left the house and went to his sister's. He told Mrs. Marilyn Campbell, 20, that he was tired of taking beatings. When things seemed to have calmed down, he went back home.

Back on Ventura Street, the Wilsons all went to bed, each in their own rooms. Bessie and Bill were tense. The boy took a loaded .22 caliber rifle to bed with him. Bob got up at about 9:00 PM. Bill heard him approaching and grabbed the rifle when his step-father entered his room "holding that big flashlight like a club." They exchanged a few brief words.

With a rifle pointed at him, Bill's last words posed a threat. "As long as you're still breathing, I'll get you." He lunged at his step-son.

"I pulled the trigger," Bill would testify, sobbing. "I didn't even aim."

Bob slumped to his knees with a bullet in his chest. Bessie Fay heard the shot and ran into her son's room. Deputies were called to the house, found a man dead, and arrested Bill on charges of homicide. After deliberating for five minutes on Thursday, September 24, the coroner's jury cleared William in the gunshot slaying of his step-father, calling the death a justifiable homicide. Bob's funeral services were held on Friday. [44]

The 2d Raiders who had served with him remembered Doctor William Benjamin "Willie" MacCracken III as a man's man and lover of the out-of-doors. He was awarded a Navy Cross in April 1943, for distinguished professional service, "extraordinary courage, and disregard of personal danger while serving as Senior Medical Officer (Attached) of the landing forces against Japanese-held Makin Island," August 17–18, 1942. He also earned a valor medal for outstanding service during the invasion of Aola Bay, Guadalcanal, on November 5, 1942.

Doctor MacCracken began an orthopedics practice in Huntington, West Virginia, on February 1, 1946, and became a successful, prominent surgeon. Early Monday morning, February 29, 1960, "Willie," aged 52, was found dying "of an accidental gunshot wound." Police reported that he had taken his own life. His wife, Myrtle May MacCracken, and his married daughter survived him. [45]

Robert William Roubideaux, 39, of Everett, Washington, was driving on the Bellevue–Renton Highway with his two boys: Billy T, 13 years old, and Raymond, 9 years old. On

Tuesday night, March 22, 1960, three miles north of Renton, a car swerved across the centerline and forced Kenneth Lee Lamott, 30, in his southbound car, onto the road's shoulder. The first car continued on its way and vanished in the night. Kenneth lost control of his auto, crossed over the centerline and smashed head-on into the northbound Roubideaux car.

The collision was like an explosion, tearing the engine of one of the vehicles from its chassis and hurtling it thirty-nine feet. Billy Roubideaux and Kenneth Lamott were killed. Robert was critically injured. Raymond was hurt, but not seriously. Robert clung to life for just over a week. On Friday, April 1, 1960, Okinawa Day, he died from the injuries suffered in the automobile accident. [46] Robert's and Billy's bodies were brought to Montana and buried together in Custer National Cemetery, Section D Site 346. Cecelia Roubideaux, 92, would be buried in Section D Site 347 beside her husband and son in 2010.

Rufus G. Mayo, 46, of Brewton, Escambia County, Alabama, had served with the 2d Raider Battalion. Around town, he was a one-time U.S. Marine hero who had fought his way through the Bougainville jungles. The companion who had been beside him in the Pacific was more famous. Caesar was the famed German shepherd, the first war canine to be wounded in combat. Rufus was Caesar's handler.

Shortly after the Marines landed on Bougainville, the dog saved PFC Mayo's life when a Japanese soldier tried to sneak up on him as he caught some sleep. A sniper wounded Caesar. Private First Class Mayo killed the attacking Japanese and the sniper. The mutual heroism of handler and war dog was national news back in the States.

Rufus' life for the next eighteen years was not much in the newspaper clippings. He moved to Houston in early 1960, working at odd jobs. He and Dick C. Vogle did some heavy drinking together on Tuesday night, May 10. Rufus was unemployed at the time, with no particular place to go. He was sleeping in the back seat of his car when Dick finally went to bed.

On Wednesday morning, the auto was still parked in front of Dick's house. The former Raider was dead. Harris County Pathologist Dr. Joseph A. Jachimczyk determined the cause of death to be acute alcoholism. [47]

✳✳✳

May 20–21, 1960. Marine Corps conventions and political campaigns could slow traffic from the VA Hospital into Chicago at times. Dick and Colonel Justice M. Chambers knew each other from CMOHS activities. "Jumping Joe," former Raider commander and Medal holder, was the second president of the Marine Corps Reserve Officers Association (MCROA). He presided over the MCROA's annual military conference and national convention in Chicago at the Palmer House. The meeting was the largest to date; 350 members made it to the Windy City.

July 17. On Sunday, at 9:00 AM, Mid-West Raiders Chapter members gathered in Fabyan Park, Geneva, west of Chicago, to hold a pre-convention rally and family picnic before heading out to Santa Monica for the August 11–14 convention.

July 25–28. The Marine Raiders tended to support President Eisenhower's administration, so their attention focused on Chicago. The Republican Party held its National Convention in the Windy City at the International Amphitheater.

September 26. On Monday evening, the nation tuned into the first-ever televised debate between major party presidential hopefuls. Vice President Richard M. Nixon and Senator John F. Kennedy discussed U.S. domestic concerns in a Chicago studio.

December 21. The Decorations and Medals Branch compiled a listing of the eight medals former Technical Sergeant Bush was authorized to wear, including a single Purple Heart for his WIA 16Apr45 on Okinawa, a good Conduct Medal with one bronze star for his Second Award, and an Asiatic–Pacific Campaign Medal with three bronze stars for his participation in the Bismarck Archipelago, Marianas, and Okinawa Gunto operations.

At the end of the year, the Raiders Association decided to relocate its headquarters from Los Angeles to 7909 S. Exchange Avenue in Chicago. The Association had yet to locate Dick in Waukegan.

January 28, 1961. Clay Gowran was a war correspondent who had served in combat with the Raiders. On Saturday night, he was at the Hotel Sherman in Chicago to cover the installation of the Raider Association's new National Headquarters and officers. Father Paul J. Redmond had arrived on Thursday night, and Clay quickly discovered that the priest was a good storyteller.

The Chicago readership was introduced to "the great piano theft" on New Hebrides Islands in early summer of 1943 when the 4th Raiders were waiting to spearhead the attack on New Georgia. [48] Clay was installed as an Honorary Raider. Father Redmond planned to reunite with the Raiders at their Galveston National Reunion.

✳✳✳

Raymond Freeman returned to Bryan, Brazos County, Texas, after the war. He and his wife Faye and their two sons resided on Route 3. The family attended the Steep Hollow Baptist Church. Ray worked with R. B. Butler Construction Company and was a member of the Bryan Carpenters Union 1855. He was knocked into a ditch while on the job on Tuesday, June 7, 1960. He was paralyzed after the accident and never really rebounded. Raymond, 43, died at 6:00 AM at his home on Wednesday, February 1, 1961. Newspapers did not report his cause of death.

"He seemed to be having difficulty dealing with life." John Henry Lock, 49, and his wife, Evelyn, were at home at 717 Westchester—a nice little house across the street from Westchester Park. They had been residents there for thirteen years. John was an unemployed truck driver.

On Tuesday afternoon, March 28, he was in the back yard, when Evelyn heard a shot at 4:44 PM and ran out of the house. She found her husband lying on the ground, a pistol lying beside him. John was dead on arrival at a local hospital from a shot in the head. Justice of the Peace W. A. Gilleland ruled the cause of death to be a self-inflicted gunshot wound. [49]

Ronald Frank Silveira, 34, had served with Dog Company, 1st Raider Battalion, and had come home from the war with a Purple Heart. He was residing at 2936 Schyler Street in Oakland's Peralta Hacienda neighborhood, earning his living as a carpenter. Donald A. Kane,

25, a service station assistant manager, and Joseph V. Maes Jr, 22, a station attendant, lived on nearby streets across Peralta Creek.

On Friday, April 21, 1961, Ron and Don got into Joe's car, apparently in a hurry. Witnesses guessed that the sedan was speeding at more than 50 mph on 14th Avenue in front of Highland Hospital when it went out of control and skidded 150 feet sideways, crashing into a power pole at E. 30th Street. The car wrapped itself around the pole, and the three men were ejected and thrown to the pavement. Ronald and Don Kane were pronounced dead at Highland Hospital. Joseph Maes survived the crash, suffering multiple abrasions and contusions. [50]

Robert Buller, 38, and his friend, George Simmons, were both fatally injured on Sunday, May 28, 1961, in a one-car accident south of Livingston, Texas, their hometown, during Memorial Day weekend.

Staff Sergeant Roy John Schwirtz, 40, had enlisted in the U.S. Marine Corps from Minneapolis at age 17. He stayed in the Marines after WWII and saw action in the Korean conflict. On Saturday, August 12, he was driving on Highway 395 in the Sweetwater Mountains of Northern California, not far from the Nevada border. Reaching Devil's Gate Pass, elevation 7,519 feet, between the Marine Corps Mountain Training Center and Bridgeport, he lost control of his vehicle.

Sergeant Schwirtz was killed in the one-car accident. He was buried in Fort Snelling National Cemetery the next Friday.

∗∗∗

August 24, 1961. Dick received good news from the Commandant. The Decorations and Medals Branch wrote to inform him that President Kennedy had signed Public Law 87-138 to go into effect on September 1, increasing the MOH monthly pension from $10 to $100. The age of eligibility was lowered from 65 to 50. He should apply for enrollment six months before his 50th birthday, should he elect to receive it. A copy of the Bill was enclosed for his information and retention. Dick would not have to wait until 1974 to apply for his pension.

Wanted: Current addresses for the following. The Raider Association was growing in membership, but understood that thousands of the Raiders who had come home after the war did not have address labels on the newsletter. *The Patch* periodically published long lists of men for whom they were searching. The Association encouraged its members to wear their Raider lapel pins and t-shirts around town and to put a Raider decal on their cars in hopes of finding other Raiders who might be neighbors.

Members in good standing sent notes to *The Patch* editor of local Raiders they had found. They also sent newspaper clippings.

∗∗∗

On Tuesday before Thanksgiving 1961, Ann Segale, having celebrated her 37th birthday two weeks earlier, reported that the love of her life, Raymond G. Segale, 41, of Seattle, was missing. His two sons and two daughters were at home waiting for him.

Ray was well known. "Hard working Ray Segale" had worn #50 on the 1939–1941 University of Oregon *Ducks* varsity football teams. In his 1940 *Oregana* yearbook on Page

83, he sat third from the right end, 2d row, in the team photo taken at Howe Field. He had coached two high school football teams in Oregon and had helped open Blanchet High School where he also coached.

The wreck of his crumpled car was found Wednesday at the foot of a 500-foot bluff twenty miles south of Bellingham. Ray's body was inside. State Patrolman Henry Dean surmised that the car had gone off Alternate U.S Highway 99 at high speed. Ann spent Thanksgiving caring for the children and planning her husband's funeral. Ray was buried on Saturday November 25. [51]

Charles E. Ashbee, 19, and his friend John R. McGowan, 18, both of 860 South Main in Akron, Ohio, had rallied to the flag in May 1942 and enlisted in the Marines. PFC Ashbee volunteered to join the 1st Raiders and fought in Company D. Following his service, he married and eventually worked for the Allis-Chalmers Company in Kansas City, Missouri. Charles, 40, was killed in an automobile accident on Friday, April 13, 1962, in Kansas City. He left behind his wife, Dolla, his parents, and a brother. He was buried in Greenlawn Cemetery, Romig Road, Akron, on Tuesday.

✳✳✳

April 15, 1962. Marine helicopters first flew into Viet Nam's Mekong Delta from the amphibious assault ship USS *Princeton*, LPH-5, on Palm Sunday. That August, the Marine Medium Helicopter squadrons began rotating in-country every four months. A gradual Marine build-up in Viet Nam followed over several years. These events would have an impact on Dick Bush.

August 2–5. When the Raiders checked into the Edgewater Beach Hotel Playhouse, Chicago was bustling. The city was celebrating Armed Forces Week, and the Internation Fair was happening. The reunion activities included pool parties, a visit to the Arlington Race Track, the evening All-Star game, a Teen-age Coke and Dancing party, the banquet, and memorial services and exhibitions from Armed Forces Day.

✳✳✳

Robert J. "Bob" Guisti, 38, of Elko, Nevada, had the right-of-way in his car at an Elko intersection on Tuesday afternoon, October 23, 1962. John Churchfield, 17, failed to yield the right-of-way, and the two cars collided. Bob was seriously injured and transported to an Elko hospital. He had been wounded twice in the Pacific and had been awarded a Purple Heart with one Gold Star. So, his wife, Mary, and their four children, held on to the hope he would pull through. Bob died Tuesday night. The teenager was cited for causing the two-car collision.

Thanksgiving always gave pause to the Silverthorne family to remember that when Spencer Victor Silverthorne Sr. was 37 years old, he had survived the night of April 14–15, 1912, and was rescued from the RMS *Titanic* sinking. That was good fortune. Thanksgiving would change for Spencer's grandchildren.

Spencer V. Silverthorne Jr., his wife, Holly, and their three sons lived in Beaver Falls, New York. Before joining the 1st Raiders, he had been a star football player at Williams College and earned a degree at Yale Law School, Class of 1942. As a first lieutenant, he was awarded the Silver Star for conspicuous gallantry and intrepidity in action against enemy forces on Okinawa. He was long a respected member of the New York business community after the war.

On Friday, November 23, 1962, after Thanksgiving with his family, Spencer boarded United Air Lines Flight 297, a four-engine Viscount turbo prop plane, with four crewmembers and twelve other passengers, including one infant. He was going to a wedding in North Carolina; the flight was en route from Newark to Atlanta with a stop at Washington. Ten miles west of Baltimore, the aircraft was in trouble.

One witness said the plane was so low he could read the name on its side, then, at 12:30 PM, it suddenly went straight down. The plane crashed into a forest just off Maryland Highway 198, between the towns of Ellicott City and Clarksville in Howard County. Three explosions resounded as the craft hit the ground and disintegrated. Wreckage was strewn over a diameter of 100 yards. The largest piece identifiable was fifteen feet long. All seventeen souls aboard perished. [52]

Yearly, newspaper headlines seemed to tell of Raiders dying in road accidents—sometimes suffering a heart attack and expiring while driving, or having a heart attack during an incident involving a driver. One occurred thirty miles south of Waukegan. Dick Bush, working at the VA, was familiar with the details.

Three days before Christmas, December 22, 1962, Chicago Police Officer Paul A. Batson, 38, patrolled with his partner, heading eastbound on West Armitage Street, not far from his own neighborhood and home. He was a five-year veteran on the force, wearing Star #10018.

A white Chevrolet convertible travelling at a high rate of speed on the wrong side of Armitage forced the officers' vehicle into the curb. The officers gave chase. The driver of the Chevy increased his speed, refusing to pull over. When the chase finally ended, the driver jumped from his convertible and raised his hands. The police officers commanded the man to turn around, but he refused.

Officer Batson used necessary force to subdue the driver and placed him under arrest. During the tussle while in the performance of his duties, Officer Batson, former 1st Battalion Raider, died of a heart attack. His "End of Watch" funeral Mass was held at Santa Maria Addolorata Catholic Church at 528 North Ada Street. He was survived by his wife, Elaine, and his three children, Phyllis Ann, Philip, and Patricia.

The Chicago Police Memorial Foundation continues to conduct services and extend tributes to P. O. Batson.

The Patch editor received newspaper clippings and obituaries throughout 1963. Many of them brought more than "a tear or two." The Raider homages began early in the year.

Norris "Doc" MacDonald, 39, was prospering in Kanab, Kane County, Utah. He married Roma Church in Las Vegas on March 25, 1946, and they had two sons. He was the owner-manager of Kanab Motor Company and had been a Kanab City Councilman. On Thursday night, January 3, 1963, he was killed in an automobile accident near Kanab.

Robert Olen "Bob" Burdett Jr., 41, had lived in California for fifteen years following his four years in the Marines. He had moved back to O'Donnell, Texas, to help care for his ill parents and had been living in Lubbock for six days with an uncle and aunt. Bob had an easy, "sunny disposition," and cigarettes seemed his only "vice." Cleaned up and well dressed in a brown suit and tie, he went out on Wednesday evening, March 13, 1963.

Sergeant Wayne LeCroy discovered his body at 2:00 AM on Thursday. He was found on his stomach in a pool of blood, shot in the back of the head on Quaker Avenue, an unlighted dirt road near 82nd Street, bordered on both sides by plowed fields. His body had new bruises on arms, hands, and right thigh, and a skinned place on the right shin, as though he had been dragged from a car, kicked, and dumped in the ditch. Last seen alone at 9:30 PM in a Tahoka Highway nightclub, he had no billfold or money. Tracks left at the scene appeared to have been left by two assailants. His uncle and girlfriend thought he could have had $50 with him.

The coroner discovered a .38 caliber bullet in the former Raider's brain and determined that he had been shot at close range. His funeral services and burial at Lamesa Memorial Park were conducted on Saturday.

For weeks, the *Lubbock Avalanche–Journal* reported details surrounding the mysterious murder. A city employee found Bob's wallet, empty of cash, before noon on Friday, March 29. Eleven years would pass. The *Avalanche–Journal* reviewed the case on Sunday morning, July 14, 1974: No Killer, No Motive In Slaying.

Some news stories also brought back images to Stella Mae Ramsden Bush—of her childhood in Michigan coal mine towns, the blackened faces of her father and two older brothers, her mother's death in 1935.

Howard Cecil Human, 39, a husband and father from Stearns, Kentucky, had been a member of the Louisville Sigma Alpha Epsilon fraternity and had graduated from the University of Kentucky with an Engineering degree in 1951. He had been a mining company general manager until 1961, then, became general superintendent of a Reel Cove Coal Mine. He was driving to a United Mine Workers of America hearing at Chattanooga and was killed when his car crashed into the rear of a gasoline truck near Jasper, Tennessee, on Friday, March 22, 1963.

William Kenneth Fowler married Gail L. Exline in Taylor County, West Virginia, on August 10, 1942. After serving with Able Company, 1st Raiders, he returned to northern West Virginia, under the Pennsylvania border, and worked in the coal mines. He and Gail had four children.

Bill, 39, along with fifty-one of his fellow miners, was deep inside the Clinchfield Coal Company Compass No. 2 mine at Dola, twelve miles northwest of Clarksburg on the Thursday night shift, April 25, 1963. [53] A coal dust or methane gas-triggered explosion came in two or three puffs at 10:57 PM, sending dust into the shafts and blowing miners off their feet as far as a mile away. Thirty workers escaped the blast unharmed, hauled up a vertical elevator shaft in a cage. Twenty-two men did not get out: all married, seventeen of them the fathers of forty-one children. Within minutes after the news circulated, relatives began gathering at the mine office near the main shaft. Gail huddled anxiously with others, waiting for word of the men sealed deep below.

Rescue crews wearing gas masks went down the mineshaft. There was no evidence of fire. At 9:00 AM, Friday, they found the first bodies of two victims in a main passageway, one-and-a-half miles from the bottom of the mine shaft. Thirty minutes later, they located a third body down the corridor.

Bill was brought to the surface on a mine car with the other two, sheets over their bodies. William Bullough was one of the three victims. His brother, Mike, would be found later. Officials reported they had suffocated.

At noon, rescuers came upon eleven more bodies in rapid succession. Hope that any of the trapped men had survived the grim disaster began to fade. The last of the twenty-two bodies was found late in the day. Only five had been taken to the surface by late Friday night. Officials expected the others to be brought outside by midnight on Saturday.

"Their Light Still Shines." More than forty years after the tragedy, family members and friends organized the building of a monument. The Honor Our Fallen Dola Miners Memorial was dedicated on September 3, 2006, and is located on WV Route 20, west of Lumberport, about one-point-five miles past Gregory's Run Road. The memorial site is in the vicinity of the Ten Mile Baptist Church. William Fowler's name is engraved on the beautiful, black granite memorial with the other twenty-one miners.

Laurence Murdock Christman, 45, was working as a flight specialist for the Manned Spacecraft Center. He accidentally shot himself and died in his Houston home on Sunday, May 5, 1963. [54]

It Came as a Shock

1963. Waukegan renamed 12th Court, an east-west street on the city's south side and a few blocks southeast of Dick's home on Marshall, to Richard E. Bush Court. The street named after him is just above the border of North Chicago and two miles from the Great Lakes Naval Station Hospital where he had recovered from his Okinawa wounds.

"It came as a shock when they told me they were going to name a street after me," Dick admitted, "but, I did, however, feel honored."

The court was developed in 1971, supporting a row of side-by-side condominiums—twenty-five addresses, in the 1600 and 1700 blocks. The street would be well known to the Waukegan and Gurnee police as a rough neighborhood where they made arrests for unlawful possession of controlled substances and robberies.

Having a street named in his honor was a pleasant shock. In June, Dick would be told about a local veteran living ten miles northwest of Waukegan. The tragedy unfolded too close to home. *That* was a nasty shock.

"Then, I pulled the trigger." Felix Bernard Ksioszk, 4th Raider Battalion, had relocated to Chicago after his discharge from the Corps. He married Frances M. Grobarek (Wirtel). Their first boy, John T., was born in 1948; their first daughter, Christine, in 1951. In 1955, the family moved forty miles north to a rural farm home on Route 2, in Antioch.

Felix was employed as a mechanic at the Outboard Marine Corporation (OMC) factory in Waukegan and was involved in making outboard boat motors and boats. Francis worked night shifts at an Antioch factory. Arlene was born to them in 1960; then, the twin boys, Steven and Michael R, joined the family on June 16, 1962.

Felix was a heavy drinker and became abusive when he was "in his cups." As John got into his teen years, the discord between father and eldest son escalated. When the teenager thought of all the things his father did to the family, he also had thoughts of killing him. [55]

Felix, 42, returned from work in Waukegan on Thursday afternoon, July 25, 1963. John, 15 years old, was on his summer break from Antioch Community High School before starting his junior year with the Class of 1965. At 103 pounds, he looked forward to competing again with the *Antiocirs* wrestling team. Father and son went on a fishing trip together. Felix started his drinking. Around midnight, Felix stopped at an Antioch tavern, where he quarreled with another patron. On the way home, John complained his father was driving too fast. Felix struck him and told him he was "stupid and a coward." John had taken enough.

Once home at Bay View Drive, Lagoona Subdivision, Felix went to bed. John went to get the 12-gauge shotgun. At 3:00 AM, the son stood sixteen feet from his sleeping father. As he would recollect to authorities in the morning, he hesitated. "At first I couldn't do it. Then, I remembered everything he did to me. I thought of all the things he did to our family. Then I pulled the trigger."

Christine, who had been at home babysitting, and the three younger children slept through the shooting. John went outside to wait for his mother and fell asleep. Once home, Francis telephoned for help, and her husband was taken to Zion-Bonton Hospital, where he was admitted at 5:09 AM for a single gunshot wound to the head. Felix died on Friday at 6:50 AM.

John, son of a Marine Raider, confessed to Assistant State's Attorney Jack Hoogasian that morning. He was arrested. Held in the Lake County Jail in Waukegan, he waited for the Grand Jury to convene, expecting to be charged with murder. The Lake County Grand Jury returned an indictment for murder before Circuit Judge Thomas J. Moran on Monday, August 5. After funeral services at Strang Funeral Home on Tuesday, Felix was buried in Mount Carmel Cemetery. In December, John was missing from the AHS wrestling squad due to "difficulties other than injuries." [56]

His brother Michael R. Ksioszk later went on to work for the Fox Lake Police Department. John was his best man when he said his vows to Mary L. Bonner at St. Peter Church, Antioch, on June 18, 1983.

The newspaper clippings sent to *The Patch* during the second half of 1963 were more sad than shocking.

William Innis Yount, 54, of Wheatland, California, had earned a Silver Star for his actions along the Numa Numa-Piva trail on Bougainville Island. He and his wife, Bertha Elinor, 44, gave Freeman Scott a lift to his home in Kerby, Oregon, on Thursday night, November 14, 1963. Their truck left a Josephine County road eight miles south of Kerby, plunged over a 600-foot embankment, and rolled 200 yards down the bank.

Freeman was injured in the crash, but managed to walk to Kerby to summon help. All he could remember of the crash was that the truck had careened end-over-end down the slope. Both William and Bertha were killed. [57] They were buried together at Golden Gate National Cemetery, San Bruno, California.

Raymond J. Nowland Jr. and Margaret Burr married during WWII. After his discharge, they resided in his hometown Charlevoix, almost as far up the west coast of Michigan a couple might call home. He was hired by the Federal Bureau of Sports Fisheries and Wildlife on April 1, 1946, and worked his way up to hatchery manager. His older, unmarried sister, Francis, 56, had spent the 1963 Christmas holiday with them. The Nowland's son, Donald, was a third year cadet at West Point Military Academy.

Francis died unexpectedly at the Kent County airport en route to Detroit. On Monday, December 30, Ray and Margaret left home for Grand Rapids and Detroit to settle Francis' estate. Their 18-year-old daughter, Linda, a high school senior, and Ensign Jon Ryan, of the USCG Cutter *Sundew*, rode as passengers in the back seat. Ray obviously had much on his mind.

Late in the day, he drove through a red light at the M-55 and M-37 intersection in Wexford County, west of Cadillac, and collided with a car driven by Eugene B. Olds of Irons. Mrs. Lila Gilbert was a passenger in Eugene's car. Raymond, 44, was dead at the scene. Margaret, 40, was taken to a Cadillac hospital and died several hours later. The four others in the wreck were injured, but survived. [58]

Dick Bush would be aware of another shockwave arriving on VA phone lines and memos that began in September 1965.

✳✳✳

Spring 1964. The first Marine ground unit was detached to Viet Nam to collect signals intelligence. By year's end, thousands of servicemen were returning from their tours in Viet Nam. The majority had not been in combat, having been in support positions in "the rear." On March 6, 1965, the White House confirmed that an advance guard of two Marine battalions was to be deployed to South Viet Nam to provide security for the U.S. airbase at Da Nang.

War casualties would soon be transferred to VA hospitals at home. By 1968, of the 83,000 patients treated daily, 4% had come home from Viet Nam. By 1971, that percentage had increased to 13% when combat units were being rotated out of Southeast Asia. Before that happened, Dick Bush witnessed firsthand what American servicemen dealt with in Viet Nam

✳✳✳

James Luther Childs Jr., 43, and his wife, Mildred, had three sons in their two-room home in Bozeman, Montana. The boys looked up to their dad, a former Raider with an easy laugh. He was a logging contractor, and strong. They had once seen him turn a car tire inside out with his bare hands. But, he had trouble with anger and had beaten the boys and their mother when he was mad about something. Mildred knew it was never about arguments.

"I never answered back," she would say. "He just got mad."

At first reported as an accident, it was not. On Saturday morning, March 21, 1964, Mildred was in the kitchen preparing breakfast coffee and toast. James went into a rage about nothing, threw the plate of toast, and started tossing it into the garbage. Then, Mildred heard the shot, looked up, and saw her youngest boy, 16 years old, standing in the doorway, holding a rifle.

The youth was accused of his father's second-degree murder. His two older brothers testified in his defense at the April trial. After deliberating for three-and-a-half hours, a jury of six men and six women acquitted David Ownes Childs of the charges against him. [59]

On Tuesday, May 5, 1964, Patrolman Ralph Kenneth King, 39, of Taunton, Bristol County, Massachusetts, and John Hickey, 28, drove ten miles south to go fishing in South Watuppa

Pond on the southeast side of Fall River. The water was choppy, and the rowboat capsized. Both men were tossed into the Watuppa. Ralph drowned and John was rescued. [60] The coroner's official determination for cause of death was "Asphyxiation by submersion."

Unmarried, Irvin C. Rogers, 42, had fought with Company B, 1st Raiders. He died in a fire at his Denver, Colorado, home on Wednesday, July 8, 1964. His body was brought to Saltville, Virginia, for funeral arrangements and burial. [61]

Will Ballard Banta, 49, native of Roswell, New Mexico, employee of Service Pipeline, was killed Saturday night, September 19, 1964, in a car accident at Levelland, Texas. His funeral was held in the First Baptist Church of Quitman. His wife, LeOndus (Robinson), 56, survived him. His son, John, 15, would enlist in the USMC, earn three Purple Hearts in Viet Nam, be nominated for a MOH, and come home to Texas a disabled lance corporal. He died at age 48.

Homer Lee Lambdin, 40, had been united in marriage to Miss Alma Henrietta Dykes on January 17, 1946. They had four daughters and resided on North 28th Street in Middlesboro, Bell County, on the southeast corner of Kentucky near the Cumberland Gap. The family attended the First Baptist Church. Homer worked as a strip mine operator. He was building a road at the Carnes Coal Company mine on a hill near Davisburg, northwest of home.

On Saturday, July 17, 1965, at 1:00 PM, he was bulldozing about 150 feet from the top of a 500-foot hill. The tracked vehicle backed over a log, threw him against a tree, and ran over his body, crushing both of his legs. The bulldozer ended up at the bottom of the hill. Homer went into shock. He was transported to Pineville Community Hospital. Before Alma could be notified and rush the twelve miles up the Log Mountain ridges, Homer died of his injuries at 2:25 PM.

✳✳✳

October 30, 1964. Dick received a letter from the Commandant informing him that the president had signed Public Law 88-651, an amendment lowering the age of eligibility for the Medal of Honor Roll from 50 to 40. Should he elect to be placed on the Roll and accept to receive the accompanying pension, he would be enrolled, effective on his 40th birthday, and begin receiving the monthly $100 special pension from the VA Regional Office in Milwaukee. Dick's 40th birthday was two months away. He submitted his letter of election and application (DD Form 1369) on December 1.

December 8. The Commandant informed Dick that he endorsed his application, and he would be placed on the pension Roll, effective on December 23. A Certificate of Eligibility would be issued to him via the VA as soon as available. The paper work took until February 1965.

For WWII veterans, New Year 1965 meant that 20-year anniversaries of the Japanese defeat on Okinawa and the Emperor's surrender were going to be celebrated in VFWs and Legion Posts. Before those dates came, the anniversary of shrapnel piercing Dick's body would be in the headlines.

February 1, 1965. Dick wrote to the Commandant. He had been informed that Mr. Miendel at the Milwaukee VA had deferred his pension claim, awaiting the required certificate.

Headquarters Marine Corps took care of the delay on February 8, notifying the VA Central Office that records substantiated Mr. Bush's claim, that he was on the Medal of Honor Pension Roll, and that the VA should act.

April 28. Newspaper reporter Joel D. Weisman interviewed the Waukegan MOH recipient. [62]

Dick had been awarded a variety of civilian honors in recognition of his community efforts. He was an appointed Waukegan Elementary School Board member. He guessed that he had received more than 500 invitations to speak since he had first met President Truman at the White House. He told the reporter a little bit about the day he earned the Medal, his years of recovering in the hospitals, how he met and married Stella, and about their two teenagers.

Judy Bush, 18, was getting ready to graduate from high school. She had developed a natural inclination to be of service to others and was registered to go on to Waukegan's St. Therese School of Nursing. Richard "Rick" Jr., 15, was finishing up his freshman year at Waukegan High School East, Home of the *Bulldogs*, Class of 1968. With war news a constant on nightly news broadcasts, Rick had already decided he wanted to attend one of the military academies after high school.

Curious, Joel asked Dick about the rewards of earning the prestigious Medal.

"I guess the main benefits I got from the award were my job and the fact that my son will automatically be able to apply to one of the service academies."

Understanding the disabling wounds Dick had suffered, the reporter asked another pertinent question. "Would you go through the war again?"

"I guess I would, because we did get peace for a little while. With my son nearing draft age I often see him in my place. Over the years I've come to realize there'll probably never be a lasting peace, but our way of life must be defended."

August 14. Dick and the United States remembered Victory over Japan Day, the day on which Japanese radio announced that an Imperial Proclamation would soon be made, accepting the terms of unconditional surrender.

September 2. Newspapers proclaimed the 20th anniversary of Japan's formal surrender aboard the USS *Missouri*, anchored in Tokyo Bay, officially ending World War II. President Truman had declared the date as V–J Day.

Two gun shots heightened the significance of the two V–J dates in 1965 for Dick, old Raiders, and the VA.

✳✳✳

Earl had made the headlines in Appleton, Wisconsin, early in his life: *Earl Wilharms Elected President of 4-H Club*. He was 10 years old when the Triangle 4-H club met Wednesday night, June 22, 1932, at Triangle School for election of officers. Mr. and Mrs. Joseph C. Wilharms were visitors at the meeting, proud to see the election of their son to president of the club. After the exercises and games, the next meeting to be held on July 6 at the home of the president was announced. [63]

Holding an office was not unusual in the Wilharms' household. As Earl grew up, Hilda Wilharms for years was chairman of various committees arranging luncheons and parties on behalf of the Appleton Women's Club. She also served a term as president of the Mt. Olive Lutheran Church Ladies Aid Society. It must have seemed so promising for young Earl. He would be in the *Post–Crescent* headlines again, after he had served proudly in the Pacific with Company C, 1st Raider Battalion—CPL Bush's unit.

On Friday, September 1, 1961, Earl published an advertisement in the *Post–Crescent*. "Custom Sheet Metal & Steel Work: Bulk Feed Tanks, Trailers & Wagons, Welding & Repairs. Earl WILHARMS and Sons, 2235 W. Wis. Appleton RE 3-3228." [64] Earl's family and his business were located at the home of his parents. Ten months later, his 12-year-old son was in a newspaper photo.

On Sunday, June 17, 1962, Chief Roland Kuehnl and five Appleton Fire Department members stood beside their Engine, admiring the work Joseph Wilharms had done so far on his racer in preparation for the upcoming July 15 Junior Chamber of Commerce Soap Box Derby. The boy half-sat on the frame of his racer. The Department was sponsoring Joe's entry. He was the son of Mrs. Earl Wilharms, Appleton. [65] Earl cheered at the Derby, but would miss out seeing his children's graduations and weddings.

Verna left him in early August 1965. She was living on the other side of Fox River, at 930 Short Street. Earl, 43, became despondent, living with his parents. On Saturday August 14, he was alone in an upstairs bedroom.

Hilda heard the shot at 4:30 PM. She ran to the bedroom to find her son dead with a wound in the upper left chest. The Outagamie Sheriff authorities responded to the call. According to County Coroner Bernard Kemps, Earl had died instantly of massive hemorrhaging caused by a self-inflicted gunshot. [66] Wichmann Funeral Home handled the arrangements for his burial in Highland Memorial Park. His son and daughter would be in the news again.

After high school, Miss Janette Louis Wilharms worked at Miller Electric Manufacturing Company. In April 1966, she, her mother, and William L. Hokenstad planned a June wedding. [67] Joseph E. Wilharms graduated from Menapha High School in 1967. Like his dad, he joined the service and went to war. He was attached to a Seabee mobile construction battalion and spent nine months' duty in Quảng Tri Province during the 1968 enemy escalations in Viet Nam. Following his return, he spent his leave with his mother, Mrs. Verna Wilharms, on Short Street. He was scheduled to report for further training at Port Hueneme, California on February 21, 1969. [68]

Russell E. Bannon Jr. was 20 years old at the outbreak of WWII. He served as a Pharmacist Mate-2 with the 1st Raiders. He married Dorothy W. Bradtmuller in Rhode Island after the war and had troubles adjusting. He had thoughts of taking his own life, made suicidal threats, was assaultive to others, and went on drinking binges. In 1954, he began seeking help and was treated for mental illness at the Brockton, Massachusetts, and Providence, Rhode Island, VA hospitals.

The psychiatric and medical communities had not formulated a diagnosis for post traumatic combat conditions, but a diagnosis had to go into the records for him to be hospitalized. Various doctors decided that Russell was a schizophrenic, undifferentiated type with no basic pathology, and was suffering from a distortion of external reality beyond a point judged normal. Over eleven years, his VA medical records grew voluminous. He was reputed to elope from hospital grounds, purchase guns, and carry knives.

Dorothy, 44, petitioned the Providence Probate Court on August 4, 1965, for the appointment of a guardian to oversee her husband's care. David A. Mcgaw, MD, doctor in charge of the patient at the Brockton VA, filed an affidavit on August 10, in support of the petition, alleging Russell "to be insane, incompetent, and incapable of taking care of himself and his estate."

Russell was permitted to leave the Brockton Veterans Hospital on Wednesday, September 1, as long as he returned for 9:30 PM bed check. He was logged missing from the hospital that night. The police and Dorothy were notified of his elopement (AWOL) status. His where-abouts all day Thursday could not be verified.

That afternoon, Russell walked into a Providence gun shop and asked James DeBartolo, the proprietor, to see some bullets; then stated he wanted to look at a gun, which James pro-vided him. The clerk was called to the rear of the store. Russell loaded the gun and put it to his temple. At approximately 3:25 PM, James started to return to the counter and saw the veteran fire the single shot into his head.

Russell, 44, was pronounced dead on arrival at Rhode Island Hospital at 3:45 PM. He was buried in Section 1, Saint Ann Cemetery, in Cranston, Providence County.

Dick Bush and the VA administrators would have Russell in mind for the next three years.

Dorothy Bannon was designated Administratrix of her husband's estate. She filed a suit under the Federal Tort Claims Act to recover damages, claiming that the negligent conduct of the VA agents, servants, and employees had resulted in Russell's death. The United States District Court D in Rhode Island weighed all the evidence and found that Dorothy had not made out a case by a preponderance of evidence. On December 3, 1968, the District Court dismissed her complaint. [69]

✳✳✳

March 15, 1966. Two days before Glasgow residents donned festive green carnations to cel-ebrate St. Patrick's Day, Clarence Bush, 68, died. He was buried beside his son, Clarence Morris. Dick's father missed out on an opportunity to repeat his opinions about volunteering.

In Washington, President Lyndon Baines Johnson insisted that the purpose of the veterans' programs was "to serve those who have served us." He asked governmental agencies to do every-thing possible to smooth and speed the transition from military service to civilian life for returning Vietnam servicemen.

Late in 1966, the VA began visiting sick and wounded servicemen at their bedsides in mili-tary hospitals. Then, the president directed the VA to take its services to the battlefield for the first time. The goal was to help the men fighting in Viet Nam before they left their posts to re-turn home to resume normal lives and education much sooner than would be normally expected.

✳✳✳

John A. Trapp, 44, had encountered post-war adjustment problems. He was divorced from his first wife and had remarried. The Cincinnati truck driver was to appear on Thursday, April 14, 1966, in Clermont County Domestic Relations Court over a dispute with his former wife. On Wednesday night, he and his second wife arrived at their apartment.

Genevieve Trapp, 45, knew that the problems with her husband's former wife had made him despondent. John went to the living room closet and pulled out a shotgun without her knowledge. She found him kneeling on the floor with the shotgun pointed at his face. In an act of love and bravery, Genevieve lunged, trying to brush the gun aside. He pulled the trig-ger, and the blast hit them both. Genevieve Trapp went to Good Samaritan Hospital with a wound to her arm. The shotgun blast had taken John's life. [70]

William Walter Hyden Jr. was a Kentucky native, seven days past his 46th birthday. Following his service in the Marines, he had located himself in California, and worked as an operating engineer. He was a member-in-good-standing of San Francisco Operating Engineers Local No. 3. He and his wife, Lois K. Hyden, resided at 3524 Midvale Avenue in Oakland.

On Friday night, September 30, 1966, he was driving west on Ygnacio Valley Road in Contra Costa County, east of Concord. Depending on the traffic, he was twenty minutes from home. Richard M. Bartels, 17, was giving his 16-year-old friend a ride and collided with Mr. Hyden's vehicle. A third car crashed into them. Both William and Richard were killed in the accident. The Highway Patrol would have to investigate the circumstances resulting in the three-car pileup. [71]

On Wednesday night, October 12, 1966, Harold Franklin McWilliams, 42, was driving along IL 42A in Tinley Park, a southwest Chicago suburb. He was a brick mason, a member of the Brick Masons Union in Herrin, and had been a Crete, Illinois, resident for five years. On a curve a half-mile south of 183rd Street, his car went out of control, skidded into oncoming traffic, and smashed head-on into Frank Borman's car.

Harold was killed in the collision. Frank was in fair condition, and his three passengers were in good condition. An ambulance arrived at the scene. Minutes after departing with Harold's body and Mr. Borman, on the way to St. James Hospital in Chicago Heights, the ambulance was involved in a collision with a car. The ambulance driver was slightly injured but not hospitalized. [72]

Dr. Wesley Bailey Van Cott (b. 1905) had his share of adjustment problems after serving with the 1st Raiders as a Navy Medical Officer (Lieutenant Commander). He was the son of a Los Angeles dentist and had married Margaret T. Thornberg in Chicago on December 23, 1929, after receiving his medical degree from Northwestern University. They had three daughters; Marion was born in 1932, Gretchen in 1937, and Nancy in 1939. The couple's tribulations first came to the attention of police on Thursday, June 3, 1948, when his estranged wife called them. [73]

The physician smashed into her apartment house. She eluded him and locked herself in her bedroom. He attempted to batter the door down with an axe, then, went home. On Friday, he allegedly barricaded himself in a bedroom and threatened to kill police if they came on his property. After they overpowered him, Dr. Van Cott was arrested and charged for assault with a deadly weapon with intent to commit murder. Reporters wrote that he was currently awaiting a court hearing on charges of shooting at police.

At liberty on Monday, he filed for divorce through his attorney in Los Angeles Superior Court, accusing Margaret, 39, of cruelty and asking the court to determine whether she was a proper person to have custody of their children. Within thirteen minutes, her attorney filed a petition on her behalf, charging cruelty, asking for custody of the children, and demanding $885 a month alimony.

The divorce was finalized. In December 1955, Wesley married Jean Liddy, 37, a woman from Iowa. They had three children together, Peter, Thomas, and Lisa. In fall 1966, Wesley, 61, was visiting his sister, Helen Van Cott, in Salt Lake City. Two hunting partners found him dead in his cabin near Fish Lake, Utah, at 1:30 AM on Friday, October 21. The family reported he had died of a heart ailment. Funeral services for the beloved husband and father were held in North Hollywood on Tuesday. [74]

✳✳✳

November 26, 1966. Eleven years had passed since Dick had attended a family wedding in Glasgow. His brother, Leroy, was 36 years old when he married Virginia M. White, 27, a young woman from Glasgow. They moved to Indianapolis and had a daughter, Peggy, who would marry a Petro boy after high school. Leroy and Virginia would have two grandchildren.

Chicago Area War Hero Goes to Viet Nam [75]

January 1967. "It takes brave men to do paperwork under combat conditions." That was what former Marine Don Maclean had to say about how times and wars had changed. "It actually has happened that soldiers have crouched in foxholes and chatted with VA reps about the GI Bill even while mortar shells were bursting about them." [76]

Dick, 41, was still a contact representative at Downey VA Hospital in North Chicago. He agreed to be a member of the first two-man team for overseas duty and go to a Viet Nam embarkation port to counsel returning military personnel on their veteran rights and to provide on-the-spot benefits information about the new GI Bill.

In January, Dick flew into Viet Nam with John P. McFadden, a WWII Bronze and Silver Star recipient from Newark, to talk to men in combat—before they were veterans. They landed at Biên Hòa Air Base, then went southeast to the sprawling Long Binh U.S. Army Base twenty-one miles outside of Saigon.

February 4. The Viet Cong attacked the Long Binh Ammunition Depot. After Charlie hit the ammo dump, they receded back into tunnels and jungle. When the noise subsided, at least 15,000 high explosive 155mm artillery projectiles had been destroyed. The following day, Dick and John sent their first report back to the head of the VA.

"Please excuse the report's typing and messy appearance because the ammunition dump next to our office blew up last night and we were blasted out of our bunks and our office at the same time.

"The ammo was blowing from 3 a.m. until noon. One of the blasts at about 9 a.m. blew the knots from the knotholes in the board walls of our shattered office and we had to take cover behind sandbags. While crouched there we gave two G.I.s information about converting their service insurance to civilian group insurance when they get discharged.

"After we finished the explanation the incongruity of the situation hit all of us and we began laughing. After the ammo stopped going off we returned to the office and it looked like a sieve with all the knotholes in the walls. So we looked around and eventually found most of the knots that had been blown out and replaced them."

After that, the team talked to about 500 individual soldiers and Marines and gave discharge presentations to eighteen large formations of servicemen. [77]

March 2. Dick gave his VA director a briefing. The Long Binh ammo depot incident seemed to be of little consequence to the Chicago area war hero. He reported that the response of GIs in Viet Nam to the new program had been most enthusiastic and recommended that VA teams continue deploying to the war zone. [78] By year's end, VA teams had counseled 220,000 fighting men in Viet Nam.

✳✳✳

James Edward Jeffries, 43, had been born in Fort Madison, on the Mississippi River, and returned to Iowa's southeast border after WWII. He worked as a barber for sixteen years, married, had two sons, then, moved in 1965 to operate a barbershop in Keokuk's Hotel Iowa.

He was at home in Hamilton on Tuesday, June 6, 1967. At about 3:30 PM, James sustained a head wound from a .38 caliber pistol. Hancock County Sheriff Jamie Rea believed the gunshot wound was self-inflicted. Where his two teenage boys were at the time of the shooting was not reported.

James was transported to Blessing Hospital in Quincy and clung to life for more than two weeks. He died on Friday afternoon, June 23. Not described as a widower, his marriage must have ended before his death, since a wife was not included as a survivor in his obituary. [79]

The 1968 New Year had passed and Colonel Lincoln N. Holdzkom, 48, looked forward to his retirement in June, after twenty-six years in the USMC: except that his son was a Marine first lieutenant serving in Viet Nam. The Colonel was a passenger on a military transport plane with eighteen other Marines on Wednesday, January 10, 1968. The airplane crashed into a 125-degree slope on Mount Tobin near Battle Mountain, Nevada. All nineteen Marines perished on the snowy mountain crag. [80] The colonel was interred at Arlington National Cemetery.

On Saturday, June 29, 1968, Walter M. Henkleman, 44, and his friend Howard Adcock, 49, both of North Bend, King County, Washington, drove ten miles northeast of Snoqualmie, near where the North Fork and South Fork of the Tuft River meet, and went fishing in Mud Lake. Walt's boat capsized and the two clung to the boat, until the former Raider tried to swim to shore. Walt drowned in the effort. After two hours, unidentified persons heard Howard's cries for help and rescued him at the boat. [81]

✳✳✳

June 30, 1968. Dick was a private man when it came to his personal life. However, some family events filled him with such pride that he took photographs to the VA to show coworkers.

On Sunday, Judy Carol Bush stood with St. Therese School of Nursing Class of 1968 and recited an oath. "I solemnly pledge myself before God and in the presence of this assembly, to live . . . as a nurse." Sandra Lentini, Jan Marshall, Maureen McCarthy, and Mary Jane Muir were among her classmates. Mary Jane was going to work at St. Therese Hospital's emergency room. [82] Judy worked as a registered nurse at the Victory Memorial Hospital in Waukegan and later at the Crown Manor Nursing Home in Zion, north of Waukegan. She married.

Dick would be a loving grandpa to two boys—Robert "Rob" and David Smith.

✳✳✳

At 6:30 AM on Friday, December 27, 1968, Thaddeus J. Czubryt, 45, of 7 Victory Terrace, was headed southbound for work in Pittsfield, Massachusetts, on icy and snow covered Route 8 with five passengers. The newspaper photographs of wrecked cars and three sets of skid marks told a grim story of a grinding crash.

Mrs. Genetta P. Yates, 48, a school teacher, veered out of her northbound lane of traffic in Lanesboro and collided head-on with Thaddeus' car. His car ended up against the guardrail.

A station wagon, unable to stop, smashed into the rear end of the car. It took a wrecker to pull the cars apart. Mrs. Yates and three of Mr. Czubryt's passengers survived, but were in critical condition with multiple fractures and contusions.

Thaddeus was wearing a seat belt and "looked pretty bad" to the first responder. He had a fractured skull, fractured right leg, collapsed chest, and multiple internal injuries. He and two of his passengers were dead on arrival at Pittsfield General and St. Luke's Hospital. [83]

✳✳✳

More Departures

February 21, 1969. Dick had a phone call from his sister, Ella, on Friday, as the Presidents' Day weekend kicked off. Their mother had lived almost three years as a widow. Lois (Wakefield) Bush, 69, had passed on. She was buried beside her husband and son in Glasgow Municipal Cemetery.

Dick continued to provide service at the VA and was a few years away from retirement. Judy was busy at the start of her nursing career, and Rick had graduated from high school the previous June. Then, Dick's marriage was "torn asunder."

In April 1971, the Social Security Office listed his former bride's name as Stella Bush Espinoza. Stella Mae had married Julio C. Espinoza and was step-mother to Maria, Carmen, Julie, and Joe. The Espinozas' home was in Gurnee, bordering the west side of Waukegan. Stella stayed that close to Dick for the rest of her life.

Dick endured.

✳✳✳

Jack W. Johnstone, 45, flew from San Juan Capistrano, California, in his blue and white, single-engine, four-seat Beechcraft *Debonair* with his wife and two passengers, Mr. and Mrs. Donald Plumb. They landed at Trumbull Airport and spent Friday night, June 13, 1969, in Groton, New Jersey. The couples took off on Saturday morning and flew north into fog and bad weather.

James V. Richey packed his wife, nine-year-old son, and two daughters, aged six years and four years, into a cream and red, four-seat Cessna and took off from Linden, New Jersey. Over Long Island Sound about a quarter mile from the Goshen Point, Connecticut, shore and four miles from New London, the two light airplanes collided at 11:00 AM. Jack's *Debonair* plunged into eighteen feet of water. The Cessna went down into fifty feet of water.

At least five persons were killed in the collision. Private boats recovered two bodies near the crash site. The Coast Guard found three bodies later in the afternoon, two of them still in one of the planes. Remnants of the planes, a wing and a seat, washed up onto a Waterford beach. Three of the victims were women.

Dr. Harold H. Irwin, New London medical examiner, checked the bodies of the four Californians and Mrs. Richey at the pier of the Underwater Sound Laboratory. The bodies of James Richey and his three children were not recovered. No survivors were found. [84]

✳✳✳

"With Respect and Honor"

August 1969. Dick Bush was one of thirteen MOH recipients from WWII, Korea, and Vietnam able to attend the Marine Corps League's Midwest Division three-day, annual fall conference in St. Louis, Missouri. The convention's theme and slogan was *With Respect and Honor*, and the League gave recognition to him, Richard K. Sorenson, Hector A. Cafferata Jr., Robert E. Simanek, Justice M. Chambers, Raymond G. Murphy, Mitchell Paige, Richard A. Pittman, Carl L. Sitter, Luther Skaggs, Jr., Albert J. Smith, Kenneth A. Walsh, and Harold E. Wilson.

The recipients presided over a wreath-laying ceremony and the dedication of a permanent plaque inside the Soldiers Memorial to commemorate the occasion. Dick took home a replica of the St. Louis Arch presented to each recipient by the League and the City of St. Louis. [85]

The Medal holders followed the progress of the Vietnam War closely, hoping for a victory, praying for the young men and women serving their country in the little backwoods country. The U.S. and South Vietnamese incursion into Cambodia in April 1970 generated various opinions. Dick had met President Nixon on several occasions and agreed with his policy of seeking to end U.S. military involvement in Viet Nam. If the Marines were not free to bring victory over the North Vietnamese, then bring them home.

As Marine forces continued to withdraw from Viet Nam throughout 1970, the 1st Marine Division conducted clear and search operations, protecting Da Nang, fighting guerrillas, and supporting pacification efforts. The 5th Marines operated around Mỹ Hiệp, An Giang Province, southwest of Da Nang. The 7th Marines conducted operations near Song Thu Bon Valley, Quảng Nam Province. The last month of Marine ground combat was April 1971. Within three months, fewer than 500 U.S. Marines remained in Viet Nam.

★★★

World War II had been over for twenty-five years, but the warriors who had fought and come home, the Old Marines, the Raiders, and their families still suffered.

On Thursday, July 2, 1970, Peter H. Naphen, 45, had some thoughts about freedom as the Independence Day weekend neared. He was recently separated from his wife, and had not long ago lost his New York job. He wrote a note to his three sons. It was late and dark when he left his home at 21 Westmere Road, Rowayton, Connecticut, and went to look out at the Atlantic Ocean, two short blocks away.

Peter's body was found floating a short distance off Rowayton Beach on Friday morning at 10:00 AM. During an autopsy, Dr. Melvin Orlins, medical examiner, disclosed the head wound. Police found the note in the Naphen home in which he told his sons he had tried to be a good father and knew their mother would take good care of them. Cause of Death was recorded as a self-inflicted pistol wound in the head. [86]

Alexander Pelsley, 52, lived in Kenosha, fifteen miles north of Dick Bush's home in Waukegan. He worked at the American Motors Corporation plant. No one witnessed what happened on Wednesday, August 19, 1970. Alex apparently fell from a forklift and suffered a skull fracture. He died at a local hospital several hours after the fatal accident. [87]

Clifford W. DeRyke, 47, lived at 538 E. Hammond St., Otsego, Michigan, under the Kalamazoo River. He was down in Portage on Saturday, May 15, 1971, when his car ran off the street and struck a utility pole. He died at the scene. [88]

Jack W. DeVault and Theodore John "Ted" Senkowski, were inducted into the Marines from Dayton, Ohio, at the same time in 1942. PFC DeVault volunteered for the 2d Raider Battalion. Both men returned home following their service in the war. The day after Christmas 1971, Sunday, Jack, 51, residing at 5 East Riverview Avenue in Dayton, died. He was buried in the Dayton National Cemetery on Thursday. [89] Ted would live a much longer life, passing away at age 89, on January 11, 2011.

Daniel Joseph Yazzie, 48, resided on the Navajo reservation at Shiprock, where the San Juan River flows through the northwest New Mexico corner. Few people off the reservation would have known that he was a Navajo Code Talker, one of the elite Raiders who had used their native language to transmit coded messages and puzzle Japanese troops on Pacific islands. Code Talkers Felix Yazzie, Joe S. Yazzie, and Robert Yazzie had all enlisted from the reservation to join the Raiders in the Pacific.

On Tuesday night, February 1, 1972, Daniel went south to Gallup. After midnight, he laid down under a parked tractor-trailer rig and fell asleep. Before he was awake, the rig departed Gallup and headed northwest on Route 264. Daniel was dragged along more than thirty miles. His mangled and unidentifiable body was found near Window Rock, Arizona. Police could not determine his identity until Friday. [90]

Joe S. Yazzie would not reconnect with the Raider Association until May 1989, when he was found on the reservation at Window Rock. "Thanks for writing to me. I thought I was forgotten completely, but you have made me proud once again." [91]

Robert Frank Lavender, 49, spent most of his life in Bromide, Oklahoma. After the war he worked as a heavy equipment operator there. He was a member of the Baptist Church and had never married. His only family was a brother and a sister who also lived in Bromide. He sustained serious injuries in an automobile accident on Monday, April 17, 1972, in Idabel. He died Wednesday. [92]

Harry Thomas Schade, 51, had been from Pennsylvania. After the war, he resided at 3726 Oak Hill, in the El Sereno neighborhood of Los Angeles, between Elephant Hill and Rose Hill Park. On Thursday, June 15, 1972, he was working on his car brakes in front of his home. The automobile began to roll down a slight incline, and he grabbed the bumper to try to stop it. Harry was dragged to a nearby guardrail and crushed to death. [93]

The Marine Raiders had been trained to do extensive patrolling behind enemy lines. When not patrolling or in battles with the enemy, they enjoyed a good caper. So, reunion conversations about old friends did not always go to accidents, murders, and funerals.

Frank A. Sturgis (born Frank Angelo Fiorini), Dog Company, 1st Raider Battalion, was one who seemed to have had covert operations in his blood. When his photograph began appearing in newspaper and magazine articles, then on television broadcasts, Raiders talked about his having turned out to be a soldier of fortune—an American mercenary with suspected ties to the Mafia organization.

After coming home from the war, Frank had served briefly on the Norfolk, Virginia, police force. He participated in the anti-Castro efforts during the Cuban Revolution of 1958, working as an undercover operative, and in the Bay of Pigs invasion failure in 1961. That might have gone unreported except for his arrest on June 17, 1972, in Washington, D.C.

Frank, aged 49 years, was caught with four others installing electronic listening devices in the National Democratic Party campaign offices at the Watergate office complex and spent fewer than two years in prison. Political historians would write about him as one of the burglars whose capture brought down the Nixon Administration. [94]

Father Paul Redmond was involved with Pasadena Chapter 29, Disabled American Veterans, caring for WWII and Vietnam War amputees at the Fort Ord Army Hospital on Monterey Bay. The Chapter commended his efforts in April 1972. He was "in charge of these men and has given them the care and concern of a close relative. He has been and is most wonderful in his treatment of these men." Four months later, he needed the care of others.

He had attended the Raiders' 30th Anniversary in San Francisco, August 10–13, 1972. After the morning memorial service at the Land's End Bridge, playing of *Taps*, the Marine Firing Squad's three volleys, and ringing of Admiral Callahan's Ship's bell on Sunday, the man-of-the-cloth headed down Hwy 1 for ministry commitments at the Fort Ord Army post hospital.

Before he reached his destination, he was in a bad, head-on freeway accident. The grisly car accident took the lives of three people. Father Redmond, 73, was hospitalized for ten days, then, went into seclusion. Manslaughter charges for the driver who had caused the accident were under investigation. The Raiders Association began raising monies to help him with his personal expenses. [95]

August 18, 1972. Although Dick Bush had not been at the Crane Naval Ammunition Depot for more than twenty years, some former neighbors remembered him and mailed short (UPI) newspaper articles found among longer columns about B-52 bomber strikes near Quảng Tri City and presidential election campaigns. On Friday, the depot's explosive ordinance disposal team conducted an orientation demonstration for sixty new employees at the remote demolition range. The "controlled explosion" shattered safetyglass viewports in a bunker killing two women and slightly injuring two other women. A military spokesman at the depot could not say if the investigation report would be made public. "Explosion Kills Two" was the sort of headline that could trigger a sudden memory of grenade blasts.

Henry L. Denault, 47, had served in WWII and the Korean War. He married Theresa Charbot, and had a son, Arthur. He retired from the military in 1963, with twenty years of honorable service. The family resided in Lisbon, Maine, northwest of Brunswick. He was gainfully employed at the Improved Machinery Company. On Sunday night, October 15, 1972, Henry was on the south end of Minot, where Mechanic Falls Road and Woodman Hill Road intersect just east of the Little Androscoggin River Bridge. The Maine state police found him there. Henry had died in a single-car crash. [96]

Reverend Armand Turgcon celebrated a 10:00 AM funeral Mass on Thursday at Holy Infant Jesus Church. Six nephews served as pallbearers. Donald Marvin, commander of Lisbon's American Legion Post 153, headed a delegation of honorary pallbearers. Henry was buried in St. Aloysius Cemetery with full military honors. The flag draping the casket was presented to his widow.

November 10, 1972. No doubt, Dick Bush had been invited to a formal dinner reception and ball to celebrate the Marine Corps' 197th Birthday. Charles A. Rowand III, 50, former 4th Battalion Raider, lived in a small bungalow at 613 Palencia Place in Lakeland, Florida, and might have planned to celebrate, also.

Early on Friday morning, Charles took his companion, Ruby Stevens, also 50 years old, for a motorcycle ride, perhaps returning to her home in Haines City. Traveling on Interstate 4, near Lake Parker, at 2:10 AM, the cycle went out of control east of U.S. 98. Both riders were thrown from the motorcycle. On the road, Charles was first run over by a car, then, some minutes later by two trucks. When the Florida Highway Patrol arrived, he was dead. Ruby was admitted to the intensive care unit at Lakeland General Hospital with multiple injuries. No charges were filed for the fatal accident.

Edward R. Wojciechowski, aged 48, 1st Raiders, died on the same day in La Mesa, California, before he and his wife, Betty, could attend the Birthday Ball in San Diego. He was buried in the Greenwood Memorial Park. The simple stone with his name has the message "Someday My Love."

The Marine Raiders Association continued to track down former battalion members. Discoveries in 1973 for two Raiders proved to be heartrending for old comrades.

John Cope "Johnie" Fisk, from Sterling City, Texas, had served honorably with the 4th Marine Raiders. War wounds and illnesses made postwar adjustments challenging and kept him crippled. He first married Lela Merle Peel from the southeast border of Arkansas. They resided in Gladewater, in eastern Texas, and had three sons: John William, Noble Kieth, and Robert Neal. The marriage ended a year or so after Robert was born.

Johnie moved up to Altus, Johnson County, North of the Arkansas River, and resided on Route 1, Postal Code 72821. He married 20-year-old Mary Catherine Ellis. Their daughter, Mary Anne "Missy" Fisk, lived only nine months, dying on September 12, 1962. The couple sought solace at Ozark Methodist Church and remained married for fewer than four more years.

On Thursday, April 28, 1966, Mary Catherine, 24 years 9 months 14 days old, was in an auto wreck on the Hwy 64 Bridge over the Slough Creek Tributary, east of Hartman. She was transported to the Clarksville Hospital. Her death was recorded to be due to multiple fractures and injuries. She was buried at Highland Cemetery in Ozark. Johnie married a third time the next year.

On June 19, 1967, he and Mrs. Carolyn Ann (Blankenship) Newman, 30, a former Army private from Ozark, went together to see Evan L. Sparks, the County Clerk at the Johnson County Courthouse. They left with a marriage license commanding any official or clergyman to solemnize the rite and publish the banns of matrimony between them. Johnie became step-father to Carolyn's two sons from a previous marriage: Shannon and Murphy.

Johnie, 48 years old, was at home on Thursday, August 16, 1973. Neighbors reported a fire. Unable to escape, the tragic blaze cost him his life. Carolyn had her husband buried beside Mary Catherine at Highland Cemetery. [97]

Glen D. Page, 52, was an experienced pilot, regularly flying his single-engine Cessna 150 between his Watsonville and Modesto, California, businesses. He owned a lucrative chinchilla ranch four miles north of Watsonville. He took off alone early on Sunday, October 28, 1973, and was witnessed apparently buzzing his ranch property. The light plane smashed into a hillside at 10:00 AM. Glen was killed in the crash.

The Federal Aviation Administration investigated the accident. No evidence of mechanical malfunction was found. An autopsy ruled out a heart attack or similar physical failure. Based on "strong evidence," Santa Cruz County Deputy Coroner Donald Davis concluded that the pilot had committed suicide. Before taking his last flight that weekend, Glen had written a Last Will and Testament in which he indicated a plan to take his own life. [98]

Although Marine Raiders Association members could understand self-inflicted deaths—they had experienced enough of them on Pacific islands—news of them, or of a suspicious death, could be troubling. What if they had stayed in closer contact after the war? Would it have made any difference?

Edwin P. Nyby was the son of Danish immigrants and a Sheridan County, Montana, man through and through. He returned to Northeastern Montana after his discharge from the Marines in the fall of 1945. He married Thelma Dahl on February 7, 1947, in Plentywood. They lived eighteen miles south of the Canadian border and twenty-four miles west of North Dakota, in a region that was mostly prairie with soil best fit for small grain production. Ed worked as a carpenter and contractor. The couple had two sons and four daughters. The children grew up and married and, by summer 1975, only one daughter remained at home with them.

The Sheridan County sheriff was dispatched to the Plentywood home on Tuesday afternoon, June 10. Ed, 52, was dead of a gunshot wound. The incident was under investigation. [99]

✳✳✳

Getting Re-acquainted

In the years that followed his retiring from the Chicago VA in 1973, Dick was generous of his time and supportive of veteran events. He regularly accepted invitations to be a guest at community programs and memorial dedications and participated in CMOHS's annual meetings, the Marine Corps Birthday Balls, and 6th Marine Division Reunions.

Dick also had more time to enjoy horses, fishing, travelling, and meeting up with his Marine buddies. He had stayed in contact with "Skull" Brewington after the war. Dick was finally able to accept Skull's invitation to come up to Alaska for some fishing R & R. [100]

Hugh had been an avid fisherman from the time he was a boy in Muncie. After a Marine friend invited him up to Anchorage and taken him fishing on the Kenai River, Skull returned to California with a vision. He and Peggy moved to Anchorage with their four children in 1959, and started Custom Design Displays Inc. in 1961. Hugh looked forward to taking the "Sheriff" fishing on the Kenai River. After his first visit in the early 1970s, Dick sojourned up to Alaska every couple of years.

The Brewington "kids" were getting into their adult years when Dick started visiting. They would know him as their dad's dearest friend, a war buddy and family friend. Skull was a different person when the "Sheriff" was in Alaska, and the entire family had a great time. The two war veterans spoke little about their combat experiences. The significance of Dick being a MOH recipient would not be apparent to Hugh's children and grandchildren until many years later. He had a knack for giving funny anecdotal renditions to factual events. Dick "was a hoot" with a sense of irrepressible humor that made everyone around him laugh. Hugh's daughter, Jennifer, would never meet anyone like him again in her life.

January 1, 1974. The *Raider Patch* had grown to be twenty-plus-pages long and had a large readership across all the states. The Association's roster had expanded to 1500 Raiders: by name, Raider unit, KIA/WIA dates, and current known addresses. At least 200 lived in the Chicago area. PFC Steven A. Koslowski, 3d Squad in a Company C platoon, 1st Battalion, and William Giboun, B/1, both lived in Waukegan near Dick.

Notices went out: If anyone knows the where abouts of any Raider not on the membership roster, the Association would appreciate the information.

August 15–18. The Raider Reunion was held at the Queen Mary Hotel in Long Beach. At their membership meeting, the veterans recognized that the number of Raiders being added to the Honor Roll every year was significant. The task to go out and contact those who were once Raiders, but perhaps were unaware of the Association's existence, was a predominant concern. The members discussed another topic serious to them. The Raiders had been a select group of WWII Marines and proved to be proud of their service. Their reputation was legendary. At their meeting, they told stories of some men who had attempted to bolster their images in their hometowns after the war by falsely claiming to have been in the Raider battalions. From time to time, one of the "unfortunates" applied for membership in the Raider Association.

Besides looking for "Lost Raiders," the Association began identifying and researching all members in the roster by the units in which they had served. Over the next eight years, investigations of obituaries, newspaper items, photos, phone calls, and letters would indicate that nineteen out of twenty claims, Association members or not, proved to be inauthentic. [101]

"Men who face and survive the trials of war together, form bonds of everlasting brotherhood that others cannot fully comprehend." [102]

November 10, 1975. The Marines held a gigantic 200th Birthday celebration in Los Angeles. General Louis Hugh Wilson Jr. from Brandon, Mississippi, was the guest of honor. He had earned a Medal of Honor for his actions on Guam in July 1944 and had just been assigned to the Commandant of the Marine Corps office on July 1. Solomon Island MOH heroes attended the celebration with him: colonels "Pappy" Boyington, Mitchell Paige, and James Swett. Hollywood celebrity Telly "Kojak" Savalas was MC of the event, and Mayor Tom Bradley attended. Forty-three Raiders and their wives were present, and the festivities provided them "a thrill a minute." [103]

Meeting the Medal holders inspired Lowell V. Bulger, Raider Association Historian and Executive Secretary, to look into the battalion records. Nine MOH recipients had served in Raider units during World War II. Three Medals had been earned before the Raiders were disbanded. Eight of the awards had been earned in WWII; one was earned in Korea. Six of the awards were posthumous. Merritt Edson, Justice M. Chambers, and Richard Bush were the three who had survived WWII. Dick was the youngest of the Raider recipients, and had been a Raider for such a short time, maybe he didn't think it appropriate to be a member. The Raider Association contacted the CMOHS to find the two Raiders still living.

Duke M. Baker, of Nacona, Texas, had married Janie Carter on March 31, 1946, in Tulare, California. In February 1949, they moved to 1507 Cherokee Street in Big Spring, Texas. Brenda and Danna Jo were their first daughters. David Brent Baker was born to them on March 23, 1956. The infant had a heart disorder and underwent surgery on Monday, June 9. The 3.5-month-old baby died on Tuesday night, June 10. Duke and Janie had one more child, Debbie, born in 1958.

On Wednesday, February 29, 1976, as the 20th anniversary of his son's death neared, Duke, 51 years old, died of an accidental electric shock in Lubbock County. Survivors included his widow and three daughters. Services were at Berea Baptist Church, and he was interred near his baby boy at Trinity Memorial Park. [104]

✳✳✳

July 29, 1976. On Thursday, Dick was among friends he had not seen for more than thirty years. He checked in at the spectacular Marines' Memorial Club and Hotel, 609 Sutter Street, in the heart of downtown Union Square in San Francisco. At the entrance lobby to the Memorial Club, he joined a group of rugged, grizzled, greying, and balding men gathered with their wives and girlfriends. They were clear-eyed, proud and erect in bearing, quick of step, and exuberant as they recognized each other. And, glad to have decided to attend the Golden Gate Raider Reunion and the 34th Anniversary Celebration. [105]

Dick and Mitchell Paige, one month from his 58th birthday, greeted each other warmly. Mitch was born in the small town of Charleroi, Pennsylvania, and had served twenty-eight years in the Corps before retiring at a colonel's rank in 1964. He was one of the eight Marines who had earned Medals of Honor on Guadalcanal. [106]

One of the Raiders presented the photograph of Mitch at the May 21, 1943, First Marine Division MOH ceremony at Balcombe, Australia, standing with A. A. Vandegrift, Merritt "Red Mike" Edson, and John Basilone, and asked him to autograph the picture.

Mitch was installed as an Honorary Raider during the reunion.

On Friday, 200 men and wives boarded buses and drove over the causeway for a royal welcome on Treasure Island in the middle of San Francisco Bay. They toured the new Navy–Marine Museum, joked at a garden party, and listened to stories at a reception. The Raiders then returned to the Marine Club at 2:00 PM for more serious drinking, bragging, and lying. The men referred to the long-time married wives as the Raiders' "loyal Shelterhalves" who had restored much faith in the institution of marriage.

Wives had a hard time understanding the devotion the Raiders showed to each other, but tolerated it, seeing the depth of genuine joy the reunions with old buddies brought into their marriages.

Old Company C comrades were happy to see that the Association had reconnected with one of their MOH recipients. [107] Dick and Mitch Paige mixed jovially with the others, "lending true heroics to the moment." Both humble and peaceful, they added their own blend of humor to the idea that other Raiders wanted to take home mementos of rubbing elbows with the "REAL CELEBRITIES OF THE MOMENT." The two recipients sat and stood with admiring veterans for hundreds of photographs. The two heroes graciously signed autographs. Bill "Chief" Dae in his Native eagle feathers headdress stood proudly beside Dick for a photo.

On Saturday afternoon at the Post Exchange, Reverend Neil V. Morley treated the Raiders to a color slide show of Honiara, the Guadalcanal battlefields, SgtMaj Jacob Vouza, and his village.

The Saturday highlight began at 6:30 PM. Over 320 people jammed the Crystal Ballroom on the eleventh floor of the Marine Club for a formal reception and banquet. At the Marine Memorial Club reception, Dick, counted among the dignitaries largely responsible for the great success of the reunion, stood for photographs.

He made a stirring and humorous speech at the banquet, lending reverence to the gathering. Green Beret's Major General Robert C. Kingston was the guest of honor speaker, and his concluding remarks brought a close to the formal banquet. The four banquet "celebrities" at the 1976 reunion stood together for a photograph.

Left to Right: Major General R. C. Kingston, Father Redmond, Colonel Paige, and Richard E. Bush. [108]

On Sunday morning, 8:00 AM, the Raiders and wives were back on buses for a short ride over the Golden Gate Bridge to Marin Island. The buses turned right off Camino Real, and the passengers disembarked at Vista Point. The morning sky was clear, and they gazed at the expanse of the bridge to Fort Winfield Scott and the Presidio across the bay. They did not come to the island to sightsee, but to remember their Dead. Father Redmond gave the eulogy at the Raider Memorial Service.

"The bodies of Marine Raiders who gave their lives for their country are scattered over land and sea in known and unknown graves. . . . They were youthful men—but no man is *too* young to die to protect the things that make life worth living—Life, Liberty, and the Pursuit of Happiness for all our citizens. . . . Brave men die once—Grant to all Marines a brave death and an honored memory."

Eighty-nine names were read—Raiders who had accepted deployment to stand guard on the streets of Heaven's scenes since the veterans had last held a Memorial Service on the deck of the Queen Mary in 1974. After *Taps* was bugled, back on the buses for a half-mile trip and a stop at the peak of the bridge. The Raiders hurled the memorial wreaths into the outgoing tide and watched them swiftly float into the Pacific Ocean.

Sporting his black beret, Joe Rosenthal, Pulitzer-Prize winning photographer of the second flag raising over Iwo Jima, attended the service to take photos. Dick stood a head taller than most in the group in Joe's photos.

The Raiders returned to the Marine's Club Sky Room on the Twelfth-Floor Flight Deck at 10:00 AM for a farewell champagne breakfast and aloha party. In their recap of the reunion weekend, all agreed: "The Raiders still drink hard, swear hard, and play hard."

Dick wrote to Lowell Bulger after the reunion. [109] Medal of Honor RAIDER "Words cannot express how much I enjoyed meeting you and so many other RAIDERS and how much I enjoyed the Reunion. . . . I have attended many reunions but I can truly say that I enjoyed this one the most. . . . It was a great honor for me to have a part in it and I will be looking forward to the next one in San Diego. . . . I think it was a great idea having the Green Beret chief, MAJ GEN ROBERT KINGSTON as Guest of Honor. . . . I liked his speech very much. . . . I am leaving for Alaska for a meeting with my good friend, HUBERT BREWINGTON, 1C. We have plans for another fishing trip. . . . WE HOPE TO GET THE BIG ONES. . . . I KNOW THEY ARE THERE."

Colonel Paige also wrote and said he thought Dick "was terrific."

The January 1977 *Raider Patch* newsletter included several photos of Dick in the hospitality room and at one of the reunion receptions with an unidentified woman.

November 10. Hedley E. LeBlanc was a truck and jeep driver and interpreter at Noumea in 1943. He was also a tunesmith with a dozen and more copyrighted songs to his credits. On January 23, 1974, he had been granted rights to nine of his compositions. EU459001 was titled "Gung Ho: March of the Marine Raiders." [110] Michael Stoner, of TV Music Company of New York, signed and distributed the Raider song. The Raider Association gave Hedley an honorary membership to the Raider ranks.

On Wednesday, Marines around the world commemorated the Corps' 201st Birthday. Hedley sent his best regards to his drinking buddies—Mitch Paige, Dick Bush, Platoon Sergeant Victor J. "Transport" Maghakian (2A), and "Wild Bill" Schwerin (2EF). [111]

December 1976. Before Christmas, Thomas P. Bartlett wrote a *Leatherneck* Magazine article reminding Marines everywhere of their "Giants of the Corps." He focused on the four Medals of Honor presented to Sixth Division Marines for combat heroism in WWII—a private, PFC, corporal, and a major from different battalions and different regiments had performed "above and beyond the call of duty." In alphabetical order, he first wrote about Richard E. Bush's actions on Mount Yae Take. [112]

$$*\,*\,*$$

The Raiders were back in touch with Dick. In addition to the *Patch* newsletter, he began receiving phone calls, letters, and newspaper clippings. He and Skull Brewington sometimes talked about how sad outcomes could be for brave men.

Sitting in wilderness, Brownville is a small Piscataquis County town in the center of Maine, north of Bangor. Surrounded by rivers, brooks, and large lakes, Route 11 provides access in and out of town. The hot, humid summers could remind George V. Martin Sr. of his days on the Pacific Islands. The typical, severe winter cold was always a reminder that he was back home. No matter the season, George loved the out-of-doors. On Thursday, January 6, 1977, he waited for the temps to get above -11°F. He went out on his snowmobile when the gauges crossed over 10°F. He was discovered by his snowmobile, dead of secondary exposure to the cold.

Frank L. Walsh had served in Norwood, Massachusetts, southwest of Boston, for twenty-eight years. He was the safety officer and a decorated, well-liked public servant on a police force of sixty men. He wrote a letter to *The Raider Patch* in late 1976, asked about other Raiders, bought some Raider mementoes, and paid two years of membership dues. [113] He ordered a Raider ring in February 1977. It seemed that he looked forward to proudly wear the ring that meant so much to fellow King Company, 3d Raiders. That changed two months later.

On Monday, April 25, his police cruiser rolled aimlessly down an isolated parking lot's gentle slope, 300 yards from the downtown police station. Frank, 52, was found at 9:30 AM, slumped against the car's headrest, fatally shot twice in the chest with his own .38 caliber, snub-nosed service revolver. State Police determined his death to have been self-inflicted.

Frank Jr. wrote to inform the Raiders of his father's death in the line of duty and of the large Police Honor Guard and more than 2,500 people who paid their respects at his services. [114] Another Raider had gone to his Valhalla.

***

January 20, 1977. Dick started out the New Year planning a trip to Washington, D.C. He attended President Jimmy Carter's inauguration. He wrote to the *Patch* to report that he had seen two Honorary Raiders Colonel Mitchell Paige and Colonel Jimmy Swett at the inaugural events. Colonel Paige also wrote that he had gotten together with Dick. "Needless to say, we don't see eye to eye with the President in his pardon of the DRAFT EVADERS and we let him know it." [115]

There had been a lot of scuttlebutt about Father Redmond's piano, the often-remembered tale among the Raiders of wartime chicanery in the New Hebrides on February 28, 1943. The Great Piano Caper garnered a lot of print space in *The Raider Patch*. Dick added a bawdy comment about the legend, spoken like a true "OLD SALT."

"I know quite a bit about stolen JEEPS but I don't know anything about a STOLEN PIANO . . . I would like to know more . . . I know this much about Pianos 'PIANOS are like WOMEN. . . . When they are NOT UPRIGHT they are GRAND.'" He ended with an acknowledgement. "I look forward to the next RAIDER PATCH." [116]

Dick sent $18.00 to the Raider Gift Store in the spring, and ordered three Raider Zippo lighters.

Corporal Chester D. Fancher, aged 54 years, called Dick early in 1977, and they talked for the first time in thirty years. Chester had stayed in the Corps for twelve years and was discharged after being wounded in Korea. He had four daughters and a son. The two friends talked about Father Redmond. Both planned to attend the 1978 reunion and hoped to see old friends. Chester also wanted to join the Raider Association and start receiving *The Patch* regularly. Bob Ferrante also contacted Dick. All three of the former Raiders were happy to learn that the Padre was still living. [117]

George Holodick, Lewis Longo, and John C. Sweeney all looked forward to seeing Dick again. First Lieutenant Joseph I. Deal, A Company, wrote in. "Great to see the picture of Dick Bush . . . He appears to be in great health."

August 22–27. The 6th Marine Division Association had its reunion in Memphis. Dick checked in at the Rivermont Hotel. James Wilson came up from Odessa, Florida. He had charged onto the Okinawa beaches on April 1, 1945, with Company A, 4th Marines. A BAR man, he and Dick were great friends. Corporal Wilson was on the island's southern end a month after his good friend had been evacuated. In front of him was a small, insignificant-looking hill, some 50 feet high and about 350 yards long. On May 18, he repeatedly fought his way up to the crest of heavily defended Sugar Loaf Hill until the Marines radioed that they had the terrible mound secured. Both Dick and James thought the Memphis get-together was a great success. [118]

September 5. Monday was Labor Day. Like Memorial Day, WWII veterans got together across the nation for hotdogs, burgers, and beer. Pam Spaulding wrote about a reunion among some Raider friends in North Vernon, Indiana. Her impressions could have described any meeting of the Old Raiders.

"There was nothing too good to be said when they talked about each other. . . . and it was good to see these men loving each other. . . . They were the BEST OF MEN in the worst of times . . . NO ONE who wasn't THERE can join this BROTHERHOOD that went through hell." [119]

The newsletter editor printed a note to all the Raider MALE CHAUVINISTS. On the November 1977 *Raider Patch* cover, a photo of the San Diego skyline and Raider Convention Headquarters, was beside another photo of a lovely, bikini-clad, college coed fishing in the San Diego surf: "WHAT RAIDERS FOUGHT FOR IN 1942."

One of Chester Fancher's daughters notified *The Patch*. Dick and Chester were not going to see each other in San Diego. Her father had had a seizure while driving home from work on Wednesday morning, April 20, and had hit the Broadway Bridge in Idaho Falls. He was in intensive care for twelve days. Two months after the car accident, he was transferred to the Portland, Oregon, VA Hospital. On June 1, 1977, Chester died of heart failure on an operating table, due to complications incurred in the accident. Linda (Fancher) Scott's letter was published in the November newsletter. [120]

Dick paid his $55 room reservation and registration fees for the July 1978 reunion. He asked for a room next to William "Chief" and Betty Dae. Also, he had talked to Jim Wilson, who also wanted a Bayside room next to his room.

January 1978. When the *Raider Patch* was mailed out, anyone who did not know about his Medal award was treated to a photograph of President Truman and Dick at the 1945 Medal presentation. The caption was informative, even though erroneous. "In WWII, 28 men were awarded the Medal of Honor for falling on an enemy grenade to shield their buddies. Only two survived the explosion . . . CPL DICK BUSH is one of those!" Dick was one of the six 1976 San Francisco Reunion dignitaries in another photo on Page 3.

"Sorry to hear about the death of Chester Fancher," Dick wrote, recalling their phone conversation and plans to attend the upcoming July reunion in San Diego. Dick finished his note, expressing his appreciation of newsletter articles. "I enjoyed the November RAIDER PATCH . . . THE "EDSON'S RIDGE" BATTLE Brief was very good." [121]

Irvin L. Cross sent the 1942, 884th PLATOON USMC SAN DIEGO photo to *The Patch* editor, pointing out Dick, who had earned the nation's highest award, Clyde Wright Jr, and Wendell P. Ela. [122] The Association duplicated the photo to send to their MOH recipient. Dick wrote back. [123]

"Was I ever surprised, I do not have a copy of this picture and I don't recall ever having seen it before. . . . THAT SURE IS A MEAN LOOKING BUNCH!! There are two other MARINE RAIDERS in the picture, which I remember from the signatures on the back . . . CLYDE WRIGHT JR, 4DQ, Blanding UT, is the 1st Marine on the left in the top row. . . . I last saw him after New Georgia on New Caledonia in 1943. . . . and WENDELL P. ELA, 4DQ, is the last Marine on the right in the 2nd row from the top."

The editor noted that Wendell was killed on Okinawa on May 21, 1945.

★★★

Getting well into their 50s, grandparenting was becoming a favored topic when the Raiders got together. Many admitted that going to reunions and reading *The Patch* was "like being 19 years old again." In more somber moments, they raised glasses to an old comrade who had passed on.

Irving T. Stratton, 56, was an Illinois Bell Telephone Company communications specialist. He and Betty (nee Bechdolt) had three sons, a daughter, and four grandchildren. Irv was a Freemason and a member of Franklin Lodge No. 25 AF in Alton. He was in an auto accident on Route 4, outside Staunton on Saturday afternoon, March 4, 1978. Taken by ambulance to Staunton Community Memorial Hospital, Irv was pronounced dead on arrival at 5:00 PM. Lodgers met at the temple on Monday evening to caravan to Brother Irving's memorial services in Gillespie. [124]

✳✳✳

July 20–23. The 36th Anniversary Raider Convention was held at the Holiday Inn at the Embarcadero in San Diego. Nearly 600 Raiders, wives, and guests attended. Four Star General Lewis W. Walt was the guest of honor. Dick "lightened the festivities with his lively wit and humor" at the Saturday night banquet. The Association members voted to present permanently-emplaced plaques to Marine bases and WWII battle sites to inspire future generations of Marines.

Richard E. Bush Day

November 10–11. Dick returned to his hometown to celebrate the 203rd Marine Corps Birthday on Friday. Kentucky and Glasgow had set aside Saturday as a tribute to their MOH recipient. Dick arrived at the Barren County Courthouse. A crowd walked up from East Public Square and found seats around the tall C.S.A. monument topped by the bronze Confederate standing "at ease" with his rifle.

The veterans of Barren County erected a bronze plaque to honor the county's two MOH men as a reminder of their heroism and self-sacrifice. Dick stepped to the microphones in front of the courthouse door and addressed the large crowd. The plaque was fixed to the brick wall to the right of the entryway.

In Commemoration of Barren County's
Two Congressional Medal of Honor Winners

First Sergeant William Logan Day
Co. E, 5th United States Cavalry

For gallant conduct during campaigns and engagements with Apaches during
1872–73.

Corporal Richard Earl Bush
First Battalion, Fourth Marines, Sixth Marine Division

For conspicuous gallantry and intrepidity during the final assault against the Japanese forces on Mt. Yae Take, Okinawa, April 16, 1945. Corporal Bush continued to lead his squad forward although painfully wounded, refusing to go to the rear until ordered to do so. Although prostrate under medical treatment, he unhesitatingly seized a Japanese hand grenade that had been tossed amongst the wounded and absorbed the explosion with his own body, thus saving his comrades.

Erected by the veterans of Barren County
as a reminder of their heroism and self-sacrifice
"Lest We Forget"

Brigadier General Albert E. Brewster, USMC, Legislative Assistant to the Commandant, officiated at the ceremony. Third Battalion Raider Robert H. Jones Jr. and his wife, Polly, of Memphis, also attended and took photographs. Bob sent some photos to *The Raider Patch* and included a summary of the events. [125]

"They put a permanent plaque on the courthouse, had a parade, a banquet and other entertainment . . . DICK was at his best and a good time was had by all. . ."

"Did you know our brother on Guam? Do you know what happened to him?" Dick's publicized visits to Glasgow were not all about "good times." He had grown accustomed to citizens approaching him when given a chance to talk about their missing loved one. Thirty-five years had passed since the telegrams had been delivered to Kentucky families. Although the status of the Missing on Guam had been changed to Killed in Action or Presumed Dead, and many graves were marked with stone cenotaphs beside parents in family plots, Richard E. Bush Day rekindled memories.

By that November, Carlisle and Eunice Batts, Mc. Lewis and Mattie Mae Cain, Andrew E. and Laura K. Kearney, James E. and Dora L. Mitchell, George W. and Lennie M. Sloan, and Walter Valentine Osborn and Rose Nell Vanmeter were all dead and buried. Two sisters still survived Argus Cain. Four sisters and two brothers survived "Andy" Kearney Jr. A brother survived Bill Mitchell. A younger sister, two younger brothers, a half-brother, and two half-sisters survived "Duck" Vanmeter. Some among the family survivors hoped one day to talk to Dick about the action on Guam.

✳✳✳

Lawrence H. Tietz, 59, from Montana, had relocated to Carrabelle, on the Florida panhandle, southwest of Tallahassee. The residents were proud of the peaceful little village with its white sand beaches on the Gulf of Mexico, saltwater fishing along the coast, and freshwater fishing on the Crooked River and New River. Larry was most proud of the letter President F. D. Roosevelt had sent him for his bravery on Florida and Guadalcanal Island with Company A, 1st Raiders.

On Saturday night, September 1, 1979, he went to his favorite watering hole. Witnesses did not describe it as an all-out brawl, but Larry got into a bar fight. He died of a heart attack afterward. His wife, Margaret, 53, arranged for his burial at sea.

✳✳✳

November 10–11, 1979. The 2,200 veterans on the Raider mailing roster celebrated the Corps' 204th Birthday. The Chicago Raiders "rolled out the red carpet" for Father Redmond and treated him "like visiting royalty" at their Birthday Ball.

The Raiders talked as much, maybe more, about current events involving young Marines as they did about their own WWII days. On the Sunday before the reunion, militant Islamic students had taken over the U.S. Embassy in Tehran, Iran, and corralled fifty-six hostages inside. It was natural for family and friends to ask former Raiders how the hostage situation should be handled. With undimmed, Gung Ho attitudes, the typical reply went something like: "Send in the Raiders to kick some Iranian ass."

The story broke that six Americans had been secretly flown from Tehran on Sunday, January 27, 1980. [126]

Father Redmond's opinion about the embassy take-over in Tehran was shared by all. "Those two Embassy Marines who helped the six embassy people escape out the back door to the Canadian Embassy and then voluntarily remained as hostages, when they too, could have escaped, should be made NATIONAL HEROES." [127]

Raider John Van Ness, from Fairfield, New Jersey, had been in Company B, 1st Raiders. He had worked in Saudi Arabia in 1978 and had many friends in Iran and Pakistan. He wrote: "America is in trouble there . . . those people are RELIGIOUS FANATICS. . . . it is a tough spot for us and some HARD DECISIONS have to be made . . ." [128]

February 15, 1980. "DEDICATED TO THOSE INTREPID MARINE RAIDERS WHO GAVE THEIR LIVES FOR THEIR COUNTRY DURING WORLD WAR II." Dick saw a photo of Lowell Bulger wearing a Drill Instructor's hat at the MCRD San Diego as he unveiled the bronze RAIDER PLAQUE that was to be dedicated on February 15, 1980. Dick sent his compliments to *The Patch* editor and remembered his boot camp experience. [129]

"You look good standing there holding our RAIDER PLAQUE under that CAMPAIGN HAT. I will be thinking of you on 15 Feb 80 during the UNVEILING CEREMONY . . . I remember how mean my D.I. was to me when I was there in BOOT CAMP in 1942 . . . They made me wear those BIG SHOES . . . See you in San Francisco in July . . ."

✳✳✳

Dorwin Fredrick Myers, 56, of Portland, Indiana, was an over-the-road trucker. On Monday, March 3, 1980, he was driving fourteen miles east of McArthur, Ohio. His semi-tractor-trailer went out of control on a sharp curve and overturned in a ditch at 1:55 PM. He was dead at the scene. Dorwin left behind his widow, Maxine (Moser), and two children.

✳✳✳

March 13. There are certain things brave men do not banter about. They understand that humor is not a balm for all aches. Hugh Brewington called Dick. Jon Eric Brewington, 27, one of Hugh and Peggy's three boys, had died. He was to be buried at Anchorage Memorial Park Cemetery.

July 17–20. As the Raiders readied for their 38th Anniversary Marine Raider Convention in San Francisco, Joe "Pappy" Clark sent in his registration for himself and his wife. He and Dick had become great friends on Guadalcanal, calling each other the Mayor and Sheriff of Tassafaronga Creek. Pappy wanted a room at the Marines Club near Dick and Ural Doax

"Red" Dickerson. All of them had been together in Charlie Company. In addition to Dick, only three others from Company C registered to attend the reunion. [130]

For Thursday arrivals, the day was "catch up day" with cable car rides and tours to Chinatown, Fisherman's Wharf, and the new Pier 39. On Friday, the Raiders embarked on the Golden Gate Bridge Ferry at 9:45 AM for a cruise around the bay. Cameras were out to capture sights of The Bridge, Fort Point, the Oakland Bay Bridge, Treasure Island, Alcatraz, San Quentin Prison, Richmond Bay Bridge, and the Naval Wire Depot. The Raiders disembarked at Larkspur Landing on Tiburon Island at 10:40 AM for a four-hour shopping and dining expedition, then boarded the ferry for a one-hour return trip to the city.

Saturday was taken up with a luncheon, viewing of actual Marine Corps WWII combat footage, cocktail hour reception, and a 7:30 PM banquet with seating arranged according to the four Raider battalions. The Raiders and guests adjourned to the 11th Floor Crystal Room at 10:00 PM for entertainment and dancing.

Sunday morning, they went to the Golden Gate National Cemetery in San Bruno for the memorial service at 9:00 AM to honor all their Raider dead. At the time of the gathering, the Association listed over 1,300 deceased Raiders on the Honor Roll. The board members were discovering old Raider deaths almost daily. The ceremony included a firing squad, a bugler sounding *Taps*, laying of a wreath, and Father Redmond's eulogy. Afterwards they attended a farewell champaign brunch.

September 23. Dick went up to Alaska for two weeks in September to visit Hugh and Peggy Brewington. They talked for a while about Jon's death. "Children are not supposed to die before their parents."

Hugh recalled meeting his bride in San Francisco after the war. She was a strong-willed and independent young woman, out of high school and attending the Fashion Design Institute of San Francisco. He was immediately drawn to her cheerful outlook and infectious laugh.

Peggy reminisced about the early war years in Cutler, Indiana, when she and her sisters, Shirley and Pat, sang on the radio as the Lenet Sisters. Her family had moved to San Francisco after the Pearl Harbor attack, where she and Pat became the first female news carriers. She and Hugh married in 1949 and started their family. They moved to Anchorage with their four children in 1959, and started their own business two years later. [131]

Hugh was a highly-respected businessman in the Anchorage community. Dick thought so highly of his friend that he encouraged Hugh to become an honorary member of the CMOHS.

Dick read through 1942 *Chevron* issues that Hugh had collected while he was at MCRD San Diego. The two talked into the nights about the interesting and historic news articles about the Guadalcanal battles that had been so much in the news while they had been boot camp recruits.

The Brewingtons had a lot of family in Anchorage. Dick enjoyed times with their daughter and son-in-law, Jennifer and Ronald Taylor, their son Ross, and their granddaughters, nephew, nieces, great-niece, and great-nephews. He had a knack for amusing the adults and amazing the grandchildren.

Dick always traveled with a spare glass eye. He would palm the spare eye, pretend to take his right eye out of its socket, and present the spare to the children. Jennifer's daughter Kelly did not discover that the eye she had seen in his palm was not his real eye until some thirty years had passed. [132]

Hugh, Peggy, and Dick were robust individuals. On Tuesday, the trio went to Sterling, on the rugged Kenai Peninsula, south of Anchorage. "Skull" had long raved about the glaciers, snow-topped mountains, bald eagles, Skilak Lake, and spectacular fishing outings on the eighty-mile-long Kenai River. The various Pacific Salmon species begin migrating up river in early July to August, returning to their spawning fisheries. The trophy Chinook (king) Salmon, world-class Sockeye (red), and feisty Coho (silver) Salmon flourished in the river. Rainbow trout and dolly varden were also abundant. Skull preferred to fish the early "first run" of the Pacific arrivals. Dick was on the peninsula at the time of the Silver Salmons' later "second run." The Chugach National Forest was beginning to change into fall colors and the leaves were dropping, along with the temperatures.

The best Silver Salmon fishing was during the morning and evening hours. Skull and Sheriff Dick, dressed in their waders and warm coats, fished with lightweight spinning rods from the banks of the brilliant blue waters of the glacially-fed Kenai. Dick wore his white, western-style cowboy hat. Peggy was along to fish and to handle equipment, rubber nets, and meals. She talked about the possible encounters with brown bears stalking the shoreline.

The day's catch was good; the fish attacking flies and bait with abandon. The Silver Salmon pulled in averaged ten to sixteen pounds. Peggy took a photo of Dick holding up two of his Silvers, and another of the two anglers holding a pole with seven salmon hanging by their jaws. Skull took a photo of Dick and Peggy with eight salmon hanging from a pole. They registered a total 800-pound catch.

"Congressional Medal of Honor Raider is out to change his 'C' Ration diet." Dick sent the three photos to the *Raider Patch* editor, who put them in the left column of a newsletter page. Sharing the page in the right column was a photograph of a 1st Battalion Raider corporal sharing an experimental doughnut with a Raider lieutenant on Guam in August 1944. [133]

Along with the fishing photographs, Dick included a note about several friends and a $50 donation to the Association. "Our Raider Ass'n is just great and I have always been proud of Being a Marine Raider."

He and Hugh had travelled together to Racine, Wisconsin, to see an old Company C friend, whom they had not seen in thirty-five years. [134] Dick had passed by Racine countless times on drives up to Milwaukee, not knowing that Victor J. Rorek resided there. The Association's effort to locate and distribute contact information for "lost" Raiders alerted Dick to the fact that Victor was living fifty minutes north of Waukegan.

Victor, 58, was overwhelmed that the Medal recipient and Skull would visit him. He reminisced about his life. He had been born in Langdon, North Dakota, with three brothers and four sisters. His parents had moved the family to Racine in 1927, when he was five years old, and that is where they had stayed. They were members of St. Stanislaus Catholic Church. Victor's wife, Genevieve, and his extended family knew how proud he was to have served in the Marines, and they joined the party to meet the old Raiders. Dick's summary of the trip to Wisconsin: "Lots of beer and booze consumed and many had a good syndrome." [135]

Dick had also heard from Bill "Chief" Dae and James Wilson about the 1980 Reunion. He concluded his note. "I plan to make the next Raider reunion."

"Some men knew the need for self-sacrifice." [136]

Once Dick was a Raider Association member, attending reunions and receiving back issues of *The Patch*, he learned of the post-war illnesses and injuries his comrades had faced. Reports and discussions had become common: adenoids, alcoholism, Alzheimer's, appendectomies, arthritis, blindness, blood clots, brain tumors, broken bones, cancer, cataracts, diabetes, emphysema, gout, heart attacks, hernias, infections, kidney and liver problems, knee and hip replacements, leukemia, limb amputations, loss of lungs, mental conditions,

multiple sclerosis, nervous breakdowns, neuritis, Paget's Disease, Parkinson's Disease, phle-
bitis, pneumonia, polio, pulmonary fibrosis, spinal surgeries, strokes, ulcers, and wheel-
chair-bound paralysis.

Besides the non-fatal, car accident involving Father Redmond, the 1970's were replete
with serious accidents. One Raider fractured his skull in an ice skating accident, and another
suffered multiple broken leg bones when his pickup truck rolled on an icy Grand Rapids,
Minnesota road. Former Colonel James Brown "was stabbed by some GOON who tried to
rob him" in May 1974. He recovered fully and did fine afterwards, but no one was sure the
same could be said about the goon. Jack Morehead, a constable in Anahuac, Texas, had only
two slugs taken out of him in 1975, which was an improvement over the previous year. John
H. "Stud" Delmage suffered a compound hip fracture, on September 15, 1976, while doing
charity church work in Hawthorne, California. In August 1977, Charles E. "Pappy" Knight,
54, fell at work in Arlington, Virginia, and shattered his left wrist. Bone splinters badly damaged his blood vessels and nerves. After two weeks in the hospital, the doctors thought amputation was less likely.

On May 23, 1978, double amputee Lyle D. Brandt, his wife, and two grandchildren were
seriously injured when a drunk driver crossed the median on a Shelton, Washington, road and
struck their car head-on. Sergeant Raymond L. Rangitsch, 57, tore up his leg in a summer 1978
accident that left him immobilized for months. At work in Vista, California, in October 1978,
Edwin H. Maczko fell twelve feet to the concrete, broke his right wrist bone, shattered his left
wrist, and ended up with casts on both forearms.

In November 1978, Fish and Game Warden Lieutenant Graydon M. "Don" Harn Jr.,
Disabled Veteran's Association and Raider Association member, happened upon a drug store
robbery attempt in Napa, California, when a man half his age held a knife to a 22-year-old
female clerk. Lieutenant Harn drew his revolver, ordered the man to freeze, and reached for
the knife. The surprised man cut him, and Lieutenant Harn hit the man with the butt of his
pistol, subduing him in the scuffle. The incident ended with the assailant handcuffed and
arrested. [137]

In August 1980, Stanley J. Bozyk broke his leg in Chicago. George B. Desmond, Dick's
Company C friend, was helping his youngest son with some home repairs in October 1980. One
of the jacks slipped and broke his right hand. He was laid up for eight weeks.

August 1981. Dick had visited the Brewingtons in Alaska. He mailed several of Skull's 1942
Chevron issues to the Raider Association with interesting and historic items/articles on the
Tulagi and Guadalcanal battles. Lowell Bulger, editor, printed one story in *The Bullsheet* section about a 1st Raider ducking for cover under a house before dawn, only to be joined by
sixteen Japanese riflemen trying to escape Leatherneck machine gunners. [138] That was the
kind of tale certain to bring recollections to other Raiders.

Spring 1982. Dick looked ahead to the July reunion. The Raiders liked San Diego as a
destination. The weather was always welcoming and entertainments were abundant. Many
reminders of their training days—as well as their liberty escapades—were also in close proximity to the Hospitality Room hangout. Dick mailed a note to the Association and enclosed
a check for $30.

"Please send a RAIDER LICENSE PLATE, Zippo Lighter, T-Shirts and a CARLSON
1942 patch to SSgt Robert Bruce Cullen of Ft Myers, FL. . . . He is a great friend of the
MARINE RAIDERS and a collector. . . . In our time he would have been a RAIDER but he

wasn't born yet . . . I will try to make the San Diego RAIDER REUNION and will see you there." [139]

Lowell Bulger reported to *The Patch* readers that Dick's purchases were not unusual. "Richard E. Bush annually orders a stock of Raider Items to give to his friends and attends our reunions regularly where he once again receives his highly prized plaudits of his great fighting buddies . . . the Raiders."

In July, Lowell noted that Richard and Colonel Justice M. Chambers were the only two surviving Raider Medal of Honor recipients—"two living examples of the SUPER-BRAVE men who made up such a large percentage of the MARINE RAIDERS."

July 29. Dick checked in at the Hospitality Room on Thursday at the resort-like Red Lion Hanalei Hotel on Hotel Circle for the four-day, 40th Anniversary Raider Reunion. As always when he attended a reunion, he was met with the applause of his "great fighting buddies."

More than 430 Raiders, wives, and guests attended. They spent the evening socializing in their own Hospitality Room bar. Some had served with Colonel Justice Marion Chambers in the 1st Marine Raider Battalion in the Pacific and were saddened to learn that "Jumping Joe" had suffered a stroke and was at Bethesda Naval Hospital.

"Their guts and courage can never be equaled." The men found old friends, socialized, even wept with joy, at the parties that went on into the wee, small hours of the night—but not as late as they once carried on in merrymaking. The Raiders recognized some changes. Keeping busy had made things easier when they had returned from the Pacific battles. Memories returned in a flash at the reunions, often those terrible moments the men had tried to forget. The thoughts of comrades in action could prove to be spine chilling. Thinking and talking about friends who had passed on often brought a pause to conversation.

"The older I get, the more tearful I get."

On Friday, at 8:00 AM, the Raiders went up to the Camp Pendleton Training Area to observe a live fire and war games. Brigadier General Leonard E. Fribourg (Ret.) was the Master of Ceremonies. The Camp Pendleton Public Affairs Office dispatched reporters and photographers to cover the day. Sergeant Patrick Guide took photos of Dick chatting with Super Marines of the 1st Recon Battalion and adjusting the sight of a 105mm Howitzer. He jotted down Dick's opinion of what he had seen.

"I think these men are ready to meet any crisis with the same professionalism and esprit de corps as we Raiders displayed in the past." [140]

Claud J. Irving, 3d Battalion Raider, was talking to LCPL Robert Andiss when Dick walked up to them. Claud congratulated Dick for earning his Medal of Honor. Dick replied. "Hell, I was just a kid then and didn't know what I was doing." [141]

Then, Sergeant Guide approached and wanted the three to pose. "Let me out of here," Claud stammered, "I'm no hero."

Sergeant Guide answered. "All you Marine Raiders are heroes to us."

To that photograph, the sergeant added the caption: MGYSGT Richard E. Bush (CMH), C/1, chats with LCPL Robert Andiss, 1st Recon Bn, 1st Mar Division, at Camp Pendleton.

After a luncheon at the NCO Club, the Raiders bused to the Tent Camp Area and toured the Edson Range Chapel. They went to Base Headquarters and stood at the plaque that had been unveiled on February 27, 1981. "DEDICATED TO ALL THOSE INTREPED MARINE RAIDERS WHO GAVE THEIR LIVES FOR THEIR COUNTRY DURING WORLD WAR II."

While Dick and Lowell Bulger were visiting, the news reached them that Colonel Chambers, 74, had died at Bethesda Naval Hospital on Thursday. [142] "This news dampened the spirits of all Raiders." The Raiders left Pendleton at 4:15 PM and reminisced during the 75-minute drive back to the hotel. The Hospitality Room opened for them at 6:00 PM. Their evening was free for a night on the town or Bay tours.

Word circulated around the Red Lion that "Jumping Joe" had died. Some recalled the 20th Annual Edson's Raider Reunion at Quantico, February 24, 1968, when General (then Colonel) L. E. Fribourg had served him the first piece of the ceremonial Raider cake. Barbara Chambers sat beside him, admiring her hero. That same year, October 12, he was at Hood College in Frederick, Maryland, for the evening opening of College Day Weekend. He gave a talk titled "Presidents and Congress: How Legislation Is Enacted." Joe said, "We are a nation of laws, and we can't have a democracy unless everyone respects the law of the land." [143]

The Raiders believed it was likely that their former Company D commander would be interred at Arlington National Cemetery. That Colonel Chambers had died, naturally reminded the Raiders of Major General Merritt Austin "Red Mike" Edson, wondering if the graves would be close to each other. [144] General Edson was buried in Section 2 at Arlington National Cemetery.

As of July 29, 1982, Dick was the only surviving Raider MOH recipient.

Saturday was busy. The Raiders took tours to Tijuana and the San Diego Zoo, then, watched a combat film and slides at the hotel. They took a short bus ride to Sea World for a 6:30 PM reception, cocktails, and light show, and were back to the hotel dining room at 7:30 PM for dinner and dancing to the Marine Base Band. Father Redmond concluded his Invocation.

"Bless us survivors tonight and every night until we, too, join Colonel Joe Chambers and his comrades in your Happy Kingdom . . . Amen."

The Raiders toasted Colonel Chambers before dinner was served. Dick addressed the attendees and, as always, "had some very interesting remarks."

The Raider's sole surviving Medal of Honor recipient, Dick Bush (4D4HQ), addressed the audience and he always had some very interesting remarks.

Dick did have friends who were not "Jarheads." One Navy sailor counted Dick among his closest friends, and whenever Dick was in the San Diego area, the two would try to get together. Chief Petty Officer John William Finn had been the principle NCO supporting the guns and weaponry on the fleet of amphibian PBYs stationed at the Kaneohe Naval Air Station, Hawaii, on December 7–8, 1941. Wounded in the chest and left foot during the Pearl Harbor surprise attack, he had earned a Medal of Honor for mounting a daring counterattack on Japanese airplanes from an improvised machine-gun position. He and Dick stayed in touch through the CMOHS. "Finn" lived about forty miles east of San Diego, near Jacumba. [145]

The Raiders held their Memorial Service at Fort Rosecrans National Cemetery on Sunday morning. The last event of the weekend was the champagne brunch at the hotel at 11:30 AM.

Announcements included reminders about Annual or Lifetime Association dues and that Reno was the overwhelming choice for the biennial Raider convention in 1984. Also,

Headquarters Marine Corps had declared Wednesday, September 29, 1982, as Marine Raider Day. A Raider plaque like the one they had seen in Camp Pendleton was to be dedicated at Quantico. All the living Raiders and their guests were invited to arrive in Quantico for a 2:00 PM base tour, a 4:00 PM Base Chapel service, and a 6:00 PM Sunset Parade plaque ceremony.

The Raiders chose Reno for their 1984 reunion and immediately encountered some scheduling snags. The summer Games of the XXIII Olympiad in Los Angeles were planned for July–August. The National Championship Air Races were to fly in September 13–16 in Reno. The Raiders decided to meet a few weeks later than usual.

Once back in Waukegan, Dick wrote a short note to Lowell Bulger. "I much appreciate your mailing those RAIDER ITEMS to Staff Sergeant Cullen in Ft. Myers, FL . . . When I told him he was mentioned in our RAIDER PATCH (July 1982, Page 20), he was happy as a Movie Star with a new divorce . . ." [146]

September 1982. *The Raider Patch* dedicated a page to Colonel Justice M. Chambers and another to Dick. [147]

January 1983. The Association had a complete Master Raider Roster File for the men who had served in the battalions, numbering about 8,500. According to the list, more than 2,000 Raiders were still alive. Including men who had "washed out" from training, there would be "no more phony Raiders" telling stories and giving interviews to newspaper reporters. The Association had copies of 106 medal citations of its most famous heroes and had identified more than 400 additional holders of combat valor awards.

September 11. The phone calls from Gardena, California, began on Sunday night. Friend to all Marine Raiders, Lowell Bulger, 62, had been a member of the Association since its inception, served as one of its early Chaplains and historical researchers and as the Executive Secretary in the 1970's, and had been *The Patch* editor on and off since 1959. He had been unable to attend the August 12 Raider Plaque presentation and ceremony at Camp Lejeune with the seventy-five Raider family, friends, and active duty dignitaries who celebrated the dedication. Dick was saddened to get the news that Lowell was dead. Inez Bulger temporarily took over her husband's Association duties and Stormy Sexton temporarily took on the Editor role.

Dick knew as well as anyone the physical and psychological impact of combat. Even after his retiring from the VA, he helped young veterans adjusting following their return from Viet Nam. He was familiar with Milwaukee's VA Medical Center and the Vet Center, north of Waukegan. The Milwaukee veterans had also organized their own very strong Vietnam Veterans Against the War (VVAW) chapter. Regular vets conducted rap groups and therapy groups, providing supportive environments for the war's veterans to get together for counselling and to discuss aspects of the war that troubled them.

Bill Bruckner lived in Milwaukee. After graduating from Messmer High School in 1964, he had joined the Marines and served in Viet Nam as a radio operator. In 1968, he spent a lot of time west of Hội An at the 5th Marines An Hoa Combat Base in Quảng Nam Province, twenty-two miles southwest of Da Nang. The base was shared with the Army of the Republic of Vietnam (ARVN) and bordered the Duc Duc Resettlement Village. The place was a notorious hot bed of enemy incursions. On Sunday, March 28, 1971, seven months after the Marines had departed An Hoa, the North Vietnam Army massacred 107 villagers and left another 135 of them seriously wounded.

Bill ran a veterans group. He had the privilege and pleasure to spend quite a bit of time with Dick. Bill found his life to be enriched knowing the remarkable Medal recipient. Dick graciously attended Bill's group as a guest. His presence, his courageous World War II exploits, and his humility and sense of humor had a lasting impact on the veterans. [148]

"It's amazing what we remember when we get together!"

September 1983. Carlton Stuart "Uppy" Upchurch was an honorary Raider from Savannah, Georgia, and a *Daily Herald* columnist. He had been in Baker Company on Okinawa and was Dick Vana's foxhole mate and great friend. Stuart attended a Chicago weekend mini-reunion of Charlie and Baker Company, 1st Raiders. The smaller reunions were popular and usually well attended, because they were generally less expensive and offered casual intimate companionship. Stuart observed that steel-glinted gaze in the old warriors' eyes and chronicled his views.

"Richard Bush was there. No one will remember Richard out there in the civilian life for too much water has gone over the dam. But we will remember him for the rest of our lives. His right hand still showed evidence of the sacrifice he made for his country and buddies. . . . Smiling and happy as ever, Richard was glad once again to be in the midst of his old buddies. His country awarded Richard Bush the Medal of Honor for his bravery. Thousands of Marines gave their lives in that battle, but Richard OFFERED his. . . . Guys like Dick Vana, Richard Bush, Father Redmond (who was always there when they needed him) cut themselves a trail straight to Heaven, in my opinion." [149]

The Raiders quipped about the two-week migration of millions of land crabs through their camps on Guadalcanal to spawn in the surf, the hot sweltering heat, jungle rot in armpits and crotches and between the toes, and bouts of malaria. Stuart was also privy to quiet, solemn conversations out of the hearing of wives and children that turned to lost companions.

"Remember the day ol' Dunham was killed?" Veterans tended to refer to comrades killed in action as "Old" no matter their age. Corporal Edward Henry Dunham, B/1/4, from 48 Oxford Boulevard, Pleasant Ridge, Michigan, had enrolled at Michigan State College for the 1941–1942 school year with the Class of 1945, but decided instead that he met the entrance standards to matriculate into the Corps' ranks. He was loved and respected by the officers and enlisted men who served with him. Corporal Dunham was a young 22-years on June 23, 1945, on Okinawa. While everyone carried M-1 and carbine rifles, he was content to carry a pistol. He had been wounded in action twice and kept returning to the fight. The third time he was wounded proved to be fatal. [150] How was he remembered?

"He was the toughest, meanest, best, friendliest guy of them all."

"Uppy" and Dick Vana had had many conversations about the Okinawa battles. Two dramatic days, in particular, remained in their minds.

The first day was the Sunday before the final assault on the Mount Yae Take fortress, before CPL Bush cradled a grenade to protect wounded Marines. Corporal Vana witnessed an event that consistently emerged in their conversations. Corporal Frederick Johnson "Fred" Arrowsmith, 21, was a college graduate from Lake Placid, New York. He had some personality conflicts with Private Julian "Roy" Godwin, 21, from Benson, North Carolina, and the two did not get along well in the squad. On April 15, 1945, a Nambu machine gun burst hit Private Godwin right in the head. Corporal Arrowsmith was the first one to get to him. As he dragged the private toward safety, a Nambu riddled him with bullets. When CPL Vana was able to reach them, the two contentious Marines were in each other's arms, covered in each other's blood, both dead.

About the second day, "Uppy" and Dick had several unanswered questions. They had come to believe the date had been around June 1, 1945. Company B and Company C had dug in on a ridge south of the Asato River. In the morning, as they made their way back to their line, the enemy unleashed "a nasty mortar barrage."

Two green, replacement Marines, cousins from Boston, hunkered down in a foxhole. There had not been enough time to get to know them well. The combat veterans knew them only as "Red" and "Eightball" Richey. A mortar shell scored a direct hit on them. Dick and "Uppy" made their way through the barrage to answer Richey's cry for help. "Red" was dead, with multiple wounds and without an arm. [151] Richey was seriously wounded in the leg. The two rescuers pulled him to a cave and started first aid until a Company C corpsman arrived.

After the war, "Uppy" and Dick believed that Richey had probably lost his leg, but had survived. Despite searching, they were never able to locate the Boston Marine they had saved.

September 6–9, 1984. Guests at the MGM Grand Hotel unfamiliar with the Corps' legends and traditions might have asked a question or two in the lobby. "What is that they say to each other?" "What does *Semper Fidelis* mean?" The guests were witnesses to a bond and loyalty few have the good fortune to experience. Almost 550 Raiders, wives, and adult children walked across the luxurious carpets in the hotel lobby. [152]

The Raiders greeted each other, smiling and laughing together. Their lives were playing out, and they remained mostly robust and skinny. There seemed to be no lines on their faces, and their expressions were without discouragement, hatred, or bitterness. They were buddies getting together, faithfully keeping a pledge made more than forty years earlier to look out for each other through the fight.

After the Sunday farewells, Raiders who had attended their first reunion expressed opinions familiar to *The Patch* readers. "I can't remember the last time I had such a good time! I definitely plan on being in D.C. for the 1986 reunion."

James Wilson and Dick kept in touch between reunions, covering the distance from Odessa to Waukegan by phone and mail. Their conversations were not always "sea tales." In spring 1985, forty years after the initial Okinawa assault, James called his good friend. He had a new grandson named after him. James Chance Wilson was born on April 1. Grandpa James was ready for anyone who made note of the baby's birth date.

"No, he wasn't born on April Fool's Day," he would say. "He was born on Okinawa Day." [153]

James kept a note he had received with Dick's signature. The cherished memento from the MOH holder was passed down in the Wilson family to his namesake.

Dick marveled at the fact that he had kept his sight, as impaired as it might be. "I think about it every day," he said, "how lucky I am." [154]

September 6–8, 1985. The weekend after Labor Day, Dick did not have far to go for the C/1/4 mini reunion. Actually, it was a 1st Raiders get-together, organized by Joe Clark, Larry Bangser, and others. Veterans of Company A, B, and C attended. Elmer A. Mapes came up from Iowa and checked into the hospitality room at O'Hara Field's Howard Johnson International Hotel. Brigadier General Fribourg was the guest speaker at the banquet and gave a nice talk about the close camaraderie among the men who served in the Corps. [155]

According to the Association's roster, the count was down to 2,116 surviving Raiders. Dick was one of 1,075 active Raider Association members who either were lifetime members or were paying annual dues. The roster included 1,041 inactive members. The Association began planning the 1986 Reunion for Washington, D.C. and asked those on *The Patch* mailing list for suggestions for speakers. Rudy Rosenquist, 3d Raider Battalion, historian, and Association board member, wrote in.

"I think we should give a spot to Dick Bush, MOH, he's great." [156]

January 1987. At year's start, the Raider Association continued its quest to locate, acknowledge, and add Raiders to the membership rolls. Determined to learn if eighty-two "Lost Raiders" were alive and kicking out there somewhere, the newsletter printed an appeal for the members to help find Raiders in their own locale. [157]

November 8. The Corps' birthday and Veterans Day approached, and the CMOHS gathered in Irvine, California, for its annual meeting. Dick, Waukegan, Illinois, was 14th in the alphabetical order of all the living WWII Medal of Honor Holders listed in the Sunday *Santa Ana Orange County Register*. [158]

September 7–11, 1988. On Wednesday, Dick checked into the New Tower Inn on Cass Street and 78th Street in Omaha, Nebraska, with the more than 300 attending the Raider Reunion. He was among the nineteen 1st Raiders greeting each other in the Hospitality Room. He was happy to introduce his companion, Nelda Moyers, to them. Nelda had celebrated her 54th birthday the week before they travelled to Omaha.

The other three battalions had much larger turnouts, and all were happy to see the MOH recipient again.

On Thursday morning, the Raiders toured the SAC Museum, then, were treated to a luncheon at the SAC Officers Club. That night, Dick went for a two-hour riverboat cruise on the Missouri River and enjoyed a buffet dinner aboard. On Friday, buses took them west to visit Father Flanagan's Boys Town. After freshening up back at the Inn, the Raiders regathered at the Dog Races for dinner and a little betting. Winnings were generously contributed to the Association funds. Shopping at the Old Market, described by waitresses to be the city's #1 attraction, took up the Saturday morning hours. Most of the afternoon was spent at the Hospitality Room swapping "Salty Sea Stories" and raising glasses to those who had passed on to guard the streets on Heaven's scenes.

The Saturday evening banquet and dance were under the stars at the Peony Park Grand Ballroom across the street from the Inn. Commandant General Alfred M. Gray Jr., the reunion's guest speaker, sat at the long head table. Dick and Nelda were at the table with the Raider Association president, three retired generals, and Father Redmond. The meal was to Dick's liking—a delicious charcoal broiled, choice Filet Mignon. Entertainment consisted of a recapping of the afternoon's miniature golf scores and a performance by master hypnotist Kirby McGill.

A photo of "Mr. and Mrs. Richard Bush" at the head table was published in a later Association newsletter. [159]

The Sunday morning memorial was conducted in the Orchard Room. Father Redmond remarked that he had never been afraid when he was with Marines. Talking about the *Invisible Medal*, he paid tribute to the unrecognized and unrewarded heroes who had either been killed or wounded and evacuated and had gone without valor medals. He recalled how he had observed extraordinary bravery over and over again by sweat stained, bone weary, "feather merchants" who believed that their country and family were worth fighting for. After the Padre's comments, the names of 163 Raiders who had been added to the deceased Honor Roll since the 1986 reunion were read.

Brunch at the Inn concluded the weekend. The servers and chefs at the hotel reported to the management and the Association president that "the Raiders were the best behaved and nicest group they ever had the privilege to serve."

September 1, 1989. Stella Mae Espinoza, aged 64, of Gurnee, Illinois, Dick's former wife, passed away on Friday. Julio handled the funeral arrangements. Her Obituary Notice noted that she was survived by her husband; a daughter, Judith Bush Smith of Gurnee; a son,

Richard E. Bush; her four married step-children; two sisters, both living in California, and five grandchildren. Helen Louise Ramsden Walton, 68, was living in Glendale, Los Angeles County, and Vera Cohn was in Santa Barbara. [160]

Friends were welcomed for a visitation on Tuesday at Ringa Funeral Home, 122 S. Milwaukee Avenue, Lake Villa, from 6:00–8:00 PM. On Wednesday, September 6, services were held at the funeral home at 9:30 AM, followed by a 10:00 AM Mass of Christian Burial at Prince of Peace Church in Libertyville. Stella was laid to rest in Ascension Catholic Cemetery; Section 7, Block 33, Lot 14, Grave 3.

October 3–9. The Raiders returned to the San Diego Hanalei Hotel for their Reunion. [161] Dick's companion, Nelda, was along with him. *The Patch* photographer snapped a picture of the casually dressed couple while at brunch.

The Raiders went to Camp Pendleton to share tales with the First Force Recon Company, watched two five-man jump teams freefall 8,000 feet, at 150 mph from an airplane and glide another 4,000 feet to a spot thirty kilometers away from where the guests were sitting. They toured the San Diego Marine Corps Recruit Depot, ate a wonderful buffet lunch at the Officers Club, and went to Tijuana to watch horse races. On their return trip from Mexico, they participated in an unexpected "sobering international experience."

"On the freeway just seconds north of the border a group of seven 'wetback' illegal immigrants barely escaped being hit by the bus as they tried to run across six lanes of the busy freeway on their way to jobs or wherever."

The Saturday dusk-to-sundown banquet was held outdoors under a tent in the parking lot. Dick and Nelda, formally dressed, took their seats at the head table with the generals and other honored guests. The November *Patch* identified Nelda as 1stBn Richard's wife. While the Raiders dined on shrimp salad, filet mignon, and dessert, the Depot Marine Band played marches and old favorites. [162]

> **"Although they are all common men,**
> **once in their lives**
> **they each did an uncommon act."** [163]

Early in 1990, the Illinois Vietnam Veterans Leadership Program sent out invitations to the 217 living MOH recipients to attend the four-day *Salute to America's Heroes* in Chicago in June. Dick sent in his RSVP, acknowledging his intention to attend. Before that tribute, there would be other heroes to whom he would salute and say goodbye.

February 2, 1990. Dick and the Brewingtons, having gotten into their sixties, had for years escaped the Illinois and Alaska winters, meeting in Florida for a month of warmth. Peggy had been planning the trip and rendezvous since after the New Year. [164] She called Dick on Friday asking him to come to Anchorage. His friend and fishing buddy, Hugh, 66, had died at home while packing for the vacation. She asked Dick to be a pallbearer.

Dick traveled to Alaska to attend the visitation held at Evergreen Memorial Chapel, on 8th and E Street. Hugh's funeral was conducted at the Maplewood Chapel of the Church of Jesus Christ of Latter Day Saints with Bishop Richard L. Clarke officiating. Dick, Ronald Taylor, Fred Robinette, Hugh's sons, Geoffrey and Ross, and his nephew, William Jr., carried the coffin from the hearse to the grave site in Anchorage Memorial Park Cemetery. The old Raider was buried two plots from Jon Brewington. The space between father and son was reserved for Peggy. [165]

March 12. Dick went to Indianapolis to stand beside his sister-in-law, Virginia Bush, and his niece, Peggy Petro. His younger brother, Levy Leroy Bush, had died. He was buried in Round Hill Cemetery. In fewer than three months, another death touched Dick's spirit.

June 1. Father Paul Redmond had forty-six years of priestly life after WWII. He distinguished himself each year with good service. The news went out to all the Marine Raiders who could find their way to the east coast. Father Redmond, aged 91, had died. He was buried in Arlington National Cemetery.

The Raider Association made sure their padre was memorialized at the Marine Raider Museum in Richmond, Virginia. The entire fifty-two page, June 1990 issue of *The Patch* was a Thank You tribute to the good Padre. The reunion photograph of Father Redmond, MajGen Kingston, Mitch Page, MOH, and Dick Bush, MOH, was on Page 10. The United States Raider Association pictorial tribute of Father Redmond, for sale at the Raider Museum Gift Shop, would go out of print in January 1993.

June 14. On Thursday, Dick was among the seventy MOH recipients who gathered in Chicago to attend the *Salute to America's Heroes*. Anne Keegan, a *Chicago Tribune* staff journalist, understood that the weekend would be the nation's largest single gathering of the Medal winners that year. She showed up to see what the Medal recipients were like. [166]

She looked across the hotel lobby at a large, congenial, affable group of men who had gathered for a drink and who all knew each other by first names. They were "a collection of Average Joes looking like anyone and everyone's husband, grandpa or neighbor." They had arrived from towns as different as Midland, Texas, Tenafly, New Jersey, and Bremerton, Washington; and, to Anne there was nothing distinctive about their facial expressions, their dress, or the way they carried themselves. Over the weekend the recipients wined, dined, laughed, went fishing, golfed, played cards, and visited with old friends. They did what a pack of men friends might be expected to do together, except for the one thing Anne had hoped to hear from them.

"They did not tell war stories."

When they all got together, they talked about jobs, homes, families, and their lives since their service. They did not talk about the nasty business of war. She learned that their looks and conversations disguised the true nature of their valor. She began collecting interviews. None of the men had been looking to win a Medal at the time of their heroic actions. They were not supermen.

"We are just common men who did the best we could a long time ago."

Nick Oresko, an Army master sergeant and World War II recipient, explained that their actions occurred not in a normal environment. "There's a lot of confusion, emotion, screaming and yelling. You can't explain it. At that moment, you're not fighting for the president or the flag, you are doing it for yourself and your buddies. . . . My heart was pumping so loud I thought the enemy could hear by heartbeat. I was mad, I was wounded, I was scared and I was dirty. It all happened in twenty minutes for me."

Anne wondered, what made the men do the heroic things they had done? None of the recipients could explain it to her. Dick Bush, perhaps, said it as well as any of the recipients who had returned home from war to be celebrated as heroes.

"I wasn't out there alone that day on Okinawa. I had Marines to my right, Marines to my left, Marines behind me and Marines overhead. I didn't earn this alone. It belongs to them, too."

September 19–23. Dick arrived at the Riviera Hotel in Las Vegas for the Raider Reunion. Bus tours carried Raiders to the Hoover Dam, the Chocolate Factory, and the Atomic Bomb test site. They took in various shows along the Vegas Strip. The guests shared notes about eating a prime rib dinner at the Silver City Casino for $3.99, seeing free circus acts at the Circus Circus, and enjoying an "all you can eat" breakfast, lunch, and dinner at the old-time Stardust. One favorite among the "white walls" (meaning those with a middle age paunch) was a half-pound hotdog and eight-ounce beer for a dollar. For those lured to the gaming capital to "roll the dice," the Excalibur, the world's largest hotel, fronted by a giant castle, proved to be enticing. The Mirage had also recently opened its doors to guests.

Twenty-one 1st Battalion Raiders smiled for the camera: front row sitting, second row of eight standing. Dick stood third from the right end in the group photo. [167]

The Association members decided at their general meeting on Saturday morning to hold reunions every year rather than every two years. The Saturday night banquet was conducted with perfection: delicious salad, filets, and desserts. There was much joking that the Mustang Ranch (a desert brothel) was up for sale at auction.

Brigadier General Thomas "Tom" Draudy was the guest of honor speaker at the banquet. He talked about the principle reason for his wanting to join the Marine Corps, a decision he never for a moment regretted. Raider stories he had heard when he was just a boy, how the Marine Raiders had given the Japanese the first real back-breaking defeat in WWII set him on his course.

"Also at the head table was old salt Richard BUSH, Congressional Medal Of Honor recipient who amused the Raiders with a story." [168]

"I never had trouble sleeping up on the front lines during combat," Dick said. "I would patiently stay awake while my foxhole buddy had the first watch and when that buddy fell asleep, I would carefully plant a kiss on the guy's lips. This so startled and surprised my buddy, that he could not fall asleep again. I'd sleep soundly until my turn on the watch, knowing my buddy was awake—and alert."

The Raiders moved rhythmically afterwards to a live dance band and WWII show tunes.

Dick attended the Sunday morning memorial service held in the Riviera's penthouse meeting room. The names of 192 Raiders deceased since the last reunion were read. Dick's Charlie Company friends, Hugh Brewington, Donald G. Carr, and Michael G. Paredes, had all joined the Raider Honor Roll. A bugler played *TAPS* following the service.

1991. The year held many reminders of Dick's bravery for the Raiders.

The January *Patch* (Page 8) printed a photo of Dick speaking at the podium at the Riviera. The March issue (Page 19) printed his full Citation along with those of six other recipients. The caption beside the July *Patch* photo (Page 2) identified the THREE FAMOUS RAIDERS: Dick Bush, Father Redmond, and Lowell Bulger, "dressed to the nines," standing shoulder to shoulder together at the reunion, smiling as if one of them had just told a joke—a characteristic for which all three of them were famous. The November issue (Page 10) printed an almost full-page photograph of Dick shaking hands with President Truman after the Medal had been placed around his neck in 1945.

Dick always put a perspective on his own heroism, often with a touch of humor or irony, especially when he was among Marines. Underneath the official photo's caption was a microwave recipe and directions for *Dick Bush Fudge*: blending sweetened condensed milk, lots of Ghirardelli chocolate chips, miniature marshmallows, vanilla, chopped walnuts, and a dash of salt.

September 3–8, 1991. The selection of Scottsdale for a reunion worked nicely. The Raiders could fit in a thorough annual checkup into their schedules at the famed Mayo clinic, and enjoy the outstanding food, booze, and Hospitality Room. Dick registered at the Marriott's Mountain Shadows Hotel with Nelda Moyer on Thursday and enjoyed a trip to the Dog Races. On Friday, they feasted at a western cookout at the Rancho Fiesta. The men selected cowboy hats and bandanas to wear for dinner. Igor's Jazz Cowboys provided the music.

An interview video with Father Redmond before he had died was featured at the Saturday banquet. The after-dinner speeches were not like those generally given at a reunion, but turned out to be "more of a rap session between buddies."

Brigadier General Jay Hubbard, a 2d Raider platoon leader, shared some "friendly barbs" with Dick, next to take the podium. Dick was able to "give as well as he got." He explained the selection of his cowboy hat before the western cookout, knowing he was going to have to eat with General Hubbard and Brigadier General Leonard E. "Len" Fribourg.

"I had better get the largest hat I could," he joked, "then, shrink my head to fit it." Dick had the audience laughing throughout his time at the podium, telling a series of jokes, tending toward the bawdy. [169]

August 20–23, 1992. Hundreds of new members had been added to the Raider Association's roster since April 1991. The members continued in their efforts to "snag and drag" lost Raiders back into the fold, using the "wonderful computers" in libraries to find possible addresses. [170] The Vice President for Membership wrote postcards, informing the addressee of the Raider Association and asking if he had been a Raider.

Before the 50th Anniversary of the Guadalcanal assault, thirteen lost Raiders contacted Archie Rackerby. Six had been in the 1st Battalion: three of them in Charlie Company. Walter M. Jacobi was living part time in New Zealand and joined the membership. Charles P. Roddy answered his post card. "I am the lost Raider you are looking for from the First Raiders. . . . Many thanks for finding me." Henry J. Wajtowicz was in poor health. He responded to the postcard inquiry. "This is the first contact from a Raider I have received since WWII." He sent in annual dues and joined the Association.

Dick attended the reunion with 425 Raiders and wives in Arlington, Virginia. Thirty-two of the Raiders represented Edson's 1st Battalion. Cecil E. McClelland looked for Dick in the Crystal Gateway Marriot hospitality room. He had also served in Charlie Company. Steven A. Koslowski from Waukegan did not attend.

On Thursday, Dick toured the White House with 250 Raiders. President George and Barb Bush were not home. Old friends liked to ask Dick how he was related to the president. On Friday, he rode on one of the five buses taking a two-hour road trip, one way, to the Raider Museum in Richmond. Major General Edison E. Scholes, Fort Bragg, U.S. Army Deputy Commanding Officer, gave a stirring address at the Museum praising the Raider's history. In the evening, Dick walked five blocks to watch the 8th & I parade and the Marine's Silent Drill Team.

The annual auction was on Saturday. There was an inspiring promotion of Rudy G. Rosenquist, Martin J. Sexton, and Robert A. Buerlein's new book, *Our Kind of War*. The bidders could purchase a hardcover copy for $35. [171] A sheet of twenty-four Raider Commemorative postage stamps was also available for $6.

Brigadier General Thomas Draudy was the speaker at the Saturday night banquet, repeating his 1990 Las Vegas appearance. He spoke about the aspect of Marine combat training that overcomes fear. "Marines fight for their buddies, not for patriotism, money or macho, but for love of their fellow Marines." The general went on to say, "This concept is expressed in your book, *Our Kind of War*, on page 249 which quotes Father Redmond on his 91st birthday." Part of Father Redmond's statement was "a family so close that each one would risk his life for another." Brigadier General Draudy concluded with a compliment to the Raiders. "Best thing about being a Raider is that you don't have to apologize for not being one." [172]

As always, the Sunday memorial services were counted as a memorable event. The Raiders bused to Arlington Cemetery and visited the graves of men they had once known. They openly shed tears of sadness, humility, and awe, remembering how young were the men who had sacrificed their futures in battles for their love of comrades. The Honor Roll was read at the Memorial Amphitheater in front of the Tomb of the Unknown Soldier. At the farewell brunch, the Association announced that the membership had decided to reinstate annual reunions, rather than biennial reunions.

Harry S. Truman

The Harry S. Truman Library was dedicated on July 6, 1957, and had held a July 4th celebration every year afterwards. The planning committee organized the 35th annual Independence Day celebration as a salute to the World War II era.

July 3, 1993. Scores of library visitors lined the path for an early-morning military parade on Saturday, cheering as war heroes, American Legion and military bands, vintage cars, and World War II airplanes passed along the route.

Among the library's honored guests were: Richard Bush, Jacklyn Lucas, and Army Master Sergeant Nicholas Oresko, who had earned his Medal for actions near Tettingen, Germany, on January 23, 1945; Charles Lindberg, the last surviving Marine who had participated in the first flag raising at Iwo Jima; Joe Rosenthal, who had taken the photo of the second flag raising; and sculptor Felix de Weldon, who had created the Marine Corps War Memorial at Arlington National Cemetery from Joe's iconic photo. [173]

Benjamin Zobrist, Truman Library and Museum Director, introduced the three recipients during the festivities. He remembered what President Truman often had said of the men who wore the Medal around their necks.

"They didn't think they were doing anything unusual. They were just doing what the situation called for."

Jack Lucas agreed and said that's how he felt about having earned the Medal on Iwo Jima. Dick Bush declined to talk about his war heroics when he was interviewed. Instead, he focused on how much he admired President Truman. So, Benjamin Zobrist provided the details from the Citation about how CPL Bush had pulled a Japanese hand grenade to himself, absorbing the charge, and saving the lives of the evacuees around him.

September 8–12. Chicago is 410 miles from Minneapolis. Approximately 200 1st Battalion Raiders lived within a 1,000-mile radius of Minneapolis. Many of them had never attended a reunion. Forty-one newly found 1st Battalion Raiders, seven from Company C, had been added to the Association directory. [174] The city seemed a perfect location to draw the 1st Raiders to a reunion.

The Raiders registered at the Radisson Hotel West on Thursday afternoon. After greeting each other at the Hospitality Room, they took a three-hour tour of downtown Minneapolis sights. Dick had a choice between the Old Log Theater and the Mystic Lake Casino for a prime rib and walleye dinner. Friday morning, 250 Raiders left the hotel at 9:00 AM to bus to Fort Snelling National Cemetery for the memorial service in a tribute to the 196 Raiders added to the Honor Roll. Sixteen of the deceased had been C/1 Raiders. Back at the hotel by noon, the Raiders departed the Radisson at 5:15 PM to board the Anson and Betsy Northrop sternwheeler for dinner, dancing, and a three-hour Mississippi riverboat cruise. The strolling Dixieland band was a hit.

Saturday was open for an all-day shopping event following the Mall of America's grand opening or more touring of the city.

"Going once, going . . ." During the auction of memorabilia, Raiders bought over 700 raffle tickets for a chance to win a commemorative Raider Stiletto. The Camillus Cutlery Company reproduction of its 1942 combat knife sat in a wood display case with a red velvet lining. The handle was cast pewter, and the USMC scroll and Camillus name were etched in gold on the blued blade. Shoppers at the Raider Museum Gift Store in Richmond could purchase the collectable knife and case at a bargain $224. Dick had been presented a gift stiletto at a previous reunion.

Following evening cocktails, Dick was a Guest of Honor at the banquet and was acknowledged for his part in making the reunion a success.

After dessert was served, the Raider Stiletto was presented to John P. Howe, 3K. He was most pleased that he had bought a $1 raffle ticket. As couples danced to the Dick Mako Orchestra, there were many discussions about whether the roast prime rib of beef au jus, prepared to perfection, or the Black Forrest cake was most outstanding.

All the reunion activities were captured on a video cassette for Raiders to pass on to friends and family.

September 18–25, 1994. Nearly 600 Raiders, wives, friends, and guests registered at the Las Vegas Gold Coast Hotel-Casino. Dick was one of twenty-eight from Illinois, Missouri, Kansas, and Nebraska. [175] The 1st Raiders, most from the east coast, attended the reunion in record numbers. Rather than playing the slots over the weekend, most of the 285 Raiders spent time socializing in the Hospitality Room and at the Leatherneck Club a few long blocks from the hotel. The names of 255 deceased Raiders were read at the Friday memorial service.

Commandant of the Marine Corps General Carl Epting Mundy Jr., principle speaker at the Saturday banquet, was proud to have his photograph taken with Dick at the head table. Directly in front of the Commandant, on top of a small mahogany table, was a Marine dress hat, a red rose in a vase, and a pair of white dress gloves, symbolizing all Marines lost in combat since 1775.

The 50th anniversary of the amphibious landing on Okinawa was approaching. Dick had accepted an invitation to go back to Okinawa in June for the 6th Marine Division 50th Anniversary Tour coordinated by the Galaxy Tours Company. The war veterans planned to place wreaths and dedicate division battle commemoration plaques at Camp Smedley D. Butler—a collection of distinct Marine camps scattered across the former Okinawan battlegrounds.

The officers and men of the United States Marine Raider Association
extend our deepest sympathy to you in this time of your bereavement.

As private as Dick was about his personal life, only those closest to him knew about his marriage and divorce and Stella's death in 1989. Little about his life was published in newspaper articles or the Raider newsletter. Hugh and Peggy Brewington knew some of the details. Dick had been there for them when their son had died. Peggy knew that Dick's daughter was struggling and did what she could to bolster his spirits. Nelda Moyer was at his side after Easter Sunday, April 16, 1995, passed. That was the same date he had pulled a grenade into his abdomen. As had been true during the war, Dick outlived others he cared about.

April 21, 1995. Judith (Bush) Smith, 47, had spent most of her days in the Waukegan area. She died at home in Gurnee on Friday. Gurnee Funeral Home arranged the private services for early on Tuesday afternoon, April 25. Robert came home from Boston, and David came from Charlottesville, Virginia. Rick Bush and his wife, Karen, came from Long Grove. Dick, of course, attended. These were Judy's survivors. Stella was also included in her obituary, which the family wished not to be published until after the funeral. Judy was buried next to her mother at Ascension Cemetery in Libertyville. The family requested that donations be made to the American Cancer Society research in Judy's name. [176]

Dick endured.

Return to a Beautiful Island

The May *Leatherneck* Magazine issue reminded the current 3d Marine Division infantrymen on Okinawa that they sweated on the same hills and rushed through the same dense subtropical bush that their predecessors had fifty years earlier. Okinawa was the keystone of the Pacific, the Far East bastion of the Corps, and a living edifice to the valor of those who had fought there. Corporal Richard E. Bush, MOH recipient, was one of them. [177]

June 16. Two months after his daughter was buried, Dick departed Chicago early on Friday for the flight to Los Angeles. He boarded the connecting flight with 140 Raiders for the return to Okinawa.

First, there was a layover on Guam to tour the battle sights and visit the new WWII *Liberators' Memorial* at the tip of Asan Point, between Agat and Orote Peninsula. The Raiders stopped to read the bronze plaques imbedded in the walkway leading to the memorial and quietly reminisced in sight of the many war relics left along the coastal regions. Across several days, they visited with village dignitaries and natives who had celebrated their victory on the island in 1944. [178]

On Tuesday, the flight from Guam terminated at Fukuoka, Japan, for a one-night layover.

June 21–25. On Wednesday, the 4:30 AM wake-up call had the veterans gathered very early on the street outside their hotel, only to experience a long delay before taking off. The last leg on Japan Airlines covered the 300 miles due south of mainland Japan in two hours. On approach to Naha International, they could look out at the sixty-seven miles of Okinawa stretching north.

"Welcome back to Okinawa." Approximately 600 Marine, Army, and Navy veterans of the battle had made the trip. Ushered through customs, friendly and warm American military men and women with their families took pictures, applauded, shook their hands, patted them on the back, and greeted them. They helped carry the baggage and escorted the veterans to the air-conditioned buses waiting to take them to the Pacific Hotel in the center of bustling Naha on the southern portion of the island. The escorts for each bus stayed with their veterans for the entire visit.

Reporters looked for Dick, Navy Hospital Apprentice 1st Class Robert Eugene Bush from Tacoma, Washington, and Army PFC Alejandro R. Ruiz Sr. from Loving, New Mexico, three

MOH recipients from the battle and long-time friends. A few veterans had not seen Dick since his evacuation from the island in 1945 and asked to have photos taken with him.

George Mandich, 69, making the tour from Chicago, had been a 6th MarDiv private on Okinawa. After twenty-eight years of working as an FBI Special Agent and retiring in 1980, he worked security for the NFL and the Chicago *Bears*. He believed that the veterans had come in their waning years for their "last hurrah."

The returning veterans relaxed for the rest of the day.

On Thursday morning, the buses left Naha and drove north toward the Asa Kawa for the dedication of the Sergeant Elbert L. Kinser Memorial Display at Camp Kinser. Dick stood with the Marines at 9:00 AM to remember the young sergeant who had thrown himself on a grenade to protect his men on May 4, 1945. Charles F. Kinser, his wife, Margaret, and his sister, Hazel, had tears in their eyes, standing on the ground near where their older brother had given his life. The veterans then toured the Battle of Okinawa Museum Display at Camp Kinser Building 107.

Next, the buses continued north toward Kadina to Camp Foster's Headquarters Building 1. Dick attended a wreath laying ceremony and flag raising memorial service at 2:30 PM. The original 6th Division flag that had flown over the island during the battle was displayed. The Honorable Walter Mondale was the key speaker. The tour ended the day in the Plaza Housing area for a welcome dinner at the Camp Butler Officers' Club. General Carl Epting Mundy Jr., 30th Commandant of the Marine Corps and guest of honor at the banquet, was pleased to shake hands and have photographs taken with Dick. The vets were bound back to the Naha hotel at 9:30 PM.

On Friday morning, Dick was on another part of the island he had not seen in 1945. The tour drove southeast to a 292-foot-high hill for the 10:00 AM unveiling of The Cornerstone of Peace Wall in the center of Mabuni Hill Park. The memorial is made up of 1,200 black granite squares, each a meter high and inscribed with more than 234,000 names of Americans, Japanese, and Okinawans (147,110 noncombatant civilians) who had died during the final battle of WWII. The day's oppressive summer heat and humidity was a reminder for the Marines of the sweat and blood they had once left in the island's soils.

Afterwards, Dick enjoyed a special Japanese luncheon in a restaurant. At 6:00 PM, the veterans attended an open house and special dinner at the Grand Castle Hotel.

The tour went to the northeast early on Saturday for the 7:00 AM Joint Morning Colors and Honors Parade at Camp Courtney, just below the Isthmus, on the Philippine Sea side of Okinawa. After a VIP breakfast with Ambassador Mundale the buses headed back toward Naha to Sugar Loaf Hill (Kirama Chiiji), sitting between old Asato and Makabe towns. A 6th Marine Division Memorial Plaque ceremony was held at 10:00 AM. That ceremony followed more than a week of controversy.

The governor of Okinawa had urged the United States to reduce its military bases on the island and objected to the wording on the planned Sugar Loaf Hill plaque. In part, the plaque read: "This is the summit of Sugar Loaf Hill, site of the costliest battle in the U.S. Marine Corps' history and hallowed ground for the two nations which fought here. . . . Survivors from both nations treasure its soil as a symbol to courageous warriors. Their spirit roams these hills." Japanese anti-war activists protested the plaque's dedication, claiming that it "glorified war." [179] Japan had also asked not to be invited to the 50th VJ Day Anniversary ceremony on August 14.

The reality that all wartime passions do not die easily was sparked during the ceremony. While one of the Japanese veterans was speaking, his companion suddenly displayed a Japanese Battle Flag. Viewed as deliberate and provocative, the action caused an immediate stir among the Raiders—several obviously very upset.

"I hated them then. I can't help but hate them again."

Returning to the Naha hotel, the visitors rested until 4:00 PM. They attended a 5:00 PM service at the 6th Division Memorial to the Marines killed on the island and a tree planting at the Garden of Remembrance. Next on the itinerary was the Camp Kinser Fifty Years of Friendship Open House, featuring "Carnival Time," complete with various entertainments, food booths, and other fun-filled activities. Dinner was served at 7:00 PM.

Sunday was spent on the East China Sea coast. In the morning, the guests toured the Naha Air Base, the beach defense positions, and the extensive underground headquarters of the Japanese admiral who had conducted the last stand on Oroku Peninsula. A 6th Marine Division Memorial Plaque dedication ceremony was held at 9:00 AM. The buses then travelled up to Camp Foster for a fabulous Sunday Brunch Buffet at the Camp Butler Officers Club.

June 26. Monday proved to be an emotion-packed day and a highlight for Dick. The Marine veterans took the longest motorcoach trip of the entire tour, driving north, half the length of the island, to Camp Schwab. Dick was back on the Ishikawa Isthmus, in the vicinity of Ora Village, Naga, Motobu Peninsula, and Mount Yae Take.

A 4th Marines' rifle company conducted an assault landing demonstration on the beach in front of the spectators at 10:00 AM. Lunch was packaged MREs. Then, Dick boarded an LVT and took a ride in the Philippine Sea. USMC correspondent Corporal Laura L. Gawecki asked him what it was like to return to the island.

"I lost a lot of friends here," Dick recalled, "and I think about them a lot. But I think a lot of us have come back to see what's happened. There's nothing wrong with that. I think Okinawa's a beautiful island."

Everyone returned to the hotel in mid-afternoon, rested, and dressed for the farewell dinner at the Camp Butler restaurant.

Tuesday was a day of rest, comradeship, and salty sea stories at the hotel.

June 28. The veterans departed at 12:15 PM on Wednesday, en route to Guam. After a four-hour layover, they flew to Honolulu. The brief two-hour stay gave time for a snack in the terminal, then, they were on their way to the Mainland. Dick landed in Los Angeles at 5:10 PM and caught his flight back to Chicago. The return to Okinawa had been a thirteen-day affair.

Dick was immediately busy. The 1st Raiders were planning for a seventh mini-reunion for the Chicago area veterans and had divided up the organizational duties. Frank Kemp and Victor Anderson took on the Company A Chairmen duties. Dick Vana and Melvin D. Heckt served as the B Company Chairmen. Larry "Bang Away At" Bangser and Dick Bush acted as C Company Chairmen.

October 13–15. The Raiders met at the Clarion O'Hare Hotel at 6810 Mannheim in Rosemont. The 120 Raiders attending the festivities and the Saturday evening banquet concluded that the planned event was a success.

1996. His hometown continued to remember and honor Dick. The Glasgow Marine Corps League (Detachment 584) began presenting the annual Richard Bush Award to individuals in recognition for their service to the community and to the country. Jerry V. Stahl, 63, a Korean War veteran and former Commandant of the Glasgow MCL Detachment, was the first to be honored with the award.

Jerry knew Dick personally, and the award meant a lot to him. He presented the second award to James Morris "Jimmy" Simmons, 69, in 1997. Jimmy was a WW II U.S. Army veteran and a retired Glasgow High School history teacher, living on Cleveland Avenue. He considered the Richard Bush Award to be at the top of his civic merit awards. Seven more veterans would receive the honor until the award was renamed the Patriot Award in 2004. [180]

October 17–19, 1997. The Raiders held an eighth mini-reunion at the Four Points Hotel at O'Hare in Chicago. Dick invited Peggy Brewington to come down from Anchorage, and Skull's fellow Raiders welcomed her. Peggy mixed comfortably among the 125 people who attended, enjoying the stories about Hugh. The Saturday evening banquet and dance was the high point, as usual. Those present considered the weekend another big success.

February 1998. *The Raider Patch* paid a special tribute to the seven Raiders awarded the nation's highest award for valor during WWII battles. The photograph of Dick receiving his Medal at the White House was on Page 2.

August 1998. The Association began to insist on further explorations on Makin Atoll for the gravesite of nineteen Marines killed during the Raider WWII night assault on the island. Medal of Honor recipient Sergeant Clyde A. Thomason was one of the missing.

October 1998. In 1997, visitors to the Illinois State Capitol, located on South 2nd Street in Springfield, found a first-floor corner display in the Statehouse east corridor fascinating. The Springfield Area Chapter of American Ex-Prisoners of War had presented the flags on either side of two permanent panels. Floodlights kept the display illuminated. "Honoring Illinois Heroes" was the title on both panels.

In October 1998, the display featured seven MOH recipients: four from WWII and three from the Vietnam War. The display included an eight-by-ten photograph of each hero and the text of his Medal Citation. Five of the recipients had served in the U.S. Army. Corporal Richard Earl Bush had a display. The second Marine was Captain Robert Hugo Dunlap. He had earned a Medal on Iwo Jima with the 1st Battalion, 26th Marines, 5th MarDiv, on February 20–21, 1945. [181]

May 28, 1999. Ipalco Enterprises, Inc. had invited all 158 living MOH recipients to Indianapolis to attend a special Memorial Day weekend. Dick and ninety-five other recipients accepted. Ipalco paid for all travel expenses, bringing them to the gala unveiling of Ipalco's new Medal of Honor Memorial in downtown on Friday.

The names of 3,410 recipients representing fifteen conflicts dating to the Civil War were etched into twenty-seven awesome curved glass panels rising above the canal that splits downtown. Every night at dusk, a sound system played stories, some narrated by the veteran who had earned the star-shaped Medal. [182]

On Saturday, Dick rode in the Indianapolis 500 Festival Parade and then completed one lap around the mile-long Indianapolis Motor Speedway track before Sunday's race. [183] The weekend holiday was an opportunity for Alene and Willie Dee to drive down from Marion and enjoy some time with Dick.

Word came that U.S. Army Air Corps WWII Medal recipient William R. Lawley Jr., 78, of Leeds, Alabama, had died that day. Then, on June 1, U.S. Army Korean War recipient, Lloyd "Scooter" Burke, 74, of Tichnor, Arkansas, died. Before autumn passed, by mid-October five more recipients had died.

John McCarthy, *The Patch* newsletter editor, felt an agitation about a lot of "flakes" and "fakes" and "fabricators" posing as former Raiders and Medal recipients. He and Dick had a conversation about "phonies literally trying to steal honored valor that they never deserved from those heroes that did." [184]

The Medal recipients knew of each other through their membership in the CMOHS. Dick and the other thirty-three surviving Marine recipients easily recognized each other at Medal conventions and reunions. He put the editor in touch with Mitchell Paige, the 80-year-old retired Marine Corps colonel who went after the frauds.

Mitchell had earned his Medal "during a night of terror on Guadalcanal that left his platoon dead around him and 920 Japanese soldiers lying on the ground." Dick's fellow recipient was the official "hound dog" for the CMOHS, checking out any and all dubious claims. He had been running down the frauds and exposing them since the 1950s. Mitchell had bagged 500 of them, confronting them at holiday parades and at military bases, often discovering them through newspaper stories and obituaries. Some of the impostors had been in the service, and some had not. [185]

Writer-director Julia Davis contacted Dick and scheduled a meeting with him. The Rock Entertainment and Fleur De Lis Film studios were collaborating on a new television series. Actor Burt Reynolds, Academy Award nominee, was at the meeting, pleased and honored to chitchat with the MOH recipient. The producers planned to script twenty-four episodes. Mitchell Paige, Everett Pope, Raymond Clausen, Harvey C. Barnum, and Smedley Darlington Butler would be other Marines featured in the series in addition to Dick.

September 4–9. Dick was in San Diego again. The Association met at the U.S. Grant Hotel and visited MCRD and Camp Pendleton. The members planned their first reunion of the new millennium for Chicago in 2000. They also appropriated $3,000 to send two Raiders to Makin Island in an urgent, final effort to find the remains of the Makin Raiders killed in action.

The 1st Raider Battalion planned to hold a mini-reunion in Chicago and asked Dick to be a speaker. All present knew that the old Marine would bring some light-hearted comments to his speech. Dick pulled out a newspaper article that he had saved several years earlier. His photo would accompany a copy of his speech reprinted in the Raider Association newsletter four months later. [186]

World War II veteran Robert J. Grady, LtCol, USAF (Ret), of Colorado Springs, had read a comment from the White House and wrote a letter to the president in a newsletter on July 30, 1994. Charlton Heston read the letter during a nationwide radio talk show broadcast in 1994. [187] The letter stayed in circulation over the years, appearing in various newspapers, like the *Cleveland Plain Dealer* in 1996.

October 9. On Saturday night, Dick stepped up to the microphone. On one hand, his remarks about the letter were definitely tongue-in-cheek; on the other hand, the irony in what he would say had a serious underpinning for many Raiders.

"I was embarrassed to read that President Clinton and his advisors have said that the older generation must learn to sacrifice as other generations have done. I knew eventually someone would ferret out our dirty little secret. We lived the lifestyle of the rich and famous all our lives. Now I know I must bare the truth of my generation. Let the Country condemn us for our selfishness.

"During the great Depression we had a hilarious time dancing to the tune of *Brother, Can You Spare a Dime?* We could choose to dine at any country's fabulous soup kitchens, often joined by our parents and siblings. Oh, those were the heady good old days of carefree self-indulgence.

"Then World War II came along and filled our cup to overflowing. We had a chance to bask on the exotic beaches of Guadalcanal, New Georgia, Guam, Iwo Jima and Okinawa; to see the capitals of Europe and to travel to such scenic spots as Bastogne, Malmedy and Monte Casino. One of the most exhilarating adventures, in the Philippines, was the stroll from Bataan to the local Japanese hotels. But the good times really rolled for those lucky devils—those lucky enough to be on the beaches of Normandy for the swimming and boating on that most pleasant June day in 1944. Unforgettable.

"Even more lucky were those who drew the holiday cruises on sleek gray ships to fun-filled spots like Midway, the Solomons, Murmansk and Iron Bottom Bay. Instead of asking, 'What can you do for your Country?', an indulgent government let us fritter away our youth wandering through the lush and lovely jungles of Guadalcanal, Bougainville, Burma and New Guinea.

"Yes, it is true. We were pampered, we were spoiled. We were spoiled rotten. We never did really grow up and realize what sacrifice meant. Some of us smoked but we didn't inhale and we didn't enjoy it. Even when we were doing something wrong, we couldn't do it right. I never thought anyone would ever find out about all that soft money we collected on Guadalcanal in exchange for our core values.

"We envy you, Mr. Clinton, the harsh lessons you learned in Little Rock, Oxford and Moscow.

"My generation is old Mr. President, and guilty, but we are repentant. Punish us for our failings, sir, that we may truly learn the meaning of Duty, Honor and Country."—Dick Bush

The speech and the mini-reunion proved to be "a Big Hit." Archibald B. Rackerby, 3d Raider Battalion, submitted Dick's speech to *The Patch*.

"I CAN'T FORGET ONE SINGLE NAME.
THOSE MEN ARE WITH ME STILL
IF I DON'T REMEMBER THEM,
I ASK YOU THEN WHO WILL?" [188]

Sergeant Robert A. Gannon, USMC

November 5. Dick and eighty-four Medal recipients were at the third traffic circle in the Riverside National Cemetery, California, across Highway 15 from the March Field Air Museum, for the dedication of the magnificent National Medal of Honor Memorial. The polished, black granite monument initially listed 3,409 names (today 3,455), alphabetically organized on wall panels according to each war, starting with the Civil War. Stunning replicas of the three distinct Medal emblems, each over three feet high, adorn one wall. When Dick stood at that wall, the Navy/Marine emblem was head high in front of him. The Army version was above his left shoulder, and the Air Force emblem was at his right hip. The monument is "a very special tribute to a very special group of men."

By 2000, Dick was one of 151 surviving Medal recipients. Having to decide which invitation to accept had become a constant in his life.

April 14, 2000. A sign near the road off Quantico Drive Circle marked the location. Dick walked up a familiar trail, winding through trees on the east side of a hill at Quantico National Cemetery on Joplin Road in Triangle, Virginia. The cemetery had been formally dedicated on May 15, 1983, and he had visited it before for various formal occasions.

The Memorial Pathway, first envisioned at the 1984 annual Raider reunion in Quantico, is located near the center of the cemetery grounds. The first of nine memorials within walking distance of each other was unveiled on a warm, sunny Sunday, August 6, 1989, morning. The 1st Marine Raider Battalion monument was dedicated at the top of a hill. The Edson's Raiders Memorial is a stone terrace with a bench overlooking the cemetery.

The Purple Heart Memorial, dedicated on August 7, 1990, sat about 400 feet away from Dick's destination. Another monument at the top of the hill, on the west side, overlooking part of the cemetery, had been dedicated by the Sixth Marine Division Association on October 5, 1995, to commemorate their 50th anniversary. The first "Striking Sixth" Memorial is a bronze plaque on a stone sitting on the ground. [189]

Dick was on the Memorial Trail for the unveiling of a second *Striking Sixth Monument* to honor the Marine division that had won the Presidential Unit Citation for its action on Okinawa. [190] Sergeant Gannon's poem *For Those Who Never Came Home* is engraved on a bronze plaque at the entryway's left side. To the right, another plaque describes the division's four regiments. The impressive memorial is a stone bench resembling an Okinawan tomb. Markers along the inside of the bench reflect the nine campaigns the regiments fought in during WWII.

In the years since covering a grenade on a Pacific island, Dick had time to think about the significance of the memorials along the pathway. He attended dedications purposely. "A nation reveals itself not only by the men it produces," he said, "but by the men it honors, the men it remembers, men like those who gave their lives on Okinawa. They must not be forgotten."

A Marine Corps reporter carefully wrote down Dick's view of going to war. Characteristic of the old Raider, he was both humble and humorous.

"I didn't want to get any medals," he said. "In fact, when my brother and I were leaving to go into the service, I didn't really want to go. I still have all the splinters in my fingernails from where they came and pulled me off the porch." In the years ahead, newspapers would periodically print a shortened quote. "I didn't want to get any medals." [191]

"He didn't really flaunt what he did."

True as that was, stories of Dick's heroics were well known to Waukegan area veterans. One was Waukegan Police Lieutenant James Sroka. As Dick got into his later years, Jim chauffeured him to various Marine events and witnessed the effect the Medal recipient had on others. Dick had "near rock star popularity among younger Marines," and they flocked to him, wanting to talk to him and listen to what he said. As often as he was asked, he graciously scripted his autograph.

June 6. The opening of the D-Day Museum (became the National World War II Museum) in New Orleans was accompanied by a parade with scores of military units and a rare B-1 bomber flyover. Dick was in New Orleans to enjoy a few drinks with friends when the museum opened a second gallery dedicated to the amphibious invasions of the Pacific War.

September 12–17. The Raider National Convention was held in Chicago for the first time since 1962. Attendance at conventions and reunions had been diminishing in previous years, and the Raider Association directors wondered if they could keep their reunions going into the new millennium. At the start of the New Year, the Association had 947 Raiders on its roster: 439 Life Members and 508 Annual Members remembering to pay their dues. Of those, 109 Raiders along with 175 wives and guests attended the Chicago Convention.

The Makin Island CILHI (Central Identification Laboratory, Hickam AFB, Hawaii) recovery team was among the invited guests. The team gave a presentation of how the Makin Raider remains were discovered. Clyde Thomason's half-brother, Hugh M. Thomason, and his wife attended the reunion. [192]

The details were familiar to all the Raiders in attendance. At 5:13 AM, on August 17, 1942, 211 Marines of LtCol Evan Carlson's 2d Raider Battalion, Companies A and B, landed on Makin Island Atoll in the Marshall Islands to overtake the Japanese garrison defending a seaplane base. The Raiders advanced against enemy snipers and machine guns, withstood two banzai charges, and depleted the forces manning the garrison.

Then, withdrawing to the waiting U.S. submarines turned problematic. The next morning ninety-three Raiders returned to the subs. Seventy-two Marines remained on the island as the Japanese sent in reinforcements. The last of the Raiders were evacuated from Makin before midnight on August 18.

Thirty Marines did not return from the Makin Island Raid. Reported USMC casualties included eighteen KIA, twelve MIA, and seventeen wounded. Nine of the missing had been unintentionally and unknowingly left behind on the island during the night withdrawal. They were captured by the Japanese, taken from the island, and beheaded on Kwajalein on October 16, 1942. Famed Olympic runner and WWII POW, Louie Zamperini, was briefly imprisoned in the same Kwajalein cell and saw the names of the nine executed Raiders carved into a wooden plank. The remains of the nine and two other missing Raiders have never been located. [193]

"Operation Due Regard." During excavation and recovery attempts, the Army's CILHI had finally discovered an unmarked mass grave on Makin in November 1999. Human remains, equipment, weapons, hand grenades, and dog tags obviously belonging to Raiders had been sent to Hawaii for identification. [194]

September 21–23. The CMOHS annual meeting was planned for Pueblo, Colorado, nicknamed "Home of Heroes." Nearly 100 recipients began arriving on Wednesday. Governor Bill Owens declared the days to be Colorado Medal of Honor week. On Thursday, at 1:30 PM, the recipients gathered in the Heroes Plaza at the Pueblo Convention Center, 320 Central Main Street, for the dedication of the Medal of Honor Memorial. The names of the 3,433 recipients across the wars were engraved on a stretch of granite walls. One highlight of the unveiling was the four bronze statues of the city's four resident recipients.

One statue was of U.S. Army Staff Sergeant Drew Dennis Dix, Vietnam War recipient. His sister-in-law repeated something he had said—a sentiment often expressed by MOH recipients.

"He said he was the person who was recognized, but there were 100,000 other men who he fought alongside who he felt were just as deserving of the honor." [195]

The recipients then went into the Convention Center grand ballroom for an open house, from 2:30–4:00 PM, to give the public a chance to meet them.

Friday's schedule was full. At 9:00 AM, the recipients started fanning out across Pueblo County to visit school children. At 2:00 PM they toured the Sangre de Cristo Arts Center's Special Military Arts Exhibits at 210 North Santa Fe Avenue. They returned to the Convention Center at 6:00 PM for the Patriot Award Dinner. The organizing committee had decided to acknowledge the contribution of sports events to military morale and had selected five distinguished sports figures to accept the Patriot Award on behalf of the athletes of their respective sports. Guests had purchased their tickets to the dinner for $300 each.

The Medal recipients presented awards to Brooks Robinson—Baseball, David "The Admiral" Robinson—Basketball, Arnold Palmer—Golf, Pat LaFontaine—Hockey, and two-time, American-born Middleweight Champion of the World, Gene Fullmer—Boxing. They awarded the "Tex" McCrary Award for Excellence in Journalism to radio broadcaster Paul Harvey and the Bob Hope Entertainment Award to editorial cartoonist and two-time Pulitzer Prize winner William Henry "Bill" Mauldin.

A Memorial Service for MOH recipients who had passed away during the previous year was outside at 10:00 AM on Saturday in Heroes Plaza. The evening social hour and banquet, put on for them at the South Union Avenue riverfront promenade on the Historic Arkansas Riverwalk, was a short walk from the Convention Center. At 8:15 PM, the city then concluded the convention with a special finale fireworks display at the Lake Elizabeth pavilion.

October 11, 2000. Season 1 of *The Medal of Honor: History of Heroes* television series with Burt Reynolds hosting debuted on Wednesday night. The sixty minute episodes, incredible stories of MOH recipients, aired monthly until September 11, 2001. The second and third episodes, broadcast on November 11 and December 11, featured Mitchell Paige and Everett Pope.

February 11, 2001. Dick's incredible story was Episode 5. [196]

July 2001. The group of young Raiders had been KIA fifty-nine years earlier in the first American offensive ground combat operations of World War II. They were finally returning home. The repatriated remains were positively identified as nineteen Marines who had fought and died and had been buried together. Sergeant Clyde A. Thomason, 28 years old, from Atlanta, Georgia, the first enlisted Marine in World War II awarded the Medal of Honor, was among the identified Raiders. Another of the Marines had been counted among the twelve Raiders missing in action.

Six families requested the return of their Raider for private burial ceremonies in their hometowns. A ceremony was planned at Arlington for the other thirteen to coincide with the 59th anniversary of the day they had died.

August 2001. The Marine Raider Association sponsored two seats in the United States Naval Academy Navy–Marine Corps Memorial Stadium, a 34,000-seat facility. Seats 8 and 10 have plaques in honor of Brigadier General Evans F. Carlson and Brigadier General Merritt A. Edson, the original Raider commanders. Jack Lengyel, Academy Director of Athletics sent thanks to the Association on August 8, 2001. He wrote ". . . it is only fitting that we honor these two great military leaders in this stadium." [197]

August 15. On Wednesday, a Marine Aerial Refueler Transport Squadron 152 KC-130 *Hercules* flew the caskets from Hickam Air Force Base to Edwards Air Force Base in southern California for a brief stop.

August 16–19. The National Raiders' D.C. Reunion was an extraordinary event. The date had been meaningfully selected. Dick assembled with the others at Reunion Headquarters at the Doubletree Hotel in Crystal City (Arlington). They were there to remember and pay tribute to the Makin Island Raiders.

Dick represented both the Raider Association and the CMOHS.

The KC-130 arrived at Andrews Air Force Base on Thursday. The Marine Band, the Ceremonial Honor Guard Platoon, the pallbearers, and fourteen black Cadillac hearses were in place to welcome the Raiders home. The aircraft taxied to a stop in front of the waiting Next-of-Kin, who watched as each flag draped casket was tenderly carried down the tailgate and placed in a hearse. Following a ceremony, the hearses departed the tarmac for the final ride to Arlington National Cemetery. The families and guests returned to the hotel.

The eight pallbearers and alternates were veterans of the original four Raider battalions.

On Thursday evening, Dick attended a reception with musicians, honor guards, pallbearers and joined in a salute to the Makin Island Raiders Next-of-Kin.

Friday morning at 9:00 AM, the Raider Memorial Services were held at the hotel. Afterwards, Dick and the Raiders boarded buses at 10:00 AM for the ride to the Fort Myers Main Chapel. The Marine Honor Guard Platoon stood in formation at "parade rest." By 11:00 AM, 620 people jammed the chapel, while another 200 stood outside for the solemn Full Honors Burial services: a tribute to all thirty Marines who gave their lives for their country on remote Makin Island.

The fourteenth "symbolic casket," holding mixed human remains too difficult to accurately identify in Hawaii and representing the thirteen waiting twenty yards from their open gravesites, was in place in front of the alter.

"Today, we are gathered to remember, respect and honor thirty young Marine Raiders." The service began with a "Call to Worship" by two chaplains. Commandant General James L. Jones addressed the standing-room-only assembly. Raider Association President Melvin D. Heckt gave a heartfelt eulogy. After the recessional hymn, the relatives, guests, and visitors boarded the buses and proceeded to the cemetery.

At 11:45 AM, under grey and misting skies, the Honor Guard snapped to "attention" and "present arms" as the casket emerged from the chapel. The six honorary pallbearers protected the flag-draped casket with a plastic cover and lifted it onto the six-horse-drawn caisson. The Honor Guard was at the head of the procession. Behind them, the Marine Band was 100 feet in front of the hearse. Behind the hearse, Commandant General Jones and the Sergeant Major of the Marine Corps led a three-abreast column of officers and honored guests.

When not playing *Onward Christian Soldier* and *The Marine Hymn*, the band kept a steady, muffled drum beat. The column marched two-point-one miles along tree-shaded roads, mostly downhill, into the winding paths of Arlington National Cemetery, to Bradley Drive and Section 60. The procession stopped across the road from Father Redmond's Gravesite 2486 in Section 66. The pallbearers carried the "symbolic casket" to its place with the others.

The silent afternoon was not disturbed.

In front of each casket, the Next-of-Kin and guests sat and stood under a temporary awning. Retired Marine Colonel Hugh Thomason, 80, sat in front of his older, half-brother's casket. Dick Bush stood behind Sergeant Clyde Thomason's family through the internment ceremony.

A lone bugler sounded *Taps*, and a 21-gun salute ended the gravesite ceremony. In the minds of all the Raiders present, their comrades at last resided in the nation's hallowed ground.

The Raiders returned to the Doubletree Hotel hospitality room at 2:00 PM to share drinks and emotional conversation about the day's services. After supper, they left on buses at 6:30 PM for a ride to the renowned Marine Barracks at the corner of 8th and I Streets, Southeast in Washington, D.C. The silent drill team awed the guests. Captain Joe B. Griffith, 81, believed to be the only surviving Marine Raider officer, was honored at the 7:30 PM evening parade.

Saturday morning at 9:00 AM, the Raiders conducted their membership meeting. Their efforts to continue searching for the still missing eleven Makin Raiders gathered momentum. At 11:00, Dick mingled with the others, including wives, at the annual Raider auction. The donated artefacts, relics, memorabilia, and weapons garnered over $1700 for the Association's general fund. More visiting at the hospitality room followed.

John McCarthy, *Patch* editor, had an opportunity to "corner" Dick for an extended interview. They did not talk about wartime heroics, his wounds, or his medals. He'd had enough of that over the years. Dick was known for his humorous and interesting stories and anecdotes. John imagined that Dick was privy to the company of many important people in very high places, that the Medal had opened many doors, and that a lot of people wanted his company. Most people found that he was really a very special person with a great sense of humor.

"Of all the "big shots" you've had a close relationship with," John wanted to know, "who was your favorite?"

Dick replied without hesitation. "Harry Truman always gave me good advice. He once asked me how many times I have to get hit on the head before I find out what is hitting me on the head." He went on, and his admiration of the president who had put the Medal of Honor around his neck was evident.

"When Admiral Nimitz returned from overseas on 5 October 1945, and landed at the Naval Air Station at Bethesda, Maryland, I was waiting for him at the White House. He was due at the White House at 10:00 AM. I wanted to go meet Nimitz when he landed, but Truman said, 'No, let him come to us.' Truman had only been President for six months, but he learned this early and used it again when he met MacArthur at Wake Island during the Korean War. MacArthur kept circling the field at Wake, waiting for Truman to land first. Truman said, 'Look at that—he keeps circling the field waiting for me to land first. He wants me to be there to greet him!' Truman told his pilot to call that plane and tell that son-of-a-bitch to get that plane on the ground."

In simple summary, Dick believed that President Truman was "some kind of Commander-in-Chief!" After he was back in Waukegan, he mailed John copies of several photos to illustrate the facts of their interview.

John McCarthy was quite fond of Dick. He found him to be a most pleasant and accommodating person and was proud to have a photo with Dick taken the day of the interview.

Dick attended "the big event" at 7:00 PM, with 534 Raiders, 250 Makin Raiders relatives, and many dignitaries. Once seated at the annual evening banquet, each guest had a choice of prime rib, salmon, or chicken. General Paul X. Kelly, USMC Commandant (Ret.), and Lieutenant General Emil R. "Buck" Bedard, USMC, were the guest speakers. The generals and surviving Makin Raiders felt honored to have their photographs taken with Dick, the last surviving Raider MOH recipient. In a photo taken during the banquet of the "stalwart group" of six who "could keep historians busy for months if they told their stories," Dick stood tall on the left flank, a head taller than the others. [198]

On Sunday morning, at their 8:00 AM farewell breakfast and brunch, Dick and the Raiders wished each other safe travels and hopes to meet again at future reunions.

November 9. Peggy Faye (Kingery) Lenet Brewington, aged 72, died on Friday. The family contacted Dick, and he went to Alaska to attend her funeral services.

Dick Bush endured.

November 12. Jefferson County had commissioned a sculptor to cast a memorial to honor Kentucky's fifty-six MOH recipients from the Civil War through the Vietnam War

(1961–1975). The six-foot bronze statue representing Army Sergeant John C. Squires, a WWII recipient from Louisville killed in action in Italy, stands on a four-foot base. On Veterans Day Monday, the Kentucky Medal of Honor Memorial was dedicated on a paved semi-circular alcove on the corner of Fifth and Jefferson streets in downtown Louisville, on the grounds of the old Jefferson County Courthouse. A plaque on the east base of the memorial is devoted to Sergeant Squires. The recipients' names are engraved on a bronze plaque on the west base of the sculpture. Marine Corps Corporal Richard E. Bush is at the top of the WWII list.

March 8, 2002. A plaque honoring the 158 Marine Raiders buried in the Punchbowl National Cemetery in Hawaii was dedicated.

August 10. Dick's former brother-in-law, Robert M. Tansey, aged 81, died Saturday at the Ohio Veteran's Home in Sandusky following a lengthy illness. David, Edward, and Thomas, Dick's nephews, buried their father in Maple Grove Cemetery, Vermilion.

September 8–15. Dick attended the 6th Marine Division Reunion, held at the Las Vegas Plaza Hotel. The next month, he went to Ohio, to say a last farewell: another of many reminders to him that sometimes loved ones leave before their time.

October 17, 2002. Mary Tansey VanDyke, aged 74, his closest sister, died on Thursday. After living in Illinois and Vermilion, she had moved to Orange Park, Florida, in 1979, where, for 18 years, she had worked as a dietician for the Orange Park Medical Center. Having returned to Ohio in 2001, she was in Lorain's New Life Hospice Center of St. Joseph following a brief illness. As per her wishes, her three sons had her laid to rest in Maple Grove Cemetery. [199]

When Dick returned to Waukegan, only Christine Russell, Alene Lois Ritter, and Clara Ella Bush, his youngest sisters, survived to remember life with him on the Hiseville farm in Kentucky.

Spring 2003. "We Raiders are becoming an endangered species . . ." *Taps* had been sounded for sixteen Raiders since the previous newsletter was mailed. The USMRA printed an appeal for help to find contact information for 102 lost Raiders from the membership roster. [200]

May 20, 2003. Dick's sister-in-law, Virginia Bush, 64, died in Indianapolis. [201]

✳✳✳

July 2. Dick's friend, PFC Glen Emery Arnold had come home from WWII with a Purple Heart, having been seriously wounded on Guam. The Association had been searching for him as far back as 1981. He was living in Dewey, Oklahoma, in the 1950s—the last time anyone had an address for him. Since 1976, he had been living on an Omaha farm.

Before *The Raider Patch* issue reached Dick in Waukegan, there was no time left to locate Glen, the only C/1 Raider left on the lost listing. Aged 78, he had died on Wednesday at the Veterans Medical Center in Fayetteville, Missouri. Glen's memorial service was held on

Saturday, July 12, and he was buried in Arlington National Cemetery Section 54, between Eisenhower Drive and Halsey Drive, a short walk from the Visitors Center entrance. [202]

✳✳✳

August 24–31. The Striking Sixth Marine Division Reunion was held at St. Petersburg, Florida. At their meetings, the members laid out some activities for 2004. They planned to have their weeklong 2004 reunion at the Millennium Maxwell House Hotel in Nashville, Tennessee, in the last week of September. A tour of historic sites in the city, a tour of the Country Music Hall of Fame, and, of course, an evening at the Grand Ole Opry made the itinerary. That the Marine Corps War Memorial on Arlington Ridge would share its 50th Birthday with the 229th Marine Corps' Birthday on November 10, 2004, was also noted.

September 19–21. MARINE CORPS RECRUIT DEPOT SAN DIEGO—The Marine Raiders of World War II, one of the Corps' most celebrated and legendary units, held their annual reunion aboard the Depot. Place: Red Lion Hanalei Hotel.

The Grim Reaper's Terrible Toll

Dick was invited to spend Memorial Day at the nation's capital to attend the dedication of the national memorial to all who had served during World War II. Veteran associations also looked forward to his attendance at reunions—two in Nashville.

Dick was among the 689 living Raiders the USMRA carried on its membership rolls. The Association had also located another 227 Lost Raiders who had never joined. Since their 2003 San Diego reunion, forty-one members had been reported deceased. Robert Bremkamp, Robert Jernigan, and David T. Rumler, C/1 Raiders, had been added to the Honor Roll since the January–February–March 2004 *Patch* issue had been mailed. [203] Dick's membership status changed before the next *Patch* went to the printer.

By mid-2004, government reports estimated that WWII veterans were dying at a daily rate of 1,056. The number of living MOH recipients had dwindled to 130. Various association newsletters would be making special mention of Dick. For one, he would appear on the Roll of Honor in *The Raider Patch* Report of Fallen Raiders.

May 19, 2004. The Raider 2004 reunion was planned for September 8–12 at the Millennium Maxwell House Hotel in Nashville. "Don't be AWOL" was the persuasion going out. Approximately 250 Sixth Marine Division veterans had registered for their September 26–October 2 reunion at the Millennium Maxwell House Hotel, and over 650 were expected to attend. [204]

Dick had been a member of The Marine Corps Law Enforcement Foundation since 1989. The Foundation was holding its 10th Annual Invitational Gala, beginning on Saturday, June 12, 2004, in Atlantic City, New Jersey. Dick had been attending the event for years. Colonel Harvey C. "Barney" Barnum Jr. (Ret.), Vietnam War MOH recipient, was preparing introductions for Dick and the nine other MOH recipients intending to attend. Only nine introductions were necessary.

Fifty-nine years after he had pulled an enemy grenade into his own body to protect other wounded Marines, Dick went to the Mayo Clinic in Minneapolis for a medical check-up. He had so much metal in his body, an MRI (magnetic resonance imaging) could not be ordered. He returned home to Waukegan.

May 29. On Saturday, the massive crowd in the National Mall, between the Lincoln Memorial and the Washington Monument, listened to the speakers at the National World War II Memorial formal dedication. The sun was bright and the temperatures cool. President George W. Bush addressed the people. At 3:10 PM, his words certainly described Dick, even though the Waukegan recipient was not present to hear them.

"These were the modest sons of a peaceful country, and millions of us are very proud to call them dad. They gave the best years of their lives to the greatest mission their country ever accepted." [205]

June 5. Dick called Army Sergeant Major Jon R. Cavaiani, Vietnam War recipient who had been attending the Law Enforcement Foundation reunions going back to 1986. Regarding the Atlantic City gala, Dick wanted his 60-year-old friend to know his plans.

"I'm coming," he told Jon.

On Sunday, newspapers reminded readers that sixty years had passed since D-Day at Normandy.

MOH Holder Richard E. Bush Dies

June 7, 2004. Richard E. Bush, 79, died in his Waukegan home on Monday. His son, Richard Jr., of Long Grove, Illinois, reported that congestive heart failure was the cause of death.

Dick's obituary was printed in the *Chicago Tribune* on Wednesday, and the "Old Breed" Marine was remembered in towns and cities across the United States. Most newspapers included that he was a WWII veteran; that he had received the Congregational Medal of Honor for valor and five Purple Hearts for injuries received in combat; that he was the loving father of Richard and grandfather of David and Rob; that he was also survived by his longtime and loving companion, Nelda Moyers; and that he had been preceded in death by his daughter, Judith Smith, and his former wife, Stella. In light of Dick's fidelity to the Corps, donations to the Marine Corps Toys for Tots were preferred. [206]

The Chicago Tribune offered an online Guest Book for Memories & Condolences. Steven and Janice Brown, of Little Rock, learned of the death from their future son-in-law, David Smith, and wrote to express their sympathy to all of Dick's friends and family. They had enjoyed learning a little about Dick's life and valor from his loving grandson.

Guy J. Cesario, of CXI Trucking in Melrose Park, left his sincere condolences at the passing of his friend's dad. On Monday, Bill Bruckner, in Milwaukee, sent his deepest sympathies and condolences to the family, recalling how Dick's life had enriched his own in the 1980s. The Guest Book remained permanently available courtesy of Barbara A. Barclay. [207]

The Wednesday *Glasgow Daily Times* printed an obituary and biography on Page 4. The headline in Waukegan's June 10 *The News Sun* read "Medal of Honor Winner Richard Bush Dies." The column reported that Dick was from Waukegan and had always been modest about receiving the nation's highest award for bravery.

The New York Times reported his death on Sunday, June 13, and the *Los Angeles Times*, on June 15. [208] The Thursday, June 17, 2004, *Washington Post* printed a long obituary on Page B05. [209]

Hendersonville, North Carolina, is separated from Glasgow by two state lines, the Great Smoky Mountains and Blue Ridge Divide, and a straight-line distance of only 220 miles. The *Hendersonville Times–News* printed a brief, four-line announcement of Richard's death in its June 17, 2004, publication.

June 10. A visitation was held on Thursday at the Gurnee Funeral Home on 4190 Old Grand Avenue from 5:00 to 8:00 PM.

June 11. Dick's funeral services with full military honors began at 11:00 AM, Friday, at the funeral home. From there, the procession carried him six miles south to Ascension Catholic Cemetery on 1920 Buckley Road in Libertyville. His remains were laid to rest in Section 7, Block 10, Lot 63, Grave 7, on the north side of Buckley Road and to the right of the entrance. The landscaping at the site, with interspaced bushes and monuments, forms a cross. Stella's and Judy's graves in Block 33 are twenty-three rows to the east.

Dick's grave is marked with a simple, flat, granite stone with gold embossed lettering. A Christian cross is in the upper left corner and the Marine MOH symbol is in the upper right corner. His grave is easy to locate in front and to the right of the Virgin Mary statue standing on a large Immaculate Heart with the engraving, I AM THE IMMACULATE CONCEPTION.

Learning of his death, many recalled conversations they had had with him. Barbara Barclay and Pat and Linda Carry were among those who would remember him over the years, thank him for his bravery, and wish him heavenly peace.

June 12. On Saturday, Barney Barnum introduced the nine MOH recipients at the Law Enforcement Foundation gala. Then he announced Dick's death. "One of our recipients who has been with us for the past 15 years passed away—Marine Corporal Richard E. Bush." He asked the recipients to stand at attention while everyone paused for a moment to remember Dick and his outstanding service to the nation. [210]

"Semper Fidelis Richard, from all of us." John McCarthy was ready to send the April–May–June 2004 *Patch* issue to the printer. He had to find a space for the headline: **Last Raider MOH Recipient Passes**. In a box at the bottom of Page 22, he wrote the Notice.

Word just received at press time of the Patch: "He was a gentleman, a Marine, and a Raider and was extremely well liked by all who had the privilege to know him. He was a loving father and grandfather. He is survived by his longtime and loving companion, Nelda Moyers."

John thought that donations to the Corps' Toys for Tots Program in Richard's memory would be appropriate. He promised that the next *Patch* issue would "offer a feature with details on the life of this great Raider Marine."

June 18. Illinois State Senator Terry Link (D) was saddened to learn of Dick's death in Waukegan. He and all the members of the Senate attending the 93rd General Assembly recognized that the old Marine's passing would be deeply felt, especially by his son, Richard (Karen) Bush; his two grandsons, David and Rob; and his longtime and loving companion, Nelda Moyers. The Senate resolved to express their deep sense of loss and wishes to extend their sincere condolences to Dick's family and friends. Agreeing that a suitable copy of the resolution should be presented to the family as an expression of their deepest sympathy, they filed a Memorial for Richard E. Bush with the Secretary. State Resolution 0596 was adopted on July 2.

"May he rest in peace." The *Striking Sixth Newsletter* editor notified readers of Dick's death in the Spring/Summer 2004 publication. The MOH recipient was one of their best-deserved special mentions. All in the Sixth Marine Division Association extended their sympathy to his family and friends. They had lost one of their best. "Bush, C-1-4, corporal, didn't have the advantage of a lifetime's written work to be his valediction, just his family and friends and the Marine Corps." [211]

September 2004. The autumn *Patch* included A Special Tribute to a Special Raider, recognizing Richard Bush as the PRIDE OF THE RAIDER MARINES. He had brought pride and honor to the Association. John McCarthy wrote of interviewing Dick at the 2001 D.C. reunion. A recent photo of "Our Hero" appeared over a column copy of his MOH Citation. John understood what Dick's passing would mean to the living Raiders.

"We'll all miss him." He summed up the tribute in a few meaningful words. "He was the genuine article." [212]

April 27, 2005. Dick's home sold by grant deed. The property was free of debt and had no legal claims against it.

Lasting Tributes

2007. Since his death, Dick has been remembered in various places. The Marine Corps Coordinating Council of Kentucky (MCCCK) was restructured from its 1991 parent charitable organization and includes Dick among the thirteen Kentucky Legends. [213]

Young Marine officers at The Basic School in Quantico walked along the sidewalks and read the standing 6th Marine Division Medal of Honor Recipients bronze marker. The Okinawa bronze sat between O'Bannon Hall and Heywood Hall. In alphabetical order, Dick's name is at the top of the six names—five Marines and one Navy corpsman—of those who had earned the Medal in the last WWII battle.

OKINAWA
SEMPER FIDELIS
DEDICATED
TO THE
6TH MARINE DIVISION
MEDAL OF HONOR
RECIPIENTS
WORLD WAR II

April 16, 2008. Wednesday was the sixty-third anniversary of Dick's MOH actions on Okinawa. The Leasing News website of Saratoga, California, printed his Citation in its *This Day in American History* article. [214]

November 11. Waukegan includes Dick among its Notable People, along with Otto Graham, Pro Football Hall of Fame quarterback for the Cleveland *Browns*, and Comedian Jack Benny, who had entertained the Marine Raider battalions on the AES-Guadalcanal radio. Another MOH recipient with ties to Waukegan is also lauded in the city on Memorial and Veterans Day holidays.

Union Army Private Orion Perseus Howe, a severely wounded, 14-year-old Civil War drummer boy, had earned his Medal at Vicksburg on May 19, 1863, two years after he had joined Company C, 55th Illinois Volunteer Regiment. On Veterans Day 2006, a diminutive bronze statue of Private Howe was unveiled at Waukegan's new Veterans Memorial Plaza, joining the WWI Dough Boy statue.

Dick received a permanent tribute on Veterans Day Tuesday, 2008, forever gaining a spot in Waukegan's history. The city hosted its annual Veterans Day Parade, starting downtown at Grand Avenue and Genesee Street at 10:30 AM. The parade passed in front of City Hall and the County Courthouse, making its way southwest to the Veterans Plaza at the corner of Washington and S. West streets.

The Plaza is a beautiful brick terrace butting up against the Waukegan River and Washington Park, where the American Legion Homer Dahringer Post 281 building was located before moving down to W. Water Street. The patriotic crowd gathered at 11:10 AM for a moment of silence and rifle salute, followed by the unveiling of a new, thirteen-foot bronze flag wall sculpture.

A new bronze plaque honoring Marine Richard E. Bush was also dedicated. The commemorative plaque lies in a large planter, above large stones taken from the old Legion Post. People who knew Dick watched the unveiling and spoke fondly of him, remembering his humble nature and popularity among younger Marines. [215]

November 11, 2009. The City of Glasgow has had its own website since 1995. Dick Bush and Diane Sawyer, journalist and TV news host, are included among its twenty-two notable natives. In 2009, nearly 14,028 residents called Glasgow home. The city, rich in military history, wanted to honor all Glasgow and Barren County citizens, living and deceased, who had served in the Armed Forces.

Beulah C. Nunn Park is on the west corner of the South Public Square and W. Washington Street, where the First Christian Church once stood—across the street from the Court House back door. The park is a quiet place, a perfect location for a monument. Glasgow dedicated the Veterans Wall of Honor on Veterans Day in the park.

The wall, honoring the men and women who fought for the country and the character and courage they exemplified, holds 1,455 black plaques. Richard E. Bush and William L. Day both are remembered with distinct Medal of Honor plaques. [216]

Spring 2010. The *Striking Sixth* newsletter featured Okinawa: 65 years ago. Laura Lacey, the Division historian, wrote an article entitled Recognition Continues To Grow of Marines' Role in the Pacific. The Sixth Marine Division had provided its share of recognized heroes, men like Richard Bush and three other recipients who inspire the current generation of Marines with their valor. [217]

James Chance Wilson was looking through *The Striking Sixth* website and saw a picture of Dick. He was reminded that his grandfather, CPL James Wilson, had been a BAR man who had survived multiple climbs up Sugar Loaf Hill and was a good friend of the MOH recipient. On April 1, 2010, his 25th birthday, he wrote to Bill Pierce, Public Relations, to let him know he had kept the note Dick had signed to his grandfather. [218]

March 15, 2012. Louisville's WDRB 41 radio broadcast the news on Thursday. A bronze plaque listing the names of Kentucky's sixty MOH recipients was to hang in the Capitol Rotunda opposite the Abraham Lincoln statue. Representative Tanya Pullin had sponsored legislation in 2011, calling for the plaque's creation. Governor Steve Beshear joined lawmakers and veterans' groups from across the Commonwealth to unveil the plaque. Three of the state's five living MOH recipients attended the ceremony: Army PFC Ernest E. West, Korean War, Army Staff Sergeant Don Jenkins, Vietnam, and USMC Sergeant Dakota Meyer, Afghanistan

War. Army Private Wilburn Kirby Ross, World War II, and Army Sergeant First Class Gary Lee Littrell, Vietnam, were unable to attend.

In two columns under the three service Medals and their blue ribbons, the ornate plaque bears the heroes' names. Seventeen are from the Civil War, including the only woman to have ever earned the Medal. Dr. Mary Edwards Walker, a combat surgeon who had entered medical service at Louisville, had not been in the military, but the officers who had served with her insisted that she had served with valor and had earned the Medal. [219]

The Medal had been earned by twelve men during the Indian Campaigns, one of whom was First Sergeant William Day, from Glasgow; three during Peacetime, three during Wars of American Expansion, including the Spanish–American War; and one during World War I. Dick's name on the plaque was among the eight from World War II. Seven Kentuckians had earned the Medal during the Korean War, eight during the Vietnam War, and one from the Iraq and Afghanistan wars.

Governor Beshear spoke at the dedication. "This symbol of their sacrifice and bravery," he said, "can now be shared with the thousands of Capitol visitors, who can pay their respects and acknowledge the amazing achievements of these individuals." [220]

Still Honored at Raider Reunions

August 13–18, 2013. MARSOC Commander Major General Mark A. Clark invited the WWII Marine Raiders to hold their annual reunion at the Hilton Wilmington Riverside, North Carolina. Andrew Koehler, Honorary 3d Battalion Raider, president of the Marine Raider Association, accepted the invitation. PFC Joseph Harrison, H/2, Banning, California, PFC Kenneth H. "Mudhole" Merrell, B/2, Phoenix, and PFC Charles H. "Chuck" Meachem Sr., K/3, Gig Harbor, Washington, former Raider Association president and co-founder of the U.S. Marine Raider Foundation, attended. [221]

No matter how many years had passed since the Pacific Island battles, the Raiders made it evident that their Marine brothers were never far from their minds.

"There's been a strong bond between us all because of what we went through," Mudhole said. "We have a lot to be thankful for. All of us. And the ones we left behind, we've never forgotten them."

"You could depend on your foxhole buddy. That was the main thing," Joe Harrison told the reporter. "The guys would give their lives for each other."

Chuck Meachem had more to say about that. "You lay in that old foxhole on a muddy rainy night, bullets flying with Jap planes coming over and dropping bombs. You knew the guy on the left-hand side of you and the right-hand side of you. They would die for you, and they knew that's exactly what you would do for them."

August 6–10, 2014. Seventy years had passed since the original Raiders had been disbanded and the name was dropped from unit designations. On Wednesday, Commandant of the Marine Corps General James F. Amos released a proclamation declaring that subordinate U.S.M.C. Forces, Special Operations Command (MARSOC) commands would be officially renamed and integrate the Marine *Raider* nickname into their titles: like Marine Raider Battalion and Marine Raider Group. MARSOC had long embraced the Marine Raider moniker and fought hard to adopt the name.

"Mudhole" Merrill, 90, a surviving Carlson's Raider, was present. "It made me cry, actually," he said, "because of what it meant to me and the Raiders still alive. It means our legacy will live on for as long as there's a United States."

As part of their annual reunion, eighteen old Raiders were at Shepherd Field aboard MCRD San Diego on Friday, August 8, during the Company D, 1st Recruit Training Battalion, Recruit Training Regiment graduation ceremony. Lieutenant Colonel Jack R. Christensen, retired Dog Company, 1st Raiders, was participating in a reunion for the first time. "It's always a good feeling," he said, "to be around Marines." [222]

That sentiment was felt by the dozens of living original Raiders: among them were Joe Harrison; Harold W. Berg, B/1, Peoria, Illinois; Buck L. Daley, A/4, Tallahassee; Dr. Byron H. Eller, C/1, Loma Linda, California; Frank J. Guidone, A/1, Vista, California; Emmitt Hays, HQ/1, Palos Hills, Illinois; Mel Heckt, A/1, Minneapolis; Chuck H. Meacham Sr., K/3; Archibald B. "Archie" Rackerby, K/3, Rough and Ready, California; Jack B. Shaffer, HQ/4, Largo, Florida; and Dick Vana, Des Plaines, Illinois.

April 16–18, 2015. Garland (Gerold) R. Carter, E/1, Theodore A. Gaskin, B/1, Charles E. Pulford, E/1, Jack Richardson, D/1, and Jim "Horse Collar" Smith, HQ/1, had been heroes, men to emulate. They viewed themselves not as heroes but as public servants. The youngest of the five 1st Raider Battalion veterans was 89 years old when they gathered aboard MCB Quantico for the 69th anniversary reunion since WWII's end.

They toured the Marine Corps Museum and Raider Hall and gathered together for several meals. Colonel David Edson, grandson of their first commanding officer, Merritt "Red Mike" Edson, attended the closing banquet. Lieutenant General Kenneth Glueck Jr. was the evening's guest of honor. During his speech, he read the names of the ten 1st Raiders who had died in the last year. The assembly observed a solemn moment of silence. Other sobering moments throughout the evening included Jack and "Horse Collar" referring to the reunion as their "final one." [223]

June 19. On Friday, Harold W. Berg, 89, Chuck Meacham Sr., 89, and "Mudhole" Merrill, 91, felt honored to attend the Camp Lejeune ceremony when the MARSOC Marines unfurled their new colors bearing the historic "Raiders" name.

August 26–30. Eight surviving World War II Raiders and their families celebrated Raider history at their annual reunion in San Antonio. Jack Christensen and "Mudhole" Merrill attended. MARSOC Raiders, celebrating their own ninth anniversary, traveled far and wide to attend.

An active duty MARSOC Raider had whittled a walking stick, including ornate WWII Raider and MARSOC insignias in the design. He donated the staff to the U.S. Marine Raider Association and Foundation for any Raider needing assistance while walking. Jack Christensen made good use of the handmade staff on trips to Lackland Air Force Base and The National Museum of the Pacific War.

Major General Joseph L. Osterman, MARSOC commander, and Sergeant Major John W. Scott, MARSOC senior enlisted advisor, attended the final night formal banquet. Staff Sergeant Brandan Lee Joseph Taylor, graduate of MARSOC's first Individual Training Course iteration, was one of the active-duty Marines invited to the Raider reunion and had been asked to speak during the dinner. He had sustained severe back, spine, and knee injuries during a winter 2014 helicopter raid in Afghanistan, including an eight-mile hike to a village using night-vision goggles. He was in San Antonio learning to walk and run with exoskeletal orthosis leg braces. He had never planned on speaking.

"But, I felt I owed them an answer on how proud we are, as MARSOC Marines, to earn the title of Marine Raider," he explained. "I spoke to them about what an honor it is to carry their legacy on with the future generation of Raiders from MARSOC." [224]

March 29, 2016. On Tuesday, Richard T. "Dick" Vana, 92, one of the last living WWII Raiders to have been a close friend of Dick Bush, died in Des Plaines. He had been one of the first members of the Mid-West Chapter when they met in Waukegan in April 1958 and had teamed up with the MOH recipient to organize the October 1995 mini-reunion in Chicago.

In the Senate's first session of the 110th Congress, on Friday, September 28, 2007, Elizabeth Dole had risen in order to recognize and honor the heroism of Dick Vana and C. Stuart "Uppy" Upchurch for their selfless and courageous actions in rescuing Private Richey during the enemy mortar attack.

Dick had been interviewed about his WWII experiences a number of times in his later years. Paul R. Meincke, of the Veterans History Project, American Folklife Center, met with him for an oral history interview and videotaping on May 26, 2004. [225] Dick had distinct memories, some lighthearted and some difficult. The interview was humorous, emotional, and tearful. He kept a handkerchief in hand to wipe away tears.

Neil O'Shea conducted an interview at the Niles Public Library on July 9, 2008, as part of the Legacy of Our Fathers Project. Dick provided Neil a copy of Dick Bush's Tribute in the autumn 2004 *Raider Patch*. [226] Jody Kopsky, Honor Flight Chicago Volunteer, interviewed Dick on August 3, 2013, in preparation of the all-expense-paid Honor Flight scheduled for June 30, 2015, to visit the Washington, D.C., WWII Memorial. Dick had looked forward to the trip and was glad to have seen the memorial. [227]

Some of the most vivid images held in his mind had occurred during his ninety-nine straight days on Okinawa. Dick relished in telling tales of Sergeant Ernest Ashworth Horsfall (died July 22, 1997), C. Stuart "Uppy" Upchurch Sr. (died July 24, 2010), John M. "Jack" Thomas, C/1, and Father Redmond. He could not fully comprehend why he had survived the battles and others in B/1/4 had died, but accepted God's hands in all things. He had seen many men die, seemingly almost daily, officers and enlisted grunts, so many of them teenagers, and all of them deserving medals for valor.

In his thoughts, Dick had kept 1stLt Thad N. Dodds, killed by an enemy bullet through the mouth on April 2, 1945. Private Frank Giglio, 18, and Pvt Chester Stanley Pas, 19, were KIA on April 14. Six were killed on April 15: 1stLt William Edward Quirk, 24, CPL Fred Arrowsmith, Pvt Roy Godwin, CPL Elroy Burton Tuttle, 18, PFC Albert Henry Dreisewerd, 24, and Pvt Carl Kaercher Jr., 18. PFC Felix Edwin Ezell, 18, was KIA on April 17. Corporal Dean Wilson Wallace, 21, and PFC Gilbert A. Brusman, 24, died on May 20. The next two days were bad: CPL James Leroy "Jimmy" Harpst, 18, PFC Ward Riker Bowers, 21, PFC Benjamin T. McBurney, 22, PFC Ira Joseph Morgan, 20, Pvt Melvin James Jennings, 19, and Pvt Robert Joseph McGee Jr., 16, all died on May 21; 2dLt William Parr Fisher, 21, PFC James Alexander Cockrum, 19, (DOW), PFC Charles Richard "Dick" Hamilton, 19, and PFC Calvin Lee Loudin, 18, were KIA on May 22. PFC George William Bannerman Jr., 22, was KIA, and Sergeant Eugene Leonus Conrad, 25, DOW on May 23. Gunnery Sergeant William Arthur Raynes, 23, was KIA on May 25, and Pvt Edward Joseph Lamberson, 25, was KIA on May 26.

"Red" was killed on June 1; PFC William Owens Betz, 23, June 4; 2dLt Charles Evan McBride and PFC Robert James "Bobby" Banker, 19, on June 6; CPL Robert Evers, 27, Pvt Glen Eugene Brinson, 27, Pvt Charles Curcuro, 29, and Pvt Leo Joseph McNulty, 29, on June 9; 2dLt William Neilson Van Aman, 23, June 10; PFC Wellington John Hall, 26, and PFC Robert George Connell, 18, DOW on June 11; Private Eugene Edward Allen, 18, June 12; Private Ralph Glorinore Fiore, 18, June 19; and CPL Edward Henry Dunham, 22, on June 23, 1945.

Of one thing Dick Vana had had no doubt. When he spoke of the bond Marines in combat felt for each other, he was speaking for generations of Marines across all wars.

"They were just a great bunch of guys. That was probably the most exciting part about the whole experience, was the, was the guys we shared together, you know. It was . . . we were really blood brothers, without any kidding. You know they'd, they'd risk their lives for you, and, I would for them. They knew that. And, and it was done time and time again."

April 4, 2016. Sergeant John Charlton Holladay, 31, Company B, 1st Marine Raiders, had been one of those great guys. A Japanese sniper had killed him during the battle at Bairoko Harbor, New Georgia Island, on July 20, 1943. He was hastily buried and Father Redmond said prayers over his grave. His remains were not recovered when the Raider Battalions departed the island at the end of August. Seventy-two years passed. His sister still hoped and nine nieces and nephews wondered. On February 24, 2015, a New Georgia farmer discovered the remains. DNA technology properly identified the Raider on July 30, 2015. Sergeant Holladay was returned to his hometown and laid to rest with military honors on his birthday in Florence National Cemetery, South Carolina.

July 19–24, 2016. The Marine Corps remembers to honor Dick Bush and the WWII Raiders. MARSOC Commander Major General Joseph L. Osterman invited the WWII Marine Raiders to the New Raider Ten Year Celebration and Change of Command at Camp Lejeune. The event was broadcast as the U.S. Marine Raider To Raider Reunion in Wilmington, North Carolina. On Thursday, there was a joint "Honor the Fallen" Ceremony for Raiders. Four original WWII Raiders attended the Celebration: Archie Rackerby, Jack Shaffer, 91, Joe Harrison, 93, and "Mudhole" Merrill. On Friday, Major General Osterman unveiled the WWII Raider Memorial which joined the MARSOC fallen Raider Memorial on the quarterdeck of MARSOC Headquarters. On Saturday, the Marine Raider Association and Foundation presided over the Marine Raider Gala/ Ball/Banquet at the Hilton Wilmington Riverside, the pinnacle event of the weekend. [228]

Living out the Raider Ethos, Seeking No Credit

Dick Bush had carried himself with a humble kind of pride—more about having been a Marine and a Raider, than it was about his Medal of Honor. His comrades carry themselves with the same dignity, even if it is with the aid of a cane, a walker, or a wheel chair.

The last among the original surviving Marine Raiders still attend reunions and celebrate sad and inspirational days. Darrell "Sarge" Ault Loveland, 93, 2/C, passed away on Wednesday, December 21, 2016, at his home in Brigham City, Utah. James "Horse Collar" Smith, 97, a member of the 1st Raider Battalion, was welcomed to Marine Corps Base Quantico's Raider Hall Martial Arts Center of Excellence on March 6, 2017, to speak with Marine Corps Embassy Security Group Marines. Two weeks later, Joseph J. Accardo, 95, an Edson Raider and Marine through and through, passed away on March 19, 2017.

Edson's Raiders held a reunion May 5–7, 2017, in Quantico, seventy-five years after the battalion of volunteers had formed up. Seven attended with family and friends.

The U.S. Marine Raider Association planned to hold their annual reunion in San Diego, August 9–11, 2017. The MARSOC Foundation was going to sponsor all WWII Raiders and companions who wanted to attend. The Raiders, widows, families, and friends were invited to reserve accommodations at the Town and Country Resort. The theme was to be in the "whimsical USO style" of the 1940s. The Raider Dinner and Dance was to feature the Lindy Sisters and Swing Dancers and DJ Misha's Big Band sounds.

Harold Berg, 91, of Peoria, Illinois, was 17 years old when he signed up for the Marines in 1942. He served in Company B, Edson's 1st Raiders. He won't be taking his wife of seventy-one years to any more reunions. Lorraine Berg, 89, died on October 27, 2016. When he is interviewed about being a WWII hero, he is firm in his reply. And his thoughts are echoes of Dick Bush and all the Raiders who came home.

"We know where the real heroes are. They are buried in areas all over the Pacific. Those are the real heroes." [229]

CHAPTER 22

That Certain Something

✳✳✳

"That certain *something* that seems to weld men together prevailed." [1]

— Staff Sergeant Donald M. Griffith, USMC, former POW

Who jumps on a grenade? Bravery is imbedded in personal character. Marines new to combat and seasoned veterans have jumped on grenades; doing so cannot be explained as an inexperienced infantryman's act. Men of varying ages have cradled grenades, so it does not reflect youth—not a matter of being too young to know better. Moreover, race, ethnicity, religion, and rank do not determine a man's willingness to protect others from shrapnel.

The men who hurled themselves onto grenades made first and lasting impressions across their lifetimes. Although often described as having been common, ordinary, and average men, they were special in many ways. The actions they demonstrated in combat reflected ingrained, personal qualities, certain traits, evident across their lifetimes, starting in childhood.

To a man, they had experienced early personal and physical challenges. They had demonstrated a pattern of putting themselves into challenging situations in which brave actions were a likely eventuality. Driven to overcome personal or perceived shortcomings, they sought to better themselves and their situations—to excel at whatever they did. They possessed resilience to adversity, contending with hardships rather than withdrawing from or submitting to them. Intensely competitive with others and within themselves, they tended to be direct in expressing thoughts, standing up for what they believed to be right, even to the point of being confrontative, always willing to fight for their own beliefs. A common tendency among them was an inclination to risk and to volunteer to go into harm's way.

As boys, they preferred action over contemplation, wanting to be in and at the forefront of the action. They did more than asked, were quick to act, acted with their own initiative when under duress, continued to push when wanting something, and did "whatever it takes" to achieve an objective. They appeared to be single-minded when an objective was in mind, accepting tasks and missions with a selfless regard for outcome. They made a difference for others.

Growing up, they were introduced to a strong spiritual or moral fabric that resulted in a sense of duty and loyalty. An innate and vigorous spirit became a distinctive characteristic of their valor and inspired others to go beyond expectations. *Esprit* came naturally.

One attribute stands out among the Marines who cradled grenades to protect comrades—seeking affiliation, which is the condition of connection, allegiance, or association. These men demonstrated both the desire to have associations with others and an ease of being amid others. They preferred the company of boys and men like themselves. Few, if any, are remembered as having been "a loner." From this preference to associate with others is affiliation derived. In a sense, it was a belonging these men sought.

WHY JUMP ON A GRENADE? Marines do not jump on grenades to prove their bravery or to appear heroic. They do not jump on grenades when alone. When a grenade lands in a lone Marine's foxhole, natural instincts take over. He either vacates the position, diving out of the hole, or he tries to throw the grenade back in the direction from which it came. Unable to do either, he might just as likely keep fighting until the detonation.

Sergeant William G. Harrell is an example. His foxhole buddy on Iwo Jima had gone to the rear to re-arm. The enemy launched a nighttime counterattack. An enemy grenade rolled into the foxhole and exploded, fracturing his thigh, and blowing off his left hand. His companion returned, joined the fight, and was wounded. Sergeant Harrell ordered him back to a safe place and stayed on the defensive perimeter alone. Exhausted and bleeding profusely, two more enemy soldiers charged at him. He shot and killed one with his pistol. The other crouching soldier dropped a grenade near his head. Sergeant Harrell grabbed the sputtering Nambu grenade with his good hand, painfully pushed it toward the assailant, and watched him obliterated in the explosion. Sergeant Harrell was evacuated at dawn. His right hand had been severed.

Marines only jump on hostile grenades when they are in the company of fellow Marines. The seventy men from the Second Nicaraguan War to Iraq and Afghanistan listed in the first pages of this book considered the presence of other Marines likely to be injured or killed in the proximity of a grenade's detonation, overcame their own instinct for self-preservation, and quickly decided in the seconds between recognition of the grenade and its explosion to cover the device with their own bodies. This selfless act is performed for one reason. The eleven who survived their wounds, maybe speaking for those who sacrificed their lives, had the same answer when asked the question.

James Bradley, author of *Flags of Our Fathers*, asked Jack Lucas why he had jumped on two grenades. The Marine veteran of Iwo Jima responded unhesitatingly.

"To save my buddies." [2]

Cradling a grenade to protect others is an extraordinary action. Yet, had they been in different circumstances, the men who jumped on grenades might just as likely charged headlong into fierce machine-gun fire or dived an airplane into the blazing turret of a ship's anti-aircraft guns to safeguard companions.

Private Raymond "Mike" Clausen, MOH recipient from Vietnam, explained his racing across a mine field to rescue other Marines in 1970. "I did it because there were troops out in the field that needed help getting out—brother Marines, if you want to call them that. We were all the same, all brothers." [3]

The readiness to give up one's life to save a buddy and ensure that others might live demonstrates a deep capacity for affiliation, camaraderie, and compassion.

"If something happens to me, these jokers will take care of me." [4]

Affiliation and esprit de corps bind Marines to one another across generations and wars. America's enemies recognize this fact. Our other Armed Service branches acknowledge it—sometimes respectfully, other times begrudgingly.

Army psychiatrist Major William F. Mayer studied the records of over 4,000 returning Americans prisoners of war who had survived three years of captivity in twelve separate North Korean POW camps. The number of repatriated soldiers was clearly fewer than the number known to have been captured. Of the 7,000 U.S. servicemen believed to have been captured, a lot of men had died. [5]

"As a matter of fact, out of every ten men captured, approximately four died in captivity. Four out of ten. Thirty-eight percent (38%) to be precise."

The American experience in communist camps had been significantly different from the prisoner behavior in Japanese and German POW camps in World War II. So different that Colonel Franklin Brooke Nihart, USMC, wrote Six Articles of Conduct at Marine Corps Headquarters in summer 1955. From this work, President Dwight D. Eisenhower issued Executive Order 10631 on August 17, 1955, establishing the Code of Conduct for all servicemen and women in combat and captivity circumstances.

Major Mayer travelled and gave speeches about the POW findings and the need for the Code of Conduct. He addressed the U.S. Army Chaplain School in Fort Slocum, New York, in February 1957 and the Freedom Forum, in Searcy, Arkansas, on April 15, 1957. After his talk at Fort Slocum, a chaplain in the audience asked a question about the Marines who had been returned to military control after being held as POWs. Major Mayer had noted that the Marines were a significant group from the standpoint of size, because, statistically, more of them had survived the camps than had Army soldiers and other captured UN troops.

In evidence was a complete roster of Marines captured in Korea, by name, rank, unit, and date. A total of 221 USMC officers and enlisted men had been captured. Of these POWs, 194 (87.7%) were returned to military control, twenty-one (9.5%) had died in captivity, and six (2.7%) were presumed dead. A little more than one out of ten Marines, twelve percent (12%), is quite different than four out of ten (38%) and deserved explanation.

Major Mayer had observed returned soldiers sitting on the Tokyo Army Hospital ward not talking to each other. That observation was repeated time and time again. No matter the camps men had been kept in, the reports were consistent. The wary soldiers seemed to want nothing to do with each other. There had been no *buddy system* among them while in captivity.

In contrast, the Army psychiatrist believed that Marines as a group had conducted themselves extremely well. They tended to have been troublesome to their captors. They had the temerity to resist any indoctrination, seemed stubbornly unbending to communist methods, and were most likely to have been segregated with the five percent (5%) of POWs held in the reactionary camps. Those were special camps for the Americans who would "not be nice" and go along with the communist brain washing efforts. The Marines had counted on each other, believing "if something happens to me, these jokers will take care of me." For Major Mayer, it came down to the discipline and morale and esprit and the attitude the Corps instilled in its members. In short, they had measured up.

"For this they deserve greatest admiration and credit."

Staff Sergeant Donald Marcel Griffith from Northwood, Ohio, was 23 years old when he was seriously wounded and captured on December 2, 1950. He was one of eight 5th Marines taken prisoner during the Chosin Reservoir breakout. Three of them died. Sergeant Griffith spent thirty-three months as a prisoner of the Chinese and North Korean Communists. He attributed the triumph of the 151 enlisted Marines who survived the POW camps to have resulted from the bond buddies establish. "That certain something that seems to weld men together prevailed more among the Marine POWs than it did with the other captured UN Troops."

That certain something, that bond, springs from affiliation.

Of the sixteen Marines who pulled grenades to their bodies to save comrades in the Korean War, Hector Albert Cafferata Jr., Duane Edgar Dewey, Robert Sidney Kennemore, and Robert Ernest Simanek recuperated from their wounds and came home. Allan Jay Kellogg Jr. was the only Marine of the twenty-three who jumped on grenades in the Vietnam War to survive. Corporal William Kyle Carpenter, 21, earned a Medal of Honor in Marjah, Helmand Province, Afghanistan, on November 21, 2010, throwing himself in front of a grenade to protect a Marine lance corporal.

Robert Sidney Kennemore, 68, died on April 26, 1989, and Hector Albert Cafferata Jr., 86, died on April 12, 2016. As of this writing, Duane E. Dewey, 85, Robert E. Simanek, 87, Allan J. Kellogg, 73, and Kyle Carpenter, 27, continue to live productively in their communities.

The lives of these six can teach many lessons about camaraderie, spirit, and resilience.

CHAPTER 1. Introduction

1. Native American shaman and author.
2. Medal of Honor Citations are available for the 3,498 recipients in all service branches. Initially, the official records were maintained in government archives and sporadically printed. In 1973, the U.S. Senate ordered that the Citations be compiled together and printed in a book, resulting in the first volume of *Committee on Veterans' Affairs, U.S. Senate, Medal of Honor Recipients: 1863–1973*, Washington, D.C.: Government Printing Office, 1973. The book was updated and reprinted in 1979. Heidi M. Peters, Information Research Specialist, compiled a report current to November 6, 2014, that covered additions and changes to the list of Medal recipients since the release of the committee print. *Medal of Honor Recipients: 1979–2014*, Congressional Research Service, December 2, 2014. The eighteen recipients who earned awards in Somalia, Afghanistan, and Iraq were included. Since that report, five additional Medals of Honor have been awarded.
3. Various family details have been derived from Missouri State Board of Health Bureau of Vital Statistics Death Certificates.
4. One source remembered that George was orphaned when both his parents were killed in a car accident.
5. Most United States Census data cited throughout this text was accessed from the *FamilySearch* site at FamilySearch.org.
6. Edna would live the longest, staying around Labadie, and becoming the family historian. She passed away at age 93, on January 8, 2004.
7. Emmett Becker graciously provided this information, in a phone conversation, September 25, 2005. A resident of Labadie and former Commander of American Legion Post 565, he was a boyhood friend of George Phillips. Tammy Kuddes and Lisa Coffman, School District of Washington, Missouri, kindly referred this author to Mr. Becker.
8. Frank McLean, Yakima Valley Genealogical Society, provided copies of Lois' obituary, death notice, and Shaw & Sons Funeral Home record in correspondence on Monday, May 22, 2017. Lester Phillips, 59, died January 1, 1976. Lois Lorraine Phillips, 57, died on November 3, 1978.
9. Frank Richard Phillips died in Pasco, Washington, on May 30, 1966, due to car accident while traveling back from Moses Lake, Washington, where he was visiting his brother Lester Phillips. Pasco Crash Kills Idaho Passenger. Washington, *Walla Walla Union–Bulletin*, Tuesday, May 31, 1966, Page 1.
10. Services for Young Mother of Two. Idaho, *Gooding Leader*, Thursday, October 25, 1944.
11. Further details of Private Phillips service are described in James H. Hallas, *Uncommon Valor on Iwo Jima: The Story of the Medal of Honor Recipients in the Marine Corps' Bloodiest Battle of WWII*, pp. 288–302.
12. Don Morfe's photograph of the monument can be viewed at findagrave.com/cgi-bin/fg.cgi?page=pv&GRid=6403426&PIpi=388305.
13. Robert E. "Bob" McLanahan died on June 1, 2003.
14. Ernie Pyle. *Brave Men*, 1944.
15. *The Raider Patch*, United States Marine Raider Association, September 1989, Page 9.
16. Philip Caputo. *A Rumor of War*. New York: Henry Holt and Company, 1977, p. 223–24.
17. *The Raider Patch*, March 1983, Page 3.
18. USMC Assistant Commandant, in Jon T. Hoffman, *Once a Legend*, Foreword, p xii.

CHAPTER 2. Given In Full Measure

1. "Fortis Cadere, Cadere Non Potest."
2. Derived from history.army.mil/moh, June 26, 2016. As of that date, seventy-six recipients remained living.
3. Derived from Marine Corps History Division, mcu.usmc.mil/historydivision/Pages/Who's%20Who/V-X/willis_jh.aspx.
4. *Once a Legend*, pp 208–209.
5. In the chapters ahead, unless otherwise noted, all exchanges with family members and other contributers were by correspondence.

CHAPTER 3. A Medal Easier To Win Than To Wear

1. *A Farewell to Arms*. New York: Charles Scribner's Sons, 1929, p. 94.
2. Joan A. Inabinet and L. Glen Inabinet. *A History of Kershaw County, South Carolina*. Columbia, SC: The University of South Carolina Press, 2010. Stephen Truesdell provided this reference in correspondence, Monday, December 7, 2015. The Truesdells have a prominent place in the history.
3. Details of the Truesdale ancestry are inconsistently recorded in various genealogies and available records. This adaptation is derived from rootsweb.ancestry.com/~sclancas/bios/truesdell_3.htm and geni.com/people/John-Truesdale/6000000006775424611. Confirmed in materials provided by Donna Truesdell, January 7, 2016. A diagram of the family generations is at the end of this chapter.
4. Which brother, James or John III, was the older of the two varies depending on the genealogy referenced. James is more often cited as the older brother.
5. Kershaw County Wills III A 192.
6. The Truesdale/Truesdell/Truesdel/Trudell surname seems to have randomly changed on birth, marriage, land transfer, and death records within and down through the generations. For simplicity sake, here the Truesdale name is continued until Donald Truesdale officially changed his name to Truesdell.
7. Which of John Henry Truesdale's children were born to Druscilla or Matilda varies depending on the genealogy referenced.
8. Lancaster County, SC, Land Records and Deeds: File R-503, 1858.
9. Family genealogies and Official Confederate Records/Rosters sometimes vary regarding service years and units.
10. Obituary. Camden Chronicle, Friday, August 15, 1919.
11. Retrieved from researchonline.net/cemetery/archive/conf_obits_pg4.pdf.
12. "South Carolina Civil War Service Records of Confederate Soldiers, 1861–1865." Database. FamilySearch. http://FamilySearch.org: accessed 2015. From "Compiled Service Records of Confederate Soldiers Who Served in Organizations from the State of South Carolina." Database. Fold3.com. http://www.fold3.com:n.d. Citing NARA microfilm publication M267. Washington, D.C.: National Archives and Records Administration, 1959.
13. Derived from tribalpages.com/tribe/familytree?uid=researchlady&surname=Truesdale.
14. Derived from the roster at sciway3.net/sc-reserves/jr/rg03sccoi.html.
15. Donna Truesdell provided most of the family history details, including photographs, starting with Zachariah and Mittie Truesdale, November 8, 2015–February 13, 2016. She kept in mind Robert Lawrence's non-fiction *They Were Strong And True*, Viking

Press, 1940, that she used in her elementary school classes each year around Thanksgiving to talk about things for which to be thankful. The author wrote about where his grandparents and parents had come from, how they had met, what they had done, and where they had lived in Minnesota. About his ancestors, he said in the Preface, "None of them were great or famous, but they were strong and good." In his Foreword he stated, "Most of it I heard as a little boy, so there may be many mistakes; perhaps I have forgotten or mixed up some of the events and people."

16. Stephen Truesdell, Monday, December 7, 2015.
17. CRIMES AND CASUALTIES. South Carolina, *The Anderson Intelligencer*, Thursday, June 7, 1888, Page 2.
18. WITH A SHOTGUN. *Camden Chronicle*, Friday, September 4, 1891. Donna Truesdell confirmed, Wednesday, January 20, 2016.
19. Derived from findagrave.com/cgibin/fg.cgi?page=cr&GSsr=41&GScid=2270531&CRid=2270531&pt=Saint Johns Methodist Cemetery&.
20. Donna Truesdell, Friday, January 15, 2016.
21. Donna Truesdell, Monday, November 9, 2015.
22. Death of Mrs. Christine Truesdale. Special to *The State*, Monday, September 23, 1907.
23. Obituary. *The State*, Friday, November 22, 1974, Page 16A.
24. Donna Truesdell, Monday, November 9, 2015. Stephen Truesdell, Thursday, November 19, 2015.
25. Later another baby, Lois' daughter, Lois Lee Clyburn, born in July 1938, lived only seven months.
26. Stephen Truesdell, Thursday, November 19, 2015.
27. Donna Truesdell, Saturday, February 13, 2016.

CHAPTER 4. *Proud to Claim the Title*

1. One is on display at National Museum of the Marine Corps in Quantico.
2. Donna Truesdell, Monday, November 9, 2015. Stephen Truesdell, Thursday, November 19, 2015. Dee remembers this story a little differently. Her father was underage, and he and grandfather walked the thirty miles to Columbia so he could lie about his age and enlist in the Army.
3. Marine Corps Order No. 32, May 3, 1919, officially changed the name "Paris" to "Parris."
4. Hash Mark. Hits and Misses… *Leatherneck* Magazine, Volume 7, Issue 37, September 1924.
5. Elmore A. Champie. *A Brief History Of The Marine Corps Recruit Depot Parris Island, South Carolina 1891–1962*, Revised Edition. Marine Corps Historical Reference Series Number 8. Washington, D.C.: Historical Branch, G-3 Division, Headquarters, U.S. Marine Corps, 1962.
6. The account of Donald Truesdale's USMC service in Nicaragua that follows relied largely on: Bernard C. Nalty, *The United States Marines in Nicaragua*; Neill Macaulay, *The Sandino Affair*; Jon T. Hoffman, *Once a Legend*; Brent Leigh Gravatt, *The Marines and the Guardia Nacional De Nicaragua 1927–1932*, Duke University Department of Political Science, 1973; and Julian C. Smith, et. al. *A Review Of The Organization And Operations Of The Guardia Nacional De Nicaragua*, Quantico, Virginia, Library of the Marine Corps, 1937, pp. 348–76.
7. Stephen Truesdell, Thursday, November 19, 2015.
8. See map at sandinorebellion.com/PhotoPgs/2Maps/Managua-127-38-32.jpg.

9. Translation of Alfred Wegener's Die Entstehung der Kontinente und Ozeane, Friedr. Vieweg & Sohn, 1915, 1920, 1922. The "continental drift" theory would not find much credibility until the late 1950s.

10. The following account is derived from Neill Macaulay, *The Sandino Affair*; C. J. Chappell's Report in Detail of Engagement at La Paz Centro; Dion Williams, Captain Richard Bell Buchanan, U. S. Marine Corps, *Marine Corps Gazette*, June 1927, Volume 12, Issue 2; and Frank Hunt Rentfrow, And In Sunny Tropic Scenes, *Leatherneck* Magazine, March 1931, Volume 14, Issue 3.

11. Unless otherwise noted, Don Truesdell's comments are from a December 1987 conversation recorded by his son-in-law, Fred Schindler, in Lugoff. Described further below. See also CHAPTER 6 Note 77.

12. Six months later, he served as a Marine aviator for a year in Nicaragua and received the Navy Cross for his "skill and devotion to duty of a high order." He retired from the Marine Corps as a Brigadier General in 1949.

13. U.S. MARINES AND NICARAGUAN LIBERALS CLASH. Iowa, *Creston Daily Advertiser*, Monday, May 16, 1927, Page 1; Douglas Bukowski. Early Conflicts, Other Lessons. *Chicago Tribune*, September 17, 1986.

14. William W. Savage Jr. They Were Called "Banana Wars". Columbia, *The State*, Sunday, September 8, 1963, Page C-1. This article is cited in Neill Macaulay, p. 44.

15. William W. Savage Jr., Page C-1.

16. Retrieved from Michael J. Schroeder, *The Sandino Rebellion Nicaragua 1927–1934*, PC-Doc 27.05.19. Chappell, Report in Detail of Engagement at La Paz Centro.

17. Julian C. Smith, et. al., pp. 23–24.

18. Holland M. Smith and Percy Finch. FMFRP 12-37, *Coral And Brass*, Washington, D.C.: Zenger Publishing Co., 1948, p. 38. General Holland McTyeire "Howlin' Mad" Smith was a veteran of the Banana Wars, at Corinto, Nicaragua, December 1909–April 1910 and of WWI Belleau Wood, with the 8th Machine Gun Company, 5th Marines.

19. U. S. MARINES ENGAGE NICARAGUAN REBELS IN BATTLE. Danville, Virginia, *The Bee*, Monday, July 18, 1927, Page 1 Headline.

20. Deaths. *Leatherneck*, November 1927, Volume 10, Issue 11.

21. Retrieved from Michael J. Schroeder, PC-Doc 27.09.08. Chappell, Report of SOMOTO Patrol.

22. At 12°51'8" north of the equator and 86°15'38" west of the Prime Meridian.

23. Stephen Truesdell, Thursday, November 19, 2015.

24. Nebraska, *The Lincoln Star*, Friday, October 14, 1927, Page 12.

25. In part, adapted from Michael J. Schroeder, PC-Doc 27.11.02. Chappell, Operations Report the QUILALI Patrol.

26. Wounded Marine Has Thrilling Tale. Pennsylvania, *Warren Morning Mirror*, Tuesday, January 10, 1928, Page One–Two. Account also based on 1st Lieutenant M. J. Gould's December 31, 1927 Engagement with Bandits report.

27. Marine Fliers Slain Fighting to the End. *New York Times,* November 9, 1927, Section 1, Page 14; TWO FLIERS SLAIN BY NICARAGUANS. Circleville, Ohio, *The Daily Union-Herald*, Wednesday, November 9, 1927, Page 1.

28. Stephen Truesdell, Thursday, November 19, 2015.

29. NICARAGUA: Marines Trapped. *Time* Magazine, Monday, January 9, 1928; Many at Nicaragua Given Citations for Bravery. Ohio, *The Canton Daily News*, Monday, January 9, 1928, Page 1.

30. Neill Macaulay, p. 103.

31. FEATURE NOTES. Pennsylvania, *Indiana Evening Gazette*, Tuesday, January 3, 1928, Pages 1–2; Pennsylvania, *Bradford Era*, Tuesday morning, January 10, 1928, Page One.

32. Neill Macaulay, p. 107.

33. Marine Hero. Iowa, *Waterloo Evening Courier*, Tuesday, January 17, 1928, Page 2; Roger W. Peard, "The *Tactics of Bush Warfare*," Infantry Journal 38, September–October 1931, pp. 408–15. Neill Macaulay, p. 101.

34. Edward W. Pickard. American Marines Bomb Nicaraguans. Iowa, *Rock Valley Bee*, January 20, 1928, Page 14.

35. He retired from the USMC as a four-star general in 1957.

36. Medal of Honor statistics can be viewed at homeofheroes.com/moh/war/1_a_main.html.

37. Private Joseph V. Kilbride, from New York City. MARINE IS KILLED IN NICARAGUA. Utah, *The Ogden Standard-Examiner*, Wednesday, May 9, 1928, Page 9.

38. AMERICAN MARINE IS KILLED IN NICARAGUA. Illinois, *Centralia Evening Sentinel*, Saturday, December 8, 1928, Page One.

39. Recent Deaths. *Leatherneck*, September 1929, Volume 12, Issue 9.

40. Officer Killed Nicaragua. New Hampshire, *Portsmouth Herald*, Wednesday, March 12, 1930, Page 7.

41. Texas, *Wichita Daily Times*, April 20, 1930, Page One.

42. Mississippi, *Biloxi Daily Herald*, June 21, 1930, Page 2.

43. Neill Macaulay, p. 174.

44. Stephen Truesdell, Thursday, November 19, 2015.

45. Ibid.

46. MARINE SERGEANT DIES. Mississippi, *Biloxi Daily Herald*, December 22, 1930, Page 10.

47. U.S. Marines Massacred in Nicaragua. *Syracuse Herald*, January 2, 1931, Page One.

48. Citations can be reviewed at homeofheroes.com/members/02_NX/citations/02_interim-nc/nc_04interim_2nicaragua.html.

49. Neill Macaulay, p. 178.

50. U.S. MARINES IN NEW SCRAP. *Burlington Hawk Eye*, Sunday, January 4, 1931, Page One.

51. THE SPIRIT OF ADVENTURE IS NOT YET DEAD. Chicago, *Suburbanite Economist*, Tuesday, February 10, 1931, Page 4.

52. Held Service for M'Carty in Nicaragua. Missouri, *Chillicothe Constitution Tribune*, Friday, February 13, 1931, Page One.

53. Telegram traffic recording the American Assistance Following the Destruction of Managua can be viewed at library.wisc.edu/FRUS/EFacs/1931v02/reference/frus.frus1931v02.i0028.pdf.

54. As happened in a series of explosions at the Campo De Marte arsenal at midnight on August 1, 1933.

55. In Plot: Sec: 7, Site: 9066-SH. Lieutenant Colonel Murray, retired, died on April 10, 1941, and was buried with his wife in Arlington, Site: 9066-RH.

56. Marine Sergeant is Killed; Former Eckman Resident. West Virginia, *Bluefield Daily Telegraph*, Sunday, April 5, 1931, Page 1.

57. Will Rogers Observes the Lighter Side Of Conditions in Stricken City of Managua. *The New York Times*, Friday, April 10, 1931, Page 26; WILL ROGERS FLIES TO CAPITAL

OF PANAMA; He Will Give Benefit Performance There to Aid Victims of Managua Earthquake. Special Cable to *The New York Times*, Sunday, April 12, 1931, Page 3.

58. Details of the following actions were derived, in part, from Julian C. Smith, et. al., pp. 348–76. Lieutenant D. L. Truesdale is cited in eight contacts quoted from the Official Contact Files of GN-2, GN-3 Section, Headquarters, Guardia Nacional De Nicaragua: #243, #244, #273, #278, #297, #350, #358, and #371.

59. IDAHO MARINE CAPTAIN FALLS BEFORE REBELS. *Salt Lake Tribune*, Sunday Morning, April 12, 1931, Page 1.

60. KILLS SANDINO AIDE IN NICARAGUA CLASH: Guardia National Reports Two skirmishes in Vicinity of Ocotal, in Northwest. *New York Times*, Friday, May 1, 1931; TWO BATTLES ARE REPORTED. South Carolina, *Florence Morning News*, Friday, May 1, 1931, Page 8.

61. 25 Years Ago. *The Hancock Herald*, Thursday, August 30, 1951, Page Eight.

62. His long USMC career up through WWII was derived from the Navy Directory: Officers of the United States Navy and Marine Corps archives at mocavo.com. Muriel relocated to Yonkers, NY, and he married a second time, to Elizabeth Jane Kline, in September 1934. Dr. Frisbie died on February 26, 1983.

63. 12 Slain in Nicaragua in Three Skirmishes. *New York Times*, Wednesday, March 16, 1932.

64. Retrieved from Michael J. Schroeder, *The Sandino Rebellion Nicaragua 1927–1934*, at sandinorebellion.com/top100pgs/Top100-p95L.html; and, Julian C. Smith, et. al., Contact #358.

65. Derived from "Extracts from personal letter of 1st. Lt. W. L. Bales, USMC, NNG, to Lt. Col. R. L. Denig, USMC, dated 20 May 1932," at sandinorebellion.com/top100pgs/Top100-p95L.html.

66. MARINE SERGEANT KILLED IN MUTINY OF NATIVE GUARDS. Louisiana, *Monroe News Star*, Thursday, April 7, 1932, Page 1.

67. Stephen Truesdell, Thursday, November 19, 2015.

68. He later served as a Lieutenant Colonel in the 3rd Marine Raider Battalion.

69. THREE AMERICANS DIE IN NICARAGUA. Missouri, *Sedalia Capital*, Saturday, April 23, 1932, Page One; Marines Hit Back. Texas, *El Paso Herald Post*, Tuesday, April 26, 1932, Page One.

70. Texas, *San Antonio Light*, Thursday, April 28, 1932, Page 14.

71. This account is adapted from F. D. Beans' April 25, 1932 Patrol Report from Quilalí to the Northern Area Commander in Ocotal. Stephen Truesdell added details, November 19, 2015.

72. Donna Truesdell, Thursday, November 12, 2015. Stephen Truesdell, Thursday, November 19, 2015.

73. Donna Truesdell, Friday, January 15, 2016.

74. Marine Sergeant Is Slain in Nicaragua. Reno, *Nevada State Journal*, Friday, July 1, 1932, Page 1.

75. DONALD TRUESDALE WAS RELEASED FROM HOSPITAL. Pennsylvania, *Lebanon Daily News*, July 22, 1932, Page 15.

76. Herbert Hoover: "Remarks on Presenting the Congressional Medal of Honor to Captain Edward V. Rickenbacker," November 6, 1930. Gerhard Peters and John T. Woolley, *The American Presidency Project*, at presidency.ucsb.edu/ws/?pid=22418.

77. Orville Simmons Killed, Plane Crash, Nicaragua. Ohio, *Hamilton Evening Journal*, Thursday, August 25, 1932, Page Fourteen.

78. Two U.S. Marines Get Hero Medals. New York, *The Brooklyn Daily Eagle*, Sunday, September 4, 1932, Page 1; Beckley, West Virginia, *Raleigh Register*, Sunday, September 4, 1932, Page 5.

79. An official casualty roster is available on Michael J. Schroader's USMC-DOCS website. See sandinorebellion.com/USMC-Docs/USMC-docs-Casualties.html page. Donald Truesdale is not included in the WIA listing.

80. Funeral Services This Afternoon in West Wateree. Special to *The State*, Sunday, January 15, 1933.

81. Couple United in Marriage At Rye By Chaplain Williams of Navy. New Hampshire, *The Portsmouth Herald*, Thursday, November 9, 1933, Page 5.

CHAPTER 5. Life Following Combat

1. *The Meditations*. Book VI, Meditation 39 in Irwin Edman, *Marcus Aurelius And His Times*, Roslyn, New York: Walter J. Black, Inc, 1945, 1973, p. 39.

2. The Butler Family, 1935.

3. Hans Schmidt. *Maverick Marine: General Smedley D. Butler and the Contradictions of American Military History*. University Press of Kentucky, 1987.

4. Stephen Truesdell, Monday, December 7, 2015.

5. Gayle Truesdell Lilly and Donna Truesdell provided a photograph of the Final Divorce Decree, Saturday, January 23, 2016.

6. Lois Monson assisted in researching William St. Clair Phillips genealogy, , Sunday, November 29, 2015.

7. Donna Truesdell, , Thursday, November 12, 2015. The composition of "Clare" and Anna's family was difficult to determine from census records. Only Gladys May is listed in the available 1910 and 1920 Census files.

8. Lois Monson, Sunday, November 29, 2015.

9. Derived from familysearch.org/ark:/61903/1:1:XHSV-738.

10. Lois Monson provided the Commonwealth of Pennsylvania, Department of Health, Bureau of Vital Statistics Death Certificate, Sunday, November 29, 2015.

11. Keesler Field News. Mississippi, *Biloxi Daily Herald*, Wednesday, July 15, 1942, Page Four.

12. Ebin joined the Lutheran Church and taught Sunday school. He married a second time to Barbara Darnell Truesdell and had three stepdaughters and a step-son; Patricia S. Lyons, Donna S. Flinn, Bobbie S. Barrs, and Carl E. Smoaks. Derived from his obituary in *The State* newspaper, August 28, 1998.

13. Donna Truesdell, Tuesday, January 5, 2016.

14. Maryland, *Cumberland Evening Times*, Wednesday, December 10, 1941, Page Four.

15. Robert J. Cressman. *A Magnificent Fight: Marines in the Battle for Wake Island*; National Archives War Casualties from World War II for Navy, Marine Corps, and Coast Guard Personnel from California, 1946, p. 203; MARINES FROM WAKE IS., CAUGHT BY JAPS, SAFE. Pennsylvania, *Chester Times*, Friday, October 23, 1942, Page 1. John Hamas died in San Diego on March 5, 1951.

16. Army and Navy Legion of Valor of the United States of America, General Orders, Volume 52, Issue 2, 1942, p. 18.

17. He earned his fourth service stripe in July 1940.

18. Leatherneck Association, Marine Corps Institute: *Leatherneck*, Volume 25, November 1942, p. 72.

19. Adapted from The American Legion at legion.org.

20. Donna Truesdell, Tuesday, January 14, 2016. Stephen Truesdell, Thursday, September 15, 2016.

21. Donna Truesdell provided details of all her siblings' births, Friday, January 15, 2016.

22. Gayle Truesdell Lilly and Donna Truesdell provided a photograph of his Discharge Certificate, Saturday, January 23, 2016.

CHAPTER 6. The Quiet Life in Kershaw County

1. Donna Truesdell, Wednesday, November 11, 2015.

2. Donna Truesdell, Wednesday January 20, 2016.

3. Stephen Truesdell, Thursday, September 15, 2016.

4. Donna Truesdell, Saturday January 23, 2016.

5. Donna Truesdell, Friday, January 15, 2016.

6. Donna Truesdell, Saturday, January 23, 2016.

7. David Jeffrey Truesdell, quoted by Martin Cahn, staff reporter. A quiet hero: Legion pays tribute to medal of honor recipient. *Chronicle–Independent*, Tuesday, September 3, 2002.

8. Stephen Truesdell, Thursday, November 19, 2015.

9. GPS is 34.2267 North, 80.7079 West.

10. Donna Truesdell, Friday, January 15, 2016.

11. Donna Truesdell, Wednesday, January 20, 2016.

12. Donna Truesdell, Saturday, February 13, 2016.

13. Stephen Truesdell, Monday, December 7, 2015.

14. Donna Truesdell, Wednesday, November 11, 2015.

15. Ibid.

16. Stephen Truesdell, Thursday, November 19, 2015.

17. Donna Truesdell, Monday, November 9, and Wednesday, November 11, 2015.

18. Stephen Truesdell, Monday, December 7, 2015.

19. Donna Truesdell, Sunday, November 8, 2015.

20. Vet Day Special in S.C. *Florence Morning News*, Sunday, November 10, 1957, Page 13.

21. Retrieved from eisenhower.archives.gov/research/online_documents/presidential_appointment_books/1958/May_1958.pdf.

22. Eisenhower Greets 216 Honor Medal Winners. Connecticut, *Bridgeport Telegram*, Saturday, May 31, 1958, Page 3.

23. Stephen Truesdell, Thursday, November 19, 2015.

24. Ibid.

25. Joan Anderson married L. Glen Inabinet around 1966. Both held History degrees and together authored *A History of Kershaw County South Carolina*.

26. Donna Truesdell, Thursday, November 12, 2015.

27. Ibid.

28. Stephen Truesdell, Monday, December 7, 2015.

29. Ibid.

30. Found in Title 36 U.S.C., Chapter 33.

31. Stephen Truesdell, Thursday, September 15, 2016.

32. Derived in part from Bill Dahl's contributions in Vladimir Bogdanov, Chris Woodstra, Stephen Thomas Erlewine, Editors, *All Music Guide to the Blues: The Definitive Guide to the Blues*, San Francisco, Backbeat Books; Third Edition, 2003.

33. Donna Truesdell in correspondence, Thursday, January 14, 2016.

34. HELL'S HOLE DISTRICT IN SOUTH CAROLINA RAIDED; 33 RUM RUNNERS CAPTURED. North Carolina, *Gastonia Daily Gazette*, Monday, September 5, 1926, Page One.

35. CONSTABLE SHOT TO DEATH IN RAID—ALLEGED SLAYER IS ALSO KILLED. South Carolina, *The Gaffney Ledger*, Saturday, July 9, 1927, Page 8.

36. Donna Truesdell, Saturday, January 23, 2016.

37. Kevin Ryan, James Cooper, and Susan Tauer. *Teaching for Student Learning: Becoming a Master Teacher*, 2d Edition. Belmont, California: Wadsworth Publishing; 2012, p. 88.

38. The Papers of Olin D. Johnston, Box 103, Folder Legislative, 1962, Supreme Court, School Prayer Decision (2 of 8), in the South Carolina Political Collections, Columbia.

39. South Carolina, *Florence Morning News*, Friday, May 3, 1963: Medal of Honor Winners Meet JFK, Page 1; State Men Are Invited For Dinner, Page 3-A.

40. Honored at White House. *Chicago Tribune*, Friday, May 3, 1963, Section 1-5; President, Medal of Honor Winners Appear Mutually Awed. Texas, *El Paso Herald–Post*, Friday, May 3, 1963, Page 6.

41. William W. Savage Jr. They Were Called "Banana Wars," Page C-1.

42. John S. Bowman, Ed. *The Vietnam War: An Almanac*. New York: World Almanac Publications, 1985.

43. Donna Truesdell, Thursday, November 12, 2015, and Saturday, February 13, 2016.

44. Varying perspectives on the events at Cam Ne are available: Jack Shulimson and Charles M. Johnson. *U.S. Marines in Vietnam: The Landing and Buildup*, pp. 62-65; Wallace Terry. *Bloods: Black Veterans of the Vietnam War: An Oral History*, pp. 1–3; Peter Brush. What Really Happened at Cam Ne. *Vietnam Magazine*, Vol. 16:2, August 2003, pp. 28–33; and library.vanderbilt.edu/central/Brush/Cam-Ne.htm.

45. Honor Medal Holders Feted. South Carolina, *Florence Morning News*, Friday, January 21, 1966, Page 11.

46. Stephen Truesdell, Thursday, November 19, 2015.

47. Ibid.

48. Ibid.

49. Charles Whitman had earlier in the day murdered his wife and mother and had killed three people inside the Tower before reaching the observation deck.

50. Stephen Truesdell, November 19, 2015.

51. Ibid.

52. Agnew To Present Medal Of Honor. North Carolina, *Kannapolis Daily Independent*, Sunday, April 19, 1970, Page Eight-A.

53. Mrs. Leila Lee, 84, of Lugoff. Obituary. *The State*, April 2, 1957; K. T. Rosborough Obituary. *The State* September 12, 1957, Page 6B; Tries Suicide At University. South Carolina, Greenwood *Index–Journal*, Saturday, October 3, 1959, Page 5; S.C. Police Probe Death Of Youth. North Carolina, *Rocky Mount Evening Telegram*, Sunday, October 4, 1959, Page 1.

54. *San Antonio Light*, Friday, June 10, 1966, Page 16.

55. Honor Medals To Houston. Texas, *Brownsville Herald*, Sunday, October 5, 1969; Army Allowed to Decline Until Trouble Arises. Texas. *Bonham Daily Favorite*, Sunday, October 12, 1969, Page 1. Page 14-A.

56. *Bonham Daily Favorite*, Sunday, October 12, 1969, Page 1.

57. Donna Truesdell, Saturday, January 23, 2016.

58. Ibid. The *JACS* article was in the June 1, 1972, Volume 94, Issue 12, pp. 4217–4222.

59. Donna Truesdell, Wednesday, November 11, 2015.

60. Donna Truesdell, Tuesday, November 10, 2015.

61. Iowa, *Fort Madison Evening Democrat*, Thursday, January 18, 1973, Page 9.

62. James Webb. *I Heard My Country Calling: A Memoir*. New York: Simon & Schuster, 2014. David Martin interview, Sunday Morning CBS News, May 25, 2014.

63. Donna Truesdell, Saturday, January 23, 2016.

64. Stephen Truesdell, Thursday, November 19, 2015, Saturday, December 10, 2016.

65. Stephen Truesdell, Sunday, November 22, 2015.

66. Richard Goldstein. Maj. Gen. Marion E. Carl, 82, Marine Air Ace in World War II. *The New York Times*, June 30, 1998.

67. Donna Truesdell, Wednesday, November 11, 2015.

68. Richard Goldstein. Richard Rocco, Medal of Honor Recipient, Is Dead at 63. *The New York Times*, Monday, November 4, 2002.

69. Derived from Henry Franklin Tribe, "Rocco, Louis Richard", American National Biography Online, February 2000, at anb.org/articles/06/06-00903.html.

70. Donna Truesdell, with photographs, Saturday, January 23, 2016.

71. Derived from the Congressional Medal Of Honor Society History at cmohs.org/society-history.php and Doug Sterner's HomeofHeroes website.

72. South Carolina, *The Gaffney Ledger*, Wednesday, August 21, 1985, Page 3; Medal of Honor Easier To Win Than To Wear. South Carolina, *Aiken Standard*, Friday, September 6, 1985, Page 3; Medal of Honor winners gather for convention. Darmstadt, Hesse, *European Stars And Stripes*, September 9, 1985, Monday, Page 5.

73. Donna Truesdell, Thursday, November 12, 2015.

74. Symbols: The decoration puts spotlight on honorees. *Santa Ana Orange County Register*, Sunday, November 8, 1987, Pages M1–17. Donald Truesdell is on Pages M4 and M16.

75. Reported in *The Raider Patch*, March 1988, Page 2. Wade H. Trepagnier Jr., aged 86, died on Thursday, August 19, 2004.

76. Stephen Truesdell, Saturday, November 21, 2015.

77. Donna Truesdell, Monday, January 11, Wednesday, January 20, 2016. Donna had the videotape transferred to a DVD disc and provided a copy on Tuesday, February 16, 2016.

78. Donna Truesdell, Tuesday, January 5, 2016.

79. Donna Truesdell, with photographs, Saturday, January 23, 2016.

80. Derived from the Journal of the House of Representatives, South Carolina General Assembly, 107th Session, 1987–1988, Thursday, February 11, 1988.

81. Donna Truesdell, Thursday, November 12, 2015.

82. Donna Truesdell, Wednesday, November 11, 2015.

83. Intolerance. Opinion page. Maryland, *Cumberland Sunday Times*, Sunday, February 14, 1993, Page 9.

84. Donna Truesdell, Thursday, November 12, 2015.

85. Donna Truesdell, Friday, February 5, 2016.

86. Donna Truesdell, Friday, January 15, 2016.

87. James Leroy Belk Post 17, 1333 Chestnut Ferry Road, Camden, South Carolina; the marker can be viewed at hmdb.org/marker.asp?marker=62200.

88. Rickie Good, Camden Archives and Museum Curator of Collections, provided photographs in correspondence, Wednesday, February 10, 2016.

89. Donna Truesdell, Thursday, November 12, 2015.

90. Medals stolen from Yorktown museum. *The State*, June 30, 2004.

91. Honoring Our Veterans: Historic Medals of Honor Restored to Place of Honor. *The FBI Newsletter*, May 28, 2004.

92. Melissa Vogt, Staff writer. TV show to focus on stolen Medals of Honor. *The Navy Times*, Friday, February 16, 2007. This broadcast could not be verified at AMW.com's archive.

93. Allyson Bird. Agents bring medals home. Charleston, SC, *The Post and Courier*, August 22, 2009; Waring Hills. FBI returns stolen Medals of Honor to museum! Patriots Point Organization, August 25, 2009.

94. Martin Cahn, staff reporter. A quiet hero: Legion pays tribute to medal of honor recipient. *Chronicle–Independent*, Tuesday, September 3, 2002.

95. Located at 34°14'00.24"N, 80°36'43.56"W.

96. The correct place-name spelling is Constancia.

97. Donna Truesdell, Thursday, November 12, 2015.

98. Stephen Truesdell, Thursday, November 19, 2015.

99. Donna Truesdell, Friday, January 15, 2016.

100. His Obituary was posted by Powers Funeral Home, 832 Ridgeway Road, Lugoff.

101. Donna Truesdell, Saturday, February 13, 2016.

102. Gary Phillips. Medal of Honor winners honored with I-20 bridge naming. *Chronicle–Independent*, Tuesday, August 26, 2014.

103. This is mentioned in only two references and has not been reported in the *Military Times* or the *Marine Corps Times* newspapers. Traditionally, the launching would have been sponsored by one of Donald's daughters, since his widow was already deceased. See Dialynn Dwyer, 10 facts about the Navy's new 'stealth' destroyer, Boston Globe Media Partners, LLC, *Boston.com*, Tuesday, December 8, 2015.

104. Lance Corporal Kyle Carpenter, Staff Sergeant Ty Michael Carter, Staff Sergeant Salvatore A. Giunta, Corporal Dakota L. Meyer, Staff Sergeant Leroy A. Petry, Staff Sergeant Ryan M. Pitts, Staff Sergeant Clinton L. Romesha, Captain William D. Swenson, and Specialist Kyle J. White.

105. All biographies are available at cmohs.org/living-recipients.php?

106. Matthew 24:6, King James Version.

107. Donna Truesdell provided a photo of Paul at Pamplona, Tuesday, July 12, 2016.

CHAPTER 7. Dynamic Upheavals

1. A lyric from his song, *Forever Young*, on his *Planet Waves* album, released 1974.

2. Sorenson family data was retrieved in part from the Find-A-Grave website, starting at findagrave.com/cgi-bin/fg.cgi?page=gr&GRid=119907901. Wendy Sorenson Thorson provided ancestry details in correspondence, Wednesday, January 13, 2016. Lahd is the surname on the couple's tombstone in the family cemetery.

3. A Sorenson family diagram is included at the end of this chapter.

4. James Sorenson, Sunday, March 13, 2016.

5. *54th Pioneer Infantry, with the Army of Occupation, Third U.S. Army* Roster Book, U.S. Army, Germany, 1919. Available at the University of Michigan Library.

6. Wendy Sorenson Thorson, Wednesday, January 13, 2016.

7. Family details were derived from U.S. Census archives. Much of the census data in this chapter was derived from mocavo.com.

8. James Sorenson, Sunday, March 13, 2016.

9. The 54th Pioneer Infantry Roster Book records his enlistment name as Frank A. Wieczorkeweicz.

10. Wendy Sorenson Thorson and James Sorenson provided background details about the family experiences on Foster Island.

11. *ANOKA COUNTY MINNESOTA: A COLLECTION OF HISTORICAL SKETCHES AND FAMILY HISTORY.* Anoka County Historical Society, 1982, p. 283. Vickie Wendel, ACHS Program Manager, and her researcher provided this reference in correspondence, Tuesday, February 23, 2016.

12. Wendy Sorenson Thorson, Wednesday, January 13, 2016.

13. Franklin Elementary stands in the same location today. Vickie Wendel, provided confirmation of various details of Rick's school years, Wednesday, November 4, 2015.

14. Wendy Sorenson Thorson, Wednesday, January 13, 2016.

15. FAMILY REUNION. Anoka *Union*, September 26, 1934. Vickie Wendel and her researcher provided, Tuesday, February 23, 2016.

16. Details regarding Bill Sorenson's life are derived from his May 25, 2010 interview with Darlene Bearl at the Anoka County Historical Society.

17. The history of Anoka High School, retrieved from anoka.k12.mn.us/Page/5363.

18. Jack Kelly, Minnesota Tornado Kills 9, Injures 200, Madison, *Wisconsin State Journal*, Monday, June 19, 1939, Page Nine; TWISTER HITS MANY TOWNS IN MINNESOTA. Iowa, *Fairfield Daily Ledger*, Monday, June 19, 1939, Page 1.

19. Vickie Wendel, Thursday, November 5, 2015.

20. *Anokan* Page Forty-four. Vickie Wendel provided a scan of the photo and details from the yearbook, November 5, 2015.

21. Craig L. Torbenson. *Tornado Magic: A History of Anoka High School Sports*, CreateSpace, 2014. Reference provided by Gwendolyn Poore, Anoka High School Activities Director, in correspondences, November 10–13, 2015. See also, anoka.k12. mn.us/Page/27744.

22. *Minneapolis Star Tribune*, Monday, October 18, 2004.

23. *The Herald*, January 1940, July 1, 1942. Vickie Wendel and her researcher provided copies of the obituary in correspondence, Tuesday, February 23, 2016.

24. From Records of the Office of War Information, 1926–1951.

25. *Popular Photography*, November 1942, Vol. 11, No. 5, pp. 76–77.

26. James Sorenson, Sunday, March 13, 2016.

CHAPTER 8. *Proud to Serve*

1. Peter Hill. California, *Van Nuys Valley News And Green Sheet*, Thursday, May 28, 1970, Front Page.

2. As told to his son James Sorenson. Provided on Sunday, March 20, 2016.

3. Ibid.

4. Ibid.

5. Ibid.

6. *Life*, Vol. 15, No. 15, October 11, 1943, pp. 126–29.

7. Of the twenty-three Marines KIA and awarded Medals of Honor for protecting others from grenades in WWII, thirteen had ships commissioned in their names.

8. *The Raider Patch*, May 1977, Page 21.

9. Trudi Hahn. Medal of honor winner Richard Sorenson dies. *Minneapolis Star Tribune*, Monday, October 18, 2004.

10. James Sorenson, Sunday, March 20, 2016.

11. Ibid.

12. Jack Lummus Enlists in Marine Corps. Lubbock, Texas, *Morning Avalanche*, January 31, 1942, Page 7.

13. Hugh Fullerton Jr. Service Dept. *Alton Evening Telegraph*, Wednesday, May 27, 1942, Page Eighteen.

14. Jeff Walker. *The Last Chalkline: The Life & Times of Jack Chevigny*, Shelbyville, Kentucky: Wasteland Press, 2012.

15. Mentioned in Richard Goldstein, A Football Giant Was a Hero at Iwo Jima, *The New York Times*, February 19, 2005.

16. All four were Killed in Action and earned medals for valor. Jack Lummus was awarded a Medal of Honor.

17. Greg H. Williams. *The Liberty Ships of World War II: A Record of the 2,710 Vessels and Their Builders, Operators and Namesakes, with a History of the Jeremiah O'Brien*. Jefferson, North Carolina: McFarland & Company, 2014.

18. Liberty Ship Defects. *Waterloo Daily Courier*, Friday, July 9, 1943, Iowa, Page 4.

19. Mississippi, *Hattiesburg American*, Monday, December 6, 1943, Page Two.

20. Rick Sorenson interview with Pat Schwabik (misspelling of her name) Anoka County Historical Society—Oral History Collection, May 28, 1991.

21. The following battle account is derived from: Robert D. Heinl, Jr. and John A. Crown, *The Marshalls: Increasing the Tempo*; S. L. A. Marshall, *Island Victory: The Battle for Kwajalein*; Naval Analysis Division, *Campaigns of the Pacific War: Chapter IX, Central Pacific Operations*; and The Fighting Fourth of World War II, *Division History, Namur: Penetrating the Outer Ring*, Marine Corps Base Camp Lejeune, North Carolina, at fightingfourth.com/namur.htm. Where noted, battle descriptions and Private Sorenson's comments are derived from later conversations he had with his son James Sorenson.

22. A tactical map can be viewed at: lapahie.com/Pictures/Navajo_Code_Talker_Burlesque-Camouflage_Map.jpg. A map showing the "Approximate Disposition of RCT 24 the Night of D-plus 1" can be viewed at Chapter 5, Namur, D-Plus 1 and 2, ibiblio.org/hyperwar/USMC/USMC-M-Marshalls/maps/USMC-M-Marshalls-9.jpg.

23. Details specific to Private Sorenson and his comments about the battle are derived, in part, from his interview with Pat Schwabik, May 28, 1991. James Sorenson added details, March 20, 2016.

24. KIA, Saipan, June 18, 1944. Posthumous Navy Cross.

25. KIA, Grand Gorge, Saipan, June 15, 1944.

26. KIA, Saipan, June 18, 1944. Posthumous Silver Star. RED BOOK at hq224usmc.com/secondroster.html.

27. James Sorenson, March 20, 2016. Private Sorenson's recollections of the battle are also adapted from Captain Phillip Thompson's interview. Medal of Honor recipient recalls island of Roi–Namur. *Hawaii Marine*, February 17, 1994, Pages A-1, A-8.

28. Captain Phillip Thompson's interview.

29. James Sorenson, March 20, 2016.

30. Ibid.

31. His Shadow Box Profile can be viewed at marines.togetherweserved.com/usmc, ID=143704.

32. James Sorenson, March 20, 2016.

33. A roster of World War II United States Marine Corps Casualties can be viewed at naval-history.net/WW2UScasaaDB-USMCbyName.htm.

34. Minnesota, *Moorhead Daily News*, Wednesday, July 19, 1944, Page 1; Marine Who Sat on Grenade. Iowa, *Waterloo Daily Courier*, Sunday, August 6, 1944, Page Seven.

35. From his medal citation, East Tennessee Veterans Memorial, at etvma.org/veterans/benjamin-s-preston-jr-7766/.

36. James Sorenson, March 20, 2016. He has an authentic Japanese Type 97 grenade with the safety fork still in place.
37. Captain Phillip Thompson's interview.

CHAPTER 9. Fragments Forever

1. Vincent H. D. Cassidy Jr. (1923–1989) composed "Defiance At Dawn" after the fight for Bloody Ridge on Guadalcanal. His poem was printed in the *Saturday Evening Post*, Vol. 216 Issue 5, July 31, 1943, Page 51. The magazine cover was a cartoon of a worried Hitler hanging wallpaper. Second Lieutenant Richard Bruce Watkins included a copy of the poem in a letter to his wife, June, on January 8, 1944.
2. Wisconsin, *Racine Journal-Times*, Thursday Afternoon, July 20, 1944, Page Seventeen.
3. From his Congressional Medal of Honor Foundation interview. Retrieved from MedalofHonorBook: Oral Histories on youtube.com/watch?v=2K1mgF2C5lU.
4. Captain Phillip Thompson's interview. Medal of Honor recipient recalls island of Roi–Namur. *Hawaii Marine*, February 17, 1994, Pages A-1, A-8.
5. James Sorenson, Sunday, March 20, 2016.
6. Ibid.
7. Captain Phillip Thompson's interview.
8. James Sorenson, March 20, 2016.
9. Corporal "Nick" Basca served as a tank commander in General George Patton's 3rd Army, 4th Armored Division. He died in France on November 11, 1944, when an anti-tank round struck his tank.
10. Technical Sergeant William K. Terry, USMC, Youngstown, Ohio. Pennsylvania, *Clearfield Progress*, Wednesday, March 22, 1944, Page 1.
11. Pennsylvania, *Bradford Era*, Thursday, November 22, 1945, Page Fourteen.
12. James Sorenson, March 20, 2016.
13. Ammunition Blast At Pearl Harbor Revealed By Navy. Kalispell, Montana, *The Daily Inter Lake*, Thursday, May 25, 1944, Page One; Pearl Harbor Blast Causes Casualties. Pennsylvania, *Somerset Daily American*, Thursday, June 15, 1944, Front Page; Gene Eric Salecher. *The Second Pearl Harbor: The West Loch Disaster, May 21, 1944*. Norman, Oklahoma: University of Oklahoma Press, 2014.
14. James Sorenson, March 20, 2016.
15. *Albert Lea Evening Tribune*, Saturday, Thursday, August 10, 1944, Page Four.
16. PLAN REBUILDING PORT CHICAGO, NAVAL BASE TOWN. Minnesota, *Brainerd Daily Dispatch*, Thursday, July 20, 1944, Page Three; Wisconsin, *Racine Journal-Times*, Thursday Afternoon, July 20, 1944, Page Seventeen.
17. Portions of the ceremony can be viewed at MedalofHonorBook: Oral Histories on youtube.com/watch?v=2K1mgF2C5lU. Brian Williams introduced a collection of oral histories of more than 100 Medal of Honor recipients. Peter Collier and Nick Del Calzo, *Medal of Honor: Portraits of Valor Beyond the Call of Duty*. See also, Richard K. Sorenson Collection, (AFC/2001/001/89779), Veterans History Project, American Folklife Center, Library of Congress.
18. James Sorenson, March 20, 2016.
19. Minnesota, *Moorhead Daily News*, Wednesday, July 19, 1944, Page 1; First Enlisted Man To Get Honor Medal. *Moorhead Daily News*, Monday, July 31, 1944, Page 1.
20. Fred (1909), Barnie (1913), Rosalee (1916), Kenneth (1918), Helen (1921), Daree (1925), Ella 1928).

21. Lois Monson assisted in searching for information regarding Joe's wife, March 5–7, 2016. Lynn Ann Rone, Joe's granddaughter, provided additional information in a phone conversation, March 23, 2016.

22. *FIREBALL* newsletter, Vol. 13, Number 1, January 2004, Page 8–9, retrieved at ozbourn.org/fireball/FIREBALLVOL13_2004/January2004.pdf.

23. Their photos can be viewed in the Company B, 1st Battalion, 23d Marines' Red Book, Camp Pendleton, 1943, at yellowfootprints.com/forums/showthread.php?t=16773.

24. OZBOURN SLIDES SATURDAY FROM IRON WORKS YARD. Maine, *Bath Independent*, Thursday, December 27, 1945, Page 1.

25. From The Bridge, *FIREBALL* newsletter, Volume 11, Number 2, April 2002, Page 1, retrieved at ozbourn.org/fireball/FIREBALLVOL11_2002/April2002.pdf.

26. This date appears on his military grave marker at Hillcrest Memorial Park, Sandoval, Illinois. Some references cite his birth year as 1920 or 1922.

27. Parents To Receive Medal Of Honor Here. Illinois, *Centralia Evening Sentinel*, Monday, July 23, 1945, Page One.

28. *Albert Lea Evening Tribune*, Wednesday, August 2, 1944, Page Seven.

29. Namur Hero Goes Home: Winner Of Medal Of Honor Leaves Base On Furlough. *Marine Corps Chevron*, Volume 3, Number 31, Saturday Morning, August 5, 1944, Page Three.

30. Marine Who Sat on Grenade. Iowa, *Waterloo Daily Courier*, Sunday, August 6, 1944, Page Seven.

31. Mary Jean Porter. Risked His Life to Save Other Marines, Colorado, *The Pueblo Chieftain*, June 29, 1995.

32. Anoka Honors Marine Hero. Minnesota, *Albert Lea Evening Tribune*, Saturday, August 5, 1944, Page Two; Home Town Welcomes Hero. Wisconsin, *Racine Journal-Times*, August 5, 1944, Page Three.

33. *Moorhead Daily News*, Tuesday, August 8, 1944, Page 1.

34. State to Honor Marine: Parade in Minneapolis Loop and Luncheon Planned for Wednesday. *Albert Lea Evening Tribune*, Monday, August 7, 1944, Page One; Tribute Paid to Rick Sorenson: State's Marine Hero Paraded Through Loop: Honor Luncheon Guest. *Albert Lea Evening Tribune*, Wednesday, August 9, 1944, Page Two.

35. Anoka Historical Society photograph viewed at startribune.com/an-officer-and-a-gentleman/129557238/.

36. Time Out for Fishing. Minnesota, *Brainerd Daily Dispatch*, Saturday, August 12, 1944, Front Page.

37. The photo can be viewed at the Minnesota Historical Society archive mnhs.org/sites/default/files/media/news/rickysorenson_1945.jpg.

38. "RICKY SORENSON" ON KATE TONIGHT. *Albert Lea Evening Tribune*, Thursday, August 10, 1944, Page Four.

39. To Broadcast Adventure That Won Medal of Honor. *Moorhead Daily News*, Tuesday, August 15, 1944, Page 8.

40. RICKY SORENSON TO BROADCAST. *Albert Lea Evening Tribune*, Wednesday, August 16, 1944, Page Four.

41. Imposter Breaks In on Convention. *Albert Lea Evening Tribune*, Monday, August 21, 1944, Page 4.

42. *Albert Lea Evening Tribune*, Monday, August 21, 1944, Page 4.

43. Ricky at Detroit Lakes. *Albert Lea Evening Tribune*, Friday, August 11, 1944, Page Four.

44. Helen Burgess. Claude Marine Receives Award Posthumously. Texas, *Amarillo Sunday News Globe*, July 22, 1945, Page 1.

45. Lois Monson assisted, finding Richard's birth certificate on file at Cook County Genealogy Records, Saturday, December 12, 2015.

46. Phyllis (Beard) Robertus attended Edison High in the same years, knew Richard, but could not find him in her *Wizard* yearbook, which primarily featured the senior class: in correspondence and phone conversation, Sunday, April 6, 2008.

47. Navy Department Lists Casualties. *Moorhead Daily News*, Tuesday, November 7, 1944, Page Three.

48. Twelve Months of Marine History: Year 169. *Leatherneck*, Volume 27, Issue 12, November 1944.

49. Bill Sorenson's May 25, 2010 interview.

50. *Moorhead Daily News*, Friday, December 8, 1944, Page 8.

51. Kenneth (1914), Robert (1916), Howard (1918), Virginia "Virgie" (1919-2006), Marcella (1922), Evelyn M (1923), Norman (1924), Mary Lou (1929), and Elaine (1931).

52. NINE KILLED OVER WEEKEND BY ACCIDENTS. Albert Lea, *The Evening Tribune*, Monday, August 28, 1933, Page Three; 1940 Minneapolis Census Ward 9, Enumeration District 89–260; Sarah Burghardt. Medal of Honor memorial unveiled. *Sun Focus*, Tuesday, October 18, 2016.

53. An Inventory of James D. LaBelle Papers at the Minnesota Historical Society can be reviewed at 2.mnhs.org/library/findaids/00754.xml.

54. Mike Nowatzki. Fargo Central alumni hold 70-year reunion. *The Fargo Forum*, June 25, 2011. Robert Thompson married after the war and lived in Chaska, MN. He helped organize the July 12–13 class reunion. By WWII's end eighteen sailors and seven Marines from Fargo had been reported KIA or DOW while a POW.

55. Paul Levy. An officer and a gentle man. *Star Tribune*, Tuesday, September 13, 2011.

56. Marine Awarded Medal of Honor Posthumously. *Moorhead Daily News*, Thursday, August 2, 1945, Page Five.

57. His post WWII history is adapted from his 1991 interview, newspaper articles, and his published obituary. Trudi Hahn. Medal of honor winner Richard Sorenson dies. *Minneapolis Star Tribune*, October 18, 2004.

58. Appointment to Positions of Contact Representative, Veterans Administration, Without Regard to the Requirements of the Civil Service Rules.

59. A/P. DESTROYER JOINS NAVY. *San Antonio Express*, Friday Morning, May 24, 1946 Page 5.

60. Obituary. St. Paul *Pioneer Press*, Saturday, May 17, 2003.

61. The marker for Yvonne, John (January 3, 1926–July 28, 2004), and daughter, Jean M. Jansen (April 8, 1958–October 11, 1972) is at Plot: N 4519.

62. Pam Sigurdson, counselor, Columbia Heights High School, provided details, Tuesday, April 8, 2008.

CHAPTER 10. Return to Civilian Life

1. King Henry V, Act II, Scene I Prologue. The Chorus.
2. Nolle Roberts. 4 Division Reunion. *Leatherneck* Magazine, Volume 31, Issue 9, September 1948. Accounts of Rick's participation in reunions and conventions in this chapter are adapted from public sources and provide just a sampling of his travel commitments.

3. James Sorenson provided copies of the photograph and dispatch, Sunday, January 22, 2017.

4. Paul Levy. An officer and a gentle man. *Star Tribune*, Tuesday, September 13, 2011.

5. Robert Sorenson described the development of the Silver Lake properties up through 2002, Sunday, January 29, 2017.

6. Two resources augment Bill Sorenson's May 25, 2010 interview: Joseph R. Owen's memoir of Baker Company, 1st Battalion, 7th Marines, *Colder Than Hell: A Marine Rifle Company at Chosin Reservoir*. New York: Ballantine Books, 1997; Terence W. Barrett. *Remembering James Edmund Johnson, USMC: Pocatello's "Number One Hero Of The Korean War."* Fargo, North Dakota: Aftermath Research, 2013.

7. Details derived from Legacy Files at koreanwar.org/html/units1/5cav.htm.

8. Jack Gallapo served as a Chicago Fire Chief and died on November 24, 2012. His obituary was published in the *Chicago Tribune*, Wednesday, November 28, 2012.

9. Watson Crumbie, from his memoir, *My Time As A Marine*, p. 17, provided in correspondence, Saturday, January 12, 2013.

10. Edwin H. Simmons, *Frozen Chosin: U.S. Marines at the Changjin Reservoir*, p. 122. Most of the non-battle casualties were frostbite injuries.

11. The daily activities of the battalions and companies were reviewed at *7th Marines Historical Diary*, January to May 1951. Retrieved at koreanwar2.org/kwp2/usmc/.

12. Over the years, the special Medal of Honor pension was adjusted for cost-of-living increases. In 2016, $1,299.61 per month above and beyond any military pensions or other benefits for which a recipient might be eligible.

13. Wendy Sorenson Thorson provided date corrections to the family genealogy, Wednesday, January 13, 2016. James Sorenson provided further details, Thursday, March 2, 2017.

14. George Henry Mallon of St. Cloud had died in 1934, the first burial in Fort Snelling National Cemetery; Lloyd Cortez Hawks of Becker died in 1953; Louis Cukela of Minneapolis, Army/USMC, died in 1956. Of the two attending the 1959 convention, Donald Eugene Rudolph died in 2006, and Mike Colalillo died in 2011.

15. Mark Stodghill. Medal of Honor recipient a down-to-earth hero. Duluth, *News–Tribune*, Tuesday, May 16, 1995.

16. 'This Is Your Life' Surprise Touches Gov. Foss to Tears. Texas, *Corpus Christi Times*, Thursday, March 8, 1956, Page 10.

17. Convention Asks to Give Ike Backing. *Brainerd Daily Dispatch*, Thursday, August 27, 1959, Page 1.

18. Marine-Veterans Schedule Reunion. Shreveport, Louisiana, *The Times*, Thursday, June 9, 1960, Page 37.

19. James Sorenson, Monday, December 26, 2016.

20. Robert Sorenson, Saturday, January 21, 2017, Wednesday, March 1, 2017.

21. Debby Sorenson Hanaway provided this detail on Tuesday, January 3, 2017.

22. *Albert Lea Evening Tribune*, Thursday, September 15, 1966, Page 1. Bill Sorenson's May 25, 2010 interview.

23. OBITUARY. *Reno Gazette–Journal*, Thursday, December 5, 2002, Page 20.

24. Marine Corps Association News. *Marine Corps Gazette*, Volume 51, Issue 8, August 1967.

25. James Sorenson, Monday, January 2, 2017.

26. "Orphan" Group Ends Existence. Butte, *Montana Standard*, Thursday, November 1, 1945, Page Eight.

27. James Sorenson, Sunday, March 20, 2016; Monday, December 26, 2016.

28. Wendy Thorson, Tuesday, January 3, 2017.

29. The helmet had a spike for field service and all other occasions. The spike was removed and replaced by a large silvered eagle when full dress was required.

30. Honor Medals To Houston. Texas, *Brownsville Herald*, Sunday, October 5, 1969, Page 14-A.

31. Programs for Memorial Day Scheduled in Valley Area. California, *Van Nuys Valley News And Green Sheet*, Thursday, May 29, 1969, Page 18.

32. Bruce Martin. With Respect and Honor. *Leatherneck Magazine*, Volume 52, Issue 8, August 1969, Pages 30–31.

33. Mary Jean Porter. Risked His Life to Save Other Marines. Colorado, *The Pueblo Chieftain*, Thursday, June 29, 1995. Robert Sorenson provided details of the Vietnam Draft in correspondence, Saturday, March 18, 2017.

34. Wendy Thorson, Tuesday, January 3, 2017.

35. Remember and honor: Pvt. Richard K. Sorenson Catamaran (FB224) dedicated. *THE KWAJALEIN HOURGLASS*, Volume 44 Number 90, Friday, November 12, 2004, Pages 6–7.

36. News of Activities. *Van Nuys* California, *The News*, Friday, May 15, 1970, Page 9-A.

37. Peter Hill. Van Nuys, California, *The Valley News And Green Sheet*, Thursday, May 28, 1970, Front Page; Valley Will Honor Fallen in 102nd Day of Remembrance. *The Valley News*, Friday, May 29, 1970, Front Page.

38. Congressional Medal of Honor Society. *Above and Beyond: A History of the Medal of Honor from the Civil War to Vietnam*, p. 235.

39. James Sorenson, March 20, 2016, December 26, 2016.

40. Ibid.

41. Huge pageant to precede Shrine game. California, *Redlands Daily Facts*, Tuesday, July 25, 1972, Page 8; Mike Rawlingson. South Wins in Rout. Pomono, *Progress–Bulletin*, Friday, July 28, 1972, Page C-2.

42. POW Adjustment to Freedom. *Nevada State Journal*, Monday, July 2, Page 7.

43. Wolfgang Saxon. DESPONDENT P.O.W. APPARENT SUICIDE. *The New York Times*, Monday, June 4, 1973, Page 7.

44. Marines at Work. *Marine Corps Gazette*, Volume 57, Issue 10, October 1973.

45. Bob Hope to Receive Patriot Award. *Redlands Daily Facts*, Thursday, April 15, 1976, Page 12.

46. The Memorial can be viewed at anok.co/tours/bunker_hills_regional_park/index.htm.

47. James Sorenson, December 26, 2016, January 2, 2017.

48. Trudi Hahn. Medal of honor winner Richard Sorenson dies. *Minneapolis Star Tribune*, Monday, October 18, 2004.

49. Hilliard E. Miller. Sentimental journey to hell and back. Colorado Springs, *Gazette Telegraph*, Sunday, May 20, 1984, Pages C1–C5.

50. WWII historic sites named. Kansas, *Hutchinson News*, Sunday, April 28, 1985, Page 9; Of Monuments and Marines. *Marine Corps Gazette*, Volume 70, Issue 7-12, July–December 1986.

51. Sheila Gideon. Visiting Marines take Roi historical tour. the *Kwajalein Hourglass,* Volume 54 Number 33, Saturday, August 17, 2013, Page 6. A recent brochure describing the STOPS along the tour can be downloaded at smdc.army.mil/2008/Historical/StaffRide/ROI-TOUR_Aug23.pdf. The pdf. includes battle photographs, a map of the tour sites, and a photograph of PFC Richard K. Sorenson 1924-2004.The Roi Namur WWII Battlefield Tour snapshots and narratives can also be viewed at pbase.com/nowhereatoll/ww2_tour_of_roi_namur.

52. Robert Sorenson, Sunday, January 22, 2017.

53. Craig Pursley. Special Report, MEDAL OF HONOR. Front Page and Page M5.

54. Robert Sorenson, Sunday, January 22, 2017.

55. War inspires marches of protest, support. *The Joplin Globe*, Monday, January 28, 1991, Page 3A.

56. H.J.Res.652—101st Congress (1989–1990) reviewed at congress.gov.

57. Derived in part from RECOGNIZING THE VETERANS GUEST HOUSE. 114th Congress, 2nd Session, *Congressional Record*, Vol. 162, No. 66—Senate Daily Edition, April 28, 2016, Page S2552.

58. James Sorenson, Friday, December 4, 2016.

59. LCFs were renamed Missile Alert Facility (MAF) in 1992 when the Strategic Air Command was inactivated.

60. James Sorenson, Monday, December 26, 2016.

61. Years after Ken had passed away, the Luger was returned to his family for safe keeping.

62. Rodger M. Brodin sculpted the statue.

63. Details and photos of the Memorial can be viewed at mementobelli.wordpress.com/2013/09/03/anoka/.

64. Vickie Wendel confirmed, Wednesday, November 4, 2015.

65. Rick Sorenson interview with Pat Schwabik, May 28, 1991.

66. Paul Levy. An officer and a gentle man. *Star Tribune*, Tuesday, September 13, 2011.

67. Legion hears about Russia trip. Louisiana, *Hammond Daily Star*, Friday, June 26, 1992, Page 5. James Sorenson confirmed, Tuesday, March 21, 2017.

68. The *Akibasan, Asakazi, Choko, Eiko, Ikuta, Kembu, Palawan, Phantom, Shoyei, Takunan,* and *Tateyama* all have *Maru* as a suffix. The translation of the Japanese word means *Beloved Merchant Ship.*

69. Captain Phillip Thompson. Medal of Honor recipient recalls island of Roi–Namur. Hawaii Marine, February 17, 1994, Pages A-1, A-8; 1994 REUNION—CENTRAL PACIFIC. *MARINE BOMBING SQUADRON SIX-THIRTEEN* newsletter, 1994. vmb613.com/reunion/1994_reunion.htm.

70. James Sorenson, Monday, December 26, 2016, Wednesday, January 4, 2017.

71. Thomas and James Sorenson provided information about their father's passport, Sunday, March 19, 2017.

72. James Zumwalt. I Was Not Going To Let Them Down. Texas, *The Kerrville Times, Parade Magazine*, Sunday, October 17, 1999, Page 14.

73. Linda D. Kozaryn. GI Joe: Man of the 20th Century. American Forces Press Service, February 25, 2000.

74. Wendy Sorenson Thorson provided the family photograph, Tuesday, February 7, 2017.

75. Bing West and Ray Smith. *The March Up: Taking Baghdad with the United States Marines.* New York: Bantam Books, 2004, p. 5.

76. Retrieved from MedalofHonorBook: Oral Histories on youtube.com/watch?v=2K1mgF2C5lU.

77. Retrieved from nevadaday.com/pages/grand-marshals/2003.htm.

78. Veterans Day celebration: Veterans are to be honored. *Reno Gazette–Journal*, Sunday, November 9, 2003, Page 6A.

79. Casualties Update: Deaths reported by the military on Saturday. Syracuse, *The Post-Standard*, Sunday, April 25, 2004, Page A-6; Michael M. Phillips. In Combat, Marine Put Theory to Test, Comrades Believe. *The Wall Street Journal*, Tuesday, May 25, 2004, Page A-1.

80. Gidget Fuentes. Medal of Honor is first for a Marine since Vietnam. *Marine Corps Times*, November 10, 2006.

81. State's lone Medal of Honor recipient dies. *Nevada Appeal*, Thursday, October 14, 2004.

82. Robert Sorenson, Sunday, February 28, 2017.

83. James Sorenson, March 20, 2016.

84. Robert Sorenson, Sunday, January 22, 2017.

85. Paul Levy. An officer and a gentle man. *Star Tribune*, Tuesday, September 13, 2011.

86. As of October 23, 2015, 143 Sorensons are interred at Fort Snelling.

87. A Medal of Honor hero ancestors from Freeborn County. *Albert Lea Tribune*, Friday, November 12, 2004.

88. James Sorenson, Monday, December 26, 2016, provided a reference to Remember and honor: Pvt. Richard K. Sorenson Catamaran (FB224) dedicated. Published in *THE KWAJALEIN HOURGLASS*, November 12, 2004, Pages 6–7. A 2011 photograph of the *Pvt. Sorenson* can be viewed at *smdc.army.mil/KWAJ/Hourglass/issues-archived/2011/03-26-11hourglass.pdf*–p. 7.

89. An Army Air Corps Technical Sergeant Ronald E. Hall (Tucson, AZ), 464 Heavy Bomber Group, 15th Army Air Force, served as a WWII photographer on B-24 Liberators. On the return trip, fifteen minutes from the target at the Ploesti, Romania oilfields, German fighters hit B-24 tail #42-50411. He was captured on June 6, 1944, with nine other crewmen. He was a POW until returned to U.S. Military Control at the end of hostilities in May 1945. Arizona, *Tucson Daily Citizen*, Friday, November 2, 1945, Page 4. See also Bill Beigel's Daily Posts. Five From the 464th Bomb Group. March 20, 2015, at ww2research.com.

90. James Sorenson, Monday, December 26, 2016.

91. Charles F. Knapp, Frank L. Pokrop, James Dee Garls, and Foster K. Cummings have since died.

92. Bill Sorenson's May 25, 2010 interview.

93. Jason Olson, Sports Editor. Anoka's ready for its first Hall of Fame class. *Union*, August 26, 2011; Anoka High Hall of Fame, Class of '11, *Star Tribune*, Tuesday September 6, 2011.

94. Paul Levy. An officer and a gentle man. *Star Tribune*, Tuesday, September 13, 2011.

95. Jason Olson, Sports Editor. Five more inductees set to join Anoka Hall of Fame. *Union*, September 3, 2014

96. Viewed at karen-illustrations.blogspot.com/2011/11/veterans-day.htm.

97. Newsletter of the Anoka County Historical Society, Vol. 43 No. 3, May–June 2013.

98. Joe Steik. Post 518 Veteran of the Month–USMC MSG Richard Keith Sorenson. *Mankato Times*, Thursday, February 5, 2015.

99. The May 12, 2015, June 9, 2015, August 11, 2015, September 8, 2015 Regular Meeting Minutes.

100. Boston Publishing Company Editors. *The Medal of Honor: A History of Service Above and Beyond*, Back Cover.

101. Mark Brunswick. Medal of Honor recipients gather in the Twin Cities this week. *Star Tribune*, Wednesday, October 5, 2016; Sarah Burghardt. Medal of Honor memorial unveiled. *Sun Focus*, October 18, 2016.

102. Olivia Alveshere. Anoka DAR publishes book on Medal of Honor recipients. *ABC Newspapers*, November 18, 2016.

103. Robert Sorenson, Sunday, January 22, 2017.

CHAPTER 11. The Hero Of Peleliu

1. From his 1863 The Poet's Tale; The Birds of Killingworth, in *Tales of a Wayside Inn*, New York: The Macmillan Company, 1917, pp 141–151.
2. E. B. Sledge. *With the Old Breed: At Peleliu and Okinawa*, p. 77.
3. Bill Sloan. *Brotherhood of Heroes: The Marines at Peleliu, 1944*, p. 311.
4. James H. Hallas. *The Devil's Anvil: The Assault on Peleliu*, pp 80–82.
5. Some references site Pennsylvania as his birthplace.
6. Camden Notes. *Philadelphia Inquirer*, Wednesday, November 30, 1910.
7. Jacquelyn Rouh Govan provided family details, December 28, 2015.
8. Wounded Yank Smothers Jap Grenade, Lives: Wounded Hero Back Home: Says Glad It Was a U.S. Grenade. Pennsylvania, *Bradford Era*, January 13, 1945, Page Twelve.
9. Recollections of Phyllis Rowland Rouh are derived from Marlyn Margulis' The Town With The Patco Station, *The Inquirer*, Sunday, August 18, 1996.
10. Kathryn Carroll, Haddon Heights High School Library Media Specialist, provided scans of selected pages of the 1935 *Senior Record Yearbook*, and the 1936 and 1937 *Garneteer* yearbooks, in correspondences, Thursday, December 17, 2015.
11. Nick Gandolfo-Lucia (HHHS '12, Haverford College). Connections Alumni Newsletter, 2012–2013, viewed at haddonheightsalumni.com/wp-content/uploads/2014/10/Alumni-2012-2013.pdf, Pages 4–5. Also, *The 1936 Garneteer* Yearbook, Page Sixty-eight.
12. Football Candidates Train for Grid Season During Summer. Haddon Heights High School, *The Scribe*, Wednesday, September 30, 1936.
13. Kathryn Carroll, Thursday, December 17, 2015.
14. Ibid.
15. Song title of 1936 composition by Richard Rodgers and Lorenz Hart.
16. Derived from ancientfaces.com/person/howard-c-rouh/154220594.
17. Ira Wolfert. *Cullier's Weekly Magazine*, September 22, 1945, p. 14.
18. Ira Wolfert, from Cullier's Weekly Magazine. Lincoln, Nebraska, *Sunday Journal And Star*, September 16, 1945, Page 5.
19. John Wukovitz. *Pacific Alamo: The Battle for Wake Island*.

CHAPTER 12. Joining the Leathernecks

1. Hector said to Andromache, his wife, in the *Iliad of Homer*, edited by Louise R. Loomis, Roslyn, New York: Walter J. Black, Inc, 1944, p. 99.
2. Ira Wolfert. *Cullier's Weekly Magazine*, September 22, 1945, p. 83.
3. Ibid.
4. Ibid.
5. The following account is adapted from Henry I. Shaw Jr., *First Offensive: The Marine Campaign for Guadalcanal*, Washington, D.C. Marine Corps Historical Center, 1992.
6. Ira Wolfert. *Cullier's Weekly Magazine*.
7. His Silver Star citation can be viewed at the MilitaryTimes Hall of Valor, valor.militarytimes.com/recipient.php?recipientid=314.
8. These stats vary depending on the source referenced.
9. Ira Wolfert. *Cullier's Weekly Magazine,* p. 84.
10. The study was published later in *Education Digest*, April 1945, Vol. 10 Issue 8, p. 31.
11. Ira Wolfert. *Cullier's Weekly Magazine,* p. 84.

12. Newspapers later misreported that he had commanded a machine-gun platoon during the New Britain campaign. In his own descriptions, he was in command of a heavy mortar platoon.

13. JERSEY MARINE HONORED: Hero at Guadalcanal, Gets Medal. *New York Times,* Sunday, July 4, 1943, Page One.

14. Details of this campaign are adapted, in parts, from two references: Frank O. Hough and John A. Crown. *The Campaign on New Britain*; Bernard C. Nalty. *Cape Gloucester: The Green Inferno.*

15. Ira Wolfert. *Cullier's Weekly Magazine,* p. 85.

16. The following account is adapted in part from Frank O. Hough, *The Seizure of Peleliu,* Historical Branch, G-3 Division, Headquarters, U.S. Marine Corps, 1950.

17. Ira Wolfert. *Cullier's Weekly Magazine,* p. 84.

18. Ibid.

CHAPTER 13. The Greatest Defiance

1. See CHAPTER 9, Note 1, *Defiance At Dawn.*

2. A lieutenant junior grade, Doc Crain, MD, was a battle surgeon. He earned a Silver Star and Purple Heart on Peleliu. He later earned a Navy Cross on Okinawa.

3. Iowa, *Boone News Republican*, Saturday, December 23, 1944, Page Five.

4. Massachusetts, *Lowell Sun*, Saturday, January 13, 1945, Page One.

5. Wounded Yank Smothers Jap Grenade, Lives: Wounded Hero Back Home; Says Glad It Was a U.S. Grenade. Pennsylvania, *Bradford Era*, January 13, 1945, Page Twelve.

6. Ira Wolfert. *Cullier's* Weekly Magazine, September 22, 1945, p. 14.

7. Texas, *Port Arthur News*, Sunday, June 3, 1945, Page 11. The broadcast can be accessed at oldtimeradiodownloads.com/drama/the-cavalcade-of-america/the-lieutenants-come-home-1945-06-04.

8. Guest list retrieved from trumanlibrary.org/calendar/main.php?currYear=1945&currMonth=6&currDay=15.

9. Truman Presents Congressional Medals of Honor. New York, *Salamanca Republican Press*, Friday, June 15, 1945, Page Six.

10. *All Hands*, The Bureau Of Naval Personnel Information Bulletin, NAVPERS-O, Number 341, August 1945, p. 57.

11. *Ibid*, p. 58.

12. Ira Wolfert, from Cullier's Weekly Magazine. Lincoln, Nebraska, *Sunday Journal And Star*, September 16, 1945, Page 5.

13. Private First Class Albert Andrew Schmid, 21, born in Philadelphia's Burholme neighborhood, fought with the 2d Battalion, 1st Marines at the Battle of the Tenaru River on Guadalcanal. On February 18, 1943, he was awarded the Navy Cross for his heroism in the early morning hours of August 22, 1942. He was the popular subject of magazine articles, books, and a 1945 movie.

14. Ira Wolfert. Lincoln, Nebraska, *Sunday Journal And Star*, September 16, 1945, Page 5.

15. This article can be viewed at unz.org/Pub/Colliers-1945sep22-00076.

16. Ira Wolfert. *Cullier's Weekly Magazine*, pps. 14, 83–85.

17. L.R. Alwood, writing for Pick Hotels Corporation's book, "Pick-Ups." An Angel Stood By. Missouri, *Sikeston Standard*, Friday, April 11, 1947, Page Eight.

18. Photo is available at static.panoramio.com/photos/large/51503437.jpg. The MOH Emblem on the monument was the Army MOH Valor Medal not the Navy/USMC Medal.

19. The stately building was later named the Overbrook Regional High School in 1958. In 1999, the borough acquired the school, now named Lindenwold Middle School. The monument and sundial remain in front of the building.

20. Medal of Honor Winner Guest Here. *Evening Annapolis Capital*, Saturday, October 8, 1949, Page 5; *The Chicago Tribune*, Sunday, October 9, 1949, Page *F Part 2–Page 3.

21. New Delaware Bridge Is Dedicated. Pennsylvania, *Chester Times*, Wednesday, August 15, 1951, Page One; Delaware Memorial Bridge Dedicated. Maryland, *Denton Journal*, Friday, August 17, 1951, Page One.

22. New Jersey, Camden *Courier–Post*, Friday, December 9, 1977, Page 13. Jacquelyn Rouh Govan provided details, Tuesday, January 26, 2016.

23. Jacquelyn Rouh Govan, Tuesday, January 26, 2016.

24. Bert Okuley. Congressional Medal Winners Remain Modest. Iowa, *Cedar Rapids Gazette*, Sunday, November 11, 1956, Page 19.

25. Tomb of Unknowns Is Decorated by Medal Of Honor Winners. Kansas, *Arkansas City Traveler*, Thursday, July 12, 1962, Page 8.

26. Pennsylvania, *Levittown Times*, Thursday, April 11, 1963, Page 3.

27. Councilwoman Cheryle Randolph-Sharpe, Did You Know? *The Lindenwold Express* Newsletter, Fall/Winter 2007, Vol. 2, Issue 2.

28. Marlyn Margulis. The Town With The Patco Station. *The Inquirer*, Sunday, August 18, 1996.

29. California, *Oakland Tribune*, Sunday, April 16, 1967, Page Two.

30. The Medal of Honor Society convention returned to Houston on October 23, 1972. The convention was held in Indiahoma, Oklahoma, August 17–20, 1976.

31. Medal of Honor Winners Recalled. Wednesday, September 17, 1969, *Kittanning Leader–Times*, Page 24; Thursday, September 18, 1969, *Kittanning Leader–Times*, Page 4.

32. Photograph retrieved from New Jersey National Guard Photograph Collection, Image No. A117.

33. Jacquelyn Rouh Govan, Monday, December 21, 2015.

34. Jason Laughlin. Lindenwold: A tree by any name. South Jersey, *Courier–Post*, Monday, October 18, 2006.

35. Jacquelyn Rouh Govan, Tuesday, March 21, 2017.

36. Carlton R. Rouh dies, Medal of Honor winner. Camden, *Courier–Post*, Friday, December 9, 1977, Page 13.

37. The numbers are derived from Home of Heroes website statistics.

38. U.S. Army Allan Masaharu Ohata, 59, World War II veteran from Honolulu, died on October 17, 1977. Following an investigation of military records and citations, President Bill Clinton presented the posthumous Medal of Honor award to his family on June 21, 2000. Jesus Santiago Duran, 28, U.S. Army Vietnam War veteran was stabbed to death in a Riverside, California, bar on February 17, 1977. President Barack Obama presented the Medal to his daughter on March 18, 2014.

39. New York, *Syracuse Post Standard*, Tuesday, October 31, 1978. Jacquelyn Rouh Govan, Tuesday, January 31, 2017.

40. Names are listed on an online Beirut Memorial in order of date of death from 1958 to 1995: at beirut-memorial.org/memory/brtnames.html.

41. PO1 Fel Barbante. Battle of Peleliu—40 Years Later. *Pacific Stars And Stripes*, Saturday, March 3, 1984, Page 7.

42. From Theodore O'Hara, *The Bivouac of the Dead*, composed in 1847.

43. Photographs can be viewed at waymarking.com/waymarks/WM4F4A_Medal_of_Honor_Memorial_Pennsauken_NJ.

44. Adapted from knightfuneralhome.net/tribute/details/8/Phyllis_L_Rouh/obituary.html; published in the *Courier–Post* on October 21, 2012.

45. Lavinia DeCastro, staff. Lindenwold recalls a hometown hero. South Jersey, *Courier–Post*, Monday, September 14, 2009.

CHAPTER 14. Defend What Is Yours

1. *Essays*, First Series, 1841, Essay VIII *Heroism*.

2. Jack's early background is primarily derived from several sources: Jack H. Lucas & D. K. Drum. *Indestructible*, 2006; Jack Lucas: Youngest Man to Win the Congressional Medal of Honor, *Life on the Pamlico*, December 2001; and *The Official Biography of Jack Lucas* compiled by the Jack Lucas Memorial Foundation at mcldeptms.org/Documents/jack_Lucas-biography.pdf. Various newspaper references are cited individually in the text.

3. *Indestructible*, p. 15.

4. *Indestructible*, p. 18.

5. Clint Johnson. *Touring the Carolinas' Civil War Sites*. Winston-Salem, NC: John F. Blair, 1996, pp. 81–85.

6. Vance and Veronica Haskett, Marion Everett. WASHINGTON COUNTY NORTH CAROLINA CEMETERIES 1769-1997, in four volumes, can be viewed at archive.org/stream/WashCoCemeteries.

7. *Indestructible*, pp. 13–15.

8. Data retrieved at familysearch.org/ark:/61903/1:1:ML3G-BXW.

9. *Indestructible*, pp. 87–88.

10. *Indestructible*, p. 180.

11. *Indestructible*, pp. 54–55.

12. *Indestructible*, p. 55.

13. *Indestructible*, p. 39.

14. Ibid.

15. Margaret Lucas at FamilySearch.org/ark:/61903/1:1:KW7Q-9R9, sheet 12B, Sixteenth Census of the United States, 1940.

16. *Indestructible*, p. 51.

17. Advertisement in Swan Quarter, *The Hyde County Herald*, Thursday, October 18,1951, Page 6.

18. *Indestructible*, p. 31.

19. *Hyde County Messenger*, Fairfield Monthly, Vol. 13, #4, April 1936.

20. *Indestructible*, p. 121.

21. *Indestructible*, p. 17.

CHAPTER 15. A Place of Grenades, Gore, Guts, and Glory

1. Scott McGaugh. *Surgeon in Blue: Jonathan Letterman, the Civil War Doctor Who Pioneered Battlefield Care*. New York: Arcade Publishing, 2013, p. 293.

2. Arthur N. Hill. Battalion on Iwo. *Marine Corps Gazette*, November 1945, Volume 29, Issue 11, Page 27; WELCOME HOME. *The Cincinnati Enquirer*, Friday, January 21, 1944, Page 6.

3. *Indestructible*, p. 29–30.

4. Charles Hocking. *Dictionary of disasters at sea during the age of steam: Including sailing ships and ships of war lost in action, 1824-1962*. Vol 1. London, United Kingdom: Lloyd's Register of Shipping, 1969.

5. SWAN QUARTER BOY KILLED IN ACTION IN NAVY. North Carolina, *The Dare County Times*, Friday, March 26, 1943, Page 4.

6. *Indestructible*, p. 53–54.

7. William Standring. The Story of Jack Lucas. *Marine Corps Magazine*, Summer 1996.

8. Amy O'Neal, Librarian, Washington County Library, provided a transcription of a September 19, 1957 *The Roanoke Beacon* story in correspondence, Friday, September 30, 2016. FUNERAL SERVICES HERE SATURDAY FOR PULP MILL WORKER: Rites at Veterans Building For Marshall L. Moore, Fatally Hurt in Accident Last Week.

9. FUNERAL HELD SUNDAY FOR SWAN QUARTER NATIVE. *Dare County Times*, Friday, January 19, 1945, Page 1.

10. Jack Lucas' account of his battle experience is described in *Indestructible*, pp. 81–112.

11. J. L. Battenfeld. Texas, *Brownsville Herald*, Tuesday, February 19, 1985, Page 22.

12. Bob Hill. Iwo Jima flags recall an era of bravery, service. *Louisville Courier–Journal*, Saturday, February 24, 2007.

CHAPTER 16.   Blessed, Lucky, or Jinxed?

1. Publius Ovidius Naso (43 BC–17 AD) was a Roman poet and philosopher. Quoted in Timothy Light and Brian Courtney Wilson (Eds), *Religion as a Human Capacity: A Festschrift in Honor of E. Thomas Lawson*, Leiden, The Netherlands: Koninklijke Brill, 2004, p. 377.

2. Jack's description of the grenade explosion is provided in *Indestructible*, pp. 101–111. Several sources are combined here with his own memoir.

3. Forty-seven service men who died in the two World Wars, Korea, and Vietnam are named on the Veteran Memorial, Washington County Courthouse lawn in downtown Plymouth.

4. National Archives. State Summary of War Casualties from World War II: Navy, Marine Corps, and Coast Guard Personnel. Viewed at archives.gov/research/military/ww2/navy-casualties/index.html.

5. Father Cormac A. Walsh. Arlington National Cemetery Website, September 18, 2004. Confirmed in *The Raiders Patch*, September 1977, Page 15. Lyric is quoted from *Sean O'Duibhir a Ghleanna*.

6. *Indestructible*, p. 104.

7. Whitman S. Bartley. *Iwo Jima: Amphibious Epic*. Historical Section, Division of Public Information Headquarters, U.S. Marine Corps, 1954, Appendix III: Casualties. Other sources estimate the number of KIA, DOW, and wounded corpsmen at 827.

8. FUNERAL SERVICES MONDAY FOR MIDDLETOWN MAN. *Dare County Times*, Friday, July 27, 1945; pg. 3.

9. *Indestructible*, pp. 131–32.

10. As he appeared on Medal of Honor: Oral Histories. Viewed at youtube.com/watch?v=_aGhPjeayJY. Uploaded on September 27, 2011.

11. Margaret Kernodle. Young Carolinian All Set To Receive Medal Of Honor From Truman. North Carolina, *Gastonia Daily Gazette*, Thursday, October 4, 1945, Page 12; Margaret Kernodle. Boy Hero to Go Back to School After Honors From President. Maryland, *Cumberland Evening Times*, Friday October 5, 1945, Page 1; Syracuse,

Herald–Journal, October 5, 1945, Page 1; Youngest Marine Gets Highest Award From President Truman. Virginia, *Pulaski Southwest Times*, October 5, 1945, Page 2; *Wisconsin Rapids Daily Tribune*, Saturday, October 6, 1945, Page 3; Margaret Kernodle. North Carolina, *Burlington Daily Times News*, Monday, October 22, 1945, Page 20.

12. Remarks at the Presentation of the Congressional Medal of Honor to Fourteen Members of the Navy and Marine Corps. File 160 reviewed at trumanlibrary.org/publicpapers/viewpapers.php?pid=169.

13. Massachusetts, *Pittsfield Berkshire Evening Eagle*, Thursday, October 4, 1945, Page 1.

14. Marine Private First Class Jacklyn H. Lucas waves from the back seat of a Jeep during Nimitz Day celebrations in New York City Oct. 9, 1945. Collection of Fleet Admiral Chester W. Nimitz, USN. NHHC Photograph Collection, NH 103870.

15. *Indestructible*, p. 141.

16. Genevieve Anton. Acts of courage changed their lives forever. *Colorado Springs Gazette*, Tuesday, July 4, 1995, Pages A1, A3.

17. Ibid.

18. Margaret Kernodle. LETTERS FLOOD TAR HEEL HERO—Lucas, Winner Of Congressional Medal, Gets 10,000 Letters In Three Weeks. *Gastonia Daily Gazette*, Monday, October 22, 1945, Page 1; North Carolina, *Burlington Daily Times News*, Monday, October 22, 1945, Page 20.

19. *Indestructible*, p. 145–46.

20. *Indestructible*, p. 37.

21. *Indestructible*, p. 149.

22. Sue Anne Pressley. War Hero's Hard Luck. *The Washington Post*, Monday, September 9, 1985.

23. Seth Kantor. RETURN TO IWO. *Syracuse Herald Journal*, February 19, 1985, Page A6.

24. *The Coastland Times* (the combined *Belhaven Pilot* and *Swan Quarter Herald*), Friday, May 7, 1948, Page 6

25. *Indestructible*, p. 15.

26. Iwo Jima Hero Says "I do." Ohio, *Norwalk Reflector Herald*, Friday, March 28, 1952, Page 1; Indiana, *Brazil Daily Times*, Wednesday, April 2, 1952, Page 4.

27. *Indestructible*, p. 55.

28. Amy O'Neal, Librarian, Washington County Library, courteously provided a copy of the NC Certificate of Death No. 24838 in correspondence, Thursday, September 29, 2016.

29. Only ten family members are buried there. Walter Moore died on May 1, 1958, and Virginia followed him on October 30, 1988. An aunt, Ruth Roseland Satterthwaite, died on Aug 10, 1972, and was the last to be buried in the cemetery. Mahlon Satterthwaite Moore, 85, outlived all in his family of origin. He died on Saturday, October 24, 2009, at his residence and was buried at Hillside Memorial Gardens. Viewed at maitlandfuneralhome.com/obituaries/Mahlon-S-Moore?obId=564884#/obituaryInfo.

30. Hero Of Iwo Jima Plans To Attend Inauguration Of John F. Kennedy. *The Wilson Daily Times*, Thursday Evening, January 19, 1961, Page 20.

31. *Indestructible*, p. 160.

32. *Indestructible*, p. 161.

33. *Indestructible*, p. 162.

34. Maryland Historic Trust survey and inventory of Prince George's County Historic Site, Survey P.G. #81A-8 was prepared by Michael F. Dwyer, Senior Park Historian, on 8-1-1974. Details and photographs are at msa.maryland.gov/megafile/msa/stagsere/se1/se5/019000/019200/019218/pdf/msa_se5_19218.pdf.

35. This account is derived from a full-page story that shared space with a short Dear Abby column. Robert Pack. Killer For Hire. *Colorado Springs Gazette*, Monday, November 26, 1984, Pages C1, C5. Also, Prosecutor Cites Tip In Arrests. Pennsylvania, *Hanover Evening Sun*, Tuesday, July 12, 1977, Page C-1.

36. Jack's account thirty years later, *Indestructible*, pp. 167–176, varies from the details reported at the time.

37. Sue Anne Pressley. War Hero's Hard Luck. *The Washington Post*, Monday, September 9, 1985.

38. Seth Kantor. Violence Haunting Hero's Life. *The Palm Beach Post*, Monday, February 18, 1985, Page A10; Seth Kantor. Tax agents relent under pressure in case of destitute war hero. Arizona, *Yuma Daily Sun*, Sunday, June 30, 1985, Page 5.

39. U.S. WAR HERO DENIES ANY PART IN DRUG RACKET. *New York Times*, Saturday, August 31, 1985. Sue Anne Pressley. War Hero's Hard Luck. *The Washington Post*, Monday, September 9, 1985. Darmstadt, Hesse, *European Stars And Stripes*, Monday, September 9, 1985, Page 5.

40. Sue Anne Pressley. Maryland Drops Marijuana Charges Against World War II Hero. *The Washington Post*, Thursday, October 24, 1985.

41. Billy Watkins. Mississippi WWII hero Jack Lucas' valor challenged by life's grit. Jackson, Mississippi, *The Clarion–Ledger*, Friday, November 7, 1997.

42. MILITARY COULDN'T KEEP THEM OUT—War turned boys into soldiers. *Colorado Springs Gazette*, Monday, May 27, 1996, Pages A1, A3. Ray D. Jackson and Susan M. Jackson, Editors, *America's Youngest Warriors*, Tempe, AZ: VUMS, 1997, pp. 139–143. Volumes 2 and 3 published in 2002 and 2006. Editions provided by Bruce Salisbury in 2009.

43. Mississippi, *Laurel Leader Call*, Wednesday, January 25, 1995, Page 1.

44. Transcript State of the Union Address at millercenter.org/president/clinton/speeches/speech-3440.

45. Ron Fournier. A true definition of courage. *Texas City Sun*, Monday, February 20, 1995, Page 1.

46. Barney Barnum, Guest Columnist, USMC recipient from Vietnam. Maryland, *Annapolis Capital*, Sunday, February 26, 1995, Page 11.

47. Bill Edwards and Dixon Boyles. Jack Lucas: Youngest Man to Win the Congressional Medal of Honor. *Life on the Pamlico*, December 2001, p. 15.

48. David Tisdale, Office of University Communications Press Release. Southern Miss History Award to Honor WWII Hero Jack Lucas. Monday, June 23, 2008.

49. Bill Edwards and Dixon Boyles. *Life on the Pamlico*, December 2001, p. 16.

50. Genevieve Anton. *Colorado Springs Gazette*, Tuesday, July 4, 1995, Pages A1, A3.

51. William Standring. The Story of Jack Lucas. *Marine Corps League Magazine*, Summer, Vol. 52, No. 2, 1996, p. 24.

52. *The Clarion–Ledger*, Friday, November 7, 1997.

53. Association Plans Reunion. Texas, *Burkburnett Informer Star*, Thursday, December 31, 1998, Page 7; Survivors sought. Granbury, *Hood County News*, Wednesday, February 10, 1999, Page 16.

54. Bill Edwards and Dixon Boyles. *Life on the Pamlico*.

55. Mississippi, *Laurel Leader Call*, Sunday, March 26, 2000, Page 3-A.

56. *Indestructible*, p. 200.

57. Ship keeps patriotism afloat. Fort Walton Beach, Florida, *Northwest Florida Daily News*, Sunday, July 1, 2001, Pages A1, A8; Pennsylvania, *Altoona Mirror*, Sunday, July 1, 2001, Page B2.

58. Bruce Kauffman. Kentucky, *Corbin Times Tribune*, Saturday, July 6, 2002, Page 4A.

59. Tim Carpenter. Kansas, *Lawrence Journal World*, Tuesday, July 22, 2003, Page 5A.

60. Glenda Taylor, John Schmid, Jack Parker. From the Frontlines of WAR. Texas, *Kerrville Daily Times*, Monday, February 21, 2005, Pages 1A, 3A.

61. *Indestructible*, p. 200.

62. Eric Talmadge. Veterans mark 60th anniversary on Iwo Jima. Alabama, *Athens News Courier*, Sunday, March 13, 2005, Page 16A.

63. James Bradley. *Flags of Our Fathers*. New York: Bantam Books, 2000, pp. 174–75.

64. Peter Collier and Nick Del Calzo, p. 164–66. Rob Novit. Book honors American heroes. South Carolina, *Aiken Standard*, Tuesday, November 22, 2005, Page 2A.

65. Chris Talbott, Associated Press. Teen WWII hero, now 80, gravely ill with cancer. *USA TODAY*, Wednesday, June 4, 2008.

66. David Revere. 26 Marine Heroes Presented With Medal of Honor Flags. *American Forces Press*, U.S. Department of Defense, August 4, 2006. William D. Moss, Defense Department photo, August 3, 2006.

67. Bob Hill. Iwo Jima flags recall an era of bravery, service: Marine from invasion to speak in Louisville. *Louisville Courier–Journal*, Saturday, February 24, 2007.

68. Chris Talbott. Writer World War II legend Jack Lucas dies. Virginia, *Winchester Star*, Saturday, June 7, 2008, Page A2.

69. Can be viewed at marines.togetherweserved.com/usmc/servlet/tws.webapp.WebApp?type=PersonExt&cmd=ShadowBoxPersonPhoto&maxphoto=16&order=Sequence_desc&ID=71433&filter=All&page=1&photoIndex=first.

70. TWS Island Storm 2008. *The Guidon* Newsletter, April 2008.

71. *Indestructible*, pp. 203–205.

72. See his August 7, 2014 comment at debbieschlussel.com/3846/jack-lucas-amazing-wwii-teen-hero-american-patriot-rip.

73. Mississippi, *Laurel Leader Call*, Sunday, May 25, 2008, Page A4.

74. Chris Talbott. Teen WWII hero, now 80, gravely ill with cancer. *USA TODAY*, Wednesday, June 4, 2008; Alabama, *Athens News Courier*, Wednesday, June 4, 2008, Page 3A.

75. Mike Fishbaugh. Leatherneck.com/forums/archive/index.php/t-66618.html.

76. Chris Talbott. Virginia, *The Winchester Star*, Saturday, June 7, 2008, Page A2.

77. Marine Corps mourns loss of hero. Headquarters Marine Corps Media Branch, HQMC Division of Public Affairs, June 6, 2008.

78. Earlesha Butler. He served honorably. Local News, *Hattiesburg American*, Friday, June 6, 2008.

79. Governor Haley Barbour set his hand and caused the Great Seal of the State of Mississippi to be affixed to Executive Order No. 997 on the 6th day of June, in the year of our Lord two thousand eight, and of the Independence of the United States of America, the two hundred and thirty-second.

80. Adapted from at debbieschlussel.com/3846/jack-lucas-amazing-wwii-teen-hero-american-patriot-rip.

81. David Tisdale, Office of University Communications Press Release. Southern Miss History Award to Honor WWII Hero Jack Lucas. Monday, June 23, 2008.

82. WTOK-TV 815 Meridian, Mississippi; David Tisdale, Monday, June 23, 2008.

83. Wes Prater. In Memory of PFC Jack Lucas 1928-2008. *The Guidon* Newsletter, June 2008. Pages 1–2.

84. Alexander Lynch. Auburndale sergeant to be featured on Veterans Day calendar. *News Chief*, Monday, November 10, 2003; Sgt. Daniel Angel. Medal of Honor Tribute presented

to Dakota Meyer, displayed at Lindsey Wilson College. mcrc.marines.mil, November 1, 2013; Carly Besser. Man Educates Others About Military Heroes. *The Washington Times*, Saturday, June 7, 2014; His mission: Knowledge. Medal of Honor winners are the focus of veteran's project. *Colorado Springs Gazette*, Sunday, June 15, 2014, Page F4.

85. 2013 Mississippi Code, Title 65 - Highways, Bridges And Ferries, Chapter 3 - State Highway System, Special Designations Of Portions Of Highway System And Bridges.

86. Mississippi WWII hero Jack Lucas' valor challenged by life's grit.

87. Two Destroyers To Be Named for Medal of Honor Recipients. Associated Press, Military. com Network, Sunday, September 18, 2016.

CHAPTER 17. Survival Rooted In Resilience

1. See CHAPTER 9, Note 1, *Defiance At Dawn*.

2. The family histories described in this account relied primarily on U.S. Census and finda-grave.com records. All census data was available at mocavo.com and FamilySearch.org.

3. *Barren County KY Deed Book D.* Retrieved at files.usgwarchives.net/ky/barren/deeds/bk-d-pg147.txt.

4. Additional family information was derived from the 1850 U.S. Census.

5. Sandra K. Gorin. *Barren County Kentucky Vital Statistics, Deaths, 1852 through 1859, 1861, 1877–1879*. Glasgow KY: Gorin Genealogical Publishing, 1994.

6. Stuart LeRoy Thayer. *Annals of the American Circus: 1848–1860, Volume 3*. Seattle: Dauven and Thayer, 1992.

7. Chorus lines from a popular Civil War song written by George F. Root in 1864 to give hope to Union prisoners of war.

8. After the war, he resided in Cave City, married, and raised a family. He is buried in King Cemetery, a small African-American cemetery on Glasgow's northwest side on the Stovall Road (Highway 685), between Dripping Springs Road and Park City-Glasgow Road.

9. He is buried in Cave City Cemetery, Barren County.

10. Frederick H. Dyer. *Compendium of the War of the Rebellion: Battles*. Reviewed at Tufts University, perseus.tufts.edu.

11. Details regarding the 11th Regiment Kentucky Volunteer Infantry retrieved from kykin-folk.com/gallatin/11regiment.txt.

12. James A. Ramage. *Rebel Raider: The Life of General John Hunt Morgan*, Lexington: University Press of Kentucky, 1986, pp. 86–106.

13. Rebel News. Indiana, *New Albany Daily Ledger*, Monday, January 3, 1862, Page 3.

14. Louisville. Indiana, *The Indianapolis Daily Journal*, Monday Morning, May 12, 1862, Page 3.

15. W.C. Sleet. To the Editor of the Recorder. Burlington, Kentucky, *The Boone County Recorder*, August 16, 1905.

16. By Telegraph. Indiana, *New Albany Daily Ledger*, Wednesday, August 20, 1862, Page 3.

17. Rebel Barbarity. Indiana, *Connersville Weekly Times*, Thursday, October 30, 1862, Page 1.

18. Shocking Murder by Morgan's Rebels. California, *Sacramento Daily Union*, Thursday, November 13, 1862, Page 2.

19. Claude Everett Bush. *Townsend Mountain*, Kentucky, 1988.

20. Not everyone took a flattering view of James and his family. The October 1872 *Lexington Observer and Reporter*, as reported by Deputy Jailor Captain Stephen G. Sharp, formerly of John Hunt Morgan's cavalry, printed A RECORD OF BLOOD—The Evil History of the Townsend Family, in the Mountains of Kentucky—Ten Years For a Foul Murder.

21. *Official Records of the Union and Confederate Armies Vol. XXIII, Part 1–Reports*, pages 365–67.

22. Carl Howell and Dixie Hibbs. *South Central Kentucky: Adair, Barren, Green, Hart, and Taylor Counties*. Charleston, South Carolina: Arcadia Publishing, 2001, p. 30; Lisa Simpson Strange. Fort Williams site of Civil War skirmish. *Glasgow Daily Times*, Sunday, April 10, 2011.

23. Indiana, *New Albany Daily Ledger*, Saturday Evening, August 6, 1864, Page 2.

24. Bold Rebel Movements in Kentucky. *New Albany Daily Ledger*, Monday, October 17, 1864, Page 2.

25. Iowa, *Burlington Daily Hawk-Eye*, Monday, October 31, 1864, Page 2.

26. Indiana, *Madison Weekly Courier*, Wednesday, November 9, 1864, Page 2. The 1850 and 1860 U. S. Census records list his given name as Charles W., son of Charles J. Fox.

27. Woodford Houchin died May 31, 1909, and was buried in Old Brownsville Cemetery. Mary died on January 11, 1938, and was the last of eight burials in the Fox Family Graveyard.

28. Indiana, *New Albany Daily Ledger*, Saturday Evening, December 31, 1864, Page 2.

29. Susan's date of birth and year of death are variously recorded. The dates on her gravestone at Blue Springs Cemetery are 1847–1934.

30. Paul R. Petersen. Knee Deep in Blood. *Quantrill at Lawrence: The Untold Story*. Pelican Publishing Company, Inc, 2011, pp. 24–30.

31. Bruce Nichols. *Guerrilla Warfare in Civil War Missouri, Volume II, 1863*. Jefferson, North Carolina: McFarland & Company, Inc., 2007, p 209.

32. *New York Times*, Monday, August 17, 1863, PAGE 8. THE KANSAS MASSACRE. *New York Times*, Monday, August 24, 1863, Page 4.

33. Indiana, *Cannelton Reporter*, Thursday, March 30, 1865, Page 1. From the *Evansville Dispatch*.

34. *New Albany Daily Ledger*, Saturday, January 21, 1865, Page 2.

35. GUERRILLA BARBARITY. Madison, *Wisconsin State Journal*, Thursday, January 26, 1865, Page 1; Ohio, *Steubenville Weekly Herald*, Wednesday, February 1, 1865, Page 1; Execution of Sue Mundy. *New Albany Daily Ledger*, Thursday, March 16, 1865, Page 1; Indiana, *Madison Courier*, Wednesday, March 22, 1865, Page 4.

36. Execution of Champ Ferguson. *Indianapolis Daily Journal*, Tuesday, October 24, 1865, Page 2.

37. Line from *The Blue And The Gray* by Francis Miles Finch (1827-1907).

38. Most of the National Archive 1890 Census population schedules were badly damaged in a devastating fire in January 1921. No fragments for the Kentucky schedule exist.

39. If acquired records are correct, William D. Bush was born in January 1878, Lou Ada in April 1880, and Eugene in August 1884. There were many farmers named George Bush in Barren during these same years. In Temple Hill, a George Bush, younger by three years, had married Margaret S. Brice from Tennessee. Another same-age George had married widow Emma C. and was raising his family on a farm outside of Glasgow.

40. The cemetery is located at coordinates N37°03.133' W085°52.867'.

41. Paul Reps and Nyogen Senzaki. *Zen Flesh Zen Bones*. Boston: Tuttle Publishing, 1998, p. 165.

42. Hidden River Cave was reopened for tourists in 1993.

43. Skeleton Of Prehistoric "Floyd Collins" Is Found. Virginia, *Danville Bee*, Wednesday Afternoon, June 19, 1935, Page 1.

44. John Enright. Tutuila in WWII: In the Cross-hairs of History–Part 1. *Samoa News*, Tuesday, March 15, 2011.

45. Derived from Adjutant General's Office, Chronological List of Actions with Indians: 1872, 1873. Can be viewed at cgsc.edu/CARL/nafziger/872XAA.pdf and cgsc.edu/CARL/nafziger/873XAA.pdf.

46. Henry Holman Dickinson is a fifth-generation descendant of William L. Day's family and provides a brief biography at so-ky.com/dickinson/book/wmday.htm. A William L. Day died on September 21, 1913, and is buried in Arlington National Cemetery, Section 17, Site: 18287. His birth date is unrecorded. This veteran served as a private in the Casual Detachment, 1st U.S. Cavalry, and is unlikely to be Barren County's Medal recipient.

47. The accounts of Raider operations were derived from several sources: Henry I. Shaw Jr. and Douglas T. Kane, Chapter 4, The Dragons Peninsula Campaign, *History of the U.S. Marine Corps in WWII, Volume II, Isolation on Rabaul*, PCN 19000262500, Historical Branch, G-3 Division, Headquarters, U.S. Marine Corps, 1963; Jon T Hoffman, 1995; Charles L. Updegraph Jr., *Special Marine Corps Units of World War II*, PCN 19000413200, Washington, D.C.: Headquarters, U.S. Marine Corps History and Museums Division, 1972; Ronnie Day, *New Georgia: The Second Battle for the Solomons*, Bloomington, Indiana: Indiana University Press, 2016.

48. USS *Robert I. Paine* (DE/DER-578), a Buckley-class destroyer escort of the United States Navy, was commissioned on February 26, 1944, in his honor.

49. An incomplete list of Marines KIA in WWII was reviewed at http://naval-history.net/WW2UScasaaDB-USMCbyNAME.htm. The names of Company C Raiders KIA in WWII were also derived from *The Raider Patch* Honor Roll, September 1976, January 1990, Pages 2–4; March 1990, Pages 19–20; May 1990, Pages 21–23; July 1990, Pages 6–7; and September 1990, Pages 23–25.

50. Joseph H. Alexander, *Edson's Raiders*, pp. 135–197. Marlin F. "Whitey" Groft and Larry Alexander, 2014.

51. United States Marine Raider Association newsletter, *The Raider Patch*, May 1978, Page 18.

52. New York, *The Brooklyn Daily Eagle*, Saturday, December 12, 1942, Page 2.

53. Myrna Oliver. Richard E. Bush, 79; Was Honored for WWII Acts, *Los Angeles Times*, June 15, 2004.

54. Comrades Say That Marine Dies in Action. *Altoona Tribune*, Tuesday, June 22, 1943, Page 5; Sgt J. J. Stark Reported Dead. Pennsylvania, *Altoona Tribune*, Friday, September 22, 1944, Page 3.

55. Herbert Edwards, Nelson A. Francisco, and Eric R. Powers, USMC Military Awards Branch, assisted with a records search. Various details of Richard's recruit experience, his USMC service, and medical history were derived from a review of his military records, as allowed by the Freedom of Information Act: coordinated by Jodi L. Foor and provided by Jason Gibbs, Archive Technician, National Personnel Records Center, St. Louis, Missouri, on November 8, 2016.

CHAPTER 18. Want *ACTION?* Join the U*S*MARINE CORPS!

1. In his eulogy for the 2d Raiders who had perished in the jungles of Guadalcanal; delivered at Camp Gung Ho on Espiritu Santo, December 1942. John Wukovits. *American Commando: Evans Carlson, His WWII Marine Raiders and America's First Special Forces Mission*. New York: New American Library, 2009, pp. 263–64.

2. Joseph H. Alexander, *Edson's Raiders*, p. 102.

3. USS *Kenneth D. Bailey* (DD-713/DDR-713), a Gearing-class destroyer, was launched on July 8, 1944.

4. United States Marine Raider Association newsletter, *The Raider Patch*, March 1980, Page 26.

5. *Raider Patch*, March 1977, Pages 14–15.

6. Sergeant Allard and eight other Raiders were taken to Kwajalein, and beheaded by his Japanese captors. Awarded the Navy Cross for his actions at Makin, his remains are still missing.

7. *Raider Patch*, No. 124, 4th Qtr, 2013, Pages 22–23; Joel Mills. Nearly 70 years after the end of WWII, a local veteran reflects on his exploits as a Marine. Idaho, *The Lewiston Tribune*, Monday, March 16, 2015.

8. William "Chief" Dae, *The Raider Patch*, May–July 1981, Page 19.

9. Daniel Yazzie, Joe S. Yazzie, Robert Yazzie, and other Code Talkers also served on Bougainville.

10. The USS *Strong* might also have been hit by a "Long Lance" torpedo launched at least 15 minutes (and three radical course changes) earlier by one of four undetected enemy destroyers in the Gulf area.

11. *Raider Patch*, March 1978, Page 12.

12. When his body was brought home, Rabbi Samuel Yalow officiated at his burial in Ahavath Achim Cemetery.

13. Francis Hepburn, *Raider Patch*, November 1989, Page 3.

14. UNCLASSIFIED details on three index cards were reviewed at chutesandskullsdotorg.files.wordpress.com/2015/07/zinkevich_new.pdf. See also, the WFI Research Group at wfirg.com/memorial_day. On December 30, PFC Zinkevich's remains were buried in Grave #6 Row #3, Plot #20 at the U.S. Government New Georgia Cemetery. Then, his remains were reported to have been reburied on November 10, 1945, in Grave #1524 in USAF Cemetery #3, Fischhafen, New Guinea. By 1948, Mrs. Zinkevich had changed her address to St. Marys Villa Nursing Home, Elmhurst, Pennsylvania, near Scranton. Rather than bringing her son's remains home to the States, in January she requested that PFC Zinkevich be interred in a permanent American military cemetery overseas. At the time, that would have been Fort William McKinley Cemetery, also known as the Manila American Cemetery and Memorial. Four years passed, then, the Field Board BuMed, Department of the Navy, reported on July 2, 1952, that a Major Discrepancy had occurred. The remains of PFC Barney Zinkevich, MCSN # 403959, had been determined to be "Non-recoverable." He was among sixty-six other missing Marines whose remains would not be recovered and identified as of 2015.

15. A "casualty" in military terms was a person lost from the unit rolls through death, wounding, injury, sickness, capture, internment, or missing in action. Casualty lists tended to include twenty percent dead and eighty percent wounded. Some KIAs started out on the wounded and missing rosters.

16. *Raider Patch*, January 1981, Page 7.

17. *Raider Patch*, November 1977, Page 4.

18. *Raider Patch*, September 1983, Page 18; *Raider Patch*, September 1979, Page 14. Stevo Popovich, died March 30, 1989, in East Hanover, New Jersey.

19. *Raider Patch*, November 1976, Page 10

20. Shawne K. Wickham. More than tradition—history on Memorial Day weekend. *New Hampshire Union Leader*, Saturday, May 26, 2012.

21. His remains were later found in 1999 and buried in North Hollywood, California.

22. Henry I. Shaw Jr. and Douglas T. Kane, *The Dragons Peninsula Campaign*, p. 145.

23. *Raider Patch*, March 1978, Page 12.

24. Farmer Near Pana Told of Son's Death in Action. *The Chicago Tribune*, Saturday, December 19, 1942; *Raider Patch*, March 1977, Page 16–17.

25. Yank Souvenir Hunters, *Marine Corps Chevron*, VoI. II, No. 43, Saturday, October 30, 1943, Page 3.

26. Adapted from 93rd Seabees Battalion, Nickel Docks Explosion, Noumea, November 1, 1943, at seabees93.net/MEM Noumea.htm.

27. *Raider Patch*, March 1979, Page 24.

28. *Life* Magazine, Volume 14, Number 5, February 1, 1943, Pages 21–27.

29. Jennifer Brewington Taylor, phone conversation, Wednesday, July 20, 2016.

30. Ibid.

31. Adapted from Martin Hadlow, *The Mosquito Network: American Military Radio in the Solomon Islands During World War II*, Broadcast Education Association, Washington, D.C.: *The Journal of Radio Studies*, Vol. 11, No. 1, 2004, pp. 73–86.

32. Henry I. Shaw Jr. and Douglas T. Kane. *History of U.S. Marine Corps Operations in World War II, Volume II: Isolation of Rabaul.* Historical Branch, G-3 Division, Headquarters U.S. Marine Corps, 1963, pp. 518–523.

33. Roger Mansell compiled a complete list of names and units available at Mansell.com, the CENTER FOR RESEARCH, ALLIED POWS UNDER THE JAPANESE. Also, Roger Mansell and Linda Goetz Holmes (Editor), *Captures: The Forgotten Men of Guam*, Annapolis, Maryland: Naval Institute Press, 2012.

34. John L. Sterling, Company K, 3d Raider Battalion, *Raider Patch*, September 1985, Page 18.

35. Jennifer Brewington Taylor, phone conversation, Wednesday, July 20, 2016.

36. The following account is derived largely from O. R. Lodge, *The Recapture of Guam*, Historical Branch, G-3 Division, Headquarters, U.S. Marine Corps, 1954.

37. Ernie Pyle. *Brave Men*, p. 118.

38. *Raider Patch*, September 1978, Page 17.

39. A roster of USMC KIA/WIA casualties on Guam can be viewed at nps.gov/wapa/learn/historyculture/guam-armed-forces-casualties.htm.

40. *Raider Patch*, May 1987, Page 13.

41. *Raider Patch*, May 1978, Page 3.

42. LT MAX BELKO LOSES LIFE IN GUAM INVASION. California, *The Fresno Bee–The Republican*, Tuesday, August 15, 1944, Page 19; Danville, Pennsylvania, *The Morning News*, Thursday, August 24, 1944, Page 5; California, *Hanford Sentinel*, Sunday, August 27, 1944, Page 1; Charles B. Blackmar. *The Princeton Class of 1942 During World War II: The Individual Stories.* Princeton, New Jersey: Princeton University, Class of 1942, 2000.

43. Michigan, *Detroit Free Press*, Thursday, September 21, 1944, Page 7.

44. *Raider Patch*, November 1980, Page 18.

45. *Raider Patch*, November 1978. Page 14.

46. *The Council Bluffs Nonpareil*, Council Bluffs, Friday, September 24, 1948, Page 13.

47. Private Butterfield went on to Tsingtao, China after the war. He was located in Seattle, WA, in 1981. *Raider Patch*, September 1981, Page 25, and November 1999, Page 10–11.

48. Navy Cross Award Citations can be viewed at homeofheroes.com/members/02_NX/citations/03_wwii-nc/nc_06wwii_usmcH.html.

49. COLORADO CITY'S "BABY MARINE" WON'T COME HOME FROM WAR. *Abilene Reporter News*, Friday Morning, September 1, 1944, Page 3.

50. PRIVATE JACK CHUDA KILLED. Iowa, *Boone News Republican*, Tuesday, October 24, 1944, Page Three; Iowa, *Council Bluffs Nonpareil*, Wednesday, November 1, 1944, Page 5.

51. Helena, Montana, *The Independent Record*, Tuesday, August 29, 1944, Page 6.

52. *Raider Patch*, May 1978, Page 13.

53. Men in Action. Kansas, *Emporia Gazette*, Wednesday, September 6, 1944, Page Five.

54. Pfc. Harold E. Lowry Killed in South Pacific Zone. Alabama, *The Cullman Banner*, Thursday, August 24, 1944, Page One; Card Of Thanks. *The Cullman Banner*, Thursday, September 14, 1944, Page 10.

55. Marine Casualties. *Marine Corps Chevron*, Volume 3, Number 32, August 12 1944, Page 13. Records of this flight vary. Second Lieutenant Howard J. Schroeder, VMSB-241, is named as the pilot of SBD 54217 and Sergeant Robert W. Carman, of Detroit, as the machine gunner; see pacificwrecks.com/aircraft/sbd/54217.html; and USN Overseas Aircraft Loss List May 1944, located at aviationarchaeology.com/src/USN/LLMay44.htm.

56. Jennifer Brewington Taylor, phone conversation, Wednesday, July 20, 2016.

57. DIES IN ACTION. Pfc. Wellbaum Dies in Action. Illinois, *The Decatur Herald*, Friday, August 18, 1944, Page 14; Don Wellbaum Rites Tuesday. *The Decatur Herald*, Sunday, January 9, 1949, Page 8; Pvt. John Wellbaum Visits Grave of His Brother on Guam. *The Decatur Daily Review*, Tuesday, May 29, 1945, Page 3.

58. Eaton Soldier Killed on Guam Expressed Faith. Colorado, *Greeley Daily Tribune*, Wednesday, September 20, 1944, Page Ten.

59. Marine Raider Killed on Guam. California, *Oakland Tribune*, Wednesday, October 18, 1944, Page 8.

60. Final Rites for Gallant Marine Held Wednesday. Smith Center, Kansas, *Smith County Pioneer*, Thursday, December 16, 1948, Page 1.

61. MARINE CASUALTIES. *Marine Corps Chevron*, Volume 3, Number 39, September 30, 1944, Page 11.

62. NAVY CASUALTIES. Texas, *Abilene Reporter News*, Friday Evening, October 13, 1944, Page Fifteen; Pfc. Alton Glenn, McLean, Is Killed. Texas, *Amarillo Daily News*, Friday Morning, November 3, 1944, Page Five; Marine Casualties: Dead. *Marine Corps Chevron*, Volume 3, Number 44, Saturday Morning, 4 November 1944, Page Fifteen; War Dead Is Returned. *Pampa Daily News*, Sunday, June 13, 1948, Page One; Funeral Today For A. L. Glenn. *Amarillo Daily News*, Tuesday, June 15, 1948, Page Two.

63. Doris Louise Wynes, his wife of 11 months, was notified after an investigation later that, on June 20, 1944, Sergeant Arthur "Duck" Vanmeter had been WIA by a gunshot wound in the back, bullet passing through his lung. After first aid, he was left in a hedgegrow and died there. His body was never recovered.

64. Elizabeth Feeney, FOR IMMEDIATE RELEASE, from Joint POW/MIA Accounting Command Public Affairs Office, JBPHH, Hawaii, Release # 12-9, May 9, 2012. Seth Robson and Wyatt Olson, WWII veteran's effort to recover MIA remains in the Pacific bears fruit, *Stars and Stripes*, Saturday, August 4, 2015.

65. His statement at his 91st birthday, March 27, 1990, in Fresno, CA. Father Paul J. Redmond tribute, *Raider Patch*, June 1990, Page 34.

CHAPTER 19. The Space Between Battles

1. Timon of Athens, Act IV, Scene III. Timon responds to Alcibiades in front of a cave.

2. Pfc Edw. Phemister: Reported Killed In South Pacific Area. Illinois, *Carbondale Free Press*, Monday, December 4, 1944, Page 1.

3. Regina Ford. Australian soldier returns long-lost dog tags to WWII vet. Arizona, *Sahuarita Sun*, Saturday, June 16, 2012; More WWII dog tags on their way back to owners. *Green Valley News*, Saturday, August 11, 2012.

4. The account of the Okinawa campaign was primarily derived from two sources: Chas. S. Nichols Jr. and Henry I. Shaw Jr., *Okinawa: Victory in the Pacific*, Washington, D.C.: Historical Branch, G-3 Division, Headquarters, U.S. Marine Corps, 1955; and, Joseph H. Alexander, 1996.

5. World War 2 - UNITED STATES MARINE CORPS CASUALTIES BY NAME at naval-history.net/WW2UScasaaDB-USMCbyNameA.htm.

6. RECREATION CENTER IS NAMED FOR LANGELOTH OFFICER. Pennsylvania, *Charleroi Mail*, Tuesday, May 29 1945. Lieutenant Dodds is buried in Section 10, Lot 72, Robinson Run Cemetery in McDonald, Allegheny County, Pennsylvania.

7. From his Sunday, July 20, 1980 Eulogy For Marine Raider Dead. *Raider Patch*, September 1980, Page 10.

8. Adapted from his citation at valor.militarytimes.com/recipient.php?recipientid=37777.

9. *Raider Patch*, September 1982, Page 13.

10. Jon T. Hoffman, *Once A Legend*, Pg 270.

11. A biographical chapter for Justice M. Chambers is included in *The Search For The Forgotten Thirty-Four*, CreateSpace, 2011, pp. 199–222.

12. Joseph H. Alexander, *Edson's Raiders*, p. 87.

13. Major John Smith interview, USMC, Bureau of Aeronautics, 10 November 1942.

14. In November 2006, his victories over Guadalcanal were first featured in the History Channel's Dogfights series.

15. *The Beta Theta Pi* magazine, Vol CXXIX, No. 4, Miami University, Spring 2002, Pg 24.

16. Arlington National Cemetery Web site, May 14, 2000.

17. Ernie Pyle, *Brave Men*, p. 4.

18. Joel D. Weisman. RICHARD E. BUSH: Won Medal Of Honor In Attack On Japanese. Illinois, *Mt. Vernon Register–News*, Wednesday, April 28, 1965, Page 2.

CHAPTER 20. Setting a Good Example

1. G. R. Thompson. The Premature Burial. *Great Short Works of Edgar Allan Poe: Poems, Tales, Criticism*. New York: Perennial Classics, 1970, p. 414.

2. The Associated Press. Death photo of war reporter Ernie Pyle found: Pentagon never released it out of deference to his widow. Viewed at Military on nbcnews.com/id/22980127, February 3, 2008.

3. *Raider Patch*, March 1980, Page 25.

4. Jennifer Brewington Taylor, phone conversation, Wednesday, July 20, 2016.

5. William Adelbert Foster's body was returned to Cleveland on October 5, 1949, and buried in Section 110 at Calvary Cemetery.

6. A biographical chapter for John Peter Fardy is included in *The Search For The Forgotten Thirty-Four*, Aftermath Research, 2011, pp. 255–283.

7. Henry J. McCormick. Playing the Game. Madison, *The Wisconsin State Journal*, Sunday, July 1, 1945, Page 17.

8. Dave Schreiner Dies of Wounds on Okinawa. *The Wisconsin State Journal*, Friday, June 29, 1945, Page One. A full account of the two deaths is presented in Terry Frei's *Third Down and a War to Go*, Madison: Wisconsin Historical Society Press, 2007.

9. As quoted in Bevin G. Cass, Ed, *History of the Sixth Marine Division*, Washington, D.C.: Infantry Journal Press, 1948, p. 178; Marines Dedicate Okinawa Cemetery. Alabama, *The Tuscaloosa News*, Wednesday, July 4, 1945, Page One.

10. The outgoing NTX message released by Col J. C. Burger was dated 29 October 1945.

11. MARINE WHO SAVES COMRADES TO GET MEDAL OF HONOR, Texas, *San Antonio Express*, Tuesday Morning, October 2, 1945, Page 6.

12. Brief details of Sergeant Harrell's life are presented in *The Search For The Forgotten Thirty-Four: Honored By The U.S. Marines, Unheralded In Their Hometowns?* Fargo, North Dakota: Aftermath Research, 2011, p. 317–18. He was awarded a Medal of Honor for a heroic defense of a company perimeter on Iwo Jima that, in part, involved a grenade exchange with an enemy assailant.

13. Millions Turn Out to Cheer Fleet Adm. Chester Nimitz for NYC Ticker-Tape Parade. *New York Times*, Wednesday, October 10, 1945.

14. Stan Watts. Maricopa County Lawyers Played Pivotal Roles in Ernesto Miranda Cases. *The Legal Nexus*, Maricopa County Bar Association, April 18, 2011.

15. Ernie Pyle, *Brave Men*, p. 318.

16. Hilliard E. Miller. Sentimental journey to hell and back. Colorado Springs, *Gazette Telegraph*, Sunday, May 20, 1984, Pages C1, C4.

17. The Raider obituaries that appear in the remainder of this chapter were extracted from newspapers or from the usmarineraiders.org/about-the-raiders/history/raider-roster/obituaries/.

18. Car Hits Bridge. Two Are Killed. Pittsfield, Massachusetts, *Berkshire County Eagle*, Wednesday, August 7, 1946, Page One.

19. Former Resident Dies In Accident. Texas, *The Brownsville Herald*, Tuesday, September 24, 1946, Page 2.

20. Des Plaines war veteran takes own life. Illinois, *The Rosell Register*, Friday, December 13, 1946, Page One.

21. The sisters named the home St. Mary Magdalen Home. It is now the Summit School, a preschool, situated on N. 8th Avenue East and Plum Street.

22. They were living at 533 North Fifty-Ninth Avenue West in 1930.

23. Lois Monsoon provided details of Stella's life and school activities, Friday, May 20, Monday, May 23, and Sunday, May 29, 2016.

24. SSN 471-20-4254.

25. June is an important month for you! *LIFE* Magazine, June 10, 1946, Page 66.

26. U.S. Department of Veterans Affairs Beneficiary Identification Records Locator Subsystem (DVA BIRLS). Lois Monsoon provided this detail, Friday, May 20, 2016.

27. Tire Blowout Is Cause of Crash. Pennsylvania, *Indiana Evening Gazette*, Tuesday, August 6, 1947, Page Five.

28. Six Persons Perish In Accidents During Weekend. Helena, Montana, *The Independent–Record*, Monday, August 18, 1947, Page Two.

29. Pennsylvania, *The Wilkes-Barre Record*, Monday, November 24, 1947, Page 12; Friday, November 28, 1947, Page 20.

30. Man Is Killed In Road Mishap. Montana, *The Billings Gazette*, Saturday, June 19, 1948, Page Six.

31. SHOOTING AT KIRKSDALE. Missouri, *Jefferson City Daily Capital News*, Friday, July 9, 1948, Page One.

32. MICHAEL MEGURA HANGS SELF IN CELL. Connecticut, *The Bridgeport Post*, Thursday, June 3, 1948, Page Seventeen.

33. CYCLIST KILLED. Jacksonville, Illinois, *The Daily Journal*, Saturday, July 10, 1948, Page Nine.

34. Pennsylvania, *The Wilkes-Barre Record*, Saturday, July 24, 1948, Page 10.

35. As complied by Decorations and Medals Branch, HqUSMC, December 21, 1960. A Purple Heart is awarded for the first wound suffered under combat conditions, but for each subsequent award an oak leaf cluster or 5/16 inch star is worn in lieu of another medal. Not more than one award will be made for more than one wound or injury received at the same instant.

CHAPTER 21. A Normal Life

1. This is a line translated from Seneca's moral letters to Lucilius. Richard M. Gummere. Epistle XC, 34. *Ad Lucilium Epistulae Morales*. Loeb Classical Library, Cambridge, Massachusetts: Harvard University Press, 1970, p. 423.

2. YOUNG PUBLISHER DIES TRYING TO SAVE GIRL. West Virginia, *Beckley Post–Herald*, Monday Morning, August 29, 1949, Page One.

3. Some later newspaper accounts cite 1946 as the year he started working for the Veterans Administration.

4. Motorcycle Crash Victim. Wisconsin, *Kenosha Evening News*, Monday, October 24, 1949, Page One.

5. ANTLERS NEWS. Oklahoma, *The Ada Evening News*, Sunday, December 2, 1951, Page 7; *The Ada Weekly News*, Thursday, December 6, 1951, Page 2.

6. Award Medal of Honor to Red Cloud, Wisconsin Indian Who Fell in Korea. *The Racine Journal–Times*, Friday Afternoon, March 30, 1951, Page 1.

7. Newark Marine. War Hero, Killed in Korea. Canandaigua, New York, *The Daily Messenger*, Thursday, December 21,1950, Page 3.

8. Faces Murder Charge of Killing Marine Home on Leave. Kentucky, *Middlesboro Daily News*, Tuesday, May 22, 1951, Page One; One Man Gets Life Another Is Freed In Kentucky Killings. Ohio, *The Cincinnati Enquirer*, Tuesday, August 21, 1951, Page 2.

9. Raider R. C. Rosenquist, Raider Colonel Martin J. "Stormy" Sexton and Honorary Raider Robert A. Buerlein. *Our Kind of War,* 1991. Authorized by the U.S. Marine Raider Association, the book includes the "Raider Roster"—a listing of all the men who had served in the Raiders in WWII.

10. An archive of PDF format newsletters is available at the Association's website at usmarineraiders.org/newsletters.htm. The October 1956 issue is the earliest available.

11. *The Patch*, November 1988, Page 22.

12. Rites for Cornish, Gunshot Victim. New York, *Syracuse Post Standard*, Saturday, December 8, 1951, Page 7.

13. Burlington, Kentucky, *The Boone County Recorder*, Thursday, January 8, 1953, Page One.

14. MEDAL OF HONOR HOLDERS CONVENE. Pennsylvania: *Greenville Record Argus*, Monday, March 16, 1953, Page 1; Texas, *Lubbock Avalanche Journal*, Wednesday, April 1, 1953, Page 4, Section 2.

15. Ex-Pen guard, Wife Are Dead. *Walla Walla Union—Bulletin*, Tuesday, September 22, 1953, Page One.

16. At Least 10 Killed In State Accidents. Alabama, *The Anniston Star*, Monday, October 5, 1953, Page 2.

17. *The Galveston Tribune*, Saturday, November 7, 1953, Page 1.

18. Warren Dowson Dies In Diving Mishap In Navy. Iowa, *The Muscatine Journal and News–Tribune*, Thursday, April 22, 1954, Page 2.

19. Two Drowned In Del Norte. *Humboldt Standard*, Monday, June 21, 1954, Page 21.

20. Oklahoma, *Ada Evening News*, Sunday, August 1, 1954, Page 9.

21. W. L. Hankins Rites Friday in Beach City. Long Beach, *The Independent*, Thursday, August 5, 1954, Page 29.

22. UNVEIL MASSIVE IWO JIMA STATUE. Illinois, *Mt. Vernon Register News*, Wednesday, November 10, 1954, Page One.

23. Born in 1927, Willie Dee Ritter died on May 1, 2012.

24. Merritt Edson is mentioned in Chapter 19, Self-Inflicted Death Before Dishonor, *The Search For The Forgotten Thirty-Four*, Aftermath Research, 2011, p. 317.

25. Fragment Kills Father of Four. California, *San Mateo Times*, Wednesday, November 9, 1955, Page One.

26. Frozen Body Of Man Found In Trailer. Alaska, *Fairbanks Daily News Miner*, Monday, December 17, 1956, Page 7; Inquest Begins. *Fairbanks Daily News Miner*, Thursday, December 20, 1956, Page 2.

27. *Raider Patch*, October 1956, Pages 1–2.

28. Illinois, *Dixon Evening Telegraph*, Monday, January 21, 1957, Page 1.

29. Joel D. Weisman. RICHARD E. BUSH: Won Medal Of Honor In Attack On Japanese. Illinois, *Mt. Vernon Register–News*, Wednesday, April 28, 1965, Page 2.

30. *Raider Patch*, May 1957, September 1957.

31. *Raider Patch*, January 1987, Page 15.

32. Joel D. Weisman. *Mt. Vernon Register News*, Wednesday, April 28, 1965, Page 2.

33. Nicholas Alajakis. New Waukegan memorials salute 2 Marines: Bush, Medlicott stand out in holiday tributes. Leatherneck.com, November 12, 2008, /forums/archive/index.php/t-73807.html.

34. Adapted from his November 11, 2013 interview at *Victor A. Sneller*: Veterans History Project of the Library of Congress.

35. *Raider Patch*, March 1958, Pages 2–3; Richard Vana interview, Veterans History Project, Niles Public Library, Illinois, July 9, 2008.

36. Kalispell, *The Daily Inter Lake*, Friday, August 23, 1957, Page 12.

37. Bloomington, Illinois, *The Pantagraph*, Friday, November 8, 1957, Page 5.

38. Marine Sergeant Is Critically Hurt In Smothering Grenade. Lumberton, NC, *The Robesonian*, Thursday, September 27, 1956, Page 1; Phoenix, *Arizona Republic*, Friday, November 29, 1957, Page 43.

39. Murder Ends Jealous Feud. Oklahoma, *The Lawton Constitution*, Monday, February 23, 1959, Page 2; *Raider Patch*, May 1980, Page 19.

40. 21 Persons Die in State. Michigan, *Holland Evening Sentinel*, Monday, June 8, 1959, Page One.

41. ADAN DROWNS NEAR RAVIA ON FAMILY FISHING TRIP. Oklahoma, *The Ada Evening News*, Sunday, July 12, 1959, Page One.

42. Louisville, *The Courier–Journal*, Saturday, August 18, 1951, Page 17.

43. Louisville, *The Courier–Journal*, Friday, August 21, 1959, Page 33; Saturday, August 22, 1959, Page 12.

44. Altadian Slain: Stepson Held. California, *Pasadena Independent*, Wednesday, September 23, 1959, Page One; Youth Cleared in Slaying. Pasadena, *Star–News*, Thursday, September 24, 1959, Page One.

45. Beckley, West Virginia, *The Raleigh Register*, Monday, February 29, 1960, Page 2.

46. Two Killed In Collision. *The Daily Chronicle*, Wednesday, March 23, 1960, Page 3; Third Victim Of Crash Dies. Walla Walla, *Union Bulletin*, Sunday, April 3, 1960, Page 5.

47. Devil Dogs. *The Raider Patch*, January 1984, Pages 6–12; Marine Hero Who Fought Beside Famed War Dog Dies. Texas, *Corpus Christi Times*, Friday, May 13, 1960, Page 5-D.

48. Clay Gowran. A Saintly Man. *The Chicago Daily Tribune*, Thursday, January 26, 1961.

49. Texas, *Corpus Christi Times*, Wednesday, March 29, 1961, Page 10.

50. Two Killed In Oakland Crash. Hayward, California, *The Daily Review*, Friday, April 21, 1961, Page 8.

51. BODY FOUND. Washington, *Port Angeles Evening News*, Friday, November 24, 1961, Page 8.

52. AIRLINER FALLS. Missouri, *St. Louis Post–Dispatch*, Friday, November 23, 1962, Page 2.

53. 22 Men Perish In Mine Near Clarksburg. West Virginia, *Bluefield Daily Telegraph*, Saturday Morning, April 27, 1963, Page One.

54. Weekend Violence Kills 35 In State. Texas, *Brownwood Bulletin*, Monday, May 6, 1963, Page 4.

55. 15-Year-Old Boy Is Charged With Shotgun Murder Of His Father. Illinois, *The Sterling Daily Gazette*, Saturday, July 27, 1963, Page 2; *The Indianapolis Star*, July 27, 1963, Page 3; Wisconsin, *Madison Capital Times*, July 27, 1963, Page 2; *Antioch News*, Thursday, August 1, 1963, Page 1; *Dixon Evening Telegraph*, Tuesday, August 6, 1963, Page 18.

56. John married, lived in Waukesha, Wisconsin, and had children, step-children, grandchildren, great-grandchildren, nieces, nephews, other relatives, and many friends. His wife Janice M. Ksioszk, 57, died in 2000. He married again to Lorna (nee Freele) Squires. He died at age 68 on December 3, 2015.

57. Oregon Toll Up to 497. Walla Walla, *Union–Bulletin*, Friday, November 15, 1963, Page One.

58. Second Person Dies of Injuries. Michigan, *Holland Evening Sentinel*, Tuesday, December 31, 1963, Page Eighteen.

59. Accused Boy Weeps At Trial. Montana, *The Billings Gazette Morning Edition*, Friday, April 10, 1964, Page 5; Youth Acquitted Of Killing Dad. *The Montana Standard and The Butte Daily Post*, Saturday, April 11, 1964, Page One.

60. Policeman Dies In Boat Mishap. New Hampshire, *Nashua Telegraph*, Wednesday, May 6, 1964, Page 9.

61. West Virginia, *Bluefield Daily Telegraph*, Friday, July 10, 1964, Page 2; Killed in Auto Wreck at Levelland. Texas, *Quitman Wood County Democrat*, Thursday, September 24, 1964, Page 1.

62. Joel D. Weisman. RICHARD E. BUSH: Won Medal Of Honor In Attack On Japanese. Illinois, *Mt. Vernon Register–News*, Wednesday, April 28, 1965, Page 2; Medal of Honor Winner Lives With Handicaps. *Mattoon Journal Gazette*, Wednesday, May 12, 1965, Page 25.

63. Wisconsin, *Appleton Post–Crescent*, Friday, June 24, 1932, Page 4.

64. The *Appleton Post–Crescent*, Page 27.

65. *Appleton Post–Crescent*, Monday, June 18, 1962, Page 30.

66. Man Dies of Gun Wound. *Appleton Post–Crescent*, Sunday, August 15, 1965, Page B1.

67. *Appleton Post–Crescent*, Sunday, April 10, 1966, Page 21.

68. News of Servicemen. *Appleton Post–Crescent*, Saturday, February 15, 1969, Page 8.

69. See BANNON v. UNITED STATES, C. A. No. 3714, 293 F. Supp. 1057 (1968). Dorothy died on September 8, 2008, and was buried with Russell. Her obituary was published in

The Providence Journal on September 10. Their marker mistakenly dates Russell's death as 1963.

70. Wife Problem Spurs Suicide. Ohio, *The Defiance Crescent–News*, Thursday, April 14, 1966, Page One.

71. Head-on Crash Kills Man, Youth. *Oakland Tribune*, Saturday, October 1, 1966, Page 2-B.

72. Headon Collision Kills One Driver. Illinois, *The Morris Daily Herald*, Thursday, October 13, 1966, Page Two.

73. Doctor Charges Cruelty. *Los Angeles Times*, Tuesday, June 8, 1948, Page 25.

74. *The Salt Lake Tribune*, Thursday, October 27, 1966, Page 14B.

75. Name Waukegan Man To Aid Viet Returnees. Illinois, *Park Forest Star*, Thursday, January 5, 1967, Page 1A–15.

76. Ibid.

77. Don Maclean. New Ways. Maryland, *Cumberland Evening Times*, Tuesday, February 28, 1967, Page 4.

78. Give Advanced Briefing to GIs On VA Benefits. Pennsylvania, *Warren Times Mirror And Observer*, Friday, March 3, 1967, Page B-8.

79. Former Local Man Sustains Gunshot Wound. Iowa, *Fort Madison Evening Democrat*, Wednesday, June 7, 1967, Page 12; James Jeffries, Keokuk barber, dies in Quincy hospital. Friday. Keokuk, Iowa, *The Daily Gate City*, Saturday, June 24, 1967, Page 10.

80. Illinois Marine Dies In Crash. Illinois, *Mt. Vernon Register–News*, Friday, January 12, 1968, Page One.

81. Three Drown Over Weekend. Walla Walla, *Union Bulletin*, Monday, July, 1, 1968, Page 7.

82. Take The Pledge To "Live As Nurses." Chicago, *The Daily Herald*, Sunday, June 30, 1968, Page 22.

83. Peggy Richardson and Charles J. Hoye. Head-on Crash Kills Three Adams Men; Leaves 3 on Critical List in Pittsfield. Massachusetts, *North Adams Transcript*, Friday, December 27, 1968, Page 1 and 3.

84. Five die as planes crash. Massachusetts, *Lowell Sunday Sun*, June 15, 1969, Page A-3.

85. Bruce Martin. With Respect and Honor. *Leatherneck* Magazine, Volume 52, Issue 8, August 1969, Pages 30–31.

86. BULLET WOUND FOUND AS CAUSE OF DEATH. Connecticut, *The Bridgeport Post*, Monday, July 6, 1970, Page Four.

87. Kenosha Worker Fatally Injured. Wisconsin, *Sheboygan Press*, Thursday, August 20, 1970, Page 20.

88. Accidents claim 24. Michigan, *The Holland Evening Sentinel*, Monday, May 17, 1971, Page Nine.

89. *The Cincinnati Enquirer*, Sunday, June 7, 1942, Page 7. *Xenia Daily Gazette*, Wednesday, December 29, 1971, Page 5.

90. Police Identify Mishap Victim. New Mexico, *Farmington Daily Times*, Friday, February 4, 1972, Page 2.

91. *The Patch*, July 1989, Page 19.

92. Obituary. Oklahoma, *The Ada Evening News*, Friday, April 21, 1972, Page 2.

93. Man Dies When Auto Pins Him To Guardrail. California, *Van Nuys News*, Sunday, June 18, 1972, Page 20A.

94. Frank Sturgis died in a Miami hospital on December 4, 1993.

95. Ray McConnell. More or Less Personal. Pasadena *Star–News*, Thursday, April 6, 1972, Page B-1; *Raider Patch*, September 1972, Page Four.

96. Maine Man Dies In Car Crash. New Hampshire, *The Portsmouth Herald*, Monday, October 16, 1972, Page 22; New Hampshire, *Nashua Telegraph*, Tuesday, October 17, 1972, Page 2, and Thursday, October 20, 1972, Page 2.

97. Carolyn Ann Fisk, 60, died on September 13, 1997, and was buried in Fayetteville National Cemetery. Lela Fisk, 86, died in 2012, outliving John and his two other wives.

98. Plane Crash Kills Pilot. Eureka, California, *The Times–Standard*, Monday, October 29, 1973, Page 3; Death Of Pilot Possibly Planned. *Independent Journal*, November 1, 1973, Page 36.

99. Montana, *The Billings Gazette*, Thursday, June 12, 1975, Page 12A.

100. Jennifer Brewington Taylor, conversation, Wednesday, July 20, 2016.

101. *Raider Patch*, March 1982. Page 8.

102. General Louis Hugh Wilson Jr., printed in *The Patch*, September 1976, Page 5.

103. *Raider Patch*, January 1976, Page 1.

104. Baker Baby Dies In Dallas Hospital. Texas, *Big Spring Daily Herald*, Wednesday, July 11, 1956, Page 8; Former B-Spring Man Dies In Lubbock. Texas, *The Abilene Reporter–News*, Thursday Morning, March 4, 1976, Page 7-C.

105. Golden Gate Raider Reunion. *The Patch*, September 1976, Page 2–3.

106. Kenneth D. Bailey, John Basilone, Harold William Bauer, Anthony Casamento, Merritt Edson, Joseph Jacob Foss, and Archibald A. Vandegrift were the other seven Marines. Medals of Honor on Guadalcanal were also awarded to U.S. Navy Norman Scott, U.S. Army, Charles W. Davis, William G. Fournier, and Lewis Hall, and U.S. Coast Guard Douglas Albert Munro.

107. *Raider Patch*, May 1977, Page 23.

108. *Raider Patch*, September 1976, Page 5.

109. *Raider Patch*, January 1977, Page 15.

110. Copyright entry numbers 458994-459001. Catalog of Copyright Entries: Third series, Volume 28, Part 5, Number 1, Section 2. Washington: Copyright Office, The Library of Congress, 1975, p. 1518.

111. *Raider Patch*, January 1977, Page 17.

112. Tom Bartlett. Giants of the Corps. *Leatherneck Magazine*, Volume 59, Issue 12, December 1976, Pages 28–29.

113. *Raider Patch*, January 1977, Page 18.

114. *Raider Patch*, July 1977, Page 19. From Frank's death to 2001, five more Norwood police officers died self-inflicted deaths. Thomas Farragher. Suicide syndrome? Six Norwood policemen have taken their own lives, and no one knows why. *Boston Globe Magazine*, Sunday, April 28, 2002, cover story, Page 12.

115. *Raider Patch*, September 1977, Page 19.

116. *Raider Patch*, May 1977, Page 18.

117. *Raider Patch*, September 1977, Page 15.

118. *Raider Patch*, January 1978. Page 20.

119. A Reunion of Marines. *Louisville Courier–Journal*, November 11, 1977, Page C6.

120. Chester Fancher, 55, dies of injuries. Obituary. *Idaho Falls Post Register*, Thursday, June 2, 1977, Page C-10.

121. *Raider Patch,* January 1978. Page 19.

122. *Raider Patch* March 1978, Page 2.

123. *Raider Patch*, March 1980, Page 26.

124. Illinois, *Alton Telegraph*, Monday, March 6, 1978, B-6, B-7.

125. Bob identified himself as an amputee from Item Company. *Raider Patch*, March 1979, Page. 16; September 1979, Page 9.

126. John M. Goshko and Michael Getler. Canada Helps Six U.S Diplomats Flee Iran. *Washington Post*, Wednesday, January 30, 1980; A wave of thanks to a neighbor for saving six diplomats from Tehran. *TIME* Magazine, February 11, 1980, the Nation section, Page 20.

127. *Raider Patch*, March 1980, Page 25.

128. *Raider Patch*, September 1980, Page 21.

129. *Raider Patch*, March 1980, Pages 2 and 26.

130. *Raider Patch*, May 1980, Page 5; July 1980, Pages 2–3.

131. Derived from her Obituary, *Anchorage Daily News*, Tuesday, November 13, 2001, and Indiana, *Delphi Carroll County Comet*, Wednesday, November 14, 2001, Page 5A.

132. Jennifer Brewington Taylor, conversation, Wednesday, July 20, 2016.

133. *Raider Patch*, January 1981, Page 13.

134. *Raider Patch*, January 1981, Page 21.

135. Victor Rorek passed away on June 11, 1986.

136. LtCol Evans F. Carlson describing the courage of the enlisted men who ensured victory on Tarawa: quoted in *Raider Patch*, March 1983, Page 2.

137. Fish and Game Patrolman Foils Attempted Robbery. *Napa Register*, November 1978. He died at his residence on September 27, 2005, aged 81.

138. *Raider Patch*, September 1981, Page 24.

139. *Raider Patch*, July 1982, Page 20.

140. *Raider Patch*, September 1982, Page 13.

141. *Raider Patch*, January 1983, Page 22.

142. Kenneth E. John, *Washington Post*, Thursday, July 29, 1982.

143. 20 Years Ago. *Frederick News Post*, Wednesday, October 13, 1982, Page B-8.

144. Colonel Chambers was buried in Section 6, off Grant Drive, near the road leading up to the Memorial Amphitheater.

145. John William Finn was Pearl Harbor's last surviving hero and lived to age 100. He died on May 27, 2010.

146. *Raider Patch*, September 1982, Page 21.

147. MEDAL OF HONOR RAIDER, Page 9; Sergeant Patrick Guide, MEDAL OF HONOR, Page 13.

148. Adapted from legacy.com/guestbooks/chicagotribune/richard-e-bush-condolences/231 1240?cid=full#sthash.LtG0nij5.dpuf.

149. *Raider Patch*, November 1983, Pages 24–25.

150. East Lansing, *Michigan State College Record*, September 1945, Vol. 50 NO. 4, Page 2.

151. Regarding the cousins, six Boston Marines were reported KIA in June. "Red" might have been Private Frederick William Gundel, 23, (June 6, 1945), PFC Robert Louis Judge, or PFC Wellington John Hall, 26, CoB, 1stBn, 4thMar, (June 11, 1945). *Marine Corps Chevron*, Volume 4, Number 31, August 11, 1945, Page 11.

152. *Raider Patch*, November 1984.

153. *Striking Sixth*, Spring 2010, Vol. 35, No. 1, Page 16.

154. Congressional Medal of Honor Society. *Above and Beyond*, p. 235.

155. *Raider Patch*, November 1985, Page 21.

156. *Raider Patch*, November 1985, Page 18.

157. *Raider Patch*, January 1987, Page 5.

158. *Santa Ana Orange County Register*, Sunday, November 8, 1987, Page M4.

159. *Raider Patch*, September 1989, Page 26.

160. *Antioch News*, Volume 103, Friday, September 8, 1989, Page 25. Christine Moraetes courteously searched generations of Ringa Funeral Home records. She provided cemetery details and a copy of the Obituary Notice with further family information, in telephone conversations and correspondence, June 24–28, 2016.

161. *Raider Patch*, November 1989.

162. *Raider Patch*, November 1989, Page 6; January 1990, Pages 17, 24, 27.

163. Anne Keegan. Medal Of Honor Veterans Shun Hero Label. *Chicago Tribune*, Monday, June 18, 1990.

164. Jennifer Brewington Taylor, phone conversation, Wednesday, July 20, 2016.

165. Peggy Faye (Kingery) Lenet Brewington, 72, died on November 9, 2001.

166. Anne Keegan. *Chicago Tribune*, Monday, June 18, 1990.

167. *Raider Patch*, November 1990, Page 7.

168. *Raider Patch*, November 1990, Page 3.

169. *Raider Patch*, January 1992, Pages 3–7.

170. *Raider Patch*, September 1992, Pages 11–12, 24.

171. *Our Kind of War*. Today, this hardcopy sells for $882 used and new for $1,300.

172. *Raider Patch*, November 1992, Page 7.

173. Forrest Martin. Truman Library honors WWII heroes. Missouri, *Independence Examiner*, Monday, July 5, 1993, Page 10A.

174. *Raider Patch*, July 1993, Pages 25–26.

175. *Raider Patch*, November 1994, Page 26.

176. Katie McLain, Adult Reference at Waukegan Public Library, searched the archive and provided a copy of the obituary on Saturday, August 6, 2016. Christine Moraetes, Ringa Funeral Home, also provided information related to Judy's funeral, Monday, July 25, 2016. *Waukegan News—Sun*, Tuesday, April 25, 1995, Page B6. *Antioch News*, Volume 109, No. 17, Friday, April 28, 1995, Page C4.

177. R. R. Keene. World War II: 50 Years Ago: Medals of Honor, Okinawa: Not a Time for Schools or Shrines. *Leatherneck Magazine*, Volume 78, Issue 5, May 1995, Pages 24–29.

178. R. R. Keene. Return to Okinawa 50 Years Later: an Expedition of Peace. *Leatherneck* Magazine, Volume 78, Issue 10, October 1995, Pages 30–37; David Allen. Heroes of the Bloody Battle and Schedule of Commemorations, *Pacific Stars and Stripes*, Sunday, June 18, 1995, Pages 10–11; Martin J. "Stormy" Sexton. Return to Okinawa. *Raider Patch*, November 1995, Pages 27–30.

179. The wording of the permanent historical marker as it now stands was rewritten.

180. Jerry V. Stahl graciously provided this information in a telephone call, April 10, 2010. Jimmy Simmons died on Thursday, March 26, 1998, at the Glasgow Health Care Center.

181. Diane Ross, Statehouse News Service. Sobering exhibits in the Statehouse this month speak volumes. Illinois, *Homewood Star*, Sunday, October 25, 1998, Page A11.

182. Two local Medal of Honor recipients recognized. Arlington Heights, *Daily Herald Suburban Chicago*, Saturday, May 29, 1999, Page 1.

183. Medal of Honor Winners. Indiana, *The Kokomo Tribune*, Saturday, May 29, 1999, Page A2.

184. John McCarthy. THE SMELL OF PHONY HEROES STINKS. *The Raider Patch*, 2006, No. 98, 4th Qtr, Page 8.

185. Michael Taylor, Staff Writer. Tracking Down False Heroes/Medal of Honor recipients go after impostors. *San Francisco Chronicle*, Monday, May 31, 1999. Mitchell Paige died on November 15, 2003.

186. DICK BUSH SPEECH. *The Raider Patch*, February 2000, Pages 16–17.

187. President Clinton Should Learn Some Real Lessons About Sacrifice. Scotch Plains-Fanwood, New Jersey, *The Times*, Thursday, June 16, 1994, Page 5. The history of the letter has been questioned and investigated.

188. Sergeant Gannon arrived at Inchon as a replacement and survived the Korean War. He wrote poetry to keep himself sane. He composed Monuments And Memories, For Those Who Never Came Home. This is the last of the seven touching stanzas.

189. The Memorial is located at 38°32.512'N, 77°21.662'W.

190. Sits at 38°32.461'N, 77°21.636'W, and can be viewed at waymarking.com/waymarks/WMB12X_The_Striking_Sixth_6th_Marine_Division.

191. Myrna Oliver. Richard E. Bush, 79; Was Honored for WWII Acts, *Los Angeles Times*, June 15, 2004.

192. *Raider Patch*, November 2000.

193. Gregg K. Kakesako. Makin Raiders get hero's burial. *Honolulu Star–Bulletin*, Wednesday, August 15, 2001. Lance Cpl. John R. Lawson III, Makin Raiders Laid to Rest. Headquarters Marine Corps: *Marine Corps News*, August 17, 2001. SEMPER FIDELIS RAIDERS: 'TILL WE MEET AGAIN... *Raider Patch*, Aug/Sept/Oct 2001. Marine Corps Raiders Home At Last, ArlingtonCemetery.net/raiders-1942.htm, Friday August 17, 2001. William Cole, 'Makin Raiders' revisited, *Honolulu Advertiser*, Monday, March 11, 2002.

194. Corporal Abigail B. LaBin, *Raider Patch*, February 2000, Page 5.

195. Pueblo unveils: Congressional Medal of Honor memorial. New Mexico, *Farmington Daily News*, Sunday, September 24, 2000, Page F6.

196. Available at imdb.com/title/tt1742884/?ref_=ttfc_ql, a Database and Amazon.com subsidiary. The series was repeated in 2012–2013 with thirty-seven episodes. Season 1, Episode 6, *U.S.M.C.*, aired on October 31, 2012.

197. *Raider Patch*, Nov–Dec 2001–Jan 2002, Page 17.

198. *Raider Patch*, Jan–Feb–March 2002, Page 10.

199. Details derived from her obituary at findagrave.com/cgi-bin/fg.cgi?page=gr&GRid=108819645.

200. *Raider Patch*, No 84, April–May–June 2003, Pages 5–6.

201. Obituary. *The Indianapolis Star*, Wednesday, May 21, 2003.

202. Missouri, *Bolivar Herald-Free Press*, Friday, July 11, 2003.

203. *Raider Patch*, No 88, April–May–June 2004, Page 4.

204. *Striking Sixth*, Vol. 29, No. 3, Spring/Summer 2004.

205. Johanna Neuman. Memorial Dedicated Amid Tears, Joy. *Los Angeles Times*, Sunday, May 30, 2004.

206. *Chicago Tribune*, June 9, 2004.

207. See at legacy.com/guestbooks/chicagotribune/richard-e-bush-condolences/2311240?cid=full#sthash.LtG0nij5.dpuf.

208. Richard Golstein. Richard E. Bush, Who Served on Okinawa, Dies at 79, *New York Times*, June 13, 2004; Myrna Oliver. Richard E. Bush, 79: Was Honored for WWII Acts, *Los Angeles Times*, June 15, 2004.

209. Adam Bernstein, Staff Writer. Obituary: Richard Bush; Medal of Honor Recipient.

210. Rudi Williams, American Forces Press Service. Nine Medal of Honor Recipients Attend Gala. *Veterans Advantage*, June 14, 2004.

211. Vol. 29, No.3, Spring/Summer 2004, Page 1.

212. *Raider Patch*, No. 89, July–Aug–Sept 2004.

213. Derived from kentuckymarines.org/index.cfm/legends/richard-e-bush

214. Retrieved from leasingnews.org/archives/April 2008/04-16-08.htm#day.

215. Nicholas Alajakis. Waukegan, *The News Sun*, Wednesday, November 12, 2008.

216. Bobbie Hayse. Glasgow Barren County Veterans Wall of Honor. *Glasgow Daily Times*, Thursday, June 5, 2014.

217. *Striking Sixth*, Vol. 35, No. 1, Page 11.

218. Mail Call. *Striking Sixth*, Vol. 35, No. 1, Page 16.

219. In 1917, Congress rescinded her award, along with 910 others. Dr. Walker refused to return hers, and wore it proudly until her death in 1919. President Jimmy Carter reinstated her Medal in 1977.

220. New Medal of Honor plaque includes local men. *Evansville Courier & Press*, Thursday, March 15, 2012.

221. Karen Carlson Loving, chair of the U.S. Marine Raider Reunion. General invites Marine Raiders to reunite here. *Wilmington Star News*, Tuesday, July 23, 2013; Holden Kurwicki. WWII Marine Raiders reunite in Wilmington. WWAYTV, Wednesday, August 14, 2013.

222. Sergeant Christina Porras. World War II Marine Raiders reunite. Marine Corps Recruit Depot San Diego *Chevron*, Friday, August 15, 2014, Page 1.

223. Eve A. Baker. Edson's Raiders hold final reunion, toast brothers in arms. *Marine Corps Base Quantico*, April 23, 2015.

224. Corporal Steven Fox. MARSOC, World War II Raiders celebrate Raider history. Camp Lejeune, NC: Marine Website, Friday, September 18, 2015.

225. Viewed at youtu.be/gn376xWWNNw, published on April 1, 2016.

226. Retrieved at evanced.nileslibrary.org/vhp/Searchable/Richard%20Vana.searchable.pdf.

227. Retrieved at honorflightchicago.org/mnu-veterans/mnu-profiles/22-cat-profiles/133-vanar. Norrine Twohey. Neighbors in the News. *Daily Herald*, Saturday, July 25, 2015.

228. Retrieved from usmarineraiders.org and facebook.com/USMarineRaiderAssociation-Foundation, May 16, 2016.

229. Andy Kravetz. Peoria man among last surviving Marine Raiders from World War II. Illinois, *Peoria Journal Star*, December 10, 2016; Obituary, *Peoria Journal Star*, Sunday, October 30, 2016.

CHAPTER 22. That Certain Something

1. Staff Sergeant Donald Marcel Griffith (1927–2016), USMC (Retired), WWII and Korean War veteran. At the battle of the Chosin Reservoir with Company F, 2d Battalion, 5th Marine Regiment, 1st Marine Division.

2. James Bradley. *Flags of Our Fathers*. New York: Bantam, 2000, p. 175.

3. Gary Reaves. Ross Perot Aids Ailing Medal of Honor Winner. Dallas, Texas, WFAA-TV, Friday, January 23, 2004.

4. The following is derived from three sources. Major William E. Mayer, U.S. Army. Brainwashing: The Ultimate Weapon. Presented at the Naval Radiological Defense Laboratory, San Francisco Naval Shipyard, October 4, 1956; James Angus MacDonald Jr. (Major, USMC). *The Problems Of U.S. Marine Corps Prisoners Of War In Korea*. Master's Thesis, University of Maryland, 1962, p. 88; Pat Meid and James M. Yingling. *U.S. Marine Operations In Korea 1950–1953: Volume V–Operations In West Korea*. Historical Division, Headquarters, U.S. Marine Corps, 1972, p. 440.

5. The Chinese Communists began publically releasing the names of American POWs in December 1951.

REFERENCES

Joseph H. Alexander. *The Final Campaign: Marines in the Victory on Okinawa*. Washington, D.C.: Marine Corps Historical Center, 1996.

Joseph H. Alexander. *The Battle History of the U.S. Marines: A Fellowship of Valor*. New York: HarperCollins Publishers, 1997.

Joseph H. Alexander. *Edson's Raiders: The 1st Marine Raider Battalion in World War II*. Annapolis, MD: Naval Institute Press, 2001.

Joseph H. Alexander. *Storm Landings: Epic Amphibious Battles in the Central Pacific*. Annapolis, MD: Naval Institute Press, 1997.

Whitman S. Bartley. *Iwo Jima, Amphibious Epic*. Nashville: Battery Press, 1997. Reprint of Historical Section, Headquarters USMC 1954 edition.

Boston Publishing Company, Editors. *The Medal of Honor: A History of Service Above and Beyond*. Minneapolis: Zenith Press, 2014.

Marc Cerasini. *Heroes: U.S. Marine Corps Medal of Honor Winners*. New York, Berkley Publishing, 2002.

John C. Chapin. *Breaching the Marianas: The Battle for Saipan*. Washington, D.C.: Marine Corps Historical Center, 1994.

George B. Clark, Editor. *United States Marine Corps Medal of Honor Recipients: A Comprehensive Registry*. Jefferson, NC: McFarland & Company, 2005.

Peter Collier and Nick Del Calzo. *Medal of Honor: Portraits of Valor Beyond the Call of Duty*. New York: Artisan, 2003. Published in collaboration with the Congressional Medal of Honor Foundation.

Congressional Medal of Honor Society. *Above and Beyond: A History of the Medal of Honor from the Civil War to Vietnam*. Boston Publishing Co., 1985.

Robert J. Cressman. *A Magnificent Fight: Marines in the Battle for Wake Island*. Washington, D.C.: History and Museums Division, Headquarters, U.S. Marine Corps, 1992.

Bruce Gamble. *The Black Sheep*. Novato, CA: Presidio Press, 1998.

Gordon D. Gayle. *Bloody Beaches: The Marines at Peleui*. Washington, D.C.: Marine Corps Historical Center, 1996.

Marlin F. "Whitey" Groft and Larry Alexander. *Bloody Ridge and Beyond: A World War II Marine's Memoir of Edson's Raiders in the Pacific*. New York: Berkley Caliber, 2014.

James H. Hallas. *The Devil's Anvil: The Assault on Peleliu*, Westport, Connecticut: Praeger Publishers, 1994.

James H. Hallas. *Uncommon Valor on Iwo Jima: The Story of the Medal of Honor Recipients in the Marine Corps' Bloodiest Battle of World War II.* Mechanicsburg, PA: Stackpole Books, 2016.

Robert D. Heinl, Jr. and John A. Crown. *The Marshalls: Increasing the Tempo.* Quantico: Historical Branch, G-3 Division, Headquarters, U.S. Marine Corps, 1954.

Jon T. Hoffman. *Chesty: The Story of Lieutenant General Lewis B. Puller.* Random House, 2001.

Jon T. Hoffman. *FROM MAKIN TO BOUGAINVILLE: Marine Raiders in the Pacific War.* Washington, D.C.: Marine Corps Historical Center, 1995.

Jon T. Hoffman. *Once a Legend: "Red Mike" Edson of the Marine Raiders.* Novato, CA: Presidio Press, 2000.

Frank O. Hough, Verle E. Ludwig, Henry I. Shaw, Jr. *Pearl Harbor to Gaudalcanal: History of the Marine Corps Operations in World War II, Volume 1.* Nashville: Battery Press, 1993. Reprint of 1958 edition.

Frank O. Hough and John A. Crown. *The Campaign on New Britain.* Historical Branch, G-3 Division, Headquarters, U.S. Marine Corps, 1952.

Victor H. Krulack. *First to Fight: An Inside View of the U.S. Marine Corps.* Annapolis, MD: Naval Institute Press, 1984.

Jack H. Lucas & D. K. Drum. *Indestructible: The Unforgettable Story of a Marine Hero at the Battle of Iwo Jima.* Cambridge, MA: Da Capo Press, 2006.

Neill Macaulay. *The Sandino Affair.* Chicago: Quadrangle Books, 1967.

S. L. A. Marshall. *Island Victory: The Battle for Kwajalein.* Rockville, Maryland: Zenger Publishing Company, 1982.

Thomas G. Miller. *Cactus Air Force.* New York: Harper and Row, 1969.

Joseph N. Mueller. *Guadalcanal 1942: The Marines Strike Back*, Oxford: Osprey Publishing, 1992.

Bernard C. Nalty. *Cape Gloucester: The Green Inferno.* Washington, D.C.: History and Museums Division, Headquarters, U.S. Marine Corps, 1995.

Bernard C. Nalty. *The United States Marines in Nicaragua*, revised edition. Washington: Government Printing Office, 1962.

Naval Analysis Division. *Campaigns of the Pacific War: Chapter IX, Central Pacific Operations.* Washington, D.C: United States Government Printing Office, 1946.

Mitchell Paige. *A Marine Named Mitch.* New York: Vantage Press, 1975.

Ernie Pyle. *Brave Men.* New York: Henry Holt and Company, Inc., 1944.

Thomas E. Ricks. *Making the Corps.* New York: Scribner, 1997.

Rudy G. Rosenquist, Martin J. Sexton, Robert A. Buerlein. *Our Kind of War: Illustrated Saga of the U.S. Marine Raiders of World War II.* Richmond, Virginia: American Historical Foundation, 1991.

Bill D. Ross. *Iwo Jima: Legacy of Valor.* New York, The Viking Press, 1976.

Edwin H. Simmons. *Frozen Chosin U.S. Marines at the Changjin Reservoir.* Washington, D.C.: Marine Corps Historical and Museum Division, Headquarters, U.S. Marine Corps, 2002.

E. B. Sledge. *With the Old Breed: At Peleliu and Okinawa.* New York: Presidio Press, 1981.

Bill Sloan. *Brotherhood of Heroes: The Marines at Peleliu, 1944—The Bloodiest Battle of the Pacific War.* New York: Simon & Schuster, 2006.

John Wukovitz. *Pacific Alamo: The Battle for Wake Island.* New York: New American Library, 2003.

About the Author

***

TERENCE W. BARRETT, PHD, SPENT seven years in the U.S. Marine Corps. He served during Desert Storm in 1991 and retired from the North Dakota National Guard after twenty years of service. Barrett is dedicated to honoring the heroism of U.S. Marines who put their lives on the line for their country.

Barrett studied at the College of Wooster and earned advanced degrees from the University of Southern California, North Dakota State University, and the University of North Dakota. He is a licensed, practicing psychologist in Fargo, North Dakota, and an instructor at North Dakota State University. He was the charter president of the North Dakota Chapter of the American Foundation for Suicide Prevention. Barrett is also a clinical consultant at the Fargo Vet Center.

Made in the USA
Columbia, SC
08 April 2022

58692089R00361